THE OFFICIAL
PRICE GUIDE TO
American
Silver
and
Silver Plate

BY
THE HOUSE OF COLLECTIBLES

We have compiled the information contained herein through a *patented computerized process* which relies primarily on a nationwide sampling of information provided by noteworthy collectible experts, auction houses and specialized dealers. This unique retrieval system enables us to provide the reader with the most current and accurate information available.

EDITOR
THOMAS E. HUDGEONS III

THIRD EDITION

THE HOUSE OF COLLECTIBLES, INC., ORLANDO, FLORIDA 32809

ACKNOWLEDGEMENTS

Sandra Matzer, for technical assistance and for lending her collection to be photographed; D. R. Nell, for technical assistance; Kathleen Perelli, Dorothy and Neal Nolan, Caroline and Ruth Asness, for editorial and/or clerical help.

PHOTO CREDITS

All photos in this book were done by Steven G. Proshan of Princeton, New Jersey, whose contribution is deeply appreciated and gratefully acknowledged.

IMPORTANT NOTICE. All of the information, including valuations, in this book has been compiled from the most reliable sources, and every effort has been made to eliminate errors and questionable data. Nevertheless the possibility of error, in a work of such immense scope, always exists. The publisher will not be held responsible for losses which may occur, in the purchase, sale, or other transaction of items, because of information contained herein. Readers who feel they have discovered errors are invited to WRITE and inform us, so they may be corrected in subsequent editions. Those seeking further information on the topics covered in this book, each of which, because of the nature of the publication, must be treated briefly, are advised to use the specialized House of Collectibles OFFICIAL GUIDES.

Published by: The House of Collectibles, Inc.
Orlando Central Park
1900 Premier Row
Orlando, FL 32809
Phone: (305) 857-9095

Printed in the United States of America

Library of Congress Catalog Card Number: 81-81771

ISBN: 0-87637-184-5 / Paperback

TABLE OF CONTENTS

LISTINGS

INTRODUCTION

For thousands of years silver has lured, beguiled, and enchanted mankind. It served as a medium of exchange in the golden days of ancient Greece, when the legends of gods and goddesses were still fresh. It has been searched for, sought after, bought, sold, and hoarded to a far greater extent than any other metal — even more than gold, because silver has been within easier reach of the public. Now that society has advanced so far, with its complex banking systems and paper investments, silver is even more respected as security. It cannot be devalued by government. And, unlike the values of almost everything else, silver's value is usually aided by inflation rather than injured.

In early America, while colonists struggled to build homes and plant crops and fend off Indian invasions, craftsmen made silverware. Silversmithing was a thriving trade in this country before the close of the 17th century. Even though America lacked a native source of silver, its smiths worked — and worked — using recycled silver, foreign coins, and bullion brought in from abroad. When native sources were eventually found, the market in silverware boomed like never before, spurred on by the Victorian zest for opulent formal dining.

We are still living in the Age of Silver. Modern silverware is chiefly factory made, but still admired and valued. Thanks to the long-standing American craft tradition, OLD silverware is available for us to enjoy, to collect, and to set aside for financial investment. It is not nearly so plentiful as it once was. Through the years, much American silverware has been exported, and large quantities have gone to their final reward in the smelter's furnace. But *so much* was made, over so long a period of time, that the onslaughts of melters and the accidents of nature cannot totally stamp it out.

Few classes of objects have been scattered so thoroughly as antique silverware. Usually it represented the most valuable possessions of its owners; so it went on the ox-cart or the canvas wagon, if the family pushed west. In hard times it was pawned, and traveled from one hand to the next. It was gambled over, and stolen, and salted away in secret hiding places. And of course the antiques market has done its part in the migrations of silverware. A serving dish made in Boston in the 1780's might have, by the 1980's, traveled back and forth across the continent dozens of times.

THE OFFICIAL 1983 PRICE GUIDE TO AMERICAN SILVER AND SILVER PLATE is a book for the collector, dealer, investor, and everyone who owns or takes an interest in silver objects. For the person who owns heirloom silver, it will give an accurate indication of its present market value, and help in settling the question: should I sell? For the hobbyist and investor, it presents a review of items now being bought and sold. It shows not only the potential for building a collection or investment but the probable costs that would be involved. Numerous photos have been provided to aid in identification, as well as descriptions of the items and advice for the buyer or seller.

At the present time, silver bullion is selling for a lower price than it did two years ago, when our second edition was published. This has led to a renaissance of the market in silver antiques and collectors' items of all kinds, as buyers now have opportunities which may never again occur. Even the silver enthusiast who has no interest in investment knows that the trade is now rich in bargains, and that items bought at today's prices could double or triple in value with the next surge of bullion activity.

APPROACHES TO COLLECTING SILVERWARE

Those unfamiliar with the world of antiques are apt to think that old silver is bought chiefly by speculators and museums. While it may not seem like a hobby item in quite the same was as stamps or coins, silverware is definitely being collected and the numbers of its collectors are growing. Many of them are pure hobbyists in the traditional sense of the term. Even in this day and age of bullion investment with its charts and graphs and "spot prices," there are buyers of silverware who are not in the least concerned about intrinsic value or what tomorrow will bring. Their delight is in the object itself, and in the enjoyment of assembling and displaying a fine collection. These individuals are, without question, the backbone of the market, as they provide a stability to counteract the unpredictable buying and selling patterns of investors.

Antique American silver certainly offers multiple opportunities for collecting, in terms of its variety, abundance, and the many ranges of price into which specimens fall. It is a hobby without geographical limits, as the antiques shops (and auction houses) in all parts of the country buy and sell silverware. But of course in a hobby such as this there are no "beginner's kits" to get one started out. The path to take, and the way to take it, must be chosen by the individual.

Quite a few collections of silverware are begun more or less by accident, without any decision to collect. The classic example is the inheritor of silver, who resolves to fill out an incomplete set and keeps on buying — until he owns twenty times as much silver as his ancestor. Then there's the chance buyer, the person who picks up a silver spoon or brush at a flea market. If the chemistry is right between the owner and the object, nothing more is necessary to spark the beginnings of a collection. And, of course, silver does have ample physical charm. It can be very appealing for collecting just because it looks handsome, even if the hobbyist has no interest in history, research, or in antiques *per se*.

Many enthusiasts of silver will buy whatever appeals to them — whatever "strikes their fancy" in the antiques shop, whether or not it fits in with items they already own. There is no harm in this, and of course it gives you the advantage of boundless selection rather than looking for one special kind of item. A miscellaneous collection CAN display very well (though this calls for a bit more ingenuity than in showing a specialized collection), and in terms of resale value there is not much sacrificed in a miscellaneous collection compared to a specialized. In short — it's up to you. Your tastes, financial circumstances, the amount of time you can put into antiques browsing, and available display space will be considerations.

If you choose to collect what appeals to you on sight, there is no need for any special plan beyond the effort to visit as many dealers as your schedule permits. You will find silverware in nearly all antiques shops. Our only word of advice is to familiarize yourself with antique silver before doing any large-scale buying. This book should help in that direction. When one builds up a collection rapidly, before learning all about the types of items he collects, he could have regrets later. The person who THINKS he has no specialist interest may be a potential specialist, in some field of silverware of which he does not know enough to take a real interest. We know of hobbyists who, upon seeing their first silver punch ladle in an antiques shop, abandoned their interest in all other silver and bought nothing but punch ladles. Silver is that way. It is a very emotional collectible.

The specialist collector has many possible roads to travel, and regardless how he chooses to proceed he will have no shortage of company. Specialist collectors are active today for every sort of silverware. There are many more specialists for spoons that for centerpiece bowls, but this is because of circumstance: centerpiece bowls are not as plentiful, cost a great deal more money and take up considerable space in storage. On the other hand, a collection of 10 or 12 fine centerpiece bowls would be much more noteworthy than 10 or 12 spoons.

The usual way to specialize is by item type; one person becomes a fork collector and another seeks out salt shakers. Probably as many as ⅔rds of all silverware hobbyists are "item specialists." One of the intrigues of an item collection is the comparison between specimens, reflecting differences in style from one era to another and from one geographical locale to another. The larger such a collection grows, the more varied it becomes, and the more educational for study purposes. But of course the hobbyist holds the controls; he can clamp limits to his collection, whenever and however he chooses. He may decide that his *spoon* collection will include nothing manufactured after 1800, or nothing made outside of New England. In this way a specialized collection become more specialized, and could be much more satisfying. The MORE specialized a collection gets, the more unique it is, as the number of collectors following the precise same approach is apt to be few. If you choose a rather offbeat type of silver as your target, say sardine forks, you might in a couple of years amass the best collection in private hands. This of course is seldom possible to say with any certainty, as the holdings of collectors are usually not publicized until after their deaths. Another good plus about being an ultra-specialist is that one gets a reputation with the dealers. They remember you and your interests, and put away things for you before the general public has the chance to buy them.

Another way to collect is by time period. This method has its followers but they are not very numerous. Most of the time-period collectors are interested in Victorian wares. In the past (before prices started getting too high), there were many collectors for early colonial silver. This is a fascinating group of wares, but much of it has gone into museums. What remains on the market is beyond the budgets of most of us. Yet another possibility is to collect by manufacturer, which can be expensive or inexpensive depending entirely on which manufacturer is selected.

THE SILVER MARKET

The silver market is a vast worldwide network of refiners, jewelry makers, industries, investors, coin dealers and collectors, and others. Each utilizes silver for his own purposes. The radio manufacturer uses it for printed circuits in transistor radios, because of its conductivity. The jewelry maker fashions it into adornments that are passed along for retail sale. Demand for silver is enormous — greater than at any previous time in history. The quantity of raw silver mined each year is no more today than it was ten years ago, about 300 million ounces annually. Yet demand is at least double. Obviously the only way that this additional demand can be met is by melting down things that were made of silver in the past — coins, tableware, decorations and miscellaneous items.

Tons upon tons of "old silver" was bought by scrap dealers in 1980 and resold to refineries. Never in the history of the silver market had so much melting been done as in 1980 — and the 1981 totals may well be even higher. Nevertheless, silver is still not coming on the market fast enough to keep in line with the demand. Therefore, its price has risen to about ten times what it was a decade ago.

As a substance of intrinsic value, like gold, silver has attracted a great many investors. Though silver has certainly been dabbled in by investors over the years, going back centuries, the first significant wave of investor buying occurred in the early to mid 1970's. This was not only generated by the gradually rising prices of silver bullion (in those days a $2 climb in a whole year, for one troy ounce, was considered very impressive), but step-ups in industrial use and projected figures on mining yields, which clearly showed that demand for silver would inevitably hike the price higher and higher. At first, investors concentrated mostly on bars or ingots of .999 fine. Later, they began buying silver bullion coins (common-date coins made of silver, in circulated condition) and various other forms of silver. With each increase in investor activity, the daily "spot" price was driven upward. This natually encouraged still more persons to invest in silver, and for those already holding it to add to their holdings. During the late 1970's, as the price climbed from $5 to $10 to $20, it became evident that silver had the ability — as an investment — to increase in value at a faster pace than the national inflation rate.

But despite the decline of 1980, and fear-mongering warnings by so-called experts that the bottom was soon to fall out, it happened to be a very good year for silver and silver investors. The market was *strong.* Industrial demand grew. Investors multiplied, not only in the U.S. but around the world. And the spot price of silver was more than twice as high, at the end of 1980, than it was at the beginning of 1979. Anyone who bought in *mid* 1979 could have sold in December of that year, or January 1980, for very enviable profits. The only individuals who "got burned" on silver were those who bought at the peak of spot in December, 1979 and January, 1980. If they sold soon thereafter, amid the chaos and confusion of rapidly tumbling prices, they lost money — possibly a very great deal of it. If they had enough courage to *hold,* they still have the chance of making a profit. There is no guarantee that silver will ever get up around the $50 per troy ounce mark again, but there is also no valid reason to believe that it couldn't or wouldn't. Nothing has changed.

Like other commodities, silver is freely traded in the financial centers of the world and "spot" prices are established for it as the result of this trading. The spot price is for one troy ounce of .999 fine silver. This is important to keep in mind. It is not for one ounce of *any other grade,* because lower grades — even the highly-respected Britannia used for top-quality flatware — are alloyed with basemetal to a greater or lesser degree. If, for example, the spot price is $20 per troy ounce and you have a full ounce of .925 sterling silver, you don't have $20 worth of silver. A deduction must be made for the proportion of alloy. We have provided formulas elsewhere in this book for calculating the values of alloyed silver, based on any spot price.

There isn't just one spot price but several of them, recorded by the various commodity exchanges of the world. The American spot price is achieved on the New York exchange, which operates Monday through Friday from 9 a.m. to 4 p.m. This price is used by many bullion brokers, scrap buyers and others in buying and selling. It may be referred to as "New York spot" or "New York close." When "New York close" is used, this can be taken to mean the price at close of trading (4 p.m., or slightly later if trading is heavy) on the *previous* day, or the *last business day* if a weekend or holiday has just occurred.

The closing price may be very different than the price at which the day's trading opened, or even quite different than the price just an hour before close. The figure changes almost constantly, though usually by small amounts, all throughout the trading day. This is an indication of the volume of buying and selling, just as with stocks and other investments that are traded on a public exchange. When the volume of buying exceeds the volume of selling, the price goes up. If there is extremely heavy buying the price will go up sharply, as brokers search frantically to find willing sellers to meet the demand. By the same token, when selling is very heavy, it is not possible for brokers to turn over (that is, resell) huge quantities as rapidly as they come in, and still maintain the same price. Thus, the price goes down; and if enough buyers do not appear, the price will go down further, until a leveling-off point is attained between buyers and sellers. When you have a great deal more of one than the other, the price will not hold steady.

Since the *London spot* is accepted as the standard for Europe and most foreign countries, U.S. brokers and dealers often refer to it, rather than New York spot. To avoid misunderstanding and confusion, the more responsible dealers do not switch back and forth between the New York and London spot but choose one or the other for their purposes and stay with it. By switching arbitrarily, it would be possible for the dealer to use whichever price was more favorable at the moment. The New York and London spot prices on bullion (silver as well as gold) are not the same. When New York closes at $23.76, London may be $23.41 or $23.98. This is because the volume is different, and the people doing the buying and selling are, largely, different also. But the two prices never get *very* far apart. You will not find silver selling for $25 in London and $20 in New York on any given day. Based just on buying and selling, this could conceivably happen; but it doesn't, because the two markets keep an eye on each other. So do the buyers and sellers. If the price starts getting appreciably higher in New York, people who would have sold on the London market switch their order to New York; and vice-versa. This drives the New York price down. If it appears that the market is being controlled, by the very close similarity in prices around the world, it *is* — but not by government. The control is placed upon it by its customers, including you if you invest in silver. It's the exact same kind of control that prevails in your neighborhood markets. When a product isn't selling, the price is reduced. When it's selling briskly, the price tends to go up. When one shop offers better terms than a competitor, it gets the business.

But, of course, the price of silver depends upon much more than simply what happens in New York and London, in a pair of commodity exchanges, between 9.00 and 4.00 five days a week. The spot price is, in a way, a reflection of what has occurred in the silver market *in the world at large,* because this (not just the daily spot) also has a tremendous influence on investors and industrial buyers. And this is not a 9-to-4 matter, but continuous, 24 hours a day, international in scope.

Some of the things that have an ultimate influence on silver prices are as follows. All of these make themselves felt in the "spot" price, because they determine to some extent whether buyers will be optimistic or pessimistic, cautions or cavallier (or, to use the Wall Street term, bearish or bullish). How quickly they have an effect is never easy to predict; it is often a matter of how rapidly investors learn of these developments, and the various details surrounding each particular case. Nor can it be flatly stated that bad news about silver, or something that could be bad for silver, always hurts investors. This just isn't so. Sometimes it can have the exact opposite result. The spot price can be driven down somewhat for a while, which allows silver to be purchased at a bargain rate. Then, sooner or later, good news comes to supplant the bad news (or perhaps the bad news is discovered to have been just a rumor anyway), the spot price rebounds, and those who bought during the slump are handsomely rewarded.

1. Gold prices. Of everything that happens or could happen in the world — economically, politically, or in any other way — the price of gold has the most direct influence on the price of silver. So far as fractional advances and declines are concerned, silver does not always rise when gold rises, nor always when gold falls. In checking the day to day spot, you will notice that some days one is up while the other is down. But these are the days of slow trading. Whenever a sizable movement occurs in the price of gold, a corresponding move is sure to follow in silver, usually immediately. Since gold is more heavily invested in than silver in terms of total cash value, it may be said that gold pulls silver along with it, up or down. When silver achieved its record price of $50 per troy ounce in January, 1980, gold was — at the same time — also at its record level. When gold began declining from that peak, silver declined with it.

This is not a modern phenomenon but has been happening throughout history, long before spot prices or any of the other present-day accourtrements of bullion trading. To show how closely the price of these two metals has been aligned throughout the ages, it was 13½-to-1 in ancient Greece (gold was worth 13½ times as much as silver), and 15-to-1 in 1792 when our Mint was established, a change of only 10% in nearly 2,000 years. Very little further change occurred until the past 10-15 years, when gold and silver began to be freely traded on the world market — not backed by currency as they had traditionally been. You will probably recall the "Silver Certificates," or notes which could be turned in for silver dollars. They were known as demand notes: the government guaranteed to pay their stated value in bullion on demand. Today, currency notes are not redeemable for anything, except what can be bought for them in the marketplace.

2. Bad economic news, such as inflation increasing, interest rates going up, gross national product going down, etc. But often these have a positive rather than negative effect on the silver market. They tend to discourage purchase of the more traditional forms of investment, and some of this money is diverted into silver.

3. U.S. balance of payments falling further in the red. This is always *good* for the silver market. It encourages foreign holders of dollars to dispose of them, and invariably some percentage of this wealth is exchanged for silver bullion.

4. War or threat of war. Usually good for bullion investment.

5. Discovery of new silver mines. Initial reaction is generally negative from investors, as this means more silver coming on the world market and the natural assumption that prices will either fall or not rise as rapidly as they might have otherwise. But such speculation is unfounded. It would be

impossible to discover enough new silver mines, and to work them at minimal operation cost, to seriously affect the price of silver. Compared to the annual world production figures (more than 300 million ounces), new mines account for very little silver.

THE CRASH OF 1980

The story of silver from the late 1979 to early 1980 was one of a remarkable climb, far surpassing anything that the most optimistic analysts thought possible, followed by a resounding crash round the world.

In two months, the spot price of silver rose more than $30. Then, in a frantic two-week period of near-hysterical selling, it dropped $30.

There were those who predicted silver would hit $100 an ounce while it was climbing; it got half that far. There were others who felt it would totally bottom out when it was falling. It didn't.

And the silver market, though a little shaken, pulled through those two weeks of "spilled bullion" alive and fairly well. Since January, 1980, the market has firmed up admirably. No, silver isn't as high today as it was at its peak. But it's shown confidence-building strength, and a lot of investors who trembled at the mention of silver a year ago are now back in the market.

Sad to say, investors were largely to blame for upsetting the silver market. Not the ordinary cool-headed investors, but big-money operators who jumped in to get on the bandwagon. They poured millions into the market and drove prices up to vastly inflated levels, from which they had to fall. The sensible investor sees the dangers of this kind of action. He saw it in late 1979, but he was powerless to do anything about it. He was trampled by an army of financial goliaths.

At one point in December, 1979, the spot price of silver was jumping ahead by as much as *$5 per day.* Increases were so swift, and so hefty, that owners were able to sell, *at handsome profits,* silver they had just purchased a month earlier. Then, when wholesale profit-taking set in, prices fell back to saner levels.

Circumstances that caused the "rush" of late 1979 still prevail and in fact have grown more pronounced: there is *more* world inflation, *more* industrial demand for silver, *fewer* articles left to be melted to obtain bullion, and just as much investor lack of confidence in stocks and other traditional investments. But the silver market is looking particulary good these days, and nobody ought to be discouraged from silver investment because of the events of late 1979 and early 1980. Since then, well over a year ago, there have been no panics or runs on bullion. Silver has re-established its solidity as an investment by showing gradual but significant advances in price. It may well be on the threshhold of more substantial increases. If they occur in a more orderly fashion this time, without the influence of overnight profiteers and media madness, they may not be followed by a sharp readjustment.

Silver simply went up *too fast* in price in the second half of 1979, to levels that even ordinary buying and selling could not have supported over a long stretch of time. Had there been no profit-takers at all, the daily spot price would have still fallen (but slower, of course), until a level was reached that reflected the *true silver market.* We have, at present, such a level. We did not have it in December, 1979 or early January, 1980, because the people who normally control silver prices — industrial users, intelligent investors and the like — lost their grip on it, or rather had it wrenched away from them by big wheeler-dealers who gambled for quick profits.

When silver was around $50 per troy ounce in January, 1980, that kind of price could only have been maintained if scores of new investors kept getting into the market, on a daily basis, without anyone selling substantial amounts. The simple *leveling-off of investment buying,* regardless of whether any selling was occurring, would have been enough to drop prices. Silver suddenly became a hungry elephant that needed hundreds of pounds of food every day to keep his strength. Without the necessary food — investment dollars — his strength waned.

Some investors profited handsomely in the bullion spill. Others lost seriously. Everybody, even the new investor just starting out today, learned something.

TYPES OF SILVER

PURE SILVER (.999 FINE)

Pure silver is bullion with all, or nearly all, adhering mineral or other matter (generally known as waste matter) removed. This is done by refiners as the raw silver comes from the mines. In its freshly mined state, silver is very far from pure; it is normally fused with miscellaneous "rock junk." The refining process is costly and this is one reason, though not the principal one, why silver increases in price.

Pure silver is made into bars, ranging in weight from one ounce upward; 30 pound bars are the largest commonly produced. They carry a fineness marking, which will be .999 or .999 + . The fineness is never given as 1.000, which would stand for absolute purity, since it cannot be guaranteed that every last trace of adhering matter has been successfully removed. In addition they should carry the refiner's name and a statement of the weight.

Pure silver is rarely made into anything but bars, or ingots (small bars). It isn't sturdy enough for use in manufacturing. Coins made of pure silver would wear down rapidly in circulation. Even with the customary addition of 10% copper, silver coins do not stand up well in circulation. Pure silver could be employed in plating, where only a thin layer of bullion is overlaid on a basemetal core; but this is seldom done, since lightly alloyed silver has the same physical appearance in terms of sheen and brilliance and can be used more inexpensively.

The belief of some beginners, that antique silverware (plates, knives, spoons, etc.) is made of pure silver, is incorrect. All of these items, no matter how splendid or valuable or how old, are made from alloyed silver, usually sterling silver.

BRITANNIA SILVER (.9584 FINE)

This is an industry term for a very high grade of silver, the highest used in manufacturing. It is made in Great Britain and carries an impressed figure of Britannia, a goddess-like female who symbolizes the British Empire. Britannia silver is 95.84% pure, meaning it contains less than 4½% alloy. It is very soft — too soft for most uses but satisfactory for tableware. You will pay more for Britannia silver than for .999 + bars because of the surcharge for workmanship. It is therefore not attractive as a bullion investment. On the other hand, older Britannia ware found in secondhand shops is occasionally priced below the silver market, raising the possibility of quick profit-making. This happens because many proprietors of antiques and secondhand shops, especially in small towns, do not keep up on the spot price of silver or do not bother to weigh their merchandise (or both). They have items bought ages ago when silver was inexpensive, which they continue to offer at the original price or a slight advance.

STERLING SILVER (.925 FINE)

Sterling is the best-known grade of silver in manufacturing, but not the highest grade; its purity is slightly less than that of Britannia, which is 95.84% against 92.5% for sterling. This negligible difference cannot be detected by the naked eye, nor can the difference in weight. However, objects made of sterling are slightly less valuable *as bullion* than those of Britannia. Whether they are less valuable overall depends upon (as stated elsewhere) their merits as possible collectors' items or other circumstances.

Sterling is normally hallmarked and/or stamped "sterling," depending on the place of origin and prevailing regulations in that country. Occasionally the marking .925 is used.

Though sterling is identified with Great Britain, mainly because of the term "pound sterling" to denote the British currency, its manufacture is just about universal. Sterling is made from the Orient to America. While it naturally varies stylistically, the value of all this merchandise is identical *as bullion,* ounce for ounce.

Origin of the word sterling is doubtful. Its use in relation to silver is of great antiquity, going back to the Middle Ages. Apparently, "silver" and "sterling" were interchangeable words at one time. It may have arisen as a means of identifying silver used by smiths in the making of plate, etc., as opposed to the slightly inferior grade used by coiners.

COIN SILVER (.900 FINE)

A misleading term, because silver coins exist with varying proportions of silver content. Coin silver is taken to mean .900, or 90% silver against a 10% basemetal alloy, which nearly always is copper. It is thus a slightly lower grade than sterling and an appreciably lower grade than Britannia. Coin siver, when marked (which it frequently isn't), will usually carry the designation "coin silver" or ".900." Antique objects of coin silver are sometimes marked "DOLLAR" or "D," to indicate their manufacture from melted dollars. Most coin silver used in the U.S. is still obtained from melted coins, all the way from dollars down to pre-clad dimes. Coin silver is attractive for manufacturers to use because it required no refining; the coins used in producing it already have the necessary alloy and need only be melted. It is cheaper to do this, than to refine out the alloy and use silver from coins to make sterling or another higher grade. Since there is no government regulation against melting and reusing U.S. coins, the practice could conceivably continue until *all* silver coins that have no collector value are depleted. But it is unlikely that this could occur, since continued melting on a large scale would gradually render common coins scarce, and they would acquire a numismatic value over and above the bullion content. How low this might take to happen, at the present rate of absorbtion, is hard to forecast.

GERMAN SILVER

A low grade silver, composed chiefly of nickel and copper and containing a small amount of silver, or an exterior silver wash that accounts for perhaps 3% of the overall weight or less. As German Silver has been manufactured for more than 150 years, the composition has changed many times along the way. It first appeared as a material used in the making of novelties and souvenirs in Bavaria, sold at a very cheap price to tourists and to the import/export trade. The motive was to achieve a substance which could retain a high surface polish and bear the general appearance of silver, or at least sufficiently to be convincing to undiscriminating persons. By around 1850 the world market was being innundated with German Silver trinkets of all descriptions. Quite frequently dealers succeeded in leading customers to believe that they were good silver. After 1890, when the law was passed in the U.S. requiring all imported merchandise to be stamped, the designation "GERMAN SILVER" showed up on countless numbers of articles, as we were then importing more goods from Germany than from any other nation. Still, devious merchants were not discouraged. They now explained to customers that "German Silver" was a special kind of silver made only in Europe and very desirable; in this way they sometimes obtained higher prices for it than for sterling. The so-called Feuchtwanger Cent, proposed for use as a government coin and circulated to some extent as a token in 1837, was made of German Silver. It should not be supposed that the manufacture of German Sivler has been confined to Germany. It is now produced worldwide, and has been for many years. The common reference to it as "low grade" silver is misleading; it should more correctly be called "no grade."

SILVER PLATE

During the 19th century, silver plating began on a large scale. The technique was known earlier but not placed to extensive use. In earlier times, customers who could not afford such articles as silverplates, utensils, and other items settled for the same designs in pewter, which was just as sturdy and not bad-looking. Then, gradually, the social revolution of Europe during the late 1700's changed public buying habits. The middle classes wanted things that the upper classes owned, or as near to them as possible. If they could not have the exact same clothing, furniture, etc., they wanted facsimilies or imitations that could not easily be detected from the real thing. Manufacturers of silverware brought out plated ware, to satisfy the vast demand for silver by persons who could not afford it. The wealthy continued to buy fine silver but for the masses — who, as always, spent a total of considerably more money — plated ware served the purpose. It looked exactly like solid silverware, the difference being only in the weight; and even that was similar enough to deceive everyone but the most astute experts.

Silver plated objects are made of basemetal, to which an exterior of good silver is bonded (generally by electroplating). The bullion invariably accounts for less than 10% of the object's weight, sometimes much less. The layer applied is as thin as practical, to withstand normal wear and tear without the underlying metal showing through. Very frequently, however, the surface will wear down and "dark spots" will appear. If desired, such items can be replated, but are often less expensive and troublesome to simply replace.

Silver plated items are sometimes bought by scrap dealers. The price paid is very low, since the quantity of silver that will be obtained after refining is hard to precisely calculate without performing elaborate tests. Therefore the dealer pays a so-called "tolerance" price, meaning he pays for the lowest quantity of silver that the item could reasonably be expected to contain. He in turn receives a tolerance price from the refinery, and the refinery profits if the article proves to contain somewhat more silver than was paid for.

ALLOYS AND SILVER

Like the other precious metals, silver in its pure state (.999 or .999 +) is quite soft and unsuitable for use in art or industry, except in instances where ruggedness is not important. Where *electrical conductivity* is vital, as in circuitry, it is usually desirable not to alloy silver as this reduces its capacity to conduct electricity.

The degree to which silver is alloyed for manufacturing depends largely upon the type of items to be made from it. Durability, appearance, and price are the three chief considerations.

Whether used to a small or great degree in any given article, copper is the standard and universal alloy for silver — just as for gold. It alloys silver splendidly. When used in small ratios it does not materially effect the color or brilliance, and just a minimal quantity lends the necessary durability. Of course, the alloying process is important in itself and must be executed correctly to achieve proper results. Since silver and copper are of very different colors in their natural state, silver being white or grey-white and copper being dark brown or red, *streaking* is inevitable if the blending is not carefully carried out. The silver will show dark streaks or cloudy areas, where the copper has not totally mixed in. Alloying must be done when the ingredients are in absolutely liquid state, and the blending cannot be rushed. Before the modern age, this was done by workers who literally churned the mixture in the manner of cream.

Silver can, of course, be alloyed with metals other than copper. This is done occasionally but is rare in the modern world, as there seems no possibility of improving on the silver/copper combination excepting for an occasional special use. There is nothing to be gained, for example, in alloying silver with brass or bronze, which themselves are largely copper. This was often done in early times, because the foundries used whatever was at hand without really caring one way or another. This is why old coins, especially those of the Romans, are found in the same denomination made from various metals or combinations of metals.

If there is a desire to whiten the color, silver can be alloyed with nickel or zinc; but the resulting product is not (in the opinion of most) as handsome, nor does it consistently polish as well as silver alloyed with copper.

Naturally, the more alloy used, the lower the grade of silver. Britannia silver contains nearly 20 parts of silver for every part of alloy, and is therefore an extremely high grade (the highest used in manufacture). So-called coin silver is .900, which means nine parts silver to one part alloy. Even though the difference between coin silver and Britannia is just .900 to .958, Britannia is *more than twice as pure as coin silver.* This is because it contains less than half as much alloy.

The lowest grade of silver to carry a fineness is .800, which contains 80% silver and 20% alloy. At this point the silver begins taking on a darker color, which could, of course, be mistaken for oxidation or failure to polish it regularly. An experienced silver handler can tell the difference in weight, too, when this much alloy is employed, unless the item is very small.

The important point for the investor or seller of scrap silver to keep in mind is that *the alloy is worthless.* You will not be paid anything for the alloy, but only the quantity of .999 + silver that can be obtained in refining. Therefore, the more alloy in an article, the less its value as bullion in relation to its overall weight. True enough, the refineries obtain a great deal of copper as a result of melting down scrap silver, and you can be sure they dispose of it profitably; but this is not considered in the price when they buy scrap objects from suppliers.

TESTING SILVER

A good deal of silver is marked and in most cases can be used to determine the exact proportion of pure bullion vs. basemetal. In the case of unmarked articles, tests must be performed to discover this information.

The object in testing silver is to determine one or more of the following:

1. Whether the item contains any silver at all, or is simply an imitation such as German Silver, polished nickel, or some other substance that gives the appearance of silver (there are numerous combinations of metals that look more or less like silver, especially to the untrained eye).

2. If the object is silver plated — that is, coated with silver but containing a core of basemetal.

3. If solid silver, the grade or quality. The "grade" is the degree to which the silver it contains has been alloyed with basemetal. If heavily alloyed, the item may be worth very little inspite of being solid silver. "Solid silver" simply means that it isn't plated; it makes no representation of the fineness.

As a general rule it can be presumed that most, or nearly all, manufactured items intended for commercial sale are not of high grade silver unless marked. It is obviously to the maker's and seller's advantage to mark high-grade items, as this increases their appeal. The only instances in which markings may not occur on good silver are custom made items and, occasionally, antiques and objets d'art fashioned by persons who were not licensed smiths or guild members. Of course, coins are unmarked, but their content is a matter of record (if the specimen is genuine).

WEIGHTED ARTICLES. In addition to the possibility that silver articles may be plated, or contain a silver coating over a basemetal core, the likelihood of *weighting* must also be investigated. In the modern era, and even dating back to the 19th century, commerical manufacturers have been notorious for weighting silver goods to give them the "feel" of being solid silver, when in fact the silver content is quite low. For example the base of a candelabra may be filled with cement, plasticene, gravel bonded with glue, or other substances. The uninformed person, coming upon such an item, places it upon a scale, discovers it to weight 3 or 4 pounds, and believes he has a fortune in silver bullion. The actual melt value, when this stuffing is extracted, will generally amount to less than 1/20th the original weight. Of course the figure varies depending on weight of stuffing material, thickness of silver, type of article and other factors. In instances where the weighting material is totally hidden by the silver exterior, so that it cannot be observed even when the object is turned upside-down, testing by specific gravity will tell if the item is wholly silver.

Table utensils can likewise be deceiving. The handle may be marked and this leads to the conclusion that the whole piece is silver, but very often it has components which are not — such as stainless steel blades on knives.

NITRIC ACID. Nitric acid has traditionally been the popular method of testing silver. It reacts to basemetal differently than to silver. If a positive reaction is obtained, proof is given that the metal is either not silver or silver heavily alloyed. The nitric acid test should be run on any article suspected of being made of low grade silver, or plated in silver. It is important to conduct such testing carefully, as laxness can cause incorrect results.

Applying nitric acid to the surface will determine if the object is made wholly of low-grade silver or non-silver, but it does not provide proof of plating. A plated item tested on its surface will give the same reaction as one made entirely of silver because the acid reacts only on the outer layer. It does not "eat in." It is therefore logical to make both tests at once: for silver content and the possibility of plating.

This is easily done on most kinds of articles. A notch or groove must be filed into the surface, down to a depth of about 1/32nd of an inch. In the case of very large or heavy objects, such as punch bowls, where plating might be thick, a deeper notch is called for. The owner's consent must be obtained before doing this. If consent cannot be obtained, and only a surface test can be performed, the item must be regarded as plated. It can, however, be tested by specific gravity, which we'll get into, if you have the equipment to do this.

Choose an inconspicuous place for filing the notch, such as the underside of a plate or the inside of a watch case. If this isn't possible, the notch should at least be placed where it won't interefere with prominent portions of design. A drop of nitric acid is placed in the notch and determination of content will be made by the acid's change in color, which will occur very quickly.

If the object is made of high grade silver, such as sterling, the acid will merely turn a greyish color. In other words it will tone down the metal a bit-but not change its basic color. Should there be a high proportion of copper alloying, a green color will appear. Whenever green is obtained you are dealing either with low grade silver or an article made chiefly of copper with the addition of enough nickel or other metal to give an appearance of silver (usually 75% copper/25% nickel).

Be certain to remove the acid as soon as possible after obtaining results, by wiping with a clean cloth. It may cause pitting to the surface or permanent discoloration if this is not done.

Dichromate acid can also be used to test silver. This is a more sophisticated approach because the dichromate solution does not merely tell if the item is silver or non-silver; it indicates the presence of several other metals, depending upon the color to which the acid-treated region turns. But dichromate acid is somewhat more difficult to get. If you can't get it from a chemist or jewelry supply house, it can be prepared in the following manner. Use care in handling ingredients; the fumes are quite toxic and serious burns can result from dichromate acid coming into contact with the skin.

Dissolve an eighth of a teaspoon of potassium dichromate in a quarter ounce of nitric acid. Place the potassium dichromate into the nitric acid, not the other way around. This should be done in a small bottle, not a dish, to contain fumes as much as possible. Stir it around gently with a glass rod until it achieves a rich burgundy color. It is then ready for use. If not to be used immediately, the bottle ought to be tightly stoppered to keep it fresh. Dichromate acid deteriorates rapidly in contact with air. In fact it will deteriorate in a stoppered container but not as quickly.

The same testing procedure outlined above is used: filing a notch and applying a drop of solution. If the article is solid silver of a high grade, the resulting color will be bright red. When applied to an item containing a large proportion of copper, it turns green — just as does nitric acid alone. If the metal is lead, the color will be yellow. Pewter gives a black color.

BULLION CONTENT OF PLATED ITEMS. It is very difficult to calculate the bullion content in plated items because thickness of plating varies. The *average* plated article contains about 2% of its weight in silver and this figure can be used as a rough guide. You need therefore to weigh it, multiply the weight by .02, and the result will be approximately its weight in bullion — but it will not be exact and a scrap dealer will not pay you on the strength of this calculation. A table fork of plated silver, weighing two ounces, would have a silver content of about 1/5th of an ounce. Of course if the article has a bone handle or any non-metallic components this method becomes even less reliable.

SPECIFIC GRAVITY. The specific gravity method is a high reliable test for determining the nature of metals and mineral substances. Everyone who buys or intends to buy gold, silver, jewels and the like should become acquainted with it.

This is a very delicate test which, if not performed to exacting standards, will not yield correct results. On the other hand its accuracy when correctly carried out is far above that of almost all other testing techniques, including those using more costly equipment.

If one plans on trading commercially in silver, it would be wise to purchase a specific gravity testing device. Otherwise a homemade substitute can be used, whose reliability will be fairly close to that of professional models.

Specific gravity is the ratio at which a material displaces water in relation to its bulk. We all know that lead sinks while cork floats in water. This proves nothing except that some substances are lighter than others, which could be determined by weighing on an ordinary (avoirupois) scale. Specific gravity goes beyond the mere difference between sink-or-float. It gives the weight of an object in relation to its *exact* size, as water fully surrounds whatever is submerged in it. It therefore measures much better than rulers or calipers. As every object of the *same material* gives the same specific gravity reading, regardless of size, the specific gravity reading easily distinguishes between (for example) silver and copper, silver and nickel, or alloys of these metals. It also helps in identifying precious stones.

A useful specific gravity scale can be concocted from an ordinary pan scale that gives readings in grams. If it gives readings in larger measures than grams it isn't suitable. In other words you cannot use a postal scale or something of that nature. Remove the pan and tie a length of string, such as thin nylon, from the pan holder, at the extreme southeast corner as the scale faces you. The string must not be long enough to touch the desk on which the scale rests. A glass tumbler about 3/4ths filled with water is then placed beneath the string. It may be necessary to set the tumbler on a low platform to achieve the right height. It has to be positioned so that the item to be tested, when tied to the string and dropped into the glass, is fully submerged but *does not touch the bottom of the glass.* If it rests upon the bottom, or even touches lightly, the test is spoiled.

As the object dangles in the glass, a reading is taken of the weight indicated on the scale. This is called the "weight in water." It does not determine specific gravity but is the main step in arriving at the figure. To get the specific gravity, the object must then be weighed on the scale in the ordinary manner, or "in air." Subtract the weight in water from the weight in air (the latter will always be a higher number), then divide the weight in air by the *loss of weight in water.* The answer will be the item's specific gravity.

Example:
Weight in water, 27.10 grams
Weight in air, 30 grams
Loss of weight in water, 2.9 grams
2.9 divided into 30 (weight in air) = 10.34 (specific gravity of the item)

The item tested in this sample, with a specific gravity reading of 10.34, was .925 sterling silver.

Depending on the accuracy of your scale you will probably only be able to get very close approximations, rather than precise readings. In this example we got a specific gravity of 10.34 and called it .925 sterling silver. This is because 10.34 is the closest on the following table to our answer. As in all of these tests and formulas there is always "visual inspection" involved and in this case the item appeared to be .925 sterling silver, so the conclusion reached after testing was obvious. It also must be kept in mind that, even using advanced equipment, specific gravity readings can vary minutely on the same grade of silver or gold. This is because the alloy material is not always exactly the same. If bronze or brass is used as an alloy instead of pure copper, .925 sterling (or any other grade of silver) made from it will not have the exact same specific gravity reading as .925 alloyed with pure copper.

SPECIFIC GRAVITIES OF METALS

German silver 8.74
.999 Silver 10.50
.925 Sterling Silver 10.31

WEIGHING SILVER

The weight of silver may be stated in troy ounces, pennyweight, or by metric division. Troy is the most common and the most universally understood by jewelers and bullion dealers. The daily spot price of silver is always given by the troy ounce. Pennyweight is much more commonly used for gold than for silver, but is included here in the event you may need to make this calculation. The reason why pennyweight is applied to gold more than to silver is that it represents a very small measure of weight; silver, being much less valuable than gold, has little value by pennyweight.

The metric system, now becoming international, has not yet penetrated into the bullion market to a very major extent and probably will not do so for a number of years.

As statements of weight may be given in grains by one dealer, grams by another, and dwt (pennyweight) by a third, it is important that anyone buying or selling silver become familiar with the equivalents, and methods of changing one to another.

AVOIRDUPOIS WEIGHT. Like troy weight, the avoirdupois system also uses pounds and ounces, but these are not equal. Avoirdupois is the common method by which just about everything — except precious metals — is weighed. Bathroom scales are avoirdupois scales. Unlike troy scales, they may be equipped with springs.

PENNYWEIGHT. Abbreviated as DWT. ("D" stands for penny, in British coinage, and "WT" for weight.) The system of weighing by pennyweight originated with English merchants of the distant past, who used pennies as counterweights on their scales. The U.S. penny weighs two pennyweight, equal to 48 grains. So it is readily apparent that pennyweight is an extremely small measure. A pennyweight is considerably less than one full ounce. But this is a useful method of weighing.

TROY WEIGHT. This is a standard system by which weights of precious metals are given all over the world. Its basic unit is the grain. Scales (using balances, not springs) for weighing items in troy measure can be had and are usually referred to as jewelers' or gemologists' scales.

WEIGHTS AND MEASURES
APOTHECARIES' WEIGHT

one grain	=	.01666 dram
20 grains	=	.33 dram
60 grains	=	one dram
480 grains	=	one apothecary ounce (8 drams)

AVOIRDUOIS WEIGHT

.0625 ounce	=	1.7719 grams
one ounce	=	28.350 grams
16 ounces	=	one pound (453.59 grams)

TROY WEIGHT.

one grain	=	.0416666 pennyweight or .648 grams
24 grains	=	one pennyweight
480 grains	=	20 pennyweights, or one troy ounce
5760 grains	=	240 pennyweights, or 12 troy ounces, or one troy pound

FORMULAS OF COVERSIONS

To change . . .
grams to pennyweights, mulitply grams by .643
pennyweights to grams, multiply pennyweights by 1.555
grams to troy ounces, multiply grams by .032
troy ounces to grams, multiply troy ounces by 31.103
pennyweights to troy ounces, divide pennyweights by 20
troy ounces to pennyweights, multiply troy ounces by 20
grains to grams, multiply grains by .0648

grams to grains, multiply grams by 15.432
avoirdupois ounces to troy ounces, multiply avoirdupois ounces by .912
troy ounces to avoirdupois. multiply troy ounces by 1.097
avoirdupois ounces to grams, multiply avoirdupois by 28.35.
grams to avoirdupois ounces, multiply grams by .035
avoirdupois pounds to kilograms, multiply avoirdupois pounds by .454
kilograms to avoirdupois pounds, multiply kilograms by 2.205
avoirdupois pounds to grains, multiply avoirdupois pounds by 7000
grains to avoirdupois pounds, multiply grains by .00014

HOW MUCH IS IT WORTH?

The value of silver bullion in any given article of silver is somewhat easier to calculate than gold, so long as the fineness is known, since silver prices are nearly always expressed by the troy ounce. This is different than with gold, where ounces are used along with pennyweights and grains. These lesser measures are not very useful with silver because of its lower value.

The daily spot price of silver is always stated in troy ounces (like the daily spot price of gold). Dealers buy and sell silver by the troy ounce. Even when more than a pound is involved, the weight in invariably expressed in troy ounces. Therefore, you need only know the weight and fineness of a silver object, and perform some simple mathematics, to arrive at the "melt value" at any given spot price.

The daily spot price is quoted for one ounce of .999 fine. If you have bars or ingots of .999 or .999 + fine, their value is obvious. You merely multiply the spot price on that day by the number of ounces in your bars or ingots. Of course, when selling you will not receive that sum, as the broker or dealer deducts a percentage of commission. With silver the percentage margin tends to be larger than with gold.

Spot price of $15 per troy ounce.
six .999 silver bars weighing 1 oz. each = 6 ounces
six X $15 = $490.00 (melt value)

If your silver is not .999 fine, it is naturally worth less than spot, but the difference in value is extremely slight if you have fine quality ware such as Britannia or sterling. Britannia is .958 and sterling .925. Since *coin silver* is .900 fine, the calculations for it are very simple — you need only deduct 10% from the weight and then multiply the resulting figure by "spot." Technically, the answer will not be precise, since the 10% of alloy (copper, usually) does not comprise exactly 10% of the weight. This is because silver and copper have slightly different weights. it is, nevertheless, accurate enough for buying and selling purposes.

Before any price calculations can be attempted, it is necessary to learn:
1. How much the article weighs, in ounces
2. What the fineness is

Good quality silver, .800 fine and over, will usually carry a marking, stamped on some inconspicuous part of its surface. If there appears to be no marking, study it closer to be certain you have not overlooked it. The marking could be extremely small — so small that a person with sub-par vision might need a magnifier to find it. Or it could be partially or totally hidden by grime, if the item has not been thoroughly cleaned. If the marking is not in numbers and/or letters, but a decorative symbol, it is probably a foreign hallmark or touchmark and suggests that the piece may be very old. As the variety of markings that can be encountered are numerous, and often very similar but with different meanings, the aid of a book on hallmarks or an expert will be needed. *Generally,* though not invariably, hallmarked silver that does not state the fineness is .925. Many dealers will buy it at .925 even if further evidence is lacking. This grade is known as "sterling."

It may be easier to understand fineness and value in the following way. Silver which has been alloyed is like a beverage into which water is added. A few drops of water and little or no difference is noticed in the taste; but as more and more is added, the beverage grows weaker. So it is with silver. The more alloy that is added, the more reduction in quality or fineness.

If you have silver which is *not marked,* tests outlined in the chapter on testing will determine whether the object contains any silver and will provide an approximate indication of the fineness. Generally speaking, though, you are likely to have a difficult time selling silver which is not marked, as many dealers prefer not to handle it. Antique items are another matter.

Once the fineness is known, the weight must be determined to calculate the article's melt value.

This can be done very easily be weighing it on any scale that gives readings in troy ounces, or on an avoirdupois scale and then converting the weight into troy ounces. To change avoirdupois ounces to troy ounces, the avoirdupois ounces are multipled by .912 (For additional conversions, see the section on "Methods of Weighing Silver.")

You now have a fineness reading plus a weight. The next step is to multiply the *fineness* by the *weight,* which will tell you the amount of .999 silver the object contains.

For example:
Tray made of coin silver, .900 fine, weighs 5 troy ounces
5 X .900 = 4.500, or 4½ troy ounces of .999 fine

You then multiply the *spot price* by this figure to arrive at the melt value:
Spot price of $15 per troy ounce
$15 X 4½ = $67.50 melt value

Now remember, when you sell to a dealer he will be buying at a discount, usually 10% to 25%. This discount is fair because, as when buying gold, the dealer must recover refining costs, pay freight or postage to the refinery, and leave himself a reasonable profit.

So, keeping this in mind, you should be able to sell your .900 silver tray to a dealer for roughly $50 to $60. This should be a fair transaction for both parties. If the offer you get is substantially lower, you ought to definitely shop around and get another dealer's price.

PRICING CONSIDERATIONS

The worth of a particular piece of silver or silver plate is determined by some combination of the following factors:

AGE

As will immediately be obvious from reading the price section, in many instances a newer, machine-produced item will be worth much more than the early hand-wrought piece of silver. While of course there are some absolutely priceless samples of early American silver, the buying public has taken a liking to ornate Victorian silver and is willing to pay more for it than for plain coin silver of an earlier age.

APPEAL

An item can be old, beautiful, well-made, and in excellent condition and still not command top dollar simply because the buying public does not take an interest in it. Right now, ornate is in. The plain (with the exception of Art Deco items) is out, and this is very much reflected in the prices. *De gustibus non est disputandum.*

AUTHENTICITY

The ease with which an item can be identified and verified has some bearing on its value, and an item which is questionable in any way is probably not a very good investment. The best approach is for collectors to assume that every item they see is a misrepresentation of one sort or another and then to "prove" to themselves that the item is legitimate.

The would-be collector must study the topic both by reading everything he/she can and by handling as much old silver as possible. Armed with facts, figures, and a "feel" for silver, the collector will hopefully be able to avoid making major mistakes.

AVAILABILITY

Any item which is readily available tends to become commonplace in the eyes of collectors and this is usually reflected in its value. It must be pointed out, however, that there is a difference between rare and obscure. Ideally, an item should be scarce enough to make the chase interesting and available enough to give the collector occasional gratification.

CONDITION

The condition of sterling and silver-plated items is of importance in determining their value. Items which are unusable or unsightly just do not command the same prices as perfect ones. When purchasing less then perfect items, mentally add in the cost of the repair. It is frequently the case that the "bargain" will turn out to be not such a bargain after all. Badly-damaged newer sterling usually ends up in the melting pot, and all sterling items listed in this book were in good condition unless otherwise stated. Silver-plated items vary considerably, so the condition of each item is listed along with its price. The following categories were used:

Mint — the item looks like it just left the store.

Excellent — the item shows no wearing-off of the silver or other damage, but the finish is not quite as perfect as on a mint item.

Good — the item shows perhaps a tiny wear spot on the heel, the finish is somewhat dulled, but otherwise the item is still attractive.

Fair — the item shows quite a bit of wear and tear but is still in usable condition.

Poor — the item is missing most of its silver and/or is damaged to the point where it is not usable without replating and/or repairs.

There are very few listings for items in poor condition, since most of it ends up in the garbage. Items in fair condition are recommended only if they are desperately needed to complete a set.

Most types of damage can be repaired, but there is always the question of whether a particular repair will exceed the value of the item. The decision to repair or not to repair is always an individual one usually based on one or all of the following considerations:

(a) Restored items are never worth quite as much as those in original condition.

(b) Unusable items are no fun, and in certain cases (e.g., loose teapot handles) can be dangerous.

(c) Repairs take time, sometimes months.

(d) Repairs can be expensive, and as already mentioned can sometimes exceed the value of the item.

(e) The item can be lost in the mail or by the repairer.

(f) On certain types of repairs worse damage may result (e.g., soldering a split may cause a larger, harder-to-fix split elsewhere on the item).

Many repairs, such as small soldering jobs, can be handled at the local jewelry store. Larger, more difficult jobs should be sent to someone who specializes in silver repairs. Fine antique silver should only be given to a craftsperson who understands and appreciates it since others tend, at the very least, to buff the living daylights out of items.

Some of the more common repairs include:

Dents—Many dents can be successfully smoothed out, but prices will vary greatly depending on how large the dent is and its accessibility. For example, a dent in the handle of a teapot would be harder to fix than one on a flat item.

Ivory or Wood Replacements—Loose or worn ivory and wood parts can be replaced in most instances, either by cannibalizing good parts from another set or with new parts. New ivory gives a peculiar look to antique items, and if at all possible yellowed ivory should be replaced with more yellowed ivory. The same is true of wooden handles — a rosewood handle should be replaced by more rosewood.

Loose or Worn Blades—The blades of most hollow-handled items are merely cemented in place, so resetting them when they come loose presents no major challenge. Some older pieces of silver, however, will have a small pin helping to hold the blade and if this is the case the pin must be removed before the blade can be re-cemented. Figure on paying no less than $12 for the simple type of operation. Since blades are so readily removed, it makes it easy to replace worn or damaged blades or to switch dinner knives to cake servers and the like. This is especially important for people who have the newer patterns which never had the wide range of items the earlier patterns had. A new dinner knife blade replacement would be no less than $30.

Missing Pieces—Replacing a missing sugar bowl lid or similar item is costly and is probably only worthwhile for very expensive items. Keep in mind that the replacement part will be held against it when the item is sold. The replacement of a missing foot to a small mustard pot recently cost $40.

Monogram Removal—A huge percentage of the available older silver bears a monogram, partly because it was once the custom for jewelry stores to offer free engraving with the purchase of silver. Some types of patterns are much likelier than others to have monograms, and collectors for whom monograms are anathema are well-advised to avoid them. (For example, Durgin "Chrysanthemum" practically screams for a monogram, while Durgin "Medallion" has no spot for a monogram on the handle.) Monogram removals can be done, although results vary considerably depending on the skill of the silversmith, the size and depth of the engraving, and the type of pattern. The removal will leave a depression in the silver, and how large a depression is left depends on how deep the monogram went. On ornate patterns, some of the design will almost invariably be taken off along with the monogram. Filling in monograms with silver solder frequently leaves a "ghost" or faint outline of the engraving. Since the solder is less pure than the sterling, the two metals will tarnish at different rates and the ghost may be very visible at times. Some monograms can be altered, e.g., the letter "P" made over into an "R" or "B". Prices quoted for one-letter monogram removal ranged from $3 to $10 depending on the type of pattern. As a rule, items which have never been monogrammed are worth the most, however an item with its monogram left on is worth more than one with a botched-up removal. In general terms, it is probably best to leave a monogram alone and make up an interesting story about how the item belonged to a great-great aunt who went down with the Titanic. The cost of engraving is rising sharply, and in years to come the monograms may well be considered as valuable additions to the items.

Refinishing—Contact with various substances will sometimes ruin the surface of an item, and refinishing may be the only solution to the problem. On antique items, however, this will remove the patina so it is a toss-up as to which would be worse, the corrosion or the lack of patina. Do not let anyone but an antiques expert work on such an item. On all items, new and old, some detailing may be lost in the refinishing process. Costs of refinishing will vary considerably.

Resilvering—Silver-plated items which have base metal showing through can be resilvered, but it must be remembered that there is a bias against resilvered antique items. Most people think that Sheffield plate should never be resilvered while other types of silver-plated items are not quite so sacrosanct. The theory is that since resilvering is an electrolytic process, any item which was originally silvered in that fashion can also be resilvered that way. Be wary of using worn plated items if copper is showing through since the copper can react with certain foods to produce disastrous results. (Remember that copper cookware is always lined with tin.) Other metals can impart a disagreealbe flavor to food or beverages. My personal opinion is that worn plated ware is ugly and I would not hesitate to have it replated.

Soldering—Repairing minor damage by soldering is usually not prohibitively expensive and if done well will not be too noticeable. Hollow-handled items must have their blades removed before soldering or else the heat build-up inside the handle will cause further damage.

Wear—Spoon bowls and fork tines will sometimes be worn on one side, usually the left since most people were right-handed. (Think of stirring a cup of tea — it isn't done with the top of the spoon but the spoon held a little to one side.) The other side of the item can usually be ground down to make the piece even, but keep in mind that the overall dimensions of the item will change. Badly worn forks must be evened up to make them usable.

MAKER

The reputation of a particular silver manufacturer can have a great effect on the value of their items. Down through the years, some companies simply had higher standards than others regarding design, quality control, etc. The net result to today's collectors is that they are going to have to pay more for Company A's products than for Company B's. It should become obvious after reading through the price section which companies are more highly prized than the others, so no attempt will be made here to rate them. The decision whether or not to invest the extra money in Company A's products rather than Company B's is an individual one. In general, if there is only a slight differential in price it is probably best to go for Company A because if it becomes necessary to sell a collection Company A's products will probably be easier to unload.

SILVERSMITHS' MARKS

The collector of American silver has one distinct advantage over those whose interests run to foreign wares: nearly all pieces of American silverware are stamped with their maker's name. This is not the case with a great deal of foreign ware, where the traditional practice was to use a combination of symbols rather than an actual name.

As silverware has been produced in this country for more than 300 years, the number of makers involved is well beyond the scope of a book such as this, which is essentially a price guide. In this chapter we have provided information on some of the more prominent manufacturers and their marks. The reader interested in doing research on this vast subject will find a wealth of material available at his public library. Still it must be pointed out that no single book is complete in this respect, and that a mark unrecorded by one author could well be identified by another. The number of totally unrecorded marks, not mentioned in any books of reference, is very small, as American silver has been a subject of investigation by museums and historians for many years.

A few words need to be said, by way of introduction to this subject for the inexperienced.

A study and knowledge of marks is of course important for the collector. But the question arises: what real effect does the mark have upon the item's value? Is the study of marks merely an aid to identification and dating, or does it possibly help in finding "sleepers" or "bargains"? This is more complex than it looks at first glance. Generally speaking, American silverware is not collected by maker. That is, few collectors set out to find specimens from the hands of certain smiths. It would be an extremely advanced hobbyist who collects in this fashion. Basically, the older antique pieces are valued and collected chiefly on merit of their age, artistry, and unusualness. Compared against these points, the name stamped upon them counts somewhat less in the price. There are, however, exceptions. If the silversmith has acquired great fame and a large collector following, such as the Reveres (father and son) of Boston, a premium is automatically placed on their creations. Any item marked REVERE — if substantiated to be authentic — will sell for two, three, or more times the value it would carry with another mark. Not many silversmiths are in that category, though, or even approaching to it. Even those whose skills were just as noteworthy as the Reveres are not usually in the "premium" class: their works are valued on individual merits, and the name itself counts for little or nothing. In the case of VERY EARLY smiths, their objects normally do carry a premium value, but this is owing more to the age than to the origin.

The only other instance in which a premium is placed on the mark is that of rare marks. Some marks are understandably much scarcer than others of their time-period, owing to various circumstances. If a mark has been recorded on just a handful of pieces, several of which are in museums and not available to the market, this provides some extra sales appeal — collectors (of all objects) are always intrigues by rarity. Nevertheless, the influence of rarity on silverware is not so potent as in many other hobbies, especially where the mark is concerned. The rarity of an OBJECT attracts much more notice than the rarity of a MARK. If, for example, some novelty article made in the 17th century turned up, of a type not generally manufactured until much later, it would command a strong price. Collectors would be more eager to buy it, than a conventional item carrying a scarce or rare mark. Why should it be is a matter of collector psychology. From the earliest days of its appeal as collectors' items, silverware's chief attraction has been physical — the quality of its manufacture. This is, perhaps, because silver IS very physical and boldly reflects the talent — or lack of talent — of its creator. The abstract considerations of a stamp or book collector, as to rarity and other points, thus have a harder time making inroads into the world of silverware. Most buyers of silverware, even the antique wares of great age, want first of all to display it just as the museums do. If the object is not physically appealing, it has at once a damaging strike against it, even though it may be historically interesting or scarce. A smaller proportion of collectors (though, it must be admitted, their ranks are swelling gradually) take a historical viewpoint, and will buy a plain or even downright badly-made article for its "background." But there are extremely few who seek out the works of particular makers, and stand ready to give a premium price for them.

Premiums for the mark can occur for regional factors. In this case, the premium (which seldom is very high, in terms of what the piece would otherwise be expected to fetch) is placed more on geographical considerations than on the maker. It has long been the case that *antique silverware* sells a bit higher in the region of its origin, than in other parts of the country: New England items sell stronger in New England, etc. But even this is not invariably the case, because in some parts of the country the collecting fervor is not as potent as in others.

Another instance of *premium for the mark* is a piece made by one of the earliest (or THE earliest) smiths in a given locality. Just as in "first editions," collectors are attracted to the works of a pioneer smith, and may willingly give an added 20% or 30% (or more) for his productions. To fall under this heading, a piece needs to be no later than the 18th century, and it must be established beyond reasonable doubt that its manufacturer was among the first silversmith in his town, country, or colony.

Never forget that silverware collectors are aesthetics. In judging value and desirability, they invariably look on the aesthetic side of the question. This is why scarcity in itself often counts for nothing, and why the hopeful seller of a scarce item is likely to be disappointed in its price. Even if you can show that a particular manufacturer was at work only six months, and that only 10 or 12 examples of his handicraft exist, you may find that prospective buyers react cooly to the item. A buyer will probably exclaim, "That maker worked only six months because he was unskilled and could not sell his products — it is therefore not a desirable piece." And, when you think about it, this line of reasoning makes some sense. Not everyone who got into silversmithing had a magic touch. Some apprentices who graduated and went off on their own simply could not make the grade. They disappeared from the trade and left little impact upon it. Why should their works deserve a better price today, than those of the smiths who were admired and patronized? This is certainly not the case in *oil painting*. Most of the Old Masters — Titian, Rembrandt, Vandyke — left behind hundreds of canvases, which are by no stretch "scarce." Yet they sell for much higher prices than the works of less celebrated artists, whose pictures might be considerably scarcer.

Unmarked pieces. Though well in the minority (thankfully), unmarked pices of American silverware will be found. Unmarked items exist from all the age groups, and of all geographical locales. Sometimes they can be attributed, even if not with strong confidence, on the basis of style. Most times they cannot be attributed, and there is nothing to be done about it. *A fairly* confident attribution is possible when the unmarked piece precisely matches a marked piece in a museum or other published collection. Even in this situation, the certainty is well short of 100%, as it was *common* for one marker to use another's products as his models and copy them inch by inch. The question then arises: why did some manufacturers fail to mark their wares? This could be the result of various factors, which the collector and historian can do no better than to guess about. An obvious motive for failure to mark products would have been the concealment of its origin, to avoid payment of taxes or perhaps keep secret an illegal source of silver bullion. Also, if an object was not of standard fineness (which, in the pre-1850 "antique" era, meant coin silver or .900), it was certainly to the smith's disadvantage to advertise himself upon it. The possibility of an unmarked item being of BELOW STANDARD FINENESS must always be considered, though the effect on value, in the case of non-bullion antique specimens, would not likely be very great. When variations are encountered from the standard .900 fineness, they will not be extreme, unless the item is an actual fake. The original buyers were not so unknowing about silver that gross frauds could be perpetrated on them.

Letting alone devious reasons for failing for mark their wares, there is yet another possibility, a much more comforting one to the collector. it is entirely conceivable that many unmarked antique pieces represent apprentice efforts, made by student smiths — who normally were apprenticed at age 13 and stayed under the master's wing 7 or 8 years. Mostly the apprentice was a helper, who looked after the furnace, brought in supplies, and swept out the shop. But at the same time he was learning the trade, and this required him to fashion some works of his own along the way. If the master considered his works worthy of the shop, he could impress them with his name. But certainly there must have been numerous cases of amateurish work done by apprentices, to which the master did not care placing his name — and of course the apprentice had no mark of his own to use. If the thing was grossly bad, it could be thrown back for melting. But if it was salable at all, the master was probably in the habit of selling it unmarked, possibly through an agent or street peddlers. There is good evidence to back this contention, as a very large number of unmarked antique silver items are rather sub-standard in quality. If the maker was in the practice of charging triple bullion value for his products, he could get away (presumably) charging double bullion value for these not-quite-brilliant apprentice jobs. It was more profitable than merely reusing the silver, which gained him nothing. And since the apprentice received no salary or other payment, aside from room and board, anything obtained over and above the bullion value was profit.

When an item of antique silverware is unmarked, the possibility also exists that its mark has been removed — which a careful examination will usually reveal, though a strong lens may be necessary. The reason for removing a mark could have been an attempt to sell a foreign-made object as American.

Counterfeit Marks. These do of course exist, as it should be unnecessary to state. Faking and counterfeiting has made inroads into every sphere of art, and silverware has not escaped. Compared to many groups of hobby items, the degree of counterfeiting in silver marks is not by any means excessive. This is largely because the counterfeiter, of today or yesterday, is limited in the value he can add to a piece by applying a false mark. Still, we would strong caution readers not to become complacent on this matter, since anyone actively collecting antique silverware is almost certain to encounter fake marks occasionally.

Most fake marks are in the nature of celebrated makers' names applied to pieces which they did not create. The Revere mark has unquestionably been faked more often than that of other American silversmith, as this is the faker's chance — his only real chance — of turning a $100 item into one salable for thousands. Revere's marks has been counterfeited for generations, long before the present enthusiasm for silver and silver-investing. The dealers see "bad" Reveres (their word for fake marks) frequently, and do their best to keep them off the market. If all pieces marked Revere were authentic, the Reveres would have needed to work 24 hour days, and lived to be advanced centenarians, to produce so much silver. Faked marks of other manufacturers are much less common, because they offer very little profit potential to the counterfeiter.

To make a faked mark more convincing, the counterfeiter will often embellish the piece with an inscription, in which the maker's name is repeated. He may disguise the item as a presentation gift from the manufacturer. This has been done repeatedly with Revere. Many silver bowls, trays, etc., have turned up, inscribed as gifts from Revere to George Washington or other notables of the time. This not only lends more support to the faked mark, it gives the object an "association" interest and would qualify it for an extremely high price — if it was genuine. Authentic works of this nature, inscribed from the manufacturer, are very unusual. When any such piece is located, it should be regarded with caution until examined by a competent expert. When this is not possible — when, for example, the item appears at a flea market or small auction — we would urge readers to clamp a tight control on their temptation to buy it.

Faked marks are sometimes easy to distinguish, sometimes not. There is no general rule — but the mere experienced the observer, the higher ratio of success he will have. *Old* faked marks are generally harder to detect than those applied recently, as the marked area has built up a surface patina similar or identical to that of the piece as a whole. In a piece which has only recently been struck with a fake mark, the marked area is apt to look different in coloration or toning than the area surrounding it. It will have a freshness and almost a gleam, as the area has not been subjected to the wear and polishing received by the adjacent surface. It may be necessary to use a magnifying lens to notice this. Of course, any thinking faker tries to cover his tracks as much as possible, and treats his faked marks to give them an aged look. When this has been skillfully done, it becomes almost impossible to detect by simple visual examination.

Variations in marks. There has never been any standard prevailing formula for silver trademarks in this country. Thus the study of marks, though fascinating to the devotee of antique silver and especially to the historian, is a field strewn with brambles and traps. Some smiths spelled out their entire names, both Christian and surname, and added their address as a part of their mark. With the passage of time this became a very prevalent approach, especially as 19th century makers often distributed their wares nationwide and were anxious that they be properly identified. But in earlier times only a handful of the smiths took pains to use such descriptive marks. Despite our regret that this was not done, we can readily understand the reasons. The 17th and 18th century silversmith was not manufacturing for the benefit of 20th century collectors. He knew nothing about silver collecting, or investing, or the headaches of today's historians. If an early silversmith was operating in a village where no competitor was active, and intended to sell his wares locally, there was hardly much motive to use an elaborate or descriptive mark. Everyone who bought his merchandise would know where it came from — and where to go if they wanted more. Thus, we find numerous colonial smiths using marks consisting of their surname only; or an abbreviation of the surname; or (worse, for us) initial letters. Even a simple initial letter suited their purpose, but it falls well short of suiting the silver researcher's.

The task of connecting these brief and often confusing marks to the smiths who used them has been — and continues to be — a detective feat of which .007 could take pride. Today, in the 1980's, the vast majority of recorded marks have been identified beyond all shadow of doubt. This has been accomplished not so much by study of the objects themselves, but by searching through early town and county directories, newspaper advertisements and the like. Very fortunately, most silversmiths advertised SOMEWHERE, and the advertisement (when it can be found) gives not only the full name but the place of business, and additionally it shows when the individual was active. In the case of smiths who did not advertise, or whose advertisements have escaped attention, information may exist in the form of invoices, letters, ledger books or miscellaneous. Historians have done miraculous work, piecing together facts on the most fragile data. But the task is not complete, and what has been thus far accomplished is not necessarily without error.

Retailers' Marks. The majority of early American silversmiths up to about 1850 were both manufacturers and retailers. Their shops included (in the European tradition) a working area, sealed off from the public, and an outer gallery or sales office in which the output was sold. As transportation improved, and especially after the laying of rail lines to connect major cities, many silversmiths not only sold direct to the public but wholesaled their wares to dealers. Usually in these cases the wholesaled items would be marked in the same fashion as those sold in the smith's shop, but the retailer might impress his own mark upon them — or the smith would impress it, on every piece intended for delivery to him. Thus these pieces carry both a manfacturer's mark and a retailer's mark. They may appear separately and unconnected, or a legend may accompany them such as SMITH, MADE FOR JONES.

For a fuller understanding of marks, please refer to our section of PSEUDO-HALLMARKS.

ABBOT, JOHN

John Abbot (1790-1850) worked at Portsmouth, New Hampshire, on the Maine border. He entered business at age 27 in 1817, taking over the established shop of Robert Gray. In addition to making silver and gold wares, Abbot sold fancy goods of various types and also did repair work. He was apparently active up to the time of his death at age 60 in 1850. At least three distinct varieties of Abbot's mark are known, in two of which the name appears as J. ABBOT and in the third as J. W. ABBOTT. Lettering is raised, in block characters against a rectangular frame, which may be lightly scalloped.

ADAM, JOHN JR.

John Adam, Jr., of Alexandria, Virginia, was the son of a silversmith. Researches into his life and work have been complicated by the fact that his father was likewise named John Adam, and that the son's name was not identified as "junior." Therefore the products of one are frequently mistaken for those of the other. We know that the younger John Adam was born in 1780. He was almost certainly apprenticed to his father, and probably started in business around 1800. The last dated mention of him occurs in 1846; no obituary notices have been traced, and we are uninformed of the year of his death. It is known, however, that he was still in the business in 1846, which gave him a career spanning c. 46 years. The usual mark is I.ADAM closely compressed, with raised lettering set in a narrow rectangle. The letter I was used to represent his name, John, rather than J, to conform with classical tradition (the Roman alphabet had no letter J — thus Julius Caesar was really Iulius). A period followed the name.

AITKEN, JOHN

Not much is known of the life of this federal-era Philadelphia manufacturer. The year of his birth is uncertain. We do know however that he was apprenticed in 1771 to a Philadelphia goldsmith. As the normal age of commencement for apprenticeship was 13, it can be estimated that he was born in or about 1758. The first notice of Aitken working independently occurs in 1785, when he was operating as a jack-of-all-trades in selling and repairing clocks, watches, and musical instruments — in addition to goldsmithing and silversmithing. His last recorded notice is dated 1814, at which time he would have been c. 56 years of age. Aitken's usual mark consists of I. AITKEN (Roman form of the letter J), in thin block capitals in which the serifs of the K and E are joined.

ALEXANDER, SAMUEL

Samuel Alexander worked as goldsmith, silversmith and jeweler in Philadelphia from the late 18th to early 19th centuries. he advertised frequently and his activities can be rather well traced from these ads, but we are not aware of the dates of his birth and death. In 1797 he was in partnership with another Philadelphia smith, a German named Christian Wiltberger. By 1800 he had gone into a new partnership, with Anthony Simmons, and this lasted for several years. In 1805 or possibly earlier he opened his own establishment, and for a number of years operated as a silversmith. Thereafter he seems to have abandoned smithing, and kept his shop strictly for the purpose of retailing wares made by others, and possibly also for repair and engraving work. The final notice of Samuel Alexander occurs in 1814. His common mark is S ALEXANDER (no period after the initial) within a plain rectangle.

ALSTYNE, JEROME

A not-very-prolific maker, Jerome Alstyne's real Christian name was Jeronimus or (in the correct European spelling) Hieronymus. He worked in New York City in the late 18th century and possibly the early 19th century, but no references to him dated later than 1797 are recorded. He was a goldsmith and silversmith, of Dutch ancestry. The name sometimes appears in advertisements as Allstyne (with two 1's), but in his mark always as Alstyne. his usual type of mark is J ALSTYNE in script letters, within a wavy frame whose contour matches that of the script. The earliest reference to Jerome Alstyne as a shop proprietor occurs in 1787, so we know that his career spanned at least one full decade.

ANDREWS, JEREMIAH

Jeremiah Andrews did far more moving about than most silversmiths of his time. His long career spanned from at least 1774, when the first notice of him appears, until after 1800, during which time he worked at New York City; Philadelphia; Augusta, Georgia; Savannah, Georgia; and finally at Norfolk, Virginia. Andrews' first recorded advertisement announces him as a jeweler *from London.* Presumably he found the New York trade crowded, and started his travels south in search of more fertile ground. Though he kept to no address very long, Andrews became a prominent and apparently a wealthy citizen. The final notice of him in business occurs in Norfolk, Virginia, in 1803, but whether this was actually his year of retirement is doubtful. He died in 1817. Andrews used various marks, the most common of which is J ANDREWS in roughly worked block letters, against a shaped rectangular frame. When working at Norfolk, he stamped the city's name on his wares, but does not seem to have ever done this in his other places of business.

ARNOLD, THOMAS

This long-lived smith spent his entire career in Newport, Rhode Island, from the second half of the 18th century to the earlier 19th century. Though Newport was not at that time a "millionaire's summer resort," as it became following the Civil War, it was a well-to-do town with ample market for silver. Arnold was born in 1739. His year of entrance into the trade is not established. The first notice of him appears in 1760. He died in 1828, aged 89, and was still in business by 1817 (aged 78), but at that point he was probably only retailing the works of other silversmiths along with general merchandise. Arnold is known to have done work for the Trinity Church in Newport. He used an unusual type of mark, which was really two marks in combination: one tool carried his initials TA in script, the other his surname ARNOLD in bold narrow block capitals. These he placed together on most of his wares, though the spacing varied; on a spoon stem, for example, the TA might occur near the terminal, while ARNOLD was halfway down or close to the bowl. No conclusive explanation can be given for his use of name plus initials. Possibly he started out using ARNOLD, then added the decorative initials for a more eye-catching appearance.

AUSTIN, JOSIAH

This 18th century Massachusetts smith was related to, and associated with, a number of others in the same profession. Born in 1719, he worked first at Charlestown and later at Boston, where the final printed reference to him appears in 1770. The year of his death is not established; it is possible he was still active at the Revolution. Austin used a number of marks, which differed considerably one from another. Among them was I.AUSTIN in gothic lettering, in which the S was shown as an F. Sometimes Austin stamped himself as J.AUSTIN, abondoning the formal or Roman style of initial for his Christian name. There are pieces of his marked simply I.A.

AYRES, SAMUEL

Samuel Ayers worked at Lexington and Danville, Kentucy, in the late 18th and early 19th centuries. Some confusion once prevailed about this manufacturer. In one form of his trademark, the name appears as SAYERS (his initial and surname compressed without period or space), leading researchers to hunt for a silversmith called Sayers. He was born in 1767 and is known to have been in business by 1790, in Lexington. At that time he was operating as a silversmith and jeweler. It is established that he remained at Lexington a considerable length of time, as the Ayers shop is listed in both the 1806 and 1818 directories of that town. At some point, perhaps around 1810, he went into parnership with John Hiter. Finally he quit Lexington, sometime in the period from 1818 to 1823, and set up at Danville, Kentucky. There he ran a smithing business with his son, T. R. J. Ayers. He died in 1824. His most frequent mark is S AYERS in script lettering, of raised letters within a shaped rectangle.

BAKER, ELEAZER

Eleazer Baker lived to 85 and had a long career in the silversmithing trade, in rural Connecticut. For most, or possibly all, of his years in business he also worked as a clock and watch maker, and as a goldsmith — one of the typical "all purpose" artisans who were more prominent in early American villages and countryside than in the larger cities. Not too much is known of his activities, as he rarely advertised. He was born in 1764 and probably was in business by the mid eighties, but the first notice of him does not appear until 1793. He died in 1849, apparently having spent all of his years in Ashford, Connecticut. Eleazer Baker's mark normally consisted of EBAKER (no space between initial and surname), in block letters within a rectagle. Sometimes he used a simple punch with initials EB.

BALDWIN, JEDEDIAH

Jedediah Baldwin worked in 4 states, in a career that spanned many years. Though a good deal is known about him, the record of his activities is far from complete. He was born in 1769. After working briefly in Norwich, Connecticut, he moved to Northampton, Massachusetts, and announced his arrival with an advertisement which stated he was *from London.* In Northampton he went into partnership with Samuel Stiles, operating as clockmakers, watchmakers, jewelers, goldsmiths and silversmiths. This association lasted about one year, followed by a partnership between Baldwin and Nathan Storrs. Papers were filed to dissolve this business on January 22, 1794. Baldwin afterward worked at Hanover, New Hampshire; Fairfield, Connecticut; Morrisville, New York; and finally at Rochester, New York. He was at Morrisville around 1820 but the length of time he spent there is questionable. His stay of residence at Rochester has been established at 11 years at least, from 1834 to 1844. In 1849 he died, aged 80. His mark was distinctive, the name BALDWIN in graceful slim block capitals against a smooth rectangular frame.

BALL, WILLIAM

A Baltimore smith, Ball worked in the late 18th and early 19th centuries. Though Baltimore was smaller than Philadelphia or New York, it had far fewer silversmiths and apparently provided a lucrative trade for those who entered the business; we can surmise this without much doubt, since few Baltimore smiths left that city to go elsewhere. Ball was born in England in 1763. At what time he arrived in America is not known. He was in business in Baltimore (in a partnership) by 1785. This partnership, with a smith named Johnson (first name not established), ended in 1790. Thereafter Ball sometimes worked alone, but was for a time engaged in another partnership, with J. S. Heald. He advertised very extensively. One of his advertisements, placed in 1795, was a want-ad for an apprentice. He died in 1815, aged 52. The common mark used by this smith is WBALL (no spacing), in block letters within a shaped rectangular frame.

BANCKER, ADRIAN

Adrian Bancker worked as a silversmith and goldsmith in colonial New York City. Like most colonial smiths of that city he was of Dutch descent. He was born in 1703 (not long after the Dutch had lost control of the city and the name changed from New Amsterdam to its present form) and apprenticed around age 15 to a Dutch goldsmith named Boelen. His association with Boelen is thought to have lasted until about 1731. Thereafter he went into business independently. He died in 1772 at the age of 69, and was still in business as late as 1766 and possibly afterward. Bancker never spelled out his name in his mark, but used the initials AB. These normally were framed in a circle or oval. The AB mark within a heart-shaped punch has been recorded, on ware dating from the period in which Bancker was active; but it has not yet been positively identified as his.

BARTHOLOMEW, ROSWELL

Roswell Bartholomew worked at Hartford, Connecticut. He was born in 1781 and was sent at age 16 (1797) to be an apprentice smith with the shop of Beach and Ward in Hartford. By 1802 Ward, one of his masters, was in partnership with Bartholomew, along with another individual known only by the initial T. This mysterious figure later quitted the partnership, and by 1804 it became simply Ward and Bartholomew. In 1809 the partners took Charles Brainard into association with them, and the three worked together until Bartholomew's death in 1830. They were more versatile than most smith, operating (in addition to a smithing trade) a hardware shop and real estate office. Presumably, Bartholomew was the only one of the partners who actually engaged in silversmithing, as the wares bear a mark consisting of his initials only: RB on a rectangular punch.

BARTON, JOSEPH

This late 18th/early 19th century smith worked at Utica, New York and Stockbridge, Massachusetts. He turned out quantities of flatware and his spoons of various sizes are well known to collectors, for their frequent appearances in the auction rooms. Barton was born in 1764 and had gone into business by 1791, as a clockmaker, goldsmith and silversmith. His first location was at Stockbridge, where he remained for a number of years. By 1804 he had removed to the central New York town of Utica and continued in business there until the time of his death in 1832, at the age of 68. At Utica he also engaged in the jewelry business. Barton was involved in several partnerships while at Utica, trading under the firm names of Barton and Smith, then Barton and Butler. His relations included a number of other silversmiths, who operated businesses of their own. Joseph Barton's mark was distinctive. It comprised his surname preceded by initial, without space or period, contained within a sawtooth rectangular frame. Instead of a raised marking, Barton's was stamped in incuse — that is, the lettering was sunk into the silver.

BAYLEY, JOHN

This early Philadelphia maker's career stretched from the colonial era until after Independence. Very little is known about him. Bayley is of course the archaic spelling of the surname *Bailey,* and it can be presumed that he was of English descent. His first advertisement appeared in 1754, and his last in 1783. This is all we have in the way of dates for Bayley's career or life, as his dates of birth and death are not recorded. His usual mark was a simple punch, I.B, in which his Christian name was Romanized to the initial I rather than J. The initials are set within a rectangle with rounded corners. Occasionally he used another mark, in which the surname is spelled out, but it appears as BAYLY rather than Bayley (the form given in his advertisements). He was apparently a very well-respected artisan with a large following of clientele.

BEDFORD, JOHN

John Bedford was one of many early eastern smiths whose entire career was spent in the same rural village, in this case Fishkill, New York. (Though the temptation of "big town" trade lured some rural smiths to the cities, most realized that the extra competition canceled out advantages.) Bedford was born in 1757. His first advertisement appeared in 1782, but he may have been active before that time. He survived to the age of 77 (1834), but it is not established whether he continued in business to the end of his life. Unquestionably his years in the trade were long, as his products appear rather frequently on the antiques market. There are several varieties of the John Bedford mark. In one it appears as J.BEDFORD, the initial letter being slightly smaller than the surname letters. There is also another interesting feature of this mark: the first three letters of the surname (BED) are somewhat thicker than the rest. Another version of this smith's mark comprises script initial letters, contained within an oval.

BEECHER, CLEMENT

Clement Beecher enjoyed an exceptionally lengthy career in the silversmithing business, spanning a number of eras in taste and carrying over from the "shop" age into that of factory production. He lived to 91 years of age. All of his years in the business were spent in Connecticut. Beecher was born during the Revolutionary War, in 1778. He was in business early, by the age of 23, as an advertisement of his appears in a Hartford newspaper from 1801. Hartford was for many years his headquarters. He worked not only as a silversmith but a jeweler, goldsmith, and brassworker. During his entire career he operated, so far as is known, individually, never entering into any partnership. Having begun life at the War of Independence, Beecher lived through the Civil War and died in 1869. It is not known at what age he left the business. Generally his mark is a simple punch with his initial letters separated by a period. C.B., enclosed in a rectangle with sawtooth border.

BENJAMIN, JOHN

The entire career of John Benjamin was confined to the colonial era. His place of residence was Stratford, Connecticut — today a short distance from New York City by modern highways, but then rural and secluded. Benjamin was born in 1699. He went into business around 1725, probably on a small scale to supply the local community. In the mid to late 1740's he is believed to have formed a partnership with Robert Fairchild, another Stratford smith. The year of his death was 1773, at age 74. John Benjamin never (it seems) used anything but initials for his mark, a simple I.B. within either an oval or rectangular frame. The letters are of block form and highly raised. Anyone interested in adding a specimen of this pioneer smith's work to their collection should have no difficulty finding one or more of his spoons on the market, as he produced a great many of them.

BILLINGS, DANIEL

Daniel Billings worked at Stonington and Preston, a pair of small Connecticut towns. Recorded details of his life and activities are sparse. He is known to have been born in 1749 and was presumably of English descent. It is established that he was active in the business by 1790, but in fact was probably engaged in silversmithing at an earlier period. He ran very few advertisements. Billings' death was not covered in any printed obituaries. The last dated mention of him occurs in 1795, but we are probably safe in concluding that he lived for some years thereafter. Billings used a mark consisting of his full surname preceded by his initial, written out in a flowing script. This is contained within a rectangle with slightly rounded corners.

BOELEN, HENRICUS

One of the pioneer silversmiths of America, Henricus Boelen worked at New York City (then governed by the Dutch and called New Amsterdam). He was a Dutchman and had a brother, Jacob, who was likewise a smith. As the Dutch were avid devotees of silverware, the New Amsterdam colony proved a lucrative headquarters for those engaged in the trade. Boelen, like his contemporaries, worked almost strictly in the Old World taste, turning out wares very similar to those of Holland. An early death put an end to what was apparently a very promising career. Boelen was born in 1661 and died in 1691. His products are understandably rare on the market, most specimens having gone into museums from the possession of old New York families. He used just a single mark, a set of linked initial letters in which the righthand portion of the H formed the ascender of the B for HB. The mark is very European in character.

BLOWERS, JOHN

John Blowers was active at Boston in the first half of the 18th century. He survived only to the age of 38 but apparently had, by that time, built up a thriving trade. He was born in 1710. At what date he went into the business is not known. Blowers is established to have been working in or before 1738, as the Boston Gazette carried an advertisement in that year, placed by a citizen who wished to recover a lost thimble made by him. Another "lost and found" ad concerning an item made by John Blowers — this time a spoon — appeared in the same publication in 1746. Two years thereafter Blowers died. His mark consisted of his surname only, without the initial letter. It was written in modified script characters without connections between the letters, and contained in a rectangle.

BONTECOU, TIMOTHY

Timothy Bontecou was one of the better known silversmiths of the 18th century, and certainly one of the most skilled and artistic among those who worked in America prior to the Revolutionary War. Born in New York City, he went to France at an early age and was there apprenticed into silversmithing. At what date he returned to America is not established, but he is known to have been at Stratford, Connecticut, by 1735. After a brief stay in that town he moved to New Haven, Connecticut, where the remainder of his long career was spent. For nearly half a century Bontecou supplied fine silverware to early New Haven society, including of course many of the officials and patrons of Yale College. He died in 1784 at the age of 91. Normally his mark consisted of his initials, separated by a rising period and enclosed within a rectangular frame with lobework decoration along the top.

BOUDO, LOUIS

Louis Boudo spent his entire career in Charleston, South Carolina. He emigrated there from Santo Domingo, where he was born in 1786. The details of his early life are not known. He was in business by 1809 and possibly earlier. At first he worked in partnership with one Maurel (first name not recorded), but this association was soon dissolved. For a number of years Boudo continued at work on his own, then in 1818 sold his business and went (apparently) into retirement. But in the following year he returned to the silversmith trade, opening up a new shop, and carried on with it until his death in 1827. He lived to the age of 41. Boudo was a skilled craftsman and left behind many notable products, but by far the most memorable is a silver map container presented to Gen. Lafayette in 1825, on the occasion of Lafayette's return to America. His mark consisted of his surname spelled out, arranged in a wavy rectangular frame.

BOYER, DANIEL

Daniel Boyer worked at Boston, both before and after the Revolution. He was born in 1725. The first record of him in the business dates from 1748, but undoubtedly he was active from before that time. We know that he worked not only as a silversmith but as a goldsmith, jeweler, and importer of jewelry and jeweler's equipment. He seldom ran advertisements. Boyer died at the age of 54 in 1779 and is known to have been active up to the time of his death, as he produced a mourning ring for a Mrs. Gorring in 1779. There are three distinct varieties of Daniel Boyer's mark: (1) The surname preceded by initial letter; (2) The surname alone, in thin block characters against a rectangular frame; (3) initial letters only, in a rectangular frame with rounded corners.

BRASHER, EPHRAIM

Ephraim Brasher, a silversmith and goldsmith of New York City, is even better known to the world of numismatics than to that of antiques: he was the manufacturer of the great "Brasher doubloon," a rare goldpiece made in 1787 which has sold at auction for close to three quarters of a million dollars. Brasher was born in 1744. It is not known at what age he entered the business. His shop, in the area of Manhattan now known as the financial district, was patronized by most of the city's prominent residents. Among his neighbors was George Washington, in the period following Washington's retirement from the military and his first term as President. For a time he was in partnership with George Alexander, the shop name being Brasher and Alexander. This association was discontinued in 1801 and Brasher went on alone, at least until 1807 — the final year in which his name appears in the city directory. He died in 1810, aged 66. Brasher used a number of different marks. These included ones in which his name was spelled out, but not preceded by an initial letter; spelled out AND preceded by an initial letter; and initial-letter punches. Brasher sometimes stamped N YORK on his products.

CAMPBELL, BENJAMIN

This maker live to the age of 94. Much more is known about his activities than about most early silversmiths, as one of his account books has been preserved. This volume includes entries for a 22 year period, beginning in 1782 and ending in 1804. It not only shows all the various types of work done by him, but the prices charged; and likewise the prices paid for supplies. Benjamin Campbell was born in 1749 and apparently entered the trade shortly prior to the Revolution, at Uniontown, Pennsylvania. He survived to 1843, but probably had retired from business long before that time. During the years encompassed by the account book he was extremely active, making silver spoons, buckles, fixing watches, cutting dies, and doing general engraving. His mark consisted of his initials, BC, on a small oval punch.

CARPENTER, JOSEPH

Joseph Carpenter worked at Norwich, Connecticut, in the years preceding and following the Revolution. He was born in 1747 and was of English descent. The exact year in which he entered the trade is not recorded. His chief specialty was silver spoons, of which he seems to have produced a great deal. These he never advertised, but in 1776 he issued a broadside poster advertising prints of the battles of Lexington and Concord. Joseph Carpenter's son, Charles, also became a silversmith, and worked both at Norwich alongside his father and later at Boston. His mark consisted of his initials, I.C, with the J of Joseph changed to an I in conformity with the traditional style. Carpenter died in the year 1804, at age 57.

CASEY, GIDEON

This early smith, who worked mainly in the colonial era, was a Rhode Islander and occupied offices in four different towns of that state, at different times. He was born in 1726. Casey had a brother, Samuel, who was likewise a silversmith, and with whom he was in partnership for a while. Gideon Casey appears to have started in the business in Newport, then went to Exeter, South Kingston, and finally Warwick. It was while at Kingston that the partnership with his brother occurred, in the early 1750's. Gideon Casey died in 1786, aged 60. In 1763, while at Warwick, his shop sustained a serious fire, which was reported in the *Boston News-Letter* (a newspaper) in October, 1764. His mark was G.CASEY in narrow block capitals, only slightly raised, set into a rectangular frame.

CHEAVENS, HENRY

This New York City manufacturer was active in the first and second quarters of the 19th century. He appears to have enjoyed a lengthy career, but the dates of his birth and death are unknown; neither are the years in which he entered and left the business. Cheavens' name is found for the first time in the New York Directory of 1810, and continued appearing in that publication until 1834. He was listed as the proprietor of a fancy goods shop, which meant, in the terminology of that time, a shop selling clocks and decorative household items. He was also a watchmaker and, of course, a silversmith. Beginning in 1832 he entered into a partnership with one John Hyde, a watchmaker. Perhaps at that date Cheavens turned his attentions solely to silversmithing. He is not heard of after 1834. Cheavens used a handsome mark, consisting of his surname and initial in distinctively sculptured block letters.

CHITTENDEN, EBENEZER

Ebenezer Chittenden had a long career as a silversmith, beginning well before the Revolution and continuing many years thereafter. All of his life was spent in Connecticut, working first at East Guilford (now known as Madison) and later at New Haven. He was born in 1726. While at East Guilford he had as his apprentice Abel Buel, who later manufactured the dies used in striking the "Connecticut coppers," a series of coins issued by the State of Connecticut prior to U.S. federal coinage. It is not known when Ebenezer Chittenden entered the business. He did no advertising and all information relating to his life and work has derived from other sources. Among the notices of him is a record of silver beakers made for a church at Meriden, Connecticut, in 1767 and 1797. He died in 1812, aged 86. Chiefly his mark consisted of a simple initial punch without a period between or following the letters, but he sometimes used one in which his surname was spelled out, E.CHITTENDEN.

CLARK, JOSEPH

Little is known of the career of Joseph Clark, who worked in the pre-Revolutionary era. He was from Massachusetts and apparently worked for a time at Saugus, Massachusetts, which had been the site of the Saugus Iron Works in the 1650's — where the first American coins were struck. He may also have worked at Lynn in the same state. Clark is believed to have entered the trade in 1737. He did no advertising which can be traced. The year of his death has not been determined. There is no evidence to indicate that he ever worked in any other profession but silversmithing. Joseph Clark used at least three different marks, which may possibly represent different business locations. One carries his surname spelled out, preceded by the initial of his Christian name, in very crudely modeled letters. Another, much better designed (and therefore presumably of later origin) reads simply CLARK, in wide block capitals. The third is an initial mark, IC, in which the J of Joseph is transformed to I.

CLEVELAND, WILLIAM

Added glamor and collecting interest attaches to the works of William Cleveland, as he was the grandfather of an American President: Grover Cleveland, who served two non-consecutive terms in the 1880's and 1890's. William Cleveland was an easterner who started in the business in Connecticut, settled later in Ohio and ended his career in the small town of Black Rock, New York. He was born in 1770. At Norwich, Connecticut, he was apprenticed to Thomas Harland. Later he was in partnership in New London, Connecticut, with John Trott. This association lasted from 1792 to 1794. From then until 1812 he carried on his own business, at which date he entered into a partnership with Samuel Post. After having returned from New London to Norwich, and spending many years there, he worked in Massachusetts and eventually quit the east for Zanesville, Ohio. From Zanesville he moved to Putnam, Ohio, and then east again, in a career which witnessed a great number of changes of location and company names. He died in 1837 at the age of 67. William Cleveland used two marks, in one of which the surname is spelled out without an initial letter and is stamped from an incuse punch (the letters sunk into the surface rather than raised). His other mark has the initials W.C, and is presumably of earlier date.

COBB, EPHRAIM

This maker was active in Massachusetts prior to the Revolutionary War. He had a fairly lengthy career. Ephriam Cobb was born in 1708 at Barnstable, Massachusetts. He was sent as apprentice to a silversmith of that town, Moody Russell. Whether Cobb set up in business at Barnstable after completing his apprenticeship is not known. If so, it was for a short duration, as he was working at Plymouth, Massachusetts, by 1735. The entire remainder of his career was spent at Plymouth. So far as can be determined, Cobb never entered into partnerships or engaged in any trade besides silversmithing. The year of his death is disputed, listed sometimes as 1775, sometimes as 1776 or 1777. His attractive mark consists of the surname spelled out, preceded by initial, in upper and lower-case characters.

COEN, DANIEL BLOOM

Daniel Bloom Coen of New York City was one of a community of Jewish silversmiths who operated in that city during the late 18th and early 19th century. Coen is an early or variant spelling of the name Cohen. Neither the years of this maker's birth or death have been recorded. We know that his active career spanned at least the years from 1787 to 1804, as he appears in all of these years in the New York City Directory. He worked as a goldsmith and silversmith. His most common mark is D.COEN in block letters, set within a rectangle. Another silversmith named Cohen was working in New York at a slightly later period, but there is no evidence of a relationship between them.

CONEY, JOHN

This historic maker is included here on grounds of fame — not because it is likely that readers will ever possess an item bearing his mark. He worked at Boston in the later 17th and early 18th centuries. Among the early colonial smiths he was certainly one of the most active. Though his products rarely occur for sale, a fair number are preserved in museums and historical societies. John Coney was born in 1656. At the age of 13 or 14 he was sent as apprentice to Hull and Sanderson, who were then engaged in striking silver coins for the colony of Massachusetts as well as in general silversmithing. It is not known in what year he entered business on his own, but a cup inscribed 1676, made by Coney, is in existence. Coney was very well patronized throughout his entire career and became a leading citizen of Boston. He died in 1722, aged 66, and is known to have been at work at least as late as 1718. Though his accomplishments were many, John Coney's chief impact on history came via one of his pupils: Paul Revere the elder was apprenticed to him, late in his career. Coney's mark was a simple IC in a shield-shaped frame, with small ornaments above and below. It was sometimes accompanied by a figure of a rabbit, as the archaic word for rabbit was "coney."

CORNELL, WALTER
Walter Cornell was born in 1729 at Providence, Rhode Island, and worked his whole career in that town. He was one of many smiths who gave Providence a reputation as a center for silverware, enhanced later by the Gorham Company. Cornell ran a watchmaking and goldsmithing business in addition to silversmithing. It is not known when he entered the trade. The year of his death was 1801, and he seems to have been active to the end. Cornell used several marks, one of which is quite distinctive as it carries the name CORNELL in block capitals against a frame with slanting sawtooth edges. In one of his other marks the initial is also given, W CORNELL, spaced widely apart from the surname and not followed by a period.

COWELL, WILLIAM
A very early maker, who was born in the 17th century and entered the business around the year 1700 or shortly thereafter. The year of his birth was 1682. Cowell had a shop with rooms above it, and rented out the rooms to travelers. Thus he operated both as silversmith and innkeeper. He died in 1736, aged 54. He seems to have been extremely active and had a circle of clientele that included a number of prominent citizens. Cowell worked all his life at Boston. He is believed to have learned the silversmithing trade from Jeremiah Dummer, also of Boston. William Cowell's son, William Jr., was also a silversmith. His mark was a simple initial punch, WC, within an oval.

DALLY, PHILIP
Philip Dally worked at New York City in the latter part of the 18th century. The year of his birth is not recorded. The first notice relating to him is dated 1780, but he may, by that time, have been engaged in the trade for a number of years. In the later 1780's he was engaged in a partnership with Jabez Halsey, in a goldsmithing and silversmithing business. This partnership was broken in 1789. It is not established whether Dally then worked independently, after breaking with Halsey. He was apparently not a very prolific maker. No references to his death have been uncovered. Dally's mark consisted of his initials, P.D, in an unusual form in which the P is smaller than the D.

DAVENPORT, JOHN
This manufacturer started work at Baltimore, then moved to Philadelphia where the remainder of his career was spent. The date of his birth is not known. The earliest reference to him is dated 1789. In 1793 he quitted

Baltimore for Philadelphia, an ambitious move in that Philadelphia was known to be well supplied with silversmiths. Apparently the shop that he ran in Baltimore continued to be operated under his name, by whomever took it over, as John Davenport is listed in the Baltimore city directories for 1795 and 1796. He died in 1801 at an undetermined age. Davenport's mark consisted of the initials I.D., the letter I representing the classical form of J for John.

DeRIEMER, PETER

A distinguished New York State smith of the 18th and 19th centuries, Peter DeRiemer boasted a number of the state's most socially prominent families among his customers — including the Van Renssalaers. He lived to the age of 96 and had a long career, though his financial success probably encouraged him to retire well before the end of his life. The first notice of Peter DeRiemer appears at Albany in 1763, when he was 25 years of age. DeRiemer was of Dutch ancestry, and his actual first name was Pieter, anglicized to Peter. In the later 1760's he made his way to New York City and stayed in the metropolis 30 years or longer. His next place of residence was Poughkeepsie, New York, and finally Hyde Park, where he died in 1834. His mark consisted of the letters PDR in thick European-style capital letters, in a faint rectangular frame.

DIXWELL, JOHN

John Dixwell was from Connecticut. He started in the business at New Haven but the lure of a "big town" clientele afterward drew him to Boston. He was born in 1681. No details of the earlier part of his life are recorded. He was in the smithing business at least as early as 1705, working as a goldsmith and silversmith. He died in 1725 at the age of 44. A number of his works have been preserved, but very rarely occur for sale on the open market. John Dixwell's mark was ID within an oval..

DOOLITTLE, AMOS

The whole career of this manufacturer was spent at Connecticut. Amos Doolittle was born in 1754 and apprenticed in the silversmithing profession to Eliakim Hitchcock of Cheshire, Connecticut, probably in the late 1760's. He is known to have been operating his own shop by 1775. Amos Doolittle worked as a goldsmith, silversmith, jeweler and engraver. He died in 1832 at the age of 78. His mark was always a set of initials, in very narrow capitals, sometimes joined and sometimes not.

DUMMER, JEREMIAH

No book on American silverware would be complete without reference to Jeremiah Dummer, though his works are not likely to come within the collector's reach. He was the first goldsmith/silversmith born on American soil. Dummer was born at Boston in 1645, 25 years after the pilgrim landing. At the age of 14 he was apprenticed to John Hull, who was not only a silversmith but the "mintmaster" of the Massachusetts Bay Colony (Hull was engaged in striking coins to alleviate the area's coin shortage). During his long career Dummer had, as apprentices, a number of youths who became notable silversmiths. He was extremely versatile, turning out silver and gold wares of all varieties. Dummer died in 1718 at the age of 73. His mark usually consisted of his initial letters in wide block capitals, within a heart-shaped frame.

DUPUY, DANIEL

This long-lived manufacturer founded what amounted to a business dynasty in his native city of Philadelphia, as a number of his descendants also went into the trade. The family became very socially prominent. Daniel Dupuy was born in 1719. It is not known when he entered the trade, but a notice (referring to him as a goldsmith) exists bearing the date of 1745. Following the Revolution he took his son, Daniel Jr., into the business with him. He was still at work as late as 1807, the year of his death, when he was 88 years of age. Dupuy habitually used a set of initials, DD, as his mark, sometimes impressed once and often twice on his wares.

EDWARDS, JOHN

John Edwards was the patriarch of a celebrated family of Boston goldsmiths and silversmiths, which left behind an impressive number of works. These are now mainly in museums but some are seen, from time to time, in the marketplace. John Edwards was born in 1671. It is believed he was apprenticed to Jeremiah Dummer, the leading Boston smith of the time. He was working on his own by 1700 and quite likely for some years before. Over the years he produced large numbers of ceremonial objects for the local churches. He died in 1746, at the age of 75. So far as is known he never ran advertisements. His mark was IE, contained in a clover or shield-like frame, sometimes capped by a crown.

EMBREE, EFFINGHAM

Effingham Embree worked at New York City in the late 18th century. He was, in addition to a silversmith, a clock and watch maker. He also advertised jewelry for sale. There is no record of the dates of his birth or death. Notice of him appears first in the New York City directory for 1789, and he continues to be listed in succeeding editions of that work until 1795. A newspaper of the time reported in 1795 that his shop was taken over by Stephen Van Wyck. Embree spelled out his surname in his mark, but did not use the first-name initial. The lettering is thin block capitals in a rectangular frame. The mark sometimes appears in combination with a letter punch reading IB. These are the initials of James Byrne (the J changed to an I), a smith with whom Embree was for a while associated. Embree also was in partnership for a time with a man named Coles.

EOFF, GARRETT

Garrett Eoff enjoyed a long and varied career in the silversmithing trade, stretching from the latter part of the 18th century until well into the 19th. All of his many years in the business were spent in New York City, but he moved about to various shop locations and was in and out of partnerships with a number of different associates. Garrett Eoff was born in 1779. A Garrett Eoff is listed as a silversmith in the New York City directory for 1789, but as THIS Garrett Eoff was then 10 years of age it is obviously a different person. Quite likely the 1789 Garrett Eoff was the father of this smith, though no information has been discovered regarding him. The younger Garrett Eoff was in business by the year of 1801, and appears continuously in the New York City directory from that date until 1845. In that year he died, at the age of 66. At first he was in partnership with Paul Howell as Eoff & Howell, then with John Conner as Eoff & Conner. His final partnership (of which record exists) was with John C. Moore as Eoff & Moore. It is known that Eoff worked as a goldsmith as well as a silversmith, but there is no record of him engaging in watch or clockmaking or any other related trades. His mark has been confusing to beginning collectors. It consists of the Christian name initial, G, compressed against the surname, EOFF, and gives the appearance of reading GEOFF. There is, however, a small period following the initial letter. The mark is contained within a rectangular punch.

ERWIN, JOHN

John Erwin's background was rather different than most of the early silversmiths, as he started out in the umbrella business. Umbrella making was not a really thriving trade in early America, because of heavy importation of umbrellas from Britain. Perhaps this is why Erwin turned his attentions to silversmithing. he did not, however, abandon umbrella making, but carried on both businesses simultaneously, and also did goldsmithing. John Erwin spent most of his life in Baltimore. The dates of his birth and death are not recorded. He appears in the directory of that city's businessmen for the first time in 1808, and apparently continued at Baltimore at least until 1820. The final years of his life are said to have been spent in the West (exact location unspecified), but it is not known whether he worked as a silversmith after leaving Baltimore. The mark of John Erwin is quite unusual. It appears as J. ERWIN, in clock capitals, without the J converted into an I as was the standard practice among silversmiths. Perhaps there was another smith active, who signed himself I. ERWIN, but no such individual has been traced..

FAIRCHILD, ROBERT

This 18th century smith's career spanned the eras before and after the War of Independence. The majority of his career was spent in Connecticut, and he then finished up in New York State. Robert Fairchild was born in 1703, in Durham, Connecticut. There is no information about the date in which he entered the business. The first record of him occurs at Durham in 1747, when he would have been 44 years of age. At that time he was possibly in the trade for 20 years or more, but did no advertising during that period. From Durham he moved to Stratford, Connecticut, an important center for silversmaking in the 18th century. He then went to New Haven, where he enjoyed his greatest success. He was a regular advertiser in the local newspaper, the *New Haven Gazette,* from 1767 to 1784. His ads announce him as a silversmith, goldsmith, and jeweler. Around 1789, when he was 86 years of age and still active in the business, he left Connecticut and settled in Pawling, New York, where he died in 1794 at 91. He generally usued an initial punchmark, RF, separated by a star instead of a period. The star occurs parellel to the second crossbar on the F. When he used a name mark, it was R. FAIRCHILD within a rectangular frame. Works of Robert Fairchild are among the most often encountered, on the antiques market, of any 18th century silversmith..

FERGUSON, JOHN

This smith worked at Philadelphia in the early part of the 19th century. The first reference to him in the business occurs in 1801. It is not known how old he was at that time, or how long he had been active. He was in partnership with Charles Moore, operating a silversmithing and goldsmithing business. This association soon dissolved and Ferguson then worked on his own. The final record of him dated from 1810. His mark consisted of the initial I (romanized from J) followed by his full surname, in stylish block capitals. There is no record of Ferguson ever using a plain initial punch-mark. To judge his surviving wares, he seems to have been a very skilled artisan who probably catered to an affluent clientele.

FISHER, THOMAS

Thomas Fisher was born in 1765. He worked first at Baltimore and then at Philadelphia, and concluded his career in the town of Easton, Pennsylvania. In addition to silversmithing he also worked as a goldsmith. He did no advertising that can be traced and consequently very little is known about him. The first reference to him appears in 1797, and the last in 1807, but quite likely his career spanned a longer period than this. The year of his death has not been established. Thomas Fisher's mark consisted of his surname in modified script form, preceded by initial. This was an "incuse" mark in which the name was sunken down into the silver, rather than raised. Incuse marks were used by a comparatively few of the early smiths, as they tended to get rubbed and worn smooth faster.

FOLSOM, JOHN

John Folsom was born in 1756 in Stratford, Connecticut. He was apprenticed early and is recorded to have been an active workman in 1770 at the age of 14. At that time he did both silversmithing and goldsmithing. For about a decade he stayed at Stratford, but, probably finding the town too well-supplied with established smiths, he moved to Albany, New York, around 1780. At Albany he enjoyed the bulk of his success, building up a clientele that included some of the more socially prominent families of that era. Around 1806 he quitted the silversmithing business and moved to Glens Falls, New York, where the remainer of his life was spent as a shopkeeper. He died in 1839 at the age of 83. john Folsom's mark was an initial punch, IF, in which the J of John was changed to an I in keeping with the long-standing tradition of the profession..

FORBES, GARRET

This New York City smith was born in 1785. He got into the business early and worked as goldsmith and silversmith. Notice of him appears in the New York City directory from 1808 until 1815. He remained in New York thereafter, where he died in 1851 at the age of 66, but no longer engaged in the smithing business. The latter part of his life was spent as an agent for the U. S. Customs, evaluating incoming goods at the Port of New York and collecting duties on them. He used two similiar marks, both reading G. FORBES, but in one there is no period following the initial. Both are in block capitals set within a rectangular frame. Since Forbes was not too long in the profession, his works are not abundant on the antiques market.

FORMAN, BENONI

Very little is known of this 19th century smith, who worked in New York State. He was active in Albany in 1813 and continues to appear in that city's directory until 1846. Thereafter he settled at Troy, New York, where the final notice of him appears in 1848. This may have been the year of his death. There is no record that he ever engaged in any other trade but silversmithing, but he seems to have run no advertisements. The oddity of his first name, Benoni, suggests that he might have been an immigrant who assumed the name of Forman to avoid being treated as a foreigner — this was not an uncommon practice for tradesmen, especially those whose names were very ethnic-sounding. His mark was an initial punch in which he incorporated his middle initial, B, to form BBF. The letters are stylishly designed and so too, generally, are the products of the maker.

FUETER, LEWIS

Lewis Fueter was active in New York City around the time of the Revolutionary War. Not a great deal is known about him. He was the son of a goldsmith and silversmith named Daniel C. Lewis. An advertisement appeared in a New York City newspaper in 1769, announcing that Daniel C. and Lewis Fueter had returned to the city. Where they returned FROM, or how long they had been absent, was not mentioned. This 1769 ad is the first printed record of Lewis Fueter, but we have no way of knowing how old he was at the time or how long he had engaged in silversmithing. In the early to mid 1770's he worked as a goldsmith and silversmith. His chief claim to fame was making a presentation piece (a silver salver) for New York Govenor Tryon, which carries an inscription dated 1773. No record of Lewis Fueter appears after 1775. His mark is L. Fueter in a flowing copperplate style of script, probably modeled from his signature. The frame of his mark is a modified rectangle, arching outward around the large initial letters.

GAITHER, JOHN

This smith was active at Alexandria, Virginie, in the early part of the 19th century. The earliest notice relating to him is a newspaper advertisement from 1809. At that time he was engaged in a partnership with G. Griffith, running a silversmithing, watchmaking, and clockmaking shop. A later advertisement (1811) announces the arrival of merchandise from New York and Philadelphia. After 1811 there is no traceable record of John Gaither. The dates of his birth and death are lost. His very distinctive mark consisted of his surname in bold block capitals preceded by his initial letter, J. GAITHER, and set against a checked background. It can be assumed from his business location that he catered chiefly to customers in Washington, D. C.

GARDINER, JOHN

John Gardiner was born at New London, Connecticut, in 1734. His apprenticeship was spent with his uncle, a local smith named Pygan Adams. By about 1750 he was working on his own, at the age of 16. His entire career was spent at New London. John Gardiner died in 1776 at the age of 42. The styles of his wares were similar to those made by his uncle. John Gardiner used both an initial punch and a mark in which his name was spelled out, J. GARDINER within a rectangular frame.

GEFFROY, NICHOLAS

Nicholas Geffroy's real name was Geoffroy. He was a French immigrant. He was born in 1761 and seems to have fled his native land during, or shortly following, the French Revolution of 1792/3. This would suggest he was a known supporter of the Bourbons, whose foes had vowed to exterminate all "royalists." Or, possibly, the Revolution had simply made for bad business. His career in America was spent at Newport, Rhode Island, where he first worked with a silversmith named Shaw and then by himself. He was listed as a silversmith, goldsmith, and watchmaker. Nicholas Geffroy died in 1839 at the age of 78. This much used a very eye-catching mark, consisting of N. GEFFROY separated not by a period but a large multi-pointed star and set within a sawtooth frame.

GERRISH, TIMOTHY

Timothy Gerrish spent his career in Portsmouth, New Hanpshire, on the Maine border. He worked in the latter part of the 18th and the early 19th centuries. He rarely advertised, but when he did he listed his occupations as silversmith and goldsmith. He was born in 1749. There is no available information on the year in which he entered the business. The first notice of him does not occur until 1796. We know that he died in 1815 at the age of 66. Much of his time seems to have been spent in spoon making. He used both an initial punchmark and a mark in which his surname is spelled out in attractive script letters of a modernistic style.

GIBBS, JOHN

John Gibbs was born in Providence, Rhode Island, and spent his entire career in that city. The year of his birth was 1751. He got into the trade at an early age and ran an advertisement in 1773, in the local newspaper, announcing himself as a silversmith, goldsmith and jeweler. Gibbs died in 1797 at the age of 48. His widow carried on the business thereafter, going into partnership with John C. Jenckes. His mark consisted of a simple J. GIBBS in swelled block capitals, within a shaped rectangular frame..

GILMAN, JOHN WARD

John Ward Gilman enjoyed a long career in the business. He was born in 1741 at Exeter, New Hampshire, and spent his entire career at that town. He was the brother of Benjamin Gilman, also a silversmith, who was his junior by more than 20 years. The first notice of him is dated 1770. He worked as a silversmith and engraver, and we know that some of his engraving was in the form of plates for sheet music to be printed from. He died in 1823 at the age of 84 and was apparently at work until very late in life. Usually the mark he used was an initial punch, IWG, in which the letters are not separated by periods and in which the I has a small bar set across its shaft.

GOELET, PHILIP

Philip Goelet worked in New York City in the first half of the 18th century. He was born in 1701. The first reference to him occurs in 1731. He ran no advertisements and left behind a comparatively small number of pieces, to judge by the infrequency with which they turn up today. He died in 1748. Philip Goelet's mark was an initial punch, PG, within an oval.

GRIGG, WILLIAM

This manufacturer had a long and quite a checkered career, not only moving about a great deal but at one point even leaving the country to practice his trade in Halifax, Nova Scotia! There is no information on the year of his birth. The first references to him occur in the middle 1760's, at which time he was established in New York City. During the Revolutionary War he was working at Albany, New York, then returned to New York City around 1778. It was in 1782 that he decided to push northward and test the business climate in Halifax. This daring move was apparently prompted by the fact that Halifax was a growing port town with a thriving fishing industry, so Grigg must have figured that it could use a silversmith. He stayed at Halifax until 1789, when he came back (for the third time) to New York City, and there spent the balance of his life. He died in 1797 at an undetermined age. He used a mark in which his surname is spelled out in flowing, thin script letters, not preceded by an initial. The mark is set within a border which conforms to the shape of the lettering. In addition, Grigg also made use of an initial punch, reading WG in very ornamental script letters.

HALL, CHARLES

Silversmith and goldsmith Charles Hall of Pennsylvania became one of the leading citizens of that colony, accumulating wealth and rising to social prominence. He was born in 1742 and was already in the trade by 1759, at age 17, working alongside his brother David Hall. He began advertising in 1765, by which time he had removed to Lancaster, Pennsylvania. The remainder of his life was spent in Lancaster, where he carried on his business and was engaged in many civic and philanthropic ventures. He died in 1783 at the age of 41. Charles Hall's mark was a simple initial punch within a rectangular frame, or, on occasion, his name spelled out in a similar style of frame.

HALSTED, BENJAMIN

This manufacturer's real name was probably Halstead. He worked in the late 18th and early 19th centuries and was engaged in a number of trades in addition to silversmithing. He was often advertised as a manufacturer of thimbles (silver ones, of course), and he is known to have done goldsmithing. Benjamin Halsted started out in business in New York City in the early 1760's. From there he moved to Elizabeth, New Jersey, and later worked his way down to Philadelphia, where he stayed for several years. He then returned to New York following the Revolutionary War and was still at work in 1794. This is the last recorded notice of him. We do not know the dates of his birth or death. His usual mark consisted of the name Halsted spelled out in script letters, within a shaped frame (the frame border styled to match the contours of the letters). Halsted was briefly in partnership with Myer Myers, a well-known Hebrew silversmith of New York City.

HAVERSTICK, WILLIAM

William Haverstick had a long career in the goldsmithing and silversmithing professions. He also worked as a jeweler. He was born in Philadelphia in 1756 and worked both there and (later) at Lancaster, Pennsylvania, which became a headquarters for silvermaking toward the close of the 18th century. His son carried on his business for him, then moved it back to Philadelphia. The printed information regarding William Haverstick is not very extensive. He did very little advertising. The year of his death was 1823, at the age of 67. The marks used by him were also used by his son, William, Jr., making it difficult to assign any particular item to one or the other. The marks are all in the form of simple initial punches. In one the letters are joined at the top and not separated by a period. In another they are not joined, and have a period between them.

HENCHMAN, DANIEL

Daniel Henchman of Boston worked in the period preceding the Revolutionary War. Born in 1730, he was apprenticed to Jacob Hurd, a noted Boston smith, and married Hurd's daughter in 1753. At that time he was probably already in the business. He did very little advertising, which makes our knowledge of his activities quite meager. Daniel Henchman died in 1775 at the age of 55. There are records of several individual items he made for special clients, including a gold mourning ring. His basic mark consisted of the name spelled out in lower case letters, within a rectangular frame. He also on occasion used an initial punch reading DH.

HITCHCOCK, ELIAKIM

This colonial and early Federal-era manufacturer was born in Cheshire, Connecticut, in 1726. He started working in that town in the 1750's or possibly earlier, then moved to New Haven. He was active as a silversmith, goldsmith and jeweler. Hitchcock did only occasional advertising and not a great deal is known about him. He died in 1788 at the age of 62. So far as has been determined, he never used a mark in which his name was spelled out, but always an initial punch. There were two types of these initial punches, one in which the initials are in squat block capitals separated by a star; and, in the other, the letters are tall, sleek, and not separated by either a star or period.

HOPKINS, JOSEPH

Joseph Hopkins spent his whole career in the town of Waterbury, Connecticut, working both before and after the Revolutionary War. He was born in 1730 but no references to him can be found until 1760. During the later 1760's and early seventies he advertised himself as a maker and dealer in plates, buckles, spoons, and silver plated wares. Joseph Hopkins died in 1801. His principal mark carried the name spelled out in modified script characters, not preceded by an initial letter. Occasionally he used an initial punch, JH, set in a rectangle.

HULBEART, PHILIP

The name of this early maker represents an archaic form of *Holbart*. He worked in Philadelphia prior to the Revolutionary War. There is no record of the year of his birth. He was probably active as early as 1750, as a goldsmith and silversmith. In the only advertisement he ran, of which any trace has turned up, Hulbeart gave his profession as goldsmith. He died in 1764. Hulbeart always used an initial punch, P.H, in which the P is somewhat smaller than the H. The likelihood is strong that he was an immigrant to this country and learned the silversmithing trade abroad.

HUTTON, ISAAC

This long-surviving smith appears to have spent his entire career in Albany, New York. For a while he was a dealer in military goods, at the time of the War of 1812, but for most of his life he made and sold silverware. He was born in 1767 and went into the trade around the age of 20, not long after the Revolutionary War. At this time he was in association with John Folsom. He died in 1855 at the age of 88, but it would appear that he retired from business quite early as no record of him appears after 1813. He may have carried on for a time in the military goods trade after leaving silversmithing. He used marks in which his surname is fully spelled out but not preceded by an initial letter, sometimes in combination with a punch reading ALBANY.

JACOB, GEORGE

George Jacobs worked at Baltimore and Philadelphia in the first half of the 19th century. He was extremely successful in the business. The large numbers of wares he turned out is evidenced by their frequent appearance on the antiques market. He was born in 1775 and the first reference to him occurs in 1800, when he is listed as a swordmaker in the Baltimore city directory. He appears continuously in the directory of that city as a silversmith from 1802 to 1845 and also appears in the Philadelphia directory beginning in 1839. Since these are overlapping dates, it has been presumed that Jacobs operated shops in both cities at the same time. He died in 1846, still engaged in the business, at the age of 71. His mark is habitually G.JACOB in block capitals set against a rectangular frame, sometimes accompanied by numeral punches whose meaning has not been ascertained.

JOHONNOT, WILLIAM

This manufacturer worked at Connecticut and Vermont in the late 18th and early 19th centuries. He was born in 1766 and was sent as an apprentice to Samuel Canfield in 1782 at the age of 16. The apprenticeship lasted five years, and for the five following years (until 1792) Johonnot plied the trade of silversmith in Middletown, Connecticut. From there he moved to Windsor, Vermont, probably because northern New England had fewer silversmiths than the southern portion. There he continued to the end of his career. The final notice of him actively engaged in business is dated 1815, but he probably carried on considerably longer. Johonnot died in 1838. His mark was always an initial punch, IW (the J changed to I to conform with the long-standing tradition of using Latinized spellings), within a sawtooth rectangular frame.

KENDALL, JAMES

James Kendall worked at Wilmington, Delaware, a town which had relatively few silversmiths (its close proximity to Philadelphia, which boasted numerous smiths, ranked it as a mediocre location). He was born in 1768 and the first notice of him comes by way of a newspaper advertisement in 1796, listing him as a silversmith and jeweler. There is very little known information on his life. He died in 1808 at the age of 40. James Kendall primarily used an initial punch as his mark, in which the J for James is switched to an I and reads IK. Specimens are known, however, in which KENDALL is spelled out.

LAMAR, MATTHIAS

Matthias Lamar was of French extraction. Whether he was an immigrant from France, or both in this country, has not been determined. His name was probably anglicized to Lamar from Lemaire. He settled in Philadelphia and appears for the first time in that city's directory in 1785, when his occupation is given as silversmith. He continued to be listed as a silversmith up to 1803, but beginning in 1804 his profession reads "tavernkeeper." He died in 1809, apparently having engaged in tavernkeeping up to the time of his death. He used a mark in which his surname is spelled out in block capitals, not preceded by an initial letter, and also initial punches. In the latter, the initials are not separated by a period and are set within a rectangular frame.

LeROUX, CHARLES

Charles LeRoux (pronounced *Sharl LeRow)* was of French ancestry. He worked in New York City in the mid-colonial era, when the silversmithing trade in that city was largely controlled by Dutch artisans. Very few examples of his work are recorded. He was born in 1689 and died in 1748. Details regarding his life are scant. His mark was an initial punch reading CR, omitting the L, within a circular frame.

LITTLE, PAUL

Paul Little had a varied career, working as a silversmith, goldsmith and the operator of a food store. He was born in 1740 in Portland, Maine, and was in business there as early as 1761. In his first venture he was in a partnership with John Butler, a goldsmith, which lasted until about 1765. From Portland he moved to Windham, Maine, and stayed there for the remainder of his life. He died in 1818. His mark is always an initial punch, sometimes containing a period between the letters and sometimes not. The mark is invariably enclosed in a rectangular border.

LORD, T.

Absolutely nothing is known about this manufacturer, as all efforts to trace him through advertisements, directories, etc., have failed. He is known to have existed only via the wares he produced, which was impressed T.LORD in bold block capitals within a rectangular frame. He apparently worked in the early part of the 19th century.

LYING, JOHN BURT

John Burt Lying worked in New York City around the time of the Revolutionary War. Not too much is known about him. The first reference to him is dated 1764 and comes by way of a newspaper advertisement. He was still at work in 1781 and died in 1785, at an undetermined age. Unlike most of the smiths of that era, he sometimes used a town mark, N.YORK, in addition to his own mark; this would consist of LYNG in block capitals, not preceded by an initial letter, or an initial punch reading IBL (the J changed to an I).

MERRIMAN, MARCUS

Marcus Merriman lived to the age of 88 and spent the whole of his long career in New Haven, Connecticut. His prolific works used to turn up frequently in the Connecticut antiques shops, but have become harder to find in recent years (not to mention more costly). He was born in 1762 and was advertising from as early as 1787, though the actual date at which he entered the business has not been established. He entered into a number of apprenticeships, mostly with persons who were general merchants rather than silversmiths. He ceased advertising in 1825 but it is believed he remained in the business for at least a while thereafter. He died in 1850. Merriman used initial punchmarks as well as a mark in which his surname is spelled out in widely spaced block capitals, in a sawtooth frame.

MILNE, EDMUND

Early American silversmiths were remarkable for surviving to very advanced ages; as a group they probably outlived all other tradespersons. Edmund Milne reached 98, living his entire lifetime in Philadelphia. He was born in 1724. The date at which he entered the profession has not been recorded. His first traceable advertisement is from 1757. Thereafter he advertised steadily, listing himself as a goldsmith, silversmith, and seller of imported English plate. In 1777 he produced a set of drinking cups for George Washington, then serving as General with the Continental Army. Milne died in 1822. It is not known when he retired from business, but the belief is that this occurred long before his death as he had apparently attained comfortable wealth. His mark is usually an initial punch, EM, in which the letters are not separated by a period. At other times he used E.MILNE within a rectangular frame.

MORSE, NATHANIEL

This historic manufacturer was engaged in engraving dies for coins, for his native colony of Massachusetts. He was noted both as a goldsmith and silversmith. Nathaniel Morse was born at Boston in 1685 and spent his entire career in that city. He learned the trade from John Coney and was in business by around 1710. His versatility showed itself not only in his table-wares but in portrait engraving, which he practiced from time to time. He died in 1748 at the age of 63. Nathaniel Morse used a number of marks, the most familiar of which is the letters NM joined together. He also sometimes marked his pieces MORS or N MORS, leaving the E off his name.

MUNSON, AMOS

Amos Munson's works are among the scarcer specimens of 18th century silver, as he lived only to the age of 32. It seems that he was quite successful as a silversmith and abundantly talented. He was born at New Haven, Connecticut, in 1753, and spent his career there. He was probably in the business by the early 1770's. Most of the existing examples of his work are spoons. He died in 1785. He never advertised, so far as can be determined, so we do not know if he engaged in other pursuits in addition to silversmithing. He used an initial punchmark, of which there are two distinct forms. In one the letters, AM, are close together and not separated by a period. In the other a period is placed between them and the letters are far apart. In both versions of Munson's mark the frame is rectangular and features sawtooth work.

MYERS, MYER

One of the legendary names in colonial American silversmithing, Myer Myers belonged to the small colony of Hebrew smiths who operated in New York City. He was the most active and successful among them, and probably inspired many others to follow the trade. Myer Myers was born in 1723. He served an apprenticeship as a silversmith in the early 1740's. He set up shop soon thereafter and continued working in New York City until 1776, a stretch of three decades. During this time he became one of the best-known smiths in the city and, in fact, in all the colonies. With the outbreak of the Revolutionary War, he considered it unsafe to remain in New York and removed to Norwalk, Connecticut, where he carried on his trade until 1780. He then went to Philadelphia briefly, and in 1783, with the war over, came back to New York. He continued in business until the time of his death in 1795, at age 72. Though very skilled in his workmanship, one of the major contributions to his success was his attention to newspaper advertising. Few smiths did as much public advertising as Myer Myers, who tried to keep his name constantly before the buyers of silverware. He used a script-type mark with his surname only, which has a very modernistic tone. Other wares of his were punched with a crest-shaped initial mark, MM. In addition to ordinary wares, Myer Myers also fashioned a large number of Jewish ceremonial objects.

NORTON, ANDREW

Andrew Norton of Goshen, Connecticut, was a tavernkeeper who also worked as a goldsmith and silversmith (this was not unique among 18th century smiths). He was born in 1765 and was in the business by 21 or 22 years of age. The history of his career is not well known, as he left behind few advertisements or personal papers. He died in 1838 at the age of 73, having spent his whole life in Goshen. Andrew Norton is known mainly for his spoons. His mark carries his surname in large narrow block capitals, preceded by initial letter. A very large period is placed after the initial, and the frame is rectangular with wavy borders at the two vertical edges.

OLIVER, ANDREW

Andrew Oliver was of French extraction. His real name was Andre Olivier. He was born in 1724 and worked at Boston, as a jeweler and silversmith. He may also have been a goldsmith as well. He died in 1776. Oliver's mark is usually A OLIVER, without a period following the initial letter, set in a rectangular frame. Occasionally he used an initial punchmark, which will be found on the stems of spoons, etc. On the whole his work is rare.

PARKER, DANIEL

Daniel Parker worked at Boston and Salem, Massachusetts, prior to the Revolutionary War. Though he lived until after the Revolution, it is believed he retired or went into another business at the war's outbreak. He was born in 1726 and was at work in Boston from around 1747, as a goldsmith and silversmith. His career at Boston lasted more than a quarter century. In 1775, undoubtedly because of the war conditions prevailing at that city, he resettled in Salem, and worked there briefly. He was a constant advertiser in the *Boston Gazette* and therefore a fairly complete record of his activities is preserved. He died in 1785. Daniel Parker used two marks, one with his surname preceded by initial letter, D.PARKER, in stout block capitals in a rectangular frame. His other mark was an initial punch, DP within an oval.

PERKINS, HOUGHTON

This colonial smith was active at Boston and Taunton, Massachusetts. Like many of the Boston silversmiths (and other tradesmen) he quitted that city during the Revolutionary War. He was likely planning to return upon the war's conclusion, but an early death at the age of 43 extinguished such hopes. Houghton Perkins was born in 1735 and was an apprentice of Jacob Hurd. It appears that his apprenticeship was served at a more mature age than was normal in the trade, from about 23 to 27. He worked both as a goldsmith and silversmith, and seems to have prospered during his relatively brief career. He died in 1778. Houghton Perkins' mark consisted of a full surname in script lettering, preceded by initial. Instead of a period, the initial was followed by a four-pointed star, and the mark was set within a rectangular frame.

PITMAN, SAUNDERS

Saunders Pitman, a silversmith of Providence, Rhode Island in the later 18th century, was also a prominent resident of that town. He was born in 1732. Nothing is known of his earlier life, except that at one time he worked as a scavenger — the equivalent to "sanitation worker." The date at which he entered the smithing profession is not recorded. During the latter part of his career he was a frequent advertiser in the local newspaper, where his occupation is given as goldsmith and silversmith. Beginning in about 1793 he entered into a partnership with Seril Dodge, another smith. He died in 1804 at the age of 72. Saunders Pitman never used an initial punchmark, so far as can be determined, but always a mark carrying his surname without initial letter. This was invariably in thin block capitals, either in a plain rectangular border or one highlighted with sawtooth rim.

POTWINE, JOHN

Though a very active smith over a long period of time (he lived to 94), the surviving works of John Potwine are scarce. They are found mostly in museums, historical societies, and churches of New England; but the diligent hobbyist might succeed in finding one or more on the open market. He was born in 1698 and started working at Boston around 1715 while still a teenager. Since he was still active in the business in the year of his death, 1792, he could claim a career of more than 75 years in silversmithing — possibly the longest of any colonial smith. He stayed at Boston until the late 1730's, when he moved to Hartford, Connecticut. Thereafter he worked at Coventry and East Windsor, also in Connecticut. His career was concluded at East Windsor. Potwine did little or no advertising, but his name appears frequently in various official records, chiefly in connection with objects he made for churches. His full mark consisted of the surname in script lettering, preceded by the initial I (changed from J to conform to tradition). This is enclosed in a rectangular border with shaped top. He also used an initial punchmark, IP, set into a shaped frame. The punchmark's shape has occasioned some speculation. Some observers think it represents a play on his name, a *pot* of *wine*. But it really looks more like a crest.

QUINTARD, PETER

Peter Quintard worked at New York City and South Norwalk, Connecticut in the middle part of the 18th century. He was possibly of Dutch or Flemish extraction. He was born in 1699 and served his apprenticeship in New York City. He was in business from about 1719. The year of his removal to South Norwalk is placed at about 1737. He finished out his career there and died in 1762 at the age of 63. While at South Norwalk he occasionally advertised in the *New Haven Gazette,* relying on a New Haven paper because South Norwalk had none of its own. Peter Quintard used an initial punchmark, PQ, the Q shaped like a backwards P. Sometimes a period separates the letters and sometimes not.

REVERE, PAUL, Jr.

The most famous of all American silversmiths, Paul Revere Jr.'s works command a higher *maker premium* on the antiques market than those of any of his contemporaries. He was extremely active and turned out a great deal of products, but generations of active collecting have sent the majority of them into museums. When offered today, it is usually only when a notable collection is brought up for auction sale. Paul Revere, Jr., also known as Paul Revere II, was the son of a goldsmith and silversmith. His father was French and his real name was Apollos Rivoire. The younger Revere was apprenticed to his father. He was born in 1735 and was working alongside his father from the 1750's. The legend of his ride through Boston to warn of approaching British troops is now chiefly relegated to folklore. He died in 1818 at the age of 83. His entire career was spent at Boston. In later life he lived in comfortable retirement, having become a very prominent citizen. His mark is either REVERE in gold block lettering set within a rectangular border, or script initials PR. These markings are different than those used by his father, so there is never any trouble in attributions.

RICHARDSON, JOSEPH, Jr.

Joseph Richardson, Jr., is the most celebrated of the old Philadelphia silversmiths. He was the son of a noted silversmith. During a long career, the younger Richardson counted many of society's and government's greats among his clients, including George Washington (who bought a teapot and waste bowl from him for $44.50 in 1796 — the equivalent of close to $500 in 1980's money). He became a prominent and respected citizen and served as assayer for the U.S. Mint, beginning in 1795. Joseph Richardson, Jr. was born in 1752. He was in the business from the early 1770's, at first in partnership with his brother, Nathaniel Richardson. This association lasted to 1790. He died in 1831 at the age of 79. A great deal of records exist by which the career of Joseph Richardson, Jr., can be chronicled, including a ledger book kept by him from 1796 until the year of his death. He always used an initial punchmark, with JR either in a rectangular or oval frame, or sometimes without frame. This differs from the punchmark of his father, who observed the old tradition among smiths and signed himself IR (changing the J to an I).

ROGERS, DANIEL

Daniel Rogers of Ipswich, Massachusetts, worked in the late 18th and early 19th centuries. He is known in the silver collecting hobby for his use of many different marks, probably the greatest variety of marks employed by any single smith. Without attempting to describe them, we would simply advise readers that any piece marked D.ROGERS, in any style of marking, is a work of this smith. Only one D. Rogers has been traced among the American silversmiths, though the variety of markings would easily lead to the conclusion that half a dozen or more were active.

ROSS, JOHN

John Ross worked at Baltimore in the latter part of the 18th century. He was born in 1756. There is no information about the date at which he entered the business. He did no advertising, but a reference to him is found in the 1796 edition of the Baltimore city directory. He died two years later. The total number of his works does not seem to have been large. He habitually used an initial punchmark, IR (the J changed to I), either separated by a period or without period, but always within a rectangular frame. The collector will probably succeed in finding some of his spoons on the market, but other works by this manufacturer are elusive.

SAYRE, JOEL

Joel Sayre worked at Southampton, Long Island (New York) and at New York City, in a career which spanned about 20 years. He was born in 1778 and was in business by 1798. After four years in Southampton he moved to New York City and for more than a decade shared a shop with his brother John, also a silversmith. They did no advertising but their business is recorded in the New York City directory between the years 1802 and 1813. In 1814 Joel began working alone and continued until his death in 1818. His mark is usually in script lettering, with the surname spelled out and preceded by the initial J (not switched to I, as so many smiths did). He also at times made use of an initial punchmark.

SHEPHERD, ROBERT

This smith worked at Albany, New York in the first half of the 19th century. He was active both as a goldsmith and silversmith and had a long career, which is fairly well documented. Robert Shepherd was born in 1781. In the earlier part of his career he was engaged in a partnership known as

Shepherd & Boyd, which lasted from about 1806 to 1830. He thereafter worked on his own, until the time of his death in 1853 at the age of 72. His mark was extremely interesting: R.SHEPHERD in very well-modeled script lettering, in a close-fitting rectangular frame with cut-outs at certain strategic points (to allow for the height of tall letters).

SIMPKINS, WILLIAM

William Simpkins worked at Boston during the colonial era. He was born in 1704 and was in business by 1728, as an advertisement of his appears in the *Boston Weekly News Letter* of that year, announcing him as a goldsmith and silversmith. How much earlier he might have entered the trade is open to speculation. He is known to have still been in business in 1770, but no references to him from a later era are found. He died in 1780 at the age of 76. Quite possible he went into retirement at the outbreak of war in Boston, rather than removing to another location at his advanced age. His mark can occur in any of three styles: a surname preceded by initial letter; surname without initial letter; and an initial punch, in which the letters are not separated by a period.

STANTON, ENOCH

Enoch Stanton worked at Stonington, Connecticut. He was born in 1745 and was probably in the business by the late 1760's. Not much is known about his activities. He died in 1781 at the age of 36, leaving behind a relatively small amount of work. His usual mark is E:STANTON in a rectangular frame, the E followed by a colon instead of a period. Sometimes he used an initial punchmark in which the letters are likewise separated by a colon, as well as an initial mark in which a period occurs between the letters.

STORRS, NATHAN

A famous and very successful silversmith, Nathan Storrs of Massachusetts and New York worked from the late 18th century well into the 19th. He was born in 1768 and got into the business at an early age, at Springfield, Massachusetts. Around 1790 he settled in New York City, then bustling with silversmiths but growing so rapidly in population that there always seemed room for "one more." Storrs was disappointed with the city and decided to return to a more rural place of business after a brief stay. He settled in Northampton, Massachusetts, and spent about 42 years in the trade there. He retired in 1833 and died six years later at the age of 71. Nathan Storrs' mark is usually N.STORRS in block capitals within a rectangular frame, but is sometimes found simply as N.S in a punchmark.

SYNG, PHILIP

Philip Syng was one of very few native Irishmen in the American silversmithing trade during our colonial era. He was born in Cork in 1676 and arrived in this country in 1714, already an accomplished smith. His destination in America was Philadelphia. The ship in which he landed docked at Annapolis, Maryland, and from there he made his way to Philadelphia. This fleeting glimpse of Annapolis made a strong impression, as he returned to that city after about a decade in Philadelphia and spent the remainder of his life there. He died in 1739, having worked as a silversmith in America for about two and a half decades. He was a regular newspaper advertiser (rare for that early period), and his ads mention that his shop was shared by Richard Warder, a maker of smoking pipes. *Syng* is the early version of the Irish surname which later was spelled *Synge,* as in the case of the novelist John Millington Synge. It was always pronounced *sing.* Philip Syng's mark was his initials, PS, crudely cut within a heart-shaped punch. No period separates the letters.

TOWNSEND, THOMAS

Thomas Townsend of Boston worked in the period preceding the Revolutionary War. He was active for 35 or more years but less is known about him than of most Boston smiths, as he never advertised. He was born in 1701 and got into the business around 1725. Townsend worked both as a goldsmith and silversmith. He seems to have retired around the early 1760's and lived until 1777. His mark was always in the form of an initial punch, with the letters separated by a period. In one version of the mark, it rests within a tall oval frame and is surmounted by a crown.

VAN DER SPIEGEL, JACOB

Jacob (or Jacobus) Van Der Spiegel was one of the early Dutch silversmiths of New York City. He was born in 1668 and served with the Dutch army assigned to New Amsterdam (New York). He appears to have entered the silversmithing trade around 1695 and was active for a little more than a decade. He died in 1708. Specimens of this manufacturer's work are extremely rare. His mark consists of his initials set against a cloverleaf punch.

VERNON, SAMUEL

Samuel Vernon was one of the early silversmiths at the town of Providence, Rhode Island, which later became one of the nation's headquarters for fine silverware. He was born in 1683 and was in the business from around 1725. His activities prior to becoming a silversmith are not recorded. He served as a Justice of the Peace in Providence. Samuel Vernon died in 1737. His works are not too often found on the market. Usually his mark consisted of the letters SV in a heart-shaped punch, with a tiny cross beneath them.

WALRAVEN, JOHN

John Walraven worked at Baltimore in the late 18th and early 19th centuries. Because the city of Baltimore regularly published a directory, the years in which its smiths were active can be pretty conclusively established. Walraven's name appears in the directory from 1795 to 1808, listing him as a silversmith and dealer in hardware. He was born in 1771 and died in 1814. When he ran newspaper ads, he referred to himself as a silversmith and goldsmith. His mark consists of his surname in slanting script letters preceded by an initial, within a shaped rectangular frame.

YOU, THOMAS

Thomas You worked at Charleston, South Carolina in the 18th century. He was born in 1735 and was in the business by 1756, as a goldsmith and silversmith. He also did importing and engraving. He was a frequent advertiser in the local newspapers. You died in 1786 at the age of 51. His mark was a crude initial punch with the letters TY inside a rectangle with rounded sides.

PSEUDO-HALLMARKS OR AMERICAN SILVERSMITHS

A pseudo-hallmark is an artificial or contrived hallmark, and is peculiar to *American* silver. It will not be found on the silverware of Great Britain, which carries authentic hallmarks. British silverware was required by governmental law to be hallmarked, as a guarantee of its fineness. This practice began centuries ago, following numerous complaints of fraud against silversmiths who misrepresented the fineness of their wares. A royal corporation was established to monitor the use of hallmarks. As it was located in the *guild hall* — the headquarters of the silversmiths' guild — the markings were thus called HALLmarks. Likenesses of animals and birds were the most commonly used.

No hallmarking laws existed in America, so the American smiths were not required to use markings. Nevertheless, many of them chose to mark their products in a manner similar to British silverware, to give them the distinction and status of British silverware. Mostly, the same types of markings were used, but occasionally some very original ones will be found.

MARKINGS ON SILVER

To identify the various types of plating combinations many pieces manufactured were stamped with letters that indicated the base metal and plating process used. Pieces were marked as follows:

EPNS — Electroplate on nickel silver
EPBM — Electroplate on Britannia Metal
EPWM — Electroplate on White Metal
EPC — Electroplate on copper
EPNS-WMM — Electroplate on nickel silver with white metal mounts.

In addition to trademark and/or the above designations, many manufacturers of plated flatware stamped the quality upon their goods. These are:

A.I — standard thickness of plating
XII — sectional plate
4 — double plating on teaspoons
6 — double plating on dessert spoons and forks
  and when found on teaspoons represents triple plating
8 — double plating on tablespoons
9 — triple plating on dessert spoons and forks
12 — triple plating on tablespoons

SELLING SILVER

There are of course numerous different kinds of silver articles, old and modern, high-grade and low, decorative and plain. To simplify matters we have grouped them into categories as follows. Any type of silver that you might possibly own should fall into one of these classifications.

1. .999 or .999 + fine silver, such as *marked* bars and ingots

2. Items of melt value — meaning the silver they contain is worth as much, or more than, the item could be sold for as merchandise. *Most* things made of silver, new and secondhand, fall in this class: common circulated coins, tableware, toilette articles, old jewelry, etc.

3. Articles of silver which have greater melt value: uncirculated or scarce-date coins, popular antiques and collectors' items, works of sculpture.

The approach to be taken in selling depends to some extent upon whether you have Category One, Category Two, or Category Three material.

All of them are salable, and there are many dealers who will gladly purchase any kind of silver you might have to offer, from a few grubby coins to a pharoah's treasure. But you are likely to do better, in terms of price and fair treatment, if you become a little choosey about selecting a buyer.

.999 or .999 + FINE SILVER. Bars and ingots, bearing a fineness marking and (preferably) the name of a refiner, are the least trouble to sell. You know beforehand exactly what they're worth, based on the day's spot price; and, what may be more important, any prospective buyer *knows that you know* what they're worth. There will not be any haggling over the price. Their value is a matter of record; how much of that value you receive depends upon the dealer's rate of commission and spot price on that day. If the dealer makes a fulltime business of buying and selling precious metals, his handling charges for .999 silver should be prominently displayed in the show window or posted inside. If the handling charge is not posted, this naturally leads to speculation that no fixed charge exists but that the percentage is changed customer-by-customer depending on how much the dealer feels he can get. You should avoid doing business with buyers of this type. Reputable dealers work off a standard handling charge and are more than content with the profits they realize from it. They treat every seller alike, whether the transaction is large or small or the seller appears to be knowledgeable or uninformed. These dealers do a tremendous volume of business, because of their reputation for fair practices, and do much better than the gypsters. The respectable dealers are just as dedicated to protecting their reputations as the fly-by-nighters are to gouging out unfair profits.

The handling charge for buying silver bullion is greater than for gold. This is true even of .999 fine, where no refining is necessary. A fair commission charge or discount on .999 bars or ingots is anywhere from 10% to 12% off "spot." In other words, if you present $500 worth of silver (according to the spot price on that day), you can expect to be paid $400 to $450. In times of rapidly soaring prices — or rapidly falling ones — dealers might adjust their commissions upward or downward to achieve (or attempt to achieve) a balanced flow of buyers and sellers. There is nothing illegal in this so long as the commission charge is posted and all customers are charged the same rate. When utter chaos occurs, as in the gold/silver stampede of January, 1980, some dealers will temporarily discontinue buying and/or selling. This, too, is their right.

ITEMS OF MELT VALUE. Coin dealers and bullion brokers will sometimes purchase miscellaneous articles of melt value. Coin dealers will obviously purchase common-date circulated coins, and pay you the spot price on that day less their handling fee. For many kinds of melt-value articles, however, you will need to find a dealer who advertises to purchase scrap silver or "anything of melt value." Such individuals were once hard to locate but in the past 1-1½ years they have been appearing in increasing numbers, and no matter where you live there should be one (probably more) very close by. The same advice given above about buying practices applies here, too. The reputable melt-value buyer advertises his prices or calculates according to spot on that day, charging a standard handling fee. There is some leeway here, however, as the scrap buyer might occasionally be purchasing unmarked or other questionable articles, and for these he is not required to pay any announced or posted sum. He takes a certain gamble on such items because the quantity of silver they contain is not positively known; he is therefore justified in making an estimated valuation, and offering a price based on this valuation. The seller is, of course, at liberty to accept or refuse it. He may wish to obtain another offer before reaching a decision. Offers for unmarked or other problem pieces will vary more than for marked silver. (An example of a "problem piece" is something made partly of silver and partly of another material, such as a fork with a bone handle, which is hard to weigh.)

Be prepared to accept a rather substantial discount from the spot price, for the dealer's handling charge. The discount on scrap items is always higher than for .999 bars or ingots, because the refinery to which the dealer resells them will not pay as much. They must go through a refining process to extract the alloy. This is costly and the cost is naturally passed along, as is always the case in business, to the public. A fair commission charge or discount on melt items is 10% to 25% off "spot." Thus, if you sell scrap silver with a bullion melt value of $500, you should receive $375.00 to $450.00

Another reason why discounts are smaller on bars and ingots is that the dealers often do not pass them along to refineries, but simply resell them to investors.

It is important, when contemplating the sale of silver as scrap bullion, that the item's overall value be considered in relation to the "melt" value.

When something is sold for melting, whatever it may be, you will be paid the current spot price on that day (if the buyer is reputable) less a discount for the buyer's commission. This is true whether the object is a coin, a silver ingot, or a chalice made in France in the 14th century. The scrap dealer buys it as scrap — nothing more.

Whether he turns around and resells it as scrap is another matter. Dealers, even if they appear totally without knowledge of art or collectors' items, are fairly adept at identifying *objects that should not be melted*. They will buy them at the melt value, but will sell them to dealers in antiques or whatever the article happens to be. All scrap merchants have friends in related trades, to whom they dispose of worthwhile items that come in. Quite a few scrap dealers run their own coin and/or antiques businesses, too, and use favorable purchases for their own stock. By buying merchandise for its scrap value, they can get it cheaper, in many instances, than they would be compelled to pay if buying from a collector.

The scrap dealer profits greatly from the simple fact that the public, at large, has a hard time distinguishing *silver that should be melted from silver that shouldn't*. This is especially true of persons who have not personally bought the objects presented, but found them in their attic or acquired them in some other way. In these cases they are likely to have no idea of the value, and may be very happy to get the "spot" price for something worth many, many times more.

There is no point asking the scrap dealer for his opinion of whether the item should be sold for melting. He is not impartial. He wants to make money on your merchandise and cannot be depended on to give a straightforward answer — assuming he has the knowledge to do this in the first place. An antiques dealer may likewise undervalue an item. The temptation to do this is very strong for some dealers (the trade as a whole is ethical — let's not have any misunderstanding) when they see that the owner is totally uninformed. If you must, as a last resort, obtain a price estimate from a dealer, you are more likely to get an accurate one by taking the right manner of approach and by getting estimates *from several dealers for comparison.* When someone goes into a shop, and admits his lack of knowledge by saying, "I have no idea what this is worth . . .," this is a red flag for the dealer to take advantage. Even if you have no idea, don't say so. Conceal your ignorance of the item's value as best as possible. The clever seller will say something like this: "I'd like to get an idea of what this would be worth *to you."* This implies that he has a good notion of the value but is simply interested in seeing what the dealer will pay. Then when a dealer asks you: "Well what do you think it's worth?" Don't give him a figure as this will put an absolute ceiling on his offer, simply ask him to make you an offer.

As far as modern manufactured objects are concerned, they can usually be sold for the melt value only. This may seem unfair, especially if you bought a dinner service for $800 and it contained, at the time $300 worth of silver. You might expect to be paid, when reselling it, the current melt value plus the difference between its original bullion value and retail price ($500). but you won't be, because that $500 represented profits to the manufacturer, wholesaler, shopkeeper and others, and none of it can be reclaimed. It's in their pockets and it's gone forever. What you have now is X amount of silver; the fact that it happens to be in the shape of saucers and forks and other objects is meaningless in most cases.

Antiques and collectors' items are another matter. If something is genuinely old, or for some special reason is out of the ordinary (if it belonged to a famous person, for example, or is a highly collectible limited edition), it could very possibly have greater than melt value. The difference between melt value and collector value cannot be shown on a chart, it all depends on the specific object, and varies from one to another. The 14th century French chalice we mentioned above might contain $2,000 worth of silver and have a collector value of $50,000 or more. Silver bookbindings (which are rare) contain extremely little silver by weight, but are very valuable because of their scarcity and artistry that went into them. A binding with 5 or 6 ounces of silver could sell for $20,000. In general, though, the difference between the melt value and collector value of antiques and art objects is not nearly this extreme. Miscellaneous silverware from the Victorian and Edwardian eras (say 1840-1910), unless very ornate, generally can be sold for about 20% more than the melt value. In other words if you have a snuffbox containing two ounces of .999 + silver (plus alloy), and the spot price is $15, you can expect to be paid about $40 for it. If it had no collector value, you would get only about $25, as the dealer would take his handling charges out. For more detailed information, refer to the following chapter on antique silver articles.

ANTIQUE SILVER ARTICLES

Because of silver's immense popularity in manufacturing and craftwork for centuries and centuries, antiques made of silver (or containing silver components) are abundant.

Their surface appearance may be slightly different than that of modern silver of the identical grade, due to the effects of age. If silver is not regularly cleaned and polished, it can lose its luster and become grimy looking. When exposed for ages to the harshness of nature, such as silver articles from shipboard or decorations from the exteriors of houses, the condition may truly be poor. Any silver item that has been buried underground for a long time (archaeological silver), or brought up from a shipwreck, is sure to show signs of its ordeal.

The melt value of these items, appearance notwithstanding, is the same as for modern silver of the same fineness and weight. It is no more and no less. But, unlike modern silver, which may be flashy and very catching to the eye, these old soldiers frequently have an added *collector value* which removes them from the melt category.

It should not be presumed that anything to which the magic word "antique" attaches is automatically very valuable. An item can be extremely old without exciting great collector interest, either because of commonness, poor workmanship, bad condition or other considerations. Some articles are very "offbeat" and appeal only to highly specialized collectors, of which there may be few in the market at any given time. An antique silver object may only be worth 10% or 20% more than the melt value — but some are worth much more.

It is important to keep in mind that an article need not fall under the definition of "antique," generally taken to mean 100 years old or older, to have *collector* value. Collectors, being unpredictable folk, sometimes value a semi-modern item higher than a very old one, because of its manufacturer, design, topical interest or for various other reasons.

With collectors' items, the quantity of silver they contain is often secondary to other considerations in arriving at a value. An article made of one ounce of .925 fine could outsell something containing three or four ounces of the same grade; it has a much lower melt value but the *other considerations* greatly enhance its price. For example, a decorative table fork made in England in the reign of George I (early 18th century) will generally contain from two to three ounces of .925 fine silver. This would mean $30-$50 worth of silver — approximately — when the spot price is in the $15-$16 category. If the workmanship is really outstanding, as it sometimes was on these specimens, it could easily have a collector value of $150.

You will find, however, that *most* antiques and collectors' items made of silver are valued *primarily for the silver.* In other words, more than 50% of their value is in the bullion. The great majority of silver articles found in ordinary antiques shops, which date no earlier than the mid 1800's and are not remarkable in workmanship, are in that class. So, too, are probably any silver antiques you have in your attic or are preserving as family heirlooms. Unless extremely old, or brilliantly made, they are likely to carry most of their value in bullion content. Obviously, if you have a punch bowl made by Paul Revere, or a salver known to have been owned by George Washington, the collector value is 20 or 30 times the bullion value or more. (But don't jump to conclusions on these things — fakes are very abundant.)

Why should this be so? Why should an object 100 or more years old, which has collector appeal, be worth only a fractional sum above the bullion value?

The answer lies mostly in the fact that bullion prices have advanced much more sharply, since mid 1979, than prices on collectors' items. When silver was $3 an ounce (not really too long ago), miscellaneous Victorian and Edwardiana made of silver was selling at *double* to *triple* the bullion value. But the premium for collector value was still just a few dollars. Today, the collector premium has risen somewhat, but it has been vastly overshadowed by advances in bullion prices.

The following may help to illustrate this:

Hairbrush containing four ounces of .999 silver (approx.), made c. 1885, sold at $25 in 1973. Silver was $3 per ounce. Item contained $12 worth (approx.) of silver, had $13 collector value — more collector value than bullion value.

Same item sells at 85.00 in 1982, with spot price of silver at $15. Item now has $60 bullion value, $25 collector value, or 2½ times as much bullion value as collector value. Collector value nearly doubled since 1973 ($13 to $25), bullion value increased more than 5 times.

There are many other factors involved, too, much too numerous to discuss at length.

Unfortunately for the owners of such material, the discount taken by dealers off their buying prices is quite high for antiques and other collectors items. In the chapter on selling silver, we pointed out that the usual discount or handling fee for melt-value objects is 10% to 25%. You receive the full spot price for these objects less 10-25%. With antiques or collectors' items, the same discount is taken from spot (even though there is no intention of shipping off your filigreed pillbox to a refiner), plus another discount — and a bigger one — from the collector value.

It usually works out something like the following.

Say you're selling the aforementioned c. 1885 silver hairbrush, which has a retail value of $125 and contains $100 worth of silver. Ten to 15% will be knocked off the bullion value, bringing that down to $85-90. From the collector value at least 50% will be shaved, making it $12.50 or less. Put them together and you get a price of $97.50-$102.50 — which means an overall discount on the item of about 20%. And you will be lucky to get away that well! Often the collector value is cut down by 75%, depending on the item, the dealer's stock, his class of cutsomers, and, perhaps, the mood he happens to be in that day. There is no standard rate of discount because collectors' items have no standard retail prices. It's all a matter of "What will you pay?"

Some devious dealers — in antiques, secondhand items and related — have reaped windfall profits from the bullion upsurge of recent months. They have devised a variety of what are strictly gimmicks, used in buying from the public, to acquire items at less than reputable dealers pay. Some will pay only the bullion value, less commission, claiming that the high price of silver makes it impossible for them "to make a larger investment." Or they may go so far as to say that old silver is less valuable than modern because of oxidizaton or some such reason, which of course is not true.

PROTECTING YOUR SILVER

Silver has long been popular with the criminal element in our society since, unlike television sets or expensive china, it is easily transported and can be rendered unidentifiable by melting it down. Although there is no

100% sure method of safeguarding a collection, there are steps which can be taken to cut down on the risks.

(a) Install a burglar alarm system. The more elaborate systems can be quite expensive and the cost must be weighed against the value of the collection. Many people install two systems, an expensive one and an inexpensive back-up.

(b) Don't display your silver where it is easily seen through windows or by repairmen or meter readers. If a stranger does see your collection, make it a point to tell them that it's cheap silver plate and not sterling. It pays not to have too much to say about your silver collection to friends and acquaintances. Although they may be perfectly honest they may also talk too much.

(c) Many well-bred burglars will call first before dropping in for a visit, so some people leave their phones off the hook if going out for only a brief while. Tighten up security a bit if there is a rash of wong number calls, since this ploy is frequently used to determine a household's schedule.

(d) Time is of the essence to thieves, so anything which slows them down is a help. Keep your silver under lock and key and hide the key. The burglar may well opt for your leather luggage or new ten-speed bike, both of which would be easier to replace than great-grandmother's silver.

(e) Rent a bank vault for infrequently used pieces of silver. There is usually enough warning that twelve people are coming for a sit-down dinner to allow for a quick trip to the bank to retrieve the silver. If frequency of use precludes this, keep a basic set around the house and store those items not likely to be needed in the vault.

Although the above information may help protect against the casual thief, there is really little or no protection against the professional burglar or against loss from fire. Adequate insurance protection can help soften the blow a bit, and it is wise to check in advance on the limits of a policy. For example, although a homeowner may have household goods covered for a total of $30,000 there might be a limit of $500 for sterling silver.

Once stolen, precious little silver is ever recovered. Keep in mind that if the police do turn up your items you will be required to prove that they are indeed yours. This is best accomplished by keeping accurate records on all silver purchases. A vague listing such as 67 pieces of Company A's "British Tyrant" may very well be inadequate for these purposes. The inventory should read something like:

Company A's "British Tyrant," 67 piece set including —
12 teaspoons (6 with monogram "P", 6 with no monogram, all in excellent condition); 1 gravy ladle (monogram "P", dent in bowl); and so on for all items in the set.

Although most stolen silver ends up in the melting pot there is no harm in wandering around the area antiques shops and flea markets just in case. The laws governing return of stolen items vary somewhat from state to state, but in many cases there can be a long wait for them. If you think you have spotted your silver call the authorities rather than trying to retrieve them yourself.

CARE AND STORAGE OF SILVER AND SILVER PLATE

It is always best to store plated or sterling flatware in a box or drawer lined with a soft cloth treated to impart resistant qualities. If you do not use it regularly it should be wrapped in tissue and sealed in plastic bags to prevent excessive tarnishing from oxidation.

Holloware, generally not used quite as often or regularly as flatware, should be stored in the same manner. This of course is a decided disadvantage if one wishes to enjoy the beauty of old silver on display. The best way is to display the pieces in a glass front cabinet that is as airtight as can be reasonably be expected of fine furniture. Tucking a few pieces of gum camphor in unobtrusive locations within the cabinet will help to retard the inevitable tarnish development.

The best method of day to day caring for silver is an immediate washing after use, in warm, soapy water, drying with a soft cloth and proper storage. It is the proper, repeated washing, tarnishing, and polishing cycle over the years that imparts the beautiful patina associated with fine old silver.

There are a number of good products on the market today for the care, cleaning and polishing of silver, but the collector must take care to use them properly.

There are liquid cleaners into which articles may be dipped, but most will not only remove the tarnish from intended areas but will also remove the tarnish in crevices and depressed areas which define the decorative details so well.

Be wary of commercially available metal cleaners with an abrasive powder ingredient. Use only cleaners recommended for silver.

GLOSSARY

Acanthus—A form of ornamentation taken from the leaf of the acanthus plant.

Ajoure—A French term applied to metalwork which is perforated, pierced, or open.

Albata—An infrequently used word for Nickel Silver or German Silver.

Alchemy—An alloy of tin and copper used to make a very high quality pewter in the 16th and 17th centuries. The word derives from the unsuccessful Dark Ages attempts to turn base metals into gold.

Alcomy—An alloy of several base metals used primarily in making buttons.

Alloy—A substance made up of two or more metals mixed while in molten form.

Alpacca—An infrequently used word for Nickel Silver or German Silver.

Aluminum Silver—A composition of aluminum and silver, usually 3 parts silver to 97 parts aluminum. The resulting alloy is harder than aluminum.

Amorini—A silver decoration consisting of cherub-like figures. Italian in origin.

Anneal—A process by which silver is repeatedly reheated after gradual cooling to keep it malleable while it is being worked. It has the added advantage of removing or reducing internal stress in the object being fashioned.

Amthemion—Honeysuckle motif inspired from classical architecture.

Applied Work—Details (spouts, handles, etc.) and decorations which have been made separately and applied to an object with solder.

Aqua Regia—A chemical widely used in the jewelry industry, especially for testing the fineness of gold. Agua regia is made of three parts hydrochloric acid and one part nitric acid.

Arabesque—A complex interwoven design from the Italian Renaissance period.

Argentine—An alloy of tin and antimony used as a base for silver plating. Sometimes used synonymously with Nickel Silver or German Silver.

Art Deco—A modernistic style which was popular in the United States in the 1920's and 1930's. It is characterized by symmetrical, rectilinear styling.

Art Nouveau—A style of the late 19th and early 20th century, characterized by curvilinear styling. The motifs and designs were frequently taken from Nature.

Assay—A test to determine whether a metal is of the required composition and quality.

Balance Scale—A scale operating solely by the balance principal, rather than by springs or the use of a sliding weight. It consists of two pans suspended on hangers, connected at the top to a horizontal bar containing a pivot at the center. When empty, the pans are at precisely equal distance from the ground. For weighing, the object(s) to be weighed are placed in one pan, and counterweights of established weight in the other. The object(s) weight is determined by the weight of counterweights needed to precisely balance it.

Base Metal—An alloy or metal of relatively low value to which a coating or plating of a more valuable metal is applied.

Beading—A border decoration consisting of small, bead-like contiguous forms. Commonly found on silver of the late 18th or early 19th centuries.

Bell Metal—A type of old Sheffield Plate consisting of a very heavy coating of silver. First introduced in 1789.

Bleeding—Term used when a silver plating was worn off in spots and the copper showing through.

Bright Cut—A form of engraved decoration whereupon a portion of the metal is removed with a bevelled cutting instrument. The result is a jewel-like faceted sparkle.

Bright Finish—Highly polished surface obtained by using jeweler's rouge on a polishing wheel.

Britannia—An alloy closely related to pewter but differing in composition. It is made up of tin, copper and antimony (as is pewter), but contains no lead as pewter does. It was frequently used as a base metal in the early days of silver plating.

Bronze—An alloy mostly composed of copper and tin.

Buffing—Polishing the surface of metal, usually with a flexible wheel, leaving a smooth, mar-free surface.

Burnishing—When silverplate is formed it is composed of crystalline forms aggregated upon the surface of the base metal. A hard tool is used to rub the surface to smooth and harden the silverplate by spreading the crystals together and forcing them into the surface irregularities of base metal. The result is a harder, more durable finish which is also more resistant to tarnishing.

Butler Finish—A dull-appearing finish obtained by buffing with a wire wheel which impacts countless tiny scratches to the surface.

Cable—A design similar to twisted rope. Derived from Norman architecture.

Cartouche—A design in the shape of a shield or scroll with curled edges.

Caryatid—A statue of a woman used as a column or base.

Cast—Formed in a mold.

Champleve—Grooves or troughs are cut into the metal surface and filled with enamel ingredients which are then melted. The surface is then usually ground smooth and polished.

Clipping—A once-prevalent method of criminally acquiring bullion, by trimming small portions from coin edges and then passing the coins at their face value. This occurred in the days of hammered coins, whose edges were not perfectly symmetrical.

Chasing—A vague general term used to describe effects produced by chisels and hammers on cold metal without the removal of any of the metal.

Cloissone—A design is applied to the surface of the object by soldering a wire or metal ribbon on edge in the desired pattern. Enamel is then poured into the network of cells, fused, and then ground and polished. The result is an enamel design with the wire or ribbon edges showing through.

Coin/Coin Silver—Term used to indicate 900 parts of silver and 100 parts of copper in 1000 parts. This is the standard previously used by American silversmiths prior to the introduction of the sterling standard. Sometimes called Pure Coin, Dollar, Standard or Premium.

Commercial Silver—999/1000 fine or higher.

Corrosion—The discoloration of patina to which old, neglected (not regulary polished) silver can fall prey results from acids or oxides acting upon chemical properties in the metal. It can generally be removed or at least diminished, by treatment with common solvent (silver cleaner). However, in the case of collectors' items hundreds of years old, such as coins or religious objects, experts generally advise against its removal.

Craig Silver—Used in making knives, similar to German Silver.

C-Scroll—A Rococo scroll design in the form of the letter "C". Frequently used to describe the shape of handles. Also called single scroll.

Cutler—One who deals in, sells, makes or repairs knives and cooking utensils.

Cutlery—Items having a cutting edge.

Dichromate—A chemical solution used for testing the composition of metal article. Dichromate is composed of potassium cishromate and nitric acid.

Domed—Spheroid type of cover first used in the early 18th Century. Frequently used on tankards, teapots, etc.

Double-Scroll—An S-shaped line, frequently used in handle design.

Draw Plates—Metal parts of a drawing bench through which wire is drawn to reduce its size or change its shape.

Electrolysis—The process of conducting an electric current by an electrolyte of charged particles. This process is used to remove silver or to deposit silver on a base metal.

Electroplate—Articles made of a base metal coated with silver by electrolysis.

Electrotype—Reproduction of an object by electroplating a wax impression.

Electrum—A natural, pale yellow alloy of gold and silver. Also an alloy made of 8 parts copper, 4 parts nickel, and 3½ parts zinc.

Embossing—Making raised designs on the surface of an object by hammering from the reverse side. Also see repousse.

Engraving—Forming a design on metal by removing or cutting away the metal. A common example of this type of work would be monogramming.

Etching—Surface decoration done with acid.

Feather Edge—A chased edge of slanting lines, sometimes used to ornament spoon handles.

Festoon—A garland of leaves or flowers hanging in a curve.

File Mark—A recessed mark left upon an object as the result of filing, to test its metallic content. File marks are occasionally found on gold coins, tested for the possibility of being counterfeit. They also appear on items that proved to be of low bullion or non-bullion content, as the majority of tested objects found to be of solid gold or silver are sent for melting.

Fineness—The degree of purity in an object of precious metal, usually expressed by hundredths in decimal form (such as .995, which means 99½ parts pure and ½ part of alloy). It may also be written in terms of a percentage; in the case of the example given, the percentage equivalent would be 99½%. The highest degree of obtainable fineness in gold or silver is expressed as .999 +, rather than 1.000, because of the impossibility of guranteeing that all minor traces of incidental metallic substances have been removed.

Fine Silver—The term applied to silver which is at least 999/1000 pure. Fine silver is too soft for most purposes.

Finial—A terminating ornament on lids, sometimes in the form of animals or flowers.

Flash Plate—Cheap, unbuffed plated ware.

Flat Chasing—Surface decoration in very low relief. Popular in England in the early 1700's.

Flatware—Term used for knives, forks, spoons, and other such items used for eating.

Fluting—A type of decoration with wide, smooth concave grooves with ridges between.

Forging—The fashioning of metal into shapes by alternate heating and hammering.

Gadroon—A border trim of reeds and flutes, sometimes referred to as knurling.

Gilding—A thin coating of gold on an item. Prior to the introduction of electroplating, the usual method of gilding was to mix gold with mercury, apply it to the object and heat it. The mercury evaporated leaving a coating of gold on the object.

German Silver—See Nickel Silver.

Gold Plated—Covered with a thin layer of gold.

Gold Wash—See Gold Plating and Gilding.

Graver—A chisel used in the engraving of silver.

Guilloche—A motif of interlaced circular forms, usually with a flower in the center.

Hallmark—The official mark used by the English to indicate items were of an acceptable nature. The term has been corrupted to mean any stamp or trademark on silver items.

Holloware—A general term applying to objects in the form of hollow vessels such as bowls, pitchers, pots and mugs.

Husks—Festoons of seeds.

Ingot—Bar of silver or other metal.

Latten—An alloy of copper, zinc and brass.

Maker's Mark—A mark, initials or name, struck on an item to indicate who made it.

Malleable—Capable of being extended or molded by being beaten with a hammer.

Matte Finish—A dull surface finish produced by light hammering.

Melt Value—The bullion value of any object containing precious metal. When sold for melting, the full price of an item's bullion content is not received but only a percentage of it. Some articles, such as gold or silver coins of key dates or mintmarks, have a higher retail or "intact" value than melt value and obviously should not be melted.

Mounts—Handles, spouts, finials, feet, etc.

Nickel Silver—An alloy of nickle, copper and zinc. Usually 65% copper, 5% to 25% copper, and 10% to 30% zinc.

Niello—Line engraving on silver which is filled in with black enamel.

Oxidizing—Application of an oxide to a metal to darken the surface. Used to heighten detail by emphasizing shadows and highlights.

Parcel-gilt—Partly gilded.

Patina—Soft luster and satiny feel on old silver usually produced by use and polishing through the years.

Planishing—Smoothing out of the hammering marks left by fashioning a piece of silver.

Plating—The covering of base metal articles with a layer of gold or silver, which may be of various thickness and grades. Presence of plating may be discovered by filing and using nitric acid, or subjecting the item to specific gravity testing.

Plique-a-jour—Translucent enamel without a backing, framed within metalwork. The effect is much like that of stained glass.

Pricking—Delicate engraving using a needle point instrument.

Pure Coin—See Coin.

Purity—The proportion of precious metal in an object vs. base metal. A purity of .900 would mean a content of 90% precious metal and 10% base metal alloy, or a ratio of 9-to-1.

Raising—Creation of a piece of hollowware from a flat sheed of silver by hammering in ever-increasing concentric circles over a series of anvils.

Repousse—A refinement of embossing where a raised design is hammered out from the inside of an object and then usually enhanced by surface chasing.

Reticulated—Piercing on rims or sides of hollowware.

Rococo—An extremely ornate, curvilinear form of decoration imitative of foliage, scrolls and shellwork. Originated in France during the reign of Louis XV.

Rolled Plate—See Sheffield Plate.

Rope Molding—A border trim which resembles a rope.

Satin Finish—A satin finish is produced in the same way as a butler finish, but leaves deeper scratches.

Scorper—Small, variously shaped chisels used in engraving.

Scrap—Material made of or containing precious metal, which has no value beyond that of its bullion content and is suitable only for melting. Old spectacle frames containing gold are an example of typical scrap.

Serrated—Toothed or notched.

Sheffield Plate—Frequently called "old Sheffield plate" to distinguish it from electroplate. Developed around 1743 by Thomas Boulsover. Made by a sheet of copper being fused with a thin sheet of silver on one or both sides. The fused sheet is then rolled down to the desired thickness.

Silver Plate—The term used to describe articles made of a base metal and then electroplated with silver. Also seen as silverplate and silver-plate. No to be confused with "Plate" as used in England when referring to solid silver items.

Silver Shield—The placing of a solid or sterling silver shield device on a piece of silver-plated ware for purposes of engraving. Some silver plate is so thin that engraving would cut though it to base metal.

Solid—When an object is referred to as solid bullion, this means it is not plated or filled but that its interior composition is identical to its exterior. No inference can be drawn, however, merely on strength of such evidence that the bullion is either heavily or lightly alloyed. "Solid gold" is not necessarily 24K.

Specific Gravity—A method of testing the composition of metallic objects, which measures their desplacement of water in relation to their bulk. Each metal element has an established specific gravity.

Spinning—Pressing a flat sheet of metal against a revolving form on a lathe so as to produce a piece of hollowware.

Spot Price—"Spot Price" is the price at which precious metal is being traded at any given time. Spot prices are always calculated on the basis of one full troy ounce and must be multiplied or divided to arrive at prices for larger or smaller quantities. The spot price is achieved in day to day trading in gold markets, just as are prices for stocks and other commodities. Generally, the London spot is used as the world barometer, after conversion from pounds to dollars.

Stamping—Using dies and hammers to strike a mark in a piece of metal. Used in decorating.

Standard—See Coin.

Sterling Silver—925 parts silver and 75 parts added metal, usually copper, to give the silver the needed strength to be worked into durable items.

Stoning—Polishing silver with a special stone made for this purpose.

Strapwork—Narrow, folded interlacing bands or straps.

Swaged—Formed by a process of rolling or hammering.

Tempering—A process of heating and cooling by which metal is strengthened.

Touch—Silversmith's mark, impressed with a die or punch.

Touchstone—A hard siliceous stone on which a piece of silver or gold of known quality can be rubbed to compare its mark with that of any item being assayed.

Trademark—Symbol or trade name marked on an item of silver to identify the manufacturer.

Vermeil—Gold plating on silver.

White Metal—An alloy made up of tin with either copper, lead, antimony or bismuth. The color of the metal will be whiter as more tin is used.

DEALER DIRECTORY

Edward G. Wilson
1802 Chesthut Street
Philadelphia, PA 19103
215-563-7369

Fine estate and antique silver; active, inactive and obsolete sterling and coin silver flatware patterns matched.

•

House of Antiques
Joseph Seigel & Chas. Kuhnline
202 N. 5th Street
Springfield, Illinois 62701
217-544-9677

Active, inactive and obsolete sterling flatware patterns.

Locator's, Inc.
908 Rock Street
Little Rock, Arkansas 72202
501-371-0858

Out-of-production patterns.

Robinson's
Box 180
Trenton, N.J. 08601

China and crystal liners for sterling holders.

Silver Antiquities
Mrs. Roz Mouber
Post Office Box 7092
Kansas City, Missouri 64113
816-333-1361

Specializing in antique and unique silver, Victorian and turn-of-the-century. Pattern matching service for ornate patterns introduced before 1910, and unusual serving pieces and hollowware.

Silver Lane Antiques
Mary Moore
Post Office Box 322
San Leandro, CA 94577
415-483-0632

Pattern matching specialist — obsolete, current and discontinued sterling flatware.

(Please include a self-addressed, stamped envelope when writing to these dealers.) The author has not personally dealt with all of them, so their inclusion here should not be taken as a recommendation. Conversely, their inclusion should not be construed as an endorsement by them of the prices and/or opinion set forth in this book. Dealers wishing to be listed in future editions of this book may write to the address in the introduction.

HOW TO USE THIS BOOK

THE OFFICIAL 1983 PRICE GUIDE TO AMERICAN SILVER & SILVER PLATE has been designed for easy use by collector, dealer, and general public. The main section lists items which fall mainly into the class of "pattern ware": that is, silver tableware and accessories produced by factories and marketed under pattern names. Another section, titled Special Items, deals with early antique silverware and articles of an unusual or antique nature. Both sections are in alphabetical format by *type of item*. Within each category the listed specimens are arranged alphabetically by manufacturer. Every effort has been made to supply adequate information for a *positive* identification, including markings, decorative style, size and weight.

To find the proper listing for any item, the item must be identified to its specific use. If you are unsure whether a fork (for example) is a dinner fork, salad fork, etc., look under each of the headings that might possibly pertain to it. Soup ladles and punch ladles are often mistaken for each other; once again the reader should consult both sections, even if he feels certain that he has correctly identified the item.

A few brief notes concerning the information in this book:

Classification of Items. Items have been classified according to the most reliable information. Sometimes, auction catalogues and dealers' lists misclassify items. The reader is urged to keep this in mind, especially in the case of objects which lend themselves to errors of this kind. *Early antique wares* have been classified by the names by which they were originally known. Prior to 1800, drinking mugs were commonly called *canns,* and we have listed them as such. This has been the standard practice in the antiques trade.

Manufacturers. Items have been attributed to manufacturers only when they bear identifiable markings. No attempts have been made to attribute unmarked pieces. Even among the most advanced experts, the success ratio of this kind of attribution is low. *Full names of makers are given when known,* even if the actual marking on the item consists only of initial letters. The reader should keep in mind that *before about 1820,* most smiths whose first names started with J (John, James, Joseph etc.) changed the initial to I in their mark. Thus, John Jones appears as IJ. This was done to achieve a more "classical" appearance, in keeping with inscriptions on architecture and monuments.

Place of Manufacture. The majority of old silverware does not carry any indication of its place of manufacture. In cases where the place of origin of early antique pieces has been established, this information is included in the listings, even if it is not actually stamped on the objects themselves.

Pattern. Pattern names are used according to the terminology of the silver industry. For early antique wares, prior to the use of standard industry patterns, each item is described to the fullest and clearest possible detail.

Dates. Silverware is almost never dated. Dates have been estimated for some of the early antique and special item pieces, based on the period in which their manufacturer was active or other pertinent information. Usually, only a very rough dating is possible.

Size. Measurements are given in inches. Items whose height exceeds their width (such as candlesticks) are measured by height; in the case of objects WIDER THAN TALL, the width is stated. In other words the stated size is always the *greatest dimension* of the object.

Weight. Weight is given in ounces, even for items which weigh more than one pound. This is because the value of silver bullion is always tabulated by ounces. When an item is marked "not weighable," this indicates it contains non-silver components and in such cases a weight reading would of course be meaningless. In a few cases, where items or sets of items contain a great deal of silver and only a minimal amount of non-silver weight, the weight HAS been indicated and identified as GROSS WEIGHT.

Values. Values stated are the current market prices at the time of going to press. In all cases a price RANGE is given, in fairness to both buyer and seller, as the price of any item — whether rare or common — is never precisely the same in every sale. Prices are *retail prices* as charged by antiques dealers and other dealers in collectors' items. When selling TO a dealer, a fair price would be somewhat less than the figures shown.

ABOUT THE PRICES IN THIS BOOK

Prices in this book were compiled from auction sale results, dealers' catalogues, and advertisements in the nationwide collector periodicals. Only the most current information was used, to reflect values at the actual time of going to press. All sales and sale offerings occured with silver in the $8-10 per ounce range (spot price), the range at which it has now stabilized for more than a year. This has been the first sustained period of price stabilization for silver bullion since the hectic market rush of 1979/80. If any sharp movement should occur in silver bullion prices, this will of course have some effect on values of silver collectibles. Values of *plated* items (which contain little silver) can be expected to remain fairly stable regardless of bullion prices. Items made of solid silver (such as sterling) are more directly influenced by the bullion market, since they have twofold value as bullion and collectors' items. The more silver a piece containes, the more its value will rise or fall with changes in bullion prices. Pieces which are rare, unusual, or of particular interest to collectors, fluctuate less in value than those sold for melting.

To give an example:

Item worth $100 with silver at $10 per ounce, whose value is $20 in bullion and $80 in collector appeal: if silver doubles in value, this item climbs to $120.

Item worth $100 with silver at $10 per ounce, whose value if $80 in bullion and $20 in collector appeal: if silver doubles in value, this item climbs to $180.

Keep apprised of the silver bullion market (reported daily in all newspapers), whether buying or selling.

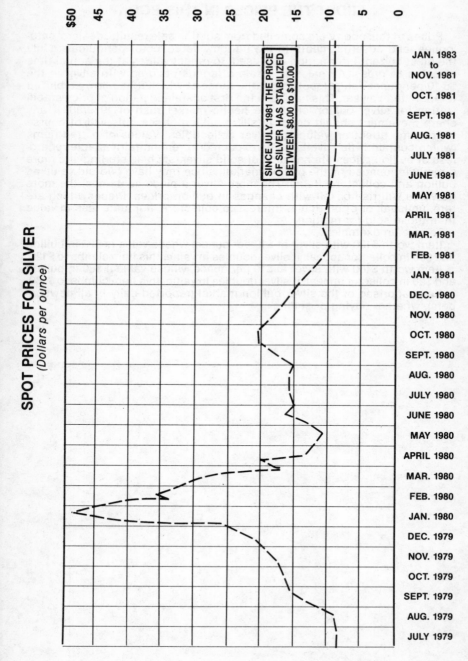

SPOT PRICES FOR SILVER
(Dollars per ounce)

SINCE JULY 1981 THE PRICE OF SILVER HAS STABILIZED BETWEEN $8.00 to $10.00

REFERENCE PUBLICATIONS

The following books may prove useful to those wanting more information about silver and plated wares. In the author's opinion, the three books which are indispensible to the collector or dealer are: (1) the Kovel directory (for identification of coin silver makers); (2) the Rainwater encyclopedia of manufacturers (for identification of later makers' marks); and (3) the Turner book (for pattern identification and general information about silver).

Abbey, Staton. *The Goldsmiths and Silversmiths Handbook.* New York: Van Nostrand, 1952.

Adams, Philip R. "The Adams-Emery Wing at the Cincinnati Art Museum: Silver." *Antiques* 89 (1966): 404-5.

American Art: 1750-1800, Towards Independence. Catalogue of an exhibition, Yale University Art Gallery, and Victoria & Albert Museum. Edited by Charles F. Montgomery and Patricia E. Kane. Boston: New York Graphic Society for the Yale University Art Gallery and the Victoria & Albert Museum, 1976.

American Art from American Collections. Catologue of an exhibition. New York: Metropolitan Museum of Art, 1963.

American Church Silver of the Seventeeth and Eighteenth Centuries with a Few Pieces of Domestic Plate. Catalogue of an exhibition. Boston: Museum of Fine Arts, 1911.

American Silver: The Work of Seventeenth and Eighteenth Centuries. Boston: Museum of Fine Arts, 1906.

American Silver and Art Treasures. Catalogue of an exhibition. London: English-Speaking Union of the Commonwealth, 1960.

Avery, C. Louise. *American Silver of the Seventeenth and Eighteenth Centuries: A Study Based on the Clearwater Collection.* New York: Metropolitan Museum of Art, 1920.

—. *Early American Silver.* New York: Century Co., 1930. Reprint ed., New York: Russell & Russell, 1968.

—. *Early New York Silver.* Catalogue of an exhibition. New York: Metropolitan Museum of Art, 1931.

Bacot, H. Parrot, and Bethany B. Lambdin. "Nineteenth-Century Silver in Natchez." *Antiques* 99 (1971) 412-17.

Banister, Judith. *Old English Silver.* New York: G. P. Putnam's Sons, 1965.

Barr, Lockwood. "Kentucky Silver and Its Makers." *Antiques* 43 (1945): 25-27.

Beckman, Elizabeth D. *Cincinnati Silvermiths, Jewelers, Watchmakers and Clockmakers.* Cincinnati: B. & B. Co., 1975.

Belknap, Henry Wyckoff. *Artists and Craftsmen of Essex County, Massachussetts.* Essex Institute, 1927.

Benson, Rita R., ed. *The Encyclopedia of Early American Silversmiths and Their Marks with a Concise Glossary of Terms.* Harrisburg, Pa.: Benson Gallery Press, 1966.

Bentley, William. *The Diary of William Bentley.* 4 vols. Salem, Mass.: Essex Institute, 1905-14.

Bigelow, David. *History of Prominent Mercantile and Manufacturing Firms in the United States.* Boston: Published by the author, 1857.

Bigelow, Francis Hill. *Historic Silver of the Colonies and Its Makers.* New York: Macmillan, 1917. Reprint ed., New York: Tudor, 1948.

Birdwell, M. M. "Kentucky Silversmiths before 1850. *"Filson Club History Quarterly* 16 (1942): 111-12.

Bishop, J. Leander. *A History of American Manufacturers from 1608 to 1860.* 2 vols. Philadelphia: Edward Young, 1861.

Bohan, Peter J. *American Gold, 1700-1860.* Catalogue of an exhibition. New Haven, Conn.: Yale University Art Gallery, 1963.

Bohan, Peter, and Philip Hammerslough. *Early Connecticut Silver, 1700-1840.* Middletown, Conn.: Wesleyan University Press, 1970.

Bollers, Albert S. *The Industrial History of the United States from the Earliest Settlements to the Present Time.* Norwich, Conn.: Henry Bill, 1879.

Bolton, Charles Knowles. *Bolton's American Armory.* Boston: F. W. Faxon, 1927.

Brown, Joan. "William Faris, Sr., His Sons, and Journeymen, Annapolis Silversmiths." *Antiques* 111 (1977): 378-85.

Buck, John H. *The Early Church Plate of Salem, Massachusetts.* Salem, Mass.: Essex Institute, 1907.

—. *Old Plate, Ecclesiatical, Decorative and Domestic: Its Makers and Marks.* New York: Gorham Manufacturing Co., 1888. New ed., New York: Gorham Manufacturing Co., 1903.

Buhler, Kathryn C. *American Silver.* Cleveland: World, 1950.

—. *American Silver, 1655-1825, in the Museum of Fine Arts, Boston.* 2 vols. Greenwich, Conn.: New York Graphic Society for the Museum of Fine Arts, Boston, 1972.

—. "John Edwards, Goldsmith, and His Progeny." *Antiques* 59 (1951): 288-92.

—. *Massachusetts Silver in the Frank L. and Louise C. Harrington Collection.* Worcester, Mass.: Barre Publishers, 1965.

—. *Mount Vernon Silver.* Mount Vernon, Va.: Mount Vernon Ladies' Association of the Union, 1957.

—. *Paul Revere, Goldsmith, 1735-1818.* Boston: Museum of Fine Arts, 1956.

—. "Silver, 1640-1820." *The Concise Encyclopedia of American Antiques,* edited by Helen Comstock, pp. 123-37, 141-44. New York: Hawthorne Books, 1965.

Buhler, Kathryn C., and Graham Hood. *American Silver: Garvan and Other Collections in the Yale University Art Gallery.* 2 vols. New Haven, Conn.: Yale University Press, 1970.

Burgess, Frederick William. *Silver, Pewter, Sheffield Plate.* New York: Tudor Publishing Co., 1937.

Burrage, Jane B. "Early Silversmiths in Vermont." *Antiques* 67 (1955): 154-55.

Burton, E. Milby. *South Carolina Silversmiths, 1690-1860.* Charleston, S. C.: Charleston Museum, 1942.

Caldwell, Benjamin H., Jr. "Tennessee Silversmiths." *Antiques* 100 (1971): 382-85, 906-13.

Carlisle, Lilian Baker. *Vermont Clock and Watchmakers, Silversmiths, and Jewelers, 1778-1878.* Burlington, Vt.: Privately printed, 1970.

Carpenter, Ralph E., Jr. *The Arts and Crafts of Newport, Rhode Island, 1640-1820.* Newport: Preservation Society of Newport County, 1954.

A Century of Alexandria, District of Columbia, and Georgetown Silver, 1750-1850. Catalogue of an exhibition. Washington, D. C.: Corcoran Gallery of Art, 1966.

Checklist of American Silversmiths' Work in Museums in the New York Metropolitan Area. New York: Metropolitan Museum of Art, 1968.

Christie, Ralph Aldrich. *Silver Sups of Colonial Middletown.* Middletown, Conn.: Privately printed, 1937.

Clark, Victor S. *History of Manufacturers in the United States.* Introduction by Henry W. Farnam. 3 vols. Rev. ed. New York: McGraw-Hill for the Carnegie Institute of Washington, 1929. Vol. 1, 1607-1860. Vol. 2, 1860-93. Vol. 3, 1803-1929.

Clark, Hermann Frederick. *John Coney, Silversmith, 1655-1722.* Introduction by Hollis French. Boston: Houghton Mifflin, 1932.

—. *John Hull, A Builder of the Bay Colony.* Portland, Maine: Southworth-Anthoensen Press, 1940.

Clarke, Hermann Frederick, and Henry Wilder Foote. *Jeremiah Dummer, Colonial Craftsman and Merchant, 1645-1718.* Foreword by E. Alfred Jones. Boston: Houghton Mifflin, 1935.

Classical America, 1815-1845. Catalogue of an exhibition. Newark, N. J.: Newark Museum, 1963.

Clearwater, Alphonso T. *American Silver: List of Unidentified Makers and Works in the Collection of Alphonso T. Clearwater.* Kingston, N. Y. 1913.

Colonial Silversmiths, Masters & Apprentices. Catalogue of an exhibition. Edited by Richard B. K. McLanathan. Introduction by Kathryn C. Buhler. Boston: Museum of Fine Arts, 1956.

Comstock, Helen. "The John Marshall Phillips Collection of Silver." In *The Connoisseur Year Book.* London, 1957.

Craig, James H. *The Arts and Crafts in North Carolina, 1699-1840.* Winston-Salem, N. C.: Museum of Early Southern Decorative Arts, Old Salem, 1965.

Crawford, Rachael B. "The Forbes Family of Silversmiths." *Antiques* 107 (1976): 730-35.

Crosby, Everett Uberto. *Books and Baskets, Signs and Silver of Old Time Nantucket.* Nantucket, Mass.: Inquirer and Mirror Press, 1940.

—. *Ninety-Five Percent Perfect.* Nantucket, Mass.: Teutankimmo Press, 1953.

—. *The Spoon Primer; or, An Easy and Pleasant Guide for Determining the Approximate Dates of the Making of Old American Silver Spoons.* Nantucket, Mass.: Inquirer and Mirror Press, 1941.

Cummings, Abbott Lowell, ed. *Rural Household Inventories, Establishing the Names, Uses and Furnishings of Rooms in the Colonial New England Home, 1675-1775.* Boston: Society for the Preservation of New England Antiquities, 1964.

Currier, Ernest M. *Early American Silversmiths, The Newbury Spoonmakers.* New York: 1929.

Currier, Ernest M. *Marks of Early American Silversmiths, List of New York City Silversmiths 1815-1841.* Portland, Me.: The Southworth-Athoensen Press, 1938; reprinted by Robert Alan Green 1970.

Curtis, George Munson. *Early Silver of Connecticut and Its Makers.* Meriden, Conn.: International Silver Co., 1913.

Cutten, George Barton. *Silversmiths of North Carolina, 1696-1850.* Raleigh, N.C.: State Department of Archives and History, 1948. Rev. ed. Raleigh, N. C.: Department of Cultural Resources, Division of Archives and History, 1973.

—. *Silversmiths of Northampton, Massachusetts, and Vicinity Down to 1850.* Hamilton, N. Y.: Colgate University Library, 1939.

—. *The Silversmiths of Georgia, Together with Watchmakers and Jewelers, 1733 to 1850.* Savannah: Pigeonhole Press, 1958.

—. *The Silversmiths of Virginia, Together with Watchmakers and Jewelers from 1694 to 1850.* Richmond: Dietz Press, 1952.

—. *The Silversmiths, Watchmakers, and Jewelers of the State of New York, Outside of New York City.* Hamilton, N. Y.: Privately printed, 1939.

—. *Ten Silversmith Families of New York State.* Albany, 1946.

Cutten, George Barton and Minnie Warren Cutten. *The Silversmiths of Utica.* Hamilton, N.Y.: Privately printed, 1938.

Dallett, Francis James. "Some Franco-American Silversmiths and Jewelers." *Antiques* 84 (1963): 706-10.

—. "The Thibaults, Philadelphia Silversmiths." *Antiques* 95 (1969): 547-49.

Darling, Sharon S., and Gail Farr Casterline. *Chicago Metalsmiths.* Chicago: Chicago Historical Society, 1977.

Darling Foundation. *New York State Silversmiths.* With supplement. Eggertsville, N. Y.: Darling Foundation of New York State Early American Silversmiths and Silver, 1964.

Davidson, Marshall B. *The American Heritage History of Colonial Antiques.* New York: American Heritage, 1967.

Davis, John D. "Antiques at Colonial Williamsburg: The Silver." *Antiques* 95 (1969): 134-37.

Day, Olive. *Rise of Manufacturing in Connecticut, 1820-1850.* New Haven: Yale University Press, 1935

Decatur, Stephen. "The Moulton Silversmiths." *Antiques* 39 (1941): 14-17.

—. "William Cario, Silversmith." *Old-Time New England* 55 (1965): 81-83.

Delieb, Eric, and Roberts, Michael. *Matthew Boulton, Master Silversmith.*

Dennis, Faith. *Three Centuries of French Domestic Silver.* 2 vols. New York: Metropolitan Museum of Art, 1960.

Dow, george Francis. *The Arts and Crafts in New England, 1704-1775: Gleanings from Boston Newspapers.* Topsfield, Mass.: Wayside press, 1927.

Dresser, Louisa. "Worcester Silversmiths and the Examples of Their Work in the Collections of the Museum." In *Worcester Art Museum Annual,* vol. 1, 1935-36. Worcester, Mass.: Worcester Art Museum, 1936.

Drinking Vessels from the Collection of the Darling Foundation for New York Silver and Its Makers. Catalogue of an exhibition. Buffalo, N. Y.: Buffalo Historical Society, 1960.

Durbin, Louise. "Samuel Kirk, Nineteenth-Century Silversmith." *Antiques* 94 (1968): 868-73.

Dyer, Walter. *Early American Craftsmen.* New York: Century Co., 1915.

Early American Silver. Catalogue of an exhibition, January 1-28, 1945. Hartford, Conn.: Wadsworth Atheneum, 1945.

Early American Silver. New York: Metropolitan Museum of Art, 1955.

Early Connecticut Silver, 1700-1830. Catalogue of an exhibition. Held in conjunction with the Connecticut Tercentenary, 1635-1935. New Haven: Yale University, Gallery of Fine Arts, 1935.

Early New England Silver Lent from the Mark Bortman Collection. Catalogue of an exhibition. Northampton, Mass.: Smith College Museum of Art, 1958.

Early Silver by New Haven Silversmiths. Catalogue of an exhibition. Introduction by John Devereux Kernan. New Haven, Conn.: New Haven Colony Historical Society, 1967.

Eckhardt, George H. *Pennsylvania Clocks and Clockmakers.* New York: Crown, 1955.

Elias Pelletreau: Long Island Silversmith and His Sources of Design. Catalogue of an exhibition. Brooklyn, N. Y.: Brooklyn Museum, 1959.

Elwell, Newton W. *Colonial Silverware of the Seventeenth and Eighteenth Centuries.* Boston: G. H. Polley, 1899.

Ensko, Robert. *Makers of Early American Silver.* New York: Published by the author, 1915.

Ensko, Stephen G. C. *American Silversmiths and Their Marks.* New York: Privately printed, 1927.

—. *American Silversmiths and Their Marks II.* New York: Robert Ensko, 1937.

—. *American Silversmiths and Their Marks III.* New York: Robert Ensko, 1948.

Fales, Martha Gandy. *American Silver in the Henry Francis du Pont Winterthur Museum.* Winterthur, Del.: The Henry Francis du Pont Wineterthur Museum, 1958.

—. "Daniel Rogers, Silversmiths." *Antiques* 91 (1967): 487-91.

—. *Early American Silver.* New York: E. P. Dutton, 1973.

—. "Joseph Richardson and Family, Philadelphia Silversmiths." *Antiques* 107 (1975): 170-77.

—. *Joseph Richardson and Family, Philadelphia Silversmiths.* Middletown, Conn.: Wesleyan University Press, 1974.

Farnham, Katherine Gross, and Callie Huger Efird. "Early Silversmiths and the Silver Trade in Georgia." *Antiques* 99 (1971): 380-85.

Flynt, Henry N. and Martha Gandy Fales. *The Heritage Foundation Collection of Silver, with Biographical Sketches of New England Silversmiths, 1625-1825.* Old Deerfield, Mass.: Heritage Foundation, 1968.

Forbes, Esther. *Paul Revere and the World He Lived In.* Boston: Houghton Mifflin, 1942.

Forbes, H. A. Crosby, John Devereux Kernan, and Ruth S. Wilkins. Chinese Export Silver, 1785-1885. Milton, Mass.: Museum of the American China Trade, 1975.

Fredymà, James P. *A Directory of Maine Silversmiths and Watch and Clock Makers.* Hanover, N.H.: Privately printed, 1972.

Fredyma, John J. *A Directory of Connecticut Silversmiths and Watch and Clock Makers.* Hanover, N. H.: Privately printed, 1973.

Fredyma, Paul J., and Marie-Louise Fredyma. *A Directory of Boston Silversmiths and Watch and Clock Makers.* Hanover, N.H.: Privately printed, 1975.

—. *A Directory of Massachusetts Silversmiths and Their Marks.* Hanover, N.H.: Privately printed, 1972.

—. *A Directory of New Hampshire Silversmiths and Their Marks.* Hanover, N.H.: Privately printed, 1971.

—. *A Directory of Rhode Island Silversmiths and Their Marks.* Hanover, N.H.: Privately printed, 1972.

—. *A Directory of Vermont Silversmiths and Their Marks.* Hanover, N.H.: Privately printed, 1974.

Freedley, Edwin T., ed. *Leading Pursuits and Leading Men: A Treatise on the Principal Trades and Manufactures in the United States.* Philadelphia: Edward Young, 1856.

French, Hollis. *Jacob Hurd and His Sons Nathaniel and Benjamin, Silversmiths, 1702-1781.* Foreword by Kathryn C. Buhler. Cambridge, Mass.: Walpole Society, 1939. Addenda, 1941.

—. *A List of Early American Silversmiths and Their Marks, with a Silver Collectors' Glossary.* New York: Walpole Society, 1917.

French, English and American Silver. Catalogue of an exhibition, June 9 to July 15, 1956. Minneapolis: Minneapolis Institute of Arts, 1956.

The French in America, 1520-1880. Catalogue of an exhibition. Detroit, Mich.: Detroit Institute of Arts, 1951.

From Colony to Nation: American Painting, Silver and Architecture from 1650 to the War of 1812. Catalogue of an exhibition, April 21 to June 19, 1949. Chicago: Art Institute of Chicago, 1949.

Gaines, Edith, ed. "Collectors' Notes: The Forbes Family, New York Silversmiths." *Antiques* 103 (1973): 561-63.

Gerstell, Vivian S. *Silversmiths of Lancaster, Pennsylvania, 1730-1850.* Lancaster: Lancaster County Historical Society, 1972.

Gibb, George Sweet. *The Whitesmiths of Taunton: A History of Reed and Barton, 1824-1943.* Cambridge, Mass.: Harvard University Press, 1943.

Gillingham, Harold E. "Ceasar Ghiselin: Philadelphia's First Gold and Silversmith, 1693-1733." *Pennsylvannia Magazine of History and Biography* 57 (1933).

—. *Indian Ornaments Made by Philadelphia Silversmiths.* New York: Museum of the American Indian, Heye Foundation, 1936.

—. "Indian Silver Ornaments." *Pennsylvannia Magazine of History and Biography* 58 (1934).

Goldsborough, Jennifer F. *Eighteenth- and Nineteenth-Century Maryland Silver in the Collection of the Baltimore Museum of Art.* Edited by Ann Boyce Harper. Baltimore: Baltimore Museum of Art, 1975.

Gorham Silver Co. *The Gorham Manufacturing Company Silversmiths.* New York: Cheltenham Press, 1900.

Goss, Elbridge Henry. *The Life of Colonel Paul Revere. 2* vols. Boston: Howard W. Spurr, 1891.

Gottesman, Rita Susswein, comp. *The Arts and Crafts in New York, 1726-1776: Advertisements and News Items from New York City Newspapers.* New York: New-York Historical Society, 1938.

—. *The Arts and Crafts in New York, 1777-1799: Advertisements and News Items from New York City Newspapers.* New York: New-York Historical Society, 1954.

—. *The Arts and Crafts in New York, 1800-1804: Advertisements and News Items from New York City Newspapers.* New York: New-York Historical Society, 1965.

Graham, James. *Early American Silver Marks.* New York: Privately printed, 1936.

Green, Robert Alan. "American Silver Trademarks." *Silver 6,* no. 4 (1973): 6-8.

—. *"Louisianna Silver, 1800-1900." Silver 8,* no. 2 (1975): 6-11.

—. *Marks of American Silversmiths.* Harrison, N. Y.: Published by the author, 1977.

—. "Notes on American Silver Trademarks and Hallmarks, 1655-1865: Their Role in the Identification Process." *Silver 8,* no. 3 (1975): 6-11.

Groce, George C., and David H. Wallace. *The New-York Historical Society's Dictionary of Artists in America, 1564-1860.* New Haven: Yale University Press, 1957.

Hammerslough, Philip. *American Silver Collected by Philip H. Hammerslough.* 3 vols. With supplements. Hartford, Conn.: Privately printed, 1958, 1960, 1965.

Hammerslough, Philip H., and Rita F. Feigenbaum. *American Silver Collected by Philip H. Hammerslough.* Vol. 4 Hartford, Conn.: Privately printed, 1973.

Harned, Henry H. "Ante-Bellum Kentucky Silver." *Antiques* 105 (1974): 818-24.

Harrington, Jessie. *Silversmiths of Delaware, 1700-1850, and Old Church Silver in Delaware.* Camden. N. J.: National Society of Colonial Dames of America in the State of Delaware, 1939.

Harvard Tercentenary Exhibition: Furniture, Silver, Pewter, Glass, Ceramics, Paintings, Prints, Together with Allied Art and Crafts of the Period, 1636-1836. Catalogue of an exhibition. Cambridge, Mass.: Harvard University Press, 1936.

Hayden, Arthur. *Chats on Old Silver.* London: Ernest Benn, 1915.

Hennessey, William C. "Silversmiths of Portsmouth." *New Hampshire Profiles 4 (1955).*

"The Henry Ford Museum: The Silver." Antiques 73 (1958): 174-77.

Hiatt, Noble W. and Lucy F. *The Silversmiths of Kentucky, 1785-1880.* Introduction by J. Winston Coleman, Jr. Louisville.: The Standard Print Co., 1954.

Hipkiss, Edwin J. *Eighteenth-Century American Arts: The M. and M. Karolik Collection.* Cambridge, Mass.: Published for the Museum of Fine Arts, Boston, by Harvard University Press, 1941.

—. *The Philip Leffingwell Spalding Collection of Early American Silver.* Cambridge, Mass.: Published for the Museum of Fine Arts, Boston, by Harvard University Press, 1943.

Hoitsma, Muriel Cutten. "Early Cleveland Silversmiths." *Antiques* 63 (1953): 130-31.

Hood, Graham. *American Silver, A History of Style, 1650-1900.* Praeger, 1971.

Hoopes, Penrose R. *Connecticut Clockmakers of the Eighteenth Century.* Hartford: Edwin Valentine Mitchell; New York: Dodd, Mead & Co., 1930.

—. *Shop Records of Daniel Burnap, Clockmaker.* Hartford: Connecticut Historical Society, 1958.

How, Mrs. G. E. P. "Seventeenth-Century English Silver and Its American Derivatives." In *Arts of the Anglo-American Community in the Seventeenth Century.* Charlottesville: University Press of Virginia, 1975.

Hughes, Graham. *Modern Silver.* New York: Crown Publishers, Inc., 1967.

Hunter, Walter C. "Old Silver Salt Spoons." *Antiques* 15 (1929): 32-33.

An Introduction to Silver. Catalogue of an exhibition, October 31, 1953, to May 9. 1954. Newark, N.J.: Newark Museum, 1953.

Jackson, Charles James. *English Goldsmiths and Their Marks: A History of the Goldsmiths and Plate Workers of England, Scotland and Ireland.* 2d ed., rev. London: Macmillan, 1921. Reprint ed., London: B. T. Batsford, 1949.

—. *Illustrated History of English Plate.* 2 vols. London: B. T. Batsford, 1911.

James, George B., Jr. *Souvenir Spoons.* Boston: A. W. Fuller, 1891.

Johnson, Philip A. "The Silversmiths of Norwich, Connecticut." *Antiques* 79 (1961): 570-71.

Jones, E. Alfred. *The Old Silver of American Churches.* Letchworth, England: National Society of Colonial Dames of America, 1913.

—. *Old Silver of Europe and America.* Philadelphia: Lippincott, 1928.

Kauffman, Henry J. "Peter Getz of Lancaster." Antiques *83 (1950): 112-13.*

Kent, Henry Watson and Florence N. Levy. *American Paintings, Furniture, Silver, and Other Objects of Arts, 1625-1825.* Catalogue of an exhibition held in conjunction with the Hudson-Fulton Celebration. New York: Metropolitan Museum of Art, 1909.

"Kentucky Silversmiths." *Silver* 5, no. 5 (1972): 10-14.

Kernan, John D., Jr. "Further Notes on Albany Silversmiths." *Antiques* 80 (1961): 60-61.

Kernan, John. "China Trade Silver." *Antiques* 90 (1966): 195-99.

Kihn, Phyllis. "Frederick Oakes, Hartford Jeweler and Gentleman Farmer." *Connecticut Historical Society Bulletin* 32 (1967): 1-15.

Kirk Silver in United States Museums. Baltimore: Samuel Kirk & Son, 1976.

Kirk Sterling - A Complete Catalog of America's Finest Sterling by America's Oldest Silversmiths. Baltimore: 1956(?).

Knittle, Rhea Mansfield. *Early Ohio Silversmiths and Pewterers, 1787-1847.* Cleveland: Calvert-Hatch Co., 1943.

Kovel, Ralph M., and Terry H. Kovel. *A Directory of American Silver, Pewter, and Silver Plate.* New York: Crown Publishers, 1961.

Langdon, John E. *American Silversmiths in British North America, 1776-1800.* Toronto: Privately printed, 1960.

—. *Canadian Silversmiths, 1700-1900.* Toronto: Privately printed 1966.

—. *Canadian Silversmiths and Their Marks, 1667-1867.* Lunenberg, Vt.: Stinehour Press, 1960.

—. *Guide to Marks on Early Canadian Silver, Eighteenth and Nineteenth Centuries.* Toronto: Ryerson Press, 1968.

Larus, Jane Bortman, *Myer Myers, Silversmith, 1723-1795.* A catalogue of the Bortman-Larus Collection of Myer Myers colonial silver. Washington, D.C.: B'nai B'rith, n.d.

Laughlin, Ledlie I. *Pewter in America.* 2 vols. Boston: Houghton Mifflin, 1940.

Loan Exhibition of Silver. Catalogue. Philadelphia: Pennsylvania Museum of Art, 1921.

McClinton, Katharine Morrison. *Collecting American Nineteenth Century Silver.* New York: Scribner's, 1968.

McCulloch, Robert, and Alice Beale. "Silversmiths of Barnstable, Massachusetts." *Antiques* 84 (1963): 72-74.

MacKay, Donald. *Silversmiths and Related Craftsmen of the Atlantic Provinces.* Halifax, Nova Scotia: Petheric Press, 1973.

Masterpieces of American Silver. Catalogue of an exhibition. Richmond: Virginia Museum of Fine Arts, 1960.

Masterpieces of New England Silver, 1650-1800. Catalogue of an exhibition. Cambridge, Mass.: Published for Yale University, Gallery of Fine Arts, by Harvard University Press, 1939.

May, Earl Chapin. *Century of Silver, 1847-1957: Connecticut Yankees and a Noble Metal.* New York: Robert M. McBride, 1947.

Meeks, E. V. *Masterpieces of New England Silver.* Cambridge, Mass.: Harvard University Press, 1939.

Merriman, Jean R. *The Mystery of John Jackson, Eighteenth-Century Silversmith: One Man or Two?* Nantucket, Mass.: Poets Corner Press, 1976.

Miller, V. Isabelle. *New York Silversmiths of the Seventeenth Century.* Catalogue of an exhibition. New York: Museum of the City of New York, 1962.

—. *Silver by New York Makers, Late Seventeenth Century to 1900.* Catalogue of an exhibition. New York: Museum of the City of New York, 1937.

Miller, William Davis. *The Silversmiths of Little Rest.* Kingston, R.I.: D. B. Updike, 1928.

Montgomery, Charles F., and Catherine H. Maxwell. "Early American Silver: Collectors, Collections, Exhibitions, Writings." In *Wapole Society Notebook 1968.* Portland, Maine: Anthoensen Press, 1969.

Natchez-Made Silver of the Nineteenth Century. Catalogue of an exhibition. Baton Rouge: Anglo-American Art Museum, Louisiana State University, 1970.

Nineteenth-Century America: Furniture and Other Decorative Arts. Catalogue of an exhibition. New York: Metropolitan Museum of Art, 1970.

Noe, Sidney P. *The New England Willow Tree Coinages of Massachusetts.* New York: American Numismatic Society, 1943.

Norman-Wilcox, Gregor. "American Silver at the Los Angeles County Museum." In *Connoisseur Year Book.* London, 1956.

Nygren, Edward J. "Edward Winslow's Sugar Boxes, Colonial Echoes of Courtly Love." *Yale University Art Gallery Bulletin* 33 (1971).

Old American and English Silver. Catalogue of an exhibition. Philadelphia: Pennsylvania Museum of Art, 1917.

Oman, Charles. *English Domestic Silver.* London: Adam & Charles Black, 1959.

Ormsbee, Thomas Hamilton. "The Craft of the Spoonmaker." *Antiques* 16 (1929): 189-92.

Paintings by Gilbert Stuart, Furniture by the Goddards and Townsends, Silver by Rhode Island Silversmiths. Catalogue of an exhibition. Providence, R.I.: Rhode Island School of Design, 1936.

Paul Revere's Boston: 1735-1818. Catalogue of an exhibition. Edited by Jonathan L. Fairbanks and Wendy A. Cooper. Boston: Published by the New York Graphic Society for the Museum of Fine Arts, 1975.

Peirce, Donald C. "Cincinnati Silversmiths." Typescript, 1974. Decorative Arts Photographic Collection, Winterthur Museum Library.

Peterson, Harold L. *American Silver Mounted Swords, 1700-1815.* Washington, D.C.: Privately printed, 1955.

—. *The American Sword, 1775-1945.* Philadelphia: Privately printed, 1955.

Philadelphia: Three Centuries of American Art. (1676-1976). Catalogue of an exhibition. Philadelphia: Philadelphia Museum of Art, 1976.

Philadelphia Silver, 1682-1800. Catalogue of an exhibition. Preface by Phoebe Phillips Prime. Text by Henry P. McIlhenny. Philadelphia: Philadelphia Museum of Art, 1956.

Phillips, John Marshall. *American Silver.* New York: Chanticleer Press, 1949.

—. *Early American Silver Selected from the Mabel Brady Garvan Collection.* Edited by Meyric R. Rogers. New Haven, Conn.: Yale University Art Gallery, 1960.

Phillips, John Marshall, Barbara N. Parker, and Kathryn C. Buhler, eds. *The Waldron Phoenix Belknap, Jr., Collection of Portraits and Silver.* Cambridge, Mass.: Published for the New-York Historical Society by Harvard University Press, 1955.

Pitkin, A. P. *Pitkin Family of America.* Hartford, Conn.: Privately printed, 1887.

Pleasants, J. Hall and Howard Sill. "Charles Oliver Bruff, Silversmith." *Antiques* 39 (1941): 309-11.

—. *Maryland Silversmiths, 1715-1830.* Baltimore: Privately printed, 1930.

Prime, Alfred Coxe, comp. *The Arts and Crafts in Philadelphia, Maryland, and South Carolina, 1721-1785: Gleanings from Newspapers.* Topsfield, Mass.: Walpole Society, 1929.

—. *The Arts and Crafts in Philadelphia, Maryland, and South Carolina, 1786-1800: Gleanings from Newspapers.* Topsfield, Mass.: Walpole Society, 1932.

Prime, Mrs. Alfred Coxe, comp. and ed. *Three Centuries of Historic Silver.* Philadelphia: Pennsylvania Society of the Colonial Dames of America, 1938.

Proper, David R. "Edmund Currier, Clockmaker." *Essex Institute Historical Collections* 101 (1965): 281-88.

Rainwater, Dorothy T. *American Silver Manufacturers.* Hanover, Pa.: Everybodys Press, 1966.

—. *Encyclopedia of American Silver Manufacturers.* New York Crown Publishers, 1975.

Rainwater, Dorothy T., ed. *Sterling Silver Holloware: Gorham Manufacturing Company, 1888; Gorham Martele, 1900; Unger Brothers, 1904.* American Historical Catalogue Collection. Princeton, N.J.: Pyne Press, 1973.

Rainwater, Dorothy T., and Donna H. Felger. *American Spoons: Souvenir and Historical.* Camden, N.J., Thomas Nelson & Sons; Hanover, Pa., Everybodys Press, 1968.

Rainwater, Dorothy T., and H. Ivan Rainwater. *American Silverplate.* Nashville, Tenn., Thomas Nelson; Hanover, Pa., Everybodys Press, 1968.

Rice, Norman S. *Albany Silver 1652-1825.* Catalogue of an exhibition. Foreword by Laurence McKinney. Introduction by Kathryn C. Buhler. Albany, N.Y.: Albany Institute of History and Art, 1964.

Rice, Norman S., and James H. Halpin. "Joseph Warford, Silversmith of Albany and Salem, New York." *Antiques* 85 (1964): 429-31.

Richardson, M. W. "A Silversmith of the Genesee Trail [John Hatch Cheadell]." *Antiques* 29 (1936): 260-61.

Roach, Ruth Hunter. *St. Louis Silversmiths.* St. Louis, Mo.: Privately printed, 1967.

—. "Silversmiths of St. Louis." *Antiques* 51 (1947): 51-53, 186-88.

Rosenbaum, Jeanette W. *Myer Myers, Goldsmith, 1723-1795.* Philadelphia: Jewish Publication Society of America, 1954.

Sabine, Julia. "Silversmiths of New Jersey, 1623-1800." *Proceedings of the New Jersey Historical Society 61 (1943).*

Schild, Joan Lynn. *Silversmiths of Rochester.* Rochester, N.Y.: Rochester Museum of Arts and Sciences, 1944.

Schwartz, Marvin D. *Collectors' Guide to Antique American Silver.* Garden City, N.Y.: Doubleday, 1975.

Sherman, Frederick Fairchild. *Early Connecticut Artists and Craftsmen.* New York: Privately printed, 1925.

Silver Used in New York, New Jersey, and the South. With a note on early New York silversmiths by R. T. Haines Halsey. Catalogue of an exhibition. New York: Metropolitan Museum of Art, 1911.

"Silversmiths of Alexandria [Virginia]." *Antiques* 47 (1945): 93-95.

Smith, Sidney Adair. "Mobile Silversmiths and Jewelers, 1820-1867." *Antiques* 99 (1971): 407-11.

—. *Mobile Silversmiths and Jewelers, 1820-1867.* Mobile, Ala.: Historic Mobile Preservation Society, 1970.

Snodin, Michael, and Gail Belden. *Collecting for Tomorrow: Spoons.* London: Pitman Publishing, 1976.

*Southern Silver Made in the South Prior to 1860.*Catalogue of an exhibition. Introduction by David B. Warren. Houston, Tex.: Museum of Fine Arts, 1968.

Spear, Dorothea E. *American Watch Papers; with a Descriptive List of the Collection in the American Antiquarian Society.* Worcester, Mass.: American Antiquarian Society, 1952.

Spinney, Frank O. "An Ingenious Yankee Craftsman [Benjamin Clark Gilman]." *Antiques* 44 (1943): 116-19.

Steele, T., & Sons. *What Shall I Buy for a Present?* Cambridge, Mass.: n.p., 1877.

Stollenwerck, Frank, and Dixie Oruh Stollenwerck. *The Stollenwerck, Chaudron and Billon Families in America.* N.p.: Privately printed, 1948.

Stow, Millicent. *American Silver.* New York: Barrows, 1950.

Stutzenberger, Albert. *The American Story in Spoons.* Louisville, Ky.: Privately printed, 1953.

Tapley, Harriet S. "The Ledger of Edward Lang, Silversmith of Salem." *Essex Institute Historical Collections* 66 (1930): 325-29.

Taylor, Gerald. *Silver.* New York: Penguin Books, 1956.

Thorn, C. Jordan. *Handbook of American Silver and Pewter Marks.* Preface by John Meredith Graham II. New York: Tudor, 1949.

Turner, Noel D. *American Silver Flatware, 1837-1910.* New York: Barnes, 1972.

Upon This Occasion: A Loan Exhibition of Important Presentation Silver Pieces from Colonial Times to Today. Newburyport, Mass.: Towle Silversmiths, 1955.

U.S. Bureau of the Census. *Digest of Accounts of Manufacturing Establishments in the United States and of Their Manufactures.* Washington, D.C., 1823.

U.S. Department of State. *Silver Supplement to the Guide to the Diplomatic Reception Rooms.* Washington, D.C.: Government Printing Office, 1973.

Utica Silver. Catalogue of an exhibition. Utica, N.Y.: Fountain Elms, Munson-Williams-Proctor Institute, 1973.

Van Hoesen, Walter Hamilton. *Crafts and Craftsmen of New Jersey.* Rutherford, N.J.: Fairleigh-Dickinson University Press, 1973.

Van Slyck, J. D. *New England Manufacturers and Manufactories.* 2 vols. Boston: Van Slyck, 1879.

Waldo, J. Curtis. *Illustrated Guide to New Orleans, Louisiana.* New Orleans: n.p., 1879.

Wenham, Edward. *The Practical Book of American Silver.* Philadelphia: Lippincott, 1949.

White, Margaret E. "European and American Silver in the Newark Museum Collections." *Museum,* n.s. 5 (Summer-Fall 1953).

White-Beekman Papers. Box 7A. New York-Historical Society Collections, New York City.

Williams, Carl M. *Silversmiths of New Jersey, 1700-1825, with Some Notice of Clockmakers Who Were Also Silversmiths.* Philadelphia: George S. MacManus, 1949.

Williams, James A. "Savannah Silver and Silversmiths." *Antiques* 91 (1967): 347-49.

Williamson, Scott Graham. *The American Craftsman.* New York: Crown Publishers, 1940.

Woodhouse, Samuel W., Jr. "Two Philadelphia Silversmiths." *Antiques* 17 (1930): 326-27.

Work in Silver and Gold by Myer Myers. Catalogue of an exhibition. Brooklyn, N.Y.: Brooklyn Museum, 1954.

Wroth, Lawrence C. *Abel Buell of Connecticut, Silversmith, Type-Founder, and Engraver.* New Haven, Conn.: Yale University Press, 1926.

Wyler, Seymour B. *The Book of Old Silver.* New York: Crown Publishers, 1937.

ASHTRAYS

Ashtrays were apparently first made of silver in 17th century Europe, probably in Holland, where pipe-smoking became a national pasttime toward the middle part of that century. Coffeehouses of that era mostly provided pewter ahstrays to their customers, or, in some cases, put barrels of sand as ash-receptacles. The pewter types were duplicated in silver, generally with extra detailing added, and found their way into the parlors of wealthy burghers and other prominent citizens. In America, silver ashtrays were not commonly made until the popularization of *cigar-smoking,* in the third quarter of the 19th century. They received a further boost from the slightly later (4th quarter of the 19th century) popularity of cigarettes. Sizes can vary greatly, as huge specimens were made for conference tables and other public or semi-public use. Corrosion of the bowl's face is, of course, frequently encountered.

Ashtray, *(sterling), Unger Bros., "Love's Dream", individual size,* 40.00 - 60.00

(Silver-Plated)	Price Range	
☐ **Barbour,** *square shape, match holder on top, ball feet, shell handle, overall embossing with human figures, good condition.*	13.50	14.50
☐ **Maker unknown,** *Civil War Centennial, 1861-1961, embossed military design, 5½" Dia.*	8.00	10.00
☐ **Maker unknown,** *figural, fly, enamel work on wings and face of fly, 6" L., 2½" H.*	22.00	25.00

(Sterling Silver)   **Price Range**
☐ **Kirk "Repousse"**, *no monogram, individual size*. 22.00   25.00

ASPARAGUS SERVERS

Asparagus, originally known as "sparrow grass," was considered an exotic delicacy in England 300 years ago — Samuel Pepys in his famous *Diary* calls attention to the occasions when he is lucky enough to get some. It was also apparently quite scarce in America up to the mid 19th century, and therefore a favorite of those who wished to avoid the commonplace. Silversmiths were seldom so presumptive as to include asparagus servers in ordinary flatware sets: but anyone could include them in his set, by buying them separately. Types were generally available matching the standard flatware patterns. Of course asparagus *could* be served with other, more common, table implements — but manufacturers wanted to sell silver, and our ancestors helped along the industry by using a different utensil for every conceivable purpose. There is no standard model of asparagus server. Some have four prongs and others five, and those with a greater or lesser number may even occasionally be found. They have in common, however, the fact that the prong terminals bend outward, for the aid of scooping. Because of their large size, these are invariably heavy objects. The large size likewise provided opportunity for considerable ornament.

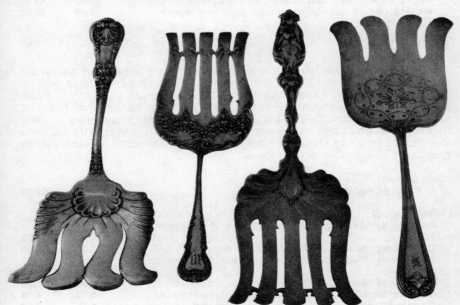

Asparagus Servers, *(L to R) (sterling), Tiffany "English King",* 50.00 - 60.00; *Durgin "Cromwell",* 40.00 - 50.00; *Whiting "Lily"* 60.00 - 70.00; *Tiffany "Colonial",* 45.00 - 50.00

	Price Range	
(Silver-Plated)		
☐ **Maker unknown,** *medallion pattern with child's face, 7" L., good condition.*	8.00	10.00
(Sterling Silver)		
☐ **Dominick & Haff "Number 10",** *no monogram.*	75.00	85.00
☐ **Frank Smith "Bostonia",** *monogram, 9½" L.*	25.00	30.00
☐ **Stieff "Rose",** *monogram.*	90.00	100.00
☐ **Stieff "Rose",** *no monogram.*	20.00	30.00
☐ **Tiffany "Chrysanthemum" tongs,** *no monogram.*	195.00	215.00
☐ **Watson "Putnam" tongs,** *monogram.*	45.00	55.00

ASPARAGUS TONGS, INDIVIDUAL

It was too much, of course, for the Victorian imagination to think of using pickle tongs or other table tongs for asparagus. As always, in that golden age of gadgets and novelties, a special tool was called for. There was really little call for asparagus tongs and relatively few seem to have been made. As collectors items they have moderate appeal today.

(Sterling Silver)		
☐ **Gorham "King George",** *monogram.*	20.00	25.00
☐ **Reed & Barton "Les Cinq Fleurs",** *no monogram.*	40.00	45.00
☐ **Whiting,** *pattern unknown, plain design, no monogram.*	18.00	20.00

BABY FORKS

Eating utensils specially designed for children are of early origin but did not come into widespread use until the mid to late 19th century. In well-to-do households, baby's forks and spoons would naturally be of silver. Available patterns were in harmony with those of each company's chief line. The specially chosen motifs for baby forks and spoons, embodying nursery themes, lend an additional charm. They also exist, however, with patterns identical to those of standard ware. The very light weights of these pieces give them a negligible bullion value.

(Coin Silver)		
☐ **C. F. Butler,** *engraved.*	30.00	32.00
(Silver-Plated)		
☐ **Community "Adam",** *child's first name and date, excellent condition.*	4.50	6.00
☐ **Community "Adam",** *monogram, fair condition.*	2.00	2.50
☐ **Community "South Seas",** *no monogram, excellent condition.*	3.50	5.50
☐ **Community "South Seas",** *no monogram, resilvered.*	5.50	6.50
☐ **Gorham "Carolina",** *no monogram, excellent condition.* ...	4.00	6.00
☐ **Gorham "Carolina",** *monogram, good condition.*	1.75	2.50
☐ **S.L. & G.H. Rogers "Webster II",** *no monogram, excellent condition.*	4.50	5.50
☐ **1847 Rogers "Persian",** *no monogram, resilvered.*	7.50	9.00

	Price Range	
☐ **1847 Rogers "Vintage"**, *monogram, fair condition.*	2.00	2.50
☐ **1847 Rogers "Vintage"**, *no monogram, excellent condition.*	4.50	6.50
☐ **Maker unknown,** *"Puss 'n Boots"design, no monogram, good condition.*	5.00	6.00

(Sterling Silver)

☐ **Dominick & Haff,** *pattern unknown, clown on handle, first name and date.*......................................	16.00	18.00
☐ **Durgin "Chrysanthemum"**, *monogram on handle, date in bowl.*	22.00	24.00
☐ **Gorham "Chantilly"**, *monogram.*......................	12.00	14.00
☐ **International "Serenity"**, *no monogram.*.................	9.00	11.00
☐ **Kirk "Repousse"**, *no monogram.*	20.00	22.00
☐ **Tiffany "Cordis"**, *no monogram.*	10.00	12.00
☐ **Unger Bros. "Cupid's Sunbeams"**, *no monogram.*.........	30.00	32.00
☐ **Wallace,** *pattern unknown, rabbit design on handle, monogram.*...	10.00	12.00

BABY SETS

(Silver-Plated)

☐ **Community "Evening Star"**, *two-piece set includes spoon and fork, no monogram, excellent condition.*............	8.00	9.00
☐ **Oneida "Avalon"**, *two-piece set includes fork and spoon, no monogram, excellent condition.*	6.50	7.50
☐ **1847 Rogers "Old Colony"**, *three-piece set includes spoon, fork, and food pusher, monogram and date, excellent condition.*	32.00	35.00

(Sterling Silver)

☐ **Gorham "Fairfax"**, *three-piece set includes food pusher, fork, and spoon, monogram.*...........................	22.00	25.00
☐ **Wallace,** *pattern unknown, rabbits on handle, three-piece set includes food pusher, fork, and spoon, no monogram.*...	18.00	20.00
☐ **Wallace,** *pattern unknown, rabbits on handle, three-piece set includes food pusher, fork, and spoon, monogram.*	28.00	30.00

BABY SPOONS

(Coin Silver)

☐ **Kirk "Repousse"**, *curled handle, monogram and date in bowl.*	34.00	36.00

(Silver-Plated)

☐ **Community "Adam"**, *curled handle, no monogram, excellent condition.*	10.00	12.00
☐ **Community "Adam"**, *long handled, no monogram, excellent condition.*	4.00	4.50
☐ **Community "Adam"**, *long handled, monogram and date, fair condition.*..	1.50	2.00

		Price Range	

☐ **Oneida "Banbury"**, *long handled, no monogram, excellent condition.* **4.00** **5.00**

☐ **Oneida "Banbury"**, *curled handle, monogram, excellent condition.* **7.00** **8.00**

☐ **Oneida "Bridal Wreath"**, *long handled, no monogram, excellent condition.* **4.00** **5.00**

☐ **Oneida "Bridal Wreath"**, *curled handle, no monogram, excellent condition.* **7.00** **8.00**

☐ **Rogers "Burgundy"**, *long handled, no monogram, good condition.* **3.50** **4.50**

☐ **Rogers "Burgundy"**, *long handled, monogram and date, fair condition.* **2.75** **3.50**

☐ **Stratford "Shakespeare"**, *long handled, no monogram, fair condition.* **1.75** **2.75**

☐ **Stratford "Shakespeare"**, *long handled, no monogram, excellent condition.* **6.00** **7.00**

☐ **Wm. A. Rogers "Chalice"**, *curled handle, excellent condition.* **8.00** **10.00**

☐ **Wm. A. Rogers "Chalice"**, *curled handle, monogram, excellent condition.* **1.50** **2.25**

☐ **Wm. A. Rogers "Chalice"**, *long handled, no monogram, excellent condition.* **4.50** **5.50**

☐ **Wm. Rogers & Son "Victorian Rose"**, *long handled, no monogram, fair condition.* **1.25** **1.75**

☐ **Wm. Rogers & Son "Victorian Rose"**, *long handled, no monogram, excellent condition.* **7.00** **8.00**

☐ **1847 Rogers "Daffodil II"**, *long handled, no monogram, excellent condition.* **4.50** **5.50**

☐ **1847 Rogers "Daffodil II"**, *long handled, no monogram, fair condition.* **1.25** **1.75**

☐ **1847 Rogers "Daffodil II"**, *curled handle, no monogram, resilvered.* **1.25** **1.75**

☐ **1847 Rogers "First Love"**, *curled handle, no monogram, excellent condition.* **8.00** **9.00**

☐ **1847 Rogers "Flair"**, *long handled, no monogram, excellent condition.* **4.00** **4.75**

☐ **1847 Rogers "Flair"**, *long handled, no monogram, excellent condition.* **4.00** **5.00**

☐ **1847 Rogers "Flair"**, *curled handle, no monogram, excellent condition.* **8.00** **9.00**

☐ **1847 Rogers "Old Colony"**, *curled handle, monogram, excellent condition.* **7.00** **8.00**

☐ **1847 Rogers "Old Colony"**, *long handled, no monogram, excellent condition.* **6.00** **7.00**

☐ **1847 Rogers "Persian"**, *curled handle, no monogram, resilvered.* **8.00** **10.00**

☐ **1847 Rogers "Persian"**, *curled handle, monogram, fair condition.* **1.75** **2.50**

☐ **1847 Rogers "Persian"**, *long handled, no monogram, excellent condition.* **8.00** **9.00**

☐ **1847 Rogers "Persian"**, *long handled, monogram, good condition.* **3.50** **5.50**

☐ **1847 Rogers "Reflection"**, *curled handle, no monogram, excellent condition.* **7.00** **8.00**

	Price Range	
☐ **1847 Rogers "Reflection"**, *long handled, no monogram, excellent condition.*	6.00	7.00
☐ **1847 Rogers "Vintage"**, *curled handle, no monogram, excellent condition.*	20.00	25.00
☐ **1847 Rogers "Vintage"**, *curled handle, monogram, excellent condition.*	20.00	22.00
☐ **1847 Rogers "Vintage"**, *long handled, no monogram, excellent condition.*	16.00	18.00
☐ **Maker unknown,** *Gerber baby food, no monogram, excellent condition.*	1.50	2.50
☐ **Maker unknown,** *hand-hammered, curled handle, no monogram.*	1.50	2.50
☐ **Maker unknown,** *"Bo Peep", curled handle, pierced work, no monogram, good condition.*	8.00	9.00
☐ **Maker unknown,** *"Huckleberry Hound", no monogram.*	4.00	5.00
☐ **Maker unknown,** *"Gerber baby food", no monogram, 4½",excellent condition.*	6.00	7.00

(Sterling Silver)

☐ **International "Royal Danish"**, *long handled, monogram.*	7.00	8.00
☐ **International "Serenity"**, *long handled, no monogram.*	5.00	6.00
☐ **Kirk "Old Maryland Engraved"**, *long handled, no monogram.*	10.00	12.00
☐ **Kirk "Repousse"**, *curled handle, no monogram.*	28.00	30.00
☐ **Kirk "Repousse"**, *long handled, no monogram.*	16.00	18.00
☐ **Oneida "Lasting Spring"**, *long handled, monogram.*	7.00	8.00
☐ **Reed & Barton "Francis I"**, *long handled, no monogram.*	10.00	12.00
☐ **Schofield "Baltimore Rose"**, *curled handle.*	18.00	20.00
☐ **Tiffany "Nursery Rhyme"**, *curled handle, gold wash bowl, monogram.*	50.00	60.00
☐ **Maker unknown,** *hand-made with Indian-type engraving on handle, curled handle, no monogram.*	12.00	14.00

BACON FORKS

The tradition of eating bacon with the fingers — a holdover of the medieval practice of eating *all* meats with the fingers — still thrives, but silversmiths have not overlooked those who wish to approach bacon more genteelly. This was never a widely produced article, because of the nature of the product. Bacon consumption was consigned almost strictly to breakfast, and only in the most fashionable households was silver used at breakfast; and, even then, there was not likely to be company, so a large supply of bacon forks was unnecessary.

(Silver-Plated)

☐ **1835 R. Wallace "Troy"**, *no monogram, excellent condition.*	20.00	22.00
☐ **Maker unknown,** *Greek key design, monogram and date.*	10.00	12.00

(Sterling Silver)

☐ **Durgin "Fairfax"**, *no monogram.*	28.00	30.00
☐ **Kirk "Repousse"**, *no monogram.*	48.00	50.00

BAR STIRRERS

Made quite extensively from the late 1800's onward, these are in rather active collector demand. They are sought not only by silver enthusiasts but those who collect liquor memorabilia, a group of hobbyists whose ranks are swelling.

(Sterling Silver)	Price Range	
☐ **International "Avalon"**, *pierced bowl, no monogram.*	28.00	30.00
☐ **Towle "Canterbury"**, *gold wash bowl, pierced bowl, no monogram.*	25.00	30.00
☐ **Whiting "Lily"**, *pierced bowl, monogram.*	48.00	50.00
☐ **Maker unknown**, *pierced bowl, gold wash bowl, monogram and date.*	18.00	20.00

BASKETS

Silver baskets, like any other type, could be carried out of doors and put to various uses. Mainly, however, they were intended as indoor ornaments for elegant households, in which would be displayed waxed fruits, ferns, or candies. Baskets lent themselves superbly to openwork decoration, which served not only as a sales factor but an additional plus to their manufacturers: openwork decor always gave the impression that you were getting more silver than you actually were. Baskets are one class of silverware which has its strong devotees, and its equally strong detractors, the latter claiming that the ruggedness of silver and delicacy of baskets do not well suit each other. It happens only rarely, but you should check for the possibility of a false base concealing a quantity of lead or other "loading."

(Silver-Plated)		
☐ **Barbour**, *fruit type, chain design handle, applied flowers on sides, satin finish with gold wash interior, excellent condition.*	100.00	110.00
☐ **Barbour**, *stationary handle, 6¼" W., overall embossed tavern scene, good condition.*	32.00	35.00
☐ **Barbour**, *9½" H., 7" W., hexagon shape, overall embossing with women, children and flowers.*	32.00	35.00
☐ **Barbour**, *sweetmeat type, glass insert with three compartments, stationary handle, ball feet, embossed scenes, good condition.*	42.00	45.00
☐ **F. B. Rogers**, *swing handle, 11" W., 5" H., pierced work all over, grapes and leaves on rim and handle, good condition.*	42.00	45.00
☐ **Middletown**, *swing handle, medallion pattern, figural feet, engraved design on interior, good condition.*	50.00	52.00
☐ **Rockford**, *bride's type, rubina glass insert with etched design, small fleck on rim, silver in good condition.*	40.00	45.00
☐ **Wm. Rogers**, *bride's type, cut glass insert, minor flecks, silver in good condition.*	200.00	225.00
☐ **Maker unknown**, *bride's type, 11" H., 11" Dia., fluted, ribbed and scalloped design, band of flowers on folded rim, silver in good condition.*	95.00	105.00

Cake Basket, *Kirk, "Repousssé" 1900, 32 ounces,* 1250.00

	Price Range	
☐ **Maker unknown,** *cake type, fair condition, no monogram. . .*	18.00	20.00
☐ **Maker unknown,** *swing handle, 5" W., 2½" H., swirled and scalloped design, ball feet, good condition. . . . .*	10.00	12.00

(Sterling Silver)

☐ **Gorham,** *date mark for 1908, Theodore B. Starr retailer mark, oval, pierced latticework, grape and vine motif on top border. . . . .*	600.00	650.00
☐ **Kirk,** *repousse flowers and ferns, 5¾" by 4" rectangle, 4" H., weight unknown.*	180.00	200.00

BEAKERS

Beakers made of silver have been more plentiful, over the years, in Europe than in the U.S. They were manufactured almost exclusively for the use of taverns and served as a receptacle for beer and ale. Their collector popularity is somewhat greater than that of most silverware, owing to the demand from collectors of tavern articles and beer-related materials. Their limited manufacture had nothing to do with cost — it derived simply from the fact that silver is not too beneficial to the flavor of beer and ale.

(Silver-Plated)

☐ **Maker unknown,** *ornate tavern scene, good condition.*	18.00	22.00

(Sterling Silver)   **Price Range**

☐ **Frank W. Smith,** *flared cylinder shape, engraved crest, set of six, 5" H., total weight 21½ oz.* 175.00   185.00

BELLS

Silver bells, in addition to being the title of a favorite Christmas tune, are also collectors' items. Those of modern origin are strictly ornamental, or made as limited editions for collectors (and investors). The earlier specimens, such as listed here, were utilitarian. The nature of this article did not lend itself well to the silver medium and therefore silver bells were not extensively made.

Call Bell, *maker unknown, dome shaped, round base, spring operated clapper,* 10.00 - 40.00

(Silver-Plated)
☐ **Maker unknown,** *wooden handle, 7" H.* 35.00   45.00
☐ **Maker unknown,** *foot-operated call bell, 3 feet, embossed trim.* 75.00   85.00

(Sterling Silver)
☐ **Reed & Barton "Pointed Antique",** *all silver, no monogram.*. 20.00   25.00
☐ **Maker unknown,** *engraved scroll design on bell, twisted handle.* 28.00   30.00

BERRY FORKS

Berry forks are not as numerous as berry *spoons,* since scooping rather than spearing has been the preferred etiquette with berries. They are, though, certainly plentiful enough to serve as the subject of a hobbyist's collection. Taking more than one berry at a time on a berry fork was considered (in Victorian times at any rate) a gross breach of table manners. Eating berries with the fingers was even worse. Berries were ranked as far more of a delicacy on the 19th century table than they are today; city dwellers often had to pay very inflated prices for them.

(Silver-Plated)
☐ **American Silver Company "Nenuphar",** *no monogram, excellent condition.* 8.00   9.00

	Price Range	
☐ **American Silver Company "Oregon"**, *no monogram, excellent condition.*	10.00	12.00
☐ **Holmes & Edwards "DeSancy"**, *no monogram, excellent condition.*	8.00	10.00
☐ **Rogers & Bro. "Laurel"**, *no monogram, excellent condition.*	9.00	10.00
☐ **Rogers & Bro. "Mystic"**, *no monogram, excellent condition.*	9.00	11.00
☐ **Rogers & Bro. "Mystic"**, *monogram, excellent condition.*	8.00	10.00
☐ **Smith "Iris"**, *no monogram, excellent condition.*	13.00	14.00
☐ **Wallace "Troy"**, *no monogram, excellent condition.*	7.00	8.00
☐ **Wm. Rogers "Arbutus"**, *monogram, excellent condition.*	10.00	12.00
☐ **Wm. Rogers "Arbutus"**, *no monogram, excellent condition.*	12.00	14.00
☐ **1835 R. Wallace "Blossom"**, *no monogram, excellent condition.*	8.00	10.00
☐ **1835 R. Wallace "Blossom"**, *no monogram, fair condition.*	3.00	4.00
☐ **1847 Rogers "Beaded"**, *no monogram, excellent condition.*	8.00	9.00
☐ **1847 Rogers "Beaded"**, *no monogram, good condition.*	5.00	7.00
☐ **Maker unknown**, *strawberry on tip, gold wash bowl, no monogram, mint condition.*	10.00	12.00
(Sterling Silver)		
☐ **Durgin "Watteau"**, *no monogram.*	13.00	15.00
☐ **Gorham "Buttercup"**, *no monogram.*	13.00	15.00
☐ **Gorham "Buttercup"**, *monogram.*	12.00	15.00
☐ **Gorham "Poppy"**, *no monogram.*	15.00	18.00
☐ **Gorham "Strasbourg"**, *no monogram.*	16.00	18.00
☐ **Gorham "Virginiana"**, *no monogram.*	15.00	17.00
☐ **Tiffany "Windham"**, *no monogram.*	12.00	15.00
☐ **Towle "Rustic"**, *no monogram.*	10.00	12.00

BERRY SPOONS

These are very abundant, and appealing to collect. Neither the bowl shapes or sizes were standard, which adds to their intrigue. Silver makers never failed to give their best flourish to specialized tableware, and berry spoons definitely got "the works." The assumption was that utensils used with a food such as berries would be examined more attentively, since the food was eaten at a leisurely pace. Berry spoons were of course standard equipment in the English silver cabinet from as long ago as the 1700's. They were not very widely made in this country until around 1850, but the ouput from then until 1900 was nothing short of prodigeous. Aside from thjeir inclusion in sets, they served as a favorite individual gift item. Nobody cared very much whether their berry spoons matched — it was one piece of silverware in which some variety could be shown. Berry spoons tend to be slightly lighter in weight than their size would indicate, good proof of the fact that *visual weighing* of silver is sometimes dangerous.

(Silver-Plated)

☐ **American Silver Company "Moselle"**, *no monogram, excellent condition.*	50.00	55.00
☐ **American Silver Company "Moselle"**, *monogram, good condition.*	30.00	35.00

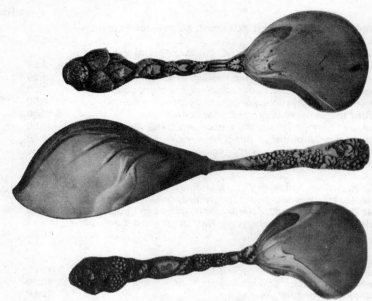

Berry Spoons, *(T to B) (sterling), Tiffany "Strawberry",* 200.00; *Tiffany "Vine",* 240.00; *Tiffany "Blackberry",* 225.00

	Price Range	
☐ **Community "Ballad",** *monogram, excellent condition.*	8.00	10.00
☐ **Community "Evening Star",** *no monogram, mint condition.* .	10.00	12.00
☐ **Community "Evening Star",** *no monogram, fair condition.* .	3.00	3.50
☐ **Community "Flight",** *no monogram, mint condition.*	6.00	7.00
☐ **Community "Georgian",** *no monogram, excellent condition.*	10.00	12.00
☐ **Community "Georgian",** *no monogram, good condition.* ...	8.00	9.00
☐ **Community "Morning Rose",** *no monogram, mint condition.*	9.00	10.00
☐ **Community "Morning Rose",** *no monogram, good condition.*	7.00	8.00
☐ **Community "Patrician",** *no monogram, good condition.* ...	10.00	12.00
☐ **Community "Patrician",** *no monogram, good condition.* ...	10.00	12.00
☐ **Community "Patrician",** *no monogram, poor condition.*	3.00	3.50
☐ **Community "Sheraton",** *no monogram, excellent condition.*	8.00	9.00
☐ **Community "Sheraton",** *no monogram, fair condition.*	2.00	2.50
☐ **Community "Silver Flower",** *no monogram, mint condition.*	7.00	8.00
☐ **Community "Silver Flower",** *no monogram, good condition.*	5.00	6.00
☐ **Community "Silver Valentine",** *no monogram, mint condition.*	8.00	9.00
☐ **Community "Silver Valentine",** *no monogram, excellent condition.*	9.00	10.00
☐ **Community "South Seas",** *no monogram, mint condition.* ...	9.00	10.00
☐ **Community "South Seas",** *no monogram, good condition.* .	6.00	7.00
☐ **Community "Tangier",** *no monogram, mint condition.*	8.00	9.00

	Price Range	
☐ Community "White Orchid", *no monogram, excellent condition.*	14.00	15.00
☐ Community "White Orchid", *no monogram, fair condition.*	3.50	4.50
☐ C. Rogers & Bro. "Victor", *no monogram, resilvered.*	13.00	15.00
☐ C. Rogers & Bro. "Victor", *no monogram, good condition.*	5.00	6.00
☐ DeepSilver "Laurel Mist", *no monogram, excellent condition.*	13.00	15.00
☐ DeepSilver "Laurel Mist", *no monogram, good condition.*	8.00	9.00
☐ DeepSilver "Wakefield", *no monogram, excellent condition.*	13.00	15.00
☐ DeepSilver "Wakefield", *fair condition*	3.00	3.50
☐ Gorham "Carolina", *no monogram, mint condition.*	9.00	10.00
☐ Gorham "Carolina", *no monogram, excellent condition.*	13.00	15.00
☐ Gorham "Kings", *no monogram, excellent condition.*	13.00	15.00
☐ Gorham "Kings", *good condition.*	9.00	10.00
☐ Harmony House "Danish Queen", *no monogram, excellent condition.*	12.00	15.00
☐ Harmony House "Serenade", *no monogram, excellent condition.*	4.00	5.00
☐ Harmony House "Serenade", *no monogram, poor condition.*	2.00	2.50
☐ Holmes & Edwards "Angelo", *no monogram, small size, excellent condition.*	25.00	28.00
☐ Holmes & Edwards "Angelo", *monogram, good condition.*	9.00	14.00
☐ Holmes & Edwards "Bright Future", *no monogram, excellent condition.*	7.00	8.00
☐ Holmes & Edwards "Bright Future", *no monogram, excellent condition.*	10.00	12.00
☐ Holmes & Edwards "Bright Future", *no monogram, pierced, good condition.*	6.00	7.00
☐ Holmes & Edwards "Carolina", *no monogram, good condition.*	4.00	5.00
☐ Holmes & Edwards "Chatsworth", *no monogram, excellent condition.*	9.00	10.00
☐ Holmes & Edwards "Chatsworth", *no monogram, excellent condition.*	13.00	15.00
☐ Holmes & Edwards "Danish Princess", *no monogram, excellent condition.*	9.00	10.00
☐ Holmes & Edwards "Danish Princess", *no monogram, good condition.*	6.00	7.00
☐ Holmes & Edwards "Lafayette", *no monogram, excellent condition.*	10.00	12.00
☐ Holmes & Edwards "Lafayette", *no monogram, excellent condition.*	13.00	15.00
☐ Holmes & Edwards "Lovely Lady", *no monogram, excellent condition.*	13.00	15.00
☐ Holmes & Edwards "Lovely Lady", *no monogram, fair condition.*	3.00	3.50
☐ Holmes & Edwards "Marina", *no monogram, excellent condition.*	12.00	14.00
☐ Holmes & Edwards "Marina", *no monogram, excellent condition.*	14.00	16.00
☐ International "Orleans", *no monogram, excellent condition.*	10.00	12.00

	Price Range	
☐ International "Orleans", *no monogram, poor condition.* ...	2.00	2.50
☐ International "Silver Tulip", *no monogram, excellent condition.*	10.00	12.00
☐ Oneida "Sheraton", *no monogram, excellent condition.* ...	8.00	9.00
☐ Oneida "Sheraton", *no monogram, excellent condition.* ...	10.00	12.00
☐ Reed & Barton "Oxford", *no monogram, resilvered.*	26.00	28.00
☐ Reed & Barton "Oxford", *no monogram, good condition.* ...	4.00	5.00
☐ Reed & Barton "Oxford", *monogram, fair condition.*	2.00	2.50
☐ Reliance "Exeter", *no monogram, excellent condition.*	10.00	12.00
☐ Reliance "Exeter", *no monogram, good condition.*	8.00	9.00
☐ Rockford "Fairoaks", *bowl engraved with acorns and leaves, no monogram, excellent condition*	18.00	20.00
☐ Rockford "Fairoaks", *no monogram, small size, good condition.*	9.00	10.00
☐ Rockford "Fairoaks", *no monogram, fair condition.*	2.50	3.50
☐ Rockford "Shell", *no monogram, fair condition.*	3.00	4.00
☐ Rockford "Shell", *no monogram, excellent condition.*	12.00	14.00
☐ Rogers "Burgundy", *no monogram, good condition.*	10.00	12.00
☐ Rogers "Burgundy", *monogram, good condition.*	5.00	6.00
☐ Rogers "Carlton", *no monogram, excellent condition.*	12.00	14.00
☐ Rogers "Carlton", *no monogram, good condition.*	6.00	7.00
☐ Rogers "Chelsea", *gold wash bowl, no monogram, excellent condition.*	12.00	14.00
☐ Rogers "Chelsea", *no monogram, fair condition.*	3.00	3.50
☐ Rogers "Croyden", *good condition*	6.00	7.00
☐ Rogers "Croyden", *no monogram, excellent condition.*	13.00	15.00
☐ Rogers "Queen Bess II", *no monogram, excellent condition.*	5.00	6.00
☐ Rogers "Queen Bess II", *no monogram, poor condition.* ...	1.75	2.50
☐ Rogers & Bro. "Daybreak", *no monogram, excellent condition.*	12.00	14.00
☐ Rogers & Bro. "Daybreak", *monogram, good condition.*	1.50	2.50
☐ Rogers & Hamilton "Raphael", *no monogram, excellent condition.*	14.00	16.00
☐ Rogers & Hamilton "Raphael", *no monogram, excellent condition.*	35.00	40.00
☐ Smith "Iris", *no monogram, excellent condition.*	13.00	15.00
☐ Smith "Iris", *no monogram, good condition.*	6.00	8.00
☐ Tudor "Friendship", *no monogram, good condition.*	7.00	8.00
☐ Tudor "Queen Bess II", *no monogram, fair condition.*	2.00	3.00
☐ Tudor "Queen Bess II", *no monogram, good condition.*	10.00	12.00
☐ Tudor "Queen Bess II", *no monogram, excellent condition.*..	14.00	16.00
☐ Wallace "Floral", *no monogram, excellent condition.*	24.00	26.00
☐ Wallace "Floral", *no monogram, good condition.*	14.00	16.00
☐ W. D. Smith "Adam", *no monogram, mint condition.*	10.00	12.00
☐ W. D. Smith "Adam", *no monogram, good condition.*	7.00	8.00
☐ Williams Bros. "Isabella", *no monogram, resilvered.*	16.00	18.00
☐ Williams Bros. "Isabella", *no monogram, excellent condition.*	16.00	18.00
☐ Wm. A. Rogers "Marcella", *no monogram, small size, excellent condition.*	14.00	16.00
☐ Wm. A. Rogers "Marcella", *no monogram, good condition.* ..	6.00	7.00
☐ Wm. A. Rogers "Meadowbrook", *no monogram, fair condition.*	2.00	3.00

	Price Range	
☐ **Wm. A. Rogers "Meadowbrook"**, *no monogram, excellent condition.*	10.00	12.00
☐ **Wm. A. Rogers "Rosalie"**, *no monogram, excellent condition.*	12.00	14.00
☐ **Wm. A. Rogers "Rosalie"**, *no monogram, good condition.* . . .	6.00	7.00
☐ **Wm. Rogers "Arbutus"**, *no monogram, excellent condition.*	20.00	22.00
☐ **Wm. Rogers "Arbutus"**, *no monogram, good condition.*	20.00	22.00
☐ **Wm. Rogers "Arbutus"**, *monogram, fair condition.*	6.00	8.00
☐ **Wm. Rogers "Bridal Bouquet"**, *no monogram, mint condition.*	6.00	8.00
☐ **Wm. Rogers "Bridal Bouquet"**, *no monogram, fair condition.*	1.25	2.00
☐ **Wm. Rogers "Debutante"**, *no monogram, excellent condition.*	10.00	12.00
☐ **Wm. Rogers "Debutante"**, *no monogram, good condition.* . .	5.00	6.00
☐ **Wm. Rogers "Flower"**, *no monogram, excellent condition.* . .	13.00	15.00
☐ **Wm. Rogers "Grand Elegance"**, *no monogram, excellent condition.*	6.00	7.00
☐ **Wm. Rogers "Grand Elegance"**, *no monogram, good condition.*	4.00	5.00
☐ **Wm. Rogers "Lincoln"**, *no monogram, excellent condition.* . .	5.00	6.00
☐ **Wm. Rogers "Magnolia"**, *no monogram, excellent condition.*	6.00	7.00
☐ **Wm. Rogers "Magnolia"**, *no monogram, fair condition.*	1.50	2.50
☐ **Wm. Rogers "Spring Charm"**, *no monogram, excellent condition.*	12.00	14.00
☐ **Wm. Rogers "Spring Charm"**, *no monogram, good condition.*	6.00	7.00
☐ **Wm. Rogers "Starlight"**, *no monogram, excellent condition.*	12.00	15.00
☐ **Wm. Rogers "Starlight"**, *no monogram, good condition.* . . .	6.00	8.00
☐ **Wm. Rogers "Treasure"**, *no monogram, excellent condition.*	14.00	15.00
☐ **Wm. Rogers "Treasure"**, *no monogram, resilvered.*	16.00	18.00
☐ **Wm. Rogers Mfg. Co. "Alhambra"**, *no monogram, good condition.*	9.00	10.00
☐ **Wm. Rogers Mfg. Co. "Alhambra"**, *no monogram, excellent condition.*	20.00	22.00
☐ **Wm. Rogers Mfg. Co. "Magnolia"**, *no monogram, good condition.*	10.00	12.00
☐ **Wm. Rogers Mfg. Co. "Magnolia"**, *monogram, good condition.*	6.00	7.00
☐ **Wm. Rogers Mfg. Co. "Opal"**, *no monogram, excellent condition.*	16.00	18.00
☐ **Wm. Rogers Mfg. Co. "Opal"**, *no monogram, mint condition.*	20.00	22.00
☐ **Wm. Rogers Mfg. Co. "York"**, *no monogram, good condition.*	18.00	20.00
☐ **Wm. Rogers Mfg. Co. "York"**, *monogram, good condition.* . . .	16.00	18.00
☐ **Wm. Rogers & Son "Floral Bouquet"**, *no monogram, excellent condition.*	12.00	14.00
☐ **Wm. Rogers & Son "Floral Bouquet"**, *no monogram, finish in excellent condition but small dent in bowl.*	8.00	9.00

	Price Range	
☐ World "Franconia", *no monogram, excellent condition.* ...	12.00	14.00
☐ World "Franconia", *no monogram, fair condition.*	2.00	3.00
☐ 1835 R. Wallace "Blossom", *no monogram, excellent condition.*	22.00	24.00
☐ 1835 R. Wallace "Blossom", *no monogram, good condition.*	12.00	14.00
☐ 1847 Rogers "Adoration", *no monogram, excellent condition.*	9.00	10.00
☐ 1847 Rogers "Avon", *no monogram, excellent condition.* ...	28.00	30.00
☐ 1847 Rogers "Berkshire", *no monogram, excellent condition.*	18.00	20.00
☐ 1847 Rogers "Berkshire", *no monogram, excellent condition.*	28.00	30.00
☐ 1847 Rogers "Berkshire", *no monogram, good condition.* ...	8.00	9.00
☐ 1847 Rogers "Berkshire", *no monogram, fair condition.*	3.00	4.00
☐ 1847 Rogers "Charter Oak", *no monogram, excellent condition.*	20.00	22.00
☐ 1847 Rogers "Charter Oak", *monogram, good condition.*	9.00	10.00
☐ 1847 Rogers "Columbia", *no monogram, resilvered.*	12.00	14.00
☐ 1847 Rogers "Columbia", *monogram, excellent condition.* .	12.00	14.00
☐ 1847 Rogers "Columbia", *no monogram, mint condition.*	28.00	30.00
☐ 1847 Rogers "Daffodil", *no monogram, excellent condition.*	12.00	14.00
☐ 1847 Rogers "Daffodil", *no monogram, fair condition.*	2.00	3.00
☐ 1847 Rogers "Daffodil II", *no monogram, excellent condition.*	12.00	14.00
☐ 1847 Rogers "Daffodil II", *no monogram, good condition.* ...	8.00	9.00
☐ 1847 Rogers "Esperanto", *no monogram, excellent condition.*	12.00	14.00
☐ 1847 Rogers "Flair", *no monogram, excellent condition.* ...	6.00	7.00
☐ 1847 Rogers "Flair", *no monogram, good condition.*	5.00	6.00
☐ 1847 Rogers "Heritage", *no monogram, excellent condition.*	7.00	8.00
☐ 1847 Rogers "Heritage", *no monogram, good condition.*	4.00	5.00
☐ 1847 Rogers "Lotus", *no monogram, excellent condition.* ..	20.00	22.00
☐ 1847 Rogers "Lotus", *monogram, excellent condition.*	16.00	18.00
☐ 1847 Rogers "Magic Rose", *no monogram, mint condition.* .	7.00	8.00
☐ 1847 Rogers "Magic Rose", *no monogram, silver in excellent condition but handle slightly bent.*	1.50	2.00
☐ 1847 Rogers "Marquise", *no monogram, excellent condition.*	13.00	15.00
☐ 1847 Rogers "Moselle", *no monogram, excellent condition.*	60.00	65.00
☐ 1847 Rogers "Moselle", *no monogram, good condition.*	28.00	30.00
☐ 1847 Rogers "Moselle", *no monogram, fair condition.*	12.00	14.00
☐ 1847 Rogers "Moselle", *monogram, good condition.*	20.00	22.00
☐ 1847 Rogers "Norfolk", *no monogram, excellent condition.*	12.00	14.00
☐ 1847 Rogers "Norfolk", *no monogram, good condition.*	6.00	7.00
☐ 1847 Rogers "Old Colony", *no monogram, excellent condition.*	17.00	18.00
☐ 1847 Rogers "Old Colony", *monogram, good condition.* ...	7.00	8.00
☐ 1847 Rogers "Portland", *monogram, excellent condition.* ..	10.00	12.00
☐ 1847 Rogers "Priscilla", *no monogram, excellent condition.*	12.00	14.00
☐ 1847 Rogers "Priscilla", *no monogram, fair condition.*	3.00	4.50
☐ 1847 Rogers "Savoy", *no monogram, excellent condition.* ...	14.00	16.00
☐ 1847 Rogers "Savoy", *monogram, good condition.*	6.00	7.00
☐ 1847 Rogers "Sharon", *no monogram, excellent condition.* ..	22.00	24.00

	Price Range	
☐ 1847 Rogers "Sharon", *monogram, excellent condition.* ...	18.00	20.00
☐ 1847 Rogers "Sharon", *no monogram, fair condition.*	3.50	4.50
☐ 1847 Rogers "Silver Lace", *no monogram, excellent condition.*	12.00	14.00
☐ 1847 Rogers "Springtime", *no monogram, excellent condition.*	7.00	8.00
☐ 1847 Rogers "Springtime", *monogram, excellent condition.*	3.00	4.00
☐ 1847 Rogers "Vesta", *no monogram, resilvered.*	14.00	16.00
☐ 1847 Rogers "Vesta", *no monogram, good condition.*	9.00	10.00
☐ 1847 Rogers "Vintage", *no monogram, excellent condition.*	26.00	28.00
☐ 1847 Rogers "Vintage", *no monogram, excellent condition.*	38.00	40.00
☐ 1847 Rogers "Vintage", *gold wash bowl, no monogram, excellent condition.*	48.00	50.00
☐ 1847 Rogers "Vintage", *monogram, fair condition.*	6.00	8.00

(Sterling Silver)

☐ Alvin "Raphael", *no monogram.*	125.00	150.00
☐ Durgin "Chrysanthemum", *no monogram, 9″ L.*	75.00	85.00
☐ Durgin "Chrysanthemum", *good monogram removal, 9″ L.* .	50.00	60.00
☐ Durgin "Chrysanthemum", *no monogram, large size.*	100.00	125.00
☐ Durgin "Watteau", *monogram, 8⅝″ L. ribbed bowl.*	65.00	75.00
☐ Gorham "King George", *monogram, 9″ L.*	35.00	40.00
☐ Gorham "Strasbourg", *monogram, 7¼″ L.*	26.00	30.00
☐ International "Bridal Veil", *no monogram.*	25.00	28.00
☐ International "Cambridge", *no monogram.*	28.00	30.00
☐ Reed & Barton "Francis I", *ribbed bowl, no monogram.*	30.00	35.00
☐ Reed & Barton "Francis I", *no monogram.*	36.00	40.00
☐ Reed & Barton "Love Disarmed", *no monogram, 8½″ L.* ...	185.00	210.00
☐ Simpson, Hall & Miller "Frontenac", *no monogram, 9″ L.* ...	60.00	85.00
☐ Tiffany "Olympian", *gold wash bowl, no monogram.*	145.00	165.00
☐ Whiting "Arabesque", *monogram and date.*	18.00	20.00
☐ Whiting "Imperial Queen", *no monogram.*	65.00	75.00
☐ Whiting "King Edward", *monogram.*	95.00	115.00

BISCUIT JARS

These are uncommon in silver, as in all metals, as metallic containers were considered injurious to the delicate flavors of biscuits and cookies. This is perhaps unfortunate, as their large size and bold shape lent very well to impressive decoration. Most specimens on the market (even in the U.S.) are foreign, and quite often the silver is low grade. Watch for "loaded" bases, which, when they occur, are invariably loaded from the INSIDE of the container with a false floor applied. This can add considerably to the weight.

(Silver-Plated)

☐ **Maker unknown,** *ovoid shape, decorated with engraved leaves, flowers and scroll design, four scroll and shell feet, lion's head handles, 7″ H., excellent condition except for small dent.*	100.00	125.00

BON BON SPOONS

These tend to be quite elegant, even to the point of exoticness sometimes, to suit the festive nature of their use. They are therefore popular with collectors of silver. Collections representing numerous styles and patterns are not difficult to assemble. Almost every antiques shop has, amid it showing of old silver, at least one specimen — and you will probably not encounter any duplicates until your collection has grown substantially.

Bon bon Spoons, *(sterling), pierced, (L to R) Tiffany "Vine",*
75.00; *Durgin "Chrysanthemum", 75.00; Tiffany "Persian", 75.00*

	Price Range	
(Silver-Plated)		
☐ **Community "Coronation",** *no monogram, mint condition...*	8.00	10.00
☐ **Community "Coronation",** *no monogram, good condition.*	7.00	8.00
☐ **Rogers & Bro. "Mystic",** *hotel insignia, excellent condition.*	20.00	22.00
☐ **1881 Rogers "Delmar",** *no monogram, excellent condition..*	3.50	4.50
(Sterling Silver)		
☐ **Blackington "Nautilus",** *pierced, no monogram.*	12.00	15.00
☐ **Dominick & Hall "Rococo",** *monogram.*	18.00	20.00
☐ **Durgin "Fairfax",** *pierced, no monogram.*	12.00	15.00
☐ **Durgin "Madame Royale",** *gold wash bowl, monogram.....*	30.00	35.00
☐ **Gorham "Chantilly",** *no monogram.*	12.00	15.00
☐ **Gorham "Etruscan",** *pierced, monogram.*	18.00	20.00
☐ **Gorham "King George",** *pierced, gold wash bowl, monogram.*	28.00	30.00
☐ **International "Wedgwood",** *no monogram.*	15.00	18.00
☐ **Lunt "Monticello",** *monogram.*	20.00	22.00

☐ **Wallace "Carthage",** *no monogram.*	18.00	20.00
☐ **Wallace "Violet",** *no monogram.*	35.00	40.00
☐ **Wallace "Violet",** *monogram.*	14.00	16.00

BON BON TONGS

Bon bon *tongs* are much less common than spoons. They were used only by the most fastidious, so far as home use is concerned, but of course were employed in shops where these delicacies were sold. The average shop specimen of the late 1800's/early 1900's is stainless steel or some other non-silver material, those of silver being used only in extremely prestigious shops. If a specimen is engraved or impressed with the shop's name, which is rare, this lends to the value somewhat.

	Price Range	
(Silver-Plated)		
☐ **Wm. A. Rogers "Glenrose"** *no monogram, excellent condition.*	12.00	14.00
(Sterling Silver)		
☐ **Gorham "Versailles",** *no monogram.*	55.00	60.00
☐ **Whiting "Lily",** *no monogram.*	40.00	45.00
☐ **Maker unknown,** *cherub and floral design, no monogram.* . . .	18.00	20.00

BOOK MARKS

Book marks were among the miscellaneous small novelties made usually of other materials, but occasionally of silver, in the 19th and earlier 20th centuries. A careful book lover would automatically shun silver book marks, and book marks of any metallic composition, since they pose a danger of harming the book. If the book is tightly compressed by being placed on a crowded shelf, the mark will create scoring lines on the paper. Nevertheless silver book marks did enjoy some popularity as gift items and simple trinkets, and are appealing to collect. The designs are very diverse, as their flat surfaces provided an excellent ground for engraving. Many are personalized. Obviously the weight is very slight.

(Sterling Silver)		
☐ **Tiffany,** *gold wash, no monogram.*	16.00	18.00
☐ **Unger Bros.,** *Art Nouveau poppy design, monogram.*	18.00	20.00
☐ **Maker unknown,** *plain design.*	6.00	8.00
☐ **Maker unknown,** *fancy engraving, monogram and date.*	8.00	10.00

BOOT HOOKS

Boot hooks made of silver were designed strictly for the wardrobe of the well-to-do — individuals who wished to have their finest of everything, even down to articles of a very inelegant utilitarian use. These devices, not to be confused with *shoe horns* (which were also sometimes made of silver, and are listed in their appropriate place in this book), were used to fasten the buttons on shoes. Because of the leather construction of shoes, a sturdier hook was necessary for the purpose than that used for clothing buttons. As buttoned boots had drifted out of popularity by World War I, it is safe to conclude that nearly all specimens of boot hooks, silver or otherwise, are of earlier origin. The majority apparently date from 1880 to about 1905.

(Sterling Silver)   Price Range

☐ **Kirk "Repousse"**, *monogram.*	38.00	40.00
☐ **Unger Bros., "Love's Voyage"**, *monogram.*	38.00	40.00
☐ **Maker unknown**, *plain design.*	14.00	16.00

BOTTLE OPENERS

As a class, bottle openers have more collector value (over and above the silver bullion value) than the vast majority of other silver novelties. This is owing to their appeal to collectors of soft-drink memorabilia, whose numbers are legion. While most specimens do not rank as first-class memorabilia, as a result of not carrying a soft-drink's brand name, they are still considered a good supplement to such a collection. It is not likely that any examples date prior to the 1880's, as soft-drink bottles were cork stopped before that time and there was no need for the modern sort of bottle opener. This likewise was true of other bottled beverages. Silver bottle openers represent a sharp contrast to those of the present time, being much sturdier and having a handle very similar to that of a knife or fork. A great variety of patterns can be found. Some wear may be encountered along the edge of the tool's "tooth" or prong, where it engaged the bottle's cap.

Bottle Opener, *(sterling), maker unknown,* 24.00

(Sterling Silver)

☐ **Frank M. Whiting,** *pattern unknown, sterling handle with stainless opener.*	28.00	30.00
☐ **Kirk "Repousse"**, *monogram.*	28.00	30.00
☐ **Kirk "Repousse"**, *no monogram.*	32.00	34.00
☐ **Maker unknown**, *scroll design, monogram.*	18.00	20.00

BOUILLON CUPS

Bouillon was in considerably greater favor with our ancestors than it is today. Recipe books of the 1800's and early 1900's never fail to include directions for preparing it, and even medical volumes of that era are high in praise of bouillon. It was prepared not only from chicken and beef, as is usually the case today, but likewise lamb, mutton, duck, goose, and even fish. Most persons used metallic cups for bouillon, believing they held heat better than chinaware or other substances. Actually this is not the case, unless the cup or other utensil has been warmed before use; but it did result in very widespread manufacture of metallic bouillon cups, including many of silver. They were generally sold in sets, a full set normally comprising a dozen and a half-set 6. One would expect them to be thick and heavy for purposes of heat-retention, but they seldom are. Two ounces is the average weight.

	Price Range	
(Silver-Plated)		
☐ **Maker unknown,** *Lenox liners with plain gold trim, ornate floral holders, set of six.*	100.00	110.00
(Sterling Silver)		
☐ **Alvin,** *openwork design, Lenox liner with plain gold trim, silver weight 1 oz.*	26.00	28.00
☐ **Alvin,** *plain silver with strap handles, Lenox liner with plain gold trim, silver weight 2 ozs.*	40.00	45.00
☐ **Barbour,** *openwork design, hollow handles, Lenox liners with plain gold trim, total silver weight 12 oz., set of six.*	250.00	275.00
☐ **Dominick & Haff,** *sterling silver, openwork design with raised floral design on rim, Lenox liners with plain gold trim, total silver weight 20 oz., set of eight.*	400.00	450.00
☐ **Dominick & Haff,** *plain design, Lenox liner with etched gold trim, weight 2½ oz.*	50.00	55.00
☐ **Dominick & Haff,** *openwork design, ornate reverse "C" handles, Lenox liner with plain gold trim, total silver weight 24 oz., set of 12.*	500.00	550.00
☐ **Durgin,** *plain design, strap handles, Lenox liners with plain gold trim, total weight 24 oz., set of 12.*	525.00	575.00
☐ **Gorham,** *plain design, strap handles, Lenox liners with plain gold trim, total weight 15 oz., set of six.*	300.00	325.00
☐ **International,** *openwork design, strap handles, weight 1½ oz., Lenox liner.*	36.00	38.00
☐ **Matthews,** *openwork design, hollow handles, Lenox liner with gold trim, total weight 16 oz., set of eight.*	350.00	375.00
☐ **Matthews,** *bright-cut work, inverted "S" handles, Lenox liners with plain gold trim, total weight 12 oz., set of six.*	250.00	275.00
☐ **Mauser,** *openwork design with ornate handles, Lenox/ C.A.C. transition mark liners, green exteriors, hand-painted-floral garlands inside, total weight 16 oz., set of six.*	450.00	485.00
☐ **Reed & Barton,** *openwork design, inverted "S" handles, Lenox liners with plain gold trim, total weight 24 oz., set of 12.*	500.00	550.00
☐ **Reed & Barton,** *plain design, squared-off hollow handles, Lenox liners with plain gold trim, total weight 16 oz., set of eight.*	350.00	375.00
☐ **Towle,** *plain silver, rolled rim, hollow handles, Lenox liners with plain gold trim, total weight 24 oz., set of 12.*	500.00	550.00
☐ **Unger Brothers,** *Art Nouveau floral design, ornate handles, Lenox liners with plain gold trim, total weight 12 oz., set of four.*	200.00	250.00

	Price Range	
☐ **Wallace**, *openwork design, inverted "S" handles, Lenox liners with plain gold trim, total weight 12 oz., set of eight.* .	240.00	265.00
☐ **Watson**, *vertical openwork design, Lenox liners with plain gold trim, total silver weight 12 oz., set of six.*	250.00	275.00
☐ **Whiting (Frank M.)**, *plain silver, strap handles, Lenox liners with plain gold trim, total silver weight 12 oz., set of six.*	250.00	275.00
☐ **Whiting Mfg. Co.**, *"Adam" pattern, Lenox liners with plain gold trim, total silver weight 12 oz., set of six.*	250.00	275.00

BOUILLON LADLES

Like silver ladles generally, those made for bouillon are very intriguing to the collector because of their large size and impressive appearance. Unfortunately they were not too extensively made, certainly in far less numbers than soup ladles. This was owing to the fact that bouillon was normally prepared in individual portions, rather than set out in a bowl and from thence ladled to cups. They are similar to soup ladles but usually a bit smaller in the bowl, and frequently have a pouring spout at the lefthand side of the bowl. You will have no trouble identifying them.

(Sterling Silver)

☐ **Lunt "Chateau"**, *no monogram*	65.00	75.00

BOUILLON SPOONS

Any household well supplied with silver tableware, in the period from about 1850 to fairly recently, was certain to own various bouillon spoons. Bouillon could just as well be taken with a soup spoon, but, even in families where strict etiquette was not practiced, the bouillon spoon made its appearance when bouillon reached the table. The bowl is slightly smaller than that of a soup spoon of the corresponding pattern but aside from this there is little recognizable difference.

(Silver-Plated)

☐ **Alvin "Classic"**, *no monogram, excellent condition*	7.00	8.00
☐ **Alvin "Classic"**, *monogram, fair condition.*	1.50	2.50
☐ **Alvin "Diana"**, *monogram, excellent condition.*	1.50	2.50
☐ **Alvin "Diana"**, *no monogram, good condition.*	2.00	3.00
☐ **Community "Georgian"**, *no monogram, excellent condition.*	3.00	4.00
☐ **Community "Georgian"**, *no monogram, fair condition.*	1.00	2.00
☐ **Community "Lady Hamilton"**, *no monogram, excellent condition.*	7.00	8.00
☐ **Community "Patrician"**, *monogram, excellent condition.*	2.00	3.00
☐ **Community "Patrician"**, *monogram, good condition.*	1.50	2.50
☐ **Community "Sheraton"**, *no monogram, excellent condition.*	7.00	8.00
☐ **Community "Sheraton"**, *no monogram, mint condition.*	8.00	9.00
☐ **Gorham "Carolina"**, *monogram, mint condition.*	4.00	5.00
☐ **Gorham "Carolina"**, *no monogram, good condition.*	2.00	3.00
☐ **Gorham "Kings"**, *monogram and date, excellent condition.*	4.50	5.00

	Price Range	
☐ Gorham "Kings", *U.S. Navy, excellent condition.*	**7.00**	**8.00**
☐ Gorham "Kings", *no monogram, mint condition.*	**8.00**	**10.00**
☐ Holmes & Edwards "Carolina", *monogram, excellent condition.*	**2.00**	**4.00**
☐ Holmes & Edwards "Carolina", *no monogram, excellent condition.*	**7.00**	**8.00**
☐ Holmes & Edwards "Orient", *no monogram, excellent condition.*	**4.00**	**5.00**
☐ Holmes & Edwards "Orient", *monogram, good condition.* ...	**1.00**	**2.00**
☐ International "Kings", *no monogram, excellent condition.* .	**3.00**	**4.00**
☐ International "Kings", *no monogram, mint condition.*	**6.00**	**7.00**
☐ National "King Edward", *no monogram, excellent condition.*	**7.00**	**8.00**
☐ National "King Edward", *no monogram, mint condition.* ...	**9.00**	**10.00**
☐ Oneida "Wildwood", *no monogram, resilvered.*	**8.00**	**9.00**
☐ Oneida "Wildwood", *no monogram, good condition.*	**3.00**	**4.00**
☐ Rogers "Ambassador", *no monogram, excellent condition.*	**4.00**	**5.00**
☐ Rogers "Florette', *no monogram, excellent condition.*	**3.00**	**4.00**
☐ Rogers "LaTouraine", *no monogram, good condition.*	**6.00**	**7.00**
☐ Rogers "LaTouraine", *monogram ghost showing through, resilvered.*	**8.00**	**10.00**
☐ Rogers "Orange Blossom", *no monogram, excellent condition.*	**7.00**	**8.00**
☐ Rogers "Orange Blossom", *no monogram, mint condition.* .	**9.00**	**10.00**
☐ Rogers & Bro. "Hostess", *no monogram, fair condition.* ...	**2.00**	**2.50**
☐ Rogers & Bro. "Hostess", *no monogram, excellent condition.*	**6.00**	**7.00**
☐ Wm. A. Rogers "Hanover", *no monogram, good condition.* .	**3.00**	**4.00**
☐ Wm. A. Rogers "Hanover", *no monogram, poor condition.* .	**2.00**	**3.00**
☐ Wm. A. Rogers "Hanover", *no monogram, excellent condition.*	**4.00**	**5.00**
☐ Wm. Rogers "Fairmount", *no monogram, excellent condition.*	**7.00**	**8.00**
☐ Wm. Rogers "Fairmount", *monogram, fair condition.*	**1.75**	**2.50**
☐ Wm. Rogers "Memory", *no monogram, excellent condition.*	**7.00**	**8.00**
☐ Wm. Rogers "Memory", *monogram, good condition.*	**2.00**	**3.00**
☐ Wm. Rogers "Orange Blossom", *no monogram, excellent condition.*	**8.00**	**10.00**
☐ Wm. Rogers "Orange Blossom", *no monogram, resilvered.* .	**8.00**	**10.00**
☐ 1835 R. Wallace "LaSalle", *no monogram, excellent condition.*	**2.00**	**3.00**
☐ 1835 R. Wallace "LaSalle", *monogram, good condition.*	**1.50**	**2.50**
☐ 1847 Rogers "Argosy", *no monogram, good condition.*	**4.00**	**5.00**
☐ 1847 Rogers "Argosy", *no monogram, fair condition.*	**2.50**	**3.50**
☐ 1847 Rogers "Avon", *monogram, excellent condition.*	**8.00**	**10.00**
☐ 1847 Rogers "Avon", *no monogram, good condition.*	**5.00**	**6.00**
☐ 1847 Rogers "Avon", *monogram, fair condition.*	**1.50**	**2.50**
☐ 1847 Rogers "Cromwell", *no monogram, excellent condition.*	**2.00**	**3.00**
☐ 1847 Rogers "Cromwell", *monogram, fair condition.*	**1.00**	**2.00**
☐ 1847 Rogers "Old Colony", *no monogram, good condition.* .	**6.00**	**7.00**
☐ 1847 Rogers "Old Colony", *no monogram, excellent condition.*	**7.00**	**8.00**
☐ 1847 Rogers "Old Colony", *no monogram, resilvered.*	**9.00**	**10.00**

Price Range

- [ ] **1847 Rogers "Queen Ann"**, *no monogram, excellent condition.* 7.00   8.00
- [ ] **1847 Rogers "Queen Ann"**, *monogram, good condition.* ... 3.00   4.00
- [ ] **1847 Rogers "Vintage"**, *no monogram, excellent condition.* 18.00   20.00
- [ ] **1847 Rogers "Vintage"**, *no monogram, good condition.*..... 16.00   18.00
- [ ] **1847 Rogers "Vintage"**, *monogram, good condition.* 5.00   6.00
- [ ] **1881 Rogers "Chippendale"**, *no monogram, excellent condition.* 7.00   8.00
- [ ] **1881 Rogers "Chippendale"**, *monogram, fair condition.*..... 1.50   2.50

(Sterling Silver)
- [ ] **Alvin "Monterey"**, *monogram.* 14.00   16.00
- [ ] **Alvin "Wellington"**, *no monogram.* 16.00   18.00
- [ ] **Alvin "Raleigh"**, *no monogram.* 18.00   20.00
- [ ] **Amston "Gladstone"**, *no monogram.* 28.00   30.00
- [ ] **Amston "Queen Mary"**, *no monogram.* 14.00   16.00
- [ ] **Baker-Manchester "Spartan"**, *no monogram.* 16.00   18.00
- [ ] **Baker-Manchester "Van Buren"**, *no monogram.* 13.00   15.00
- [ ] **Blackington "Verona"**, *gold wash bowl, no monogram.* 10.00   12.00
- [ ] **Concord Silversmiths "America"**, *no monogram.* 16.00   18.00
- [ ] **Dimes "Irish Antique Engraved"**, *monogram.* 13.00   15.00
- [ ] **Dominick & Haff "Acanthus"**, *monogram.* 13.00   15.00
- [ ] **Dominick & Haff "Kings"**, *monogram and date.* 14.00   16.00
- [ ] **Dominick & Haff "New Kings"**, *no monogram.*............ 16.00   18.00
- [ ] **Durgin "Fairfax"**, *no monogram 5½" L.* 10.00   12.00
- [ ] **Durgin "Medallion"**, *no monogram₂*..................... 34.00   36.00
- [ ] **Fessenden "McKinley"**, *no monogram.* 18.00   20.00
- [ ] **Fessenden "Newport"**, *no monogram.*.................... 18.00   20.00
- [ ] **Frank Smith "Chippendale"**, *no monogram.* 16.00   18.00
- [ ] **Gorham "Etruscan"**, *no monogram.* 23.00   25.00
- [ ] **Gorham "Huguenot"**, *no monogram.* 22.00   24.00
- [ ] **Gorham "King George"**, *no monogram.* 26.00   28.00
- [ ] **Graff, Washbourne & Dunn "French Border, Hand Chased"**, *no monogram.* 23.00   25.00
- [ ] **International "Edgewood"**, *no monogram.*................ 16.00   18.00
- [ ] **International "Kingston"**, *no monogram.* 12.00   14.00
- [ ] **Kirk "Calvert"**, *no monogram.* 13.00   15.00
- [ ] **Lunt "Chatelaine"**, *no monogram.*...................... 14.00   16.00
- [ ] **Manchester "Mary Warren"**, *monogram.* 14.00   16.00
- [ ] **Mount Vernon "Pointed Antique"**, *monogram.* 8.00   10.00
- [ ] **Reed & Barton "Marlborough"**, *monogram.* 12.00   14.00
- [ ] **Tiffany "Flemish"**, *no monogram.* 10.00   12.00
- [ ] **Tiffany "Hampton"**, *monogram.* 16.00   18.00
- [ ] **Tiffany "Marquise"**, *no monogram.*..................... 20.00   22.00
- [ ] **Towle "Georgian"**, *no monogram set of 12.* 200.00   235.00

BOWLS

The extent of bowls manufactured of silver is so extensive that we cannot, in this book, attempt to give more than basic representative listings. The specimens listed here are of a general type, not designed for a special use, but ELSEWHERE IN THE BOOK will be found listings for bowls of designated use. These could roughly be termed "ornamental bowls," and were not at all uncommon in the Victorian, Edwardian, and even in the somewhat later household. They could simply be placed out in view — for example on the dining table when it was not in use — and lend an ornamental touch to the decor. Or they could serve as a receptacle for real or waxed fruits, candies, etc. The silver bowl of the 19th century descended from ancestors going back far into history. This was one article that early silversmiths were frequently called on to make — long before the world knew of berry spoons, bouillon cups or most later silverware. Designs are very diverse, and, as can be expected, so too are the sizes and WEIGHTS. Even on bowls of approximately the same size, the weights can vary substantially because of different thicknesses of silver used by the manufacturer. There was no "standard" bowl, so each specimen found on the market must be approached singally and investigated for its own individual characteristics. LOADING (adding to the weight by the addition of lead, sand or other substance) is not uncommon in bowls. This will generally be concealed by a false floor, rather than a false underside.

Bowl, *(sterling), Tiffany "Blackberry", 17½ ounces,* 425.00

(Silver-Plated)	Price Range	
☐ **Meriden,** *ornate, Art Nouveau styling, monogram, 10" Dia. silver in good condition.*	35.00	40.00
☐ **Maker unknown,** *Victorian styling, lion's head handles, movable rings in lions' mouths, raised on four paw feet, monogram, silver in good condition.*	60.00	65.00
☐ **Maker unknown,** *plain Paul Revere shape, no monogram, excellent condition.*	25.00	28.00

(Sterling Silver)	Price Range	
☐ **Gorham,** *berry type, applied fruit border, 10" Dia., weight unknown.*	180.00	200.00
☐ **Randahl,** *"Chicago", monogram.*	45.00	60.00
☐ **Webster,** *gadroon banding, 4½" top Dia., 2½" bottom Dia., 3½" H., weight unknown, dented.*	8.00	10.00
☐ **Maker unknown,** *Art Deco styling, c. 1930, 6½" Dia., weight 10 oz., vertical engraved lines.*	75.00	85.00

(Sterling Silver and China)		
☐ **Kirk,** *Lenox, Paul Revere style, Lenox liner with gold banding, 6" Dia., silver weight 5 oz.*	100.00	120.00

BREAD KNIVES

Bakery and other commercially-sold bread came in solid unsliced loaves until the first quarter of the 20th century. The baker would of course slice your bread as a courtesy, but few customers wished to have this done, believing that the flavor and keeping qualities would be impaired. So the bread knife was standard equipment in all households. To cut bread, and especially *newly baked bread,* which tends to be spongy, a large sharp knife is necessary. The silver bread knives are sometimes a little larger than those of stainless steel or other materials: this is probably because anyone who could afford silver was concerned about labor-saving, and an extra-large bread knife did the job better. Even after getting on the antiques market and going through collections, some specimens retain the lethalness of their sharpened blade, so APPROACH WITH CAUTION.

(Silver-Plated)		
☐ **1847 Rogers "Vintage"** *no monogram, 14½" L., excellent condition.*	65.00	70.00

(Sterling Silver)		
☐ **Gorham "King George",** *monogram.*	55.00	60.00
☐ **Gorham,** *pattern unknown, monogram.*	55.00	60.00

BREAD SERVING SETS

Bread serving sets provided a dining knife and fork in addition to a bread knife, with which slices were taken from the loaf. They sometimes also consisted of serving trays. This was not a common article for the silverware manufacturers, owing to limited public demand. Bread was, of course, universally consumed, but was so standard and common that it seemed hardly to warrant any special attention. As collectors' items, bread serving sets do not rank in a very high category. They are so difficult to find, or assemble piecemeal, that most would-be collectors lose interest before getting far.

(Sterling Silver)		
☐ **Gorham,** *floral pattern, fork and knife, c. 1890.*	110.00	120.00

BREAD TRAYS

These are serving trays on which the full loaf of bread was brought to the table, and were a necessity in well-appointed households. Normally the sides are built up somewhat and slope inward, to add ornamental appeal. This, however, made slicing more challenging than if the tray was absolutely flat; and often you will find scratches on the sides of bread trays, caused by the edge of the bread knife. Being more or less standard in size, bread trays were much more suitable for home-baked loaves than those bought from the bakery, which might be of a large size or unusual shape.

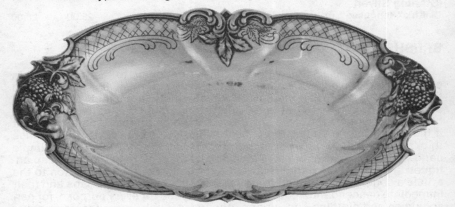

Bread Tray, *Tiffany "Blackberry", 14 ounces,* 335.00

	Price	Range
(Silver-Plated)		
☐ **1847 Rogers "Flair",** *no monogram, excellent condition.* . . .	28.00	30.00
☐ **Maker's mark worn,** *Art Nouveau styling with woman with flowing hair, pierced borders, resilvered.*	38.00	40.00
☐ **Maker unknown,** *plain design, rolled rim, monogram, poor condition.*	3.00	4.50
(Sterling Silver)		
☐ **Gorham,** *pierced border, monogram in center, 10 oz.*	125.00	150.00

BREAKFAST KNIVES

A splendid example of the lengths to which the proper Victorians carried their ideal of *a specific table implement for every possible table use.* There was no such thing as the multi-purpose knife. A knife, like everything else on the table, had its certain function and perish the mere suggestion of not having the proper type ready at the proper moment. The concept behind *breakfast knives* was that foodstuffs normally served at breakfast did not require the strenuous cutting of supper meats — therefore a breakfast knife ought to be daintier and lighter and more easily manageable. This was quite fine if the meal consisted of scrambled eggs or pancakes, but breakfast knives looked very out of character if ham or sausage made an appearance. Do not make the assumption that breakfast knives necessarily have dull edges; this is not always so.

(Silver-Plated)
           Price Range

☐ **Gorham "Kings"**, *no monogram, excellent condition*....... 3.00   4.00
☐ **Gorham "Kings"**, *U.S. Navy, good condition*.............. 3.00   4.00
☐ **Wm. Rogers Eagle "Kings"**, *hollow handled, hotel name, excellent condition*.................................... 3.00   4.00

(Sterling Silver)
☐ **Kirk "Repousse"**, *no monogram*...................... 26.00   28.00

BRUSHES

    Brushes have, especially within recent years, come to the front ranks in popularity among silver articles. Collectors are extremely fond of them and there is no mystery why: there is excellent variety in brushes, in sizes and styles, and of course in patterns. Brushes are more decorative than most other silverware, as the large silver head could be turned to pure ornament if the manufacturer so desired. It could likewise be built up to an immense thickness, and carry artwork in high relief, which was often done. Simple hand-weighing of silver brushes (specimens that you might locate in an antiques store) will reveal that the weight if often very great in relation to the article's comparatively small overall size. Of course the Victorians and their immediate descendants required elegant brushes for every purpose, for personal use and clothing and various other uses, so the manufacturers never hesitated to bring out full lines of them. In judging the COLLECTOR value of a silver brush, some estimate must be made of the age, as the earlier specimens tend to be valued more highly, and of the artistic quality of the decoration. It is not unusual for an especially fine one — old and well-made — to sell for three or even four times the melt value of its silver bullion content. If the bristles are not intact this draws somewhat from the value.

(Sterling Silver)
☐ **Durgin**, *repousse floral design, man's hat brush, oval shape, monogram*.................................... 16.00   18.00
☐ **Gorham**, *floral pattern, hair brush, no monogram*.......... 18.00   20.00
☐ **Kirk "Repousse"**, *clothes brush, monogram*.............. 65.00   75.00
☐ **Unger Bros. "He Loves Me"**, *military brush, no monogram, bristles in good condition.* 40.00   45.00
☐ **Unger Bros. "Love's Voyage"**, *clothes brush, monogram.* ... 40.00   45.00
☐ **Maker unknown**, *figural pig clothes brush, no monogram, 4½ " L*.. 10.00   12.00
☐ **Maker unknown**, *clothes brush, plain design, monogram.* ... 16.00   18.00
☐ **Maker unknown**, *set of three, Art Nouveau lady with flowing hair, no monogram.* 70.00   80.00

BUTTER DISHES

The simple plastic articles which now serve this purpose, on most tables, pale before the elaborate silver butter dishes of yesteryear. The butter dish as a species of tableware is not as antique as might be imagined. It developed only in the 19th century, as the earlier practice was to keep butter in tubs rather than forming it into bars or sticks. Of course the dish must be lidded to act as a preservative and also keep the butter from melting, so far as tradition has dictated. In fact neither purpose was accomplished by the lid, but it added extra ornament and that alone might have been a reasonable excuse for having it. The finial atop butter dish lids is sometimes a little gem of designing and may, often, be the most endearing feature of the whole article. When butter dishes are lacking the lid their value as collectors' pieces is sharply reduced, though in terms of "melt value" it is still (as always) a matter of weight and silver content.

Butter Dish, *Gorham "Medallion", coin silver, 21 ounces,* 465.00

	Price Range	
(Silver-Plated)		
☐ **Meriden,** *dome type, pineapple finial, ornate embossed design, liner missing, resilvered.*	25.00	28.00
☐ **Tufts,** *round dome type, ornate chasing on lid, liner present, monogram, good condition.*	22.00	24.00
☐ **Maker unknown,** *revolving lid fits into bottom section, liner present, monogram, good condition.*	14.00	16.00
(Sterling Silver)		
☐ **International,** *small open type, lattice work design, Lenox liner with gold trim.*	18.00	20.00
☐ **Kirk,** *cow finial, underplate and pierced liner, plain design, monogram.*	195.00	215.00
☐ **Reed & Barton,** *rectangular modern type, gadroon banding on rims, monogram.*	65.00	75.00

BUTTER KNIVES (MASTER)

As collectors use the term, a *butter knife* is the utensil with which butter is sliced from the stick or bar. The utensil used in spreading butter on bread, etc., is correctly known as a *butter spreader,* and these are listed following the present section.

Consequently the butter knife is somewhat larger and weightier than the spreader, since it had more of a task to do. It had to be rather wide, for tackling a thick bar of butter. It needed also to be fairly sturdy, in the event (though this was hardly desirable) that the butter was thoroughly chilled and solid. There are various common shapes, the most common being the cleaver variety which resembles a butcher's cleaver in miniature. The variety in shapes, and of course in patterns, has rendered the butter knife quite popular as a collectors' item.

As a further safeguard against confusing butter knives and spreaders, the former are often referred to as butter MASTER knives.

Master Butter Knives, *(L to R) (sterling), Tiffany "Chrysanthemum",* 60.00; *Simpson, Hall & Miller "Frontenac",* 50.00; *Tiffany "Wave Edge",* 60.00; *Durgin "Chrysanthemum",* 30.00

(Coin Silver)	Price Range	
☐ C. Stakesman.	23.00	25.00

(Silver-Plated)

☐ Alvin "Brides' Bouquet", *no monogram, excellent condition.*	5.00	6.00
☐ Alvin "Bride's Bouquet", *no monogram, fair condition.*	1.00	2.00
☐ Alvin "Diana", *no monogram, excellent condition.*	5.00	6.00

	Price Range	
☐ Alvin "Diana", *no monogram, good condition*............	4.00	5.00
☐ Alvin "George Washington", *no monogram, excellent condition*...	5.00	6.00
☐ Alvin "George Washington", *no monogram, good condition*..	4.00	5.00
☐ Alvin "Louisiana", *no monogram, excellent condition*......	5.00	6.00
☐ Alvin "Louisiana", *no monogram, good condition*.	4.00	5.00
☐ Alvin "Victory", *no monogram, excellent condition*.	3.00	4.00
☐ Alvin "Victory", *no monogram, excellent condition*.	5.00	6.00
☐ American Silver Co. "Moselle", *no monogram, fair condition*...	10.00	12.00
☐ American Silver Co. "Moselle", *no monogram, excellent condition*...	10.00	18.00
☐ American Silver Co. "Rosalie", *no monogram, good condition*...	4.00	5.00
☐ American Silver Co. "Rosalie", *no monogram, excellent condition*...	5.00	6.00
☐ Benedict "Shell", *twisted handle, no monogram, good condition*...	7.00	8.00
☐ Boardman "Medallion", *flat-handled, no monogram, poor condition*...	2.00	3.00
☐ Community "Adam", *no monogram, excellent condition*. ..	5.00	6.00
☐ Community "Adam", *no monogram, good condition*.	3.00	4.00
☐ Community "Adam", *no monogram, excellent condition*. ..	2.00	3.00
☐ Community "Avalon", *no monogram, excellent condition*. .	3.00	4.00
☐ Community "Avalon", *no monogram, good condition*.	3.00	4.00
☐ Community "Ballad", *no monogram, mint condition*.	3.00	4.00
☐ Community "Ballad", *no monogram, excellent condition*. ..	5.00	6.00
☐ Community "Bedford", *no monogram, excellent condition*..	4.00	5.00
☐ Community "Bird of Paradise", *no monogram, excellent condition*...	5.00	6.00
☐ Community "Bird of Paradise", *no monogram, good condition*...	4.00	5.00
☐ Community "Bird of Paradise", *no monogram, excellent condition*...	6.00	7.00
☐ Community "Coronation", *no monogram, mint condition*...	2.00	3.00
☐ Community "Coronation", *no monogram, excellent condition*...	5.00	6.00
☐ Community "Coronation", *no monogram, good condition*. .	4.00	5.00
☐ Community "Deauville", *no monogram, excellent condition*...	3.00	4.00
☐ Community "Deauville", *no monogram, excellent condition*...	3.00	4.00
☐ Community "Deauville", *no monogram, excellent condition*...	5.00	6.00
☐ Community "Enchantment", *no monogram, excellent condition*...	5.00	6.00
☐ Community "Enchantment", *no monogram, good condition*...	4.00	5.00
☐ Community "Evening Star", *no monogram, good condition*.	4.00	5.00
☐ Community "Evening Star", *no monogram, excellent condition*...	3.00	4.00
☐ Community "Flight", *no monogram, excellent condition*. ..	5.00	6.00

Price Range

☐ Community "Flower de Luce", *monogram, excellent condition.* 3.00   4.00

☐ Community "Flower de Luce", *no monogram, excellent condition.* 5.00   6.00

☐ Community "Forever", *no monogram, excellent condition.* . 3.00   4.00

☐ Community "Forever", *no monogram, excellent condition.* . 5.00   6.00

☐ Community "Georgian", *no monogram, excellent condition.* 1.00   2.00

☐ Community "Georgian", *no monogram, fair condition.* 1.50   2.50

☐ Community "Georgian", *no monogram, excellent condition.* 5.00   6.00

☐ Community "Grosvenor", *monogram, excellent condition.* . 3.00   4.00

☐ Community "Grosvenor", *no monogram, excellent condition.* 4.00   5.00

☐ Community "King Cedric", *no monogram, excellent condition.* 5.00   6.00

☐ Community "King Cedric", *no monogram, poor condition.* . 1.00   2.00

☐ Community "Lady Hamilton", *no monogram, excellent condition.* 5.00   6.00

☐ Community "Lady Hamilton", *no monogram, good condition.* 5.00   6.00

☐ Community "Lady Hamilton", *no monogram, good condition.* 3.00   4.00

☐ Community "Lady Hamilton", *no monogram, fair condition.* 1.50   2.50

☐ Community "Linda", *no monogram, excellent condition.* . . . 5.00   6.00

☐ Community "Linda", *no monogram, good condition.* 3.00   4.00

☐ Community "Louis XVI", *no monogram, excellent condition.* 5.00   6.00

☐ Community "Louis XVI", *no monogram, good condition.* . . . 4.00   5.00

☐ Community "Louis XVI", *monogram, excellent condition.* . . 1.00   2.00

☐ Community "Milady", *no monogram, excellent condition.* . . 5.00   6.00

☐ Community "Milady", *no monogram, good condition.* 4.00   5.00

☐ Community "Milady", *no monogram, fair condition.* 1.00   2.00

☐ Community "Modjeska", *no monogram, excellent condition.* 4.00   5.00

☐ Community "Modjeska", *no monogram, fair condition.* 1.00   2.00

☐ Community "Morning Star", *no monogram, excellent condition.* 5.00   6.00

☐ Community "Morning Star", *no monogram, good condition.* 4.00   5.00

☐ Community "Morning Star", *no monogram, fair condition.* . 1.50   2.50

☐ Community "Noblesse", *no monogram, excellent condition.* 5.00   6.00

☐ Community "Noblesse", *monogram, excellent condition.* . . 2.50   3.50

☐ Community "Noblesse", *no monogram, good condition.* . . . 4.00   5.00

☐ Community "Patrician", *no monogram, excellent condition.* 5.00   6.00

☐ Community "Patrician", *no monogram, good condition.* . . . 4.00   5.00

☐ Community "Paul Revere", *no monogram, excellent condition.* 5.00   6.00

☐ Community "Paul Revere", *no monogram, poor condition.* . 1.00   2.00

☐ Community "Silver Flowers", *no monogram, excellent condition.* 5.00   6.00

☐ Community "Silver Flowers", *no monogram, fair condition.* 1.00   2.00

☐ Community "South Seas", *no monogram, excellent condition.* 5.00   6.00

	Price Range	
☐ Community "South Seas", *no monogram, good condition.* .	4.00	5.00
☐ Embassy "Bouquet", *no monogram, excellent condition.* ..	5.00	6.00
☐ Embassy "Bouquet", *no monogram, good condition.*......	4.00	5.00
☐ Fortune "Fortune", *no monogram, excellent condition.*	5.00	6.00
☐ Fortune "Fortune", *no monogram, fair condition.*.........	1.50	2.50
☐ Gorham "Carolina", *no monogram, mint condition.*	2.00	3.00
☐ Gorham "Cavalier", *no monogram, excellent condition.* ...	3.00	4.00
☐ Gorham "Empire", *no monogram, excellent condition.*	3.00	4.00
☐ Gorham "Empire", *monogram, excellent condition.*........	2.00	3.00
☐ Gorham "Lady Caroline", *no monogram, excellent condition.*..	5.00	6.00
☐ Gorham "Lady Caroline", *no monogram, good condition.* ..	4.00	5.00
☐ Gorham "Regent", *no monogram, excellent condition.*	5.00	6.00
☐ Gorham "Regent", *no monogram, poor condition.*	1.00	2.00
☐ Gorham "Vanity Fair", *no monogram, excellent condition.* .	5.00	6.00
☐ Hall, Elton & Co. "Eastlake", *no monogram, excellent condition.*..	8.00	10.00
☐ Hall, Elton & Co., "Italian" *no monogram, excellent condition.*...	5.00	6.00
☐ Hall, Elton & Co. "Italian", *no monogram, excellent condition.*..	6.00	7.00
☐ Harmony House "Serenade", *no monogram, excellent condition.*...	3.00	4.00
☐ Harmony House "Serenade", *no monogram, excellent condition.*...	5.00	6.00
☐ Harmony House "Serenade", *good condition.*.............	4.00	5.00
☐ Hartford "Lyonnaise", *no monogram, excellent condition.* .	12.00	14.00
☐ Holmes, Booth & Haydens "Japanese", *no monogram, excellent condition.*....................................	6.00	7.00
☐ Holmes & Edwards "Century", *no monogram, excellent condition.*..	5.00	6.00
☐ Holmes & Edwards "Century", *no monogram, good condition.*...	4.00	5.00
☐ Holmes & Edwards "Charm", *no monogram, excellent condition.*..	5.00	6.00
☐ Holmes & Edwards "Charm", *no monogram, resilvered.* ...	—	7.00
☐ Holmes & Edwards "Danish Princess", *no monogram, excellent condition.*....................................	3.00	6.00
☐ Holmes & Edwards "Danish Princess", *no monogram, excellent condition.*....................................	5.00	6.00
☐ Holmes & Edwards "Danish Princess", *no monogram, good condition.*..	4.00	5.00
☐ Holmes & Edwards "First Lady", *no monogram, excellent condition.*...	5.00	6.00
☐ Holmes & Edwards "First Lady", *no monogram, fair condition.*..	1.50	2.50
☐ Holmes & Edwards "Flower", *twisted handle, no monogram, excellent condition.*	7.00	8.00
☐ Holmes & Edwards "Flower", *twisted handle, monogram, excellent condition.*..................................	3.00	4.00
☐ Holmes & Edwards "Irving", *no monogram, excellent condition.*..	7.00	8.00
☐ Holmes & Edwards "LaFayette", *twisted handle, no monogram, excellent condition.*	7.00	8.00

Price Range

- ☐ Holmes & Edwards "LaFayette", *no monogram, good condition.* 4.00   5.00
- ☐ Holmes & Edwards "Leader", *twisted handle, engraved blade, no monogram, excellent condition.* 8.00   9.00
- ☐ Holmes & Edwards "Lovely Lady", *no monogram, excellent condition.* 1.00   2.00
- ☐ Holmes & Edwards "Lovely Lady", *no monogram, silver in excellent condition but deep nick on blade.* 2.00   3.00
- ☐ Holmes & Edwards "Lovely Lady", *no monogram, excellent condition.* 4.00   5.00
- ☐ Holmes & Edwards "Orient", *no monogram, excellent condition.* 9.00   10.00
- ☐ Holmes & Edwards "Orient", *monogram, good condition.* . . . 4.00   5.00
- ☐ Holmes & Edwards "Pageant", *no monogram, excellent condition.* 5.00   6.00
- ☐ Holmes & Edwards "Pageant", *no monogram, fair condition.* 1.50   2.50
- ☐ Holmes & Edwards "Romance II", *no monogram, excellent condition.* 4.00   5.00
- ☐ Holmes & Edwards "Romance II", *no monogram, excellent condition.* 5.00   6.00
- ☐ Holmes & Edwards "Rosemary", *no monogram, excellent condition.* 10.00   12.00
- ☐ Holmes & Edwards "Queen Anne", *no monogram, excellent condition.* 3.00   5.00
- ☐ Holmes & Edwards "Silver Fashion", *no monogram, excellent condition.* 5.00   6.00
- ☐ Holmes & Edwards "Silver Fashion", *no monogram, good condition.* 4.00   5.00
- ☐ Holmes & Edwards "Spring Garden", *no monogram, excellent condition.* 5.00   6.00
- ☐ Holmes & Edwards "Spring Garden", *no monogram, poor condition.* 1.00   2.00
- ☐ Holmes & Edwards "Triumph", *no monogram, excellent condition.* 14.00   16.00
- ☐ Holmes & Edwards "Unique", *no monogram, excellent condition.* 4.00   5.00
- ☐ Holmes & Edwards "Unique", *no monogram, fair condition.* 1.50   2.50
- ☐ International "Silver Tulip", *no monogram, fair condition.* . . . 4.00   5.00
- ☐ International "Silver Tulip", *no monogram, excellent condition.* 2.00   3.00
- ☐ Marion "Camden", *no monogram, excellent condition.* 5.00   6.00
- ☐ National "King Edward", *no monogram, excellent condition.* . . . . —   6.00
- ☐ National "King Edward", *no monogram, good condition.* 4.00   5.00
- ☐ Nobility "Caprice", *no monogram, excellent condition.* 5.00   6.00
- ☐ Nobility "Caprice", *no monogram, fair condition.* 1.50   2.50
- ☐ Nobility "Royal Rose", *no monogram, excellent condition.* . . 5.00   6.00
- ☐ Nobility "Royal Rose", *no monogram, good condition.* 4.00   5.00
- ☐ Old Company Plate "Signature", *monogram, excellent condition.* 3.00   4.00
- ☐ Oneida "Avalon", *flat-handled, no monogram, excellent condition.* 1.00   2.00
- ☐ Oneida "Avalon", *no monogram, good condition.* 2.00   3.00

	Price Range	

☐ **Oneida "Exeter"**, *twisted handle, no monogram, mint condition.* 5.00 6.00

☐ **Oneida "Exeter"**, *twisted handle, no monogram, excellent condition.* 5.00 6.00

☐ **Oneida "Flower de Luce"**, *flat handled, no monogram, excellent condition.* 5.00 6.00

☐ **Oneida "Flower de Luce"**, *flat-handled, no monogram, excellent condition.* 8.00 9.00

☐ **Oneida "Flower de Luce"**, *flat-handled, no monogram, fair condition.* 2.00 3.00

☐ **Oneida "Jamestown"**, *monogram, excellent condition.* 2.00 3.00

☐ **Oneida "Louis XVI"**, *no monogram, excellent condition.* . . . 1.50 2.50

☐ **Oneida "Narcissus"**, *no monogram, excellent condition.* . . 8.00 10.00

☐ **Oneida "Primrose"**, *no monogram, excellent condition.* . . . 1.00 2.00

☐ **Prestige "Grenoble"**, *no monogram, excellent condition.* . . 5.00 6.00

☐ **Prestige "Grenoble"**, *no monogram, good condition.* 4.00 5.00

☐ **R.C. Co. "Isabella"**, *twisted handle, no monogram, excellent condition.* 10.00 12.00

☐ **R.C. Co. "Manchester"**, *twisted handle, no monogram, fair condition.* 5.00 6.00

☐ **Reed & Barton "Commonwealth"**, *monogram, excellent condition.* 1.00 2.00

☐ **Reed & Barton "Gem"**, *no monogram, excellent condition.* . . 10.00 12.00

☐ **Reed & Barton "Gem"**, *no monogram, resilvered.* 2.00 3.00

☐ **Reed & Barton "Jewell"**, *twisted handle, no monogram, fair condition.* 5.00 6.00

☐ **Reed & Barton "Jewell"**, *twisted handle, no monogram, good condition.* 6.00 8.00

☐ **Reed & Barton "Maid of Honor"**, *no monogram, excellent condition.* 5.00 6.00

☐ **Reed & Barton "Maid of Honor"**, *no monogram, good condition.* 4.00 5.00

☐ **Reed & Barton "Manor"** , *twisted handle, no monogram, excellent condition.* 9.00 10.00

☐ **Reed & Barton "Manor"**, *twisted handle, no monogram, fair condition.* 1.00 2.00

☐ **Reed & Barton "Manor"**, *twisted handle, no monogram, excellent condition.* 7.00 8.00

☐ **Reed & Barton "Modern Art"**, *no monogram, excellent condition.* 9.00 10.00

☐ **Reed & Barton "Olive"**, *no monogram, excellent condition.* . . 3.00 4.00

☐ **Reed & Barton "Oxford"**, *flat-handled, no monogram, excellent condition.* 10.00 11.00

☐ **Reed & Barton "Oxford"**, *twisted handle, no monogram, fair condition.* 3.00 4.00

☐ **Reed & Barton "Poppy"**, *twisted handle, no monogram, excellent condition.* 10.00 12.00

☐ **Reed & Barton "Rembrandt"**, *no monogram, excellent condition.* 4.00 5.00

☐ **Reed & Barton "Shell"**, *no monogram, excellent condition.* . . 8.00 10.00

☐ **Reed & Barton "Sierra"**, *no monogram, excellent condition.* 5.00 6.00

☐ **Reed & Barton "Sierra"**, *no monogram, good condition.* . . . 4.00 5.00

☐ **Reed & Barton "Sierra"**, *monogram, excellent condition.* . . 2.00 3.00

	Price Range	

☐ **Reed & Barton "Threaded"**, *twisted handle, no monogram, excellent condition.*................................. 3.00 4.00

☐ **Reed & Barton "Unique"**, *no monogram, excellent condition.*................................... 8.00 10.00

☐ **Reliance "Exeter"**, *no monogram, excellent condition.* 9.00 10.00

☐ **Reliance "Exeter"**, *no monogram, good condition.*......... 6.00 7.00

☐ **Reliance "Kenwood"**, *twisted handle, no monogram, excellent condition.*................................. 8.00 9.00

☐ **Reliance "Kenwood"**, *twisted handle, no monogram, good condition.*... 5.00 6.00

☐ **Reliance "Wildwood"**, *twisted handle, no monogram, excellent condition.*................................. 10.00 12.00

☐ **Rogers "Burgundy"**, *no monogram, excellent condition.* ... 5.00 6.00

☐ **Rogers "Burgundy"**, *no monogram, good condition.* 4.00 5.00

☐ **Rogers "Carlton"**, *no monogram, excellent condition.* 9.00 10.00

☐ **Rogers "Carlton"**, *no monogram, good condition.* 5.00 6.00

☐ **Rogers "Clinton"**, *no monogram, excellent condition.* 6.00 7.00

☐ **Rogers "Clinton"**, *no monogram, fair condition.* 1.00 2.00

☐ **Rogers "Kensington"**, *twisted handle, no monogram, excellent condition.*................................. 8.00 9.00

☐ **Rogers "Kensington"**, *twisted handle, no monogram, good condition.*... 6.00 7.00

☐ **Rogers "Margate"**, *no monogram, excellent condition.* 5.00 6.00

☐ **Rogers "Margate"**, *no monogram, excellent condition.* 4.00 5.00

☐ **Rogers "Mayflower"**, *twisted handle, no monogram, excellent condition.*................................. 9.00 10.00

☐ **Rogers "Mayflower"**, *twisted handle, no monogram, good condition.*... 7.00 8.00

☐ **Rogers "Newport"**, *twisted handle, monogram, excellent condition.*... 10.00 12.00

☐ **Rogers "Newport"**, *twisted handle, no monogram, excellent condition.*................................. 11.00 13.00

☐ **Rogers "Oval Thread"**, *excellent condition.* 4.00 5.00

☐ **Rogers "Pansy"**, *twisted handle, no monogram, excellent condition.*... 13.00 15.00

☐ **Rogers "Princess"**, *no monogram, fair condition.* 1.00 2.00

☐ **Rogers "Queen Bess II"**, *no monogram, excellent condition.*... 1.00 2.00

☐ **Rogers "Shell"**, *twisted handle, engraved blade, no monogram, good condition.*............................... 8.00 10.00

☐ **Rogers "Shell"**, *twisted handle, no monogram, excellent condition.*... 7.00 8.00

☐ **Rogers "Shell"**, *no monogram, poor condition.* 1.00 2.00

☐ **Rogers "Tipped"**, *twisted handle, no monogram, excellent condition.*... 7.00 8.00

☐ **Rogers "Tipped"**, *twisted handle, monogram, excellent condition.* 6.00 7.00

☐ **Rogers & Bro. "Aldine"**, *twisted handle, no monogram, excellent condition.*................................. 8.00 9.00

☐ **Rogers & Bro. "Aldine"**, *twisted handle, no monogram, good condition.*... 5.00 6.00

☐ **Rogers & Bro. "Daybreak"**, *no monogram, excellent condition.*... 5.00 6.00

☐ **Rogers & Bro. "Daybreak"**, *no monogram, good condition.* .. 4.00 5.00

	Price Range	
☐ Rogers & Bro. "Mystic", *no monogram, excellent condition.*	11.00	12.00
☐ Rogers & Bro. "Mystic", *twisted handle, monogram, resilvered.*	10.00	11.00
☐ Rogers & Bro. "New Century", *twisted handle, monogram, excellent condition.*	7.00	8.00
☐ Rogers & Bro. "New Century", *twisted handle, monogram, fair condition.*	4.00	5.00
☐ Rogers & Bro. "Tuxedo", *twisted handle, no monogram, excellent condition.*	10.00	12.00
☐ Rogers & Bro. "Tuxedo", *twisted handle, no monogram, poor condition.*	1.00	2.00
☐ Rogers & Bro. "Vesta", *no monogram, excellent condition.*	10.00	12.00
☐ Rogers & Hamilton "Aldine", *monogram, excellent condition.*	10.00	12.00
☐ Rogers & Hamilton "Burgundy", *no monogram, good condition.*	3.00	4.00
☐ Rogers & Hamilton "Marquise", *no monogram, excellent condition.*	3.00	4.00
☐ Rogers & Hamilton "Monarch", *twisted handle, no monogram, good condition.*	8.00	9.00
☐ Rogers & Hamilton "Raphael", *no monogram, excellent condition.*	14.00	16.00
☐ S.L. & G.H. Rogers "Countess II", *no monogram, excellent condition.*	5.00	6.00
☐ S.L. & G.H. Rogers "Countess II", *no monogram, good condition.*	4.00	5.00
☐ S.L. & G.H. Rogers "Encore", *no monogram, excellent condition.*	4.00	5.00
☐ S.L. & G.H. Rogers "English Garden", *excellent condition.*	5.00	6.00
☐ S.L. & G.H. Rogers "English Garden", *no monogram, fair condition.*	1.00	2.00
☐ S.L. & G.H. Rogers "Kingston", *no monogram, excellent condition.*	5.00	6.00
☐ S.L. & G.H. Rogers "Laureate", *no monogram, excellent condition.*	5.00	6.00
☐ S.L. & G.H. Rogers "Laureate", *no monogram, good condition.*	4.00	5.00
☐ S.L. & G.H. Rogers "Thor", *no monogram, excellent condition.*	5.00	6.00
☐ S. Rogers "Webster I", *twisted handle, no monogram, excellent condition.*	9.00	10.00
☐ Stratford "Starlight", *no monogram, excellent condition.*	5.00	6.00
☐ Stratford "Starlight", *no monogram, good condition.*	4.00	5.00
☐ Towle "Engraved", *no monogram, excellent condition.*	7.00	8.00
☐ Towle "Engraved", *no monogram, good condition.*	5.00	6.00
☐ Tudor "Duchess", *no monogram, excellent condition.*	5.00	6.00
☐ Tudor "Duchess", *no monogram, good condition.*	4.00	5.00
☐ Tudor "Enchantment", *no monogram, good condition.*	3.00	4.00
☐ Tudor "Fortune", *no monogram, excellent condition.*	5.00	6.00
☐ Tudor "Queen Bess I", *no monogram, good condition.*	4.00	5.00
☐ Tudor "Sweetbriar", *no monogram, excellent condition.*	5.00	6.00
☐ Tudor "Sweetbriar", *no monogram, good condition.*	4.00	5.00
☐ Wallace "Blossom", *twisted handle, monogram, excellent condition.*	8.00	10.00

	Price Range	
☐ **Wallace "Blossom",** *twisted handle, no monogram, excellent condition.*	15.00	16.00
☐ **Wallace "Floral",** *twisted handle, no monogram, excellent condition.*	15.00	16.00
☐ **Wallace "Sonata",** *no monogram, excellent condition.*	5.00	6.00
☐ **Wallace "Sonata",** *no monogram, good condition.*	4.00	5.00
☐ **W.D. Smith "Adam",** *no monogram, excellent condition.*	2.00	3.00
☐ **Whiting "New Honeysuckle",** *flat-handled, no monogram, excellent condition.*	10.00	12.00
☐ **Williams Bros. "Isabella",** *twisted handle, no monogram, excellent condition,*	12.00	14.00
☐ **Williams Bros. "Isabella",** *no monogram, poor condition.*	8.00	9.00
☐ **Williams Bros. "Vineyard",** *no monogram, excellent condition.*	9.00	10.00
☐ **Wm. A. Rogers "Carnation",** *flat-handled, no monogram, fair condition.*	6.00	7.00
☐ **Wm. A. Rogers "Carnation",** *flat-handled, no monogram, excellent condition.*	10.00	12.00
☐ **Wm. A. Rogers "Country Lane",** *no monogram, excellent condition.*	5.00	6.00
☐ **Wm. A. Rogers "Country Lane",** *no monogram, good condition.*	4.00	5.00
☐ **Wm. A. Rogers "Garland",** *no monogram, excellent condition.*	3.00	4.00
☐ **Wm. A. Rogers "Garland",** *no monogram, excellent condition.*	5.00	6.00
☐ **Wm. A. Rogers "Imperial",** *twisted handle, no monogram, excellent condition.*	9.00	10.00
☐ **Wm. A. Rogers "Imperial",** *twisted handle, no monogram, good condition.*	8.00	9.00
☐ **Wm. A. Rogers "LaConcorde",** *twisted handle, no monogram, excellent condition.*	11.00	12.00
☐ **Wm. A. Rogers "LaConcorde",** *twisted handle, no monogram, good condition.*	7.00	8.00
☐ **Wm. A. Rogers "LaConcorde",** *twisted handle, monogram, mint condition.*	7.00	8.00
☐ **Wm. A. Rogers "LaConcorde",** *twisted handle, no monogram, poor condition.*	1.00	2.00
☐ **Wm. A. Rogers "Lady Stuart",** *no monogram, excellent condition.*	5.00	6.00
☐ **Wm. A. Rogers "LaVigne",** *no monogram, excellent condition.*	18.00	20.00
☐ **Wm. A. Rogers "LaVigne",** *no monogram, fair condition.*	5.00	6.00
☐ **Wm. A. Rogers "Margate",** *no monogram, excellent condition.*	5.00	6.00
☐ **Wm. A. Rogers "Meadowbrook",** *no monogram, excellent condition.*	5.00	6.00
☐ **Wm. A. Rogers "Meadowbrook",** *no monogram, good condition.*	4.00	5.00
☐ **Wm. A. Rogers "Narcissus",** *no monogram, poor condition.*	7.00	8.00
☐ **Wm. A. Rogers "Narcissus",** *no monogram, good condition.*	10.00	12.00
☐ **Wm. A. Rogers "Paramount",** *no monogram, excellent condition.*	5.00	6.00

	Price Range	
☐ **Wm. A. Rogers "Paramount"**, *no monogram, good condition.*	4.00	5.00
☐ **Wm. A. Rogers "Raleigh"**, *twisted handle, no monogram, excellent condition.*	7.00	8.00
☐ **Wm. A. Rogers "Raleigh"**, *twisted handle, no monogram, good condition.*	6.00	7.00
☐ **Wm. Rogers "Arbutus"**, *twisted handle, no monogram, excellent condition.*	10.00	12.00
☐ **Wm. Rogers "Arbutus"**, *twisted handle, no monogram, good condition.*	9.00	10.00
☐ **Wm. Rogers "Arbutus"**, *twisted handle, monogram, fair condition.*	5.00	6.00
☐ **Wm. Rogers "Ardsley"**, *twisted handle, no monogram, excellent condition.*	9.00	10.00
☐ **Wm. Rogers "Argyle"**, *twisted handle, no monogram, excellent condition.*	9.00	10.00
☐ **Wm. Rogers "Athens"**, *no monogram, resilvered.*	6.00	7.00
☐ **Wm. Rogers "Athens"**, *no monogram, excellent condition.*	7.00	8.00
☐ **Wm. Rogers "Beloved"**, *no monogram, excellent condition.*	5.00	6.00
☐ **Wm. Rogers "Beloved"**, *no monogram, good condition.*	4.00	5.00
☐ **Wm. Rogers "Beloved"**, *no monogram, fair condition.*	1.00	2.00
☐ **Wm. Rogers "Berwick"**, *no monogram, excellent condition.*	14.00	16.00
☐ **Wm. Rogers "Berwick"**, *no monogram, good condition.*	10.00	12.00
☐ **Wm. Rogers "Bridal Bouquet"**, *no monogram, mint condition.*	4.00	5.00
☐ **Wm. Rogers "Carlton"**, *no monogram, excellent condition.*	9.00	10.00
☐ **Wm. Rogers "Carlton"**, *no monogram, fair condition.*	2.00	3.00
☐ **Wm. Rogers "Carnation"**, *no monogram, good condition.*	9.00	10.00
☐ **Wm. Rogers "Carrollton"**, *no monogram, excellent condition.*	8.00	9.00
☐ **Wm. Rogers "Carrollton"**, *no monogram, excellent condition.*	9.00	10.00
☐ **Wm. Rogers "Debutante"**, *no monogram, excellent condition.*	4.00	5.00
☐ **Wm. Rogers "Debutante"**, *no monogram, good condition.*	3.00	4.00
☐ **Wm. Rogers "Devonshire"**, *no monogram, excellent condition.*	5.00	6.00
☐ **Wm. Rogers "Devonshire"**, *no monogram, good condition.*	4.00	5.00
☐ **Wm. Rogers "Fairoaks"**, *no monogram, fair condition.*	5.00	6.00
☐ **Wm. Rogers "Fidelis"**, *no monogram, excellent condition.*	5.00	6.00
☐ **Wm. Rogers "Fidelis"**, *no monogram, good condition.*	4.00	5.00
☐ **Wm. Rogers "Florida"**, *twisted handle, no monogram, excellent condition.*	8.00	9.00
☐ **Wm. Rogers "LaConcorde"**, *no monogram, excellent condition.*	12.00	14.00
☐ **Wm. Rogers "LaConcorde"**, *no monogram, fair condition.*	3.00	4.00
☐ **Wm. Rogers "Magnolia"**, *no monogram, excellent condition.*	4.00	5.00
☐ **Wm. Rogers "Mayfair"**, *no monogram, excellent condition.*	5.00	6.00
☐ **Wm. Rogers "Mayfair"**, *no monogram, fair condition.*	1.00	2.00
☐ **Wm. Rogers "Precious Mirror"**, *no monogram, excellent condition.*	5.00	6.00
☐ **Wm. Rogers "Precious Mirror"**, *no monogram, good condition.*	4.00	5.00

Price Range

☐ **Wm. Rogers "Puritan"**, *twisted handle, no monogram, excellent condition.* 4.00   5.00
☐ **Wm. Rogers "Shell"**, *no monogram, excellent condition.* . . . 5.00   6.00
☐ **Wm. Rogers "Sherwood"**, *no monogram, excellent condition.* 16.00   18.00
☐ **Wm. Rogers "Sherwood"**, *no monogram, good condition.* . . 10.00   12.00
☐ **Wm. Rogers "Treasure"**, *no monogram, excellent condition.* 1.00   2.00
☐ **Wm. Rogers "Treasure"**, *no monogram, excellent condition.* 5.00   6.00
☐ **Wm. Rogers "Westminister"**, *twisted handle, no monogram, excellent condition.* 12.00   14.00
☐ **Wm. Rogers Eagle "Berwick"**, *no monogram, excellent condition.* 12.00   14.00
☐ **Wm. Rogers Mfg. Co. "Arbutus"**, *twisted handle, no monogram, excellent condition.* 8.00   9.00
☐ **Wm. Rogers Mfg. Co. "Camelot"**, *no monogram, excellent condition.* 5.00   6.00
☐ **Wm. Rogers Mfg. Co. "Camelot"**, *no monogram, good condition.* 4.00   5.00
☐ **Wm. Rogers Mfg. Co. "Clinton"**, *twisted handle, no monogram, excellent condition.* 3.00   4.00
☐ **Wm. Rogers Mfg. Co. "Clinton"**, *twisted handle, no monogram, good condition.* 4.00   5.00
☐ **Wm. Rogers Mfg. Co. "Countess"**, *no monogram, good condition.* 2.00   3.00
☐ **Wm. Rogers Mfg. Co. "Daisy"**, *twisted handle, no monogram, excellent condition.* 7.00   8.00
☐ **Wm. Rogers Mfg. Co. "Jubilee"**, *no monogram, excellent condition.* 5.00   6.00
☐ **Wm. Rogers Mfg. Co. "Magnolia"**, *no monogram, excellent condition.* 5.00   6.00
☐ **Wm. Rogers Mfg. Co. "Oval Thread"**, *no monogram, excellent condition.* 2.00   3.00
☐ **Wm. Rogers Mfg. Co. "Rose"**, *no monogram, excellent condition.* 7.00   8.00
☐ **Wm. Rogers Mfg. Co. "Sovereign"**, *no monogram, excellent condition.* 5.00   6.00
☐ **Wm. Rogers Mfg. Co. "Sovereign"**, *no monogram, good condition.* 4.00   5.00
☐ **Wm. Rogers & Son "Arbutus"**, *no monogram, excellent condition.* 8.00   9.00
☐ **Wm. Rogers & Son "Arbutus"**, *no monogram, good condition.* 8.00   9.00
☐ **Wm. Rogers & Son "Daisy"**, *no monogram, excellent condition.* 9.00   10.00
☐ **Wm. Rogers & Son "Florida"**, *no monogram, excellent condition.* 9.00   10.00
☐ **Wm. Rogers & Son "Florida"**, *no monogram, good condition.* 8.00   9.00
☐ **Wm. Rogers & Son "Flower"**, *no monogram, excellent condition.* 9.00   10.00
☐ **Wm. Rogers & Son "Flower"**, *no monogram, good condition.* 8.00   9.00

Price Range

☐ **Wm. Rogers & Son "LaFrance"**, *no monogram, excellent condition.*	5.00	6.00
☐ **Wm. Rogers & Son "LaFrance"**, *no monogram, good condition.*	4.00	5.00
☐ **Wm. Rogers & Son "Oxford"**, *twisted handle, no monogram, excellent condition.*	9.00	10.00
☐ **Wm. Rogers & Son "Oxford"**, *twisted handle, no monogram, fair condition.*	5.00	6.00
☐ **Wm. Rogers & Son "Primrose II"**, *no monogram, excellent condition.*	5.00	6.00
☐ **Wm. Rogers & Son "Primrose II"**, *no monogram, good condition.*	4.00	5.00
☐ **Wm. Rogers & Son "Primrose II"**, *fair condition.*	1.00	2.00
☐ **Wm. R. Rogers "Juliette"**, *no monogram, mint condition.*	2.00	3.00
☐ **1835 R. Wallace "Buckingham"**, *no monogram, good condition.*	6.00	7.00
☐ **1835 R. Wallace "Buckingham"**, *no monogram, fair condition.*	3.00	4.00
☐ **1835 R. Wallace "Cardinal"**, *flat-handled, no monogram, excellent condition.*	5.00	6.00
☐ **1835 Wallace "Cardinal"**, *flat-handled, no monogram, good condition.*	4.00	5.00
☐ **1835 R. Wallace "Cardinal"**, *no monogram, fair condition.*	4.00	5.00
☐ **1835 R. Wallace "Floral"**, *no monogram, excellent condition.*	10.00	12.00
☐ **1847 Rogers "Adoration"**, *no monogram, excellent condition.*	4.00	5.00
☐ **1847 Rogers "Adoration"**, *no monogram, good condition.*	4.00	5.00
☐ **1847 Rogers "Ancestral"**, *no monogram, good condition.*	4.00	5.00
☐ **1847 Rogers "Anniversary"**, *no monogram, fair condition.*	1.00	2.00
☐ **1847 Rogers "Arcadian"**, *twisted handle, no monogram, good condition.*	12.00	14.00
☐ **1847 Rogers "Assyrian"**, *twisted handle, no monogram, excellent condition.*	12.00	14.00
☐ **1847 Rogers "Assyrian"**, *flat-handled, no monogram, excellent condition.*	10.00	11.00
☐ **1847 Rogers "Avon"**, *twisted handle, no monogram, excellent condition.*	12.00	14.00
☐ **1847 Rogers "Avon"**, *twisted handle, no monogram, excellent condition.*	26.00	28.00
☐ **1847 Rogers "Berkshire"**, *twisted handle, no monogram, excellent condition.*	11.00	12.00
☐ **1847 Rogers "Berkshire"**, *twisted handle, no monogram, excellent condition.*	12.00	14.00
☐ **1847 Rogers "Charter Oak"**, *twisted handle, no monogram, excellent condition.*	13.00	14.00
☐ **1847 Rogers "Charter Oak"**, *twisted handle, no monogram, excellent condition.*	15.00	16.00
☐ **1847 Rogers "Columbia"**, *twisted handle, no monogram, excellent condition.*	13.00	14.00
☐ **1847 Rogers "Cromwell"**, *no monogram, excellent condition.*	3.00	4.00
☐ **1847 Rogers "Daffodil"**, *no monogram, excellent condition.*	4.00	5.00
☐ **1847 Rogers "Daffodil II"**, *excellent condition.*	5.00	6.00

	Price Range	

☐ **1847 Rogers "Dundee"**, *twisted handle, no monogram, excellent condition*. 10.00 12.00

☐ **1847 Rogers "Esperanto"**, *no monogram, excellent condition*. 5.00 6.00

☐ **1847 Rogers "Esperanto"**, *no monogram, mint condition*. . . 4.00 5.00

☐ **1847 Rogers "Eternally Yours"**, *no monogram, excellent condition*. 4.00 5.00

☐ **1847 Rogers "Eternally Yours"**, *no monogram, excellent condition*. 5.00 6.00

☐ **1847 Rogers "First Love"**, *no monogram, excellent condition*. 3.00 4.00

☐ **1847 Rogers "First Love"**, *no monogram, excellent condition*. 5.00 6.00

☐ **1847 Rogers "Flair"**, *no monogram, excellent condition*. . . . 3.00 4.00

☐ **1847 Rogers "Gothic"**, *no monogram, excellent condition*. . 7.00 8.00

☐ **1847 Rogers "Gothic"**, *no monogram, fair condition*. 1.00 2.00

☐ **1847 Rogers "Gothic"**, *monogram, excellent condition*. 4.00 5.00

☐ **1847 Rogers "Grecian"**, *flat-handled, no monogram, excellent condition*. 11.00 12.00

☐ **1847 Rogers "Grecian"**, *twisted handle, no monogram, excellent condition*. 4.00 5.00

☐ **1847 Rogers "Heraldic"**, *no monogram, excellent condition*. 3.00 4.00

☐ **1847 Rogers "Laurel"**, *twisted handle, no monogram, excellent condition*. 8.00 13.00

☐ **1847 Rogers "Legacy"**, *no monogram, excellent condition*. . 5.00 6.00

☐ **1847 Rogers "Legacy"**, *no monogram, good condition*. . . . 4.00 5.00

☐ **1847 Rogers "Lily (Embossed)"**, *no monogram, excellent condition*. 12.00 13.00

☐ **1847 Rogers "Lorne"**, *no monogram, excellent condition*. . . 12.00 13.00

☐ **1847 Rogers "Lorne"**, *monogram, excellent condition*. 9.00 10.00

☐ **1847 Rogers "Lorne"**, *twisted handle, no monogram, excellent condition*. 12.00 13.00

☐ **1847 Rogers "Lorne"**, *twisted handle, no monogram, good condition*. 7.00 8.00

☐ **1847 Rogers "Lotus"**, *no monogram, excellent condition*. . . 12.00 13.00

☐ **1847 Rogers "Lotus"**, *twisted handle, monogram, excellent condition*. 6.00 7.00

☐ **1847 Rogers "Lotus"**, *twisted handle, no monogram, excellent condition*. 12.00 13.00

☐ **1847 Rogers "Lovelace"**, *no monogram, good condition*. . . . 4.00 5.00

☐ **1847 Rogers "Lovelace"**, *no monogram, excellent condition*. 5.00 6.00

☐ **1847 Rogers "Magic Rose"**, *no monogram, excellent condition*. 5.00 6.00

☐ **1847 Rogers "Marquise"**, *no monogram, excellent condition*. 5.00 6.00

☐ **1847 Rogers "Moline"**, *twisted handle, no monogram, excellent condition*. 7.00 8.00

☐ **1847 Rogers "Moselle"**, *flat-handled, no monogram, excellent condition*. 26.00 28.00

☐ **1847 Rogers "Moselle"**, *no monogram, excellent condition*. 25.00 26.00

☐ **1847 Rogers "Newport"**, *twisted handle, no monogram, excellent condition*. 6.00 7.00

	Price Range	
☐ **1847 Rogers "Newport"**, *twisted handle, monogram, fair condition.*	2.00	3.00
☐ **1847 Rogers "Newport"**, *twisted handle, no monogram, excellent condition.*	9.00	10.00
☐ **1847 Rogers "Old Colony"**, *no monogram, excellent condition.*	3.00	4.00
☐ **1847 Rogers "Old Colony"**, *no monogram, excellent condition.*	4.00	5.00
☐ **1847 Rogers "Old Colony"**, *no monogram, excellent condition.*	5.00	6.00
☐ **1847 Rogers "Persian"**, *twisted handle, no monogram, good condition.*	8.00	9.00
☐ **1847 Rogers "Persian"**, *twisted handle, no monogram, excellent condition.*	7.00	8.00
☐ **1847 Rogers "Persian"**, *no monogram, excellent condition.*	8.00	9.00
☐ **1847 Rogers "Portland"**, *twisted handle, no monogram, excellent condition.*	9.00	10.00
☐ **1847 Rogers "Portland"**, *twisted handle, no monogram, good condition.*	8.00	9.00
☐ **1847 Rogers "Portland"**, *twisted handle, monogram, good condition.*	3.00	4.00
☐ **1847 Rogers "Reflection"**, *no monogram, excellent condition.*	4.00	5.00
☐ **1847 Rogers "Remembrance"**, *no monogram, excellent condition.*	5.00	6.00
☐ **1847 Rogers "Remembrance"**, *no monogram, fair condition.*	1.00	2.00
☐ **1847 Rogers "Remembrance"**, *no monogram, mint condition.*	3.00	4.00
☐ **1847 Rogers "Saratoga"**, *twisted handle, no monogram, excellent condition.*	9.00	10.00
☐ **1847 Rogers "Savoy"**, *twisted handle, no monogram, excellent condition.*	9.00	10.00
☐ **1847 Rogers "Sharon"**, *no monogram, excellent condition.* . .	18.00	20.00
☐ **1847 Rogers "Silhouette"**, *no monogram, excellent condition.*	5.00	6.00
☐ **1847 Rogers "Silver Lace"**, *no monogram, excellent condition.*	5.00	6.00
☐ **1847 Rogers "Vesta"**, *twisted handle, no monogram, excellent condition.*	8.00	9.00
☐ **1847 Rogers "Vesta"**, *twisted handle, no monogram, fair condition.*	4.00	5.00
☐ **1847 Rogers "Vesta"**, *twisted handle, no monogram, excellent condition.*	8.00	9.00
☐ **1847 Rogers "Vintage"**, *twisted handle, monogram, excellent condition.*	10.00	12.00
☐ **1847 Rogers "Vintage"**, *twisted handle, no monogram, mint condition.*	26.00	28.00
☐ **1847 Rogers "Vintage"**, *twisted handle, no monogram, excellent condition.*	18.00	20.00
☐ **1847 Rogers "Vintage"**, *twisted handle, no monogram, excellent condition.*	12.00	14.00
☐ **1847 Rogers "Vintage"**, *twisted handle, no monogram, fair condition.*	6.00	7.00

	Price Range	
☐ **1847 Rogers "Vintage"**, *twisted handle, no monogram, poor condition.*	3.00	4.00
☐ **1881 Rogers "Briar Rose"**, *no monogram, excellent condition.*	12.00	14.00
☐ **1881 Rogers "Capri"**, *no monogram, excellent condition.*	5.00	6.00
☐ **1881 Rogers "Capri"**, *no monogram, good condition.*	4.00	5.00
☐ **1881 Rogers "Chevron"**, *no monogram, excellent condition.*	5.00	6.00
☐ **1881 Rogers "Chevron"**, *no monogram, good condition.*	4.00	5.00
☐ **1881 Rogers "Coronet"**, *no monogram, excellent condition.*	4.00	5.00
☐ **1881 Rogers "Coronet"**, *no monogram, good condition.*	4.00	5.00
☐ **1881 Rogers "Flirtation"**, *no monogram, excellent condition.*	5.00	6.00
☐ **1881 Rogers "Flirtation"**, *no monogram, good condition.*	4.00	5.00
☐ **1881 Rogers "Godetia"**, *no monogram, excellent condition.*	8.00	10.00
☐ **1881 Rogers "Grecian"**, *twisted handle, no monogram, excellent condition.*	9.00	10.00
☐ **1881 Rogers "Grecian"**, *twisted handle, no monogram, good condition.*	8.00	9.00
☐ **1881 Rogers "LaVigne"**, *no monogram, fair condition.*	5.00	7.00
☐ **1881 Rogers "LaVigne"**, *no monogram, excellent condition.*	9.00	10.00
☐ **1881 Rogers "Scotia"**, *no monogram, excellent condition.*	4.00	5.00
☐ **1881 Rogers "Scotia"**, *twisted handle, no monogram, good condition.*	7.00	8.00

(Sterling Silver)

☐ **Alvin "Romantique"**, *flat-handled, no monogram.*	14.00	16.00
☐ **Durgin "Fairfax"**, *monogram.*	16.00	18.00
☐ **Fine Arts "Processional"**, *flat-handled, no monogram.*	14.00	16.00
☐ **Frank Smith "Chippendale"**, *no monogram.*	14.00	16.00
☐ **Gorham "Greenbrier"**, *flat-handled, no monogram.*	14.00	16.00
☐ **Gorham "Imperial Chrysanthemum"**, *no monogram.*	16.00	18.00
☐ **Gorham "Luxembourg"**, *no monogram.*	18.00	20.00
☐ **Gorham "Maryland"**, *monogram.*	13.00	15.00
☐ **Gorham "Versailles"**, *flat-handled, no monogram.*	16.00	18.00
☐ **Gorham "Willow"**, *hollow-handled, no monogram.*	14.00	16.00
☐ **International" Bridal Veil"**, *flat-handled, no monogram.*	12.00	13.00
☐ **International "Fontaine"**, *flat-handled, no monogram.*	16.00	18.00
☐ **International "Frontenac"**, *no monogram.*	16.00	18.00
☐ **International "Grand Regency"**, *no monogram.*	15.00	17.00
☐ **International "Joan of Arc"**, *no monogram.*	14.00	16.00
☐ **Internatonal "Royal Danish"**, *flat-handled, no monogram.*	14.00	16.00
☐ **International "Swan Lake"**, *flat-handled, no monogram.*	13.00	15.00
☐ **Manchester "Amarylis"**, *no monogram.*	14.00	16.00
☐ **Oneida "Heiress"**, *flat-handled, no monogram.*	13.00	15.00
☐ **Oneida "Heiress"**, *flat-handled.*	10.00	12.00
☐ **Oneida "Lasting Spring"**, *flat-handled, no monogram.*	13.00	15.00
☐ **Reed & Barton "Francis I"**, *hollow-handled, no monogram.*	14.00	16.00
☐ **Reed & Barton "Spanish Baroque"**, *hollow-handled, no monogram.*	14.00	16.00
☐ **Royal Crest "Castle Rose"**, *flat-handled, no monogram.*	13.00	15.00
☐ **Simpson, Hall & Miller "Frontenac"**, *no monogram.*	30.00	32.00
☐ **Simpson, Hall & Miller "Frontenac"**, *no monogram.*	24.00	26.00
☐ **Towle "Cambridge"**, *no monogram*	10.00	12.00
☐ **Towle "Georgian"**, *no monogram.*	24.00	26.00

	Price Range	
□ **Towle "Kings"**, *no monogram.*	26.00	28.00
□ **Towle "Madeira"**, *flat-handled, no monogram.*	14.00	16.00
□ **Towle "Mary Chilton"**, *monogram.*	13.00	15.00
□ **Towle "Old Colonial"**, *no monogram.*	30.00	32.00
□ **Towle "Old English"**, *gold wash blade, monogram.*	16.00	18.00
□ **Towle "Spanish Provincial"**, *hollow-handled, no monogram.*	14.00	16.00
□ **Towle "Vespera"**, *hollow-handled, no monogram.*	10.00	12.00
□ **Wallace "Grand Colonial"**, *no monogram.*	13.00	15.00
□ **Wallace "Louvre"**, *no monogram.*	18.00	20.00
□ **Westmoreland "John & Priscilla"**, *flat-handled, no monogram.*	14.00	16.00
□ **Maker unknown**, *engraved blade, shell motif on handle, monogram and date.*	16.00	18.00
□ **Maker unknown**, *engraved gold wash blade, figural cow on handle, monogram.*	18.00	20.00
□ **Maker unknown**, *floral repousse design on handle, no monogram.*	16.00	18.00
□ **Maker unknown**, *Art Nouveau floral design, monogram and date.*	18.00	20.00

BUTTER PATS

Perhaps the height of delicacy was reached on tables with the silver butter pat, a tiny rectangular dish for individual slices of butter. The pat of butter was rested upon this dish after being taken with the butter *knife,* and before being transferred to the butter *spreader* — a carefully arranged process for the simple action of buttering one's bread. Most of the silver butter pats are quite decorative, with floral engraving or something similar. Their small size makes them very convenient to store and display, and perhaps for this reason their popularity among hobbyists has grown. They will require some searching out, as this is not an article found in all the antiques shops. But if you choose to collect butter pats and are diligent in quest of them, there should be no barrier to forming a good collection.

(Silver-Plated)

□ **Gorham,** *embossed floral rim, monogram in center, excellent condition set of six.*	26.00	28.00
□ **Maker unknown,** *ornate Art Nouveau floral pattern, monogram.*	6.00	8.00

(Sterling Silver)

□ **Gorham,** *round, rolled rim, monogram and date in center, set of six.*	50.00	60.00
□ **Kirk "Repousse"**, *no monogram.*	18.00	20.00
□ **Maker unknown,** *scalloped rim with openwork, monogram in center.*	6.00	7.00
□ **Maker unknown,** *square, gadroon border, monogram in center, set of 12.*	55.00	65.00

BUTTON HOOKS

(Sterling Silver)   Price Range

- ☐ **Maker unknown,** *plain design* 10.00   12.00
- ☐ **Maker unknown,** *ornate design* 12.00   14.00

CAKE BREAKERS

The cake breaker stands as a memorial to the age of elegant dining, when a meal was orchestrated like a symphony and everything was supposed to flow in perfect harmony. If one merely sliced through a cake, with a cake knife (these are listed later on,) a delicate or especially moist cake was apt to become squashed in the process. This could be avoided — and of course the fastidious hostess wished to avoid such a thing at all costs — by use of the cake breaker. This ingenious tool consisted of a row of long (usually about 4″) teeth affixed to a curved handle. When pressed smartly into the cake (there was a bit of technique involved,) the spaces between each tooth or prong prevented squashing. The pieces could then be removed by a slight turn of the implement, which literally "broke" it away from the cake. Or this operation could serve merely as a preliminary to knife-slicing, to prepare the cake slice for the coup-de-grace to follow. Users of cake breakers who did NOT follow up with a knife made the following claim: the cake slice had a more natural and inviting appearance, rather than the harsh smoothness of a knife cut. The fact that these implements are no longer in general use adds to their charm as antiques, and their design is of course attention-getting.

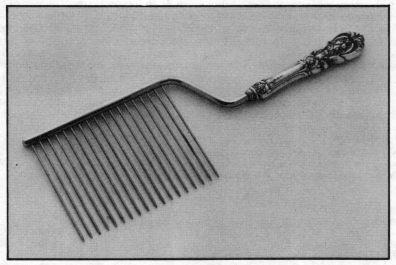

Cake Breaker, *(sterling), Reed & Barton "Frances I",* 28.00

(Sterling Silver)

- ☐ **Gorham "King George",** *monogram* 34.00   36.00
- ☐ **Reed & Barton "Francis I"** 40.00   45.00
- ☐ **Towle "Spanish Provincial",** *no monogram* 30.00   32.00

CAKE STANDS

Though the cake stand (in stainless steel or other material) carries on in restaurants and occasionally at formal dinners, its common household use is a thing of the past. Nevertheless, everyone is quite familiar with it. The obvious question to be asked is: why have cake stands been provided with a stem to elevate them, rather than resting squarely upon the table? The answer is apparently found in ancient tradition, in which (going back hundreds of years) the prime foodstuffs at any occasion were brought to table in a *grand entrance.* The cook or servant carried them aloft from the kitchen; and the elevated cake stand is, perhaps, symbolic of the procession cake once received in its way to the dining hall. In any event, cake stands are attractive and varied in their designs, and inviting to collect for the hobbyist whose means are somewhat above the average. Because of their heavy weight and considerable silver content, they will invariably be expensive even if the particular specimen has little else to recommend it. LOADING of the base (from beneath) is not at all unusual in cake stands and must be a consideration of anyone examining a specimen. Because of the customarily hollow bases, loading can be carried out to an extreme degree, adding as much as an extra six ounces to a piece that originally weighed only twelve ounces.

Cake Stand, *Tiffany, 39 ounces, 12½" Dia., 5½" H.,* 925.00

(Silver-Plated)	Price Range	
☐ **Meriden,** *Art Nouveau design, excellent condition*	80.00	90.00
☐ **Wm. A. Rogers,** *ornate vintage pattern, monogram and date in center, 11" Dia., 7" H., good condition*	50.00	60.00
☐ **Maker unknown,** *gadroon borders, 10" Dia., excellent condition*	18.00	20.00

(Sterling Silver)	Price Range	
☐ **Gorham,** c. 1908, pierced and engraved with vines and grapes, monogram, 10" Dia., 12 oz.	65.00	75.00
☐ **Tiffany,** pierced and reticulated trim, weight 29 oz.	600.00	675.00
☐ **Maker unknown,** c. 1910, applied ribbons and flowers swags, 10½" Dia., 14 oz.	75.00	85.00

CALLING CARD CASES

Naturally the Victorian gentleman (and lady) carried on his person as much fine goldware and silverware as his purse allowed. There was hardly a limit to the extent to which a fondness for silver could be indulged, as every novelty and gadget was available in silver. Calling card cases were slipped usually into the vest pocket opposite one's watch. It was impressive enough to offer someone a printed calling card, but even more impressive if extracted from a silver case. Since the calling card has gone out of fashion in America, we should explain what it was. This was similar to a business card, of small size, and nearly always of thick white paper. Instead of carrying a business address or advertisement, it simply stated the individual's name and SOMETIMES, but no always, his address. There was rarely any printed message. Calling cards were used as a means of introduction and, especially, to be left with the butler when you had made an unsuccessful effort to visit the master of the house. "He left his calling card," is a line in more novels than one would want to remember.

(Sterling Silver)

☐ **Gorham,** etched scroll design, monogram	20.00	25.00
☐ **Maker unknown,** beautifully engraved with floral butterfly design, no monogram	28.00	30.00
☐ **Maker unknown,** engraved vertical lines, raised monogram	18.00	20.00
☐ **Maker unknown,** embossed hunting scene, birds and hunter in background	34.00	36.00

CANDELABRA

The technical definition of these is a candlestick with branches, into which a minimum of two (and an unlimited maximum) of candles may be set. They have long been a forte of the silvermaker's art, and rate, in the finer examples, among the grandest of all silver creations. There is no doubting that silver candelabra date back at least as far as the ancient Roman Empire, while candelabra in general have even earlier beginnings. They have been manufactured continuously for a period of roughly 2,000 years, in all quarters of the western hemisphere. Their decorative heights were reached in Spain, France and Italy in the period from about 1475 to 1600. Later generations took these specimens as their models and tried to copy them, with mixed results. American silver candelabra were made in the colonial era, by all the smiths who were then active, and a simple native style based on puritan English evolved. In the 19th century and especially the latter part of that century, the Victorian-inspired revivals of earlier styles brought new waves of interest in silver candelabra. By around 1900 they were beginning to be fitted with wiring for electricity, but this hardly diminished their physical allure. It was not uncommon for candelabra to have detachable branches. It was considered more *in the mode* to detach branches, when subtle lighting was desired, than to remove candles or leave them unlighted. It cannot be too strongly stated that caution and discretion must be used in buying candelabra. Fakes of the costlier specimens are encountered but, even more frequently than this, loaded specimens whose weights have been increased one-quarter or one-half times over the original weight.

Candleabra, *maker unknown, detachable branches, central standard and five branches, leaf and scroll design,* 350.00

(Silver-Plated)	Price Range	
☐ **Rogers "Victorian Rose"**, *no monogram, good condition, pair*	100.00	110.00
☐ **Maker unknown**, *detachable sconces and branches, square base, raised and chased leaf and scroll design, c. 1860, 24" H., pair*	325.00	350.00
☐ **Maker unknown**, *detachable sconces and branches, square base, raised and chased leaf and scroll design, c. 1860, 24" H., pair*	325.00	350.00
☐ **Maker unknown**, *detachable branches, central standard and four branches, plain design, no monogram, good condition, pair*	125.00	135.00

(Sterling Silver)

☐ **Gorham,** *c. 1883, domed foot, bulbous stem with flowers, scrolls and shells, upper section has four scroll branches*

	Price Range	
and central standard, detachable bobeches, 24″ H. bases weighted, total weight of upper sections 210 ounces, pair	4200.00	4650.00
☐ **Gorham,** *three-light type, upper section detachable, weighted, pair*	145.00	165.00
☐ **Maker unknown,** *candelabra, sterling silver, two branches and central standard, 7¾″ H., weighted, pair*	80.00	90.00

CANDLE SNUFFERS

Here we have an item which, by its very nature, provides an obvious link with the past. Candle snuffers therefore enjoy added popularity with hobbyists, perhaps more than they would warrant if the article was designed for some less romantic use. As can be appreciated, candle snuffers go back quite far into history, though their use is probably not nearly so old as that of candles themselves. There are various alternatives to extinguishing a candle, the most direct being of course to blow upon it; and blowing out a flame seems so natural and obvious, that one might wonder why a utensil for the purpose was necessary. In large households, there would be numerous candles burning at evening, some of them in inconvenient places — on high cupboards or in chandeliers. These could be extinguished without any difficulty by using the candle snuffer, which was provided with a long handle for getting at hard-to reach candles. A simple cone device was attached to the end, which, when gently rested atop a candle prevented circulation of air and thereby eclipsed the flame. As the cone's interior was graduated in width, it could be used for any size of household candle. The huge candles of churches required special candle snuffers, which are also collectors' items but which space does not permit us to list.

(Silver-Plated)

☐ **Meriden,** *embossed floral design, no monogram, good condition*	10.00	12.00
☐ **Maker unknown,** *9¾″ L., reproduction of 1700 shape*	7.00	8.00

(Sterling Silver)

☐ **Gorham "Chantilly",** *ebony handle*	12.00	15.00
☐ **Gorham,** *plain design*	8.00	9.00

CANDLESTICKS

Silver candlesticks were manufactured in America from the very earliest days of colonial silversmithing (1600's,) and became one of the smithy's best sellers throughout the whole 18th century. Of course the average laboring family contented itself with pewter or brass, but there was ample demand for fine silver candlesticks. Every well-to-do home had them; and quite a few die-hards continued using them, at least on special occasions, well after the invention of more modern lighting apparatus. The original colonists fleeing from England brought over numerous candlesticks amongst their "plate," and these served as the models for native smiths when work of that nature began here. Unfortunately a large percentage of antique and potentially very valuable candlesticks have been destroyed over the years. As late as the inauguration of the U.S. Mint for coinage (1792,) America was without a native source of silver. Hence, old silverware by the pound was being recycled to obtain the bullion, a situation not too unlike that which prevails today. Candlesticks have adopted so many styles and patterns that any discussion, in a book of this nature, would be pointless. It is a very vast subject, even restricting oneself purely to those of American origin. As a collectors' item the silver candlestick is not immensely popular, but its use in decoration brings about many additional sales. LOADING of old silver candlesticks, with liquified lead, gravel, or other material, has been common. This may be done at the base, if the base is hollow; or into the neck, if the neck is hollow. Loading is not always the result of treacherous intent. Some candlesticks were manufactured with weighted bases, so they were in less danger of being upset.

Candlesticks, *Gorham sterling, weighted base, c. 1907, pair,* 500.00

(Sterling Silver)	Price Range	
☐ **Maker unknown,** *6" T., overall elaborate design, enamel trim, pair*	50.00	60.00

CARD TRAYS

These small receptables were used for business cards, in places of business, placed generally near the cash register where a departing customer might take one; or for calling cards, in private homes, where they would be conspicuously placed on a low table near the main entrance (usually near the umbrella stand and hatrack.) It was not really essential that they be decorative but the majority of specimens are, and constitute an intriguing group of collectors' items.

Card Tray, *maker unknown,*
c. 1865-1880, scalloped rim
with plain and floral design,
`200.00`

(Silver-Plated)	Price Range	
□ **Meriden,** *scalloped rim with scroll design, monogram, excellent condition*	8.00	10.00
□ **Maker unknown,** *tiny cherubs on rim, monogram, good condition*	12.00	14.00
□ **Maker unknown,** *plain design with rolled rim, monogram, date and birthday greeting in center, excellent condition* ..	8.00	10.00
(Sterling Silver)		
□ **Shreve & Co. retailer,** *applied rim, raised monogram*	26.00	28.00
□ **Maker unknown,** *applied rose on one edge, monogram*	14.00	16.00

CARVING FORKS

The name is confusing, as if a carving fork could serve the purpose of a carving knife. Its association with carving extended only to the point of being used in conjuction with the carving knife: the fork was held in the left hand, the carving knife in the right hand, and meat (as carved) was speared on the carving fork and conveyed to the serving platter. Carving forks are larger in size than table forks and customarily have but two prongs or tines, with specially sharp tips (for spearing.) When made of silver, the handle may be of another material, such as bone; or the reverse may be the case, i.e., a silver handle and a stainless steel blade. There are, however, many specimens in which the entire fork is silver, so these should not be regarded as curiosities or rarities.

(Silver-Plated)

□ **Community "Flower de Luce", no monogram, fair condition**	6.00	7.00

CARVING KNIVES

The carving knife of medieval Europe was the sword or dagger worn by the knight; later this evolved into a special table implement. Most of those encountered on the American antiques market will be of American manufacture and date from the late 1800's well into the present century, though some foreign specimens and an occasional early piece turn up. There are few common characteristics of carving knives, aside from their large size and the sharpness of the blade (which may have dulled over the years, but do not take this for granted!). They are quite good-looking and have been favorites of many collectors. They display especially well on colored velvet in a well-lighted case or cabinet.

(Silver-Plated)	**Price Range**	
☐ **Alvin "Bride's Bouquet",** *no monogram, good condition* ...	8.00	10.00
☐ **Wm. Rogers Mfg. Co. "Reflection",** *no monogram, good condition*	8.00	9.00
☐ **Maker unknown,** *vintage pattern, no monogram, excellent condition*	8.00	9.00
(Sterling Silver)		
☐ **Durgin "Dauphine,"** *no monogram, poultry size*	30.00	34.00

CARVING SETS

Carving sets typically consisted of one carving knife and one carving fork, but occasionally two forks were provided (rarely two knives.) Most manufacturers supplied them in gift boxes but they are not easily found in the original boxes any longer. The better class boxes were made of cedar wood, lined with velvet or sateen.

(Silver-Plated)		
☐ **Alvin "Diana,"** *three-piece, no monogram, excellent condition*	16.00	18.00
☐ **Community "Bird of Paradise,"** *two-piece, no monogram, excellent condition*	20.00	22.00
☐ **Community "Bird of Paradise,"** *two-piece, no monogram, poultry size, no monogram, excellent condition*	45.00	50.00
☐ **Community "Silver Flower,"** *two-piece, no monogram, mint condition*	16.00	18.00
☐ **Gorham "Richmond,"** *two-piece, no monogram, excellent condition*	20.00	22.00
☐ **Nobility "Royal Rose,"** *three-piece, no monogram, large, excellent condition*	40.00	45.00
☐ **Rogers "Empire,"** *two-piece, no monogram, excellent condition*	30.00	35.00
☐ **Wallace "Floral,"** *two-piece, new tines and blade, no monogram, excellent condition*	45.00	50.00
☐ **Wallace "Louvre,"** *three-piece, no monogram, excellent condition*	20.00	22.00
☐ **Wm. Rogers "Beloved,"** *two-piece, no monogram, small, excellent condition*	28.00	30.00
☐ **Wm. Rogers "Berwick,"** *three-piece, no monogram, fair condition*	26.00	28.00
☐ **Wm. R. Rogers "Juliette,"** *two-piece, no monogram, mint condition*	16.00	18.00
☐ **1835 R. Wallace "Buckingham,"** *three-piece, no monogram, good condition*	36.00	40.00
☐ **Maker unknown,** *15½" knife, stag handles, excellent condition*	36.00	40.00
(Sterling Silver)		
☐ **Frank Smith "Chippendale,"** *three-piece, no monogram, roast size*	65.00	75.00
☐ **Gorham "Cambridge,"** *two-piece, no monogram, small*	35.00	40.00
☐ **Gorham "Old French,"** *three-piece, monogram*	70.00	80.00
☐ **Gorham "Old French,"** *two-piece, monogram, poultry size* .	50.00	55.00
☐ **International "Brandon,"** *three-piece, no monogram*	40.00	45.00
☐ **International "Wedgwood,"** *two-piece, no monogram*	28.00	30.00

	Price Range	

☐ **Kirk "Repousse,"** *two-piece, no monogram, roast size, carbon steel blade and tines* 65.00 75.00
☐ **Lunt "Monticello,"** *two piece, no monogram, steak size* ... 38.00 40.00
☐ **Reed & Barton "Francis I,"** *three-piece, no monogram* 80.00 90.00
☐ **Simpson, Hall & Miller "Frontenac,"** *three-piece, carbon steel blade and tines, no monogram* 160.00 180.00
☐ **Stieff "Rose,"** *two-piece, no monogram, steak size, carbon blade* 28.00 30.00
☐ **Wallace "Violet,"** *two-piece, monogram* 40.00 50.00

CARVING STEELS

(Silver-Plated)

☐ **Wm. Rogers Mfg. Co. "Alhambra,"** *no monogram, excellent condition* 8.00 10.00
☐ **1835 R. Wallace "Joan,"** *no monogram, excellent condition* 16.00 18.00
☐ **1847 Rogers "Vintage,"** *no monogram, 12½" L., excellent condition* 32.00 35.00

CASTORS

These are small buckets, the framework made (in this case) of silver and the receptable itself of glass. Specimens wholly of silver were manufac-

Castor, *maker unknown, c. 1880, 4 bottle castor with leaf design on holder,* 90.00

tured but are extremely rare. Castors were used for serving pickles, pickled vegetables, and other fare of that sort. A spice-and-brine solution was placed in the castor, just as in the pickle barrel at the grocery store, and thoroughly permeated the dining room. Castors were nearly always sold with a pair of tongs, with which to remove and distribute the contents, but most specimens traveling on the antiques market have long since become separated from their tongs. The large size of castors has been a strike against them in the collectors' market, but they are really rather impressive looking and probably deserve greater attention.

(Silver-Plated)   **Price Range**

☐ **Hartford Silver Company,** *pickle type, with matching tongs, 11½" H., daisy and button pressed glass insert*	60.00	70.00
☐ **Meriden,** *pickle type, no tongs, elaborate design in silver, rosette and cane pattern glass*	50.00	55.00
☐ **Maker unknown,** *pickle type, cranberry shading to clear glass insert in inverted thumbprint pattern, few small flecks on glass insert*	165.00	175.00
☐ **Maker unknown,** *five-hole condiment type, 15" H., replacement bottles all matching, silver plating in good condition* .	55.00	65.00
☐ **Maker unknown,** *pickle type, no tongs, beaded glass insert, ornate engraving and embossing on lid, silver plating in fair condition*	40.00	50.00
☐ **Maker unknown,** *pickle type, no tongs, clear rosette and cane pattern insert, ornate design in silver, plating in good condition*	40.00	50.00

CENTERPIECES

The centerpieces was a bowl or tray, of no special standard shape, intended to serve as the focal point on a formal dining table. It is still in use today but it seems to merely linger on as a reminder of the days of elegant dining. It became a requisite of the well-ordered table in the 1700's. If silver tableware was being used, the centerpiece mandatorily was silver also. It could be immensely large, as much as two feet in length or circumference, or quite small, to suit the table's size. On state occasions the tables of royalty were adorned with centerpieces nearly the size of bathtubs. Though the centerpiece's purpose was chiefly decorative, it could serve as a receptable for fruits or other foodstuffs. In the later 19th century and in the 20th, these were mostly waxed imitations rather than the real thing — not for lack of availability, but because waxed fruit would not be eaten and thereby spoil the carefully devised arrangement. Centerpieces designed as holders for flowers are less numerous; a tall centerpiece was considered unfavorable, most of the time, as it acted as a kind of blockade on the table. This of course could be useful if guests who were not on cordial terms were seated directly opposite each other.

(Silver-Plated)

☐ **Pairpoint,** *three hoof feet, no monogram, 5½" Dia., cut glass insert, good condition*	55.00	65.00
☐ **Maker unknown,** *silver-plated base with rope handle, griffins supports pink glass dish, molded floral decoration on glass, four scroll feet, 12" Dia., good condition*	105.00	135.00

(Sterling Silver)	Price Range	
☐ **Gorham,** *Art Nouveau styling, 1905 date mark, rectangular shape, chased poppies on border, monogram in center, 16" W., weight 37 oz.*	500.00	525.00
☐ **Maker unknown,** *Art Nouveau styling with applied lily pads and flowers, stems meet to form handle, c. 1900, 14½" L., weight 129 oz.*	1700.00	1800.00

CHAMBERSTICKS

Chambersticks are candlesticks designed not for use on the dining table, but for area lighting in general. In days before more advanced lighting equipment they were of course in very widespread use and came in various sizes, shapes and motifs. The chambersticks served also as a portable light, to be taken along when going upstairs to bed or descending into the cellar, or putting out the cat. It normally had a small curved finger-grip to facilitate carrying and was quite light in weight. Chambersticks were in use in America from almost the earliest colonial times — at any rate from at least as early as 1660 — until the mid 19th century. They continued to be manufactured thereafter, but their place was gradually taken by the whale-oil lamp and then by the kerosene lamp. Silver specimens are far less plentiful than those of pewter, while chambersticks in wrought iron are the most numerous of all.

(Silver-Plated)		
☐ **Meriden,** *ornate floral design, monogram and date, good condition*	24.00	26.00
☐ **Maker unknown,** *plain design, no monogram, excellent condition*	10.00	12.00
☐ **Maker unknown,** *engraved scenic design, excellent condition*	14.00	16.00
(Sterling Silver)		
☐ **Howard & Co.,** *hammered finish, no monogram*	85.00	95.00
☐ **Maker unknown,** *plain design, no monogram*	45.00	50.00

CHEESE KNIVES

It did not suit the Victorian imagination (which was, in some respects, boundless) that a knife should be merely a knife. For each cutting purpose there must be a specially designed, specially named knife: and the world would stop spinning if it failed to appear on the table during the appropriate course. The cheese knife was a bit less frivolous than some other knives of our ancestors' tables. It was easier to cut a neat slice of cheese — especially hard cheese such as gouda or one of the other imports — if your knife sported a wide blade. And the blade could of course be used to lift the cheese, if it was wide, after slicing. Cheese knives were made in quite a variety. Though cheese remained in strong popularity in the 20th century, the use of a specific knife for cutting it did not, and gradually the cheese knife dwindled in production.

(Silver-Plated) Price Range

- ☐ Community "Berkley Square," *no monogram, excellent condition* 6.00 7.00
- ☐ Community "Berkley Square," *no monogram, good condition* 5.00 6.00
- ☐ Holmes & Edwards "Lovely Lady," *no monogram, excellent condition* 14.00 15.00
- ☐ Holmes & Edwards "Lovely Lady," *monogram, poor condition* 1.00 2.00
- ☐ Holmes & Edwards "May Queen," *no monogram, mint condition* 6.00 7.00
- ☐ Holmes & Edwards "Pearl," *no monogram, resilvered* 16.00 18.00
- ☐ Holmes & Edwards "Pearl," *monogram, excellent condition* 8.00 15.00
- ☐ Rockford "Whittier," *no monogram, excellent condition* ... 4.00 5.00
- ☐ Rockford "Whittier," *monogram, fair condition* 1.00 2.00
- ☐ Rogers & Hamilton "Raphael," *no monogram, excellent condition* 26.00 28.00
- ☐ Rogers & Hamilton "Raphael," *no monogram, resilvered* .. 30.00 35.00
- ☐ Sears "Rose," *no monogram, excellent condition* 10.00 12.00
- ☐ 1847 Rogers "Vintage," *no monogram, mint condition* 36.00 38.00
- ☐ 1847 Rogers "Vintage," *monogram, good condition* 18.00 20.00

(Sterling Silver)

- ☐ Gorham "King George," *monogram* 22.00 25.00
- ☐ Gorham "King George," *no monogram* 22.00 25.00
- ☐ International "Wedgwood," *no monogram* 8.00 10.00
- ☐ Stieff "Rose," *no monogram* 16.00 18.00

CHEESE SCOOPS

No all types of cheese submit well to slicing. So the careful hostess needed to keep on hand, in addition to cheese *knives* (see above,) a supply of cheese *scoops*. These handy devices, formed as miniature shovels, went into service when cottage cheese or other loose-curd cheeses appeared at table. Generally the cheese would be presented in a tub or bowl, with the scoop protruding from it; at a large gathering the practice was to pass around this tub (with the scoop) from guest to guest. At a small table where all could reach the cheese tub, it merely remained near the center. When cheese scoops were not at hand, various substitutes were called to play from the silverware arsenal, especially soup and bouillon ladles; but formal etiquette dictated that cheese be scooped with a cheese scoop and nothing else. When made of sterling silver, or other solid silver of a high grade, they carry a fairly substantial bullion value owing to their size.

(Silver-Plated)

- ☐ Wm. Rogers Mfg. Co. "Arbutus," *no monogram, resilvered* . 13.00 15.00
- ☐ Wm. Rogers Mfg. Co. "Arbutus," *monogram ghost showing through resilvering* 14.00 16.00
- ☐ Wm. Rogers Mfg. Co. "Arbutus," *no monogram, mint condition* 16.00 18.00

Cheese Scoops, *(L to R) (sterling), Reed & Barton "Trajan",* 50.00;
Wm. Gale, pattern unknown, 65.00; *Durgin "Chrysanthemum",* 75.00

(Sterling Silver)	Price Range	
☐ **Blackington "Nautilus,"** *no monogram*	28.00	30.00
☐ **Gorham "Buttercup,"** *no monogram*	55.00	60.00
☐ **Gorham "Buttercup,"** *monogram*	90.00	95.00
☐ **Whiting "Dresden,"** *enamel work on handle, no monogram* 6¹/₈"	40.00	55.00
☐ **Whiting "Lily,"** *monogram*	85.00	95.00

CHIPPED BEEF SERVERS

These are forks, whose use will not be very apparent to anyone except a collector of tableware — or someone whose memory extends back 50 or 60 years. The heyday of chipped beef has long since passed (though it can still be had, in vacuum sealed jars, in supermarkets.) Around the turn of the century, and for a while thereafter, there was hardly a restaurant whose luncheon fare did not include chipped beef. This is salted and cured beef, cut into thin slices — sometimes smoked and sometimes not. As a result of curing it dries out and tends to crumble easily, thus the name *chipped* beef. The ideal serving fork was one which could separate the slices without too much trouble and convey them to one's plate whole. Even the best chipped beef servers did not accomplish this all of the time. As a collectors' item they rank in the moderately popular class.

(Silver-Plated)	Price Range	
☐ Community "Adam," *no monogram, good condition*	8.00	10.00
☐ Holmes & Edwards "Carolina," *no monogram, good condition*	7.00	8.00
☐ Holmes & Edwards "Lafayette," *no monogram, excellent condition*	10.00	12.00
☐ Wm. Rogers "Arbutus," *no monogram, excellent condition*	12.00	14.00
☐ Wm. Rogers "Arbutus," *monogram, good condition*	4.00	5.00
☐ Wm. Rogers "Blenheim," *no monogram, excellent condition*	6.00	7.00
☐ 1847 Rogers "Avon," *monogram, excellent condition*	10.00	11.00
☐ 1847 Rogers "Berkshire," *no monogram, excellent condition*	12.00	14.00
☐ 1847 Rogers "Berkshire," *no monogram, resilvered*	18.00	20.00
☐ 1847 Rogers "First Love," *no monogram, excellent condition*	9.00	11.00
☐ 1847 Rogers "Sharon," *no monogram, excellent condition* .	12.00	14.00
☐ 1847 Rogers "Vintage," *no monogram, excellent condition*	20.00	22.00

CHOCOLATE CUPS

Silver chocolate cups are not too numerous, the traditional belief (over the years) being that chocolate tasted better when served in ceramic vessels. Some very attractive ones were, however, made, usually with a silver exterior and an inner lining of ceramic or other earthenware. Chocolate cups wholly of silver are quite rare and especially so in terms of American manufacture. As far as the half silver/half china type are concerned, there was simply not enough demand for them to encourage large-scale production. Even the wealthier classes customarily took their chocolate in ceramic cups, regardless how much silver adorned the table. As with other articles made partially of silver and partially of another substance, precise determination of the *bullion value* is impossible.

(Sterling Silver and China)		
☐ Stieff "Rose" pattern, *Lenox liner with gold trim 4 ozs.*	45.00	55.00

CHOCOLATE MUDDLERS

(Silver-Plated)		
☐ 1847 Rogers "Vintage," *no monogram, mint condition*	35.00	40.00
☐ Maker unknown, *floral pattern, no monogram, excellent condition*	14.00	16.00

(Sterling Silver)		
☐ Gorham "Buttercup," *no monogram*	30.00	35.00
☐ Towle "Old Newbury," *no monogram*	20.00	25.00
☐ Wallace "Irian," *gold wash bowl, no monogram, 7¾" L.* ...	70.00	80.00

CHOCOLATE SPOONS

Chocolate was introduced into society (via the cocoa bean of Latin America) in continental Europe, as a beverage. By the mid 1700's it had become a very popular breakfast drink in most parts of Europe and especially in England; the English had been drinking tea at breakfast for the previous 100 years and were glad for a change. Often it was taken as a breakfast in itself, or along with buttered rolls (nobody was counting calories then, or knew the meaning of the word.) It was rarely served if eggs, meats, etc., comprised the breakfast. The popularity of hot chocolate endured throughout the 19th century. It was always homemade in the Victorian kitchen, from melted chocolate bricks, not from syrups or powders. For stirring and sipping, a special spoon was of course in order, more spherical in the bowl than a teaspoon. Since chocolate drinking (though not necessarily chocolate EATING) was somewhat more widespread abroad, many of the chocolate spoons found in antique shops are foreign-made. An extremely varied collection is possible, with a little hunting.

(Silver-Plated)		**Price Range**
☐ **Williams "Louvre,"** no monogram, excellent condition	4.00	5.00
☐ **Maker unknown,** Art Nouveau styling, no monogram, excellent condition	5.00	6.00
(Sterling Silver)		
☐ **Simpson, Hall & Miller "Frontenac,"** no monogram	12.00	15.00
☐ **Stieff "Rose,"** no monogram	10.00	12.00

CHOCOLATE POTS

Recipe books and how-to-be-a-good-housewife books of the 19th century repeatedly warned against heating chocolate in metallic pots — the flavor would not be as good, and domestic bliss was apt to be threatened. Never-

Chocolate Pot,
Dominick and Haff,
c. 1880, 37 ounces, 2000.00

theless a fair number of silver chocolate pots were manufactured. How much actual use they saw is questionable. The sizes and weights vary quite a bit, and as with any item of this type there is some possibility of LOADING (adding to the weight with lead or crushed stones.)

(Silver-Plated)	Price Range	
☐ **Wilcox,** *Art Nouveau swirled design, monogram and date,* *good condition*	70.00	80.00
☐ **Maker unknown,** *plain design, wooden handle at right angle to spout, monogram and date*	35.00	40.00

CHRISTMAS CARDS

Even when silver was much less costly than today, silver Christmas cards were only occasionally made. This was the kind of flamboyant novelty that appealed to a limited class. Despite the beauty of silver and the engraved decoration the lack of color seemed unfitting in a Christmas card. As collectors' items, silver Christmas cards are really too uncommon to form a hobby in themselves.

(Sterling Silver)		
☐ **Maker unknown,** *rectangular, engraved winter scene on front of card, name, date and Christmas greeting on reverse, weight unknown*	35.00	40.00

CHRISTMAS SPOONS

(Silver-Plated)		
☐ **Wm. Rogers Mfg. Co.,** *holly leaves and berries, monogram and date*	8.00	10.00
☐ **Maker unknown,** *Santa Claus on end of handle, no monogram, excellent condition*	7.00	8.00

(Sterling Silver)		
☐ **Gorham,** *1973*	16.00	18.00
☐ **Gorham,** *1974*	16.00	18.00
☐ **Gorham,** *1976*	16.00	18.00
☐ **Gorham,** *1978*	16.00	18.00
☐ **Gorham,** *1978*	16.00	18.00
☐ **Gorham,** *1979*	16.00	18.00
☐ **Gorham,** *1979*	16.00	18.00
☐ **Gorham,** *demitasse size*	5.00	6.00
☐ **Gorham,** *demitasse size*	8.00	10.00
☐ **Maker unknown,** *teaspoon size with Santa Claus handle*	18.00	20.00
☐ **Maker unknown,** *teaspoon size with Christmas tree handle*	18.00	20.00

CHRISTMAS TREE ORNAMENTS

(Silver-Plated)		
☐ **Gorham,** *1979 Christmas Ball, Santa's Surprise*	18.00	22.00
☐ **International,** *Angel*	6.00	7.00
☐ **International,** *Holly*	6.00	7.00
☐ **International,** *1974 Santa*	3.00	4.00
☐ **International,** *1976 Santa*	3.00	4.00
☐ **International,** *1977 Santa*	3.00	4.00
☐ **International,** *1978 Santa*	3.00	4.00

Christmas Ornaments, *Gorham,*
complete set, see text for prices.

	Price Range	
☐ **Kirk,** *musical bell type, plays "Deck the Halls," 1979*	14.00	16.00
☐ **Kirk,** *musical bell type, plays "White Christmas," 1978*	15.00	17.00
☐ **Oneida,** *snowflake chime*	1.00	2.00
☐ **Oneida,** *angel mobile*	1.00	2.00
☐ **Oneida,** *ball mobile*	1.00	2.00
☐ **Oneida,** *bird mobile*	1.00	2.00
☐ **Oneida,** *Santa mobile*	1.00	2.00
☐ **Oneida,** *Madonna*	1.00	2.00
☐ **Oneida,** *reindeer*	1.00	2.00
☐ **Oneida,** *crown teardrop*	6.00	7.00
☐ **Oneida,** *joy teardrop*	6.00	7.00
☐ **Oneida,** *Madonna teardrop*	6.00	7.00
☐ **Oneida,** *partridge teardrop*	6.00	7.00
☐ **Oneida,** *star teardrop*	6.00	7.00
☐ **Reed & Barton,** *1976 First Edition Holly Ball*	46.00	52.00
☐ **Reed & Barton,** *1976 First Edition Holly Ball*	18.00	22.00
☐ **Reed & Barton,** *1977 Holly Ball*	14.00	16.00
☐ **Reed & Barton,** *1977 Holly Ball*	40.00	45.00
☐ **Reed & Barton,** *1978 Holly Ball*	11.00	13.00
☐ **Reed & Barton,** *1978 Holly Ball*	14.00	16.00
☐ **Reed & Barton,** *1979 Holly Ball*	12.00	14.00
☐ **Reed & Barton,** *1979 Holly Ball*	12.00	14.00
☐ **Reed & Barton,** *1977 pair of snowflakes*	14.00	16.00
☐ **Reed & Barton,** *1977 pair of snowflakes*	14.00	16.00
☐ **Reed & Barton,** *1977 pair of snowflakes*	30.00	35.00
☐ **Reed & Barton,** *1978 pair of snowflakes*	10.00	12.00
☐ **Reed & Barton,** *1978 pair of snowflakes*	13.00	15.00
☐ **Reed & Barton,** *1979 pair of snowflakes*	10.00	12.00

	Price Range	

☐ **Reed & Barton,** *1979 pair of snowflakes* .... | 10.00 | 12.00
☐ **Reed & Barton,** *1977 Twelve Days of Christmas, Turtle Dove and Partridge* .... | 14.00 | 16.00
☐ **Reed & Barton,** *1977 Twelve Days of Christmas, Turtle Dove and Partridge* .... | 16.00 | 18.00
☐ **Reed & Barton,** *1978 Twelve Days of Christmas, Colly Bird and French Hen* .... | 14.00 | 16.00
☐ **Reed & Barton,** *1978 Twelve Days of Christmas, Colly Bird and French Hen* .... | 16.00 | 18.00
☐ **Reed & Barton,** *1979 Twelve Days of Christmas, Geese a Laying and Five Gold Rings* .... | 14.00 | 16.00
☐ **Reed & Barton,** *1979 Twelve Days of Christmas, Geese a Laying and Five Gold Rings* .... | 16.00 | 18.00
☐ **Wallace,** *1971 First Edition bell* .... | 225.00 | 250.00
☐ **Wallace,** *1972 bell* .... | 48.00 | 52.00
☐ **Wallace,** *1973 bell* .... | 30.00 | 35.00
☐ **Wallace,** *1974 bell* .... | 18.00 | 22.00
☐ **Wallace,** *1975 bell* .... | 18.00 | 20.00
☐ **Wallace,** *1976 bell* .... | 26.00 | 28.00
☐ **Wallace,** *1977 bell* .... | 16.00 | 18.00
☐ **Wallace,** *1978 bell* .... | 16.00 | 18.00
☐ **Wallace,** *1979 bell* .... | 12.00 | 14.00
☐ **Wallace,** *1979 bell* .... | 14.00 | 16.00

(Sterling Silver)

☐ **Gorham,** *Angel* .... | 12.00 | 14.00
☐ **Gorham,** *Angel* .... | 12.00 | 15.00
☐ **Gorham,** *1975 Angel with Trumpet* .... | 16.00 | 18.00
☐ **Gorham,** *1978 Children Around Tree* .... | 14.00 | 16.00
☐ **Gorham,** *1978 Children Around Tree* .... | 15.00 | 18.00
☐ **Gorham,** *Choirboys* .... | 12.00 | 14.00
☐ **Gorham,** *Choirboys* .... | 12.00 | 14.00
☐ **Gorham,** *Drummer Boy* .... | 12.00 | 14.00
☐ **Gorham,** *Drummer Boy* .... | 12.00 | 14.00
☐ **Gorham,** *1976 Locomotive* .... | 13.00 | 15.00
☐ **Gorham,** *1976 Locomotive* .... | 16.00 | 18.00
☐ **Gorham,** *Partridge in a Pear Tree* .... | 40.00 | 45.00
☐ **Gorham,** *1973 Peace Dove* .... | 13.00 | 15.00
☐ **Gorham,** *1973 Peace Dove* .... | 16.00 | 18.00
☐ **Gorham,** *pierced ball* .... | 10.00 | 12.00
☐ **Gorham,** *pierced dove* .... | 10.00 | 12.00
☐ **Gorham,** *pierced lantern* .... | 10.00 | 12.00
☐ **Gorham,** *pierced tree* .... | 10.00 | 12.00
☐ **Gorham,** *1974 Reindeer* .... | 14.00 | 16.00
☐ **Gorham,** *1974 Reindeer* .... | 16.00 | 18.00
☐ **Gorham,** *Santa* .... | 12.00 | 14.00
☐ **Gorham,** *Santa* .... | 12.00 | 14.00
☐ **Gorham,** *1979 Santa with Sled* .... | 13.00 | 15.00
☐ **Gorham,** *1979 Santa with Sled* .... | 16.00 | 18.00
☐ **Gorham,** *Santa's Helper (Elf)* .... | 12.00 | 14.00
☐ **Gorham,** *Santa's Helper (Elf)* .... | 12.00 | 14.00
☐ **Gorham,** *1970 Snowflake, first edition* .... | 45.00 | 48.00
☐ **Gorham,** *1970 Snowflake, first edition* .... | 100.00 | 120.00
☐ **Gorham,** *1971 Snowflake* .... | 16.00 | 18.00

	Price Range	
☐ **Gorham,** *1971 Snowflake*	26.00	28.00
☐ **Gorham,** *1972 Snowflake*	12.00	14.00
☐ **Gorham,** *1972 Snowflake*	20.00	22.00
☐ **Gorham,** *1972 Snowflake*	20.00	22.00
☐ **Gorham,** *1973 Snowflake*	14.00	16.00
☐ **Gorham,** *1973 Snowflake*	15.00	17.00
☐ **Gorham,** *1973 Snowflake*	16.00	18.00
☐ **Gorham,** *1974 Snowflake*	12.00	14.00
☐ **Gorham,** *1974 Snowflake*	13.00	15.00
☐ **Gorham,** *1974 Snowflake*	15.00	17.00
☐ **Gorham,** *1975 Snowflake*	12.00	14.00
☐ **Gorham,** *1975 Snowflake*	13.00	15.00
☐ **Gorham,** *1975 Snowflake*	16.00	18.00
☐ **Gorham,** *1976 Snowflake*	12.00	14.00
☐ **Gorham,** *1976 Snowflake*	14.00	16.00
☐ **Gorham,** *1976 Snowflake*	14.00	16.00
☐ **Gorham,** *1977 Snowflake*	12.00	14.00
☐ **Gorham,** *1977 Snowflake*	14.00	16.00
☐ **Gorham,** *1977 Snowflake*	16.00	18.00
☐ **Gorham,** *1978 Snowflake*	13.00	15.00
☐ **Gorham,** *1978 Snowflake*	13.00	15.00
☐ **Gorham,** *1978 Snowflake*	13.00	15.00
☐ **Gorham,** *1978 Snowflake*	13.00	15.00
☐ **Gorham,** *1979 Snowflake*	14.00	16.00
☐ **Gorham,** *1979 Snowflake*	22.00	25.00
☐ **Gorham,** *1979 Snowflake*	24.00	26.00
☐ **Gorham,** *1979 Snowflake*	24.00	26.00
☐ **Gorham,** *complete set of Snowflakes 1970 through 1979* ...	185.00	200.00
☐ **Gorham,** *1979 Snowflake Miniature*	16.00	18.00
☐ **Gorham,** *1979 Snowflake Miniature*	18.00	20.00
☐ **Gorham,** *1979 Snowflake Miniature*	18.00	20.00
☐ **Gorham,** *Snowman*	18.00	20.00
☐ **Gorham,** *Snowman*	20.00	22.00
☐ **Gorham,** *1977 St. Nick*	23.00	25.00
☐ **Gorham,** *1977 St. Nick*	24.00	26.00
☐ **Gorham,** *three-dimensional carousel*	20.00	22.00
☐ **Gorham,** *three-dimensional carousel*	20.00	25.00
☐ **Gorham,** *three-dimensional rocking horse*	18.00	20.00
☐ **Gorham,** *three-dimensional rocking horse*	20.00	22.00
☐ **Gorham,** *three-dimensional steam engine*	18.00	20.00
☐ **Gorham,** *three-dimensional steam engine*	20.00	22.00
☐ **Gorham,** *three-dimensional treasure chest*	20.00	22.00
☐ **Gorham,** *three-dimensional treasure chest*	20.00	22.00
☐ **Gorham,** *Two Turtle Doves*	38.00	40.00
☐ **Gorham,** *Waiting for Christmas*	12.00	14.00
☐ **Gorham,** *Waiting for Christmas*	14.00	16.00
☐ **International,** *Four Colly Birds*	20.00	22.00
☐ **International,** *Three French Hens*	20.00	22.00
☐ **Lunt,** *1972, First Edition*	18.00	20.00
☐ **Lunt,** *1973*	18.00	20.00
☐ **Lunt,** *"Deck the Halls"*	10.00	12.00
☐ **Lunt,** *1979, "Joy to the World"*	8.00	10.00
☐ **Reed & Barton,** *1971 Christmas Cross, vermeil, first edition*	40.00	45.00
☐ **Reed & Barton,** *1971 Christmas Cross, vermeil, first edition*	50.00	60.00

	Price Range	
☐ **Reed & Barton,** *1971 Christmas Cross, first edition*	45.00	48.00
☐ **Reed & Barton,** *1972 Christmas Cross*	18.00	20.00
☐ **Reed & Barton,** *1972 Christmas Cross*	28.00	30.00
☐ **Reed & Barton,** *1972 Christmas Cross*	30.00	35.00
☐ **Reed & Barton,** *1973 Christmas Cross*	12.00	14.00
☐ **Reed & Barton,** *1973 Christmas Cross*	16.00	18.00
☐ **Reed & Barton,** *1973 Christmas Cross*	28.00	30.00
☐ **Reed & Barton,** *1973 Christ Cross*	26.00	28.00
☐ **Reed & Barton,** *1974 Christmas Cross, vermeil*	28.00	30.00
☐ **Reed & Barton,** *1974 Christmas Cross, vermeil*	28.00	30.00
☐ **Reed & Barton,** *1974 Christmas Cross*	23.00	25.00
☐ **Reed & Barton,** *1974 Christmas Cross*	23.00	25.00
☐ **Reed & Barton,** *1975 Christmas Cross*	10.00	12.00
☐ **Reed & Barton,** *1975 Christmas Cross*	16.00	18.00
☐ **Reed & Barton,** *1975 Christmas Cross*	23.00	25.00
☐ **Reed & Barton,** *1976 Christmas Cross, vermeil*	28.00	30.00
☐ **Reed & Barton,** *1976 Christmas Cross*	10.00	12.00
☐ **Reed & Barton,** *1976 Christmas Cross*	16.00	18.00
☐ **Reed & Barton,** *1976 Christmas Cross*	23.00	25.00
☐ **Reed & Barton,** *1977 Christmas Cross, vermeil*	28.00	30.00
☐ **Reed & Barton,** *1977 Christmas Cross*	10.00	12.00
☐ **Reed & Barton,** *1977 Christmas Cross*	10.00	12.00
☐ **Reed & Barton,** *1977 Christmas Cross*	15.00	17.00
☐ **Reed & Barton,** *1977 Christmas Cross*	23.00	25.00
☐ **Reed & Barton,** *1978 Christmas Cross*	10.00	12.00
☐ **Reed & Barton,** *1978 Christmas Cross*	13.00	15.00
☐ **Reed & Barton,** *1978 Christmas Cross*	20.00	22.00
☐ **Reed & Barton,** *1979 Christmas Cross, vermeil*	14.00	16.00
☐ **Reed & Barton,** *1979 Christmas Cross*	10.00	12.00
☐ **Reed & Barton,** *1979 Christmas Cross*	10.00	12.00
☐ **Reed & Barton,** *1979 Christmas Cross*	10.00	12.00
☐ **Reed & Barton,** *1976 Star, first edition*	30.00	35.00
☐ **Reed & Barton,** *1977 Star*	7.00	8.00
☐ **Reed & Barton,** *1978 Star, vermeil*	8.00	9.00
☐ **Reed & Barton,** *1978 Star*	7.00	8.00
☐ **Reed & Barton,** *1978 Star*	10.00	12.00
☐ **Reed & Barton,** *1978 Star*	28.00	30.00
☐ **Reed & Barton,** *1979 Star*	7.00	8.00
☐ **Reed & Barton,** *1979 Star*	8.00	9.00
☐ **Stieff,** *Angel with Trumpet, 1978 Smithsonian Institute Series*	9.00	10.00
☐ **Towle,** *1978 Melodies Medallion, first edition*	10.00	12.00
☐ **Towle,** *1978 Melodies Medallion, first edition*	13.00	15.00
☐ **Towle,** *1971 Twelve Days of Christmas, "Partridge in Pear Tree," first edition*	250.00	300.00
☐ **Towle,** *1972 Twelve Days of Christmas, "Two Turtle Doves"*	40.00	50.00
☐ **Towle,** *1973 Twelve Days of Christmas, "Three French Hens"*	22.00	24.00
☐ **Towle,** *1974 Twelve Days of Christmas, "Four Colly Birds"* .	16.00	18.00
☐ **Towle,** *1975 Twelve Days of Christmas, "Five Gold Rings"* .	8.00	9.00
☐ **Towle,** *1975 Twelve Days of Christmas, "Five Gold Rings"* .	8.00	9.00
☐ **Towle,** *1975 Twelve Days of Christmas, "Five Gold Rings"* .	20.00	22.00
☐ **Towle,** *1976 Twelve Days of Christmas, "Geese a Laying"* .	12.00	14.00
☐ **Towle,** *1976 Twelve Days of Christmas, "Geese a Laying"* .	16.00	18.00

	Price Range	
☐ **Towle,** *1977 Twelve Days of Christmas, "Seven Swans Swimming"*	10.00	12.00
☐ **Towle,** *1977 Twelve Days of Christmas, "Seven Swan Swimming"*	10.00	12.00
☐ **Towle,** *1978 Twelve Days of Christmas, "Eight Maids Milking"*	10.00	12.00
☐ **Towle,** *1978 Twelve Days of Christmas, "Eight Maids Milking"*	10.00	12.00
☐ **Towle,** *1978 Twelve Days of Christmas, "Eight Maids Milking"*	20.00	22.00
☐ **Towle,** *1979 Twelve Days of Christmas, "Nine Ladies Dancing"*	10.00	12.00
☐ **Towle,** *1979 Twelve Days of Christmas, "Nine Ladies Dancing"*	12.00	15.00
☐ **Wallace,** *1972 Peace Dove medallion*	8.00	10.00
☐ **Wallace,** *1974 Peace Dove medallion*	8.00	10.00
☐ **Wallace,** *1974 Peace Dove medallion*	10.00	12.00

(Sterling on Crystal)

☐ **Sterling America,** *1970 Yule Log*	12.00	14.00
☐ **Sterling America,** *1979 Partridge*	10.00	12.00

CIGARETTE CASES

Silver cigarette cases began to be made almost as soon as commercially packaged cigarettes came into popularity, around 1880. For a long while it was definitely a mark of low rank to carry one's cigarette in the manufacturer's package. Anyone with class — or pretensions to it — immediately transferred his cigarettes into his own personal carrying case, which also contained matches (there were no portable lighters yet) and generally bore his monogram. Cigarette cases were nearly always ornamental and often had very novel designs. Since just about everybody wanted one, they were put out in a variety of materials and price ranges. Stainless steel usually served for those who could not afford silver, and with a little imagination it could be mistaken for silver — especially if the light was dim. Silver specimens will be found in which carved or painted ivory has been inlaid, or other very artistic work performed. Most of these are European creations, sold there and likewise imported into the U.S. market. Some truly splendid ones were made in the period from about 1890 to 1905 and have sold for hundreds of dollars. The examples listed here are domestic.

(Silver-Plated)

☐ **Maker unknown,** *design with Lady Godiva, no monogram, excellent condition*	40.00	42.00

(Sterling Silver)

☐ **Gorham,** *plain design, original flannel bag, weight 4 ozs.* ..	35.00	40.00
☐ **Maker unknown,** *no monogram*	26.00	30.00

COASTERS

The thought that heat or moisture from drinking vessels might mar furniture finishes did not cross anyone's mind until about 200 years ago. And even then, it was only, for a long while, in the most opulent homes that coasters would be seen. Their general use dates from the middle part of the

19th century, and they have of course continued on into the present day — in plastic, wood, stainless steel and other materials. Silver specimens are not abundantly common but you will encounter them on the antique markets. Some are rather large and even elaborate in certain cases. It is not unusual for the dish of a silver coaster to be supported by a crystal base, serving as a kind of elegant pedestal. Coasters of this description were intended mainly for wine glasses.

(Sterling Silver)	Price Range	
☐ **Shiebler "Chrysanthemum,"** *wine coaster size, sterling rim and wooden bottom, 1 3/4 " H., 5 3/8 " Dia.*	160.00	175.00
☐ **Frank Whiting,** *sterling rim on crystal base cut in swirled star design, set of six*	28.00	30.00
☐ **Maker unknown,** *sterling rim with beaded edge, crystal bottom cut in star design, set of six*	8.00	10.00

COCKTAIL FORKS

The cocktail fork is one silver utensil whose use is seldom unrecognized. Actually cocktail forks are of more recent origin than cocktails, for the standard procedure in earlier times was simply to tilt and tap the glass, after drinking, to dislodge the olive or cherry. Naturally this struck the genteel Victorians as barbaric, and the special dainty fork for spearing one's olive or cherry came into existence. Few silver articles were manufactured in such profusion in the later 19th century and the 20th. It was one item of silverware that almost everybody could afford to have, since the silver content was negligible and the price, therefore, very low. They have become favorite collectibles; they display very well and can even be housed in albums if the hobbyist desires.

(Silver-Plated)		
☐ **Community "Adam",** *no monogram, excellent condition*	3.00	4.00
☐ **Community "Adam",** *no monogram, excellent condition*	4.00	5.00
☐ **Community "Adam",** *monogram, fair condition, set of twelve*	13.00	14.00
☐ **Community "Bird of Paradise",** *no monogram, excellent condition*	9.00	10.00
☐ **Community "Bird of Paradise",** *monogram, good condition*	3.00	4.00
☐ **Community "Coronation",** *no monogram, good condition*	4.00	5.00
☐ **Community "Coronation",** *no monogram, excellent condition*	7.00	8.00
☐ **Community "Coronation",** *monogram, excellent condition*	5.00	6.00
☐ **Community "Enchantment",** *no monogram, excellent condition*	4.00	5.00
☐ **Community "Enchantment",** *no monogram, resilvered*	8.00	9.00
☐ **Community "Enchantment",** *monogram, good condition*	4.00	5.00
☐ **Community "Flower de Luce",** *no monogram, excellent condition*	8.00	9.00
☐ **Community "Flower de Luce",** *no monogram, excellent condition*	10.00	12.00
☐ **Community "Grosvenor",** *no monogram, excellent condition*	5.00	6.00
☐ **Community "Grosvenor",** *no monogram, resilvered*	9.00	10.00
☐ **Community "June",** *no monogram, excellent condition*	1.00	2.00
☐ **Community "June",** *monogram, good condition*	1.00	2.00

	Price Range	

□ Community **"King Cedric"**, *no monogram, excellent condition* 7.00 8.00

□ Community **"King Cedric"**, *no monogram, fair condition* .. 1.00 2.00

□ Community **"King Cedric"**, *no monogram, resilvered* 8.00 9.00

□ Community **"Lady Hamilton"**, *no monogram, good condition* 4.00 5.00

□ Community **"Lady Hamilton"**, *no monogram, excellent condition* 7.00 8.00

□ Community **"Lady Hamilton"**, *monogram, good condition* . 5.00 6.00

□ Community **"Louis XVI"**, *no monogram, excellent condition* 7.00 8.00

□ Community **"Louis XVI"**, *monogram, excellent condition* .. 6.00 7.00

□ Community **"Milady"**, *no monogram, excellent condition* .. 7.00 8.00

□ Community **"Milady"**, *monogram, excellent condition* 6.00 7.00

□ Community **"Milady"**, *no monogram, good condition* 4.00 5.00

□ Community **"Patrician"**, *no monogram, excellent condition* 7.00 8.00

□ Community **"Patrician"**, *no monogram, poor condition* 1.00 2.00

□ Community **"Randolph"**, *no monogram, good condition* ... 4.00 5.00

□ Community **"Randolph"**, *no monogram, resilvered* 9.00 10.00

□ Community **"Silver Flower"**, *no monogram, excellent condition* 7.00 8.00

□ Community **"Silver Flower"**, *no monogram, mint condition* 3.00 4.00

□ Community **"Song of Autumn"**, *no monogram, mint condition* 5.00 6.00

□ Community **"Song of Autumn"**, *no monogram, excellent condition* 7.00 8.00

□ Community **"Tangier"**, *no monogram, mint condition* 3.00 4.00

□ Community **"Tangier"**, *no monogram, good condition* 3.00 4.00

□ Court **"Court"**, *no monogram, good condition* 4.00 5.00

□ Court **"Court"**, *no monogram, resilvered* 9.00 10.00

□ Gorham **"Cavalier"**, *no monogram, excellent condition* 3.00 4.00

□ Gorham **"Cavalier"**, *no monogram, good condition* 1.00 2.00

□ Gorham **"Kings"**, *no monogram, excellent condition* 5.00 6.00

□ Gorham **"Kings"**, *U.S. Navy, excellent condition* 7.00 8.00

□ Gorham **"Saxony"**, *no monogram, excellent condition* 6.00 7.00

□ Gorham **"Saxony"**, *no monogram, excellent condition* 8.00 9.00

□ Gorham **"Stanhope"**, *no monogram, excellent condition* .. 7.00 8.00

□ Hall, Elton & Company **"Eastlake"**, *no monogram, mint condition* 7.00 8.00

□ Hall, Elton & Company **"Eastlake"**, *no monogram, excellent condition* 6.00 7.00

□ Holmes & Edwards **"Century"**, *monogram, excellent condition* 3.00 4.00

□ Holmes & Edwards **"Century"**, *no monogram, excellent condition* 7.00 8.00

□ Holmes & Edwards **"Danish Princess"**, *no monogram, excellent condition* 4.00 5.00

□ Holmes & Edwards **"Danish Princess"**, *no monogram, fair condition* 1.00 2.00

□ Holmes & Edwards **"Japanese"**, *no monogram, mint condition* 13.00 14.00

□ Holmes & Edwards **"Japanese"**, *no monogram, excellent condition* 8.00 9.00

□ Holmes & Edwards **"Youth"**, *no monogram, excellent condition* 7.00 8.00

	Price Range	
☐ Holmes & Edwards "Youth", *no monogram, good condition*	4.00	5.00
☐ International "Kings", *no monogram, excellent condition* .	3.00	4.00
☐ International "Kings", *monogram, fair condition*	1.50	2.50
☐ National "King Edward", *no monogram, excellent condition*	7.00	8.00
☐ Nobility "Royal Rose", *no monogram, excellent condition* .	7.00	8.00
☐ Nobility "Royal Rose", *no monogram, resilvered*	9.00	10.00
☐ Oneida "Flower de Luce", *no monogram, excellent condition*	6.00	7.00
☐ Oneida "Flower de Luce", *monogram, good condition*	4.00	5.00
☐ Oneida "Wildwood", *no monogram, excellent condition* ...	8.00	9.00
☐ Oneida "Wildwood", *monogram, excellent condition*	5.00	6.00
☐ Paragon "Rose", *no monogram, excellent condition*	6.00	7.00
☐ Paragon "Rose", *monogram, good condition*	1.50	2.50
☐ Paragon "Sweet Pea", *no monogram, excellent condition* .	5.00	6.00
☐ Paragon "Sweet Pea", *monogram, good condition*	3.00	4.00
☐ Reed & Barton "Carlton", *no monogram, mint condition* ...	7.00	8.00
☐ Reed & Barton "Carlton", *no monogram, excellent condition*	6.00	7.00
☐ Reed & Barton "Kings", *no monogram, excellent condition*	3.00	4.00
☐ Reed & Barton "Kings", *no monogram, excellent condition*	8.00	9.00
☐ Reed & Barton "Modern Art", *no monogram, excellent condition*	4.00	5.00
☐ Reed & Barton, *monogram, excellent condition*	4.00	5.00
☐ Reed & Barton "Oxford", *no monogram, excellent condition*	6.00	7.00
☐ Reed & Barton "Oxford", *no monogram, excellent condition*	10.00	12.00
☐ Reliance "Exeter", *no monogram, good condition*	6.00	7.00
☐ Reliance "Exeter", *no monogram, excellent condition*	8.00	9.00
☐ Reliance "Wildwood", *no monogram, excellent condition* .	8.00	9.00
☐ Reliance "Wildwood", *monogram, fair condition*	1.50	2.50
☐ Rogers "Alhambra", *no monogram, excellent condition* ...	4.00	5.00
☐ Rogers "Alhambra", *no monogram, resilvered*	8.00	9.00
☐ Rogers "Beaded", *no monogram, good condition*	4.00	5.00
☐ Rogers "Beaded", *monogram, excellent condition*	4.00	5.00
☐ Rogers "Carlton", *no monogram, excellent condition*	7.00	8.00
☐ Rogers "Carlton", *monogram, excellent condition*	3.00	4.00
☐ Rogers "Grenoble", *no monogram, excellent condition* ...	10.00	12.00
☐ Rogers "Grenoble", *no monogram, fair condition*	1.00	2.00
☐ Rogers & Bro. "Aldine", *no monogram, mint condition*	6.00	7.00
☐ Rogers & Bro. "Aldine", *no monogram, mint condition*	8.00	9.00
☐ Rogers & Bro. "Cromwell", *no monogram, mint condition* ..	2.00	3.00
☐ Rogers & Bro. "Daybreak", *no monogram, excellent condition*	7.00	8.00
☐ Rogers & Bro. "Daybreak", *monogram, excellent condition*	6.00	7.00
☐ Rogers & Bro. "Hostess", *no monogram, excellent condition*	7.00	8.00
☐ Rogers & Bro. "Hostess", *monogram, good condition*	1.00	2.00
☐ Rogers & Bro. "Mystic", *no monogram, excellent condition*	4.00	5.00
☐ Rogers & Bro. "Mystic", *no monogram, resilvered*	9.00	10.00
☐ Rogers & Bro. "Siren", *no monogram, excellent condition* .	14.00	16.00
☐ Rogers & Bro. "Siren", *monogram, good condition*	5.00	7.00
☐ Rogers & Bro. "Thistle", *no monogram, excellent condition*	4.00	5.00
☐ Rogers & Bro. "Thistle", *no monogram, excellent condition*	8.00	9.00
☐ Rogers & Hamilton "Alhambra", *no monogram, excellent condition*	6.00	7.00

Price Range

☐ Rogers & Hamilton "Alhambra", *no monogram, excellent condition*	8.00	9.00
☐ Rogers & Hamilton "Alhambra", *no monogram, fair condition*	1.00	2.00
☐ Rogers & Hamilton "Alhambra", *monogram, excellent condition*	6.00	7.00
☐ Rogers & Hamilton "Marquise", *no monogram, excellent condition*	4.00	5.00
☐ Rogers & Hamilton "Marquise", *no monogram, excellent condition*	5.00	6.00
☐ Rogers & Hamilton "Raphael", *no monogram, excellent condition*	4.00	5.00
☐ Rogers & Hamilton "Raphael", *no monogram, mint condition*	12.00	14.00
☐ Rogers & Hamilton "Raphael", *no monogram, excellent condition*	9.00	10.00
☐ Sears "Adele", *no monogram, excellent condition*	8.00	9.00
☐ S.L. & G.H. Rogers "Countess", *no monogram, excellent condition*	7.00	8.00
☐ S.L. & G.H. Rogers "Countess II", *no monogram, mint condition*	8.00	9.00
☐ S.L. & G.H. Rogers "English Garden", *no monogram, excellent condition*	7.00	8.00
☐ S.L. & G.H. Rogers "Jefferson", *no monogram, excellent condition*	7.00	8.00
☐ S.L. & G.H. Rogers "Jefferson", *monogram, good condition*	3.00	4.00
☐ S.L. & G.H. Rogers "Laureate", *no monogram, excellent condition*	7.00	8.00
☐ S.L. & G.H. Rogers "Laureate", *no monogram, fair condition*	1.00	2.00
☐ S.L. & G.H. Rogers "Lexington", *no monogram, excellent condition*	6.00	7.00
☐ S.L. & G.H. Rogers "Lexington", *no monogram, mint condition*	8.00	9.00
☐ S.L. & G.H. Rogers "Thor", *no monogram, excellent condition*	7.00	8.00
☐ S.L. & G.H. Rogers "Thor", *no monogram, mint condition* ..	9.00	10.00
☐ Stratford "Lilyta", *no monogram, excellent condition*	10.00	12.00
☐ Towle "Arbutus", *no monogram, excellent condition*	6.00	7.00
☐ Towle "Arbutus", *no monogram, excellent condition*	8.00	9.00
☐ Towle "Priscilla", *no monogram, excellent condition*	6.00	7.00
☐ Towle "Priscilla", *no monogram, mint condition*	8.00	9.00
☐ Tudor "Baronet", *no monogram, excellent condition*	1.00	2.00
☐ Tudor "Baronet", *monogram, fair condition*	1.00	2.00
☐ Tudor "Bridal Wreath", *no monogram, excellent condition* .	8.00	9.00
☐ Tudor "Bridal Wreath", *monogram, good condition*	4.00	5.00
☐ Tudor "Bridal Wreath", *monogram, fair condition*	1.00	2.00
☐ Tudor "Queen Bess II", *no monogram, excellent condition* .	6.00	7.00
☐ Tudor "Queen Bess II", *no monogram, mint condition*	8.00	9.00
☐ Wallace "Floral", *no monogram, excellent condition*	8.00	9.00
☐ Wallace "Floral", *no monogram, good condition*	5.00	6.00
☐ W. F. Rogers Mfg. "Mistletoe", *no monogram, excellent condition*	7.00	8.00
☐ Williams Bros. "Isabella", *no monogram, good condition* ..	4.00	5.00

	Price Range	
☐ Wm. A. Rogers "Country Lane", *no monogram, excellent* condition	7.00	8.00
☐ Wm. A. Rogers "Country Lane", *monogram, excellent condition*	7.00	8.00
☐ Wm. A. Rogers "Hanover", *no monogram, excellent condition*	3.00	4.00
☐ Wm. A. Rogers "Hanover", *no monogram, excellent condition*	4.00	5.00
☐ Wm. A. Rogers "LaConcorde", *no monogram, excellent* condition	6.00	7.00
☐ Wm. A. Rogers "LaConcorde", *no monogram, excellent* condition	9.00	10.00
☐ Wm. A. Rogers "Malibu", *no monogram, excellent condition*	7.00	8.00
☐ Wm. A. Rogers "Malibu", *no monogram, mint condition* ...	8.00	9.00
☐ Wm. A. Rogers "Mary Lee", *no monogram, excellent condition*	7.00	8.00
☐ Wm. A. Rogers "Mary Lee", *no monogram, mint condition* .	8.00	9.00
☐ Wm. A. Rogers "Meadowbrook", *no monogram, excellent* condition	7.00	8.00
☐ Wm. A. Rogers "Meadowbrook", *no monogram, fair condition*	1.00	2.00
☐ Wm. A. Rogers "Narcissus", *no monogram, excellent condition*	6.00	7.00
☐ Wm. A. Rogers "Narcissus", *monogram, good condition* ..	5.00	6.00
☐ Wm. A. Rogers "Narcissus", *no monogram, excellent condition*	8.00	9.00
☐ Wm. A. Rogers "Rosalie", *no monogram, excellent condition*	7.00	8.00
☐ Wm. A. Rogers "Rosalie", *no monogram, good condition* ..	4.00	5.00
☐ Wm. A. Rogers "Yale I", *no monogram, excellent condition*	5.00	6.00
☐ Wm. A. Rogers "Yale I", *no monogram, excellent condition*	7.00	8.00
☐ Wm. A. Rogers "Beloved", *no monogram, excellent condition*	7.00	8.00
☐ Wm. A. Rogers "Beloved", *no monogram, excellent condition*	8.00	9.00
☐ Wm. A. Rogers "California Blossom", *no monogram, excellent condition*	1.00	2.00
☐ Wm. A. Rogers "Carrollton", *no monogram, excellent condition*	3.00	4.00
☐ Wm. A. Rogers "Carrollton", *monogram, good condition* ..	1.50	2.50
☐ Wm. Rogers "Fair Lady", *monogram, excellent condition* ..	7.00	8.00
☐ Wm. Rogers "Fair Lady", *no monogram, mint condition* ...	8.00	9.00
☐ Wm. Rogers "Hostess", *no monogram, excellent condition*	7.00	8.00
☐ Wm. Rogers "Memory", *no monogram, excellent condition*	6.00	7.00
☐ Wm. Rogers "Regent", *no monogram, excellent condition*	7.00	8.00
☐ Wm. Rogers "Regent", *monogram, good condition*	2.00	3.00
☐ Wm. Rogers "Treasure", *no monogram, excellent condition*	7.00	8.00
☐ Wm. Rogers "Treasure", *no monogram, mint condition* ...	8.00	9.00
☐ Wm. Rogers "Tuxedo", *no monogram, excellent condition* .	6.00	7.00
☐ Wm. Rogers "Tuxedo", *monogram, mint condition*	7.00	8.00
☐ Wm. Rogers "Arbutus", *no monogram, excellent condition*	10.00	12.00
☐ Wm. Rogers "Arbutus", *no monogram, resilvered*	14.00	16.00

	Price Range	
☐ Wm. Rogers "Arbutus", *no monogram, poor condition*	1.00	2.00
☐ Wm. Rogers Mfg. Co. "Berwick", *no monogram, mint condition*	4.00	5.00
☐ Wm. Rogers Mfg. Co. "Berwick", *monogram, mint condition*	5.00	6.00
☐ Wm. Rogers Mfg. Co. "Grand Elegance", *no monogram, excellent condition*	7.00	8.00
☐ Wm. Rogers Mfg. Co. "Grand Elegance", *no monogram, good condition*	4.00	5.00
☐ Wm. Rogers Mfg. Co. "Jubilee", *no monogram, excellent condition*	7.00	8.00
☐ Wm. Rogers Mfg. Co. "Jubilee", *monogram, excellent condition*	5.00	6.00
☐ Wm. Rogers & Son "Daisy", *no monogram, good condition*	6.00	7.00
☐ Wm. Rogers & Son "Daisy", *no monogram, excellent condition*	8.00	9.00
☐ Wm. Rogers & Son "Victorian Rose", *no monogram, excellent condition*	7.00	8.00
☐ 1835 R. Wallace "Kings", *no monogram, excellent condition*	7.00	8.00
☐ 1847 Rogers "Ancestral", *no monogram, excellent condition*	7.00	8.00
☐ 1847 Rogers "Ancestral", *monogram, excellent condition* .	6.00	7.00
☐ 1847 Rogers "Anniversary", *no monogram, excellent condition*	7.00	8.00
☐ 1847 Rogers "Anniversary", *monogram, poor condition* ...	1.00	2.00
☐ 1847 Rogers "Anniversary", *no monogram, resilvered*	8.00	10.00
☐ 1847 Rogers "Arcadian", *no monogram, excellent condition*	10.00	12.00
☐ 1847 Rogers "Arcadian", *monogram, good condition*	5.00	6.00
☐ 1847 Rogers "Assyrian Head", *no monogram, good condition*	6.00	7.00
☐ 1847 Rogers "Assyrian Head", *no monogram, mint condition*	10.00	12.00
☐ 1847 Rogers "Avalon", *no monogram, excellent condition* .	7.00	8.00
☐ 1847 Rogers "Avalon", *no monogram, good condition*	2.00	3.00
☐ 1847 Rogers "Avon", *no monogram, excellent condition* ...	7.00	8.00
☐ 1847 Rogers "Avon", *monogram, excellent condition*	6.00	7.00
☐ 1847 Rogers "Berkshire", *no monogram, excellent condition*	9.00	10.00
☐ 1847 Rogers "Berkshire", *no monogram, mint condition* ...	10.00	12.00
☐ 1847 Rogers "Berkshire", *no monogram, excellent condition*	10.00	12.00
☐ 1847 Rogers "Berkshire", *no monogram, excellent condition*	12.00	14.00
☐ 1847 Rogers "Berkshire", *monogram, excellent condition* .	10.00	12.00
☐ 1847 Rogers "Charter Oak", *no monogram, excellent condition*	10.00	12.00
☐ 1847 Rogers "Charter Oak", *monogram, excellent condition*	15.00	17.00
☐ 1847 Rogers "Charter Oak", *no monogram, mint condition* .	18.00	20.00
☐ 1847 Rogers "Columbia", *no monogram, excellent condition*	2.00	3.00
☐ 1847 Rogers "Columbia", *no monogram, mint condition* ...	5.00	6.00
☐ 1847 Rogers "Cromwell", *no monogram, excellent condition*	2.00	3.00

	Price Range	

	Price Range	
☐ **1847 Rogers "Eternally Yours"**, *no monogram, excellent* condition	9.00	10.00
☐ **1847 Rogers "Eternally Yours"**, *no monogram, good condition*	5.00	6.00
☐ **1847 Rogers "Flair"**, *no monogram, excellent condition* ...	4.00	5.00
☐ **1847 Rogers "Flair"**, *monogram, good condition*	2.00	3.00
☐ **1847 Rogers "Floral"**, *no monogram, excellent condition* ..	10.00	12.00
☐ **1847 Rogers "Floral"**, *monogram, mint condition*	10.00	12.00
☐ **1847 Rogers "Heritage"**, *no monogram, excellent condition*	4.00	5.00
☐ **1847 Rogers "Heritage"**, *no monogram, fair condition*	1.00	2.00
☐ **1847 Rogers "Her Majesty"**, *no monogram, excellent condition*	3.00	4.00
☐ **1847 Rogers "Legacy"**, *no monogram, excellent condition* .	7.00	8.00
☐ **1847 Rogers "Legacy"**, *monogram, good condition*	1.00	2.00
☐ **1847 Rogers "Leilani"**, *no monogram, mint condition*	4.00	5.00
☐ **1847 Rogers "Leilani"**, *no monogram, mint condition*	5.00	6.00
☐ **1847 Rogers "Magic Rose"**, *no monogram, mint condition* .	4.00	5.00
☐ **1847 Rogers "Magic Rose"**, *monogram, good condition* ...	1.50	2.50
☐ **1847 Rogers "Marquise"**, *no monogram, excellent condition*	7.00	8.00
☐ **1847 Rogers "Marquise"**, *monogram, excellent condition* ..	6.00	7.00
☐ **1847 Rogers "Moselle"**, *no monogram, mint condition*	32.00	35.00
☐ **1847 Rogers "Moselle"**, *monogram, good condition*	10.00	12.00
☐ **1847 Rogers "Moselle"**, *monogram, fair condition*	3.00	4.00
☐ **1847 Rogers "Old Colony"**, *no monogram, excellent condition*	10.00	12.00
☐ **1847 Rogers "Old Colony"**, *monogram, excellent condition*	14.00	15.00
☐ **1847 Rogers "Priscilla"**, *no monogram, excellent condition*	7.00	8.00
☐ **1847 Rogers "Priscilla"**, *monogram, good condition*	1.00	2.00
☐ **1847 Rogers "Remembrance"**, *no monogram, excellent* condition	7.00	8.00
☐ **1847 Rogers "Remembrance"**, *no monogram, good condition*	4.00	5.00
☐ **1847 Rogers "Remembrance"**, *no monogram, excellent* condition	8.00	9.00
☐ **1847 Rogers "Sharon"**, *excellent condition*	5.00	6.00
☐ **1847 Rogers "Sharon"**, *no monogram, excellent condition* .	6.00	7.00
☐ **1847 Rogers "Shrewsbury"**, *no monogram, excellent condition*	8.00	9.00
☐ **1847 Rogers "Shrewsbury"**, *no monogram, good condition*	6.00	7.00
☐ **1847 Rogers "Vesta"**, *no monogram, excellent condition* ..	9.00	10.00
☐ **1847 Rogers "Vesta"**, *no monogram, good condition*	7.00	8.00
☐ **1847 Rogers "Vintage"**, *no monogram, excellent condition*	14.00	16.00
☐ **1847 Rogers "Vintage"**, *no monogram, excellent condition*	20.00	22.00
☐ **1847 Rogers "Vintage"**, *no monogram, resilvered*	26.00	28.00
☐ **1847 Rogers "Vintage"**, *no monogram, mint condition*	30.00	32.00
☐ **1847 Rogers "#2 Embossed"**, *no monogram, excellent condition*	4.00	5.00
☐ **1847 Rogers "#2 Embossed"**, *no monogram, mint condition*	6.00	7.00
☐ **1881 Rogers "Baroque Rose"**, *no monogram, mint condition*	3.00	4.00
☐ **1881 Rogers "Baroque Rose"**, *no monogram, excellent condition*	6.00	7.00

	Price Range	
☐ **1881 Rogers "LaVigne"**, *no monogram, excellent condition*	18.00	20.00
☐ **1881 Rogers "LaVigne"**, *no monogram, mint condition*	18.00	20.00
☐ **1881 Rogers "LaVigne"**, *monogram*	7.00	8.00
☐ **1881 Rogers "LaVigne"**, *no monogram, excellent condition*	16.00	18.00

(Sterling Silver)

☐ **Blackington & Co. "Sunflower"**, *no monogram, set of 12* ...	100.00	120.00
☐ **Durgin "Crysanthemum"**, *no monogram*	26.00	28.00
☐ **Fessenden "Langdon"**, *monogram*	10.00	12.00
☐ **Gorham "Cambridge"**, *monogram*	8.00	9.00
☐ **Gorham "Chantilly"**, *no monogram*	9.00	10.00
☐ **Gorham "English Gadroon"**, *monogram*	10.00	12.00
☐ **Gorham "Imperial Chrysanthemum"**, *no monogram*	10.00	12.00
☐ **International "Frontenac"**, *no monogram*	12.00	15.00
☐ **Lunt "Mt. Vernon"**, *no monogram*	9.00	10.00
☐ **Reed & Barton "Francis I"**, *no monogram*	10.00	12.00
☐ **Reed & Barton "LaParisienne"**, *no monogram*	10.00	12.00
☐ **Schofield "Baltimore Rose"**, *no monogram*	12.00	14.00
☐ **Simpson, Hall & Miller "Frontenac"**, *no monogram*	16.00	18.00
☐ **Simpson, Hall & Miller "Frontenac"**, *no monogram*	28.00	30.00
☐ **Wallace "Normandie"**, *monogram*	10.00	12.00
☐ **Watson "King George"**, *monogram*	10.00	12.00
☐ **Watson "Mt. Vernon"**, *monogram*	8.00	10.00
☐ **Whiting "Louis XV"**, *monogram*	8.00	10.00
☐ **Whiting "Louis XV"**, *no monogram*	12.00	15.00

COCKTAIL SHAKERS

These are not too often found in silver, but (as imagined) there was a certain market for them among individuals who wanted nothing but the best in everything. Of course silver contributed nothing to the flavor of the cocktail, but that was scarcely a consideration; nor was the fact that nine in ten onlookers automatically mistook a silver cocktail shaker for a stainless steel. Most specimens on the market date from the 1920's and 1930's. If there are dents — which frequently is the case, as cocktail shakers have thin walls — the value is diminshed.

(Silver-Plated and Crystal)

☐ **Hawkes crystal,** *cocktail shaker, silver-plated lid with glass body, slight wear on silver, signed*	20.00	22.00

COFFEEPOTS

Coffee was introduced into Europe in the 1600's and became immediately popular, to such extent that coffee houses (to serve the brew ready-made, along with foodstuffs if desired) opened all across the continent and especially in England, Ireland and Scotland. Tobacco smoking became popular at the same time, so the coffee house served as a refuge for indulging in both. Coffee making was approached as a fine art in the past, and even up to the fairly recent past. Coffee beans were bought whole at the market, out of huge canvas sacks, and ground at home — the browser amongst antiques has surely seen many early coffee grinders. Everything involved in the operation of coffee making was attended with care, and nearly everybody had their own opinions — often carefully guarded family secrets — on how best to do it. An absolutely clean coffeepot was one of the essentials. Metal was, therefore, generally preferred over porous materials. Because some individuals used rather bizarre cleaning techniques (lemon oil and vinegar, for example), the interiors of silver coffeepots are usually corroded to some extent. The prime era of the silver coffeepot in America lasted from about 1840 to 1890, but many specimens on the market are later. Colonial and early federal examples are of course the most highly prized. For these the collector may need to consult a specialist dealer or keep tabs on the auction scene.

Coffee Pot, *Tiffany and Company, part of five piece set, weight of set is 130 ounces, set price 4650.00*

(Silver-Plated)	Price Range	
☐ **Maker unknown,** *Victorian styling, tapered cylinder shape, fruit and floral swags engraved on body and lid, monogram, 8" H., excellent condition*	55.00	65.00
(Sterling Silver)		
☐ **Kalo,** *c. 1920, tall neck, ivory knop and handle insulators, 11" H., weight 27 oz.*	260.00	280.00
☐ **Webster & Son,** *repousse rose and leaf design, 9" H., footed*	42.00	50.00

COFFEE SETS
(Silver-Plated)

Price Range

☐ **Barbour,** *includes pot, creamer and sugar bowl, pedestal design, ornate floral and shell motif, gold wash interiors, monograms, good condition* 80.00   90.00

☐ **International,** *includes pot, creamer and sugar, and tray, flower and scroll borders, monogram and date, good condition* 140.00   150.00

(Sterling Silver)

☐ **Gorham "Plymouth",** *includes coffeepot, sugar and creamer, c. 1916, no monogram* 425.00   450.00

☐ **Maker unknown,** *Turkish shape, includes coffeepot, sugar and creamer, pot 8¼" H.* 26.00   28.00

☐ **Maker unknown,** *plain design, includes coffeepot, sugar and creamer, monogram, pot 6¾" H.* 250.00   275.00

☐ **Maker unknown,** *repousse design, with scalloped rims, open sugar, no monogram, coffeepot 8¼" H., sugar and creamer with gold wash interiors* 475.00   500.00

COFFEE SPOONS

Teaspoons can easily double for use with coffee, but to not have a specific utensil for this purpose would have seemed unfitting to our ancestors. The glory of silver was not its versatility but the very reverse of it — the fact that, with table silver, one could build a menagerie of decorative items in the excuse that each one served a designated function. This of course is all to the hobbyist's benefit, as it has placed hundreds of articles of silverware on today's antiques trade. Patterns found on coffee spoons are in general corresponding to those of tea spoons.

(Coin Silver)

☐ **Kirk "Repousse",** *no monogram* 22.00   24.00

(Silver-Plated)

☐ **Alvin "Brides Bouquet",** *monogram, excellent condition* . .   3.00   4.00

☐ **Alvin "Brides Bouquet",** *no monogram, excellent condition*   4.00   5.00

☐ **Community "Bird of Paradise",** *no monogram, excellent condition* 6.00   7.00

☐ **Community "Bird of Paradise",** *no monogram, fair condition* 1.00   2.00

☐ **Gorham "Providence",** *no monogram, excellent condition* .   5.00   6.00

☐ **Gorham "Providence",** *monogram, fair condition* 1.50   2.50

☐ **Holmes & Edwards "Carolina",** *no monogram, excellent condition* 4.00   5.00

☐ **Holmes & Edwards "Carolina",** *monogram, excellent condition* 2.00   3.00

☐ **Holmes & Edwards "Spring Garden",** *no monogram, good condition* 2.00   3.00

☐ **Holmes & Edwards "Spring Garden",** *no monogram, excellent condition* 5.00   6.00

☐ **Holmes & Edwards "Youth",** *no monogram, excellent condition* 5.00   6.00

☐ **Holmes & Edwards "Youth",** *no monogram, fair condition* .   1.00   2.00

☐ **Oxford "Narcissus",** *no monogram, fair condition* 1.00   2.00

	Price Range	
☐ Oxford "Narcissus", *no monogram, excellent condition* . . .	7.00	8.00
☐ Oxford "Narcissus", *monogram, excellent condition*	3.00	4.00
☐ Stratford "Shakespeare", *no monogram*	3.00	4.00
☐ Stratford "Shakespeare", *no monogram, excellent condition*	5.00	6.00
☐ Tudor "Royal York", *no monogram, good condition*	1.00	2.00
☐ Tudor "Royal York", *no monogram, excellent condition* . . .	5.00	6.00
☐ Wm. Rogers "Berwick", *no monogram, good condition*	4.00	5.00
☐ Wm. Rogers "Berwick", *monogram, fair condition*	1.50	2.50
☐ Wm. Rogers "Fairoaks", *no monogram, excellent condition*	5.00	6.00
☐ 1835 R. Wallace "Blossom", *monogram, excellent condition*	3.00	4.00
☐ 1847 Rogers "Old Colony", *monogram, mint condition*	5.00	6.00
☐ 1847 Rogers "Remembrance", *no monogram, good condition*	3.00	4.00
☐ 1847 Rogers "Remembrance", *no monogram, excellent condition*	4.00	5.00
☐ 1847 Rogers "Vintage", *no monogram, mint condition*	10.00	12.00

(Sterling Silver)

☐ Durgin "Hunt Club", *no monogram*	6.00	7.00
☐ Gorham "Luxembourg", *monogram*	11.00	13.00
☐ Gorham, *pattern unknown, monogram, set of six*	28.00	30.00
☐ International "Avalon", *monogram*	14.00	16.00
☐ International "Pine Tree", *no monogram*	10.00	12.00
☐ Kirk, *unknown plain pattern, monogram, set of six*	34.00	36.00
☐ Reed & Barton "Love Disarmed", *no monogram*	36.00	38.00
☐ Reed & Barton "Love Disarmed", *no monogram, bowl needs reshaping*	14.00	16.00
☐ Simpson, Hall & Miller "Frontenac", *no monogram*	10.00	12.00
☐ Towle "Old Colonial", *no monogram*	10.00	12.00
☐ Whiting "Empire", *no monogram*	9.00	11.00
☐ Whiting "Lily", *monogram*	9.00	11.00
☐ Whiting "Lily", *no monogram*	13.00	15.00
☐ Maker unknown, *ornate floral pattern, no monogram*	8.00	9.00

COLD MEAT FORKS

Did Victorian zest for diversity in silverware actually extend to the point of using certain forks for hot meat and certain others for cold? In a way it did. "Cold meat" was the 19th century terminology for what we now call "luncheon meat," or, more colloquially, "cold cuts." At that time, sliced cold luncheon meat was a new addition to the table. The sheer novelty of it won favor for it in the highest of high society (which happened to the lowly hotdog, too, when it was introduced into Britain from America). The general use of the cold meat fork was to transfer slices from the serving platter to one's dish. Many different types were made.

(Silver-Plated)

☐ Alvin "Diana", *no monogram, excellent condition*	12.00	14.00
☐ Alvin "Diana", *no monogram, good condition*	8.00	9.00
☐ Alvin "Diana", *no monogram, fair condition*	5.00	6.00
☐ American Silver Company "Berlin", *no monogram, excellent condition*	4.00	5.00

	Price Range	
☐ Community "Adam", *no monogram, good condition*	9.00	11.00
☐ Community "Adam", *no monogram, good condition*	10.00	11.00
☐ Community "Avalon", *no monogram, good condition*	11.00	13.00
☐ Community "Avalon", *no monogram, fair condition*	8.00	9.00
☐ Community "Ballad", *no monogram, mint condition*	6.00	7.00
☐ Community "Ballad", *no monogram, excellent condition* ..	8.00	9.00
☐ Community "Bedford", *no monogram, mint condition*	6.00	7.00
☐ Community "Bird of Paradise", *no monogram, excellent condition*	12.00	14.00
☐ Community "Bird of Paradise", *no monogram, good condition*	9.00	10.00
☐ Community "Coronation", *no monogram, good condition* .	8.00	9.00
☐ Community "Coronation", *no monogram, mint condition* ..	9.00	10.00
☐ Community "Coronation", *no monogram, excellent condition*	14.00	15.00
☐ Community "Enchantment", *no monogram, excellent condition*	14.00	15.00
☐ Community "Enchantment", *no monogram, good condition*	10.00	11.00
☐ Community "Evening Star", *no monogram, excellent condition*	9.00	10.00
☐ Community "Evening Star", *no monogram, good condition*	11.00	13.00
☐ Community "Evening Star", *no monogram, fair condition* ..	3.00	4.00
☐ Community "Forever", *no monogram, excellent condition* .	14.00	15.00
☐ Community "Forever", *no monogram, good condition*	6.00	7.00
☐ Community "Flight", *no monogram, mint condition*	6.00	7.00
☐ Community "Flight", *no monogram, excellent condition* ..	12.00	13.00
☐ Community "Georgian", *no monogram, excellent condition*	7.00	8.00
☐ Community "Georgian", *no monogram, excellent condition*	12.00	14.00
☐ Community "Georgian", *no monogram, good condition* ...	8.00	9.00
☐ Community "King Cedric", *no monogram, good condition* .	11.00	13.00
☐ Community "King Cedric", *no monogram, fair condition* ..	6.00	7.00
☐ Community "Lady Hamilton", *no monogram, excellent condition*	14.00	15.00
☐ Community "Lady Hamilton", *no monogram, good condition*	9.00	11.00
☐ Community "Milady", *no monogram, excellent condition* ..	12.00	14.00
☐ Community "Milady", *no monogram, good condition*	4.00	5.00
☐ Community "Modjeska", *no monogram, good condition* ...	9.00	10.00
☐ Community "Modjeska", *no monogram, fair condition*	4.00	5.00
☐ Community "Morning Rose", *no monogram, mint condition*	6.00	7.00
☐ Community "Morning Rose", *no monogram, excellent condition*	14.00	15.00
☐ Community "Morning Star", *no monogram, mint condition*	8.00	9.00
☐ Community "Morning Star", *no monogram, excellent condition*	13.00	14.00
☐ Community "Noblesse", *monogram, excellent condition* ..	6.00	7.00
☐ Community "Patrician", *no monogram, excellent condition*	7.00	8.00
☐ Community "Patrician", *monogram, excellent condition* ..	2.00	3.00
☐ Community "Patrician", *no monogram, good condition* ...	11.00	13.00
☐ Community "Patrician", *no monogram, excellent condition*	13.00	15.00
☐ Community "Paul Revere", *no monogram, excellent condition*	7.00	8.00
☐ Community "Paul Revere", *no monogram, excellent condition*	13.00	15.00

	Price Range	
☐ **Community "Paul Revere"**, *no monogram, fair condition* . .	3.00	4.00
☐ **Community "Sheraton"**, *no monogram, excellent condition*	7.00	8.00
☐ **Community "Silver Flowers"**, *no monogram, excellent condition*	13.00	15.00
☐ **Community "Silver Flowers"**, *no monogram, excellent condition*	10.00	12.00
☐ **Community "Silver Sands"**, *no monogram, mint condition* .	6.00	7.00
☐ **Community "Silver Sands"**, *no monogram, excellent condition*	12.00	14.00
☐ **Community "Silver Valentine"**, *no monogram, mint condition*	7.00	8.00
☐ **Community "South Seas"**, *no monogram, excellent condition*	13.00	15.00
☐ **Community "South Seas"**, *no monogram, poor condition* . .	1.00	2.00
☐ **Community "South Seas"**, *no monogram, fair condition* . . .	3.00	4.00
☐ **Community "Tangier"**, *no monogram, mint condition*	6.00	7.00
☐ **Community "Tangier"**, *no monogram, excellent condition* .	13.00	15.00
☐ **Community "White Orchid"**, *no monogram, mint condition*	6.00	7.00
☐ **Community "White Orchid"**, *no monogram, excellent condition*	13.00	15.00
☐ **Community "White Orchid"**, *no monogram, excellent condition*	10.00	12.00
☐ **Community "White Orchid"**, *no monogram, fair condition* .	2.00	3.00
☐ **DeepSilver "Laurel Mist"**, *no monogram, excellent condition*	13.00	15.00
☐ **DeepSilver "Wakefield"**, *no monogram, excellent condition*	13.00	15.00
☐ **DeepSilver "Wakefield"**, *no monogram, fair condition*	2.00	3.00
☐ **Gorham "Carolina"**, *no monogram, mint condition*	8.00	9.00
☐ **Gorham "Carolina"**, *no monogram, excellent condition* . . .	13.00	15.00
☐ **Gorham "Providence"**, *no monogram, fair condition*	2.00	3.00
☐ **Harmony House "Serenade"**, *no monogram, excellent condition*	4.00	5.00
☐ **Harmony House "Serenade"**, *no monogram, excellent condition*	12.00	13.00
☐ **Holmes & Edwards "Carolina"**, *no monogram, good condition*	12.00	13.00
☐ **Holmes & Edwards "Carolina"**, *no monogram, fair condition*	2.00	3.00
☐ **Holmes & Edwards "Century"**, *no monogram, good condition*	12.00	13.00
☐ **Holmes & Edwards "Century"**, *no monogram, excellent condition*	14.00	15.00
☐ **Holmes & Edwards "Charm"**, *no monogram, excellent condition*	14.00	15.00
☐ **Holmes & Edwards "Charm"**, *no monogram, good condition*	5.00	6.00
☐ **Holmes & Edwards "Danish Princess"**, *no monogram, excellent condition*	14.00	15.00
☐ **Holmes & Edwards "Danish Princess"**, *no monogram, excellent condition*	9.00	11.00
☐ **Holmes & Edwards "Danish Princess"**, *no monogram, fair condition*	2.00	3.00
☐ **Holmes & Edwards "Dolly Madison"**, *no monogram, excellent condition*	6.00	7.00

	Price Range	
☐ Holmes & Edwards "Dolly Madison", *no monogram, excellent condition*	13.00	14.00
☐ Holmes & Edwards "Lafayette", *no monogram, excellent condition*	8.00	9.00
☐ Holmes & Edwards "Orient", *no monogram, excellent condition*	8.00	9.00
☐ Holmes & Edwards "Orient", *no monogram, fair condition*	2.00	3.00
☐ Holmes & Edwards "Triumph", *no monogram, excellent condition*	2.00	3.00
☐ International "Orleans", *no monogram, excellent condition*	9.00	11.00
☐ International "Silver Tulip", *no monogram, excellent condition*	6.00	7.00
☐ International "Silver Tulip", *no monogram, excellent condition*	11.00	13.00
☐ National "King Edward", *no monogram, excellent condition*	14.00	15.00
☐ Nobility "Royal Rose", *no monogram, excellent condition*	14.00	15.00
☐ Nobility "Royal Rose", *no monogram, good condition*	8.00	9.00
☐ Oneida "Bridal Wreath", *no monogram, excellent condition*	12.00	14.00
☐ Oneida "Bridal Wreath", *no monogram, good condition*	7.00	9.00
☐ Oneida "Flower de Luce", *no monogram, excellent condition*	14.00	15.00
☐ Oneida "Flower de Luce", *no monogram, good condition*	7.00	8.00
☐ Oneida "Flower de Luce", *no monogram, good condition*	10.00	12.00
☐ Oneida "Jamestown", *monogram, excellent condition*	4.00	5.00
☐ Oneida "Louis XVI", *no monogram, excellent condition*	7.00	8.00
☐ Oneida "Louis XVI", *no monogram, good condition*	7.00	8.00
☐ Oxford "Narcissus", *no monogram, excellent condition*	9.00	10.00
☐ Oxford "Narcissus", *no monogram, excellent condition*	14.00	15.00
☐ Oxford "Narcissus", *no monogram, fair condition*	4.00	5.00
☐ R.C. Co. "Isabella", *no monogram, excellent condition*	16.00	18.00
☐ Reed & Barton "Carlton", *no monogram, fair condition*	7.00	8.00
☐ Reed & Barton "Carlton", *no monogram, excellent condition*	14.00	16.00
☐ Reed & Barton "Jewell", *no monogram, excellent condition*	12.00	14.00
☐ Reed & Barton "Jewell", *no monogram, good condition*	10.00	12.00
☐ Reed & Barton "Oxford", *no monogram, excellent condition*	10.00	12.00
☐ Reed & Barton "Oxford", *no monogram, good condition*	8.00	9.00
☐ Reed & Barton "Sheffield", *no monogram, excellent condition*	15.00	17.00
☐ Reed & Barton "Sheffield", *no monogram, fair condition*	4.00	5.00
☐ Reed & Barton "Thistle", *no monogram, excellent condition*	13.00	15.00
☐ Reed & Barton "Tiger Lily", *no monogram, excellent condition*	24.00	26.00
☐ Rockford "Fairoaks", *no monogram, excellent condition*	12.00	14.00
☐ Rockford "Fairoaks", *no monogram, good condition*	8.00	9.00
☐ Rogers "Alhambra", *no monogram, excellent condition*	10.00	14.00
☐ Rogers "Alhambra", *no monogram, excellent condition*	14.00	15.00
☐ Rogers "Burgundy", *no monogram, excellent condition*	14.00	15.00
☐ Rogers "Burgundy", *no monogram, good condition*	11.00	13.00
☐ Rogers "Carlton", *no monogram, excellent condition*	13.00	15.00
☐ Rogers "Carlton", *no monogram, good condition*	10.00	12.00
☐ Rogers "Croyden", *no monogram, good condition*	7.00	8.00
☐ Rogers "Croyden", *no monogram, excellent condition*	9.00	10.00
☐ Rogers "Desire", *no monogram, excellent condition*	14.00	15.00

	Price Range	
☐ Rogers "Desire", *no monogram, poor condition*	1.00	2.00
☐ Rogers "Grenoble", *no monogram, good condition*	13.00	15.00
☐ Rogers "Grenoble", *no monogram, fair condition*	3.00	4.00
☐ Rogers "Kensington", *no monogram, mint condition*	9.00	10.00
☐ Rogers "Kensington", *no monogram, good condition*	8.00	9.00
☐ Rogers "Mayflower", *no monogram, excellent condition* ..	12.00	14.00
☐ Rogers "Vendome", *no monogram, excellent condition* ...	12.00	14.00
☐ Rogers "Vendrome", *no monogram, good condition*	6.00	7.00
☐ Rogers & Bro. "Aldine", *no monogram, excellent condition*	12.00	14.00
☐ Rogers & Bro. "Cromwell", *no monogram, excellent condition*	3.00	4.00
☐ Rogers & Bro. "Daybreak", *no monogram, excellent condition*	13.00	15.00
☐ Rogers & Bro. "Daybreak", *no monogram, good condition* .	12.00	13.00
☐ Rogers & Bro. "Flemish", *no monogram, excellent condition*	12.00	13.00
☐ Rogers & Bro. "Flemish", *no monogram, excellent condition*	12.00	14.00
☐ Rogers & Bro. "Florette", *no monogram, excellent condition*	16.00	18.00
☐ Rogers & Bro. "Florette", *no monogram, excellent condition*	26.00	28.00
☐ Rogers & Bro. "Laurel", *no monogram, excellent condition*	3.00	4.00
☐ Rogers & Bro. "Laurel", *no monogram, excellent condition*	3.00	4.00
☐ Rogers & Bro. "Navarre", *no monogram, excellent condition*	10.00	12.00
☐ Rogers & Bro. "Navarre", *no monogram, good condition* ..	10.00	12.00
☐ Rogers & Bro. "New Century", *no monogram, excellent condition*	10.00	12.00
☐ Rogers & Bro. "New Century", *no monogram, excellent condition*	12.00	14.00
☐ Rogers & Bro. "New Century", *no monogram, fair condition*	3.00	4.00
☐ Rogers & Hamilton "Raphael", *no monogram, excellent condition*	13.00	15.00
☐ Rogers & Hamilton "Raphael", *no monogram, excellent condition*	24.00	26.00
☐ Rogers & Hamilton "Raphael", *no monogram, good condition*	13.00	15.00
☐ Rogers & Hamilton "Raphael", *monogram, good condition*	8.00	9.00
☐ Rogers & Hamilton "Raphael", *no monogram, fair condition*	5.00	6.00
☐ Rogers & Hamilton "Raphael", *no monogram, poor condition*	1.00	2.00
☐ S.L. & G.H. Rogers "Arcadia", *no monogram, excellent condition*	12.00	14.00
☐ S.L. & G.H. Rogers "Encore", *no monogram, excellent condition*	7.00	8.00
☐ S.L. & G.H. Rogers "Encore", *no monogram, excellent condition*	12.00	14.00
☐ S.L. & G.H. Rogers "English Garden", *no monogram, excellent condition*	12.00	14.00
☐ S.L. & G.H. Rogers "English Garden", *no monogram, good condition*	8.00	9.00

Price Range

☐ **S.L. & G.H. Rogers "Lakewood"**, *no monogram, good condition* 12.00   13.00

☐ **S.L. & G.H. Rogers "Lakewood"**, *no monogram, excellent condition* 12.00   14.00

☐ **S.L. & G.H. Rogers "Lexington"**, *no monogram, good condition* 12.00   14.00

☐ **S.L. & G.H. Rogers "Lexington"**, *no monogram, excellent condition* 12.00   14.00

☐ **S.L. & G.H. Rogers "Webster I"**, *no monogram, fair condition* 6.00   7.00

☐ **S.L. & G.H. Rogers "Webster I"**, *no monogram, excellent condition* 10.00   12.00

☐ **S.L. & G.H. Rogers "Webster II"**, *no monogram, excellent condition* 14.00   15.00

☐ **S.L. & G.H. Rogers "Webster II"**, *no monogram, good condition* 12.00   13.00

☐ **S.L. & G.H. Rogers "Webster II"**, *no monogram, fair condition* 1.00   2.00

☐ **Stratford "Lilytha"**, *no monogram, excellent condition* 11.00   13.00

☐ **Stratford "Lilytha"**, *no monogram, good condition* 10.00   12.00

☐ **Towle "Arundel"**, *no monogram, excellent condition* 16.00   18.00

☐ **Towle "Byfield"**, *no monogram, mint condition* 5.00   6.00

☐ **Towle "Byfield"**, *no monogram, fair condition* 2.00   3.00

☐ **Towle "Chester"**, *no monogram, excellent condition* 8.00   9.00

☐ **Towle "Chester"**, *no monogram, good condition* 8.00   9.00

☐ **Tudor "Bridal Wreath"**, *monogram, mint condition* 7.00   9.00

☐ **Tudor "Duchess"**, *no monogram, excellent condition* 10.00   12.00

☐ **Tudor "Duchess"**, *no monogram, good condition* 8.00   10.00

☐ **Tudor "Queen Bess II"**, *no monogram, excellent condition* . 12.00   14.00

☐ **Tudor "Queen Bess II"**, *no monogram, good condition* 12.00   16.00

☐ **Tudor "Queen Bess II"**, *no monogram, fair condition* 3.00   4.00

☐ **Tudor "Sweetbriar"**, *no monogram, excellent condition* ... 10.00   12.00

☐ **Tudor "Sweetbriar"**, *no monogram, good condition* 8.00   9.00

☐ **Tudor "Together"**, *no monogram, mint condition* 8.00   9.00

☐ **Tudor "Together"**, *no monogram, good condition* 8.00   9.00

☐ **Wallace "Floral"**, *no monogram, excellent condition* 24.00   26.00

☐ **Wallace "Southgate"**, *no monogram, excellent condition* .. 12.00   14.00

☐ **Wallace "Southgate"**, *no monogram, fair condition* 3.00   4.00

☐ **W.D. Smith "Adam"**, *monogram, excellent condition* 6.00   7.00

☐ **W.D. Smith "Adam"**, *no monogram, fair condition* 2.00   3.00

☐ **Williams Bros. "Isabella"**, *no monogram, excellent condition* 15.00   17.00

☐ **Williams Bros. "Isabella"**, *no monogram, excellent condition* 18.00   20.00

☐ **Wm. A. Rogers "Chalice"**, *monogram, excellent condition* . 12.00   14.00

☐ **Wm. A. Rogers "Chalice"**, *no monogram, good condition* .. 10.00   12.00

☐ **Wm. A. Rogers "LaVigne"**, *no monogram, good to excellent condition* 26.00   28.00

☐ **Wm. A. Rogers "LaVigne"**, *no monogram, good condition* . 14.00   16.00

☐ **Wm. A. Rogers "LaVigne"**, *no monogram, fair condition* ... 8.00   10.00

☐ **Wm. A. Rogers "LaRonnie"**, *no monogram, excellent condition* 12.00   14.00

☐ **Wm. A. Rogers "LaRonnie"**, *no monogram, good condition* 8.00   12.00

	Price Range	
☐ Wm. A. Rogers "Malibu", *no monogram, excellent condition*	12.00	14.00
☐ Wm. A. Rogers "Malibu", *no monogram, good condition*	8.00	10.00
☐ Wm. A. Rogers "Meadowbrook", *no monogram, excellent condition*	3.00	4.00
☐ Wm. A. Rogers "Meadowbrook", *no monogram, excellent condition*	10.00	12.00
☐ Wm. A. Rogers "Meadowbrook", *no monogram, good condition*	8.00	10.00
☐ Wm. A. Rogers "Meadowbrook", *no monogram, fair condition*	1.00	2.00
☐ Wm. A. Rogers "Old South", *no monogram, excellent condition*	12.00	14.00
☐ Wm. A. Rogers "Rendezvous", *no monogram, excellent condition*	12.00	14.00
☐ Wm. A. Rogers "Rosalie", *no monogram, excellent condition*	12.00	14.00
☐ Wm. A. Rogers "Rosalie", *good condition*	8.00	9.00
☐ Wm. A. Rogers "Warwick", *no monogram, excellent condition*	12.00	14.00
☐ Wm. A. Rogers "Warwick", *no monogram, fair condition*	2.00	3.00
☐ Wm. Rogers "Arbutus", *no monogram, excellent condition*	15.00	18.00
☐ Wm. Rogers "Arbutus", *no monogram, fair condition*	4.00	5.00
☐ Wm. Rogers "Berwick", *no monogram, excellent condition*	18.00	20.00
☐ Wm. Rogers "Berwick", *no monogram, good condition*	14.00	15.00
☐ Wm. Rogers "Berwick", *monogram, good condition*	5.00	6.00
☐ Wm. Rogers "Bridal Bouquet", *no monogram, excellent condition*	8.00	9.00
☐ Wm. Rogers "Cordova", *no monogram, good condition*	13.00	15.00
☐ Wm. Rogers "Cromwell", *no monogram, excellent condition*	3.00	4.00
☐ Wm. Rogers "Debutante", *no monogram, excellent condition*	13.00	15.00
☐ Wm. Rogers "Exquisite", *no monogram, excellent condition*	13.00	15.00
☐ Wm. Rogers "Exquisite", *no monogram, good condition*	10.00	12.00
☐ Wm. Rogers "Fair Lady", *no monogram, excellent condition*	10.00	12.00
☐ Wm. Rogers "Fair Lady", *no monogram, fair condition*	3.00	4.00
☐ Wm. Rogers "Flower", *no monogram, excellent condition*	11.00	13.00
☐ Wm. Rogers "Grand Elegance", *no monogram, excellent condition*	8.00	9.00
☐ Wm. Rogers "Hostess", *no monogram, good condition*	10.00	12.00
☐ Wm. Rogers "Hostess", *no monogram, excellent condition*	12.00	14.00
☐ Wm. Rogers "Magnolia", *no monogram, excellent condition*	4.00	5.00
☐ Wm. Rogers "Magnolia", *no monogram, fair condition*	2.00	3.00
☐ Wm. Rogers "Mayfair", *no monogram, excellent condition*	13.00	15.00
☐ Wm. Rogers "Mayfair", *no monogram, good condition*	10.00	12.00
☐ Wm. Rogers "Spring Charm", *no monogram, excellent condition*	13.00	15.00
☐ Wm. Rogers "Starlight", *no monogram, excellent condition*	13.00	15.00
☐ Wm. Rogers "Treasure", *no monogram, excellent condition*	13.00	15.00

	Price Range	

☐ **Wm. Rogers "Treasure"**, *no monogram, good condition* . . .   11.00   13.00

☐ **Wm. Rogers Eagle "Berwick"**, *no monogram, excellent condition* 24.00   26.00

☐ **Wm. Rogers Eagle "Cedric"**, *monogram, excellent condition* 13.00   15.00

☐ **Wm. Rogers Eagle "Cedric"**, *no monogram, good condition*   14.00   16.00

☐ **Wm. Rogers Mfg. Co. "Alhambra"**, *monogram, good condition* 12.00   14.00

☐ **Wm. Rogers Mfg. Co. "Alhambra"**, *no monogram, excellent condition* 26.00   28.00

☐ **Wm. Rogers Mfg. Co. "Grand Elegance"**, *no monogram, good condition* 10.00   12.00

☐ **Wm. Rogers Mfg. Co. "Grand Elegance"**, *no monogram, excellent condition* 12.00   14.00

☐ **Wm. Rogers Mfg. Co. "Grand Elegance"**, *no monogram, fair condition* 1.00   2.00

☐ **Wm. Rogers Mfg. Co. "Kensington"**, *no monogram, excellent condition* 4.00   5.00

☐ **Wm. Rogers Mfg. Co. "Kensington"**, *no monogram, excellent condition* 10.00   12.00

☐ **Wm. Rogers Mfg. Co. "Magnolia"**, *no monogram, good condition* 10.00   12.00

☐ **Wm. Rogers Mfg. Co. "Magnolia"**, *no monogram, fair condition* 1.00   2.00

☐ **Wm. Rogers Mfg. Co. "Puritan"**, *no monogram, excellent condition* 6.00   7.00

☐ **Wm. Rogers Mfg. Co. "Sovereign"**, *no monogram, excellent condition* 12.00   14.00

☐ **Wm. Rogers Mfg. Co. "Sovereign"**, *no monogram, good condition* 4.00   5.00

☐ **Wm. Rogers & Son "Arbutus"**, *no monogram, good condition* 11.00   13.00

☐ **Wm. Rogers & Son "Arbutus"**, *no monogram, excellent condition* 13.00   15.00

☐ **Wm. Rogers & Son "Arbutus"**, *no monogram, mint condition* 16.00   18.00

☐ **Wm. Rogers & Son "Floral Bouquet"**, *no monogram, excellent condition* 13.00   15.00

☐ **Wm. Rogers & Son "Floral Bouquet"**, *no monogram, good condition* 8.00   10.00

☐ **Wm. Rogers & Son "Oxford"**, *no monogram, excellent condition* 12.00   14.00

☐ **Wm. Rogers & Son "Oxford"**, *monogram, excellent condition* 6.00   8.00

☐ **Wm. Rogers & Son "Oxford"**, *no monogram, good condition* 10.00   12.00

☐ **Wm. Rogers & Son "Primrose"**, *no monogram, fair condition* 4.00   5.00

☐ **Wm. Rogers & Son "Primrose I"**, *no monogram, good condition* 9.00   11.00

☐ **Wm. Rogers & Son "Primrose II"**, *no monogram, good condition* 10.00   12.00

☐ **Wm. Rogers & Son "Primrose II"**, *no monogram, excellent condition* 12.00   14.00

	Price Range	
☐ World "Franconia", *no monogram, excellent condition*	12.00	14.00
☐ 1835 R. Wallace "Floral", *no monogram, good condition* ..	18.00	20.00
☐ 1835 R. Wallace "Floral", *no monogram, excellent condition*	18.00	20.00
☐ 1835 R. Wallace "Floral", *monogram, excellent condition* ..	15.00	17.00
☐ 1835 R. Wallace "Joan", *monogram, good condition*	8.00	10.00
☐ 1835 R. Wallace "Joan", *no monogram, gold wash tines, mint condition*	18.00	20.00
☐ 1835 R. Wallace "Laurel", *no monogram, fair condition* ...	5.00	6.00
☐ 1835 R. Wallace "Laurel", *no monogram, good condition* ..	11.00	13.00
☐ 1847 Rogers "Ancestral", *no monogram, excellent condition*	13.00	15.00
☐ 1847 Rogers "Ancestral", *no monogram, good condition* ..	11.00	13.00
☐ 1847 Rogers "Anniversary", *no monogram, excellent condition*	13.00	15.00
☐ 1847 Rogers "Anniversary", *no monogram, good condition*	10.00	12.00
☐ 1847 Rogers "Argosy'", *no monogram, excellent condition*	12.00	14.00
☐ 1847 Rogers "Assyrian Head", *monogram, good condition*	10.00	12.00
☐ 1847 Rogers "Assyrian Head", *no monogram, excellent condition*	24.00	26.00
☐ 1847 Rogers "Assyrian Head", *no monogram, good condition*	18.00	20.00
☐ 1847 Rogers "Assyrian Head", *no monogram, fair condition*	7.00	9.00
☐ 1847 Rogers "Avon", *no monogram, excellent condition* ...	16.00	18.00
☐ 1847 Rogers "Avon", *no monogram, good condition*	14.00	16.00
☐ 1847 Rogers "Berkshire", *no monogram, excellent condition*	16.00	18.00
☐ 1847 Rogers "Berkshire", *no monogram, excellent condition*	18.00	22.00
☐ 1847 Rogers "Berkshire", *no monogram, good condition* ..	14.00	16.00
☐ 1847 Rogers "Berkshire", *monogram, good condition*	8.00	10.00
☐ 1847 Rogers "Berkshire", *monogram, fair condition*	5.00	6.00
☐ 1847 Rogers "Berkshire", *monogram, poor condition*	2.00	3.00
☐ 1847 Rogers "Charter Oak", *no monogram, resilvered* ...	15.00	18.00
☐ 1847 Rogers "Charter Oak", *no monogram, excellent condition*	16.00	18.00
☐ 1847 Rogers "Charter Oak", *no monogram, good condition*	11.00	13.00
☐ 1847 Rogers "Charter Oak", *no monogram, excellent condition*	18.00	20.00
☐ 1847 Rogers "Charter Oak", *no monogram, excellent condition*	18.00	20.00
☐ 1847 Rogers "Charter Oak", *no monogram, excellent condition*	28.00	30.00
☐ 1847 Rogers "Charter Oak", *no monogram, good condition*	18.00	22.00
☐ 1847 Rogers "Charter Oak", *no monogram, fair condition* ..	7.00	8.00
☐ 1847 Rogers "Charter Oak", *no monogram, poor condition* .	2.00	3.00
☐ 1847 Rogers "Continental", *no monogram, excellent condition*	7.00	8.00
☐ 1847 Rogers "Daffodil", *no monogram, good condition*	7.00	8.00
☐ 1847 Rogers "Daffodil", *no monogram, excellent condition*	10.00	12.00
☐ 1847 Rogers "Daffodil", *no monogram, excellent condition*	10.00	12.00
☐ 1847 Rogers "Daffodil II", *no monogram, excellent condition*	12.00	14.00

	Price Range	

☐ **1847 Rogers "Daffodil II"**, *no monogram, good condition* .. 10.00 12.00
☐ **1847 Rogers "Esperanto"**, *no monogram, excellent condition* 10.00 12.00
☐ **1847 Rogers "Esperanto"**, *no monogram, poor condition* .. 1.00 2.00
☐ **1847 Rogers "Eternally Yours"**, *no monogram, excellent condition* 14.00 15.00
☐ **1847 Rogers "Eternally Yours"**, *no monogram, good condition* 10.00 12.00
☐ **1847 Rogers "Faneuil"**, *no monogram, excellent condition* 12.00 14.00
☐ **1847 Rogers "Faneuil"**, *no monogram, excellent condition* 12.00 14.00
☐ **1847 Rogers "Flair"**, *no monogram, excellent condition* ... 6.00 7.00
☐ **1847 Rogers "Flair"**, *monogram, excellent condition* 4.00 5.00
☐ **1847 Rogers "Flair"**, *no monogram, excellent condition* ... 12.00 14.00
☐ **1847 Rogers "Floral"**, *no monogram, good condition* 14.00 16.00
☐ **1847 Rogers "Floral"**, *no monogram, excellent condition* .. 28.00 30.00
☐ **1847 Rogers "Floral"**, *no monogram, good condition* 16.00 18.00
☐ **1847 Rogers "Floral"**, *no monogram, fair condition* 7.00 8.00
☐ **1847 Rogers "Grand Heritage"**, *no monogram, excellent condition* 5.00 6.00
☐ **1847 Rogers "Heraldic"**, *no monogram, excellent condition* 8.00 10.00
☐ **1847 Rogers "Legacy"**, *no monogram, excellent condition* . 12.00 14.00
☐ **1847 Rogers "Legacy"**, *no monogram, good condition* 12.00 14.00
☐ **1847 Rogers "Louvain"**, *no monogram, excellent condition*. 12.00 14.00
☐ **1847 Rogers "Magic Rose"**, *no monogram, mint condition* . 6.00 7.00
☐ **1847 Rogers "Magic Rose"**, *no monogram, excellent condition* 12.00 14.00
☐ **1847 Rogers "Norfolk"**, *no monogram, mint condition* 10.00 12.00
☐ **1847 Rogers "Old Colony"**, *no monogram, excellent condition* 10.00 12.00
☐ **1847 Rogers "Old Colony"**, *no monogram, excellent condition* 12.00 13.00
☐ **1847 Rogers "Old Colony"**, *no monogram, excellent condition* 22.00 25.00
☐ **1847 Rogers "Old Colony"**, *no monogram, good condition* . 10.00 12.00
☐ **1847 Rogers "Old Colony"**, *no monogram, fair condition* ... 2.00 8.00
☐ **1847 Rogers "Queen Ann"**, *no monogram, excellent condition* 12.00 14.00
☐ **1847 Rogers "Reflection"**, *no monogram, excellent condition* 10.00 12.00
☐ **1847 Rogers "Reflection"**, *no monogram, good condition* .. 8.00 9.00
☐ **1847 Rogers "Sharon"**, *monogram, excellent condition* 18.00 20.00
☐ **1847 Rogers "Sharon"**, *no monogram, excellent condition* . 22.00 25.00
☐ **1847 Rogers "Vesta"**, *no monogram, excellent condition* .. 12.00 14.00
☐ **1847 Rogers "Vintage"**, *no monogram, resilvered* 18.00 20.00
☐ **1847 Rogers "Vintage"**, *no monogram, excellent condition* . 18.00 22.00
☐ **1847 Rogers "Vintage"**, *no monogram, mint condition* 22.00 24.00
☐ **1847 Rogers "Vintage"**, *no monogram, excellent condition* . 22.00 24.00
☐ **1847 Rogers "Vintage"**, *no monogram, excellent condition* . 28.00 30.00
☐ **1881 Rogers "Capri"**, *no monogram, excellent condition* ... 12.00 14.00
☐ **1881 Rogers "Capri"**, *no monogram, good condition* 10.00 12.00
☐ **1881 Rogers "Chippendale"**, *no monogram, excellent condition* 12.00 14.00
☐ **1881 Rogers "Chippendale"**, *no monogram, fair condition* . 4.00 5.00

	Price Range	

☐ **1881 Rogers "Flirtation"**, *no monogram, excellent condition* 9.00 11.00
☐ **1881 Rogers "Flirtation"**, *no monogram, excellent condition* 10.00 12.00
☐ **1881 Rogers "Grecian"**, *no monogram, good condition* 10.00 12.00
☐ **1881 Rogers "LaVigne"**, *no monogram, excellent condition* 24.00 26.00
☐ **1881 Rogers "LaVigne"**, *no monogram, excellent condition* 20.00 22.00
☐ **1881 Rogers "LaVigne"**, *no monogram, good condition* 16.00 18.00
☐ **1881 Rogers "LaVigne"**, *no monogram, fair condition* 3.00 4.00
☐ **1881 Rogers "Plantation"**, *no monogram, excellent condition* 12.00 14.00
☐ **1881 Rogers "Proposal"**, *no monogram, excellent condition* 14.00 16.00
☐ **1881 Rogers "Proposal"**, *no monogram, good condition* ... 10.00 12.00

(Sterling Silver)

☐ **Alvin "Bridal Rose"**, *no monogram, 7⅝" L.* 50.00 60.00
☐ **Alvin "Maryland"**, *monogram* 16.00 18.00
☐ **Dominick & Haff "Rococo"**, *monogram, 8⅝" L.* 45.00 55.00
☐ **Fine Arts "Processional"**, *no monogram* 30.00 32.00
☐ **Gorham "Buttercup"**, *no monogram* 38.00 40.00
☐ **Gorham "Chantilly"**, *monogram* 30.00 32.00
☐ **Gorham "Chantilly"**, *no monogram* 42.00 44.00
☐ **Gorham "Etruscan"**, *no monogram, 7⅛" L.* 38.00 40.00
☐ **Gorham "Lancaster"**, *monogram* 25.00 28.00
☐ **Gorham "Lancaster"**, *no monogram* 37.00 39.00
☐ **Gorham "Poppy"**, *no monogram* 30.00 32.00
☐ **Gorham "Rondo"**, *no monogram* 28.00 30.00
☐ **Gorham "Rondo"**, *monogram* 26.00 28.00
☐ **International "Crystal"**, *no monogram* 40.00 42.00
☐ **International "Royal Danish"**, *no monogram* 40.00 42.00
☐ **International "Silver Melody"**, *no monogram* 36.00 38.00
☐ **Kirk "Repousse"**, *monogram* 30.00 32.00
☐ **Reed & Barton "Francis I"**, *monogram and date 1907* 85.00 88.00
☐ **Reed & Barton "Marlborough"**, *monogram* 30.00 32.00
☐ **Simpson, Hall & Miller "Frontenac"**, *no monogram, 9" L.* ... 62.00 64.00
☐ **Towle "Georgian"**, *no monogram* 42.00 45.00
☐ **Wallace "Corinthian"**, *no monogram* 26.00 38.00
☐ **Wallace "Grand Baroque"**, *no monogram* 75.00 80.00
☐ **Westmoreland "John & Priscilla"**, *no monogram* 30.00 32.00
☐ **Whiting "Dorothy Vernon"**, *monogram* 40.00 42.00
☐ **Maker unknown,** *plain pattern, no monogram* 20.00 24.00

COMBS

It would have been difficult to find a giftshop or mail-order catalogue, in the period from roughly 1870 to about World War I, which did not offer an array of silver combs — both sterling silver and plated. The belief was widespread that silver, being a conductor of electricity, was beneficial to the scalp and hair. This theory proved to be erroneous; but undoubtedly silver combs would have enjoyed ample popularity in any event. Their standing with collectors has remained fairly high over the years. When any of the teeth are bent, the value is somewhat lessened.

(Sterling Silver)	Price	Range
☐ **Stieff "Rose",** *new insert, monogram*	24.00	26.00
☐ **Tiffany,** *plain design, tortoise insert in good condition*	24.00	26.00
☐ **Maker unknown,** *plain design, monogram*	8.00	10.00

COMPACTS

These now universally used articles were just coming into popularity during the height of silverware manufacture in this country. There are, therefore, not nearly so many specimens as might have otherwise existed, if the compact was of earlier origin. Portable cosmetic supplies were, on the whole, rare before the late 1800's, but their sales reached astronomical levels just a few decades later. When ordering from a dealer by mail, it is important to keep in mind that not all antique silver compacts are wholly made of silver. Some merely have a silver frame, inset with tortoiseshell or other decorative material; or the frame may be of bone with an engraved and perhaps monogrammed silver panel on the lid. When the original silver-handled applicator brushes are still present, this increases the value.

(Sterling Silver)

☐ **Tiffany,** *trimmed with 14K gold*	28.00	30.00

COMPOTES

Compotes are fruit bowls set upon pedestals. Their table use over the years has in no way been restricted to fruit, but this is their chief function, and in fact they will sometimes be found described as "fruit bowls." The compote, especially if it contained a Bacchanalian array of fruits, often served as a substitute for a formal centerpiece on dining tables. And there was no law against serving muffins, cakes or other foodstuffs in them. Compotes were already in widespread use by the 18th century. Some highly

Compote, *(sterling), maker unknown, 17½ ounces,* 325.00

exquisite types came from the earlier manufacturers, and by and large these were copied throughout the later eras. The size and shape of the compote gave more play to the designer and artisan than was generally the case with table silver. The sides, for example, could be either pierced or closed, and the piece could be styled to give an impression of frilly delicacy or Renaissance classicism. They range considerably in size and weight. Always take care to make a close examination, as compotes are notorious for LOADING — fradulent raising of the weight by adding lead or other stuffing matter into the base. Many were, additionally, manufactured with weighted bases. A *heavy* compote whose weight derives *wholly* from silver is not often found.

(Silver-Plated)   **Price Range**

☐ **Maker unknown,** *Art Nouveau styling, standing maiden holding a bird, flowers, and the bowl of the compote, 8" H.* .   140.00   150.00

(Sterling Silver)

☐ **Kirk "Repousse",** *no monogram, pair* 100.00   120.00
☐ **Kirk "Repousse",** *monogram, 5" Dia., pair* 80.00   100.00
☐ **Sterling Silver Mfg. Co.,** *pierced design on rim, monogram, 8⅞" Dia., 6" T., not weighted, 12 oz.* 80.00   90.00

CONDIMENT LADLES

Surely a "dated" class of wares, condiment ladles go back to the time when mustard, ketchup, etc., appeared on the table in tubs and were spooned out. This practice of laying out condiments, which has ancient origins, persisted in fashionable homes long after bottled condiments were available at the grocery. Strange though it may sound, the impression-minded hostess shook out the contents of her ketchup bottles into tubs, rather than allowing commercial packages to appear on her table. This also served to suggest that they were homemade. By around 1920 the condiment ladle was decidedly on the downswing in popularity and few companies put them out thereafter.

(Silver-Plated)

☐ **Maker unknown,** *monogram, 5", fair condition* 3.00   4.00

(Sterling Silver)

☐ **Donimick & Haff "Madelaine",** *monogram, excellent condition* 22.00   24.00

CONDIMENT SETS

These, which bear no relation to the above (condiment ladles), usually consisted of two or more dishes, along with a cheese slicer and pickle fork. However the accessories occasionally varied, depending on what happened to be fashionable at the moment. Condiment sets have never been popular with collectors.

(Sterling Silver)

☐ **Whiting,** *four piece set includes two glass dishes with sterling rims, sterling cheese knife and pickle fork, all in floral repousse pattern* 14.00   16.00

CORKSCREWS

These have come in for heavy demand and the prices are quite high in relation to the silver content — largely because corkscrew collecting (not just the silver ones but those of other materials as well) has become a growing hobby. Corkscrews are collected alone by some enthusiasts and as adjuncts, by others, to larger collections focusing on the history and usage of wine. Because of this widespread interest, there seems little doubt that the market will continue firm. The number of American-made silver corkscrews to be found in antique shops is less than those of foreign manufacture. French and German specimens are well in the lead, and there are also many from Great Britain. Corkscrews are of very early origins but not so early as is sometimes supposed. Those who place them in the Roman era are ignorant of the fact that wine bottles were NOT corked in the ancient world, but stopped with pebbles rolled in tar or wax. Undoubtedly the corkscrew did not originate until late medieval times, and was not in widespread use until about 1600. Wine was not sold in bottles at shops until after that date, if we exclude the wine of the ancient world. Since an aura of elegance surrounded wine, the corkscrew must, too, be elegant, and many very opulent specimens were made. Even the European museums, which sometimes are old-fashioned in their collecting tastes, have added corkscrews to their galleries.

(Sterling Silver)	Price Range	
☐ **Kirk,** *rose and foliage embossed design*	30.00	32.00
☐ **Maker unknown,** *plain design, monogram*	10.00	12.00

CORN HOLDERS

The ghosts of all etiquette commentators would stalk anyone rash enough to pick up corn in the fingers. This, however, was precisely the way corn was eaten for approximately 200 years. Even those who felt barbaric, in handling corn with the fingers, had no real alternative. One method of escape was to cut the kernels from the cob, after the corn was served. But this, too, was messy, and extremely time-consuming. The solution came with the corn *holder,* an ingenious little device or really a set of devices, consisting of small handles set with a spearpoint. The cob could be skewered on them, and handled in a manner that would not offend anyone's sense of propriety. Naturally the handle lent itself to shaping in artistic or novelty forms, and vast numbers of types were brought out. These were generally retailed in sets, of either twelve or six, and came in attractive boxes.

(Silver-Plated)		
☐ **Maker unknown,** *ornate floral pattern, stainless blades, set of 12 in silk-lined box, no monogram, mint condition*	80.00	90.00
(Sterling Silver)		
☐ **Gorham "Chantilly",** *stainless blades, no monogram, pair* .	24.00	26.00

CRACKER SCOOPS

Two distinct types of cracker scoops are found on the antiques market. The first is the large size, common to the grocery store of yesteryear, with which crackers were taken out of wood barrels to be weighed (they were always sold by the weight). This type was not made of silver, except perhaps on a very rare occasion for an especially swank store. The other variety, which is considerably smaller in size, was made for table use to scoop crackers out of a bowl into one's soup. Picking them up with the fingers was considered unsanitary as well as inelegant.

(Silver-Plated)	Price Range	
☐ Rogers "Alhambra", *monogram, good condition*	10.00	12.00
☐ S.L. & G.H. Rogers "Presentation", *no monogram, excellent condition*	16.00	18.00
☐ 1847 Rogers "Persian", *no monogram, excellent condition*	18.00	20.00
(Sterling Silver)		
☐ Gorham "Chantilly", *no monogram*	80.00	90.00
☐ Tiffany "English King", *pierced, monogram*	180.00	195.00

CREAMERS

Creamers, or small pitchers for cream that made their appearance at the table along with coffee or tea, have been made of silver since the colonial era. They are sometimes very ornate and their vairety, in styles and designs, is vast indeed.

(Coin Silver)		
☐ Kirk "Repousse", *monogram and date, 2½" T.*	70.00	75.00
(Silver-Plated)		
☐ Meriden, *raided on four hoof feet, monogram, excellent condition*	40.00	45.00
☐ Maker unknown, *ornate Victorian scroll and flower design, monogram, fair condition*	10.00	12.00
(Sterling Silver)		
☐ Maker unknown, *cow shape, milk pours through cow's mouth, no monogram*	180.00	200.00

CREAM LADLES

Strawberries and cream, peaches and cream — in fact ANYTHING and cream scored a huge success on the 19th century table. Cream itself was not an innovation of that era. It dated back considerably farther, and in 17th century Europe was often used as a breakfast in itself, without fruit or other trappings. At that time it was sold "loose" and the customer brought his own container to the shop. When 19th century Americans purchased cream from the grocery it came in wide-mouthed glass bottles, and this is where the cream ladle came into play, to scoop it out from the bottle for serving. Alternatively, the whole contents of the cream bottle could be poured into a serving bowl, as was done on more formal occasions — but still the trusty ladle did the finishing job.

(Silver-Plated)		
☐ Alvin "Lily", *no monogram, excellent condition*	8.00	10.00
☐ Alvin "Lily", *no monogram, resilvered*	14.00	16.00
☐ American Silver Company "Franconia", *no monogram, excellent condition*	6.00	7.00

	Price Range	
☐ **American Silver Company "Lawrence"**, *no monogram, excellent condition*	8.00	10.00
☐ **American Silver Company "Lawrence"**, *no monogram, good condition*	5.00	6.00
☐ **American Silver Company "Moselle"**, *no monogram, excellent condition*	20.00	22.00
☐ **Community "Adam"**, *no monogram, excellent condition* ..	12.00	14.00
☐ **Community "Adam"**, *monogram, fair condition*	2.00	3.00
☐ **Community "Bird of Paradise"**, *no monogram, excellent condition*	11.00	13.00
☐ **Community "Bird of Paradise"**, *monogram, excellent condition*	10.00	12.00
☐ **Community "Coronation"**, *no monogram, excellent condition*	5.00	6.00
☐ **Community "Coronation"**, *no monogram, good condition* .	2.00	3.00
☐ **Community "Grosvenor"**, *no monogram, excellent condition*	7.00	8.00
☐ **Community "Grosvenor"**, *no monogram, excellent condition*	12.00	14.00
☐ **Community "Louis XVI"**, *no monogram, excellent condition*	12.00	14.00
☐ **Community "Louis XVI"**, *monogram, good condition*	4.00	5.00
☐ **Community "Patrician"**, *no monogram, good condition* ...	10.00	12.00
☐ **Community "Patrician"**, *monogram, excellent condition* ..	10.00	12.00
☐ **Community "Patrician"**, *no monogram, excellent condition*	10.00	12.00
☐ **Community "Sheraton"**, *no monogram, excellent condition*	10.00	12.00
☐ **Community "Sheraton"**, *monogram, fair condition*	2.00	3.00
☐ **Holmes & Edwards "DeSancy"**, *no monogram, mint condition*	7.00	8.00
☐ **Holmes & Edwards "DeSancy"**, *monogram, fair condition* .	1.00	2.00
☐ **Holmes & Edwards "Jamestown"**, *no monogram, excellent condition*	12.00	14.00
☐ **Holmes & Edwards "Pearl"**, *no monogram, excellent condition*	4.00	5.00
☐ **Oneida "Bridal Wreath"**, *no monogram, excellent condition*	10.00	12.00
☐ **Oneida "Bridal Wreath"**, *monogram, good condition*	3.00	4.00
☐ **Oneida "Kenwood"**, *no monogram, excellent condition* ...	4.00	5.00
☐ **Oneida "Kenwood"**, *monogram, fair condition*	2.00	3.00
☐ **Oneida "Louis XVI"**, *no monogram, good condition*	2.00	3.00
☐ **Oneida "Louis XVI'**, *monogram, excellent condition*	6.00	7.00
☐ **Pairpoint "Arlington"**, *no monogram, excellent condition* ..	20.00	22.00
☐ **Pairpoint "Arlington"**, *monogram, fair condition*	5.00	6.00
☐ **Reed & Barton "Carlton"**, *no monogram, excellent condition*	5.00	6.00
☐ **Reed & Barton "Fiddle"**, *no monogram, excellent condition*	5.00	6.00
☐ **Reed & Barton "Fiddle"**, *no monogram, excellent condition*	9.00	11.00
☐ **Reed & Barton "Maid of Honor"**, *no monogram, excellent condition*	12.00	14.00
☐ **Reed & Barton "Oxford"**, *no monogram, excellent condition*	10.00	12.00
☐ **Reed & Barton "Oxford"**, *no monogram, excellent condition*	18.00	20.00
☐ **Reliance "Bridal Rose"**, *no monogram, good condition*	10.00	12.00
☐ **Reliance "Bridal Rose"**, *no monogram, mint condition*	14.00	16.00
☐ **Reliance "Wildwood"**, *no monogram, excellent condition* .	14.00	16.00
☐ **Reliance "Wildwood"**, *no monogram, good condition*	5.00	6.00

	Price Range	
☐ Rockford "Fair Oaks", *no monogram, excellent condition* .	10.00	12.00
☐ Rockford "Fair Oaks", *no monogram, mint condition*	4.00	5.00
☐ Rogers "Beaded", *no monogram, excellent condition*	7.00	8.00
☐ Rogers "Beaded", *monogram, good condition*	3.00	4.00
☐ Rogers "Carlton", *no monogram, excellent condition*	10.00	12.00
☐ Rogers "Croyden", *no monogram, excellent condition*	7.00	8.00
☐ Rogers "Croyden", *monogram, good condition*	3.00	4.00
☐ Rogers "Newport", *monogram, excellent condition*	14.00	16.00
☐ Rogers "Newport", *no monogram, excellent condition*	16.00	18.00
☐ Rogers & Bro. "Columbia", *monogram, excellent condition*	24.00	26.00
☐ Rogers & Bro. "Columbia", *no monogram, good condition* .	6.00	7.00
☐ Rogers & Bro. "Flemish", *monogram, excellent condition* .	6.00	7.00
☐ Rogers & Bro. "Newport", *no monogram, excellent condition*	5.00	6.00
☐ Rogers & Bro. "Thistle", *no monogram, good condition* . . .	7.00	8.00
☐ Rogers & Bro. "Thistle", *no monogram, excellent condition*	12.00	14.00
☐ Rogers & Bro. "Tuxedo", *no monogram, good condition* . . .	3.00	4.00
☐ Rogers & Bro. "Tuxedo", *gold wash bowl, no monogram, good condition*	7.00	8.00
☐ Rogers & Hamilton "Alhambra", *no monogram, excellent condition*	18.00	20.00
☐ Rgoers & Hamilton "Alhambra", *no monogram, fair condition*	4.00	5.00
☐ Rogers & Hamilton "Raphael", *no monogram, excellent condition*	10.00	12.00
☐ Rogers Mfg. Co. "Triumph", *no monogram, good condition*	10.00	12.00
☐ S.L. & G.H. Rogers "Thor", *no monogram, excellent condition*	10.00	12.00
☐ Towle "Victor", *no monogram, mint condition*	10.00	12.00
☐ Towle "Victor", *no monogram, excellent condition*	8.00	9.00
☐ Tudor "Baronet", *no monogram, good condition*	4.00	5.00
☐ Williams Bros. "Vineyard", *scalloped bowl, no monogram, excellent condition*	14.00	16.00
☐ Wm. A. Rogers "Chalice", *no monogram, excellent condition*	12.00	14.00
☐ Wm. A. Rogers "Elberon", *no monogram, excellent condition*	8.00	10.00
☐ Wm. A. Rogers "Garland", *no monogram, mint condition* . .	5.00	6.00
☐ Wm. A. Rogers "Grenoble", *no monogram, mint condition* .	10.00	12.00
☐ Wm. A. Rogers "Marcell", *no monogram, fair condition* . . .	10.00	12.00
☐ Wm. Rogers & Son "Arbutus", *no monogram, excellent condition*	12.00	14.00
☐ Wm. Rogers & Son "Arbutus", *no monogram, mint condition*	18.00	20.00
☐ Wm. Rogers "Argyle", *monogram, excellent condition*	4.00	5.00
☐ Wm. Rogers & Son "Oxford", *no monogram, excellent condition*	16.00	18.00
☐ Wm. Rogers Mfg. Co. "Grand Elegance", *no monogram, excellent condition*	12.00	14.00
☐ Wm. Rogers Mfg. Co. "Magnolia", *no monogram, excellent condition*	9.00	10.00
☐ World "Franconia", *no monogram, excellent condition*	12.00	14.00
☐ World "Moselle", *no monogram, excellent condition*	34.00	36.00

	Price Range	
☐ World "Moselle", *monogram, fair condition*	7.00	8.00
☐ 1835 R. Wallace "Cardinal", *no monogram, excellent condition*	32.00	35.00
☐ 1847 Rogers "Ancestral", *no monogram, excellent condition*	12.00	14.00
☐ 1847 Rogers "Ancestral", *no monogram, poor condition* . . .	2.50	3.50
☐ 1847 Rogers "Anniversary", *no monogram, excellent condition*	12.00	14.00
☐ 1847 Rogers "Avon", *no monogram, excellent condition* . . .	14.00	16.00
☐ 1847 Rogers "Berkshire", *no monogram, excellent condition*	15.00	17.00
☐ 1847 Rogers "Charter Oak", *no monogram, excellent condition*	19.00	21.00
☐ 1847 Rogers "Charter Oak", *no monogram, mint condition* .	24.00	26.00
☐ 1847 Rogers "Cromwell", *no monogram, excellent condition*	4.00	5.00
☐ 1847 Rogers "First Love", *no monogram, good condition* . .	4.00	5.00
☐ 1847 Rogers "Lorne", *no monogram, excellent condition* . .	8.00	10.00
☐ 1847 Rogers "Lotus", *no monogram, excellent condition* . .	16.00	18.00
☐ 1847 Rogers "Lotus", *no monogram, good condition*	6.00	8.00
☐ 1847 Rogers 'Louvain", *no monogram, excellent condition* .	10.00	12.00
☐ 1847 Rogers "Newport", *no monogram, excellent condition*	10.00	12.00
☐ 1847 Rogers "Newport", *no monogram, excellent condition*	16.00	18.00
☐ 1847 Rogers "Olive", *no monogram, excellent condition* . . .	20.00	22.00
☐ 1847 Rogers "Princess", *no monogram, excellent condition*	24.00	26.00
☐ 1847 Rogers "Vintage", *no monogram, excellent condition*	26.00	28.00
☐ 1847 Rogers "Vintage", *monogram, good condition*	7.00	9.00
☐ 1881 Rogers "Linden", *no monogram, excellent condition* .	10.00	12.00
☐ 1881 Rogers "Surf Club", *no monogram, good condition* . .	10.00	12.00
☐ 1881 Rogers "Surf Club", *no monogram, excellent condition*	10.00	12.00
☐ Maker unknown, *"Sweet Clover Condensed Milk", good condition*	3.00	4.00

(Sterling Silver)

☐ Baker/Manchester "Poppy", *no monogram*	34.00	36.00
☐ Durgin "Fairfax", *no monogram*	18.00	20.00
☐ Gorham "Buttercup", *no monogram*	18.00	20.00
☐ Gorham "Cambridge", *monogram*	22.00	24.00
☐ Gorham "Luxembourg", *monogram*	18.00	20.00
☐ Gorham "Plymouth", *no monogram*	15.00	17.00
☐ Lunt "Monticello", *monogram*	22.00	24.00
☐ Manchester "Mary Warren", *no monogram*	18.00	20.00
☐ Randahl, *no monogram*	40.00	45.00
☐ Towle "Old Colonial", *monogram*	45.00	48.00
☐ Tuttle "Onslow", *no monogram*	37.00	39.00
☐ Wallace "Normandie", *no monogram*	37.00	39.00

CREAM SOUP SPOONS

In the age of elegant and etiquette-ordained dining, soup spoons were divided up into two categories (as in this book). There was the simple or standard soup spoon, and then the *cream soup spoon,* for use with cream soups or any soup having a thick broth and little chewable content. Essentially the cream soup spoon had a slightly shallower bowl than a regular soup spoon, but aside from this they were not easily told apart. The practice of using two different spoons for soups continued after many of the other eccentricities of the Victorian dining table died off — therefore their numbers on the antiques market are legion.

(Silver-Plated)	Price Range	
☐ **Alvin "Cameo"**, *no monogram, excellent condition*	6.00	7.00
☐ **Alvin "Cameo"**, *monogram, excellent condition*	2.00	3.00
☐ **Alvin "Diana"**, *monogram, excellent condition*	2.00	3.00
☐ **Alvin "Diana"**, *no monogram, good condition*	3.00	4.00
☐ **American Silver "Berlin"**, *no monogram, excellent condition*	2.00	3.00
☐ **American Silver "Berlin"**, *no monogram, good condition* . .	3.00	4.00
☐ **Community "Adam"**, *no monogram, excellent condition* . .	6.00	7.00
☐ **Community "Adam"**, *no monogram, good condition*	4.00	5.00
☐ **Community "Bird of Paradise"**, *no monogram, excellent condition*	6.00	7.00
☐ **Community "Bird of Paradise"**, *no monogram, poor condition*	1.00	2.00
☐ **Community "Coronation"**, *no monogram, excellent condition*	6.00	7.00
☐ **Community "Coronation"**, *no monogram, mint condition* . .	4.00	5.00
☐ **Community "Coronation"**, *no monogram, fair condition* . . .	1.00	2.00
☐ **Community "Forever"**, *no monogram, excellent condition* .	6.00	7.00
☐ **Community "Forever"**, *no monogram, good condition*	5.00	6.00
☐ **Community "Forever"**, *no monogram, fair condition*	2.00	3.00
☐ **Community "King Cedric"**, *no monogram, excellent condition*	6.00	7.00
☐ **Community "King Cedric"**, *no monogram, excellent condition*	6.00	7.00
☐ **Community "Lady Hamilton"**, *no monogram, fair condition*	1.00	2.00
☐ **Community "Lady Hamilton"**, *no monogram, excellent condition*	6.00	7.00
☐ **Community "Lady Hamilton"**, *no monogram, good condition*	5.00	6.00
☐ **Community "Lady Hamilton"**, *no monogram, fair condition*	1.00	2.00
☐ **Community "Milady"**, *no monogram, excellent condition* . .	6.00	7.00
☐ **Community "Milady"**, *no monogram, excellent condition* . .	4.00	5.00
☐ **Community "Milady"**, *no monogram, good condition*	3.00	4.00
☐ **Community "Morning Star"**, *no monogram, excellent condition*	6.00	7.00
☐ **Community "Morning Star"**, *no monogram, excellent condition*	6.00	7.00
☐ **Community "Morning Star"**, *no monogram, good condition*	3.00	4.00
☐ **Community "Noblesse"**, *no monogram, excellent condition*	6.00	7.00
☐ **Community "Noblesse"**, *no monogram, good condition* . . .	5.00	6.00
☐ **Community "Noblesse"**, *no monogram, fair condition*	1.00	2.00
☐ **Community "Patrician"**, *no monogram, excellent condition*	6.00	7.00
☐ **Community "Patrician"**, *no monogram, good condition* . . .	5.00	6.00
☐ **Community "Paul Revere"**, *no monogram, good condition* .	5.00	6.00
☐ **Community "Paul Revere"**, *no monogram, good condition* .	3.00	4.00
☐ **Community "Paul Revere"**, *no monogram, excellent condition*	4.00	5.00
☐ **Community "Randolph"**, *no monogram, good condition* . . .	4.00	5.00

	Price Range	
☐ Community "Randolph", *no monogram, good condition* ...	5.00	6.00
☐ Community "Sheraton", *no monogram, excellent condition*	6.00	7.00
☐ Community "Sheraton", *no monogram, good condition* ...	5.00	6.00
☐ Community "Sheraton", *fair condition*	1.00	2.00
☐ Community "South Seas", *no monogram, good condition* .	2.00	3.00
☐ Community "South Seas", *no monogram, excellent condition*	6.00	7.00
☐ Community "White Orchid", *no monogram, excellent condition*	6.00	7.00
☐ Community "White Orchid", *no monogram, good condition*	5.00	6.00
☐ Gorham "Cavalier", *no monogram, excellent condition*	6.00	7.00
☐ Gorham "Cavalier", *no monogram, good condition*	3.00	4.00
☐ Gorham "Invitation", *no monogram, excellent condition* ..	6.00	7.00
☐ Gorham "Invitation", *no monogram, good condition*	3.00	4.00
☐ Gorham "Lady Caroline", *no monogram, excellent condition*	6.00	7.00
☐ Gorham "Lady Caroline", *no monogram, good condition* ..	3.00	4.00
☐ Heirloom "Cardinal", *no monogram, good condition*	6.00	7.00
☐ Holmes & Edwards "Century", *no monogram, excellent condition*	6.00	7.00
☐ Holmes & Edwards "Century", *no monogram, good condition*	5.00	6.00
☐ Holmes & Edwards "Century", *no monogram, fair condition*	1.00	2.00
☐ Holmes & Edwards "Danish Princess", *no monogram, excellent condition*	6.00	7.00
☐ Holmes & Edwards "Danish Princess", *no monogram, good condition*	5.00	6.00
☐ Holmes & Edwards "Danish Princess", *no monogram, fair condition*	1.00	2.00
☐ Holmes & Edwards "Danish Princess", *no monogram, fair condition*	1.00	2.00
☐ Holmes & Edwards "Orient", *no monogram, poor condition*	2.00	3.00
☐ Holmes & Edwards "Silver Fashion", *no monogram, excellent condition*	6.00	7.00
☐ Holmes & Edwards "Silver Fashion", *no monogram, excellent condition*	6.00	7.00
☐ Holmes & Edwards "Youth", *no monogram, fair condition* .	1.00	2.00
☐ Holmes & Edwards "Youth", *no monogram, poor condition*	1.00	2.00
☐ International "Orleans", *no monogram, mint condition*	4.00	5.00
☐ International "Orleans", *no monogram, excellent condition*	6.00	7.00
☐ International "Silver Tulip", *no monogram, excellent condition*	4.00	5.00
☐ King Edward "Cavalcade", *no monogram, excellent condition*	6.00	7.00
☐ King Edward "Cavalcade", *no monogram, good condition* .	5.00	6.00
☐ King Edward "Moss Rose", *no monogram, excellent condition*	6.00	7.00
☐ King Edward "Moss Rose", *no monogram, poor condition* .	1.00	2.00
☐ National "Embossed", *no monogram, fair condition*	1.00	2.00
☐ National "Embossed", *no monogram, good condition*	4.00	5.00
☐ National "Embossed", *no monogram, good condition*	5.00	6.00
☐ National "King Edward", *no monogram, excellent condition*	6.00	7.00
☐ Nobility "Royal Rose", *no monogram, excellent condition* .	6.00	7.00
☐ Nobility "Royal Rose", *no monogram, excellent condition* .	6.00	7.00

	Price Range	
☐ Oneida "Avalon", *no monogram, excellent condition*	3.00	4.00
☐ Oneida "Avalon", *no monogram, good condition*	5.00	6.00
☐ Oneida "Cereta", *no monogram, excellent condition*	4.00	5.00
☐ Oneida "Cereta", *no monogram, excellent condition*	6.00	7.00
☐ Oneida "Clarion", *no monogram, excellent condition*	5.00	6.00
☐ Oneida "Clarion", *no monogram, excellent condition*	5.00	6.00
☐ Prestige "Grenoble", *no monogram, excellent condition* ..	6.00	7.00
☐ Prestige "Grenoble", *no monogram, fair condition*	1.00	2.00
☐ Reed & Barton "Maid of Honor", *no monogram, excellent condition*	6.00	7.00
☐ Reed & Barton "Maid of Honor", *no monogram, good condition*	5.00	6.00
☐ Rockford "Louvre", *no monogram, excellent condition*	5.00	6.00
☐ Rogers "Gracious", *no monogram, excellent condition*	6.00	7.00
☐ Rogers "Inspiration", *no monogram, excellent condition* ..	6.00	7.00
☐ Rogers "Inspiration", *no monogram, fair condition*	1.00	2.00
☐ Rogers "Navarre", *no monogram, excellent condition*	6.00	7.00
☐ Rogers "Navarre", *no monogram, good condition*	5.00	6.00
☐ Rogers "Victorian Rose", *no monogram, excellent condition*	3.00	4.00
☐ Rogers & Bro. "Daybreak", *no monogram, excellent condition*	6.00	7.00
☐ Rogers & Bro. "Daybreak", *no monogram, fair condition* ..	1.00	2.00
☐ Rogers & Bro. "Flemish", *no monogram, excellent condition*	6.00	7.00
☐ Rogers & Bro. "Flemish", *no monogram, fair condition*	1.00	2.00
☐ Rogers & Bro. "Thistle", *no monogram, good condition* ...	5.00	6.00
☐ Rogers & Bro. "Thistle", *no monogram, excellent condition*	8.00	9.00
☐ Rogers & Hamilton "Alhambra", *no monogram, mint condition*	10.00	12.00
☐ Rogers & Hamilton "Alhambra", *no monogram, good condition*	5.00	6.00
☐ Rogers & Hamilton "Alhambra", *no monogram, fair condition*	3.00	4.00
☐ Sears "Rose", *monogram, good condition*	3.00	4.00
☐ S.L. & G.H. Rogers "Minerva", *no monogram, excellent condition*	5.00	6.00
☐ S.L. & G.H. Rogers "Minerva", *no monogram, good condition*	5.00	6.00
☐ S.L. & G.H. Rogers "Thor", *no monogram, fair condition* ...	1.00	2.00
☐ S.L. & G.H. Rogers "Thor", *no monogram, good condition* .	5.00	6.00
☐ S.L. & G.H. Rogers "Thor", *no monogram, excellent condition*	6.00	7.00
☐ S.L. & G.H. Rogers "Violet", *no monogram, good condition*	6.00	7.00
☐ S.L. & G.H. Rogers "Violet", *no monogram, excellent condition*	7.00	8.00
☐ Towle "Byfield", *no monogram, mint condition*	4.00	5.00
☐ Towle "Byfield", *no monogram, fair condition*	1.00	2.00
☐ Towle "Londonderry", *no monogram, mint condition*	4.00	5.00
☐ Towle "Londonderry", *no monogram, good condition*	4.00	5.00
☐ Tudor "Queen Bess II", *no monogram, excellent condition* .	6.00	7.00
☐ Tudor "Queen Bess II", *no monogram, good condition*	5.00	6.00
☐ Tudor "Queen Bess II", *no monogram, fair condition*	1.00	2.00
☐ Tudor "Sweetbriar", *no monogram, excellent condition* ...	6.00	7.00

		Price Range	
☐ Tudor "Sweetbriar", *no monogram, good condition*		5.00	6.00
☐ Tudor "Sweetbriar", *no monogram, fair condition*		1.00	2.00
☐ Wallace "Kings", *U.S. Navy monogram, excellent condition*		4.00	5.00
☐ Wallace "Kings", *no monogram, excellent condition*		6.00	7.00
☐ W. D. Smith "Adam", *monogram, excellent condition*		3.00	4.00
☐ W. D. Smith "Adam", *no monogram, excellent condition* ...		6.00	7.00
☐ W. D. Smith "Adam", *no monogram, fair condition*		1.00	2.00
☐ William Bros. "Queen Elizabeth", *no monogram, excellent condition*		3.00	4.00
☐ William Bros. "Queen Elizabeth", *no monogram, excellent condition*		6.00	7.00
☐ Wm. A. Rogers "Carnation", *no monogram, excellent condition*		7.00	8.00
☐ Wm. A. Rogers "Carnation", *no monogram, fair condition* .		1.00	2.00
☐ Wm. A. Rogers "Garland", *no monogram, good condition* .		3.00	4.00
☐ Wm. A. Rogers "Garland", *no monogram, good condition* .		5.00	6.00
☐ Wm. A. Rogers "Grenoble", *no monogram, fair condition* ..		1.00	2.00
☐ Wm. A. Rogers "Grenoble", *no monogram, excellent condition*		7.00	8.00
☐ Wm. A. Rogers "Lady Drake", *no monogram, excellent condition*		6.00	7.00
☐ Wm. A. Rogers "Lady Drake", *no monogram, good condition*		5.00	6.00
☐ Wm. A. Rogers "Lady Stuart", *no monogram, excellent condition*		6.00	7.00
☐ Wm. A. Rogers "Lady Stuart", *no monogram, fair condition*		1.00	2.00
☐ Wm. A. Rogers "Malibu", *no monogram, excellent condition*		6.00	7.00
☐ Wm. A. Rogers "Malibu", *no monogram, good condition* ...		5.00	6.00
☐ Wm. A. Rogers "Malibu", *no monogram, fair condition*		1.00	2.00
☐ Wm. A. Rogers "Margate", *no monogram, excellent condition*		6.00	7.00
☐ Wm. A. Rogers "Margate", *no monogram, good condition* .		5.00	6.00
☐ Wm. A. Rogers "Meadowbrook", *no monogram, excellent condition*		6.00	7.00
☐ Wm. A. Rogers "Meadowbrook", *good condition*		5.00	6.00
☐ Wm. A. Rogers "Meadowbrook", *no monogram, fair condition*		1.00	2.00
☐ Wm. A. Rogers "Paramount", *no monogram, excellent condition*		6.00	7.00
☐ Wm. A. Rogers "Paramount", *no monogram, fair condition*		1.00	2.00
☐ Wm. A. Rogers "Rendezvous", *no monogram, excellent condition*		5.00	6.00
☐ Wm. A. Rogers "Rosalie", *no monogram, excellent condition*		6.00	7.00
☐ Wm. A. Rogers "Rosalie", *no monogram, good condition* ..		5.00	6.00
☐ Wm. A. Rogers "Rosalie", *no monogram, fair condition* ...		1.00	2.00
☐ Wm. Rogers "Berwick", *no monogram, excellent condition*		7.00	8.00
☐ Wm. Rogers "Berwick", *no monogram, good condition*		6.00	7.00
☐ Wm. Rogers "Debutante", *no monogram, excellent condition*		6.00	7.00
☐ Wm. Rogers "Debutante", *no monogram, good condition* ..		4.00	5.00

	Price Range	
☐ Wm. Rogers "Debutante", *no monogram, fair condition* ...	1.00	2.00
☐ Wm. Rogers "Exquisite", *no monogram, excellent condition* ...	6.00	7.00
☐ Wm. Rogers "Exquisite", *no monogram, good condition* ...	5.00	6.00
☐ Wm. Rogers "Fairoaks", *no monogram, good condition* ...	5.00	6.00
☐ Wm. Rogers "Fairoaks", *no monogram, fair condition*	1.00	2.00
☐ Wm. Rogers "Fidelis", *no monogram, excellent condition* .	6.00	7.00
☐ Wm. Rogers "Fidelis", *no monogram, good condition*	5.00	6.00
☐ Wm. Rogers "Fidelis", *no monogram, fair condition*	1.00	2.00
☐ Wm. Rogers "Lufberry", *no monogram, excellent condition*	5.00	6.00
☐ Wm. Rogers "Lufberry", *no monogram, fair condition*	1.00	2.00
☐ Wm. Rogers "Lufberry", *no monogram, excellent condition*	6.00	7.00
☐ Wm. Rogers "Mayfair", *no monogram, good condition*	5.00	6.00
☐ Wm. Rogers "Orange Blossom", *no monogram, excellent condition* ...	8.00	10.00
☐ Wm. Rogers "Orange Blossom", *no monogram, good condition* ...	7.00	8.00
☐ Wm. Rogers "Oxford", *no monogram, excellent condition* .	4.00	5.00
☐ Wm. Rogers "Oxford", *no monogram, fair condition*	1.00	2.00
☐ Wm. Rogers "Paris", *no monogram, excellent condition* ...	6.00	7.00
☐ Wm. Rogers "Paris", *no monogram, good condition*	5.00	6.00
☐ Wm. Rogers "Treasure", *no monogram, fair condition*	1.00	2.00
☐ Wm. Rogers "Tuxedo", *no monogram, excellent condition* .	7.00	8.00
☐ Wm. Rogers "Tuxedo", *no monogram, good condition*	6.00	7.00
☐ Wm. Rogers Mfg. Co. "Alhambra", *no monogram, excellent condition* ...	4.00	5.00
☐ Wm. Rogers Mfg. Co. "Alhambra", *no monogram, excellent condition* ...	6.00	7.00
☐ Wm. Rogers Mfg. Co. "Arbutus", *monogram, good condition* ...	2.00	3.00
☐ Wm. Rogers Mfg. Co. "Arbutus", *no monogram, excellent condition* ...	7.00	8.00
☐ Wm. Rogers Mfg. Co. "Arbutus", *no monogram, fair condition* ...	2.00	3.00
☐ Wm. Rogers Mfg. Co. "Magnolia", *no monogram, excellent condition* ...	6.00	7.00
☐ Wm. Rogers Mfg. Co. "Magnolia", *no monogram, good condition* ...	5.00	6.00
☐ Wm. Rogers Mfg. Co. "Reflection", *no monogram, excellent condition* ...	6.00	7.00
☐ Wm. Rogers Mfg. Co. "Reflection", *no monogram, fair condition* ...	1.00	2.00
☐ Wm. Rogers Mfg. Co. "Talisman", *no monogram, excellent condition* ...	6.00	7.00
☐ Wm. Rogers Mfg. Co. "Talisman", *no monogram, good condition* ...	5.00	6.00
☐ Wm. Rogers & Son "Primrose", *no monogram, excellent condition* ...	6.00	7.00
☐ Wm. Rogers & Son "Primrose", *no monogram, good condition* ...	5.00	6.00
☐ Wm. Rogers & Son "Victorian Rose", *no monogram, good condition* ...	4.00	5.00

	Price Range	

☐ **1835 R. Wallace "Anjou"**, *no monogram, excellent condition* 3.00 4.00

☐ **1835 R. Wallace "Buckingham"**, *monogram, excellent condition* 2.00 3.00

☐ **1835 R. Wallace "Buckingham"**, *no monogram, excellent condition* 6.00 7.00

☐ **1835 R. Wallace "Cardinal"**, *no monogram, excellent condition* 6.00 7.00

☐ **1847 Rogers "Avon"**, *no monogram, excellent condition* ... 6.00 7.00

☐ **1847 Rogers "Avon"**, *no monogram, good condition* 5.00 6.00

☐ **1847 Rogers "Avon"**, *no monogram, fair condition* 1.00 2.00

☐ **1847 Rogers "Berkshire"**, *no monogram, excellent condition* 10.00 12.00

☐ **1847 Rogers "Berkshire"**, *no monogram, good condition* .. 8.00 9.00

☐ **1847 Rogers "Berkshire"**, *no monogram, fair condition* 3.00 4.00

☐ **1847 Rogers "Charter Oak"**, *no monogram, resilvered* 10.00 12.00

☐ **1847 Rogers "Charter Oak"**, *no monogram, good condition* 9.00 10.00

☐ **1847 Rogers "Charter Oak"**, *no monogram, fair condition* .. 2.00 3.00

☐ **1847 Rogers "Daffodil"**, *no monogram, good condition* 3.00 4.00

☐ **1847 Rogers "Daffodil"**, *no monogram, good condition* 5.00 6.00

☐ **1847 Rogers "Daffodil II"**, *no monogram, excellent condition* 6.00 7.00

☐ **1847 Rogers "Daffodil II"**, *no monogram, good condition* .. 5.00 6.00

☐ **1847 Rogers "Eternally Yours"**, *no monogram, excellent condition* 6.00 7.00

☐ **1847 Rogers "Eternally Yours"**, *no monogram, good condition* 5.00 6.00

☐ **1847 Rogers "First Love"**, *excellent condition* 6.00 7.00

☐ **1847 Rogers "First Love"**, *no monogram, fair condition* ... 1.00 2.00

☐ **1847 Rogers "Flair"**, *no monogram, excellent condition* ... 3.00 4.00

☐ **1847 Rogers "Heraldic"**, *no monogram, fair condition* 1.50 2.50

☐ **1847 Rogers "Heraldic"**, *no monogram, good condition* ... 3.00 4.00

☐ **1847 Rogers "Heraldic"**, *no monogram, excellent condition* 6.00 7.00

☐ **1847 Rogers "Magic Rose"**, *no monogram, excellent condition* 6.00 7.00

☐ **1847 Rogers "Magic Rose"**, *no monogram, good condition* 5.00 6.00

☐ **1847 Rogers "Marquise"**, *no monogram, excellent condition* 6.00 7.00

☐ **1847 Rogers "Marquise"**, *no monogram, good condition* .. 5.00 6.00

☐ **1847 Rogers "Moselle"**, *no monogram, good condition* 22.00 25.00

☐ **1847 Rogers "Moselle"**, *no monogram, fair condition* 6.00 7.00

☐ **1847 Rogers "Moselle"**, *no monogram, resilvered* 28.00 30.00

☐ **1847 Rogers "Reflection"**, *no monogram, excellent condition* 4.00 5.00

☐ **1847 Rogers "Reflection"**, *no monogram, fair condition* ... 1.00 2.00

☐ **1847 Rogers "Remembrance"**, *no monogram, excellent condition* 6.00 7.00

☐ **1847 Rogers "Remembrance"**, *no monogram, mint condition* 7.00 8.00

☐ **1847 Rogers "Springtime"**, *no monogram, excellent condition* 3.00 4.00

☐ **1847 Rogers "Vintage"**, *no monogram, excellent condition* 10.00 12.00

☐ **1847 Rogers "Vintage"**, *no monogram, excellent condition* 10.00 12.00

	Price Range	
☐ **1847 Rogers "Vintage"**, *no monogram, excellent condition*	14.00	16.00
☐ **1847 Rogers "Vintage"**, *no monogram, excellent condition*	18.00	20.00
☐ **1847 Rogers "Vintage"**, *no monogram, good condition*	12.00	14.00
☐ **1847 Rogers "Vintage"**, *no monogram, fair condition*	4.00	5.00
☐ **1847 Rogers "Vintage"**, *no monogram, poor condition*	1.00	2.00
☐ **1881 Rogers "Capri"**, *no monogram, excellent condition* ..	6.00	7.00
☐ **1881 Rogers "Capri"**, *no monogram, good condition*	5.00	6.00

(Sterling Silver)

	Price Range	
☐ **Alvin "Chateau Rose"**, *no monogram*	14.00	16.00
☐ **Alvin "Majestic"**, *monogram*	16.00	18.00
☐ **Alvin "Romantique"**, *no monogram*	12.00	14.00
☐ **Durgin "Fairfax"**, *monogram, 6⅞" L.*	14.00	16.00
☐ **Durgin "Louis XV"**, *monogram*	12.00	14.00
☐ **Fine Arts "Processional"**, *no monogram*	12.00	14.00
☐ **Frank Smith "Fiddle Thread"**, *no monogram*	22.00	24.00
☐ **Gorham "Buckingham"**, *no monogram*	16.00	18.00
☐ **Gorham "Buttercup"**, *no monogram*	16.00	18.00
☐ **Gorham "Chantilly"**, *monogram*	12.00	14.00
☐ **Gorham "Chantilly"**, *no monogram*	12.00	14.00
☐ **Gorham "English Gadroon"**, *no monogram*	14.00	16.00
☐ **Gorham "English Gadroon"**, *monogram*	14.00	16.00
☐ **Gorham "Greenbrier"**, *no monogram*	14.00	16.00
☐ **Gorham "Lancaster Rose"**, *monogram*	16.00	18.00
☐ **Gorham "Lancaster Rose"**, *no monogram*	20.00	22.00
☐ **Gorham "Newcastle"**, *monogram*	18.00	20.00
☐ **Gorham "Old French"**, *monogram, 6¼" L.*	16.00	18.00
☐ **Gorham "Old French"**, *monogram, 6¾" L.*	18.00	20.00
☐ **Gorham "Rondo"**, *no monogram*	12.00	14.00
☐ **International "Courtship"**, *no monogram*	12.00	14.00
☐ **International "Courtship"**,	12.00	14.00
☐ **International "Crystal"**, *no monogram*	16.00	18.00
☐ **International "Edgewood"**,	17.00	19.00
☐ **International "Royal Danish"**, *no monogram*	12.00	14.00
☐ **Kirk "Repousse"**, *monogram, 6¼" L.*	17.00	19.00
☐ **Lunt "Mignonette"**, *no monogram*	12.00	14.00
☐ **Manchester "Vogue"**, *no monogram*	12.00	14.00
☐ **Reed & Barton "Francis I"**, *no monogram*	14.00	16.00
☐ **Reed & Barton "Francis I"**, *no monogram*	19.00	21.00
☐ **Reed & Barton "Marlborough"**, *no monogram*	15.00	17.00
☐ **Royal Crest "Castle Rose"**, *no monogram*	12.00	14.00
☐ **Sears & Son, pattern unknown,** *no monogram*	6.00	7.00
☐ **Stieff "Rose"**, *monogram, 6½" L.*	18.00	20.00
☐ **Stieff "Rose"**, *monogram, 6⅛" L.*	17.00	19.00
☐ **Tiffany "English King"**, *monogram*	22.00	24.00
☐ **Tiffany "Hampton"**, *no monogram*	18.00	20.00
☐ **Towle "Chippendale"**, *no monogram*	12.00	14.00
☐ **Towle "Chippendale"**, *monogram*	10.00	12.00
☐ **Towle "French Provincial"**,	12.00	13.00
☐ **Towle "Madeira"**, *no monogram*	14.00	16.00
☐ **Towle "Old Colonial"**, *no monogram*	12.00	14.00
☐ **Towle "Old Colonial"**, *no monogram*	26.00	28.00
☐ **Towle "Rambler Rose"**, *monogram*	15.00	17.00
☐ **Towle "Silver Flutes"**, ...	12.00	14.00

	Price Range	
☐ **Wallace "Grande Baroque"**, *no monogram, 6¼″ L.*	18.00	20.00
☐ **Wallace "Rosepoint"**, *no monogram*	12.00	14.00
☐ **Westmoreland "John & Priscilla"**, *no monogram*	13.00	15.00
☐ **Westmoreland "Milburn Rose"**, *no monogram*	12.00	14.00
☐ **Whiting "Imperial Queen"**, *monogram*	21.00	23.00
☐ **Whiting "Lily"**, *no monogram*	38.00	40.00

CRUETS

These vessels for oil and vinegar, brought to the table when salads were served, were primarily made of glass. Silver specimens are not very common, and, even when found, are very rarely WHOLLY of silver. The base and stopper may be of silver, but the body of the vessel is glass — one reason being to avoid confusion of the contents. Cruets were almost always sold in sets, and when found in matching sets they carry a slight premium value. But individual specimens are certainly collectible, and may even be preferable to a hobbyist interested in assembling as many different patterns and shapes as possible.

(Sterling and Crystal)

☐ **Maker unknown**, *vinegar, base and stopper, crystal body cut in prism design*	26.00	28.00
☐ **Maker unknown**, *vinegar and oil, etched crystal bottoms with sterling stoppers, both bottles signed Hawkes, silver not marked, monograms on lids*	70.00	75.00

CRUMBERS

(Silver-Plated)

☐ **Frary & Clark "Landers"**, *etched blade, no monogram, 16″ L., excellent condition*	42.00	45.00
☐ **Gorham "Winthrop"**, *no monogram, excellent condition* ...	30.00	32.00
☐ **Reed & Barton "Modern Art"**, *no monogram, mint condition*	60.00	65.00
☐ **Rogers & Bro. "Monarch"**, *no monogram, excellent condition*	30.00	32.00
☐ **Rogers & Hamilton "Monarch"**, *no monogram, excellent condition*	12.00	14.00
☐ **St. Louis Silver**, *pattern unknown, vintage design, no monogram, excellent condition*	30.00	35.00
☐ **1847 Rogers "Persian"**, *no monogram, mint condition*	23.00	25.00

(Sterling Silver)

☐ **Howard & Co.**, *pattern unknown, plain design, monogram* .	56.00	58.00
☐ **Kirk "Repousse"**, *earliest mark, no monogram*	125.00	150.00

CRUMB TRAYS

(Silver-Plated)

☐ **Maker unknown**, *Art Nouveau lily pattern, good condition* .	13.00	15.00

CUCUMBER SERVERS

Cucumbers, originally called "cow cumbers," the origin of which is obscure, were very highly regarded in early times. They were not cut into salads or pickled but eaten whole along with a meal. Gradually the cucumber sellers became more inventive and pickling began. But, even thereafter, the plain unadulterated cucumber still made its appearance at the table, generally in the summer season. Most Victorians (and their successors) simply grasped cucumbers with pickle tongs, but technically this was not correct. If one was eating an unpickled cucumber, it was properly picked up with a device called a cucumber server. They have the contour of shovels with flattened scoops. Though the cucumber server is rather an oddity in the world of silver, these can be interesting to collect. Some very ornate specimens have been made, combining moulding with pierced work and sometimes also with engraving. Since the cucumber server endured no hard wear in use — it contacted nothing hot or abrasive — the state of preservation is usually excellent.

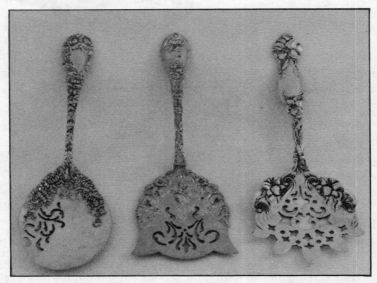

Cucumber Servers, (L to R) (sterling), Durgin "Chrysanthemum", 45.00; Durgin "Dauphin", 40.00; Simpson, Hall & Miller "Frontenac", 42.00

(Sterling Silver)	Price Range	
☐ Whiting "Imperial Queen", *monogram*	40.00	42.00

CUPS

Cups for hot beverages (tea, coffee, etc.) were only rarely made of silver, as novelties or to compliment huge services. In actual use they were always unpopular, the general opinion being that they spoiled the flavor of the beverage. This was true of metallic drinking cups in general. So, even on the tables of society's elite, where everything else was glittering silver, ceramic cups came out when coffee or tea was served. It must be assumed that many, if not most, silver drinking cups were sold as souvenirs or merely as decorations. There is not much potenial in collecting them.

Child Cup, *maker unknown, curved sides with scroll design around bottom,* 20.00

(Silver-Plated)	Price Range	
☐ **Maker unknown,** *repousse design with dolphin handle, no monogram, fair condition*	23.00	25.00
☐ **Maker unknown,** *embossed bike-riding scene, dated 1900, fair condition*	10.00	12.00

CUPS AND SAUCERS

(Silver-Plated)

☐ **Pairpoint,** *cup and saucer, nautical engraving, good condition*	64.00	68.00
☐ **Victor Silver,** *cup and saucer, beaded rims, monogram*	50.00	55.00

CUTICLE KNIVES

These devices, for manicuring the fingernails, were only occasionally made of silver. They came in sets which included, in addition to the cuticle knife or stick, a small scissors, a filing rasp, and sometimes other accessories as well. Cuticle knives were not used for cutting but for pushing back the cuticle, therefore they are misnamed. The present-day equivalent is the wooden "orange stick." Silver cuticle knives are often monogrammed. They are probably not suitable as a collection in themselves, as the quantity available in antique shops is very small, but could possibly serve as an adjunct to a collection of some related types of silver (cosmetics articles for example).

(Sterling Silver)

☐ **Unger Bros. "He Loves Me",** *monogram*	36.00	38.00
☐ **Maker unknown,** *floral and scroll design, monogram*	8.00	9.00

DARNING EGGS

This contrivance saved many a pin-prick for the seamstresses of yesteryear. When clothing was to be mended, the darning egg was slipped beneath the torn area — rather than the hand. Darning eggs were shaped very much like eggs, usually a bit larger than a hen's egg. The common variety, sold by the multi thousands everywhere, was made of wood. Metallic darning eggs were not simply a novelty — they had one specific advantage over wood. Should the needle slip and hit the egg, it would merely skim over a metallic surface, whereas it could be bent by wood. Silver darning eggs will occasionally be found on the antiques market. There was never any wholesale manufacture of them, and one can only suppose that the majority of specimens made saw no use whatsoever. Anyone who could afford a silver darning egg could also likely afford someone to do the family's sewing. They are extremely attractive and very popular with collectors, and the regret is that more are not available.

(Sterling Silver Handled)	Price Range	
☐ **Maker unknown,** *plain design, monogram*	10.00	12.00
☐ **Maker unknown,** *repousse floral design, monogram*	24.00	26.00

DEMITASSE CUPS AND SAUCERS

Americans adopted the demitasse cup from England, which in turn had adopted it from France. Afternoon tea — a devotedly-observed ritual for many years — was not complete without the demitasse cup, usually of tea but often of other beverages. Its capacity was supposed to be ½ that of a standard cup but it sometimes varied. When made of silver, demitasse cups invariably had ceramic liners to protect the beverage's flavor and (to some extent) retain heat. These were always sold in sets, and are more valuable in sets than the sum value of a set's individual components. However, a hobbyist interested in building a show of many different patterns would probably want individual examples only.

(Sterling Silver and Lenox)

☐ **Alvin,** *cup and saucer, Lenox liner with plain gold trim, total silver weight 1½ oz.*	34.00	36.00
☐ **Alvin,** *cup and saucer, Lenox liner with plain gold trim, openwork design on silver, total silver weight 1½ oz.*	34.00	36.00
☐ **Bailey, Banks and Biddle retailer,** *cup and saucer, no maker's mark, Lenox liner with plain gold trim, silver plain with rolled rims and hollow handle, total silver weight 15 oz., set of six*	300.00	325.00
☐ **Barbour Silver Co.,** *cup and saucer, Lenox liner pink with pencil line gold trim, silver with filigree openwork design and rolled rims, total silver weight 15 oz., set of six*	300.00	325.00
☐ **Dominick & Haff,** *cup and saucer, Lenox liner with plain gold trim, ornate rose design on silver, silver weight 36 oz.* . .	725.00	750.00
☐ **Dominick & Haff,** *cup and saucer, Lenox liner with plain gold trim, silver with geometric openwork, hollow handle, total silver weight 20 ozs., set of eight*	400.00	425.00
☐ **Durgin,** *cup and saucer, Lenox liner with plain gold trim, silver with openwork design, 2 oz.*	40.00	45.00
☐ **Durgin,** *cup and saucer, Lenox liner with plain gold trim, hammered finish on silver, strap handle, total silver weight 12 oz., set of six*	250.00	275.00
☐ **Gorham,** *cup and saucer, Lenox liner with plain gold trim, silver plain with hollow handle, total silver weight 30 oz., set of 12*	625.00	650.00

	Price Range	

☐ **Gorham,** *cup and saucer, Lenox liner pink with gold trim, openwork design on holder, strap handle, total silver weight 15 oz., set of six* 300.00   325.00

☐ **Hickok-Matthews,** *cup and saucer, Lenox liner with etched gold trim, silver with raised floral design, pierced rim, hollow handle, total silver weight 36 oz., set of 12* 725.00   750.00

☐ **International,** *cup and saucer, Lenox liner with plain gold trim, openwork design on silver, hollow handle, total silver weight 24 oz., set of 12* 520.00   570.00

☐ **Lunt,** *cup and saucer, Lenox liner with plain gold trim, hammered finish on silver, strap handle, total silver weight 24 oz., set of 12* 525.00   575.00

☐ **Reed & Barton,** *cup and saucer, Lenox liner with raised enamel work and gold trim, silver plain with rolled rims and strap handle, total silver weight, 5 oz., pair* 100.00   120.00

☐ **Schofield,** *cup and saucer, Lenox liner with plain gold trim, silver plain with hollow handle, 3½ oz.* 65.00   70.00

☐ **Tiffany,** *cup and saucer, Lenox liner with etched gold trim, silver with allover etched design, silver weight 4 oz.* 70.00   80.00

DEMITASSE SPOONS

The demitasse cup (see above), smaller than a regulation drinking cup, required a spoon in proportion to its size. Hence these are lightweight, delicate, and appealing to many collectors.

(Coin Silver)

☐ **Albert Coles,** *New York City, c. 1850, twisted handle* 10.00   12.00

☐ **Kirk,** *pattern unknown, c. 1846-1861, engraved work* 8.00   10.00

☐ **Kirk "Repousse",** *ealiest mark, no monogram* 30.00   32.00

(Silver-Plated)

☐ **American Silver Co. "Moselle",** *no monogram, excellent condition* 12.00   14.00

☐ **American Silver Co. "Moselle",** *monogram, good condition* 4.00   5.00

☐ **Community "Bird of Paradise",** *no monogram, excellent condition* 4.00   5.00

☐ **Community "Bird of Paradise",** *no monogram, excellent condition* 5.00   6.00

☐ **Community "Coronation",** *no monogram, excellent condition* 6.00   7.00

☐ **Community "Coronation",** *no monogram, good condition* . 3.00   4.00

☐ **Community "Evening Star",** *no monogram, excellent condition* 7.00   8.00

☐ **Community "Evening Star",** *monogram, fair condition* 1.00   2.00

☐ **Community "Forever",** *no monogram, excellent condition* . 7.00   8.00

☐ **Community "Forever",** *no monogram, good condition* 4.00   5.00

☐ **Community "Georgian",** *no monogram, excellent condition* 7.00   8.00

☐ **Community "Georgian",** *no monogram, fair condition* 1.00   2.00

☐ **Community "Lady Hamilton",** *no monogram, excellent condition* 7.00   8.00

☐ **Community "Lady Hamilton",** *no monogram, excellent condition* 7.00   8.00

☐ **Community "Morning Rose",** *no monogram, mint condition* 4.00   5.00

	Price Range	
☐ Community "Patrician", *no monogram, excellent condition*	7.00	8.00
☐ Community "Patrician", *no monogram, good condition* ...	6.00	7.00
☐ Community "Randolph", *no monogram, good condition* ...	3.00	4.00
☐ Community "Randolph", *no monogram, excellent condition*	7.00	8.00
☐ Community "South Seas", *no monogram, excellent condition*	7.00	8.00
☐ Community "South Seas", *no monogram, mint condition* ..	7.00	8.00
☐ Community "White Orchid", *no monogram, excellent condition*	7.00	8.00
☐ Community "White Orchid", *no monogram, fair condition* .	1.00	2.00
☐ Community "Winsome", *no monogram, excellent condition*	7.00	8.00
☐ Crown "Cuban", *no monogram, excellent condition*	5.00	6.00
☐ Glastonbury Silver Co. "Leona", *no monogram, fair condition*	1.00	2.00
☐ Glastonbury Silver Co. "Leona", *no monogram, good condition*	3.00	4.00
☐ Gorham "Shelburne", *no monogram, excellent condition* ..	4.00	5.00
☐ Holmes & Edwards "Century", *no monogram, excellent condition*	7.00	8.00
☐ Holmes & Edwards "Century", *no monogram, good condition*	2.00	3.00
☐ Holmes & Edwards "Danish Princess", *no monogram, excellent condition*	4.00	5.00
☐ Holmes & Edwards "Danish Princess", *no monogram, fair condition*	1.00	2.00
☐ Holmes & Edwards "Pearl", *monogram, excellent condition*	4.00	5.00
☐ Holmes & Edwards "Pearl", *no monogram, excellent condition*	7.00	8.00
☐ Holmes & Edwards "Queen Anne", *no monogram, excellent condition*	3.00	4.00
☐ Holmes & Edwards "Queen Anne", *no monogram, good condition*	2.00	3.00
☐ International "Moritz", *no monogram, excellent condition* .	4.00	5.00
☐ International "Moritz", *no monogram, fair condition*	1.00	2.00
☐ National "King Edward", *no monogram, excellent condition*	7.00	8.00
☐ National "King Edward", *no monogram, good condition* ...	3.00	4.00
☐ Oxford "Narcissus", *no monogram, resilvered*	5.00	6.00
☐ Oxford "Narcissus", *no monogram, fair condition*	1.00	2.00
☐ Oxford "Narcissus", *no monogram, excellent condition* ...	6.00	7.00
☐ Oxford "Narcissus", *no monogram, good condition*	4.00	5.00
☐ Prestige "Grenoble", *no monogram, good condition*	4.00	5.00
☐ Prestige "Grenoble", *no monogram, fair condition*	1.00	2.00
☐ Reed & Barton "Cecil", *monogram, excellent condition* ...	2.00	3.00
☐ Reed & Barton "Commonwealth", *monogram, excellent condition*	1.00	2.00
☐ Reed & Barton "Maid of Honor", *no monogram, excellent condition*	6.00	7.00
☐ Reed & Barton "Maid of Honor", *no monogram, good condition*	2.00	3.00
☐ Reed & Barton "Rex", *no monogram, excellent condition* ..	7.00	8.00
☐ Reed & Barton "Rex", *no monogram, fair condition*	1.00	2.00
☐ Reed & Barton "Seville", *gold wash bowl, monogram, mint condition*	3.00	4.00
☐ Reed & Barton "Seville", *no monogram, excellent condition*	6.00	7.00

	Price Range	
☐ Reed & Barton "Tiger Lily", *no monogram, excellent condition*	5.00	6.00
☐ Reed & Barton "Tiger Lily", *no monogram, good condition*	4.00	5.00
☐ Reed & Barton "Vendome", *monogram, gold wash bowl, excellent condition*	2.00	3.00
☐ Reliance "Wildwood", *no monogram, excellent condition*	4.00	5.00
☐ Reliance "Wildwood", *no monogram, fair condition*	1.00	2.00
☐ Rockford "Fairoaks", *no monogram, excellent condition*	3.00	4.00
☐ Rockford "Fairoaks", *no monogram, excellent condition*	7.00	8.00
☐ Rogers "Alhambra", *monogram, excellent condition*	45.00	5.00
☐ Rogers "Alhambra", *no monogram, good condition*	3.00	4.00
☐ Rogers "Burgundy", *no monogram, good condition*	4.00	5.00
☐ Rogers "Burgundy", *no monogram, excellent condition*	7.00	8.00
☐ Rogers "Carlton", *no monogram, excellent condition*	7.00	8.00
☐ Rogers "Carlton", *monogram, excellent condition*	2.00	3.00
☐ Rogers "Clinton", *no monogram, excellent condition*	6.00	7.00
☐ Rogers "Clinton", *no monogram, good condition*	5.00	6.00
☐ Rogers "Navarre", *no monogram, excellent condition*	5.00	6.00
☐ Rogers "Newport", *no monogram, excellent condition*	5.00	6.00
☐ Rogers "Newport", *no monogram, good condition*	3.00	4.00
☐ Rogers "Orange Blossom", *no monogram, excellent condition*	7.00	8.00
☐ Rogers "Orange Blossom", *no monogram, good condition*	3.00	4.00
☐ Rogers "Orange Blossom", *no monogram, fair condition*	1.00	2.00
☐ Rogers & Bro. "Columbia", *monogram, excellent condition, set of six in original presentation box*	65.00	75.00
☐ Rogers & Bro. "Columbia", *no monogram, excellent condition*	11.00	13.00
☐ Rogers & Bro. "Siren", *no monogram, gold wash bowl, excellent condition*	10.00	12.00
☐ Rogers & Bro. "Thistle", *no monogram, excellent condition*	4.00	5.00
☐ Rogers & Bro. "Thistle", *no monogram, excellent condition*	7.00	8.00
☐ Rogers & Hamilton "Cardinal", *no monogram, excellent condition*	4.00	5.00
☐ Stratford "Shakespeare", *no monogram, excellent condition*	3.00	4.00
☐ Towle "Engraved", *gold wash bowl, no monogram, excellent condition*	5.00	6.00
☐ Towle "Engraved", *no monogram, good condition*	5.00	6.00
☐ Towle "Log Cabin", *no monogram, excellent condition*	8.00	9.00
☐ W. D. Smith Co. "Adam", *no monogram, excellent condition*	2.00	3.00
☐ W. D. Smith Co. "Adam", *no monogram, excellent condition*	7.00	8.00
☐ Williams Bros. "Isabella", *no monogram, excellent condition*	4.00	5.00
☐ Wm. A. Rogers "Garland", *no monogram, excellent condition*	3.00	4.00
☐ Wm. A. Rogers "Garland", *no monogram, fair condition*	1.00	2.00
☐ Wm. A. Rogers "Garland", *no monogram, good condition*	3.00	4.00
☐ Wm. A. Rogers "Hanover", *no monogram, resilvered*	3.00	4.00
☐ Wm. A. Rogers "Hanover", *no monogram, excellent condition*	5.00	6.00
☐ Wm. A. Rogers "Meadowbrook", *no monogram, excellent condition*	7.00	8.00

	Price Range	
☐ **Wm. A. Rogers "Meadowbrook"**, *monogram, excellent condition*	2.00	3.00
☐ **Wm. A. Rogers "Narcissus"**, *no monogram, poor condition*	7.00	8.00
☐ **Wm. A. Rogers "Narcissus"**, *monogram, good condition* ..	10.00	12.00
☐ **Wm. Rogers "Arbutus"**, *no monogram, excellent condition*	6.00	7.00
☐ **Wm. Rogers "Arbutus"**, *no monogram, good condition*	5.00	6.00
☐ **Wm. Rogers "Athens"**, *no monogram, excellent condition* .	4.00	5.00
☐ **Wm. Rogers "Athens"**, *no monogram, good condition*	4.00	5.00
☐ **Wm. Rogers "Tuxedo"**, *no monogram, excellent condition* .	6.00	7.00
☐ **Wm. Rogers "Tuxedo"**, *monogram, excellent condition* ...	4.00	5.00
☐ **Wm. Rogers Mfg. Co. "Alhambra"**, *monogram, resilvered* ..	3.00	4.00
☐ **Wm. Rogers Mfg. Co. "Alhambra"**, *no monogram, excellent condition*	7.00	8.00
☐ **Wm. Rogers Mfg. Co. "Arbutus"**, *monogram, good condition*	4.00	5.00
☐ **Wm. Rogers Mfg. Co. "Arbutus"**, *no monogram, good condition*	5.00	6.00
☐ **Wm. Rogers Mfg. Co. "Daisy"**, *no monogram, excellent condition*	4.00	5.00
☐ **Wm. Rogers Mfg. Co. "Daisy"**, *no monogram, good condition*	3.00	4.00
☐ **Wm. Rogers Mfg. Co. "Lady Densmore"**, *no monogram, excellent condition*	7.00	8.00
☐ **Wm. Rogers & Son "Arbutus"**, *no monogram, excellent condition*	7.00	8.00
☐ **1835 R. Wallace "Cardinal"**, *no monogram, excellent condition*	7.00	8.00
☐ **1835 R. Wallace "Cardinal"**, *monogram, excellent condition*	3.00	4.00
☐ **1835 R. Wallace "Floral"**, *no monogram, good condition* ..	2.00	3.00
☐ **1935 R. Wallace "Floral"**, *no monogram, excellent condition*	8.00	10.00
☐ **1947 Rogers "Assyrian"**, *no monogram, excellent condition*	7.00	8.00
☐ **1847 Rogers "Assyrian"**, *no monogram, fair condition*	2.00	3.00
☐ **1847 Rogers "Assyrian"**, *no monogram, excellent condition*	8.00	10.00
☐ **1847 Rogers "Assyrian Head"**, *no monogram, resilvered* ..	4.00	5.00
☐ **1847 Rogers "Avon"**, *no monogram, excellent condition* ...	8.00	9.00
☐ **1847 Rogers "Avon"**, *no monogram, good condition*	4.00	5.00
☐ **1847 Rogers "Avon"**, *no monogram, excellent condition* ...	8.00	9.00
☐ **1847 Rogers "Avon"**, *no monogram, mint condition*	18.00	20.00
☐ **1847 Rogers "Berkshire"**, *no monogram, excellent condition*	7.00	8.00
☐ **1847 Rogers "Berkshire"**, *no monogram, excellent condition*	8.00	9.00
☐ **1847 Rogers "Berkshire"**, *monogram, excellent condition* .	4.00	5.00
☐ **1847 Rogers "Charter Oak"**, *monogram, good condition* ...	2.00	3.00
☐ **1847 Rogers "Charter Oak"**, *monogram, fair condition*	1.00	2.00
☐ **1847 Rogers "Charter Oak"**, *no monogram, excellent condition*	10.00	12.00
☐ **1847 Rogers "Charter Oak"**, *no monogram, excellent condition*	12.00	14.00
☐ **1847 Rogers "Columbia"**, *no monogram, resilvered*	6.00	7.00
☐ **1847 Rogers "Columbia"**, *no monogram, excellent condition*	8.00	9.00
☐ **1847 Rogers "Columbia"**, *monogram, fair condition*	2.00	3.00

	Price Range	
☐ **1847 Rogers "Coral"**, *no monogram, good condition*	6.00	7.00
☐ **1847 Rogers "Coral"**, *no monogram, excellent condition* . .	8.00	9.00
☐ **1847 Rogers "Cromwell"**, *no monogram, excellent condition*	3.00	4.00
☐ **1847 Rogers "Daffodil"**, *no monogram, good condition*	2.00	3.00
☐ **1847 Rogers "Daffodil"**, *no monogram, excellent condition*	8.00	10.00
☐ **1847 Rogers "Dundee"**, *no monogram, excellent condition*	4.00	5.00
☐ **1847 Rogers "Esperanto"**, *no monogram, mint condition* . .	4.00	5.00
☐ **1847 Rogers "Eternally Yours"**, *no monogram, excellent condition*	4.00	5.00
☐ **1847 Rogers "Flair"**, *no monogram, excellent condition* . . .	7.00	8.00
☐ **1847 Rogers "Flair"**, *no monogram, good condition*	4.00	5.00
☐ **1847 Rogers "Linden"**, *no monogram, excellent condition* .	4.00	5.00
☐ **1847 Rogers "Linden"**, *no monogram, fair condition*	1.00	2.00
☐ **1847 Rogers "Lotus"**, *no monogram, excellent condition* . .	6.00	7.00
☐ **1847 Rogers "Lotus"**, *no monogram, excellent condition* . .	8.00	9.00
☐ **1847 Rogers "Magic Rose"**, *no monogram, excellent condition*	7.00	8.00
☐ **1847 Rogers "Magic Rose"**, *no monogram, good condition*	4.00	5.00
☐ **1847 Rogers "Old Colony"**, *monogram, excellent condition*	2.00	3.00
☐ **1847 Rogers "Portland"**, *no monogram, good condition* . . .	7.00	8.00
☐ **1847 Rogers "Portland"**, *no monogram, fair condition*	1.00	2.00
☐ **1847 Rogers "Queen Ann"**, *no monogram, excellent condition*	7.00	8.00
☐ **1847 Rogers "Queen Ann"**, *monogram, excellent condition*	3.00	4.00
☐ **1847 Rogers "Ruby"**, *no monogram, excellent condition* . . .	6.00	7.00
☐ **1847 Rogers "Ruby"**, *no monogram, excellent condition* . . .	7.00	8.00
☐ **1847 Rogers "Savoy"**, *excellent condition*	4.00	5.00
☐ **1847 Rogers "Sharon"**, *no monogram, excellent condition* .	6.00	7.00
☐ **1847 Rogers "Sharon"**, *monogram, excellent condition* . . .	3.00	4.00
☐ **1847 Rogers "Sharon"**, *no monogram, excellent condition* .	8.00	9.00
☐ **1847 Rogers "Vesta"**, *no monogram, excellent condition* . .	7.00	8.00
☐ **1847 Rogers "Vintage"**, *no monogram, good condition*	5.00	6.00
☐ **1847 Rogers "Vintage"**, *no monogram, excellent condition*	10.00	12.00
☐ **1847 Rogers "Vintage"**, *no monogram, gold wash bowl, mint condition*	12.00	14.00
☐ **Maker unknown**, *U.S. Navy kings pattern, fair condition* . . .	1.00	2.00

(Sterling Silver)

	Price Range	
☐ **Alvin "Miss America"**, *no monogram*	4.00	5.00
☐ **Alvin "Bridal Rose"**, *monogram*	12.00	14.00
☐ **Durgin "Chrysanthemum"**, *monogram*	18.00	20.00
☐ **Durgin "Fairfax"**, *no monogram*	4.00	5.00
☐ **Durgin "Fairfax"**, *no monogram*	7.00	8.00
☐ **Durgin "Sheaf of Wheat"**, *no monogram*	12.00	15.00
☐ **Gorham "Buttercup"**, *no monogram*	8.00	9.00
☐ **Gorham "Colonial"**, *no monogram*	4.00	5.00
☐ **Gorham "Imperial Chrysanthemum"**, *gold wash bowl, date and monogram*	10.00	12.00
☐ **Gorham "Imperial Chrysanthemum"**, *gold wash bowl, no monogram*	12.00	14.00
☐ **Gorham "Old French"**, *monogram*	8.00	9.00
☐ **Gorham "Plymouth"**, *monogram*	5.00	6.00
☐ **Gorham "Raphael"**, *no monogram*	6.00	7.00

	Price Range	
☐ Gorham "Strasbourg", *no monogram*	7.00	8.00
☐ Gorham "Versailles", *gold wash bowl, no monogram*	13.00	15.00
☐ International "Joan of Arc", *no monogram*	8.00	9.00
☐ International "Royal Danish", *monogram*	6.00	7.00
☐ International "Royal Danish", *no monogram*	9.00	10.00
☐ Manchester "Amarylis", *monogram*	8.00	9.00
☐ Oneida "Heiress", *no monogram*	10.00	11.00
☐ Reed & Barton "Francis I", *no monogram*	10.00	12.00
☐ Reed & Barton "Francis I", *no monogram*	12.00	14.00
☐ Reed & Barton "Francis I", *no monogram*	14.00	16.00
☐ Reed & Barton "Hawthorne", *no monogram*	8.00	9.00
☐ Tiffany "Beekman", *monogram*	10.00	12.00
☐ Tiffany "English King", *monogram*	10.00	12.00
☐ Tiffany "Renaissance", *no monogram*	18.00	20.00
☐ Towle "King Richard", *no monogram*	13.00	15.00
☐ Towle "Madeira", *no monogram*	10.00	12.00
☐ Tuttle "Onslow", *no monogram*	12.00	14.00
☐ Wallace "Irving", *no monogram*	8.00	9.00
☐ Whiting "Honeysuckle", *no monogram*	10.00	12.00
☐ Whiting "Imperial", *no monogram*	8.00	9.00
☐ Whiting "Louis XV", *monogram*	10.00	11.00
☐ Maker unknown, *enamel work*	9.00	10.00

DESK SETS

Desk Set, *maker unknown, blotter, pen holder on tray, covered inkwell, calendar holder,* 90.00

(Sterling Silver)

☐ **Maker unknown,** *includes rocker blotter, tray with sealing wax burner, holder for pen, bowl with pen wiper and round covered inkwell with glass liner*	100.00	110.00

DESSERT SPOONS

As is often the case with table silver, "dessert spoons" does not clearly indicate the use to which articles were placed. They were not used for all types of desserts, and certainly never for fruit unless the hostess was blundering. When fruits appeared at dessert, they were eaten with a *fruit spoon. Dessert spoons* were used chiefly for puddings, custards and the like, and occasionally for mushy cakes. They have a shallow circular bowl.

(Coin Silver)	Price Range	
☐ **Shoemaker,** *Philadephia, c. 1840, fiddle-back pattern with wheat design*	34.00	36.00
☐ **Twedy & Barrows,** *location unknown, fiddle-back pattern with basket of flowers, pair*	70.00	75.00

(Silver-Plated)

☐ **American Silver Company "Moselle",** *no monogram, excellent condition*	10.00	12.00
☐ **American Silver Company "Moselle",** *monogram, fair condition*	4.00	5.00
☐ **American Silver Company "Nenuphar",** *no monogram, excellent condition*	3.00	4.00
☐ **Community "Ballad",** *no monogram, excellent condition* ..	4.00	5.00
☐ **Community "Ballad",** *monogram, good condition*	3.00	4.00
☐ **Community "Coronation",** *no monogram, mint condition* ..	5.00	6.00
☐ **Community "Coronation",** *no monogram, excellent condition*	5.00	6.00
☐ **Community "Flight",** *no monogram, mint condition*	5.00	6.00
☐ **Community "Flight",** *no monogram, fair condition*	1.00	2.00
☐ **Community "Lady Hamilton",** *no monogram, good condition*	3.00	4.00
☐ **Community "Lady Hamilton",** *no monogram, excellent condition*	5.00	6.00
☐ **Community "Morning Rose",** *no monogram, mint condition*	4.00	5.00
☐ **Community "Morning Rose",** *no monogram, good condition*	1.00	2.00
☐ **Community "Noblesse",** *no monogram, excellent condition*	3.00	4.00
☐ **Community "Patrician",** *no monogram, excellent condition*	3.00	4.00
☐ **Community "Patrician",** *no monogram, good condition* ...	2.00	3.00
☐ **Community "Silver Flower",** *no monogram, mint condition*	4.00	5.00
☐ **Community "Silver Flower",** *monogram, good condition* ...	1.00	2.00
☐ **Community "Silver Sands",** *no monogram, mint condition* .	4.00	5.00
☐ **Community "Sands",** *no monogram, poor condition*	1.00	2.00
☐ **Community "Silver Valentine",** *no monogram, mint condition*	4.00	5.00
☐ **Community "South Seas",** *no monogram, good condition* .	1.00	2.00
☐ **Community "Tangier",** *no monogram, mint condition*	4.00	5.00
☐ **Community "White Orchid",** *no monogram, excellent condition*	4.00	5.00
☐ **Community "White Orchid",** *no monogram, good condition*	2.00	3.00
☐ **Gorham "Winthrop",** *no monogram, mint condition*	4.00	5.00
☐ **Gorham "Winthrop",** *no monogram, good condition*	1.00	2.00
☐ **Harmony House "Classic Filigree",** *no monogram, excellent condition*	1.50	2.50
☐ **Harmony House "Maytime",** *no monogram, excellent condition*	1.00	2.00
☐ **Harmony House "Serenade",** *no monogram, excellent condition*	1.00	2.00
☐ **Heirloom "Cardinal",** *no monogram, excellent condition* ..	4.00	5.00
☐ **Heirloom "Cardinal",** *monogram, mint condition*	3.00	4.00
☐ **Holmes & Edwards "Danish Princess",** *no monogram, excellent condition*	4.00	5.00
☐ **Holmes & Edwards "Lovely Lady",** *no monogram, mint condition*	4.00	5.00

Price Range

☐ Holmes & Edwards "Lovely Lady", *no monogram, excellent condition*	34.00	4.00
☐ Holmes & Edwards "May Queen", *no monogram, mint condition*	4.00	5.00
☐ Holmes & Edwards "May Queen", *no monogram, good condition*	2.00	3.00
☐ Holmes & Edwards "Orient", *no monogram, excellent condition*	5.00	6.00
☐ Holmes & Edwards "Orient", *no monogram, fair condition* .	1.00	2.00
☐ Oneida "Flower de Luce", *no monogram, resilvered*	6.00	7.00
☐ Oneida "Flower de Luce", *no monogram, good condition* ..	3.00	4.00
☐ Oneida "Louis XVI", *no monogram, fair condition*	1.00	2.00
☐ Oneida "Louis XVI", *no monogram, good condition*	3.00	4.00
☐ Reed & Barton "Oxford", *no monogram, excellent condition*	4.00	5.00
☐ Reed & Barton "Oxford", *no monogram, fair condition*	1.00	2.00
☐ R.C. Co. "Isabella", *no monogram, excellent condition*	5.00	6.00
☐ R.C. Co. "Isabella", *no monogram, good condition*	3.00	4.00
☐ Rogers "Norfolk", *no monogram, excellent condition*	4.00	5.00
☐ Rogers "Queen Bess II", *no monogram, excellent condition*	1.00	2.00
☐ Rogers & Bro. "Assyrian", *no monogram, excellent condition*	6.00	7.00
☐ Rogers & Bro. "Cromwell", *no monogram, excellent condition*	3.00	4.00
☐ Rogers & Bro. "Laurel", *no monogram, fair condition*	1.00	2.00
☐ Rogers & Bro. "Tuxedo", *no monogram, fair condition*	2.00	3.00
☐ Rogers & Bro. "Tuxedo", *monogram, excellent condition* ..	7.00	8.00
☐ Rogers & Hamilton "Marquise", *no monogram, excellent condition*	4.00	5.00
☐ S.L. & G.H. Rogers "English Garden", *no monogram, excellent condition*	3.00	4.00
☐ S.L. & G.H. Rogers "Violet", *no monogram, excellent condition*	6.00	7.00
☐ Towle "Chester", *no monogram, good condition*	1.00	2.00
☐ Tudor "Bridal Wreath", *no monogram, mint condition*	4.00	5.00
☐ Tudor "Mary Stuart", *no monogram, excellent condition* ..	3.00	4.00
☐ Tudor "Together", *no monogram, mint condition*	4.00	5.00
☐ W.D. Smith "Adam", *monogram, excellent condition*	2.00	3.00
☐ W.D. Smith "Adam', *no monogram, good condition*	2.00	3.00
☐ Williams Bros. "Isabella", *no monogram, resilvered*	6.00	7.00
☐ Wm. A. Rogers "Debutante", *no monogram, excellent condition*	3.00	4.00
☐ Wm. A. Rogers "Debutante", *monogram, fair condition* ...	1.00	2.00
☐ Wm. Rogers "Arbutus", *no monogram, excellent condition*	5.00	6.00
☐ Wm. Rogers "Arbutus", *no monogram, good condition*	2.00	3.00
☐ Wm. Rogers "Beloved", *no monogram, excellent condition*	4.00	5.00
☐ Wm. Rogers "Exquisite", *no monogram, excellent condition*	4.00	5.00
☐ Wm. Rogers "Exquisite", *no monogram, poor condition* ...	1.00	2.00
☐ Wm. Rogers "Treasure", *no monogram, excellent condition*	3.00	4.00
☐ Wm. Rogers Mfg. Co. "Alhambra", *no monogram, fair condition*	2.00	3.00
☐ Wm. Rogers Mfg. Co. "Arbutus", *no monogram, fair condition*	1.00	2.00

	Price Range	
☐ Wm. Rogers Mfg. Co. "Arbutus", *no monogram, excellent condition*	8.00	9.00
☐ Wm. Rogers Mfg. Co. "Berwick", *no monogram, excellent condition*	5.00	6.00
☐ Wm. Rogers Mfg. Co. "Berwick", *no monogram, good condition*	3.00	4.00
☐ Wm. Rogers Mfg. Co. "York", *no monogram, good condition*	2.00	3.00
☐ 1835 R. Wallace "Astoria", *no monogram, excellent condition*	2.00	3.00
☐ 1835 R. Wallace "Joan", *no monogram, excellent condition*	3.00	4.00
☐ 1835 R. Wallace "Joan", *no monogram, fair condition*	1.00	2.00
☐ 1847 Rogers "Adoration", *no monogram, excellent condition*	5.00	6.00
☐ 1847 Rogers "Adoration", *no monogram, good condition*	2.00	3.00
☐ 1847 Rogers "Berkshire", *no monogram, excellent condition*	7.00	8.00
☐ 1847 Rogers "Berkshire", *no monogram, resilvered*	6.00	7.00
☐ 1847 Rogers "Charter Oak", *no monogram, resilvered*	6.00	7.00
☐ 1847 Rogers "Charter Oak", *no monogram, excellent condition*	8.00	9.00
☐ 1847 Rogers "Charter Oak", *no monogram, good condition*	4.00	5.00
☐ 1847 Rogers "Columbia", *no monogram, excellent condition*	7.00	8.00
☐ 1847 Rogers "Columbia", *no monogram, good condition*	4.00	5.00
☐ 1847 Rogers "Columbia", *no monogram, fair condition*	1.00	2.00
☐ 1847 Rogers "Daffodil", *no monogram, excellent condition*	4.00	5.00
☐ 1847 Rogers "Daffodil", *monogram, good condition*	2.00	3.00
☐ 1847 Rogers "Esperanto", *no monogram, mint condition*	4.00	5.00
☐ 1847 Rogers "Esperanto", *no monogram, excellent condition*	4.00	5.00
☐ 1847 Rogers "First Love", *no monogram, excellent condition*	3.00	4.00
☐ 1847 Rogers "Flair", *no monogram, excellent condition*	3.00	4.00
☐ 1847 Rogers "Gothic", *no monogram, excellent condition*	3.00	4.00
☐ 1847 Rogers "Heritage", *no monogram, excellent condition*	5.00	6.00
☐ 1847 Rogers "Louvain", *no monogram, poor condition*	1.00	2.00
☐ 1847 Rogers "Magic Rose", *no monogram, excellent condition*	2.00	3.00
☐ 1847 Rogers "Magic Rose", *no monogram, mint condition*	3.00	4.00
☐ 1847 Rogers "Moline", *no monogram, excellent condition*	3.00	4.00
☐ 1847 Rogers "Moselle", *no monogram, excellent condition*	14.00	16.00
☐ 1847 Rogers "Moselle", *no monogram, excellent condition*	18.00	20.00
☐ 1847 Rogers "Moselle", *no monogram, fair condition*	5.00	6.00
☐ 1847 Rogers "Newport", *no monogram, resilvered*	4.00	5.00
☐ 1847 Rogers "Newport", *no monogram, good condition*	2.00	3.00
☐ 1847 Rogers "Old Colony", *no monogram, excellent condition*	3.00	4.00
☐ 1847 Rogers "Remembrance", *no monogram, good condition*	2.00	3.00
☐ 1847 Rogers "Remembrance", *no monogram, mint condition*	5.00	6.00
☐ 1847 Rogers "Sharon", *no monogram, excellent condition*	4.00	5.00
☐ 1847 Rogers "Springtime", *no monogram, good condition*	2.00	3.00

	Price Range	
☐ **1847 Rogers "Vintage"**, *no monogram, good condition*	8.00	9.00
☐ **1847 Rogers "Vintage"**, *no monogram, poor condition*	3.00	4.00
☐ **1847 Rogers "Vintage"**, *no monogram, excellent condition*	10.00	12.00
☐ **1881 Rogers "Coronet"**, *no monogram, good condition*	3.00	4.00
☐ **1881 Rogers "Flirtation"**, *no monogram, excellent condition*	3.00	4.00
☐ **1881 Rogers "LaVigne"**, *no monogram, fair condition*	3.00	4.00
☐ **1881 Rogers "LaVigne"**, *no monogram, excellent condition*	8.00	10.00

(Sterling Silver)

☐ **Alvin "Orange Blossom"**, *monogram and date*	22.00	24.00
☐ **Kirk "Repousse"**, *no monogram*	16.00	18.00
☐ **Reed & Barton "LaParisienne"**, *monogram*	20.00	22.00
☐ **Towle "Cambridge"**, *no monogram*	10.00	12.00
☐ **Wendt "Kings"**, *monogram*	18.00	20.00

DINNER FORKS

In silverware terminology, the *dinner fork* is equivalent to the standard dining table fork. It is not simply called a fork becuase the world of silver includes other types of forks. In households where proper etiquette was observed, the dinner fork was restricted to use at that meal, while the luncheon table was supplied with *luncheon forks.* The presumption (not always true, but presumptions weigh heavily where etiquette is concerned) was that luncheon foods were of a lighter character and therefore better suited to a more streamlined fork. The dinner fork, which had to go into battle against potentially leathery meats, needed to be somewhat brawnier. Usually when someone says he collects silver forks and makes no further distinction, he means dinner forks. They exist in numbers beyond reckoning and will be found in every antiques shops, and in most outlets for general household merchandise. Their overall commonness should not induce anyone to believe that ALL speicmens are of low collector value. As the listings indicate, some are worth twice or three times as much as others; while especially old or fine examples can go for much, much more. In 18th century England, souvenir forks were occasionally made and these, very richly ornamented, have brought as much as $100 apiece.

(Coin Silver)

☐ **Hood & Tobey**, *c. 1848, monogram*	12.00	15.00

(Silver-Plated)

☐ **Alvin "Bouquet"**, *excellent condition*	2.00	3.00
☐ **Alvin "Bouquet"**, *no monogram, good condition*	2.00	3.00
☐ **Alvin "Diana"**, *monogram, excellent condition*	1.00	2.00
☐ **Alvin "Molly Stark"**, *monogram, good condition*	1.00	2.00
☐ **American Silver Co. "Corona"**, *no monogram, excellent condition*	3.00	4.00
☐ **American Silver Co. "Corona"**, *no monogram, fair condition*	1.00	2.00
☐ **American Silver Co. "Wildflower"**, *no monogram, excellent condition*	5.00	6.00
☐ **American Silver Co. "Wildflower"**, *no monogram, good condition*	4.00	5.00
☐ **American Silver Co. "Wildflower"**, *no monogram, fair condition*	1.00	2.00

Price Range

☐ **Benedict Mfg. Co. "Continental"**, *no monogram, good condition* 2.00 3.00
☐ **Community "Adam"**, *no monogram, excellent condition* .. 3.00 4.00
☐ **Community "Adam"**, *no monogram, good condition* 3.00 4.00
☐ **Community "Adam"**, *hollow-handled, no monogram, fair condition* 1.00 2.00
☐ **Community "Bird of Paradise"**, *no monogram, excellent condition* 4.00 5.00
☐ **Community "Bird of Paradise"**, *no monogram, good condition* 3.00 4.00
☐ **Community "Bird of Paradise"**, *no monogram, excellent condition* 5.00 6.00
☐ **Community "Bird of Paradise"**, *no monogram, good condition* 3.00 4.00
☐ **Community "Coronation"**, *no monogram, mint condition* .. 5.00 6.00
☐ **Community "Coronation"**, *no monogram, good condition* . 4.00 5.00
☐ **Community "Coronation"**, *viande style, no monogram, fair condition* 3.00 4.00
☐ **Community "Coronation"**, *no monogram, fair condition* ... 3.00 4.00
☐ **Community "Coronation"**, *no monogram, excellent condition* 5.00 6.00
☐ **Community "Coronation"**, *no monogram, good condition* . 4.00 5.00
☐ **Community "Deauville"**, *no monogram, excellent condition* 5.00 6.00
☐ **Community "Deauville"**, *no monogram, excellent condition* 3.00 4.00
☐ **Community "Enchantment"**, *no monogram, excellent condition* 5.00 6.00
☐ **Community "Enchantment"**, *no monogram, good condition* 4.00 5.00
☐ **Community "Evening Star"**, *no monogram, excellent condition* 5.00 6.00
☐ **Community "Evening Star"**, *no monogram, good condition* 4.00 5.00
☐ **Community "Flower de Luce"**, *no monogram, excellent condition* 5.00 6.00
☐ **Community "Flower de Luce"**, *hollow-handled, no monogram, good condition* 6.00 7.00
☐ **Community "Forever"**, *no monogram, excellent condition* . 5.00 6.00
☐ **Community "Forever"**, *no monogram, good condition* 4.00 5.00
☐ **Community "Georgian"**, *no monogram, excellent condition* 2.00 3.00
☐ **Community "Georgian"**, *no monogram, excellent condition* 5.00 6.00
☐ **Community "Grosvenor"**, *monogram, excellent condition* . 2.00 3.00
☐ **Community "Grosvenor"**, *no monogram, good condition* .. 2.00 3.00
☐ **Community "Grosvenor"**, *no monogram, excellent condition* 3.00 4.00
☐ **Community "Grosvenor"**, *no monogram, excellent condition* 3.00 4.00
☐ **Community "Grosvenor"**, *no monogram, good condition* .. 3.00 4.00
☐ **Community "King Cedric"**, *viande style, no monogram, good condition* 4.00 5.00
☐ **Community "King Cedric"**, *viande style, no monogram, fair condition* 1.00 2.00
☐ **Community "King Cedric"**, *no monogram, good condition* . 4.00 5.00
☐ **Community "Lady Hamilton"**, *no monogram, excellent condition* 5.00 6.00
☐ **Community "Lady Hamilton"**, *no monogram, good condition* 4.00 5.00

Price Range

☐ Community "Lady Hamilton", *no monogram, poor condition* 1.00   2.00
☐ Community "Louis XVI", *hollow-handled, monogram, excellent condition* 3.00   4.00
☐ Community "Louis XVI", *hollow-handled, no monogram, good condition* 2.00   3.00
☐ Community "Louis XVI", *no monogram, excellent condition*   5.00   6.00
☐ Community "Louis XVI", *no monogram, good condition* ... 4.00   5.00
☐ Community "Louis XVI", *monogram, excellent condition* .. 2.00   3.00
☐ Community "Milady", *no monogram, good condition* 4.00   5.00
☐ Community "Milady", *no monogram, fair condition* 1.00   2.00
☐ Community "Morning Rose", *no monogram, excellent condition* 5.00   6.00
☐ Community "Morning Rose", *no monogram, good condition* 4.00   5.00
☐ Community "Morning Star", *no monogram, good condition*   2.00   3.00
☐ Community "Morning Star", *no monogram, fair condition* . 1.00   2.00
☐ Community "Morning Star", *viande style, no monogram, good condition* 4.00   5.00
☐ Community "Noblesse", *viande style, no monogram, good condition* 4.00   5.00
☐ Community "Noblesse", *viande style, monogram, excellent condition* 1.00   2.00
☐ Community "Noblesse", *no monogram, excellent condition*   3.00   4.00
☐ Community "Patrician", *monogram, excellent condition* .. 1.00   2.00
☐ Community "Patrician", *no monogram, excellent condition*   3.00   4.00
☐ Community "Patrician", *no monogram, excellent condition*   5.00   6.00
☐ Community "Patrician", *no monogram, good condition* ... 4.00   5.00
☐ Community "Paul Revere", *no monogram, excellent condition* 5.00   6.00
☐ Community "Paul Revere", *no monogram, good condition* . 4.00   5.00
☐ Community "Paul Revere", *no monogram, fair condition* .. 1.00   2.00
☐ Community "Sheraton", *hollow-handled, no monogram, excellent condition* 7.00   8.00
☐ Community "Sheraton", *hollow-handled, no monogram, good condition* 5.00   6.00
☐ Community "Sheraton", *no monogram, excellent condition*   5.00   6.00
☐ Community "Sheraton", *no monogram, good condition* ... 4.00   5.00
☐ Community "Silver Sands", *no monogram, excellent condition* 6.00   7.00
☐ Community "Silver Sands", *no monogram, good condition*   4.00   5.00
☐ Community "Silver Sands", *monogram, excellent condition*   2.00   3.00
☐ Community "South Seas", *no monogram, mint condition* .. 4.00   5.00
☐ Community "South Seas", *no monogram, good condition* . 4.00   5.00
☐ Community "South Seas", *no monogram, fair condition* ... 1.00   2.00
☐ Community "White Orchid", *no monogram, mint condition* 4.00   5.00
☐ Community "White Orchid", *no monogram, excellent condition* 5.00   6.00
☐ Court "Court", *no monogram, excellent condition* 3.00   4.00
☐ DeepSilver "Laurel Mist", *no monogram, excellent condition* 5.00   6.00

	Price Range	
☐ DeepSilver "Laurel Mist", *no monogram, good condition* ..	4.00	5.00
☐ DeepSilver "Triumph", *no monogram, excellent condition* .	5.00	6.00
☐ DeepSilver "Triumph", *no monogram, good condition*	4.00	5.00
☐ DeepSilver "Triumph", *no monogram, fair condition*	1.00	2.00
☐ Derby "Harvard", *no monogram, excellent condition*	4.00	5.00
☐ Derby "Harvard", *no monogram, good condition*	2.00	3.00
☐ E.H.H. Smith "Oak", *no monogram, excellent condition* ...	2.00	3.00
☐ Embassy "Bouquet", *no monogram, excellent condition* ..	4.00	5.00
☐ Embassy "Bouquet", *no monogram, good condition*	3.00	4.00
☐ Fortune "Fortune", *no monogram, excellent condition*	5.00	6.00
☐ Fortune "Fortune", *no monogram, good condition*	4.00	5.00
☐ Gorham "Carolina", *no monogram, excellent condition* ...	4.00	5.00
☐ Gorham "Carolina", *no monogram, good condition*	4.00	5.00
☐ Gorham "Empire", *no monogram, excellent condition*	3.00	4.00
☐ Gorham "Empire", *no monogram, fair condition*	1.00	2.00
☐ Gorham "Kings", *monogram, excellent condition*	3.00	4.00
☐ Gorham "Kings", *no monogram, excellent condition*	6.00	7.00
☐ Gorham "Kings", *no monogram, excellent condition*	7.00	8.00
☐ Gorham "Lady Caroline", *no monogram, excellent condition*	5.00	6.00
☐ Gorham "Lady Caroline", *no monogram, good condition* ..	4.00	5.00
☐ Gorham "New Elegance", *no monogram, good condition* ..	4.00	5.00
☐ Gorham "New Elegance", *no monogram, fair condition* ...	1.00	2.00
☐ Gorham "Richmond", *no monogram, excellent condition* ..	7.00	8.00
☐ Gorham "Richmond", *no monogram, good condition*	6.00	7.00
☐ Gorham "Shelburne", *no monogram, poor condition*	2.00	3.00
☐ Gorham "Vanity Fair", *no monogram, excellent condition* .	2.00	3.00
☐ Hall, Elton & Co. "Orient", *no monogram, mint condition* ..	5.00	6.00
☐ Hall, Elton & Co. "Orient", *no monogram, fair condition* ...	1.00	2.00
☐ Harmony House "Maytime", *no monogram, excellent condition*	2.00	3.00
☐ Holmes & Edwards "Century", *no monogram, good condition*	4.00	5.00
☐ Holmes & Edwards "Danish Princess", *no monogram, excellent condition*	4.00	5.00
☐ Holmes & Edwards "Danish Princess", *no monogram, good condition*	2.00	3.00
☐ Holmes & Edwards "First Lady", *no monogram, excellent condition*	5.00	6.00
☐ Holmes & Edwards "First Lady", *no monogram, good condition*	4.00	5.00
☐ Holmes & Edwards "Lovely Lady", *monogram, excellent condition*	2.00	3.00
☐ Holmes & Edwards "Lovely Lady", *no monogram, excellent condition*	2.00	3.00
☐ Holmes & Edwards "Lovely Lady", *no monogram, excellent condition*	5.00	6.00
☐ Holmes & Edwards "Lovely Lady", *no monogram, good condition*	4.00	5.00
☐ Holmes & Edwards "Lovely Lady", *viande style, no monogram, excellent condition*	2.00	3.00
☐ Holmes & Edwards "May Queen", *no monogram, mint condition*	4.00	5.00

Price Range

☐ **Holmes & Edwards "Nassau"**, *no monogram, excellent condition*	3.00	4.00
☐ **Holmes & Edwards "Nassau"**, *no monogram, good condition*	3.00	5.00
☐ **Holmes & Edwards "Orient"**, *no monogram, resilvered*	4.00	5.00
☐ **Holmes & Edwards "Orient"**, *no monogram, fair condition* .	1.00	2.00
☐ **Holmes & Edwards "Romance II"**, *no monogram, excellent condition*	3.00	4.00
☐ **Holmes & Edwards "Rosemary"**, *no monogram, excellent condition*	3.00	4.00
☐ **Holmes & Edwards "Spring Garden"**, *no monogram, excellent condition*	5.00	6.00
☐ **Holmes & Edwards "Spring Garden"**, *no monogram, fair condition*	1.00	2.00
☐ **Holmes & Edwards "Woodsong"**, *no monogram, excellent condition*	5.00	6.00
☐ **Holmes & Edwards "Woodsong"**, *no monogram, good condition*	4.00	5.00
☐ **International "Beacon Hill"**, *no monogram, excellent condition*	5.00	6.00
☐ **International "Beacon Hill"**, *no monogram, good condition*	4.00	5.00
☐ **International "Charmaine"**, *no monogram, excellent condition*	5.00	6.00
☐ **International "Charmaine"**, *no monogram, good condition*	4.00	5.00
☐ **International "Kings"**, *monogram, excellent condition*	4.00	5.00
☐ **International "Silver Tulip"**, *viande style, no monogram, excellent condition*	1.00	2.00
☐ **International "Silver Tulip"**, *viande style, no monogram, excellent condition*	4.00	5.00
☐ **International "Silver Tulip"**, *viande style, no monogram, good condition*	3.00	4.00
☐ **International "Triumph"**, *viande style, no monogram, mint condition*	2.00	3.00
☐ **King Edward "Moss Rose"**, *viande style, no monogram, excellent condition*	5.00	6.00
☐ **King Edward "Moss Rose"**, *viande style, no monogram, good condition*	4.00	5.00
☐ **National "King Edward"**, *viande style, no monogram, excellent condition*	5.00	6.00
☐ **National "King Edward"**, *viande style, no monogram, good condition*	4.00	5.00
☐ **Niagara Falls Silver Co. "Adams"**, *monogram, excellent condition*	5.00	6.00
☐ **Niagara Falls Silver Co. "Colonial"**, *no monogram, excellent condition*	1.00	2.00
☐ **Niagara Falls Silver Co. "Colonial"**, *no monogram, poor condition*	1.00	2.00
☐ **Nobility "Caprice"**, *viande style, no monogram, excellent condition*	5.00	6.00
☐ **Nobility "Caprice"**, *viande style, no monogram, good condition*	4.00	5.00
☐ **Nobility "Reverie"**, *viande style, no monogram, fair condition*	1.00	2.00

Price Range

☐ **Nobility "Royal Rose"**, *viande style, no monogram, fair condition* 1.00 2.00
☐ **Old Company Plate "Signature"**, *monogram, excellent condition* 2.00 3.00
☐ **Oneida "Avalon"**, *no monogram, good condition* 2.00 3.00
☐ **Oneida "Avalon"**, *no monogram, fair condition* 1.00 2.00
☐ **Oneida "Bridal Wreath"**, *no monogram, good condition* ... 4.00 5.00
☐ **Oneida "Clarion"**, *no monogram, excellent condition* . 5.00 6.00
☐ **Oneida "Clarion"**, *no monogram, good condition* 4.00 5.00
☐ **Oneida "Flower de Luce"**, *no monogram, excellent condition* 10.00 12.00
☐ **Oneida "Flower de Luce"**, *no monogram, good condition* .. 7.00 8.00
☐ **Oneida "Jamestown"**, *monogram, excellent condition* 1.00 2.00
☐ **Oneida "Louis XVI"**, *no monogram, excellent condition* ... 3.00 4.00
☐ **Oneida "Louis XVI"**, *hollow-handled, no monogram, excellent condition* 2.00 3.00
☐ **Oneida "Sheraton"**, *no monogram, good condition* 1.00 3.00
☐ **Oneida "Wildwood"**, *no monogram, good condition* 3.00 4.00
☐ **Oneida "Wildwood"**, *hollow-handled, no monogram, fair condition* 3.00 4.00
☐ **Prestige "Grenoble"**, *viande style, no monogram, excellent condition* 5.00 6.00
☐ **Prestige "Grenoble"**, *viande style, no monogram, good condition* 4.00 5.00
☐ **Prestige "Grenoble"**, *viande style, no monogram, fair condition* 1.00 2.00
☐ **Reed & Barton "Beaded"**, *no monogram, mint condition* ... 1.00 2.00
☐ **Reed & Barton "Carlton"**, *no monogram, fair condition* 1.00 2.00
☐ **Reed & Barton "Carlton"**, *no monogram, mint condition* ... 5.00 6.00
☐ **Reed & Barton "Fiddle"**, *no monogram, excellent condition* 4.00 5.00
☐ **Reed & Barton "Jewell"**, *no monogram, excellent condition* 5.00 6.00
☐ **Reed & Barton "Jewell"**, *no monogram, good condition* ... 4.00 5.00
☐ **Reed & Barton "Maid of Honor"**, *no monogram, excellent condition* 5.00 6.00
☐ **Reed & Barton "Maid of Honor"**, *no monogram, good condition* 4.00 5.00
☐ **Reed & Barton "Manor"**, *no monogram, good condition* ... 4.00 5.00
☐ **Reed & Barton "Manor"**, *fair condition* 1.00 2.00
☐ **Reed & Barton "Modern Art"**, *no monogram, excellent condition* 7.00 8.00
☐ **Reed & Barton "Modern Art"**, *no monogram, excellent condition* 8.00 9.00
☐ **Reed & Barton "Olive"**, *monogram, excellent condition* ... 2.00 3.00
☐ **Reed & Barton "Orient"**, *no monogram, excellent condition* 3.00 4.00
☐ **Reed & Barton "Oxford"**, *no monogram, excellent condition* 2.00 3.00
☐ **Reed & Barton "Oxford"**, *no monogram, excellent condition* 3.00 4.00
☐ **Reed & Barton "Pearl"**, *no monogram, excellent condition* . 10.00 12.00
☐ **Reed & Barton "Pearl"**, *no monogram, mint condition* 10.00 12.00
☐ **Reed & Barton "Shell"**, *no monogram, excellent condition* . 2.00 3.00
☐ **Reed & Barton "Sierra"**, *no monogram, excellent condition* 5.00 6.00
☐ **Reed & Barton "Sierra"**, *no monogram, good condition* 4.00 5.00
☐ **Reed & Barton "Sierra"**, *no monogram, fair condition* 1.00 2.00
☐ **Reliance "Briar Rose"**, *no monogram, excellent condition* . 4.00 5.00

	Price Range	
☐ **Reliance "Bridal Rose"**, *no monogram, excellent condition*	5.00	6.00
☐ **Reliance "Bridal Rose"**, *no monogram, good condition*	4.00	5.00
☐ **Reliance "Exeter"**, *no monogram, excellent condition*	5.00	6.00
☐ **Reliance "Exeter"**, *no monogram, fair condition*	1.00	2.00
☐ **Reliance "Wildwood"**, *no monogram, excellent condition* .	7.00	8.00
☐ **Reliance "Wildwood"**, *no monogram, good condition*	2.00	8.00
☐ **Rockford "Fairoaks"**, *no monogram, excellent condition* ..	4.00	5.00
☐ **Rockford "Fairoaks"**, *no monogram, fair condition*	1.00	2.00
☐ **Rogers "Alhambra"**, *no monogram, excellent condition* ...	12.00	14.00
☐ **Rogers "Alhambra"**, *no monogram, poor condition*	1.00	2.00
☐ **Rogers "Ambassador"**, *monogram, excellent condition* ...	4.00	5.00
☐ **Rogers "Ambassador"**, *no monogram, excellent condition*	5.00	6.00
☐ **Rogers "Burgundy"**, *no monogram, excellent condition* ...	5.00	6.00
☐ **Rogers "Burgundy"**, *no monogram, good condition*	4.00	5.00
☐ **Rogers "Burgundy"**, *no monogram, fair condition*	1.00	2.00
☐ **Rogers "Carlton"**, *no monogram, excellent condition*	5.00	6.00
☐ **Rogers "Carlton"**, *no monogram, good condition*	4.00	5.00
☐ **Rogers "Desire"**, *viande style, no monogram, excellent condition*	5.00	6.00
☐ **Rogers "Desire"**, *viande style, no monogram, good condition*	4.00	5.00
☐ **Rogers "Desota"**, *no monogram, excellent condition*	5.00	6.00
☐ **Rogers "Desota"**, *no monogram, good condition*	4.00	5.00
☐ **Rogers "Garland"**, *viande style, no monogram, excellent condition*	5.00	6.00
☐ **Rogers "Garland"**, *viande style, no monogram, good condition*	4.00	5.00
☐ **Rogers "Gracious"**, *viande style, no monogram, excellent condition*	5.00	6.00
☐ **Rogers "Gracious"**, *viande style, no monogram, good condition*	4.00	5.00
☐ **Rogers "Grenoble"**, *monogram, excellent condition*	7.00	8.00
☐ **Rogers "Grenoble"**, *no monogram, excellent condition* ...	10.00	12.00
☐ **Rogers "Inspiration"**, *viande style, no monogram, good condition*	4.00	5.00
☐ **Rogers "Inspiration"**, *no monogram, fair condition*	1.00	2.00
☐ **Rogers "Ivy"**, *no monogram, poor condition*	1.00	2.00
☐ **Rogers "LaConcord"**, *no monogram, excellent condition* ..	4.00	5.00
☐ **Rogers "LaConcord"**, *no monogram, excellent condition* ..	5.00	6.00
☐ **Rogers "LaTouraine"**, *no monogram, excellent condition* ..	5.00	6.00
☐ **Rogers "LaTouraine"**, *no monogram, good condition*	4.00	5.00
☐ **Rogers "Lexington"**, *no monogram, excellent condition* ...	5.00	6.00
☐ **Rogers "Lexington"**, *no monogram, good condition*	4.00	5.00
☐ **Rogers "Lexington"**, *no monogram, fair condition*	1.00	2.00
☐ **Rogers "Margate"**, *no monogram, excellent condition*	5.00	6.00
☐ **Rogers "Margate"**, *no monogram, fair condition*	1.00	2.00
☐ **Rogers "Navarre"**, *no monogram, excellent condition*	6.00	7.00
☐ **Rogers "Navarre"**, *no monogram, good condition*	5.00	6.00
☐ **Rogers "Navarre"**, *monogram, excellent condition*	2.00	3.00
☐ **Rogers "Precious"**, *viande style, no monogram, excellent condition*	5.00	6.00
☐ **Rogers "Precious"**, *viande style, no monogram, good condition*	4.00	5.00

	Price Range	
☐ **Rogers "Queen Bess II"**, *no monogram, excellent condition*	1.00	2.00
☐ **Rogers "Silver"**, *no monogram, fair condition*	1.00	2.00
☐ **Rogers & Bro. "Aldine"**, *no monogram, good condition*	2.00	3.00
☐ **Rogers & Bro. "Assyrian Head"**, *no monogram, excellent condition*	16.00	18.00
☐ **Rogers & Bro. "Assyrian Head"**, *no monogram, fair condition*	1.00	2.00
☐ **Rogers & Bro. "Crown"**, *no monogram, good condition*	2.00	3.00
☐ **Rogers & Bro. "Daybreak"**, *no monogram, excellent condition*	5.00	6.00
☐ **Rogers & Bro. "Flemish"**, *no monogram, excellent condition*	5.00	6.00
☐ **Rogers & Bro. "Flemish"**, *no monogram, excellent condition*	5.00	6.00
☐ **Rogers & Bro. "Flemish"**, *no monogram, fair condition*	1.00	2.00
☐ **Rogers & Bro. "Laurel"**, *no monogram, fair condition*	1.00	2.00
☐ **Rogers & Bro. "Modern Rose"**, *viande style, no monogram, excellent condition*	5.00	6.00
☐ **Rogers & Bro. "Modern Rose"**, *viande style, no monogram, good condition*	4.00	5.00
☐ **Rogers & Bro. "Mystic"**, *no monogram, excellent condition*	4.00	5.00
☐ **Rogers & Bro. "Mystic"**, *no monogram, resilvered*	5.00	6.00
☐ **Rogers & Bro. "Siren"**, *no monogram, good condition*	3.00	4.00
☐ **Rogers & Bro. "Siren"**, *no monogram, excellent condition* .	7.00	8.00
☐ **Rogers & Hamilton "Aldine"**, *no monogram, excellent condition*	3.00	4.00
☐ **Rogers & Hamilton "Alhambra"**, *monogram, excellent condition*	5.00	6.00
☐ **Rogers & Hamilton "Raphael"**, *no monogram, excellent condition*	8.00	9.00
☐ **Rogers & Hamilton "Raphael"**, *no monogram, good condition*	5.00	6.00
☐ **Rogers, Smith & Co. "Arcadian"**, *no monogram, good condition*	5.00	6.00
☐ **Rogers, Smith & Co. "Lorne"**, *no monogram, fair condition*	3.00	4.00
☐ **S.L. & G.H. Rogers "Arcadia"**, *no monogram, good condition*	2.00	3.00
☐ **S.L. & G.H. Rogers "Countess II"**, *no monogram, excellent condition*	5.00	6.00
☐ **S.L. & G.H. Rogers "Countess II"**, *no monogram, good condition*	4.00	5.00
☐ **S.L. & G.H. Rogers "English Gardens"**, *no monogram, excellent condition*	5.00	6.00
☐ **S.L. & G.H. Rogers "English Gardens"**, *no monogram, good condition*	4.00	5.00
☐ **S.L. & G.H. Rogers "Minerva"**, *no monogram, excellent condition*	5.00	6.00
☐ **S.L. & G.H. Rogers "Minerva"**, *no monogram, poor condition*	1.00	2.00
☐ **S.L. & G.H. Rogers "Minerva"**, *no monogram, fair condition*	1.00	2.00
☐ **S.L. & G.H. Rogers "Presentation"**, *viande style, no monogram, excellent condition*	4.00	5.00
☐ **S.L. & G.H. Rogers "Princess"**, *no monogram, excellent condition*	4.00	5.00

	Price Range	

☐ **S.L. & G.H. Rogers "Princess"**, *no monogram, excellent condition* 5.00   6.00

☐ **S.L. & G.H. Rogers "Silver Rose"**, *viande style, no monogram, excellent condition* 5.00   6.00

☐ **S.L. & G.H. Rogers "Silver Rose"**, *viande style, no monogram, fair condition* 1.00   2.00

☐ **S.L. & G.H. Rogers "Webster I"**, *no monogram, excellent condition* 3.00   4.00

☐ **Towle "Arbutus"**, *no monogram, excellent condition* 4.00   5.00

☐ **Towle "Chester"**, *no monogram, excellent condition* 4.00   5.00

☐ **Towle "Chester"**, *no monogram, excellent condition* 3.00   4.00

☐ **Towle "Chester"**, *no monogram, excellent condition* 5.00   6.00

☐ **Tudor "Baronet"**, *no monogram, excellent condition* 4.00   5.00

☐ **Tudor "Duchess"**, *no monogram, excellent condition* 5.00   6.00

☐ **Tudor "Duchess"**, *no monogram, good condition* 4.00   5.00

☐ **Tudor "Duchess"**, *no monogram, fair condition* 1.00   2.00

☐ **Tudor "Enchantment"**, *no monogram, excellent condition* . 4.00   5.00

☐ **Tudor "Enchantment"**, *no monogram, fair condition* 1.00   2.00

☐ **Tudor "Queen Bess II"**, *no monogram, good condition* 4.00   5.00

☐ **Tudor "Queen Bess II"**, *no monogram, fair condition* 1.00   2.00

☐ **Tudor "Queen Bess II"**, *no monogram, poor condition* 1.00   2.00

☐ **Wallace "Floral"**, *no monogram, excellent condition* 5.00   6.00

☐ **Wallace "Portland"**, *no monogram, excellent condition* ... 2.00   3.00

☐ **Wallace "Sonata"**, *viande style, no monogram, excellent condition* 5.00   6.00

☐ **Wallace "Sonata"**, *viande style, no monogram, good condition* 4.00   5.00

☐ **Wallace "Sonata"**, *viande style, no monogram, fair condition* 1.00   2.00

☐ **W.D. Smith "Adam"**, *no monogram, mint condition* 3.00   4.00

☐ **Williams Bros. "Isabella"**, *no monogram, excellent condition* 5.00   6.00

☐ **Williams Bros. "Isabella"**, *no monogram, fair condition* ... 1.00   2.00

☐ **Williams Bros. "Isabella"**, *no monogram, poor condition* .. 1.00   2.00

☐ **Williams Bros. "Norma"**, *no monogram, excellent condition* 3.00   4.00

☐ **Williams Bros. "Pearl"**, *no monogram, excellent condition* . 10.00   12.00

☐ **Williams Bros. "Queen Elizabeth"**, *no monogram, excellent condition* 3.00   4.00

☐ **Wm. Rogers "Beloved"**, *viande style, no monogram, excellent condition* 5.00   6.00

☐ **Wm. Rogers "Beloved"**, *viande style, no monogram, good condition* 4.00   5.00

☐ **Wm. Rogers "Beloved"**, *no monogram, excellent condition* 3.00   4.00

☐ **Wm. Rogers "Chester"**, *no monogram, excellent condition* 5.00   6.00

☐ **Wm. Rogers "Chester"**, *no monogram, excellent condition* 4.00   5.00

☐ **Wm. Rogers "Cotillion"**, *no monogram, excellent condition* 5.00   6.00

☐ **Wm. Rogers "Cotillion"**, *no monogram, good condition* ... 1.00   2.00

☐ **Wm. Rogers "Debutante"**, *viande style, no monogram, good condition* 3.00   4.00

☐ **Wm. Rogers "Debutante"**, *viande style, no monogram, fair condition* 1.00   2.00

☐ **Wm. Rogers "Debutante"**, *viande style, no monogram, poor condition* 1.00   2.00

	Price Range	
☐ **Wm. Rogers "Devonshire"**, *no monogram, excellent condition*	5.00	6.00
☐ **Wm. Rogers "Devonshire"**, *no monogram, good condition* .	4.00	5.00
☐ **Wm. Rogers "Exquisite"**, *viande style, no monogram, excellent condition*	5.00	6.00
☐ **Wm. Rogers "Exquisite"**, *viande style, no monogram, good condition*	4.00	5.00
☐ **Wm. Rogers "Exquisite"**, *no monogram, excellent condition*	5.00	6.00
☐ **Wm. Rogers "Exquisite"**, *no monogram, good condition* ...	4.00	5.00
☐ **Wm. Rogers "Fairoaks"**, *no monogram, excellent condition*	5.00	6.00
☐ **Wm. Rogers "Fairoaks"**, *no monogram, good condition* ...	4.00	5.00
☐ **Wm. Rogers "Fidelis"**, *viande style, no monogram, excellent condition*	5.00	6.00
☐ **Wm. Rogers "Fidelis"**, *viande style, no monogram, good condition*	4.00	5.00
☐ **Wm. Rogers "Fidelis"**, *viande style, no monogram, fair condition*	1.00	2.00
☐ **Wm. Rogers "Grenoble"**, *excellent condition*	5.00	6.00
☐ **Wm. Rogers "Hostess"**, *no monogram, fair condition*	1.00	2.00
☐ **Wm. Rogers "Imperial"**, *viande style, no monogram, excellent condition*	5.00	6.00
☐ **Wm. Rogers "LaConcorde"**, *no monogram, excellent condition*	6.00	7.00
☐ **Wm. Rogers "LaConcorde"**, *no monogram, fair condition* .	1.00	2.00
☐ **Wm. Rogers "Lufberry"**, *no monogram, excellent condition*	4.00	5.00
☐ **Wm. Rogers "Mayfair"**, *no monogram, excellent condition* .	5.00	6.00
☐ **Wm. Rogers "Mayfair"**, *no monogram, good condition*	4.00	5.00
☐ **Wm. Rogers "Memory"**, *no monogram, good condition*	4.00	5.00
☐ **Wm. Rogers "Memory"**, *viande style, no monogram, excellent condition*	5.00	6.00
☐ **Wm. Rogers "Memory"**, *viande style, no monogram, good condition*	4.00	5.00
☐ **Wm. Rogers "Memory"**, *viande style, no monogram, fair condition*	1.00	2.00
☐ **Wm. Rogers "Mountain Rose"**, *no monogram, excellent condition*	6.00	7.00
☐ **Wm. Rogers "Mountain Rose"**, *no monogram, fair condition*	1.00	2.00
☐ **Wm. Rogers "Orange Blossom"**, *no monogram, excellent condition*	7.00	8.00
☐ **Wm. Rogers "Orange Blossom"**, *no monogram, fair condition*	2.00	3.00
☐ **Wm. Rogers "Paris"**, *no monogram, good condition*	4.00	5.00
☐ **Wm. Rogers "Paris"**, *no monogram, fair condition*	1.00	2.00
☐ **Wm. Rogers "Precious Mirror"**, *no monogram, excellent condition*	5.00	6.00
☐ **Wm. Rogers "Precious Mirror"**, *no monogram, good condition*	4.00	5.00
☐ **Wm. Rogers "Precious Mirror"**, *no monogram, fair condition*	1.00	2.00
☐ **Wm. Rogers "Regent"**, *viande style, no monogram, excellent condition*	5.00	6.00

Price Range

☐ **Wm. Rogers "Regent"**, *viande style, no monogram, good condition*	4.00	5.00
☐ **Wm. Rogers "Starlight"**, *no monogram, excellent condition*	5.00	6.00
☐ **Wm. Rogers "Starlight"**, *no monogram, good condition* . . .	4.00	5.00
☐ **Wm. Rogers "Treasure"**, *viande style, no monogram, excellent condition*	5.00	6.00
☐ **Wm. Rogers "Treasure"**, *viande style, no monogram, good condition*	4.00	5.00
☐ **Wm. Rogers "Treasure"**, *no monogram, excellent condition*	5.00	6.00
☐ **Wm. Rogers "Treasure"**, *no monogram, good condition* . . .	4.00	5.00
☐ **Wm. Rogers "Victorian Rose"**, *no monogram, mint condition*	4.00	5.00
☐ **Wm. Rogers "Victory"**, *viande style, no monogram, good condition*	4.00	5.00
☐ **Wm. Rogers "Victory"**, *viande style, no monogram, fair condition*	1.00	2.00
☐ **Wm. Rogers Eagle "Kings"**, *hotel name, excellent condition*	4.00	5.00
☐ **Wm. Rogers Mfg. Co. "Alhambra"**, *no monogram, good condition*	3.00	4.00
☐ **Wm. Rogers Mfg. Co. "Alhambra"**, *no monogram, excellent condition*	3.00	4.00
☐ **Wm. Rogers Mfg. Co. "Arbutus"**, *no monogram, excellent condition*	7.00	8.00
☐ **Wm. Rogers Mfg. Co. "Arbutus"**, *monogram, good condition*	3.00	4.00
☐ **Wm. Rogers Mfg. Co. "Argyle"**, *no monogram, good condition*	1.00	2.00
☐ **Wm. Rogers Mfg. Co. "Berwick"**, *no monogram, excellent condition*	6.00	7.00
☐ **Wm. Rogers Mfg. Co. "Camelot"**, *no monogram, excellent condition*	5.00	6.00
☐ **Wm. Rogers Mfg. Co. "Camelot"**, *no monogram, good condition*	4.00	5.00
☐ **Wm. Rogers Mfg. Co. "Chatham"**, *no monogram, excellent condition*	5.00	6.00
☐ **Wm. Rogers Mfg. Co. "Chatham"**, *no monogram, good condition*	4.00	5.00
☐ **Wm. Rogers Mfg. Co. "Countess"**, *no monogram, resilvered*	5.00	6.00
☐ **Wm. Rogers Mfg. Co. "Daisy"**, *no monogram, excellent condition*	4.00	5.00
☐ **Wm. Rogers Mfg. Co. "Florida"**, *no monogram, excellent condition*	3.00	4.00
☐ **Wm. Rogers Mfg. Co. "Geneva"**, *no monogram, excellent condition*	3.00	4.00
☐ **Wm. Rogers Mfg. Co. "Grape"**, *no monogram, good condition*	3.00	4.00
☐ **Wm. Rogers Mfg. Co. "Inheritance"**, *no monogram, excellent condition*	6.00	7.00
☐ **Wm. Rogers Mfg. Co. "Jubilee"**, *no monogram, excellent condition*	5.00	6.00
☐ **Wm. Rogers Mfg. Co. "Magnolia"**, *no monogram, excellent condition*	5.00	6.00
☐ **Wm. Rogers Mfg. Co. "Magnolia"**, *no monogram, good condition*	4.00	5.00

	Price Range	

☐ **Wm. Rogers Mfg. Co. "Magnolia"**, *no monogram, fair condition* . . . . 1.00 / 2.00

☐ **Wm. Rogers Mfg. Co. "Oak"**, *no monogram, resilvered* . . . . 5.00 / 6.00

☐ **Wm. Rogers Mfg. Co. "Reflection"**, *viande style, no monogram, excellent condition* . . . . 5.00 / 6.00

☐ **Wm. Rogers Mfg. Co. "Reflection"**, *viande style, no monogram, good condition* . . . . 4.00 / 5.00

☐ **Wm. Rogers Mfg. Co. "Regent"**, *monogram, excellent condition* . . . . 5.00 / 6.00

☐ **Wm. Rogers Mfg. Co. "Sovereign"**, *no monogram, excellent condition* . . . . 5.00 / 6.00

☐ **Wm. Rogers Mfg. Co. "Sovereign"**, *no monogram, good condition* . . . . 4.00 / 5.00

☐ **Wm. Rogers Mfg. Co. "Talisman"**, *viande style, no monogram, excellent condition* . . . . 5.00 / 6.00

☐ **Wm. Rogers Mfg. Co. "Talisman"**, *viande style, no monogram, good condition* . . . . 4.00 / 5.00

☐ **Wm. Rogers Mfg. Co. "Thistle"**, *no monogram, mint condition* . . . . 4.00 / 5.00

☐ **Wm. Rogers & Son "April"**, *no monogram, excellent condition* . . . . 5.00 / 6.00

☐ **Wm. Rogers & Son "April"**, *no monogram, good condition* . 4.00 / 5.00

☐ **Wm. Rogers & Son "Flower"**, *no monogram, fair condition* . 2.00 / 3.00

☐ **Wm. Rogers & Son "Oxford"**, *no monogram, excellent condition* . . . . 5.00 / 6.00

☐ **Wm. Rogers & Son "Oxford"**, *no monogram, good condition* 4.00 / 5.00

☐ **Wm. Rogers & Son "Spring Flower"**, *no monogram, excellent condition* . . . . 5.00 / 6.00

☐ **Wm. Rogers & Son "Spring Flower"**, *no monogram, excellent condition* . . . . 4.00 / 5.00

☐ **Wm. Rogers & Son "Chalice"**, *no monogram, excellent condition* . . . . 5.00 / 6.00

☐ **Wm. A. Rogers "Chalice"**, *no monogram, good condition* . . 4.00 / 5.00

☐ **Wm. A. Rogers "Country Lane"**, *no monogram, excellent condition* . . . . 5.00 / 6.00

☐ **Wm. A. Rogers "Country Lane"**, *no monogram, good condition* . . . . 4.00 / 5.00

☐ **Wm. A. Rogers "Elmore"**, *no monogram, excellent condition* . . . . 5.00 / 6.00

☐ **Wm. A. Rogers "Garland"**, *no monogram, excellent condition* . . . . 3.00 / 4.00

☐ **Wm. A. Rogers "Grenoble"**, *no monogram, excellent condition* . . . . 7.00 / 8.00

☐ **Wm. A. Rogers "Grenoble"**, *no monogram, good condition* 6.00 / 7.00

☐ **Wm. A. Rogers "Hanover"**, *no monogram, resilvered* . . . . . . 7.00 / 8.00

☐ **Wm. A. Rogers "Hanover"**, *no monogram, excellent condition* . . . . 7.00 / 8.00

☐ **Wm. A. Rogers "LaConcorde"**, *no monogram, good condition* . . . . 3.00 / 4.00

☐ **Wm. A. Rogers "LaConcorde"**, *no monogram, excellent condition* . . . . 3.00 / 4.00

☐ **Wm. A. Rogers "LaConcorde"**, *no monogram, excellent condition* . . . . 5.00 / 6.00

Price Range

☐ **Wm. A. Rogers "LaConcorde"**, *no monogram, poor condition*	1.00	2.00
☐ **Wm. A. Rogers "Lady Drake"**, *viande style, no monogram, excellent condition*	5.00	6.00
☐ **Wm. A. Rogers "Lady Drake"**, *viande style, no monogram, good condition*	4.00	5.00
☐ **Wm. A. Rogers "Lady Stuart"**, *no monogram, excellent condition*	5.00	6.00
☐ **Wm. A. Rogers "Lady Stuart"**, *no monogram, good condition*	4.00	5.00
☐ **Wm. A. Rogers "Lady Stuart"**, *no monogram, fair condition*	1.00	2.00
☐ **Wm. A. Rogers "LaVigne"**, *no monogram, excellent condition*	8.00	10.00
☐ **Wm. A. Rogers "LaVigne"**, *no monogram, mint condition* . .	8.00	10.00
☐ **Wm. A. Rogers "Malibu"**, *no monogram, excellent condition*	5.00	6.00
☐ **Wm. A. Rogers "Malibu"**, *no monogram, good condition* . . .	4.00	5.00
☐ **Wm. A. Rogers "Marcella"**, *no monogram, good condition* .	1.00	2.00
☐ **Wm. A. Rogers "Margate"**, *no monogram, excellent condition*	5.00	6.00
☐ **Wm. A. Rogers "Margate"**, *no monogram, good condition* .	4.00	5.00
☐ **Wm. A. Rogers "Meadowbrook"**, *viande style, no monogram, excellent condition*	5.00	6.00
☐ **Wm. A. Rogers "Meadowbrook"**, *viande style, no monogram, fair condition*	1.00	2.00
☐ **Wm. A. Rogers "Meadowbrook"**, *no monogram, excellent condition*	5.00	6.00
☐ **Wm. A. Rogers "Meadowbrook"**, *no monogram, good condition*	4.00	5.00
☐ **Wm. A. Rogers "Mystic"**, *monogram, excellent condition* . .	2.00	3.00
☐ **Wm. A. Rogers "Mystic"**, *no monogram, excellent condition*	5.00	6.00
☐ **Wm. A. Rogers "Mystic"**, *no monogram, good condition* . . .	4.00	5.00
☐ **Wm. A. Rogers "Mystic"**, *no monogram, fair condition*	1.00	2.00
☐ **Wm. A. Rogers "Paramount"**, *no monogram, excellent condition*	5.00	6.00
☐ **Wm. A. Rogers "Paramount"**, *no monogram, good condition*	4.00	5.00
☐ **Wm. A. Rogers "Paramount"**, *viande style, no monogram, excellent condition*	5.00	6.00
☐ **Wm. A. Rogers "Paramount"**, *viande style, no monogram, good condition*	4.00	5.00
☐ **Wm. A. Rogers "Raleigh"**, *no monogram, excellent condition*	3.00	4.00
☐ **Wm. A. Rogers "Rendezvous"**, *viande style, no monogram, excellent condition*	5.00	6.00
☐ **Wm. A. Rogers "Rendezvous"**, *viande style, no monogram, good condition*	4.00	5.00
☐ **Wm. A. Rogers "Rosalie"**, *no monogram, excellent condition*	5.00	6.00
☐ **Wm. A. Rogers "Rosalie"**, *no monogram, good condition* . .	4.00	5.00
☐ **1835 R. Wallace "Abbey"**, *no monogram, excellent condition*	5.00	6.00
☐ **1835 R. Wallace "Abbey"**, *no monogram, good condition* . .	4.00	5.00

	Price Range	
☐ 1835 R. Wallace "Blossom", *no monogram, excellent condition*	3.00	4.00
☐ 1835 R. Wallace "Buckingham", *no monogram, excellent condition*	5.00	6.00
☐ 1835 R. Wallace "Buckingham", *monogram, excellent condition*	2.00	3.00
☐ 1835 R. Wallace "Joan", *no monogram, good condition*	2.00	3.00
☐ 1847 Rogers "Adoration", *no monogram, excellent condition*	4.00	5.00
☐ 1847 Rogers "Adoration", *no monogram, poor condition*	1.00	2.00
☐ 1847 Rogers "Ambassador", *no monogram, excellent condition*	5.00	6.00
☐ 1847 Rogers "Ambassador", *no monogram, good condition*	4.00	5.00
☐ 1847 Rogers "Ancestral", *no monogram, excellent condition*	5.00	6.00
☐ 1847 Rogers "Ancestral", *no monogram, good condition*	4.00	5.00
☐ 1847 Rogers "Anniversary", *no monogram, excellent condition*	5.00	6.00
☐ 1847 Rogers "Anniversary", *no monogram, good condition*	4.00	5.00
☐ 1847 Rogers "Anniversary", *no monogram, fair condition*	1.00	2.00
☐ 1847 Rogers "Arcadian", *no monogram, excellent condition*	7.00	8.00
☐ 1847 Rogers "Arcadian", *no monogram, good condition*	5.00	6.00
☐ 1847 Rogers "Arcadian", *no monogram, fair condition*	1.00	2.00
☐ 1847 Rogers "Argosy", *no monogram, excellent condition*	3.00	4.00
☐ 1847 Rogers "Armenian", *no monogram, good condition*	3.00	4.00
☐ 1847 Rogers "Assyrian", *no monogram, excellent condition*	2.00	3.00
☐ 1847 Rogers "Avon", *no monogram, good condition*	5.00	6.00
☐ 1847 Rogers "Avon", *no monogram, good condition*	5.00	6.00
☐ 1847 Rogers "Avon", *no monogram, excellent condition*	5.00	6.00
☐ 1847 Rogers "Berkshire", *no monogram, excellent condition*	6.00	7.00
☐ 1847 Rogers "Berkshire", *no monogram, good condition*	2.00	3.00
☐ 1847 Rogers "Berkshire", *no monogram, excellent condition*	7.00	8.00
☐ 1847 Rogers "Berkshire", *no monogram, good condition*	4.00	5.00
☐ 1847 Rogers "Berkshire", *no monogram, excellent condition*	5.00	6.00
☐ 1847 Rogers "Charter Oak", *no monogram, resilvered*	9.00	10.00
☐ 1847 Rogers "Charter Oak", *no monogram, good condition*	5.00	6.00
☐ 1847 Rogers "Charter Oak", *no monogram, fair condition*	6.00	7.00
☐ 1847 Rogers "Charter Oak", *monogram, excellent condition*	7.00	8.00
☐ 1847 Rogers "Charter Oak", *monogram, good condition*	5.00	6.00
☐ 1847 Rogers "Columbia", *no monogram, resilvered*	10.00	12.00
☐ 1847 Rogers "Columbia", *no monogram, good condition*	7.00	8.00
☐ 1847 Rogers "Continental", *no monogram, excellent condition*	5.00	6.00
☐ 1847 Rogers "Continental", *no monogram, good condition*	4.00	5.00
☐ 1847 Rogers "Crown", *no monogram, good condition*	7.00	8.00
☐ 1847 Rogers "Daffodil", *no monogram, excellent condition*	5.00	6.00
☐ 1847 Rogers "Daffodil II", *viande style, no monogram, excellent condition*	5.00	6.00
☐ 1847 Rogers "Daffodil II", *viande style, no monogram, good condition*	1.00	2.00

	Price Range	

☐ **1847 Rogers "Daffodil II"**, *no monogram, excellent condition* 5.00 6.00
☐ **1847 Rogers "Daffodil II"**, *no monogram, good condition* .. 4.00 5.00
☐ **1847 Rogers "Embossed"**, *no monogram, fair condition* ... 1.00 2.00
☐ **1847 Rogers "Esperanto"**, *no monogram, excellent condition* 5.00 6.00
☐ **1847 Rogers "Esperanto"**, *no monogram, good condition* .. 4.00 5.00
☐ **1847 Rogers "Eternally Yours"**, *viande style, no monogram, excellent condition* 5.00 6.00
☐ **1847 Rogers "Eternally Yours"**, *viande style, no monogram, good condition* 4.00 5.00
☐ **1847 Rogers "Eternally Yours"**, *no monogram, excellent condition* 5.00 6.00
☐ **1847 Rogers "Eternally Yours"**, *no monogram, good condition* 4.00 5.00
☐ **1847 Roger "Faneuil"**, *no monogram, excellent condition* . 3.00 4.00
☐ **1847 Rogers "First Love"**, *viande style, no monogram, excellent condition* 6.00 7.00
☐ **1847 Rogers "First Love"**, *no monogram, fair condition* ... 1.00 2.00
☐ **1847 Rogers "Flair"**, *no monogram, excellent condition* ... 3.00 4.00
☐ **1847 Rogers "Flair"**, *no monogram, excellent condition* ... 5.00 6.00
☐ **1847 Rogers "Flair"**, *no monogram, good condition* 4.00 5.00
☐ **1847 Rogers "Floral"**, *monogram, excellent condition* 7.00 8.00
☐ **1847 Rogers "Floral"**, *no monogram, excellent condition* .. 8.00 10.00
☐ **1847 Rogers "Grecian"**, *no monogram, good condition* 1.00 2.00
☐ **1847 Rogers "Heraldic"**, *no monogram, excellent condition* 3.00 4.00
☐ **1847 Rogers "Heraldic"**, *no monogram, good condition* ... 3.00 4.00
☐ **1847 Rogers "Heraldic"**, *no monogram, poor condition* 1.00 2.00
☐ **1847 Rogers "Her Majesty"**, *no monogram, excellent condition* 2.00 3.00
☐ **1847 Rogers "Legacy"**, *viande style, no monogram, excellent condition* 5.00 6.00
☐ **1847 Rogers "Legacy"**, *viande style, no monogram, good condition* 4.00 5.00
☐ **1847 Rogers "Leilani"**, *no monogram, excellent condition* . 5.00 6.00
☐ **1847 Rogers "Leilani"**, *no monogram, good condition* 4.00 5.00
☐ **1847 Rogers "Lorne"**, *monogram, mint condition* 5.00 6.00
☐ **1847 Rogers "Lorne"**, *monogram, good condition* 1.00 2.00
☐ **1847 Rogers "Lorne"**, *no monogram, good condition* 1.00 2.00
☐ **1847 Rogers "Lorne"**, *no monogram, fair condition* 1.00 2.00
☐ **1847 Rogers "Lovelace"**, *viande style, no monogram, excellent condition* 5.00 6.00
☐ **1847 Rogers "Lovelace"**, *viande style, no monogram, good condition* 4.00 5.00
☐ **1847 Rogers "Lovelace"**, *no monogram, excellent condition* 5.00 6.00
☐ **1847 Rogers "Magic Rose"**, *no monogram, excellent condition* 5.00 6.00
☐ **1847 Rogers "Magic Rose"**, *no monogram, good condition* 4.00 5.00
☐ **1847 Rogers "Marquise"**, *no monogram, excellent condition* 5.00 6.00
☐ **1847 Rogers "Marquise"**, *no monogram, good condition* .. 4.00 5.00
☐ **1847 Rogers "Moline"**, *no monogram, excellent condition* . 2.00 3.00
☐ **1847 Rogers "Moselle"**, *hollow-handled, no monogram, fair condition* 20.00 22.00

		Price Range	
☐ **1847 Rogers "Moselle"**, *no monogram, excellent condition*		18.00	20.00
☐ **1847 Rogers "Moselle"**, *no monogram, excellent condition*		18.00	20.00
☐ **1847 Rogers "Newport"**, *no monogram, resilvered*		5.00	6.00
☐ **1847 Rogers "Newport"**, *no monogram, excellent condition*		5.00	6.00
☐ **1847 Rogers "Newport"**, *no monogram, good condition* ...		3.00	4.00
☐ **1847 Rogers "Newport"**, *no monogram, fair condition*		1.00	2.00
☐ **1847 Rogers "Norfolk"**, *no monogram, excellent condition* .		5.00	6.00
☐ **1847 Rogers "Norfolk"**, *no monogram, good condition*		4.00	5.00
☐ **1847 Rogers "No. 77"**, *no monogram, excellent condition* ..		1.00	2.00
☐ **1847 Rogers "Old Colony"**, *no monogram, excellent condition*		4.00	5.00
☐ **1847 Rogers "Old Colony"**, *hollow-handled, no monogram, good condition*		6.00	7.00
☐ **1847 Rogers "Old Colony"**, *no monogram, excellent condition*		6.00	7.00
☐ **1847 Rogers "Old Colony"**, *no monogram, good condition* .		4.00	5.00
☐ **1847 Rogers "Old Colony"**, *no monogram, good condition* .		4.00	5.00
☐ **1847 Rogers "Olive"**, *no monogram, excellent condition* ...		5.00	6.00
☐ **1847 Rogers "Persian"**, *no monogram, excellent condition*		6.00	7.00
☐ **1847 Rogers "Reflection"**, *no monogram, excellent condition*		4.00	5.00
☐ **1847 Rogers "Reflection"**, *no monogram, fair condition* ...		1.00	2.00
☐ **1847 Rogers "Remembrance"**, *no monogram, mint condition*		4.00	5.00
☐ **1847 Rogers "Remembrance"**, *no monogram, excellent condition*		5.00	6.00
☐ **1847 Rogers "Saratoga"**, *no monogram, excellent condition*		5.00	6.00
☐ **1847 Rogers "Saratoga"**, *no monogram, good condition* ...		4.00	5.00
☐ **1847 Rogers "Savoy"**, *no monogram, good condition*		2.00	3.00
☐ **1847 Rogers "Sharon"**, *no monogram, excellent condition* .		5.00	6.00
☐ **1847 Rogers "Sharon"**, *no monogram, good condition*		3.00	4.00
☐ **1847 Rogers "Sharon"**, *no monogram, fair condition*		1.00	2.00
☐ **1847 Rogers "Silver Lace"**, *no monogram, excellent condition*		5.00	6.00
☐ **1847 Rogers "Silver Lace"**, *no monogram, good condition* .		4.00	5.00
☐ **1847 Rogers "Siren"**, *no monogram, excellent condition* ...		4.00	5.00
☐ **1847 Rogers "Vesta"**, *no monogram, resilvered*		6.00	7.00
☐ **1847 Rogers "Vesta"**, *no monogram, excellent condition* ..		4.00	5.00
☐ **1847 Rogers "Vesta"**, *no monogram, good condition*		2.00	3.00
☐ **1847 Rogers "Vintage"**, *no monogram, good condition*		6.00	7.00
☐ **1847 Rogers "Vintage"**, *no monogram, fair condition*		3.00	4.00
☐ **1847 Rogers "Vintage"**, *no monogram, excellent condition*		8.00	10.00
☐ **1847 Rogers "Vintage"**, *hollow-handled, no monogram, excellent condition)*		16.00	18.00
☐ **1847 Rogers "Vintage"**, *no monogram, good condition*		7.00	8.00
☐ **1847 Rogers "Vintage"**, *no monogram, excellent condition*		5.00	7.00
☐ **1847 Rogers "Vintage"**, *monogram, good condition*		5.00	6.00
☐ **1847 Rogers "Vintage"**, *no monogram, good condition*		7.00	8.00
☐ **1847 Rogers "Vintage"**, *hollow-handled, no monogram, excellent condition*		16.00	18.00
☐ **1847 Rogers "Vintage"**, *no monogram, excellent condition*		6.00	7.00
☐ **1847 Rogers "Vintage"**, *monogram, good condition*		5.00	6.00

	Price Range	

- [ ] **1847 Rogers "Vintage"**, *no monogram, good condition* 5.00 6.00
- [ ] **1847 Rogers "Vintage"**, *no monogram, fair condition* 4.00 5.00
- [ ] **1881 Rogers "Briar Rose"**, *no monogram, excellent condition* 2.00 3.00
- [ ] **1881 Rogers "Capri"**, *no monogram, excellent condition* .. 5.00 6.00
- [ ] **1881 Rogers "Capri"**, *no monogram, good condition* 4.00 5.00
- [ ] **1881 Rogers "Chippendale"**, *no monogram, excellent condition* 5.00 6.00
- [ ] **1881 Rogers "Chippendale"**, *no monogram, good condition* 4.00 5.00
- [ ] **1881 Rogers "Flirtation"**, *no monogram, excellent condition* 3.00 4.00
- [ ] **1881 Rogers "Grecian"**, *no monogram, fair condition* 1.00 2.00
- [ ] **1881 Rogers "LaVigne"**, *no monogram, excellent condition* 6.00 7.00
- [ ] **1881 Rogers "LaVigne"**, *no monogram, good condition* ... 4.00 5.00
- [ ] **1881 Rogers "LaVigne"**, *no monogram, fair condition* 3.00 4.00
- [ ] **1881 Rogers "LaVigne"**, *no monogram, excellent condition* 5.00 6.00
- [ ] **1881 Rogers "LaVigne"**, *no monogram, good condition* ... 4.00 5.00
- [ ] **1881 Rogers "Leyland"**, *no monogram, fair condition* 1.00 2.00

(Sterling Silver)

- [ ] **Alvin "Chateau Rose"**, *7⅞" long, no monogram* 16.00 18.00
- [ ] **Alvin "Majestic"**, *monogram* 22.00 24.00
- [ ] **Blackington "Scroll & Bead"**, *no monogram* 30.00 32.00
- [ ] **Dominick & Haff "Louis XIV"**, *(old style), no monogram* ... 16.00 18.00
- [ ] **Dominick & Haff "Renaissance"**, *monogram* 18.00 20.00
- [ ] **Durgin "Bead"**, *monogram* 16.00 18.00
- [ ] **Durgin "Chrysanthemum"**, *no monogram* 42.00 45.00
- [ ] **Durgin "Fairfax"**, *no monogram, 7⅞" L.* 18.00 20.00
- [ ] **Durgin "Louis XV"**, *monogram* 18.00 20.00
- [ ] **Frank Smith "Fiddle Thread"**, *no monogram* 30.00 32.00
- [ ] **Gorham "Buckingham"**, *no monogram* 18.00 20.00
- [ ] **Gorham "Cambridge"**, *no monogram* 16.00 18.00
- [ ] **Gorham "Camellia"**, *no monogram* 8.00 9.00
- [ ] **Gorham "Chesterfield"**, *no monogram* 14.00 16.00
- [ ] **Gorham "Fairfax"**, *no monogram, 7⅞" L.* 18.00 20.00
- [ ] **Gorham "Greenbrier"**, *no monogram* 14.00 16.00
- [ ] **Gorham "Imperial Chrysanthemum"**, *no monogram* 16.00 18.00
- [ ] **Gorham "Lancaster Rose"**, *monogram* 22.00 24.00
- [ ] **Gorham "Marguerite"**, *no monogram* 20.00 22.00
- [ ] **Gorham "Newcastle"**, *monogram* 18.00 20.00
- [ ] **Gorham "Old French"**, *no monogram* 10.00 12.00
- [ ] **Gorham "Plymouth"**, *monogram* 17.00 19.00
- [ ] **Gorham "Poppy"**, *monogram* 18.00 20.00
- [ ] **Gorham "Sovereign"**, *no monogram* 10.00 12.00
- [ ] **Gorham "Strasbourg"**, *old and heavy, monogram* 18.00 20.00
- [ ] **Gorham "Strasbourg"**, *no monogram* 18.00 20.00
- [ ] **Gorham "Tulleries"**, *monogram, 7⅞" L.* 17.00 19.00
- [ ] **Gorham "Versailles"**, *no monogram* 28.00 30.00
- [ ] **International "Brandon"**, ... 16.00 18.00
- [ ] **International "Edgewood"**, ... 20.00 22.00
- [ ] **International "Frontenac"**, *no monogram* 28.00 30.00
- [ ] **International "Joan of Arc"**, *no monogram* 17.00 19.00
- [ ] **International "Minuet"**, *no monogram, extra heavy* 17.00 19.00
- [ ] **International "Trianon"**, *monogram* 16.00 18.00

	Price Range	
☐ Kirk "Quadrille", *monogram*	18.00	20.00
☐ Lunt "Mt. Vernon", *no monogram, 7¼" L.*	14.00	16.00
☐ Reed & Barton "Majestic", *monogram, 7⅛" L.*	17.00	19.00
☐ Reed & Barton "Marlborough", *monogram*	17.00	19.00
☐ Shiebler "American Beauty", *monogram*	14.00	16.00
☐ Simpson, Hall & Miller "Frontenac", *no monogram*	22.00	24.00
☐ Tiffany "English King", ...	28.00	30.00
☐ Tiffany "Flemish", *monogram,*	26.00	28.00
☐ Tiffany "Hampton", *monogram,*	25.00	27.00
☐ Tiffany "Persian", *monogram*	36.00	38.00
☐ Tiffany "Wave Edge", *no monogram*	26.00	28.00
☐ Tiffany "Wave Edge", *monogram*	22.00	24.00
☐ Towle "Georgian", *no monogram*	16.00	18.00
☐ Towle "Georgian", *no monogram*	22.00	24.00
☐ Towle "Kings", *no monogram*	30.00	32.00
☐ Towle "Virginia Carvel", *monogram, 7⅛" L.*	16.00	18.00
☐ Wallace "Grande Baroque", *no monogram, 7½" L.*	24.00	26.00
☐ Wallace "Grande Colonial", *no monogram*	16.00	18.00
☐ Wallace "Normandie", *monogram*	17.00	19.00
☐ Whiting "Imperial Queen", *monogram*	30.00	32.00
☐ Whiting "Ivy", *monogram, large*	28.00	30.00
☐ Whiting "Louis XV", *monogram*	17.00	19.00
☐ Whiting "Louis XV", *monogram*	17.00	19.00
☐ Whiting "Louis XV", *monogram*	18.00	20.00

DINNER KNIVES

The comments made regarding dinner forks basically apply as well to dinner knives. A flimsy knife would not do for cutting meats, though it might serve well in other uses; thus the silver manufacturers put out a variety of knives, all for designated purposes. Dinner knives may be wholly of silver, or have a silver blade attached to a bone (or other) handle. Or the reverse may be the case: the handle may be silver, and the blade stainless steel, which became more and more prevalent in the 20th century. Another variation, not nearly so noticeable but interesting, is that some specimens are smooth-bladed while others have serrated or saw-tooth blades. Which to select was a toss-up for the hostess. If she provided her guests with saw-tooth dinner knives, it suggested that the meat was going to require some carpentry work; but if she laid out smooth-bladed dinner knives and the meat was tough, this was an even worse situation. There are probably more collectors of dinner knives than of any other single class of silver tableware.

(Silver-Plated)

☐ Alvin "Diana", *monogram, excellent condition*	1.00	2.00
☐ Alvin "Diana", *no monogram, fair condition*	1.00	2.00
☐ Alvin "Molly Stark", *monogram, good condition*	1.00	2.00
☐ Alvin "Molly Stark", *no monogram, fair condition*	1.00	2.00
☐ American Silver Company "Moselle", *no monogram, excellent condition*	16.00	18.00
☐ American Silver Company "Moselle", *no monogram, good condition*	12.00	14.00
☐ American Silver Company "Moselle", *no monogram, fair condition*	7.00	8.00

	Price Range	
☐ **American Silver Company "Moselle"**, *no monogram, poor condition*	3.00	4.00
☐ **Benedict Mfg. Co. "Continental"**, *monogram, poor condition*	1.00	2.00
☐ **Benedict Mfg. Co. "Continental"**, *no monogram, good condition*	3.00	4.00
☐ **Community "Adam"**, *flat-handled, no monogram, good condition*	2.00	3.00
☐ **Community "Adam"**, *flat-handled, no monogram, excellent condition*	5.00	6.00
☐ **Community "Bird of Paradise"**, *no monogram, good condition*	3.00	4.00
☐ **Community "Bird of Paradise"**, *no monogram, good condition*	4.00	5.00
☐ **Community "Bird of Paradise"**, *no monogram, excellent condition*	6.00	7.00
☐ **Community "Bird of Paradise"**, *flat-handled, no monogram, good condition*	1.00	2.00
☐ **Community "Bird of Paradise"**, *flat-handled, no monogram, excellent condition*	5.00	6.00
☐ **Community "Coronation"**, *viande style, no monogram, excellent condition*	6.00	7.00
☐ **Community "Coronation"**, *viande style, no monogram, fair condition*	2.00	3.00
☐ **Community "Coronation"**, *viande style, no monogram, mint condition*	5.00	6.00
☐ **Community "Coronation"**, *no monogram, excellent condition*	6.00	7.00
☐ **Community "Coronation"**, *no monogram, fair condition* ...	1.00	2.00
☐ **Community "Deauville"**, *no monogram, excellent condition*	3.00	4.00
☐ **Community "Deauville"**, *no monogram, excellent condition*	6.00	7.00
☐ **Community "Deauville"**, *no monogram, good condition* ...	3.00	4.00
☐ **Community "Enchantment"**, *no monogram, excellent condition*	6.00	7.00
☐ **Community "Enchantment"**, *no monogram, fair condition* .	1.00	2.00
☐ **Community "Enchantment"**, *flat-handled, no monogram, good condition*	2.00	3.00
☐ **Community "Enchantment"**, *flat-handled, no monogram, excellent condition*	5.00	6.00
☐ **Community "Flower de Luce"**, *no monogram, excellent condition*	6.00	7.00
☐ **Community "Flower de Luce"**, *no monogram, good condition*	2.00	3.00
☐ **Community "Forever"**, *no monogram, excellent condition* .	6.00	7.00
☐ **Community "Forever"**, *no monogram, fair condition*	1.00	2.00
☐ **Community "Georgian"**, *no monogram, excellent condition*	3.00	4.00
☐ **Community "Georgian"**, *no monogram, good condition* ...	5.00	6.00
☐ **Community "Georgian"**, *no monogram, excellent condition*	3.00	4.00
☐ **Community "Georgian"**, *no monogram, good condition* ...	5.00	6.00
☐ **Community "Georgian"**, *no monogram, fair condition*	1.00	2.00
☐ **Community "Grosvenor"**, *no monogram, excellent condition*	4.00	5.00
☐ **Community "Grosvenor"**, *monogram, excellent condition* .	2.00	3.00
☐ **Community "Grosvenor"**, *no monogram, good condition* ..	4.00	5.00

	Price Range	
☐ Community **"Grosvenor"**, *no monogram, excellent condition*	6.00	7.00
☐ Community **"Grosvenor"**, *no monogram, fair condition*	1.00	2.00
☐ Community **"Grosvenor"**, *flat-handled, no monogram, excellent condition*	3.00	4.00
☐ Community **"Grosvenor"**, *flat-handled, no monogram, good condition*	1.00	2.00
☐ Community **"King Cedric"**, *viande style, no monogram, excellent condition*	6.00	7.00
☐ Community **"King Cedric"**, *viande style, no monogram, good condition*	5.00	6.00
☐ Community **"King Cedric"**, *viande style, no monogram, fair condition*	1.00	2.00
☐ Community **"Lady Hamilton"**, *flat-handled, no monogram, good condition*	2.00	3.00
☐ Community **"Lady Hamilton"**, *flat-handled, no monogram, excellent condition*	4.00	5.00
☐ Community **"Lady Hamilton"**, *flat-handled, no monogram, fair condition*	1.00	2.00
☐ Community **"Lady Hamilton"**, *viande style, no monogram, fair condition*	1.00	2.00
☐ Community **"Lady Hamilton"**, *viande style, no monogram, excellent condition*	6.00	7.00
☐ Community **"Lady Hamilton"**, *no monogram, good condition*	2.00	3.00
☐ Community **"Lady Hamilton"**, *no monogram, good condition*	6.00	7.00
☐ Community **"Louis XVI"**, *monogram, excellent condition*	3.00	4.00
☐ Community **"Louis XVI"**, *no monogram, good condition*	3.00	4.00
☐ Community **"Louis XVI"**, *no monogram, fair condition*	1.00	2.00
☐ Community **"Milady"**, *no monogram, good condition*	5.00	6.00
☐ Community **"Milady"**, *no monogram, excellent condition*	6.00	7.00
☐ Community **"Milady"**, *no monogram, fair condition*	1.00	2.00
☐ Community **"Morning Star"**, *viande style, no monogram, good condition*	5.00	6.00
☐ Community **"Morning Star"**, *viande style, no monogram, excellent condition*	6.00	7.00
☐ Community **"Morning Star"**, *viande style, no monogram, fair condition*	1.00	2.00
☐ Community **"Noblesse"**, *monogram, excellent condition*	3.00	4.00
☐ Community **"Noblesse"**, *no monogram, good condition*	5.00	6.00
☐ Community **"Noblesse"**, *no monogram, excellent condition*	6.00	7.00
☐ Community **"Noblesse"**, *viande style, monogram, excellent condition*	2.00	3.00
☐ Community **"Noblesse"**, *viande style, no monogram, good condition*	5.00	6.00
☐ Community **"Noblesse"**, *viande style, no monogram, fair condition*	1.00	2.00
☐ Community **"Patrician"**, *flat-handled, no monogram, fair condition*	1.00	2.00
☐ Community **"Patrician"**, *no monogram, excellent condition*	3.00	4.00
☐ Community **"Patrician"**, *monogram, excellent condition*	1.00	2.00
☐ Community **"Patrician"**, *no monogram, excellent condition*	6.00	7.00
☐ Community **"Patrician"**, *no monogram, good condition*	5.00	6.00

	Price Range	
☐ Community "Paul Revere", *no monogram, good condition* .	5.00	6.00
☐ Community "Paul Revere", *no monogram, excellent condition*	6.00	7.00
☐ Community "Sheraton", *no monogram, good condition* ...	5.00	6.00
☐ Community "Sheraton", *no monogram, fair condition*	1.00	2.00
☐ Community "Sheraton", *no monogram, excellent condition*	6.00	7.00
☐ Community "Sheraton", *flat-handled, no monogram, excellent condition*	3.00	4.00
☐ Community "Sheraton", *flat-handled, no monogram, good condition*	2.00	3.00
☐ Community "Silver Flowers", *no monogram, excellent condition*	6.00	7.00
☐ Community "Silver Flowers", *no monogram, good condition*	3.00	4.00
☐ Community "South Seas", *no monogram, excellent condition*	6.00	7.00
☐ Community "South Seas", *no monogram, mint condition* ..	5.00	6.00
☐ Community "South Seas", *no monogram, fair condition* ...	1.00	2.00
☐ Community "White Orchid", *no monogram, mint condition*	4.00	5.00
☐ Community "White Orchid", *no monogram, fair condition* .	1.00	2.00
☐ Court "Court", *flat-handled, no monogram, excellent condition*	1.00	2.00
☐ Court "Court", *flat-handled, no monogram, good condition*	1.00	2.00
☐ DeepSilver "Laurel Mist", *no monogram, excellent condition*	6.00	7.00
☐ DeepSilver "Laurel Mist", *no monogram, good condition* ..	3.00	4.00
☐ DeepSilver "Laurel Mist", *no monogram, fair condition*	1.00	2.00
☐ Embassy "Bouquet", *no monogram, excellent condition* ..	5.00	6.00
☐ Fortune "Fortune", *flat-handled, no monogram, excellent condition*	2.00	3.00
☐ Fortune "Fortune", *flat-handled, no monogram, fair condition*	1.00	2.00
☐ Gorham "Empire", *flat-handled, no monogram, excellent condition*	3.00	4.00
☐ Gorham "Empire", *flat-handled, no monogram, excellent condition*	5.00	6.00
☐ Gorham "Invitation", *no monogram, fair condition*	1.00	2.00
☐ Gorham "Kings", *monogram, excellent condition*	9.00	10.00
☐ Gorham "Kings", *monogram, excellent condition*	11.00	12.00
☐ Gorham "Lady Caroline", *no monogram, excellent condition*	6.00	7.00
☐ Gorham "Lady Caroline", *no monogram, good condition* ..	4.00	5.00
☐ Gorham "New Elegance", *no monogram, excellent condition*	6.00	7.00
☐ Gorham "Richmond", *no monogram, excellent condition* ..	7.00	8.00
☐ Gorham "Richmond", *no monogram, fair condition*	1.00	2.00
☐ Gorham "Vanity Fair", *no monogram, excellent condition* .	2.00	3.00
☐ Gorham "Vanity Fair", *no monogram, good condition*	2.00	3.00
☐ Gorham "Winthrop", *monogram, excellent condition*	4.00	5.00
☐ Harmony House "Maytime", *no monogram, excellent condition*	2.00	3.00
☐ Harmony House "Maytime", *no monogram, fair condition* .	1.00	2.00
☐ Harmony House "Maytime", *no monogram, poor condition*	1.00	2.00
☐ Heirloom "Cardinal", *no monogram, good condition*	7.00	8.00

	Price Range	
☐ **Heirloom "Cardinal"**, *flat-handled, viande style, no monogram, good condition*	1.00	2.00
☐ **Holmes & Edwards "Bright Future"**, *no monogram, good condition*	4.00	5.00
☐ **Holmes & Edwards "Bright Future"**, *no monogram, fair condition*	1.00	2.00
☐ **Holmes & Edwards "Carolina"**, *no monogram, good condition*	5.00	6.00
☐ **Holmes & Edwards "Carolina"**, *no monogram, excellent condition*	6.00	7.00
☐ **Holmes & Edwards "Carolina"**, *no monogram, fair condition*	1.00	2.00
☐ **Holmes & Edwards "Century"**, *monogram, excellent condition*	1.00	2.00
☐ **Holmes & Edwards "Century"**, *no monogram, excellent condition*	6.00	7.00
☐ **Holmes & Edwards "Century"**, *no monogram, good condition*	4.00	5.00
☐ **Holmes & Edwards "Danish Princess"**, *no monogram, good condition*	5.00	6.00
☐ **Holmes & Edwards "Danish Princess"**, *no monogram, excellent condition*	6.00	7.00
☐ **Holmes & Edwards "Danish Princess"**, *no monogram, excellent condition*	4.00	5.00
☐ **Holmes & Edwards "Danish Princess"**, *no monogram, fair condition*	1.00	2.00
☐ **Holmes & Edwards "First Lady"**, *no monogram, excellent condition*	6.00	7.00
☐ **Holmes & Edwards "First Lady"**, *no monogram, good condition*	3.00	4.00
☐ **Holmes & Edwards "First Lady"**, *no monogram, fair condition*	1.00	2.00
☐ **Holmes & Edwards "Lovely Lady"**, *no monogram, excellent condition*	3.00	4.00
☐ **Holmes & Edwards "Lovely Lady"**, *no monogram, fair condition*	1.00	2.00
☐ **Holmes & Edwards "Lovely Lady"**, *no monogram, excellent condition*	6.00	7.00
☐ **Holmes & Edwards "Lovely Lady"**, *monogram, excellent condition*	2.00	3.00
☐ **Holmes & Edwards "Lovely Lady"**, *viande style, no monogram, mint condition*	4.00	5.00
☐ **Holmes & Edwards "Lovely Lady"**, *viande style, no monogram, good condition*	1.00	2.00
☐ **Holmes & Edwards "May Queen"**, *viande style, no monogram, mint condition*	4.00	5.00
☐ **Holmes & Edwards "May Queen"**, *viande style, no monogram, fair condition*	1.00	2.00
☐ **Holmes & Edwards "Orient"**, *flat-handled, no monogram, excellent condition*	3.00	4.00
☐ **Holmes & Edwards "Orient"**, *flat-handled, no monogram, good condition*	2.00	3.00

Price Range

☐ Holmes & Edwards "Orient", *flat-handled, no monogram, good condition*	2.00	3.00
☐ Holmes & Edwards "Romance II", *no monogram, excellent condition*	3.00	4.00
☐ Holmes & Edwards "Silver Fashion", *no monogram, good condition*	4.00	5.00
☐ Holmes & Edwards "Spring Garden", *no monogram, excellent condition*	4.00	5.00
☐ Holmes & Edwards "Spring Garden", *no monogram, good condition*	5.00	6.00
☐ Holmes & Edwards "Spring Garden", *no monogram, excellent condition*	6.00	7.00
☐ Holmes & Edwards "Youth", *no monogram, excellent condition*	6.00	7.00
☐ Holmes & Edwards "Youth", *no monogram, good condition*	3.00	4.00
☐ Holmes & Edwards "Youth", *no monogram, fair condition*	1.00	2.00
☐ King Edward "Moss Rose", *viande style, no monogram, excellent condition*	6.00	7.00
☐ International "Beacon Hill", *no monogram, excellent condition*	6.00	7.00
☐ International "Beacon Hill", *no monogram, good condition*	3.00	4.00
☐ International "Kings", *no monogram, excellent condition*	3.00	4.00
☐ International "Kings", *no monogram, good condition*	3.00	4.00
☐ International "Orleans", *no monogram, excellent condition*	3.00	4.00
☐ International "Orleans", *no monogram, good condition*	2.00	3.00
☐ International "Silver Tulip", *viande style, no monogram, excellent condition*	4.00	5.00
☐ National "Embossed", *no monogram, fair condition*	1.00	2.00
☐ National "Embossed", *no monogram, excellent condition*	5.00	6.00
☐ National "King Edward", *viande style, no monogram, excellent condition*	6.00	7.00
☐ National "King Edward", *viande style, no monogram, good condition*	3.00	4.00
☐ Niagara Falls Silver Co. "Adams", *flat-handled, monogram, good condition*	2.00	3.00
☐ Niagara Falls Silver Co. "Adams", *no monogram, excellent condition*	2.00	3.00
☐ Nobility "Caprice", *viande style, no monogram, excellent condition*	6.00	7.00
☐ Nobility "Caprice", *viande style, no monogram, fair condition*	1.00	2.00
☐ Nobility "Reverie", *viande style, no monogram, excellent condition*	6.00	7.00
☐ Nobility "Reverie", *viande style, no monogram, good condition*	3.00	4.00
☐ Old Company Plate "Signature", *monogram, excellent condition*	2.00	3.00
☐ Old Company Plate "Signature", *no monogram, excellent condition*	5.00	6.00
☐ Oneida "Avalon", *no monogram, good condition*	3.00	4.00
☐ Oneida "Avalon", *no monogram, excellent condition*	5.00	6.00
☐ Oneida "Bridal Wreath", *no monogram, excellent condition*	6.00	7.00

	Price Range	
☐ Oneida "Bridal Wreath", *no monogram, good condition* ...	3.00	4.00
☐ Oneida "Clarion", *no monogram, excellent condition*	6.00	7.00
☐ Oneida "Clarion", *no monogram, fair condition*	1.00	2.00
☐ Oneida "Flower de Luce", *no monogram, excellent condition*	8.00	10.00
☐ Oneida "Flower de Luce", *no monogram, fair condition* ...	2.00	3.00
☐ Oneida "Flower de Luce", *no monogram, poor condition* ..	1.00	2.00
☐ Oneida "Jamestown", *monogram, excellent condition*	2.00	3.00
☐ Oneida "Jamestown", *no monogram, good condition*	3.00	4.00
☐ Oneida "Louis XVI", *no monogram, mint condition*	4.00	5.00
☐ Oneida "Louis XVI", *monogram, excellent condition*	2.00	3.00
☐ Oneida "Sheraton", *no monogram, good condition*	2.00	3.00
☐ Prestige "Grenoble", *viande style, no monogram, fair condition*	1.00	2.00
☐ Prestige "Grenoble", *viande style, no monogram, good condition*	4.00	5.00
☐ Reed & Barton "Jewell", *flat-handled, no monogram, poor condition*	1.00	2.00
☐ Reed & Barton "Maid of Honor", *no monogram, excellent condition*	6.00	7.00
☐ Reed & Barton "Maid of Honor", *no monogram, good condition*	3.00	4.00
☐ Reed & Barton, *"Rembrandt", long handled, no monogram, good condition*	4.00	5.00
☐ Reed & Barton "Sierra", *no monogram, excellent condition*	6.00	7.00
☐ Reed & Barton "Sierra", *no monogram, good condition*	5.00	6.00
☐ Reed & Barton "Tiger Lily", *no monogram, excellent condition*	3.00	4.00
☐ Reliance "Briar Rose", *no monogram, excellent condition* .	8.00	9.00
☐ Reliance "Bridal Rose", *no monogram, excellent condition*	6.00	7.00
☐ Reliance "Exeter", *flat-handled, no monogram, good condition*	1.00	2.00
☐ Reliance "Exeter", *flat-handled, no monogram, fair condition*	1.00	2.00
☐ Reliance "Wildwood", *flat-handled, no monogram, good condition*	3.00	4.00
☐ Reliance "Wildwood", *no monogram, excellent condition* .	9.00	10.00
☐ Reliance "Wildwood", *no monogram, fair condition*	3.00	4.00
☐ Rockford "Fairoaks", *no monogram, excellent condition* ..	6.00	7.00
☐ Rockford "Fairoaks", *no monogram, good condition*	4.00	5.00
☐ Rogers "Alhambra", *no monogram, excellent condition* ...	9.00	10.00
☐ Rogers "Alhambra", *no monogram, fair condition*	3.00	4.00
☐ Rogers "Ambasador", *no monogram, excellent condition* .	5.00	6.00
☐ Rogers "Ambassador", *monogram, excellent condition* ...	4.00	5.00
☐ Rogers "Ambassador", *monogram, fair condition*	1.00	2.00
☐ Rogers "Burgundy", *no monogram, good condition*	5.00	6.00
☐ Rogers "Burgundy", *no monogram, excellent condition* ...	6.00	7.00
☐ Rogers "Burgundy", *no monogram, fair condition*	1.00	2.00
☐ Rogers "Desota", *no monogram, excellent condition*	6.00	7.00
☐ Rogers "Desota", *no monogram, good condition*	3.00	4.00
☐ Rogers "Inspiration", *viande style, no monogram, excellent condition*	6.00	7.00
☐ Rogers "Inspiration", *viande style, no monogram, good condition*	5.00	6.00

Price Range

☐ **Rogers "Inspiration"**, *viande style, no monogram, fair condition* 1.00 2.00
☐ **Rogers "Inspiration"**, *no monogram, excellent condition* .. 6.00 7.00
☐ **Rogers "Inspiration"**, *no monogram, good condition* 5.00 6.00
☐ **Rogers "Inspiration"**, *no monogram, fair condition* 1.00 2.00
☐ **Rogers "Margate"**, *no monogram, excellent condition* 6.00 7.00
☐ **Rogers "Margate"**, *no monogram, excellent condition* 6.00 7.00
☐ **Rogers "Margate"**, *no monogram, good condition* 4.00 5.00
☐ **Rogers "Navarre"**, *no monogram, excellent condition* 7.00 8.00
☐ **Rogers "Margate"**, *no monogram, good condition* 5.00 6.00
☐ **Rogers "Margate"**, *no monogram, good condition* 4.00 5.00
☐ **Rogers "Navarre"**, *no monogram, excellent condition* 7.00 8.00
☐ **Rogers "Navarre"**, *no monogram, good condition* 5.00 6.00
☐ **Rogers "Navarre"**, *no monogram, fair condition* 2.00 3.00
☐ **Rogers "Precious"**, *viande style, no monogram, excellent condition* 6.00 7.00
☐ **Rogers "Precious"**, *viande style, no monogram, good condition* 2.00 3.00
☐ **Rogers & Bro. "Assyrian Head"**, *no monogram, new blade, resilvered* 18.00 20.00
☐ **Rogers & Bro. "Assyrian Head"**, *no monogram, good condition* 8.00 9.00
☐ **Rogers & Bro. "Columbia"**, *no monogram, new blade, resilvered* 16.00 18.00
☐ **Rogers & Bro. "Cromwell"**, *no monogram, mint condition* .. 2.00 3.00
☐ **Rogers & Bro. "Daybreak"**, *no monogram, excellent condition* 6.00 7.00
☐ **Rogers & Bro. "Daybreak"**, *no monogram, good condition* . 3.00 4.00
☐ **Rogers & Bro. "Flemish"**, *no monogram, mint condition* ... 6.00 7.00
☐ **Rogers & Bro. "Flemish"**, *no monogram, fair condition* 1.00 2.00
☐ **Rogers & Bro. "Modern Rose"**, *viande style, no monogram, excellent condition* 6.00 7.00
☐ **Rogers & Bro. "Modern Rose"**, *viande style, no monogram, good condition* 3.00 4.00
☐ **Rogers & Bro. "Mystic"**, *no monogram, excellent condition* 7.00 8.00
☐ **Rogers & Bro. "Mystic"**, *no monogram, good condition* ... 4.00 5.00
☐ **Rogers & Bro. "New Century"**, *no monogram, fair condition* 2.00 3.00
☐ **Rogers & Hamilton "Aldine"**, *no monogram, excellent condition* 4.00 5.00
☐ **Rogers & Hamilton "Aldine"**, *no monogram, fair condition* . 1.00 2.00
☐ **Rogers & Hamilton "Alhambra"**, *flat-handled, no monogram, good condition* 6.00 7.00
☐ **Rogers & Hamilton "Raphael"**, *no monogram, excellent condition* 10.00 12.00
☐ **Rogers & Hamilton "Raphael"**, *no monogram, good condition* 7.00 8.00
☐ **Rogers & Hamilton "Raphael"**, *no monogram, fair condition* 3.00 4.00
☐ **S.L. & G.H. Rogers "Countess II"**, *no monogram, excellent condition* 6.00 7.00
☐ **S.L. & G.H. Rogers "Countess II"**, *no monogram, good condition* 3.00 4.00

	Price Range	
☐ **S.L. & G.H. Rogers "Minerva"**, *no monogram, good condition*	6.00	7.00
☐ **S.L. & G.H. Rogers "Minerva"**, *no monogram, fair condition*	3.00	4.00
☐ **S.L. & G.H. Rogers "Silver Rose"**, *viande style, no monogram, fair condition*	1.00	2.00
☐ **S.L. & G.H. Rogers "Silver Rose"**, *viande style, no monogram, good condition*	3.00	4.00
☐ **S.L. & G.H. Rogers "Violet"**, *no monogram, good condition*	5.00	6.00
☐ **Towle "Grenoble"**, *no monogram, good condition*	5.00	6.00
☐ **Towle "Grenoble"**, *no monogram, excellent condition*	7.00	8.00
☐ **Towle "Grenoble"**, *no monogram, good condition*	4.00	5.00
☐ **Tudor "Bridal Wreath"**, *no monogram, excellent condition*	6.00	7.00
☐ **Tudor "Bridal Wreath"**, *no monogram, good condition*	3.00	4.00
☐ **Tudor "Bridal Wreath"**, *no monogram, mint condition*	3.00	4.00
☐ **Tudor "Duchess"**, *flat-handled, no monogram, excellent condition*	1.00	2.00
☐ **Tudor "Duchess"**, *flat-handled, no monogram, fair condition*	1.00	2.00
☐ **Tudor "Elaine"**, *no monogram, excellent condition*	6.00	7.00
☐ **Tudor "Elaine"**, *no monogram, fair condition*	1.00	2.00
☐ **Tudor "Enchantment"**, *no monogram, excellent condition*	5.00	6.00
☐ **Tudor "Enchantment"**, *no monogram, good condition*	3.00	4.00
☐ **Tudor "Queen Bess II"**, *flat-handled, no monogram, good condition*	1.00	2.00
☐ **Tudor "Queen Bess II"**, *no monogram, good condition*	5.00	6.00
☐ **Tudor "Queen Bess II"**, *no monogram, fair condition*	1.00	2.00
☐ **Wallace "Holland"**, *no monogram, excellent condition*	9.00	10.00
☐ **Wallace "Holland"**, *no monogram, fair condition*	2.00	7.00
☐ **Wallace "Sonata"**, *viande style, no monogram, excellent condition*	6.00	7.00
☐ **Wallace "Sonata"**, *viande style, no monogram, fair condition*	1.00	2.00
☐ **W.D. Smith "Adam"**, *flat-handled, no monogram, fair condition*	1.00	2.00
☐ **W.D. Smith "Adam"**, *monogram, excellent condition*	2.00	3.00
☐ **W.D. Smith "Adam"**, *no monogram, excellent condition*	6.00	7.00
☐ **Williams Bros. "Queen Elizabeth"**, *no monogram, excellent condition*	3.00	4.00
☐ **Williams Bros. "Vineyard"**, *no monogram, good condition*	7.00	8.00
☐ **Williams Bros. "Vineyard"**, *no monogram, excellent condition*	11.00	12.00
☐ **Williams Bros. "Vineyard"**, *no monogram, good condition*	6.00	7.00
☐ **Wm. A. Rogers "Artistic"**, *viande style, no monogram, excellent condition*	6.00	7.00
☐ **Wm. A. Rogers "Chalice"**, *no monogram, good condition*	5.00	6.00
☐ **Wm. A. Rogers "Chalice"**, *no monogram, excellent condition*	6.00	7.00
☐ **Wm. A. Rogers "Country Lane"**, *no monogram, good condition*	1.00	2.00
☐ **Wm. A. Rogers "Debutante"**, *no monogram, excellent condition*	3.00	4.00
☐ **Wm. A. Rogers "Grenoble"**, *flat-handled, excellent condition*	3.00	4.00

	Price Range	
☐ **Wm. A. Rogers "Grenoble"**, *flat-handled, no monogram, excellent condition*	6.00	7.00
☐ **Wm. A. Rogers "Hanover"**, *no monogram, blade in poor condition, handle in good condition*	2.00	3.00
☐ **Wm. A. Rogers "Hanover"**, *no monogram, blade in poor condition, handle in fair condition*	1.00	2.00
☐ **Wm. A. Rogers "Lady Drake"**, *viande style, no monogram, fair condition*	1.00	2.00
☐ **Wm. A. Rogers "Lady Drake"**, *viande style, no monogram, good condition*	3.00	4.00
☐ **Wm. A. Rogers "Lady Drake"**, *viande style, no monogram, excellent condition*	3.00	4.00
☐ **Wm. A. Rogers "Lady Stuart"**, *no monogram, excellent condition*	6.00	7.00
☐ **Wm. A. Rogers "Lady Stuart"**, *no monogram, good condition*	3.00	4.00
☐ **Wm. A. Rogers "LaVigne"**, *flat-handled, no monogram, mint condition*	7.00	8.00
☐ **Wm. A. Rogers "LaVigne"**, *flat-handled, no monogram, excellent condition*	7.00	8.00
☐ **Wm. A. Rogers "Malibu"**, *flat-handled, no monogram, excellent condition*	1.00	2.00
☐ **Wm. A. Rogers "Margate"**, *flat-handled, no monogram, excellent condition*	1.00	2.00
☐ **Wm. A. Rogers "Meadowbrook"**, *viande style, no monogram, excellent condition*	6.00	7.00
☐ **Wm. A. Rogers "Meadowbrook"**, *viande style, no monogram, fair condition*	1.00	2.00
☐ **Wm. A. Rogers "Meadowbrook"**, *no monogram, excellent condition*	6.00	7.00
☐ **Wm. A. Rogers "Meadowbrook"**, *no monogram, good condition*	3.00	4.00
☐ **Wm. A. Rogers "Mystic"**, *no monogram, good condition* . . .	5.00	6.00
☐ **Wm. A. Rogers "Mystic"**, *no monogram, fair condition*	2.00	3.00
☐ **Wm. A. Rogers "Paramount"**, *flat-handled, no monogram, excellent condition*	1.00	2.00
☐ **Wm. A. Rogers "Paramount"**, *flat-handled, no monogram, fair condition*	1.00	2.00
☐ **Wm. A. Rogers "Paramount"**, *viande style, no monogram, excellent condition*	6.00	7.00
☐ **Wm. A. Rogers "Paramount"**, *viande style, no monogram, good condition*	2.00	4.00
☐ **Wm. A. Rogers "Rendezvous"**, *viande style, no monogram, excellent condition*	6.00	7.00
☐ **Wm. A. Rogers "Rendezvous"**, *viande style, no monogram, fair condition*	1.00	2.00
☐ **Wm. A. Rogers "Rosalie"**, *no monogram, excellent condition*	6.00	7.00
☐ **Wm. A. Rogers "Rosalie"**, *no monogram, mint condition* . .	8.00	9.00
☐ **Wm. Rogers "Beloved"**, *no monogram, excellent condition*	4.00	5.00
☐ **Wm. Rogers "Beloved"**, *no monogram, good condition*	4.00	5.00
☐ **Wm. Rogers "Beloved"**, *viande style, no monogram, excellent condition*	6.00	7.00

	Price Range	
☐ Wm. Rogers "Beloved", *viande style, no monogram, fair condition*	1.00	2.00
☐ Wm. Rogers "Berwick", *no monogram, good condition*	7.00	8.00
☐ Wm. Rogers "Berwick", *no monogram, excellent condition*	8.00	10.00
☐ Wm. Rogers "Berwick", *no monogram, fair condition*	3.00	4.00
☐ Wm. Rogers "Berwick", *no monogram, blade bent, silver in excellent condition*	1.00	2.00
☐ Wm. Rogers "Cotillion", *no monogram, excellent condition*	6.00	7.00
☐ Wm. Rogers "Cotillion", *no monogram, good condition* ...	3.00	4.00
☐ Wm. Rogers "Cotillion", *viande style, no monogram, excellent condition*	6.00	7.00
☐ Wm. Rogers "Debutante", *viande style, no monogram, good condition*	4.00	5.00
☐ Wm. Rogers "Debutante", *viande style, no monogram, fair condition*	1.00	2.00
☐ Wm. Rogers "Devonshire", *no monogram, excellent condition*	6.00	7.00
☐ Wm. Rogers "Devonshire", *no monogram, good condition* .	3.00	4.00
☐ Wm. Rogers "Exquisite", *viande style, no monogram, excellent condition*	6.00	7.00
☐ Wm. Rogers "Exquisite", *viande style, no monogram, good condition*	3.00	4.00
☐ Wm. Rogers "Exquisite", *no monogram, good condition* ...	5.00	6.00
☐ Wm. Rogers "Exquisite", *no monogram, fair condition*	1.00	2.00
☐ Wm. Rogers "Fairoaks", *no monogram, excellent condition*	6.00	7.00
☐ Wm. Rogers "Fairoaks", *no monogram, good condition* ...	2.00	3.00
☐ Wm. Rogers "Fidelis", *viande style, no monogram, excellent condition*	6.00	7.00
☐ Wm. Rogers "Fidelis", *viande style, no monogram, poor condition*	1.00	2.00
☐ Wm. Rogers "Hostess", *no monogram, good condition* ...	5.00	6.00
☐ Wm. Rogers "Hostess", *no monogram, fair condition*	1.00	2.00
☐ Wm. Rogers "Hostess", *no monogram, handle in excellent condition, blade nicked*	1.00	2.00
☐ Wm. Rogers "Imperial", *viande style, no monogram, good condition*	5.00	6.00
☐ Wm. Rogers "Imperial", *viande style, no monogram, excellent condition*	6.00	7.00
☐ Wm. Rogers "Louisiana", *no monogram, excellent condition*	6.00	7.00
☐ Wm. Rogers "Louisiana", *no monogram, good condition* ..	3.00	4.00
☐ Wm. Rogers "Lufberry", *no monogram, excellent condition*	4.00	5.00
☐ Wm. Rogers "Lufberry", *no monogram, fair condition*	1.00	2.00
☐ Wm. Rogers "Memory", *no monogram, fair condition*	1.00	2.00
☐ Wm. Rogers "Memory", *no monogram, good condition*	4.00	5.00
☐ Wm. Rogers "Memory", *viande style, no monogram, good condition*	5.00	6.00
☐ Wm. Rogers "Memory", *viande style, no monogram, fair condition*	1.00	2.00
☐ Wm. Rogers "Mountain Rose", *no monogram, excellent condition*	7.00	8.00

	Price Range	
☐ **Wm. Rogers "Mountain Rose",** *no monogram, good condition*	4.00	5.00
☐ **Wm. Rogers "Precious Mirror",** *no monogram, good condition*	5.00	6.00
☐ **Wm. Rogers "Precious Mirror",** *no monogram, excellent condition*	6.00	7.00
☐ **Wm. Rogers "Precious Mirror",** *no monogram, good condition*	4.00	5.00
☐ **Wm. Rogers "Starlight",** *no monogram, excellent condition*	6.00	7.00
☐ **Wm. Rogers "Starlight",** *no monogram, fair condition*	1.00	2.00
☐ **Wm. Rogers "Treasure",** *viande style, no monogram, excellent condition*	6.00	7.00
☐ **Wm. Rogers "Treasure",** *viande style, no monogram, fair condition*	1.00	2.00
☐ **Wm. Rogers "Treasure",** *no monogram, excellent condition*	6.00	7.00
☐ **Wm. Rogers "Treasure",** *no monogram, good condition* ...	4.00	5.00
☐ **Wm. Rogers "Victory",** *viande style, no monogram, good condition*	5.00	6.00
☐ **Wm. Rogers "Victory",** *viande style, no monogram, fair condition*	1.00	2.00
☐ **Wm. Rogers Mfg. Co. "Alhambra",** *no monogram, good condition*	7.00	8.00
☐ **Wm. Rogers Mfg. Co. "Alhambra",** *no monogram, excellent condition*	3.00	4.00
☐ **Wm. Rogers Mfg. Co. "Alhambra",** *flat-handled, no monogram, excellent condition*	2.00	3.00
☐ **Wm. Rogers Mfg. Co. "Arbutus",** *no monogram, excellent condition*	18.00	20.00
☐ **Wm. Rogers Mfg. Co. "Arbutus",** *no monogram, fair condition*	7.00	8.00
☐ **Wm. Rogers Mfg. Co. "Arbutus",** *no monogram, good condition*	14.00	16.00
☐ **Wm. Rogers Mfg. Co. "Berwick",** *flat-handled, no monogram, excellent condition*	2.00	3.00
☐ **Wm. Rogers Mfg. Co. "Berwick",** *flat-handled, no monogram, fair condition*	1.00	2.00
☐ **Wm. Rogers Mfg. Co. "Berwick",** *no monogram, excellent condition*	8.00	10.00
☐ **Wm. Rogers Mfg. Co. "Berwick",** *no monogram, resilvered* .	14.00	16.00
☐ **Wm. Rogers Mfg. Co. "Berwick",** *no monogram, fair condition*	2.00	3.00
☐ **Wm. Rogers Mfg. Co. "Camelot",** *no monogram, excellent condition*	6.00	7.00
☐ **Wm. Rogers Mfg. Co. "Camelot",** *no monogram, good condition*	3.00	4.00
☐ **Wm. Rogers Mfg. Co. "Jubilee",** *no monogram, excellent condition*	6.00	7.00
☐ **Wm. Rogers Mfg. Co. "Jubilee",** *no monogram, good condition*	3.00	4.00
☐ **Wm. Rogers Mfg. Co. "Magnolia",** *viande style, no monogram, good condition*	5.00	6.00
☐ **Wm. Rogers Mfg. Co. "Magnolia",** *no monogram, excellent condition*	6.00	7.00

	Price Range	

☐ **Wm. Rogers Mfg. Co. "Magnolia"**, *no monogram, good condition* .... 2.00 — 3.00

☐ **Wm. Rogers Mfg. Co. "Regent"**, *monogram, excellent condition* .... 4.00 — 5.00

☐ **Wm. Rogers Mfg. Co. "Revelation"**, *viande style, no monogram, excellent condition* .... 6.00 — 7.00

☐ **Wm. Rogers Mfg. Co. "Revelation"**, *viande style, monogram, good condition* .... 1.00 — 2.00

☐ **Wm. Rogers Mfg. Co. "Sovereign"**, *flat-handled, no monogram, excellent condition* .... 3.00 — 4.00

☐ **Wm. Rogers Mfg. Co. "Talisman"**, *viande style, no monogram, good condition* .... 5.00 — 6.00

☐ **Wm. Rogers Mfg. Co. "Talisman"**, *viande style, no monogram, good condition* .... 4.00 — 5.00

☐ **Wm. Rogers & Son "April"**, *viande style, no monogram, good condition* .... 5.00 — 6.00

☐ **Wm. Rogers & Son "Arbutus"**, *flat-handled, no monogram, good condition* .... 4.00 — 5.00

☐ **Wm. Rogers & Son "Arbutus"**, *flat-handled, no monogram, fair condition* .... 2.00 — 3.00

☐ **Wm. Rogers & Son "Arbutus"**, *no monogram, excellent condition* .... 16.00 — 18.00

☐ **Wm. Rogers & Son "Arbutus"**, *no monogram, good condition* .... 10.00 — 12.00

☐ **Wm. Rogers & Son "California Blossom"**, *viande style, no monogram, excellent condition* .... 5.00 — 6.00

☐ **Wm. Rogers & Son "California Blossom"**, *viande style, no monogram, good condition* .... 4.00 — 5.00

☐ **Wm. Rogers & Son "Flower"**, *flat-handled, no monogram, good condition* .... 3.00 — 4.00

☐ **Wm. Rogers & Son "Flower"**, *flat-handled, no monogram, fair condition* .... 1.00 — 2.00

☐ **1835 R. Wallace "Abbey"**, *no monogram, excellent condition* .... 6.00 — 7.00

☐ **1835 R. Wallace "Abbey"**, *no monogram, good condition* .. 3.00 — 4.00

☐ **1835 R. Wallace "Buckingham"**, *no monogram, excellent condition* .... 5.00 — 6.00

☐ **1835 R. Wallace "Buckingham"**, *no monogram, good condition* .... 2.00 — 3.00

☐ **1835 R. Wallace "Buckingham"**, *no monogram, fair condition* .... 1.00 — 2.00

☐ **1835 R. Wallace "Floral"**, *no monogram, good condition* .. 5.00 — 6.00

☐ **1835 R. Wallace "Floral"**, *no monogram, excellent condition* .... 9.00 — 10.00

☐ **1835 R. Wallace "Kings"**, *no monogram, good condition* ... 5.00 — 6.00

☐ **1835 R. Wallace "Kings"**, *no monogram, fair condition* ... 1.00 — 2.00

☐ **1847 Rogers "Ancestral"**, *no monogram, excellent condition* .... 6.00 — 7.00

☐ **1847 Rogers "Ancestral"**, *no monogram, good condition* .. 4.00 — 5.00

☐ **1847 Rogers "Anniversary"**, *no monogram, excellent condition* .... 6.00 — 7.00

☐ **1847 Rogers "Anniversary"**, *no monogram, fair condition* .. 1.00 — 2.00

	Price Range	
☐ **1847 Rogers "Anniversary"**, *flat-handled, no monogram, excellent condition*	1.00	2.00
☐ **1847 Rogers "Anniversary"**, *flat-handled, no monogram, fair condition*	1.00	2.00
☐ **1847 Rogers "Argosy"**, *flat-handled, no monogram, excellent condition*	2.00	3.00
☐ **1847 Rogers "Argosy"**, *no monogram, excellent condition* .	9.00	10.00
☐ **1847 Rogers "Argosy"**, *no monogram, fair condition*	1.00	2.00
☐ **1847 Rogers "Avon"**, *no monogram, fair condition*	6.00	7.00
☐ **1847 Rogers "Avon"**, *no monogram, good condition*	9.00	10.00
☐ **1847 Rogers "Avon"**, *no monogram, excellent condition* ...	14.00	16.00
☐ **1847 Rogers "Berkshire"**, *no monogram, good condition* ..	5.00	6.00
☐ **1847 Rogers "Berkshire"**, *no monogram, poor condition* ...	2.00	3.00
☐ **1847 Rogers "Berkshire"**, *no monogram, good condition* ..	9.00	10.00
☐ **1847 Rogers "Berkshire"**, *no monogram, excellent condition*	14.00	16.00
☐ **1847 Rogers "Berkshire"**, *no monogram, good condition* ..	8.00	10.00
☐ **1847 Rogers "Berkshire"**, *no monogram, fair condition*	4.00	5.00
☐ **1847 Rogers "Charter Oak"**, *no monogram, good condition*	6.00	7.00
☐ **1847 Rogers "Charter Oak"**, *no monogram, resilvered*	10.00	12.00
☐ **1847 Rogers "Charter Oak"**, *no monogram, fair condition* ..	10.00	12.00
☐ **1847 Rogers "Charter Oak"**, *no monogram, resilvered*	10.00	12.00
☐ **1847 Rogers "Charter Oak"**, *no monogram, mint condition* .	16.00	18.00
☐ **1847 Rogers "Charter Oak"**, *flat-handled, no monogram, good condition*	2.00	3.00
☐ **1847 Rogers "Charter Oak"**, *flat-handled, no monogram, excellent condition*	4.00	5.00
☐ **1847 Rogers "Charter Oak"**, *flat-handled, no monogram, good condition*	4.00	5.00
☐ **1847 Rogers "Columbia"**, *no monogram, mint condition* ...	16.00	18.00
☐ **1847 Rogers "Columbia"**, *no monogram, good condition* ..	8.00	10.00
☐ **1847 Rogers "Columbia"**, *no monogram, fair condition*	3.00	4.00
☐ **1847 Rogers "Cromwell"**, *no monogram, excellent condition*	3.00	4.00
☐ **1847 Rogers "Daffodil"**, *no monogram, good condition*	5.00	6.00
☐ **1847 Rogers "Daffodil"**, *no monogram, excellent condition*	9.00	10.00
☐ **1847 Rogers "Daffodil"**, *no monogram, fair condition*	1.00	2.00
☐ **1847 Rogers "Daffodil II"**, *viande style, no monogram, excellent condition*	6.00	7.00
☐ **1847 Rogers "Daffodil II"**, *viande style, no monogram, good condition*	3.00	4.00
☐ **1847 Rogers "Daffodil II"**, *no monogram, excellent condition*	6.00	7.00
☐ **1847 Rogers "Esperanto"**, *no monogram, excellent condition*	6.00	7.00
☐ **1847 Rogers "Esperanto"**, *no monogram, fair condition* ...	1.00	2.00
☐ **1847 Rogers "Eternally Yours"**, *no monogram, good condition*	5.00	6.00
☐ **1847 Rogers "Eternally Yours"**, *no monogram, excellent condition*	6.00	7.00
☐ **1847 Rogers "Eternally Yours"**, *no monogram, fair condition*	1.00	2.00
☐ **1847 Rogers "Eternally Yours"**, *viande style, no monogram, excellent condition*	6.00	7.00

	Price Range	

☐ **1847 Rogers "Eternally Yours"**, *viande style, no monogram, fair condition* 1.00 2.00

☐ **1847 Rogers "First Love"**, *no monogram, excellent condition* 3.00 4.00

☐ **1847 Rogers "First Love"**, *no monogram, good condition* .. 5.00 6.00

☐ **1847 Rogers "First Love"**, *no monogram, fair condition* ... 1.00 2.00

☐ **1847 Rogers "First Love"**, *viande style, no monogram, fair condition* 1.00 2.00

☐ **1847 Rogers "First Love"**, *viande style, no monogram, good condition* 5.00 6.00

☐ **1847 Rogers "Flair"**, *no monogram, excellent condition* ... 4.00 5.00

☐ **1847 Rogers "Flair"**, *no monogram, good condition* 3.00 4.00

☐ **1847 Rogers "Floral"**, *no monogram, resilvered* 16.00 18.00

☐ **1847 Rogers "Floral"**, *no monogram, good condition* 8.00 10.00

☐ **1847 Rogers "Heraldic"**, *no monogram, excellent condition* 7.00 8.00

☐ **1847 Rogers "Heraldic"**, *no monogram, fair condition* 2.00 3.00

☐ **1847 Rogers "Heritage"**, *no monogram, excellent condition* 7.00 8.00

☐ **1847 Rogers "Heritage"**, *no monogram, mint condition* 8.00 9.00

☐ **1847 Rogers "Her Majesty"**, *flat-handled, no monogram, excellent condition* 2.00 3.00

☐ **1847 Rogers "Her Majesty"**, *flat-handled, no monogram, good condition* 2.00 3.00

☐ **1847 Rogers "Legacy"**, *viande style, no monogram, excellent condition* 6.00 7.00

☐ **1847 Rogers "Legacy"**, *viande style, no monogram, good condition* 3.00 4.00

☐ **1847 Rogers "Leilani"**, *no monogram, good condition* 5.00 6.00

☐ **1847 Rogers "Leilani"**, *no monogram, excellent condition* . 6.00 7.00

☐ **1847 Rogers "Leilani"**, *no monogram, mint condition* 2.00 3.00

☐ **1847 Rogers "Leyland"**, *flat-handled, no monogram, fair condition* 1.00 2.00

☐ **1847 Rogers "Louvain"**, *no monogram, good condition* 5.00 6.00

☐ **1847 Rogers "Louvain"**, *no monogram, excellent condition* 6.00 7.00

☐ **1847 Rogers "Lovelace"**, *no monogram, good condition* ... 5.00 6.00

☐ **1847 Rogers "Lovelace"**, *no monogram, excellent condition* 6.00 7.00

☐ **1847 Rogers "Lovelace"**, *no monogram, fair condition* 1.00 2.00

☐ **1847 Rogers "Lovelace"**, *viande style, no monogram, good condition* 5.00 6.00

☐ **1847 Rogers "Lovelace"**, *viande style, no monogram, excellent condition* 6.00 7.00

☐ **1847 Rogers "Magic Rose"**, *no monogram, excellent condition* 6.00 7.00

☐ **1847 Rogers "Magic Rose"**, *no monogram, good condition* 5.00 6.00

☐ **1847 Rogers "Marquise"**, *viande style, no monogram, excellent condition* 6.00 7.00

☐ **1847 Rogers "Marquise"**, *viande style, no monogram, fair condition* 1.00 2.00

☐ **1847 Rogers "Marquise"**, *flat-handled, no monogram, excellent condition* 3.00 4.00

☐ **1847 Rogers "Marquise"**, *flat-handled, no monogram, fair condition* 1.00 2.00

☐ **1847 Rogers "Marquise"**, *no monogram, excellent condition* 6.00 7.00

☐ **1847 Rogers "Marquise"**, *no monogram, fair condition* 1.00 2.00

	Price Range	

☐ **1847 Rogers "Moselle"**, *no monogram, mint condition* 24.00 26.00
☐ **1847 Rogers "Moselle"**, *no monogram, excellent condition* 26.00 28.00
☐ **1847 Rogers "Moselle"**, *no monogram, fair condition* 6.00 7.00
☐ **1847 Rogers "Old Colony"**, *no monogram, excellent condition* 6.00 7.00
☐ **1847 Rogers "Old Colony"**, *monogram, excellent condition* 5.00 6.00
☐ **1847 Rogers "Old Colony"**, *no monogram, good condition* . 9.00 10.00
☐ **1847 Rogers "Old Colony"**, *monogram, good condition* 1.00 2.00
☐ **1847 Rogers "Old Colony"**, *no monogram, good condition* . 5.00 6.00
☐ **1847 Rogers "Old Colony"**, *no monogram, excellent condition* 6.00 7.00
☐ **1847 Rogers "Old Colony"**, *flat-handled, no monogram, excellent condition* 2.00 3.00
☐ **1847 Rogers "Portland"**, *monogram, excellent condition* .. 4.00 5.00
☐ **1847 Rogers "Queen Ann"**, *flat-handled, no monogram, good condition* 2.00 3.00
☐ **1847 Rogers "Queen Ann"**, *flat-handled, no monogram, fair condition* 1.00 2.00
☐ **1847 Rogers "Reflection"**, *no monogram, good condition* .. 4.00 5.00
☐ **1847 Rogers "Reflection"**, *no monogram, excellent condition* 5.00 6.00
☐ **1847 Rogers "Reflection"**, *no monogram, fair condition* ... 1.00 2.00
☐ **1847 Rogers "Remembrance"**, *viande style, no monogram, excellent condition* 6.00 7.00
☐ **1847 Rogers "Remembrance"**, *viande style, no monogram, good condition* 5.00 6.00
☐ **1847 Rogers "Remembrance"**, *no monogram, good condition* 4.00 5.00
☐ **1847 Rogers "Remembrance"**, *no monogram, excellent condition* 6.00 7.00
☐ **1847 Rogers "Remembrance"**, *no monogram, fair condition* 1.00 2.00
☐ **1847 Rogers "Savoy"**, *flat-handled, no monogram, excellent condition* 2.00 3.00
☐ **1847 Rogers "Savoy"**, *flat-handled, no monogram, fair condition* 1.00 2.00
☐ **1847 Rogers "Sharon"**, *flat-handled, no monogram, excellent condition* 3.00 4.00
☐ **1847 Rogers "Sharon"**, *no monogram, good condition* 6.00 7.00
☐ **1847 Rogers "Silver Lace"**, *no monogram, excellent condition* 6.00 7.00
☐ **1847 Rogers "Vintage"**, *flat-handled, no monogram, excellent condition* 3.00 4.00
☐ **1847 Rogers "Vintage"**, *flat-handled, no monogram, fair condition* 2.00 3.00
☐ **1847 Rogers "Vintage"**, *no monogram, excellent condition* 16.00 18.00
☐ **1847 Rogers "Vintage"**, *no monogram, fair condition* 4.00 5.00
☐ **1847 Rogers "Vintage"**, *no monogram, blade worn, handle in good condition* 9.00 10.00
☐ **1881 Rogers "Capri"**, *no monogram, good condition* 5.00 6.00
☐ **1881 Rogers "Capri"**, *no monogram, fair condition* 1.00 2.00
☐ **1881 Rogers "Enchantment"**, *no monogram, good condition* 4.00 5.00
☐ **1881 Rogers "Flirtation"**, *no monogram, excellent condition* 3.00 4.00

	Price Range	
☐ **1881 Rogers "Flirtation"**, *no monogram, good condition* ..	3.00	4.00
☐ **1881 Rogers "LaVigne"**, *flat-handled, no monogram, blade slightly worn, handle in good condition*	1.00	2.00
☐ **1881 Rogers "LaVigne"**, *flat-handled, no monogram, excellent condition*	4.00	5.00
☐ **1881 Rogers "Surf Club"**, *viande style, no monogram, excellent condition*	6.00	7.00
☐ **1881 Rogers "Surf Club"**, *viande style, no monogram, good condition*	5.00	6.00
☐ **1881 Rogers "Surf Club"**, *viande style, no monogram, fair condition*	1.00	2.00

(Sterling Silver)

☐ **Alvin "Maryland"**, *no monogram, old silver plated blades in good condition*	8.00	10.00
☐ **Dominick & Haff "Louis XIV"**, *old style, no monogram*	12.00	15.00
☐ **Durgin "Chrysanthemum"**, *no monogram*	30.00	32.00
☐ **Frank Smith "Fiddle Thread"**, *no monogram*	22.00	25.00
☐ **Frank M. Whiting "Georgian Scroll"**, *no monogram, 9¼" L.*	10.00	12.00
☐ **Gorham "Buckingham"**, *no monogram*	14.00	16.00
☐ **Gorham "Buttercup"**, *no monogram*	10.00	12.00
☐ **Gorham "Buttercup"**, *monogram*	8.00	10.00
☐ **Gorham "Buttercup"**, *silver-plated old style blade, no monogram, good condition*	10.00	12.00
☐ **Gorham "Cambridge"**, *silver-plated old style blade, no monogram*	12.00	15.00
☐ **Gorham "Camelia"**, *no monogram*	20.00	22.00
☐ **Gorham "Chantilly"**, *monogram*	22.00	24.00
☐ **Gorham "Chesterfield"**, *monogram*	8.00	10.00
☐ **Gorham "Etruscan"**, *monogram*	10.00	12.00
☐ **Gorham "Fairfax"**, *stainless blade, no monogram*	10.00	12.00
☐ **Gorham "Fairfax"**, *no monogram, 9⅜" L., old silver-plated blade in very good condition*	10.00	12.00
☐ **Gorham "Imperial Chrysanthemum"**, *silver-plated blade in fair condition*	8.00	10.00
☐ **Gorham "Lancaster Rose"**, *stainless blade, no monogram*	18.00	20.00
☐ **Gorham "Versailles"**	18.00	20.00
☐ **International "Blossomtime"**, *monogram*	8.00	10.00
☐ **International "Brandon"**	10.00	12.00
☐ **International "Edgewood"**	17.00	19.00
☐ **International "Richelieu"**, *monogram*	10.00	12.00
☐ **International "Stratford"**	16.00	18.00
☐ **International "Trianon"**, *monogram*	10.00	12.00
☐ **Kirk "Quadrille"**, *monogram*	14.00	16.00
☐ **Kirk "Repousse"**, *new blade, no monogram*	14.00	16.00
☐ **Lunt "Mignonette"**, *no monogram*	8.00	10.00
☐ **Lunt "Mt. Vernon"**, *no monogram, old silver-plated blade in fair condition*	8.00	10.00
☐ **Oneida "King Cedric"**, *no monogram*	10.00	12.00
☐ **Reed & Barton "Marlborough"**, *no monogram, old silver-plated blade in poor condition*	8.00	10.00
☐ **Tiffany "English King"**	16.00	18.00
☐ **Tiffany "Hampton"**, *monogram*	18.00	20.00
☐ **Tiffany "Winthrop"**, *monogram*	18.00	20.00

	Price Range	
☐ **Towle "Fontana"**, *no monogram*	8.00	10.00
☐ **Towle "Georgian"**, *no monogram, old silver-plated blade in good condition*	14.00	16.00
☐ **Towle "Kings"**, *no monogram*	24.00	26.00
☐ **Towle "Lafayette"**, *French blade, no monogram*	10.00	12.00
☐ **Wallace "Grand Colonial"**, *no monogram*	12.00	14.00
☐ **Wallace "Normandie"**, *monogram*	8.00	10.00
☐ **Wallace "Rose"**, *no monogram*	8.00	10.00
☐ **Wallace "Washington"**, *stainless French-type blade, monogram*	10.00	12.00
☐ **Whiting "King Edward"**, *plated blade*	8.00	10.00
☐ **Whiting "Lily"**, *no monogram, original blade in good condition*	32.00	36.00
☐ **Whiting "Louis XV"**, *plated blade*	7.00	9.00
☐ **Wilcox & Everston "Cloeta"**, *no monogram, old silver blade in fair condition*	6.00	8.00

DRESSER SETS

These are a bit challenging to study and collect, as the contents vary from one set to another. Some are quite modest, consisting of only a few basic articles, while others are elaborate and were expensive even when new (in the days of .90 or $1 per ounce prices for silver). Dresser sets are an example of the advanced merchandising skills of the 19th century. Why sell a customer one item at a time, when a set could be sold — along with an irresistible container that added to the price? Every variety, novelty and "dime" store sold dresser sets, but the common sort were not made of silver. Those of silver were obtainable in the better class shops and through mail-order catalogues (both Sears Roebuck and Montgomery Ward sold them for many years). The values depend not only upon the maker, pattern, and the number of items included, but on the types of items included, so no general rules can be given. If a hairbrush is included, its weight will count somewhat towards determining the overall value.

(Silver-Plated)

☐ **Maker unknown**, , *includes mirror and brush, Art Nouveau styling with woman's head with flowing hair, monogram, good condition*	50.00	60.00

(Sterling Silver)

☐ **Dominick & Haff**, *nine-piece set includes lady's comb, hair brush (replacement insert), hand mirror, puff jar (crystal with sterling lid), nail buffer, pin tray, clothes brush, man's military brush, and two whisk brooms, overall repousse design, monograms*	500.00	550.00
☐ **Foster & Bros.**, *six-piece set includes hair brush (replacement insert), comb, mirror, nail file, cuticle knife, and button hook, Art Nouveau design with playing children, no monograms, excellent condition*	350.00	375.00
☐ **Gorham**, *c. 1900, seven-piece set includes pair of brushes, mirror, nail file, button hook, comb and pin tray*	50.00	60.00
☐ **Kirk "Repousse"**, *three-piece set includes hand mirror, brush and comb, monogram, excellent condition*	275.00	300.00
☐ **Tiffany**, *seven pieces (unspecified), no monogram*	125.00	150.00

EGG CUPS

The soft boiled egg was, in the past, a very popular breakfast item, much more so than today. It yielded at least two classes of collectors' items, the egg *timer* and of course the egg *cup*. Egg cups were far from a frilly luxury: soft-boiled eggs are not very convenient to manage without an egg cup. They are still being made but today's are mostly of plastic. Silver egg cups were sold in sets and singally. When sold in sets they were often accompanied by a tray. Egg cups have acquired a substantial collector following. Occasionally, oversized specimens are found. These are novelties intended for use in displaying the large decorative porcelain Easter eggs of the 19th century.

Egg Coddler, *Wm. Gale, 1856, 13¾" H, 29 ounces,* 1750.00

(Sterling Silver)

	Price Range	
☐ **Maker unknown,** *two soft-boiled size cups on small tray, plain design, gadroon borders, total weight 5 oz.*	35.00	45.00
☐ **Maker unknown,** *embossed floral design on rims, monogram, soft-boiled size, pair*	20.00	22.00

(Sterling Silver and China)

☐ **Reed & Barton,** *4" T., R&B shape #1145, Lenox liner with gold trim on rim*	28.00	30.00

EGG SPOONS

The soft boiled egg (see preceding entry) needed of course to be eaten with a special spoon. In this case — unlike the situation with so much "specialty" tableware — there was a real purpose to be served. To reduce fuss to a minimum, the egg spoon required a bowl with diagonally-shaped front, almost like a spade, for cracking the shell and removing it. If this was attempted with a rounded-bowl spoon, the egg was apt to be totally crushed.

(Coin Silver)	Price Range	
☐ **Maker unknown**, *fiddle pattern, monogram*	16.00	18.00
(Silver-Plated)		
☐ **1847 Rogers "Berkshire"**, *no monogram, excellent condition*	14.00	16.00
☐ **Maker unknown**, *ornate grape and leaf design, no monogram, excellent condition*	10.00	12.00
(Sterling Silver)		
☐ **Alvin "Nuremburg"**, *no monogram*	14.00	16.00
☐ **Gorham "Bird's Nest"**, *c. 1885, no monogram*	35.00	40.00
☐ **Kirk "Repousse"**, *no monogram*	24.00	26.00
☐ **Wendt "Florentine"**, *no monogram*	6.00	7.00

ENTREE DISHES

Though modern silver entree dishes are large and weighty, their predecessors were nothing short of huge; and the farther one goes back into history, the bigger they get. An entree dish of the 15th or 16th century (the name was not used then, but the function was the same) might support a roast boar's head with all the trimmings, or an entire side of veal. On stately occasions it was carried in procession into the dining hall, sometimes to the accompaniment of music. At major banquets there would be various entree dishes, each bearing its different delicacy. These early entree dishes are museum pieces, only occasionally passing through the open market. However the selection of 19th century examples, and those of the 20th, is certainly ample. The size of entree dishes and the important role they played at table demanded lavish decoration; some are masterpieces indeed. Aside from this, the weight gives them a considerable melt value. Those made up to the mid 19th century usually weighed at least four pounds and often five or six.

(Silver-Plated)		
☐ **Maker unknown**, *ornate scroll and floral engraving, monogram, good condition*	45.00	55.00
(Sterling Silver)		
☐ **Ball, Black & Co.**, *oval, Greek key and beaded borders, crest, motto and date, bird finials, c. 1860, 11½" W., pair, total weight 84 oz.*	600.00	625.00
☐ **Grogan Co.**, *gadroon rim, oval shape, 14¼" L., weight 29 oz.*	140.00	165.00
☐ **Watson**, *reticulated holder on four scroll feet, Lenox liner with hand-painted tiny roses on lid, gold trim, silver weight 11 oz.*	115.00	135.00

EWERS

Technically speaking, a ewer is a slender bucket-like vessel, with one or two handles (usually one), intended for *water*. On the Victorian table they usually contained water chilled with chunks of ice (the ice *cube* had not yet come into the world). However, they were also put to various other uses, in dispensing beverages like lemonade, etc. The basic form of the ewer is derived from terracotta vessels of ancient Greece, also used for water. Silver makers often let their imaginations go rampant on ewers, creating works with classical spirit and sculptural effects. Those of the 1830-1860 era tend to be more ornate and heavier than later specimens, though *occasional* examples of a really exceptional nature were made later. They went into the homes of the Morgans, Wideners, Rockefellers and other social giants of the time. When purchasing silver ewers, be on the lookout for LOADING as this is a common problem. Old ewers are so heavy to begin with that even an extra TWENTY or THIRTY OUNCES of loading often go unnoticed.

(Sterling Silver) Price Range

☐ **Gorham,** *chased and engraved grape motifs on body and handle, c. 1900, 17" H., weight 63 oz.* 750.00 800.00

FIGURINES

Before the era of limited edition silver figurines, manufacturers brought out silver figurines or statuettes for the giftware and interior decoration markets. In terms of a fine art medium, silver saw very limited use. Few sculptors casted their works in silver, even those of small size. The antique silver figurines found on today's market cannot really be classified as artworks, though they are sometimes inspired by famous works of art — representing them in miniature. We have seen, for example, Rodin's *The Thinker* as a silver figurine. Mostly, however, they have topical or even novelty themes. It would not be unreasonable to suspect that some were intended more as paperweights than anything else. In the case of topical subjects, the topic — such as an Old West theme — can lend extra value. *Prices tend to vary more widely on silver figurines than on most silver objects.* We suggest a careful approach in buying.

(Silver-Plated)

☐ **Maker unknown,** *pheasant, 10" beak to tail, good condition*   40.00   50.00

(Sterling Silver)

☐ **Maker unknown,** *baby buggy* 35.00   45.00
☐ **Maker unknown,** *buffalo, 5¼" L.* 200.00   235.00
☐ **Maker unknown,** *sitting cat, 2"x3"* 85.00   90.00
☐ **Maker unknown,** *cowboys, assorted poses, average 2" H., group of three* 12.00   14.00
☐ **Maker unknown,** *kangaroo* 60.00   65.00
☐ **Maker unknown,** *lion, 4 oz.* 80.00   85.00

FISH FORKS

The basic characteristics of fish forks are that the tines or teeth are shorter than in a standard dinner fork and the fork itself is USUALLY a bit wider — because of the flakiness of some types of fish. An untrained eye would easily mistake them for dinner forks, however.

(Silver-Plated)

☐ **Community "Adam",** *monogram, good condition* 4.00   5.00
☐ **Community "Adam",** *no monogram, excellent condition* . .   6.00   7.00

	Price Range	
☐ Gorham "Kings", *gold wash tines, monogram, excellent condition*	5.00	6.00
☐ Gorham "Kings", *U.S. Navy monogram, good condition*	3.00	4.00
☐ Rogers "Princess", *no monogram, excellent condition*	7.00	8.00
☐ Rogers "Princess", *monogram, fair condition*	2.00	3.00
☐ Wm. A. Rogers "Abington", *no monogram, mint condition*	6.00	7.00
☐ Wm. A. Rogers "Abington", *monogram, good condition*	3.00	4.00
☐ Wm. Rogers Mfg. Co. "Arbutus", *no monogram, excellent condition*	18.00	20.00
☐ Wm. Rogers Mfg. Co. "Arbutus", *monogram, poor condition*	1.00	2.00
☐ 1847 Rogers "Berkshire", *monogram, excellent condition*	14.00	16.00
☐ 1847 Rogers "Berkshire", *no monogram, mint condition*	18.00	20.00
☐ 1847 Rogers "Old Colony", *no monogram, excellent condition*	14.00	16.00
☐ 1847 Rogers "Old Colony", *no monogram, fair condition*	2.00	3.00
☐ 1847 Rogers "Persian", *gold wash tines, no monogram, excellent condition*	18.00	20.00
☐ 1847 Rogers "Vintage", *no monogram, good condition*	12.00	14.00
☐ 1847 Rogers "Vintage", *monogram, fair condition*	2.00	3.00

(Sterling Silver)

☐ Gorham "Chantilly", *no monogram*	16.00	18.00
☐ Gorham "Lancaster Rose", *monogram*	20.00	22.00
☐ Gorham "Lancaster Rose", *no monogram*	8.00	10.00
☐ Gorham "Marie Antoinette", *no monogram*	16.00	18.00
☐ Gorham "Newcastle", *monogram*	14.00	16.00
☐ Gorham "Newcastle", *no monogram*	18.00	20.00
☐ Gorham "Old French", *monogram, 7½" L.*	18.00	20.00
☐ Gorham "Old French", *no monogram, 7½" L.*	18.00	20.00
☐ Gorham "Versailles", *monogram*	17.00	19.00
☐ Oneida "Heiress", *no monogram*	10.00	12.00
☐ Oneida "Heiress", *monogram*	16.00	18.00
☐ Reed & Barton "Francis I", *no monogram*	16.00	18.00
☐ Reed & Barton "Francis I", *monogram*	16.00	18.00
☐ Reed & Barton "Trajan", *no monogram*	20.00	22.00
☐ Towle "Old Colonial", *no monogram*	12.00	14.00
☐ Watson "Altair", *no monogram*	16.00	18.00
☐ Whiting "Bead", *no monogram*	14.00	16.00
☐ Whiting "Imperial Queen", *no monogram*	18.00	20.00
☐ Whiting "Louis XV", *no monogram, 6½" L.*	17.00	19.00

FISH KNIVES

A bit lighter in weight than regulation dinner knives, and seldom found with serrated or saw-tooth blades — on the assumption that fish was easier to cut than meat.

(Silver-Plated)

☐ 1847 Rogers "Vintage", *monogram and date, excellent condition*	16.00	18.00

(Sterling Silver)

☐ Durgin "Chrysanthemum", *no monogram*	28.00	30.00
☐ Gorham "Newcastle", *bad monogram removal with replacement monogram*	12.00	15.00

FISH SERVING FORKS

These can be extremely handsome and deserve greater collecting attention than they have received. Fish serving forks are broad and usually four-tined, the outer two tines being (generally) thicker than those between. They were ideal for pierced or openwork decoration, and are found in numerous styles. Those on the U.S. antiques market are mostly domestic specimens (as listed below). Some foreign will be found and these are, at times, truly exquisite, and certainly deserving to be added to one's collection. The foreign makers had a long lead in this department, as fish enjoyed a much more widespread use on European tables in the 18th and 19th centuries than it did in America.

	Price Range	
(Silver-Plated)		
☐ **American Silver Company "Tours"**, *no monogram, excellent condition*	16.00	18.00
(Sterling Silver)		
☐ **Towle "Old Colonial"**, *monogram, 9⅛" L.*	65.00	75.00

FISH SERVING SETS

These are immensely appealing, as both the utensils they contain — a serving fork and a fish slice (never call it a slicer!) — are large and impressive. The *fish slice* is without doubt one of the most attractive items of all table silver, not to mention one of the more ingenious. For many years, prior to development of the fish slice, fish slicing was virtually impossible to perform in a convenient way. The fish slice is used to serve fish on to individual dishes. On one side it consists of a slightly curving blade, similar to a Turkish sword, with which the cooked fish was cut. The other side is formed as a shallow bowl with a lip or margin. After cutting, the slice was slid under the cut portion, using it as a scoop. Its design prevented the morsel from slipping off (a common problem before the age of the fish slice), as the uten-

Fish Serving Set, *(sterling silver), Reed & Barton "Love Disarmed",* *16 ounces,* 575.00

sil could be tilted slightly to the bowl side and thereby use the bowl to "catch" it. The combined weights of the two utensils in fish serving sets are usually in the neighborhood of one pound or more. Their collector value never fails to exceed the melt value, by at least double and often triple or more, except in the case of damaged specimens.

(Sterling Silver)	Price Range	
☐ **Gorham "King George"**, *monogram and date*	150.00	175.00
☐ **Shiebler "Sandringham"**, *slice has plated blade with engraving, no monogram*	40.00	45.00

FISH SETS

A fish *set* is not the same as a fish *serving set* (see above category). It is, rather, a set of utensils with which to *eat* fish, and consists of fish knives and fish forks. Occasionally, serving equipment is also included. But whenever fish knives and fish forks are present in the set, it is automatically termed a fish set, since these are never found in fish serving sets. The standard number of knives and forks in such a set is six.

(Silver-Plated)		
☐ **1847 Rogers "Old Colony"**, *six individual forks and six flat-handled individual knives, monogram and date, excellent condition except for one bent fork tine*	80.00	90.00
☐ **Maker unknown**, *Victorian, c. 1880, ivory handles, includes six individual fish knives and six individual fish forks, plus 9" fish slice*	50.00	55.00

(Sterling Silver)		
☐ **Towle "Old Colonial"**, *12 individual forks and 12 individual flat-handled all-sterling knives, monograms*	550.00	600.00

FISH SLICES

(Silver-Plated)		
☐ **American Silver Co. "Beaded"**, *scalloped edges, no monogram, excellent condition*	18.00	20.00
☐ **American Silver Co. "Beaded"**, *no monogram, excellent condition*	30.00	35.00
☐ **Hall, Elton & Co. "Italian"**, *no monogram, resilvered*	14.00	16.00
☐ **Hall, Elton & Co. "Italian"**, *monogram, good condition*	12.00	14.00
☐ **Hall, Elton & Co. "Medallion"**, *engraving and openwork on blade, monogram, excellent condition*	30.00	32.00
☐ **Hall, Elton & Co. "Medallion"**, *engraving and openwork on blade, monogram, excellent condition*	55.00	60.00
☐ **Reed & Barton, pattern unknown**, *Art Nouveau styling, half-nude woman on handle, engraved flowers and birds on blade, good condition*	36.00	38.00
☐ **Rogers & Bro. "Assyrian Head"**, *no monogram, good condition*	30.00	32.00
☐ **Rogers & Bro. "Assyrian Head"**, *no monogram, excellent condition*	45.00	50.00
☐ **Wallace "Joan"**, *no monogram, excellent condition*	26.00	28.00
☐ **Wallace "Joan"**, *no monogram, resilvered*	40.00	45.00
☐ **1835 R. Wallace "Joan"**, *no monogram, mint condition*	14.00	16.00
☐ **1847 Rogers "Assyrian Head"**, *monogram, good condition*	16.00	18.00

Fish Slices, *(T to B) (sterling), Tiffany "Chrysanthemum", 135.00; Tiffany "Palm",120.00; Simpson, Hall & Miller "Frontenac", 125.00*

	Price Range	
☐ **1847 Rogers "Assyrian Head"**, *no monogram, excellent condition*	50.00	60.00
☐ **1847 Rogers "Berkshire"**, *no monogram, fair condition*	35.00	40.00
☐ **1847 Rogers "Berkshire"**, *monogram, excellent condition*	50.00	55.00
☐ **1847 Rogers "Old Colony"**, *monogram, mint condition*	45.00	50.00
☐ **1847 Rogers "Old Colony"**, *no monogram, good condition*	22.00	25.00
☐ **1847 Rogers "Savoy"**, *no monogram, excellent condition*	26.00	28.00
☐ **1847 Rogers "Sharon"**, *no monogram, excellent condition*	23.00	25.00
☐ **1847 Rogers "Sharon"**, *no monogram, fair condition*	10.00	12.00
☐ **1847 Rogers "Vintage"**, *monogram, poor condition*	8.00	10.00
☐ **1847 Rogers "Vintage"**, *no monogram, good condition*	40.00	45.00
☐ **1847 Rogers "Vintage"**, *no monogram, mint condition*	55.00	65.00

(Sterling Silver)

☐ **Gorham "Isis"**, *no monogram, 13" L., pierced and engraved blade*	175.00	195.00
☐ **Reed & Barton "Francis I"**, *no monogram*	80.00	90.00
☐ **Tiffany "Beekman"**, *monogram, 12" L.*	125.00	135.00
☐ **Tiffany "Wave Edge"**, *applied design on handle, monogram,*	165.00	175.00

FIVE O'CLOCK SPOONS

(Silver-Plated)

☐ **Community "Lady Hamilton"**, *no monogram, excellent condition*	4.00	5.00
☐ **Community "Lady Hamilton"**, *no monogram, good condition*	2.00	3.00

	Price Range	
☐ **Gorham "Bradford"**, *no monogram, excellent condition* . . .	4.00	5.00
☐ **Gorham "Bradford"**, *no monogram, fair condition*	1.00	2.00
☐ **Rogers & Bro. "Tuxedo"**, *no monogram, good condition* . . .	1.00	2.00
☐ **Rogers & Bro. "Tuxedo"**, *no monogram, mint condition* . . .	5.00	6.00
☐ **1847 Rogers "Assyrian"**, *no monogram, excellent condition*	4.00	5.00
☐ **1847 Rogers "Assyrian"**, *no monogram, mint condition* . . .	8.00	10.00

(Sterling Silver)

☐ **Gorham "Lancaster"**, *no monogram*	8.00	10.00
☐ **Gorham "Lancaster Rose"**, *no monogram*	8.00	10.00
☐ **Gorham "Old French"**, *monogram*	8.00	10.00
☐ **Gorham "Poppy"**, *no monogram*	7.00	8.00
☐ **Gorham "Poppy"**, *(old), monogram*	10.00	12.00
☐ **Gorham "Strasbourg"**, *no monogram*	8.00	10.00
☐ **Lunt "Mt. Vernon"**, *monogram and dated 1901*	8.00	10.00
☐ **Towle "Canterbury"**, *no monogram*	8.00	9.00

FLATWARE SETS

The standard definition of *flatware* is *eating utensils* (knives, forks, spoons). In flatware SETS, however, one will not find any predictable assortment of utensils. There will be knives, forks, and spoons; but there may be any quantity of the three; and the set could include various specialty items such as soup spoons, cheese knives, fish forks, etc. In a small set, one would expect dinner forks, dinner knives, and teaspoons. The approach of manufacturers in putting up these sets changed over the years, and this is where the confusion enters in. Most of the early flatware sets, before about 1880, are quite large and were intended mainly as wedding gifts for the well-to-do. Later, when the middle classes began setting their sights on silver, makers supplemented their lines with small sets, often very small. The retail price was cut further by packaging them in less ornate boxes, often plain cedar wood. The large sets in desirable patterns are valuable when complete. When found incomplete, which of course is usually the case, the missing components can sometimes be picked up later on and the set finished off. This can lend a bit of extra excitement to collecting.

(Coin Silver)

☐ **Lewis Kimball and J.N. Lindsay & Company,** *c. 1860, leaf and scroll pattern, includes eight tablespoons, four dinner forks, 10 entree forks, monogram, length of dinner fork 7⅝" L., total weight 34 oz.*	185.00	195.00

(Silver-Plated)

☐ **Community "Bird of Paradise"**, *30 pieces, set includes six teaspoons, six tablespoons, six dinner forks, six salad forks, six dinner knives, butter knife and sugar shell, no monogram, excellent condition*	100.00	110.00
☐ **Community "Silver Valentine"**, *40 piece service for eight, set includes eight four-piece place settings (dinner knife, dinner fork, teaspoon and salad fork), three serving spoons, gravy ladle, sugar shell, lemon fork, butter knife and cold meat fork, no monogram, mint condition*	140.00	150.00

	Price Range	

☐ **Community "Silver Valentine"**, *40 piece service for eight, set includes eight five-piece place settings (dinner knife, dinner fork, teaspoon, salad fork, and oval soup spoons), no serving pieces, no monogram, mint condition* **125.00 135.00**

☐ **Community "Tangier"**, *26 pieces, set includes five dinner knives, five dinner forks, five teaspoons, five salad forks, gravy ladle, butter knife, sugar shell, and three serving spoons, no monogram, mint condition* **80.00 90.00**

☐ **Holmes & Edwards "Exquisite"**, *50 piece set, includes eight five-piece place settings (dinner fork, dinner knife, teaspoon, salad fork, cream soup spoon), plus four cocktail forks and six serving pieces (gravy ladle, sugar shell, butter knife, olive spoon, and two serving spoons), monogram, excellent condition* **130.00 140.00**

☐ **Reed & Barton "Jewell"**, *total 26 pieces, includes six four-piece place settings (luncheon fork, luncheon knife, teaspoon, and oval soup spoon), plus two servers (serving spoon and sugar shell), no monogram, excellent condition* . **40.00 45.00**

☐ **Wm. A.Rogers "LaConcorde"**, *total 26 pieces, includes six four-piece place setting (dinner fork, flat-handled dinner knives, tablespoons, and teaspoons) plus two servers (master butter and sugar shell), no monogram, in original box, mint condition* **230.00 240.00**

☐ **Wm. Rogers "Arbutus"**, *total 24 pieces, includes six four-piece place settings (dinner fork, dinner knife, teaspoon and oval soup spoon), monogram, fair condition* **60.00 70.00**

☐ **Wm. Rogers "Bridal Bouquet"**, *total 50 items, includes 16 teaspoons, eight salad forks, eight dinner knives, eight dinner forks, eight dessert spoons, two serving spoons, no monogram, mint condition* **170.00 180.00**

☐ **Wm. Rogers "Orange Blossom"**, *total 37 items, includes six dinner knives, 12 dinner forks, six teaspoons, six fruit spoons, and seven tablespoons, monogram, good condition* **70.00 80.00**

☐ **1847 Rogers "Moselle"**, *total 21 pieces, includes six three-piece place settings (luncheon knife, luncheon fork and teaspoon) plus three serving pieces (sugar shell, butter knife and gravy ladle), no monogram, good condition* **150.00 160.00**

☐ **1847 Rogers "Old Colony"**, *total 80 items, includes 12 six-piece place settings (dinner knife, dinner fork, teaspoon, salad fork, cream soup spoon and butter spreader) plus eight serving pieces (gravy ladle, sugar shell, master butter, pickle fork, three serving spoons, and bonbon spoon), no monogram, includes original chest, excellent condition* . . . **150.00 160.00**

☐ **1847 Rogers "Vintage"**, *total 21 pieces, includes six three-piece place settings (dinner knife, dinner fork, teaspoon) plus three servers (sugar shell, butter knife, pickle fork), no monogram, good condition* **140.00 150.00**

☐ **1847 Rogers "Vintage"**, *total 36 pieces, includes 12 dinner knives, 12 dinner forks, and 12 teaspoons, monogram, good condition* **180.00 200.00**

☐ **1881 Rogers "Tempo"**, *total 32 pieces, includes five six-piece place settings (dinner knife, dinner fork, teaspoon, salad fork, oval soup spoon, and butter spreader) and two*

Price Range

serving pieces (cold meat fork and gravy ladle), no monogram, mint condition 40.00   45.00

(Sterling Silver)

☐ **Alvin "Chateau Rose"**, total 41 pieces, includes eight five-piece place settings, (dinner fork, dinner knife, salad fork, cream soup spoon) and gravy ladle, no monogram 525.00   550.00

☐ **Durgin "Chrysanthemum"**, 320 items, set includes twenty-four each fish forks, oyster forks, seafood forks, sherbert forks, soup spoons, bouillon spoons, parfait spoons, custard spoons, dinner knives, fish knives, 21 teaspoons, 21 demitasse spoons, 21 luncheon knives, and 13 serving pieces, weighable silver 400 oz. 10,000.00   11,000.00

☐ **Easterling "American Classic"**, total 76 pieces, includes 12 six-piece place settings (dinner knife, dinner fork, salad fork, teaspoon, soup spoon, and butter spreader) plus four serving pieces (unspecified), no monogram 900.00   950.00

☐ **Gorham "Dolly Madison"**, total 96 pieces, includes 12 eight-piece place settings (dinner knife, dinner fork, teaspoon, salad fork, cream soup spoon, butter spreader, cocktail fork and dessert spoon), plus six serving pieces (sugar shell, gravy ladle, butter knife, pickle fork, and two serving spoons), monogram 1,000.00   1,200.00

☐ **Gorham "English Gadroon"**, total 48 pieces, includes eight six-piece place settings (dinner fork, dinner knife, teaspoon, oval soup spoon, salad fork, and butter spreader), no monogram 500.00   600.00

☐ **Gorham "Etruscan"**, total 61 pieces, includes 12 knives, 12 forks, 12 salad forks, 11 teaspoons, five demitasse spoons, master butter knife, sugar shell, pastry server, two serving spoons, carving set, and salad set, monogram 400.00   450.00

☐ **Gorham "Versailles"**, total 210 pieces, includes 12 dinner knives, 12 dinner forks, 14 luncheon forks, 14 luncheon knives, 14 cake forks, 14 salad forks, 14 oyster forks, 14 tablespoons, 14 cream soup spoons, 18 teaspoons, 18 orange spoons, 18 bouillon spoons, 18 grapefruit spoons, seven butter knives, five fruit knives, and four serving pieces, monogram, total weighable silver 195 oz. 3000.00   3250.00

☐ **Gorham "Versailles"**, total 40 pieces, includes 12 entree forks, 10 dinner forks, 10 tablespoons, eight round soup spoons, monogram, total weight 77 oz. 500.00   600.00

☐ **International "Courtship"**, total 92 pieces, includes 12 seven-piece place setting (place fork, place knife, salad fork, teaspoon, cream soup, butter spreader, iced tea), plus nine serving pieces (master butter, sugar shell, jelly server, gravy ladle, pickle fork, cold meat fork, and three serving spoons), no monogram 1200.00   1400.00

☐ **International "Frontenac"**, total 90 items, includes 12 dinner forks, 12 dinner knives, 12 flat handled butter spreaders, 12 salad forks, 12 cream soups, 24 teaspoons, 12 cocktail forks, no monogram 1500.00   1600.00

☐ **International "Silver Rhythm"**, total 20 items, six three-piece place settings (place fork, place knife and teaspoon) plus butter knife and sugar shell, no monogram 200.00   250.00

	Price Range	

☐ **National "Overture"**, *total 61 pieces, includes 12 five-piece place settings (place fork, place knife, teaspoon, salad fork, round soup spoon) plus sugar shell, no monogram* 575.00   600.00

☐ **Reed & Barton "Francis I"**, *total 167 pieces, includes 24 cream soups, 12 place knives, 12 luncheon knives, 24 teaspoons, 12 place forks, 12 luncheon forks, 12 hollow-handled butter spreaders, 12 salad forks, 12 demitasse spoons, 12 fruit spoons, 12 seafood forks, salad serving fork and spoon, punch ladle, three-piece carving set, cake server, three vegetable serving spoons, berry spoon, no monogram*   3000.00   3250.00

☐ **Royal Crest "Castle Rose"**, *40 items, includes eight five-piece place settings (dinner fork, dinner knife, teaspoon, salad fork, oval soup spoon), no monogram* 175.00   200.00

☐ **Stieff "Rose"**, *total 82 items, includes eight nine-piece place settings (dinner fork, dinner knife, teaspoon, oval soup spoon, salad fork, iced teaspoon, butter spreader, demitasse spoon and cocktail fork), plus 10 serving pieces (gravy ladle, sugar shell, butter knife, pickle fork, cold meat fork, salad serving set, and three vegetable serving spoons), monogram* 1600.00   1800.00

☐ **Towle "Georgian"**, *total 73 pieces, includes 12 each teaspoons, dinner forks, dinner knives, salad forks, cream soup spoons, flat-handled butter spreaders, plus a cake server, no monogram* 1200.00   1500.00

☐ **Towle "Louis XIV"**, *total 108 includes 16 hollow handled dinner knives (old style blades), 15 dinner forks, 12 salad forks, 23 teaspoons, eight oval soup spoons, six cream soup spoons, six cocktail forks, six flat-handled butter spreaders, four melon spoons, three tablespoons, one cold meat fork, one sugar shell, four iced teaspoons, one master butter knife, one large roast carving set, monogram* 600.00   700.00

☐ **Wallace "Evening Mist"**, *total 24 pieces, includes seven hollow-handled dinner knives, five dinner forks, six salad forks, six teaspoons, one sugar shell and one butter knife, no monogram* 80.00   90.00

☐ **Westmoreland "Lady Hilton"**, *total 41 pieces, includes eight four-piece place settings (dinner knife, dinner fork, teaspoon, cream soup spoon), plus six salad forks and three serving pieces (gravy ladle, sugar shell, butter knife), no monogram* 450.00   500.00

☐ **Whiting "Louis XV"**, *total 23 pieces, includes seven luncheon forks, four cream soup spoons, four ice cream forks, and eight teaspoons, monogram* 450.00   475.00

FOOD PUSHERS

Of course the proper Victorians would not think of anything so gross as using bread or crackers to trap an elusive food particle on their plate. There was a special utensil for just such emergencies — called a food *pusher*. It was correctly held in the left hand while the right held one's fork. These are of course scarce as they were not included in the majority of flatware sets. However, the relatively slight collecting enthusiasm for them has kept prices modest.

(Silver-Plated)   Price Range

- [ ] **Community "Evening Star"**, *no monogram, excellent condition* .... 10.00 | 12.00
- [ ] **Oneida "Avalon"**, *no monogram, excellent condition* ..... 10.00 | 12.00
- [ ] **Rogers "Alhambra"**, *no monogram, excellent condition* ... 12.00 | 14.00
- [ ] **Rogers & Bro. "Mystic"**, *no monogram, excellent condition* 12.00 | 14.00
- [ ] **Rogers & Bro. "Mystic"**, *no monogram, excellent condition* 15.00 | 17.00
- [ ] **Wm. Rogers "Berwick"**, *no monogram, excellent condition* 14.00 | 16.00
- [ ] **1847 Rogers "Old Colony"**, *monogram and date, excellent condition* .... 12.00 | 14.00
- [ ] **1847 Rogers "Vintage"**, *no monogram, good condition* .... 7.00 | 8.00
- [ ] **1847 Rogers "Vintage"**, *no monogram, resilvered* .... 18.00 | 20.00
- [ ] **Maker unknown**, *"Little Bo Peep", ring handle, no monogram, good condition* .... 12.00 | 14.00

(Sterling Silver)

- [ ] **Gorham "Buttercup"**, *monogram and date in bowl* .... 10.00 | 12.00
- [ ] **Reed & Barton "LaParisienne"**, *no monogram* .... 10.00 | 12.00
- [ ] **Tiffany "Cordis"**, *no monogram* .... 10.00 | 12.00
- [ ] **Unger Bros. "Cupid's Sunbeams"**, *monogram* .... 40.00 | 42.00
- [ ] **Wallace**, *pattern unknown, rabbits on handle, no monogram* .... 10.00 | 12.00

FRIED CHICKEN TONGS

These large impressive utensils can be extremely handsome, depending on design. Some very splendid ones have been made, comprising (for example) creative motifs in which modeled chicken claws support the tongs' graspers. The popularity of chicken today has brought increased popularity to fried chicken tongs as a collectible. The infrequency with which they were produced by yesterday's silversmiths bears witness to the low regard in which chicken — fried or in any other form — was held by the genteel. This attitude has certainly changed and tongs are definitely an "in" collectible. Their heft and bulk results in a considerable melt value, but their prices are quite a bit higher than "melt" because of the strong hobbyist interest. On the whole these are rising in price faster than any other silver table accessories.

Fried Chicken Tongs, *(sterling), Tiffany "Vine",* 195.00

(Sterling Silver)	Price Range	
☐ **Whiting,** *pattern unknown, scales on "legs" and chicken claw ends*	125.00	135.00

FRUIT KNIVES

Fruit knives are a little dainter than knives for use with meat, but no less sharp. The tip is pointed for puncturing the skins of certain fruits before slicing or peeling. Their vast variety of designs, easy availability and low prices have made fruit knives a favorite with collectors of silver tableware.

(Silver-Plated)

☐ **Community 'Louis XVI",** *monogram, excellent condition* ..	6.00	7.00
☐ **Frary & Clark "Kings",** *no monogram, excellent condition* .	6.00	7.00
☐ **Frary & Clark "Kings",** *monogram, fair condition*	1.00	2.00
☐ **Oneida "Primrose",** *no monogram, excellent condition*	1.00	2.00
☐ **Rogers & Hamilton "Alhambra",** *no monogram, excellent condition*	6.00	7.00
☐ **Rogers & Hamilton "Alhambra",** *monogram, good condition*	2.00	3.00
☐ **Williams Bros. "Isabella",** *no monogram, excellent condition*	7.00	8.00
☐ **Williams Bros. "Isabella",** *monogram, good condition*	3.00	4.00
☐ **Wm. Rogers & Son "Arbutus",** *no monogram, good condition*	7.00	8.00
☐ **W. Rogers "Orange Blossom",** *no monogram, excellent condition*	8.00	9.00
☐ **W. Rogers "Orange Blossom",** *monogram, fair condition* ..	1.00	2.00
☐ **1835 R. Wallace "Joan",** *excellent condition*	2.00	3.00
☐ **1835 R. Wallace "Joan",** *no monogram, fair condition*	1.00	2.00
☐ **1835 R. Wallace "Laurel",** *no monogram, excellent condition*	8.00	9.00
☐ **1835 R. Wallace "Laurel",** *monogram, good condition*	4.00	5.00
☐ **1847 Rogers "Columbia",** *no monogram, mint condition* ...	18.00	20.00
☐ **1847 Rogers "Columbia",** *no monogram, good condition* ..	6.00	7.00
☐ **1847 Rogers "Embossed",** *no monogram, fair condition* ...	2.00	3.00
☐ **1847 Rogers "Embossed",** *monogram, excellent condition*	6.00	7.00
☐ **1847 Rogers "Embossed",** *no monogram, excellent condition*	8.00	9.00
☐ **1847 Rogers "Grecian",** *no monogram, mint condition*	2.00	3.00
☐ **1847 Rogers "Grecian",** *no monogram, fair condition*	1.00	2.00
☐ **1847 Rogers "Grecian",** *no monogram, resilvered*	5.00	6.00
☐ **1847 Rogers "Kings",** *no monogram, excellent condition* ..	6.00	7.00
☐ **1847 Rogers "Kings",** *monogram, mint condition*	8.00	9.00
☐ **1847 Rogers "Plain",** *no monogram, excellent condition* ...	1.00	2.00
☐ **1847 Rogers "Vesta",** *no monogram, good condition*	7.00	8.00

(Sterling Silver)

☐ **Gorham "Cambridge",** *silver-plated blade, no monogram* ..	10.00	12.00
☐ **Gorham,** *bronze handles with sterling blades, each handle with different design of people and animals, blades engraved on both sides with Oriental motifs, no monograms, set of twelve*	275.00	300.00

	Price Range	
☐ **Shreve & Co.,** *mother of pearl handle*	6.00	7.00
☐ **Maker unknown,** *mother of pearl handles, ornate engraving on blades, no monogram*	8.00	9.00

FRUIT SPOONS

Silverware manufacturers tended to place greater decoration on utensils used for desserts than on other flatware. Apparently the feeling was that diners consumed dessert more leisurely, and would therefore take more notice of the table equipment. Fruit spoons are most appealing to collect, with their array of creative ornamentation. The bowl comes out to a spade-like point, for spearing into fruits that required hacking and cutting. There is, however, some variation to be found in the bowl shapes, and this adds a touch of extra collecting interest.

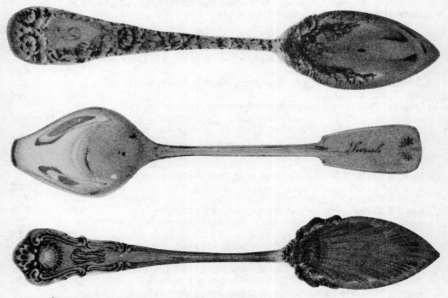

Fruit Spoons, *(T to B) (sterling), Durgin "Chrysanthemum", 36.00; Tiffany "Palm", 30.00; Durgin "New Queens", 28.00*

(Silver-Plated)

☐ **Alvin "Bride's Bouquet",** *orange type, no monogram, excellent condition*	8.00	9.00
☐ **Alvin "Bride's Bouquet",** *orange type, monogram, fair condition*	2.00	3.00
☐ **American Silver Co. "Nenuphar",** *orange type, no monogram, mint condition*	10.00	12.00
☐ **American Silver Co. "Nenuphar",** *orange type, monogram, good condition*	4.00	5.00
☐ **Community "Flight",** *grapefruit type, no monogram, mint condition*	4.00	5.00

	Price Range	
☐ Community "Flight", *grapefruit type, monogram, good condition*	2.00	3.00
☐ Community "Flower de Luce", *no monogram, excellent condition*	9.00	10.00
☐ Community "Flower de Luce", *no monogram, good condition*	5.00	6.00
☐ Community "Lady Hamilton", *no monogram, fair condition*	2.00	3.00
☐ Community "Lady Hamilton", *no monogram, good condition*	5.00	6.00
☐ Community "Morning Rose", *grapefruit type, no monogram, mint condition*	5.00	6.00
☐ Community "Morning Rose", *no monogram, good condition*	4.00	5.00
☐ Hamilton "St. Paul", *no monogram, fair condition*	2.00	3.00
☐ Hamilton "St. Paul", *monogram, excellent condition*	4.00	5.00
☐ Holmes & Edwards "Century", *no monogram, good condition*	2.00	3.00
☐ Holmes & Edwards "Century", *no monogram, excellent condition*	7.00	8.00
☐ Oneida "Avalon", *grapefruit type, no monogram, excellent condition*	7.00	8.00
☐ Oneida "Wildwood", *grapefruit type, no monogram, excellent condition*	8.00	10.00
☐ Oneida "Wildwood", *grapefruit type, no monogram, fair condition*	2.00	3.00
☐ R.C. Co. "Isabella", *grapefruit type, no monogram, excellent condition*	7.00	8.00
☐ Reed & Barton "Oxford", *orange type, no monogram, excellent condition*	7.00	8.00
☐ Reed & Barton "Oxford", *orange type, no monogram, excellent condition*	7.00	8.00
☐ Reed & Barton "Poppy", *no monogram, excellent condition*	7.00	8.00
☐ Reed & Barton "Poppy", *no monogram, fair condition*	3.00	4.00
☐ Rogers "Alhambra", *grapefruit type, no monogram, excellent condition*	6.00	7.00
☐ Rogers "Alhambra", *grapefruit type, monogram, excellent condition*	6.00	7.00
☐ Rogers "Orange Blossom", *no monogram, good condition*	4.00	5.00
☐ Rogers "Orange Blossom", *no monogram, fair condition*	1.00	2.00
☐ Rogers "Orange Blossom", *no monogram, excellent condition*	5.00	6.00
☐ Rogers "Sunkist", *no monogram, fair condition*	1.00	2.00
☐ Rogers "Sunkist", *no monogram, excellent condition*	5.00	6.00
☐ Rogers & Bro. "Crest", *no monogram, good condition*	7.00	8.00
☐ Rogers & Bro. "Crest", *grapefruit type, no monogram, good condition*	4.00	5.00
☐ Rogers & Bro. "Mystic", *no monogram, excellent condition*	9.00	10.00
☐ Rogers & Bro. "Mystic", *monogram, excellent condition*	6.00	7.00
☐ Rogers & Bro. "Mystic", *no monogram, fair condition*	2.00	3.00
☐ Rogers & Bro. "Savoy", *orange type, monogram, excellent condition*	7.00	8.00
☐ Rogers & Bro. "Thistle", *no monogram, excellent condition*	4.00	5.00
☐ Rogers & Bro. "Thistle", *no monogram, excellent condition*	7.00	8.00

	Price Range	
☐ **Rogers & Hamilton "Alhambra"**, *orange type, no monogram, excellent condition*	8.00	9.00
☐ **W.D. Smith "Adams"**, *no monogram, excellent condition* ..	3.00	4.00
☐ **Williams Bros. "Vineyard"**, *grapefruit type, no monogram, excellent condition*	8.00	9.00
☐ **Williams Bros. "Vineyard"**, *grapefruit type, monogram, excellent condition*	6.00	7.00
☐ **Wm. A. Rogers "Grenoble"**, *orange type, no monogram, good condition*	3.00	4.00
☐ **Wm. A. Rogers "Grenoble"**, *orange type, no monogram, excellent condition*	10.00	12.00
☐ **Wm. A. Rogers "Hanover"**, *grapefruit type, no monogram, resilvered*	6.00	7.00
☐ **Wm. A. Rogers "Hanover"**, *grapefruit type, monogram, excellent condition*	8.00	9.00
☐ **Wm. Rogers "Orange"**, *grapefruit type, no monogram, good condition*	7.00	8.00
☐ **Wm. Rogers "Orange"**, *grapefruit type, no monogram, excellent condition*	9.00	10.00
☐ **Wm. Rogers "Orange"**, *grapefruit type, no monogram, fair condition*	1.00	2.00
☐ **Wm. Rogers "Orange Blossom"**, *no monogram, good condition*	4.00	5.00
☐ **Wm. Rogers "Orange Blossom"**, *no monogram, fair condition*	2.00	3.00
☐ **Wm. Rogers "Orange Blossom"**, *no monogram, excellent condition*	8.00	9.00
☐ **Wm. Rogers "Tuxedo"**, *grapefruit type, no monogram, excellent condition*	8.00	9.00
☐ **Wm. Rogers "Tuxedo"**, *grapefruit type, no monogram, good condition*	5.00	6.00
☐ **Wm. Rogers Mfg. Co. "Alhambra"**, *monogram, good condition*	5.00	6.00
☐ **Wm. Rogers Mfg. Co. "Alhambra"**, *no monogram, excellent condition*	7.00	8.00
☐ **Wm. Rogers Mfg. Co. "Alhambra"**, *no monogram, excellent condition*	7.00	8.00
☐ **Wm. Rogers Mfg. Co. "Arbutus"**, *no monogram, excellent condition*	11.00	12.00
☐ **Wm. Rogers Mfg. Co. "Arbutus"**, *orange type, monogram, good condition*	8.00	9.00
☐ **Wm. Rogers Mfg. Co. "Arbutus"**, *orange type, no monogram, fair condition*	2.00	3.00
☐ **Wm. Rogers Mfg. Co. "York"**, *orange type, no monogram, excellent condition*	8.00	9.00
☐ **Wm. Rogers Mfg. Co. "York"**, *orange type, no monogram, fair condition*	2.00	3.00
☐ **Wm. Rogers & Son "April"**, *no monogram, fair condition* ..	6.00	7.00
☐ **Wm. Rogers & Son "April"**, *no monogram, excellent condition*	9.00	10.00
☐ **World "Somerset"**, *no monogram, excellent condition*	8.00	9.00
☐ **World "Somerset"**, *monogram, good condition*	3.00	4.00
☐ **1835 R. Wallace "Laurel"**, *no monogram, good condition* ..	5.00	6.00
☐ **1835 R. Wallace "Laurel"**, *monogram, excellent condition* .	8.00	9.00

	Price Range	
☐ 1847 Rogers "Anniversary", *no monogram, excellent condition*	7.00	8.00
☐ 1847 Rogers "Anniversary", *no monogram, fair condition*	1.00	2.00
☐ 1847 Rogers "Charter Oak", *orange type, no monogram, excellent condition*	18.00	20.00
☐ 1847 Rogers "Charter Oak", *orange type, no monogram, fair condition*	4.00	5.00
☐ 1847 Rogers "Charter Oak", *no monogram, mint condition*	22.00	24.00
☐ 1847 Rogers "Charter Oak", *grapefruit type, no monogram, good condition*	16.00	18.00
☐ 1847 Rogers "Columbia", *grapefruit type, no monogram, excellent condition*	18.00	20.00
☐ 1847 Rogers "Columbia", *no monogram, excellent condition*	12.00	15.00
☐ 1847 Rogers "Columbia", *no monogram, good condition*	9.00	10.00
☐ 1847 Rogers "Columbia", *monogram, good condition*	6.00	7.00
☐ 1847 Rogers "First Love", *no monogram, excellent condition*	9.00	10.00
☐ 1847 Rogers "First Love", *no monogram, good condition*	5.00	6.00
☐ 1847 Rogers "Floral", *no monogram, excellent condition*	12.00	14.00
☐ 1847 Rogers "Floral", *no monogram, good condition*	7.00	8.00
☐ 1847 Rogers "Heritage", *no monogram, excellent condition*	5.00	6.00
☐ 1847 Rogers "Heritage", *no monogram, good condition*	2.00	3.00
☐ 1847 Rogers "Old Colony", *no monogram, poor condition*	1.00	2.00
☐ 1847 Rogers "Old Colony", *no monogram, excellent condition*	8.00	9.00
☐ 1847 Rogers "Queen Ann", *no monogram, excellent condition*	7.00	8.00
☐ 1847 Rogers "Savoy", *no monogram, excellent condition*	7.00	8.00
☐ 1847 Rogers "Savoy", *no monogram, good condition*	4.00	5.00
☐ 1847 Rogers "Savoy", *no monogram, fair condition*	1.00	2.00
☐ 1847 Rogers "Sharon", *no monogram, good condition*	7.00	8.00
☐ 1847 Rogers "Sharon", *no monogram, fair condition*	1.00	2.00
☐ 1847 Rogers "Sharon", *grapefruit type, no monogram, excellent condition*	5.00	6.00
☐ 1847 Rogers "Vintage", *grapefruit type, monogram, excellent condition*	12.00	14.00
☐ 1847 Rogers "Vintage", *grapefruit type, no monogram, excellent condition*	14.00	16.00
☐ 1847 Rogers "Vintage", *no monogram, resilvered*	18.00	20.00
☐ 1847 Rogers "Vintage", *no monogram, excellent condition*	18.00	20.00
☐ 1881 Rogers "Grecian", *grapefruit type, no monogram, excellent condition*	5.00	6.00
☐ 1881 Rogers "Grecian", *no monogram, fair condition*	1.00	2.00

(Sterling Silver)

	Price Range	
☐ Alvin "Raphael", *citrus type, no monogram*	28.00	30.00
☐ Dominick & Haff "Rococo", *grapefruit type, no monogram*	12.00	15.00
☐ Dominick & Haff "Rococo", *grapefruit type, no monogram, gold wash bowl*	12.00	15.00
☐ Durgin "DuBarry", *grapefruit, gold wash bowl, monogram*	18.00	20.00
☐ Durgin "Watteau", *orange type, no monogram*	8.00	10.00
☐ Gorham "Chantilly", *grapefruit type, no monogram*	12.00	15.00

	Price Range	
☐ **Gorham "Hindostanee"**, *orange type, gold wash bowl, no monogram*	10.00	12.00
☐ **Gorham "Lancaster Rose"**, *grapefruit type, no monogram* .	12.00	14.00
☐ **Gorham "Strasbourg"**, *grapefruit type, monogram*	10.00	12.00
☐ **Gorham "Versailles"**, *grapefruit type, no monogram*	18.00	20.00
☐ **Lunt "Mt. Vernon"**, *grapefruit type, no monogram*	10.00	12.00
☐ **Reed & Barton "Francis I"**, *grapefruit type, ribbed bowl, no monogram*	16.00	18.00
☐ **Reed & Barton "Les Six Fleurs"**, *citrus type, no monogram*	18.00	20.00
☐ **Simpson, Hall & Miller "Frontenac"**, *grapefruit type, no monogram*	18.00	20.00
☐ **Towle "Mary Chilton"**, *melon type, monogram*	12.00	14.00
☐ **Maker unknown**, *orange type, gold wash bowl, dated 1892, monogram*	17.00	19.00

GLOVE STRETCHERS

Another example (of the many to be found in silverware) of the luxurious articles once manufactured for those who "had everything." Costly gloves were not merely laid away in a drawer when not in use — they might get out of shape and perish the thought of attending a gala affair wearing baggy gloves! To avoid this social embarrassment, one's gloves were kept upon an apparatus called a glove stretcher, which was modeled after a human hand. In the case of leather gloves, they reduced wrinkling after the gloves had just been worn in rainy weather. Glove stretchers are so highly specialized and so seldom offered for sale that few hobbyists concentrate their attentions upon them. But they are rather attractive and, needless to say, display well. Being hollow, the silver content is not very high. Be careful before buying, as specimens giving the appearance of silver could be stainless steel.

(Sterling Silver)

☐ **Tiffany**, *7½" L., floral repousse design*	40.00	42.00
☐ **Whiting "Lily"**, *monogram*	80.00	90.00

GOBLETS

These were only occasionally made of silver, as it was awkward to line them in ceramic and unlined silver goblets detract (in the opinion of most people) from the flavor of beverages. Of course in *very* early times, before the period dealt with here, silver was universally accepted for drinking vessels and goblets were commonly made of it. This was when the LOOK of a table setting was deemed more important than the enjoyment of eating and drinking. Silver goblets cannot be recommended as a specialty for the collector, but you may care to include one or two in a general collection. Sometimes souvenir specimens are found; these were intended more as decorations than anything else.

(Coin Silver)

☐ **W. Adams, New York**, *dated 1884*	125.00	135.00

(Silver-Plated)

☐ **Crescent Silver Co.**, *vintage pattern, cocktail shape, 5½" H., mint condition, set of six*	55.00	65.00

(Sterling Silver)   **Price Range**

☐ **Gorham,** *plain design, 5" H., weighted base* 75.00   85.00
☐ **Maker unknown,** *plain, no monogram, pair* 80.00   90.00

GRAPE SHEARS

Artistic ability was considered a valuable quality in a cook, 50 to 100 years ago. The well-appointed table was not to be plied with good food, but food elegantly prepared and set out. When the motif called for halved grapes, they were cut with a special device known as grape shears. These are scissors with short blades, specially contoured to do justice to a grape — parting it in two without crushing.

Grape Shears, *(sterling), Tiffany "Olympian",* 300.00

(Silver-Plated)

☐ **Maker unknown,** *rope design, good condition* 35.00   40.00
☐ **Maker unknown,** *vintage pattern, good condition* 40.00   45.00

(Sterling Silver)

☐ **Gorham,** *dolphin handles, steel blades, no monogram* 40.00   45.00
☐ **Unger Bros.,** *sterling handles with steel blades, ornate floral design on handles, no monogram* 60.00   65.00
☐ **Unger Bros.,** *sterling handles with steel blades, ornate floral design on handles, dents on handles* 40.00   45.00

GRAVY BOATS

These have a handle at one end and a pouring lip at the other, enabling them to be used without a ladle. However the careful hostess usually did provide a ladle, laid in the boat with its handle resting across the pouring lip. The name derives because they resemble (to someone with imagination) the hull of a sailing ship. Due to their size, those made of sterling silver have a rather substantial bullion content, but these are not suitable articles for melting unless damaged. Their attractiveness when displayed lends gravy boats a strong collector appeal.

Gravy Boat, *silver-plated, maker unknown, Greek Key design,* 65.00

(Silver-Plated)	Price Range	
☐ **Maker unknown,** *ornate embossed floral design, monogram, good condition*	25.00	30.00
(Sterling Silver)		
☐ **Gorham,** *similar to the silver-plated one shown in photo, weight 10 oz.*	80.00	90.00
☐ **Maker unknown,** *Georgian styling, monogram, weight 7 oz.*	70.00	75.00

GRAVY LADLES

Ladles in general enjoy good popularity on the collectibles market, and gravy ladles rank high in the group. The large impressive size of gravy ladles (though not as big as punch ladles) and their handsome designing make them ideal for a hobbyist's display. A very great variety exists, and if one exhausts the American specimens — which is not too likely — an equally wide range of foreign gravy ladles will be found in the antiques outlets.

(Silver-Plated)		
☐ **American Silver Company "Lawrence",** *no monogram, excellent condition*	11.00	12.00
☐ **American Silver Company "Moselle",** *no monogram, excellent condition*	16.00	18.00
☐ **Community "Adam",** *no monogram, good condition*	9.00	10.00
☐ **Community "Adam",** *no monogram, excellent condition* ..	14.00	15.00
☐ **Community "Ballad",** *no monogram, mint condition*	7.00	8.00
☐ **Community "Ballad",** *no monogram, excellent condition* ..	6.00	7.00

Gravy Ladles, *(L to R) (sterling), Tiffany "English King",* 120.00; *Gorham "Fountainbleu",* 105.00; *Gorham "Morning Glory",* 135.00; *Tiffany "Chrysanthemum",* 150.00

	Price Range	
☐ **Community "Bird of Paradise",** *no monogram, excellent condition*	14.00	15.00
☐ **Community "Bird of Paradise",** *no monogram, good condition*	12.00	13.00
☐ **Community "Coronation",** *no monogram, excellent condition*	12.00	13.00
☐ **Community "Coronation",** *no monogram, mint condition*	16.00	18.00
☐ **Community "Enchantment",** *no monogram, excellent condition*	14.00	15.00
☐ **Community "Evening Star",** *no monogram, poor condition*	4.00	5.00
☐ **Community "Evening Star",** *no monogram, excellent condition*	14.00	15.00
☐ **Community "Flight",** *no monogram, mint condition*	7.00	8.00
☐ **Community "Forever",** *no monogram, excellent condition*	14.00	15.00
☐ **Community "Georgian",** *no monogram, excellent condition*	7.00	8.00
☐ **Community "Georgian",** *no monogram, good condition*	10.00	12.00
☐ **Community "Grosvenor",** *no monogram, excellent condition*	7.00	8.00
☐ **Community "Grosvenor",** *no monogram, excellent condition*	12.00	13.00
☐ **Community "Morning Rose",** *no monogram, mint condition*	7.00	8.00
☐ **Community "Morning Star",** *no monogram, good condition*	12.00	13.00
☐ **Community "Patrician",** *no monogram, excellent condition*	14.00	15.00
☐ **Community "Sheraton",** *no monogram, excellent condition*	7.00	8.00
☐ **Community "Sheraton",** *no monogram, mint condition*	13.00	12.00
☐ **Community "Silver Flowers",** *no monogram, excellent condition*	14.00	15.00

For collectors of good reading.

- All the latest bestsellers
- Antiques and collectibles
- Bargain books
- Children's books
- Cooking ■ Crafts
- Health and fitness
- House and garden
- Travel

...and many more—thousands in all. Plus gift certificates, special ordering, and one of the best magazine selections you'll find anywhere.

Waldenbooks

Price Range

☐ **Community "South Seas",** *no monogram, excellent condition* 14.00   15.00
☐ **C. Rogers "Lenox",** *no monogram, excellent condition* 12.00   13.00
☐ **Gorham "Carolina",** *no monogram, mint condition* 9.00   10.00
☐ **Gorham "Carolina",** *no monogram, mint condition* 10.00   12.00
☐ **Gorham "Cavalier",** *no monogram, excellent condition* 8.00   9.00
☐ **Gorham "Cavalier",** *no monogram, good condition* 6.00   7.00
☐ **Gorham "Richmond",** *no monogram, excellent condition* ..   7.00   8.00
☐ **Gorham "Vanity Fair",** *no monogram, excellent condition* .   14.00   15.00
☐ **Gorham "Vanity Fair",** *no monogram, good condition* 6.00   7.00
☐ **Harmony House "Classic Filigree",** *no monogram, excellent condition* 1.00   2.00
☐ **Harmony House "Serenade",** *no monogram, excellent condition* 4.00   5.00
☐ **Holmes & Edwards "Chatsworth",** *no monogram, excellent condition* 9.00   10.00
☐ **Holmes & Edwards "Danish Princess",** *no monogram, excellent condition* 9.00   10.00
☐ **Holmes & Edwards "Danish Princess",** *no monogram, excellent condition* 12.00   14.00
☐ **Holmes & Edwards "DeSancy",** *no monogram, excellent condition* 10.00   12.00
☐ **Holmes & Edwards "DeSancy",** *no monogram, mint condition* 15.00   16.00
☐ **Holmes & Edwards "First Lady",** *no monogram, excellent condition* 14.00   15.00
☐ **Holmes & Edwards "Lovely Lady",** *no monogram, excellent condition* 14.00   15.00
☐ **Holmes & Edwards "May Queen",** *no monogram, excellent condition* 3.00   4.00
☐ **Holmes & Edwards "May Queen",** *no monogram, mint condition* 8.00   9.00
☐ **Holmes & Edwards "May Queen",** *no monogram, excellent condition* 10.00   12.00
☐ **Holmes & Edwards "Spring Garden",** *no monogram, excellent condition* 14.00   15.00
☐ **International "Coventry",** *no monogram, mint condition* ...   5.00   6.00
☐ **International "Silver Tulip",** *no monogram, excellent condition* 4.00   5.00
☐ **National "King Edward",** *no monogram, good condition* ...   5.00   6.00
☐ **Old Company Plate "Signature",** *monogram, excellent condition* 8.00   9.00
☐ **Oneida "Bridal Wreath",** *monogram, fair condition* 1.00   2.00
☐ **Oneida "Louis XVI",** *no monogram, good condition* 10.00   12.00
☐ **Oneida "Sheraton",** *monogram, excellent condition* 8.00   10.00
☐ **Paragon "Bridal Wreath",** *no monogram, excellent condition* 3.00   4.00
☐ **Prestige "Grenoble",** *no monogram, excellent condition* ..   14.00   15.00
☐ **Reed & Barton "Oxford",** *monogram, good condition* 6.00   7.00
☐ **Reed & Barton "Sierra",** *no monogram, good condition* 10.00   12.00
☐ **Reed & Barton "Sierra",** *no monogram, mint condition* 14.00   16.00
☐ **Rockford "Fairoaks",** *no monogram, excellent condition* ..   10.00   12.00
☐ **Rockford "Rosemary",** *no monogram, excellent condition* .   12.00   14.00
☐ **Rockford "Rosemary",** *no monogram, mint condition* 14.00   16.00

	Price Range	
☐ Rockford "Whittier", *no monogram, excellent condition* . . .	4.00	5.00
☐ Rockford "Whittier", *monogram, fair condition*	3.00	4.00
☐ Rogers "Alhambra", *no monogram, excellent condition* . . .	16.00	18.00
☐ Rogers "Ambassador", *no monogram, excellent condition*	9.00	10.00
☐ Rogers "Ambassador", *no monogram, good condition*	4.00	5.00
☐ Rogers "Mayflower", *no monogram, fair condition*	8.00	10.00
☐ Rogers "Norfolk", *no monogram, excellent condition* .	14.00	16.00
☐ Rogers "Queen Bess", *no monogram, excellent condition* .	4.00	5.00
☐ Rogers "Queen Bess", *no monogram, mint condition*	8.00	10.00
☐ Rogers & Bro. "Crest", *no monogram, excellent condition* .	16.00	18.00
☐ Rogers & Bro. "Crest", *no monogram, excellent condition* .	30.00	32.00
☐ Rogers & Bro. "Cromwell", *no monogram, mint condition* . .	7.00	8.00
☐ Rogers & Bro. "Flemish", *no monogram, excellent condition*	9.00	10.00
☐ Rogers & Bro. "Flemish", *no monogram, good condition* . .	6.00	7.00
☐ Rogers & Bro. "Mystic", *no monogram, excellent condition*	16.00	18.00
☐ Rogers & Bro. "Mystic", *no monogram, good condition* . . .	12.00	13.00
☐ Rogers & Bro. "Mystic", *monogram, excellent condition* . .	14.00	15.00
☐ Rogers & Bro. "Navarre", *no monogram, resilvered* .	10.00	12.00
☐ Rogers & Bro. "Navarre", *monogram, good condition*	5.00	6.00
☐ Rogers & Bro. "Siren", *no monogram, good condition*	8.00	9.00
☐ Rogers & Bro. "Siren", *no monogram, excellent condition* .	12.00	15.00
☐ Rogers & Bro. "Thistle", *no monogram, good condition* . . .	10.00	12.00
☐ Rogers & Bro. "Thistle", *no monogram, excellent condition*	16.00	18.00
☐ Rogers & Hamilton "Alhambra", *no monogram, excellent condition*	20.00	22.00
☐ Rogers & Hamilton "Alhambra", *no monogram, excellent condition*	35.00	40.00
☐ Rogers & Hamilton "Marquise", *no monogram, excellent condition*	6.00	7.00
☐ Royal "Rose", *no monogram, resilvered*	7.00	8.00
☐ S.L. & G.H. Rogers "English Garden", *no monogram, excellent condition*	5.00	6.00
☐ Stratford "Shakespeare", *no monogram, good condition* . .	12.00	13.00
☐ Tudor "Bridal Wreath", *no monogram, mint condition*	9.00	10.00
☐ Tudor "Enchantment", *no monogram, excellent condition* .	12.00	13.00
☐ Tudor "Mary Stuart", *no monogram, excellent condition* . .	14.00	15.00
☐ Tudor "Queen Bess II", *no monogram, good condition*	12.00	13.00
☐ Tudor "Queen Bess II", *no monogram, excellent condition* .	14.00	15.00
☐ Tudor "Together", *no monogram, mint condition*	7.00	8.00
☐ Wallace "Floral", *monogram, excellent condition*	18.00	20.00
☐ Wallace "Floral", *no monogram, mint condition*	26.00	28.00
☐ W.D. Smith "Adam", *no monogram, excellent condition* . . .	6.00	7.00
☐ Williams Bros. "Isabella", *no monogram, excellent condition*	13.00	14.00
☐ Williams Bros. "Isabella", *no monogram, excellent condition*	4.00	5.00
☐ Williams Bros. "Norwood", *gold wash bowl, no monogram, excellent condition*	24.00	26.00
☐ Wm. A. Rogers "Abington", *no monogram, mint condition* .	3.00	4.00
☐ Wm. A. Rogers "Arundel", *monogram, good condition*	2.00	3.00
☐ Wm. A. Rogers "Garland", *no monogram, good condition* .	10.00	12.00
☐ Wm. A. Rogers "Garland", *no monogram, mint condition* . .	16.00	18.00

	Price Range	
☐ Wm. A. Rogers "Hanover", *no monogram, excellent condition*	7.00	8.00
☐ Wm. A. Rogers "Juliette", *no monogram, mint condition* ..	7.00	8.00
☐ Wm. A. Rogers "Meadowbrook", *no monogram, excellent condition*	10.00	12.00
☐ Wm. A. Rogers "Meadowbrook", *no monogram, good condition*	10.00	11.00
☐ Wm. A. Rogers "Meadowbrook", *no monogram, excellent condition*	14.00	15.00
☐ Wm. A. Rogers "Rosalie", *no monogram, good condition* ..	12.00	13.00
☐ Wm. A. Rogers "Rosalie", *no monogram, excellent condition*	14.00	15.00
☐ Wm. Rogers "Berwick", *no monogram, excellent condition*	16.00	18.00
☐ Wm. Rogers "Berwick", *no monogram, good condition*	10.00	11.00
☐ Wm. Rogers "Bridal Bouquet", *no monogram, mint condition*	7.00	8.00
☐ Wm. Rogers "Debutante", *no monogram, excellent condition*	12.00	13.00
☐ Wm. Rogers "Debutante", *no monogram, good condition* ..	8.00	9.00
☐ Wm. Rogers "Debutante", *monogram, fair condition*	2.00	3.00
☐ Wm. Rogers "Fairoaks", *no monogram, good condition* ...	11.00	12.00
☐ Wm. Rogers "Fairoaks", *no monogram, excellent condition*	14.00	15.00
☐ Wm. Rogers "Fascination", *no monogram, excellent condition*	14.00	15.00
☐ Wm. Rogers "Florida", *no monogram, excellent condition* .	17.00	18.00
☐ Wm. Rogers "Laurel", *no monogram, excellent condition* ..	7.00	8.00
☐ Wm. Rogers "Melrose", *no monogram, excellent condition*	14.00	15.00
☐ Wm. Rogers "Orange Blossom", *no monogram, excellent condition*	16.00	18.00
☐ Wm. Rogers "Spring Charm", *no monogram, good condition*	14.00	15.00
☐ Wm. Rogers "Tuxedo", *no monogram, excellent condition* .	26.00	28.00
☐ Wm. Rogers "Tuxedo", *no monogram, fair condition*	5.00	6.00
☐ Wm. Rogers & Son "Arbutus", *no monogram, excellent condition*	14.00	15.00
☐ Wm. Rogers Mfg. Co. "Arbutus", *monogram, good condition*	10.00	12.00
☐ Wm. Rogers Mfg. Co. "Arbutus", *no monogram, advertising slogan in bowl, good condition*	10.00	12.00
☐ Wm. Rogers Mfg. Co. "Arbutus", *no monogram, excellent condition*	15.00	17.00
☐ Wm. Rogers Mfg. Co. "Berwick", *monogram, excellent condition*	12.00	14.00
☐ Wm. Rogers Mfg. Co. "Berwick", *no monogram, excellent condition*	16.00	18.00
☐ Wm. Rogers Mfg. Co. "Clinton", *no monogram, excellent condition*	1.00	2.00
☐ Wm. Rogers Mfg. Co. "Magnolia", *no monogram, fair condition*	3.00	4.00
☐ World "Nenuphar", *no monogram, excellent condition*	16.00	18.00
☐ 1835 R. Wallace "Abbey", *no monogram, excellent condition*	12.00	14.00
☐ 1835 R. Wallace "Anjou", *monogram, excellent condition* .	5.00	6.00

Price Range

☐ **1835 R. Wallace "Anjou"**, *no monogram, excellent condition* 8.00   9.00

☐ **1835 R. Wallace "Cardinal"**, *no monogram, excellent condition* 32.00   34.00

☐ **1847 Rogers "Anniversary"**, *no monogram, excellent condition* 12.00   14.00

☐ **1847 Rogers "Argosy"**, *no monogram, excellent condition* . 12.00   14.00

☐ **1847 Rogers "Avon"**, *no monogram, excellent condition* ... 12.00   14.00

☐ **1847 Rogers "Avon"**, *no monogram, excellent condition* ... 16.00   18.00

☐ **1847 Rogers "Avon"**, *no monogram, good condition* 10.00   12.00

☐ **1847 Rogers "Berkshire"**, *no monogram, excellent condition* 16.00   18.00

☐ **1847 Rogers "Berkshire"**, *no monogram, mint condition* ... 26.00   28.00

☐ **1847 Rogers "Berkshire"**, *monogram, excellent condition* . 9.00   10.00

☐ **1847 Rogers "Berkshire"**, *no monogram, good condition* .. 16.00   18.00

☐ **1847 Rogers "Charter Oak"**, *gold wash bowl, monogram, excellent condition* 18.00   20.00

☐ **1847 Rogers "Charter Oak"**, *no monogram, excellent condition* 14.00   16.00

☐ **1847 Rogers "Cromwell"**, *no monogram, excellent condition* 12.00   13.00

☐ **1847 Rogers "Daffodil"**, *no monogram, good condition* 10.00   12.00

☐ **1847 Rogers "Flair"**, *no monogram, excellent condition* ... 7.00   8.00

☐ **1847 Rogers "Floral"**, *no monogram, good condition* 16.00   18.00

☐ **1847 Rogers "Floral"**, *monogram, excellent condition* 20.00   22.00

☐ **1847 Rogers "Grand Heritage"**, *no monogram, excellent condition* 3.00   4.00

☐ **1847 Rogers "Grecian"**, *no monogram, resilvered* 16.00   18.00

☐ **1847 Rogers "Heraldic"**, *no monogram, fair condition* 6.00   7.00

☐ **1847 Rogers "Lorne"**, *no monogram, excellent condition* . 9.00   11.00

☐ **1847 Rogers "Lorne"**, *no monogram, excellent condition* .. 10.00   12.00

☐ **1847 Rogers "Magic Rose"**, *no monogram, mint condition* . 6.00   7.00

☐ **1847 Rogers "Marquise"**, *no monogram, excellent condition* 14.00   15.00

☐ **1847 Rogers "Marquise"**, *no monogram, fair condition* 4.00   5.00

☐ **1847 Rogers "Newport"**, *no monogram, excellent condition* 11.00   12.00

☐ **1847 Rogers "Newport"**, *no monogram, good condition* ... 10.00   12.00

☐ **1847 Rogers "Old Colony"**, *no monogram, excellent condition* 14.00   16.00

☐ **1847 Rogers "Old Colony"**, *no monogram, good condition* . 8.00   10.00

☐ **1847 Rogers "Old Colony"**, *no monogram, excellent condition* 12.00   14.00

☐ **1847 Rogers "Persian"**, *no monogram, excellent condition* 7.00   8.00

☐ **1847 Rogers "Persian"**, *no monogram, mint condition* 14.00   16.00

☐ **1847 Rogers "Reflection"**, *no monogram, excellent condition* 11.00   12.00

☐ **1847 Rogers "Remembrance"**, *no monogram, fair condition* 8.00   9.00

☐ **1847 Rogers "Remembrance"**, *no monogram, excellent condition* 12.00   14.00

☐ **1847 Rogers "Sharon"**, *no monogram, excellent condition* . 16.00   18.00

☐ **1847 Rogers "Sharon"**, *monogram, excellent condition* ... 16.00   18.00

☐ **1847 Rogers "Silver Lace"**, *no monogram, excellent condition* 12.00   14.00

☐ **1847 Rogers "Springtime"**, *no monogram, excellent condition* 7.00   8.00

	Price Range	
☐ **1847 Rogers "Vintage"**, *monogram, excellent condition* ...	12.00	14.00
☐ **1847 Rogers "Vintage"**, *no monogram, excellent condition*	26.00	28.00
☐ **1847 Rogers "Vintage"**, *monogram, excellent condition* ...	20.00	22.00
☐ **1847 Rogers "Vintage"**, *no monogram, mint condition*	35.00	40.00
☐ **1847 Rogers "Vintage"**, *no monogram, good condition*	12.00	14.00
☐ **1881 Rogers "Plantation"**, *no monogram, good condition* ..	2.00	3.00
☐ **Maker unknown**, *fiddle pattern, monogram, date, excellent condition*	5.00	6.00
☐ **Maker unknown**, *ornate Art Nouveau pattern, excellent condition*	8.00	9.00
☐ **Maker unknown**, *cherub on handle, good condition*	6.00	7.00
☐ **Maker unknown**, *kings pattern, excellent condition*	7.00	8.00

(Sterling Silver)

☐ **Fine Arts "Processional"**, *no monogram*	34.00	38.00
☐ **Frank Smith "Fiddle Thread"**, *no monogram*	38.00	42.00
☐ **Gorham "Chantilly"**, *no monogram*	38.00	40.00
☐ **Gorham "Etruscan"**, *no monogram*	19.00	21.00
☐ **Gorham "Etruscan"**, *monogram*	9.00	11.00
☐ **Gorham "Etruscan"**, *monogram*	20.00	23.00
☐ **Gorham "Fairfax"**, *monogram*	32.00	36.00
☐ **Gorham "Luxembourg"**, *no monogram*	28.00	30.00
☐ **Gorham "Norfolk"**, *no monogram*	4.00	5.00
☐ **International "Baronial"**, *monogram*	20.00	22.00
☐ **International "Crystal"**, *no monogram*	50.00	55.00
☐ **Lunt "Eloquence"**, *no monogram*	34.00	38.00
☐ **Roger, Lunt & Bowlen "Monticello"**, *no monogram*	27.00	30.00
☐ **Stieff "Willamsburg Shell"**, *no monogram*	43.00	48.00
☐ **Tiffany "Antique Engraved"**, *no monogram*	40.00	45.00
☐ **Tiffany "Atlantis"**, *no monogram*	70.00	75.00
☐ **Tiffany "Lap Over Edge"**, *monogram 7½" L., engraved acorns and oak leaves*	160.00	180.00
☐ **Towle "Chippendale"**, *no monogram*	32.00	35.00
☐ **Towle "Kings"**, *no monogram*	43.00	48.00
☐ **Towle "Old Colonial"**, *no monogram*	38.00	42.00
☐ **Westmoreland "John & Priscilla"**, *no monogram*	40.00	45.00
☐ **Whiting "Bead"**, *monogram*	34.00	38.00
☐ **Whiting "Imperial Queen"**, *no monogram*	43.00	48.00
☐ **Whiting "Louis XV"**, *no monogram*	32.00	36.00
☐ **Whiting "Pompadour"**, *no monogram*	32.00	36.00
☐ **Maker unknown**, *repousse design, no monogram*	27.00	30.00

HEM GAUGES

These are rulers, normally of three inches length, used for one of the trickiest of seamstressing tasks: making certain the hem of a garment is equal width all around. To judge by sight is dangerous, and even pinning and chalking leaves some margin for error. With a hem guage, the sewer is as secure as a scout with a compass. Of course, these were only rarely made of silver, as the usual type came in wood, bone, or plastic. They are not suitable for melting.

(Silver-Plated)

☐ **Maker unknown**, *plain design, monogram, good condition* .	6.00	7.00

Price Range

(Sterling Silver)

☐ **Unger Bros.,** *Art Nouveau design, monogram, 3" L.*	40.00	45.00
☐ **Webster,** *plain design, no monogram*	34.00	38.00
☐ **Webster,** *embossed floral design, no monogram*	34.00	38.00

HONEY LADLES

A quite scarce article, because (a) honey did not frequently appear on tables where silverware would be used, and (b) when it did, it was often not served in pots (see entry below) and therefore a ladle was unnecessary. You are not apt to get far collecting these, but they ARE handsome enough and curious enough to repay the time spent searching for them. Many more British specimens exist than American. We do not include the British ones here for space considerations, but the interested hobbyist will want to give them some attention.

(Coin Silver)

☐ **Peter Krider,** *c. 1850-1860, gold wash bowl, engraved work on handle*	25.00	27.00

HONEY POTS

Since honey and silver are not favorable companions (silver has an effect on the flavor, as with most liquid or semi-liquid foodstuffs), honey pots are but half silver: a silver lid surmounting a ceramic bowl. The never-say-die collector is content with just the lids, but of course the whole article (lid plus bowl) carries a much higher value. In any event these are not common. Since exposure to air over long periods of time turns honey stale, honey pots were never as popular as capped containers.

(Sterling Silver and China)

☐ **Maker unknown,** *Lenox bottom with applied bees decorated in gold, Lenox shape #894, minor flecks on bees' wings*	34.00	38.00
☐ **Maker unknown,** *Lenox bottom with applied bees decorated in gold, Lenox shape #894, perfect*	60.00	65.00

HORS D'OEUVRES PICKS

Nothing could be more aptly named than the hors d'oeuvre pick: it is precisely that, a miniature version of an icepick but of course a good deal more elegant when made of silver. Since there was no telling what the hors d'oeuvre board might comprise, an all-purpose spearing instrument was called for. This still did not, however, insure against social embarrassment, as a slippery hors d'oeuvre could work free from the pick in an instant. Real dexterity was necessary in handling hors d'oeuvre picks. As a collectible they have some popularity.

(Sterling Silver)

☐ **Maker unknown,** *sword-shaped with dolphin handles, set of six in original box*	23.00	25.00

HORSERADISH SPOONS

When horseradish appeared on the Victorian table, it had its own bowl and of course its own serving spoon set in the bowl, and was passed about the table to each diner. The spoon bowls are predictably small: who could consume a great supply of the stuff at any one sitting?

(Sterling Silver)	Price Range	
☐ Gorham "Cambridge", *no monogram*	18.00	20.00

HUMIDORS

These have only on occasion been made wholly of silver, though quite a few examples exist with silver lids and wooden or ceramic bowls. Silver, being non-porous like other metals, is not a suitable material for tobacco humidors; tobaccos stored therein are apt to acquire a mustiness. Lining the interior with cork or other substance helps somewhat but a humidor made entirely of non-metallic material is preferable. Silver humidors are, though, very attractive and might please the hobbyist much more than the pipe smoker. Heraldic engravings are often found on them. The European continent is a better hunting ground for these, than our domestic antiques shops.

(Silver-Plated)		
☐ Meriden, *embossed design, monogram, good condition* ...	43.00	48.00

HURRICANE LAMPS

Though of older origin, these received their popular name in the earlier days of electricity. Storms frequently put out the power supply, and it was handy to have oil or kerosene lamps for such an emergency. Later specimens are of course rigged for current, and today we find many of the older ones redone with electrical wiring, too. The amount of silver they comprise is very small, consisting often of merely the base.

(Silver-Plated)		
☐ Maker unknown, *etched design on glass, pair*	21.00	23.00

(Sterling Silver)		
☐ Gorham, *cut glass handles, 12" H., pair*	43.00	48.00

ICE CREAM FORKS

Ice cream is one of comparatively few foodstuffs correctly eaten with spoon or fork. Far more ice cream spoons have been made than forks, but you will encounter both on the collectibles market. Forks are of course for those who prefer their ice cream solidly frozen. The ideal solution, the spoon with teeth cut into the bowl, was not developed until the era of plastics.

(Silver-Plated)		
☐ Alvin "Molly Stark", *no monogram, excellent condition*	3.00	4.00
☐ Community "Sheraton", *no monogram, excellent condition*	7.00	8.00
☐ Community "Sheraton", *monogram, good condition*	2.00	3.00
☐ Holmes & Edwards "Century", *no monogram, excellent condition*	9.00	10.00
☐ Holmes & Edwards "Century", *monogram, fair condition* ..	1.00	2.00
☐ Wm. Rogers "Orange Blossom", *fair condition*	4.00	5.00

	Price Range	

☐ **Wm. Rogers "Orange Blossom",** *no monogram, excellent condition* 12.00 14.00
☐ **Wm. Rogers Mfg. Co. "Argyle",** *no monogram, excellent condition* 13.00 15.00
☐ **Wm. Rogers Mfg. Co. "Argyle",** *monogram, excellent condition* 9.00 10.00
☐ **1835 R. Wallace "Blossom",** *no monogram, excellent condition* 10.00 12.00
☐ **1835 R. Wallace "Blossom",** *no monogram, fair condition* . 3.00 4.00
☐ **1847 Rogers "Ancestral",** *no monogram, excellent condition* 10.00 12.00
☐ **1847 Rogers "Ancestral",** *monogram, fair condition* 2.00 3.00
☐ **1847 Rogers "Anniversary",** *no monogram, good condition* 4.00 5.00
☐ **1847 Rogers "Anniversary",** *no monogram, excellent condition* 8.00 9.00
☐ **1847 Rogers "Priscilla",** *no monogram, excellent condition* 8.00 9.00
☐ **1847 Rogers "Vintage",** *no monogram, mint condition* 13.00 15.00
☐ **1847 Rogers "Vintage",** *monogram, excellent condition* ... 12.00 14.00
☐ **1847 Rogers "Vintage",** *monogram, fair condition* 7.00 8.00

(Sterling Silver)

☐ **Alvin "Richmond",** *no monogram* 10.00 12.00
☐ **Alvin "Richmond",** *monogram* 11.00 13.00
☐ **Durgin "Dolly Madison",** *monogram* 8.00 9.00
☐ **Gorham "Buttercup",** *no monogram* 22.00 24.00
☐ **Gorham "King George",** *no monogram* 6.00 7.00
☐ **Gorham "King George",** *monogram and date, older and heavier than above listing* 6.00 7.00
☐ **Gorham "St. Dunstan Chased",** *monogram* 6.00 7.00
☐ **International "Pine Tree",** *no monogram* 11.00 13.00
☐ **Reed & Barton "Hepplewhite",** *no monogram* 13.00 15.00
☐ **S.S.M.C. "LaTosca",** *no monogram, mint condition set of 12* 135.00 150.00
☐ **Tiffany "English King",** *1885-1891 markings, no monogram* 27.00 30.00
☐ **Tiffany "English King",** *bad monogram removal* 13.00 15.00
☐ **Tiffany "Shell & Thread",** *no monogram* 6.00 7.00
☐ **Towle "Seville",** *no monogram* 6.00 7.00
☐ **Towle "Seville",** *monogram* 6.00 7.00
☐ **Whiting "Lily",** *no monogram* 32.00 36.00
☐ **Whiting "Louis XV",** *no monogram* 16.00 18.00
☐ **Whiting "Louis XV",** *monogram* 7.00 8.00

ICE CREAM SERVERS

These are also known as ice cream *knives;* server is the correct term but is much less descriptive, as it could well be mistaken for some kind of scoop. Among the collecting community, ice cream servers rank very high. Their diversity in size and shape, and especially in design, coupled with their undeniable impressiveness in display makes for a winning combination. There are hardly any more decorative silver collectibles than ice cream servers. Specimens turn up in which the entire blade is decorated, sometimes with handwrought engraving. Undoubtedly such special pieces were intended as gift items. So far as the use of a KNIFE in serving ice cream is concerned, this harks back to the age of homemade ice cream when it was brought to the table in a log or loaf, solidly frozen. However, the blades are not too sharp (but they ARE thick).

Ice Cream Knives, *(T to B) (sterling), Tiffany "Strawberry",* 150.00; *S.D. Brower & Son (1832-1854),* 120.00

	Price Range	
(Silver-Plated)		
☐ **S.L. & G.H. Rogers "Presentation",** *master spoon, no monogram, excellent condition*	16.00	18.00
☐ **1847 Rogers "Persian",** *knife, engraved blade, monogram, excellent condition*	14.00	16.00
(Sterling Silver)		
☐ **Gorham, "Domestic",** *knife, no monogram*	45.00	50.00
☐ **Gorham "Ivy",** *no monogram*	45.00	50.00
☐ **Wood & Hughes "Viola",** *two-piece set, 10" knife and 9" spoon, no monogram*	68.00	75.00

ICE CREAM SPOONS

Ice cream was known well before the age of refrigeration, thanks to the old-fashioned icebox (supplied with ice blocks from *ice-houses,* found in every town and village 100 years ago). It was being served in P.T. Barnum's Museum in New York as early as the 1840's. The ice cream *cone* was introduced at the St. Louis World's Fair in 1904. Prior to the cone — which of course was not fashionable for a social gathering at any rate — one ate ice cream with a spoon, and a special spoon for the purpose was in order. The bowl is rather deep and the shape more circular than oval. The popularity of ice cream in itself has helped along the collecting enthusiasm for ice cream forks and other related collectibles.

(Silver-Plated)

	Price Range	
☐ Community "Adam", *no monogram, fair condition*	1.00	2.00
☐ Court "Court", *no monogram, excellent condition*	7.00	8.00
☐ Oneida "Primrose", *no monogram, excellent condition*	1.00	2.00
☐ Oneida "Primrose", *monogram, good condition*	1.00	2.00
☐ Reed & Barton "Modern Art", *gold wash bowl, no monogram, excellent condition*	6.00	7.00
☐ Rogers "Clinton", *no monogram, excellent condition*	6.00	7.00
☐ Rogers & Hamilton "Raphael", *no monogram, excellent condition*	12.00	13.00
☐ S.L. & G.H. Rogers "Presentation", *no monogram, excellent condition*	6.00	7.00
☐ S.L. & G.H. Rogers "Presentation", *monogram, good condition*	3.00	4.00
☐ Wm. A. Rogers "LaConcorde", *no monogram, excellent condition*	24.00	26.00
☐ 1847 Rogers "Vintage", *no monogram, resilvered*	18.00	20.00

(Sterling Silver)

☐ Gorham "Chantilly", *monogram*	12.00	15.00

ICED TEA SPOONS

Here is one table utensil whose identity is seldom mistaken. The iced tea spoon is characterized by its extra-long handle, but aside from this it differs in no way from a common teaspoon. The available selection is nothing short of overwhelming, as iced tea has been with us for well over a century.

(Silver-Plated)

	Price Range	
☐ American Silver Company "Rosalie", *no monogram, excellent condition*	5.00	6.00
☐ American Silver Company "Rosalie", *no monogram, fair condition*	1.00	2.00
☐ Community "Adam", *no monogram, excellent condition* . .	7.00	8.00
☐ Community "Adam", *no monogram, good condition*	4.00	5.00
☐ Community "Bird of Paradise", *no monogram, excellent condition*	9.00	10.00
☐ Community "Bird of Paradise", *no monogram, good condition*	7.00	8.00
☐ Community "Evening Star", *no monogram, good condition*	7.00	8.00
☐ Community "Evening Star", *no monogram, excellent condition*	7.00	8.00
☐ Community "Flight", *no monogram, mint condition*	4.00	5.00
☐ Community "Grosvenor", *no monogram, good condition* . .	8.00	9.00
☐ Community "Grosvenor", *no monogram, excellent condition*	9.00	10.00
☐ Community "Louis XVI", *no monogram, excellent condition*	9.00	10.00
☐ Community "Louis XVI", *monogram, excellent condition* . .	4.00	5.00
☐ Community "Louis XVI", *no monogram, good condition* . . .	4.00	5.00
☐ Community "Milady", *no monogram, excellent condition* . .	9.00	10.00
☐ Community "Milady", *no monogram, fair condition*	1.00	2.00
☐ Community "Morning Rose", *no monogram, mint condition*	4.00	5.00
☐ Community "Morning Rose", *no monogram, good condition*	2.00	3.00
☐ Community "Patrician", *no monogram, excellent condition*	5.00	6.00

	Price Range	
☐ Community "Patrician", *no monogram, excellent condition*	9.00	10.00
☐ Community "Patrician", *no monogram, good condition* ...	5.00	6.00
☐ Community "Paul Revere", *no monogram, good condition* .	6.00	7.00
☐ Community "Paul Revere", *no monogram, excellent condition*	9.00	10.00
☐ Community "Paul Revere", *no monogram, fair condition* ..	1.00	2.00
☐ Community "Sheraton", *no monogram, fair condition*	3.00	4.00
☐ Community "Sheraton", *no monogram, good condition* ...	5.00	6.00
☐ Community "Silver Artistry", *no monogram, excellent condition*	9.00	10.00
☐ Community "Silver Artistry", *no monogram, good condition*	4.00	5.00
☐ Community "Silver Valentine", *no monogram, mint condition*	3.00	4.00
☐ Community "Song of Autumn", *no monogram, mint condition*	5.00	6.00
☐ Community "Song of Autumn", *monogram, good condition*	2.00	3.00
☐ Community "Tangier", *no monogram, mint condition*	4.00	5.00
☐ Community "White Orchid", *no monogram, excellent condition*	7.00	8.00
☐ Community "White Orchid", *no monogram, excellent condition*	9.00	10.00
☐ Community "White Orchid", *no monogram, good condition*	4.00	5.00
☐ Harmony House "Danish Queen", *no monogram, excellent condition*	7.00	8.00
☐ Harmony House "Danish Queen", *no monogram, good condition*	2.00	3.00
☐ Holmes & Edwards "Century", *no monogram, excellent condition*	7.00	8.00
☐ Holmes & Edwards "Century", *no monogram, good condition*	5.00	6.00
☐ Holmes & Edwards "Danish Princess", *no monogram, good condition*	7.00	8.00
☐ Holmes & Edwards "Danish Princess", *no monogram, excellent condition*	9.00	10.00
☐ Holmes & Edwards "Danish Princess", *no monogram, fair condition*	1.00	2.00
☐ Holmes & Edwards "Woodsong", *no monogram, excellent condition*	7.00	8.00
☐ Holmes & Edwards "Woodsong", *no monogram, mint condition*	8.00	9.00
☐ Holmes & Edwards "Youth", *no monogram, excellent condition*	7.00	8.00
☐ Holmes & Edwards "Youth", *monogram, excellent condition*	3.00	4.00
☐ International "Orleans", *no monogram, excellent condition*	4.00	5.00
☐ International "Triumph", *no monogram, mint condition* ...	3.00	4.00
☐ National "Embossed", *no monogram, fair condition*	1.00	2.00
☐ National "Embossed", *no monogram, good condition*	4.00	5.00
☐ National "King Edward", *no monogram, excellent condition*	7.00	8.00
☐ National "King Edward", *no monogram, fair condition*	1.00	2.00
☐ Nobility "Royal Rose", *no monogram, excellent condition* .	9.00	10.00
☐ Oneida "Avalon", *no monogram, excellent condition*	3.00	4.00
☐ Oneida "Avalon", *no monogram, good condition*	4.00	5.00
☐ Oneida "Bridal Wreath", *no monogram, excellent condition*	7.00	8.00

	Price Range	
☐ Prestige "Grenoble", *no monogram, excellent condition* ..	9.00	10.00
☐ Prestige "Grenoble", *no monogram, good condition*	7.00	8.00
☐ Prestige "Grenoble", *no monogram, fair condition*	2.00	3.00
☐ Reed & Barton "Sierra", *no monogram, excellent condition*	9.00	10.00
☐ Reed & Barton "Sierra", *no monogram, good condition*	4.00	5.00
☐ Rogers "Desire", *no monogram, excellent condition*	7.00	8.00
☐ Rogers "Desire", *monogram, excellent condition*	3.00	4.00
☐ Rogers "Orange Blossom", *no monogram, excellent condition*	11.00	13.00
☐ Rogers "Orange Blossom", *no monogram, good condition* .	6.00	7.00
☐ Rogers "Queen Bess II", *no monogram, excellent condition*	1.00	2.00
☐ Rogers "Vendome", *no monogram, excellent condition* ...	7.00	8.00
☐ Rogers "Vendome", *no monogram, good condition*	3.00	4.00
☐ Rogers & Bro. "Daybreak", *no monogram, excellent condition*	7.00	8.00
☐ Rogers & Bro. "Daybreak", *no monogram, fair condition* ..	1.00	2.00
☐ Rogers & Bro. "Daybreak", *no monogram, poor condition* .	1.00	2.00
☐ S.L. & G.H. Rogers "English Garden", *no monogram, excellent condition*	7.00	8.00
☐ S.L. & G.H. Rogers "English Garden", *monogram, excellent condition*	2.00	3.00
☐ S.L. & G.H. Rogers "Thor", *no monogram, good condition* .	6.00	7.00
☐ S.L. & G.H. Rogers "Thor", *no monogram, excellent condition*	7.00	8.00
☐ Tudor "Duchess", *no monogram, excellent condition*	7.00	8.00
☐ Tudor "Duchess", *monogram, poor condition*	1.00	2.00
☐ Tudor "Enchantment", *no monogram, excellent condition* .	6.00	7.00
☐ Tudor "Enchantment", *no monogram, fair condition*	1.00	2.00
☐ Tudor "Queen Bess II", *no monogram, mint condition*	10.00	11.00
☐ Tudor "Queen Bess II", *no monogram, excellent condition* .	7.00	8.00
☐ Tudor "Queen Bess II", *no monogram, fair condition*	1.00	2.00
☐ Tudor "Skyline", *no monogram, good condition*	5.00	6.00
☐ Wallace "Hudson", *no monogram, excellent condition*	2.00	3.00
☐ Wallace "Kings", *no monogram, excellent condition*	4.00	5.00
☐ Wallace "Kings", *no monogram, fair condition*	1.00	2.00
☐ Williams Bros. "Isabella", *no monogram, excellent condition*	12.00	14.00
☐ Williams Bros. "Isabella", *no monogram, good condition* ..	9.00	10.00
☐ Williams Bros. "Queen Elizabeth", *no monogram, excellent condition*	3.00	4.00
☐ Williams Bros. "Queen Elizabeth", *no monogram, fair condition*	1.00	2.00
☐ Wm. A. Rogers "Chalice", *no monogram, good condition* ..	5.00	6.00
☐ Wm. A. Rogers "Chalice", *no monogram, excellent condition*	6.00	7.00
☐ Wm. A. Rogers "Country Lane", *no monogram, excellent condition*	7.00	8.00
☐ Wm. A. Rogers "Country Lane", *no monogram, fair condition*	1.00	2.00
☐ Wm. A. Rogers "Garland", *no monogram, excellent condition*	5.00	6.00
☐ Wm. A. Rogers "Lady Stuart", *no monogram, excellent condition*	9.00	10.00

Price Range

☐ **Wm. A. Rogers "Lady Stuart"**, *no monogram, good condi-*
tion 5.00 6.00
☐ **Wm. A. Rogers "Lido"**, *no monogram, good condition* 6.00 7.00
☐ **Wm. A. Rogers "Lido"**, *no monogram, fair condition* 1.00 2.00
☐ **Wm. A. Rogers "Malibu"**, *no monogram, excellent condi-*
tion 9.00 10.00
☐ **Wm. A. Rogers "Malibu"**, *no monogram, good condition* ... 4.00 5.00
☐ **Wm. A. Rogers "Meadowbrook"**, *no monogram, excellent*
condition 7.00 8.00
☐ **Wm. A. Rogers "Meadowbrook"**, *no monogram, good con-*
dition 6.00 7.00
☐ **Wm. A. Rogers "Meadowbrook"**, *no monogram, fair condi-*
tion 1.00 2.00
☐ **Wm. A. Rogers "Raleigh"**, *no monogram, excellent condi-*
tion 4.00 5.00
☐ **Wm. A. Rogers "Raleigh"**, *no monogram, fair condition* ... 1.00 2.00
☐ **Wm. A. Rogers "Rosalie"**, *no monogram, excellent condi-*
tion 9.00 10.00
☐ **Wm. A. Rogers "Rosalie"**, *no monogram, good condition* .. 5.00 6.00
☐ **Wm. A. Rogers "Valley Rose"**, *no monogram, excellent con-*
dition 7.00 8.00
☐ **Wm. A. Rogers "Valley Rose"**, *no monogram, fair condition* 1.00 2.00
☐ **Wm. Rogers "Beloved"**, *no monogram, good condition* 6.00 7.00
☐ **Wm. Rogers "Beloved"**, *no monogram, excellent condition* 8.00 9.00
☐ **Wm. Rogers "Beloved"**, *no monogram, fair condition* 1.00 2.00
☐ **Wm. Rogers "Devonshire"**, *no monogram, excellent condi-*
tion 7.00 8.00
☐ **Wm. Rogers "Devonshire"**, *no monogram, good condition* . 6.00 7.00
☐ **Wm. Rogers "Devonshire"**, *no monogram, fair condition* .. 1.00 2.00
☐ **Wm. Rogers "Fairoaks"**, *no monogram, good condition* ... 7.00 8.00
☐ **Wm. Rogers "Fairoaks"**, *no monogram, excellent condition* 8.00 9.00
☐ **Wm. Rogers "Lufberry"**, *no monogram, excellent condition* 1.00 2.00
☐ **Wm. Rogers "Mayfair"**, *no monogram, good condition* 7.00 8.00
☐ **Wm. Rogers "Mayfair"**, *no monogram, fair condition* 1.00 2.00
☐ **Wm. Rogers "Mayfair"**, *no monogram, excellent condition* . 8.00 9.00
☐ **Wm. Rogers "Precious Mirror"**, *no monogram, good condi-*
tion 6.00 7.00
☐ **Wm. Rogers "Precious Mirror"**, *no monogram, excellent*
condition 8.00 9.00
☐ **Wm. Rogers "Precious Mirror"**, *no monogram, fair condi-*
tion 1.00 2.00
☐ **Wm. Rogers "Treasure"**, *no monogram, excellent condition* 8.00 9.00
☐ **Wm. Rogers "Treasure"**, *no monogram, good condition* ... 4.00 5.00
☐ **Wm. Rogers Mfg. Co. "Alhambra"**, *no monogram, good*
condition 5.00 6.00
☐ **Wm. Rogers Mfg. Co. "Alhambra"**, *no monogram, excellent*
condition 9.00 11.00
☐ **Wm. Rogers Mfg. Co. "Avalon"**, *no monogram, good condi-*
tion 1.00 2.00
☐ **Wm. Rogers Mfg. Co. "Sovereign"**, *no monogram, excellent*
condition 7.00 8.00
☐ **Wm. Rogers Mfg. Co. "Sovereign"**, *no monogram, good*
condition 4.00 5.00
☐ **1835 R. Wallace "Troy"**, *no monogram, good condition* 3.00 4.00

	Price Range	
☐ 1835 R. Wallace "Troy", *no monogram, excellent condition*	9.00	10.00
☐ 1847 Rogers "Ancestral", *no monogram, excellent condition*	9.00	10.00
☐ 1847 Rogers "Ancestral", *no monogram, fair condition*	2.00	3.00
☐ 1847 Rogers "Anniversary", *no monogram, excellent condition*	9.00	10.00
☐ 1847 Rogers "Anniversary", *no monogram, good condition*	7.00	8.00
☐ 1847 Rogers "Anniversary", *no monogram, fair condition* ..	2.00	3.00
☐ 1847 Rogers "Daffodil", *no monogram, excellent condition*	6.00	7.00
☐ 1847 Rogers "Daffodil", *no monogram, excellent condition*	7.00	8.00
☐ 1847 Rogers "Daffodil", *no monogram, good condition*	5.00	6.00
☐ 1847 Rogers "Daffodil II", *no monogram, excellent condition*	9.00	10.00
☐ 1847 Rogers "Daffodil II", *no monogram, good condition* ..	4.00	5.00
☐ 1847 Rogers "Eternally Yours", *no monogram, excellent condition*	5.00	6.00
☐ 1847 Rogers "Eternally Yours", *no monogram, excellent condition*	9.00	10.00
☐ 1847 Rogers "Eternally Yours", *no monogram, good condition*	5.00	6.00
☐ 1847 Rogers "First Love", *no monogram, excellent condition*	9.00	10.00
☐ 1847 Rogers "First Love", *no monogram, good condition* ..	4.00	5.00
☐ 1847 Rogers "Legacy", *no monogram, excellent condition* .	9.00	10.00
☐ 1847 Rogers "Legacy", *no monogram, poor condition*	1.00	2.00
☐ 1847 Rogers "Leilani", *no monogram, excellent condition* .	3.00	4.00
☐ 1847 Rogers "Magic Rose", *no monogram, mint condition* .	5.00	6.00
☐ 1847 Rogers "Queen Ann", *no monogram, excellent condition*	7.00	8.00
☐ 1847 Rogers "Queen Ann", *no monogram, fair condition* ..	1.00	2.00
☐ 1847 Rogers "Remembrance", *no monogram, mint condition*	5.00	8.00
☐ 1847 Rogers "Remembrance", *no monogram, excellent condition*	9.00	10.00
☐ 1847 Rogers "Springtime", *no monogram, excellent condition*	7.00	8.00
☐ 1847 Rogers "Springtime", *no monogram, fair condition* ..	1.00	2.00
☐ 1881 Rogers "Baroque Rose", *no monogram, mint condition*	3.00	4.00
☐ 1881 Rogers "Baroque Rose", *no monogram, excellent condition*	9.00	10.00
☐ 1881 Rogers "Enchantment", *no monogram, good condition*	6.00	7.00
☐ 1881 Rogers "Enchantment", *no monogram, fair condition*	2.00	3.00
☐ 1881 Rogers "Flirtation", *no monogram, excellent condition*	2.00	3.00

(Sterling Silver)

☐ Alvin "Romantique", *no monogram*	12.00	14.00
☐ Durgin "Fairfax", 7⅞" L., *no monogram*	14.00	16.00
☐ Frank Smith "Fiddle Thread", *no monogram*	22.00	24.00
☐ Frank Smith "Chippendale", *no monogram*	12.00	14.00
☐ Frank Smith "Chippendale", *no monogram*	7.00	8.00
☐ Gorham "Buckingham", *no monogram*	12.00	14.00

	Price Range	
☐ Gorham "Buttercup", *no monogram*	14.00	16.00
☐ Gorham "Chantilly", *no monogram*	14.00	16.00
☐ Gorham "King George", *monogram*	13.00	15.00
☐ Gorham "Old French", *monogram*	12.00	14.00
☐ International "Prelude", *monogram*	12.00	14.00
☐ International "1810", *monogram*	12.00	14.00
☐ Reed & Barton "Dorothy Quincy", *no monogram*	11.00	13.00
☐ Towle "Georgian", *no monogram*	24.00	27.00
☐ Whiting "Lily", *no monogram*	28.00	30.00

ICE TONGS

Whenever silver ice tongs are mentioned, reference is of course made to utensils used in picking up ice cubes or chunks — not to the large iceman's tongs for carrying blocks of ice (these were never, because of their strictly industrial use, made of so glamorous a metal as silver). Here the manufacturers could let their designing skills go wild as there was no prescribed type to be followed — so long as the tongs were capable of grasping, they could be of any form. Thus we find types representing shells, claws, pitchforks, spades, and even human fingers. Generally — but far from invariably — one side of the tong was bowl-like and closed, the other featuring some kind of openwork design. Even the stems are treated in many different ways. Ice tongs were being made as early as the 1700's but the hobbyist stands little chance of discovering specimens before about 1830 on the open market.

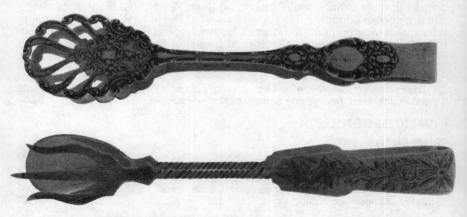

Ice Tongs, *(T to B) (sterling), Wallace "Lucerne", 75.00; Hall, Hewson & Brower (Albany, New York, c. 1850), 90.00*

(Silver-Plated)

☐ Community "Adam", *no monogram, excellent condition* ..	16.00	18.00
☐ Holmes & Edwards "Carolina", *no monogram, good condition*	12.00	14.00
☐ Rogers "Newport", *no monogram, excellent condition*	32.00	36.00
☐ Rogers "Newport", *monogram, fair condition*	2.00	3.00

	Price Range	
☐ **Wm. Rogers Mfg. Co. "Regent",** *no monogram, excellent condition*	12.00	15.00
☐ **1847 Rogers "Avon",** *9½" L., no monogram, excellent condition*	20.00	22.00
☐ **1847 Rogers "Old Colony",** *monogram, fair condition*	8.00	9.00
☐ **1847 Rogers "Persian",** *9½" L., claw and pierced spoon ends, no monogram, excellent condition*	90.00	100.00
☐ **1847 Rogers "Vintage",** *no monogram, good condition*	28.00	32.00
☐ **Maker unknown,** *ornate floral pattern, pierced ends, no monogram, excellent condition*	14.00	16.00

(Sterling Silver)

☐ **Dominick & Haff "Century",** *pierced spoon type ends, monogram*	54.00	60.00
☐ **Dominick & Haff "Century",** *no monogram*	54.00	60.00
☐ **Gorham "King George",** *pierced spoon type ends, monogram*	95.00	105.00
☐ **Wallace "Rose",** *pierced fork and spoon ends, no monogram*	45.00	50.00
☐ **Whiting "Lily",** *pierced spoon ends, no monogram*	90.00	100.00

INKWELLS

The desk (whether home or office) with every Victorian convenience naturally sported the best in inkwells. These would either be entirely of silver, or silver in combination with glass. The shapes and style are so diverse that we cannot begin describing them. A visit to the antiques shops will provide an education into silver inkwells. These have quite high collector value, since competition comes from two directions: the silver collectors, and (a larger group) collectors of inkwells. They make very appealing displays when grouped together.

(Silver-Plated)

☐ **Tiffany Studios,** *pine needle design on white glass, 5½"* ..	80.00	90.00
☐ **Maker unknown,** *figural, dog's head, hat is inkwell cover* ..	50.00	55.00

INVALID SPOONS

(Silver-Plated)

☐ **Maker unknown,** *good condition*	12.00	14.00

(Sterling Silver)

☐ **Webster,** *egg-shaped bowl, curled handle, monogram*	52.00	57.00
☐ **Maker unknown,** *no monogram*	25.00	27.00

JAM POTS

The standard material for jam pots over the years has been ceramic. Even when made of silver, like the specimens listed here, the bowl was lined with ceramic for its preservative qualities. You will also sometimes find jam pots in which the bowl is wholly ceramic and the lid silver — but take care in these cases, as the item might be a "marriage" of two unrelated pieces. When the holder and liner are inseperable, as is usually the case, determination of the bullion content is impossible.

(Sterling Silver and China)	**Price Range**	
☐ *Sterling holder with Lenox liner, hand-painted strawberries, Watson openwork holder with handle and silver lid*	**54.00**	**60.00**
☐ *Sterling holder with Lenox liner, hand-painted insects, Tiffany holder with lid with openwork design*	**50.00**	**55.00**

JELLY SERVERS

A jelly server is a spoon with a rather long handle, the overall length normally in the range of 6¾″ to 7¾″, but specimens both shorter and longer will sometimes turn up. They were an indispensible accessory to every table in the later Victorian, Edwardian, and slightly later eras, going up to about 1930; and of course they are still made today, for those who carry on the traditions of table etiquette. The bowls are circular and not deep.

(Silver-Plated)

☐ **Community "Adam"**, *no monogram, excellent condition* . .	8.00	9.00
☐ **Community "Adam"**, *no monogram, good condition*	4.00	5.00
☐ **Community "Bird of Paradise"**, *no monogram, excellent condition*	12.00	13.00
☐ **Community "Bird of Paradise"**, *monogram, excellent condition*	7.00	8.00
☐ **Community "Coronation"**, *no monogram, excellent condition*	9.00	10.00
☐ **Community "Coronation"**, *no monogram, good condition* .	6.00	7.00
☐ **Community "King Cedric"**, *no monogram, excellent condition*	1.00	2.00
☐ **Community "King Cedric"**, *no monogram, excellent condition*	7.00	8.00
☐ **Community "King Cedric"**, *no monogram, good condition* .	5.00	6.00
☐ **Community "Enchantment"**, *no monogram, excellent condition*	10.00	11.00
☐ **Community "Enchantment"**, *no monogram, good condition*	7.00	8.00
☐ **Community "Enchantment"**, *no monogram, fair condition* .	2.00	3.00
☐ **Community "Evening Star"**, *no monogram, excellent condition*	9.00	10.00
☐ **Community "Lady Hamilton"**, *no monogram, excellent condition*	7.00	8.00
☐ **Community "Lady Hamilton"**, *no monogram, good condition*	4.00	5.00
☐ **Community "Lady Hamilton"**, *monogram, good condition* .	1.00	2.00
☐ **Community "Morning Star"**, *no monogram, good condition*	3.00	4.00
☐ **Community "Morning Star"**, *no monogram, good condition*	7.00	8.00
☐ **Community "Morning Star"**, *pierced, no monogram, excellent condition*	9.00	10.00
☐ **Community "Morning Star"**, *no monogram, excellent condition*	7.00	8.00
☐ **Community "Patrician"**, *no monogram, excellent condition*	9.00	10.00
☐ **Community "Paul Revere"**, *no monogram, excellent condition*	9.00	10.00
☐ **Community "Paul Revere"**, *no monogram, fair condition* . .	1.00	2.00
☐ **Community "South Seas"**, *pierced, no monogram, excellent condition*	7.00	8.00
☐ **Community "South Seas"**, *no monogram, good condition* .	3.00	4.00

	Price Range	
☐ **Community "Spanish Crown"**, *pierced, no monogram, excellent condition*	9.00	10.00
☐ **Community "Spanish Crown"**, *no monogram, excellent condition*	7.00	8.00
☐ **Community "White Orchid"**, *no monogram, good condition*	7.00	8.00
☐ **Community "White Orchid"**, *no monogram, fair condition*	2.00	3.00
☐ **C. Rogers & Bros. "Imperial"**, *no monogram, excellent condition*	9.00	10.00
☐ **C. Rogers & Bros. "Imperial"**, *no monogram, excellent condition*	10.00	12.00
☐ **Holmes & Edwards "Century"**, *no monogram, excellent condition*	9.00	10.00
☐ **Holmes & Edwards "Century"**, *monogram, excellent condition*	4.00	5.00
☐ **Holmes & Edwards "Danish Princess"**, *no monogram, excellent condition*	5.00	6.00
☐ **Holmes & Edwards "Danish Princess"**, *no monogram, excellent condition*	7.00	8.00
☐ **Holmes & Edwards "Danish Princess"**, *no monogram, good condition*	4.00	5.00
☐ **Holmes & Edwards "DeSancy"**, *no monogram, good condition*	7.00	8.00
☐ **Holmes & Edwards "DeSancy"**, *no monogram, excellent condition*	7.00	8.00
☐ **Holmes & Edwards "Jamestown"**, *no monogram, excellent condition*	9.00	11.00
☐ **Holmes & Edwards "Jamestown"**, *monogram, excellent condition*	4.00	5.00
☐ **Holmes & Edwards "Lovely Lady"**, *no monogram, excellent condition*	9.00	10.00
☐ **Holmes & Edwards "Lovely Lady"**, *no monogram, poor condition*	1.00	2.00
☐ **Holmes & Edwards "May Queen"**, *no monogram, mint condition*	2.00	3.00
☐ **Oneida "Sheraton"**, *no monogram, good condition*	4.00	5.00
☐ **Oneida "Sheraton"**, *no monogram, excellent condition*	9.00	10.00
☐ **Reed & Barton "Oxford"**, *no monogram, excellent condition*	10.00	12.00
☐ **Reed & Barton "Oxford"**, *no monogram, mint condition*	21.00	23.00
☐ **Rockford "Lancaster"**, *no monogram, excellent condition*	18.00	20.00
☐ **Rogers "Empire"**, *no monogram, excellent condition*	9.00	10.00
☐ **Queen Bess II"**, *no monogram, excellent condition*	1.00	2.00
☐ **Towle "Arbutus"**, *no monogram, excellent condition*	10.00	14.00
☐ **Towle "Arbutus"**, *no monogram, excellent condition*	20.00	24.00
☐ **Tudor "Enchantment"**, *no monogram, excellent condition*	7.00	8.00
☐ **Tudor "Enchantment"**, *no monogram, good condition*	5.00	6.00
☐ **Tudor "Queen Bess II"**, *no monogram, excellent condition*	9.00	10.00
☐ **Tudor "Queen Bess II"**, *monogram, good condition*	4.00	5.00
☐ **Wm. A. Rogers "Meadowbrook"**, *no monogram, good condition*	7.00	8.00
☐ **Wm. A. Rogers "Meadowbrook"**, *no monogram, excellent condition*	9.00	10.00
☐ **Wm. A. Rogers "Meadowbrook"**, *no monogram, fair condition*	2.00	3.00

	Price Range	

☐ **Wm. A. Rogers "Old South"**, *pierced, no monogram, excellent condition* 9.00 10.00
☐ **Wm. A. Rogers "Old South"**, *pierced, no monogram, good condition* 6.00 7.00
☐ **Wm. Rogers "Imperial"**, *no monogram, excellent condition* 9.00 10.00
☐ **Wm. Rogers "Imperial"**, *monogram, excellent condition* ... 4.00 5.00
☐ **Wm. Rogers "Treasure"**, *no monogram, excellent condition* 9.00 10.00
☐ **Wm. Rogers Mfg. Co. "Legion"**, *no monogram, excellent condition* 9.00 10.00
☐ **Wm. Rogers Mfg. Co. "Legion"**, *no monogram, fair condition* 2.00 3.00
☐ **Wm. Rogers Mfg. Co. "Legion"**, *no monogram, good condition* 9.00 10.00
☐ **Wm. Rogers & Son "Sea Spray"**, *no monogram, good condition* 5.00 6.00
☐ **Wm. Rogers & Son "Sea Spray"**, *monogram, good condition* 2.00 3.00
☐ **World "Franconia"**, *no monogram, excellent condition* 12.00 14.00
☐ **World "Franconia"**, *no monogram, good condition* 7.00 8.00
☐ **1835 R. Wallace "Troy"**, *scalloped blade, no monogram, excellent condition* 20.00 22.00
☐ **1835 R. Wallace "Troy"**, *no monogram, good condition* 10.00 13.00
☐ **1847 Rogers "Ancestral"**, *no monogram, excellent condition* 9.00 10.00
☐ **1847 Rogers "Anniversary"**, *no monogram, good condition* 3.00 4.00
☐ **1847 Rogers "Anniversary"**, *no monogram, good condition* 7.00 8.00
☐ **1847 Rogers "Anniversary"**, *slotted, no monogram, excellent condition* 9.00 10.00
☐ **1847 Rogers "Anniversary"**, *no monogram, excellent condition* 9.00 10.00
☐ **1847 Rogers "Argosy"**, *no monogram, excellent condition* . 9.00 10.00
☐ **1847 Rogers "Argosy"**, *no monogram, mint condition* 10.00 12.00
☐ **1847 Rogers "Avon"**, *no monogram, excellent condition* ... 18.00 20.00
☐ **1847 Rogers "Avon"**, *monogram, excellent condition* 8.00 9.00
☐ **1847 Rogers "Avon"**, *no monogram, fair condition* 4.00 5.00
☐ **1847 Rogers "Berkshire"**, *no monogram, excellent condition* 32.00 36.00
☐ **1847 Rogers "Berkshire"**, *no monogram, excellent condition* 24.00 27.00
☐ **1847 Rogers "Berkshire"**, *no monogram, excellent condition* 22.00 24.00
☐ **1847 Rogers "Berkshire"**, *no monogram, good condition* .. 14.00 16.00
☐ **1847 Rogers "Berkshire"**, *monogram, fair condition* 5.00 6.00
☐ **1847 Rogers "Daffodil II"**, *no monogram, excellent condition* 9.00 10.00
☐ **1847 Rogers "Daffodil II"**, *no monogram, fair condition* ... 2.00 3.00
☐ **1847 Rogers "Esperanto"**, *pierced, no monogram, excellent condition* 9.00 10.00
☐ **1847 Rogers "Esperanto"**, *pierced, monogram, excellent condition* 4.00 5.00
☐ **1847 Rogers "Flair"**, *pierced, no monogram, excellent condition* 9.00 10.00
☐ **1847 Rogers "Flair"**, *no monogram, good condition* 6.00 7.00

Price Range

☐ **1847 Rogers "Grand Heritage"**, *no monogram, excellent condition* 5.00   6.00
☐ **1847 Rogers "Grand Heritage"**, *no monogram, fair condition* 2.00   4.00
☐ **1847 Rogers "Heraldic"**, *no monogram, fair condition* 1.00   2.00
☐ **1847 Rogers "Laurel Mist"**, *no monogram, excellent condition* 9.00   10.00
☐ **1847 Rogers "Laurel Mist"**, *no monogram, good condition* . 4.00   5.00
☐ **1847 Rogers "Leilani"**, *pierced, no monogram, excellent condition* 9.00   10.00
☐ **1847 Rogers "Leilani"**, *no monogram, excellent condition* . 9.00   10.00
☐ **1847 Rogers "Lovelace"**, *no monogram, excellent condition* 9.00   10.00
☐ **1847 Rogers "Magic Rose"**, *no monogram, excellent condition* 9.00   10.00
☐ **1847 Rogers "Magic Rose"**, *no monogram, good condition* 4.00   5.00
☐ **1847 Rogers "Marquise"**, *no monogram, excellent condition* 10.00   13.00
☐ **1847 Rogers "Marquise"**, *no monogram, mint condition* ... 14.00   16.00
☐ **1847 Rogers "Old Colony"**, *no monogram, excellent condition* 12.00   14.00
☐ **1847 Rogers "Old Colony"**, *no monogram, good condition* . 16.00   18.00
☐ **1847 Rogers "Old Colony"**, *no monogram, fair condition* .. 4.00   5.00
☐ **1847 Rogers "Old Colony"**, *no monogram, poor condition* . 1.00   2.00
☐ **1847 Rogers "Remembrance"**, *pierced, no monogram, excellent condition* 9.00   10.00
☐ **1847 Rogers "Remembrance"**, *no monogram, fair condition* 3.00   4.00
☐ **1847 Rogers "Sharon"**, *no monogram, excellent condition* . 12.00   14.00
☐ **1847 Rogers "Vintage"**, *no monogram, mint condition, in original presentation box* 28.00   30.00
☐ **1847 Rogers "Vintage"**, *no monogram, good condition* 12.00   14.00

(Sterling Silver)

☐ **Durgin "Essex"**, *7¼" L., no monogram* 20.00   22.00
☐ **Durgin "Fairfax"**, *no monogram* 15.00   17.00
☐ **Gorham "Chantilly"**, *no monogram* 13.00   15.00
☐ **Gorham "English Gadroon"**, *no monogram* 12.00   14.00
☐ **Gorham "Greenbrier"**, *monogram* 12.00   14.00
☐ **Gorham "Greenbrier"**, *no monogram* 14.00   16.00
☐ **Gorham "Tuileries"**, *no monogram* 12.00   15.00
☐ **International "Abbotsford"**, *7" L., no monogram* 8.00   10.00
☐ **International "Angelique"**, *monogram* 10.00   13.00
☐ **Oneida "Lasting Spring"**, *no monogram* 10.00   13.00
☐ **Oneida "Lasting Spring"**, *monogram* 12.00   14.00
☐ **Reed & Barton "Francis I"**, *no monogram* 16.00   18.00
☐ **Reed & Barton "Les Cinq Fleurs"**, *7" L., monogram* 10.00   12.00
☐ **Stieff "Rose"**, *no monogram* 13.00   15.00
☐ **Stieff "Rose"**, *no monogram* 18.00   20.00
☐ **Wallace "Carthage"**, *no monogram* 10.00   13.00
☐ **Whiting "Louis XV"**, *no monogram* 12.00   14.00
☐ **Maker unknown**, , *ornate pattern with blackberries on handle, gold wash blade, pierced, monogram and dated 1901* .. 16.00   18.00

JEWEL BOXES

These of course follow no standard size or design. They were made in all types, from very small to quite large. Some are quite gimmicky with compartments-within-compartments, folding doors, etc. Generally the drawers are velvet lined. Silver jewel boxes are attractive, some exceptionally so, but the space they take up in display has held down their collecting popularity slightly. Many specimens are brought on the antiques market by non-collectors who simply want to use them for storing jewelry. Though it sounds odd, jewel boxes can be "loaded": that is, weighted with the addition of lead or other weighting material applied in a false base.

Jewerly Box, *Gorham, made 1915, original velvet lining, bottom is cardboard, 7"x7"x2¹⁵⁄₁₆", 22 ounces,* 450.00

(Silver-Plated)	Price Range	
☐ **Reed & Barton,** *5" x 11" high, round shape, three sections for various types of jewelry, elaborate medallion and scroll design, silver in excellent condition, small dent on lid*	280.00	310.00
☐ **Victor Silver,** *footed 7" oval, cherubs with musical instruments, monogram, good condition*	30.00	34.00
☐ **Maker unknown,** *hinged lid, floral design*	24.00	27.00
☐ **Maker unknown,** *10" x 12" x 3" H., overall embossed floral design, silk-lined*	20.00	22.00
☐ **Maker unknown,** *10" x 4½", ladies and cherubs*	24.00	27.00

JEWELRY

The range of silver jewelry is far too extensive to explore in depth in a general book such as this. Interested readers are referred to *The Official Price Guide to Antique Jewelry,* available in bookshops or at $9.95 plus $1.00 shipping from The House of Collectibles, 1900 Premier Row, Orlando, Florida 32809.

(Sterling Silver)	Price Range	
☐ **Bracelet,** *World War II, "Flying Victory", decorated with the flags of the "Big Four" countries done in enamel*	8.00	10.00
☐ **Bracelet,** *slip-on bangle type*	1.00	2.00
☐ **Brooch,** *Gorham, hand-hammered finish with flower in center*	36.00	40.00
☐ **Clip,** *marquisite*	8.00	10.00
☐ **Concha belt,** *Navajo, 10 floral medallions, pierced decoration, pierced square buckle, thin hide strap, 28½" L.*	100.00	115.00
☐ **Cuff links,** *oval shape, no monogram*	7.00	8.00
☐ **Earrings,** *Art Nouveau styling, woman with garnet*	8.00	9.00
☐ **Earrings,** *oval, scrollwork*	7.00	8.00
☐ **Earrings,** *Tiny thimbles*	1.00	2.00
☐ **Necklace,** *Navajo, squash blossom, 20 squash blossoms and naja pendant, 25½" L.*	72.00	80.00
☐ **Necklace,** *Navajo, squash blossom, 14 squash blossoms and naja pendant with inset turquoise stone, 17½" L.*	100.00	115.00
☐ **Necklace,** *Navajo, squash blossom, 20 blossoms all inset with turquoise stone, on double bead strand, naja pendant, 27" L.*	155.00	175.00
☐ **Pendant,** *whistle with devil design*	12.00	14.00
☐ **Pendant,** *large, triangular, knight on a horse*	8.00	9.00
☐ **Pin,** *Gorham, spoon*	6.00	7.00
☐ **Pin,** *Unger Bros., "Evangeline", holly leaf shape, ⅜" W., Evangeline's face in center of leaf*	57.00	63.00
☐ **Pin,** *Scottie dog*	3.00	4.00
☐ **Pin,** *calla lily, 3" W.*	8.00	9.00
☐ **Ring,** *cross*	4.00	5.00
☐ **Ring,** *man's, tortoise trim*	4.00	5.00
☐ **Ring,** *coiled snake*	3.00	4.00
☐ **Ring,** *set with jade*	3.00	4.00
☐ **Ring,** *frog on lily pad*	7.00	8.00
☐ **Ring,** *wolf's head with garnet in mouth*	8.00	9.00
☐ **Ring,** *squirrel eating a nut*	7.00	8.00
☐ **Ring,** *frog*	7.00	8.00
☐ **Ring,** *Art Nouveau styling with woman's profile*	7.00	8.00
☐ **Ring,** *dinner type, three small garnets*	8.00	9.00
☐ **Ring,** *oval amethyst stone*	9.00	10.00
☐ **Ring,** *turtle with head sticking up*	7.00	8.00
☐ **Ring,** *Egyptian motif with garnet*	7.00	8.00
☐ **Ring,** *tragedy/comedy face*	4.00	5.00
☐ **Ring,** *bulldog's face*	7.00	8.00
☐ **Ring,** *Art Nouveau styling, woman with garnet stone*	7.00	8.00
☐ **Slide,** *owl's head, garnet eyes*	3.00	4.00
☐ **Slide,** *Art Nouveau styling with woman's profile*	3.00	4.00
☐ **Slide,** *Etruscan dome*	3.00	4.00

LETTER OPENERS

Letter openers do not have very early origins. They were made necessary (or, at any rate, useful) only when letters began to be sent in envelopes, which dates from around 1850. Prior to that time, the universal practice was to fold the letter into a small packet, and seal up the edges with wax. These early letters could easily be broken open without use of any tool. Nevertheless, despite being manufactured for only a bit more than 100 years, droves of letter openers exist, in uncountable sizes and styles. They were a mandatory article for every office and well-to-do home, and a popular gift when one was stumped for ideas. In addition to the giftshop varieties of silver letter openers, many souvenir specimens will be found. A huge collection could be built up, if one wanted to concentrate on silver letter openers. Since the handles could follow any form, manufacturers dug deep into their imaginations for motifs. You will also find some incorporating novelty devices such as thermometers, rulers, compasses, and whatnot.

Letter Opener, *(sterling), maker unknown,* 75.00

		Price Range	
(Sterling Silver)			
☐ **Maker unknown,** *miniature sword, engraved work*		15.00	17.00
☐ **Maker unknown,** *plain design*		8.00	9.00
☐ **Maker unknown,** *Art Nouveau styling, pierced handle with lady's head in heart*		54.00	60.00

LETTUCE FORKS

It may be hard to imagine lettuce being served alone, not as part of a salad (when, of course, it would be properly eaten with a salad fork). But keep in mind that many foodstuffs taken for granted today were not necessarily as common in the 19th century. Farm produce was often on the verge of spoilage by the time it reached some city markets. A hostess who could present crisp lettuce was justly proud of it.

(Silver-Plated)			
☐ **Rockford "Rosemary",** *no monogram, excellent condition* .		20.00	22.00
☐ **Rockford "Rosemary",** *monogram, fair condition*		5.00	6.00
☐ **1835 R. Wallace "Cardinal",** *no monogram, excellent condition*		18.00	21.00
☐ **1835 R. Wallace "Cardinal",** *no monogram, excellent condition*		22.00	25.00
☐ **1835 R. Wallace "Cardinal",** *no monogram, excellent condition*		22.00	25.00

	Price Range	
☐ 1835 R. Wallace "Joan", *no monogram, excellent condition*	20.00	22.00
☐ 1835 R. Wallace "Troy", *no monogram, excellent condition*	20.00	22.00
☐ 1847 Rogers "Priscilla", *no monogram, excellent condition*	27.00	30.00

(Sterling Silver)

☐ Alvin "Raphael", *no monogram*	90.00	100.00
☐ Gorham "Lancaster", *no monogram*	40.00	45.00
☐ Gorham "Lancaster Rose", *monogram*	45.00	50.00
☐ Gorham "Plymouth", *no monogram*	38.00	42.00
☐ Gorham "Strasbourg", *no monogram*	65.00	72.00
☐ Kirk "Repousse", *no monogram*	54.00	60.00
☐ Towle "Canterbury", *gold wash tines, no monogram*	54.00	60.00
☐ Towle "Old Newbury", *no monogram*	32.00	36.00

LOBSTER CRACKERS

This was an implement along the lines of a nutcracker, but without the fame of having served as the subject of a ballet. Mankind ate lobsters for several thousand years before any special tool to crack them was developed. But it WAS a great convenience; many hostesses hesitated to serve lobster because of the labor it would mean to guests. Lobster crackers are strong and sturdy, and their bullion content is greater than would appear from their size. The novelty of them adds to their collecting appeal.

(Silver-Plated)

☐ Rogers & Bro. "Assyrian Head", *no monogram, excellent condition*	75.00	85.00

LOVING CUPS

Loving cups, or trophies in the form of vases with a handle at each side, were more frequently made of silver than any other material. Those dating from the late 19/early 20th centuries are very numerous. Prices vary widely, not only because of variations in size and weight but according to the inscriptions. Any loving cup with a potent topical interest — one presented to the winner of a sporting event for example — will sell at a premium price. The term "loving cup" derives from the twin handles, which suggest that two parties seated opposite could drink from the same vessel; but it is doubtful that any loving cups were ever used in that manner. Be wary of specimens that seem heavy for their size, as they could be weighted. If the cup is mounted on a wooden or other non-silver base, this must of course be removed prior to weighing.

(Silver-Plated)

☐ Van Bergh Silver Co., *Masonic emblems, city and date*	62.00	68.00

LUNCHEON FORKS

Luncheon forks were a bit lighter than dinner forks, on the presumption that they would not be going into battle against formidable meats. Actually the difference between luncheon and dinner forks is so slight that a single type could have served just as well. But that would have meant less silverware for the manufactures to sell — so obviously the makers supported the rule of "a utensil for every specific occasion."

(Silver-Plated)   **Price Range**

☐ **Alvin "Diana"**, *no monogram, fair condition*	1.00	2.00
☐ **Alvin "Diana"**, *no monogram, excellent condition*	6.00	7.00
☐ **Alvin "Diana"**, *no monogram, mint condition*	7.00	8.00
☐ **Alvin "Molly Stark"**, *no monogram, excellent condition*	5.00	6.00
☐ **American Silver Co. "Moselle"**, *no monogram, excellent condition*	12.00	13.00
☐ **American Silver Co. "Moselle"**, *no monogram, good condition*	9.00	11.00
☐ **American Silver Co. "Moselle"**, *no monogram, poor condition*	3.00	4.00
☐ **Benedict Mfg. Co. "Continental"**, *no monogram, good condition*	3.00	4.00
☐ **Benedict Mfg. Co. "Continental"**, *monogram, excellent condition*	3.00	4.00
☐ **Community "Evening Star"**, *viande style, no monogram, excellent condition*	5.00	6.00
☐ **Community "Evening Star"**, *viande style, fair condition* ...	1.00	2.00
☐ **Community "Flower de Luce"**, *no monogram, good condition*	6.00	7.00
☐ **Community "Flower de Luce"**, *no monogram, good condition*	6.00	7.00
☐ **Community "Milady"**, *no monogram, excellent condition* ..	5.00	6.00
☐ **Community "Milady"**, *viande style, no monogram, excellent condition*	4.00	5.00
☐ **Community "Milady"**, *viande style, no monogram, fair condition*	1.00	2.00
☐ **Community "Morning Rose"**, *no monogram, mint condition*	4.00	5.00
☐ **Community "Morning Rose"**, *no monogram, good condition*	1.00	2.00
☐ **Community "Morning Star"**, *viande style, no monogram, good condition*	2.00	3.00
☐ **Community "Patrician"**, *no monogram, good condition* ...	1.00	2.00
☐ **Community "Patrician"**, *no monogram, excellent condition*	3.00	4.00
☐ **Community "Sheraton"**, *no monogram, excellent condition*	6.00	7.00
☐ **Community "Sheraton"**, *monogram, good condition*	1.00	2.00
☐ **Community "South Seas"**, *no monogram, good condition* .	3.00	4.00
☐ **Community "Tangier"**, *no monogram, mint condition*	3.00	4.00
☐ **Gorham "Cavalier"**, *no monogram, excellent condition*	3.00	4.00
☐ **Gorham "Shelburne"**, *no monogram, poor condition*	3.00	4.00
☐ **Harmony House "Classic Filigree"**, *no monogram, excellent condition*	3.00	4.00
☐ **Harmony House "Serenade"**, *no monogram, excellent condition*	3.00	4.00
☐ **Heirloom "Cardinal"**, *no monogram, excellent condition* ..	5.00	6.00
☐ **Holmes & Edwards "Century"**, *no monogram, excellent condition*	5.00	6.00
☐ **Holmes & Edwards "Century"**, *no monogram, good condition*	3.00	4.00
☐ **Holmes & Edwards "Charm"**, *no monogram, excellent condition*	5600	6.00
☐ **Holmes & Edwards "Charm"**, *no monogram, fair condition*	1.00	2.00
☐ **Holmes & Edwards "Dolly Madison"**, *no monogram, good condition*	4.00	5.00

	Price Range	

- [ ] **Holmes & Edwards "Dolly Madison"**, *no monogram, excellent condition* 6.00   7.00
- [ ] **Holmes & Edwards "Lovely Lady"**, *viande style, no monogram, excellent condition* 5.00   6.00
- [ ] **Holmes & Edwards "Lovely Lady"**, *viande style, no monogram, fair condition* 1.00   2.00
- [ ] **Holmes & Edwards "Pageant"**, *no monogram, excellent condition* 5.00   6.00
- [ ] **Holmes & Edwards "Pageant"**, *no monogram, good condition* 3.00   4.00
- [ ] **Holmes & Edwards "Pearl"**, *no monogram, resilvered* 7.00   8.00
- [ ] **Oneida "Avalon"**, *no monogram, poor condition* 1.00   2.00
- [ ] **Oneida "Avalon"**, *no monogram, fair condition* 2.00   3.00
- [ ] **Oneida "Beverly"**, *no monogram, excellent condition* 2.00   3.00
- [ ] **Oneida "Louis XVI"**, *no monogram, excellent condition* ... 3.00   4.00
- [ ] **R.C. Co. "Isabella"**, *no monogram, excellent condition* 4.00   5.00
- [ ] **R.C. Co. "Isabella"**, *no monogram, good condition* 3.00   4.00
- [ ] **Reed & Barton "Oxford"**, *no monogram, excellent condition* 3.00   4.00
- [ ] **Reed & Barton "Oxford"**, *no monogram, fair condition* 2.00   3.00
- [ ] **Reed & Barton "Roman Medallion"**, *no monogram, resilvered* 7.00   8.00
- [ ] **Reed & Barton "Roman Medallion"**, *no monogram, fair condition* 3.00   4.00
- [ ] **Reed & Barton "Tiger Lily"**, *monogram, excellent condition* 2.00   3.00
- [ ] **Rogers "Queen Bess II"**, *no monogram, excellent condition* 3.00   4.00
- [ ] **Rogers "Queen Bess II"**, *no monogram, fair condition* 1.00   2.00
- [ ] **Rogers "Shell"**, *no monogram, excellent condition* 2.00   3.00
- [ ] **Rogers "Shell"**, *no monogram, good condition* 2.00   3.00
- [ ] **Rogers "Vendome"**, *no monogram, fair condition* 1.00   2.00
- [ ] **Rogers "Vendome"**, *no monogram, good condition* 3.00   4.00
- [ ] **Rogers "Victorian Rose"**, *no monogram, excellent condition* 3.00   4.00
- [ ] **Rogers "Victorian Rose"**, *no monogram, fair condition* 1.00   2.00
- [ ] **Rogers & Bro. "Assyrian"**, *no monogram, excellent condition* 3.00   4.00
- [ ] **Rogers & Bro. "Cromwell"**, *no monogram, excellent condition* 3.00   4.00
- [ ] **Rogers & Bro. "Crest"**, *no monogram* 3.00   4.00
- [ ] **Rogers & Bro. "Crest"**, *no monogram, good condition* 3.00   4.00
- [ ] **Rogers & Bro. "Siren"**, *no monogram, good condition* 7.00   8.00
- [ ] **Rogers & Bro. "Siren"**, *no monogram, fair condition* 3.00   4.00
- [ ] **Rogers & Hamilton "Cardinal"**, *no monogram, excellent condition* 2.00   3.00
- [ ] **Rogers & Hamilton "Marquise"**, *no monogram, excellent condition* 4.00   5.00
- [ ] **Rogers & Hamilton "Tudor"**, *no monogram, excellent condition* 7.00   8.00
- [ ] **Rogers & Hamilton "Tudor"**, *no monogram, fair condition* . 2.00   3.00
- [ ] **S.L. & G.H. Rogers "Arcadia"**, *no monogram, good condition* 2.00   3.00
- [ ] **S.L. & G.H. Rogers "English Garden"**, *monogram, excellent condition* 2.00   3.00
- [ ] **S.L. & G.H. Rogers "Jasmine"**, *no monogram, excellent condition* 3.00   4.00

	Price Range	
☐ Smith "Iris", *no monogram, fair condition*	3.00	4.00
☐ Tudor "Mary Stuart", *no monogram, excellent condition* . .	3.00	4.00
☐ Wallace "Alamo", *no monogram, excellent condition*	3.00	4.00
☐ Wallace "Alamo", *no monogram, fair condition*	1.00	2.00
☐ Wm. A. Rogers "Carnation", *no monogram, excellent condition*	4.00	5.00
☐ Wm. A. Rogers "Carnation", *no monogram, good condition*	3.00	4.00
☐ Wm. A. Rogers "Hanover", *no monogram, excellent condition*	4.00	5.00
☐ Wm. A. Rogers "LaVigne", *no monogram, silver in good condition, tines worn*	6.00	7.00
☐ Wm. Rogers "Avalon", *no monogram, excellent condition* .	3.00	4.00
☐ Wm. Rogers "Carrollton", *no monogram, excellent condition*	3.00	4.00
☐ Wm. Rogers "Exquisite", *viande style, no monogram, excellent condition*	3.00	4.00
☐ Wm. Rogers "Exquisite", *no monogram, excellent condition*	3.00	4.00
☐ Wm. Rogers "French", *no monogram, fair condition*	1.00	2.00
☐ Wm. Rogers "Mayfair", *no monogram, excellent condition* .	5.00	6.00
☐ Wm. Rogers "Treasure", *viande style, no monogram, excellent condition*	3.00	4.00
☐ Wm. Rogers Eagle "Cordova", *no monogram, excellent condition*	5.00	6.00
☐ Wm. Rogers Mfg. Co. "Alhambra", *no monogram, fair condition*	1.00	2.00
☐ Wm. Rogers Mfg. Co. "Arbutus", *no monogram, excellent condition*	6.00	7.00
☐ Wm. Rogers Mfg. Co. "Arbutus", *no monogram, excellent condition*	7.00	8.00
☐ Wm. Rogers Mfg. Co. "Berwick", *monogram, excellent condition*	6.00	7.00
☐ Wm. Rogers Mfg. Co. "Berwick", *no monogram, excellent condition*	7.00	8.00
☐ Wm. Rogers Mfg. Co. "Berwick", *no monogram, fair condition*	3.00	4.00
☐ Wm. Rogers Mfg. Co. "Regent", *monogram, excellent condition*	3.00	4.00
☐ 1835 R. Wallace "Blossom", *no monogram, excellent condition*	1.00	2.00
☐ 1835 R. Wallace "Cardinal", *no monogram, excellent condition*	6.00	7.00
☐ 1835 R. Wallace "Cardinal", *no monogram, excellent condition*	7.00	8.00
☐ 1835 R. Wallace "Floral", *no monogram, good condition* . .	5.00	6.00
☐ 1835 R. Wallace "Floral", *no monogram, fair condition*	3.00	4.00
☐ 1847 Rogers "Adoration", *no monogram, excellent condition*	4.00	5.00
☐ 1847 Rogers "Adoration", *no monogram, good condition* . .	4.00	5.00
☐ 1847 Rogers "Ancestral", *no monogram, excellent condition*	5.00	6.00
☐ 1847 Rogers "Ancestral", *no monogram, good condition* . .	4.00	5.00
☐ 1847 Rogers "Ancestral", *no monogram, fair condition*	3.00	4.00
☐ 1847 Rogers "Arcadian", *no monogram, resilvered*	8.00	9.00

Price Range

☐ 1847 Rogers "Arcadian", *no monogram, excellent condition*	8.00	9.00
☐ 1847 Rogers "Arcadian", *no monogram, good condition* ...	5.00	6.00
☐ 1847 Rogers "Armenian", *monogram, excellent condition* .	3.00	4.00
☐ 1847 Rogers "Avon", *no monogram, good condition*	1.00	2.00
☐ 1847 Rogers "Berkshire", *monogram, fair condition*	3.00	4.00
☐ 1847 Rogers "Berkshire", *no monogram, good condition* ..	6.00	7.00
☐ 1847 Rogers "Charter Oak", *no monogram, good silver condition, tines worn*	6.00	7.00
☐ 1847 Rogers "Charter Oak", *no monogram, good condition*	7.00	8.00
☐ 1847 Rogers "Charter Oak", *no monogram, resilvered*	8.00	9.00
☐ 1847 Rogers "Charter Oak", *no monogram*	7.00	8.00
☐ 1847 Rogers "Charter Oak", *no monogram, fair condition* ..	4.00	5.00
☐ 1847 Rogers "Charter Oak", *monogram, fair condition*	2.00	3.00
☐ 1847 Rogers "Columbia", *no monogram, excellent condition*	7.00	8.00
☐ 1847 Rogers "Columbia", *no monogram, fair condition*	4.00	5.00
☐ 1847 Rogers "Cromwell", *no monogram, excellent condition*	3.00	4.00
☐ 1847 Rogers "Crown", *no monogram, poor condition*	2.00	3.00
☐ 1847 Rogers "First Love", *viande style, no monogram, excellent condition*	5.00	6.00
☐ 1847 Rogers "Floral", *monogram, mint condition*	9.00	11.00
☐ 1847 Rogers "Grecian", *no monogram, good condition*	1.00	2.00
☐ 1847 Rogers "Heritage", *viande style, no monogram, mint condition*	4.00	5.00
☐ 1847 Rogers "Heritage", *viande style, no monogram, mint condition*	7.00	8.00
☐ 1847 Rogers "Lorne", *no monogram, good condition*	1.00	2.00
☐ 1847 Rogers "Louvain", *no monogram, good condition*	3.00	4.00
☐ 1847 Rogers "Magic Rose", *no monogram, excellent condition*	2.00	3.00
☐ 1847 Rogers "Moselle", *no monogram, mint condition*	15.00	18.00
☐ 1847 Rogers "Moselle", *no monogram, good condition*	10.00	13.00
☐ 1847 Rogers "Moselle", *no monogram, fair condition*	6.00	7.00
☐ 1847 Rogers "Moselle", *monogram, fair condition*	4.00	5.00
☐ 1847 Rogers "Old Colony", *no monogram, fair condition* ..	1.00	2.00
☐ 1847 Rogers "Old Colony", *no monogram, excellent condition*	9.00	10.00
☐ 1847 Rogers "Persian", *no monogram, good condition*	1.00	2.00
☐ 1847 Rogers "Saratoga", *no monogram, excellent condition*	4.00	5.00
☐ 1847 Rogers "Savoy", *no monogram, excellent condition* ..	3.00	4.00
☐ 1847 Rogers "Vintage", *no monogram, good condition*	7.00	8.00
☐ 1847 Rogers "Vintage", *no monogram, excellent condition*	9.00	10.00
☐ 1847 Rogers "Vintage", *no monogram, resilvered*	10.00	13.00
☐ 1847 Rogers "Vintage", *no monogram, fair condition*	3.00	4.00
☐ 1847 Rogers "Vintage", *no monogram, poor condition*	3.00.00	4.00
☐ 1847 Rogers "Vintage", *no monogram, silver in good condition, tines worn*	4.00	5.00
☐ 1881 Rogers "Chippendale", *no monogram, excellent condition*	5.00	6.00
☐ 1881 Rogers "Coronet", *no monogram, good condition*	4.00	5.00
☐ 1881 Rogers "Godetia", *no monogram, excellent condition*	5.00	6.00

	Price Range	
☐ 1881 Rogers "Grecian", *no monogram, fair condition*	1.00	2.00
☐ 1881 Rogers "Scotia", *no monogram, excellent condition* .	5.00	6.00
☐ 1881 Rogers "Surf Club", *viande style, no monogram, excellent condition*	2.00	3.00

(Sterling Silver)

☐ Alvin "Chateau Rose", *no monogram*	16.00	18.00
☐ Alvin "Old Orange Blossom", *monogram and date*	24.00	28.00
☐ Alvin "Majestic", *monogram*	20.00	22.00
☐ Alvin "Romantique", *no monogram*	14.00	16.00
☐ Blackington "Scroll & Bead", *no monogram*	27.00	30.00
☐ Dominick & Haff "King", *monogram*	22.00	24.00
☐ Durgin "Chrysanthemum", *monogram*	33.00	36.00
☐ Durgin "Fairfax", *7¼" L., no monogram*	18.00	21.00
☐ Durgin "Louis XV", *no monogram*	16.00	18.00
☐ Durgin "Louis XV", *monogram*	10.00	13.00
☐ Fine Arts "Processional", *no monogram*	14.00	17.00
☐ Frank Smith "Chippendale", *no monogram*	14.00	17.00
☐ Frank Smith "Fiddle Thread", *no monogram*	27.00	30.00
☐ Frank Smith "Newport Shell", *no monogram*	25.00	28.00
☐ Gorham "Buttercup", *monogram*	18.00	20.00
☐ Gorham "Cambridge", *monogram*	7.00	8.00
☐ Gorham "Chantilly", *no monogram*	15.00	17.00
☐ Gorham "Cromwell", *7" L., monogram*	16.00	18.00
☐ Gorham "English Gadroon", *monogram*	15.00	17.00
☐ Gorham "Etruscan", *monogram*	13.00	15.00
☐ Gorham "Fairfax", *no monogram*	13.00	15.00
☐ Gorham "Greenbrier", *no monogram*	15.00	17.00
☐ Gorham "Imperial Chrysanthemum", *no monogram*	23.00	25.00
☐ Gorham "Lancaster", *no monogram*	18.00	20.00
☐ Gorham "Lancaster", *monogram*	15.00	19.00
☐ Gorham "Lancaster Rose", *monogram*	15.00	18.00
☐ Gorham "Lancaster Rose", *no monogram*	18.00	20.00
☐ Gorham "LaScala", *no monogram*	18.00	21.00
☐ Gorham "Newcastle", *monogram*	16.00	18.00
☐ Gorham "Old French", *monogram*	16.00	19.00
☐ Gorham "Old French", *no monogram*	18.00	20.00
☐ Gorham "Rosette", *7" L., monogram*	18.00	20.00
☐ Gorham "Sovereign", *no monogram*	18.00	20.00
☐ Gorham "Versailles", *no monogram*	13.00	15.00
☐ Gorham "Versailles", *no monogram*	16.00	18.00
☐ Gorham "Willow", *no monogram*	15.00	17.00
☐ International "Angelique", *no monogram*	16.00	18.00
☐ International "Angelique", *monogram*	16.00	18.00
☐ International "Avalon", *monogram*	22.00	24.00
☐ International "Bridal Veil", *no monogram*	15.00	17.00
☐ International "Courtship", *no monogram*	15.00	17.00
☐ International "Courtship", ...	15.00	17.00
☐ International "Crystal", *no monogram*	16.00	18.00
☐ International "Edgewood", *no monogram*	20.00	22.00
☐ International "Fontaine", *monogram*	16.00	18.00
☐ International "Frontenac", *monogram and date*	28.00	30.00
☐ International "Frontenac", *monogram*	9.00	10.00
☐ International "Joan of Arc", *no monogram*	16.00	18.00

	Price Range	
☐ International "Royal Danish", *no monogram*	16.00	18.00
☐ International "Silver Melody", *no monogram*	16.00	18.00
☐ International "Swan Lake", *no monogram*	16.00	18.00
☐ International 'Vision", *no monogram*	13.00	15.00
☐ International "Wild Rose", *no monogram*	15.00	17.00
☐ Kirk "Repousse", *7¼" L., monogram*	13.00	15.00
☐ Kirk "Repousse", *no monogram*	18.00	20.00
☐ Lunt "Eloquence", *no monogram*	14.00	16.00
☐ Lunt "Mt. Vernon", *monogram*	18.00	20.00
☐ Lunt "Sweetheart", *no monogram*	12.00	14.00
☐ Manchester "Vogue", *no monogram*	14.00	16.00
☐ Oneida "Belle Rose"*no monogram*	12.00	14.00
☐ Oneida "Heiress", *no monogram*	14.00	16.00
☐ Oneida "Heiress", *monogram*	13.00	15.00
☐ Oneida "Lasting Spring", *no monogram*	12.00	14.00
☐ Oneida "Martinique", *no monogram*	14.00	16.00
☐ Oneida "Rubiayat", *no monogram*	14.00	16.00
☐ Oneida "Silver Rose", *no monogram*	14.00	16.00
☐ Reed & Barton "Francis I", *no monogram*	20.00	22.00
☐ Reed & Barton "Les Cinq Fleurs", *no monogram*	18.00	20.00
☐ Reed & Barton "Hampton Court", *no monogram*	16.00	18.00
☐ Reed & Barton "LaParisienne", *monogram*	9.00	10.00
☐ Reed & Barton "LaReine", *no monogram*	10.00	13.00
☐ Reed & Barton "Majestic", *7¼" L., monogram*	15.00	17.00
☐ Reed & Barton "Marlborough", *monogram*	15.00	17.00
☐ Simpson, Hall & Miller "Frontenac", *no monogram*	18.00	21.00
☐ Tiffany "Chrysanthemum", *monogram*	18.00	20.00
☐ Tiffany "Colonial", *6¾" L., no monogram*	22.00	25.00
☐ Tiffany "English King", *no monogram*	25.00	27.00
☐ Tiffany "English King", *monogram*	10.00	13.00
☐ Tiffany "Flemish", *monogram*	16.00	18.00
☐ Tiffany "Palm", *no monogram*	20.00	22.00
☐ Tiffany "Renaissance", *no monogram*	18.00	20.00
☐ Tiffany "Wave Edge", *monogram*	25.00	27.00
☐ Towle "Chippendale", *no monogram*	14.00	16.00
☐ Towle "French Provincial", *monogram*	15.00	17.00
☐ Towle "French Provincial", *no monogram*	16.00	18.00
☐ Towle "Georgian", *no monogram*	13.00	15.00
☐ Towle "Georgian", *no monogram*	22.00	25.00
☐ Towle "King Richard", *no monogram*	16.00	18.00
☐ Towle "Kings", *no monogram*	25.00	28.00
☐ Towle "Laureate", *no monogram*	18.00	20.00
☐ Towle "Madeira", *no monogram*	14.00	16.00
☐ Towle "Old Master", *no monogram*	20.00	22.00
☐ Towle "Old Master", *monogram*	16.00	18.00
☐ Towle "Silver Flutes", *no monogram*	14.00	16.00
☐ Wallace "Grand Colonial", *no monogram*	15.00	17.00
☐ Wallace "Princess Mary", *no monogram*	15.00	17.00
☐ Wallace "Waverly", *monogram*	16.00	18.00
☐ Watson-Newell "Bacchante", *no monogram*	27.00	30.00
☐ Watson-Newell "Phoebe", *no monogram*	25.00	27.00
☐ Wendt "Bird", *no monogram*	10.00	12.00
☐ Wendt "Kings", *monogram*	9.00	10.00
☐ Westmoreland "John and Priscilla", *no monogram*	16.00	18.00

	Price Range	
☐ **Westmoreland "Milburn Rose",** *no monogram*	16.00	18.00
☐ **Westmoreland "Milburn Rose",** *no monogram*	16.00	18.00
☐ **Whiting "Imperial Queen",** *monogram*	10.00	12.00
☐ **Whiting "Imperial Queen",** *no monogram*	12.00	14.00
☐ **Whiting "King Edward",** *no monogram*	13.00	15.00
☐ **Whiting "Louis XV",** *6⁷⁄₈₀ L., monogram*	15.00	17.00
☐ **Whiting "Louis XV",** *7″ L., monogram*	15.00	17.00
☐ **Whiting "Madame Jumel",** *monogram*	18.00	21.00

LUNCHEON KNIVES

A very popular area of silver collectibles. So many were melted during the Great Silver Crush of 1970/80 that these once common items show real promise of becoming at least mildly scarce.

(Silver-Plated)

☐ **Alvin "Diana",** *no monogram, good condition*	5.00	6.00
☐ **Alvin "Diana",** *no monogram, excellent condition*	8.00	9.00
☐ **Alvin "Molly Stark",** *no monogram, excellent condition*	6.00	7.00
☐ **Alvin "Molly Stark",** *no monogram, good condition*	3.00	4.00
☐ **American Silver Co. "Moselle",** *no monogram, fair condition*	8.00	9.00
☐ **American Silver Co. "Moselle",** *no monogram, excellent condition*	24.00	26.00
☐ **American Silver Co. "Moselle",** *no monogram, good condition*	12.00	14.00
☐ **Community "Evening Star",** *viande style, no monogram, excellent condition*	5.00	6.00
☐ **Community "Evening Star",** *viande style, no monogram, fair condition*	1.00	2.00
☐ **Community "Flower de Luce",** *no monogram, excellent condition*	6.00	7.00
☐ **Community "Flower de Luce",** *no monogram, good condition*	4.00	5.00
☐ **Community "Milady",** *no monogram, excellent condition* . .	5.00	6.00
☐ **Community "Milady",** *viande style, no monogram, excellent condition*	5.00	6.00
☐ **Community "Milady",** *viande style, no monogram, fair condition*	1.00	2.00
☐ **Community "Morning Rose",** *no monogram, mint condition*	4.00	5.00
☐ **Community "Morning Rose",** *no monogram, good condition*	3.00	4.00
☐ **Community "Morning Star",** *viande style, no monogram, good condition*	2.00	3.00
☐ **Community "Morning Star",** *viande style, no monogram, excellent condition*	6.00	7.00
☐ **Community "Patrician",** *no monogram, excellent condition*	6.00	7.00
☐ **Community "Patrician",** *no monogram, good condition* . . .	5.00	6.00
☐ **Community "Patrician",** *no monogram, fair condition*	1.00	2.00
☐ **Community "Sheraton",** *no monogram, good condition* . . .	3.00	4.00
☐ **Community "Sheraton",** *monogram, good condition*	1.00	2.00
☐ **Community "South Seas",** *no monogram, good condition* .	2.00	3.00
☐ **Community "South Seas",** *no monogram, good condition* .	3.00	4.00
☐ **Community "Tangier",** *no monogram, good condition*	1.00	2.00

	Price Range	
☐ Community "Tangier", *no monogram, mint condition*	3.00	4.00
☐ Gorham "Carolina", *no monogram, mint condition*	6.00	7.00
☐ Gorham "Carolina", *no monogram, good condition*	3.00	4.00
☐ Gorham "Winthrop", *no monogram, excellent condition* . . .	1.00	2.00
☐ Harmony House "Classic Filigree", *no monogram, excellent condition*	1.00	2.00
☐ Harmony House "Serenade", *no monogram, excellent condition*	3.00	4.00
☐ Heirloom "Cardinal", *no monogram, good condition*	4.00	5.00
☐ Holmes & Edwards "American Beauty Rose", *no monogram, fair condition*	7.00	8.00
☐ Holmes & Edwards "American Beauty Rose", *no monogram, poor condition*	1.00	2.00
☐ Holmes & Edwards "Century", *no monogram, excellent condition*	6.00	7.00
☐ Holmes & Edwards "Century", *no monogram, good condition*	4.00	5.00
☐ Holmes & Edwards "Charm", *no monogram, excellent condition*	6.00	7.00
☐ Holmes & Edwards "Dolly Madison", *no monogram, excellent condition*	6.00	7.00
☐ Holmes & Edwards "Dolly Madison", *no monogram, fair condition*	1.00	2.00
☐ Holmes & Edwards "Lovely Lady", *viande style, no monogram, excellent condition*	6.00	7.00
☐ Holmes & Edwards "Lovely Lady", *viande style, no monogram, good condition*	3.00	4.00
☐ Holmes & Edwards "Marina", *no monogram, good condition*	6.00	7.00
☐ Holmes & Edwards "Pageant", *no monogram, excellent condition*	6.00	7.00
☐ Holmes & Edwards "Pageant", *no monogram, fair condition*	1.00	2.00
☐ Oneida "Avalon", *no monogram, excellent condition*	1.00	2.00
☐ Oneida "Flower de Luce", *no monogram, fair condition* . . .	4.00	5.00
☐ Oneida "Flower de Luce", *no monogram, excellent condition*	9.00	11.00
☐ Oneida "Louis XVI", *no monogram, excellent condition* . . .	3.00	4.00
☐ Reed & Barton "Tiger Lily", *monogram, excellent condition*	4.00	5.00
☐ Reed & Barton "Tiger Lily", *no monogram*	6.00	7.00
☐ Reliance "Wildwood", *no monogram, good condition*	5.00	6.00
☐ Reliance "Wildwood", *no monogram, poor condition*	1.00	2.00
☐ Rogers "Alhambra", *no monogram, fair condition*	4.00	5.00
☐ Rogers "Alhambra", *no monogram, excellent condition* . . .	9.00	10.00
☐ Rogers "Queen Bess II", *flat-handled, no monogram, excellent condition*	2.00	3.00
☐ Rogers & Bro. "Cromwell", *no monogram, mint condition* . .	2.00	4.00
☐ Rogers & Bro. "Cromwell", *no monogram, fair condition* . . .	2.00	3.00
☐ Rogers & Bro. "Florette", *no monogram, excellent condition*	2.00	3.00
☐ Rogers & Bro. "Florette", *no monogram, fair condition*	1.00	2.00
☐ Rogers & Hamilton "Marquise", *no monogram, mint condition*	4.00	5.00

Price Range

	Price Range	
☐ Rogers & Hamilton "Marquise", *no monogram, excellent condition*	4.00	5.00
☐ Rogers & Hamilton "Tudor", *no monogram, excellent condition*	9.00	10.00
☐ Rogers & Hamilton "Tudor", *no monogram, good condition*	6.00	7.00
☐ S.L. & G.H. "Daisy", *flat-handled, no monogram, excellent condition*	5.00	6.00
☐ S.L. & G.H. Rogers "Daisy", *flat-handled, no monogram, good condition*	3.00	4.00
☐ S.L. & G.H. Rogers "English Garden", *viande style, monogram, excellent condition*	3.00	4.00
☐ S.L. & G.H. Rogers "Jasmine", *no monogram, excellent condition*	3.00	4.00
☐ S.L. & G.H. Rogers "Jasmine", *no monogram, fair condition*	1.00	2.00
☐ Smith "Iris", *no monogram, fair condition*	2.00	3.00
☐ Smith "Iris", *no monogram, resilvered*	9.00	10.00
☐ Smith "Iris", *no monogram, good condition*	5.00	6.00
☐ Tudor "Mary Stuart", *flat-handled, no monogram, excellent condition*	1.00	2.00
☐ Tudor "Mary Stuart", *flat-handled, no monogram, poor condition*	1.00	2.00
☐ Wm. A. Rogers "Violet", *no monogram, good condition* ...	3.00	4.00
☐ Wm. A. Rogers "Violet", *no monogram, poor condition*	1.00	2.00
☐ Wm. A. Rogers "Violet", *no monogram, excellent condition*	9.00	10.00
☐ Wm. Rogers "Avalon", *no monogram, excellent condition* .	3.00	4.00
☐ Wm. Rogers "Mayfair", *no monogram, excellent condition* .	6.00	7.00
☐ Wm. Rogers "Mayfair", *no monogram*	3.00	4.00
☐ Wm. Rogers "Treasure", *viande style, no monogram, excellent condition*	2.00	3.00
☐ Wm. Rogers "Treasure", *viande style, no monogram, fair condition*	1.00	2.00
☐ Wm. Rogers Mfg. Co. "Berwick", *no monogram, handle in excellent condition, blade in good condition*	4.00	5.00
☐ Wm. Rogers Mfg. Co. "Berwick", *no monogram, excellent condition*	8.00	9.00
☐ Wm. Rogers Mfg. Co. "Berwick", *no monogram, fair condition*	3.00	4.00
☐ Wm. Rogers & Son "LaFrance", *no monogram, excellent condition*	6.00	7.00
☐ Wm. Rogers & Son "LaFrance", *no monogram, good condition*	4.00	5.00
☐ 1835 Wallace "Cardinal", *flat-handled, no monogram, excellent condition*	5.00	6.00
☐ 1835 Wallace "Cardinal", *hollow-handled, no monogram, excellent condition*	8.00	9.00
☐ 1835 Wallace "Floral", *no monogram, handle in excellent condition but needs new blade*	3.00	4.00
☐ 1835 Wallace "Floral", *monogram, excellent condition*	12.00	14.00
☐ 1835 Wallace "Floral", *no monogram, fair condition*	4.00	5.00
☐ 1847 Rogers "Ancestral", *no monogram, good condition* ..	6.00	7.00
☐ 1847 Rogers "Ancestral", *no monogram, excellent condition*	9.00	10.00
☐ 1847 Rogers "Berkshire", *no monogram, good condition* ..	5.00	6.00
☐ 1847 Rogers "Berkshire", *no monogram, resilvered*	10.00	13.00

Price Range

☐ **1847 Rogers "Berkshire"**, *no monogram, excellent condition* 9.00 11.00
☐ **1847 Rogers "Charter Oak"**, *no monogram, excellent condition new blades* 9.00 10.00
☐ **1847 Rogers "Charter Oak"**, *no monogram, excellent condition old style blades in excellent condition* 12.00 14.00
☐ **1847 Rogers "Charter Oak"**, *no monogram, good condition* 8.00 9.00
☐ **1847 Rogers "Charter Oak"**, *monogram, good condition* ... 5.00 6.00
☐ **1847 Rogers "Floral"**, *no monogram, excellent condition* .. 12.00 14.00
☐ **1847 Rogers "Floral"**, *no monogram, excellent condition* .. 11.00 12.00
☐ **1847 Rogers "Heraldic"**, *no monogram, excellent condition* 7.00 8.00
☐ **1847 Rogers "Heraldic"**, *no monogram, good condition* ... 5.00 6.00
☐ **1847 Rogers "Magic Rose"**, *no monogram, excellent condition* 3.00 4.00
☐ **1847 Rogers "Magic Rose"**, *no monogram, fair condition* .. 1.00 2.00
☐ **1847 Rogers "Moselle"**, *no monogram, mint condition* 23.00 25.00
☐ **1847 Rogers "Moselle"**, *no monogram, good condition* ... 12.00 14.00
☐ **1847 Rogers "Moselle"**, *no monogram, fair condition* 7.00 8.00
☐ **1847 Rogers "Old Colony"**, *flat-handled, no monogram, excellent condition* 1.00 2.00
☐ **1847 Rogers "Old Colony"**, *no monogram, fair condition* .. 1.00 2.00
☐ **1847 Rogers "Old Colony"**, *monogram, fair condition* 1.00 2.00
☐ **1847 Rogers "Cromwell"**, *monogram, excellent condition* . 1.00 2.00
☐ **1847 Rogers "Remembrance"**, *viande style, no monogram, mint condition* 5.00 6.00
☐ **1847 Rogers "Remembrance"**, *viande style, no monogram, good condition* 4.00 5.00
☐ **1847 Rogers "Vintage"**, *no monogram, good condition* 10.00 13.00
☐ **1847 Rogers "Vintage"**, *no monogram, excellent condition* 14.00 16.00
☐ **1847 Rogers "Vintage"**, *monogram, good condition* 6.00 7.00
☐ **1847 Rogers "Vintage"**, *no monogram, poor condition* 2.00 3.00
☐ **1847 Rogers "Vintage"**, *no monogram, resilvered, new blades* 14.00 16.00
☐ **1847 Rogers "Vintage"**, *no monogram, handle in excellent condition, blade worn* 9.00 10.00
☐ **1881 Rogers "Coronet"**, *no monogram, good condition, old style blade* 2.00 3.00
☐ **1881 Rogers "Coronet"**, *no monogram, old style blade* 9.00 10.00
☐ **1881 Rogers "Surf Club"**, *viande style, no monogram, excellent condition* 4.00 5.00

(Sterling Silver)

☐ **Alvin "Chateau Rose"**, *no monogram* 14.00 16.00
☐ **Alvin "Majestic"**, *monogram* 16.00 19.00
☐ **Alvin "Old Orange Blossom"**, *monogram and date* 18.00 21.00
☐ **Alvin "Romantique"**, *no monogram* 12.00 14.00
☐ **Dominick & Haff "#10"**, *plated blade, monogram* 6.00 7.00
☐ **Durgin "Chrysanthemum"**, *no monogram* 27.00 30.00
☐ **Frank Smith "Fiddle Thread"**, *no monogram* 20.00 23.00
☐ **Frank Smith "Newport Shell"**, *no monogram* 23.00 25.00
☐ **Frank Smith "Newport Shell"**, *monogram* 18.00 21.00
☐ **Gorham "Buttercup"**, *stainless blade, monogram* 8.00 9.00
☐ **Gorham "Buttercup"**, *old style silver-plated blade in excellent condition, no monogram* 10.00 13.00

	Price Range	
☐ Gorham "Cambridge", *no monogram*	10.00	12.00
☐ Gorham "Camellia", *no monogram*	10.00	13.00
☐ Gorham "Chantilly", *no monogram*	9.00	11.00
☐ Gorham "Chantilly", *old style silver-plated blade in good condition, monogram*	10.00	12.00
☐ Gorham "Chantilly", *old style silver-plated blade in good condition, no monogram*	13.00	15.00
☐ Gorham "Chantilly", *no monogram*	15.00	17.00
☐ Gorham "Greenbrier", *no monogram*	14.00	16.00
☐ Gorham "LaScala", *no monogram*	15.00	17.00
☐ Gorham "Versailles", *old style blade in good condition, no monogram*	18.00	21.00
☐ Gorham "Willow", *no monogram*	10.00	13.00
☐ International "Bridal Veil", *no monogram*	12.00	14.00
☐ International "Courtship", *no monogram*	10.00	13.00
☐ International "Courtship", *no monogram*	12.00	14.00
☐ International "Frontenac", *monogram and date*	20.00	23.00
☐ International "Frontenac", *stainless blade, monogram*	9.00	11.00
☐ International "Pine Tree", *no monogram*	12.00	15.00
☐ International "Royal Danish", *no monogram*	14.00	16.00
☐ International "Royal Danish", *monogram*	9.00	11.00
☐ International "Silver Melody", *no monogram*	14.00	16.00
☐ International "Stratford", *monogram*	10.00	12.00
☐ International "Swan Lake", *no monogram*	10.00	13.00
☐ International "Wild Rose", *no monogram*	10.00	13.00
☐ Kirk "Repousse", *old style blade, no monogram*	16.00	18.00
☐ Kirk "Repousse", *9" L., monogram*	15.00	17.00
☐ Lunt "Eloquence", *no monogram*	15.00	17.00
☐ Lunt "Mount Vernon", *old style silver-plated blade in bad condition, monogram*	6.00	7.00
☐ Lunt "Mount Vernon", *monogram*	14.00	16.00
☐ Lunt "Sweetheart", *no monogram*	10.00	12.00
☐ Manchester "Vogue", *no monogram*	12.00	14.00
☐ Oneida "Belle Rose", *no monogram*	10.00	12.00
☐ Oneida "Lasting Spring", *no monogram*	11.00	13.00
☐ Oneida "Lasting Spring", *no monogram*	11.00	13.00
☐ Reed & Barton "Francis I", *no monogram*	18.00	20.00
☐ Reed & Barton "Francis I", *no monogram*	10.00	12.00
☐ Reed & Barton "Hampton Court", *no monogram*	12.00	14.00
☐ Royal Crest "Castle Rose", *no monogram*	12.00	14.00
☐ Simpson, Hall & Miller "Frontenac", *old style silver-plated blade in good condition, no monogram*	16.00	18.00
☐ Stieff "Rose", *old style blade, no monogram*	8.00	9.00
☐ Tiffany "Colonial", *old style silver-plated blade in excellent condition, no monogram*	22.00	24.00
☐ Towle "Chippendale", *no monogram*	12.00	14.00
☐ Towle "French Provincial", *no monogram*	12.00	14.00
☐ Towle "Kings", *no monogram*	22.00	24.00
☐ Towle "Laureate",	14.00	16.00
☐ Towle "Silver Flutes", *no monogram*	12.00	14.00
☐ Towle "Vespera", *no monogram*	12.00	14.00
☐ Wallace "Rosepoint", *monogram, 9" L.*	9.00	11.00
☐ Wallace "Violet", *stainless blade, no monogram*	11.00	13.00

Price Range

- ☐ **Wallace "Washington"**, *old style silver-plated blade in good condition, monogram* 9.00   11.00
- ☐ **Westmoreland "John & Priscilla"**, *no monogram* 14.00   16.00
- ☐ **Westmoreland "Milburn Rose"**, *no monogram* 14.00   16.00
- ☐ **Whiting "Imperial Queen"**, *no monogram* 10.00   12.00
- ☐ **Whiting "King Edward"**, *plated blade fair condition monogram* 6.00   7.00
- ☐ **Whiting "Lily"**, *silver plated blade in fair condition monogram* 32.00   35.00
- ☐ **Whiting "Louis XV"**, *plated blade monogram* 6.00   7.00
- ☐ **Whiting "Madame Jumel"**, *monogram* 14.00   16.00

MACARONI SERVERS

Don't confuse macaroni with spaghetti: these were made for dishing out things like "elbows" and other macaroni favorites, from serving bowl to plate. They're of large size and considerable bullion content, but generally are not in the "melt" or "scrap" class because of their collector premium value. Macaroni servers come in many styles, having in common the pierced bowl (which accomplished a final draining, if the initial draining in the kitchen had been incomplete). Sometimes the bowl is covered in gold wash, as gold color was considered a better contrast against the stark whiteness of macaroni than was silver.

(Silver-Plated)

- ☐ **1847 Rogers "Vintage"**, *monogram and date, good condition* 40.00   45.00
- ☐ **Maker unknown**, *Art Nouveau floral design, no monogram, good condition* 32.00   36.00

(Sterling Silver)

- ☐ **Gorham "Rouen"**, *no monogram, gold wash bowl* 60.00   65.00

MATCH SAFES

A match safe is simply a carrying case for wooden matches. These are very small — designed to slip into the pocket — and were almost as abundant at one time as cigarette lighters are today. They began to be made in large quantity around 1880 when packaged cigarettes became popular and continued well into the 20th century. Collectors are most interested in the older specimens and those carrying especially handsome designs. Monograms are of course common on match safes, as are full names and even engraved heraldic designs. Scenic and other engravings are likewise found. Jewelers usually bought these plain (at very low wholesale prices, in batches) and added the lid engravings themselves, thereby enabling them to retail at a steep mark-up. Since the engravings are all hand work, they vary a great deal in artistic quality and choice of subject matter. Some have lid insets of other materials: tortoise-shell, bone, jade, mother-of-pearl, even hand-painted ivory.

Match Safe, *maker unknown,*
beaver motif lid,
maple leaf motif container,
shield for initials, 250.00

(Sterling Silver)	**Price Range**	
☐ **Gorham,** *engraved floral design all over, monogram*	22.00	24.00
☐ **Kirk,** *Art Nouveau design all over, no monogram*	30.00	33.00
☐ **Kirk,** *plain design, no monogram, 1⁵/₈″, no monogram*	18.00	21.00
☐ **Kirk "Repousse",** *no monogram, 2¼″*	23.00	27.00
☐ **Tiffany,** *plain design, monogram*	22.00	25.00
☐ **Maker unknown,** *embossed floral design, no monogram* ...	22.00	24.00
☐ **Maker unknown,** *plain design, monogram*	8.00	9.00
☐ **Maker unknown,** *dated 1885, all over engraving in scroll and*		
floral design, monogram	18.00	21.00

MIRRORS

In ancient times, before the invention of glass mirrors, mirrors were made wholly of metal — either copper or silver — and served the purpose surprisingly well (in fact some specimens are still reflective, when dug from archaeological sites!) The silver mirrors listed here are the hand-held variety (wall mirrors in silver were made, but are far less plentiful). The large reverse side provided a superb vehicle for decoration, and makers took every advantage of it. Many specimens have designs in high relief, with detailed work of a very excellent quality. The artistic merits count very much toward the value, as does total silver content. If possible the glass should be removed for weighing, but, usually, this cannot be done and hence the mirror's exact bullion content can only be estimated. Old silver mirrors will often need a careful cleaning, as grime is apt to have imbedded itself into the recesses of the design. The more complex the design, the more difficult it will be to remove built-up grime.

(Silver-Plated)	**Price Range**	
☐ **Maker unknown,** *Art Nouveau lady with flowing hair, original mirror in fair condition, plating in good condition, no monogram*	25.00	27.00
☐ **Maker unknown,** *Art Nouveau lady with cherub, original mirror in excellent condition, plating in excellent condition* ...	54.00	60.00
(Sterling Silver)		
☐ **Tiffany,** *plain design, no monogram, 9" x 12"*	60.00	65.00
☐ **Tiffany,** *plain design, no monogram, 9" x 12½"*	70.00	80.00

MUFFINEERS

Muffineer, *(sterling), Gorham,* 4 ounces, 105.00

(Silver-Plated)		
☐ **Maker unknown,** *ornate floral embossed design, gold wash lid, monogram and date (1902), excellent condition*	27.00	30.00
☐ **Maker unknown,** *plain Georgian styling, monogram, good condition*	14.00	16.00
(Sterling Silver)		
☐ **Maker unknown,** *Greek key design, monogram*	38.00	42.00

MUGS

Ceramic has been far more popular for mugs, even among those who could afford the best. Juvenile and souvenir types will be found.

(Silver-Plated)   Price Range

- ☐ **Meriden,** *baby chicks engraved around, child size, 3" H.,
  good condition* 23.00   25.00
- ☐ **Meriden,** *gold wash interior, monogram, child's size* 8.00   9.00
- ☐ **Oneida,** *etch design, child's size, good condition* 6.00   7.00
- ☐ **Oneida,** *plain design, no monogram, child's size, good con-
  dition* 3.00   4.00
- ☐ **Maker unknown,** *monogram, child's size, 2¾" x 2¼"* 8.00   9.00
- ☐ **Maker unknown,** *"Mary Had a Little Lamb" motif, child's
  size, good condition* 11.00   13.00

(Sterling Silver)

- ☐ **International,** *plain design, monogram and date, gold wash
  interior, child's size* 25.00   27.00

MUSH SETS

The traditional christening gift of yesteryear was a mush set. It was to be put aside until the child got a bit older, and could enjoy the delights of *mush.* Called gruel in Britain, mush was the all-purpose term for cooked cereals: farina, oatmeal and the like. Mush sets consisted of (at the least) a bowl and saucer, sometimes with the addition of a mug. They reached their apex of popularity in the late 1800's and were often decorated with nursery-rhyme motifs or other illustrations — designed of course to take baby's mind off the tasteless food he was being fed.

(Silver-Plated)

- ☐ **Wm. A. Rogers,** *includes plate and bowl, decorated with
  alphabet and "Hey, Diddle, Diddle" verse, good condition* . 80.00   90.00
- ☐ **Maker unknown,** *includes mug, plate and bowl, decorated
  with "Mary Had a Little Lamb" scene and verse, child's first
  name and date (1899), excellent condition* 78.00   85.00
- ☐ **Maker unknown,** *includes mug, plate and bowl, plain
  design, child's first name, fair condition* 16.00   18.00

MUSTACHE CUPS

In the second half of the 19th century American males of all ages took to growing mustaches. The common practice then was to use mustache wax, and this presented some inconvenience when drinking from an ordinary cup: a soggy mustache and wax in one's beverage. Necessity being the mother of invention, the *mustache cup* was developed: an ordinary drinking cup with an insert at the top, designed to keep mustache and beverage from contacting each other. These were normally made of ceramic but some in silver will be located. The insert will either be fixed, or reversable to suit a righthanded or lefthanded person. Mustache cups (silver and others) are a hobby in themselves, and have been popular on the collecting beat for many years. Therefore the prices are not in line with those of other silver drinking vessels: you are paying a premium because of the overall demand.

(Sterling Silver)

- ☐ **Maker Unknown,** *insert can be switched to make cup right
  or left-handed, monogram* 68.00   75.00

NAPKIN RINGS

The collectors of napkin rings are legion, and have been active for many, many years. Napkin rings are found in a variety of materials, silver being only one of them: stainless steel, bone, ivory, wood, tortoise-shell, etc. Prices are higher on silver napkin rings than on most silver objects of comparable size and ornament, because of the collector activity. It is an ideal group for specialization, thanks to the diversity of designs, the minimal storage space required, and the obvious display potential. Napkin rings fitted over tightly rolled cloth napkins and were standard fare in the place settings of one to three generations ago. They were not only sold individually but in sets, sometimes in velvet lined boxes. When the box is present and well preserved this adds to the value. The auction scene is well worth watching if you collect silver napkin rings: occasionally a big collection goes up for sale.

Napkin Rings, *coin silver, maker unknown, pair in original box,* 180.00

(Silver-Plated)	Price Range	
☐ **Barbour,** *rectangular base with applied flowers and leaves*	100.00	115.00
☐ **Derby,** *figural, bird and egg and wishbone, 1¾" H., 3¼" L., excellent condition*	70.00	76.00
☐ **Derby,** *figural, bird holding ring on its wings*	90.00	100.00
☐ **Derby,** *figural, rectangular base with applied leaves and branches, fox holding ring on its back, good condition*	100.00	100.00
☐ **Derby,** *figural, square base with four ball feet, saddle forms ring, polo mallets at each corner, applied leaves on top* ...	120.00	135.00
☐ **Hamilton,** *figural, sitting bear holding ring in its arms, good condition*	105.00	120.00
☐ **Mayo,** *ring held by ocean waves*	120.00	135.00
☐ **Meriden,** *figural, ring on back of sphinx*	75.00	85.00
☐ **Meriden,** *nude cherub in top hat*	90.00	100.00

Price Range

☐ **Meriden,** *figural, large pheasant on its side* . . . . | 100.00 | 110.00
☐ **Meriden,** *figural, griffin holding ring* . . . . | 60.00 | 68.00
☐ **Meriden,** *figure, kneeling child holding ring on knee* . . . . . . | 45.00 | 50.00
☐ **Middleton,** *figural, cherub holding ring* . . . . | 100.00 | 110.00
☐ **Rockford,** *figural, ring on top of bird's tail, cherub sitting on ring holding silver reins from bird's mouth* . . . . | 200.00 | 225.00
☐ **Rockford,** *figural, vase by side of ring, woman standing next to vase* . . . . | 135.00 | 150.00
☐ **Rockford,** *figural, rectangular base raised on four ball feet, leaves and flower bud along side of ring, bug on flower bud* | 100.00 | 110.00
☐ **Sampson,** *figural, two fans holding the ring, engraved work on fans* . . . . | 80.00 | 90.00
☐ **Tufts,** *figural, dog standing by side of ring, rectangular base* . . . . | 105.00 | 120.00
☐ **Tufts ,** *figural, baby in cradle, excellent condition* . . . . | 225.00 | 250.00
☐ **Tufts ,** *figural, mouse by side of ring, rectangular base* . . . . | 110.00 | 125.00
☐ **Wilcox,** *figural, oval base with scalloped rim, raised on four ball feet, two foxes on either side of ring reaching for bunch of grapes on top of ring, excellent condition* . . . . | 130.00 | 145.00
☐ **Wilcox,** *figural, ring on top of sled* . . . . | 75.00 | 85.00
☐ **Wilcox,** *figural, oval base with scalloped edge, raised on four ball feet, two cherubs sitting on either side of the ring* . | 105.00 | 120.00
☐ **Wilcox,** *ring mounted on 8" long tray, engraved "Best Wishes" with an applied wishbone, excellent condition* . . . | 36.00 | 40.00
☐ **Maker unknown,** *figural, ring on back of hunting dog, dog has bird in its mouth, excellent condition* . . . . | 56.00 | 62.00
☐ **Maker unknown,** *figural, bird on perch, $3^7/_8$" tall* . . . . | 60.00 | 68.00
☐ **Maker unknown,** *figural, standing goat* . . . . | 75.00 | 85.00
☐ **Maker unknown,** *figural, cherub with bird* . . . . | 60.00 | 68.00
☐ **Maker unknown,** *figural, lily pad with bud* . . . . | 36.00 | 40.00
☐ **Maker unknown,** *figural, eagle, good condition* . . . . | 38.00 | 42.00
☐ **Maker unknown,** *figural, emu and kangaroo* . . . . | 60.00 | 68.00
☐ **Maker unknown,** *figural, baby chicks on either side of ring, footed base* . . . . | 105.00 | 120.00
☐ **Maker unknown,** *figural, stag with ring on its back, 3¾" H.* | 100.00 | 110.00
☐ **Maker unknown, Kate Greenaway,** *good condition* . . . . | 80.00 | 90.00
☐ **Maker unknown,** *figural, squirrel eating nuts* . . . . | 60.00 | 68.00
☐ **Maker unknown,** *figural, stork, excellent condition* . . . . | 54.00 | 60.00
☐ **Maker unknown,** *figural, sitting dog with glass eyes, chasing on rings* . . . . | 60.00 | 68.00
☐ **Maker unknown,** *figural, young girl with fish in a basket, paddle base, 7½" H., good condition* . . . . | 210.00 | 235.00
☐ **Maker unknown,** *figural, rabbit playing horn, resilvered* . . . . | 120.00 | 135.00
☐ **Maker unknown,** *figural, small dog houses on either side of ring, dogs peering out of houses, good condition* . . . . | 68.00 | 75.00
☐ **Maker unknown,** *figural, mouse on top of ring, ring shaped like cheese barrel* . . . . | 100.00 | 110.00
☐ **Maker unknown,** *figural, ring on seat of chair* . . . . | 80.00 | 90.00
☐ **Maker unknown,** *figural, leaf base, cherub by side of ring, butterfly on top of the ring, good condition* . . . . | 140.00 | 155.00
☐ **Maker unknown,** *figural, large horseshoe* . . . . | 40.00 | 45.00
☐ **Maker unknown,** *figural, small horseshoe, engraved "Good Luck"* . . . . | 40.00 | 45.00

Price Range

☐ **Maker unknown,** *figural, tennis racquet leaning against ring, tennis ball on top good condition* 58.00   63.00
☐ **Maker unknown,** *figural, two wishbones supporting ring, engraved "Best Wishes", excellent condition* 54.00   60.00
☐ **Maker unknown,** *dog with ring on its back* 90.00   100.00
☐ **Maker unknown,** *figural, pageboys holding trumpets* 100.00   115.00
☐ **Maker unknown,** *figural, cherub standing by side of ring* ... 72.00   80.00
☐ **Maker unknown,** *figural, parrot by side of ring* 100.00   110.00
☐ **Maker unknown,** *figural, horseshoe by side of ring* 65.00   72.00
☐ **Maker unknown,** *figural, lily and pad by side of ring, leaf base* 80.00   90.00
☐ **Maker unknown,** *rope borders and engraved with first name* 8.00   9.00
☐ **Maker unknown,** *applied flowers and leaves* 33.00   36.00
☐ **Maker unknown,** *engraved with llama, good condition* 18.00   20.00
☐ **Maker unknown,** *baby's engraved with Mary and little lamb* 8.00   9.00

(Sterling Silver)

☐ **Gorham,** *overall embossed floral design, engraved with first name* 24.00   27.00
☐ **Gorham,** *embossed floral borders, engraved with first name* 19.00   21.00
☐ **Lebolt,** *rectangular shape, monogram* 25.00   28.00
☐ **Marshall Field retailer, maker unknown,** *rectangular shape, raised monogram* 25.00   28.00
☐ **Randahl,** *oval shape, no monogram* 25.00   28.00
☐ **Randahl,** *oval shape, monogram* 24.00   27.00
☐ **Stieff "Rose",** *all over repousse work, no monogram* 27.00   30.00
☐ **Stieff "Rose",** *c. 1925, hand-chased repousse design, monogram* 24.00   27.00
☐ **Tiffany,** *plain, round shape, monogram* 12.00   14.00
☐ **Unger Bros. "Love's Dream",** *medallion design monogram* . 68.00   75.00
☐ **Unger Bros. "Love's Dream",** *no monogram* 65.00   72.00
☐ **Maker unknown,** *applied flowers* 33.00   37.00
☐ **Maker unknown,** *rope borders, chasing and engraving with bright-cut floral work, engraved with woman's first name* .. 19.00   21.00
☐ **Maker unknown,** *chasing and engraving in pseudo-Arabic style, engraved with first name* 19.00   21.00
☐ **Maker unknown,** *banding of raised tiny shield on borders, engraved floral designs, engraved woman's first name* 20.00   22.00
☐ **Maker unknown,** *banding of raised tiny shields on borders, engraved floral designs, engraved woman's first name* 18.00   20.00
☐ **Maker unknown,** *banding of raised small flowers on border, engraved with woman's first name* 16.00   18.00
☐ **Maker unknown,** *braided borders, overall engraving and chasing in geometric and floral patterns, engraved with first name* 22.00   25.00
☐ **Maker unknown,** *oval shape, plain, narrow, monogram* 5.00   6.00
☐ **Maker unknown,** *square shape, hammered finish, engraved with first name* 13.00   15.00

NUT DISHES

Nuts were treated a good deal more ceremoniously by our ancestors than they are today: placed into ornate dishes rather than cello vending-machine bags. There was no standard size, style or shape for silver nut dishes — a boon of course for the collector, as this means more variety. Of course, none of them reached huge proportions — several inches across the bowl is large for any specimen. Usually they were mounted on pedestal bases, for no other reason than that the classical revival was in swing during the Victoria age. Classicism meant pedestaled bases wherever possible, on furniture too! Some of the Tiffany silver nut dishes are a pure delight, but prices are not for the budget-minded.

Nut Dish, *(sterling), Tiffany, Union Square markings,* 325.00

(Silver-Plated)	Price Range	
☐ **Beacon Silver Company,** *squirrel on erose rim, pedestal base, 2¼″ Dia.*	20.00	22.00
☐ **Meriden,** *nut dish, silver-plated, pierced design, no monogram, good condition*	9.00	11.00
(Sterling Silver)		
☐ **Gorham,** *plain octagonal shape, set of four, monogram*	45.00	50.00
☐ **Gorham,** *repousse floral design, no monogram*	13.00	15.00

NUT PICKS

These are small toothpick-like devices, sharply pointed at the tip, with which nuts were speared from the nut *dish* (see above entry). Though extensively made, they were not 100% effective with all types of nuts. The more solid kinds, such as Brazils, repulsed all efforts at spearing and had to be picked up in other ways. Nut picks are usually collected only by those specializing in nut accessories. They display very nicely and are no trouble in terms of space.

(Silver-Plated)	Price Range	
☐ Gorham "Empire", *no monogram, excellent condition*	2.00	3.00
☐ Hartford "Lyonnaise", *no monogram, excellent condition* .	2.00	3.00
☐ Reed & Barton "Gem", *no monogram, excellent condition* .	8.00	9.00
☐ Reed & Barton "Pearl", *no monogram, excellent condition* .	9.00	11.00
☐ Reed & Barton "Tiger Lily", *no monogram, excellent condition*	8.00	9.00
☐ Rogers "Princess", *no monogram, excellent condition*	3.00	4.00
☐ Rogers & Bro. "Flemish", *no monogram, excellent condition*	8.00	9.00
☐ S.L. & G.H. Rogers "Princess", *no monogram, excellent condition*	14.00	16.00
☐ 1847 Rogers "Assyrian", *no monogram, excellent condition*	5.00	6.00
☐ 1847 Rogers "Crown", *no monogram, excellent condition* .	3.00	4.00
☐ 1847 Rogers "Dundee", *no monogram, excellent condition*	3.00	4.00
☐ 1847 Rogers "Embossed", *no monogram, excellent condition*	6.00	7.00
☐ 1847 Rogers "Embossed", *no monogram, excellent condition*	3.00	4.00
☐ 1847 Rogers "Laurel", *no monogram, excellent condition* ..	4.00	5.00
☐ 1847 Rogers "Old Colony", *no monogram, good condition* .	7.00	8.00
☐ 1847 Rogers "Olive", *monogram, excellent condition*	5.00	6.00
☐ 1847 Rogers "Persian", *monogram, excellent condition* ...	5.00	6.00
☐ 1847 Rogers "Persian", *no monogram, excellent condition*	6.00	7.00
☐ 1847 Rogers "Saratoga", *no monogram, excellent condition*	3.00	4.00
(Sterling Silver)		
☐ Gorham "Ivy", *c. 1867, no monogram, set of six*	52.00	57.00
☐ Gorham "Versailles", *no monogram*	22.00	24.00
☐ Towle "Old Newbury", *no monogram*	8.00	9.00
☐ Maker unknown, *sterling silver and mother of pearl, set of 12*	30.00	33.00

NUT SETS

These include a nut scoop, nut picks, and (sometimes but not always) nut dish(es) and spoons. Their relative scarcity, compared against the big popularity of nuts in earlier days, shows that most people preferred to assemble their own sets rather than buying them off the counter.

(Sterling Silver)		
☐ Tiffany, *squirrel on end of rustic handle picks, ends are gold washed, 5" L., with 12" nut scoop with similar design, total weight 22 oz., no monogram*	650.00	720.00

NUT SPOONS

Also (and really more descriptively) called nut *scoops,* these served to transfer nuts from a storage container to nut *dishes.* They were not used in eating nuts, and therefore the term *spoon* can be confusing. The bowls are wide, not too deep but with rather tall sides to prevent spillout. They encompass numerous designs, including heart shaped, shell, etc. Some nut spoon bowls are solid, others enhanced with pierced-work ornament. Nut spoons have a strong collector following. The short handles should insure against anyone mistaking them for ladles.

Nut Spoons, *(L to R) (sterling), Gorham "Mythologique",* 18.00; *Tiffany floral pattern,* 40.00; *Whiting "Imperial Queen",* 21.00

(Silver-Plated)

	Price Range	
☐ **Community "Coronation",** *no monogram, excellent condition*	7.00	8.00
☐ **Community "Coronation",** *monogram, good condition*	2.00	3.00
☐ **Community "Milady",** *no monogram, excellent condition*	9.00	10.00
☐ **Gorham "King",** *monogram, good condition*	3.00	4.00
☐ **National "King Edward",** *no monogram, excellent condition*	8.00	9.00
☐ **National "Rose & Leaf",** *no monogram, excellent condition*	7.00	8.00
☐ **William Bros. "Queen Elizabeth",** *no monogram, excellent condition*	4.00	5.00
☐ **Wm. A. Rogers "Rendezvous",** *no monogram, excellent condition*	9.00	10.00
☐ **1847 Rogers "Berkshire",** *no monogram, good condition*	5.00	6.00
☐ **1847 Rogers "Berkshire",** *no monogram, mint condition*	12.00	14.00
☐ **1847 Rogers "Persian",** *no monogram, resilvered*	11.00	13.00
☐ **1847 Rogers "Vintage",** *no monogram, mint condition*	9.00	11.00
☐ **1847 Rogers "Vintage",** *monogram*	5.00	6.00

(Sterling Silver)

☐ **Durgin "Chrysanthemum",** *bad monogram removal*	16.00	18.00
☐ **Gorham "Chantilly",** *no monogram*	22.00	24.00
☐ **Gorham "King George",** *gold wash bowl, no monogram*	20.00	22.00
☐ **Stieff "Rose",** *no monogram*	22.00	24.00

OLIVE FORKS

Olive forks have two tines, sometimes of ordinary fork style and sometimes shaped as arrow points at the tips. This latter style arose as an effort to keep the olive from slipping off the fork.

(Silver-Plated)

		Price Range
☐ **Alvin "Bride's Bouquet"**, *long-handled, no monogram, excellent condition*	10.00	12.00
☐ **Community "Patrician"**, *no monogram, excellent condition*	7.00	8.00
☐ **Smith "Iris"**, *no monogram, excellent condition*	6.00	7.00
☐ **Wm. A. Rogers "Elmore"**, *no monogram, excellent condition*	3.00	4.00
☐ **Wm. Rogers "Arbutus"**, *no monogram, excellent condition*	8.00	9.00
☐ **1847 Rogers "Lotus"**, *no monogram, excellent condition* ..	9.00	11.00

(Sterling Silver)

☐ **Wallace "Number 80"**, *no monogram*	12.00	14.00
☐ **Maker Unknown**, *floral repousse design, no monogram* ...	12.00	14.00

OLIVE SETS

An olive *set* consisted (almost always) of one spoon and one fork, enclosed in a box. This was chiefly a gift item, for individuals who already owned a table service in that pattern but lacked olive utensils. When one or the other is missing, you can calculate the value as that of the remaining specimen and forget about the box.

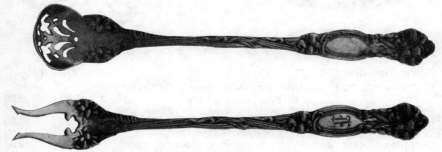

Olive and Pickle Set, *Tiffany "Wave Edge"*, 120.00

(Silver-Plated)

☐ **1847 Rogers "Vintage"**, *fork and spoon in original box, no monogram, mint condition*	33.00	36.00

OLIVE SPOONS

Olive spoons made of silver are very ornate and intriguing to collect. Unfortunately there are not a great deal of them on the market. The bowls take many shapes, but all have in common the traditional pierced-work, which allowed the olive to be picked up without any accompanying juices. Not only do they vary in bowl styles but in overall length.

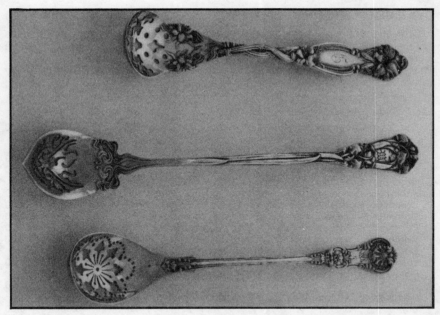

Olive Spoons, *(T to B) (sterling), Simpson, Hall & Miller "Frontenac",* 40.00; *Durgin "Iris", 48.00; Tiffany "English King", 60.00*

(Silver-Plated)	Price Range	
☐ **Benedict Mfg. Co. "Continental"**, *no monogram, excellent condition*	14.00	16.00
☐ **Community "Patrician"**, *no monogram, excellent condition*	3.00	4.00
☐ **Rockford "Fairoaks"**, *long handled, no monogram, excellent condition*	3.00	4.00
☐ **Wm. Rogers "Ashland"**, *long handled, no monogram, excellent condition*	6.00	7.00
☐ **1847 Rogers "Vintage"**, *long handled, no monogram, mint condition*	63.00	70.00

(Sterling Silver)		
☐ **Durgin "Fairfax"**, *pierced, no monogram*	16.00	18.00
☐ **Durgin "Fairfax"**, *gold wash bowl, pierced, monogram*	20.00	23.00
☐ **Gorham "Chantilly"**, *long handled, no monogram*	24.00	27.00
☐ **International "Wedgwood"**, *no monogram*	15.00	17.00
☐ **Kirk "Repousse"**, *pierced bowl, no monogram*	30.00	33.00
☐ **Lunt "Monticello"**, *monogram*	35.00	38.00
☐ **Stieff "Rose"**, *pierced, no monogram*	12.00	14.00
☐ **Towle "Canterbury"**, *gold wash pierced bowl, no monogram, 8¾" L.*	24.00	27.00
☐ **Towle "Windsor (Plain)"**, *pierced, monogram*	13.00	15.00
☐ **Unger Bros. "Narcissus"**, *bowl, no monogram, 6¼" L.*	24.00	27.00
☐ **Whiting "Louis XV"**, *no monogram*	16.00	18.00

OVAL SOUP SPOONS

One of mankind's oldest foods, soup was drunk for thousands of years before etiquette reared its head and brought forth the soup spoon. These were of course manufactured in profuse numbers, as they continue to be. There is no way of completing a collection of this kind, but the opportunity to make fresh discoveries and build a really large collection is a strong inducement.

	Price Range	
(Coin Silver)		
☐ **Deming & Gundlach,** *Hartford, Connecticut, monogram* ...	18.00	20.00
(Silver Plated)		
☐ **Alvin "Diana",** *no monogram, excellent condition*	5.00	6.00
☐ **Alvin "Diana",** *no monogram, good condition*	4.00	5.00
☐ **American Silver Co. "Moselle",** *no monogram, excellent condition*	10.00	13.00
☐ **Community "Adam",** *no monogram, excellent condition* ..	3.00	4.00
☐ **Community "Adam",** *no monogram, good condition*	3.00	4.00
☐ **Community "Avalon",** *no monogram, good condition*	4.00	5.00
☐ **Community "Avalon",** *no monogram, fair condition*	1.00	2.00
☐ **Community "Bird of Paradise",** *no monogram, excellent condition*	5.00	6.00
☐ **Community "Bird of Paradise",** *no monogram, good condition*	3.00	4.00
☐ **Community "Coronation",** *no monogram, excellent condition*	5.00	6.00
☐ **Community "Coronation",** *no monogram, good condition* .	4.00	5.00
☐ **Community "Coronation",** *no monogram, mint condition* ..	4.00	5.00
☐ **Community "Coronation",** *no monogram, poor condition* ..	1.00	2.00
☐ **Community "Evening Star",** *no monogram, excellent condition*	5.00	6.00
☐ **Community "Evening Star",** *no monogram, excellent condition*	1.00	2.00
☐ **Community "Forever",** *no monogram, excellent condition* .	5.00	6.00
☐ **Community "Forever",** *no monogram, good condition*	4.00	5.00
☐ **Community "Forever",** *no monogram, fair condition*	1.00	2.00
☐ **Community "Georgian",** *no monogram, excellent condition*	5.00	6.00
☐ **Community "Georgian",** *no monogram, good condition* ...	4.00	5.00
☐ **Community "King Cedric",** *no monogram, excellent condition*	5.00	6.00
☐ **Community "King Cedric",** *no monogram, good condition* .	4.00	5.00
☐ **Community "King Cedric",** *no monogram, fair condition* ..	1.00	2.00
☐ **Community "Lady Hamilton",** *no monogram, excellent condition*	5.00	6.00
☐ **Community "Lady Hamilton",** *no monogram, good condition*	4.00	5.00
☐ **Community "Lady Hamilton",** *no monogram, good condition*	5.00	6.00
☐ **Community "Milady",** *no monogram, excellent condition* ..	5.00	6.00
☐ **Community "Milady",** *no monogram, good condition*	4.00	5.00
☐ **Community "Milady",** *no monogram, fair condition*	1.00	2.00
☐ **Community "Morning Star",** *no monogram, excellent condition*	5.00	6.00
☐ **Community "Morning Star",** *no monogram, good condition*	4.00	5.00

	Price Range	
☐ Community **"Morning Star"**, *no monogram, poor condition*	1.00	2.00
☐ Community **"Morning Star"**, *no monogram, fair condition* .	1.00	2.00
☐ Community **"Noblesse"**, *no monogram, excellent condition*	5.00	6.00
☐ Community **"Noblesse"**, *no monogram, good condition* ...	4.00	5.00
☐ Community **"Noblesse"**, *monogram, excellent condition* ..	1.00	2.00
☐ Community **"Patrician"**, *no monogram, excellent condition*	5.00	6.00
☐ Community **"Patrician"**, *no monogram, good condition* ...	4.00	5.00
☐ Community **"Patrician"**, *no monogram, fair condition*	1.00	2.00
☐ Community **"Silver Flowers"**, *no monogram, excellent condition*	5.00	6.00
☐ Community **"Silver Flowers"**, *no monogram, good condition*	4.00	5.00
☐ Community **"Silver Sands"**, *no monogram, mint condition* .	6.00	7.00
☐ Community **"Silver Sands"**, *no monogram, excellent condition*	5.00	6.00
☐ Community **"Silver Sands"**, *no monogram, good condition*	4.00	5.00
☐ Community **"Silver Sands"**, *no monogram, fair condition* ..	1.00	2.00
☐ Community **"Silver Sands"**, *monogram, excellent condition*	2.00	3.00
☐ Community **"South Seas"**, *no monogram, mint condition* ..	4.00	5.00
☐ Community **"South Seas"**, *no monogram, excellent condition*	5.00	6.00
☐ Community **"South Seas"**, *no monogram, good condition* .	4.00	5.00
☐ Community **"White Orchid"**, *no monogram, excellent condition*	5.00	6.00
☐ Community **"White Orchid"**, *no monogram, good condition*	4.00	5.00
☐ Community **"White Orchid"**, *no monogram, fair condition* .	1.00	2.00
☐ Court **"Court"**, *no monogram, excellent condition*	2.00	3.00
☐ DeepSilver **"Laurel Mist"**, *no monogram, excellent condition*	5.00	6.00
☐ DeepSilver **"Laurel Mist"**, *no monogram, good condition* ..	4.00	5.00
☐ Gorham **"New Elegance"**, *no monogram, excellent condition*	5.00	6.00
☐ Gorham **"New Elegance"**, *no monogram, good condition* ..	4.00	5.00
☐ Gorham **"Regent"**, *no monogram, excellent condition*	4.00	5.00
☐ Gorham **"Regent"**, *no monogram, excellent condition*	5.00	6.00
☐ Gorham **"Royal"**, *monogram, excellent condition*	2.00	3.00
☐ Holmes, Booth & Hayden **"Japanese"**, *no monogram, fair condition*	1.00	2.00
☐ Holmes & Edwards **"Carolina"**, *no monogram, excellent condition*	5.00	6.00
☐ Holmes & Edwards **"Carolina"**, *no monogram, good condition*	4.00	5.00
☐ Holmes & Edwards **"Century"**, *no monogram, excellent condition*	5.00	6.00
☐ Holmes & Edwards **"Century"**, *no monogram, good condition*	4.00	5.00
☐ Holmes & Edwards **"Century"**, *no monogram, fair condition*	1.00	2.00
☐ Holmes & Edwards **"Charm"**, *no monogram, excellent condition*	5.00	6.00
☐ Holmes & Edwards **"Charm"**, *no monogram, good condition*	4.00	5.00
☐ Holmes & Edwards **"Charm"**, *no monogram, fair condition*	1.00	2.00

	Price Range	
☐ **Holmes & Edwards "Danish Princess"**, *no monogram, excellent condition*	5.00	6.00
☐ **Holmes & Edwards "Danish Princess"**, *no monogram, excellent condition*	4.00	5.00
☐ **Holmes & Edwards "Danish Princess"**, *no monogram, good condition*	3.00	4.00
☐ **Holmes & Edwards "First Lady"**, *no monogram, excellent condition*	5.00	6.00
☐ **Holmes & Edwards "First Lady"**, *no monogram, good condition*	4.00	5.00
☐ **Holmes & Edwards "Lovely Lady"**, *no monogram, excellent condition*	5.00	6.00
☐ **Holmes & Edwards "Lovely Lady"**, *monogram, excellent condition*	2.00	3.00
☐ **Holmes & Edwards "Lovely Lady"**, *no monogram, good condition*	4.00	5.00
☐ **Holmes & Edwards "Lovely Lady"**, *no monogram, fair condition*	1.00	2.00
☐ **Holmes & Edwards "Pageant"**, *no monogram, excellent condition*	5.00	6.00
☐ **Holmes & Edwards "Pageant"**, *no monogram, good condition*	4.00	5.00
☐ **Holmes & Edwards "Rosemary"**, *no monogram, excellent condition*	2.00	3.00
☐ **Holmes & Edwards "Spring Garden"**, *no monogram, excellent condition*	5.00	6.00
☐ **Holmes & Edwards "Spring Garden"**, *no monogram, good condition*	4.00	5.00
☐ **Holmes & Edwards "Spring Garden"**, *no monogram, fair condition*	1.00	2.00
☐ **International "Silver Tulip"**, *no monogram, excellent condition*	4.00	5.00
☐ **Nobility "Royal Rose"**, *no monogram, excellent condition* .	5.00	6.00
☐ **Nobility "Royal Rose"**, *no monogram, good condition*	4.00	5.00
☐ **Nobility "Windsong"**, *no monogram, excellent condition* ..	5.00	6.00
☐ **Nobility "Windsong"**, *no monogram, good condition*	4.00	5.00
☐ **Oneida "Clarion"**, *no monogram, good condition*	4.00	5.00
☐ **Oneida "Clarion"**, *no monogram, fair condition*	1.00	2.00
☐ **Pairpoint "Mistletoe"**, *no monogram, excellent condition* .	6.00	7.00
☐ **Prestige "Grenoble"**, *no monogram, excellent condition* ..	5.00	6.00
☐ **Prestige "Grenoble"**, *no monogram, good condition*	4.00	5.00
☐ **Prestige "Grenoble"**, *no monogram, fair condition*	1.00	2.00
☐ **Reed & Barton "Rex"**, *no monogram, excellent condition* ..	6.00	7.00
☐ **Reed & Barton "Sierra"**, *no monogram, excellent condition*	5.00	6.00
☐ **Reed & Barton "Sierra"**, *no monogram, good condition*	4.00	5.00
☐ **Reed & Barton "Sierra"**, *no monogram, fair condition*	1.00	2.00
☐ **R.C. Co. "Manchester"**, *no monogram, excellent condition*	5.00	6.00
☐ **R.C. Co. "Manchester"**, *no monogram, good condition*	4.00	5.00
☐ **R.C. Co. "Isabella"**, *no monogram, excellent condition*	7.00	8.00
☐ **Reliance "Wildwood"**, *excellent condition*	5.00	6.00
☐ **Reliance "Wildwood"**, *no monogram, good condition*	4.00	5.00
☐ **Rogers "Beauty"**, *no monogram, excellent condition*	5.00	6.00
☐ **Rogers "Beauty"**, *no monogram, good condition*	4.00	5.00

	Price Range	

☐ **Rogers "Burgundy",** *no monogram, excellent condition* ... 5.00 6.00
☐ **Rogers "Burgundy",** *no monogram, good condition* 4.00 5.00
☐ **Rogers "Burgundy",** *no monogram, fair condition* 1.00 2.00
☐ **Rogers "Desire",** *no monogram, excellent condition* 5.00 6.00
☐ **Rogers "Desire",** *no monogram, good condition* 4.00 5.00
☐ **Rogers "Desota",** *no monogram, excellent condition* 5.00 6.00
☐ **Rogers "Desota",** *no monogram, good condition* 4.00 5.00
☐ **Rogers "Garland",** *no monogram, excellent condition* 5.00 6.00
☐ **Rogers "Garland",** *no monogram, good condition* 4.00 5.00
☐ **Rogers "Inspiration",** *no monogram, excellent condition* .. 5.00 6.00
☐ **Rogers "Inspiration",** *no monogram, good condition* 4.00 5.00
☐ **Rogers "Navarre",** *no monogram, excellent condition* 5.00 6.00
☐ **Rogers "Navarre",** *no monogram, fair condition* 1.00 2.00
☐ **Rogers "Precious",** *no monogram, excellent condition* 5.00 6.00
☐ **Rogers "Precious",** *no monogram, good condition* 4.00 5.00
☐ **Rogers "Queen Bess II",** *no monogram, excellent condition* 3.00 4.00
☐ **Rogers & Bro. "Modern Rose",** *no monogram, excellent condition* 5.00 6.00
☐ **Rogers & Bro. "Modern Rose",** *no monogram, good condition* 4.00 5.00
☐ **Rogers & Bro. "Mystic",** *no monogram, excellent condition* 5.00 6.00
☐ **Rogers & Bro. "Mystic",** *no monogram, good condition* ... 5.00 6.00
☐ **Rogers & Hamilton "Alhambra",** *no monogram, excellent condition* 6.00 7.00
☐ **Rogers & Hamilton "Alhambra",** *no monogram, good condition* 4.00 5.00
☐ **Rogers & Hamilton "Majestic",** *no monogram, excellent condition* 2.00 3.00
☐ **Rogers & Hamilton "Raphael",** *no monogram, excellent condition* 9.00 11.00
☐ **Rogers & Hamilton "Raphael",** *no monogram, fair condition* 2.00 3.00
☐ **S.L. & G.H. Rogers "Countess II",** *no monogram, excellent condition* 5.00 6.00
☐ **S.L. & G.H. Rogers "Countess II",** *no monogram, good condition* 4.00 5.00
☐ **S.L. & G.H. Rogers "Jasmine",** *no monogram, excellent condition* 5.00 6.00
☐ **S.L. & G.H. Rogers "Jasmine",** *no monogram, excellent condition* 2.00 3.00
☐ **S.L. & G.H. Rogers "Kingston",** *no monogram, excellent condition* 5.00 6.00
☐ **S.L. & G.H. Rogers "Kingston",** *no monogram, good condition* 4.00 5.00
☐ **S.L. & G.H. Rogers "Minerva",** *no monogram, excellent condition* 6.00 7.00
☐ **S.L. & G.H. Rogers "Minerva",** *no monogram, good condition* 5.00 6.00
☐ **S.L. & G.H. Rogers "Minerva",** *no monogram, fair condition* 2.00 3.00
☐ **S.L. & G.H. Rogers "Thor",** *no monogram, excellent condition* 5.00 6.00
☐ **S.L. & G.H. Rogers "Thor",** *no monogram, good condition* . 4.00 5.00

	Price Range	
☐ Stratford "Shakespeare", *no monogram, excellent condition*	5.00	6.00
☐ Stratford "Shakespeare", *no monogram, good condition* ..	4.00	5.00
☐ Tudor "Elaine", *no monogram, fair condition*	1.00	2.00
☐ Tudor "Enchantment", *no monogram, excellent condition* .	4.00	5.00
☐ Tudor "Fantasy", *no monogram, excellent condition*	5.00	6.00
☐ Tudor "Fantasy", *no monogram, good condition*	4.00	5.00
☐ Tudor "Queen Bess II", *no monogram, excellent condition* .	6.00	7.00
☐ Tudor "Queen Bess II", *no monogram, good condition*	5.00	6.00
☐ Wallace "Sonata", *no monogram, excellent condition*	5.00	6.00
☐ Wallace "Sonata", *no monogram, good condition*	4.00	5.00
☐ Wm. A. Rogers "Chalice", *no monogram, excellent condition*	5.00	6.00
☐ Wm. A. Rogers "Chalice", *no monogram, good condition* ..	4.00	5.00
☐ Wm. A. Rogers "Country Lane", *no monogram, excellent condition*	5.00	6.00
☐ Wm. A. Rogers "Country Lane", *no monogram, good condition*	4.00	5.00
☐ Wm. A. Rogers "LaConcorde", *no monogram, excellent condition*	5.00	6.00
☐ Wm. A. Rogers "LaVigne", *no monogram, excellent condition*	8.00	9.00
☐ Wm. A. Rogers "Malibu", *no monogram, excellent condition*	5.00	6.00
☐ Wm. A. Rogers "Malibu", *no monogram, good condition* ...	4.00	5.00
☐ Wm. A. Rogers "Meadowbrook", *no monogram, excellent condition*	5.00	6.00
☐ Wm. A. Rogers "Meadowbrook", *no monogram, good condition*	4.00	5.00
☐ Wm. A. Rogers "Paramount", *no monogram, excellent condition*	5.00	6.00
☐ Wm. A. Rogers "Paramount", *no monogram, good condition*	4.00	5.00
☐ Wm. A. Rogers "Rendezvous", *excellent condition*	5.00	6.00
☐ Wm. A. Rogers "Rendezvous", *no monogram, good condition*	4.00	5.00
☐ Wm. Rogers "Alhambra", *monogram, good condition*	1.00	2.00
☐ Wm. Rogers "Beloved", *no monogram, excellent condition*	5.00	6.00
☐ Wm. Rogers "Beloved", *no monogram, good condition*	4.00	5.00
☐ Wm. Rogers "Berwick", *no monogram, good condition*	4.00	5.00
☐ Wm. Rogers "Berwick", *no monogram, fair condition*	1.00	2.00
☐ Wm. Rogers "Chester", *no monogram, excellent condition*	5.00	6.00
☐ Wm. Rogers "Chester", *no monogram, good condition*	4.00	5.00
☐ Wm. Rogers "Cotillion", *no monogram, excellent condition*	5.00	6.00
☐ Wm. Rogers "Cotillion", *no monogram, good condition* ...	4.00	5.00
☐ Wm. Rogers "Exquisite", *no monogram, excellent condition*	5.00	6.00
☐ Wm. Rogers "Exquisite", *no monogram, good condition* ...	4.00	5.00
☐ Wm. Rogers "Exquisite", *no monogram, fair condition*	1.00	2.00
☐ Wm. Rogers "Hostess", *no monogram, excellent condition*	5.00	6.00
☐ Wm. Rogers "Hostess", *no monogram, good condition* ...	4.00	5.00
☐ Wm. Rogers "Imperial", *no monogram, excellent condition*	5.00	6.00
☐ Wm. Rogers "Imperial", *no monogram, good condition*	4.00	5.00

	Price Range	

☐ **Wm. Rogers "Louisiana"**, *no monogram, excellent condition* 5.00 6.00
☐ **Wm. Rogers "Louisiana"**, *no monogram, good condition* .. 4.00 5.00
☐ **Wm. Rogers "Melrose"**, *no monogram, excellent condition* 5.00 6.00
☐ **Wm. Rogers "Melrose"**, *no monogram, good condition* 4.00 5.00
☐ **Wm. Rogers "Memory"**, *no monogram, excellent condition* 4.00 5.00
☐ **Wm. Rogers "Memory"**, *no monogram, good condition* 2.00 3.00
☐ **Wm. Rogers "Precious Mirror"**, *no monogram, excellent condition* 5.00 6.00
☐ **Wm. Rogers "Precious Mirror"**, *no monogram, good condition* 4.00 5.00
☐ **Wm. Rogers "Precious Mirror"**, *no monogram, fair condition* 1.00 2.00
☐ **Wm. Rogers "Starlight"**, *no monogram, excellent condition* 5.00 6.00
☐ **Wm. Rogers "Starlight"**, *no monogram, good condition* ... 4.00 5.00
☐ **Wm. Rogers "Treasure"**, *no monogram, excellent condition* 5.00 6.00
☐ **Wm. Rogers "Treasure"**, *no monogram, good condition* ... 4.00 5.00
☐ **Wm. Rogers Mfg. Co. "Jubilee"**, *no monogram, excellent condition* 5.00 6.00
☐ **Wm. Rogers Mfg. Co. "Jubilee"**, *no monogram, good condition* 4.00 5.00
☐ **Wm. Rogers Mfg. Co. "Jubilee"**, *no monogram, fair condition* 1.00 2.00
☐ **Wm. Rogers Mfg. Co. "Magnolia"**, *no monogram, excellent condition* 5.00 6.00
☐ **Wm. Rogers Mfg. Co. "Magnolia"**, *no monogram, good condition* 4.00 5.00
☐ **Wm. Rogers Mfg. Co. "Reflection"**, *no monogram, excellent condition* 6.00 7.00
☐ **Wm. Rogers Mfg. Co. "Reflection"**, *no monogram, good condition* 5.00 6.00
☐ **Wm. Rogers Mfg. Co. "Reflection"**, *no monogram, fair condition* 1.00 2.00
☐ **Wm. Rogers Mfg. Co. "Revelation"**, *no monogram, excellent condition* 6.00 7.00
☐ **Wm. Rogers Mfg. Co. "Revelation"**, *no monogram, good condition* 5.00 6.00
☐ **Wm. Rogers Mfg. Co. "Talisman"**, *no monogram, excellent condition* 5.00 6.00
☐ **Wm. Rogers Mfg. Co. "Talisman"**, *no monogram, good condition* 4.00 5.00
☐ **Wm. Rogers Mfg. Co. "Talisman"**, *no monogram, fair condition* 1.00 2.00
☐ **Wm. Rogers & Son "April"**, *no monogram, excellent condition* 5.00 6.00
☐ **Wm. Rogers & Son "April"**, *no monogram, good condition* . 4.00 5.00
☐ **Wm. Rogers & Son "Arbutus"**, *no monogram, fair condition* 1.00 2.00
☐ **Wm. Rogers & Son "Daisy"**, *no monogram, excellent condition* 5.00 6.00
☐ **Wm. Rogers & Son "Daisy"**, *no monogram, good condition* 4.00 5.00
☐ **Wm. Rogers & Son "Daisy"**, *no monogram, fair condition* .. 1.00 2.00
☐ **Wm. Rogers & Son "Florida"**, *no monogram, excellent condition* 5.00 6.00

	Price Range	
☐ **Wm. Rogers & Son "Florida"**, *no monogram, good condition*	4.00	5.00
☐ **Wm. Rogers & Son "Oxford"**, *no monogram, excellent condition*	5.00	6.00
☐ **Wm. Rogers & Son "Oxford"**, *no monogram, good condition*	4.00	5.00
☐ **World "Somerset"**, *no monogram, excellent condition*	5.00	6.00
☐ **1835 R. Wallace "Abbey"**, *no monogram, excellent condition*	5.00	6.00
☐ **1835 R. Wallace "Abbey"**, *no monogram, good condition* ..	4.00	5.00
☐ **1835 R. Wallace "Joan"**, *no monogram, excellent condition*	5.00	6.00
☐ **1835 R. Wallace "Joan"**, *no monogram, good condition* ...	4.00	5.00
☐ **1847 Rogers "Ancestral"**, *no monogram, excellent condition*	5.00	6.00
☐ **1847 Rogers "Ancestral"**, *no monogram, good condition* ..	4.00	5.00
☐ **1847 Rogers "Ancestral"**, *no monogram, fair condition*	1.00	2.00
☐ **1847 Rogers "Avon"**, *no monogram, excellent condition* ...	5.00	6.00
☐ **1847 Rogers "Avon"**, *no monogram, good condition*	4.00	5.00
☐ **1847 Rogers "Avon"**, *no monogram, fair condition*	1.00	2.00
☐ **1847 Rogers "Berkshire"**, *no monogram, good condition* ..	5.00	6.00
☐ **1847 Rogers "Berkshire"**, *no monogram, excellent condition*	8.00	9.00
☐ **1847 Rogers "Berkshire"**, *no monogram, poor condition* ...	1.00	2.00
☐ **1847 Rogers "Charter Oak"**, *no monogram, excellent condition*	9.00	10.00
☐ **1847 Rogers "Charter Oak"**, *no monogram, fair condition* ..	3.00	4.00
☐ **1847 Rogers "Cromwell"**, *no monogram, good condition* ..	1.00	2.00
☐ **1847 Rogers "Daffodil II"**, *no monogram, excellent condition*	5.00	6.00
☐ **1847 Rogers "Daffodil II"**, *no monogram, good condition* ..	4.00	5.00
☐ **1847 Rogers "Daffodil II"**, *no monogram, fair condition* ...	1.00	2.00
☐ **1847 Rogers "Eternally Yours"**, *no monogram, excellent condition*	5.00	6.00
☐ **1847 Rogers "Eternally Yours"**, *no monogram, excellent condition*	5.00	6.00
☐ **1847 Rogers "Eternally Yours"**, *no monogram, good condition*	4.00	5.00
☐ **1847 Rogers "Eternally Yours"**, *no monogram, fair condition*	1.00	2.00
☐ **1847 Rogers "First Love"**, *no monogram, excellent condition*	3.00	4.00
☐ **1847 Rogers "First Love"**, *no monogram, fair condition* ...	4.00	5.00
☐ **1847 Rogers "First Love"**, *no monogram, fair condition* ...	2.00	3.00
☐ **1847 Rogers "Her Majesty"**, *no monogram, excellent condition*	5.00	6.00
☐ **1847 Rogers "Lotus"**, *no monogram, excellent condition* ..	5.00	6.00
☐ **1847 Rogers "Lotus"**, *no monogram, good condition*	4.00	5.00
☐ **1847 Rogers "Lotus"**, *no monogram, fair condition*	1.00	2.00
☐ **1847 Rogers "Lovelace"**, *no monogram, excellent condition*	5.00	6.00
☐ **1847 Rogers "Lovelace"**, *no monogram, good condition* ...	4.00	5.00
☐ **1847 Rogers "Marquise"**, *no monogram, excellent condition*	5.00	6.00
☐ **1847 Rogers "Marquise"**, *no monogram, good condition* ..	4.00	5.00
☐ **1847 Rogers "Moselle"**, *no monogram, excellent condition*	16.00	18.00

	Price Range	
☐ **1847 Rogers "Moselle",** *no monogram, poor condition*	6.00	7.00
☐ **1847 Rogers "Newport",** *no monogram, excellent condition*	7.00	8.00
☐ **1847 Rogers "Newport",** *no monogram, good condition* ...	5.00	6.00
☐ **1847 Rogers "Newport",** *no monogram, fair condition*	1.00	2.00
☐ **1847 Rogers "Old Colony",** *no monogram, excellent condition*	6.00	7.00
☐ **1847 Rogers "Old Colony",** *no monogram, excellent condition*	6.00	7.00
☐ **1847 Rogers "Old Colony",** *no monogram, resilvered*	6.00	7.00
☐ **1847 Rogers "Reflection",** *no monogram, excellent condition*	5.00	6.00
☐ **1847 Rogers "Reflection",** *no monogram, good condition* ..	3.00	4.00
☐ **1847 Rogers "Reflection",** *no monogram, fair condition* ...	1.00	2.00
☐ **1847 Rogers "Remembrance",** *no monogram, excellent condition*	5.00	6.00
☐ **1847 Rogers "Remembrance",** *no monogram, good condition*	4.00	5.00
☐ **1847 Rogers "Silver Lace",** *no monogram, excellent condition*	5.00	6.00
☐ **1847 Rogers "Silver Lace",** *no monogram, good condition* .	4.00	5.00
☐ **1847 Rogers "Vintage",** *no monogram, excellent condition*	8.00	9.00
☐ **1847 Rogers "Vintage",** *no monogram, fair condition*	2.00	3.00
☐ **1881 Rogers "Capri",** *no monogram, excellent condition* ..	5.00	6.00
☐ **1881 Rogers "Capri",** *no monogram, good condition*	4.00	5.00
☐ **1881 Rogers "Capri",** *no monogram, fair condition*	1.00	2.00
☐ **1881 Rogers "Godetia",** *no monogram, excellent condition*	5.00	6.00
☐ **1881 Rogers "Godetia",** *no monogram, good condition*	4.00	5.00
☐ **1881 Rogers "LaVigne",** *no monogram, fair condition*	1.00	2.00
☐ **1881 Rogers "Surf Club",** *no monogram, excellent condition*	3.00	4.00
☐ **1881 Rogers "Surf Club",** *no monogram, excellent condition*	5.00	6.00
☐ **1881 Rogers "Surf Club",** *no monogram, good condition* ..	4.00	5.00

(Sterling Silver)

☐ **Alvin "Majestic",** *monogram*	16.00	18.00
☐ **Dominick & Haff "King",** *monogram*	16.00	18.00
☐ **Durgin "Louis XV",** *monogram*	14.00	16.00
☐ **Gorham "Blithe Spirit",** *no monogram*	12.00	14.00
☐ **Gorham "Buttercup",** *no monogram*	10.00	12.00
☐ **Gorham "Chantilly",** *monogram*	14.00	16.00
☐ **Gorham "Colonial",** *no monogram*	16.00	18.00
☐ **Gorham "Lancaster",** *monogram*	12.00	14.00
☐ **Gorham "LaScala",** *monogram*	16.00	18.00
☐ **Gorham "Plymouth",** *monogram*	16.00	18.00
☐ **Gorham "Willow",** *monogram*	12.00	14.00
☐ **International "Fontaine",** *no monogram*	16.00	18.00
☐ **International "Frontenac",** *no monogram*	11.00	13.00
☐ **International "Grand Regency",** *no monogram*	11.00	13.00
☐ **International "Joan of Arc",** *no monogram*	14.00	16.00
☐ **International "Pine Tree",** *no monogram*	12.00	14.00
☐ **International "Silver Melody",** *no monogram*	13.00	15.00
☐ **International "Swan Lake",** *no monogram*	13.00	15.00

	Price Range	
☐ International "Vision", *no monogram*	12.00	14.00
☐ Lunt "Mt. Vernon", *monogram*	14.00	17.00
☐ Oneida "Rubiayat", *no monogram*	12.00	14.00
☐ Reed & Barton "Hampton Court", *monogram*	14.00	16.00
☐ Reed & Barton "Majestic", *monogram*	14.00	17.00
☐ Reed & Barton "Savannah", *monogram*	18.00	20.00
☐ Simpson, Hall & Miller "Frontenac", *no monogram*	25.00	27.00
☐ Tiffany "English King", *monogram*	22.00	24.00
☐ Tiffany "Hampton", *monogram*	23.00	25.00
☐ Towle "Country Manor", *no monogram*	12.00	14.00
☐ Towle "Esplanade", *no monogram*	11.00	13.00
☐ Towle "Laureate", *no monogram*	12.00	14.00
☐ Towle "Old Colonial", *no monogram*	14.00	17.00
☐ Towle "Spanish Provincial", *no monogram*	14.00	17.00
☐ Towle "Vespera", *no monogram*	14.00	16.00
☐ Wallace "Royal Rose", *no monogram*	11.00	13.00
☐ Whiting "Imperial Queen", *no monogram*	14.00	17.00

OYSTER LADLES

These were used for ladling oyster stew from the serving pot into individual cups or bowls. Oyster stew was an extremely popular dish in this country from the period immediately following the Civil War up to the early 1900's. For a while it was ignored by society, since it had the reputation of being cheap and common. This view soon changed, and while restaurants were serving their standard oyster stews for 5¢ or less per cup, the well-to-do fixed elegant versions served up to the accompaniment of fine silver.

(Silver-Plated)

☐ Reed & Barton "Tiger Lily", *no monogram, mint condition,* *12" L.*	62.00	68.00
☐ Reed & Barton "Tiger Lily", *no monogram, fair condition,* *12" L.*	22.00	24.00
☐ Rogers "Alhambra", *no monogram, excellent condition* ...	36.00	40.00
☐ Rogers "Alhambra", *no monogram, good condition*	18.00	20.00
☐ Rogers & Bro. "Aldine", *no monogram, excellent condition,* *11½" L.*	36.00	40.00
☐ Rogers & Bro. "Assyrian Head", *no monogram, excellent* *condition*	54.00	60.00
☐ S.L. & G.H. Rogers "Arcadia", *no monogram, excellent con-* *dition*	15.00	17.00
☐ S.L. & G.H. Rogers "Arcadia", *no monogram, fair condition*	3.00	4.00
☐ Towle "Norwood", *no monogram, excellent condition,* *10¼" L.*	20.00	22.00
☐ Williams Bros. "Verona", *no monogram, excellent condi-* *tion*	16.00	18.00
☐ Wm. A. Rogers "Plymouth", *no monogram, excellent condi-* *tion*	36.00	40.00
☐ Wm. Rogers & Son "Oxford", *no monogram, excellent con-* *dition*	55.00	62.00
☐ Wm. Rogers & Son "Oxford", *no monogram, good condition*	22.00	24.00
☐ Wm. Rogers Eagle "Cedric", *no monogram, good condition*	18.00	21.00
☐ 1847 Rogers "Arcadia", *no monogram, excellent condition,* *9½" L.*	18.00	20.00

Price Range

☐ **1847 Rogers "Berkshire",** *no monogram, mint condition* . . .	50.00	54.00
☐ **1847 Rogers "Berkshire",** *no monogram, good condition* . .	28.00	32.00
☐ **1847 Rogers "Berkshire",** *no monogram, in original box, in mint condition*	62.00	68.00
☐ **1847 Rogers "Columbia",** *no monogram, excellent condition*	55.00	62.00
☐ **1847 Rogers "Columbia",** *monogram, fair condition*	11.00	13.00
☐ **1847 Rogers "Newport",** *no monogram, excellent condition*	36.00	40.00
☐ **1847 Rogers "Newport",** *monogram, good condition*	32.00	36.00
☐ **1847 Rogers "Savoy",** *no monogram, good condition*	26.00	28.00
☐ **1847 Rogers "Savoy",** *no monogram, excellent condition* . .	36.00	40.00
☐ **1847 Rogers "Vintage",** *no monogram, mint condition*	65.00	72.00
☐ **1847 Rogers "Vintage",** *no monogram, mint condition, 11" L.*	67.00	75.00
☐ **1847 Rogers "Vintage",** *good condition*	36.00	40.00
☐ **1881 Rogers "LaVigne",** *no monogram, resilvered*	90.00	100.00
☐ **1881 Rogers "LaVigne",** *monogram, fair condition*	32.00	36.00

OYSTER SERVERS

(Silver-Plated)

☐ **Pairpoint "Clifton",** *no monogram, excellent condition*	50.00	55.00
☐ **1847 Rogers "Vintage",** *monogram, excellent condition* . . .	52.00	58.00
☐ **Maker unknown,** *lily of the valley design, no monogram, mint condition*	36.00	40.00

(Sterling Silver)

☐ **Tiffany "Beekman",** *monogram*	120.00	135.00

PASTE JARS

Even so lowly a commodity as paste went into elegant containers, in homes of the well-to-do (and of course in offices as well). The silver in paste jars is usually confined to the base and lid, or only to the lid — the actual container itself being made of glass. This was white library paste, a little thinner probably than the modern version of it. It was applied with a brush resembling a shaving brush, attached to the underside of the lid. One can't expect the brush to be in very good condition. Its bristles will be solidified with caked paste, unless the specimens has passed through the hands of a collector or dealer who took the pains to clean it up. If the bristles are natural hair, which ought to be the case with an old brush, turpentine mixed with a little linseed oil ought to clean them fairly well. They will not end up looking "as new."

(Sterling Silver and Crystal)

☐ **Maker unknown,** *etched design in crystal, floral design on sterling silver lid, attached brush, no monogram*	30.00	33.00
☐ **Maker unknown,** *plain crystal bottom, floral design on sterling silver lid, original brush, monogram*	36.00	40.00
☐ **Maker unknown,** *plain crystal bottom, plain lid, original brush, no monogram*	36.00	40.00

PASTRY/DESSERT FORKS

Most pastries were not customarily eaten with the fingers but with a special fork, a little shorter at the head but wider than a dinner fork. This gave the option of spearing each piece, or balancing it upon the fork. The average overall length is 5½″ to 6″.

(Silver-Plated)	Price Range	
☐ **Community "Coronation"**, *no monogram, excellent condition*	7.00	8.00
☐ **Community "Coronation"**, *no monogram, good condition*	6.00	7.00
☐ **Community "Patrician"**, *no monogram, excellent condition*	8.00	9.00
☐ **Community "Patrician"**, *no monogram, fair condition*	2.00	3.00
☐ **Pilgrim Silver Co. "Peerless"**, *no monogram, mint condition*	6.00	7.00
☐ **Rogers "Alhambra"**, *no monogram, excellent condition*	5.00	6.00
☐ **Rogers "Carlton"**, *no monogram, excellent condition*	6.00	7.00
☐ **Rogers "Carlton"**, *no monogram, good condition*	4.00	5.00
☐ **Rogers & Bros. "Mystic"**, *no monogram, excellent condition*	5.00	6.00
☐ **Wm. A. Rogers "Carnation"**, *no monogram, excellent condition*	11.00	13.00
☐ **Wm. A. Rogers "LaVigne"**, *no monogram, fair condition*	10.00	12.00
☐ **Wm. A. Rogers "Lenora"**, *no monogram, good condition*	7.00	8.00
(Sterling Silver)		
☐ **Alvin "Evangeline"**, *monogram*	9.00	10.00
☐ **Gorham "Chantilly"**, *no monogram, 5¾″ L.*	14.00	16.00
☐ **Gorham "Lancaster"**, *monogram*	14.00	16.00
☐ **Gorham "Plymouth"**, *no monogram*	14.00	16.00
☐ **Wallace "Violet"**, *monogram*	24.00	27.00
☐ **Whiting "Imperial Queen"**, *twisted tines, no monogram*	19.00	21.00
☐ **Whiting "Imperial Queen"**, *no monogram*	16.00	19.00

PASTRY SERVERS

Among the most eye-appealing of all silver table articles are pastry servers. Their use was not confined to restaurants and bakeries, though commercial establishments certainly used pastry servers to a large extent.

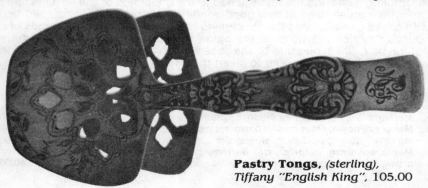

Pastry Tongs, *(sterling),*
Tiffany "English King", 105.00

At the home table, pastry was (if the serving was done according to proper form) brought out on a large flat tray, and from there transferred to individual dishes or platters with the pastry server. It was not touched by the hand — either of the server or the consumer, who ate it with a pastry/dessert fork (see above entry). Though pastry servers are technically in the category of "tongs," they are much sleeker and less cumbersome than food tongs in general (because, of course, pastry was light and easy to manage with tongs).

	Price Range	
(Coin Silver)		
☐ **Albert Coles "Kenilworth"**, *c. 1860, lady's head on handle* .	68.00	75.00
(Silver Plated)		
☐ **Community "Coronation"**, *pie type, no monogram, excellent condition*	12.00	14.00
☐ **Community "Coronation"**, *pie type, pierced blade, no monogram, excellent condition*	10.00	12.00
☐ **Community "Enchantment"**, *pie type, no monogram, excellent condition*	12.00	14.00
☐ **Community "Enchantment"**, *pie type, no monogram, excellent condition*	14.00	16.00
☐ **Community "Evening Star"**, *pie type, no monogram, excellent condition*	16.00	19.00
☐ **Community "Evening Star"**, *pie type, monogram, fair condition*	3.00	4.00
☐ **Community "Flight"**, *pie type, no monogram, excellent condition*	6.00	7.00
☐ **Community "Flight"**, *pie type, no monogram, mint condition*	9.00	10.00
☐ **Community "Milady"**, *pie type, pierced blade, no monogram, excellent condition*	10.00	12.00
☐ **Community "Milady"**, *pie type, pierced blade, no monogram, excellent condition*	12.00	14.00
☐ **Community "Morning Rose"**, *pie type, no monogram, mint condition*	7.00	8.00
☐ **Community "Morning Rose"**, *pie type, pierced blade, no monogram, excellent condition*	12.00	14.00
☐ **Community "Patrician"**, *master pastry fork type, no monogram, excellent condition*	16.00	18.00
☐ **Community "Patrician"**, *pie type, pierced blade, no monogram, excellent condition*	12.00	14.00
☐ **Community "Silver Flower"**, *pie type, no monogram, mint condition*	8.00	9.00
☐ **Community "Silver Sands"**, *pie type, no monogram, mint condition*	6.00	7.00
☐ **Community "Silver Valentine"**, *pie type, no monogram, mint condition*	6.00	7.00
☐ **Community "Silver Valentine"**, *pie type, no monogram, excellent condition*	7.00	8.00
☐ **Community "South Seas"**, *pie type, no monogram, excellent condition*	11.00	13.00
☐ **Community "Tangier"**, *no monogram, mint condition*	7.00	8.00
☐ **Community "Tangier"**, *no monogram, good condition*	3.00	4.00
☐ **Community "White Orchid"**, *pie type, no monogram, mint condition*	7.00	8.00

Price Range

☐ **Fortune "Fortune"**, *pie type, pierced blade, no monogram, excellent condition*	11.00	13.00
☐ **Gorham "Shelburne"**, *pie type, no monogram, excellent condition*	7.00	8.00
☐ **Hall, Elton & Co. "Italian"**, *tart type, no monogram, excellent condition*	20.00	22.00
☐ **Hall, Elton & Co. "Italian"**, *pie type, no monogram, excellent condition*	22.00	25.00
☐ **Hall, Elton & Co. "Italian"**, *pie type, no monogram, excellent condition*	36.00	40.00
☐ **Harmony House "Serenade"**, *pie type, no monogram, excellent condition*	5.00	6.00
☐ **Heirloom "Cardinal"**, *pie type, no monogram, excellent condition*	12.00	13.00
☐ **Holmes & Edwards "Lovely Lady"**, *pie type, pierced blade, no monogram, excellent condition*	11.00	13.00
☐ **Holmes & Edwards "Lovely Lady"**, *pie type, pierced blade, no monogram, good condition*	5.00	6.00
☐ **International "Happy Anniversary"**, *pie type, no monogram, excellent condition*	3.00	4.00
☐ **International "Silver Tulip"**, *pie type, pierced blade, no monogram, excellent condition*	5.00	6.00
☐ **International "Silver Tulip"**, *pie type, pierced blade, no monogram, excellent condition*	12.00	13.00
☐ **National "King Edward"**, *pie type, pierced blade, no monogram, excellent condition*	12.00	13.00
☐ **National "Rose & Leaf"**, *pie server, slotted blade, no monogram, excellent condition*	8.00	9.00
☐ **National "Rose & Leaf"**, *pie type, no monogram, excellent condition*	5.00	6.00
☐ **Prestige "Grenoble"**, *pie type, no monogram, excellent condition*	12.00	13.00
☐ **Prestige "Grenoble"**, *pie type, no monogram, excellent condition*	7.00	8.00
☐ **Reliance "Wildwood"**, *pie type, no monogram, poor condition*	5.00	6.00
☐ **Reed & Barton "Carlton"**, *pie type, no monogram, fair condition*	7.00	8.00
☐ **Reed & Barton "Olive"**, *no monogram, resilvered*	16.00	18.00
☐ **Rogers "Burgundy"**, *pie type, slotted blade, no monogram, good condition*	5.00	6.00
☐ **Rogers "Olive"**, *pie type, no monogram, excellent condition*	11.00	13.00
☐ **Rogers & Bro. "Assyrian Head"**, *pie type, no monogram, excellent condition*	24.00	26.00
☐ **Rogers & Bro. "Assyrian Head"**, *pie type, no monogram, mint condition*	45.00	50.00
☐ **Rogers & Bro. "Flemish"**, *pie type, no monogram, excellent condition*	9.00	11.00
☐ **Rogers & Bro. "Flemish"**, *pie type, no monogram, excellent condition*	12.00	14.00
☐ **S.L. & G.H. Rogers "Faun"**, *pie type, pierced blade, no monogram, excellent condition*	12.00	14.00
☐ **S.L. & G.H. Rogers "Faun"**, *pie type, pierced blade, no monogram, good condition*	6.00	7.00

Price Range

☐ **S.L. & G.H. Rogers "Kingston"**, *pie type, pierced blade, no monogram, excellent condition* 10.00 12.00

☐ **Towle "Norwood"**, *pie type, no monogram, excellent condition* 12.00 14.00

☐ **Towle "Norwood"**, *pie type, no monogram, mint condition* . 20.00 22.00

☐ **Towle "Victor"**, *pie type, no monogram, poor condition* . . . 6.00 7.00

☐ **Towle "Victor"**, *pie type, pierced blade, no monogram, excellent condition* 12.00 14.00

☐ **Tudor "Bridal Wreath"**, *pie type, no monogram, mint condition* 9.00 11.00

☐ **Tudor "Bridal Wreath"**, *pie type, no monogram, good condition* 3.00 4.00

☐ **Tudor "Fortune"**, *pie type, pierced blade, no monogram, fair condition* 4.00 5.00

☐ **Tudor "Queen Bess II"**, *pie type, slotted blade, no monogram, good condition* 11.00 13.00

☐ **Tudor "Queen Bess II"**, *pie type, pierced blade, no monogram, excellent condition* 12.00 14.00

☐ **Tudor "Together"**, *pie type, no monogram, mint condition* . 7.00 8.00

☐ **Tudor "Winsome"**, *pie type, slotted, no monogram, good condition* 5.00 6.00

☐ **Wallace "Floral"**, *pie type, no monogram, excellent condition* 18.00 20.00

☐ **Wm. A. Rogers "Jennifer"**, *pie type, pierced blade, no monogram, fair condition* 4.00 5.00

☐ **Wm. A. Rogers "Jennifer"**, *pie type, pierced blade, no monogram, excellent condition* 12.00 14.00

☐ **Wm. A. Rogers "Lenora"**, *pie type, no monogram, excellent condition* 13.00 15.00

☐ **Wm. A. Rogers "Meadowbrook"**, *pie type, pierced blade, no monogram, excellent condition* 11.00 13.00

☐ **Wm. A. Rogers "Meadowbrook"**, *pie type, pierced blade, monogram, fair condition* 2.00 3.00

☐ **Wm. Rogers "Arbutus"**, *pie type, no monogram, excellent condition* 18.00 20.00

☐ **Wm. Rogers "Arbutus"**, *pie type, no monogram, mint condition* 16.00 20.00

☐ **Wm. Rogers "Berkshire"**, *pie type, no monogram, excellent condition* 20.00 23.00

☐ **Wm. Rogers "Berkshire"**, *pie type, no monogram, poor condition* 3.00 4.00

☐ **Wm. Rogers "Bridal Bouquet"**, *pie type, no monogram, mint condition* 6.00 7.00

☐ **Wm. Rogers "Devonshire"**, *pie type, no monogram, excellent condition* 12.00 14.00

☐ **Wm. Rogers "Devonshire"**, *pie type, no monogram, good condition* 6.00 7.00

☐ **Wm. Rogers "Fair Lady"**, *pie type, no monogram, excellent condition* 11.00 13.00

☐ **Wm. Rogers "Fair Lady"**, *pie type, pierced blade, no monogram, excellent condition* 13.00 15.00

☐ **Wm. Rogers "Hostess"**, *pie type, pierced blade, no monogram, excellent condition* 11.00 13.00

	Price Range	

☐ **Wm. Rogers "Hostess",** *pie type, pierced blade, monogram, good condition* 5.00 6.00

☐ **Wm. Rogers "Magnolia",** *pie type, no monogram, excellent condition* 4.00 5.00

☐ **Wm. Rogers "Magnolia",** *pie type, no monogram, mint condition* 13.00 14.00

☐ **Wm. Rogers "Orange Blossom",** *pie type, no monogram, excellent condition* 20.00 23.00

☐ **Wm. Rogers "Spring Charm",** *pie type, slotted blade, no monogram, excellent condition* 12.00 14.00

☐ **Wm. Rogers "Spring Charm",** *pie type, slotted blade, monogram, good condition* 3.00 4.00

☐ **Wm. Rogers "Treasure",** *pie type, slotted blade, no monogram, good condition* 10.00 12.00

☐ **Wm. Rogers "Treasure",** *pie type, slotted blade, no monogram, excellent condition* 12.00 14.00

☐ **Wm. Rogers Mfg. Co. "Alhambra",** *pie type, hollow handle, no monogram, excellent condition* 10.00 12.00

☐ **Wm. Rogers Mfg. Co. "Alhambra",** *pie type, monogram, good condition* 11.00 13.00

☐ **Wm. Rogers Mfg. Co. "Arbutus",** *pie type, monogram, good condition* 14.00 16.00

☐ **Wm. Rogers Mfg. Co. "Arbutus",** *pie type, no monogram, excellent condition* 18.00 20.00

☐ **Wm. Rogers Mfg. Co. "Berwick",** *pie type, no monogram, good condition* 13.00 15.00

☐ **Wm. Rogers Mfg. Co. "Berwick",** *cake type, monogram, excellent condition* 16.00 18.00

☐ **Wm. Rogers Mfg. Co. "Grand Elegance",** *pie type, pierced blade, no monogram, excellent condition* 12.00 14.00

☐ **Wm. Rogers Mfg. Co. "Grand Elegance",** *cake type, pierced blade, no monogram, excellent condition* 12.00 14.00

☐ **Wm. Rogers Mfg. Co. "Magnolia",** *cake type, pierced blade, no monogram, good condition* 10.00 12.00

☐ **Wm. Rogers "Magnolia",** *pie type, no monogram, excellent condition* 12.00 14.00

☐ **Wm. Rogers Mfg. Co. "Magnolia",** *pie type, monogram, fair condition* 3.00 4.00

☐ **1835 R. Wallace "Abbey",** *cake type, no monogram, excellent condition* 12.00 14.00

☐ **1835 R. Wallace "Abbey",** *pie type, pierced blade, no monogram, excellent condition* 13.00 15.00

☐ **1835 R. Wallace "Anjou",** *cake type, hollow-handled, no monogram, excellent condition* 15.00 17.00

☐ **1835 R. Wallace "Anjou",** *cake type, no monogram, good condition* 3.00 4.00

☐ **1835 R. Wallace "Cardinal",** *pie type, no monogram, excellent condition* 10.00 12.00

☐ **1835 R. Wallace "Cardinal",** *pie type, no monogram, excellent condition* 16.00 18.00

☐ **1847 Rogers "Anniversary",** *pie type, no monogram, excellent condition* 7.00 8.00

	Price Range	
☐ **1847 Rogers "Anniversary"**, *cake type, pierced blade, no monogram, excellent condition*	12.00	14.00
☐ **1847 Rogers "Assyrian Head"**, *pie type, monogram, good condition*	14.00	16.00
☐ **1847 Rogers "Assyrian Head"**, *cake type, pierced blade, no monogram, mint condition*	18.00	20.00
☐ **1847 Rogers "Avon"**, *cake type, no monogram, excellent condition*	20.00	23.00
☐ **1847 Rogers "Avon"**, *pie type, pierced blade, no monogram, excellent condition*	25.00	27.00
☐ **1847 Rogers "Berkshire"**, *pie type, no monogram, excellent condition*	14.00	17.00
☐ **1847 Rogers "Berkshire"**, *pie type, no monogram, fair condition*	16.00	19.00
☐ **1847 Rogers "Berkshire"**, *pie type, no monogram, excellent condition*	25.00	28.00
☐ **1847 Rogers "Columbia"**, *pie type, no monogram, resilvered*	19.00	21.00
☐ **1847 Rogers "Columbia"**, *cake type, no monogram, excellent condition*	22.00	25.00
☐ **1847 Rogers "Eternally Yours"**, *pie type, pierced blade, no monogram, excellent condition*	17.00	19.00
☐ **1847 Rogers "Eternally Yours"**, *pie type, pierced blade, monogram, fair condition*	3.00	4.00
☐ **1847 Rogers "Grand Heritage"**, *pie type, pierced blade, no monogram, excellent condition*	4.00	5.00
☐ **1847 Rogers "Grand Heritage"**, *pie type, small, pierced blade, no monogram, excellent condition*	2.00	3.00
☐ **1847 Rogers "Heritage"**, *pie type, no monogram, mint condition*	9.00	10.00
☐ **1847 Rogers "Heritage"**, *pie type, no monogram, mint condition*	9.00	11.00
☐ **1847 Rogers "Heritage"**, *cake type, no monogram, excellent condition*	9.00	11.00
☐ **1847 Rogers "Leilani"**, *pie type, no monogram, excellent condition*	12.00	14.00
☐ **1847 Rogers "Leilani"**, *cake type, no monogram, excellent condition*	12.00	14.00
☐ **1847 Rogers "Magic Rose"**, *pie type, no monogram, mint condition*	7.00	8.00
☐ **1847 Rogers "Magic Rose"**, *pie type, no monogram, poor condition*	1.00	2.00
☐ **1847 Rogers "Persian"**, *pie type, no monogram, excellent condition*	18.00	21.00
☐ **1847 Rogers "Persian"**, *pie type, pierced blade, no monogram, mint condition*	25.00	27.00
☐ **1847 Rogers "Persian"**, *pie type, no monogram, excellent condition*	15.00	17.00
☐ **1847 Rogers "Reflection"**, *pie type, no monogram, excellent condition*	10.00	12.00
☐ **1847 Rogers "Reflection"**, *cake type, no monogram, excellent condition*	11.00	13.00

	Price Range	

☐ **1847 Rogers "Vintage"**, *cake type, no monogram, mint condition* 45.00 50.00

☐ **1847 Rogers "Vintage"**, *cake type, no monogram, excellent condition* 36.00 40.00

☐ **1847 Rogers "Vintage"**, *pie type, pierced blade, no monogram, mint condition* 35.00 39.00

☐ **1881 Rogers "Plymouth"**, *pie type, no monogram, excellent condition* 9.00 10.00

(Sterling Silver)

☐ **Alvin "Apollo"**, *pie type, no monogram* 36.00 40.00

☐ **Durgin "Madame Royale"**, *pierced blade, no monogram* ... 40.00 45.00

☐ **Durgin "Madame Royale"**, *pie type, etched blade, no monogram* 75.00 85.00

☐ **Gorham "King George"**, *pie type, no monogram* 40.00 45.00

☐ **Gorham "Strasbourg"**, *pie type, no monogram* 28.00 31.00

☐ **International "Grand Regency"**, *cake type, no monogram* . 12.00 14.00

☐ **International "Silver Melody"**, *cake type, no monogram* ... 16.00 18.00

☐ **International "Wedgwood"**, *no monogram* 15.00 17.00

☐ **Kalo**, *raised monogram* 95.00 105.00

☐ **Lunt "Eloquence"**, *cake type, no monogram* 15.00 17.00

☐ **Reed & Barton "Francis I"**, *cake type, no monogram* 45.00 50.00

☐ **Tiffany "Flemish"**, *pie type, no monogram* 100.00 110.00

☐ **Towle "Georgian"**, *no monogram* 27.00 30.00

☐ **Towle "Madeira"**, *cake type, no monogram* 15.00 17.00

☐ **Towle "Old Colonial"**, *no monogram* 27.00 30.00

☐ **Watson-Newell "Lily"**, *monogram* 16.00 18.00

☐ **Whiting "Keystone"**, *cake type, no monogram* 45.00 50.00

☐ **Whiting "Lily"**, *8½ ", all sterling, no monogram* 100.00 110.00

PEA SERVERS

Their spherical shape and small size has made peas one of the problem foods of the table for many years. They — more than any other food — inspired the *food pusher* (see entry in this book), as peas alone on a plate can be extremely elusive. In serving peas, no ordinary utensil could be depended on to do the job. Something special was needed and of course the ever-resourceful silverware makers supplied it, in the form of the pea server. This was a ladle with pierced-work bowl, the bowl moderately deep and the sides built up to prevent escape of peas on their way to the dinner plate. Actually the pea server was used not only with common green peas but beans of all kind.

(Silver-Plated)

☐ **Holmes & Edwards "Waldorf"**, *no monogram, excellent condition* 20.00 23.00

(Sterling Silver)

☐ **Dominick & Haff "Number 10"**, *monogram* 68.00 75.00

PENCIL CASES

Today's hobbyist is likely to think of collectible pencil cases in terms of those bearing likenesses of Disney characters, Presley, the Beatles and so forth. Pencil cases in silver have been made and were, in fact, rather plentiful at one time. This was a favorite novelty of the 1870/1920 period. The lids often carry engraved designs and the price will depend somewhat of the skillfulness (or lack of it) in the artwork. Monograms, full names, and even heraldic bearings are found on silver pencil cases. What you will seldom find in them are *pencils,* which have long since disappeared from their cases and are floating around by themselves on the antique markets.

	Price Range	
(Silver-Plated)		
☐ **Maker unknown,** *etched lines, monogram and date*	11.00	13.00
(Sterling Silver)		
☐ **Gorham,** *engraved floral design, monogram*	27.00	30.00
☐ **Maker unknown,** *plain design, monogram and date*	25.00	27.00

PENCILS

Writing equipment made of silver is so extensive, covering a time period extending right up to today, that we cannot attempt to do the subject full justice. This is a collecting topic in itself; most of the buyers are either pen hobbyists or pencil hobbyists (or both), rather than collectors of silverware. It is a very refined hobby, insofar as specific values have been laid down for nearly every make and model of writing tool going well back into the 1800's. For this reason, the shopper is apt to find some good bargains as well as some outrageously overpriced specimens, when he browses among the shops of general antiques merchants. You are advised to consult *The Official Price Guide to Antiques & Other Collectibles,* published by The House of Collectibles.

(Sterling Silver)		
☐ **Eversharp,** *engraved design, no monogram*	22.00	24.00
☐ **Eversharp,** *plain design, Florentine finish, no monogram* .:	18.00	21.00

PENS

(Sterling Silver)		
☐ **Waterman's Ideal,** *plain design*	8.00	9.00
☐ **Maker unknown,** *gold wash banding*	9.00	10.00

PERFUME BOTTLES

Glass containers have almost always been used for perfumes. Silver perfume bottles are really glass bottles with silver stoppers. They can be very ornate, in some cases designed so that the stopper is twice the height of the bottle. The stoppers (which can be collected by themselves, sans bottles) come in more types than could be named in a thick book. Not many restrained ones will be found. Manufacturers felt that if someone could afford silver, they could afford and appreciate artistic design too. Readers interested in perfume bottles should consult *The Official Guide to Bottles Old & New,* sold in bookshops or available at $9.95 plus $1 shipping from The House of Collectibles, 1900 Premier Row, Orlando, Fla. 32809.

(Sterling Silver and Crystal)		
☐ **Maker unknown,** *sterling silver and crystal, ornate floral sterling lid, cut crystal bottom, several small flecks on crystal*	27.00	30.00

Perfume Bottle, *DJE, England,
cut glass motif, repoussé,
one end on hinge
and one end screws,* 125.00

PICKLE FORKS

Pickles go back much farther into history than one might think, as does the pickling of foodstuffs in general. The pickle barrel was standard at American grocery shops by the mid 18th century, perhaps earlier. This is one of many foodstuffs which genteel society had doubts about, for a while, then finally accepted with open arms. Social recognition of the pickle brought forth the pickle fork, a long-handle fork with good spearing tines that would not just lift the pickle but hold it securely. Average length is from 7″ to 7¾″.

(Silver-Plated)	Price Range	
☐ Alvin "Bride's Bouquet", *long handled, no monogram, excellent condition*	12.00	14.00
☐ Alvin "Bride's Bouquet", *long handled, no monogram, good condition*	9.00	11.00
☐ Community "Adam", *no monogram, excellent condition* . .	11.00	13.00
☐ Community "Adam", *no monogram, good condition*	9.00	11.00
☐ Community "Adam", *monogram, excellent condition*	8.00	9.00
☐ Community "Adam", *monogram, fair condition*	2.00	3.00
☐ Community "Avalon", *long handled, no monogram, excellent condition*	12.00	14.00
☐ Community "Avalon", *long handled, no monogram, poor condition*	1.00	2.00

Price Range

☐ Community "Bird of Paradise", *no monogram, excellent condition*	9.00	11.00
☐ Community "Bird of Paradise", *no monogram, good condition*	5.00	6.00
☐ Community "Evening Star", *no monogram, excellent condition*	7.00	8.00
☐ Community "Evening Star", *no monogram, excellent condition*	9.00	10.00
☐ Community "Flower de Luce", *long handled, no monogram, excellent condition*	18.00	20.00
☐ Community "Flower de Luce", *long handled, no monogram, good condition*	16.00	18.00
☐ Community "Flower de Luce", *long handled, no monogram, fair condition*	5.00	6.00
☐ Community "Flower de Luce", *long handled, monogram, fair condition*	1.00	2.00
☐ Community "Georgian", *long handled, no monogram, excellent condition*	7.00	8.00
☐ Community "Georgian", *long handled, no monogram, excellent condition*	14.00	16.00
☐ Community "Georgian", *long handled, no monogram, good condition*	11.00	13.00
☐ Community "Georgian", *long handled, no monogram, fair condition*	4.00	5.00
☐ Community "Lady Hamilton", *no monogram, excellent condition*	9.00	11.00
☐ Community "Lady Hamilton", *no monogram, good condition*	7.00	8.00
☐ Community "Lady Hamilton", *no monogram, good condition*	6.00	7.00
☐ Community "Patrician", *no monogram, excellent condition*	9.00	10.00
☐ Community "Patrician", *no monogram, good condition*	4.00	5.00
☐ Community "Sheraton", *long handled, no monogram, excellent condition*	16.00	18.00
☐ Community "Sheraton", *long handled, monogram, excellent condition*	8.00	9.00
☐ Community "Silver Flowers", *no monogram, excellent condition*	7.00	8.00
☐ Community "South Seas", *no monogram, excellent condition*	4.00	5.00
☐ Community "South Seas", *no monogram, fair condition*	1.00	2.00
☐ E.H.H. Smith "Holly", *long handled, no monogram, excellent condition*	18.00	20.00
☐ E.H.H. Smith "Holly", *long handled, no monogram, poor condition*	1.00	2.00
☐ Hall, Elton & Co. "Eastlake", *long handled, no monogram, excellent condition*	16.00	18.00
☐ Holmes & Edwards "Carolina", *no monogram, excellent condition*	9.00	10.00
☐ Holmes & Edwards "Carolina", *no monogram, good condition*	7.00	8.00
☐ Holmes & Edwards "Charm", *no monogram, excellent condition*	9.00	10.00

Price Range

☐ Holmes & Edwards "Charm", *no monogram, good condition* 3.00   4.00

☐ Holmes & Edwards "Danish Princess", *no monogram, excellent condition* 7.00   8.00

☐ Holmes & Edwards "Jamestown", *no monogram, good condition* 9.00   10.00

☐ Holmes & Edwards "Jamestown", *no monogram, fair condition* 1.00   2.00

☐ Holmes & Edwards "Lovely Lady", *no monogram, excellent condition* 9.00   10.00

☐ Holmes & Edwards "Lovely Lady", *no monogram, poor condition* 1.00   2.00

☐ Holmes & Edwards "May Queen", *no monogram, excellent condition* 7.00   8.00

☐ Holmes & Edwards "May Queen", *no monogram, excellent condition* 9.00   10.00

☐ Oneida "Flower de Luce", *long handled, no monogram, excellent condition* 7.00   8.00

☐ Oneida "Flower de Luce", *long handled, no monogram, good condition* 7.00   8.00

☐ Oneida "Wildwood", *long handled, no monogram, excellent condition* 14.00   16.00

☐ Oneida "Wildwood", *long handled, no monogram, fair condition* 3.00   4.00

☐ Prestige "Grenoble", *no monogram, excellent condition* .. 9.00   10.00

☐ Prestige "Grenoble", *no monogram, good condition* 7.00   8.00

☐ Reed & Barton "Maid of Honor", *no monogram, excellent condition* 9.00   10.00

☐ Reed & Barton "Maid of Honor", *no monogram, good condition* 7.00   8.00

☐ Reed & Barton "Oxford", *long handled, no monogram, excellent condition* 11.00   13.00

☐ Reed & Barton "Oxford", *long handled, no monogram, excellent condition* 15.00   17.00

☐ Reed & Barton "Pearl", *long handled, no monogram, excellent condition* 12.00   14.00

☐ Reed & Barton "Pearl", *long handled, no monogram, good condition* 10.00   12.00

☐ Reliance "Bridal", *long handled, no monogram, excellent condition* 12.00   14.00

☐ Rogers "Newport", *no monogram, excellent condition* 12.00   14.00

☐ Rogers & Bro. "Assyrian Head", *no monogram, excellent condition* 27.00   30.00

☐ Wm. Rogers "Berwick", *no monogram, excellent condition* 12.00   14.00

☐ Wm. Rogers "Berwick", *no monogram, good condition* 9.00   11.00

☐ Wm. Rogers "Exquisite", *no monogram, excellent condition* 9.00   10.00

☐ Wm. Rogers "Exquisite", *no monogram, good condition* ... 7.00   8.00

☐ Wm. Rogers "Mayfair", *long handled, no monogram, excellent condition* 12.00   14.00

☐ Wm. Rogers "Mayfair", *long handled, monogram, excellent condition* 6.00   7.00

☐ Wm. Rogers "Melrose", *no monogram, fair condition* 3.00   4.00

Price Range

☐ **Wm. Rogers "Orange Blossom"**, *long handled, no monogram, excellent condition*	15.00	18.00
☐ **Wm. Rogers "Orange Blossom"**, *long handled, no monogram, poor condition*	1.00	2.00
☐ **Wm. Rogers "Spring Charm"**, *no monogram, excellent condition*	9.00	10.00
☐ **Wm. Rogers "Spring Charm"**, *no monogram, good condition*	7.00	8.00
☐ **Wm. Rogers "Yale"**, *no monogram, excellent condition* ...	11.00	13.00
☐ **Wm. Rogers "Yale"**, *no monogram, good condition*	9.00	11.00
☐ **Wm. A. Rogers "Garland"**, *no monogram, excellent condition*	3.00	4.00
☐ **Wm. A. Rogers "Lenora"**, *twisted handle, no monogram, excellent condition*	16.00	18.00
☐ **Wm. A. Rogers "Lenora"**, *long handled, no monogram, mint condition*	11.00	13.00
☐ **Wm. Rogers & Son "Arbutus"**, *long handled, no monogram, excellent condition*	12.00	14.00
☐ **Wm. Rogers & Son "Arbutus"**, *long handled, no monogram, good condition*	9.00	11.00
☐ **Wm. Rogers Mfg. Co. "Berwick"**, *no monogram, excellent condition*	16.00	18.00
☐ **Wm. Rogers Mfg. Co. "Berwick"**, *no monogram, fair condition*	5.00	6.00
☐ **1847 Rogers "Avon"**, *no monogram, good condition*	11.00	13.00
☐ **1847 Rogers "Avon"**, *no monogram, fair condition*	5.00	6.00
☐ **1847 Rogers "Charter Oak"**, *long handled, no monogram, excellent condition*	16.00	18.00
☐ **1847 Rogers "Charter Oak"**, *long handled, no monogram, excellent condition*	24.00	26.00
☐ **1847 Rogers "Charter Oak"**, *long handled, no monogram, mint condition*	26.00	28.00
☐ **1847 Rogers "Charter Oak"**, *long handled, no monogram, fair condition*	7.00	8.00
☐ **1847 Rogers "Daffodil"**, *no monogram, excellent condition*	6.00	7.00
☐ **1847 Rogers "Daffodil II"**, *no monogram, excellent condition*	9.00	10.00
☐ **1847 Rogers "Daffodil II"**, *no monogram, good condition* ..	8.00	9.00
☐ **1847 Rogers "Esperanto"**, *no monogram, excellent condition*	9.00	10.00
☐ **1847 Rogers "Esperanto"**, *no monogram, poor condition* ..	1.00	2.00
☐ **1847 Rogers "Eternally Yours"**, *no monogram, excellent condition*	11.00	13.00
☐ **1847 Rogers "Eternally Yours"**, *no monogram, good condition*	9.00	11.00
☐ **1847 Rogers "Eternally Yours"**, *no monogram, poor condition*	1.00	2.00
☐ **1847 Rogers "Flair"**, *no monogram, excellent condition* ...	3.00	4.00
☐ **1847 Rogers "Grand Heritage"**, *no monogram, excellent condition*	5.00	6.00
☐ **1847 Rogers "Heraldic"**, *no monogram, excellent condition*	7.00	8.00
☐ **1847 Rogers "Heraldic"**, *no monogram, good condition* ...	7.00	8.00
☐ **1847 Rogers "Heritage"**, *no monogram, mint condition*	4.00	5.00

	Price Range	
☐ 1847 Rogers "Leilani", *no monogram, mint condition*	6.00	7.00
☐ 1847 Rogers "Lorne", *long handled, no monogram, excellent condition*	10.00	12.00
☐ 1847 Rogers "Lorne", *long handled, no monogram, good condition*	9.00	10.00
☐ 1847 Rogers "Louvain", *no monogram, excellent condition*	9.00	10.00
☐ 1847 Rogers "Louvain", *no monogram, good condition*	7.00	8.00
☐ 1847 Rogers "Magic Rose", *no monogram, excellent condition*	5.00	6.00
☐ 1847 Rogers "Old Colony", *long handled, no monogram, excellent condition*	12.00	14.00
☐ 1847 Rogers "Old Colony", *long handled, no monogram, excellent condition*	18.00	20.00
☐ 1847 Rogers "Old Colony", *long handled, no monogram, good condition*	10.00	13.00
☐ 1847 Rogers "Remembrance", *no monogram, excellent condition*	9.00	10.00
☐ 1847 Rogers "Remembrance", *no monogram, good condition*	7.00	8.00
☐ 1847 Rogers "Saratoga", *no monogram, excellent condition*	5.00	6.00
☐ 1847 Rogers "Saratoga", *no monogram, good condition* ...	9.00	10.00
☐ 1847 Rogers "Savoy", *long handled, no monogram, excellent condition*	20.00	22.00
☐ 1847 Rogers "Savoy", *long handled, no monogram, good condition*	13.00	15.00
☐ 1847 Rogers "Sharon", *long handled, no monogram, excellent condition*	18.00	20.00
☐ 1847 Rogers "Sharon", *long handled, no monogram, good condition*	12.00	14.00
☐ 1847 Rogers "Vintage", *long handled, no monogram, excellent condition*	22.00	25.00
☐ 1847 Rogers "Vintage", *long handled, no monogram, excellent condition*	36.00	40.00
☐ 1847 Rogers "Vintage", *long handled, no monogram, good condition*	25.00	28.00
☐ 1847 Rogers "Vintage", *long handled, no monogram, fair condition*	9.00	10.00
☐ 1847 Rogers "Vintage", *long handled, monogram, excellent condition*	15.00	17.00
☐ 1881 Rogers "LaVigne", *long handled, no monogram, excellent condition*	16.00	18.00
☐ 1881 Rogers "Plymouth", *long handled, no monogram, excellent condition*	12.00	14.00

(Sterling Silver)

☐ Alvin "Chateau Rose", *no monogram*	10.00	12.00
☐ Alvin "Monterey", *long handled, no monogram*	22.00	24.00
☐ Dominick & Haff "Renaissance", *7¼" L., monogram*	9.00	10.00
☐ Gorham "Buttercup", *no monogram*	13.00	15.00
☐ Gorham "Greenbrier", *no monogram*	11.00	13.00
☐ International "Silver Melody", *no monogram*	10.00	12.00
☐ International "Wedgwood", *no monogram*	15.00	17.00
☐ Reed & Barton "Majestic", *no monogram*	20.00	23.00

	Price Range	
☐ **Stieff "Rose",** *no monogram*	9.00	10.00
☐ **Stieff "Rose",** *no monogram*	10.00	12.00
☐ **Towle "Madeira",** *no monogram*	11.00	13.00

PICTURE FRAMES

Silver picture frames were never popular. Metallic picture frames have been very extensively made, as large heavy canvases do not go very well in wooden frames — but most are bronze with gold-gilt coating. We have the era of Louis XIV to thank for that, when nearly everything in the home was gold gilded, including the walls. Silver picture frames were occasionally made in America in the Victorian era and slightly later. They never caught on.

(Sterling Silver)

☐ **Kirk,** *small, shell and leaf design in relief*	50.00	57.00
☐ **Lebolt,** *15½" H., 10" across, plain design*	190.00	210.00
☐ **Reed & Barton,** *6" H., oval shape, plain design*	12.00	14.00
☐ **Maker unknown,** *two ball feet, easel back and hanger, opening 3¾" H., 2½" across, engraved floral design*	23.00	27.00

PILL BOXES

Any visitor to museums has seen the elegant pill boxes of the past. These small containers, intended to be slipped into pocket or purse with the least inconvenience, are sometimes wonderful works of art. Specimens can be found in gold and silver, with finely enameled lids on which portraits or scenes are painted, in carved ivory, and a great range of other materials. Thus the pill box has become a special favorite of collectors. Silver specimens are avidly sought, but usually as an adjunt to a general collection of pill boxes rather than to form a collection in themselves. Lids are either hinged or removeable. It is difficult to give general suggestions about pill box buying or collecting, as you will encounter so many diverse types. Just be sure that what appears to be silver is indeed silver and not "German silver" or some other imitation, as wares of that kind were heavily imported.

(Silver-Plated)

☐ **Pairpoint,** *monogram*	30.00	33.00

(Sterling Silver)

☐ **Frank M. Whiting,** *floral repousse design on hinged lid, 2" diameter, monogram*	43.00	48.00
☐ **Maker unknown,** *hand-chased floral repousse design, hinged lid, 1¾" diameter, no monogram*	40.00	45.00
☐ **Maker unknown,** *ornate relief design, 1" by 1¼" H., no monogram*	13.00	15.00

PIN CUSHIONS

Naturally it is only the base of silver pin cushions that are silver, but a fair amount of silver can be involved depending on whether the base is solid or hollow. Tricksters take the hollow ones, fill them with lead or sculptor's clay, then plate over the bottom in silver. This increases the weight considerably.

(Silver-Plated)   **Price Range**

☐ **Tiffany,** *good condition, monogram*	70.00	76.00
☐ **Maker unknown,** *figural, large bird, good condition*	30.00	33.00
☐ **Maker unknown,** *figural, dolphin, good condition*	16.00	18.00
☐ **Maker unknown,** *plain design, excellent condition*	12.00	14.00

(Sterling Silver)

☐ **Reed & Barton,** *small, heart-shaped, velvet in bad condition*	33.00	37.00
☐ **Maker unknown,** *oval, scalloped rim, velvet in excellent condition*	27.00	30.00

PIN DISHES

These are small trays for pins, on which the pins were laid out during sewing. However, unless someone was blessed with very sharp eyesight, the pins blended right in with the dish. For this reason, silver pin dishes never became overly popular. Some have black velvet or other plush insets at the top, which was the ideal solution to this dilemma.

(Silver Plated)

☐ **Maker unknown,** *ornate Art Nouveau floral design, monogram and date 1901, good condition*	12.00	14.00
☐ **Maker unknown,** *plain design, monogram, good condition*	2.00	3.00

(Sterling Silver)

☐ **International,** *floral design, monogram*	10.00	12.00
☐ **Maker unknown,** *repousse floral design on border, monogram in center, two oz.*	27.00	30.00

PITCHERS

Silver pitchers are very attractive — ideal items to collect and display. But they were not too popular for actual use, and for this reason the quantity manufactured was modest at best. They range in size depending on the intended contents (milk pitchers, for example, being larger than those for syrup), and also depending on whether the item was intended for a public eating place or home use. The designs are sometimes highly ornate and sometimes starkly plain. When a very plain one is found, the conclusion to be drawn is that it was intended to be engraved with heraldic arms, or other engraving, but never was. Pewter pitchers are more numerous than silver, so be wary of mistaking the former for the latter. *Foreign made* silver pitchers are considerably more abundant on the market than American.

(Silver-Plated)

☐ **Barbour Bros.,** *syrup size, tavern scenes, reed-wrapped handle*	24.00	27.00
☐ **Maker unknown,** *syrup size, attached under-plate, dated 1856, beading on rim, cherub finial, ornate handle*	52.00	58.00
☐ **Maker unknown,** *plain design, monogram, ice guard on lip, good condition*	27.00	30.00
☐ **Maker unknown,** *ornate chased design on cherubs, flowers and trees, mask spout, gargoyle handle, ice guard on lip, some slight wear spots*	68.00	75.00

Milk Pitcher, *(sterling), Tiffany*
6½ ounces, 8" H., 140.00

(Sterling Silver)	**Price Range**	
☐ **Baltimore Silversmiths,** *water size, hand-chased repousse design in floral pattern, applied handle with grapes and leaves, 9" T., c. 1903, weight 30 oz., monogram*	450.00	500.00
☐ **Black, Starr & Frost,** *spherical body and cylindrical top, plain design, 7½" H., monogram, 18 oz.*	135.00	150.00
☐ **Gorham,** *c. 1908, spherical shape, beading on mid-section, scroll handle, 7" H., weight 14 oz.*	120.00	135.00
☐ **Tiffany,** *c. 1895, pyriform with embossed and chased scroll, flower and lattice-work design, cartouche with monogram, 10" H., weight 45 oz.*	650.00	725.00

(Sterling Silver and Crystal)

☐ **Maker unknown,** *sterling silver and crystal, bulbous shape, deeply cut melon rib design, star on bottom, 6½" H., 2" sterling collar, spout and hinged lid*	40.00	45.00

PLACE FORKS

On a properly set table, each place must be accompanied by (in addition to a platter) a knife, fork and spoon. Today, in our modern era of casual dining, these are the actual utensils employed at the meal. Going back 100 years, the "place" utensils were not necessarily those to be used — they merely set the stage. Special utensils for use with each course and each type of food then appeared thereafter. Hence, the silverware makers brought out special "place" knives, forks and spoons. A place fork was very much like a dinner fork. It served the purpose of a dinner fork excellently.

But it was a breach of etiquette to use it, if the hostess gave you a dinner fork when the main course was served. If this all seems peculiar, keep in mind that a formal or even semi-formal dinner of the 1880's was treated as an *event* which must be perfectly orchestrated. In society, each hostess was in competition against her contemporaries to bring off the best dinners. These things were reported on in the newspaper.

(Silver-Plated)

	Price Range	
☐ Community "Ballad", *no monogram, excellent condition* ..	3.00	4.00
☐ Community "Ballad", *no monogram, mint condition*	3.00	4.00
☐ Community "Silver Flower", *no monogram, mint condition*	4.00	5.00
☐ Community "Silver Flower", *no monogram, excellent condition*	3.00	4.00
☐ Community "Silver Sands", *no monogram, mint condition* .	3.00	4.00
☐ Community "Silver Sands", *no monogram, good condition*	2.00	3.00
☐ Community "Silver Valentine", *no monogram, mint condition*	3.00	4.00
☐ Community "Silver Valentine", *no monogram, fair condition*	1.00	3.00
☐ Community "Song of Autumn", *no monogram, mint condition*	3.00	4.00
☐ Community "Song of Autumn", *no monogram, good condition*	1.00	2.00
☐ Rogers & Bro. "Daybreak", *no monogram, excellent condition*	3.00	4.00
☐ Rogers & Bro. "Daybreak", *no monogram, good condition* .	2.00	3.00
☐ Tudor "Together", *no monogram, mint condition*	3.00	4.00
☐ Tudor "Together", *no monogram, excellent condition*	3.00	4.00
☐ 1847 Rogers "Esperanto", *no monogram, mint condition* ..	4.00	5.00
☐ 1847 Rogers "Magic Rose", *no monogram*	4.00	5.00
☐ 1847 Rogers "Springtime", *no monogram, excellent condition*	3.00	4.00

(Sterling Silver)

☐ Gorham "Blithe Spirit", *monogram*	16.00	18.00
☐ Gorham "Chantilly", *no monogram*	16.00	19.00
☐ Gorham "Fairfax", *7½" L., no monogram*	17.00	19.00
☐ International "1810", *monogram*	16.00	18.00
☐ International "Grand Regency", *no monogram*	15.00	17.00
☐ Oneida "Botticelli", *no monogram*	16.00	18.00
☐ Reed & Barton "Francis I", *no monogram*	18.00	20.00
☐ Reed & Barton "Old Virginia", *no monogram*	16.00	18.00
☐ Reed & Barton "Spanish Baroque", *no monogram*	16.00	18.00
☐ Towle "Country Manor", *no monogram*	16.00	18.00
☐ Towle "Kings", *no monogram*	24.00	27.00
☐ Towle "Spanish Provincial", *no monogram*	20.00	22.00
☐ Towle "Spanish Provincial", *monogram*	17.00	19.00
☐ Wallace "Royal Rose", *no monogram*	15.00	17.00

PLACE KNIVES

See the comments above in reference to place forks.

(Silver-Plated)

☐ Community "Ballad", *no monogram, mint condition*	3.00	4.00
☐ Community "Ballad", *no monogram, good condition*	1.00	2.00

	Price Range	
☐ Community "Silver Flower", *no monogram, mint condition*	4.00	5.00
☐ Community "Silver Sands", *no monogram, mint condition* .	3.00	4.00
☐ Community "Silver Valentine", *no monogram, mint condition*	4.00	5.00
☐ Community "Silver Valentine", *no monogram, good condition*	1.00	2.00
☐ Community "Song of Autumn", *no monogram, mint condition*	4.00	5.00
☐ Rogers & Bro. "Daybreak", *no monogram, mint condition* ..	6.00	7.00
☐ Rogers & Bro. "Daybreak", *no monogram, excellent condition*	4.00	5.00
☐ 1847 Rogers "Esperanto", *no monogram, mint condition* ..	4.00	5.00
☐ 1847 Rogers "Esperanto", *no monogram, excellent condition*	3.00	4.00
☐ 1847 Rogers "Magic Rose", *no monogram, mint condition* .	4.00	5.00
☐ 1847 Rogers "Magic Rose", *no monogram, fair condition* ..	1.00	3.00
☐ 1847 Rogers "Springtime", *no monogram, excellent condition*	4.00	5.00
☐ 1847 Rogers "Springtime", *no monogram, resilvered*	6.00	7.00

(Sterling Silver)

☐ Gorham "Blithe Spirit", *no monogram*	13.00	15.00
☐ Gorham "Blithe Spirit", *no monogram, damaged blade*	9.00	11.00
☐ Gorham "Buttercup", *no monogram*	14.00	16.00
☐ Gorham "Chantilly", *no monogram*	14.00	16.00
☐ Gorham "Lansdown", *monogram*	16.00	18.00
☐ International "Avalon", *monogram*	22.00	25.00
☐ International "Grand Regency", *no monogram*	12.00	14.00
☐ International "Monticello", *no monogram*	13.00	16.00
☐ Oneida "Botticelli", *no monogram*	13.00	15.00
☐ Reed & Barton "Francis I", *no monogram*	18.00	20.00
☐ Reed & Barton "Renaissance", *no monogram*	16.00	18.00
☐ Reed & Barton "Old Virginia", *no monogram*	13.00	15.00
☐ Reed & Barton "Spanish Baroque", *no monogram*	13.00	15.00
☐ Towle "Country Manor", *no monogram*	13.00	15.00
☐ Towle "Spanish Provincial", *no monogram*	13.00	16.00
☐ Wallace "Grand Colonial", *no monogram*	12.00	14.00

PLACE SETTINGS

These were sold in sets consisting of various pieces, with different components for luncheon or dinner settings.

(Silver-Plated)

☐ **S.L. & G.H. Rogers "English Garden"**, *seven pieces, includes dinner knife, dinner fork, teaspoon, salad fork, oval soup spoon, butter spreader, and iced tea spoon, no monogram, mint condition*	40.00	45.00
☐ **1847 Rogers "Daffodil II"**, *six pieces, includes luncheon fork, luncheon knife, cream soup spoon, teaspoon, butter spreader, and salad fork, monogram, good condition*	20.00	22.00
☐ **1847 Rogers "Old Colony"**, *seven pieces, includes dinner knife, dinner fork, teaspoon, cream soup spoon, dessert spoon, salad fork, butter spreader, no monogram, resilvered*	40.00	45.00

		Price Range

☐ **1847 Rogers "Vintage"**, *five pieces, includes dinner knife, dinner fork, teaspoon, salad fork and oval soup spoon, monogram, good condition* 24.00   27.00

(Sterling Silver)

☐ **Gorham "King George"**, *nine pieces, includes dinner knife, dinner fork, teaspoon, salad fork, cream soup spoon, butter spreader, iced tea spoon, demitasse spoon and cocktail fork, monogram and dated 1902, knife blade original silver-plated one in excellent condition* 190.00   210.00

☐ **International "Frontenac"**, *seven pieces, includes dinner knife, dinner fork, cream soup spoon, teaspoon, salad fork, butter spreader, and cocktail fork, monogram* 115.00   130.00

☐ **International "Old Rhapsody"**, *three pieces, includes place fork, place knife and teaspoon, no monogram* 45.00   50.00

☐ **International "Valencia"**, *three pieces, includes luncheon fork, luncheon knife and teaspoon, no monogram* 43.00   48.00

☐ **Lunt "Mt. Vernon"**, *six pieces, includes dinner fork, dinner knife, teaspoon, salad fork, oval soup spoon, and cocktail fork, monogram* 86.00   96.00

☐ **Reed & Barton "Cameo"**, *six pieces, includes dinner fork, dinner knife, teaspoon, salad fork, oval soup spoon, and butter spreader, no monogram* 100.00   110.00

☐ **Reed & Barton "Love Disarmed"**, *six pieces, includes luncheon fork, luncheon knife, teaspoon, salad fork, place spoon, flat-handled butter spreader, monogram and date, excellent condition* 170.00   300.00

☐ **Whiting "Madame Jumel"**, *seven pieces includes dinner knife, dinner fork, teaspoon, salad fork, oval soup spoon, butter spreader, and iced tea spoon, monogram* 95.00   105.00

PLACE SPOONS

See the comments above in reference to place forks.

(Silver-Plated)

☐ **Community "Silver Artistry"**, *no monogram, excellent condition* 3.00   4.00

☐ **Community "Silver Artistry"**, *monogram, fair condition* ... 1.00   2.00

☐ **C. Rogers & Bro. "Victor"**, *no monogram, excellent condition* 2.00   3.00

☐ **Oneida "Wildwood"**, *no monogram, good condition* 3.00   4.00

☐ **Oneida "Wildwood"**, *no monogram, resilvered* 7.00   8.00

☐ **Paragon "Sweet Pea"**, *no monogram, excellent condition* . 4.00   5.00

☐ **Paragon "Sweet Pea"**, *monogram, good condition* 2.00   3.00

☐ **Reed & Barton "Tiger Lily"**, *monogram, excellent condition* 3.00   4.00

☐ **Rogers & Bro. "Siren"**, *no monogram, resilvered* 8.00   9.00

☐ **S.L. & G.H. Rogers "Webster I"**, *no monogram, excellent condition* 2.00   3.00

☐ **Wm. Rogers "Victorian Rose"**, *no monogram, excellent condition* 3.00   4.00

☐ **Wm. Rogers Mfg. Co. "Venetian"**, *no monogram, good condition* 2.00   3.00

☐ **1835 R. Wallace "Stuart"**, *monogram, mint condition* 2.00   3.00

	Price Range	
☐ **1835 R. Wallace "Stuart"**, *no monogram, excellent condition*	3.00	4.00
☐ **1847 Rogers "Persian"**, *no monogram, good condition*	1.00	2.00
☐ **1847 Rogers "Vintage"**, *no monogram, good condition*	5.00	6.00
☐ **1847 Rogers "Vintage"**, *no monogram, resilvered*	8.00	9.00
(Sterling Silver)		
☐ **Alvin "Maryland"**, *monogram*	9.00	11.00
☐ **Lunt "Mt. Vernon"**, *monogram*	16.00	18.00
☐ **Whiting "Louis XV"**, *monogram*	15.00	17.00
☐ **Whiting "Madame Jumel"**, *monogram*	18.00	20.00

PLATES

Silver plates have been made in much greater quantities than these listings would suggest. All have identifying names according to their use, and the majority listed in this book are grouped by these identifying names. General collectors of silver plates are rare: nearly everybody specializes for sake of narrowing down the target somewhat, either by (a) plates designed for a special use, or (b) those made by a certain manufacturer, or in a certain pattern. When the term *silver plate* is found in older books, especially British books, it refers not only to plates but silver tableware in general. Taking things a step farther, *silver plate* can also mean a coating of silver applied to a copper or other metallic article.

(Silver-Plated)

☐ **Maker unknown**, *6" diameter, bread and butter type, fair condition, some knife marks, set of 12*	30.00	33.00

(Sterling Silver)

☐ **Gorham**, *5¾" diameter, bread and butter type, ornate applied rims, set of 11, total weight 40 oz.*	390.00	435.00
☐ **Gorham**, *7" diameter, dessert or salad size, ornate wide borders, set of eight, weight 50 oz.*	500.00	550.00

PLATTERS

In the world of tableware a platter is always a *serving* platter, never something from which to eat. They come in numerous sizes and of course an endless array of patterns. The larger ones, particularly those which are thick as well as wide, can be very impressive. Silver platters have an ancient history, and, so far as America is concerned, were made in this country from the earliest days of domestic silversmithing. Specimens a yard across exist, but these are so rare as to be found mainly in museums. On the market you will not often encounter them more than 24". There is no average size nor even an average shape; the basic shape was oval, but many liberties were taken with it to suit the specifics of different patterns. Platters are automatically thought of as "melt" objects by many people. Many of them, even in mint condition, carry very little premium collector value; however, one should investigate the individual specimen's value before selling it as scrap. If the premium value is very slight — say 10% or 15% above "melt" — a dealer (whether in antiques or bullion) will only pay you the melt value.

	Price Range	
(Silver-Plated)		
☐ **Maker unknown,** *some cuts on top surface, some wear spots*	20.00	22.00
☐ **International,** *well-and-tree type, rolled rim, good condition* .	24.00	27.00
(Sterling Silver)		
☐ **International,** *oval, stylized leaf rim, monogram in center, 18¼" L., 27 oz.*	210.00	235.00

PORRINGERS

These are cups or (if you prefer) bowls with handles, in which "porridge" was served. Porridge, a British expression adopted early in America, was not necessarily always a breakfast food. In early times, anything was likely to be made into porridge, as the old rhyme "peas porridge hot" testifies. Undoubtedly the porridge bowl was the last resting place for the cupboard's leftovers. Until fairly recently the term gruel was used of hot breakfast cereal, rather than porridge. Nevertheless we can be fairly sure that most owners of American-made silver porringers used them for oatmeal, farina, grits and the like. This is not really a plentiful article in silver, probably because the social classes preferred more stately foods at breakfast.

(Silver-Plated)		
☐ **Maker unknown,** *plain with pierced handle, monogram*	10.00	12.00
(Sterling Silver)		
☐ **Kirk,** *plain design, pierced handle, monogram, weight six oz.*	50.00	54.00
☐ **Reed & Barton,** *plain design, pierced handle, no monogram, weight five oz.*	34.00	38.00
☐ **Maker unknown,** *plain design, pierced handle, monogram and date, weight five oz.*	54.00	60.00

POWDER JARS

Like perfume jars, these have glass bowls surmounted with silver stoppers. The values depend much more on the artistry than on bullion content. Various types will be found, most of which date to the second half of the 19th century. It was not an article which any manufacturer brought out in great abundance, but many different manufacturers made them. They appeared in the fashionable giftshops of great-grandma's time.

(Sterling and Crystal)		
☐ **Maker unknown,** *sterling and crystal, 5" diameter, plain crystal, beading on silver lid*	22.00	24.00
☐ **Maker unknown,** *sterling and crystal, cane cutting on crystal, star bottom, repousse animal and flower design on sterling lid*	100.00	115.00

PRESERVE PADDLES

These are aptly named: they resemble miniature paddles. They served their purpose ideally, much better than a spoon, as they could spread the preserve. Preserve paddles are wider than knives and the blades (if we can call them that) are shorter, with slim handles of medium length. The overall length ranges usually from about 7" to 8". Though many accessories of the

Victorian table were clearly unnecessary, the preserve paddle was not one of them. Today's version is in stainless steel or, more often, disposable plastic.

(Silver-Plated)	**Price Range**	
☐ Holmes & Edwards "Chatsworth", *monogram, excellent condition*	7.00	8.00
☐ Rogers "Alhambra", *no monogram, excellent condition* ...	11.00	13.00
☐ Rogers "Alhambra", *monogram, good condition*	5.00	6.00
☐ Rogers & Hamilton "Raphael", *no monogram, good condition*	13.00	15.00
☐ 1847 Rogers "Berwick", *no monogram, excellent condition*	14.00	16.00
☐ 1847 Rogers "Persian", *no monogram, excellent condition*	10.00	12.00
☐ 1847 Rogers "Vintage", *no monogram, mint condition*	20.00	22.00
☐ 1847 Rogers "Vintage", *monogram, fair condition*	6.00	7.00
☐ 1847 Rogers "Vintage", *no monogram, good condition*	7.00	8.00
(Sterling Silver)		
☐ Durgin "Chrysanthemum", *monogram*	45.00	50.00
☐ Reed & Barton "Les Cinq Fleurs", *7¾", no monogram*	18.00	20.00
☐ Tiffany "Colonial", *no monogram*	45.00	50.00

PUNCH BOWLS AND PUNCH SETS

Punch bowls are the largest articles of silverware for the table. They vary greatly in size and can reach weights of well over 100 ounces — specimens are recorded with weights of as much as 300 ounces, but these hardly ever appear for sale on the market. Since punch was meant for festive occasions, the

Punch Bowl, *Tiffany "Chrysanthemum," c. 1895, diameter 17", 114 ounces, 6500.00*

punch bowl was designed to reflect the festive atmosphere. With so much space available for decoration on punch bowls, the manufacturers could turn them into stunning works of art — or leave them virtually plain, for owners to have decorated in the style they preferred. Many carry engraved heraldic arms and passed down from one generation to another in a family. Punch sets consist of the bowl plus a ladle and, normally, a dozen cups, but the number of cups can vary. Hooks were usually set around the bowl rim, on which the cups hung. The buyer should beware of "loaded" specimens, whose weight has been increased by filling up a hollow base. Even when the bases were not actually hollow, there was usually enough space at the bottom to introduce some loading material. In an already-heavy article such as this, loading is more difficult to detect, especially if it has not been overdone — an extra 10 ounces in an object of 100 ounces is apt to go unnoticed.

(Coin Silver) Price Range

☐ **Eoff & Shepherd,** c. 1850, embossed and chased basketweave design, rope rim, cartouche with monogram and crest, three dolphin supports, undulating base, 9¾" H., 11" diameter across top, with nonmatching ladle by Wm. B. North (New York, c. 1820), applied wheat motif, ladle 13¾" L., total weight 61 ozs. 1,500.00   1,650.00

(Silver-Plated)

☐ **Maker unknown,** pedestal base, ornate shell motif, with 12 pedestal cups, undertray and ladle, monogram and date on bowl, all in excellent condition, bowl capacity three gallons . . 245.00   270.00

(Silver-Plated and Crystal)

☐ **Maker unknown,** c. 1880, Victorian styling, swirled glass with vertical cut ribs, silver-plated mask and scroll feet, lid with pineapple knop, 15" H. 100.00   115.00

(Sterling Silver)

☐ **Maker Unknown,** late Victorian, ornate design, monogram and date, weight 100 oz. 2,150.00   2,375.00

PUNCH LADLES

These have long ranked among the most popular silver collectors' items, and with ample reason. Their huge sizes make for a very impressive display. English specimens dating as early as the 1700's will be found on the market, but those of American manufacture are nearly always 19th century or later. There is a definite scarcity factor with punch ladles; they were made as accessories to punch bowls, which comparatively few households owned. Even the well-stocked dealers in silver collectibles seldom can offer more than a few specimens at any given time. This, coupled with their substantial bullion content, would seem to place them in a favorable category not only for collecting but investing. The *lengths* of punch ladles vary considerably. Smaller ones are sometimes mistaken for soup ladles; there is no foolproof way of telling them apart.

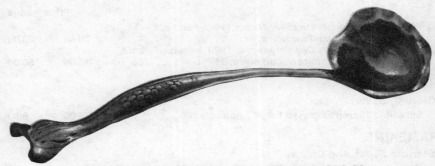

Punch Ladle, *(sterling), Gorham "Martele",* 720.00

(Silver-Plated)

	Price Range	
☐ Rogers & Bro. "Crown", *11½" handle, no monogram, excellent condition*	54.00	60.00
☐ Rogers & Hamilton "Alhambra", *no monogram, good condition*	60.00	66.00
☐ S.L. & G.H. Rogers "Puritan", *no monogram, excellent condition*	27.00	30.00
☐ Wm. Rogers Mfg. Co. "Chevallier", *13" L., 4½" bowl, monogram and date, resilvered*	44.00	48.00
☐ 1847 Rogers "Daffodil", *no monogram, mint condition*	75.00	85.00

(Sterling Silver)

☐ Gorham "Colonial", *no monogram*	95.00	105.00
☐ Gorham "Marie Antoinette", *no monogram*	135.00	150.00
☐ Gorham "Newcastle", *no monogram*	135.00	150.00
☐ Reed & Barton "Francis I", *monogram*	350.00	390.00
☐ Wood & Hughes "Medallion", *17" L., trifoil bowl, no monogram*	200.00	225.00

PURSES

The Victorian/Edwardian lady whose dining table glistened with silver, and whose dressing table abounded in silver accessories, could also use a silver *purse* if she wished. Manufacturers catered to the admirers of silver in every conceivable way. Silver purses were intended of course for use on formal occasions. They remained popular well into the age of Art Deco, and in fact were probably more popular then than previously. They are usually quite small, the majority designed to be held in the hand rather than carried on a strap. Collectors of silver purses take a special interest in those with interior compartments, the more (and the more offbeat) the better. These are difficult to find in unblemished condition.

(Sterling Silver)

☐ Unger Bros. "Love's Dream", *mesh body with snap top closure, "Love's Dream" medallion on each side, 5" x 8½", engraved with first name, chain handle*	225.00	250.00
☐ Unger Bros., *heavy scroll engraving on both sides, includes coin and bill holders, mirror, pencil, writing pad, has chain handle*	54.00	60.00

	Price Range	
☐ **Whiting & Davis,** *ornate silver frame, chain handle, 6¾" L., 5" W., colorful enamel work*	20.00	23.00
☐ **Maker unknown,** *Art Deco styling, c. 1930, engraved frame, mesh handle, blue stone thumb piece, 6¾" L.*	45.00	50.00

RAMEKIN FORKS
(Sterling Silver)

☐ **Schofield "Scroll Engraved Edge",** *monogram*	7.00	8.00

RAMEKINS
(Sterling Silver and China)

☐ **Gorham and Lenox,** *sterling silver and china, ornate holders with attached underplate, hand-painted Lenox liners with gold filigree work, C.A.C. transition mark on liners, Gorham date mark for 1899, total silver weight 30 oz., set of six*	270.00	200.00
☐ **International and Lenox,** *sterling silver and china, holders have teaspoon type handles, openwork design, Lenox liners with plain gold trim, set of twelve, total silver weight 30 oz.*	250.00	275.00
☐ **Tiffany and Lenox,** *sterling silver and china, holder has openwork and rolled rim, no handle, Lenox liner with plain gold trim, silver weight 2 oz.*	18.00	20.00

RATTLES

The infant of yesteryear whose playthings included a silver rattle was a privileged character indeed — though not in a position to relish this status symbol. Very few silver baby rattles were made. There was little call for them, as even parents who *could* afford silver rattles for their offspring usually bought the ordinary kinds. Obviously, silver did not make for a better rattle or a more contented baby: it simply provided a means for

Baby Rattle, *(sterling), Tiffany, mother-of-pearl handle,* 180.00

extravagant parents to showcase their wealth. But, as collectors' items, they ARE attractive and unusual, and deserve some claim on the hobbyist's attention.

(Sterling Silver)	Price Range	
☐ **Maker unknown,** *sterling silver with mother-of-pearl handle, jingle bell on one end, ring on the other, twisted stem, several tiny dents, monogram and date*	16.00	18.00

RELISH FORKS

Both forks and spoons were made for use with relish, and the careful hostess always provided both. Either served the purpose; the choice of which to use depended on whether or not the relish *juice* appealed to you. They have not yet made any significant inroads with collectors.

(Silver-Plated)		
☐ **1881 Rogers "LaVigne",** *no monogram, excellent condition*	16.00	18.00

RELISH SPOONS

(Silver-Plated)		
☐ **Community "Flight",** *no monogram, mint condition*	5.00	6.00
☐ **Rogers "Alhambra",** *no monogram, excellent condition* ...	6.00	7.00
☐ **1847 Rogers "Flair",** *no monogram, excellent condition* ...	3.00	4.00
☐ **1847 Rogers "Heritage",** *no monogram, mint condition*	3.00	4.00
☐ **1847 Rogers "Old Colony",** *no monogram, resilvered*	7.00	8.00
☐ **1847 Rogers "Remembrance",** *no monogram, good condition*	4.00	5.00

(Sterling Silver)		
☐ **Maker unknown,** *Art Nouveau floral pattern, gold wash bowl*	16.00	19.00

RELISH TRAYS

These were used not only in homes but restaurants. They usually have recesses along the rim, for resting the relish fork or spoon.

(Silver-Plated)		
☐ **Community "Noblesse",** *monogram, excellent condition* ..	12.00	13.00
☐ **Maker unknown,** *ornate floral rim, monogram, good condition*	25.00	28.00

SALAD FORKS

Salads, though long served in Europe and elsewhere, did not become popular in America until late in the 19th century. Our ancestors had, for some reason, an inherent dislike of raw vegetables. By around 1890 salads had worked their way sufficiently into public favor to bring forth a multitude of accessories. Every silverware manufacturer put them out, in every existing pattern. Salad forks are a bit lighter than dinner forks, because, in the world of silverware, the character of the utensil was supposed to match the character of the food. Even with the countless thousands destroyed during the Great Silver Melt of 1979/80, salad forks are still very plentiful on the market.

(Silver-Plated)	Price Range	
☐ Alvin "Bride's Bouquet", *no monogram, excellent condition*	8.00	9.00
☐ Alvin "Cameo", *no monogram, excellent condition*	6.00	7.00
☐ Alvin "Cameo", *no monogram, good condition*	4.00	5.00
☐ Alvin "Cameo", *no monogram, good condition*	4.00	5.00
☐ Alvin "Cameo", *no monogram, good condition*	2.00	3.00
☐ Alvin "Diana", *no monogram, excellent condition*	6.00	7.00
☐ Alvin "Diana", *no monogram, good condition*	5.00	6.00
☐ Alvin "Diana", *no monogram, poor condition*	1.00	2.00
☐ Community "Adam", *no monogram, excellent condition* ..	4.00	5.00
☐ Community "Adam", *monogram, good condition*	3.00	4.00
☐ Community "Adam", *no monogram, excellent condition* ..	6.00	7.00
☐ Community "Adam", *monogram, excellent condition*	3.00	4.00
☐ Community "Adam", *monogram, fair condition*	1.00	2.00
☐ Community "Ballad", *no monogram, excellent condition* ..	4.00	5.00
☐ Community "Ballad", *no monogram, good condition*	3.00	4.00
☐ Community "Bedford", *no monogram, good condition*	4.00	5.00
☐ Community "Bedford", *no monogram, fair condition*	1.00	2.00
☐ Community "Beverly", *no monogram, excellent condition* .	6.00	7.00
☐ Community "Beverly", *no monogram, good condition*	5.00	6.00
☐ Community "Beverly", *no monogram, fair condition*	1.00	2.00
☐ Community "Bird of Paradise", *no monogram, excellent condition*	4.00	5.00
☐ Community "Bird of Paradise", *no monogram, excellent condition*	6.00	7.00
☐ Community "Bird of Paradise", *no monogram, good condition*	5.00	6.00
☐ Community "Bird of Paradise", *no monogram, poor condition*	1.00	2.00
☐ Community "Classic", *no monogram, excellent condition* .	6.00	7.00
☐ Community "Classic", *no monogram, good condition*	5.00	6.00
☐ Community "Coronation", *no monogram, excellent condition*	5.00	6.00
☐ Community "Coronation", *no monogram, good condition* .	4.00	5.00
☐ Community "Coronation", *no monogram, fair condition* ...	1.00	2.00
☐ Community "Deauville", *no monogram, excellent condition*	3.00	4.00
☐ Community "Deauville", *no monogram, excellent condition*	6.00	7.00
☐ Community "Deauville", *no monogram, good condition* ...	5.00	6.00
☐ Community "Deauville", *no monogram, fair condition*	1.00	2.00
☐ Community "Enchantment", *no monogram, excellent condition*	6.00	7.00
☐ Community "Enchantment", *no monogram, good condition*	5.00	6.00
☐ Community "Enchantment", *monogram, good condition* ..	2.00	3.00
☐ Community "Evening Star", *no monogram, excellent condition*	6.00	7.00
☐ Community "Evening Star", *no monogram, good condition*	5.00	6.00
☐ Community "Evening Star", *no monogram, fair condition* ..	1.00	2.00
☐ Community "Georgian", *no monogram, excellent condition*	3.00	4.00
☐ Community "Georgian", *no monogram, good condition* ...	4.00	5.00
☐ Community "Grosvenor", *no monogram, excellent condition*	4.00	5.00
☐ Community "Grosvenor", *no monogram, good condition* ..	3.00	4.00
☐ Community "Grosvenor", *no monogram, fair condition*	1.00	2.00
☐ Community "Grosvenor", *monogram, excellent condition* .	2.00	3.00

Price Range

☐ Community "King Cedric", *no monogram, excellent condition*	6.00	7.00
☐ Community "King Cedric", *no monogram, good condition*	5.00	6.00
☐ Community "King Cedric", *no monogram, poor condition*	1.00	2.00
☐ Community "Lady Hamilton", *no monogram, good condition*	4.00	5.00
☐ Community "Lady Hamilton", *no monogram, excellent condition*	6.00	7.00
☐ Community "Lady Hamilton", *no monogram, good condition*	4.00	5.00
☐ Community "Lady Hamilton", *no monogram, fair condition*	1.00	2.00
☐ Community "Louis XVI", *no monogram, excellent condition*	6.00	7.00
☐ Community "Louis XVI", *no monogram, good condition*	5.00	6.00
☐ Community "Louis XVI", *no monogram, fair condition*	2.00	3.00
☐ Community "Milady", *no monogram, excellent condition*	4.00	5.00
☐ Community "Milady", *no monogram, excellent condition*	6.00	7.00
☐ Community "Milady", *no monogram, good condition*	5.00	6.00
☐ Community "Milady", *no monogram, fair condition*	1.00	2.00
☐ Community "Morning Rose", *no monogram, mint condition*	4.00	5.00
☐ Community "Morning Rose", *no monogram, excellent condition*	6.00	7.00
☐ Community "Morning Rose", *no monogram, good condition*	5.00	6.00
☐ Community "Morning Star", *no monogram, excellent condition*	4.00	5.00
☐ Community "Morning Star", *no monogram, good condition*	3.00	4.00
☐ Community "Morning Star", *no monogram, fair condition*	1.00	2.00
☐ Community "Noblesse", *monogram, excellent condition*	3.00	4.00
☐ Community "Noblesse", *no monogram, excellent condition*	6.00	7.00
☐ Community "Noblesse", *no monogram, good condition*	5.00	6.00
☐ Community "Noblesse", *monogram, excellent condition*	2.00	3.00
☐ Community "Noblesse", *monogram, fair condition*	1.00	2.00
☐ Community "Patrician", *no monogram, excellent condition*	4.00	5.00
☐ Community "Patrician", *no monogram, excellent condition*	6.00	7.00
☐ Community "Patrician", *no monogram, good condition*	5.00	6.00
☐ Community "Patrician", *no monogram, fair condition*	1.00	2.00
☐ Community "Paul Revere", *no monogram, excellent condition*	6.00	7.00
☐ Community "Paul Revere", *no monogram, good condition*	5.00	6.00
☐ Community "Paul Revere", *no monogram, fair condition*	1.00	2.00
☐ Community "Paul Revere", *no monogram, poor condition*	1.00	2.00
☐ Community "Sheraton", *no monogram, excellent condition*	4.00	5.00
☐ Community "Sheraton", *no monogram, excellent condition*	6.00	7.00
☐ Community "Sheraton", *no monogram, good condition*	4.00	5.00
☐ Community "Sheraton", *no monogram, fair condition*	1.00	2.00
☐ Community "Silver Artistry", *no monogram, excellent condition*	6.00	7.00
☐ Community "Silver Artistry", *no monogram, good condition*	5.00	6.00
☐ Community "Silver Artistry", *no monogram, fair condition*	1.00	2.00
☐ Community "Silver Flowers", *no monogram, mint condition*	5.00	6.00
☐ Community "Silver Flowers", *no monogram, excellent condition*	6.00	7.00
☐ Community "Silver Flowers", *no monogram, good condition*	5.00	6.00

	Price Range	
☐ Community **"Silver Flowers"**, *no monogram, fair condition*	1.00	2.00
☐ Community **"Silver Sands"**, *no monogram, excellent condition*	4.00	5.00
☐ Community **"Silver Sands"**, *no monogram, good condition*	5.00	6.00
☐ Community **"Silver Sands"**, *no monogram, poor condition*	1.00	2.00
☐ Community **"Silver Valentine"**, *no monogram, excellent condition*	4.00	5.00
☐ Community **"Silver Valentine"**, *no monogram, fair condition*	1.00	2.00
☐ Community **"Song of Autumn"**, *no monogram, excellent condition*	4.00	5.00
☐ Community **"Song of Autumn"**, *no monogram, good condition*	3.00	4.00
☐ Community **"South Seas"**, *no monogram, excellent condition*	4.00	5.00
☐ Community **"South Seas"**, *no monogram, good condition*	2.00	3.00
☐ Community **"South Seas"**, *no monogram, fair condition*	1.00	2.00
☐ Community **"Tangier"**, *no monogram, excellent condition*	4.00	5.00
☐ Community **"Tangier"**, *no monogram, good condition*	5.00	6.00
☐ Community **"Tangier"**, *no monogram, fair condition*	2.00	3.00
☐ Community **"Tangier"**, *no monogram, poor condition*	1.00	2.00
☐ Community **"Tangier"**, *monogram, fair condition*	1.00	2.00
☐ Community **"White Orchid"**, *no monogram, excellent condition*	6.00	7.00
☐ Community **"White Orchid"**, *no monogram, good condition*	5.00	6.00
☐ Community **"White Orchid"**, *no monogram, poor condition*	1.00	2.00
☐ Community **"White Orchid"**, *no monogram, silver in excellent condition but tines bent*	1.00	2.00
☐ DeepSilver **"Laurel Mist"**, *no monogram, excellent condition*	6.00	7.00
☐ DeepSilver **"Laurel Mist"**, *no monogram, good condition*	5.00	6.00
☐ DeepSilver **"Laurel Mist"**, *no monogram, fair condition*	1.00	2.00
☐ DeepSilver **"Triumph"**, *no monogram, excellent condition*	6.00	7.00
☐ DeepSilver **"Triumph"**, *no monogram, good condition*	5.00	6.00
☐ DeepSilver **"Triumph"**, *no monogram, fair condition*	2.00	3.00
☐ DeepSilver **"Triumph"**, *no monogram, poor condition*	1.00	2.00
☐ Embassy **"Bouquet"**, *no monogram, excellent condition*	6.00	7.00
☐ Embassy **"Bouquet"**, *no monogram, good condition*	5.00	6.00
☐ Embassy **"Bouquet"**, *fair condition*	1.00	2.00
☐ Fortune **"Fortune"**, *no monogram, excellent condition*	6.00	7.00
☐ Fortune **"Fortune"**, *no monogram, good condition*	5.00	6.00
☐ Fortune **"Fortune"**, *no monogram, fair condition*	1.00	2.00
☐ Gorham **"Empire"**, *no monogram, excellent condition*	5.00	6.00
☐ Gorham **"Empire"**, *monogram, fair condition*	1.00	2.00
☐ Gorham **"New Elegance"**, *no monogram, excellent condition*	6.00	7.00
☐ Gorham **"New Elegance"**, *no monogram, good condition*	5.00	6.00
☐ Gorham **"New Elegance"**, *no monogram, fair condition*	1.00	2.00
☐ Gorham **"Providence"**, *no monogram, excellent condition*	3.00	4.00
☐ Gorham **"Shelburne"**, *no monogram, excellent condition*	4.00	5.00
☐ Gorham **"Shelburne"**, *no monogram, good condition*	3.00	4.00
☐ Gorham **"Vanity Fair"**, *no monogram, excellent condition*	6.00	7.00
☐ Gorham **"Vanity Fair"**, *no monogram, good condition*	4.00	5.00
☐ Gorham **"Vanity Fair"**, *no monogram, fair condition*	1.00	2.00

Price Range

☐ Gorham "Vanity Fair", *no monogram, good condition*	4.00	5.00
☐ Gorham "Vanity Fair", *no monogram, fair condition*	1.00	2.00
☐ Gorham "Westminster", *no monogram, excellent condition*	6.00	7.00
☐ Gorham "Westminster", *no monogram, good condition* . . .	5.00	6.00
☐ Gorham "Westminster", *no monogram, fair condition*	1.00	2.00
☐ Gorham "Winthrop", *no monogram, excellent condition* . . .	4.00	5.00
☐ Gorham "Winthrop", *no monogram, poor condition*	1.00	2.00
☐ Harmony House "Serenade", *no monogram, excellent condition*	4.00	5.00
☐ Heirloom "Cardinal", *no monogram, excellent condition* . .	6.00	7.00
☐ Heirloom "Cardinal", *no monogram, good condition*	5.00	6.00
☐ Heirloom "Cardinal", *no monogram, fair condition*	2.00	3.00
☐ Holmes & Edwards "Carolina", *no monogram, excellent condition*	5.00	6.00
☐ Holmes & Edwards "Carolina", *no monogram, good condition*	4.00	5.00
☐ Holmes & Edwards "Century", *no monogram, excellent condition*	6.00	7.00
☐ Holmes & Edwards "Century", *no monogram, good condition*	5.00	6.00
☐ Holmes & Edwards "Century", *no monogram, fair condition*	1.00	2.00
☐ Holmes & Edwards "Century", *no monogram, poor condition*	1.00	2.00
☐ Holmes & Edwards "Century", *monogram, excellent condition*	2.00	3.00
☐ Holmes & Edwards "Danish Princess", *no monogram, excellent condition*	4.00	5.00
☐ Holmes & Edwards "Danish Princess", *no monogram, excellent condition*	6.00	7.00
☐ Holmes & Edwards "Danish Princess", *no monogram, good condition*	5.00	6.00
☐ Holmes & Edwards "Danish Princess", *no monogram, fair condition*	1.00	2.00
☐ Holmes & Edwards "DeSancy", *no monogram, excellent condition*	6.00	7.00
☐ Holmes & Edwards "DeSancy", *no monogram, good condition*	5.00	6.00
☐ Holmes & Edwards "DeSancy", *no monogram, fair condition*	1.00	2.00
☐ Holmes & Edwards "Lovely Lady", *no monogram, excellent condition*	6.00	7.00
☐ Holmes & Edwards "Lovely Lady", *no monogram, good condition*	5.00	6.00
☐ Holmes & Edwards "Lovely Lady", *monogram, excellent condition*	3.00	4.00
☐ Holmes & Edwards "May Queen", *no monogram, excellent condition*	5.00	6.00
☐ Holmes & Edwards "May Queen", *no monogram, poor condition*	1.00	2.00
☐ Holmes & Edwards "Orient", *no monogram, excellent condition*	7.00	8.00
☐ Holmes & Edwards "Orient", *no monogram, good condition*	6.00	7.00
☐ Holmes & Edwards "Romance", *no monogram, good condition*	3.00	4.00

	Price Range	

☐ Holmes & Edwards "Rosemary", *no monogram, excellent condition* 4.00 5.00

☐ Holmes & Edwards "Spring Garden", *no monogram, excellent condition* 6.00 7.00

☐ Holmes & Edwards "Spring Garden", *no monogram, good condition* 6.00 7.00

☐ Holmes & Edwards "Spring Garden", *no monogram, fair condition* 1.00 2.00

☐ Holmes & Edwards "Youth", *no monogram, excellent condition* 6.00 7.00

☐ Holmes & Edwards "Youth", *no monogram, good condition* 5.00 6.00

☐ International "Orleans", *no monogram, excellent condition* 4.00 5.00

☐ International "Silver Tulip", *no monogram, excellent condition* 5.00 6.00

☐ King Edward "Moss Rose", *no monogram, excellent condition* 6.00 7.00

☐ King Edward "Moss Rose", *no monogram, good condition* . 5.00 6.00

☐ King Edward "Moss Rose", *no monogram, fair condition* .. 1.00 2.00

☐ Landers, Frary & Clark "Farmington", *no monogram, excellent condition* 3.00 4.00

☐ Melody "Melody", *no monogram, excellent condition* 5.00 6.00

☐ Melody "Melody", *no monogram, good condition* 4.00 5.00

☐ National "King Edward", *no monogram, excellent condition* 6.00 7.00

☐ National "King Edward", *no monogram, good condition* ... 5.00 6.00

☐ Nobility "Wind Song", *no monogram, excellent condition* . 3.00 4.00

☐ Old Company Plate "Signature", *no monogram, excellent condition* 4.00 5.00

☐ Oneida "Avalon", *no monogram, excellent condition* 4.00 5.00

☐ Oneida "Bridal Wreath", *no monogram, excellent condition* 6.00 7.00

☐ Oneida "Bridal Wreath", *no monogram, good condition* ... 5.00 6.00

☐ Oneida "Clarion", *no monogram, excellent condition* 5.00 6.00

☐ Oneida "Clarion", *no monogram, fair condition* 1.00 2.00

☐ Oneida "Flower de Luce", *no monogram, excellent condition* 8.00 9.00

☐ Oneida "Flower de Luce", *no monogram, good condition* .. 7.00 8.00

☐ Oneida "Flower de Luce", *monogram, excellent condition* . 6.00 7.00

☐ Oneida "Jamestown", *no monogram, excellent condition* . 4.00 5.00

☐ Oneida "Jamestown", *monogram, excellent condition* 2.00 3.00

☐ Oneida "Primrose", *no monogram, excellent condition* 4.00 5.00

☐ Oneida "Wildwood", *no monogram, excellent condition* ... 12.00 14.00

☐ Oneida "Wildwood", *monogram, excellent condition* 8.00 9.00

☐ Prestige "Grenoble", *no monogram, excellent condition* .. 6.00 7.00

☐ Prestige "Grenoble", *no monogram, good condition* 6.00 7.00

☐ R.C. Co. "Orleans II", *no monogram, excellent condition* .. 6.00 7.00

☐ R.C. Co. "Orleans II", *no monogram, good condition* 5.00 6.00

☐ Reed & Barton "Belmont", *no monogram, excellent condition* 4.00 5.00

☐ Reed & Barton "Belmont", *no monogram, fair condition* ... 1.00 2.00

☐ Reed & Barton "Dresden Rose", *no monogram, excellent condition* 6.00 7.00

☐ Reed & Barton "Dresden Rose", *no monogram, good condition* 5.00 6.00

☐ Reed & Barton "Dresden Rose", *no monogram, fair condition* 1.00 2.00

	Price Range	
☐ Reed & Barton "Fiddle", *no monogram, excellent condition*	5.00	6.00
☐ Reed & Barton "Fiddle", *no monogram, fair condition*	1.00	2.00
☐ Reed & Barton "Maid of Honor", *no monogram, excellent condition*	6.00	7.00
☐ Reed & Barton "Maid of Honor", *no monogram, good condition*	5.00	6.00
☐ Reed & Barton "Maid of Honor", *no monogram, fair condition*	1.00	2.00
☐ Reed & Barton "Sheffield", *no monogram, excellent condition*	7.00	8.00
☐ Reed & Barton "Sheffield", *no monogram, good condition* .	6.00	7.00
☐ Reed & Barton "Sierra", *no monogram, excellent condition*	7.00	8.00
☐ Reed & Barton "Sierra", *no monogram, good condition*	6.00	7.00
☐ Reed & Barton "Sierra", *no monogram, fair condition*	2.00	3.00
☐ Reed & Barton "Thistle", *no monogram, excellent condition*	10.00	13.00
☐ Reed & Barton "Thistle", *no monogram, good condition* . . .	10.00	13.00
☐ Reed & Barton "Thistle", *no monogram, fair condition*	4.00	5.00
☐ Reed & Barton "Tiger Lily", *no monogram, excellent condition*	7.00	8.00
☐ Reed & Barton "Tiger Lily", *no monogram, good condition* .	6.00	7.00
☐ Reed & Barton "Tiger Lily", *monogram, fair condition*	3.00	4.00
☐ Reliance "Exeter", *no monogram, excellent condition*	6.00	7.00
☐ Reliance "Exeter", *no monogram, good condition*	5.00	6.00
☐ Reliance "Wildwood", *no monogram*	9.00	11.00
☐ Reliance "Wildwood", *no monogram, fair condition*	3.00	4.00
☐ Rockford "Whittier", *no monogram, excellent condition* . . .	3.00	4.00
☐ Rockford "Whittier", *no monogram, good condition*	4.00	5.00
☐ Rogers "Alhambra", *no monogram, excellent condition* . . .	8.00	9.00
☐ Rogers "Alhambra", *no monogram, good condition*	7.00	8.00
☐ Rogers "Alhambra", *no monogram, poor condition*	1.00	2.00
☐ Rogers "Ambassador", *monogram, excellent condition* . . .	3.00	4.00
☐ Rogers "Burgundy", *no monogram, excellent condition* . . .	6.00	7.00
☐ Rogers "Burgundy", *no monogram, good condition*	5.00	6.00
☐ Rogers "Burgundy", *no monogram, fair condition*	1.00	2.00
☐ Rogers "Clinton", *no monogram, excellent condition*	6.00	7.00
☐ Rogers "Clinton", *monogram, fair condition*	1.00	2.00
☐ Rogers "Desire", *no monogram, excellent condition*	6.00	7.00
☐ Rogers "Desire", *no monogram, good condition*	5.00	6.00
☐ Rogers "Desota", *no monogram, excellent condition*	6.00	7.00
☐ Rogers "Desota", *no monogram, good condition*	5.00	6.00
☐ Rogers "Inspiration", *no monogram, excellent condition* . .	6.00	7.00
☐ Rogers "Inspiration", *no monogram, fair condition*	1.00	2.00
☐ Rogers "LaConcorde", *no monogram, excellent condition* .	12.00	14.00
☐ Rogers "LaConcorde", *no monogram, good condition*	10.00	13.00
☐ Rogers "LaTouraine", *no monogram, excellent condition* . .	6.00	7.00
☐ Rogers "LaTouraine", *monogram, excellent condition*	2.00	3.00
☐ Rogers "Nuart", *no monogram, excellent condition*	6.00	7.00
☐ Rogers "Nuart", *no monogram, poor condition*	1.00	2.00
☐ Rogers "Orange Blossom", *no monogram, excellent condition*	7.00	8.00
☐ Rogers "Orange Blossom", *monogram, good condition* . . .	4.00	5.00
☐ Rogers "Precious", *no monogram, excellent condition*	6.00	7.00
☐ Rogers "Precious", *no monogram, good condition*	5.00	6.00

	Price Range	
☐ Rogers "Precious", *monogram, fair condition*	1.00	2.00
☐ Rogers "Queen Bess II", *no monogram, excellent condition*	3.00	4.00
☐ Rogers "Queen Bess II", *no monogram, poor condition* ...	1.00	2.00
☐ Rogers "Vendome", *no monogram, excellent condition* ...	6.00	7.00
☐ Rogers "Vendome", *no monogram, good condition*	5.00	6.00
☐ Rogers & Bro. "Daybreak", *no monogram, excellent condition*	3.00	4.00
☐ Rogers & Bro. "Daybreak", *no monogram, excellent condition*	6.00	7.00
☐ Rogers & Bro. "Daybreak", *monogram, good condition*	2.00	3.00
☐ Rogers & Bro. "Modern Rose", *no monogram, excellent condition*	5.00	6.00
☐ Rogers & Bro. "Modern Rose", *no monogram, good condition*	4.00	5.00
☐ Rogers & Bro. "Mystic", *no monogram, excellent condition*	7.00	8.00
☐ Rogers & Bro. "Mystic", *no monogram, good condition* ...	5.00	6.00
☐ Rogers & Bro. "Mystic", *no monogram, fair condition*	2.00	3.00
☐ Rogers & Bro. "Mystic", *monogram, excellent condition* ...	3.00	4.00
☐ Rogers & Bro. "Thistle", *no monogram, excellent condition*	9.00	10.00
☐ Rogers & Hamilton "Aldine", *no monogram, excellent condition*	8.00	9.00
☐ Rogers & Hamilton "Aldine", *no monogram, good condition*	7.00	8.00
☐ Rogers & Hamilton "Aldine", *monogram, excellent condition*	7.00	8.00
☐ Rogers & Hamilton "Alhambra", *no monogram, good condition*	6.00	7.00
☐ Rogers & Hamilton "Doric", *no monogram, excellent condition*	8.00	9.00
☐ Rogers & Hamilton "Doric", *no monogram, good condition*	7.00	8.00
☐ Rogers & Hamilton "Marquise", *no monogram, excellent condition*	4.00	5.00
☐ Rogers & Hamilton "Marquise", *monogram, poor condition*	1.00	2.00
☐ Rogers & Hamilton "Raphael", *no monogram, excellent condition*	15.00	17.00
☐ Rogers Mfg. Co. "Triumph", *no monogram, excellent condition*	6.00	7.00
☐ Rogers Mfg. Co. "Triumph", *no monogram, good condition*	5.00	6.00
☐ Rogers Mfg. Co. "Triumph", *no monogram, fair condition* ..	1.00	2.00
☐ S.L. & G.H. Rogers "Countess II", *no monogram, excellent condition*	6.00	7.00
☐ S.L. & G.H. Rogers "Countess II", *no monogram, good condition*	5.00	6.00
☐ S.L. & G.H. Rogers "Countess II", *no monogram, fair condition*	1.00	2.00
☐ S.L. & G.H. Rogers "English Garden", *no monogram, excellent condition*	4.00	5.00
☐ S.L. & G.H. Rogers "English Garden", *no monogram, good condition*	3.00	4.00
☐ S.L. & G.H. Rogers "English Garden", *no monogram, excellent condition*	6.00	7.00
☐ S.L. & G.H. Rogers "English Garden", *no monogram, good condition*	5.00	6.00
☐ S.L. & G.H. Rogers "Faun", *no monogram, excellent condition*	6.00	7.00

	Price Range	
☐ S.L. & G.H. Rogers "Faun", *no monogram, good condition* .	5.00	6.00
☐ S.L. & G.H. Rogers "Faun", *no monogram, fair condition* ..	1.00	2.00
☐ S.L. & G.H. Rogers "Jasmine", *no monogram, excellent condition*	4.00	5.00
☐ S.L. & G.H. Rogers "Presentation", *no monogram, excellent condition*	6.00	7.00
☐ S.L. & G.H. Rogers "Presentation", *no monogram, good condition*	5.00	6.00
☐ S.L. & G.H. Rogers "Presentation", *no monogram, fair condition*	1.00	2.00
☐ S.L. & G.H. Rogers "Silver Rose", *no monogram, excellent condition*	6.00	7.00
☐ S.L. & G.H. Rogers "Silver Rose", *no monogram, good condition*	5.00	6.00
☐ S.L. & G.H. Rogers "Silver Rose", *no monogram, fair condition*	1.00	2.00
☐ S.L. & G.H. Rogers "Thor", *no monogram, excellent condition*	6.00	7.00
☐ S.L. & G.H. Rogers "Thor", *no monogram, good condition* .	5.00	6.00
☐ S.L. & G.H. Rogers "Thor", *no monogram, fair condition* ...	1.00	2.00
☐ S.L. & G.H. Rogers "Viking", *no monogram, excellent condition*	6.00	7.00
☐ S.L. & G.H. Rogers "Viking", *no monogram, good condition*	5.00	6.00
☐ Stratford "Cotillion", *no monogram, excellent condition* ..	6.00	7.00
☐ Stratford "Cotillion", *no monogram, good condition*	5.00	6.00
☐ Stratford "Cotillion", *no monogram, fair condition*	1.00	2.00
☐ Stratford "Shakespeare", *no monogram, excellent condition*	4.00	5.00
☐ Stratford "Shakespeare", *no monogram, excellent condition*	6.00	7.00
☐ Stratford "Shakespeare", *no monogram, good condition* ..	5.00	6.00
☐ Tudor "Baronet", *no monogram, excellent condition*	3.00	4.00
☐ Tudor "Bridal Wreath", *no monogram, excellent condition* .	4.00	5.00
☐ Tudor "Bridal Wreath", *no monogram, excellent condition* .	6.00	7.00
☐ Tudor "Bridal Wreath", *no monogram, good condition*	5.00	6.00
☐ Tudor "Duchess", *no monogram, excellent condition*	5.00	6.00
☐ Tudor "Duchess", *no monogram, fair condition*	1.00	2.00
☐ Tudor "Enchantment", *no monogram, excellent condition* .	5.00	6.00
☐ Tudor "June", *no monogram, excellent condition*	6.00	7.00
☐ Tudor "June", *no monogram, good condition*	5.00	6.00
☐ Tudor "June", *no monogram, fair condition*	1.00	2.00
☐ Tudor "Queen Bess II", *no monogram, excellent condition* .	6.00	7.00
☐ Tudor "Queen Bess II", *no monogram, good condition*	5.00	6.00
☐ Tudor "Queen Bess II", *no monogram, fair condition*	1.00	2.00
☐ Tudor "Together", *no monogram, excellent condition*	4.00	5.00
☐ Wallace "Cardinal", *no monogram, excellent condition* ...	5.00	6.00
☐ Wallace "Floral", *no monogram, excellent condition*	16.00	18.00
☐ Wallace "Floral", *no monogram, good condition*	12.00	14.00
☐ Wallace "Floral", *monogram, good condition*	8.00	9.00
☐ Wallace "Floral", *monogram, poor condition*	1.00	2.00
☐ Wallace "Laurel", *no monogram, excellent condition*	4.00	5.00
☐ Wallace "Sonata", *no monogram, excellent condition*	6.00	7.00
☐ Wallace "Sonata", *no monogram, good condition*	5.00	6.00
☐ Wallace "Sonata", *no monogram, fair condition*	1.00	2.00

	Price Range	
☐ W.D. Smith "Adam", *monogram, excellent condition*	4.00	5.00
☐ W.D. Smith "Adam", *no monogram, excellent condition* . . .	5.00	6.00
☐ Wm. A. Rogers "Ardsley", *no monogram, excellent condition*	6.00	7.00
☐ Wm. A. Rogers "Chalice", *no monogram, excellent condition*	6.00	7.00
☐ Wm. A. Rogers "Chalice", *no monogram, good condition* . .	5.00	6.00
☐ Wm. A. Rogers "Chalice", *no monogram, fair condition* . . .	1.00	2.00
☐ Wm. A. Rogers "Country Lane", *no monogram, excellent condition*	6.00	7.00
☐ Wm. A. Rogers "Country Lane", *no monogram, good condition*	5.00	6.00
☐ Wm. A. Rogers "Country Lane", *no monogram, fair condition*	1.00	2.00
☐ Wm. A. Rogers "Debutante", *no monogram, excellent condition*	4.00	5.00
☐ Wm. A. Rogers "Garland", *no monogram, excellent condition*	4.00	5.00
☐ Wm. A. Rogers "Grenoble", *no monogram, excellent condition*	5.00	6.00
☐ Wm. A. Rogers "Helena", *no monogram, excellent condition*	7.00	8.00
☐ Wm. A. Rogers "Lady Stuart", *no monogram, excellent condition*	6.00	7.00
☐ Wm. A. Rogers "Lady Stuart", *no monogram, good condition*	5.00	6.00
☐ Wm. A. Rogers "Lady Stuart", *no monogram, fair condition*	1.00	2.00
☐ Wm. A. Rogers "Malibu", *no monogram, excellent condition*	6.00	7.00
☐ Wm. A. Rogers "Malibu", *no monogram, good condition* . . .	5.00	6.00
☐ Wm. A. Rogers "Malibu", *no monogram, fair condition*	1.00	2.00
☐ Wm. A. Rogers "Mystic", *no monogram, excellent condition*	6.00	7.00
☐ Wm. A. Rogers "Mystic", *no monogram, good condition* . . .	5.00	6.00
☐ Wm. A. Rogers "Mystic", *no monogram, fair condition* . . .	1.00	2.00
☐ Wm. A. Rogers "Paramount", *no monogram, excellent condition*	6.00	7.00
☐ Wm. A. Rogers "Paramount", *no monogram, excellent condition*	6.00	7.00
☐ Wm. A. Rogers "Paramount", *no monogram, good condition*	5.00	6.00
☐ Wm. A. Rogers "Paramount", *no monogram, fair condition*	1.00	2.00
☐ Wm. A. Rogers "Rendezvous", *no monogram, excellent condition*	6.00	7.00
☐ Wm. A. Rogers "Rendezvous", *no monogram, good condition*	5.00	6.00
☐ Wm. A. Rogers "Rendezvous", *no monogram, fair condition*	1.00	2.00
☐ Wm. A. Rogers "Rosalie", *no monogram, excellent condition*	6.00	7.00
☐ Wm. A. Rogers "Rosalie", *no monogram, good condition* . .	5.00	6.00
☐ Wm. A. Rogers "Rosalie", *no monogram, fair condition* . . .	1.00	2.00
☐ Wm. A. Rogers "Valley Rose", *no monogram, excellent condition*	6.00	7.00
☐ Wm. A. Rogers "Valley Rose", *no monogram, good condition*	5.00	6.00

	Price Range	
☐ Wm. A. Rogers "Valley Rose", *no monogram, fair condition*	1.00	2.00
☐ Wm. A. Rogers "Valley Rose", *no monogram, poor condition*	1.00	2.00
☐ Wm. Rogers "Beloved", *no monogram, excellent condition*	6.00	7.00
☐ Wm. Rogers "Beloved", *no monogram, good condition*	5.00	6.00
☐ Wm. Rogers "Beloved", *no monogram, fair condition*	1.00	2.00
☐ Wm. Rogers "Berwick", *no monogram, excellent condition*	9.00	10.00
☐ Wm. Rogers "Berwick", *no monogram, good condition*	7.00	8.00
☐ Wm. Rogers "Berwick", *monogram, good condition*	4.00	5.00
☐ Wm. Rogers "Berwick", *monogram, fair condition*	1.00	3.00
☐ Wm. Rogers "Carrollton", *no monogram, excellent condition*	4.00	5.00
☐ Wm. Rogers "Carrollton", *no monogram, good condition* ..	4.00	5.00
☐ Wm. Rogers "Cotillion", *no monogram, excellent condition*	6.00	7.00
☐ Wm. Rogers "Cotillion", *no monogram, fair condition*	1.00	2.00
☐ Wm. Rogers "Debutante", *no monogram, excellent condition*	6.00	7.00
☐ Wm. Rogers "Debutante", *no monogram, good condition* ..	5.00	6.00
☐ Wm. Rogers "Debutante", *no monogram, fair condition* ...	1.00	2.00
☐ Wm. Rogers "Exquisite", *no monogram, excellent condition*	4.00	5.00
☐ Wm. Rogers "Exquisite", *no monogram, good condition* ...	4.00	5.00
☐ Wm. Rogers "Exquisite", *no monogram, good condition* ...	5.00	6.00
☐ Wm. Rogers "Exquisite", *no monogram, fair condition*	1.00	2.00
☐ Wm. Rogers "Fairoaks", *no monogram, excellent condition*	6.00	7.00
☐ Wm. Rogers "Fairoaks", *no monogram, excellent condition*	6.00	7.00
☐ Wm. Rogers "Fairoaks", *no monogram, good condition* ...	5.00	6.00
☐ Wm. Rogers "Fairoaks", *no monogram, fair condition*	1.00	2.00
☐ Wm. Rogers "Gardenia", *no monogram, excellent condition*	3.00	4.00
☐ Wm. Rogers "Hostess", *no monogram, excellent condition*	6.00	7.00
☐ Wm. Rogers "Hostess", *no monogram, good condition* ...	5.00	6.00
☐ Wm. Rogers "Hostess", *no monogram, poor condition*	1.00	2.00
☐ Wm. Rogers "Imperial", *no monogram, excellent condition*	6.00	7.00
☐ Wm. Rogers "Imperial", *no monogram, good condition*	5.00	6.00
☐ Wm. Rogers "Imperial", *no monogram, fair condition*	1.00	2.00
☐ Wm. Rogers "Louisiana", *no monogram, excellent condition*	6.00	7.00
☐ Wm. Rogers "Louisiana", *no monogram, good condition* ..	5.00	6.00
☐ Wm. Rogers "Louisiana", *no monogram, fair condition*	1.00	2.00
☐ Wm. Rogers "Mayfair", *no monogram, excellent condition* .	6.00	7.00
☐ Wm. Rogers "Mayfair", *no monogram, good condition*	5.00	6.00
☐ Wm. Rogers "Mayfair", *no monogram, fair condition*	1.00	2.00
☐ Wm. Rogers "Melrose", *no monogram, excellent condition*	4.00	5.00
☐ Wm. Rogers "Memory", *no monogram, excellent condition*	6.00	7.00
☐ Wm. Rogers "Memory", *no monogram, good condition*	5.00	6.00
☐ Wm. Rogers "Memory", *no monogram, poor condition*	1.00	2.00
☐ Wm. Rogers "Mountain Rose", *no monogram, excellent condition*	7.00	8.00
☐ Wm. Rogers "Mountain Rose", *no monogram, good condition*	5.00	6.00
☐ Wm. Rogers "Mountain Rose", *no monogram, fair condition*	1.00	2.00
☐ Wm. Rogers "Nuart", *no monogram, excellent condition* ..	4.00	5.00
☐ Wm. Rogers "Nuart", *no monogram, good condition*	3.00	4.00

	Price Range	
☐ Wm. Rogers "Orange Blossom", *no monogram, excellent condition*	13.00	15.00
☐ Wm. Rogers "Orange Blossom", *no monogram, good condition*	11.00	13.00
☐ Wm. Rogers "Orange Blossom", *no monogram, poor condition*	1.00	2.00
☐ Wm. Rogers "Orange Blossom", *monogram, excellent condition*	8.00	9.00
☐ Wm. Rogers "Precious Mirror", *no monogram, excellent condition*	6.00	7.00
☐ Wm. Rogers "Precious Mirror", *no monogram, good condition*	5.00	6.00
☐ Wm. Rogers "Precious Mirror", *no monogram, fair condition*	1.00	2.00
☐ Wm. Rogers "Treasure", *no monogram, excellent condition*	6.00	7.00
☐ Wm. Rogers "Treasure", *no monogram, good condition* ...	5.00	6.00
☐ Wm. Rogers "Treasure", *monogram, excellent condition* ..	3.00	4.00
☐ Wm. Rogers "Treasure", *monogram, good condition*	3.00	4.00
☐ Wm. Rogers "Victory", *no monogram, excellent condition* .	6.00	7.00
☐ Wm. Rogers "Victory", *no monogram, good condition*	5.00	6.00
☐ Wm. Rogers Mfg. Co. "Alhambra", *monogram, excellent condition*	6.00	7.00
☐ Wm. Rogers Mfg. Co. "Alhambra", *no monogram, good condition*	7.00	8.00
☐ Wm. Rogers Mfg. Co. "Alhambra", *no monogram, fair condition*	3.00	4.00
☐ Wm. Rogers Mfg.Co. "Berwick", *no monogram, excellent condition*	7.00	8.00
☐ Wm. Rogers Mfg. Co. "Daisy", *no monogram, excellent condition*	5.00	6.00
☐ Wm. Rogers Mfg. Co. "Daisy", *no monogram, good condition*	4.00	5.00
☐ Wm. Rogers Mfg. Co. "Magnolia", *no monogram, excellent condition*	6.00	7.00
☐ Wm. Rogers Mfg. Co. "Magnolia", *no monogram, good condition*	5.00	6.00
☐ Wm. Rogers Mfg. Co. "Oak", *no monogram, excellent condition*	7.00	8.00
☐ Wm. Rogers Mfg. Co. "Puritan", *no monogram, excellent condition*	3.00	4.00
☐ Wm. Rogers Mfg. Co. "Regent", *no monogram, excellent condition*	6.00	7.00
☐ Wm. Rogers Mfg. Co. "Revelation", *no monogram, excellent condition*	6.00	7.00
☐ Wm. Rogers Mfg. Co. "Revelation", *no monogram, good condition*	5.00	6.00
☐ Wm. Rogers Mfg. Co. "Revelation", *no monogram, fair condition*	1.00	2.00
☐ Wm. Rogers Mfg. Co. "Sovereign", *no monogram, excellent condition*	6.00	7.00
☐ Wm. Rogers Mfg. Co. "Sovereign", *no monogram, good condition*	5.00	6.00
☐ Wm. Rogers Mfg. Co. "Sovereign", *no monogram, fair condition*	1.00	2.00

	Price Range	
☐ **Wm. Rogers Mfg. Co. "Talisman"**, *no monogram, excellent condition*	6.00	7.00
☐ **Wm. Rogers Mfg. Co. "Talisman"**, *no monogram, good condition*	5.00	6.00
☐ **Wm. Rogers Mfg. Co. "Talisman"**, *no monogram, fair condition*	1.00	2.00
☐ **Wm. Rogers & Son "Arbutus"**, *no monogram, fair condition*	1.00	2.00
☐ **Wm. Rogers & Son "Spring Flower"**, *no monogram, excellent condition*	6.00	7.00
☐ **Wm. Rogers & Son "Spring Flower"**, *no monogram, good condition*	5.00	6.00
☐ **Wm. Rogers & Son "Spring Flower"**, *no monogram, fair condition*	1.00	2.00
☐ **Wm. Rogers & Son "LaFrance"**, *no monogram, excellent condition*	6.00	7.00
☐ **Wm. Rogers & Son "LaFrance"**, *no monogram, good condition*	5.00	6.00
☐ **Wm. Rogers & Son "LaFrance"**, *no monogram, fair condition*	1.00	2.00
☐ **Wm. Rogers & Son "LaFrance"**, *monogram, excellent condition*	2.00	3.00
☐ **Wm. Rogers & Son "Victorian Rose"**, *no monogram, excellent condition*	6.00	7.00
☐ **Wm. Rogers & Son "Victorian Rose"**, *no monogram, good condition*	5.00	6.00
☐ **Wm. Rogers & Son "Victorian Rose"**, *no monogram, fair condition*	1.00	2.00
☐ **Williams Bros. "Queen Elizabeth"**, *no monogram, excellent condition*	4.00	5.00
☐ **World "Roanoke"**, *no monogram, excellent condition*	6.00	7.00
☐ **World "Somerset"**, *no monogram, excellent condition*	6.00	7.00
☐ **1835 R. Wallace "Abbey"**, *no monogram, excellent condition*	6.00	7.00
☐ **1835 R. Wallace "Abbey"**, *no monogram, good condition*	5.00	6.00
☐ **1835 R. Wallace "Abbey"**, *no monogram, fair condition*	1.00	2.00
☐ **1835 R. Wallace "Blossom"**, *monogram, excellent condition*	9.00	11.00
☐ **1835 R. Wallace "Blossom"**, *no monogram, excellent condition*	12.00	14.00
☐ **1835 R. Wallace "Blossom"**, *no monogram, good condition*	10.00	13.00
☐ **1835 R. Wallace "Blossom"**, *no monogram, fair condition*	4.00	5.00
☐ **1835 R. Wallace "Buckingham"**, *no monogram, excellent condition*	6.00	7.00
☐ **1835 R. Wallace "Buckingham"**, *no monogram, good condition*	5.00	6.00
☐ **1835 R. Wallace "Buckingham"**, *no monogram, fair condition*	1.00	2.00
☐ **1835 R. Wallace "Cardinal"**, *no monogram, excellent condition*	10.00	13.00
☐ **1835 R. Wallace "Cardinal"**, *no monogram, fair condition*	5.00	6.00
☐ **1847 Rogers "Adoration"**, *no monogram, excellent condition*	4.00	5.00
☐ **1847 Rogers "Adoration"**, *no monogram, excellent condition*	6.00	7.00

	Price Range	
☐ 1847 Rogers "Ancestral", *no monogram, excellent condition*	6.00	7.00
☐ 1847 Rogers "Ancestral", *no monogram, good condition* ..	5.00	6.00
☐ 1847 Rogers "Ancestral", *no monogram, fair condition*	1.00	2.00
☐ 1847 Rogers "Anniversary", *no monogram, excellent condition*	6.00	7.00
☐ 1847 Rogers "Anniversary", *no monogram, good condition*	5.00	6.00
☐ 1847 Rogers "Anniversary", *no monogram, fair condition* ..	1.00	2.00
☐ 1847 Rogers "Avon", *no monogram, excellent condition* ...	10.00	13.00
☐ 1847 Rogers "Charter Oak", *no monogram, excellent condition*	22.00	24.00
☐ 1847 Rogers "Charter Oak", *no monogram, good condition*	16.00	19.00
☐ 1847 Rogers "Charter Oak", *no monogram, fair condition* ..	8.00	9.00
☐ 1847 Rogers "Charter Oak", *monogram, excellent condition*	20.00	22.00
☐ 1847 Rogers "Charter Oak", *monogram, good condition* ...	10.00	13.00
☐ 1847 Rogers "Columbia", *no monogram, excellent condition*	28.00	31.00
☐ 1847 Rogers "Columbia", *no monogram, fair condition*	10.00	13.00
☐ 1847 Rogers "Columbia", *monogram, fair condition*	9.00	11.00
☐ 1847 Rogers "Columbia", *monogram, poor condition*	5.00	6.00
☐ 1847 Rogers "Daffodil", *no monogram, excellent condition*	7.00	8.00
☐ 1847 Rogers "Daffodil", *no monogram, good condition*	6.00	7.00
☐ 1847 Rogers "Daffodil", *no monogram, fair condition*	2.00	3.00
☐ 1847 Rogers "Daffodil", *no monogram, poor condition*	1.00	2.00
☐ 1847 Rogers "Esperanto", *no monogram, excellent condition*	6.00	7.00
☐ 1847 Rogers "Esperanto", *no monogram, good condition* ..	5.00	6.00
☐ 1847 Rogers "Esperanto", *no monogram, fair condition* ...	1.00	2.00
☐ 1847 Rogers "Esperanto", *monogram, good condition*	2.00	3.00
☐ 1847 Rogers "Esperanto", *monogram, fair condition*	1.00	2.00
☐ 1847 Rogers "Eternally Yours", *no monogram, excellent condition*	6.00	7.00
☐ 1847 Rogers "Eternally Yours", *no monogram, good condition*	5.00	6.00
☐ 1847 Rogers "Eternally Yours", *no monogram, fair condition*	1.00	2.00
☐ 1847 Rogers "Flair", *no monogram, excellent condition* ...	4.00	5.00
☐ 1847 Rogers "Flair", *no monogram, excellent condition* ...	6.00	7.00
☐ 1847 Rogers "Flair", *no monogram, good condition*	5.00	6.00
☐ 1847 Rogers "Flair", *no monogram, poor condition*	1.00	2.00
☐ 1847 Rogers "Floral", *no monogram, excellent condition* ..	24.00	27.00
☐ 1847 Rogers "Floral", *no monogram, good condition*	21.00	24.00
☐ 1847 Rogers "Floral", *no monogram, fair condition*	11.00	13.00
☐ 1847 Rogers "Floral", *no monogram, poor condition*	4.00	5.00
☐ 1847 Rogers "Floral", *monogram, excellent condition*	17.00	19.00
☐ 1847 Rogers "Floral", *monogram, good condition*	9.00	11.00
☐ 1847 Rogers "Grecian", *no monogram, excellent condition*	7.00	8.00
☐ 1847 Rogers "Grecian", *no monogram, poor condition*	1.00	2.00
☐ 1847 Rogers "Heraldic", *no monogram, excellent condition*	4.00	3.00
☐ 1847 Rogers "Heraldic", *no monogram, good condition* ...	5.00	6.00
☐ 1847 Rogers "Heraldic", *no monogram, fair condition*	2.00	3.00
☐ 1847 Rogers "Leilani", *no monogram, excellent condition* .	6.00	7.00
☐ 1847 Rogers "Leilani", *no monogram, good condition*	5.00	6.00
☐ 1847 Rogers "Leilani", *no monogram, fair condition*	1.00	2.00

	Price Range	
☐ 1847 Rogers "Lovelace", *no monogram*	6.00	7.00
☐ 1847 Rogers "Lovelace", *no monogram, good condition*	5.00	6.00
☐ 1847 Rogers "Lovelace", *no monogram, fair condition*	1.00	2.00
☐ 1847 Rogers "Magic Rose", *no monogram, excellent condition*	4.00	5.00
☐ 1847 Rogers "Magic Rose", *no monogram, fair condition*	1.00	2.00
☐ 1847 Rogers "Old Colony", *no monogram, excellent condition*	8.00	9.00
☐ 1847 Rogers "Old Colony", *no monogram, good condition*	7.00	8.00
☐ 1847 Rogers "Old Colony", *no monogram, fair condition*	2.00	3.00
☐ 1847 Rogers "Old Colony", *no monogram, poor condition*	1.00	2.00
☐ 1847 Rogers "Old Colony", *monogram, excellent condition*	4.00	5.00
☐ 1847 Rogers "Old Colony", *monogram, fair condition*	1.00	2.00
☐ 1847 Rogers "Queen Anne", *no monogram, excellent condition*	6.00	7.00
☐ 1847 Rogers "Reflection", *no monogram, excellent condition*	6.00	7.00
☐ 1847 Rogers "Reflection", *no monogram, good condition*	5.00	6.00
☐ 1847 Rogers "Reflection", *no monogram, fair condition*	1.00	2.00
☐ 1847 Rogers "Remembrance", *no monogram, excellent condition*	5.00	6.00
☐ 1847 Rogers "Remembrance", *no monogram, good condition*	4.00	5.00
☐ 1847 Rogers "Sharon", *no monogram, excellent condition*	7.00	8.00
☐ 1847 Rogers "Sharon", *good condition*	6.00	7.00
☐ 1847 Rogers "Sharon", *no monogram, fair condition*	2.00	3.00
☐ 1847 Rogers "Silver Lace", *no monogram, excellent condition*	6.00	7.00
☐ 1847 Rogers "Silver Lace", *no monogram, good condition*	5.00	6.00
☐ 1847 Rogers "Silver Lace", *no monogram, fair condition*	1.00	2.00
☐ 1847 Rogers "Springtime", *no monogram, excellent condition*	6.00	7.00
☐ 1847 Rogers "Springtime", *no monogram, poor condition*	1.00	2.00
☐ 1847 Rogers "Vintage", *no monogram, excellent condition*	22.00	25.00
☐ 1847 Rogers "Vintage", *no monogram, good condition*	20.00	22.00
☐ 1847 Rogers "Vintage", *no monogram, fair condition*	10.00	12.00
☐ 1847 Rogers "Vintage", *no monogram, poor condition*	6.00	7.00
☐ 1881 Rogers "Capri", *no monogram, excellent condition*	6.00	7.00
☐ 1881 Rogers "Capri", *no monogram, good condition*	5.00	6.00
☐ 1881 Rogers "Chevron", *no monogram, excellent condition*	6.00	7.00
☐ 1881 Rogers "Chevron", *no monogram, good condition*	5.00	6.00
☐ 1881 Rogers "Chevron", *no monogram, fair condition*	1.00	2.00
☐ 1881 Rogers "Chippendale", *no monogram, excellent condition*	6.00	7.00
☐ 1881 Rogers "Chippendale", *no monogram, good condition*	5.00	6.00
☐ 1881 Rogers "Chippendale", *no monogram, fair condition*	1.00	2.00
☐ 1881 Rogers "Flirtation", *no monogram, excellent condition*	4.00	5.00
☐ 1881 Rogers "Grecian", *no monogram, excellent condition*	6.00	7.00
☐ 1881 Rogers "Grecian", *no monogram, good condition*	5.00	6.00
☐ 1881 Rogers "Grecian", *monogram, good condition*	2.00	3.00
☐ 1881 Rogers "Proposal", *no monogram, excellent condition*	6.00	7.00
☐ 1881 Rogers "Proposal", *no monogram, good condition*	5.00	6.00

	Price Range	
☐ **1881 Rogers "Proposal"**, *no monogram, fair condition*	1.00	2.00
☐ **1881 Rogers "Surf Club"**, *no monogram, excellent condition*	4.00	5.00
☐ **1881 Rogers "Surf Club"**, *no monogram, good condition* ..	3.00	4.00

(Sterling Silver)

	Price Range	
☐ **Alvin "Chateau Rose"**, *no monogram*	16.00	18.00
☐ **Alvin "Old Orange Blossom"**, *monogram*	17.00	21.00
☐ **Alvin "Romantique"**, *no monogram*	16.00	18.00
☐ **Alvin "Touraine"**, *monogram*	14.00	16.00
☐ **Blackington "Scroll & Bead"**, *no monogram*	26.00	29.00
☐ **Durgin "Fairfax"**, *6⅛" L.*	13.00	15.00
☐ **Fine Arts "Processional"**, *no monogram*	13.00	15.00
☐ **Frank Smith "Fiddle Thread"**, *no monogram*	26.00	29.00
☐ **Frank Smith "Newport Shell"**, *no monogram*	25.00	28.00
☐ **Gorham "Blithe Spirit"**, *no monogram*	15.00	17.00
☐ **Gorham "Buckingham"**, *no monogram*	18.00	20.00
☐ **Gorham "Chantilly"**, *5¾" L., monogram*	14.00	16.00
☐ **Gorham "Chantilly"**, *no monogram*	15.00	17.00
☐ **Gorham "English Gadroon"**, *no monogram*	14.00	16.00
☐ **Gorham "English Gadroon"**	13.00	15.00
☐ **Gorham "Fairfax"**, *6½" L., no monogram*	14.00	16.00
☐ **Gorham "Greenbrier"**, *no monogram*	16.00	18.00
☐ **Gorham "King Edward"**, *no monogram*	15.00	17.00
☐ **Gorham "Lancaster"**, *monogram*	14.00	16.00
☐ **Gorham "LaScala"**, *no monogram*	19.00	21.00
☐ **Gorham "Melrose"**, *monogram*	15.00	17.00
☐ **Gorham "Norfolk"**, *no monogram*	8.00	9.00
☐ **Gorham "Old French"**, *6" L., monogram*	14.00	16.00
☐ **Gorham "Rondo"**, *no monogram*	14.00	16.00
☐ **Gorham "Sovereign"**, *no monogram*	15.00	17.00
☐ **International "Angelique"**, *monogram*	13.00	15.00
☐ **International "Courtship"**, *no monogram*	13.00	15.00
☐ **International "Courtship"**, *no monogram*	14.00	16.00
☐ **International "Edgewood"**, *no monogram*	18.00	20.00
☐ **International "Fontaine"**, *no monogram*	16.00	18.00
☐ **International "Frontenac"**, *monogram*	22.00	24.00
☐ **International "Grand Regency"**, *no monogram*	15.00	17.00
☐ **International "Joan of Arc"**, *no monogram*	14.00	16.00
☐ **International "Minuet"**, *no monogram*	12.00	14.00
☐ **International "Royal Danish"**, *no monogram*	15.00	17.00
☐ **International "Swan Lake"**	15.00	17.00
☐ **International "Trianon"**, *monogram*	12.00	14.00
☐ **International "Wild Rose"**, *monogram*	12.00	14.00
☐ **International "Wild Rose"**, *no monogram*	14.00	16.00
☐ **Kirk "Repousse"**, *no monogram*	19.00	21.00
☐ **Lunt "Eloquence"**, *no monogram*	16.00	18.00
☐ **Lunt "Mignonette"**, *no monogram*	12.00	14.00
☐ **Lunt "Monticello"**, *monogram*	19.00	31.00
☐ **Lunt "Mt. Vernon"**, *no monogram*	14.00	16.00
☐ **Lunt "Mt. Vernon"**, *no monogram*	14.00	16.00
☐ **Lunt "Sweetheart Rose"**, *no monogram*	11.00	13.00
☐ **Manchester "Vogue"**, *no monogram*	13.00	15.00
☐ **Oneida "Botticelli"**, *no monogram*	14.00	17.00

	Price Range	
☐ Oneida "Heiress", *no monogram*	13.00	15.00
☐ Oneida "Heiress", *monogram*	10.00	13.00
☐ Reed & Barton "Francis I", *monogram*	19.00	21.00
☐ Reed & Barton "French Renaissance", *no monogram*	18.00	20.00
☐ Reed & Barton "Georgian Rose", *no monogram*	10.00	13.00
☐ Reed & Barton "Hampton Court", *no monogram*	14.00	17.00
☐ Reed & Barton "Marlborough", *monogram*	14.00	16.00
☐ Reed & Barton "Old Virginia", *no monogram*	15.00	17.00
☐ Reed & Barton "Spanish Baroque", *no monogram*	15.00	17.00
☐ Schofield "Baltimore Rose", *monogram*	26.00	29.00
☐ Stieff "Corsage", *no monogram*	13.00	15.00
☐ Stieff "Rose", *monogram*	16.00	19.00
☐ Tiffany "Flemish", *monogram*	16.00	19.00
☐ Tiffany "Hampton", *monogram*	25.00	28.00
☐ Towle "Canterbury", *gold wash tines, no monogram*	22.00	24.00
☐ Towle "Chippendale", *no monogram*	13.00	15.00
☐ Towle "Country Manor", *no monogram*	15.00	17.00
☐ Towle "Esplanade", *no monogram*	13.00	15.00
☐ Towle "Fontana", *no monogram*	12.00	14.00
☐ Towle "French Provincial", *no monogram*	14.00	16.00
☐ Towle "Georgian", *no monogram*	24.00	27.00
☐ Towle "Georgian", *no monogram*	24.00	27.00
☐ Towle "Kings", *no monogram*	24.00	27.00
☐ Towle "Laureate", *no monogram*	15.00	17.00
☐ Towle "Old Colonial", *no monogram*	22.00	25.00
☐ Towle "Rambler Rose", *monogram*	14.00	16.00
☐ Towle "Spanish Provincial", *no monogram*	18.00	20.00
☐ Towle "Virginia Carvel", *monogram*	12.00	14.00
☐ Wallace "Grande Baroque", *no monogram*	18.00	20.00
☐ Wallace "Normandie", *monogram*	14.00	16.00
☐ Wallace "Rosepoint", *no monogram*	12.00	14.00
☐ Wallace "Royal Rose", *no monogram*	14.00	16.00
☐ Westmoreland "Milburn Rose", *no monogram*	15.00	17.00
☐ Whiting "King Albert", *monogram*	12.00	14.00
☐ Whiting "Lily", *no monogram*	32.00	36.00
☐ Whiting "Madame Jumel", *no monogram*	12.00	14.00
☐ Whiting "Madame Jumel", *no monogram*	18.00	20.00
☐ Whiting "Madame Jumel", *monogram*	16.00	18.00

SALAD SERVING FORKS

Salad serving forks are of course considerably larger than salad forks (see above), and while the basic patterns are alike they tend to be more ornamental. Considerably fewer were manufactured, as the hostess could get along with one serving fork even if the dining room was swelled with guests. Salad serving forks have four long tines and a shoulder which slopes slightly or, sometimes, not at all. The tines were not for piercing, but simply to hold the salad in place against the serving spoon until it safely reached the plate.

(Silver-Plated)

☐ **Community "Coronation"**, *no monogram, excellent condition*	8.00	9.00
☐ **Holmes & Edwards "Woodsong"**, *no monogram, excellent condition*	8.00	9.00

		Price Range	
☐ Wm. Rogers "Yale I", *no monogram, excellent condition* ..		11.00	13.00
☐ Wm. Rogers "Yale I", *monogram, excellent condition*		7.00	8.00
☐ Wm. Rogers Mfg. Co. "El California", *no monogram, excellent condition*		11.00	13.00
☐ 1835 R. Wallace "Joan", *no monogram, good condition* ...		12.00	14.00
☐ 1847 Rogers "Avon", *no monogram, excellent condition* ...		36.00	40.00
☐ 1847 Rogers "Avon", *no monogram, mint condition, in original box*		36.00	40.00
☐ 1847 Rogers "Vintage", *no monogram, excellent condition*		36.00	40.00
☐ 1847 Rogers "Vintage", *monogram, fair condition*		8.00	9.00

(Sterling Silver)

☐ Gorham "Norfolk", *monogram*		38.00	42.00
☐ Reed & Barton "Francis I", *no monogram*		75.00	85.00

SALAD SERVING SETS

These consisted of one fork and one spoon. Some were packaged in elegant boxes and of course command a higher price when the box is present. The spoon and fork were usually of equal length from tip to tip. There was a reason for providing two utensils of wholly different nature for serving salads. This allowed a salad to be served with more or less juice, as desired, depending on whether the spoon or fork was placed underneath.

Salad Serving Set, *(sterling), Whiting, twisted peony pattern,* 180.00

(Silver-Plated)

☐ Holmes & Edwards "May Queen", *two-piece, no monogram, mint condition*		16.00	18.00
☐ Holmes & Edwards "Woodsong", *two-piece, no monogram, good condition*		20.00	23.00
☐ Holmes & Edwards "Woodsong", *two-piece, no monogram, excellent condition*		25.00	28.00
☐ Wm. Rogers "Tuxedo", *two-piece, no monogram, excellent condition*		50.00	54.00

Price Range

- ☐ **Wm. Rogers "Tuxedo"**, *two-piece, no monogram, fair condition* 16.00   18.00
- ☐ **1847 Rogers "Daffodil"**, *two-piece, no monogram, excellent condition* 20.00   22.00
- ☐ **1847 Rogers "Daffodil"**, *two-piece, no monogram, mint condition* 28.00   32.00
- ☐ **1847 Rogers "Old Colony"**, *two-piece, monogram, excellent condition* 18.00   20.00
- ☐ **1847 Rogers "Persian"**, *two-piece, no monogram, mint condition, in original silk-lined presentation box* 60.00   68.00

(Sterling Silver)

- ☐ **Alvin "Bridal Rose"**, *two-piece, 7⅞" L., no monogram* 50.00   55.00
- ☐ **Alvin "Raphael"**, *two-piece, 9" L., no monogram* 250.00   275.00
- ☐ **Dominick & Haff "Broad Antique"**, *two-piece, 8¾" L., no monogram* 37.00   41.00
- ☐ **Gorham "Buttercup"**, *two-piece, medium size, monogram* . 80.00   90.00
- ☐ **Gorham "Imperial Chrysanthemum"**, *two-piece, large size, monogram* 130.00   145.00
- ☐ **Marshall Field retailer**, *two-piece, large size, applied flowers on hand-hammered surface* 105.00   120.00
- ☐ **Reed & Barton "Francis I"**, *two-piece, large size, pierced spoon bowl, no monogram* 165.00   180.00
- ☐ **Reed & Barton "LaComtesse"**, *two-piece, 7½" L., monogram* 22.00   25.00
- ☐ **Reed & Barton "Love Disarmed"**, *two-piece, gold wash bowl and tines, no monogram* 380.00   420.00
- ☐ **Simpson, Hall & Miller "Frontenac"**, *two-piece, no monogram* 165.00   180.00
- ☐ **Wallace "Kings"**, *two-piece, small size, no monogram* 70.00   80.00
- ☐ **Watson, Newell & Co. "Victoria"**, *two-piece, small size, no monogram* 34.00   38.00
- ☐ **Whiting "Dresden"**, *two-piece, large size, no monogram* ... 135.00   150.00

SALAD SERVING SPOONS

Salad serving spoons have large bowls, usually somewhat rectangular, and rather shallow. They run from restrained to lavishly ornamental in decoration. The highspot on deluxe specimens is the underside of the bowl, which may carry a combination of molded and engraved work. Salad serving spoons display very well and have become favorites of specialist collectors. The available selection is more than ample, to keep any hobbyist busy. The average length is 7½" to 8½".

(Silver-Plated)

- ☐ **Holmes & Edwards "May Queen"**, *no monogram, excellent condition* 11.00   13.00
- ☐ **1847 Rogers "Daffodil"**, *no monogram, excellent condition* 11.00   13.00
- ☐ **1847 Rogers "Newport"**, *no monogram, excellent condition* 15.00   17.00
- ☐ **1847 Rogers "Newport"**, *no monogram, excellent condition* 16.00   18.00
- ☐ **1847 Rogers "Old Colony"**, *no monogram, excellent condition* 16.00   18.00
- ☐ **1847 Rogers "Persian"**, *no monogram, mint condition* 25.00   28.00
- ☐ **1847 Rogers "Vintage"**, *no monogram, excellent condition* 33.00   36.00

(Sterling Silver) Price Range

☐ **Alvin "Bridal Rose",** *monogram* 28.00   32.00
☐ **Gorham "Chantilly",** *gold wash bowl, no monogram* 40.00   45.00
☐ **Gorham "King George",** *gold wash bowl, monogram and*
    date 40.00   45.00
☐ **Gorham "Strasbourg",** *no monogram* 40.00   45.00

SALT AND PEPPER SHAKERS

A perennial favorite, these have been manufactured in silver since the 17th century in Europe and at least as early as the 18th in America. The shapes are very diverse, without any standard or traditional approach, and this of course lends to the appeal of a collection. Salt and pepper shakers have been made wholly of silver, and also (as included in our listings) of a combination of silver and porcelain — to satisfy those who believed silver might hurt the flavor of the contents. Values on the whole are high, as these are collected not only by specialists in silver but by collectors of salt and pepper sets.

Salt and Pepper Set, *(sterling), Shiebler, hand-chased, blue cobalt liners in salt dips, includes two salts and two peppers,* 240.00

(Silver-Plated)

☐ **Community "Ascot",** *no monogram, good condition* 7.00   8.00

(Sterling Silver)

☐ **Gorham,** *barrel shape, plain, 2" H., dent on one* 6.00   7.00
☐ **Maker unknown,** *individual size, repousse design, several*
    dents 6.00   7.00

(Sterling and China)

☐ **Maker unknown,** *cruet shape, silver caps and snap-on*
    bases, Lenox liners, pair 25.00   27.00

Price Range

☐ **Maker unknown,** *sterling and china, sterling lids and tiny tray, Lenox bodies*	30.00	33.00
☐ **Maker unknown,** *sterling lids, Lenox tray and bodies*	20.00	23.00

SALT DIP AND PEPPER SHAKER SETS

At the same time that silverware manufacturers were putting out salt and pepper shakers (see above), they continued catering to the "old school" crowd which preferred its salt in dips. A salt dip is simply a small bowl, from which salt is taken with a spoon and sprinkled on one's food. Though they could be used for pepper as well, it was usually considered more desirable for pepper to be covered up. Thus, the combination set consisting of a salt dip and pepper shaker. In addition, sets also included a salt spoon.

(Sterling Silver)

☐ **Baltimore Sterling Silver Co.,** *three pieces, pepper shaker 4¼" T., open salt dip 2¼" diameter, matching spoon, overall repousse floral design, c. 1895*	90.00	100.00
☐ **Kirk "Repousse",** *four piece set, two 4½" T. pepper shakers, two 2½" diameter salt dip, all items on three small feet, early marks, monogram*	200.00	225.00
☐ **Stieff "Rose",** *four piece set, two 4¼" pepper shakers, two salt dips, all items on three small scroll feet, no monogram*	210.00	235.00

SALT DIPS

The practice of leaving salt exposed on the table, in an open receptacle, during meals dates back hundred of years. Before the salt spoon, it was taken by the pinch in the fingers — or one would simply DIP his food directly in it, hence the name. In the late Middle Ages and going up to about 1600 A.D., salt was consumed in quantities that would make a 20th century diner whince. It was used almost exclusively with meats, and undoubtedly the liberal use was intended to hide the unpleasant flavor of meats that had spoiled (which was, in those pre-refrigeration times, a constant problem). Salt dips are so small that the uninitiated sometimes mistakes them for candle holders.

(Sterling Silver)

☐ **Graff & Washbourne,** *c. 1880, 2¾"*	42.00	47.00
☐ **Tiffany,** *footed base, hammered finish, two tiny handles, gold wash interior*	38.00	43.00
☐ **Webster,** *no monogram, set of four*	35.00	39.00
☐ **Wilcox,** *c. 1870, hexagon shape, 1½" H., footed base*	30.00	33.00
☐ **Maker unknown,** *cobalt liner, salt spoon, no monogram* . . .	22.00	24.00
☐ **Maker unknown,** *grape and leaf design, 2⅜" H., clear glass liner*	28.00	32.00
☐ **Maker unknown,** *shell motif*	9.00	11.00
☐ **Maker unknown,** *1" T., 1½" diameter, includes salt spoon* .	9.00	11.00

SALT SHAKER AND PEPPER MILL SETS

Another concession to the fastidious diner was the *pepper mill,* a small box with a crank which dispensed pepper as the crank was turned. It made for more colorful and folksy dining, but the pepper mill never could quite stand up to the pepper shaker in popularity. As collectors' pieces there are few silver items so appealing; one can only regret that a larger variety was not made. These sets often came in decorative boxes.

(Sterling Silver)

	Price Range	
☐ **Tiffany,** *monogram*	27.00	30.00
☐ **Maker unknown,** *vasiform shape*	16.00	19.00

SALT SPOONS

These were used in conjunction with salt dips (see above). They have small circular bowls, not very deep.

(Coin Silver)

☐ **Maker J. Shaffner,** *c. 1840, fiddle back pattern*	9.00	11.00

(Silver-Plated)

☐ **Holmes & Edwards "Leader"** *no monogram, excellent condition*	9.00	11.00
☐ **Holmes & Edwards "Leader",** *no monogram, mint condition*	10.00	12.00
☐ **Reed & Barton "Olive",** *monogram ghost showing through, resilvered*	7.00	8.00
☐ **1847 Rogers "Persian",** *no monogram, excellent condition*	25.00	27.00
☐ **1847 Rogers "Saratoga",** *no monogram, good condition* ...	9.00	11.00

(Sterling Silver)

☐ **Durgin "Colfax",** *no monogram*	8.00	9.00
☐ **Gorham "Colonial",** *no monogram*	9.00	11.00
☐ **Gorham, pattern unknown,** *no monogram*	6.00	7.00
☐ **Maker unknown,** *floral pattern*	8.00	9.00
☐ **Maker unknown,** *repousse floral pattern*	8.00	9.00

SALVERS

These accessories were used much more plentifully in Great Britain than in America; hence, most specimens found on the U.S. antiques market prove to be of British manufacture. Salvers were rather large flat trays. They were NOT used at the table. In noble households, etiquette dictated that the butler or maid could not hand things (such as letters that just arrived) to their employers. They must instead place the object on a salver, from which My Lord or My Lady could take it. This practice dated back to a medieval belief that the hands of a nobleman should not touch those of a commoner. It became afterwards — like shaking hands to show that they held no weapons — merely a formality. Many salvers are extremely decorative, though the American versions are not usually as good as the foreign.

(Coin Silver)

☐ **Wm. Forbes,** *made for Ball, Black & Co., New York, mid-19th c., circular, engraved crest in center, surrounded by engraved flowers, grape motif on rim, four feet, 13" diameter, 30 oz.*	675.00	750.00

SARDINE FORKS

Sardines traditionally had a reputation of being a cheap, common food of European peasants. But like many other foodstuffs in that category, they developed into a social fad in the 19th century. Vacuum canning brought them into even greater popularity. Silverware manufacturers were quick to bring out special forks for use with sardines.

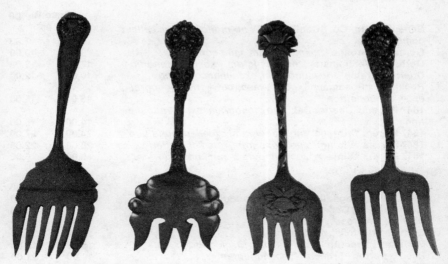

Sardine Forks, *(L to R) (sterling),* Frank Smith *"Newport Shell",* 21.00; *Dominick & Haff "New Kings",* 27.00; *Whiting twisted peony design,* 27.00; *Reed & Barton "Trajan",* 24.00

(Silver-Plated)

	Price Range	
☐ **Wm. Rogers "Melody"**, *no monogram, excellent condition* .	16.00	18.00
☐ **Maker unknown**, *sardine on tip, no monogram, excellent condition*	14.00	16.00

(Sterling Silver)

☐ **Alvin "Raphael"**, *no monogram*	60.00	66.00
☐ **Baker/Manchester "Poppy"**, *gold wash tines, no monogram*	45.00	50.00
☐ **Gorham, "Cambridge"**, *no monogram*	30.00	33.00
☐ **Gorham "Chantilly"**, *monogram*	35.00	39.00
☐ **Gorham "Lancaster"**, *monogram*	15.00	17.00
☐ **Gorham "Norfolk"**, *gold wash tines, no monogram*	28.00	32.00
☐ **Gorham "Plymouth"**, *monogram*	19.00	21.00
☐ **Kirk "Repousse"**, *no monogram*	50.00	57.00
☐ **Unger Bros. "Douvaine"**, *no monogram*	35.00	39.00
☐ **Whiting "Louis XV"**, *no monogram*	12.00	14.00

SAUCE LADLES

These did not follow any standard size. Among the sauces with which they were used was ketchup, even long after it was being commercially sold in bottles. A hostess who wished to give the impression that it was home-made poured it into a bowl before serving, and nobody was the wiser. There has always been a rather active market for sauce ladles, though they are smaller and not as attention-getting as punch ladles or soup ladles.

(Silver-Plated)

☐ **American Silver Co. "Oregon"**, *no monogram, excellent condition*	6.00	7.00

	Price Range	
☐ **Benedict Mfg. Co. "Continental"**, *no monogram, excellent condition*	6.00	7.00
☐ **Gorham "Carolina"**, *no monogram, mint condition*	9.00	10.00
☐ **Gorham "Westminster"**, *no monogram, excellent condition*	17.00	19.00
☐ **Oneida "Avalon"**, *no monogram, excellent condition*	10.00	12.00
☐ **Rockford "Rosemary"**, *gold wash bowl, no monogram, excellent condition*	13.00	15.00
☐ **1847 Rogers "Charter Oak"**, *no monogram, excellent condition*	14.00	16.00
☐ **1847 Rogers "Vintage"**, *no monogram, excellent condition*	24.00	27.00
☐ **1847 Rogers "Vintage"**, *no monogram, good condition*	20.00	22.00
☐ **1847 Rogers "Vintage"**, *no monogram, fair condition*	5.00	6.00
(Sterling Silver)		
☐ **Alvin "Monterey"**, *no monogram*	22.00	24.00
☐ **Alvin "Old Orange Blossom"**, *no monogram*	30.00	33.00
☐ **Gorham "King George"**	14.00	16.00
☐ **Gorham "Melrose"**, *no monogram*	12.00	14.00
☐ **Gorham "Norfolk"**, *monogram*	20.00	23.00
☐ **Gorham "Plymouth"**, *gold wash bowl, monogram*	16.00	18.00
☐ **Reed & Barton "Francis I"**, *no monogram*	19.00	21.00
☐ **Simpson, Hall & Miller "Frontenac"**, *no monogram*	40.00	45.00
☐ **Simpson, Hall & Miller "Warwick"**, *gold wash bowl, no monogram*	16.00	19.00
☐ **Stieff "Rose"**, *no monogram*	16.00	18.00
☐ **Stieff "Rose"**, *no monogram*	25.00	27.00
☐ **Tiffany "Palm"**, *no monogram*	40.00	45.00
☐ **Towle "Mary Chilton"**, *no monogram*	14.00	16.00
☐ **Maker unknown**, *engraved handle and bowl, decorated with dainty floral sprays*	13.00	15.00

SCISSORS

Among the many household accessories made of silver were scissors. They cut no better than those of stainless steel or other metals, but in physical appearance it was hardly any contest. Silver scissors have become a great favorite of collectors, not only because of the variety in decoration but in styles and sizes. The majority of those manufactured were sewing scissors or others of small size, but with some search you will find every possible type of scissors in silver. Many novelty specimens exist, such as the head of a bird for handles and the beak for blades.

(Sterling Silver)

☐ **Maker unknown**, *embroidery type, steel blades with ornate handles*	13.00	15.00
☐ **Maker unknown**, *embroidery type, steel blades with plain handles*	10.00	12.00
☐ **Maker unknown**, *sewing type, steel blades with ornate silver handles in the form of branches wrapped in vines and leaves, extremely good detailing*	21.00	23.00

SERVING FORKS

These all-purpose utensils were used in serving various kinds of foods. A good deal larger than dinner forks, they show the different patterns to much better advantage. The lengths are not standard, ranging anywhere from about 8″ to 10″; nor is the number of tines, or even the general shape. Therefore a collection can reflect a good deal of diversify. Serving forks were marketed separately by the manufacturers, and also in sets with serving spoons.

(Silver-Plated)	Price Range	
☐ **Hall, Elton & Co. "Orient"**, *no monogram, mint condition, in original box*	28.00	32.00
☐ **Hall, Elton & Co. "Orient"**, *monogram, fair condition*	3.00	4.00
☐ **Oneida "Jamestown"**, *monogram, excellent condition*	10.00	12.00
☐ **Rockford "Fairoaks"**, *no monogram, good condition*	9.00	10.00
☐ **Rockford "Fairoaks"**, *no monogram, mint condition*	18.00	20.00
☐ **Wm. A. Rogers "Hanover"**, *no monogram, excellent condition*	36.00	40.00
☐ **1847 Rogers "Daffodil"**, *no monogram, excellent condition*	20.00	22.00
☐ **1847 Rogers "First Love"**, *no monogram, good condition* ..	7.00	8.00
☐ **1847 Rogers "First Love"**, *no monogram, engraved work on tines, mint condition*	26.00	29.00
☐ **1847 Rogers "Old Colony"**, *no monogram, excellent condition*	17.00	19.00
☐ **1847 Rogers "Old Colony"**, *monogram, good condition*	8.00	9.00
☐ **1847 Rogers "Persian"**, *no monogram, mint condition, in original silk-lined box*	25.00	27.00
☐ **1847 Rogers "Vintage"**, *no monogram, resilvered*	33.00	36.00
☐ **1847 Rogers "Vintage"**, *no monogram, excellent condition*	30.00	33.00
☐ **1847 Rogers "Vintage"**, *monogram, fair condition*	8.00	9.00
(Sterling Silver)		
☐ **Frank M. Whiting "Adams"**, *five tines, no monogram*	40.00	45.00
☐ **Gorham "Colonial"**, *four tines, no monogram*	33.00	36.00
☐ **Gorham "King George"**, *five tines, gold wash on tines, monogram and date*	80.00	87.00
☐ **Kalo**, *raised monogram*	95.00	105.00
☐ **Kirk "Repousse"**, *10″ L., 6 tines, early mark, no monogram*	135.00	150.00
☐ **Reed & Barton "Trajan"**, *five tines, no monogram*	48.00	54.00
☐ **Stieff "Williamsburg Shell"**, *10″ L., five tines, no monogram*	30.00	35.00
☐ **Tiffan "English King"**, *five tines, no monogram*	60.00	66.00
☐ **Wallace "Irian"**, *five tines, very wide, no monogram*	80.00	87.00
☐ **Wallace "Rose"**, *8½″ L., five tines, monogram*	33.00	36.00

SERVING SPOONS

A huge field, ideal for the collector because of its rich variety in sizes, shapes and patterns. Bowls of serving spoons may be circular, oval, spade-shaped or even rectangular; they may be solid or pierced. This arises from the fact that serving spoons were made for use with many different foods. Those with a great deal of pierced-work in the bowls (for use in draining) are considered the most handsome. They make excellent displays. Fortunately for the collector, there is no shortage of silver serving spoons on today's antique markets.

Vegetable Serving Spoons, *(sterling), pierced, (L to R) Tiffany "Peapod",* 180.00; *Tiffany "Audubon",* 165.00; *Reed & Barton "Trajan",* 135.00; *J.P. & S.M. Knowles "Argo",* 105.00

(Coin Silver)	Price Range	
☐ R. & W. Wilson "Fiddle Thread", *monogram*	24.00	27.00
(Silver-Plated)		
☐ Alvin "Diana", *no monogram, excellent condition*	7.00	8.00
☐ Alvin "Diana", *no monogram, good condition*	6.00	7.00
☐ Alvin "Molly Stark", *no monogram, excellent condition*	7.00	8.00
☐ Alvin "Molly Stark", *monogram, good condition*	1.00	2.00
☐ Community "Bird of Paradise", *no monogram, excellent condition*	7.00	8.00
☐ Community "Bird of Paradise", *no monogram, good condition*	6.00	7.00
☐ Community "Bird of Paradise", *no monogram, fair condition*	1.00	2.00
☐ Community "Classic", *no monogram, good condition*	2.00	4.00
☐ Community "Classic", *no monogram, poor condition*	1.00	2.00
☐ Community "Coronation", *no monogram, excellent condition*	7.00	8.00
☐ Community "Coronation", *no monogram, good condition*	6.00	7.00
☐ Community "Coronation", *no monogram, fair condition*	1.00	2.00
☐ Community "Deauville", *no monogram, excellent condition*	7.00	8.00
☐ Community "Deauville", *no monogram, good condition*	5.00	6.00
☐ Community "Enchantment", *no monogram, excellent condition*	7.00	8.00
☐ Community "Enchantment", *no monogram, good condition*	6.00	7.00
☐ Community "Enchantment", *no monogram, fair condition*	1.00	2.00

Price Range

- Community **"Enchantment"**, *pierced, no monogram, excellent condition* 7.00 8.00
- Community **"Enchantment"**, *pierced, no monogram, fair condition* 1.00 2.00
- Community **"Georgian"**, *no monogram, excellent condition* 7.00 8.00
- Community **"Georgian"**, *no monogram, good condition* ... 6.00 7.00
- Community **"Lady Hamilton"**, *no monogram, excellent condition* 8.00 9.00
- Community **"Lady Hamilton"**, *no monogram, good condition* 6.00 7.00
- Community **"Louis XVI"**, *monogram, excellent condition* .. 2.00 3.00
- Community **"Louis XVI"**, *no monogram, excellent condition* 7.00 8.00
- Community **"Milady"**, *no monogram, excellent condition* .. 6.00 7.00
- Community **"Milady"**, *no monogram, fair condition* 2.00 3.00
- Community **"Morning Star"**, *no monogram, excellent condition* 8.00 9.00
- Community **"Morning Star"**, *no monogram, good condition* 5.00 6.00
- Community **"Patrician"**, *no monogram, excellent condition* 7.00 8.00
- Community **"Patrician"**, *no monogram, good condition* ... 6.00 7.00
- Community **"Patrician"**, *monogram, good condition* 2.00 3.00
- Community **"Paul Revere"**, *no monogram, excellent condition* 7.00 8.00
- Community **"Paul Revere"**, *no monogram, good condition* . 6.00 7.00
- Community **"Silver Flowers"**, *no monogram, excellent condition* 7.00 8.00
- Community **"Silver Flowers"**, *no monogram, good condition* 6.00 7.00
- Community **"Silver Flowers"**, *pierced, no monogram, excellent condition* 7.00 8.00
- Community **"Silver Flowers"**, *pierced, no monogram, good condition* 5.00 6.00
- Community **"South Seas"**, *no monogram, excellent condition* 7.00 8.00
- Community **"South Seas"**, *no monogram, fair condition* ... 1.00 2.00
- Fortune **"Fortune"**, *no monogram, excellent condition* 7.00 8.00
- Fortune **"Fortune"**, *no monogram, good condition* 4.00 5.00
- Gorham **"Kings"**, *no monogram, excellent condition* 7.00 8.00
- Gorham **"Kings"**, *no monogram, good condition* 6.00 7.00
- Gorham **"Kings"**, *monogram, excellent condition* 3.00 4.00
- Gorham **"New Elegance"**, *no monogram, excellent condition* 7.00 8.00
- Gorham **"New Elegance"**, *no monogram, good condition* .. 6.00 7.00
- Holmes, Booth & Haydens **"Japanese"**, *no monogram, fair condition* 1.00 2.00
- Holmes & Edwards **"Century"**, *no monogram, good condition* 6.00 7.00
- Holmes & Edwards **"Century"**, *no monogram, fair condition* 1.00 2.00
- Holmes & Edwards **"Danish Princess"**, *no monogram, excellent condition* 7.00 8.00
- Holmes & Edwards **"Danish Princess"**, *no monogram, good condition* 6.00 7.00
- Holmes & Edwards **"Lovely Lady"**, *no monogram, excellent condition* 7.00 8.00

	Price Range	
☐ Holmes & Edwards "Lovely Lady", *no monogram, good condition*	6.00	7.00
☐ Holmes & Edwards "May Queen", *no monogram, excellent condition*	7.00	8.00
☐ Holmes & Edwards "May Queen", *no monogram, good condition*	6.00	7.00
☐ Holmes & Edwards "Spring Garden", *no monogram, excellent condition*	7.00	8.00
☐ Holmes & Edwards "Spring Garden", *no monogram, good condition*	4.00	5.00
☐ Holmes & Edwards "Youth", *no monogram, excellent condition*	7.00	8.00
☐ Holmes & Edwards "Youth", *no monogram, good condition*	6.00	7.00
☐ International "Silver Tulip", *no monogram, excellent condition*	6.00	7.00
☐ International "Silver Tulip", *no monogram, good condition*	5.00	6.00
☐ International "Silver Tulip", *pierced, no monogram, excellent condition*	6.00	7.00
☐ International "Silver Tulip", *pierced, no monogram, good condition*	4.00	5.00
☐ King Edward "Cavalcade", *no monogram, excellent condition*	7.00	8.00
☐ King Edward "Cavalcade", *no monogram, good condition* .	6.00	7.00
☐ King Edward "Moss Rose", *no monogram, excellent condition*	7.00	8.00
☐ King Edward "Moss Rose", *no monogram, good condition* .	6.00	7.00
☐ National "Embossed", *no monogram, excellent condition* .	7.00	8.00
☐ National "Embossed", *no monogram, fair condition*	1.00	2.00
☐ National "King Edward", *no monogram, excellent condition*	7.00	8.00
☐ National "King Edward", *no monogram, good condition* ...	6.00	7.00
☐ Nobility "Royal Rose", *no monogram, excellent condition* .	7.00	8.00
☐ Nobility "Royal Rose", *no monogram, good condition*	6.00	7.00
☐ Old Company Plate "Signature", *monogram, excellent condition*	3.00	4.00
☐ Old Company Plate "Signature", *no monogram, fair condition*	1.00	2.00
☐ Oneida "Banbury", *no monogram, excellent condition*	7.00	8.00
☐ Oneida "Banbury", *no monogram, good condition*	6.00	7.00
☐ Oneida "Bridal Wreath", *no monogram, excellent condition*	7.00	8.00
☐ Oneida "Bridal Wreath", *no monogram, good condition* ...	6.00	7.00
☐ Paragon, unknown grape pattern, *no monogram, fair condition*	3.00	4.00
☐ Prestige "Grenoble", *no monogram, excellent condition* ..	7.00	8.00
☐ Prestige "Grenoble", *no monogram, good condition*	6.00	7.00
☐ Prestige "Grenoble", *no monogram, fair condition*	1.00	2.00
☐ Reed & Barton "Jewell", *no monogram, excellent condition*	7.00	8.00
☐ Reed & Barton "Jewell", *no monogram, good condition* ...	6.00	7.00
☐ Reed & Barton "Jewell", *no monogram, fair condition*	1.00	2.00
☐ Reliance "Exeter", *no monogram, excellent condition*	7.00	8.00
☐ Reliance "Exeter", *no monogram, good condition*	6.00	7.00
☐ Reliance "Exeter", *no monogram, fair condition*	1.00	2.00
☐ Rogers "Burgundy", *no monogram, excellent condition* ...	7.00	8.00
☐ Rogers "Burgundy", *no monogram, good condition*	6.00	7.00
☐ Rogers "Burgundy", *no monogram, fair condition*	1.00	2.00

Price Range

☐ Rogers **"Carlton"**, *no monogram, excellent condition*	7.00	8.00
☐ Rogers **"Carlton"**, *no monogram, good condition*	6.00	7.00
☐ Rogers **"Carlton"**, *no monogram, fair condition*	1.00	2.00
☐ Rogers **"Desire"**, *no monogram, excellent condition*	7.00	8.00
☐ Rogers **"Desire"**, *no monogram, good condition*	6.00	7.00
☐ Rogers **"Garland"**, *no monogram, excellent condition*	7.00	8.00
☐ Rogers **"Garland"**, *no monogram, good condition*	6.00	7.00
☐ Rogers **"Gracious"**, *no monogram, excellent condition*	7.00	8.00
☐ Rogers **"Gracious"**, *no monogram, good condition*	6.00	7.00
☐ Rogers **"Grenoble"**, *no monogram, excellent condition* . . .	8.00	9.00
☐ Rogers **"Grenoble"**, *no monogram, good condition*	6.00	7.00
☐ Rogers **"Grenoble"**, *monogram, excellent condition*	7.00	8.00
☐ Rogers **"Grenoble"**, *monogram, good condition*	2.00	3.00
☐ Rogers **"Inspiration"**, *no monogram, excellent condition* . .	7.00	8.00
☐ Rogers **"Inspiration"**, *no monogram, good condition*	6.00	7.00
☐ Rogers **"Inspiration"**, *no monogram, fair condition*	2.00	3.00
☐ Rogers **"LaTouraine"**, *no monogram, excellent condition* . .	7.00	8.00
☐ Rogers **"LaTouraine"**, *no monogram, good condition*	6.00	7.00
☐ Rogers **"Lexington"**, *no monogram, excellent condition* . . .	7.00	8.00
☐ Rogers **"Lexington"**, *no monogram, good condition*	6.00	7.00
☐ Rogers **"Lexington"**, *no monogram, fair condition*	1.00	2.00
☐ Rogers **"Milton"**, *no monogram, excellent condition*	7.00	8.00
☐ Rogers **"Milton"**, *no monogram, good condition*	6.00	7.00
☐ Rogers **"Precious"**, *no monogram, excellent condition*	7.00	8.00
☐ Rogers **"Precious"**, *no monogram, good condition*	6.00	7.00
☐ Rogers **"Shell"**, *no monogram, excellent condition*	7.00	8.00
☐ Rogers **"Shell"**, *no monogram, good condition*	6.00	7.00
☐ Rogers **"Tipped"**, *no monogram, excellent condition*	5.00	6.00
☐ Rogers **"Tipped"**, *no monogram, fair condition*	1.00	2.00
☐ Rogers & Bro. **"Daybreak"**, *no monogram, excellent condition*	7.00	8.00
☐ Rogers & Bro. **"Daybreak"**, *no monogram, good condition* .	6.00	7.00
☐ Rogers & Bro. **"Modern Rose"**, *no monogram, excellent condition*	7.00	8.00
☐ Rogers & Bro. **"Modern Rose"**, *no monogram, good condition*	6.00	7.00
☐ Rogers & Bro. **"New Grecian"**, *monogram, excellent condition*	1.00	2.00
☐ S.L. & G.H. Rogers **"English Garden"**, *no monogram, excellent condition*	7.00	8.00
☐ S.L. & G.H. Rogers **"English Garden"**, *no monogram, good condition*	6.00	7.00
☐ S.L. & G.H. Rogers **"Minerva"**, *no monogram, excellent condition*	8.00	9.00
☐ S.L. & G.H. Rogers **"Minerva"**, *no monogram, fair condition*	2.00	3.00
☐ Tudor **"Queen Bess II"**, *no monogram, excellent condition* .	7.00	8.00
☐ Tudor **"Queen Bess II"**, *no monogram, good condition*	6.00	7.00
☐ Tudor **"Queen Bess II"**, *no monogram, fair condition*	1.00	2.00
☐ Tudor **"Queen Bess II"**, *pierced, no monogram, good condition*	6.00	7.00
☐ Tudor **"Queen Bess II"**, *pierced, no monogram, fair condition*	1.00	2.00
☐ Wallace **"Sonata"**, *no monogram, excellent condition*	7.00	8.00
☐ Wallace **"Sonata"**, *no monogram, good condition*	6.00	7.00

	Price Range	
☐ Wallace "Sonata", *no monogram, fair condition*	**1.00**	**2.00**
☐ **Wm. A. Rogers "Artistic"**, *no monogram, excellent condition*	**7.00**	**8.00**
☐ **Wm. A. Rogers "Artistic"**, *no monogram, good condition* ..	**6.00**	**7.00**
☐ **Wm. A. Rogers "Chalice"**, *slotted, no monogram, excellent condition*	**7.00**	**8.00**
☐ **Wm. A. Rogers "Chalice"**, *slotted, no monogram, good condition*	**6.00**	**7.00**
☐ **Wm. A. Rogers "Gala"**, *no monogram, excellent condition* .	**7.00**	**8.00**
☐ **Wm. A. Rogers "Gala"**, *no monogram, good condition*	**6.00**	**7.00**
☐ **Wm. A. Rogers "Gala"**, *pierced, no monogram, excellent condition*	**7.00**	**8.00**
☐ **Wm. A. Rogers "LaConcorde"**, *no monogram, mint condition*	**9.00**	**10.00**
☐ **Wm. A. Rogers "Lady Stuart"**, *no monogram, excellent condition*	**7.00**	**8.00**
☐ **Wm. A. Rogers "Lady Stuart"**, *no monogram, good condition*	**6.00**	**7.00**
☐ **Wm. A. Rogers "Meadowbrook"**, *no monogram, excellent condition*	**7.00**	**8.00**
☐ **Wm. A. Rogers "Meadowbrook"**, *no monogram, fair condition*	**1.00**	**2.00**
☐ **Wm. A. Rogers "Rendezvous"**, *no monogram, excellent condition*	**7.00**	**8.00**
☐ **Wm. A. Rogers "Rendezvous"**, *no monogram, good condition*	**6.00**	**7.00**
☐ **Wm. A. Rogers "Rendezvous"**, *no monogram, fair condition*	**1.00**	**2.00**
☐ **Wm. A. Rogers "Rosalie"**, *no monogram, excellent condition*	**7.00**	**8.00**
☐ **Wm. A. Rogers "Rosalie"**, *no monogram, good condition* ..	**6.00**	**7.00**
☐ **Wm. Rogers "Beloved"**, *no monogram, excellent condition*	**7.00**	**8.00**
☐ **Wm. Rogers "Beloved"**, *no monogram, good condition*	**6.00**	**7.00**
☐ **Wm. Rogers "Beloved"**, *no monogram, fair condition*	**1.00**	**2.00**
☐ **Wm. Rogers "Cotillion"**, *no monogram, excellent condition*	**7.00**	**8.00**
☐ **Wm. Rogers "Cotillion"**, *no monogram, good condition* ...	**6.00**	**7.00**
☐ **Wm. Rogers "Debutante"**, *no monogram, good condition* ..	**6.00**	**7.00**
☐ **Wm. Rogers "Debutante"**, *no monogram, fair condition* ...	**1.00**	**2.00**
☐ **Wm. Rogers "Devonshire"**, *no monogram, excellent condition*	**7.00**	**8.00**
☐ **Wm. Rogers "Devonshire"**, *no monogram, good condition* .	**6.00**	**7.00**
☐ **Wm. Rogers "Exquisite"**, *no monogram, excellent condition*	**7.00**	**8.00**
☐ **Wm. Rogers "Exquisite"**, *no monogram, good condition* ...	**6.00**	**7.00**
☐ **Wm. Rogers "Exquisite"**, *no monogram, fair condition*	**1.00**	**2.00**
☐ **Wm. Rogers "Hostess"**, *no monogram, excellent condition*	**7.00**	**8.00**
☐ **Wm. Rogers "Hostess"**, *no monogram, good condition* ...	**6.00**	**7.00**
☐ **Wm. Rogers "Mayfair"**, *no monogram, excellent condition* .	**7.00**	**8.00**
☐ **Wm. Rogers "Mayfair"**, *no monogram, good condition*	**6.00**	**7.00**
☐ **Wm. Rogers "Memory"**, *no monogram, good condition*	**6.00**	**7.00**
☐ **Wm. Rogers "Memory"**, *no monogram, fair condition*	**1.00**	**2.00**
☐ **Wm. Rogers "Treasure"**, *no monogram, excellent condition*	**7.00**	**8.00**
☐ **Wm. Rogers "Treasure"**, *no monogram, good condition* ...	**6.00**	**7.00**
☐ **Wm. Rogers Mfg. Co. "Camelot"**, *no monogram, excellent condition*	**7.00**	**8.00**

Price Range

☐ **Wm. Rogers Mfg. Co. "Camelot"**, *no monogram, good condition*	6.00	7.00
☐ **Wm. Rogers & Son "April"**, *no monogram, excellent condition*	7.00	8.00
☐ **Wm. Rogers & Son "April"**, *no monogram, good condition* .	6.00	7.00
☐ **Wm. Rogers & Son "Arbutus"**, *no monogram, excellent condition*	7.00	8.00
☐ **Wm. Rogers & Son "Arbutus"**, *no monogram, good condition*	6.00	7.00
☐ **Wm. Rogers & Son "Arbutus"**, *no monogram, fair condition*	1.00	2.00
☐ **Wm. Rogers & Son "Flower"**, *no monogram, good condition*	6.00	7.00
☐ **Wm. Rogers & Son "Flower"**, *no monogram, poor condition*	1.00	2.00
☐ **Wm. Rogers & Son "Oxford"**, *no monogram, excellent condition*	7.00	8.00
☐ **Wm. Rogers & Son "Oxford"**, *no monogram, good condition*	6.00	7.00
☐ **Wm. Rogers & Son "Oxford"**, *no monogram, fair condition* .	1.00	2.00
☐ **World "Nenuphar"**, *no monogram, excellent condition*	8.00	9.00
☐ **World "Nenuphar"**, *no monogram, good condition*	5.00	6.00
☐ **World "Nenuphar"**, *no monogram, fair condition*	1.00	2.00
☐ **1835 R. Wallace "Joan"**, *no monogram, excellent condition*	8.00	9.00
☐ **1835 R. Wallace "Joan"**, *no monogram, fair condition*	1.00	2.00
☐ **1847 Rogers "Ancestral"**, *no monogram, excellent condition*	7.00	8.00
☐ **1847 Rogers "Ancestral"**, *no monogram, good condition* ..	6.00	7.00
☐ **1847 Rogers "Anniversary"**, *no monogram, excellent condition*	7.00	8.00
☐ **1847 Rogers "Anniversary"**, *no monogram, good condition*	6.00	7.00
☐ **1847 Rogers "Anniversary"**, *no monogram, fair condition* ..	1.00	2.00
☐ **1847 Rogers "Berkshire"**, *no monogram, excellent condition*	7.00	8.00
☐ **1847 Rogers "Berkshire"**, *no monogram, good condition* ..	6.00	7.00
☐ **1847 Rogers "Berkshire"**, *no monogram, fair condition* ...	1.00	2.00
☐ **1847 Rogers "Columbia"**, *no monogram, excellent condition*	7.00	8.00
☐ **1847 Rogers "Columbia"**, *no monogram, good condition* ..	6.00	7.00
☐ **1847 Rogers "Columbia"**, *no monogram, fair condition*	1.00	2.00
☐ **1847 Rogers "Eternally Yours"**, *no monogram, excellent condition*	6.00	7.00
☐ **1847 Rogers "Eternally Yours"**, *no monogram, good condition*	5.00	6.00
☐ **1847 Rogers "Eternally Yours"**, *no monogram, fair condition*	1.00	2.00
☐ **1847 Rogers "First Love"**, *no monogram, excellent condition*	7.00	8.00
☐ **1847 Rogers "First Love"**, *no monogram, good condition* ..	6.00	7.00
☐ **1847 Rogers "Leilani"**, *pierced, no monogram, excellent condition*	5.00	6.00
☐ **1847 Rogers "Leilani"**, *no monogram, excellent condition* .	7.00	8.00
☐ **1847 Rogers "Lovelace"**, *no monogram, excellent condition*	7.00	8.00
☐ **1847 Rogers "Lovelace"**, *no monogram, good condition* ...	6.00	7.00
☐ **1847 Rogers "Marquise"**, *no monogram, excellent condition*	7.00	8.00
☐ **1847 Rogers "Marquise"**, *no monogram, good condition* ..	6.00	7.00
☐ **1847 Rogers "Marquise"**, *no monogram, fair condition*	2.00	3.00

	Price Range	
☐ 1847 Rogers "Old Colony", *no monogram, excellent condition*	7.00	8.00
☐ 1847 Rogers "Old Colony", *monogram, good condition....*	2.00	3.00
☐ 1847 Rogers "Portland", *no monogram, excellent condition*	7.00	8.00
☐ 1847 Rogers "Portland", *no monogram, good condition* ...	6.00	7.00
☐ 1847 Rogers "Portland", *no monogram, fair condition*	1.00	2.00
☐ 1847 Rogers "Reflection", *no monogram, excellent condition*	9.00	11.00
☐ 1847 Rogers "Reflection", *pierced, no monogram, good condition*	6.00	7.00
☐ 1847 Rogers "Reflection", *no monogram, good condition* ..	3.00	4.00
☐ 1847 Rogers "Remembrance", *slotted, no monogram, excellent condition*	7.00	8.00
☐ 1847 Rogers "Remembrance", *slotted, no monogram, good condition*	6.00	7.00
☐ 1847 Rogers "Remembrance", *slotted, no monogram, fair condition*	1.00	2.00
☐ 1847 Rogers "Saratoga", *no monogram, excellent condition*	7.00	8.00
☐ 1847 Rogers "Saratoga", *no monogram, good condition* ...	5.00	6.00
☐ 1847 Rogers "Saratoga", *no monogram, poor condition* ...	1.00	2.00
☐ 1847 Rogers "Silver Lace", *pierced, no monogram, excellent condition*	7.00	8.00
☐ 1847 Rogers "Silver Lace", *pierced, no monogram, good condition*	6.00	7.00
☐ 1847 Rogers "Vintage", *no monogram, excellent condition*	8.00	9.00
☐ 1847 Rogers "Vintage", *no monogram, good condition*	7.00	8.00
☐ 1847 Rogers "Vintage", *no monogram, excellent condition*	12.00	14.00
☐ 1881 Rogers "Capri", *no monogram, excellent condition* ..	7.00	8.00
☐ 1881 Rogers "Capri", *no monogram, good condition*	6.00	7.00
☐ 1881 Rogers "LaVigne", *no monogram, excellent condition*	8.00	9.00
☐ 1881 Rogers "LaVigne", *no monogram, good condition* ...	7.00	8.00
☐ 1881 Rogers "Scotia", *no monogram, excellent condition* .	7.00	8.00
☐ 1881 Rogers "Scotia", *no monogram, good condition*	6.00	7.00

(Sterling Silver)

☐ Alvin "Morning Glory", *no monogram*	35.00	39.00
☐ Durgin "Fairfax", *8⅜" L., monogram*	43.00	48.00
☐ Frank Smith "Newport Shell", *7½" L., pierced bowl, no monogram*	30.00	33.00
☐ Gorham "Buttercup", *gold wash bowl, no monogram*	38.00	42.00
☐ Gorham, *chrysanthemum pattern, 9" L., bright-cut floral bowl, no monogram*	28.00	32.00
☐ Gorham "Kings", *gold wash bowl worn, monogram*	30.00	34.00
☐ Gorham "Lancaster", *monogram*	27.00	30.00
☐ Gorham "Medallion", *no monogram*	54.00	60.00
☐ Gorham "Old French", *8½" L., monogram*	21.00	23.00
☐ Gorham "Plymouth", *small, gold wash bowl, monogram* ..	18.00	20.00
☐ Gorham "Versailles", *pierced, no monogram*	65.00	72.00
☐ International "Fontaine", *no monogram*	40.00	44.00
☐ International "Trianon", *large, no monogram*	24.00	27.00
☐ Kirk "Repousse", *9½" L., no monogram*	71.00	81.00
☐ Oneida "Heiress", *no monogram*	27.00	30.00

	Price Range	
☐ Reed & Barton "Marlborough", *monogram*	36.00	40.00
☐ Schofield "Baltimore Rose", *9⅜" L., no monogram*	28.00	32.00
☐ Shiebler "American Beauty", *vegetable size, no monogram*	43.00	48.00
☐ Shiebler, *Art Nouveau design, no monogram*	23.00	25.00
☐ Tiffany "English King", *five tines, no monogram*	60.00	66.00
☐ Wallace "Irian", *five tines, very wide, no monogram*	80.00	87.00
☐ Wallace "Rose", *8½" L., five tines, monogram*	33.00	36.00
☐ Towle "Old Colonial", *no monogram*	16.00	18.00
☐ Towle "Rambler Rose", *pierced, monogram*	24.00	26.00
☐ Wallace "Grande Baroque", *pierced, no monogram*	54.00	60.00
☐ Wallace "Grande Baroque", *8¾" L., no monogram*	38.00	42.00
☐ Watson-Newell "Phoebe", *pierced, no monogram*	60.00	66.00
☐ Whiting "Imperial Queen", *long, no monogram*	54.00	60.00
☐ Wood & Hughes "Venetian", *deep bowl, 9" L., bright cut* *work and gold wash bowl, in original box*	90.00	100.00
☐ Maker unknown, *scroll pattern, monogram*	28.00	32.00

SHAVING MUGS

These are all quite old; the majority of those found on the market date from about 1880 to 1925. Before shaving cream came in aerosol cans, it had to be prepared by the user, by mixing shaving soap (cake or liquid) in boiling water. Shaving soap was designed to produce a thick frothy lather. While shaving, the lather was kept in a shaving mug, and transferred from the mug to one's face with a shaving brush. Most shaving mugs were made of porcelain, but some silver ones did come on the market. Their values are rather high, because of overall interest in shaving mugs and other shaving accessories (silver and otherwise). Those with engraved topical motifs are always worth a premium.

Shaving Mug, *maker unknown, c. 1890, single-handled cup with matching brush, flower motif,* 90.00

(Silver-Plated)

☐ Maker unknown, *4½" T., good condition*	45.00	50.00
☐ Maker unknown, *4¼" T., ornate embossed floral design,* *monogram*	54.00	60.00

SHERBERTS
(Sterling Silver)   Price Range
- ☐ **Kirk "Repousse",** *set of 12* 925.00   1,025.00

SHOE HORNS

Shoe horns were among the many novelties made of silver in the late 19th and early 20th centuries. Like letter openers, the handles lent themselves to all manner of creative design work. Specimens will be found in which the handles comprise heads of animals and people, floral motifs, seashells, and many other types. Imitations — often in styles that were even MORE novel — were made in German Silver (nickel). It's important to check and make certain that you're getting the real thing.

(Sterling Silver)
- ☐ **Gorham,** *ornate design, no monogram* 8.00   10.00
- ☐ **Tiffany,** *repousse handle* 40.00   45.00
- ☐ **Whiting "Lily of the Valley",** *design extends down onto horn, monogram* 40.00   45.00
- ☐ **Maker unknown,** *plain design, 8½" L., no monogram* 10.00   12.00

SHOVELS

No, our ancestors were not so enamored of silver that they used it in making snow shovels. Silver shovels were a table accessory, a type of serving spoon used in picking up ornery foods that a common serving spoon could not handle. They were also widely used in shops, in weighing out foodstuffs sold by the pound.

(Coin Silver)
- ☐ **R. & W. Wilson,** *8¼", strawberries on bowl, monogram* 72.00   80.00

(Sterling Silver)
- ☐ **Watson-Newell "Bacchante",** *no monogram, pierced work* . 40.00   45.00

SILENT BUTLERS
(Silver-Plated)
- ☐ **Reed & Barton,** *wooden handle, coat of arms design on lid, good condition* 40.00   45.00
- ☐ **Maker unknown,** *ornate embossed floral design, monogram and dated 1901, good condition* 45.00   50.00

SMOKE SETS

These varied considerably in the accessories included, and in their design. The more typical smoke sets featured a cigar holder, cigarette holder and match holder. They were placed on the library or den table, to which the gentlemen retired after dining. This long-standing social custom — of men heading into a separate room for group-smoking — was based on the belief that ladies in the company disliked tobacco smoke more than they liked the company of men. Often a smoke set's holders were fashioned into small barrels of graduated sizes: the largest for cigars, the next largest for cigarettes, the smallest for matches. The matches were of course of the wood variety. Smoke sets were sometimes placed on rotating bases.

(Silver-Plated)   Price Range

☐ **Tufts,** *round ashtray, match holder and cigar holder, Indian figures on sides of all pieces* 160.00   180.00

☐ **Maker unknown,** *cigarette barrel, cigar barrel and match barrel on wheel barrel with moving wheels* 145.00   160.00

SOAP DISHES

These were only occasionally made of silver, and are not plentiful enough on the market to be actively collected. General collectors of antique silverware sometimes buy them, as examples of the lengths to which manufacturers went in producing novelties. The designs vary quite a bit. Some are made to resemble the cast-iron bathtubs of their day, resting on ball-and-claw feet. Though our ancestors had vast admiration for silver wares, it apparently was not strong enough to lend much popularity to silver soap dishes.

(Sterling Silver)

☐ **Maker unknown,** *ball feet, 6¼" x 6", monogram* 35.00   39.00

☐ **Maker unknown,** *covered, travel type, etched geometric design, raised monogram* 54.00   60.00

SODA SPOONS

Soda spoons have become much more widely manufactured in recent years, but the usual material is stainless steel. Those made of silver are not common, while specimens in sterling silver (as opposed to plated) are hardly ever found. Their function made a graceful shape necessary: a long tapering handle, to reach the ice cream nestled at the bottom of an ice cream soda. Not too many people made ice cream sodas at home, and this is the reason for the scarcity of silver soda spoons. Drugstore soda fountains simply did not go to the extremes of using silver accessories.

(Silver-Plated)

☐ **Wm. A. Rogers "Lenora",** *no monogram, resilvered* 18.00   20.00

SOUP LADLES

Soup ladles rank very close to — or perhaps on a par with — punch ladles in their popularity as collectors' items. A strict comparison would reveal that punch ladles are somewhat more alluring physically; but soup ladles have the important advantage of being far more plentiful on the market, and hence can be built up into a much larger and more diversified collection. Every household that had silver table service had at least one silver soup ladle. The finer restaurants also used them. There is no "average" size or weight — and this contributes to their appeal. Some specimens are as small as 10", while others measure 17" or even more. Why such diversity? Because fashion dictated that the size of the soup ladle should at least roughly agree with the size of the soup tureen. If one had an oversized tureen, it was considered unseemly to reach into it with a short-handled ladle. The bowl shapes of soup ladles vary greatly: rounds, ovals, and rectangulars will be found, along with many modifications of these basic shapes. There are few silver articles which display so handsomely.

Soup Ladle, *(sterling), Tiffany "Audubon", gold wash bowl,* 450.00

(Coin Silver)	Price Range	
☐ **Duhme "Medallion",** *16½ " L., gold wash bowl, fluted and scalloped bowl*	200.00	225.00
(Silver-Plated)		
☐ **American Silver Co. "Berlin",** *no monogram, excellent condition*	25.00	27.00
☐ **Bailey, Banks & Biddle "Fiddle",** *no monogram, excellent condition*	25.00	27.00
☐ **Community "Flower de Luce",** *no monogram, excellent condition*	38.00	42.00
☐ **Community "Flower de Luce",** *monogram, fair condition* ..	18.00	20.00
☐ **Holmes & Edwards "Orient",** *no monogram, excellent condition*	48.00	54.00
☐ **Holmes & Edwards "Orient",** *no monogram, mint condition, in original presentation box*	56.00	62.00
☐ **Oneida "Kenwood",** *10½ " L., no monogram, excellent condition*	20.00	22.00
☐ **Oneida, pattern unknown,** *roses on handle, 10¾" L., monogram, excellent condition*	22.00	24.00
☐ **Reed & Barton "Italian",** *large size, no monogram, excellent condition*	35.00	40.00
☐ **Reed & Barton "LeLouvre",** *no monogram, good condition* .	62.00	68.00
☐ **Reed & Barton "Oxford",** *12" L., no monogram, poor condition*	27.00	27.00
☐ **Rockford "Rosemary",** *no monogram, excellent condition* .	35.00	40.00
☐ **Rockford "Rosemary",** *no monogram, good condition*	17.00	19.00
☐ **Rogers "Newport",** *no monogram, excellent condition*	48.00	54.00
☐ **Rogers & Bro. "Assyrian Head",** *no monogram, excellent condition*	56.00	62.00
☐ **Rogers & Bro. "Assyrian Head",** *12" L., no monogram, excellent condition*	100.00	115.00
☐ **Rogers & Bro. "Assyrian Head",** *10" L., no monogram, excellent condition*	67.00	75.00
☐ **Rogers & Bro. "Garland",** *no monogram, excellent condition*	56.00	62.00
☐ **Rogers & Bro. "Garland",** *monogram, good condition*	18.00	20.00
☐ **Wallace "Astoria",** *no monogram, fair condition*	25.00	27.00
☐ **W.D. Smith "Adam",** *no monogram, mint condition*	23.00	25.00

Price Range

☐ Wm. A. Rogers "Raleigh", *no monogram, excellent condition*	40.00	45.00
☐ Wm. A. Rogers "Rendezvous", *no monogram, excellent condition*	56.00	62.00
☐ Wm. Rogers Mfg. Co. "Arbutus", *11½" L., no monogram, excellent condition*	53.00	58.00
☐ Wm. Rogers Mfg. Co. "Arbutus", *no monogram, excellent condition*	75.00	85.00
☐ 1847 Rogers "Berkshire", *no monogram, excellent condition*	36.00	40.00
☐ 1847 Rogers "Berkshire", *monogram, good condition*	36.00	40.00
☐ 1847 Rogers "Berkshire", *monogram, excellent condition*	67.00	75.00
☐ 1847 Rogers "Dundee", *no monogram, excellent condition*	62.00	68.00
☐ 1847 Rogers "Etruscan", *no monogram, excellent condition*	33.00	36.00
☐ 1847 Rogers "Gothic", *no monogram, resilvered*	33.00	36.00
☐ 1847 Rogers "Newport", *no monogram, good condition*	56.00	62.00
☐ 1847 Rogers "Savoy", *no monogram, excellent condition*	62.00	68.00
☐ 1847 Rogers "Vintage", *no monogram, excellent condition*	80.00	90.00
☐ 1847 Rogers "Vintage", *no monogram, excellent condition*	100.00	115.00
☐ 1847 Rogers "Vintage", *monogram, good condition*	45.00	50.00
☐ 1881 Rogers "LaVigne", *no monogram, resilvered*	70.00	80.00
☐ 1881 Rogers "LaVigne", *no monogram, mint condition, in original silk-lined presentation box*	95.00	105.00
☐ Maker unknown, *pearl handled, monogram in bowl, fair condition*	6.00	7.00
☐ Maker unknown, *plain with shell design on top, excellent condition*	45.00	50.00

(Sterling Silver)

☐ Durgin "Dauphin", *monogram*	190.00	210.00
☐ Gorham "Imperial Chrysanthemum", *engraved bowl, 15½" L., no monogram*	190.00	210.00
☐ Gorham "Imperial Chrysanthemum", *monogram*	215.00	240.00
☐ Gorham "Isis", *no monogram*	190.00	210.00
☐ Gorham "Isis", *monogram*	245.00	270.00
☐ Gorham "King George", *monogram and date, gold wash bowl*	190.00	210.00
☐ John Wendt "Tuscan", *14¼" L., monogram*	50.00	56.00
☐ Schofield "Rose", *hand-chased, 15" L., no monogram*	215.00	240.00
☐ Wallace "Peony", *15" L., no monogram*	125.00	140.00
☐ Wallace "Peony", *monogram*	145.00	160.00
☐ Whiting "Arabesque", *monogram*	150.00	165.00
☐ Wood & Hughes "Daisy", *gold wash bowl, 16" L., no monogram*	135.00	150.00

THE STORY OF SPOONS

Spoon collecting began when our ancestors began eating with something other than their fingers. The first recorded spoonmaker, listed in the Book of Exodus, is Bezalel, a worker in gold, silver and brass. Early spoons were fashioned from shells, carved from wood, ivory, made from metals, or whatever man's mind could devise.

Collecting the really ancient spoons is nearly impossible since most of them have not survived. Existing specimens are beyond the reach of the average person, in ancient graves or kings' palaces and museums.

The first spoons crafted in America were very simple. The first patent was obtained in 1844. By 1849 silversmiths were beginning to make all kinds, sizes and shapes of spoons. Apostle and birthday spoons go back to the 1300's in Europe. The souvenir spoons craze hit the United States in 1890.

WHAT TYPES OF SPOONS SHOULD YOU COLLECT?

Collect the types of spoons everyone likes. They have pictures in the bowls or engraving, fancy handles with figures or historical information. They are *souvenir types commemorating an event or place.*

Spoons made of silver have always been prized possessions. The giving of spoons for gifts is well established. In Europe at baptism it was common to give the child a spoon, or a set of spoons, birthdate spoons or a set of Apostle spoons.

Many old spoons are still available. You may want to specialize in one type. What may happen is that you begin with one category and end up with a general collection or more than one category. This occurs when you are a trader, a gift receiver or a bargain buyer. There is nothing wrong with this approach. It differs from many hobbies in this respect. You can chart your own course.

You settle on a category by deciding that you want to collect only sterling spoons. You may decide that you want to collect only sterling spoons with enameling on them. That is a more defined category. You are the boss here. A few possibilities will be listed so that you may know what is available and what sort of a choice you want to make. What you can find in your area may be a determining factor until you discover that you can mail order from everywhere. The sky and your pocketbook then become the limit.

1. Series collecting. Included in this category would be the newspaper sales promotion series by several different silver companies, the American Presidential series, State series, etc.

2. Set collecting. Sets are a group of spoons issued at the same time such as the actor or actress sets, Dionne quintuplets, Campbell Kids, Apostles, holidays, American heroes and patriots, American composers, Disney spoons, etc.

3. States and cities. Collecting spoons from a certain city or state. The choice will be limited if a city is chosen, unless a large city such as New York, Los Angeles, Chicago, etc. is the target.

4. Content collecting - Sterling, silverplate, pewter, China, brass, copper, bone, clay and shell spoons are available. The collecting could be determined by content along with another consideration.

5. **Designer or manufacturer.** Designs by an individual or a specific company. Spoons were designed by craftsmen just as designer dressmakers, etc.

6. **Oddity.** Full standing figures, heads, engraving, enamelling, pictures in the bowls such as mountains, famous people, animals, skylines, etc.

7. **World's Fairs** - The first spoon issued by a fair was in 1893.

8. **Events** - Olympics, moon landings, space flights, holidays, etc., etc.

9. **Historical events.** Could include war and military spoons.

10. **Advertising.** These were promotional spoons such as newspaper spoons, and advertising products such as Log Cabin syrup, watches, foods, tea, peanuts, etc.

11. **Regional.** Spoons from a geographical location such as the west, south, parks, rivers, mountains, etc.

12. **Foreign** - Many foreign spoons are available in the United States, but we do not have the space to deal with them here.

WHERE TO FIND THEM

You can begin by casually announcing your intention to collect spoons to your relatives and friends. Ask them to be on the lookout for you and then follow up on their leads. They may have some in their drawer, too. Hang up a spoon rack with a couple of spoons on it and you probably will begin receiving them as gifts on special occasions if you express your interest in them.

Check secondhand stores and thrift shops. Look in antique stores. Run an ad in the paper saying you will buy old spoons. You won't get many that way, but a few. The ads are a good way to get that missing series spoon. Run your own ad to buy a specific spoon and see what you get.

Attend garage sales, auctions, and estate sales. Go to flea markets. Keep looking for souvenir spoons on your vacation.

Subscribe to antique or silver magazines. Check magazines for ads. You will find plenty of spoons to buy, even though the supply of spoons has decreased considerably since the January 1980 meltdown.

An antique dealer in your town will probably look for spoons for you once he knows you are a collector. Check the section under buying for instructions on how to communicate with a dealer.

Check classified ads in any newspaper or magazine you pick up and see if silver is advertised. You may find better prices in small out of the way antique stores, but not always.

Send for spoon price lists that you see advertised. This is an excellent way to learn pricing in addition to seeing if there are spoons you want to buy. Compare prices.

BUYING AND SELLING

The price of spoons is about as low as it will be, right now. They do not come down in price very much regardless of the price of silver. Now is the time to be buying while the silver market is "soft." Buy sterling in preference to plate unless it is a series, or especially attractive. Older spoons will not cost you much more than the new ones. Newer spoons will have to be held longer for profit.

Learn prices and compare before you begin active buying. Look at the prices for spoons whether you are buying or not. You will begin to see a price pattern. Remember, however, that you may not have a second chance to find a specific spoon. You may have to pay slightly more for a rarer spoon, especially when buying from a dealer who knows about spoons.

If you are working with a dealer, be sure to tell them what you want and approximately what you will pay for a spoon, or set. Dealers won't buy items for you if you refuse them after they have purchased them with you in mind. Have a clear understanding with your dealer, particularly if you intend for him to buy in your behalf. Be really specific. For instance, "Mary, I will buy any spoon you find with an Indian on it, if it is a sterling demitasse and doesn't cost over $20. I can buy only one spoon at a time, so if you find more than one, please don't buy them for me unless you understand that I can buy only about one a month. Also, the Indian should be a head or a full standing figure. I already have one with a head and war bonnet from Colorado so I wouldn't be interested in another."

Believe me, if Mary finds a full standing figure from New York for $20 or less you had better buy it, or Mary isn't going to bother with you again. If Mary finds any full standing figure of anything for $20 or less, even if you have a dozen, you should snap it up as an investment. Full standing figures are scarce.

When you are ready to sell, look again for ads in magazines, particularly trade magazines where there are requests for spoons. Answer the ads. Run your own sale ad. Mail order can be very profitable. A dealer can only pay you a portion of the value since he must make a profit.

If you have enough to sell, you can give them to large auction houses with a good reputation, to sell for you. If you do that, remember to put a reserve on what you will sell for, so that you don't sustain a loss.

Flea markets are also a selling source. You may get to know other collectors who will buy from you.

Remember to keep a list of what you pay for spoons so that you don't accidently sell for less than you paid. This will also show you how your spoons are growing in value.

DISPLAYING YOUR COLLECTION

Spoon racks are decorative and fairly inexpensive. They do not protect silver from dust, tarnish or theft.

Locked wall cases with glass doors prevent dust, tarnish and petty theivery but are not deterrent to the determined thief who will break the glass.

Silver chests are a good protection against tarnish and dust. They are also easy for a burglar to steal.

One or two displays of your least valuable spoons is all that you should allow yourself to show. The rest of your silver should be treated like the valuable commodity it is.

Would you leave coins or paper money lying about? Don't tempt someone with a glittering display of silver. Why have it then? Because it is an investment that retains and increases its value.

The storage place should be a safety deposit box, or ingenious fire-proof hiding place in your home. Under the bed, in closets, under the mattress, under the davenport and other related places just won't do if you have your house ransacked or it burns. Burying it in the yard is not advisable either.

SPOONS AND MORE SPOONS

Daniel Low, jeweler and silversmith, opened a shop in Salem, Massachusetts in 1867. In 1887, he took a trip to Europe to buy "fine wares" for his rapidly growing business. Mr. Low observed that souvenir spoons were popular in Europe. On his return, he discussed with his son, Seth Low, the feasibility of making American souvenir spoons. Why not a Witch Spoon as a souvenir of Salem and the witchcraft story?

Seth designed the spoon and it was advertised in a national magazine. The magazine ad brought 1500 orders and thousands were sold to tourists and the North Shore summer colony.

Several other designs were made for Daniel Low. A leaflet illustrating the spoons was sent to customers who ordered from the magazine advertisement. It was successful. Another booklet was published including jewelry and silver. Daniel Low was in the mail order business. Catalogs are still available today from the company. A new Witch Spoon is being offered. Five or six years ago a sterling spoon was offered at $5. Last year the same spoon was $10. It is now $19, giving you an idea of the increase of interest in commemorative spoons.

A variety of shapes in Witch Spoons was developed at the turn of the century. They were offered in two patterns and included teaspoons, orange spoons, coffee spoons, bonbon tongs, sugar spoons, berry forks, sardine forks and a paper knife. The coffee spoon (sterling) sold for $1.75. The price was $3.00 for a sugar spoon with a gold washed bowl.

Spoon collecting was going full bent by the time of the Columbian Exposition in 1893 in Chicago. A little caution needs to be exercised with these spoons. Check the back for a hallmark, U.S. Sterling. Be aware that this is a company and not the silver content. Don't pay a sterling price for it. There is a nice variety from this fair.

People were traveling considerably at the turn of the century, buying souvenir spoons to keep or give for gifts. It is interesting to note that not too many spoons from a city or state of origin are found in the same place, the result of the traveler taking them home with him. Eastern spoons can be found in the west. Less western spoons can be found in the east. This probably indicates the direction of travel. There seem to be more Colorado spoons available than other states, possibly because of the silver mining. Idaho has been the largest silver mining state in the United States, but the availability of the spoons is considerably less. Many Montana spoons will be made of copper, advertising the copper capital of the United States.

The first World War curtailed travel and spoon collecting. Souvenir spoon companies went out of business and other silversmiths turned to items more in demand.

About 1915 Moses Annenberg of Chicago decided to attempt to raise newspaper circulation by offering silver plated States spoons for about 15¢ and a coupon cut from a newspaper or magazine.

The promotion was an instant success and millions of the spoons were manufactured. International Silver Co. was the first producer.

Other promotions were begun by Oneida, Community, Wallace and Sons, Wm. Rogers, and Federal State Silver Co., making advertising spoons as state seals and presidential series.

The Rogers presidential series was manufactured from the 1930's through the time of John F. Kennedy's term in office.

Spoons picturing actors and actresses along with Florida tourist spoons appeared from 1925 to 1930, but the depression ended the revival attempt.

SETS

Souvenir Spoons - Sets
Price Range

☐ **Apostle Spoons,** *souvenir, 12 apostles and the Master, sterling silver Franklin Mint limited edition, name and symbol on reverse, Apostle's Creed in bowls; Rodney Winfield, designer and sculptor. In original case.* **585.00   780.00**

Apostle spoons appeared in Europe early in the 15th century. Pre-Christian silversmiths frequently adorned their utensils with figures of their gods. It is thought that the figure of an Apostle on the handle of a spoon may have had its origin with these utensils.

Only the rich owned a spoon, or spoons, during the Middle Ages (500-1500 A.D.). They were usually gold or silver and each guest carried his own spoon to a meal in a velvet pouch. This tradition extended far into the 14th century. Silver spoons were treasured keepsakes, customarily willed to grandchildren, children or other relatives or special friends.

Apostle spoons were introduced in England about 1450 as christening gifts. These sets contain 13 spoons, one for Christ and one each for the 12 Apostles. If the godparents were financially able, a full set was presented to the child. A single spoon was otherwise presented. The spoon was usully the Apostle whose anniversary came closest to the baby's christenening date or birth, or for whom the child was named.

Although popular for nearly 200 years, only five complete sets are in existence today. Some sets were made in the 1800's.

Rodney Winfield is the designer and sculptor of the above set. His works appears in private collections, in churches and public building throughout the country, including the Washington Cathedral in Washington, D. C., the International Building in San Francisco, Christ Church in St. Louis and Good Samaritan Hospital in Mt. Vernon, Illinois. The master design was sculptured for each spoon directly in silver instead of clay, the process usually used by sculptors. The metal is sculptured from the back to accentuate the finely detailed bas-relief of the design.

Each Apostle is holding the emblem or symbol with which he is traditionally associated, either the insignia or office or the sign of his martyrdom. His name and symbol are also carved into the reverse of the spoon. St. Peter holds two keys, symbolizing the keys to Heaven. St. Andrew is depicted with the saltire, or X-shaped, cross on which he was crucified. St. James the Greater carries a pilgrim's staff, symbolic of his journeys, while St. John holds the cup of sorrow. St. Philip has a basket containing loaves of bread. St. James the Less carries a fuller's club, the clay-working instrument with which he was beaten to death. St. Thomas holds the spear with which he was martyred. St. Bartholomew's symbol is a knife, which was used to flay him before his crucifixion. St. Matthew's purse represents his position as tax collector. St. Simon Zelotes, the fisherman, has an oar and net containing fish. St. Matthias, who took Judas's place, has an axe, the symbol of his martyrdom. St. Jude the carpenter carries a square, symbol of his trade.

The bowl of each spoon has a portion of the Apositles' Creed etched into it. The creed is completed in the set of 12 spoons. Christ, the master spoon, holds the orb and cross. The bowl has the two Greek letters which are the monogram of Christ.

☐ **Zodiac,** *souvenir, Franklin Mint set of 12, sterling silver, limited edition, teaspoon, signature edition, Gemini, designer, Richard Baldwin; Virgo, Ernest Lauser; Pisces, Hal Faulkner; Scorpio, Ceasar Rufo; Aquarius, Richard Baldwin; Cancer, Ceasar Rufo; Leo, Anthony Jones; Taurus, Philip Nathan; Sagittarius, Philip Nathan; Libra, Ernest Lauser; Aries, Anthony Jones. Zodiac signs on front, signature of designer on reverse, in original case* . . . .

☐ **Presidential Set,** *teaspoons, silver plate, Wm. Rogers for International Silver Company, face on handle tip, name running down handle, picture in bowl relating to president. In original case. Price for each.* 8.00   10.00

This presidential set was originally designed to increase newspaper sales. The set was available until the last eight to ten years, offered for purchase one spoon at a time. A case was available for the entire collection. The last spoon offered was President Kennedy, in gold color.

These spoons were originally offered at 25¢ and a coupon taken from a newspaper or magazine to increase their circulation. Later the price rose to $3.50 and up. The spoons were popular and were issued later for their own attraction, not related particularly to increasing circulations in periodicals. Five of the presidents are pictured as well as President Kennedy; Andrew Jackson, 1829-1837, Battle of New Orleans in the bowl; James A. Garfield, 1881-1881, birthplace Grange, Ohio in bowl; Franklin D. Roosevelt, 1933-1945, Social Security Act in bowl; Grover Cleveland, 1885-1887 & 1893-1897, Interstate Commerce 1887 in bowl; Chester A. Arthur, 1881-1885, Civil Service Act 1883 in bowl; and President John F. Kennedy, 1961-1963, gold washed, globe of world with space ship circling, "Friendship" in bowl

☐ **State Seal,** *souvenir spoons, teaspoon, extra heavy silver plate on 18% nickel silver base, Wallace A + 1, patented. Henry L. Wallace, Wallingford, Conn. June 1, 1915 (U. S. Pat. No.47,414) "E. Pluribus Unum" on handle* 8.00   12.00

These spoons were made for distribution by R. H. Macy & Co. at 11% each with a coupon. Pictured are New York, Pennsylvania, Arizona, Washington and California. All of the states are available. The handles have the state, top of handle state seal, and plain bowls.

☐ **State Seal** *series, souvenir spoons, teaspoons, Grosvenor N. Allen, Oneida, NY, March 9, 1915 (U. S. Patent No 47065) Oneida Community A1X plate. Seal at top, state on handle, plain bowls.*   8.00   12.00

These spoons were also part of a newspaper advetising campaign started about 1913 by Moses Annenberg, Chicago, Ill. They were originally offered at two for 25¢ or 12½¢ per spoon with a coupon, on January 17,1915. One Sunday or three daily paper coupons were required.

☐ **State Seal,** *souvenir spoons, teaspoon, Golden Rod, Gustave Strohhaker, Wallingford, Conn., Fmb. 23, 1915, Patent No. 47017, February 23, 1915. Eagle on handle tip, state, and goldenrod down handle, plain bowls. Wm. Rogers & Son, mfg. by International Silver Company, Meriden, Conn.* 8.00   12.00

Anneberg first approached the International Silver Company in about 1913. For 15¢ and a newspaper coupon these silver plated spoons of the states could be obtained. News dealers received ½ to 2 cents per spoon as well as the increased circulation. The response was overwhelming. Dessert spoons and sugar shells were manufactured as well, apparently in smaller quantities since they are generally unavailable.

	Price Range	
☐ Dessert and sugar shells, same pattern as above	15.00	18.50
☐ State Seal series, teaspoon, plate, Interstate Silver Co. Wyoming.	6.00	8.00

Apostle Spoon, *one of twelve,* 585.00 - 780.00 *per set.*

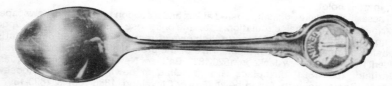

Zodiac, *one of twelve, Gemini,* 480.00 - 600.00 *per set.*

Presidential Set, *James A. Garfield,* 8.00 - 10.00 *ea.*

State Seal, *"Washington" on handle,* 8.00 - 10.00 *ea.*

State Seal, *"Ohio", on handle,* 8.00 - 12.00 ea.

State Seal, *"Idaho",* 8.00 - 12.00 ea.

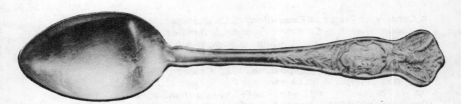

State Seal, *"Wyoming", State Seal on Tip,* 6.00 - 8.00 ea.

Souvenir Spoons · World's Fair

	Price Range	
☐ **1893 World's Fair,** *Columbian Exposition 1492-1893, Chicago, Illinois Plate, demitasse, Standard Co. Machinery Hall in bowl.*	**12.00**	**20.00**
☐ **1893 World's Fair,** *Columbian Exposition 1492-1893, Chicago, Illinois plate, demitasse, Standard Co. Capitol Washington, D. C. in bowl.*	**12.00**	**20.00**
☐ **1893 World's Fair,** *Columbian Exposition 1492-1893, Chicago, Illinois plate, demitasse, A-1 Coin Silver Co. plain bowl.*	**10.00**	**15.00**

These spoons were made to commemorate the discovery of America by Christopher Columbus at the Columbian Exposition, 1893, held at Chicago, Illinois. They brought spoon collecting into focus, triggering souvenir spoons of all types, shapes and for every holiday and occasion. Mrs. Potter Palmer was chosen President of the Board of Lady Managers of the Fair. The architectural work was primarily done by Daniel Burnham. The Spanish government provided a replica of the Santa Maria. Replicas of the Nina, Pinta and Santa Maria sailed from Spain in 1892 to New York harbor for the fair in 1893. Many other spoons are available, such as a bust of Mrs. Palmer, the buildings, the arch, totem pole etc.

Price Range

☐ **Louisana Purchase Exposition,** *April 30-December 1, 1904,*
teaspoon, plate, steamboat on handle tip, St. Louis 1904 on han-
dle, Cascade Gardens in bowl. 12.00   17.50

☐ **Louisiana Purchase Exposition,** *"St. Louis Exposition",*
demitasse, plate, Palace of Machinery in bowl 8.00   12.00

☐ **Louisiana Purchase Exposition,** *"St. Louis Exposition",*
demitasse, plate, Palace of Varied Industries in bowl 8.00   12.00

☐ **Lewis & Clark Exposition 1905,** *Portland, Oregon, teaspoon,*
silver plate, Lewis & Clark on handle tip, Mt. Hood, 1805-1905
and Columbia river salmon on handle, Forestry Building, Lewis &
Clark Exposition, Portland, Oregon 1905, picture of Forestry
Building in bowl. 12.00   15.00

☐ **Alaska-Yukon-Pacific Exposition,** *teaspoon, silver plate,*
Stratford Silver Co. AXI, Lilies on handle, Exposition 1909,
Manufacturers Building, Seattle, Washington in bowl. 8.00   12.50

☐ **San Francisco World's Fair 1915,** *demitasse, silver plate, of-*
ficial souvenir, Jewel tower on handle, San Francisco 1915 han-
dle, plain bowl, seal on reverse. 8.00   10.00

☐ **A Century of Progress Exposition,** *1933, Chicago, Illinois*
teaspoon, silver plate, Woman's head on handle tip, Century of
Progress Chicago on handle, Administration Building in bowl.
Wm. A. Rogers. 8.00   15.00

☐ **A Century of Progress Exposition,** *1933, Chicago, Illinois,*
teaspoon, silverplate, Century of Progress on handle tip, Clara
Lu'N Em on handle, Science Court in bowl, Winthrop silver-
plate. 8.00   15.00

☐ **A Century of Progress Exposition,** *1933, Chicago, Illinois,*
teaspoon, silverplate, Black Partridge Indian head on handle
tip, Hall of Science and Century of Progress on handle, Fort
Dearborn 1833-1934, Chicago in bowl. Century silverplate. .   8.00   15.00

☐ **A Century of Progress Exposition,** *1933, Chicago, Illinois,*
teaspoon, silverplate, Official-Tower on handle tip, A Cen-
tury of Progress on handle, plain bowl. Green Duck Co.
Chicago. 8.00   15.00
   "A Century of Progress" exposition commemmorated Chicago's 100th an-
niversary. It was held in Chicago in 1933 and 1934. Chicago's growth from Fort Dearborn
to a huge city was portrayed in this fair.

☐ **California PAC Intl. Exposition,** *1935, San Diego, California,*
teaspoon, silverplate, seal on handle tip, San Diego 1935 and
tower, California PAC Intl. Exposition on handle, plain bowl.   8.00   15.00

☐ **New York World's Fair,** *1939, teaspoon, silverplate, Theme*
Building 1939 on handle tip, New York World's Fair on handle,
plain bowl. Exposition silverplate co. 8.00   15.00
   This fair centered around the "World of Tomorrow". Long Island marshes were
filled for a fair site. Trylon and perisphere were its symbols.

☐ **Golden Gate International Exposition,** *1939, teaspoon, sil-*
verplate, tower, Golden Gate 1939 on handle tip, International
Exposition on handle, plain bowl. 8.00   15.00

Price Range

☐ **Golden Gate International Exposition,** *San Francisco 1940, demitasse, sterling, Tower 1940 on handle tip, Golden Gate picture with San Francisco on handle, plain bowl.* 10.00   15.00

☐ **Seattle World's Fair,** *1962, Century 21 Exposition, demitasse, sterling, Space Needle 21 on handle tip, Seattle World's Fair on handle, plain bowl.* 10.00   15.00

☐ **Japanese Expo** *1970, demitasse, EPNS, Globe in hands on handle tip, "Osaka" in bowl. Made in Holland.* 4.00   6.00

☐ **World's Fair, Spokane, Washinton,** *1974, demitasse, sterling.*   10.00   15.00

Louisiana Purchase Exposition, *St. Louis 1904 on handle,* 12.00 - 17.50

Lewis and Clark Exposition 1905, *Portland, Oregon,* 12.00 - 15.00

San Francisco World's Fair 1915, 8.00 - 10.00

World's Fair, *Spokane, Washington, 1974,* 10.00 - 15.00

War Spoons
Price Range

☐ **Captain C. E. Clark USN,** *teaspoon, silverplate, beaded handle, U.S. Battleship Oregon, 10288 tons, picture in bowl. Standard Co.* 8.00 15.00

☐ **Rear Admiral Sampson,** *teaspoon, silverplate, beaded handle, Heroic Crew of the Merrimac, with a list of the crew members and June 3, 1898, Santiago De Cuba in bowl. Standard Co.* 8.00 15.00

☐ **Captain Sigsbee,** *demitasse, silverplate, shield, anchor, twisted rope handle, picture U.S. Battleship Maine "Blown up in Havana Harbor, Feb. 15, 1898," Crown Silver Plate Co.* 6.00 8.00

☐ **Commodore Dewey,** *demitasse, silverplate, beaded handle, Flagship Olympia, Battle of Manila, May 1, 1898 in bowl. Standard Co.* 6.00 8.00

☐ **Battleship Baltimore,** *demitasse, silverplate, Horse's head, horseshoe, "Good Luck" on handle, picture on bowl, extra coin silverplate.* 8.00 12.00

These spoons all honor and commemorate the Spanish-American War of 1898, waged between Spain and the United States. The war begin in Manila Bay in the Philippines and in Cuba. The U.S.S. Maine was sunk in Havana Harbar by an explosion whose cause was not determined. Theodore Roosevelt led the assault on San Juan Hill. This series is also available in sterling.

Captain Sigsbee, *demitasse,* 6.00 - 8.00

Souvenir Spoons - Advertising

☐ **Betty Lou,** *teaspoon, silverplate, Betty Lou in relief on handle top, "Betty Lou" on handle, plain bowl. Carlton Silver Co.* 8.00 12.50

☐ **Campbell's Soup,** *soup spoon, silverplate, Campbell's Kid, boy, in relief on handle top, plain bowl. International Silver.* 18.00 22.00

☐ **Campbell's Soup,** *soup spoon, silverplate, Campbell's Kid, girl in relief on handle top, plain bowl. International Silver.* . 18.00 22.00

Price Range

☐ **Huckleberry Hound,** *cereal spoon, silverplate, Huckleberry Hound in relief on handle tip, "Huckleberry Hound" on handle, plain bowl. H. B. P. Old Company Plate IS. (Cereal promotion.)* 8.00   15.00

☐ **Gerber's Baby Food,** *3½ " baby spoon, plate, Gerber baby on handle tip, plain bowl, Gerber's on reverse. Winthrop Silver Plate Co.* 4.00   8.00

☐ **Malta-Vita,** *teaspoon, plate, Malta-Vita character on handle with wheat, "Malta-Vita" in bowl. Wm. Rogers.* 8.00   15.00

☐ **Mary Poppins,** *sugar spoon, plate, Mary Poppins on handle top, sugar bowl, Wm. A. Rogers, Oneida Ltd., 1964 Walt Disney Productions.* 15.00   20.00

Mary Poppins was an English nanny from the novel by P. L. Travers, made into a movie by Walt Disney. The subject was ideal for a souvenir spoon, as the movie's hit song was "A Spoonful of Sugar."

☐ **Peek's Tea,** *teaspoon, plate, Eagle on handle tip. "In God We Trust," President Wilson, "Wilson" on handle, plain bowl. Wm. Rogers.* 8.00   15.00

This spoon was offered at 10¢ and a coupon from Peek's Tea. It was also available in sterling for 15¢. With one coupon from each two-ounce package of Peek's Perfect Tea, a spoon was available.

☐ **Rolex-Bucherer Watches,** *demitasse, heavy plate, Rolex, tree, Bucherer Watches on handle top, Interlaken on handle, picture Swiss mountains in bowl. B 100 12.* 10.00   15.00

☐ **Towle's Log Cabin Syrup,** *demitasse, plate, Towle's Log Cabin in relief on handle, tree trunk handle, gold wash bowl. Roof line extends beyond chimney on left side. Cabin door open.* 9.00   13.00

☐ **Towle's Log Cavin Syrup,** *teaspoon, plate, Towle's Log Cabin pictured on handle top, flower handle, plain bowl. Towle, St. Paul, U.S.A. Pat. Jan 14, '08. on reverse.* 10.00   15.00

Patrick Towle's maple syrup was marketed in a hand-made log-cabin-shaped tin. The cans had paper labels with the trade name "Towle's Log Cabin Maple Syrup." The tines were later painted and the spoons were attached or given with the purchase of a can of syrup as a sales promotion.

The newspaper spoons listed in sets are actually a part of the advertising spoon section, spoons which were produced to promote products other than the spoons themselves. The number of spoons made places them more readily in the set category.

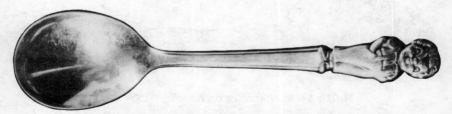

Campbell's Soup, *Boy on handle top,* 18.00 - 22.00

Campbell's Soup, *Girl on handle top,* 18.00 - 22.00

Huckleberry Hound, *cereal promotion,* 8.00 - 15.00

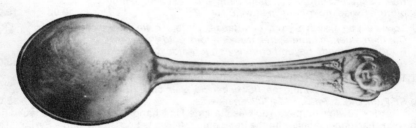

Gerber's Baby Food, 4.00 - 8.00

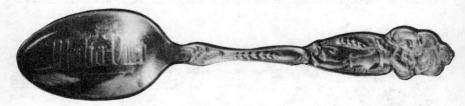

Malta Vita, *character on handle,* 8.00 - 15.00

Towle's Log Cabin Syrup, 10.00 - 15.00

Souvenir Spoons — Christmas

Price Range

☐ **Christmas, 1969,** *demitasse, silverplate, gold wash, Wreath "Noel 1969" on handle top, stars on handle, enamel dove "Peace" in bowl.* 4.00   6.00

☐ **Christmas, 1978,** *demitasse, sterling silver, Wreath, two children with candles on handle top, hands in prayer, "1978" in bowl.* 8.00   12.00

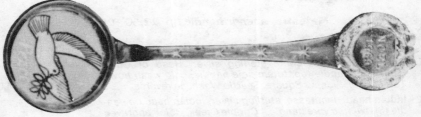

Christmas, 1969, *demitasse,* 4.00 - 6.00

Souvenir Spoons · Fish & Boats

☐ *Fish and Paddle handle, in relief, demitasse, sterling silver, Albuquerque, N.M. in gold washed bowl.* 17.50   21.00

☐ *Salmon Fish handle, in relief, teaspoon, sterling silver, Catalina Island, Cal. engraved in gold washed bowl.* 35.00   37.50

☐ *Tuna Fish handle, teaspoon, sterling silver, picture Avalon, Catalina Island in bowl, glass bottom boat, flying fish on reverse.* 25.00   27.50

☐ *Leaping Fish handle, teaspoon, sterling silver, picture lighthouse, Greenport, Long Island.* 17.50   20.00

☐ *Majestic, teaspoon, sterling silver, Anchor handle tip, twisted wire handle, gold washed bowl, picture sailing ship, Majestic in bowl.* 22.50   25.00

Avalon, Catalina Island, *Tuna Fish handle,* 25.00 - 27.50

Majestic, *anchor handle tip,* 22.50 - 25.00

Souvenir Spoons · Indians	Price Range	
☐ **Chief Seattle,** *teaspoon, sterling silver, Head of Chief Seattle on handle top, totem pole handle, gold wash bowl. Totem Pole, Pioneer Square, Seattle Wash. on reverse*	30.00	35.00
☐ **Indian head,** *demitasse, sterling silver, Indian head on handle tip, twisted wire handle, "Cripple Creek, Colo" engraved in bowl*	17.50	25.00
☐ **Indian head,** *war bonnet, teaspoon, sterling silver, Indian head in relief, corn, tepee handle, "Malvern, Va." ornate engraving in bowl. '06 on reverse*	45.00	50.00
☐ **Indian head,** *side view war bonnet, demitasse, sterling silver, crossed axes, buffalo, flower handle, picture Spokane Falls, flour mill, bridge, "Spokane Falls, Spokane, Wash" in bowl*	17.50	25.00
☐ **Indian head,** *full war bonnet, face view, demitasse, sterling silver, quiver, arrows, axe, snow shoes on handle, gold washed bowl, engraved, "Lewistown, Idaho"*	20.00	25.00

Chief Seattle, 30.00 - 35.00

Indian Head, *demitasse, full war bonnet,* 20.00 - 25.00

Souvenir Spoons - Liberty

	Price Range	
☐ **Independence Hall,** *demitasse, silver plate, Independence Hall on handle top, designed handle, Liberty bell in bowl. (1976 for bicentennial).*	5.00	7.50
☐ **Liberty Bell,** *demitasse, silver plate, Liberty bell on handle top, designed handle, plain bowl. 1976.*	4.50	7.00
☐ **Seal, E. Pluribus Unum,** *demitasse, silver plate, eagle and shield, designed handle, 1776 USA 1976 (bicentennial), Liberty bell in bowl.*	5.00	7.50
☐ **Statue of Liberty,** *demitasse, silver plate, State of Liberty on handle top, designed handle, Liberty Bell in bowl.*	5.00	7.50

Independence Hall, *demitasse,* 5.00 - 7.00

Souvenir Spoons - Lodges

☐ **Elks,** *teaspoon, sterling silver, B.P.O.E. clock held by elk's head and horns, holly and berries on handle, Lodge No. 1168, picture lodge, Medford, Oregon "Dedicated Sept 23, 1915" on reverse.* 20.00   25.00

    The Benevolent and Protective Order of the Elks was organized 1868 in New York City. It claims a membership of over a million members. Its purpose is to promote educational opportunities and charity. A national Elks Home for the Aged is maintained also.

☐ **Lion's Club,** *teaspoon, sterling silver, lion on handle top, twisted wire handle, head with wings at base, lion in bowl.* . 20.00   22.50

    The Lion's Club promotes sight and hearing for children among other charitable activities, usually for local needs.

☐ **Masonic, O.E.S.,** *demitasse, sterling, gold wash bowl, Star Symbol on handle top, "Ruth" O.E.S. on handle, Seal of Order of Eastern Star on handle top, reverse.* 15.00   22.50

☐ **Masonic,** *teaspoon, sterling silver, symbols on handle top, symbols on handle, Masonic sign at base, Masonic Temple pictured, Sioux Falls, South Dakota in bowl.* 25.00   27.50

Price Range

☐ **Masonic,** *teaspoon, sterling silver, symbols on handle top,*
Masonic Temple pictured, Indianapolis in bowl. W.R. on reverse.   **20.00**   **22.50**

    The Eastern Star is composed of women relatives of Masons, introduced to the
United States about 1876, originating from France. Masons were introduced to the
United States around 1730. Approximately 15 United States presidents have been a
member of this organization.

Masonic, *O.E.S., demitasse,* 15.00

Masonic, *Masonic Temple, Indianapolis in bowl,* 20.00 - 22.50

Souvenir Spoons - Space Ships

☐ *Space ship, demitasse, silver plate, space ship circling the*
earth on handle top, twisted handle, "Borman, Lovel, Anders,
1968" in bowl. **8.00**   **10.00**

☐ **Moon Landing,** *demitasse, silver plate, picture moon landing on*
handle top, twisted handle, "Armstrong, Collins, Aldrin,
7-20-68" in bowl. **8.00**   **10.00**

☐ **Apollo 12,** *demitasse, silver plate, Gordon, Conrad, Bean, Nov*
19-20, 1969 on handle top, twisted handle, plain bowl. **8.00**   **10.00**

☐ **Apollo 13,** *demitasse, silver plate, John Swigert, James*
Lovell, Fred Haise - courage, drama, ingenuity, on handle top,
twisted handle, plain bowl. **8.00**   **10.00**

☐ **Apollo 14,** *demitasse, silver plate, Stuart A. Roosa, Edgar D.*
Mitchell, Allan B. Shepard, Moon Landing, Feb. 5, 1971. Plain
bowl. **8.00**   **10.00**

Apollo 12, *demitasse,* 8.00 - 10.00

Souvenir Spoons - States

Price Range

☐ **Alaska,** *demitasse, sterling silver, Mt. McKinley, Bear Totem, on handle top, "Alaska" on handle, plain bowl.* 17.50   22.50

☐ **Alaska,** *Totem Pole demitasse, sterling silver, A. B. Mt. Skagway, Alaska in bowl. "Indian Totem Pole Alaska" on reverse.* 20.00   22.50

☐ **Alaska,** *Totem Pole, demitasse, silver plate, plain bowl.* 5.00   7.00

☐ **Alaska,** *Totem Pole, demitasse, copper, Face Mt. picture in bowl, "Face Mountain, Skagway, Alaska," "Indian Totem Pole".* 9.00   11.00

☐ **Arizona,** *teaspoon, copper, Grand Canyon picture on handle, "Grand Canyon Arizona", plain bowl.* 12.00   15.00

☐ **California,** *teaspoon, sterling silver, seal, California, bear, grapes, other fruit, poppies on handle, "Needles" engraved in bowl.* 33.50   35.00

☐ **California,** *teaspoon, sterling silver, Golden Gate skyline on handle, picture Golden Gate in bowl, "Golden Gate, San Francisco Bay", P & B Sterling Co.* 45.00   50.00

☐ **California,** *teaspoon, sterling silver, designed handle, pointed, fluted bowl "San Jose" engraved.* 37.50   40.00

☐ **California,** *teaspoon, sterling silver, Leland Stanford Junior University 1891, Phi Beta Kappa, plain bowl, '16 on reverse.* 20.00   27.50

☐ **California,** University of California, demitasse, sterling silver, seal "Universitas Californiensis in unum versi, Let There Be Light - 1868", wire twisted handle, plain bowl. 16.00   18.50

☐ **California,** *demitasse, sterling silver, covered wagon, oxen, steer head, "Death Valley, Cal" on handle, plain bowl.* 10.00   15.00

☐ **California,** *teaspoon, sterling silver, Fruit cut out, "Los Angeles" on handle, plain bowl.* 8.00   10.00

☐ **Canada,** *demitasse, sterling silver, enamel crown and maple leaf, "Canada" flower handle, picture city hall.* 15.00   17.50

☐ **Canada,** *demitasse, sterling silver, gold wash, Crown, seal "We Prosper by Sea and Land", picture of Empress in bowl, "U.S.S. Empress of India, Vancouver, B.C.".* 15.00   17.50

☐ **Canada,** *demitasse, silver plate, gold wash, Maple leaf enamel, Vancouver, heart shaped bowl, "Canada".* 6.50   9.50

☐ **Chicago,** *teaspoon, sterling, The Fort Dearborn Massacre in detail, Indians at base capturing girl, picture Fort Dearborn in handle, "Chicago 1832", C. D. Peacock designer, Historic, Official Chicago, on reverse, extra heavy.* 60.00   80.00

☐ **Chicago,** *teaspoon, sterling silver, Indian head on handle, "Chicago" in script on handle, picture Ft. Dearborn, "Ft. Dearborn 1830" in bowl.* 17.50   22.50

☐ **Chicago,** *teaspoon, sterling silver, Art Institute, Court House, Government Building, "Chicago" on handle, plain bowl.* 12.00   15.00

☐ **Colorado,** *teaspoon, sterling silver, "Colorado" in large letters in handle, seal, miners, flower, donkey in letters, picture state capitol in bowl, "State Capitol, Denver, Colo.", mountain, bridge, mining on handle reverse.* 45.00   50.00

Alaska, *Totem Pole, demitasse,* 20.00 - 22.50

California, *teaspoon, Golden Gate Skyline,* 45.00 - 50.00

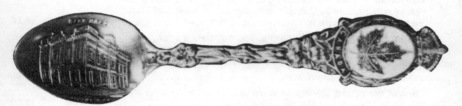

Canada, *demitasse, maple leaf enamel,* 6.50 - 9.50

Colorado, *teaspoon, State Capitol in bowl* 45.00 - 50.00

Price Range

☐ **Colorado,** *teaspoon, sterling silver, Mining scene down handle, large letters, "Colorado", smelter and mining scene on reverse.* 37.50   40.00

☐ **Colorado,** *teaspoon, sterling silver, Indian Swastic, feather headdress, "Swastika" on handle, "Colorado Springs" engraved in bowl.* 30.00   37.50

☐ **Colorado,** *demitasse, sterling silver, enamel flower and leaves on handle, gold was bowl, "Colo. Springs, Colo." engraved in bowl.* 17.50   22.00

☐ **Florida,** *demitasse, sterling silver, Palm Trees on handle, "Florida", plain bowl.* 8.00   10.00

☐ **Honolulu,** *demitasse, sterling silver, Flower handle, picture engraved Diamond Head, "Diamond Head, Honolulu" in bowl. Flowers on handle reverse.* 17.50   20.00

☐ **Idaho,** *teaspoon, copper, dam, potatoes, skiing, "Idaho" on handle, picture state capitol in bowl "State Capitol, Idaho", Craters of the Moon, falls, etc. on reverse.* 6.00   8.00

☐ **Idaho,** *demitasse, sterling silver, shield, Shoshone Falls, lumberjack, "Idaho" on handle, picture state capitol in bowl, "State Capitol, Boise, Idaho". Picture mining on reverse.* 15.00   17.50

☐ **Iowa,** *teaspoon, sterling silver, Flower handle, gold wash bowl, brilliant engraving, picture court hourse, "Court House, Cherokee, Ia.".* 22.50   30.00

☐ **Illinois,** *demitasse, sterling silver, twisted handle, "Streator, Ill" in handle, 17th Mch, 1892 on reverse.* 15.00   17.50

☐ **Kentucky,** *teaspoon, sterling silver, designed handle, brilliant cut engraving, picture entrance to cave, "Entrance to Mammoth Cave, Ky.".* 22.50   30.00

☐ **Maine,** *demitasse, sterling silver, gold wash, shield, "Maine" on handle top, designed handle, brilliant engraved picture in bowl, Poland Spring House, "The Poland Spring House, So. Poland, Maine", elaborate scroll work on reverse.* 17.50   22.00

☐ **Massachusetts,** *demitasse, sterling silver, The Hue, Boston Public Library on handle tip, Paul Revere 1776, Old South Church, beans, on handle, picture "State House, Boston, Mass" in bowl.* 17.50   20.00

☐ **Mexico,** *demitasse, sterling silver, Eagle, "Republic Mexico" on handle, bullfights, "Recuerdo De Mexico" bullfight scene in bowl, "Corrida De Toros, Mexico". Donkey, watercarrier on reverse.* 10.00   12.50

☐ **Michigan,** *teaspoon, sterling silver, designed handle, brilliant cut picture, "High School, Northville, Minn.".* 20.00   25.00

☐ **Minnesota,** *demitasse, sterling silver, "Irene" flowers on handle, picture "High School, Canby, Minn" in bowl.* 10.00   12.00

☐ **Montana,** *teaspoon, sterling silver, "Oro Y Plata", picture, smelter, beef, miner, "Montana" on handle, brilliant gold wash bowl, "Great Falls, Mont." engraved.* 32.50   40.00

Colorado, *teaspoon, "Swastica" on handle,* 30.00 - 37.50

Idaho, *teaspoon, State Capitol in bowl,* 6.00 - 8.00

Minnesota, *demitasse,* 10.00 - 12.00

Montana, *teaspoon, "Great Falls" engraved,* 32.50 - 40.00

Price Range

☐ **Montana,** *teaspoon, copper, full standing figure Indian, designs on handle, "Helena, Mont" in bowl.* ... 27.50 30.00

☐ **Montana,** *teaspoon, copper, designed handle, picture "Broadwater Natatorium, Helena, Mont." in bowl.* ... 15.00 17.50

☐ **Montana,** *teaspoon, copper, designed handle, picture "Richest Hill in the World, Butte, Mont.".* ... 10.00 15.00

☐ **Montana,** *teaspoon, copper, State Capitol in relief on handle, "Helena, Mont". Plain bowl.* ... 8.00 10.00

☐ **Montana,** *teaspoon, copper, Indian head, corn on handle, picture, Anaconda Mine, Butte, Montana in bowl.* ... 9.00 11.00

☐ **Montana,** *demitasse, sterling silver, full standing figure miner with gold pan on handle, picture, "Washoe Smelter, Anaconda, Mont." in bowl. Miner's back on reverse.* ... 30.00 35.00

☐ **Montana,** *demitasse, copper, Miner and donkey on handle, "Virginia City, Mont", plain bowl.* ... 5.00 7.00

☐ **Montana,** *demitasse, copper, Indian, war bonnet, corn, on handle, picture, "School of Mines, Butte, Mont." (1890's).* ... 15.00 17.50

☐ **Montana,** *demitasse, copper, Horseshoe, clover swastika, "Good Luck" on handle, picture, "Masonic Temple, Butte, Mont.". Clover and swastika on reverse.* ... 15.00 17.50

☐ **Nebraska,** *teaspoon, sterling silver, Flower handle, brilliant cut picture, "Govt Bldg, Trans Miss, Ex. Omaha, Neb.", Flowers on handle reverse.* ... 25.00 27.50

☐ **New Jersey,** *teaspoon, sterling silver, Mosquitoes pon, cattails on handle, picture boat race, "Asbury Park, NJ.", boating scene, cattails on reverse.* ... 25.00 27.50

☐ **New York,** *teaspoon, sterling silver, Seal, Niagara Falls, "New York" on handle, gold wash bowl, brilliant cut engraving, picture "House of Gov. Huggins, Olean".* ... 25.00 30.00

☐ **New York,** *teaspoon, sterling silver, Gorham Buttercup pattern, brilliant gold washed bowl, deep cut engraved picture "Minnehaha Falls".* ... 27.50 32.00

☐ **North Dakota,** *demitasse, sterling silver, Rooster on handle, fancy engraving "Leal, N.D." in handle.* ... 10.00 12.50

☐ **Ohio,** *teaspoon, sterling silver, ornate flower handle, brilliant gold wash bowl, deep cut engraving, picture "M. E. Church, Findlay, O.", ornate flowers on reverse.* ... 30.00 35.00

☐ **Oregon,** *teaspoon, sterling silver, carnations on handle, gold wash bowl, brilliant deep cut engraved picture, "High School, Lebanon, Ore.", carnations on reverse.* ... 30.00 35.00

☐ **Oregon,** *teaspoon, sterling silver, Eagle, State seal, capitol, "Oregon" on handle, "Coquille" engraved in bowl.* ... 17.50 25.00

☐ **Oregon,** *teaspoon, sterling silver, State seal, Portland Rose, "Oregon" on handle, picture "Mt. Hood, 11932 Ft. Portland, Or." in bowl.* ... 22.50 27.50

Montana, *teaspoon, "Butte" in bowl,* 9.00 - 11.00

Oregon, *teaspoon, "Mt. Hood" in bowl,* 22.50 - 27.50

Oregon, *demitasse, Eagle Seal,* 18.00 - 22.00

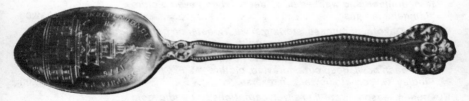

Pennsylvania, *teaspoon,* 20.00 - 25.00

	Price Range	

☐ **Oregon,** *demitasse, sterling silver, State Capitol, roses, seal, "Rooster Rock", "Oregon" on handle, engraved picture "Church of The Redeemer, Pendleton, Ore.", small scene on reverse.* **15.00** **17.50**

☐ **Oregon,** *demitasse, sterling silver, Eagle, seal, fish, etc. "Oregon" on handle, gold wash bowl, brilliant deep cut engraving, picture "Mt. Hood, The Dalles, Or. Alt 11934 Ft.".* **18.00** **22.00**

☐ **Oregon,** *demitasse, sterling silver, two Indian figures in relief, "Coming of the White Man", "Portland, Ore." on handle, plain bowl.* **10.00** **15.00**

☐ **Oregon,** *demitasse, sterling silver, flower handle, gold wash picture, "Court House, Roseburg, Ore.".* **10.00** **15.00**

☐ **Pennsylvania,** *teaspoon, sterling, design handle, brilliant gold wash bowl, deep cut engraving, picture, "Episcopal Church, Coudersport, Pa." Sept, 1, 1887 on reverse.* **37.50** **42.50**

☐ **Pennsylvania,** *teaspoon, sterling silver, flower, beaded handle, gold wash bowl, picture "Independence Hall, Philadelphia, Pa. 1776".* **20.00** **25.00**

☐ **Pennsylvania,** *demitasse, sterling silver, full standing figure, William Penn, plain bowl, "Philadelphia" engraved on reverse.* **30.00** **35.00**

☐ **Rhode Island,** *demitasse, sterling silver, ornate raised lettering "Providence" in handle.* **10.00** **15.00**

☐ **Tennessee,** *demitasse, sterling silver, design handle, picture "Old Capitol, Knoxville, Tenn. 1796-1811".* **17.50** **23.50**

☐ **Tennessee,** *demitasse, sterling silver, gold washed, cut-out "Athens Tenn" on handle, twisted, heart-shaped bowl.* **32.50** **40.00**

☐ **Texas,** *teaspoon, sterling silver, wreath, star, longhorn head, "Dallas", confederate monument, "Confederate Monument" on handle, Cowboy on bucking horse in bowl, "Stick To Your Saddle". Courthouse, post office, library, "Joseph Linz and Bros." on reverse, heavy.* **40.00** **45.00**

☐ **Utah,** *teaspoon, sterling silver, heavy, Moroni, "Salt Lake City" on handle, brilliant gold wash bowl, picture Mormon Temple. "Territory of Utah, 1850" on reverse.* **60.00** **70.00**

☐ **Washington,** *teaspoon, sterling silver, head of Washington, shipyards, salmon, wavy handle, "Washington", brilliant gold wash bowl, picture, "State Capitol, Olympia, Wash." Indian head, panning gold, star fish on reverse.* **30.00** **35.00**

☐ **Washington,** *teaspoon, sterling silver, ornate flower handle, brilliant gold wash bowl, picture engraved, "Upper Falls, Spokane, Wash.".* **27.50** **30.00**

☐ **Washington,** *teaspoon, sterling silver, head of Washington, fish, fir tree, "Washington" on handle, engraved picture in bowl "Mt. Baker, 11000 Ft. Bellingham, Wash.".* **25.00** **27.50**

☐ **Washington,** *teaspoon, sterling silver, Poppy handle, gold wash bowl, brilliant cut picture engraved, "Mt. Baker, Everett, Wash." Poppies on reverse.* **25.00** **27.50**

Utah, *teaspoon, Mormon Temple in bowl,* 60.00 - 70.00

Washington, *teaspoon, "Upper Falls" in bowl,* 27.50 - 30.00

Washington, *teaspoon, "Mt. Tacoma" on bowl,* 25.00 - 27.50

Washington, *demitasse, Indian designs on handle,* 10.00 - 11.50

Price Range

☐ **Washington,** *teaspoon, sterling silver, cut-out flower handle, oval gold washed bowl, picture engraved, "Mt. Tacoma, 14444 Ft."* 25.00   27.50

☐ **Washington,** *demitasse, sterling silver, pine cones on handle, picture "Spokane Falls, Spokane, Wash." in handle.* 15.00   17.50

☐ **Washington,** *demitasse, copper, enamel picture, Mt. St. Helens, Washington on handle, Indian designs on handle and in bowl.*   10.00   11.50

☐ **Yellowstone Park,** *teaspoon, sterling silver, picture, "Grotto Geyser" on handle, "Yellowstone Park", plain bowl.* 17.50   20.00

☐ **Yellowstone Park,** *teaspoon, sterling silver, gold wash, Twin Bears, "Yellowstone" on handle, plain bowl.* 22.50   27.50

☐ **Yellowstone Park,** *teaspoon, silver plate, deer, "A Family Group", "Yellowstone Park" on handle, plain bowl.* 10.00   12.00

Souvenir Spoons - Miscellaneous

☐ **Dwight D. Eisenhower,** *demitasse, silver plate, Bust of Eisenhower, twisted handle, plain bowl.* 6.50   8.00

☐ **Mary Baker Eddy,** *large teaspoon, sterling, Crown, picture Mary Baker Eddy, "Mary Baker Eddy", picture "Pleasant View" in handle, Crown, roses, "Not matter but mind satisfieth" on reverse, extra heavy.* 92.50   114.00

☐ *Mother, teaspoon, sterling silver, "Mother" beaded handle, brilliant cut picture of a home in bowl, 1857-1896 on reverse.* 50.00   57.50

☐ *Sunflower, teaspoon, sterling silver, cut-out sunflower with unusual center, leaves, gold wash bowl.* 30.00   35.00

☐ *Salem Witch, teaspoon, sterling silver, Witch on broomstick, house of Seven Gables, Daniel Low. Plain bowl.* 19.00   22.00

Mary Baker Eddy, *teaspoon,* 92.50 - 114.00

SPATULA SERVERS

No, spatula servers were NOT intended for serving spatulas; the name is used to draw a distinction between them and kitchen spatulas (used in preparation of food rather than in serving). They have a wide, long, dull blade; a neck which rises vertically from the blade; and a handle which is either horizontal or inclining at approximately 45 degrees. In use, the blade was to be slid beneath a portion of food and lifted. They could correctly be used in serving wedges of pie, cake, cheese, etc. — even though special utensils were available for these purposes. By turning the spatula on its side, the blade could be used as a knife in cutting, though it was never kept very sharp. Spatula servers vary in size.

	Price Range	
(Silver-Plated)		
☐ **Rogers Bro. Mfg. Co. "Tuscan"**, *etched blade, monogram,*		
resilvered	19.00	21.00
(Sterling Silver)		
☐ **Tiffany "Broom Corn"**, *monogram*	120.00	135.00

STEAK KNIVES

It may be comforting to know that our ancestors had just as frequent problems with tough steaks as we do. The steak knife was the indispensable diner's weapon, for going into combat against balky meat cuts. The thoughtful hostess always provided a steak knife, even when occasion did not seem to demand it; far better to let the knife go unused, than risk the mortification of a guest having to ASK for one. Today's version of the steak knife invariably has a row of saw-teeth, but this was not always the case with their predecessors of the 19th and earlier 20th century. Sometimes the early steak knife was just a bit heavier in the blade than a common dinner knife, and of course it was intended to be kept razor sharp. But all the sharpness in the world could not always conquer leathery meats, so gradually the saw-tooth knife became standard. Still, nature got the better of art: what could be CUT could not necessarily be CHEWED. Steak knives enjoy moderate collecting popularity.

(Silver-Plated)		
☐ **Community "Silver Valentine"**, *no monogram, mint condi-*		
tion	3.00	4.00
☐ **Rogers "Victorian Rose"**, *no monogram, excellent condi-*		
tion	4.00	5.00
☐ **Wm. Rogers Eagle "Kings"**, *hotel name, excellent condition*	5.00	6.00
(Sterling Silver)		
☐ **Gorham "Cambridge"**, *no monogram*	13.00	15.00
☐ **Gorham "King George"**, *monogram and date*	16.00	18.00
☐ **Kirk "Repousse"**, *no monogram*	16.00	18.00
☐ **Wallace "Grande Baroque"**, *blade needs replacement, no*		
monogram	14.00	16.00
☐ **Wallace "Grande Baroque"**, *no monogram*	16.00	18.00

STEINS

Except when supplied with porcelain bodies, which often was the case, silver steins were intended more as ornamental decorations than for actual use. Even the staunchest admirers of silver agreed that beverages drunk from pure silver vessels lost something in flavor. American silversmiths were probably encouraged to make them, because of the extensive sale of imported specimens which began around 1890. Most of the imports were, however, not sterling or even silver plated, but made of "German silver" (nickel). Some of the imports served as models, as did, apparently, earlier steins in pewter. They were often retailed with undecorated sides, to be engraved with the owner's crest of arms. Jewelers did this work. Silver steins are sometimes included in general collections of steins but, other than that, their popularity as collectors' items is well short of overwhelming.

(Silver-Plated)

	Price Range	
☐ **Maker unknown,** *plain design, monogram, excellent condition*	20.00	22.00
☐ **Maker unknown,** *ornate scroll and floral design, wooden handle*	62.00	68.00

(Sterling and China)

☐ *Stein, sterling lid with Lenox body, hand-painted soccer player in monochromatic blues, Lenox transition mark, no silver mark*	165.00	180.00
☐ *Stein, sterling lid with Lenox body, hand-painted Indian in full color on pale tan background, Lenox transition mark, Gorham silver mark*	195.00	215.00

STRING HOLDERS

Is the silver string holder the ultimate length to which manufacturers reached, in offering wares of every type to lovers of silver? We leave the reader to draw his own conclusions. Silver string holders were normally fitted with glass bodies, to show how much string remained on the pool. They were intended to be hung, and their usual post was at the cash register in shops, where parcels were packed up. Bakeries, butchers, and most general merchandise shops used them — as many still do. However the usual sort were made of stainless steel, or other non-silver materials.

(Sterling and Cut Glass)

☐ **Gorham,** *sterling with cut glass, ornate cutting in glass, pierced silver*	80.00	87.00
☐ **Maker unknown,** *sterling and cut crystal, cane cutting in glass, pierced silver*	68.00	75.00

STUFFING SPOONS

The practice of stuffing turkeys and other fowl had very early beginnings in America. Though turkeys are not native to Europe, the art of stuffing was based on European tradition and more precisely on an ancient Scottish dish: haggis. For at least 500 years, no foreigner's visit to Scotland has been complete without an introduction to haggis: the bladder of a cow, stuffed with meats and other ingredients, which swells in cooking and bursts open ceremoniously when an incision is made. Stuffed turkeys do not — for better or worse — react in this way. Stuffing spoons are a bit too specialized to draw a really large collector following, but can be good "conversation piece" in a general collection of silverware.

(Silver-Plated)

☐ **1847 Rogers "Vintage",** *monogram and date, excellent condition*	58.00	64.00

(Sterling Silver)   **Price Range**

☐ **Kirk "Repousse",** *9½" L., monogram*	105.00	120.00
☐ **Reed & Barton "Les Cinq Fleurs",** *monogram*	120.00	135.00
☐ **Reed & Barton "Les Cinq Fleurs",** *no monogram*	140.00	155.00
☐ **Reed & Barton,** *pattern unknown, monogram and date*	45.00	50.00
☐ **Shiebler "Cupids",** *no monogram*	80.00	90.00
☐ **Wendt,** *pattern unknown, bird on handle, monogram*	135.00	150.00

SUGAR AND CREAMER SETS

These were sold in large numbers, but the majority of sets have become separated through the years and their components turn up individually on the market. Due to the odd shapes of these items they were not usually put up in decorative boxes.

Sugar and Creamer, *Dominick and Haff, 1907, 35 ounces,* 1350.00

(Silver-Plated)

☐ **Wm. Rogers Eagle,** *footed, good condition*	11.00	13.00
☐ **Maker unknown,** *on small tray, grape and vine decoration,*		
good condition	21.00	23.00

(Sterling Silver)

☐ **Jacobi & Jenkins,** *repousse design*	80.00	90.00
☐ **Kalo,** *simple design, hammered finish, 3½" H., weight*		
10 oz.	95.00	105.00

SUGAR BOWLS

The popularity of silver sugar bowls (in terms of table use — not collector esteem) faded rather early. They had been widely made in England from the 1600's and domestically from the 1700's, but porcelain made inroads upon them and won over most of the public by around 1850. It wasn't a matter of cost; many people were convinced that sugar kept in silver bowls acquired a metallic flavor. In general this opinion prevailed toward all delicately-flavored foodstuffs. But the manufacturers did not totally drop silver sugar bowls from their lines: there was a place for everything in the retail market, where silver was concerned. Most silver sugar bowls found on the U.S. antique markets are foreign-made. Those of extra large size (which are rare) were not necessarily designed for restaurant use, but possibly for banqueting tables where many guests were present.

(Coin Silver)   **Price Range**

☐ **Wood & Hughes,** *c. 1850, basket type, boat-shaped body with chased scroll cartouches and flowers, applied rim, twisted swing handle, rectangular base, 6" L., weight 8½ oz.* 110.00   125.00

SUGAR SHELLS

Sugar shells, so-called because of the shell-like shape of the bowl, were the spoons with which sugar was transferred from the bowl to one's drinking cup or glass. Despite the name, however, it should not be presumed that all specimens bear shell-shaped bowls, as this is certainly not the case. Faced with the sort of demand that existed for sugar spoons, manufacturers could not allow their creative energies to run on just one track. Hence you will find specimens of various types, not to mention a huge array of patterns.

(Coin Silver)

☐ **Butler & McCarthy,** *c. 1845* 25.00   28.00
☐ **Duhme & Co.,** *sugar shell, coin silver, c. 1860* 25.00   28.00
☐ **Duhme & Co.,** *c. 1860, handle bent* 16.00   18.00
☐ **Farrington & Hunnewell,** *c. 1840* 25.00   28.00
☐ **W.W. Child,** *c. 1830* 25.00   28.00

(Silver-Plated)

☐ **Alvin "Cameo",** *no monogram, excellent condition* 5.00   6.00
☐ **Clark & Sawyer,** *pattern unknown, beaded edge, scroll work, monogram, excellent condition* 4.00   5.00
☐ **Community "Adam",** *no monogram, excellent condition* 5.00   6.00
☐ **Community "Adam",** *no monogram, good condition* 4.00   5.00
☐ **Community "Adam",** *no monogram, fair condition* 1.00   2.00
☐ **Community "Avalon",** *no monogram, excellent condition* . .   5.00   6.00
☐ **Community "Avalon",** *no monogram, good condition* 4.00   5.00
☐ **Community "Avalon",** *no monogram, poor condition* 1.00   2.00
☐ **Community "Ballad",** *no monogram, mint condition* 2.00   3.00
☐ **Community "Ballad",** *no monogram, good condition* 4.00   5.00
☐ **Community "Bedford",** *no monogram, excellent condition* .   5.00   6.00
☐ **Community "Bedford",** *no monogram, good condition* 4.00   5.00
☐ **Community "Bird of Paradise",** *no monogram, excellent condition* 5.00   6.00
☐ **Community "Bird of Paradise",** *no monogram, excellent condition* 6.00   7.00
☐ **Community "Bird of Paradise",** *no monogram, good condition* 4.00   5.00
☐ **Community "Bird of Paradise",** *no monogram, fair condition* 1.00   2.00
☐ **Community "Coronation",** *no monogram, mint condition* . .   3.00   4.00
☐ **Community "Coronation",** *no monogram, excellent condition* 5.00   6.00

	Price Range	
☐ Community "Coronation", *no monogram, good condition* .	4.00	5.00
☐ Community "Deauville", *no monogram, excellent condition*	3.00	4.00
☐ Community "Deauville", *no monogram, excellent condition*	5.00	6.00
☐ Community "Deauville", *no monogram, good condition* ...	4.00	5.00
☐ Community "Enchantment", *no monogram, excellent condition*	5.00	6.00
☐ Community "Enchantment", *no monogram, fair condition* .	1.00	2.00
☐ Community "Evening Star", *no monogram, excellent condition*	4.00	5.00
☐ Community "Evening Star", *no monogram, good condition*	4.00	5.00
☐ Community "Flight", *no monogram, mint condition*	4.00	5.00
☐ Community "Flower de Luce", *no monogram, excellent condition*	5.00	6.00
☐ Community "Flower de Luce", *no monogram, good condition*	4.00	5.00
☐ Community "Flower de Luce", *no monogram, fair condition*	2.00	3.00
☐ Community "Forever", *no monogram, excellent condition* .	5.00	6.00
☐ Community "Forever", *no monogram, good condition*	4.00	5.00
☐ Community "Georgian", *no monogram, excellent condition*	4.00	5.00
☐ Community "Georgian", *no monogram, good condition* ...	4.00	5.00
☐ Community "Grosvenor", *no monogram, excellent condition*	4.00	5.00
☐ Community "Grosvenor", *no monogram, good condition* ..	4.00	5.00
☐ Community "Hampton Court", *no monogram, excellent condition*	3.00	4.00
☐ Community "Hampton Court", *no monogram, poor condition*	1.00	2.00
☐ Community "King Cedric", *no monogram, excellent condition*	3.00	4.00
☐ Community "King Cedric", *no monogram, fair condition* ..	1.00	2.00
☐ Community "Lady Hamilton", *no monogram, excellent condition*	5.00	6.00
☐ Community "Lady Hamilton", *no monogram, fair condition*	1.00	2.00
☐ Community "Lady Hamilton", *monogram, fair condition* ..	1.00	2.00
☐ Community "Louis XVI", *monogram, excellent condition* ..	3.00	4.00
☐ Community "Louis XVI", *no monogram, excellent condition*	5.00	6.00
☐ Community "Louis XVI", *no monogram, fair condition*	1.00	2.00
☐ Community "Louis XVI", *no monogram, good condition* ...	4.00	5.00
☐ Community "Milady", *no monogram, excellent condition* ..	3.00	4.00
☐ Community "Milady", *no monogram, excellent condition* ..	5.00	6.00
☐ Community "Milady", *no monogram, good condition*	4.00	5.00
☐ Community "Modjeska", *no monogram, excellent condition*	5.00	6.00
☐ Community "Modjeska", *no monogram, good condition* ...	4.00	5.00
☐ Community "Morning Rose", *no monogram, excellent condition*	5.00	6.00
☐ Community "Morning Rose", *no monogram, good condition*	4.00	5.00
☐ Community "Morning Star", *no monogram, excellent condition*	5.00	6.00
☐ Community "Morning Star", *no monogram, good condition*	4.00	5.00
☐ Community "Morning Star", *no monogram, fair condition* .	1.00	2.00
☐ Community "Noblesse", *no monogram, excellent condition*	4.00	5.00
☐ Community "Noblesse", *no monogram, excellent condition*	5.00	6.00
☐ Community "Noblesse", *no monogram, good condition* ...	4.00	5.00

	Price Range	
☐ Community "Noblesse", *monogram, excellent condition* ..	2.00	3.00
☐ Community "Patrician", *no monogram, excellent condition*	5.00	6.00
☐ Community "Patrician", *no monogram, good condition* ...	4.00	5.00
☐ Community "Patrician", *no monogram, fair condition*	1.00	2.00
☐ Community "Paul Revere", *no monogram, excellent condition*	5.00	6.00
☐ Community "Paul Revere", *no monogram, good condition* .	4.00	5.00
☐ Community "Paul Revere", *no monogram, fair condition* ..	1.00	2.00
☐ Community "Sheraton", *no monogram, excellent condition*	5.00	6.00
☐ Community "Sheraton", *no monogram, good condition* ...	4.00	5.00
☐ Community "Sheraton", *no monogram, fair condition*	1.00	2.00
☐ Community "Silver Artistry", *no monogram, excellent condition*	4.00	5.00
☐ Community "Silver Artistry", *no monogram, excellent condition*	5.00	6.00
☐ Community "Silver Artistry", *no monogram, good condition*	4.00	5.00
☐ Community "Silver Flower", *no monogram, good condition*	3.00	4.00
☐ Community "Silver Flower", *no monogram, excellent condition*	5.00	6.00
☐ Community "Silver Flower", *no monogram, fair condition* .	1.00	2.00
☐ Community "Silver Sands", *no monogram, mint condition* .	3.00	4.00
☐ Community "Silver Sands", *no monogram, fair condition* ..	1.00	2.00
☐ Community "Silver Valentine", *no monogram, good condition*	1.00	2.00
☐ Community "South Seas", *no monogram, good condition* .	3.00	4.00
☐ Community "South Seas", *no monogram, excellent condition*	5.00	6.00
☐ Community "South Seas", *no monogram, fair condition* ...	1.00	2.00
☐ Community "Tangier", *no monogram, mint condition*	4.00	5.00
☐ Community "White Orchid", *no monogram, mint condition*	4.00	5.00
☐ Community "White Orchid", *no monogram, excellent condition*	5.00	6.00
☐ Community "White Orchid", *no monogram, good condition*	4.00	5.00
☐ C. Rogers "Imperial", *no monogram, excellent condition* ..	6.00	7.00
☐ C. Rogers "Imperial", *no monogram, good condition*	5.00	6.00
☐ Gorham "Carolina", *no monogram, mint condition*	6.00	7.00
☐ Gorham "Carolina", *no monogram, fair condition*	1.00	2.00
☐ Gorham "Empire", *no monogram, excellent condition*	4.00	5.00
☐ Gorham "Empire", *no monogram, good condition*	4.00	5.00
☐ Gorham "Lady Caroline", *no monogram, excellent condition*	5.00	6.00
☐ Gorham "Lady Caroline", *no monogram, good condition* ..	4.00	5.00
☐ Harmony House "Maytime", *no monogram, excellent condition*	3.00	4.00
☐ Harmony House "Maytime", *no monogram, good condition*	3.00	4.00
☐ Harmony House "Serenade", *no monogram, excellent condition*	5.00	6.00
☐ Harmony House "Serenade", *no monogram, good condition*	4.00	5.00
☐ Holmes & Edwards "American Beauty Rose", *no monogram, resilvered*	9.00	11.00
☐ Holmes & Edwards "Century", *no monogram, excellent condition*	5.00	6.00

	Price Range	

☐ Holmes & Edwards "Century", *no monogram, good condition* 4.00 5.00
☐ Holmes & Edwards "Century", *no monogram, fair condition* 1.00 2.00
☐ Holmes & Edwards "Charm", *no monogram, excellent condition* 5.00 6.00
☐ Holmes & Edwards "Charm", *no monogram, good condition* 4.00 5.00
☐ Holmes & Edwards "Danish Princess", *no monogram, excellent condition* 5.00 6.00
☐ Holmes & Edwards "Danish Princess", *no monogram, good condition* 4.00 5.00
☐ Holmes & Edwards "Danish Princess", *no monogram, poor condition* 1.00 2.00
☐ Holmes & Edwards "Danish Princess", *monogram, good condition* 1.00 2.00
☐ Holmes & Edwards "Jac Rose", *no monogram, excellent condition* 7.00 8.00
☐ Holmes & Edwards "Jac Rose", *no monogram, fair condition* 2.00 3.00
☐ Holmes & Edwards "Lovely Lady", *no monogram, excellent condition* 4.00 5.00
☐ Holmes & Edwards "Lovely Lady", *no monogram, excellent condition* 5.00 6.00
☐ Holmes & Edwards "Lovely Lady", *no monogram, good condition* 4.00 5.00
☐ Holmes & Edwards "Lovely Lady", *fair condition* 1.00 2.00
☐ Holmes & Edwards "Lovely Lady", *monogram, good condition* 1.00 3.00
☐ Holmes & Edwards "Marina", *no monogram, excellent condition* 6.00 7.00
☐ Holmes & Edwards "Marina", *no monogram, good condition* 5.00 6.00
☐ Holmes & Edwards "Marina", *no monogram* 1.00 2.00
☐ Holmes & Edwards "Pageant", *no monogram, excellent condition* 5.00 6.00
☐ Holmes & Edwards "Pageant", *no monogram, good condition* 4.00 5.00
☐ Holmes & Edwards "Romance II", *no monogram, excellent condition* 4.00 5.00
☐ Holmes & Edwards "Romance II", *no monogram, fair condition* 1.00 2.00
☐ Holmes & Edwards "Spring Garden", *no monogram, excellent condition* 5.00 6.00
☐ Holmes & Edwards "Spring Garden", *no monogram, good condition* 4.00 5.00
☐ Holmes & Edwards "Unique", *no monogram, excellent condition* 12.00 14.00
☐ Holmes & Edwards "Unique", *no monogram, fair condition* 4.00 5.00
☐ Holmes & Edwards "Unique", *monogram, poor condition* .. 1.00 2.00
☐ International "Laurel Mist", *no monogram, excellent condition* 4.00 5.00
☐ International "Laurel Mist", *no monogram, fair condition* .. 1.00 2.00
☐ International "Orleans", *no monogram, mint condition* 3.00 4.00

Price Range

☐ International "Silver Tulip", *no monogram, excellent condition*	4.00	5.00
☐ International "Silver Tulip", *no monogram, fair condition*	1.00	2.00
☐ King Edward "Moss Rose", *no monogram, excellent condition*	5.00	6.00
☐ King Edward "Moss Rose", *no monogram, good condition*	4.00	5.00
☐ National "King Edward", *no monogram, excellent condition*	5.00	6.00
☐ National "King Edward", *no monogram, good condition*	4.00	5.00
☐ Niagara Falls Silver Co. "Adams", *monogram, excellent condition*	5.00	6.00
☐ Nobility "Royal Rose", *no monogram, excellent condition*	5.00	6.00
☐ Nobility "Royal Rose", *no monogram, good condition*	4.00	5.00
☐ Nobility "Royal Rose", *no monogram, fair condition*	1.00	2.00
☐ Old Company Plate "Signature", *no monogram, excellent condition*	5.00	6.00
☐ Old Company Plate "Signature", *monogram, excellent condition*	2.00	3.00
☐ Oneida "Avalon", *no monogram, excellent condition*	5.00	6.00
☐ Oneida "Avalon", *no monogram, good condition*	4.00	5.00
☐ Oneida "Clarion", *no monogram, excellent condition*	5.00	6.00
☐ Oneida "Clarion", *no monogram, good condition*	4.00	5.00
☐ Oneida "Clarion", *no monogram, fair condition*	1.00	2.00
☐ Oneida "Kenwood", *no monogram, excellent condition*	6.00	7.00
☐ Oneida "Kenwood", *no monogram, poor condition*	1.00	2.00
☐ Oneida "New Era", *no monogram, excellent condition*	7.00	8.00
☐ Oneida "New Era", *no monogram, good condition*	5.00	6.00
☐ Oneida "New Era", *no monogram, fair condition*	1.00	2.00
☐ Oneida "Primrose", *no monogram, excellent condition*	4.00	5.00
☐ Oneida "Primrose", *no monogram, poor condition*	1.00	2.00
☐ Oxford "Narcissus", *no monogram, excellent condition*	9.00	10.00
☐ Oxford "Narcissus", *no monogram, good condition*	6.00	7.00
☐ Pairpoint "Essex", *no monogram, excellent condition*	7.00	10.00
☐ Pairpoint "Essex", *no monogram, fair condition*	3.00	4.00
☐ Prestige "Grenoble", *no monogram, excellent condition*	5.00	6.00
☐ Prestige "Grenoble", *no monogram, good condition*	4.00	5.00
☐ Prestige "Grenoble", *no monogram, fair condition*	1.00	2.00
☐ R.C. Co. "Orleans II", *no monogram, excellent condition*	4.00	5.00
☐ R.C. Co. "Orleans II", *no monogram, fair condition*	1.00	2.00
☐ Reed & Barton "Alden", *no monogram, excellent condition*	4.00	5.00
☐ Reed & Barton "Alden", *no monogram, fair condition*	1.00	2.00
☐ Reed & Barton "Belmont", *no monogram, excellent condition*	8.00	9.00
☐ Reed & Barton "Belmont", *no monogram, poor condition*	1.00	2.00
☐ Reed & Barton "Fiddle", *no monogram, excellent condition*	6.00	7.00
☐ Reed & Barton "Fiddle", *monogram, good condition*	2.00	3.00
☐ Reed & Barton "Gem", *no monogram, excellent condition*	6.00	7.00
☐ Reed & Barton "Gem", *monogram, excellent condition*	4.00	5.00
☐ Reed & Barton "Gem", *monogram, poor condition*	1.00	2.00
☐ Reed & Barton "Kings", *no monogram, mint condition*	11.00	13.00
☐ Reed & Barton "Kings", *no monogram, good condition*	5.00	6.00
☐ Reed & Barton "Manor", *no monogram, excellent condition*	5.00	6.00
☐ Reed & Barton "Manor", *no monogram, good condition*	4.00	5.00
☐ Reed & Barton "Oxford", *no monogram, excellent condition*	9.00	11.00
☐ Reed & Barton "Oxford", *no monogram, fair condition*	1.00	2.00

	Price Range	
☐ Reed & Barton "Unique", *no monogram, excellent condition*	7.00	8.00
☐ Reed & Barton "Unique", *no monogram, good condition* ...	5.00	6.00
☐ Reed & Barton "Unique", *no monogram, fair condition*	1.00	2.00
☐ Reliance "Bridal Rose", *no monogram, excellent condition*	5.00	6.00
☐ Reliance "Bridal Rose", *no monogram, good condition*	4.00	5.00
☐ Reliance "Bridal Rose", *no monogram, fair condition*	1.00	2.00
☐ Reliance "Exeter", *no monogram, excellent condition*	5.00	6.00
☐ Reliance "Exeter", *no monogram, good condition*	4.00	5.00
☐ Rogers "Alhambra", *no monogram, excellent condition* ...	7.00	8.00
☐ Rogers "Alhambra", *no monogram, good condition*	5.00	6.00
☐ Rogers "Ambassador", *no monogram, excellent condition*	4.00	5.00
☐ Rogers "Ambassador", *no monogram, good condition*	3.00	4.00
☐ Rogers "Ambassador", *no monogram, fair condition*	1.00	2.00
☐ Rogers "Carlton", *no monogram, excellent condition*	5.00	6.00
☐ Rogers "Carlton", *no monogram, good condition*	4.00	5.00
☐ Rogers "Clinton", *no monogram, excellent condition*	5.00	6.00
☐ Rogers "Clinton", *no monogram, good condition*	4.00	5.00
☐ Rogers "Clinton", *monogram, good condition*	1.00	2.00
☐ Rogers "Crown", *no monogram, excellent condition*	4.00	5.00
☐ Rogers "Crown", *no monogram, good condition*	3.00	4.00
☐ Rogers "Desire", *no monogram, excellent condition*	5.00	6.00
☐ Rogers "Desire", *no monogram, good condition*	4.00	5.00
☐ Rogers "Desire", *no monogram, fair condition*	1.00	2.00
☐ Rogers "Inspiration", *no monogram, excellent condition* ..	5.00	6.00
☐ Rogers "Inspiration", *no monogram, good condition*	4.00	5.00
☐ Rogers "Inspiration", *no monogram, poor condition*	1.00	2.00
☐ Rogers "Margate", *no monogram, excellent condition*	5.00	6.00
☐ Rogers "Margate", *no monogram, good condition*	4.00	5.00
☐ Rogers "Olive", *no monogram, excellent condition*	4.00	5.00
☐ Rogers "Olive", *no monogram, fair condition*	1.00	2.00
☐ Rogers "Oval", *no monogram, excellent condition*	3.00	4.00
☐ Rogers "Precious", *no monogram, excellent condition*	5.00	6.00
☐ Rogers "Precious", *no monogram, good condition*	4.00	5.00
☐ Rogers "Queen Bess II", *no monogram, excellent condition*	1.00	2.00
☐ Rogers "Shell", *monogram, poor condition*	2.00	3.00
☐ Rogers "Victorian Rose", *no monogram, excellent condition*	3.00	4.00
☐ Rogers & Bro. "Assyrian", *no monogram, excellent condition*	8.00	9.00
☐ Rogers & Bro. "Assyrian", *no monogram, good condition* ..	8.00	9.00
☐ Rogers & Bro. "Assyrian", *no monogram, mint condition* ..	20.00	22.00
☐ Rogers & Bro. "Columbia", *no monogram, excellent condition*	20.00	22.00
☐ Rogers & Bro. "Columbia", *monogram, excellent condition*	10.00	12.00
☐ Rogers & Bro. "Columbia", *monogram, good condition*	7.00	8.00
☐ Rogers & Bro. "Daybreak", *no monogram, excellent condition*	5.00	6.00
☐ Rogers & Bro. "Daybreak", *no monogram, good condition* .	4.00	5.00
☐ Rogers & Bro. "Daybreak", *no monogram, fair condition* ..	1.00	2.00
☐ Rogers & Bro. "Laurel", *no monogram, excellent condition*	5.00	6.00
☐ Rogers & Bro. "Laurel", *no monogram, good condition*	4.00	5.00
☐ Rogers & Bro. "New Century", *no monogram, excellent condition*	11.00	13.00

Price Range

☐ Rogers & Bro. "New Century", *no monogram, good condition*	9.00	11.00
☐ Rogers & Bro. "New Century", *monogram, good condition* .	6.00	7.00
☐ Rogers & Bro. "Siren", *no monogram, excellent condition* .	16.00	18.00
☐ Rogers & Bro. "Siren", *no monogram, good condition*	12.00	14.00
☐ Rogers & Bro. "Siren", *no monogram, poor condition*	2.00	3.00
☐ Rogers & Hamilton "Alhambra", *no monogram, excellent condition*	14.00	16.00
☐ Rogers & Hamilton "Alhambra", *monogram, poor condition*	2.00	3.00
☐ Rogers & Hamilton "Cardinal", *no monogram, excellent condition*	8.00	9.00
☐ Rogers & Hamilton "Cardinal", *no monogram, fair condition*	2.00	3.00
☐ Rogers & Hamilton "Marquise", *no monogram, excellent condition*	4.00	5.00
☐ Rogers & Hamilton "Marquise", *no monogram, good condition*	4.00	5.00
☐ Rogers & Hamilton "Raphael", *gold wash bowl, no monogram, excellent condition*	16.00	18.00
☐ Rogers & Hamilton "Raphael", *no monogram, fair condition*	3.00	4.00
☐ Rogers Mfg. Co. "Triumph", *no monogram, excellent condition*	5.00	6.00
☐ Rogers Mfg. Co. "Triumph", *no monogram, good condition*	4.00	5.00
☐ Rogers Mfg. Co. "Triumph", *no monogram, fair condition* . .	1.00	2.00
☐ S.L. & G.H. Rogers "Arcadia", *no monogram, excellent condition*	11.00	13.00
☐ S.L. & G.H. Rogers "Arcadia", *no monogram, good condition*	9.00	11.00
☐ S.L. & G.H. Rogers "Countess II, *no monogram, excellent condition*	5.00	6.00
☐ S.L. & G.H. Rogers "Countess II", *no monogram, good condition*	4.00	5.00
☐ S.L. & G.H. Rogers "Countess II", *no monogram, fair condition*	1.00	2.00
☐ S.L. & G.H. Rogers "Encore", *no monogram, excellent condition*	5.00	6.00
☐ S.L. & G.H. Rogers "Encore", *no monogram, good condition*	4.00	5.00
☐ S.L. & G.H. Rogers "Encore", *no monogram, fair condition* .	1.00	2.00
☐ S.L. & G.H. Rogers "English Garden", *no monogram, excellent condition*	5.00	6.00
☐ S.L. & G.H. Rogers "English Garden", *no monogram, good condition*	4.00	5.00
☐ S.L. & G.H. Rogers "English Garden", *no monogram, fair condition*	1.00	2.00
☐ S.L. & G.H. Rogers "Kingston", *no monogram, excellent condition*	5.00	6.00
☐ S.L. & G.H. Rogers "Kingston", *no monogram, good condition*	4.00	5.00
☐ S.L. & G.H. Rogers "Kingston", *no monogram, fair condition*	1.00	2.00
☐ S.L. & G.H. Rogers "Puritan", *no monogram, excellent condition*	7.00	8.00
☐ S.L. & G.H. Rogers "Puritan", *no monogram, poor condition*	1.00	2.00

	Price Range	
☐ **S.L. & G.H. Rogers "Thor"**, *no monogram, excellent condition*	5.00	6.00
☐ **S.L. & G.H. Rogers "Thor"**, *no monogram, good condition*	4.00	5.00
☐ **S.L. & G.H. Rogers "Thor"**, *no monogram, fair condition*	1.00	2.00
☐ **S.L. & G.H. Rogers "Thor"**, *no monogram, poor condition*	1.00	2.00
☐ **Towle "Engraved"**, *no monogram, excellent condition*	7.00	8.00
☐ **Towle "Engraved"**, *no monogram, good condition*	5.00	6.00
☐ **Towle "Engraved"**, *no monogram, fair condition*	2.00	3.00
☐ **Tudor Plate "Bridal Wreath"**, *no monogram, mint condition*	4.00	5.00
☐ **Tudor Plate "Bridal Wreath"**, *no monogram, excellent condition*	5.00	6.00
☐ **Tudor Plate "Bridal Wreath"**, *no monogram, good condition*	4.00	5.00
☐ **Tudor Plate "Duchess"**, *no monogram, excellent condition*	4.00	5.00
☐ **Tudor Plate "Duchess"**, *no monogram, excellent condition*	5.00	6.00
☐ **Tudor Plate "Duchess"**, *no monogram, good condition*	4.00	5.00
☐ **Tudor Plate "Fortune"**, *no monogram, excellent condition*	5.00	6.00
☐ **Tudor Plate "Fortune"**, *no monogram, good condition*	4.00	5.00
☐ **Tudor Plate "Fortune"**, *no monogram, fair condition*	1.00	2.00
☐ **Tudor Plate "Queen Bess II"**, *no monogram, excellent condition*	6.00	7.00
☐ **Tudor Plate "Queen Bess II"**, *no monogram, good condition*	5.00	6.00
☐ **Tudor Plate "Queen Bess II"**, *no monogram, excellent condition*	5.00	6.00
☐ **Tudor Plate "Queen Bess II"**, *no monogram, good condition*	4.00	5.00
☐ **Tudor Plate "Queen Bess II"**, *no monogram, fair condition*	1.00	2.00
☐ **Tudor Plate "Sweetbriar"**, *no monogram, excellent condition*	5.00	6.00
☐ **Tudor Plate "Sweetbriar"**, *no monogram, good condition*	4.00	5.00
☐ **Tudor Plate "Sweetbriar"**, *no monogram, fair condition*	1.00	2.00
☐ **Tudor Plate "Together"**, *no monogram, mint condition*	3.00	4.00
☐ **Tudor Plate "Together"**, *no monogram, excellent condition*	5.00	6.00
☐ **Wallace "Floral"**, *gold wash bowl, no monogram, excellent condition*	16.00	18.00
☐ **Wallace "Floral"**, *no monogram, excellent condition*	12.00	14.00
☐ **Wallace "Floral"**, *no monogram, good condition*	9.00	10.00
☐ **Wallace "Sonata"**, *no monogram, excellent condition*	5.00	6.00
☐ **Wallace "Sonata"**, *no monogram, good condition*	4.00	5.00
☐ **Wallace "Sonata"**, *no monogram, fair condition*	1.00	2.00
☐ **W.D. Smith "Adam"**, *no monogram, excellent condition*	2.00	3.00
☐ **W.D. Smith "Adam"**, *no monogram, excellent condition*	5.00	6.00
☐ **W.D. Smith "Adam"**, *no monogram, poor condition*	1.00	2.00
☐ **William Bros. "Queen Elizabeth"**, *no monogram, excellent condition*	4.00	5.00
☐ **William Bros. "Queen Elizabeth"**, *no monogram, good condition*	4.00	5.00
☐ **William Bros. "Isabella"**, *no monogram, excellent condition*	11.00	13.00
☐ **William Bros. "Isabella"**, *no monogram, poor condition*	1.00	2.00
☐ **Wm. A. Rogers "Carnation"**, *no monogram, excellent condition*	10.00	13.00
☐ **Wm. A. Rogers "Carnation"**, *no monogram, good condition*	9.00	12.00
☐ **Wm. A. Rogers "Chalice"**, *no monogram, excellent condition*	5.00	6.00
☐ **Wm. A. Rogers "Chalice"**, *no monogram, good condition*	4.00	5.00
☐ **Wm. A. Rogers "Chalice"**, *no monogram, fair condition*	1.00	2.00

	Price Range	

☐ **Wm. A. Rogers "Country Lane"**, *no monogram, excellent condition* 5.00 6.00

☐ **Wm. A. Rogers "Country Lane"**, *no monogram, good condition* 4.00 5.00

☐ **Wm. A. Rogers "Country Lane"**, *no monogram, fair condition* 1.00 2.00

☐ **Wm. A. Rogers "Elmore"**, *no monogram, excellent condition* 9.00 11.00

☐ **Wm. A. Rogers "Elmore"**, *no monogram, fair condition* 2.00 3.00

☐ **Wm. A. Rogers "Garland"**, *no monogram, excellent condition* 5.00 6.00

☐ **Wm. A. Rogers "Greylock"**, *no monogram, excellent condition* 4.00 5.00

☐ **Wm. A. Rogers "Greylock"**, *no monogram, good condition* . 4.00 5.00

☐ **Wm. A. Rogers "LaConcorde"**, *no monogram, excellent condition* 7.00 8.00

☐ **Wm. A. Rogers "LaConcorde"**, *no monogram, good condition* 6.00 7.00

☐ **Wm. A. Rogers "LaConcorde"**, *no monogram, fair condition* 2.00 3.00

☐ **Wm. A. Rogers "Lady Stuart"**, *no monogram, excellent condition* 5.00 6.00

☐ **Wm. A. Rogers "Lady Stuart"**, *no monogram, good condition* 4.00 5.00

☐ **Wm. A. Rogers "Lady Stuart"**, *no monogram, fair condition* 1.00 2.00

☐ **Wm. A. Rogers "LaVigne"**, *no monogram, excellent condition* 16.00 18.00

☐ **Wm. A. Rogers "LaVigne"**, *no monogram, good condition* . 9.00 11.00

☐ **Wm. A. Rogers "LaVigne"**, *no monogram, fair condition* ... 3.00 4.00

☐ **Wm. A. Rogers "LaVigne"**, *monogram, good condition* 5.00 6.00

☐ **Wm. A. Rogers "Linden"**, *no monogram, excellent condition* 7.00 8.00

☐ **Wm. A. Rogers "Linden"**, *no monogram, poor condition* ... 1.00 2.00

☐ **Wm. A. Rogers "Marcella"**, *no monogram, excellent condition* 5.00 6.00

☐ **Wm. A. Rogers "Marcella"**, *no monogram, good condition* . 4.00 5.00

☐ **Wm. A. Rogers "Margate"**, *no monogram, excellent condition* 5.00 6.00

☐ **Wm. A. Rogers "Margate"**, *no monogram, good condition* . 4.00 5.00

☐ **Wm. A. Rogers "Margate"**, *no monogram, fair condition* ... 1.00 2.00

☐ **Wm. A. Rogers "Meadowbrook"**, *no monogram, excellent condition* 5.00 6.00

☐ **Wm. A. Rogers "Meadowbrook"**, *no monogram, good condition* 4.00 5.00

☐ **Wm. A. Rogers "Narcissus"**, *no monogram, excellent condition* 9.00 10.00

☐ **Wm. A. Rogers "Narcissus"**, *no monogram, good condition* 5.00 6.00

☐ **Wm. A. Rogers "Paramount"**, *no monogram, excellent condition* 5.00 6.00

☐ **Wm. A. Rogers "Paramount"**, *no monogram, good condition* 4.00 5.00

☐ **Wm. A. Rogers "Paramount"**, *no monogram, fair condition* 1.00 2.00

☐ **Wm. A. Rogers "Rendezvous"**, *no monogram, excellent condition* 5.00 6.00

	Price Range	
☐ **Wm. A. Rogers "Rendezvous"**, *no monogram, good condition*	4.00	5.00
☐ **Wm. A. Rogers "Rosalie"**, *no monogram, excellent condition*	5.00	6.00
☐ **Wm. A. Rogers "Rosalie"**, *no monogram, good condition* ..	4.00	5.00
☐ **Wm. A. Rogers "Rosalie"**, *no monogram, poor condition* ..	1.00	2.00
☐ **Wm. A. Rogers "Standish"**, *no monogram, excellent condition*	4.00	5.00
☐ **Wm. A. Rogers "Standish"**, *no monogram, fair condition* ..	1.00	2.00
☐ **Wm. R. Rogers "Juliette"**, *no monogram, excellent condition*	5.00	6.00
☐ **Wm. R. Rogers "Juliette"**, *monogram, fair condition*	1.00	2.00
☐ **Wm. Rogers "Arbutus"**, *no monogram, excellent condition*	7.00	8.00
☐ **Wm. Rogers "Arbutus"**, *no monogram, good condition*	6.00	7.00
☐ **Wm. Rogers "Arbutus"**, *monogram, fair condition*	1.00	2.00
☐ **Wm. Rogers "Athens"**, *no monogram, excellent condition* .	7.00	8.00
☐ **Wm. Rogers "Athens"**, *no monogram, mint condition*	8.00	9.00
☐ **Wm. Rogers "Berwick"**, *no monogram, excellent condition*	16.00	18.00
☐ **Wm. Rogers "Berwick"**, *no monogram, good condition*	11.00	13.00
☐ **Wm. Rogers "Berwick"**, *no monogram, fair condition*	7.00	8.00
☐ **Wm. Rogers "Bridal Bouquet"**, *no monogram, excellent condition*	4.00	5.00
☐ **Wm. Rogers "Bridal Bouquet"**, *no monogram, good condition*	4.00	5.00
☐ **Wm. Rogers "Cotillion"**, *no monogram, excellent condition*	5.00	6.00
☐ **Wm. Rogers "Cotillion"**, *no monogram, good condition* ...	4.00	5.00
☐ **Wm. Rogers "Cotillion"**, *no monogram, fair condition*	5.00	6.00
☐ **Wm. Rogers "Debutante"**, *no monogram, excellent condition*	4.00	5.00
☐ **Wm. Rogers "Debutante"**, *no monogram, good condition* ..	1.00	2.00
☐ **Wm. Rogers "Devonshire"**, *no monogram, excellent condition*	5.00	6.00
☐ **Wm. Rogers "Devonshire"**, *no monogram, good condition* .	4.00	5.00
☐ **Wm. Rogers "Devonshire"**, *no monogram, fair condition* ..	1.00	2.00
☐ **Wm. Rogers "Exquisite"**, *no monogram, excellent condition*	5.00	6.00
☐ **Wm. Rogers "Exquisite"**, *no monogram, good condition* ...	4.00	5.00
☐ **Wm. Rogers "Exquisite"**, *no monogram, fair condition*	1.00	2.00
☐ **Wm. Rogers "Fair Oaks"**, *no monogram, excellent condition*	5.00	6.00
☐ **Wm. Rogers "Fair Oaks"**, *no monogram, good condition* ..	4.00	5.00
☐ **Wm. Rogers "Fair Oaks"**, *no monogram, fair condition*	1.00	2.00
☐ **Wm. Rogers "Fidelis"**, *no monogram, excellent condition* .	5.00	6.00
☐ **Wm. Rogers "Fidelis"**, *no monogram, good condition*	4.00	5.00
☐ **Wm. Rogers "Fidelis"**, *no monogram, fair condition*	1.00	2.00
☐ **Wm. Rogers "Grenoble"**, *no monogram, excellent condition*	10.00	13.00
☐ **Wm. Rogers "Grenoble"**, *no monogram, good condition* ...	9.00	10.00
☐ **Wm. Rogers "Grenoble"**, *no monogram, fair condition*	3.00	4.00
☐ **Wm. Rogers "Hostess"**, *no monogram, excellent condition*	5.00	6.00
☐ **Wm. Rogers "Hostess"**, *no monogram, good condition* ...	4.00	5.00
☐ **Wm. Rogers "Imperial"**, *no monogram, excellent condition*	5.00	6.00
☐ **Wm. Rogers "Imperial"**, *no monogram, good condition*	4.00	5.00
☐ **Wm. Rogers "Imperial"**, *no monogram, fair condition*	1.00	2.00

	Price Range	
☐ Wm. Rogers "LaConcorde", *no monogram, excellent condition*	12.00	14.00
☐ Wm. Rogers "LaConcorde", *no monogram, fair condition*	5.00	6.00
☐ Wm. Rogers "LaConcorde", *monogram, poor condition*	1.00	2.00
☐ Wm. Rogers "Lufberry", *no monogram, excellent condition*	4.00	5.00
☐ Wm. Rogers "Lufberry", *no monogram, good condition*	3.00	4.00
☐ Wm. Rogers "Lufberry", *no monogram, fair condition*	1.00	2.00
☐ Wm. Rogers "Mayfair", *no monogram, excellent condition*	5.00	6.00
☐ Wm. Rogers "Mayfair", *no monogram, good condition*	4.00	5.00
☐ Wm. Rogers "Mayfair", *no monogram, fair condition*	1.00	2.00
☐ Wm. Rogers "Melrose", *no monogram, excellent condition*	4.00	5.00
☐ Wm. Rogers "Melrose", *no monogram, excellent condition*	5.00	6.00
☐ Wm. Rogers "Memory", *no monogram, excellent condition*	5.00	6.00
☐ Wm. Rogers "Memory", *no monogram, good condition*	4.00	5.00
☐ Wm. Rogers "Memory", *no monogram, fair condition*	1.00	2.00
☐ Wm. Rogers "Precious Mirror", *no monogram, excellent condition*	5.00	6.00
☐ Wm. Rogers "Precious Mirror", *no monogram, good condition*	4.00	5.00
☐ Wm. Rogers "Precious Mirror", *no monogram, fair condition*	1.00	2.00
☐ Wm. Rogers "Treasure", *no monogram, excellent condition*	2.00	3.00
☐ Wm. Rogers "Treasure", *no monogram, excellent condition*	5.00	6.00
☐ Wm. Rogers "Treasure", *no monogram, good condition*	4.00	5.00
☐ Wm. Rogers "Treasure", *no monogram, fair condition*	1.00	2.00
☐ Wm. Rogers "Westminster", *no monogram, excellent condition*	9.00	11.00
☐ Wm. Rogers "Westminster", *no monogram, fair condition*	2.00	3.00
☐ Wm. Rogers Mfg. Co. "Alhambra", *monogram, good condition*	8.00	9.00
☐ Wm. Rogers Mfg. Co. "Alhambra", *no monogram, excellent condition*	12.00	14.00
☐ Wm. Rogers Mfg. Co. "Arbutus", *no monogram, excellent condition*	7.00	8.00
☐ Wm. Rogers Mfg. Co. "Arbutus", *no monogram, good condition*	6.00	7.00
☐ Wm. Rogers Mfg. Co. "Arbutus", *no monogram, fair condition*	3.00	4.00
☐ Wm. Rogers Mfg. Co. "Avalon", *no monogram, excellent condition*	5.00	6.00
☐ Wm. Rogers Mfg. Co. "Avalon", *no monogram, good condition*	4.00	5.00
☐ Wm. Rogers Mfg. Co. "Avalon", *no monogram, fair condition*	3.00	4.00
☐ Wm. Rogers Mfg. Co. "Camelot", *no monogram, excellent condition*	5.00	6.00
☐ Wm. Rogers Mfg. Co. "Camelot", *no monogram, good condition*	4.00	5.00
☐ Wm. Rogers Mfg. Co. "Camelot", *no monogram, fair condition*	1.00	2.00
☐ Wm. Rogers Mfg. Co. "Grand Elegance", *no monogram, excellent condition*	5.00	6.00
☐ Wm. Rogers Mfg. Co. "Grand Elegance", *no monogram, good condition*	4.00	5.00

	Price Range	
☐ **Wm. Rogers Mfg. Co. "Grand Elegance"**, *no monogram, excellent condition*	5.00	6.00
☐ **Wm. Rogers Mfg. Co. "Magnolia"**, *scalloped bowl, no monogram, excellent condition*	7.00	8.00
☐ **Wm. Rogers Mfg. Co. "Magnolia"**, *scalloped bowl, monogram, good condition*	2.00	3.00
☐ **Wm. Rogers Mfg. Co. "Magnolia"**, *no monogram, excellent condition*	5.00	6.00
☐ **Wm. Rogers Mfg. Co. "Magnolia"**, *no monogram, good condition*	4.00	5.00
☐ **Wm. Rogers Mfg. Co. "Magnolia"**, *no monogram, fair condition*	1.00	2.00
☐ **Wm. Rogers Mfg. Co. "Reflection"**, *no monogram, excellent condition*	5.00	6.00
☐ **Wm. Rogers Mfg. Co. "Reflection"**, *no monogram, good condition*	4.00	5.00
☐ **Wm. Rogers Mfg. Co. "Reflection"**, *no monogram, poor condition*	1.00	2.00
☐ **Wm. Rogers Mfg. Co. "Talisman"**, *no monogram, excellent condition*	5.00	6.00
☐ **Wm. Rogers Mfg. Co. "Talisman"**, *no monogram, good condition*	4.00	5.00
☐ **Wm. Rogers Mfg. Co. "Talisman"**, *no monogram, fair condition*	1.00	2.00
☐ **Wm. Rogers & Son "Arbutus"**, *no monogram, excellent condition*	5.00	6.00
☐ **Wm. Rogers & Son "Arbutus"**, *no monogram, good condition*	4.00	5.00
☐ **Wm. Rogers & Son "LaFrance"**, *no monogram, excellent condition*	5.00	6.00
☐ **Wm. Rogers & Son "LaFrance"**, *no monogram, good condition*	4.00	5.00
☐ **Wm. Rogers & Son "LaFrance"**, *no monogram, fair condition*	1.00	2.00
☐ **Wm. Rogers & Son "Oxford"**, *no monogram, excellent condition*	6.00	7.00
☐ **Wm. Rogers & Son "Oxford"**, *no monogram, good condition*	5.00	6.00
☐ **Wm. Rogers & Son "Oxford"**, *no monogram, poor condition*	1.00	2.00
☐ **Wm. Rogers & Son "Primrose II"**, *no monogram, excellent condition*	5.00	6.00
☐ **Wm. Rogers & Son "Primrose II"**, *no monogram, good condition*	4.00	5.00
☐ **Wm. Rogers & Son "Primrose II"**, *no monogram, fair condition*	1.00	2.00
☐ **Wm. Rogers & Son "Spring Flower"**, *no monogram, excellent condition*	5.00	6.00
☐ **Wm. Rogers & Son "Spring Flower"**, *no monogram, good condition*	4.00	5.00
☐ **Wm. Rogers & Son "Spring Flower"**, *no monogram, poor condition*	1.00	2.00
☐ **Wm. Rogers & Son "Victorian Rose"**, *no monogram, excellent condition*	5.00	6.00
☐ **Wm. Rogers & Son "Victorian Rose"**, *no monogram, good condition*	4.00	5.00

Price Range

☐ **Wm. Rogers & Son "Victorian Rose"**, *no monogram, poor condition*	1.00	2.00
☐ **1835 R. Wallace "Abbey"**, *no monogram, excellent condition*	5.00	6.00
☐ **1835 R. Wallace "Abbey"**, *no monogram, good condition* ..	4.00	5.00
☐ **1835 R. Wallace "Abbey"**, *no monogram, fair condition* ...	1.00	2.00
☐ **1835 R. Wallace "Buckingham"**, *no monogram, excellent condition*	5.00	6.00
☐ **1835 R. Wallace "Buckingham"**, *no monogram, good condition*	4.00	5.00
☐ **1835 R. Wallace "Buckingham"**, *no monogram, fair condition*	1.00	2.00
☐ **1835 R. Wallace "Buckingham"**, *monogram, excellent condition*	2.00	3.00
☐ **1835 R. Wallace "Joan"**, *no monogram, excellent condition*	5.00	6.00
☐ **1835 R. Wallace "Joan"**, *no monogram, good condition* ...	4.00	5.00
☐ **1835 R. Wallace "Joan"**, *no monogram, fair condition*	2.00	3.00
☐ **1835 R. Wallace "Kings"**, *scalloped bowl, no monogram, excellent condition*	6.00	7.00
☐ **1835 R. Wallace "Kings"**, *scalloped bowl, no monogram, good condition*	5.00	6.00
☐ **1847 Rogers "Adoration"**, *no monogram, excellent condition*	4.00	5.00
☐ **1847 Rogers "Adoration"**, *no monogram, good condition* ..	3.00	4.00
☐ **1847 Rogers "Ancestral"**, *no monogram, excellent condition*	5.00	6.00
☐ **1847 Rogers "Ancestral"**, *no monogram, good condition* ..	4.00	5.00
☐ **1847 Rogers "Ancestral"**, *monogram, good condition*	3.00	4.00
☐ **1847 Rogers "Anniversary"**, *no monogram, excellent condition*	5.00	6.00
☐ **1847 Rogers "Anniversary"**, *no monogram, good condition*	4.00	5.00
☐ **1847 Rogers "Anniversary"**, *no monogram, fair condition* ..	1.00	2.00
☐ **1847 Rogers "Argosy"**, *no monogram, excellent condition* .	4.00	5.00
☐ **1847 Rogers "Argosy"**, *no monogram, good condition*	2.00	3.00
☐ **1847 Rogers "Argosy"**, *no monogram, fair condition*	1.00	2.00
☐ **1847 Rogers "Assyrian"**, *no monogram, excellent condition*	9.00	10.00
☐ **1847 Rogers "Assyrian"**, *no monogram, excellent condition*	13.00	15.00
☐ **1847 Rogers "Assyrian"**, *monogram, good condition*	7.00	8.00
☐ **1847 Rogers "Assyrian"**, *monogram, poor condition*	2.00	3.00
☐ **1847 Rogers "Avon"**, *no monogram, excellent condition* ...	9.00	11.00
☐ **1847 Rogers "Avon"**, *no monogram, excellent condition* ...	11.00	13.00
☐ **1847 Rogers "Avon"**, *no monogram, good condition*	8.00	11.00
☐ **1847 Rogers "Avon"**, *no monogram, poor condition*	1.00	2.00
☐ **1847 Rogers "Berkshire"**, *no monogram, excellent condition*	13.00	15.00
☐ **1847 Rogers "Berkshire"**, *no monogram, good condition* ..	10.00	12.00
☐ **1847 Rogers "Berkshire"**, *no monogram, fair condition*	4.00	5.00
☐ **1847 Rogers "Charter Oak"**, *no monogram, resilvered*	20.00	22.00
☐ **1847 Rogers "Charter Oak"**, *no monogram, excellent condition*	18.00	20.00
☐ **1847 Rogers "Charter Oak"**, *no monogram, good condition*	11.00	13.00
☐ **1847 Rogers "Charter Oak"**, *no monogram, fair condition* ..	5.00	6.00
☐ **1847 Rogers "Charter Oak"**, *monogram, fair condition*	5.00	6.00

	Price Range	
☐ **1847 Rogers "Columbia"**, *no monogram, excellent condition*	13.00	15.00
☐ **1847 Rogers "Columbia"**, *no monogram, good condition* ..	11.00	13.00
☐ **1847 Rogers "Columbia"**, *no monogram, fair condition*	3.00	4.00
☐ **1847 Rogers "Continental"**, *no monogram, excellent condition*	5.00	6.00
☐ **1847 Rogers "Continental"**, *no monogram, good condition*	4.00	5.00
☐ **1847 Rogers "Continental"**, *no monogram, fair condition* ..	1.00	2.00
☐ **1847 Rogers "Daffodil"**, *no monogram, excellent condition*	6.00	7.00
☐ **1847 Rogers "Daffodil"**, *no monogram, good condition*	5.00	6.00
☐ **1847 Rogers "Daffodil"**, *no monogram, fair condition*	2.00	3.00
☐ **1847 Rogers "Daffodil II"**, *no monogram, excellent condition*	5.00	6.00
☐ **1847 Rogers "Daffodil II"**, *no monogram, good condition* ..	4.00	5.00
☐ **1847 Rogers "Daffodil II"**, *no monogram, fair condition* ...	1.00	2.00
☐ **1847 Rogers "Eternally Yours"**, *no monogram, excellent condition*	3.00	4.00
☐ **1847 Rogers "Eternally Yours"**, *no monogram, excellent condition*	5.00	6.00
☐ **1847 Rogers "Eternally Yours"**, *no monogram, fair condition*	2.00	3.00
☐ **1847 Rogers "First Love"**, *no monogram, excellent condition*	5.00	6.00
☐ **1847 Rogers "First Love"**, *no monogram, good condition* ..	4.00	5.00
☐ **1847 Rogers "First Love"**, *no monogram, fair condition* ...	1.00	2.00
☐ **1847 Rogers "First Love"**, *good condition*	2.00	3.00
☐ **1847 Rogers "Flair"**, *no monogram, excellent condition* ...	3.00	4.00
☐ **1847 Rogers "Flair"**, *no monogram, excellent condition* ...	5.00	6.00
☐ **1847 Rogers "Flair"**, *no monogram, good condition*	4.00	5.00
☐ **1847 Rogers "Flair"**, *no monogram, poor condition*	1.00	2.00
☐ **1847 Rogers "Floral"**, *no monogram, excellent condition* ..	11.00	13.00
☐ **1847 Rogers "Floral"**, *no monogram, good condition*	9.00	11.00
☐ **1847 Rogers "Floral"**, *no monogram, fair condition*	5.00	6.00
☐ **1847 Rogers "Heraldic"**, *no monogram, excellent condition*	3.00	4.00
☐ **1847 Rogers "Heraldic"**, *no monogram, fair condition*	1.00	2.00
☐ **1847 Rogers "Heritage"**, *no monogram, good condition* ...	3.00	4.00
☐ **1847 Rogers "Heritage"**, *no monogram, poor condition* ...	1.00	2.00
☐ **1847 Rogers "Laurel"**, *no monogram, excellent condition* ..	6.00	7.00
☐ **1847 Rogers "Laurel"**, *no monogram, good condition*	5.00	6.00
☐ **1847 Rogers "Legacy"**, *no monogram, excellent condition* .	5.00	6.00
☐ **1847 Rogers "Legacy"**, *no monogram, good condition* ...	4.00	5.00
☐ **1847 Rogers "Legacy"**, *no monogram, fair condition*	1.00	2.00
☐ **1847 Rogers "Linden"**, *no monogram, excellent condition* .	11.00	13.00
☐ **1847 Rogers "Lorne"**, *no monogram, excellent condition* ..	6.00	7.00
☐ **1847 Rogers "Lorne"**, *no monogram, good condition*	4.00	5.00
☐ **1847 Rogers "Lorne"**, *monogram, excellent condition*	4.00	5.00
☐ **1847 Rogers "Lorne"**, *monogram, good condition*	2.00	3.00
☐ **1847 Rogers "Lotus"**, *no monogram, excellent condition* ..	8.00	9.00
☐ **1847 Rogers "Lotus"**, *monogram, excellent condition*	5.00	6.00
☐ **1847 Rogers "Lotus"**, *monogram, fair condition*	2.00	3.00
☐ **1847 Rogers "Louvain"**, *no monogram, excellent condition*	5.00	6.00
☐ **1847 Rogers "Louvain"**, *no monogram, good condition*	4.00	5.00
☐ **1847 Rogers "Magic Rose"**, *mint condition*	3.00	4.00

Price Range

	Price Range	
☐ 1847 Rogers "Magic Rose", *no monogram, excellent condition*	5.00	6.00
☐ 1847 Rogers "Magic Rose", *no monogram, good condition*	4.00	5.00
☐ 1847 Rogers "Marquise", *no monogram, excellent condition*	5.00	6.00
☐ 1847 Rogers "Marquise", *no monogram, good condition* ..	4.00	5.00
☐ 1847 Rogers "Marquise", *no monogram, fair condition*	1.00	2.00
☐ 1847 Rogers "Moselle", *no monogram, excellent condition*	32.00	36.00
☐ 1847 Rogers "Moselle", *monogram, good condition*	22.00	24.00
☐ 1847 Rogers "Moselle", *monogram, poor condition*	5.00	6.00
☐ 1847 Rogers "Newport", *no monogram, excellent condition*	15.00	17.00
☐ 1847 Rogers "Newport", *no monogram, good condition* ...	10.00	12.00
☐ 1847 Rogers "Newport", *no monogram, fair condition*	3.00	4.00
☐ 1847 Rogers "Old Colony", *no monogram, excellent condition*	9.00	11.00
☐ 1847 Rogers "Remembrance", *no monogram, excellent condition*	5.00	6.00
☐ 1847 Rogers "Remembrance", *no monogram, good condition*	4.00	5.00
☐ 1847 Rogers "Remembrance", *no monogram, fair condition*	1.00	2.00
☐ 1847 Rogers "Salem", *no monogram, excellent condition* ..	5.00	6.00
☐ 1847 Rogers "Salem", *no monogram, good condition*	4.00	5.00
☐ 1847 Rogers "Salem", *no monogram, fair condition*	1.00	2.00
☐ 1847 Rogers "Savoy", *no monogram, resilvered*	11.00	13.00
☐ 1847 Rogers "Savoy", *no monogram, excellent condition* ..	8.00	9.00
☐ 1847 Rogers "Savoy", *no monogram, poor condition*	1.00	2.00
☐ 1847 Rogers "Sharon", *no monogram, excellent condition* .	8.00	9.00
☐ 1847 Rogers "Sharon", *no monogram, good condition*	7.00	8.00
☐ 1847 Rogers "Vintage", *no monogram, excellent condition*	20.00	22.00
☐ 1847 Rogers "Vintage", *no monogram, good condition*	10.00	12.00
☐ 1847 Rogers "Vintage", *no monogram, fair condition*	4.00	7.00
☐ 1847 Rogers "Vintage", *monogram, good condition*	7.00	9.00
☐ 1847 Rogers "Vintage", *monogram, fair condition*	3.00	6.00
☐ 1881 Rogers "Capri", *no monogram, excellent condition* ..	5.00	6.00
☐ 1881 Rogers "Capri", *no monogram, good condition*	4.00	5.00
☐ 1881 Rogers "Chippendale", *no monogram, excellent condition*	5.00	6.00
☐ 1881 Rogers "Chippendale", *no monogram, good condition*	4.00	5.00
☐ 1881 Rogers "Chippendale", *no monogram, fair condition* .	1.00	2.00
☐ 1881 Rogers "Coronet", *no monogram, excellent condition*	4.00	5.00
☐ 1881 Rogers "Coronet", *no monogram, fair condition*	1.00	2.00
☐ 1881 Rogers "Flirtation", *no monogram, excellent condition*	3.00	4.00
☐ 1881 Rogers "Grape", *monogram, good condition*	5.00	6.00
☐ 1881 Rogers "Grecian", *no monogram, excellent condition*	5.00	6.00
☐ 1881 Rogers "Grecian", *no monogram, good condition*	4.00	5.00
☐ 1881 Rogers "LaVigne", *no monogram, excellent condition*	11.00	13.00
☐ 1881 Rogers "LaVigne", *no monogram, good condition*	9.00	11.00
☐ 1881 Rogers "LaVigne", *no monogram, poor condition*	2.00	3.00
☐ 1881 Rogers "Leyland", *no monogram, excellent condition*	7.00	8.00
☐ 1881 Rogers "Leyland", *no monogram, good condition*	6.00	7.00
☐ 1881 Rogers "Proposal", *no monogram, excellent condition*	5.00	6.00
☐ 1881 Rogers "Proposal", *no monogram, good condition* ...	4.00	5.00
☐ 1881 Rogers "Scotia", *no monogram, excellent condition* .	5.00	6.00

	Price Range	
☐ **1881 Rogers "Scotia"**, *no monogram, good condition*	4.00	5.00
☐ **1881 Rogers "Scotia"**, *no monogram, fair condition*	1.00	2.00

(Sterling Silver)

☐ **Alvin "Chateau Rose"**, *no monogram*	14.00	16.00
☐ **Alvin "Raphael"**, *no monogram*	52.00	57.00
☐ **Durgin "Chrysanthemum"**, *no monogram*	35.00	39.00
☐ **Durgin "Chrysanthemum"**, *no monogram*	40.00	45.00
☐ **Durgin "Fairfax"**, *monogram*	16.00	18.00
☐ **Frank Smith "Fiddle Thread"**, *no monogram*	26.00	29.00
☐ **Gorham "Bird's Nest"**	120.00	135.00
☐ **Gorham "Blithe Spirit"**, *no monogram*	12.00	14.00
☐ **Gorham "Buttercup"**, *no monogram*	14.00	16.00
☐ **Gorham "Chantilly"**, *no monogram*	16.00	18.00
☐ **Gorham "Chantilly"**, *monogram*	13.00	15.00
☐ **Gorham "Chantilly"**, *monogram*	16.00	18.00
☐ **Gorham "Greenbrier"**, *no monogram*	16.00	18.00
☐ **Gorham "Greenbrier"**, *monogram*	14.00	16.00
☐ **Gorham "Lancaster"**, *no monogram*	10.00	12.00
☐ **Gorham "Lancaster Rose"**, *no monogram*	16.00	18.00
☐ **Gorham "Luxembourg"**, *monogram*	15.00	17.00
☐ **Gorham, pattern unknown**, *no monogram*	10.00	13.00
☐ **International "Bridal Veil"**, *no monogram*	10.00	12.00
☐ **International "Crystal"**, *no monogram*	14.00	16.00
☐ **International "Frontenac"**, *no monogram*	22.00	24.00
☐ **International "Joan of Arc"**, *no monogram*	14.00	16.00
☐ **International "Prelude"**, *monogram*	14.00	16.00
☐ **International "Silver Melody"**, *no monogram*	10.00	13.00
☐ **International "Wedgwood"**, *no monogram*	16.00	18.00
☐ **Kirk "Repousse"**, *monogram*	16.00	19.00
☐ **Lunt "Eloquence"**, *monogram*	14.00	16.00
☐ **Lunt "Monticello"**, *monogram*	22.00	24.00
☐ **Lunt "William and Mary"**, *monogram*	15.00	17.00
☐ **Oneida "Martinique"**, *no monogram*	12.00	14.00
☐ **Oneida "Silver Rose"**, *no monogram*	12.00	14.00
☐ **Reed & Barton "Francis I"**, *no monogram*	15.00	17.00
☐ **Reed & Barton "LaReine"**, *no monogram*	13.00	15.00
☐ **Reed & Barton "L'Elegant"**, *no monogram*	20.00	22.00
☐ **Reed & Barton "Marlborough"**, *no monogram*	16.00	18.00
☐ **Reed & Barton "Savannah"**, *no monogram*	17.00	19.00
☐ **Simpson, Hall & Miller "Frontenac"**, *no monogram*	24.00	27.00
☐ **Stieff "Rose"**, *no monogram*	13.00	15.00
☐ **Towle "Aristocrat"**, *no monogram*	10.00	12.00
☐ **Towle "Georgian"**, *no monogram*	26.00	29.00
☐ **Towle "Kings"**, *no monogram*	26.00	29.00
☐ **Towle "Madeira"**, *no monogram*	14.00	16.00
☐ **Towle "Old Colonial"**, *monogram*	10.00	12.00
☐ **Towle "Old Colonial"**, *no monogram*	26.00	29.00
☐ **Towle "Rambler"**, *monogram*	14.00	16.00
☐ **Towle "Silver Flutes"**, *monogram*	12.00	14.00
☐ **Towle "Spanish Provincial"**, *no monogram*	14.00	16.00
☐ **Wallace "Irian"**, *no monogram*	24.00	27.00
☐ **Wallace "Louvre"**, *no monogram*	23.00	25.00
☐ **Wallace "Princess Mary"**, *no monogram*	14.00	16.00

	Price Range	
☐ **Wallace "St. George"**, *no monogram*	15.00	17.00
☐ **Westmoreland "John & Priscilla"**, *no monogram*	13.00	15.00
☐ **Westmoreland "Milburn Rose"**, *no monogram*	12.00	14.00
☐ **Whiting "Adam"**, *monogram*	10.00	13.00
☐ **Whiting "Bead"**, *monogram*	17.00	20.00
☐ **Whiting "Imperial Queen"**, *no monogram*	19.00	21.00

SUGAR SIFTERS

These large, good-looking utensils are often mistaken for strainers, because of their pierced bowls. Since they have not been in active use for many years, their purpose may puzzle the collector. Actually they had at least two purposes in connection with sugar. In early times, most households did their marketing less frequently than today, and bought non-perishables in very large supplies. Sugar was commonly bought in 10 or 20 pounds sacks, and might be kept for a month or longer. If the atmosphere was humid, it was sure to clot. In transferring it from the sack to sugar bowl, the *sugar sifter* insured that no clots came along (these were eventually mashed up, when all the loose sugar had been used — or, in households where cost not an object, discarded). Another use was in sprinkling granulated sugar over doughnuts or pastries.

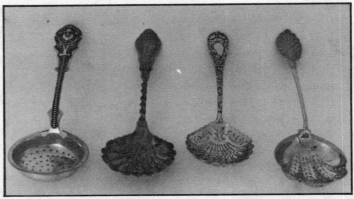

Sugar Sifters, *(L to R) (sterling), Wood & Hughes "Medallion", 75.00; Albert Coles, pattern unknown, 75.00; Durgin "Chrysanthemum", 90.00; Gorham "Grecian", 80.00*

(Silver-Plated)

☐ **Community "Bird of Paradise"**, *no monogram, excellent condition*	11.00	13.00
☐ **Community "Grosvenor"**, *no monogram, excellent condition*	11.00	13.00
☐ **Community "Paul Revere"**, *no monogram, excellent condition*	10.00	12.00
☐ **Holmes & Edwards "Rosemary"**, *no monogram, excellent condition*	18.00	21.00
☐ **Holmes & Edwards "Waldorf"**, *no monogram, excellent condition*	23.00	26.00

	Price Range	
☐ **Wm. Rogers "Magnolia"**, *no monogram, excellent condition*	10.00	13.00
☐ **1847 Rogers "Lorne"**, *no monogram, excellent condition*	14.00	17.00
(Sterling Silver)		
☐ **Dominick & Haff "Acanthus"**, *no monogram, 7 1/8" L.*	14.00	18.00
☐ **Gorham "Lancaster"**, *no monogram*	36.00	39.00

SUGAR TONGS

Cubed sugar was manufactured as early as the 1700's, and used both in households and public eating places. The object was to provide convenience in handling as well as portions of a standard size. Naturally this required the use of a special utensil, especially as the earlier sugar cubes did not have paper wrappers. Tongs, similar to pickle tongs but a good deal smaller, were introduced, and became a fixture on every well-appointed table. These were made in virtually every country of the western world, and are far more numerous as antiques than a non-collector might guess. You will not very often find an 18th century specimen; when you do, the odds are strong that it will be British. Sugar tongs vary quite a bit in length, and of course in treatment of the "claws" — which often are indeed represented as claws, of birds, reptiles, etc.

Sugar Tongs, *(L to R) (sterling), Gorham "Morning Glory",* 27.00; *Alvin "Bridal Rose",* 30.00; *Whiting "Lily",* 36.00; *Simpson, Hall & Miller "Frontenac",* 33.00

(Silver-Plated)

☐ **Community "Avalon"**, *no monogram, excellent condition*	25.00	27.00
☐ **Community "Bird of Paradise"**, *no monogram, excellent condition*	18.00	20.00
☐ **Community "Grosvenor"**, *no monogram, excellent condition*	11.00	13.00

	Price Range	

☐ **Community "Lady Hamilton"**, *no monogram, good condition* 8.00 9.00
☐ **Community "Patrician"**, *no monogram, excellent condition* 23.00 25.00
☐ **Gorham "Kings"**, *hotel name, excellent condition, 4" L.* ... 14.00 16.00
☐ **Gorham "Kings"**, *no monogram, excellent condition* 18.00 20.00
☐ **Hartford "Lyonnaise"**, *no monogram, excellent condition* . 6.00 7.00
☐ **Holmes & Edwards "Jamestown"**, *no monogram, excellent condition* 21.00 23.00
☐ **Holmes & Edwards "Lovely Lady"**, *no monogram, excellent condition* 20.00 22.00
☐ **Holmes & Edwards "Masterpiece"**, *no monogram, excellent condition* 21.00 23.00
☐ **Holmes & Edwards "Newport"**, *no monogram, excellent condition* 21.00 23.00
☐ **Reed & Barton "Cecil"**, *no monogram, excellent condition, 4" L.* 18.00 20.00
☐ **Reliance "Exeter"**, *no monogram, excellent condition* 22.00 25.00
☐ **Rogers "Shell"**, *no monogram, excellent condition* 16.00 18.00
☐ **Rogers "Windsor"**, *no monogram, excellent condition, 5" L.* 8.00 9.00
☐ **Rogers & Bro. "Assyrian Head"**, *no monogram, excellent condition, 6" L.* 36.00 40.00
☐ **Rogers & Bro. "Columbia"**, *no monogram, excellent condition, 4" L.* 40.00 43.00
☐ **Rogers & Bro. "Siren"**, *no monogram, excellent condition* . 21.00 23.00
☐ **Rogers & Hamilton "Alhambra"**, *no monogram, excellent condition, 5" L.* 25.00 27.00
☐ **Tudor "Queen Bess II"**, *no monogram, excellent condition* . 18.00 20.00
☐ **Wm. A Rogers "Glenrose"**, *no monogram, excellent condition* 16.00 18.00
☐ **Wm. A. Rogers "Meadowbrook"**, *no monogram, excellent condition* 21.00 23.00
☐ **Wm. Rogers "Abington"**, *no monogram, good condition* ... 7.00 8.00
☐ **Wm. Rogers "Countess"**, *no monogram, excellent condition* 11.00 13.00
☐ **Wm. Rogers "Cromwell"**, *no monogram, excellent condition, 4" L.* 10.00 12.00
☐ **Wm. Rogers "Geneva"**, *no monogram, excellent condition* . 8.00 9.00
☐ **1847 Rogers "Assyrian Head"**, *claw ends, no monogram, good condition, 5" L.* 19.00 21.00
☐ **1847 Rogers "Assyrian"**, *claw ends, no monogram, excellent condition* 26.00 28.00
☐ **1847 Rogers "Berkshire"**, *no monogram, excellent condition* 21.00 23.00
☐ **1847 Rogers "Berkshire"**, *no monogram, excellent condition* 24.00 27.00
☐ **1847 Rogers "Lorne"**, *monogram, excellent condition* 16.00 18.00
☐ **1847 Rogers "Louis XV"**, *demitasse size, no monogram, excellent condition* 8.00 9.00
☐ **1847 Rogers "Lovelace"**, *no monogram, excellent condition* 21.00 23.00
☐ **1847 Rogers "Old Colony"**, *no monogram, excellent condition, 4½" L.* 30.00 32.00
☐ **1847 Rogers "Saratoga"**, *no monogram, excellent condition* 11.00 13.00

(Sterling Silver)

	Price Range	
☐ Durgin "Fairfax", *no monogram*	14.00	16.00
☐ Gorham "Cambridge", *no monogram*	21.00	23.00
☐ Gorham "Chantilly", *no monogram*	27.00	29.00
☐ Gorham "Chantilly", *no monogram*	15.00	17.00
☐ Gorham "Lancaster", *no monogram*	15.00	17.00
☐ Simpson, Hall & Miller "Frontenac", *no monogram, 5" L.*	30.00	33.00
☐ Tiffany "Colonial", *gold ends, no monogram, 4" L.*	54.00	60.00
☐ Tiffany "Faneuil", *no monogram*	11.00	13.00
☐ Tiffany "Grammercy", *no monogram*	16.00	18.00
☐ Tiffany "Saratoga", *1870-1891 era, no monogram*	22.00	25.00
☐ Towle "Aristocrat", *no monogram*	9.00	10.00
☐ Towle "French Provincial", *monogram*	15.00	17.00
☐ Unger Bros. "Douvaine", *no monogram*	25.00	27.00
☐ Wallace "Puritan", *monogram*	18.00	20.00
☐ Whiting "Imperial Queen", *monogram*	22.00	24.00

TABLESPOONS

Few silver articles are so universal as the tablespoon, which, if its listings in this book reflected its overall abundance on the market, would fill at least ¼th the volume. Even the household which lacked silver tableware in general often had silver tablespoons; they were inexpensive enough to be within reach of nearly everybody. Specimens of U.S. manufacture as early as the 17th century exist but are mainly in museums and historical societies. Those of the 18th are plentiful enough to come within the hobbyist's grasp, and represent one of his few opportunities to own American silverware of the 1700's. Take care, though: many 18th century tablespoons are pewter, and could be mistaken for silver at a quick glance. When "coin silver" was used at this time, it was not obtained by melting U.S. coins (of which there were none), but probably the Spanish 8 reales and 4 reales pieces and possibly the French silver ecu, all of which circulated in the colonial era.

(Coin Silver)

☐ Hood & Tobey, *c. 1848, monogram*	16.00	19.00
☐ Jacob Sargent, Hartford, Connecticut, *c. 1761*	22.00	25.00
☐ Rogers Bro., *monogram*	22.00	25.00
☐ Twedy & Barrowss, *fiddleback pattern, basket of flowers on handle*	40.00	45.00

(Silver-Plated)

☐ Alvin "Diana", *no monogram, excellent condition*	7.00	8.00
☐ Alvin "Diana", *no monogram, good condition*	6.00	7.00
☐ Alvin "Diana", *no monogram, fair condition*	1.00	2.00
☐ Alvin "Diana", *monogram, excellent condition*	1.00	2.00
☐ American Silver Co. "Moselle", *no monogram, excellent condition*	12.00	14.00
☐ American Silver Co. "Moselle", *no monogram, good condition*	9.00	11.00
☐ American Silver Co. "Moselle", *no monogram, fair condition*	1.00	2.00
☐ American Silver Co. "Wildflower", *no monogram, resilvered*	8.00	9.00
☐ American Silver Co. "Wildflower", *no monogram, good condition*	4.00	5.00

	Price Range	

☐ **American Silver Co. "Wildflower"**, *no monogram, good condition* 4.00 5.00

☐ **Community "Adam"**, *no monogram, excellent condition* .. 4.00 5.00

☐ **Community "Adam"**, *no monogram, good condition* 4.00 5.00

☐ **Community "Adam"**, *no monogram, fair condition* 2.00 3.00

☐ **Community "Avalon"**, *no monogram, excellent condition* .. 4.00 5.00

☐ **Community "Avalon"**, *no monogram, good condition* 3.00 4.00

☐ **Community "Avalon"**, *monogram "ghost", resilvered* 4.00 5.00

☐ **Community "Ballad"**, *no monogram, excellent condition* .. 4.00 5.00

☐ **Community "Ballad"**, *no monogram, good condition* 3.00 4.00

☐ **Community "Ballad"**, *no monogram, excellent condition* .. 4.00 5.00

☐ **Community "Ballad"**, *pierced, monogram, poor condition* . 1.00 2.00

☐ **Community "Bird of Paradise"**, *no monogram, excellent condition* 5.00 6.00

☐ **Community "Bird of Paradise"**, *no monogram, good condition* 4.00 5.00

☐ **Community "Coronation"**, *no monogram, excellent condition* 6.00 7.00

☐ **Community "Coronation"**, *no monogram, good condition* . 5.00 6.00

☐ **Community "Coronation"**, *no monogram, fair condition* ... 2.00 3.00

☐ **Community "Coronation"**, *pierced, no monogram, excellent condition* 7.00 8.00

☐ **Community "Coronation"**, *pierced, no monogram, good condition* 5.00 6.00

☐ **Community "Coronation"**, *pierced, no monogram, poor condition* 1.00 2.00

☐ **Community "Evening Star"**, *no monogram, excellent condition* 5.00 6.00

☐ **Community "Evening Star"**, *no monogram, good condition* 4.00 5.00

☐ **Community "Evening Star"**, *no monogram, fair condition* .. 1.00 2.00

☐ **Community "Georgian"**, *no monogram, excellent condition* 4.00 5.00

☐ **Community "Georgian"**, *no monogram, good condition* ... 4.00 5.00

☐ **Community "Grosvenor"**, *monogram, excellent condition* . 3.00 4.00

☐ **Community "Grosvenor"**, *no monogram, fair condition* 2.00 3.00

☐ **Community "Grosvenor"**, *no monogram, mint condition* ... 7.00 8.00

☐ **Community "Lady Hamilton"**, *no monogram, good condition* 4.00 5.00

☐ **Community "Lady Hamilton"**, *no monogram, good condition* 5.00 6.00

☐ **Community "Morning Rose"**, *no monogram, mint condition* 4.00 5.00

☐ **Community "Morning Rose"**, *pierced, no monogram, excellent condition* 6.00 7.00

☐ **Community "Morning Rose"**, *pierced, no monogram, good condition* 5.00 6.00

☐ **Community "Morning Rose"**, *no monogram, good condition* 4.00 5.00

☐ **Community "Morning Star"**, *no monogram, fair condition* . 1.00 2.00

☐ **Community "Patrician"**, *no monogram, excellent condition* 4.00 5.00

☐ **Community "Patrician"**, *no monogram, good condition* ... 4.00 5.00

☐ **Community "Silver Flower"**, *pierced, no monogram, mint condition* 4.00 5.00

☐ **Community "Silver Flower"**, *pierced, no monogram, fair condition* 1.00 2.00

☐ **Community "Silver Flower"**, *no monogram, mint condition* 4.00 5.00

	Price Range	
☐ Community "Silver Sands", *no monogram, mint condition* .	4.00	5.00
☐ Community "Silver Sands", *pierced, no monogram, mint condition*	5.00	6.00
☐ Community "Silver Sands", *pierced, no monogram, good condition*	5.00	6.00
☐ Community "Silver Sands", *pierced, no monogram, resilvered*	6.00	7.00
☐ Community "Song of Autumn", *no monogram, mint condition*	4.00	5.00
☐ Community "Song of Autumn", *no monogram, fair condition*	1.00	2.00
☐ Community "South Seas", *no monogram, mint condition* ..	6.00	7.00
☐ Community "South Seas", *no monogram, good condition* .	5.00	6.00
☐ Community "Tangier", *no monogram, mint condition*	4.00	5.00
☐ Community "Tangier", *no monogram, excellent condition* .	4.00	5.00
☐ Community "White Orchid", *no monogram, mint condition*	4.00	5.00
☐ Community "White Orchid", *no monogram, good condition*	5.00	6.00
☐ Community "White Orchid", *pierced, no monogram, mint condition*	4.00	5.00
☐ Derby "Roman", *monogram, good condition*	2.00	3.00
☐ Derby "Roman", *no monogram, good condition*	4.00	5.00
☐ Gorham "Carolina", *no monogram, excellent condition* ...	4.00	5.00
☐ Gorham "Carolina", *no monogram, good condition*	3.00	4.00
☐ Gorham "Carolina", *no monogram, poor condition*	1.00	2.00
☐ Gorham "Cavalier", *no monogram, excellent condition*	4.00	5.00
☐ Gorham "Cavalier", *no monogram, good condition*	4.00	5.00
☐ Gorham "Cavalier", *no monogram, fair condition*	1.00	2.00
☐ Gorham "Empire", *no monogram, excellent condition*	4.00	5.00
☐ Gorham "Empire", *no monogram, good condition*	4.00	5.00
☐ Gorham "Regent", *no monogram, mint condition*	4.00	5.00
☐ Gorham "Regent", *monogram, good condition*	2.00	3.00
☐ Hall & Elton "Fiddle", *no monogram, excellent condition* ..	4.00	3.00
☐ Hall & Elton "Fiddle", *monogram, good condition*	1.00	2.00
☐ Hall & Elton "Orient", *monogram, excellent condition*	2.00	3.00
☐ Hall & Elton "Orient", *no monogram, excellent condition* ..	6.00	7.00
☐ Hall & Elton "Orient", *no monogram, fair condition*	1.00	2.00
☐ Harmony House "Classic Filigree", *no monogram, excellent condition*	4.00	5.00
☐ Harmony House "Classic Filigree", *no monogram, good condition*	4.00	5.00
☐ Harmony House "Serenade", *no monogram, excellent condition*	4.00	5.00
☐ Harmony House "Serenade", *monogram, good condition* ..	1.00	2.00
☐ Holmes & Edwards "Danish Princess", *no monogram, excellent condition*	4.00	5.00
☐ Holmes & Edwards "Danish Princess", *no monogram, good condition*	4.00	5.00
☐ Holmes & Edwards "Orient", *no monogram, excellent condition*	4.00	5.00
☐ Holmes & Edwards "Orient", *no monogram, poor condition*	1.00	2.00
☐ Holmes & Edwards "Orient", *no monogram, silver in excellent condition, dent in bowl*	1.00	2.00
☐ Holmes & Edwards "Pearl", *monogram, excellent condition*	2.00	3.00

	Price Range	
☐ Holmes & Edwards "Pearl", *no monogram, excellent condition*	5.00	6.00
☐ Holmes & Edwards "Rosemary", *no monogram, excellent condition*	3.00	4.00
☐ Holmes & Edwards "Rosemary", *no monogram, good condition*	4.00	5.00
☐ International "Orleans", *no monogram, excellent condition*	4.00	5.00
☐ International "Orleans", *no monogram, good condition* ...	3.00	4.00
☐ International "Silver Tulip", *pierced, no monogram, excellent condition*	3.00	4.00
☐ International "Silver Tulip", *pierced, no monogram, good condition*	3.00	4.00
☐ Niagara Falls Silver Co. "Adams", *monogram, excellent condition*	5.00	6.00
☐ Niagara Falls Silver Co. "Adams", *no monogram, good condition*	4.00	5.00
☐ Niagara Falls Silver Co. "Elberon", *no monogram, excellent condition*	4.00	5.00
☐ Niagara Falls Silver Co. "Elberon", *no monogram, good condition*	4.00	5.00
☐ Oneida "Avalon", *no monogram, excellent condition*	4.00	5.00
☐ Oneida "Avalon", *no monogram, poor condition*	1.00	2.00
☐ Oneida "Flower de Luce", *no monogram, excellent condition*	8.00	9.00
☐ Oneida "Flower de Luce", *no monogram, good condition* ..	5.00	6.00
☐ Oneida "Flower de Luce", *no monogram, fair condition* ...	1.00	2.00
☐ Oneida "Jamestown", *no monogram, excellent condition* .	10.00	12.00
☐ Oneida "Jamestown", *no monogram, fair condition*	2.00	3.00
☐ Oneida "Louis XVI", *no monogram, excellent condition* ...	6.00	7.00
☐ Oneida "Louis XVI", *no monogram, good condition*	4.00	6.00
☐ Oneida "Louis XVI", *no monogram, good condition except for slight bend in handle*	1.00	2.00
☐ Oneida "Wildwood", *no monogram, excellent condition* ...	4.00	5.00
☐ Oneida "Wildwood", *no monogram, excellent condition* ...	5.00	6.00
☐ Oneida "Wildwood", *no monogram, excellent condition* ...	4.00	5.00
☐ Oneida "Wildwood", *no monogram, fair condition*	1.00	2.00
☐ Paragon "Sweet Pea", *no monogram, excellent condition* .	5.00	6.00
☐ Paragon "Sweet Pea", *no monogram, good condition*	3.00	4.00
☐ Paragon "Sweet Pea", *no monogram, fair condition*	1.00	2.00
☐ Reed & Barton "Carlton", *no monogram, excellent condition*	4.00	5.00
☐ Reed & Barton "Carlton", *no monogram, good condition* ..	3.00	4.00
☐ Reed & Barton "Oxford", *no monogram, excellent condition*	6.00	7.00
☐ Reed & Barton "Oxford", *no monogram, good condition* ...	4.00	5.00
☐ Reed & Barton "Oxford", *no monogram, fair condition*	1.00	2.00
☐ Reed & Barton "Oxford", *no monogram, good condition* ...	6.00	7.00
☐ Reed & Barton "Oxford", *no monogram, poor condition* ...	1.00	2.00
☐ Rockford "Louvre", *no monogram, excellent condition*	11.00	13.00
☐ Rockford "Louvre", *no monogram, fair condition*	4.00	5.00
☐ Rockford "Louvre", *no monogram, poor condition*	2.00	3.00
☐ Rogers "Alhambra", *no monogram, excellent condition* ...	7.00	8.00
☐ Rogers "Alhambra", *no monogram, excellent condition* ...	5.00	6.00
☐ Rogers "Alhambra", *no monogram, poor condition*	2.00	3.00

Price Range

☐ Rogers "Ambassador", *no monogram, excellent condition*	4.00	5.00
☐ Rogers "Ambassador", *no monogram, good condition*	4.00	5.00
☐ Rogers "Chevalier", *no monogram, excellent condition* ...	4.00	5.00
☐ Rogers "Chevalier", *no monogram, good condition*	4.00	5.00
☐ Rogers "LaConcord", *no monogram, excellent condition* ..	4.00	5.00
☐ Rogers "LaConcord", *no monogram, good condition*	3.00	4.00
☐ Rogers "Norfolk", *no monogram, excellent condition*	4.00	5.00
☐ Rogers "Norfolk", *no monogram, fair condition*	1.00	2.00
☐ Rogers "Precious", *no monogram, excellent condition*	4.00	5.00
☐ Rogers "Precious", *no monogram, good condition*	4.00	5.00
☐ Rogers "Queen Bess II", *no monogram, excellent condition*	4.00	5.00
☐ Rogers "Queen Bess II", *no monogram, good condition* ...	4.00	5.00
☐ Rogers "Victorian Rose", *no monogram, excellent condition*	4.00	5.00
☐ Rogers "Victorian Rose", *no monogram, good condition* ..	3.00	4.00
☐ Rogers "Victorian Rose", *pierced, no monogram, excellent condition*	6.00	7.00
☐ Rogers "Victorian Rose", *pierced, no monogram, good condition*	3.00	4.00
☐ Rogers & Bro. "Assyrian", *no monogram, excellent condition*	6.00	7.00
☐ Rogers & Bro. "Assyrian", *no monogram, resilvered*	9.00	11.00
☐ Rogers & Bro. "Assyrian Head", *no monogram, excellent condition*	15.00	17.00
☐ Rogers & Bro. "Assyrian Head", *no monogram, resilvered* .	12.00	14.00
☐ Rogers & Bro. "Assyrian Head", *no monogram, good condition*	9.00	11.00
☐ Rogers & Bro. "Assyrian Head", *no monogram, poor condition*	2.00	3.00
☐ Rogers & Bro. "Cromwell", *no monogram, mint condition* ..	5.00	6.00
☐ Rogers & Bro. "Cromwell", *no monogram, fair condition* ...	1.00	2.00
☐ Rogers & Bro. "Crown", *no monogram, excellent condition*	4.00	5.00
☐ Rogers & Bro. "Crown", *no monogram, good condition*	2.00	3.00
☐ Rogers & Bro. "Crown", *no monogram, fair condition*	1.00	2.00
☐ Rogers & Bro. "Flemish", *no monogram, excellent condition*	8.00	9.00
☐ Rogers & Bro. "Flemish", *no monogram, good condition* ..	7.00	8.00
☐ Rogers & Bro. "Flemish", *no monogram, good condition* ..	6.00	7.00
☐ Rogers & Bro. "Laurel", *no monogram, excellent condition*	6.00	7.00
☐ Rogers & Bro. "Laurel", *no monogram, good condition*	4.00	5.00
☐ Rogers & Bro. "Laurel", *no monogram, fair condition*	2.00	3.00
☐ Rogers & Bro. "Mystic", *no monogram, excellent condition*	4.00	5.00
☐ Rogers & Bro. "Mystic", *no monogram, good condition* ...	4.00	5.00
☐ Rogers & Bro. "Mystic", *no monogram, fair condition*	1.00	2.00
☐ Rogers & Bro. "Navarre", *no monogram, mint condition* ...	6.00	7.00
☐ Rogers & Bro. "Navarre", *no monogram, good condition* ..	5.00	6.00
☐ Rogers & Bro. "New Century", *no monogram, excellent condition*	7.00	8.00
☐ Rogers & Bro. "New Century", *no monogram, excellent condition*	8.00	9.00
☐ Rogers & Bro. "New Century", *no monogram, good condition*	6.00	7.00
☐ Rogers & Hamilton "Raphael", *no monogram, excellent condition*	7.00	8.00

Price Range

☐ Rogers & Hamilton "Raphael", *no monogram, excellent condition*	9.00	10.00
☐ Rogers & Hamilton "Raphael", *no monogram, good condition*	6.00	7.00
☐ S.L. & G.H. Rogers "English Garden", *monogram, excellent condition*	3.00	4.00
☐ S.L. & G.H. Rogers "English Garden", *no monogram, excellent condition*	6.00	7.00
☐ Stratford "Lilytha", *no monogram, excellent condition*	8.00	9.00
☐ Stratford "Lilytha", *no monogram, poor condition*	2.00	3.00
☐ Tudor "Friendship", *no monogram, excellent condition* ...	3.00	4.00
☐ Tudor "Friendship", *no monogram, excellent condition* ...	6.00	7.00
☐ Tudor "Mary Stuart", *no monogram, excellent condition* ..	4.00	5.00
☐ Tudor "Mary Stuart", *no monogram, good condition*	4.00	5.00
☐ Tudor "Together", *no monogram, mint condition*	4.00	5.00
☐ Tudor "Together", *pierced, no monogram, excellent condition*	6.00	7.00
☐ Tudor "Together", *pierced, no monogram, good condition* .	5.00	6.00
☐ Wallace "Floral", *no monogram, excellent condition*	8.00	9.00
☐ Wallace "Floral", *no monogram, excellent condition*	11.00	13.00
☐ Wallace "Floral", *no monogram, good condition*	6.00	7.00
☐ W.D. Smith "Adam", *no monogram, excellent condition* ...	6.00	7.00
☐ W.D. Smith "Adam", *monogram, excellent condition*	3.00	4.00
☐ W.D. Smith "Adam", *no monogram, fair condition*	1.00	2.00
☐ Wm. Rogers "Melrose", *no monogram, excellent condition*	4.00	5.00
☐ Wm. Rogers "Melrose", *no monogram, fair condition*	1.00	2.00
☐ Wm. Rogers Mfg. Co. "Regent", *no monogram, mint condition*	5.00	6.00
☐ Wm. Rogers Mfg. Co. "Regent", *no monogram, good condition*	4.00	5.00
☐ Wm. A. Rogers "Debutante", *no monogram, excellent condition*	4.00	5.00
☐ Wm. A. Rogers "Debutante", *no monogram, fair condition* .	1.00	2.00
☐ Wm. A. Rogers "Debutante", *monogram, poor condition* ..	1.00	2.00
☐ Wm. A. Rogers "Elmore", *no monogram, excellent condition*	5.00	6.00
☐ Wm. A. Rogers "Elmore", *no monogram, good condition* ..	5.00	6.00
☐ Wm. A. Rogers "Garland", *no monogram, excellent condition*	5.00	6.00
☐ Wm. A. Rogers "Garland", *no monogram, good condition* .	5.00	6.00
☐ Wm. A. Rogers "Grenoble", *no monogram, excellent condition*	7.00	8.00
☐ Wm. A. Rogers "Grenoble", *no monogram, fair condition* ..	4.00	5.00
☐ Wm. A. Rogers "Grenoble", *no monogram, good condition*	6.00	7.00
☐ Wm. A. Rogers "Hanover", *no monogram, resilvered*	7.00	8.00
☐ Wm. A. Rogers "Hanover", *no monogram, fair condition* ...	4.00	5.00
☐ Wm. A. Rogers "Hanover", *no monogram, good condition* .	6.00	7.00
☐ Wm. A. Rogers "LaConcorde", *no monogram, resilvered* ..	8.00	9.00
☐ Wm. A. Rogers "LaConcorde", *no monogram, fair condition*	3.00	4.00
☐ Wm. A. Rogers "LaConcorde", *no monogram, good condition*	5.00	6.00
☐ Wm. A. Rogers "LaConcorde", *no monogram, excellent condition*	8.00	9.00

	Price Range	
☐ **Wm. A. Rogers "LaVigne",** *no monogram, good condition* .	5.00	6.00
☐ **Wm. A. Rogers "LaVigne",** *no monogram, excellent condition*	9.00	10.00
☐ **Wm. A. Rogers "LaVigne",** *no monogram, mint condition* ..	10.00	11.00
☐ **Wm. A. Rogers "Marcella",** *no monogram, good condition* .	3.00	4.00
☐ **Wm. A. Rogers "Violet",** *no monogram, excellent condition*	7.00	8.00
☐ **Wm. A. Rogers "Violet",** *no monogram, fair condition*	1.00	2.00
☐ **Wm. R. Rogers "Juliette",** *no monogram, excellent condition*	4.00	5.00
☐ **Wm. R. Rogers "Juliette",** *pierced, no monogram, excellent condition*	4.00	5.00
☐ **Wm. R. Rogers "Juliette",** *pierced, no monogram, good condition*	4.00	5.00
☐ **Wm. Rogers "Beloved",** *no monogram, excellent condition*	4.00	5.00
☐ **Wm. Rogers "Beloved",** *no monogram, good condition*	4.00	5.00
☐ **Wm. Rogers "Beloved",** *no monogram, fair condition*	1.00	2.00
☐ **Wm. Rogers "Carrollton",** *no monogram, excellent condition*	4.00	5.00
☐ **Wm. Rogers "Carrollton",** *no monogram, good condition* ...	3.00	4.00
☐ **Wm. Rogers "Exquisite",** *no monogram, excellent condition*	4.00	5.00
☐ **Wm. Rogers "Exquisite",** *no monogram, good condition* ...	4.00	5.00
☐ **Wm. Rogers "Oxford",** *monogram, good condition*	2.00	3.00
☐ **Wm. Rogers "Oxford",** *no monogram, excellent condition* .	7.00	8.00
☐ **Wm. Rogers "Oxford",** *no monogram, fair condition*	1.00	2.00
☐ **Wm. Rogers "Treasure",** *no monogram, excellent condition*	4.00	5.00
☐ **Wm. Rogers "Treasure",** *no monogram, good condition* ...	4.00	5.00
☐ **Wm. Rogers Eagle "Melrose",** *no monogram, good condition*	3.00	4.00
☐ **Wm. Rogers Mfg. Co. "Alhambra",** *no monogram, excellent condition*	4.00	5.00
☐ **Wm. Rogers Mfg. Co. "Alhambra",** *no monogram, good condition*	3.00	4.00
☐ **Wm. Rogers Mfg. Co. "Arbutus",** *monogram, good condition*	4.00	5.00
☐ **Wm. Rogers Mfg. Co. "Arbutus",** *no monogram, good condition*	5.00	6.00
☐ **Wm. Rogers Mfg. Co. "Berwick",** *no monogram, resilvered* .	4.00	5.00
☐ **Wm. Rogers Mfg. Co. "Berwick",** *no monogram, excellent condition*	8.00	9.00
☐ **Wm. Rogers Mfg. Co. "Countess",** *no monogram, excellent condition*	4.00	5.00
☐ **Wm. Rogers Mfg. Co. "Florida",** *no monogram, excellent condition*	4.00	5.00
☐ **Wm. Rogers Mfg. Co. "Florida",** *no monogram, good condition*	3.00	5.00
☐ **Wm. Rogers Mfg. Co. "Florida",** *no monogram, poor condition*	1.00	2.00
☐ **1835 R. Wallace,** *unknown floral pattern, monogram, fair condition*	1.00	2.00
☐ **1847 Rogers "Adoration",** *no monogram, excellent condition*	4.00	5.00
☐ **1847 Rogers "Adoration",** *no monogram, good condition* ..	5.00	6.00

Price Range

☐ 1847 Rogers "Arcadian", *no monogram, excellent condition*	7.00	8.00
☐ 1847 Rogers "Arcadian", *no monogram, fair condition*	3.00	4.00
☐ 1847 Rogers "Arcadian", *no monogram, poor condition* ...	1.00	2.00
☐ 1847 Rogers "Assyrian", *monogram, excellent condition* ..	7.00	8.00
☐ 1847 Rogers "Avon", *no monogram, good condition*	4.00	5.00
☐ 1847 Rogers "Avon", *no monogram, fair condition*	2.00	3.00
☐ 1847 Rogers "Berkshire", *no monogram, resilvered*	7.00	8.00
☐ 1847 Rogers "Berkshire", *no monogram, excellent condition*	9.00	10.00
☐ 1847 Rogers "Berkshire", *no monogram, good condition* ..	8.00	9.00
☐ 1847 Rogers "Berkshire", *no monogram, fair condition*	2.00	3.00
☐ 1847 Rogers "Charter Oak", *monogram, good condition* ...	5.00	6.00
☐ 1847 Rogers "Charter Oak", *monogram, bowl tip rounded off to eliminate wear spot, resilvered*	5.00	6.00
☐ 1847 Rogers "Charter Oak", *no monogram, resilvered*	9.00	10.00
☐ 1847 Rogers "Charter Oak", *no monogram, excellent condition*	8.00	9.00
☐ 1847 Rogers "Columbia", *no monogram, resilvered*	10.00	11.00
☐ 1847 Rogers "Columbia", *no monogram, excellent condition*	8.00	9.00
☐ 1847 Rogers "Columbia", *no monogram, resilvered*	9.00	10.00
☐ 1847 Rogers "Columbia", *monogram, excellent condition* .	7.00	8.00
☐ 1847 Rogers "Daffodil", *no monogram, excellent condition*	7.00	8.00
☐ 1847 Rogers "Daffodil", *no monogram, good condition* ...	6.00	7.00
☐ 1847 Rogers "Daffodil", *no monogram, fair condition*	2.00	3.00
☐ 1847 Rogers "Esperanto", *no monogram, excellent condition*	4.00	5.00
☐ 1847 Rogers "Esperanto", *pierced, no monogram, excellent condition*	4.00	5.00
☐ 1847 Rogers "Esperanto", *no monogram, good condition* ..	4.00	5.00
☐ 1847 Rogers "First Love", *no monogram, excellent condition*	4.00	5.00
☐ 1847 Rogers "First Love", *no monogram, good condition* ..	4.00	5.00
☐ 1847 Rogers "Flair", *no monogram, excellent condition* ...	4.00	5.00
☐ 1847 Rogers "Flair", *no monogram, fair condition*	1.00	2.00
☐ 1847 Rogers "Flair", *pierced, no monogram, excellent condition*	4.00	5.00
☐ 1847 Rogers "Flair", *pierced, no monogram, good condition*	4.00	5.00
☐ 1847 Rogers "Floral", *no monogram, excellent condition* ..	11.00	13.00
☐ 1847 Rogers "Floral", *no monogram, fair condition*	2.00	3.00
☐ 1847 Rogers "Floral", *no monogram, poor condition*	1.00	2.00
☐ 1847 Rogers "Floral", *monogram, excellent condition*	7.00	8.00
☐ 1847 Rogers "Garland", *pierced, no monogram, excellent condition*	4.00	5.00
☐ 1847 Rogers "Garland", *pierced, no monogram, good condition*	5.00	6.00
☐ 1847 Rogers "Grand Heritage", *no monogram, excellent condition*	4.00	5.00
☐ 1847 Rogers "Grand Heritage", *no monogram, excellent condition*	6.00	7.00
☐ 1847 Rogers "Grecian", *no monogram, excellent condition*	4.00	5.00
☐ 1847 Rogers "Grecian", *no monogram, fair condition*	1.00	2.00
☐ 1847 Rogers "Heraldic", *no monogram, excellent condition*	4.00	5.00

	Price Range	
☐ **1847 Rogers "Heraldic"**, *no monogram, poor condition*	**1.00**	**2.00**
☐ **1847 Rogers "Heritage"**, *pierced, no monogram, excellent condition*	**5.00**	**6.00**
☐ **1847 Rogers "Heritage"**, *pierced, no monogram, mint condition*	**6.00**	**7.00**
☐ **1847 Rogers "Heritage"**, *pierced, no monogram, fair condition*	**2.00**	**3.00**
☐ **1847 Rogers "Heritage"**, *pierced, no monogram, poor condition*	**1.00**	**2.00**
☐ **1847 Rogers "Lorne"**, *no monogram, excellent condition* ..	**7.00**	**8.00**
☐ **1847 Rogers "Lorne"**, *no monogram, good condition*	**6.00**	**7.00**
☐ **1847 Rogers "Lorne"**, *no monogram, fair condition*	**1.00**	**2.00**
☐ **1847 Rogers "Magic Rose"**, *no monogram, excellent condition*	**5.00**	**6.00**
☐ **1847 Rogers "Magic Rose"**, *no monogram, good condition*	**4.00**	**5.00**
☐ **1847 Rogers "Magic Rose"**, *no monogram, fair condition* ..	**1.00**	**2.00**
☐ **1847 Rogers "Magic Rose"**, *pierced, no monogram, excellent condition*	**6.00**	**7.00**
☐ **1847 Rogers "Magic Rose"**, *pierced, no monogram, poor condition*	**1.00**	**2.00**
☐ **1847 Rogers "Moline"**, *no monogram, excellent condition* .	**4.00**	**5.00**
☐ **1847 Rogers "Moline"**, *no monogram, good condition*	**4.00**	**5.00**
☐ **1847 Rogers "Moline"**, *no monogram, fair condition*	**1.00**	**2.00**
☐ **1847 Rogers "Moselle"**, *no monogram, resilvered*	**19.00**	**21.00**
☐ **1847 Rogers "Moselle"**, *no monogram, excellent condition*	**14.00**	**16.00**
☐ **1847 Rogers "Moselle"**, *no monogram, good condition*	**16.00**	**18.00**
☐ **1847 Rogers "Moselle"**, *no monogram, fair condition*	**4.00**	**5.00**
☐ **1847 Rogers "Moselle"**, *no monogram, poor condition*	**3.00**	**4.00**
☐ **1847 Rogers "Old Colony"**, *no monogram, poor condition* .	**1.00**	**2.00**
☐ **1847 Rogers "Old Colony"**, *no monogram, good condition* .	**4.00**	**5.00**
☐ **1847 Rogers "Old Colony"**, *no monogram, excellent condition*	**5.00**	**6.00**
☐ **1847 Rogers "Old Colony"**, *monogram, good condition*	**2.00**	**3.00**
☐ **1847 Rogers "Old Colony"**, *monogram and date, mint condition*	**5.00**	**6.00**
☐ **1847 Rogers "Persian"**, *no monogram, good condition*	**7.00**	**8.00**
☐ **1847 Rogers "Persian"**, *no monogram, fair condition*	**2.00**	**3.00**
☐ **1847 Rogers "Persian"**, *no monogram, poor condition*	**1.00**	**2.00**
☐ **1847 Rogers "Remembrance"**, *no monogram, mint condition*	**6.00**	**7.00**
☐ **1847 Rogers "Remembrance"**, *no monogram, excellent condition*	**6.00**	**7.00**
☐ **1847 Rogers "Saratoga"**, *no monogram, excellent condition*	**4.00**	**5.00**
☐ **1847 Rogers "Saratoga"**, *no monogram, good condition* ...	**4.00**	**5.00**
☐ **1847 Rogers "Saratoga"**, *no monogram, fair condition*	**1.00**	**2.00**
☐ **1847 Rogers "Sharon"**, *monogram, excellent condition* ...	**5.00**	**6.00**
☐ **1847 Rogers "Sharon"**, *no monogram, excellent condition* .	**8.00**	**9.00**
☐ **1847 Rogers "Springtime"**, *no monogram, excellent condition*	**4.00**	**5.00**
☐ **1847 Rogers "Springtime"**, *no monogram, good condition* .	**4.00**	**5.00**
☐ **1847 Rogers "Vintage"**, *no monogram, good condition*	**9.00**	**11.00**
☐ **1847 Rogers "Vintage"**, *no monogram, fair condition*	**4.00**	**5.00**

	Price Range	
☐ 1847 Rogers "Vintage", *no monogram, good condition*	9.00	11.00
☐ 1847 Rogers "Vintage", *no monogram, excellent condition*	12.00	14.00
☐ 1847 Rogers "Vintage", *no monogram, resilvered*	14.00	16.00
☐ 1847 Rogers "Vintage", *no monogram, fair condition*	5.00	6.00
☐ 1847 Rogers "Vintage", *monogram, fair condition*	4.00	5.00
☐ 1847 Rogers "Vintage", *monogram, poor condition*	2.00	3.00
☐ 1847 Rogers "Vintage", *monogram, poor condition*	2.00	3.00
☐ 1881 Rogers "LaVigne", *no monogram, excellent condition*	6.00	7.00
☐ 1881 Rogers "LaVigne", *no monogram, mint condition*	7.00	8.00
☐ 1881 Rogers "LaVigne", *no monogram, good condition* ...	6.00	7.00
☐ 1881 Rogers "LaVigne", *no monogram, fair condition*	2.00	3.00
☐ 1881 Rogers "LaVigne", *no monogram, poor condition*	1.00	2.00

(Sterling Silver)

☐ Dominick & Haff "Renaissance", *monogram*	38.00	42.00
☐ Dominick & Haff "Renaissance", *pierced, monogram*	40.00	45.00
☐ Durgin "Fairfax", *8½" L., no monogram*	27.00	30.00
☐ Durgin "Fairfax", *8½" L., no monogram*	30.00	33.00
☐ Durgin "New Vintage", *monogram*	27.00	30.00
☐ Frank Smith "Chippendale", *no monogram*	19.00	21.00
☐ Frank Smith "Fiddle Thread", *pierced, no monogram*	38.00	42.00
☐ Frank Smith "Fiddle Thread", *no monogram*	38.00	42.00
☐ Frank Whiting "Palm", *8" L., monogram*	27.00	30.00
☐ Gorham "Blithe Spirit", *no monogram*	33.00	36.00
☐ Gorham "Chantilly", *no monogram*	35.00	38.00
☐ Gorham "Chantilly", *no monogram*	32.00	36.00
☐ Gorham "Etruscan", *monogram*	27.00	30.00
☐ Gorham "Fairfax", *8⅜" L., no monogram*	28.00	31.00
☐ Gorham "Imperial Chrysanthemum", *monogram*	22.00	24.00
☐ Gorham "Imperial Chrysanthemum", *no monogram*	22.00	24.00
☐ Gorham "King George", *monogram*	36.00	40.00
☐ Gorham "Lancaster Rose", *monogram*	26.00	29.00
☐ Gorham "Luxembourg", *monogram*	30.00	34.00
☐ Gorham "Medallion", *no monogram*	27.00	30.00
☐ Gorham "Newcastle", *monogram*	24.00	27.00
☐ Gorham "Norfolk", *monogram*	30.00	33.00
☐ Gorham "Plymouth", *monogram*	24.00	27.00
☐ Gorham "Versailles", *no monogram*	33.00	36.00
☐ International "Angelique", *pierced, monogram*	33.00	36.00
☐ International "Avalon", *monogram*	42.00	47.00
☐ International "Bridal Veil", *no monogram*	28.00	31.00
☐ International "Courtship", *no monogram*	29.00	32.00
☐ International "Courtship", *no monogram*	30.00	34.00
☐ International "Crystal", *pierced, no monogram*	36.00	40.00
☐ International "Crystal", *no monogram*	32.00	36.00
☐ International "Edgewood",	40.00	45.00
☐ International "Fontaine", *no monogram*	34.00	38.00
☐ International "Irene", *no monogram*	25.00	27.00
☐ International "Kenilworth", ...	22.00	24.00
☐ International "Royal Danish", *pierced, no monogram*	36.00	40.00
☐ International "Royal Danish", *no monogram*	32.00	36.00
☐ Lunt "Mt. Vernon", *8½" L., no monogram*	20.00	22.00
☐ Manchester "Vogue", *no monogram*	30.00	33.00
☐ Oneida "Lasting Spring", *no monogram*	27.00	30.00

	Price Range	
☐ Reed & Barton "Francis I", *large, no monogram*	45.00	50.00
☐ Reed & Barton "LaReine", *monogram*	27.00	30.00
☐ Reed & Barton "Les Six Fleurs", *no monogram*	25.00	27.00
☐ Reed & Barton "Marlborough", *no monogram*	30.00	33.00
☐ Reed & Barton "Savannah", *no monogram*	36.00	40.00
☐ Simpson, Hall & Miller "Frontenac", *no monogram*	27.00	30.00
☐ Tiffany "Persian", *monogram*	18.00	20.00
☐ Tiffany "Renaissance", *no monogram*	19.00	21.00
☐ Tiffany "Wave Edge", *large, no monogram*	14.00	16.00
☐ Towle "Chippendale", *no monogram*	27.00	30.00
☐ Towle "French Provincial", *monogram*	33.00	36.00
☐ Towle "Georgian", *no monogram*	38.00	42.00
☐ Towle "Georgian", *no monogram*	27.00	30.00
☐ Towle "Georgian", *monogram and date*	27.00	30.00
☐ Towle "Kings", *pierced, no monogram*	40.00	45.00
☐ Towle "Old Colonial", *no monogram*	38.00	42.00
☐ Towle "Old Colonial", *pierced, no monogram*	38.00	42.00
☐ Whiting "Grecian", *no monogram*	20.00	23.00
☐ Whiting "Imperial Queen", *no monogram*	40.00	45.00
☐ Whiting "Imperial Queen", *no monogram*	14.00	16.00
☐ Whiting "Imperial Queen", *no monogram*	20.00	23.00
☐ Whiting "Ivy", *monogram*	36.00	39.00
☐ Whiting "King Albert", *monogram*	19.00	21.00
☐ Whiting "Lily", *no monogram*	42.00	48.00
☐ Whiting "Louis XV", *8⅛" L., monogram*	23.00	26.00
☐ Whiting "Madame Jumel", *no monogram*	20.00	23.00
☐ Maker unknown, *plain pattern, no monogram*	34.00	38.00

TALC SHAKERS

Designed for dispensing talcum powder or similar products, talc shakers never got got far on the commercial market. When packaged talcum powder was first brought out, talc shakers made sense, as the original store packages were nothing but screw-cap cans. When transferred from this into a talc shaker, use was far more convenient. Very soon, however, the powder makers saw the error of their ways and began putting up talcum powder in shake-top cans. Though the store cans were not silver, they were very colorfully printed and few people objected to using them "as is." Thus the market for silver talc shakers was dealt a crushing blow.

(Sterling Silver)

☐ Maker unknown, *plain shape with beading on top and bottom rims, monogram*	22.00	25.00

(Sterling and Crystal)

☐ Maker unknown, *sterling and crystal, strawberry diamond cutting on crystal, repousse floral design and beaded rim on sterling top*	68.00	75.00

TEA AND COFFEE SERVICES

There were so many variations, in terms of the components supplied in tea and coffee service sets, that any attempt to describe them would be useless. They ranged greatly in opulence, too, from very simple patterns in lightweight silver to services fit for royalty. When these are listed for sale by a retail dealer, the total weight is customarily stated, and the difference between bullion value and the dealer's selling price serves as an indication of artistic merit and collector appeal. Often the difference is relatively slight, no more than 20% or 30% above "spot," but for an especially elegant service the price could be double its bullion value. Tea and coffee services were melted profusely when the value of silver went skyrocketing between October, 1979 and January, 1980. Generally speaking, a dealer will pay some kind of premium — even if VERY slight — for any better-than-average service, over and above the bullion value. Be careful of "loading," as these sets offer wonderful opportunity for such practices. With at least two and possibly three large pieces involved (two pots and a kettle), modest loading here and there could add several extra pounds to the aggregate weight.

(Silver-Plated)   **Price Range**

☐ **International,** *six-piece set includes coffeepot, teapot, sugar, creamer, waste bowl, and tray, good condition, plain design, monogram* 95.00   105.00

☐ **Maker unknown,** *four-piece set includes coffeepot, teapot, sugar and creamer, monogram, good condition* 80.00   90.00

(Sterling Silver)

☐ **Amston Silver Co.,** *five-piece set includes teapot, coffeepot, sugar, creamer and waste bowl, early 20th c., hand-chased with scrolls and flowers, pierced and chased footed bases, coffee 9½" H., total weight 96 oz.* 1,000.00   1,125.00

☐ *Two pieces marked P.L. Krider Co., four marked J.E. Caldwell & Co., Philadelphia, six-piece set includes teapot, coffeepot, hot water pot, creamer, covered sugar, and waste bowl, repousse design, twig handles, child-shaped finials, coffeepot 10" H., total weight 153 oz.* 5,350.00   5,850.00

☐ **Gorham,** *six-piece set includes coffeepot, tea kettle on stand, covered sugar, creamer, waste bowl and two-handled tray, c. 1922, engraved and chased with fruit, shells, and strapwork, ivory insulators, coffeepot 8½" H., tray 29" L., total weight 225 oz.* 2,520.00   2,800.00

☐ **Gorham,** *seven-piece set includes coffeepot, teapot, creamer, covered sugar, hot water kettle and stand, wast bowl, and handled tray, foliate chasing, total weight 258 oz.* 4,350.00   4,825.00

☐ **Gorham,** *six-piece set includes coffeepot, tea kettle on stand, covered sugar, creamer and waste bowl, decorated with ribbons and scrolls, c. 1916, total weight 162 oz.* 3,400.00   3,775.00

☐ **Harris & Shafer,** *seven-piece set includes teapot, coffeepot, kettle on stand, covered sugar, creamer, waste bowl and two-handled tray, c. 1900, pyriform shape, floral chasing, footed bases with flowers, floral knops, tray has floral rim and handles, diaper pattern center, coffeepot 10¾" H., total weight 347 oz.* 8,325.00   9,250.00

☐ **International,** *seven-piece set includes coffeepot, teapot, kettle on stand, covered sugar, creamer, waste bowl and two-handled tray, "Charleroi" pattern, embossed and chased flowers, scrolls and foliage, applied borders, coffeepot 10¾" H., tray 25¼" L., total weight 222 oz.* 2,225.00   2,475.00

☐ **Kirk,** *five-piece set includes teapot, coffeepot, tea kettle, covered sugar and creamer, "Repousse" pattern, turn-of-the-century markings* 3,500.00   3,900.00

Tea, Coffee Set, *Wm. Gale and Son, "Medallion,"*
1862, 82 ounces, 3500.00

Price Range

☐ **Ritter & Sullivan,** *four-piece set includes teapot, coffeepot, sugar and creamer, repousse design* 800.00 900.00

☐ **Shreve, Crump & Low (Boston), retailers,** *sterling silver, six-piece set includes teapot, coffeepot, kettle on stand, covered sugar, creamer and waste bowl, early 20th c., coffee pot 9¾" H., total weight 127 oz.* 1,080.00 1,200.00

☐ **Stieff,** *five-piece set includes teapot, coffeepot, sugar bowl, creamer and waste bowl, floral repousse design, coffeepot 8½" H., total weight 91 oz, with silver-plated tray, 29" handle to handle* 3,400.00 3,775.00

☐ **Stieff,** *six-piece set includes teapot, coffeepot, covered sugar, creamer, waste bowl and tea caddy, with silver-plated tray, repousse design with applied floral borders, no monogram, total silver weight 108 oz.* 4,500.00 5,000.00

☐ **Theodore B. Starr (New York City), retailer,** *sterling silver, six-piece set includes coffeepot, teapot, tea kettle on stand, covered sugar, creamer, waste bowl, and two-handled tray, c. 1910, chased and engraved with floral and foliate designs, similar decoration on handles, rims and bases, coffeepot 11" H., tray 32" handle to handle, total weight 363 oz.* 4,450.00 4,950.00

☐ **Tiffany,** *six-piece set includes coffeepot, teapot, kettle on stand, covered sugar, creamer and waste bowl, silver-plated matching tray, c. 1920, rectangular shape, no monograms, coffeepot 9" H., total silver weight 143 oz.* ... 3,000.00 3,300.00

☐ **Tiffany,** *nine-piece set includes coffeepot, teapot, hot water pot, creamer, covered sugar, waste bowl, pair of salt and pepper shakers, rectangular tray, c. 1880, floral and foliate chasing, coffeepot 7¾" H., total weight 90 oz.* 2,350.00 2,600.00

☐ **Maker unknown,** *Bailey, Banks & Biddle Co. retailer, c. 1920, seven-piece set includes coffeepot, teapot, kettle on stand, covered sugar, creamer, waste bowl, and two-handled tray, fluted shield shape bodies, square plinth bases, urn-shaped knops, engraved bands of foliage on bodies and bases, coffeepot 12" H., tray 28" L., total weight 280 oz.* 2,675.00 2,975.00

TEA CADDIES

These are small cannisters in which tea leaves were kept prior to use. Fads for exotic teas prevailed in olden times, just as today; so the well-stocked larder would have many tea caddies, each containing a different blend. Daring souls even concocted their own, by mixing some of one blend and some of another. This is essentially what the domestic tea companies did in the 19th century, taking imported teas and mixing them together with various recipes to tempt the public's taste. Tea caddies are often very handsomely decorated, and were frequently used for other kitchen purposes beside storage of tea. Their walls are thin and the weight is considerably less than one would estimate from their size.

Tea Caddy, *(sterling),*
Bailey, Banks & Biddle,
5 ounces, 120.00

(Silver-Plated)	Price	Range
☐ Meriden, *embossed leaves and branches, hunting scene,* *excellent condition*	54.00	60.00
☐ **Maker unknown,** *ornate engraved design, monogram and* *date*	25.00	27.00
(Sterling Silver)		
☐ **Kirk,** *plain design, monogram weight 4 oz.*	48.00	54.00
☐ **Maker unknown,** *hammered finish, raised monogram*	45.00	50.00

TEA INFUSERS

In a sense these were the forerunners of the tea *bag.* Boiling tea in the common manner led to tea leaves in one's cup. While this was ideal for reading fortunes, it was objectionable to many people. A solution was the *tea infuser,* a small container, pierced with holes, which could be filled with tea and suspended into the kettle for brewing. They were not without their drawbacks: tea took longer to brew when an infuser was used, and, in the opinion of those with sensitive tastebuds, acquired a hint of metallic flavor. Generally, tea infusers were used with ceramic kettles rather than metal, to avoid metallic flavor. They achieved some popularity but never put the old-fashioned teapot out of business. It is important to keep in mind that tea infusers were NEVER — unlike tea bags — used in making tea in individual cups; they were always used in kettles. Since no standard shape was necessary, the makers could, and did, let their imaginations go wild. Some were made in the likeness of miniature teapots. Tea infusers are intriguing to collect, but, unfortunately, not a great many are to be found. If the chain is missing this detracts from the value.

Tea Infusers, *(L to R) (sterling),* makers unknown, 36.00 - 36.00, and 45.00

(Silver-Plated)

☐ 1847 Rogers "Olive", *no monogram, excellent condition* ...	18.00	20.00

(Sterling Silver)

☐ **Durgin "Fairfax",** *spoon type, no monogram*	20.00	22.00
☐ **Gorham "Buttercup",** *no monogram*	90.00	100.00
☐ **Gorham "Cambridge",** *no monogram*	45.00	50.00
☐ **Gorham,** *ball type, overall repousse rose design*	40.00	45.00
☐ **Kirk "Repousse",** *ball type*	60.00	66.00
☐ **Tiffany "Richelieu",** *spoon type, no monogram*	95.00	105.00
☐ **Maker unknown,** *ball type, shaped like World War II submarine*	72.00	80.00

TEA KNIVES

Domestically made teas were nearly always packaged loose, in boxes or bags. Those imported into the U.S. market in the 19th and early 20th centuries, especially teas of Chinese, Tibetan and Manchurian origins, often came in solid bricks or cakes and had to be cut with a knife. The practice of selling tea in brick fashion is, in the Orient, of extremely ancient origins. The makers impressed their signs and symbols in it, along with decorative pictures. Tea bricks were occasionally used as money, as they carried fixed values, and are avidly collected by enthusiasts of "odd and curious money."

(Silver-Plated)

☐ 1847 Rogers "Persian", *no monogram, excellent condition*	2.00	3.00
☐ 1847 Rogers "Persian", *no monogram, good condition*	2.00	3.00

(Sterling Silver)

☐ **Maker unknown,** *king pattern, monogram and date*	11.00	13.00

TEAPOTS

We can scarcely do justice, in our brief space, to this immense group of objects. Teapots have been made in silver since the beginnings of tea drinking popularity (the 17th century), and have reflected all styles from then until now. They will be found in classical revival and all its branches, in Louis XIV, and many native American designs. Some specimens were elegantly decorated before leaving the manufacturer's hands. Others went on sale with plain undecorated sides, to be engraved with the purchaser's coat-of-arms and family name. They vary in size and weight, too, though the variations are much more noticeable in teapots of the 19th century than those of the 20th. The impressive silver specimens served as models for manufacturers putting out teapots in stainless steel.

Tea Kettle, *silver-plated, maker unknown, Victorian era,* 90.00

(Silver-Plated)

☐ **Wilcox,** *bright-cut decoration, mint condition* 28.00   34.00

☐ **Maker unknown,** *pedestal base, 10" H., finial of grapes and leaves, more grapes on handle and spout, excellent condition* 32.00   36.00

☐ **Maker unknown,** *round-bodied, engraved with scroll design, monogram* 65.00   72.00

(Sterling Silver)

☐ **Maker unknown,** *plain pattern, weight 12 oz.* 200.00   225.00

TEA SETS

Tea sets generally consisted of three pieces: a teapot, creamer and sugar bowl. Retailing in sets pre-dates the era of factory production. Most of the remarks made in connection with tea and coffee services (see above) apply equally here.

Three-piece Tea Set, coin silver, *J. & I. Cox (New York, c. 1840), total weight 61 ounces,* 1075.00

(Silver-Plated)
☐ **Maker unknown,** *engraved ornate design, includes teapot, sugar and creamer, monogram, fair condition* 30.00   33.00

(Sterling Silver)
☐ **Tiffany,** *c. 1860's, Empire styling, ovoid body on paw feet with cherub supports, chased handles and spouts, chased in foliage design, applied banding of acanthus leaves on rims, includes teapot, tea kettle on stand, sugar bowl with swing handle, and waste bowl (no creamer), teapot 9½" H., total weight 117 oz.* 1,620.00   1,800.00
☐ **Unger Bros.,** *repousse design in Art Nouveau style, includes teapot, sugar and creamer, teapot 7½" H., sugar and creamer each 4" H., weight unknown* 350.00   390.00
☐ **Maker unknown,** *fluted Georgian shape, c. 1900, includes teapot, sugar and creamer, teapot 3¾" H., sugar 2¾" H., weight unknown* 175.00   195.00
☐ **Maker unknown,** *c. 1930, Art Deco styling, includes teapot, covered creamer, covered sugar, matching oval tray, stylized leaf knops, tray 20½" L., total weight 98 oz.* 825.00   925.00

TEASPOONS

Here the available selection is so huge that the collector can well afford to specialize in one way or another. Among the most popular specialties are very early American-made silver teaspoons, of the colonial age and slightly later; and those sold in topical sets, each handle carrying a different design relating to some central theme. We are certainly all familiar with apostle spoons, which originated in Europe centuries ago and seem to have provided the impetus for all spoon "sets." Since the average spoon set is 12, makers have sought out themes which agree to that number: signs of the zodiac and months of the year are perfect. There are of course also many non-topical spoons, representing the diverse patterns used by silver manufacturers during the 19th and 20th centuries. Their low price, easy availability, and suitability for storage and display have ranked teaspoons near the forefront of hobbyist favor.

Zodiac Teaspoons, *(sterling), Watson-Newell, set of 12,* 275.00

(Coin Silver)

☐ Bailey, Portland, Maine, *c. 1835, monogram*	15.00	17.00
☐ Brasier, Philadelphia, *c. 1800, fiddleback*	54.00	60.00
☐ Burnham, *monogram*	15.00	17.00
☐ Getz, Lancaster, Pennsylvania, *c. 1780's, oval tip pattern, wear*	40.00	45.00
☐ Kinsley, Cincinnati, Ohio, *c. 1840's, monogram*	13.00	15.00
☐ Miller, Boston, *c. 1850, monogram*	13.00	15.00
☐ Olmsted, Farmington, Connecticut, *c. 1810, monogram* ...	22.00	25.00
☐ Prescott, Keeseville, New York, *c. 1820's, monogram*	8.00	9.00
☐ Shoemaker, Philadelphia, Pennsylvania, *c. 1830's, fiddleback*	10.00	13.00
☐ Story, ...	15.00	17.00
☐ Ward & Bartholomew, Hartford, Connecticut, *c. 1800's, fiddle thread & shell, monogram*	14.00	16.00
☐ White, New York City, *c. 1790's, oval tip, monogram*	40.00	45.00
☐ Maker's mark rubbed, *fiddleback, monogram*	6.00	7.00

(Silver-Plated)	Price Range	
☐ Alvin "Bride's Bouquet", *no monogram, excellent condition*	4.00	5.00
☐ Alvin "Bride's Bouquet", *no monogram, good condition* ...	3.00	4.00
☐ Alvin "Bride's Bouquet", *no monogram, fair condition*	1.00	2.00
☐ Alvin "Diana", *no monogram, excellent condition*	4.00	5.00
☐ Alvin "Diana", *no monogram, good condition*	3.00	4.00
☐ Alvin "Diana", *no monogram, fair condition*	1.00	2.00
☐ Alvin "Diana", *monogram, excellent condition*	1.00	2.00
☐ Alvin "Molly Stark", *no monogram, excellent condition*	4.00	5.00
☐ Alvin "Molly Stark", *no monogram, good condition*	3.00	4.00
☐ Alvin "Molly Stark", *monogram, good condition*	1.00	2.00
☐ American Silver Co. "Camelot", *no monogram, excellent condition*	2.00	3.00
☐ American Silver Co. "Camelot", *monogram, excellent condition*	1.00	2.00
☐ American Silver Co. "Rosalie", *no monogram, excellent condition*	4.00	5.00
☐ American Silver Co. "Rosalie", *no monogram, fair condition*	1.00	2.00
☐ American Silver Co. "Tours", *no monogram, excellent condition*	2.00	3.00
☐ American Silver Co. "Tours", *no monogram, good condition*	2.00	3.00
☐ Community "Adam", *no monogram, excellent condition* ..	2.00	3.00
☐ Community "Adam", *no monogram, excellent condition* ..	4.00	5.00
☐ Community "Adam", *no monogram, good condition*	3.00	4.00
☐ Community "Adam", *no monogram, fair condition*	1.00	2.00
☐ Community "Ballad", *no monogram, mint condition*	3.00	4.00
☐ Community "Ballad", *no monogram, excellent condition* ..	4.00	5.00
☐ Community "Ballad", *no monogram, good condition*	3.00	4.00
☐ Community "Ballad", *no monogram, fair condition*	1.00	2.00
☐ Community "Beverly", *no monogram, excellent condition* .	4.00	5.00
☐ Community "Beverly", *no monogram, good condition*	3.00	4.00
☐ Community "Beverly", *no monogram, fair condition*	1.00	2.00
☐ Community "Bird of Paradise", *no monogram, excellent condition*	4.00	5.00
☐ Community "Bird of Paradise", *no monogram, good condition*	2.00	3.00
☐ Community "Bird of Paradise", *no monogram, fair condition*	1.00	2.00
☐ Community "Bird of Paradise", *monogram, good condition*	1.00	2.00
☐ Community "Bird of Paradise", *monogram, fair condition* .	1.00	2.00
☐ Community "Coronation", *no monogram, excellent condition*	4.00	5.00
☐ Community "Coronation", *no monogram, good condition* .	3.00	4.00
☐ Community "Coronation", *no monogram, fair condition* ...	1.00	2.00
☐ Community "Coronation", *no monogram, poor condition* ..	1.00	2.00
☐ Community "Deauville", *no monogram, excellent condition*	4.00	5.00
☐ Community "Deauville", *no monogram, good condition* ...	3.00	4.00
☐ Community "Deauville", *no monogram, fair condition*	1.00	2.00
☐ Community "Enchantment", *no monogram, excellent condition*	4.00	5.00
☐ Community "Enchantment", *no monogram, good condition*	3.00	4.00
☐ Community "Enchantment", *no monogram, fair condition* .	1.00	2.00
☐ Community "Evening Star", *no monogram, excellent condition*	4.00	5.00
☐ Community "Evening Star", *no monogram, good condition*	3.00	4.00

	Price Range	
☐ Community **"Evening Star"**, *no monogram, fair condition* ..	1.00	2.00
☐ Community **"Evening Star"**, *monogram, good condition* ...	1.00	2.00
☐ Community **"Flight"**, *no monogram, good condition*	2.00	3.00
☐ Community **"Flight"**, *no monogram, fair condition*	1.00	2.00
☐ Community **"Georgian"**, *no monogram, excellent condition*	6.00	7.00
☐ Community **"Georgian"**, *no monogram, good condition* ...	5.00	6.00
☐ Community **"Georgian"**, *no monogram, good condition* ...	1.00	2.00
☐ Community **"Georgian"**, *no monogram, poor condition*	1.00	2.00
☐ Community **"Grosvenor"**, *no monogram, excellent condition*	2.00	3.00
☐ Community **"Grosvenor"**, *monogram, excellent condition* .	1.00	2.00
☐ Community **"Grosvenor"**, *monogram, fair condition*	1.00	2.00
☐ Community **"King Cedric"**, *no monogram, excellent condition*	4.00	5.00
☐ Community **"King Cedric"**, *no monogram, good condition* .	3.00	4.00
☐ Community **"Lady Hamilton"**, *no monogram, good condition*	3.00	4.00
☐ Community **"Lady Hamilton"**, *no monogram, poor condition*	1.00	2.00
☐ Community **"Lady Hamilton"**, *no monogram, excellent condition*	4.00	5.00
☐ Community **"Lady Hamilton"**, *no monogram, good condition*	3.00	4.00
☐ Community **"Louis XVI"**, *no monogram, good condition* ...	2.00	3.00
☐ Community **"Louis XVI"**, *no monogram, fair condition*	1.00	2.00
☐ Community **"Milady"**, *no monogram, excellent condition* ..	2.00	3.00
☐ Community **"Milady"**, *no monogram, good condition*	2.00	3.00
☐ Community **"Milady"**, *no monogram, excellent condition* ..	4.00	5.00
☐ Community **"Milady"**, *no monogram, fair condition*	1.00	2.00
☐ Community **"Morning Rose"**, *no monogram, mint condition*	2.00	3.00
☐ Community **"Morning Rose"**, *no monogram, excellent condition*	4.00	5.00
☐ Community **"Morning Rose"**, *no monogram, good condition*	3.00	4.00
☐ Community **"Morning Rose"**, *no monogram, poor condition*	1.00	2.00
☐ Community **"Morning Star"**, *no monogram, excellent condition*	4.00	5.00
☐ Community **"Morning Star"**, *no monogram, good condition*	3.00	4.00
☐ Community **"Morning Star"**, *no monogram, fair condition* .	1.00	2.00
☐ Community **"Noblesse"**, *no monogram, excellent condition*	2.00	3.00
☐ Community **"Noblesse"**, *no monogram, excellent condition*	4.00	5.00
☐ Community **"Noblesse"**, *no monogram, good condition* ...	3.00	4.00
☐ Community **"Noblesse"**, *no monogram, fair condition*	1.00	2.00
☐ Community **"Noblesse"**, *monogram, excellent condition* ..	2.00	3.00
☐ Community **"Patrician"**, *no monogram, excellent condition*	2.00	3.00
☐ Community **"Patrician"**, *monogram, excellent condition* ..	1.00	2.00
☐ Community **"Patrician"**, *no monogram, excellent condition*	4.00	5.00
☐ Community **"Patrician"**, *no monogram, good condition* ...	3.00	4.00
☐ Community **"Patrician"**, *no monogram, fair condition*	1.00	2.00
☐ Community **"Paul Revere"**, *no monogram, excellent condition*	4.00	5.00
☐ Community **"Paul Revere"**, *no monogram, good condition* .	3.00	4.00
☐ Community **"Paul Revere"**, *no monogram, fair condition* ..	1.00	2.00
☐ Community **"Randolph"**, *no monogram, excellent condition*	4.00	5.00

Price Range

☐ Community "Randolph", *no monogram, good condition* ...	3.00	4.00
☐ Community "Randolph", *no monogram, fair condition*	1.00	2.00
☐ Community "Sheraton", *no monogram, excellent condition*	4.00	5.00
☐ Community "Sheraton", *no monogram, good condition* ...	3.00	4.00
☐ Community "Sheraton", *no monogram, fair condition*	1.00	2.00
☐ Community "Sheraton", *monogram, excellent condition* ..	2.00	3.00
☐ Community "Silver Artistry", *no monogram, mint condition*	4.00	5.00
☐ Community "Silver Artistry", *no monogram, good condition*	3.00	4.00
☐ Community "Silver Artistry", *no monogram, fair condition* .	1.00	2.00
☐ Community "Silver Flowers", *no monogram, mint condition*	4.00	5.00
☐ Community "Silver Flowers", *no monogram, good condition*	3.00	4.00
☐ Community "Silver Flowers", *no monogram, poor condition*	1.00	2.00
☐ Community "Silver Sands", *no monogram, excellent condition*	4.00	5.00
☐ Community "Silver Sands", *no monogram, good condition*	3.00	4.00
☐ Community "Silver Sands", *no monogram, fair condition* ..	1.00	2.00
☐ Community "Silver Sands", *monogram, excellent condition*	2.00	3.00
☐ Community "Silver Valentine", *no monogram, mint condition*	3.00	4.00
☐ Community "Silver Valentine", *no monogram, excellent condition*	4.00	5.00
☐ Community "Silver Valentine", *no monogram, fair condition*	1.00	2.00
☐ Community "Song of Autumn", *no monogram, mint condition*	4.00	5.00
☐ Community "Song of Autumn", *no monogram, good condition*	3.00	4.00
☐ Community "Song of Autumn", *no monogram, fair condition*	1.00	2.00
☐ Community "South Seas", *no monogram, excellent condition*	4.00	5.00
☐ Community "South Seas", *no monogram, good condition* .	3.00	4.00
☐ Community "South Seas", *no monogram, poor condition* ..	1.00	2.00
☐ Community "Tangier", *no monogram, mint condition*	3.00	4.00
☐ Community "Tangier", *no monogram, good condition*	2.00	3.00
☐ Community "Twilight", *no monogram, excellent condition* .	4.00	5.00
☐ Community "Twilight", *no monogram, good condition*	3.00	4.00
☐ Community "Twilight", *no monogram, fair condition*	1.00	2.00
☐ Community "White Orchid", *no monogram, mint condition*	3.00	4.00
☐ Community "White Orchid", *no monogram, excellent condition*	4.00	5.00
☐ Community "White Orchid", *no monogram, good condition*	3.00	4.00
☐ Community "White Orchid", *no monogram, fair condition* .	1.00	2.00
☐ Community "White Orchid", *no monogram, poor condition*	1.00	2.00
☐ DeepSilver "Laurel Mist", *no monogram, excellent condition*	4.00	5.00
☐ DeepSilver "Laurel Mist", *no monogram, good condition* ..	3.00	4.00
☐ DeepSilver "Laurel Mist", *no monogram, poor condition* ...	1.00	2.00
☐ Derby "Lily", *no monogram, excellent condition*	4.00	5.00
☐ Derby "Lily", *monogram, fair condition*	1.00	2.00
☐ Embassy "Bouquet", *no monogram, excellent condition* ..	4.00	5.00
☐ Embassy "Bouquet", *no monogram, good condition*	3.00	4.00

	Price Range	

☐ **Fortune "Fortune"**, *no monogram, excellent condition* 4.00 5.00
☐ **Fortune "Fortune"**, *no monogram, good condition* 4.00 5.00
☐ **Fortune "Fortune"**, *no monogram, fair condition* 1.00 2.00
☐ **Gorham "Cavalier"**, *no monogram, excellent condition* 2.00 3.00
☐ **Gorham "Cavalier"**, *no monogram, excellent condition* 4.00 5.00
☐ **Gorham "Cavalier"**, *no monogram, good condition* 3.00 4.00
☐ **Gorham "Cavalier"**, *no monogram, fair condition* 1.00 2.00
☐ **Gorham "Empire"**, *no monogram, good condition* 3.00 4.00
☐ **Gorham "Empire"**, *no monogram, fair condition* 1.00 2.00
☐ **Gorham "Empire"**, *monogram, good condition* 1.00 2.00
☐ **Gorham "Kings"**, *no monogram, excellent condition* 4.00 5.00
☐ **Gorham "Kings"**, *no monogram, good condition* 3.00 4.00
☐ **Gorham "Kings"**, *U.S. Navy marks, good condition* 3.00 4.00
☐ **Gorham "Roman"**, *monogram, excellent condition* 5.00 6.00
☐ **Gorham "Roman"**, *monogram, good condition* 4.00 5.00
☐ **Hall, Elton & Co. "Lyonnaise"**, *no monogram, excellent condition* 4.00 5.00
☐ **Hall, Elton & Co. "Lyonnaise"**, *no monogram, fair condition* 1.00 2.00
☐ **Harmony House "Maytime"**, *no monogram, excellent condition* 2.00 3.00
☐ **Harmony House "Maytime"**, *no monogram, good condition* 1.00 2.00
☐ **Harmony House "Maytime"**, *no monogram, fair condition* . 1.00 2.00
☐ **Harmony House "Serenade"**, *no monogram, excellent condition* 2.00 3.00
☐ **Harmony House "Serenade"**, *no monogram, good condition* 2.00 3.00
☐ **Heirloom "Cardinal"**, *no monogram, excellent condition* .. 4.00 5.00
☐ **Heirloom "Cardinal"**, *no monogram, good condition* 3.00 4.00
☐ **Heirloom "Cardinal"**, *no monogram, fair condition* 1.00 2.00
☐ **Holmes & Edwards "Carolina"**, *no monogram, excellent condition* 4.00 5.00
☐ **Holmes & Edwards "Carolina"**, *no monogram, good condition* 4.00 5.00
☐ **Holmes & Edwards "Carolina"**, *no monogram, fair condition* 1.00 2.00
☐ **Holmes & Edwards "Century"**, *no monogram, excellent condition* 4.00 5.00
☐ **Holmes & Edwards "Century"**, *no monogram, good condition* 3.00 4.00
☐ **Holmes & Edwards "Century"**, *no monogram, fair condition* 1.00 2.00
☐ **Holmes & Edwards "Charm"**, *no monogram, excellent condition* 4.00 5.00
☐ **Holmes & Edwards "Charm"**, *no monogram, good condition* 3.00 4.00
☐ **Holmes & Edwards "Charm"**, *no monogram, fair condition* 1.00 2.00
☐ **Holmes & Edwards "Danish Princess"**, *no monogram, excellent condition* 2.00 3.00
☐ **Holmes & Edwards "Danish Princess"**, *no monogram, excellent condition* 4.00 5.00
☐ **Holmes & Edwards "Danish Princess"**, *no monogram, good condition* 3.00 4.00
☐ **Holmes & Edwards "Danish Princess"**, *no monogram, fair condition* 1.00 2.00

Price Range

☐ Holmes & Edwards "Hostess", *no monogram, excellent condition*	4.00	5.00
☐ Holmes & Edwards "Hostess", *no monogram, good condition*	3.00	4.00
☐ Holmes & Edwards "Hostess", *no monogram, fair condition*	1.00	2.00
☐ Holmes & Edwards "Imperial", *no monogram, excellent condition*	4.00	5.00
☐ Holmes & Edwards "Imperial", *no monogram, good condition*	3.00	4.00
☐ Holmes & Edwards "Imperial", *no monogram, fair condition*	1.00	2.00
☐ Holmes & Edwards "Liberty", *no monogram, excellent condition*	6.00	7.00
☐ Holmes & Edwards "Lovely Lady", *no monogram, good condition*	2.00	3.00
☐ Holmes & Edwards "Lovely Lady", *no monogram, excellent condition*	4.00	5.00
☐ Holmes & Edwards "Lovely Lady", *no monogram, good condition*	3.00	4.00
☐ Holmes & Edwards "Lovely Lady", *no monogram, fair condition*	1.00	2.00
☐ Holmes & Edwards "May Queen", *no monogram, excellent condition*	2.00	3.00
☐ Holmes & Edwards "May Queen", *no monogram, mint condition*	3.00	4.00
☐ Holmes & Edwards "May Queen", *no monogram, excellent condition*	4.00	5.00
☐ Holmes & Edwards "May Queen", *no monogram, good condition*	3.00	4.00
☐ Holmes & Edwards "May Queen", *no monogram, fair condition*	1.00	2.00
☐ Holmes & Edwards "Orient", *no monogram, excellent condition*	5.00	6.00
☐ Holmes & Edwards "Orient", *no monogram, good condition*	4.00	5.00
☐ Holmes & Edwards "Orient", *no monogram, fair condition* .	1.00	2.00
☐ Holmes & Edwards "Pageant", *no monogram, excellent condition*	4.00	5.00
☐ Holmes & Edwards "Pageant", *no monogram, good condition*	3.00	4.00
☐ Holmes & Edwards "Pageant", *no monogram, fair condition*	1.00	2.00
☐ Holmes & Edwards "Queen Anne", *no monogram, fair condition*	1.00	2.00
☐ Holmes & Edwards "Romance II", *no monogram, excellent condition*	2.00	3.00
☐ Holmes & Edwards "Romance II", *no monogram, fair condition*	1.00	2.00
☐ Holmes & Edwards "Rosemary", *no monogram, excellent condition*	4.00	5.00
☐ Holmes & Edwards "Rosemary", *no monogram, good condition*	3.00	4.00
☐ Holmes & Edwards "Rosemary", *no monogram, fair condition*	1.00	2.00

Price Range

- [ ] Holmes & Edwards "Silver Fashion", *no monogram, excellent condition* 4.00 5.00
- [ ] Holmes & Edwards "Silver Fashion", *no monogram, good condition* 3.00 4.00
- [ ] Holmes & Edwards "Silver Fashion", *no monogram, fair condition* 1.00 2.00
- [ ] Holmes & Edwards "Spring Garden", *no monogram, excellent condition* 2.00 3.00
- [ ] Holmes & Edwards "Spring Garden", *no monogram, excellent condition* 4.00 5.00
- [ ] Holmes & Edwards "Spring Garden", *no monogram, good condition* 3.00 4.00
- [ ] Holmes & Edwards "Spring Garden", *no monogram, fair condition* 1.00 2.00
- [ ] Holmes & Edwards "Spring Garden", *no monogram, poor condition* 1.00 2.00
- [ ] Holmes & Edwards "Unique", *no monogram, good condition* 2.00 3.00
- [ ] Holmes & Edwards "Unique", *no monogram, fair condition* 1.00 2.00
- [ ] Holmes & Edwards "Youth", *no monogram, excellent condition* 4.00 5.00
- [ ] Holmes & Edwards "Youth", *no monogram, good condition* 3.00 4.00
- [ ] International "Beacon Hill", *no monogram, excellent condition* 4.00 5.00
- [ ] International "Kings", *hotel name, excellent condition* 7.00 8.00
- [ ] International "Kings", *no monogram, excellent condition* . 2.00 3.00
- [ ] International "Kings", *no monogram, poor condition* 1.00 2.00
- [ ] International "Orleans", *no monogram, excellent condition* 3.00 4.00
- [ ] International "Orleans", *no monogram, excellent condition* 4.00 5.00
- [ ] International "Silver Tulip", *no monogram, excellent condition* 1.00 2.00
- [ ] International "Silver Tulip", *no monogram, excellent condition* 4.00 5.00
- [ ] International "Silver Tulip", *no monogram, fair condition* .. 1.00 2.00
- [ ] International "Triumph", *no monogram, mint condition* ... 3.00 4.00
- [ ] International "Triumph", *no monogram, good condition* ... 3.00 4.00
- [ ] International "Triumph", *no monogram, fair condition* 1.00 2.00
- [ ] King Edward "Holiday", *no monogram, excellent condition* 4.00 5.00
- [ ] King Edward "Holiday", *no monogram, good condition* ... 3.00 4.00
- [ ] King Edward "Holiday", *no monogram, fair condition* 1.00 2.00
- [ ] King Edward "Moss Rose", *no monogram, excellent condition* 4.00 5.00
- [ ] King Edward "Moss Rose", *no monogram, good condition* . 3.00 4.00
- [ ] King Edward "Moss Rose", *no monogram, fair condition* .. 1.00 2.00
- [ ] National "King Edward", *no monogram, excellent condition* 4.00 5.00
- [ ] National "King Edward", *no monogram, good condition* ... 3.00 4.00
- [ ] National "King Edward", *no monogram, fair condition* 1.00 2.00
- [ ] Niagara Falls Silver Co. "Colonial", *no monogram, excellent condition* 3.00 4.00
- [ ] Niagara Falls Silver Co. "Colonial", *no monogram, mint condition* 4.00 5.00
- [ ] Niagara Falls Silver Co. "Colonial", *no monogram, fair condition* 1.00 2.00

Price Range

☐ Niagara Falls Silver Co. "Wild Rose", *no monogram, mint condition*	4.00	5.00
☐ Niagara Falls Silver Co. "Wild Rose", *no monogram, excellent condition*	2.00	3.00
☐ Niagara Falls Silver Co. "Wild Rose", *no monogram, good condition*	1.00	2.00
☐ Niagara Falls Silver Co. "Wild Rose", *no monogram, fair condition*	1.00	2.00
☐ Nobility "Reverie", *no monogram, excellent condition*	4.00	5.00
☐ Nobility "Reverie", *no monogram, good condition*	3.00	4.00
☐ Nobility "Reverie", *no monogram, fair condition*	1.00	2.00
☐ Nobility "Royal Rose", *no monogram, excellent condition*	4.00	5.00
☐ Nobility "Royal Rose", *no monogram, good condition*	3.00	4.00
☐ Nobility "Royal Rose", *no monogram, fair condition*	1.00	2.00
☐ Old Company Plate "Signature", *no monogram, excellent condition*	4.00	5.00
☐ Old Company Plate "Signature", *no monogram, good condition*	3.00	4.00
☐ Old Company Plate "Signature", *no monogram, fair condition*	1.00	2.00
☐ Old Company Plate "Signature", *monogram, excellent condition*	3.00	4.00
☐ Oneida "Avalon", *no monogram, excellent condition*	4.00	5.00
☐ Oneida "Avalon", *no monogram, good condition*	4.00	5.00
☐ Oneida "Avalon", *no monogram, fair condition*	1.00	2.00
☐ Oneida "Beverly", *no monogram, excellent condition*	3.00	4.00
☐ Oneida "Beverly", *no monogram, fair condition*	1.00	2.00
☐ Oneida "Bridal Wreath", *no monogram, excellent condition*	4.00	5.00
☐ Oneida "Bridal Wreath", *no monogram, good condition*	3.00	4.00
☐ Oneida "Bridal Wreath", *no monogram, fair condition*	1.00	2.00
☐ Oneida "Bridal Wreath", *no monogram, excellent condition*	4.00	5.00
☐ Oneida "Bridal Wreath", *no monogram, good condition*	3.00	4.00
☐ Oneida "Bridal Wreath", *no monogram, fair condition*	1.00	2.00
☐ Oneida "Cereta", *no monogram, fair condition*	3.00	4.00
☐ Oneida "Clarion", *no monogram, excellent condition*	4.00	5.00
☐ Oneida "Clarion", *no monogram, good condition*	3.00	4.00
☐ Oneida "Clarion", *no monogram, fair condition*	1.00	2.00
☐ Oneida "Flower de Luce", *no monogram, good condition*	4.00	5.00
☐ Oneida "Flower de Luce", *no monogram, fair condition*	1.00	2.00
☐ Paragon "Sweet Pea", *no monogram, excellent condition*	3.00	4.00
☐ Paragon "Sweet Pea", *no monogram, good condition*	2.00	3.00
☐ Plymouth "Jewel", *no monogram, fair condition*	1.00	2.00
☐ Prestige "Grenoble", *no monogram, excellent condition*	4.00	5.00
☐ Prestige "Grenoble", *no monogram, good condition*	3.00	4.00
☐ Prestige "Grenoble", *no monogram, fair condition*	1.00	2.00
☐ R.C. Co. "Isabella", *no monogram, excellent condition*	3.00	4.00
☐ R.C. Co. "Isabella", *no monogram, good condition*	2.00	3.00
☐ R.C. Co. "Orleans II", *no monogram, excellent condition*	4.00	5.00
☐ R.C. Co. "Orleans II", *no monogram, good condition*	3.00	4.00
☐ R.C. Co. "Orleans II", *no monogram, fair condition*	1.00	2.00
☐ R.C. Co. "Rose", *no monogram, excellent condition*	4.00	5.00
☐ R.C. Co. "Rose", *no monogram, good condition*	3.00	4.00
☐ R.C. Co. "Rose", *no monogram, fair condition*	1.00	2.00

	Price Range	
☐ Reed & Barton "Carlton", *no monogram, excellent condition*	4.00	5.00
☐ Reed & Barton "Carlton", *no monogram, good condition* ..	3.00	4.00
☐ Reed & Barton "Carlton", *no monogram, fair condition*	1.00	2.00
☐ Reed & Barton "Fiddle", *no monogram, excellent condition*	4.00	5.00
☐ Reed & Barton "Fiddle", *no monogram, fair condition*	1.00	2.00
☐ Reed & Barton "Jewell", *no monogram, excellent condition*	4.00	5.00
☐ Reed & Barton "Jewell", *no monogram, good condition* ...	3.00	4.00
☐ Reed & Barton "Jewell", *no monogram, fair condition*	1.00	2.00
☐ Reed & Barton "Maid of Honor", *no monogram, excellent condition*	4.00	5.00
☐ Reed & Barton "Maid of Honor", *no monogram, good condition*	3.00	4.00
☐ Reed & Barton "Maid of Honor", *no monogram, fair condition*	1.00	2.00
☐ Reed & Barton "Manor", *no monogram, excellent condition*	4.00	5.00
☐ Reed & Barton "Manor", *no monogram, good condition* ...	3.00	4.00
☐ Reed & Barton "Manor", *no monogram, fair condition*	1.00	2.00
☐ Reed & Barton "Modern Art", *no monogram, excellent condition*	4.00	5.00
☐ Reed & Barton "Modern Art", *no monogram, good condition*	3.00	4.00
☐ Reed & Barton "Modern Art", *no monogram, fair condition*	1.00	2.00
☐ Reed & Barton "Olive", *no monogram, excellent condition* .	3.00	4.00
☐ Reed & Barton "Olive", *no monogram, good condition*	2.00	3.00
☐ Reed & Barton "Oxford", *no monogram, excellent condition*	3.00	4.00
☐ Reed & Barton "Oxford", *no monogram, good condition* ...	2.00	3.00
☐ Reed & Barton "Oxford", *no monogram, fair condition*	1.00	2.00
☐ Reed & Barton "Sierra", *no monogram, excellent condition*	4.00	5.00
☐ Reed & Barton "Sierra", *no monogram, good condition*	3.00	4.00
☐ Reed & Barton "Sierra", *no monogram, fair condition*	1.00	2.00
☐ Reed & Barton "Threaded", *no monogram, excellent condition*	3.00	4.00
☐ Reed & Barton "Threaded", *no monogram, good condition*	2.00	3.00
☐ Reed & Barton "Tiger Lily", *no monogram, mint condition* .	5.00	6.00
☐ Reed & Barton "Tiger Lily", *no monogram, fair condition* ..	1.00	2.00
☐ Reed & Barton "Tiger Lily", *no monogram, poor condition* .	1.00	2.00
☐ Reliance "Exeter", *no monogram, excellent condition*	4.00	5.00
☐ Reliance "Exeter", *no monogram, good condition*	3.00	4.00
☐ Reliance "Exeter", *no monogram, fair condition*	1.00	2.00
☐ Reliance "Exeter", *monogram, mint condition*	3.00	4.00
☐ Reliance "Wildwood", *no monogram, excellent condition* .	4.00	5.00
☐ Reliance "Wildwood", *excellent condition*	5.00	6.00
☐ Reliance "Wildwood", *no monogram, good condition*	4.00	5.00
☐ Reliance "Wildwood", *no monogram, fair condition*	1.00	2.00
☐ Rockford "Fairoaks", *no monogram, excellent condition* ..	4.00	5.00
☐ Rockford "Fairoaks", *no monogram, good condition*	3.00	4.00
☐ Rockford "Fairoaks", *no monogram, fair condition*	1.00	2.00
☐ Rockford "Puritan Engraved", *no monogram, excellent condition*	4.00	5.00
☐ Rockford "Puritan Engraved", *no monogram, good condition*	3.00	4.00
☐ Rockford "Puritan Engraved", *no monogram, fair condition*	1.00	2.00
☐ Rockford "Rose", *no monogram, excellent condition*	3.00	4.00

	Price Range	
☐ Rockford "Rose", *no monogram, fair condition*	1.00	2.00
☐ Rogers "Alhambra", *no monogram, excellent condition* ...	7.00	8.00
☐ Rogers "Alhambra", *no monogram, good condition*	6.00	7.00
☐ Rogers "Alhambra", *no monogram, fair condition*	2.00	3.00
☐ Rogers "Alhambra", *no monogram, poor condition*	2.00	3.00
☐ Rogers "Ambassador", *no monogram, excellent condition*	2.00	3.00
☐ Rogers "Ambassador", *no monogram, fair condition*	1.00	2.00
☐ Rogers "Burgundy", *no monogram, excellent condition* ...	4.00	5.00
☐ Rogers "Burgundy", *no monogram, good condition*	3.00	4.00
☐ Rogers "Burgundy", *no monogram, fair condition*	1.00	2.00
☐ Rogers "Carlton", *no monogram, good condition*	2.00	3.00
☐ Rogers "Cromwell II", *no monogram, excellent condition* ..	4.00	5.00
☐ Rogers "Cromwell II", *no monogram, good condition*	3.00	4.00
☐ Rogers "Cromwell II", *no monogram, fair condition*	1.00	2.00
☐ Rogers "Croydon", *no monogram, excellent condition*	2.00	3.00
☐ Rogers "Croydon", *no monogram, fair condition*	1.00	2.00
☐ Rogers "Desire", *no monogram, excellent condition*	4.00	5.00
☐ Rogers "Desire", *no monogram, good condition*	3.00	4.00
☐ Rogers "Desire", *no monogram, fair condition*	1.00	2.00
☐ Rogers "Desota", *no monogram, excellent condition*	4.00	5.00
☐ Rogers "Desota", *no monogram, good condition*	3.00	4.00
☐ Rogers "Desota", *no monogram, fair condition*	1.00	2.00
☐ Rogers "Garland", *no monogram, excellent condition*	4.00	5.00
☐ Rogers "Garland", *no monogram, good condition*	3.00	4.00
☐ Rogers "Garland", *no monogram, fair condition*	1.00	2.00
☐ Rogers "Gracious", *no monogram, excellent condition*	5.00	6.00
☐ Rogers "Gracious", *no monogram, good condition*	4.00	5.00
☐ Rogers "Gracious", *no monogram, fair condition*	1.00	2.00
☐ Rogers "Grenoble", *no monogram, excellent condition* ...	7.00	8.00
☐ Rogers "Grenoble", *no monogram, good condition*	5.00	6.00
☐ Rogers "Grenoble", *no monogram, fair condition*	2.00	3.00
☐ Rogers "Grenoble", *no monogram, poor condition*	1.00	2.00
☐ Rogers "Inspiration", *no monogram, excellent condition* ..	5.00	6.00
☐ Rogers "Inspiration", *no monogram, good condition*	4.00	5.00
☐ Rogers "Inspiration", *no monogram, fair condition*	1.00	2.00
☐ Rogers "LaConcorde", *no monogram, good condition*	8.00	9.00
☐ Rogers "LaConcorde", *no monogram, poor condition*	2.00	3.00
☐ Rogers "LaTouraine", *no monogram, excellent condition* ..	4.00	5.00
☐ Rogers "LaTouraine", *no monogram, good condition*	3.00	4.00
☐ Rogers "LaTouraine", *no monogram, fair condition*	1.00	2.00
☐ Rogers "Manhattan", *no monogram, excellent condition* ..	4.00	5.00
☐ Rogers "Manhattan", *no monogram, good condition*	3.00	4.00
☐ Rogers "Manhattan", *no monogram, fair condition*	1.00	2.00
☐ Rogers "Newport", *no monogram, excellent condition*	3.00	4.00
☐ Rogers "Newport", *no monogram, good condition*	3.00	4.00
☐ Rogers "Nuart", *no monogram, excellent condition*	5.00	6.00
☐ Rogers "Nuart", *no monogram, good condition*	4.00	5.00
☐ Rogers "Nuart", *no monogram, fair condition*	1.00	2.00
☐ Rogers "Nuart", *no monogram, poor condition*	1.00	2.00
☐ Rogers "Precious", *no monogram, excellent condition*	4.00	5.00
☐ Rogers "Precious", *no monogram, good condition*	3.00	4.00
☐ Rogers "Precious", *no monogram, fair condition*	1.00	2.00
☐ Rogers "Queen Bess II", *no monogram, excellent condition*	2.00	3.00
☐ Rogers "Queen Bess II", *no monogram, fair condition*	1.00	2.00

	Price Range	

☐ Rogers "Vendome", *no monogram, excellent condition* ...	5.00	6.00
☐ Rogers "Vendome", *no monogram, fair condition*	1.00	2.00
☐ Rogers "Victorian Rose", *no monogram, excellent condition*	3.00	4.00
☐ Rogers "Victorian Rose", *no monogram, fair condition*	1.00	2.00
☐ Rogers & Bro. "Assyrian Head", *no monogram, excellent condition*	15.00	17.00
☐ Rogers & Bro. "Assyrian Head", *no monogram, good condition*	12.00	14.00
☐ Rogers & Bro. "Assyrian Head", *no monogram, poor condition*	3.00	4.00
☐ Rogers & Bro. "Columbia", *monogram, excellent condition*	8.00	9.00
☐ Rogers & Bro. "Columbia", *no monogram, fair condition* ..	2.00	3.00
☐ Rogers & Bro. "Crest", *no monogram, excellent condition* .	1.00	2.00
☐ Rogers & Bro. "Crest", *no monogram, fair condition*	1.00	2.00
☐ Rogers & Bro. "Daybreak", *no monogram, excellent condition*	2.00	3.00
☐ Rogers & Bro. "Daybreak", *no monogram, fair condition* ..	1.00	2.00
☐ Rogers & Bro. "Flemish", *no monogram, excellent condition*	5.00	6.00
☐ Rogers & Bro. "Flemish", *no monogram, good condition* ..	3.00	4.00
☐ Rogers & Bro. "Flemish", *no monogram, fair condition*	1.00	2.00
☐ Rogers & Bro. "Flemish", *monogram, poor condition*	1.00	2.00
☐ Rogers & Bro. "Florette", *no monogram, excellent condition*	4.00	5.00
☐ Rogers & Bro. "Florette", *no monogram, good condition* ..	3.00	4.00
☐ Rogers & Bro. "Florette", *no monogram, fair condition*	1.00	2.00
☐ Rogers & Bro. "Modern Rose", *no monogram, excellent condition*	4.00	5.00
☐ Rogers & Bro. "Modern Rose", *no monogram, good condition*	3.00	4.00
☐ Rogers & Bro. "Modern Rose", *no monogram, fair condition*	1.00	2.00
☐ Rogers & Bro. "Mystic", *no monogram, excellent condition*	4.00	5.00
☐ Rogers & Bro. "Mystic", *no monogram, fair condition*	1.00	2.00
☐ Rogers & Bro. "New Century", *no monogram, excellent condition*	3.00	4.00
☐ Rogers & Bro. "New Century", *no monogram, good condition*	2.00	3.00
☐ Rogers & Bro. "New Century", *no monogram, fair condition*	1.00	2.00
☐ Rogers & Bro. "Siren", *no monogram, resilvered*	7.00	8.00
☐ Rogers & Bro. "Siren", *no monogram, fair condition*	1.00	2.00
☐ Rogers & Hamilton "Cardinal", *no monogram, good condition*	2.00	3.00
☐ Rogers & Hamilton "Cardinal", *no monogram, fair condition*	1.00	2.00
☐ Rogers & Hamilton "Marquise", *no monogram, mint condition*	4.00	5.00
☐ Rogers & Hamilton "Marquise", *no monogram, good condition*	3.00	4.00
☐ Rogers & Hamilton "Raphael", *no monogram, excellent condition*	9.00	10.00
☐ Rogers & Hamilton "Raphael", *no monogram, good condition*	3.00	4.00

	Price Range	
☐ **Rogers & Hamilton "Raphael"**, *no monogram, fair condition*	1.00	2.00
☐ **Rogers, Smith & Co. "Lorne"**, *no monogram, good condition*	4.00	5.00
☐ **S.L. & G.H. Rogers "Countess II"**, *no monogram, excellent condition*	4.00	5.00
☐ **S.L. & G.H. Rogers "Countess II"**, *no monogram, good condition*	3.00	4.00
☐ **S.L. & G.H. Rogers "Countess II"**, *no monogram, fair condition*	1.00	2.00
☐ **S.L. & G.H. Rogers "Daisy"**, *no monogram, fair condition* ..	1.00	2.00
☐ **S.L. & G.H. Rogers "Encore"**, *no monogram, excellent condition*	3.00	4.00
☐ **S.L. & G.H. Rogers "Encore"**, *no monogram, good condition*	2.00	3.00
☐ **S.L. & G.H. Rogers "Encore"**, *no monogram, fair condition* .	1.00	2.00
☐ **S.L. & G.H. Rogers "English Garden"**, *no monogram, excellent condition*	2.00	3.00
☐ **S.L. & G.H. Rogers "English Garden"**, *no monogram, excellent condition*	4.00	5.00
☐ **S.L. & G.H. Rogers "English Garden"**, *no monogram, good condition*	3.00	4.00
☐ **S.L. & G.H. Rogers "English Garden"**, *no monogram, fair condition*	1.00	2.00
☐ **S.L. & G.H. Rogers "Jasmine"**, *no monogram, excellent condition*	2.00	3.00
☐ **S.L. & G.H. Rogers "Jasmine"**, *no monogram, good condition*	3.00	4.00
☐ **S.L. & G.H. Rogers "Jasmine"**, *no monogram, fair condition*	1.00	2.00
☐ **S.L. & G.H. Rogers "Lexington"**, *no monogram, excellent condition*	4.00	5.00
☐ **S.L. & G.H. Rogers "Lexington"**, *no monogram, good condition*	3.00	4.00
☐ **S.L. & G.H. Rogers "Lexington"**, *no monogram, fair condition*	1.00	2.00
☐ **S.L. & G.H. Rogers "Minerva"**, *no monogram, excellent condition*	5.00	6.00
☐ **S.L. & G.H. Rogers "Minerva"**, *no monogram, good condition*	4.00	5.00
☐ **S.L. & G.H. Rogers "Minerva"**, *no monogram, fair condition*	1.00	2.00
☐ **S.L. & G.H. Rogers "Orchid"**, *no monogram, excellent condition*	3.00	4.00
☐ **S.L. & G.H. Rogers "Orchid"**, *no monogram, good condition*	2.00	3.00
☐ **S.L. & G.H. Rogers "Orchid"**, *monogram, excellent condition*	3.00	4.00
☐ **S.L. & G.H. Rogers "Orchid"**, *monogram, poor condition* ..	1.00	2.00
☐ **S.L. & G.H. Rogers "Silver Rose"**, *no monogram, excellent condition*	4.00	5.00
☐ **S.L. & G.H. Rogers "Silver Rose"**, *no monogram, good condition*	3.00	4.00
☐ **S.L. & G.H. Rogers "Silver Rose"**, *no monogram, fair condition*	1.00	2.00
☐ **Stratford "Carmen"**, *no monogram, excellent condition* ...	2.00	3.00
☐ **Stratford "Carmen"**, *no monogram, fair condition*	1.00	2.00

	Price Range	
☐ Stratford "Shakespeare", *no monogram, excellent condition*	4.00	5.00
☐ Stratford "Shakespeare", *no monogram, good condition*	3.00	4.00
☐ Stratford "Shakespeare", *no monogram, fair condition*	1.00	2.00
☐ Towle "Chester", *no monogram, good condition*	3.00	4.00
☐ Towle "Chester", *no monogram, fair condition*	1.00	2.00
☐ Tudor Plate "Bridal Wreath", *no monogram, mint condition*	4.00	5.00
☐ Tudor Plate "Bridal Wreath", *no monogram, good condition*	3.00	4.00
☐ Tudor Plate "Bridal Wreath", *no monogram, fair condition*	1.00	2.00
☐ Tudor Plate "Duchess", *no monogram, excellent condition*	4.00	5.00
☐ Tudor Plate "Duchess", *no monogram, good condition*	3.00	4.00
☐ Tudor Plate "Duchess", *no monogram, fair condition*	1.00	2.00
☐ Tudor Plate "Enchantment", *no monogram, excellent condition*	2.00	3.00
☐ Tudor Plate "Enchantment", *no monogram, excellent condition*	4.00	5.00
☐ Tudor Plate "Enchantment", *no monogram, good condition*	3.00	4.00
☐ Tudor Plate "Enchantment", *no monogram, fair condition*	1.00	2.00
☐ Tudor Plate "Enchantment", *no monogram, poor condition*	1.00	2.00
☐ Tudor Plate "Friendship", *no monogram, excellent condition*	4.00	5.00
☐ Tudor Plate "Friendship", *no monogram, good condition*	3.00	4.00
☐ Tudor Plate "Friendship", *no monogram, fair condition*	1.00	2.00
☐ Tudor Plate "Mary Stuart", *no monogram, excellent condition*	4.00	5.00
☐ Tudor Plate "Mary Stuart", *no monogram, good condition*	3.00	4.00
☐ Tudor Plate "Mary Stuart", *no monogram, fair condition*	1.00	2.00
☐ Tudor Plate "Queen Bess II", *no monogram, excellent condition*	4.00	5.00
☐ Tudor Plate "Queen Bess II", *no monogram, good condition*	3.00	4.00
☐ Tudor Plate "Queen Bess II", *no monogram, fair condition*	1.00	2.00
☐ Tudor Plate "Sweetbriar", *no monogram, excellent condition*	4.00	5.00
☐ Tudor Plate "Sweetbriar", *no monogram, good condition*	3.00	4.00
☐ Tudor Plate "Sweetbriar", *no monogram, fair condition*	1.00	2.00
☐ Tudor Plate "Together", *no monogram, mint condition*	4.00	5.00
☐ Tudor Plate "Together", *no monogram, good condition*	3.00	4.00
☐ Tudor Plate "Together", *no monogram, fair condition*	1.00	2.00
☐ Wallace "Floral", *no monogram, excellent condition*	8.00	9.00
☐ Wallace "Floral", *no monogram, good condition*	6.00	7.00
☐ Wallace "Floral", *no monogram, fair condition*	2.00	3.00
☐ Wallace "Floral", *monogram, excellent condition*	7.00	8.00
☐ Wallace "Floral", *monogram, poor condition*	1.00	2.00
☐ Wallace "Hudson", *no monogram, excellent condition*	2.00	3.00
☐ Wallace "Hudson", *monogram, excellent condition*	1.00	2.00
☐ Wallace "Kings", *no monogram, excellent condition*	4.00	5.00
☐ Wallace "Kings", *no monogram, good condition*	2.00	3.00
☐ Wallace "Kings", *U.S. Navy monogram, excellent condition*	2.00	3.00
☐ Wallace "Sonata", *no monogram, excellent condition*	4.00	5.00
☐ Wallace "Sonata", *no monogram, good condition*	3.00	4.00
☐ Wallace "Sonata", *no monogram, fair condition*	1.00	2.00
☐ W.D. Smith "Adam", *no monogram, good condition*	2.00	3.00
☐ W.D. Smith "Adam", *monogram, excellent condition*	4.00	5.00
☐ W.D. Smith "Adam", *monogram, mint condition*	4.00	5.00

	Price Range	
☐ **W.D. Smith "Adam",** *monogram, poor condition*	1.00	2.00
☐ **Williams Bros. "Isabella",** *no monogram, good condition* ..	3.00	4.00
☐ **Williams Bros. "Isabella",** *no monogram, excellent condition*	4.00	5.00
☐ **Williams Bros. "Isabella",** *no monogram, fair condition* ...	1.00	2.00
☐ **Williams Bros. "Queen Elizabeth",** *no monogram, excellent condition*	4.00	5.00
☐ **Williams Bros. "Queen Elizabeth",** *no monogram, fair condition*	1.00	2.00
☐ **Williams Bros. "Verona",** *no monogram, excellent condition*	2.00	3.00
☐ **Williams Bros. "Verona",** *no monogram, good condition* ..	2.00	3.00
☐ **Williams Bros. "Verona",** *no monogram, fair condition*	1.00	2.00
☐ **Williams Bros. "Vineyard",** *no monogram, resilvered*	8.00	9.00
☐ **Williams Bros. "Vineyard",** *no monogram, good condition* .	5.00	6.00
☐ **Wm. A. Rogers "Artistic",** *no monogram, excellent condition*	4.00	5.00
☐ **Wm. A. Rogers "Artistic",** *no monogram, good condition* ..	3.00	4.00
☐ **Wm. A. Rogers "Artistic",** *no monogram, fair condition*	1.00	2.00
☐ **Wm. A. Rogers "Artistic",** *no monogram, poor condition* ..	1.00	2.00
☐ **Wm. A. Rogers "Carnation",** *no monogram, excellent condition*	4.00	5.00
☐ **Wm. A. Rogers "Carnation",** *no monogram, fair condition* .	2.00	3.00
☐ **Wm. A. Rogers "Carnation",** *no monogram, excellent condition*	5.00	6.00
☐ **Wm. A. Rogers "Chalice",** *no monogram, excellent condition*	4.00	5.00
☐ **Wm. A. Rogers "Chalice",** *no monogram, good condition* ..	3.00	4.00
☐ **Wm. A. Rogers "Chalice",** *no monogram, fair condition* ...	1.00	2.00
☐ **Wm. A. Rogers "Country Lane",** *no monogram, excellent condition*	4.00	5.00
☐ **Wm. A. Rogers "Country Lane",** *no monogram, good condition*	3.00	4.00
☐ **Wm. A. Rogers "Country Lane",** *no monogram, fair condition*	1.00	2.00
☐ **Wm. A. Rogers "Garland",** *no monogram, excellent condition*	3.00	4.00
☐ **Wm. A. Rogers "Garland",** *no monogram, excellent condition*	3.00	4.00
☐ **Wm. A. Rogers "Garland",** *no monogram, fair condition* ...	1.00	2.00
☐ **Wm. A. Rogers "Grenoble",** *no monogram, excellent condition*	5.00	6.00
☐ **Wm. A. Rogers "Grenoble",** *no monogram, good condition*	4.00	5.00
☐ **Wm. A. Rogers "Grenoble",** *no monogram, fair condition* ..	1.00	2.00
☐ **Wm. A. Rogers "Grenoble",** *no monogram, excellent condition*	4.00	5.00
☐ **Wm. A. Rogers "Hanover",** *no monogram, fair condition* ...	1.00	2.00
☐ **Wm. A. Rogers "LaConcorde",** *no monogram, good condition*	4.00	5.00
☐ **Wm. A. Rogers "LaConcorde",** *no monogram, excellent condition*	5.00	6.00
☐ **Wm. A. Rogers "LaConcorde",** *no monogram, good condition*	4.00	5.00

	Price Range	
☐ **Wm. A. Rogers** "LaConcorde", *no monogram, excellent condition*	5.00	6.00
☐ **Wm. A. Rogers** "LaConcorde", *no monogram, good condition*	3.00	4.00
☐ **Wm. A. Rogers** "Lady Drake", *no monogram, excellent condition*	4.00	5.00
☐ **Wm. A. Rogers** "Lady Drake", *no monogram, good condition*	3.00	4.00
☐ **Wm. A. Rogers** "Lady Drake", *no monogram, fair condition*	1.00	2.00
☐ **Wm. A. Rogers** "Lady Stuart", *no monogram, excellent condition*	4.00	5.00
☐ **Wm. A. Rogers** "Lady Stuart", *no monogram, good condition*	3.00	4.00
☐ **Wm. A. Rogers** "Lady Stuart", *no monogram, fair condition*	1.00	2.00
☐ **Wm. A. Rogers** "LaVigne", *no monogram, excellent condition*	8.00	9.00
☐ **Wm. A. Rogers** "LaVigne", *no monogram, fair condition* ...	4.00	5.00
☐ **Wm. A. Rogers** "LaVigne", *monogram, poor condition*	1.00	2.00
☐ **Wm. A. Rogers** "Lenora", *no monogram, fair condition*	3.00	4.00
☐ **Wm. A. Rogers** "Malibu", *no monogram, excellent condition*	4.00	5.00
☐ **Wm. A. Rogers** "Malibu", *no monogram, good condition* ...	3.00	4.00
☐ **Wm. A. Rogers** "Malibu", *no monogram, fair condition*	1.00	2.00
☐ **Wm. A. Rogers** "Marcella", *no monogram, good condition* .	4.00	5.00
☐ **Wm. A. Rogers** "Margate", *no monogram, excellent condition*	4.00	5.00
☐ **Wm. A. Rogers** "Margate", *no monogram, good condition* .	3.00	4.00
☐ **Wm. A. Rogers** "Margate", *no monogram, fair condition* ...	1.00	2.00
☐ **Wm. A. Rogers** "Meadowbrook", *no monogram, excellent condition*	4.00	5.00
☐ **Wm. A. Rogers** "Meadowbrook", *no monogram, good condition*	3.00	4.00
☐ **Wm. A. Rogers** "Meadowbrook", *no monogram, fair condition*	1.00	2.00
☐ **Wm. A. Rogers** "Rendezvous", *no monogram, excellent condition*	4.00	5.00
☐ **Wm. A. Rogers** "Rendezvous", *no monogram, good condition*	3.00	4.00
☐ **Wm. A. Rogers** "Rendezvous", *no monogram, fair condition*	1.00	2.00
☐ **Wm. A. Rogers** "Rosalie", *no monogram, excellent condition*	5.00	6.00
☐ **Wm. A. Rogers** "Rosalie", *no monogram, good condition* ..	4.00	5.00
☐ **Wm. A. Rogers** "Rosalie", *no monogram, fair condition* ...	1.00	2.00
☐ **Wm. A. Rogers** "Valley Rose", *no monogram, excellent condition*	4.00	5.00
☐ **Wm. A. Rogers** "Valley Rose", *no monogram, good condition*	3.00	4.00
☐ **Wm. A. Rogers** "Valley Rose", *no monogram, fair condition*	1.00	2.00
☐ **Wm. A. Rogers** "Violet", *no monogram, excellent condition*	2.00	3.00
☐ **Wm. A. Rogers** "Violet", *fair condition*	1.00	2.00
☐ **Wm. A. Rogers** "Warwick", *no monogram, excellent condition*	4.00	5.00
☐ **Wm. A. Rogers** "Warwick", *no monogram, good condition* .	3.00	4.00
☐ **Wm. A. Rogers** "Warwick", *no monogram, fair condition* ..	1.00	2.00

Price Range

☐ **Wm. Rogers "Avalon"**, *no monogram, excellent condition* .	3.00	4.00
☐ **Wm. Rogers "Avalon"**, *no monogram, good condition*	2.00	3.00
☐ **Wm. Rogers "Avalon"**, *no monogram, fair condition*	1.00	2.00
☐ **Wm. Rogers "Beloved"**, *no monogram, excellent condition*	3.00	4.00
☐ **Wm. Rogers "Beloved"**, *no monogram, excellent condition*	4.00	5.00
☐ **Wm. Rogers "Beloved"**, *no monogram, fair condition*	1.00	2.00
☐ **Wm. Rogers "Cedric"**, *no monogram, excellent condition* .	4.00	5.00
☐ **Wm. Rogers "Cedric"**, *no monogram, good condition*	3.00	4.00
☐ **Wm. Rogers "Cordova"**, *no monogram, excellent condition*	4.00	5.00
☐ **Wm. Rogers "Cordova"**, *no monogram, good condition* . . .	3.00	4.00
☐ **Wm. Rogers "Cordova"**, *no monogram, fair condition*	1.00	2.00
☐ **Wm. Rogers "Cotillion"**, *no monogram, excellent condition*	4.00	5.00
☐ **Wm. Rogers "Cotillion"**, *no monogram, good condition* . . .	3.00	4.00
☐ **Wm. Rogers "Cotillion"**, *no monogram, fair condition*	1.00	2.00
☐ **Wm. Rogers "Debutante"**, *no monogram, excellent condition*	4.00	5.00
☐ **Wm. Rogers "Debutante"**, *no monogram, good condition* . .	3.00	4.00
☐ **Wm. Rogers "Debutante"**, *no monogram, fair condition* . . .	1.00	2.00
☐ **Wm. Rogers "Devonshire"**, *no monogram, excellent condition*	3.00	4.00
☐ **Wm. Rogers "Devonshire"**, *no monogram, good condition* .	2.00	3.00
☐ **Wm. Rogers "Exquisite"**, *no monogram, excellent condition*	2.00	3.00
☐ **Wm. Rogers "Exquisite"**, *no monogram, excellent condition*	4.00	5.00
☐ **Wm. Rogers "Exquisite"**, *no monogram, good condition* . . .	3.00	4.00
☐ **Wm. Rogers "Exquisite"**, *no monogram, fair condition*	1.00	2.00
☐ **Wm. Rogers "Fidelis"**, *no monogram, excellent condition* .	4.00	5.00
☐ **Wm. Rogers "Fidelis"**, *no monogram, good condition*	3.00	4.00
☐ **Wm. Rogers "Fidelis"**, *no monogram, fair condition*	1.00	2.00
☐ **Wm. Rogers "Geneva"**, *no monogram, excellent condition* .	4.00	5.00
☐ **Wm. Rogers "Geneva"**, *no monogram, good condition*	3.00	4.00
☐ **Wm. Rogers "Geneva"**, *no monogram, fair condition*	1.00	2.00
☐ **Wm. Rogers "Grenoble"**, *no monogram, excellent condition*	3.00	4.00
☐ **Wm. Rogers "Imperial"**, *no monogram, excellent condition*	4.00	5.00
☐ **Wm. Rogers "Imperial"**, *no monogram, good condition*	3.00	4.00
☐ **Wm. Rogers "Imperial"**, *no monogram, fair condition*	1.00	2.00
☐ **Wm. Rogers "Kensington"**, *no monogram, excellent condition*	4.00	5.00
☐ **Wm. Rogers "LaConcorde"**, *no monogram, excellent condition*	4.00	5.00
☐ **Wm. Rogers "LaConcorde"**, *no monogram, poor condition*	1.00	2.00
☐ **Wm. Rogers "Louisiana"**, *no monogram, excellent condition*	4.00	5.00
☐ **Wm. Rogers "Louisiana"**, *no monogram, good condition* . .	3.00	4.00
☐ **Wm. Rogers "Louisiana"**, *no monogram, fair condition*	1.00	2.00
☐ **Wm. Rogers "Lufberry"**, *no monogram, excellent condition*	4.00	5.00
☐ **Wm. Rogers "Lufberry"**, *no monogram, good condition* . . .	3.00	4.00
☐ **Wm. Rogers "Lufberry"**, *no monogram, fair condition*	1.00	2.00
☐ **Wm. Rogers "Mayfair"**, *no monogram, excellent condition* .	4.00	5.00
☐ **Wm. Rogers "Mayfair"**, *no monogram, good condition*	3.00	4.00
☐ **Wm. Rogers "Mayfair"**, *no monogram, fair condition*	1.00	2.00
☐ **Wm. Rogers "Melrose"**, *no monogram, excellent condition*	2.00	3.00
☐ **Wm. Rogers "Memory"**, *no monogram, excellent condition*	5.00	6.00

	Price Range	
☐ Wm. Rogers "Memory", *no monogram, good condition*	3.00	4.00
☐ Wm. Rogers "Memory", *no monogram, fair condition*	1.00	2.00
☐ Wm. Rogers "Mountain Rose", *no monogram, excellent condition*	5.00	6.00
☐ Wm. Rogers "Mountain Rose", *no monogram, good condition*	4.00	5.00
☐ Wm. Rogers "Oxford", *no monogram, good condition*	2.00	3.00
☐ Wm. Rogers "Pickwick", *no monogram, excellent condition*	4.00	5.00
☐ Wm. Rogers "Pickwick", *no monogram, good condition* . . .	3.00	4.00
☐ Wm. Rogers "Pickwick", *no monogram, fair condition*	1.00	2.00
☐ Wm. Rogers "Precious Mirror", *no monogram, excellent condition*	5.00	6.00
☐ Wm. Rogers "Precious Mirror", *no monogram, good condition*	4.00	5.00
☐ Wm. Rogers "Precious Mirror", *no monogram, fair condition*	1.00	2.00
☐ Wm. Rogers "Shell", *no monogram, excellent condition* . . .	2.00	3.00
☐ Wm. Rogers "Shell", *no monogram, fair condition*	1.00	2.00
☐ Wm. Rogers "Starlight", *no monogram, excellent condition*	4.00	5.00
☐ Wm. Rogers "Starlight", *no monogram, good condition* . . .	3.00	4.00
☐ Wm. Rogers "Starlight", *no monogram, fair condition*	1.00	2.00
☐ Wm. Rogers "Treasure", *no monogram, excellent condition*	2.00	3.00
☐ Wm. Rogers "Treasure", *no monogram, excellent condition*	4.00	5.00
☐ Wm. Rogers "Treasure", *no monogram, good condition* . . .	3.00	4.00
☐ Wm. Rogers "Treasure", *no monogram, fair condition*	1.00	2.00
☐ Wm. Rogers "Victorian Rose", *no monogram, mint condition*	4.00	5.00
☐ Wm. Rogers "Victorian Rose", *no monogram, fair condition*	1.00	2.00
☐ Wm. Rogers Mfg. Co. "Arbutus", *no monogram, mint condition*	6.00	7.00
☐ Wm. Rogers Mfg. Co. "Arbutus", *no monogram, good condition*	3.00	4.00
☐ Wm. Rogers Mfg. Co. "Arbutus", *no monogram, fair condition*	1.00	2.00
☐ Wm. Rogers Mfg. Co. "Avalon", *no monogram, excellent condition*	4.00	5.00
☐ Wm. Rogers Mfg. Co. "Avalon", *no monogram, good condition*	3.00	4.00
☐ Wm. Rogers Mfg. Co. "Avalon", *no monogram, fair condition*	1.00	2.00
☐ Wm. Rogers Mfg. Co. "Berwick", *no monogram, resilvered* .	8.00	9.00
☐ Wm. Rogers Mfg. Co. "Chevalier", *no monogram, good condition*	2.00	3.00
☐ Wm. Rogers Mfg. Co. "Daisy", *no monogram, excellent condition*	3.00	4.00
☐ Wm. Rogers Mfg. Co. "Florida", *no monogram, mint condition*	4.00	5.00
☐ Wm. Rogers Mfg. Co. "Florida", *no monogram, fair condition*	1.00	2.00
☐ Wm. Rogers Mfg. Co. "Grape", *monogram, good condition*	3.00	4.00
☐ Wm. Rogers Mfg. Co. "Inheritance", *no monogram, excellent condition*	4.00	5.00
☐ Wm. Rogers Mfg. Co. "Inheritance", *no monogram, good condition*	3.00	4.00

Price Range

☐ Wm. Rogers Mfg. Co. "Inheritance", *no monogram, fair condition*	1.00	2.00
☐ Wm. Rogers Mfg. Co. "Inheritance", *no monogram, poor condition*	1.00	2.00
☐ Wm. Rogers Mfg. Co. "Ivanhoe", *no monogram, excellent condition*	4.00	5.00
☐ Wm. Rogers Mfg. Co. "Ivanhoe", *no monogram, good condition*	3.00	4.00
☐ Wm. Rogers Mfg. Co. "Ivanhoe", *no monogram, fair condition*	1.00	2.00
☐ Wm. Rogers Mfg. Co. "Magnolia", *no monogram, excellent condition*	4.00	5.00
☐ Wm. Rogers Mfg. Co. "Magnolia", *no monogram, good condition*	3.00	4.00
☐ Wm. Rogers Mfg. Co. "Magnolia", *no monogram, fair condition*	1.00	2.00
☐ Wm. Rogers Mfg. Co. "Regent", *no monogram, excellent condition*	6.00	7.00
☐ Wm. Rogers Mfg. Co. "Regent", *monogram, excellent condition*	4.00	5.00
☐ Wm. Rogers Mfg. Co. "Revelation", *no monogram, excellent condition*	4.00	5.00
☐ Wm. Rogers Mfg. Co. "Revelation", *no monogram, good condition*	3.00	4.00
☐ Wm. Rogers Mfg. Co. "Revelation", *no monogram, fair condition*	1.00	2.00
☐ Wm. Rogers Mfg. Co. "Sovereign", *no monogram, excellent condition*	4.00	5.00
☐ Wm. Rogers Mfg. Co. "Sovereign", *no monogram, good condition*	3.00	4.00
☐ Wm. Rogers Mfg. Co. "Sovereign", *no monogram, fair condition*	1.00	2.00
☐ Wm. Rogers Mfg. Co. "Talisman", *no monogram, excellent condition*	4.00	5.00
☐ Wm. Rogers Mfg. Co. "Talisman", *no monogram, good condition*	3.00	4.00
☐ Wm. Rogers Mfg. Co. "Talisman", *no monogram, fair condition*	1.00	2.00
☐ Wm. Rogers Mfg. Co. "Thistle", *no monogram, good condition*	4.00	5.00
☐ Wm. Rogers Mfg. Co. "Thistle", *no monogram, fair condition*	1.00	2.00
☐ Wm. Rogers & Son "Arbutus", *no monogram, excellent condition*	4.00	5.00
☐ Wm. Rogers & Son "Arbutus", *no monogram, good condition*	3.00	4.00
☐ Wm. Rogers & Son "Arbutus", *no monogram, fair condition*	1.00	2.00
☐ Wm. Rogers & Son "April", *no monogram, excellent condition*	4.00	5.00
☐ Wm. Rogers & Son "April", *no monogram, good condition*	3.00	4.00
☐ Wm. Rogers & Son "April", *no monogram, fair condition*	1.00	2.00
☐ Wm. Rogers & Son "Daisy", *no monogram, good condition*	2.00	3.00
☐ Wm. Rogers & Son "Flower", *no monogram, good condition*	4.00	5.00
☐ Wm. Rogers & Son "Flower", *no monogram, fair condition*	1.00	2.00

	Price Range	

☐ **Wm. Rogers & Son "LaFrance"**, *no monogram, excellent condition*	4.00	5.00
☐ **Wm. Rogers & Son "LaFrance"**, *no monogram, good condition*	3.00	4.00
☐ **Wm. Rogers & Son "LaFrance"**, *no monogram, fair condition*	1.00	2.00
☐ **Wm. Rogers & Son "Rose"**, *no monogram, good condition* .	2.00	3.00
☐ **Wm. Rogers & Son "Rose"**, *no monogram, fair condition* ..	1.00	2.00
☐ **Wm. Rogers & Son "Victorian Rose"**, *no monogram, excellent condition*	4.00	5.00
☐ **Wm. Rogers & Son "Victorian Rose"**, *no monogram, good condition*	3.00	4.00
☐ **Wm. Rogers & Son "Victorian Rose"**, *no monogram, fair condition*	1.00	2.00
☐ **World "Moselle"**, *no monogram, good condition*	7.00	8.00
☐ **World "Moselle"**, *monogram, good condition*	5.00	6.00
☐ **World "Roanoke"**, *no monogram, excellent condition*	4.00	5.00
☐ **World "Roanoke"**, *no monogram, good condition*	3.00	4.00
☐ **World "Roanoke"**, *no monogram, fair condition*	1.00	2.00
☐ **1835 R. Wallace "Abbey"**, *no monogram, excellent condition*	4.00	5.00
☐ **1835 R. Wallace "Abbey"**, *no monogram, good condition* ..	3.00	4.00
☐ **1835 R. Wallace "Abbey"**, *no monogram, fair condition* ...	1.00	2.00
☐ **1835 R. Wallace "Anjou"**, *no monogram, excellent condition*	3.00	4.00
☐ **1835 R. Wallace "Anjou"**, *no monogram, fair condition*	1.00	2.00
☐ **1835 R. Wallace "Blossom"**, *no monogram, good condition*	4.00	5.00
☐ **1835 R. Wallace "Blossom"**, *monogram, good condition* ..	2.00	3.00
☐ **1835 R. Wallace "Buckingham"**, *no monogram, excellent condition*	4.00	5.00
☐ **1835 R. Wallace "Buckingham"**, *monogram, excellent condition*	2.00	3.00
☐ **1835 R. Wallace "Floral"**, *no monogram, excellent condition*	7.00	8.00
☐ **1835 R. Wallace "Floral"**, *no monogram, good condition* ..	5.00	6.00
☐ **1835 R. Wallace "Floral"**, *no monogram, fair condition*	1.00	2.00
☐ **1835 R. Wallace "Joan"**, *no monogram, excellent condition*	4.00	5.00
☐ **1835 R. Wallace "Joan"**, *no monogram, good condition* ...	3.00	4.00
☐ **1835 R. Wallace "Joan"**, *no monogram, fair condition*	1.00	2.00
☐ **1835 R. Wallace "Troy"**, *no monogram, good condition*	3.00	4.00
☐ **1835 R. Wallace "Troy"**, *no monogram, excellent condition*	3.00	4.00
☐ **1835 R. Wallace "Troy"**, *no monogram, excellent condition*	4.00	5.00
☐ **1847 Rogers "Troy"**, *monogram, mint condition*	3.00	5.00
☐ **1847 Rogers "Adoration"**, *no monogram, good condition* ..	3.00	4.00
☐ **1847 Rogers "Adoration"**, *no monogram, fair condition* ...	1.00	2.00
☐ **1847 Rogers "Adoration"**, *no monogram, poor condition* ..	1.00	2.00
☐ **1847 Rogers "Ancestral"**, *no monogram, excellent condition*	4.00	5.00
☐ **1847 Rogers "Ancestral"**, *no monogram, good condition* ..	3.00	4.00
☐ **1847 Rogers "Ancestral"**, *no monogram, fair condition*	1.00	2.00
☐ **1847 Rogers "Anniversary"**, *no monogram, excellent condition*	4.00	5.00
☐ **1847 Rogers "Anniversary"**, *no monogram, good condition*	3.00	4.00
☐ **1847 Rogers "Anniversary"**, *no monogram, fair condition* ..	1.00	2.00

	Price Range	
☐ 1847 Rogers "Arcadian", *no monogram, excellent condition*	6.00	7.00
☐ 1847 Rogers "Arcadian", *no monogram, good condition* . . .	4.00	5.00
☐ 1847 Rogers "Arcadian", *no monogram, fair condition*	1.00	2.00
☐ 1847 Rogers "Argosy", *no monogram, excellent condition* .	3.00	4.00
☐ 1847 Rogers "Argosy", *no monogram, good condition*	3.00	4.00
☐ 1847 Rogers "Argosy", *monogram, good condition*	2.00	3.00
☐ 1847 Rogers "Avon", *no monogram, excellent condition* . . .	4.00	5.00
☐ 1847 Rogers "Avon", *no monogram, good condition*	3.00	4.00
☐ 1847 Rogers "Avon", *no monogram, good condition*	3.00	4.00
☐ 1847 Rogers "Avon", *no monogram, excellent condition* . . .	3.00	5.00
☐ 1847 Rogers "Avon", *no monogram, excellent condition* . . .	4.00	5.00
☐ 1847 Rogers "Berkshire", *no monogram, excellent condition*	5.00	6.00
☐ 1847 Rogers "Berkshire", *no monogram, good condition* . .	3.00	4.00
☐ 1847 Rogers "Berkshire", *no monogram, excellent condition*	6.00	7.00
☐ 1847 Rogers "Berkshire", *no monogram, resilvered*	7.00	8.00
☐ 1847 Rogers "Berkshire", *no monogram, good condition* . .	6.00	7.00
☐ 1847 Rogers "Charter Oak", *no monogram, resilvered*	7.00	8.00
☐ 1847 Rogers "Charter Oak", *monogram, good condition* . . .	4.00	5.00
☐ 1847 Rogers "Charter Oak", *no monogram, excellent condition*	6.00	7.00
☐ 1847 Rogers "Charter Oak", *no monogram, good condition*	5.00	6.00
☐ 1847 Rogers "Charter Oak", *no monogram, poor condition* .	2.00	3.00
☐ 1847 Rogers "Charter Oak", *no monogram, good condition*	7.00	8.00
☐ 1847 Rogers "Charter Oak", *no monogram, fair condition* . .	3.00	4.00
☐ 1847 Rogers "Columbia", *no monogram, excellent condition*	12.00	14.00
☐ 1847 Rogers "Columbia", *no monogram, good condition* . .	10.00	12.00
☐ 1847 Rogers "Columbia", *no monogram, fair condition*	3.00	4.00
☐ 1847 Rogers "Continental", *no monogram, excellent condition*	4.00	5.00
☐ 1847 Rogers "Continental", *no monogram, good condition*	3.00	4.00
☐ 1847 Rogers "Continental", *no monogram, fair condition* . .	1.00	2.00
☐ 1847 Rogers "Cromwell", *no monogram, excellent condition*	3.00	4.00
☐ 1847 Rogers "Cromwell", *no monogram, fair condition*	1.00	2.00
☐ 1847 Rogers "Daffodil", *no monogram, good condition*	4.00	5.00
☐ 1847 Rogers "Daffodil", *excellent condition*	5.00	6.00
☐ 1847 Rogers "Daffodil II", *no monogram, excellent condition*	4.00	5.00
☐ 1847 Rogers "Daffodil II", *no monogram, good condition* . .	3.00	4.00
☐ 1847 Rogers "Daffodil II", *no monogram, fair condition* . . .	1.00	2.00
☐ 1847 Rogers "Dundee", *no monogram, excellent condition*	4.00	5.00
☐ 1847 Rogers "Dundee", *no monogram, fair condition*	1.00	2.00
☐ 1847 Rogers "Embossed", *no monogram, excellent condition*	4.00	5.00
☐ 1847 Rogers "Embossed", *no monogram, good condition* .	3.00	4.00
☐ 1847 Rogers "Embossed", *no monogram, fair condition* . . .	1.00	2.00
☐ 1847 Rogers "Esperanto", *no monogram, excellent condition*	4.00	5.00
☐ 1847 Rogers "Esperanto", *no monogram, good condition* . .	3.00	4.00
☐ 1847 Rogers "Esperanto", *no monogram, fair condition* . . .	1.00	2.00

		Price Range	

- [ ] **1847 Rogers "Eternally Yours"**, *no monogram, excellent condition* 4.00 5.00
- [ ] **1847 Rogers "Eternally Yours"**, *no monogram, good condition* 3.00 4.00
- [ ] **1847 Rogers "Eternally Yours"**, *no monogram, fair condition* 1.00 2.00
- [ ] **1847 Rogers "Faneuil"**, *no monogram, excellent condition* 4.00 5.00
- [ ] **1847 Rogers "First Love"**, *no monogram, excellent condition* 3.00 4.00
- [ ] **1847 Rogers "First Love"**, *no monogram, good condition* .. 2.00 3.00
- [ ] **1847 Rogers "First Love"**, *no monogram, excellent condition* 4.00 5.00
- [ ] **1847 Rogers "First Love"**, *no monogram, good condition* .. 3.00 4.00
- [ ] **1847 Rogers "First Love"**, *no monogram, fair condition* ... 1.00 2.00
- [ ] **1847 Rogers "Flair"**, *no monogram, mint condition* 4.00 5.00
- [ ] **1847 Rogers "Flair"**, *no monogram, excellent condition* ... 3.00 4.00
- [ ] **1847 Rogers "Flair"**, *no monogram, excellent condition* ... 4.00 5.00
- [ ] **1847 Rogers "Flair"**, *no monogram, good condition* 3.00 4.00
- [ ] **1847 Rogers "Flair"**, *no monogram, fair condition* 1.00 2.00
- [ ] **1847 Rogers "Floral"**, *no monogram, excellent condition* .. 7.00 8.00
- [ ] **1847 Rogers "Floral"**, *no monogram, good condition* 5.00 6.00
- [ ] **1847 Rogers "Floral"**, *no monogram, excellent condition* .. 9.00 11.00
- [ ] **1847 Rogers "Floral"**, *no monogram, fair condition* 4.00 5.00
- [ ] **1847 Rogers "Gothic"**, *no monogram, excellent condition* . 2.00 3.00
- [ ] **1847 Rogers "Grecian"**, *no monogram, mint condition* 3.00 4.00
- [ ] **1847 Rogers "Grecian"**, *no monogram, good condition* 2.00 3.00
- [ ] **1847 Rogers "Grecian"**, *no monogram, fair condition* 1.00 2.00
- [ ] **1847 Rogers "Heraldic"**, *no monogram, good condition* ... 3.00 4.00
- [ ] **1847 Rogers "Heritage"**, *no monogram, mint condition* 4.00 5.00
- [ ] **1847 Rogers "Laurel"**, *no monogram, excellent condition* .. 5.00 6.00
- [ ] **1847 Rogers "Laurel"**, *no monogram, good condition* 4.00 5.00
- [ ] **1847 Rogers "Laurel"**, *no monogram, fair condition* 1.00 2.00
- [ ] **1847 Rogers "Laurel"**, *monogram, excellent condition* 3.00 4.00
- [ ] **1847 Rogers "Leilani"**, *no monogram, mint condition* 4.00 5.00
- [ ] **1847 Rogers "Lorne"**, *no monogram, excellent condition* .. 3.00 4.00
- [ ] **1847 Rogers "Lorne"**, *no monogram, good condition* 3.00 4.00
- [ ] **1847 Rogers "Lorne"**, *no monogram, fair condition* 1.00 2.00
- [ ] **1847 Rogers "Lotus"**, *no monogram, good condition* 5.00 6.00
- [ ] **1847 Rogers "Louvain"**, *no monogram, excellent condition* 4.00 5.00
- [ ] **1847 Rogers "Louvain"**, *no monogram, good condition* 3.00 4.00
- [ ] **1847 Rogers "Louvain"**, *no monogram, fair condition* 1.00 2.00
- [ ] **1847 Rogers "Lovelace"**, *no monogram, excellent condition* 4.00 5.00
- [ ] **1847 Rogers "Lovelace"**, *no monogram, good condition* ... 3.00 4.00
- [ ] **1847 Rogers "Lovelace"**, *no monogram, fair condition* 1.00 2.00
- [ ] **1847 Rogers "Magic Rose"**, *no monogram, mint condition* . 4.00 5.00
- [ ] **1847 Rogers "Magic Rose"**, *no monogram, excellent condition* 2.00 3.00
- [ ] **1847 Rogers "Magic Rose"**, *no monogram, excellent condition* 4.00 5.00
- [ ] **1847 Rogers "Magic Rose"**, *no monogram, good condition* 3.00 4.00
- [ ] **1847 Rogers "Magic Rose"**, *no monogram, fair condition* .. 1.00 2.00
- [ ] **1847 Rogers "Marquise"**, *no monogram, excellent condition* 4.00 5.00
- [ ] **1847 Rogers "Marquise"**, *no monogram, good condition* .. 3.00 4.00

	Price Range	
☐ **1847 Rogers "Moselle"**, *no monogram, excellent condition*	**11.00**	**13.00**
☐ **1847 Rogers "Moselle"**, *no monogram, good condition*	**9.00**	**11.00**
☐ **1847 Rogers "Moselle"**, *no monogram, fair condition*	**3.00**	**4.00**
☐ **1847 Rogers "Moselle"**, *no monogram, resilvered*	**13.00**	**15.00**
☐ **1847 Rogers "Newport"**, *no monogram, resilvered*	**5.00**	**6.00**
☐ **1847 Rogers "Newport"**, *no monogram, excellent condition*	**4.00**	**5.00**
☐ **1847 Rogers "Newport"**, *no monogram, good condition* ...	**3.00**	**4.00**
☐ **1847 Rogers "Newport"**, *no monogram, fair condition*	**2.00**	**3.00**
☐ **1847 Rogers "Norfolk"**, *no monogram, excellent condition* .	**4.00**	**5.00**
☐ **1847 Rogers "Norfolk"**, *no monogram, good condition*	**3.00**	**4.00**
☐ **1847 Rogers "Norfolk"**, *no monogram, fair condition*	**1.00**	**2.00**
☐ **1847 Rogers "Old Colony"**, *no monogram, excellent condition*	**5.00**	**6.00**
☐ **1847 Rogers "Old Colony"**, *no monogram, excellent condition*	**4.00**	**5.00**
☐ **1847 Rogers "Old Colony"**, *no monogram, good condition* .	**3.00**	**4.00**
☐ **1847 Rogers "Old Colony"**, *monogram, good condition*	**1.00**	**2.00**
☐ **1847 Rogers "Old Colony"**, *no monogram, resilvered*	**7.00**	**8.00**
☐ **1847 Rogers "Old Colony"**, *no monogram, excellent condition*	**5.00**	**6.00**
☐ **1847 Rogers "Old Colony"**, *no monogram, good condition* .	**3.00**	**4.00**
☐ **1847 Rogers "Old Colony"**, *monogram, excellent condition*	**4.00**	**5.00**
☐ **1847 Rogers "Persian"**, *no monogram, excellent condition*	**5.00**	**6.00**
☐ **1847 Rogers "Portland"**, *no monogram, excellent condition*	**4.00**	**5.00**
☐ **1847 Rogers "Portland"**, *no monogram, good condition* ...	**3.00**	**4.00**
☐ **1847 Rogers "Portland"**, *no monogram, fair condition*	**1.00**	**2.00**
☐ **1847 Rogers "Princess"**, *no monogram, good condition* ...	**3.00**	**4.00**
☐ **1847 Rogers "Priscilla"**, *no monogram, excellent condition*	**4.00**	**5.00**
☐ **1847 Rogers "Priscilla"**, *no monogram, good condition* ...	**3.00**	**4.00**
☐ **1847 Rogers "Priscilla"**, *no monogram, fair condition*	**1.00**	**2.00**
☐ **1847 Rogers "Queen Ann"**, *no monogram, excellent condition*	**3.00**	**4.00**
☐ **1847 Rogers "Queen Ann"**, *no monogram, excellent condition*	**7.00**	**8.00**
☐ **1847 Rogers "Reflection"**, *no monogram, excellent condition*	**4.00**	**5.00**
☐ **1847 Rogers "Reflection"**, *no monogram, good condition* ..	**3.00**	**4.00**
☐ **1847 Rogers "Reflection"**, *no monogram, fair condition* ...	**1.00**	**2.00**
☐ **1847 Rogers "Remembrance"**, *no monogram, excellent condition*	**3.00**	**4.00**
☐ **1847 Rogers "Remembrance"**, *no monogram, excellent condition*	**4.00**	**5.00**
☐ **1847 Rogers "Remembrance"**, *no monogram, good condition*	**3.00**	**4.00**
☐ **1847 Rogers "Remembrance"**, *no monogram, fair condition*	**1.00**	**2.00**
☐ **1847 Rogers "Ruby"**, *no monogram, excellent condition* ...	**4.00**	**5.00**
☐ **1847 Rogers "Saratoga"**, *no monogram, excellent condition*	**4.00**	**5.00**
☐ **1847 Rogers "Saratoga"**, *no monogram, good condition* ...	**3.00**	**4.00**
☐ **1847 Rogers "Saratoga"**, *no monogram, fair condition*	**1.00**	**2.00**
☐ **1847 Rogers "Savoy"**, *no monogram, good condition*	**2.00**	**3.00**
☐ **1847 Rogers "Savoy"**, *no monogram, fair condition*	**1.00**	**2.00**
☐ **1847 Rogers "Sharon"**, *no monogram, excellent condition* .	**6.00**	**7.00**
☐ **1847 Rogers "Sharon"**, *no monogram, good condition*	**5.00**	**6.00**

	Price Range	
☐ 1847 Rogers "Sharon", *monogram, excellent condition* ...	4.00	5.00
☐ 1847 Rogers "Silver Lace", *no monogram, excellent condition*	4.00	5.00
☐ 1847 Rogers "Silver Lace", *no monogram, good condition* .	3.00	4.00
☐ 1847 Rogers "Silver Lace", *no monogram, fair condition* ...	1.00	2.00
☐ 1847 Rogers "Siren", *no monogram, good condition*	5.00	6.00
☐ 1847 Rogers "Siren", *no monogram, fair condition*	2.00	3.00
☐ 1847 Rogers "Springtime", *no monogram, excellent condition*	4.00	5.00
☐ 1847 Rogers "Springtime", *no monogram, good condition* .	3.00	4.00
☐ 1847 Rogers "Springtime", *no monogram, fair condition* ..	1.00	2.00
☐ 1847 Rogers "Vintage", *no monogram, resilvered*	7.00	8.00
☐ 1847 Rogers "Vintage", *no monogram, good condition*	4.00	5.00
☐ 1847 Rogers "Vintage", *no monogram, excellent condition*	7.00	8.00
☐ 1847 Rogers "Vintage", *no monogram, good condition*	5.00	6.00
☐ 1847 Rogers "Vintage", *no monogram, poor condition*	4.00	5.00
☐ 1847 Rogers "Vintage", *no monogram, resilvered*	7.00	8.00
☐ 1847 Rogers "Vintage", *monogram, good condition*	4.00	5.00
☐ 1847 Rogers "Vintage", *no monogram, resilvered*	7.00	8.00
☐ 1847 Rogers "Vintage", *no monogram, good condition*	5.00	6.00
☐ 1847 Rogers "Vintage", *no monogram, fair condition*	4.00	5.00
☐ 1847 Rogers "Vintage", *monogram, good condition*	2.00	3.00
☐ 1847 Rogers "Vintage", *no monogram, resilvered*	9.00	10.00
☐ 1847 Rogers "Vintage", *no monogram, excellent condition*	8.00	9.00
☐ 1847 Rogers "Vintage", *no monogram, good condition*	7.00	8.00
☐ 1847 Rogers "Vintage", *monogram, excellent condition* ...	7.00	8.00
☐ 1847 Rogers "Vintage", *monogram, good condition*	6.00	7.00
☐ 1881 Rogers "Beverly", *no monogram, good condition*	1.00	2.00
☐ 1881 Rogers "Briar Rose", *no monogram, excellent condition*	4.00	5.00
☐ 1881 Rogers "Briar Rose", *no monogram, good condition* .	3.00	4.00
☐ 1881 Rogers "Coronet", *no monogram, excellnt condition* .	3.00	4.00
☐ 1881 Rogers "Coronet", *no monogram, good condition*	2.00	3.00
☐ 1881 Rogers "Enchantment", *no monogram, excellent condition*	4.00	5.00
☐ 1881 Rogers "Enchantment", *no monogram, good condition*	3.00	4.00
☐ 1881 Rogers "Enchantment", *no monogram, fair condition*	1.00	2.00
☐ 1881 Rogers "Flirtation", *no monogram, excellent condition*	2.00	3.00
☐ 1881 Rogers "Godetia", *no monogram, excellent condition*	3.00	4.00
☐ 1881 Rogers "Grecian", *no monogram, excellent condition*	4.00	5.00
☐ 1881 Rogers "Grecian", *no monogram, good condition*	3.00	4.00
☐ 1881 Rogers "Janet", *no monogram, good condition*	3.00	4.00
☐ 1881 Rogers "Janet", *no monogram, poor condition*	1.00	2.00
☐ 1881 Rogers "LaVigne", *no monogram, excellent condition*	5.00	6.00
☐ 1881 Rogers "LaVigne", *no monogram, fair condition*	3.00	4.00
☐ 1881 Rogers "LaVigne", *no monogram, poor condition*	1.00	2.00
☐ 1881 Rogers "LaVigne", *no monogram, resilvered*	7.00	8.00
☐ 1881 Rogers "LaVigne", *no monogram, good condition* ...	4.00	5.00
☐ 1881 Rogers "Plymouth", *no monogram, good condition* ..	3.00	4.00
☐ 1881 Rogers "Plymouth", *no monogram, fair condition*	1.00	2.00
☐ 1881 Rogers "Scandanavia", *no monogram, excellent condition*	4.00	5.00

	Price Range	
☐ 1881 Rogers "Scandanavia", *no monogram, good condition*	3.00	4.00
☐ 1881 Rogers "Scandanavia", *no monogram, fair condition* .	1.00	2.00
☐ 1881 Rogers "Surf Club", *no monogram, excellent condition*	2.00	3.00

(Sterling Silver)

☐ Alvin "Chateau Rose", *no monogram*	11.00	13.00
☐ Alvin "Majestic", *monogram*	10.00	12.00
☐ Alvin "Maryland", *monogram*	10.00	12.00
☐ Alvin "Maryland", *monogram*	10.00	12.00
☐ Alvin "Old Orange Blossom", *monogram and date*	18.00	20.00
☐ Alvin "Raphael", *monogram*	11.00	13.00
☐ Alvin "Touraine", *monogram*	10.00	12.00
☐ Alvin "Touraine", *monogram*	11.00	13.00
☐ Blackington "Scroll & Bead", *no monogram*	19.00	21.00
☐ Dominick & Haff "Blossom", *monogram*	14.00	15.00
☐ Dominick & Haff "Imperial", *monogram*	14.00	16.00
☐ Dominick & Haff "King", *monogram*	11.00	13.00
☐ Dominick & Haff "Louis XIV", *old styling, no monogram* ...	9.00	11.00
☐ Durgin "Fairfax", *5¾" L., no monogram*	9.00	11.00
☐ Durgin "Fairfax", *monogram*	10.00	12.00
☐ Fine Arts "Processional", *no monogram*	9.00	11.00
☐ Frank Smith "Chippendale", *no monogram*	9.00	11.00
☐ Frank Smith "Fiddle Thread", *no monogram*	20.00	22.00
☐ Frank Smith "Newport Shell", *no monogram*	20.00	22.00
☐ Frank Whiting "Orleans", *no monogram, date*	9.00	12.00
☐ Gorham "Blithe Spirit", *no monogram*	9.00	11.00
☐ Gorham "Buckingham", *no monogram*	9.00	11.00
☐ Gorham "Buttercup", *no monogram*	11.00	13.00
☐ Gorham "Buttercup", *no monogram*	16.00	18.00
☐ Gorham "Camellia", *no monogram*	9.00	11.00
☐ Gorham "Chantilly", *monogram*	8.00	9.00
☐ Gorham "Chantilly", *monogram*	10.00	12.00
☐ Gorham "Chantilly", *no monogram*	10.00	12.00
☐ Gorham "Chantilly", *no monogram*	10.00	12.00
☐ Gorham "Chantilly", *monogram*	9.00	11.00
☐ Gorham "Classic Bouquet", *monogram*	10.00	13.00
☐ Gorham "Colonial", *no monogram*	8.00	9.00
☐ Gorham "Cluny", *monogram*	7.00	8.00
☐ Gorham "Etruscan", *no monogram*	9.00	11.00
☐ Gorham "Etruscan", *monogram*	9.00	11.00
☐ Gorham "Fairfax", *no monogram*	10.00	12.00
☐ Gorham "Greenbrier", *no monogram*	9.00	11.00
☐ Gorham "Hunt Club", *no monogram*	9.00	11.00
☐ Gorham "Imperial Chrysanthemum", *no monogram*	9.00	10.00
☐ Gorham "Imperial Chrysanthemum", *monogram*	9.00	11.00
☐ Gorham "Jac Rose", *no monogram*	7.00	8.00
☐ Gorham "Lancaster", *monogram*	10.00	12.00
☐ Gorham "Lancaster Rose", *no monogram*	11.00	13.00
☐ Gorham "LaScala", *no monogram*	13.00	15.00
☐ Gorham "Maryland", *no monogram*	8.00	9.00
☐ Gorham "Medici", *no monogram*	11.00	13.00
☐ Gorham "Newcastle", *monogram*	10.00	12.00
☐ Gorham "Norfolk", *no monogram*	9.00	10.00

		Price Range
☐ Gorham "Plymouth", *monogram*	8.00	9.00
☐ Gorham "Plymouth", *monogram*	10.00	12.00
☐ Gorham "Poppy", *(old), monogram*	11.00	13.00
☐ Gorham "Poppy", *monogram*	6.00	7.00
☐ Gorham "Raphael", *no monogram*	5.00	6.00
☐ Gorham "Rondo", *no monogram*	10.00	12.00
☐ Gorham "Sovereign", *no monogram*	10.00	13.00
☐ Gorham "Sovereign", *monogram*	9.00	11.00
☐ Gorham "Strasbourg", *monogram*	11.00	13.00
☐ Gorham "Tuileries", *no monogram*	9.00	11.00
☐ Gorham "Versailles", *no monogram*	16.00	18.00
☐ Gorham "Willow", *no monogram*	9.00	11.00
☐ Gorham "Zodiac", *no monogram, set of 12*	210.00	235.00
☐ International "Abbotsford", *monogram*	9.00	11.00
☐ International "Angelique", *monogram*	9.00	11.00
☐ International "Avalon", *monogram*	16.00	18.00
☐ International "Brandon", *no monogram*	10.00	11.00
☐ International "Cambridge", *monogram*	9.00	11.00
☐ International "Courtship", *no monogram*	9.00	11.00
☐ International "DuBarry", *no monogram*	12.00	14.00
☐ International "Frontenac", *monogram and date*	13.00	15.00
☐ International "Frontenac", *no monogram*	7.00	8.00
☐ International "Georgian Maid", *no monogram*	7.00	8.00
☐ International "Grand Regency", *no monogram*	11.00	13.00
☐ International "Joan of Arc", *no monogram*	10.00	12.00
☐ International "Masterpiece", *no monogram*	10.00	13.00
☐ International "Monticello", *no monogram*	10.00	13.00
☐ International "Prelude", *monogram*	9.00	11.00
☐ International "Royal Danish", *no monogram*	9.00	11.00
☐ International "Spring Glory", *no monogram*	5.00	6.00
☐ International "Stratford", *monogram*	10.00	12.00
☐ International "Swan Lake", *no monogram*	9.00	11.00
☐ International "Vision", *no monogram*	9.00	11.00
☐ International "Wild Rose", *no monogram*	9.00	11.00
☐ Kirk "Quadrille", *monogram*	12.00	14.00
☐ Kirk "Repousse', *no monogram*	10.00	12.00
☐ Lunt "Chateau", *monogram*	9.00	10.00
☐ Lunt "Delacourt", *no monogram*	11.00	13.00
☐ Lunt "Eloquence", *no monogram*	11.00	13.00
☐ Lunt "Floral Lace", *no monogram*	10.00	12.00
☐ Lunt "Mignonette", *no monogram*	9.00	11.00
☐ Lunt "Mt. Vernon", *no monogram*	10.00	13.00
☐ Lunt "Nellie Curtis", *monogram*	10.00	12.00
☐ Lunt "Pynchon", *no monogram*	9.00	10.00
☐ Lunt "Sweetheart Rose", *no monogram*	9.00	11.00
☐ Manchester "Vogue", *no monogram*	9.00	11.00
☐ Marshall Field, *hammered finish with applied grapevine motif*	40.00	45.00
☐ Oneida "Belle Rose", *no monogram*	9.00	11.00
☐ Oneida "Botticelli", *no monogram*	12.00	14.00
☐ Oneida "Heiress", *no monogram*	9.00	10.00
☐ Oneida "Heiress", *no monogram*	9.00	11.00
☐ Oneida "Lasting Spring", *no monogram*	8.00	10.00
☐ Oneida "Lasting Spring", *no monogram*	9.00	11.00

	Price Range	
☐ Oneida "Martinique", *no monogram*	9.00	11.00
☐ Oneida "Silver Rose", *no monogram*	9.00	11.00
☐ Oneida "Silver Rose", *monogram*	8.00	10.00
☐ Reed & Barton "Francis I", *no monogram*	12.00	14.00
☐ Reed & Barton "Georgian Rose", *no monogram*	9.00	11.00
☐ Reed & Barton "Hampton Court", *no monogram*	10.00	12.00
☐ Reed & Barton "Itaglio", *monogram*	9.00	11.00
☐ Reed & Barton "LaContessa", *monogram*	9.00	11.00
☐ Reed & Barton "LaPerle", *no monogram*	10.00	12.00
☐ Reed & Barton "LaSplendide", *monogram and date*	11.00	13.00
☐ Reed & Barton "Les Cinq Fleurs", *monogram*	10.00	12.00
☐ Reed & Barton "Les Cinq Fleurs", *no monogram*	13.00	15.00
☐ Reed & Barton "Les Six Fleurs", *no monogram*	10.00	12.00
☐ Reed & Barton "Love Disarmed", *monogram*	40.00	45.00
☐ Reed & Barton "Marlborough", *monogram*	7.00	8.00
☐ Reed & Barton "Marlborough", *no monogram*	14.00	16.00
☐ Reed & Barton "Old Virginia", *no monogram*	10.00	13.00
☐ Reed & Barton "Spanish Baroque", *no monogram*	10.00	13.00
☐ Reed & Barton "Spanish Baroque", *no monogram*	10.00	13.00
☐ Rogers "Mt. Vernon", *monogram*	10.00	13.00
☐ Royal Crest "Castle Rose", *no monogram*	9.00	11.00
☐ Shiebler "Fiorito", *monogram*	19.00	21.00
☐ Shiebler, pattern unknown, *Art Nouveau floral design*	17.00	19.00
☐ Shreve & Co., pattern unknown, *Art Deco styling, no monogram*	27.00	30.00
☐ Simpson, Hall & Miller "Frontenac", *no monogram*	9.00	11.00
☐ Simpson, Hall & Miller "Frontenac", *extra heavy, no monogram*	10.00	12.00
☐ Simpson, Hall & Miller "Trumbull", *monogram*	7.00	8.00
☐ Tiffany "Beekman", *monogram*	6.00	7.00
☐ Tiffany "Colonial", *no monogram*	9.00	10.00
☐ Tiffany "English King", *no monogram*	14.00	16.00
☐ Tiffany "English King", *monogram*	14.00	16.00
☐ Tiffany "Flemish", *monogram*	12.00	14.00
☐ Tiffany "Flemish", *no monogram*	9.00	10.00
☐ Tiffany "Grammercy", *no monogram*	9.00	11.00
☐ Tiffany "Hampton", *monogram*	10.00	13.00
☐ Tiffany "Marquise", *monogram*	6.00	7.00
☐ Tiffany "Persian", *monogram*	7.00	8.00
☐ Towle "Canterbury", *no monogram*	9.00	11.00
☐ Towle "Chippendale", *no monogram*	9.00	11.00
☐ Towle "Country Manor", *no monogram*	10.00	13.00
☐ Towle "El Grande", *monogram*	10.00	13.00
☐ Towle "Esplanade", *monogram*	9.00	11.00
☐ Towle "Fontana", *no monogram*	9.00	11.00
☐ Towle "French Provincial", *nomonogram*	9.00	11.00
☐ Towle "Georgian", *no monogram*	12.00	14.00
☐ Towle "Georgian", *no monogram*	19.00	21.00
☐ Towle "Georgian", *monogram*	5.00	6.00
☐ Towle "King Richard", *no monogram*	11.00	13.00
☐ Towle "Kings", *no monogram*	11.00	13.00
☐ Towle "Kings", *no monogram*	19.00	21.00
☐ Towle "Laureate", *no monogram*	11.00	13.00
☐ Towle "Madeira", *no monogram*	10.00	12.00

	Price Range	
☐ Towle "Old Colonial", *no monogram*	13.00	15.00
☐ Towle "Old Colonial", *no monogram*	20.00	23.00
☐ Towle "Old English", *monogram*	9.00	11.00
☐ Towle "Old Master", *monogram*	10.00	12.00
☐ Towle "Silver Flutes", *no monogram*	9.00	11.00
☐ Towle "Spanish Provincial", *no monogram*	10.00	12.00
☐ Towle "Virginia Carvel", *monogram*	10.00	12.00
☐ Tuttle "Onslow", *no monogram*	5.00	6.00
☐ Unger Bros. "He Loves Me", *no monogram*	24.00	27.00
☐ Unger Bros. "He Loves Me", *no monogram*	24.00	27.00
☐ Unger Bros. "He Loves Me", *gold wash bowl, monogram* ..	27.00	30.00
☐ Unger Bros. "Love's Dream", *no monogram*	27.00	30.00
☐ Unger Bros., pattern unknown, *Art Nouveau, no monogram*	36.00	39.00
☐ Wallace "Grande Baroque", *no monogram*	12.00	14.00
☐ Wallace "Lucerne", *monogram*	8.00	10.00
☐ Wallace "Lucerne", *no monogram*	9.00	11.00
☐ Wallace "Lucerne", *monogram*	11.00	13.00
☐ Wallace "Rosepoint", *no monogram*	10.00	12.00
☐ Wallace "Rosepoint", *monogram*	8.00	10.00
☐ Wallace "Royal Rose", *no monogram*	9.00	11.00
☐ Wallace "Violet", *monogram*	4.00	5.00
☐ Wallace "Waverly", *monogram*	10.00	12.00
☐ Wallace "Waverly", *no monogram*	11.00	13.00
☐ Wallace "Zodiac", *set of 12*	145.00	160.00
☐ Watson "Mt. Vernon", *no monogram*	7.00	8.00
☐ Watson, pattern unknown, *flower, monogram*	15.00	17.00
☐ Watson-Newell "Bacchante", *no monogram*	25.00	27.00
☐ Watson-Newell "Cherub", *monogram*	13.00	15.00
☐ Watson-Newell "Phoebe", *no monogram*	19.00	21.00
☐ Westmoreland "John & Priscilla", *no monogram*	10.00	12.00
☐ Westmoreland "Milburn Rose", *no monogram*	10.00	12.00
☐ Whiting "Egyptian", *no monogram*	10.00	12.00
☐ Whiting "Imperial Queen", *monogram*	12.00	14.00
☐ Whiting "Imperial Queen", *monogram*	5.00	6.00
☐ Whiting "Ivy", *monogram removed*	10.00	12.00
☐ Whiting "King Albert", *no monogram*	10.00	12.00
☐ Whiting "King Albert", *monogram*	9.00	11.00
☐ Whiting "Lily", *monogram*	8.00	9.00
☐ Whiting "Louis XV", *no monogram*	11.00	13.00
☐ Whiting "Louis XV", *monogram*	12.00	14.00
☐ Whiting "Madame Jumel"	12.00	14.00
☐ Whiting "Plain Tip", *no monogram*	12.00	14.00
☐ Whiting "Radiant", *no monogram*	10.00	12.00
☐ Wood & Hughes "Venetian", *monogram*	11.00	13.00
☐ Wood & Hughes "Undine", *no monogram*	9.00	10.00
☐ Maker unknown, *rose on tip, gold wash bowl*	8.00	9.00
☐ Maker unknown, *plique a jour, swirled handle, 4" L.*	18.00	20.00
☐ Maker unknown, *fish handle with enamel trim*	9.00	11.00

TEA STRAINERS

Almost an "unknown" among silverware collectibles, because of their infrequent appearances in sales, tea strainers deserve better recognition. Though their use was not too glamorous a one, their physical appearance suggests just the opposite: few silver objects are as handsome, or as interestingly varied in shapes and designs. Today's simple mesh tea strainers represent a mere shadow of their precedessors' brilliance, with extra-wide lips on the bowls and decoration spilling over on to the handle in many specimens. Silver tea strainers are a delight to collect and an excellent specialty: every collection of them is unique.

Tea Strainers, *(L to R) (sterling),* Stieff *"Rose",* 120.00; Galt Bros. *"repousse" design with ebony handle,* 150.00; Alvin *"Bridal Rose",* 120.00

(Silver-Plated)

☐ **Wm. Rogers, pattern unknown,** *floral border, no monogram, good condition*	11.00	13.00

(Sterling Silver)

☐ **Kirk "Repousse",** *double-handled type*	54.00	60.00
☐ **Lebolt**	45.00	50.00
☐ **Whiting,** *long-handled, scalloped and beaded rim*	33.00	36.00
☐ **Maker unknown,** *wooden handle*	13.00	15.00

TEA URNS

(Silver-Plated)

☐ **Maker unknown,** *spherical body, scroll and floral chasing in intricate pattern, rectangular base with four scroll feet. 14" H.*	—	170.00

TEETHING RINGS
(Sterling Silver)

	Price Range	
☐ **Maker unknown**, *mother of pearl with sterling bell, in original box, engraving on bell*	—	30.00

TERRAPIN FORKS

Terrapin, or sea turtle, became a prized delicacy in the U.S. in the late 19th century, though its consumption was (for geographical reasons) confined mostly to the East Coast. For a while, all prestigeous restaurants featured terrapin on their menus, and many ambitious hostesses whipped up the dish at home — even though few recipe books gave any hint how to prepare it! Of course the occasion was not complete unless terrapin was consumed with terrapin forks. Obviously these were not made in any vast numbers, but are an interesting curiosity and well worth the collector's notice.

(Silver-Plated)

☐ **Maker unknown**, *ornate floral pattern, monogram and date, good condition*	3.00	4.00

(Sterling Silver)

☐ **Gorham "King George"**, *monogram*	26.00	29.00
☐ **Whiting "Lily"**, *no monogram*	36.00	39.00

THERMOMETER HOLDERS

These were used in conjunction with thermometers for recording room temperature. Generally they were placed inconspicuously in the dining room — but with a handsome silver holder there was nothing to be ashamed of if one's thermometer happened to be seen. The tops are either pierced or provided with a hanging loop.

(Silver-Plated)

☐ **Maker unknown**, *small cherubs on each corner, fair condition*	11.00	13.00

(Sterling Silver)

☐ **Maker unknown**, *hand-chased floral repousse design, replacement thermometer, loop handle, monogram*	80.00	90.00

THIMBLE HOLDERS

These accessories to the sewing kits of grandma and great-grandma's time were more often made of stainless steel or nickel, but silver ones do turn up.

(Silver-Plated)

☐ **Meriden**, *ornate floral design, good condition*	20.00	22.00

(Sterling Silver)

☐ **Maker unknown**, *pierced design, cylindrical shape*	33.00	36.00

THIMBLES

These indispensible sewing aids were made not only in silver, but occasionally gold; and sometimes silver with a gold wash. Designs are very diverse, in spite of the very dimunitive size. Prices are considerably higher than the bullion content would warrant, because thimble collecting (silver specimens as well as others) is a hobby in itself. The European antique shops are marvelous hunting grounds, if silver thimbles are your topic of interest. The maker's name seldom appears on them, and their patterns do not, of course, conform with those of tableware. Many unusual, novelty, and even souvenir types will be found. They can present problems in dating, as they offer so little evidence on which to draw conclusions.

(Silver-Plated)	**Price Range**	
☐ **Maker unknown,** *gold wash, in original leather case*	18.00	20.00

(Sterling Silver)		
☐ **Maker unknown,** *engraved scenic design*	20.00	23.00
☐ **Maker unknown,** *engraved scenic design on border*	8.00	9.00
☐ **Maker unknown,** *engraved scenic design on border*	14.00	16.00
☐ **Maker unknown,** *hand-crafted ornate design*	2.00	3.00
☐ **Maker unknown,** *copper band, etched design on copper* ...	2.00	3.00
☐ **Maker unknown,** *heavy and ornate*	9.00	11.00

TOAST FORKS

Toast forks, small and dainty, were used to spear small pieces of toast (cut from slices into croutons) and dip them into soups or broths. They turn up only occasionally on the collectibles market.

(Sterling Silver)		
☐ **Durgin,** *pattern unknown, plain design, no monogram*	45.00	50.00

TOMATO SERVERS

Though tomatoes have been used as a foodstuff in Europe for several thousands of years, tomato servers are not of very early origin. Like many other accessories which appeared on the Victorian table, they served to satisfy the concerned hostesses need to use correct utensils at all times.

(Silver-Plated)		
☐ **Community "Beverly",** *no monogram, excellent condition* .	12.00	14.00
☐ **Community "Bird of Paradise",** *no monogram, excellent condition*	18.00	20.00
☐ **Community "Bird of Paradise",** *monogram, excellent condition*	14.00	16.00
☐ **Community "Grosvenor",** *no monogram, excellent condition*	13.00	15.00
☐ **Community "Grosvenor",** *monogram, good condition*	9.00	11.00
☐ **Community "Morning Rose",** *no monogram, mint condition*	7.00	8.00
☐ **Community "Sheraton",** *no monogram, excellent condition*	9.00	10.00
☐ **Community "Sheraton",** *no monogram, good condition* ...	11.00	13.00
☐ **Community "Silver Sands",** *no monogram, mint condition* .	6.00	7.00
☐ **Heirloom "Cardinal",** *no monogram, excellent condition* ..	12.00	14.00
☐ **Holmes & Edwards "Century",** *no monogram, excellent condition*	17.00	19.00
☐ **Holmes & Edwards "First Lady",** *no monogram, excellent condition*	16.00	18.00
☐ **Holmes & Edwards "Lovely Lady",** *no monogram, excellent condition*	20.00	22.00

	Price Range	

☐ Holmes & Edwards "Lovely Lady", *monogram, good condition*	9.00	10.00
☐ Holmes & Edwards "Rosemary", *no monogram, excellent condition*	27.00	30.00
☐ Nobility "Royal Rose", *no monogram, good condition*	8.00	9.00
☐ Nobility "Royal Rose", *no monogram, excellent condition*	16.00	18.00
☐ Oneida "Clarion", *no monogram, excellent condition*	10.00	12.00
☐ Rogers "Orange Blossom", *no monogram, excellent condition*	20.00	22.00
☐ Rogers & Bro. "Flemish", *no monogram, excellent condition*	10.00	12.00
☐ Rogers & Bro. "Siren", *no monogram, fair condition*	24.00	26.00
☐ R. Wallace "Cardinal", *no monogram, excellent condition*	20.00	22.00
☐ Tudor "Baronet", *no monogram, good condition*	8.00	9.00
☐ Tudor "Skyline", *no monogram, excellent condition*	11.00	13.00
☐ S.L. & G.H. Rogers "Encore", *no monogram, excellent condition*	10.00	12.00
☐ S.L. & G.H. Rogers "Minerva", *no monogram, excellent condition*	12.00	14.00
☐ S.L. & G.H. Rogers "Minerva", *no monogram, excellent condition*	14.00	16.00
☐ W.D. Smith Silver Co. "Adam", *no monogram, excellent condition*	7.00	8.00
☐ Wm. A. Rogers "Lido", *no monogram, good condition*	10.00	12.00
☐ Wm. A. Rogers "Rosalie", *no monogram, excellent condition*	16.00	18.00
☐ Wm. Rogers "Fair Lady", *no monogram, excellent condition*	10.00	12.00
☐ Wm. Rogers "Mountain Rose", *no monogram, excellent condition*	11.00	13.00
☐ Wm. Rogers "Precious Mirror", *no monogram, excellent condition*	16.00	18.00
☐ Wm. Rogers Mfg. Co. "Laurel", *no monogram, excellent condition*	11.00	13.00
☐ 1847 Rogers "Anniversary", *no monogram, excellent condition*	11.00	13.00
☐ 1847 Rogers "Charter Oak", *no monogram, excellent condition*	42.00	47.00
☐ 1847 Rogers "Charter Oak", *no monogram, good condition*	36.00	40.00
☐ 1847 Rogers "Flair", *no monogram, excellent condition*	42.00	47.00
☐ 1847 Rogers "Charter Oak", *no monogram, good condition*	36.00	40.00
☐ 1847 Rogers "Flair", *no monogram, excellent condition*	10.00	12.00
☐ 1847 Rogers "Heraldic", *no monogram, excellent condition*	14.00	16.00
☐ 1847 Rogers "Laurel", *no monogram, good condition*	5.00	6.00
☐ 1847 Rogers "Louvain", *no monogram, excellent condition*	9.00	11.00
☐ 1847 Rogers "Magic Rose", *no monogram, mint condition*	9.00	11.00

(Sterling Silver)

☐ Blackington & Co., pattern unknown, *pierced, no monogram*	36.00	40.00
☐ Dominick & Haff "Mazarin", *8" L., monogram*	22.00	24.00
☐ Durgin "Vintage", *no monogram*	24.00	27.00
☐ Gorham "Buttercup", *no monogram*	60.00	66.00

	Price Range	
☐ **Gorham "Chantilly"**, *pierced, monogram*	22.00	24.00
☐ **Gorham "Rondo"**, *no monogram*	60.00	66.00

TOOTHPICK HOLDERS

The place of toothpicks was taken, in very early times, by the point of a knife-blade. Since their introduction, toothpicks have never stood in any danger of going out of style — even though manufacturers have tried to popularize substitutes. Toothpick holders are especially appealing. The designs are either ornate or bizarre, with a distinct leaning toward novelty: almost as if the toothpick holder had to, by eye-catching appearance, make an excuse for its presence on the table. They can be collected topically: animals on toothpick holders, etc. Not too many of the collectors' shops have them, but with some searching they can be found.

(Silver-Plated)

☐ **Pairpoint**, *figural, rat by side of holder, "This is the rat that ate the malt" engraving*	54.00	60.00
☐ **Tufts**, *figural, boy riding bicycle, has toothpick holder on his back*	160.00	180.00
☐ **Maker unknown**, *figural, buffalo*	75.00	85.00
☐ **Maker unknown**, *figural, baby chick*	16.00	18.00
☐ **Maker unknown**, *figural, porcupine, good condition*	36.00	40.00

TOOTHPOWDER JARS

Toothpowder was used before toothpaste. Of course the majority of purchasers used it directly from the commercial carton, but those not satisfied with the store carton could transfer its contents into a gleaming silver toothpowder jar. These had their heyday on the market from about 1880 to 1920, giving way thereafter to the almost universal preference for toothpaste . . . for which silver containers were impossible!

(Sterling Silver)

☐ **Maker unknown**, *floral repousse design, monogram*	40.00	45.00
☐ **Maker unknown**, *engraved vertical lines, monogram*	22.00	24.00

TOYS

A comprehensive survey of all toys utilizing silver in one way or another would make an interesting study. But this is, of course, well beyond the scope of our book. We can only comment that toys have, from time to time, been made of silver, and that they have mainly been toys for the very young. A larger proportion of silver toys will be found among the playthings of early Europe than early America.

(Sterling Silver)

☐ **Maker unknown**, *yo-yo, plain design, no monogram*	13.00	15.00

TRAVEL CUPS

Travel cups were a monument to the inventive genius of the 19th century: collapsible drinking cups that could be slipped in the pocket. Today the travel cup is still with us, but the modern version is more likely to be made of plastic. Even when first introduced, silver was not the usual material, but stainless steel. Only a comparatively few were produced in silver. But even the existence of these few in silver shows that, where silver was concerned, out of sight was definitely not out of mind.

(Silver-Plated)

☐ **Pairpoint,** *in original box, no monogram, good condition* ..   **9.00**   **11.00**

TRAYS

Trays whose use can be assigned to specific purposes have been listed elsewhere in this book, in their proper alphabetical places. Here we list a few trays of the all-purpose variety, of which every silverware manufacturer produced at least several. Even many purchasers who demanded specific tablewares for specific uses would gladly use a tray for various purposes — serving meat or drink, or even passing around snacks at an afternoon tea. Nor was their use necessarily restricted to foodstuffs. A large tray of the type here pictured could be brought to the gentleman of the house in the morning, laden with kettle of boiling water and shaving equipment. The general belief of the public, that trays have no hobbyist value, leads to destruction of many for the bullion content. We would suggest that the advice of a competent authority be sought, before selling any old tray as scrap silver. It is certainly true that an antique dealer will not pay a premium over melt value for the majority of silver trays, but exceptions occur. If a tray is truly old, well designed, and soundly preserved, it should command at least 10% or possibly 15% over "melt" when sold to a dealer.

Tray, *(sterling), Dominick & Haff, monogram, 15" handle to handle, 25 ounces, c. 1875,* 450.00

(Silver-Plated)

☐ **Reed & Barton,** *square, Georgian styling, scrolls and flowers in relief, ribbing on inner rim, excellent condition* ..   **30.00**   **34.00**

☐ **Maker unknown,** *round, 14" diameter, ornate rim and handles, divided glass insert, excellent condition* **28.00**   **32.00**

☐ **maker unknown,** *rectangular, 17" handle to handle, plain design, excellent condition* **30.00**   **34.00**

☐ **Maker unknown,** *gallery type, 15" x 1¼" H., mint condition*   **19.00**   **21.00**

(Sterling Silver)

	Price Range	
☐ **Gorham,** *8½" L., reeded rim, no monogram*	27.00	30.00
☐ **Kalo,** *c. 1920, plain shape, round, hammered finish, 12" diameter, 21 oz.*	180.00	200.00
☐ **Maker unknown,** *made for Bailey, Banks & Biddle Co., Philadelphia, c. 1908, rectangular, 24½" L., pierced gallery border, crest and motto in center, 145 oz.*	1850.00	2050.00

UMBRELLA HANDLES

These are often very decorative and appealing, as they encompass many topical subjects — birds, fish, human figures and faces, etc. The problem in collecting them is that the majority are still attached to the umbrella body, for which the hobbyist — even if he has no interest in umbrellas beyond their handles — must pay a premium. Then a storage difficulty arises, often prompting collectors to remove the handles and discard the remainder of the umbrella, especially if its condition is poor and has not weighed much in the price. Sometimes old handles are found applied to new shafts and fabric, but this hardly makes sense as the owner could not wish to actually use such a specimen.

(Sterling Silver)

☐ **Maker unknown,** *repousse design, 7" L., with new umbrella*	62.00	70.00
☐ **Maker unknown,** *scroll design, 6½" L., with old umbrella in bad condition*	9.00	11.00

VASES

Though silver has never been as popular for vases as ceramic, the precedent for silver vases is extremely old, going back into classical antiquity. The objection to them in modern times is that the expense involved is not repaid by their decorative qualities, as ceramic vases (which can be painted) are much more colorful. Chiefly the use of silver vases has been confined to moble households, and especially those in which a strong family tradition for heraldry has prevailed — as the sides of vases were ideal for engraving coats of arms. Unless a vase is extremely plain or in damaged condition, its value as a collectors' item will exceed its bullion or melt value.

(Sterling Silver)

☐ **Gorham,** *8½" H., not weighted, engraved work and openwork*	285.00	315.00
☐ **International "Orchid",** *5" H., weight unknown*	36.00	40.00
☐ **Maker unknown,** *J.E. Caldwell & Co., Philadelphia, Pa., retailer, c. 1896, flared cylindrical shape, pierced and applied floral motifs on top, base and mid-section, 18" H., 57 ozs.*	775.00	860.00
☐ **Maker unknown,** *trumpet shape, 12" H., 6" diameter at top, weight unknown*	40.00	45.00

WAFFLE SERVERS

The large size and interesting shapes of waffle servers has helped promote them as collectors' items. They are not plentiful enough to form the basis of a large collection.

(Sterling Silver)	Price Range	
☐ Gorham "Buttercup", *no monogram*	60.00	66.00
☐ Towle "Paul Revere", *no monogram*	36.00	39.00
☐ Whiting "Lily", *no monogram*	100.00	115.00

WATCHES

Watches can only be touched upon briefly in a general work of this nature. Obviously the number of silver watches made over the years was staggering, and their values cannot be judged by any single set of standards. Many considerations are involved: the maker, age, quantity of silver, quality of movement, condition, etc. In general, old silver watches which were expensive originally have risen in value quicker than cheaper ones: a specimen retailed in 1900 at $8.50 might today be at $200, while one sold for $2.50 is likely to be in the $40-50 range on today's market. This is of course a rough guide only.

(coin silver)		
☐ American Watch Co., 18S, *fancy coin silver case, key-wind, key set, 17 jewels, Bartlett Model, solid balance wheel, stock number 669,664, running condition*	24.00	27.00
☐ Elgin, 18S, *heavy coin silver hunting case, J.T. Ryerson Model, stock number 252,192, solid balance wheel, excellent running condition*	40.00	44.00
☐ Waltham, 18S, *coin silver, heavy coin silver case, 11-15 jewels, key-wind, key set, Samuel Richards model, excellent running condition*	33.00	36.00

(Sterling Silver)		
☐ Addison, *fancy sterling case, not running*	19.00	21.00
☐ Elgin, *15 jewel, sterling and gold inlaid case*	105.00	120.00
☐ Rockford, *fancy engraved swing-open case, key wind, running condition*	40.00	43.00
☐ Waltham, 18S, *16 jewel, sterling case in mint condition*	36.00	40.00
☐ Waltham, *17 jewels, sterling case, running condition*	26.00	29.00

WHISK BROOMS

More of these were made in silver than you might think. There will either be embossed or engraved designs, or a combination of the two. Condition of the broom hairs counts slightly in the value.

(Silver-Plated)		
☐ Meriden, *ornate embossed floral design, no monogram, excellent condition*	8.00	9.00

(Sterling Silver)		
☐ Maker unknown, *small size, plain design*	3.00	4.00

YOUTH SETS

These are sets of a knife, fork and spoon, made for the use of young children. They were intended as the utensils with which the child learned to use untensils, and in progressive homes were introduced as early as possible.

Many carry either a monogram or the child's first name spelled out. As can be expected, the knives are not very sharp, and in terms of size the articles in a youth set are smaller than their adult equivalents.

	Price Range	
(Silver-Plated)		
☐ **Community "Coronation"**, *three-piece set, no monogram, good condition*	30.00	32.00
☐ **Community "Coronation"**, *two-piece set, no monogram, good condition*	8.00	9.00
☐ **C. Rogers & Bros. A-1**, *pattern unknown, very ornate, two-piece set, no monogram, excellent condition*	10.00 12.00	
☐ **Tudor "Queen Bess II"**, *three-piece set, no monogram, excellent condition*	16.00	18.00
☐ **Tudor "Queen Bess II"**, *two-piece set, monogram, good condition*	7.00	8.00
☐ **Williams Bros. "Isabella"**, *two-piece set, no monogram, excellent condition*	16.00	18.00
☐ **Williams Bros. "Isabella"**, *three-piece set, no monogram, excellent condition*	22.00	24.00
☐ **1847 Rogers "Berkshire"**, *two-piece set, monogram, excellent condition*	9.00	11.00
☐ **1847 Rogers "Berkshire"**, *three-piece set, no monogram, resilvered*	21.00	23.00
☐ **1847 Rogers "Berkshire"**, *three-piece set, monogram, fair condition*	5.00	6.00
☐ **1847 Rogers "Charter Oak"**, *two-piece set, no monogram, good condition*	17.00	19.00
☐ **1847 Rogers "Charter Oak"**, *three-piece set, no monogram, good condition*	18.00	20.00
☐ **1847 Rogers "Flair"**, *two-piece set, no monogram, excellent condition*	7.00	8.00
☐ **1847 Rogers "Flair"**, *three-piece set, no monogram, good condition*	14.00	16.00
☐ **1847 Rogers "Remembrance"**, *two-piece set, no monogram, good condition*	8.00	10.00
☐ **1847 Rogers "Remembrance"**, *three-piece set, no monogram, resilvered*	24.00	27.00
☐ **1881 Rogers "Flirtation"**, *three-piece set, no monogram, excellent condition*	11.00	13.00
☐ **1881 Rogers "Flirtation"**, *three-piece set, monogram, poor condition*	3.00	4.00
(Sterling Silver)		
☐ **Dominick & Haff "Renaissance"**, *three-piece set, knife flat-handled, engraved with child's name and date*	40.00	45.00
☐ **Gorham "Fairfax"**, *three-piece set, monogram and date* . . .	24.00	27.00
☐ **International "Bridal Veil"**, *three-piece set, no monogram* .	30.00	34.00
☐ **Reed & Barton "Francis I"**, *three-piece set, no monogram* .	36.00	39.00
☐ **Simpson, Hall & Miller "Frontenac"**, *three-piece set, silver-plated blades, monogram*	52.00	57.00

ALVIN COMPANY, THE

PATTERNS	CURRENT STATUS
Albemarle	available
Antique	special order only
Antique No. 8	special order only
Apollo	special order only
Avila	available
Bridal Bouquet	available
Bridal Rose	special order only
Cellini	special order only
Chapel Bells	special order only
Chased Romantique	available
Chateau Rose	available
Chippendale, new	special order only
Chippendale, old	special order only
Delaware	discontinued
Della Robbia	special order only
Duquesne	special order only
Edward VII	discontinued
Eternal Rose	available
Evangeline	special order only
Evangeline, No. 7	special order only
Flander, new	special order only
Flanders, old	special order only
Fleur de Lis	special order only
Florence Nightingale	special order only
Florentine	discontinued
Francis I	special order only
French Scroll	available
Gainsborough	special order only
Hamilton	special order only
Hampton	special order only
Jenny Lind	discontinued
Josephine	special order only
Kenmore	special order only
Lace	discontinued
Lady Beatrice	special order only
Lorna Doone	special order only
Lorraine	discontinued
Majestic	discontinued
Marie Antoinette	special order only
Marseilles	special order only
Maryland	special order only
Maryland, hammered	special order only
Mastercraft	special order only
Maytime	special order only
Melrose	discontinued
Miss Alvin	special order only
Miss America	special order only
Modern Colonial	special order only
Molly Stark	special order only
Monterey	discontinued
Morning Glory	special order only
Nuremburg	special order only

PATTERNS	CURRENT STATUS
Orange Blossom, new	special order only
Orange Blossom, old	special order only
Orient	discontinued
Pirouette	available
Prince Eugene	available
Raleigh	special order only
Raphael	discontinued
Regent	special order only
Richmond	special order only
Roanoke	special order only
Romantique	special order only
Rosecrest	special order only
Shenandoah	special order only
Sorrento	discontinued
Southern Charm	available
Spring Bud	available
Star Blossom	special order only
Suffolk	special order only
Viking	discontinued
Virginia	special order only
Vivaldi	available
Wellington	discontinued
Wm. Penn	special order only
Wm. Penn, No 7	special order only
Winchester	special order only

AMSTON SILVER COMPANY

PATTERNS	CURRENT STATUS
American Colonial	special order only
Arcadia	special order only
Athene	special order only
Champlain	special order only
Colonial Rose	special order only
Duncan Phyfe	special order only
Ecstasy	special order only
Empire	special order only
Gladstone	special order only
Puritan	special order only
Queen Mary	special order only
Tyrolean	special order only

CONCORD SILVERSMITHS CORPORATION

PATTERNS	CURRENT STATUS
America	discontinued
Colonial	discontinued
Concord (formerly Yankee Clipper	special order only
Crusader	special order only
Danish	special order only
Old Hampshire	special order only

DOMINICK & HAFF

PATTERNS	CURRENT STATUS
Acanthus	*discontinued*
Alexandra	*discontinued*
Basket-of-Flowers	*special order only*
Basket Weave	*special order only*
Blossom	*discontinued*
Broad Antique	*discontinued*
Century	*special order only*
Charles II	*discontinued*
Chippendale	*discontinued*
Contempora	*special order only*
Cupid	*discontinued*
Eastlake	*special order only*
Fiddle Antique	*discontinued*
Gothic	*discontinued*
Grape	*discontinued*
Imperial	*discontinued*
Labors of Cupid (formely Nineteen Hundred)	*available*
La France	*special order only*
La Salle	*special order only*
La Salle, chased	*special order only*
Lexington	*special order only*
Louis XIV	*special order onl*
Louis XIV, old style	*discontinue*
Louis XVI	*special order onl*
Louis, old style	*discontinued*
Madeleine	*special order only*
Marie Antoinette	*special order only*
Marie Antoinette, chased	*special order only*
Marie Antoinette, chased x 96	*special order only*
Martha Washington	*special order only*
Mayfair	*special order only*
Mayfair, engraved	*special order only*
Mayflower	*discontinued*
Mazarin	*special order only*
Medallion	*discontinued*
New King	*special order only*
Old Basket of Flowers	*discontinued*
Old English Antique	*special order only*
Old English Antique, No. 1	*special order only*
Plain Antique	*discontinued*
Pointed Antique, hammered	*available*
Pointed Antique, No. 2, engraved	*special order only*
Pointed Antique, No. 3, engraved	*special order only*
Priscilla	*special order only*
Queen Anne, No. 11, engraved	*special order only*

PATTERNS	CURRENT STATUS
Queen Anne, No. 15, engraved	*special order only*
Queen Anne, No. 18, engraved	*special order only*
Queen Anne, plain	*special order only*
Queen Elizabeth	*special order only*
Rattail Antique	*special order only*
Renaissance	*discontinued*
Rococo	*discontinued*
"1776"	*discontinued*
Shannon	*special order only*
Shell	*special order only*
Tipt Antique	*discontinued*
Tipt Fiddle Antique	*discontinued*
Tradition	*special order only*
Victoria	*discontinued*
Virginia	*special order only*
Virginia No. 19, engraved	*special order only*
Virginia No. 20, engraved	*special order only*
Washington	*special order only*
Yorktown (formely F25)	*special order only*

FESSENDEN & COMPANY

PATTERNS	CURRENT STATUS
Alice	*discontinued*
Antique	*discontinued*
Avon	*discontinued*
Daisy	*discontinued*
Graeco	*discontinued*
Greenwich	*discontinued*
Langdon	*discontinued*
La Provence	*discontinued*
Marie Louise	*discontinued*
McKinley	*discontinued*
Narcissus	*discontinued*
Newport	*discontinued*
Old Boston, hand hammered	*discontinued*
Old Rose	*discontinued*
Tremont	*discontinued*
Tulip	*discontinued*

FRANK M. WHITING & COMPANY

PATTERNS	CURRENT STATUS
Adams	*special order only*
Antique	*special order only*
Antique B	*special order only*
Autumn	*special order only*
Colonial Antique	*special order only*

PATTERNS	CURRENT STATUS
Crystal	special order only
Damascus	special order only
Esther	special order only
Genoa	special order only
George III	special order only
Georgian Shell	special order only
Gothic	special order only
Governor Winthrop	special order only
Hagie	special order only
Helena 1st	special order only
Josephine	special order only
Kings Court (formerly Neapolitan)	special order only
Lily, engraved	special order only
Lily (formerly Floral)	special order only
Marquis	special order only
Narcissus	special order only
Orleans	special order only
Palm	special order only
Pearl	special order only
Plain Tip	special order only
Princess Ingrid	available
Roderic	special order only
Rose, engraved	special order only
Rose of Sharon	available
Shell	special order only
Silver Song	special order only
Talisman Rose	special order only
Troubadour	special order only
Victoria (formerly Florence)	special order only
Wheat, engraved	special order only

FRANK SMITH SILVER COMPANY

PATTERNS	CURRENT STATUS
Adrienne	discontinued
American Chippendale (formerly Chippendale) Division of R. Blackinton & Co.	available
Antique	discontinued
Baronial	discontinued
Bead	discontinued
Beverly	discontinued
Bostonia	discontinued
Cambodia	discontinued
Century	discontinued
Chippendale, old	discontinued
Classic American, Division of R. Blackinton & Co.	available
Classic Beauty	discontinued
Colbert	discontinued

PATTERNS	CURRENT STATUS
Colonial, hand hammered, Division of R. Blackinton & Co.	available
Countess	discontinued
Crystal	special order only
Federal Cotillion (formerly Edward VII) Division of R. Blackinton & Co.	available
Fiddle	discontinued
Fiddle Shell (formerly Alden) Division of R. Blackinton & Co.	available
Fiddle Thread (formerly French Thread) Division of R. Blackinton & Co.	available
French Antique	discontinued
George VI (formerly Richfield)	discontinued
Georgian Garland (formerly Isleworth) Division of R. Blackinton & Co.	available
Golden Age	discontinued
Ivanhoe	discontinued
Ivy	discontinued
Kensington	discontinued
Laurel	discontinued
Lincoln, engraved	discontinued
Lincoln K, engraved	discontinued
Lion	discontinued
L. Kraft	discontinued
Martha Randolph	discontinued
Martha Washington	discontinued
Mayfair	discontinued
Mayflower	discontinued
Mayflower, hand chased	discontinued
M. W. Lily	discontinued
M. W. Star	discontinued
Newport Shell (formerly Puritan) Division of R. Blackinton & Co.	available
No. 2	discontinued
No. 4	discontinued
No. 9, engraved	discontinued
No. 10	discontinued
No. 12	discontinued
No. 14	discontinued
No. 15	discontinued
Oak	discontinued
Paul Revere, engraved	discontinued
Pilgrim	discontinued
Priscilla	discontinued
Salem	discontinued
Shell	discontinued
Tokay	discontinued
Tulipan	discontinued
Vergennes	discontinued

PATTERNS	CURRENT STATUS
V. Kraft . . . . *discontinued*
Windsor . . . . *discontinued*
Winslow . . . . *discontinued*
Woodily, Divison of R. Blackinton & Co. .
available

GORHAM

PATTERNS	CURRENT STATUS
Acanthus, *c. 1891* . . . . *discontinued*
Adam, *c. 1906* . . . . *special order only*
Albemarle, *c. 1894*. . . . *special order only*
Albion, *Durgin Division,*
c. 1880 . . . . *discontinued*
Alcazar, *Durgin Division,*
c. 1885 . . . . *discontinued*
Alhambra, *c. 1880* . . . . *discontinued*
Andante, *c. 1963*. . . . . *available*
Angelo, *c. 1870* . . . . *discontinued*
Antique, *Durgin Division*
c. 1880 . . . . *discontinued*
Antique, *c. 1880*. . . . . . *special order only*
Antique, chased, *c. 1885* . . *discontinued*
Antique Engraved 1, *c. 1880* . . . .
. . . . *special order only*
Antique Engraved 2, *c. 1880* . . . .
. . . . *special order only*
Antique Engraved 3, *c. 1880* . . . .
. . . . *special order only*
Antique Engraved 4, *c. 1880* . . . .
. . . . *special order only*
Antique Engraved 5, *c. 1880* . . . .
. . . . *special order only*
Antique Engraved 6, *c. 1880* . . . .
. . . . *special order only*
Antique Engraved 7, *c. 1880* . . . .
. . . . *special order only*
Antique Engraved 8, *c. 1880* . . . .
. . . . *special order only*
Antique Engraved 9, *c. 1880* . . . .
. . . . *special order only*
Antique Engraved 10, *c. 1880* . . . .
. . . . *special order only*
Antique Engraved 11, *c. 1880* . . . .
. . . . *special order only*
Antique Engraved 12, *c. 1880* . . . .
. . . . *special order only*
Antique Engraved 15, *c. 1880* . . . .
. . . . *special order only*
Antique, hammered, *c. 1880* . . . .
. . . . *special order only*
Antique, hammered and applied, *c. 1880*
. . . . *special order only*

PATTERNS	CURRENT STATUS
Antique Lily, engraved, *Whiting Division*
c. 1885 . . . . *special order only*
Antique M-2, engraved, *Whiting Division*
c. 1885 . . . . *special order only*
Antique Rosette, *Whiting Division* . . . . .
c. 1880 . . . . *discontinued*
Antique Sheaf, *Durgin Division,*
c. 1895 . . . . *special order only*
Antique Tip, *Whiting Division,*
c. 1880. . . . .
. . . . *discontinued*
Apostles, large, *c. 1890* . . . *discontinued*
Apostles, small, *c. 1890* . . . *discontinued*
Arabesque, *Whiting Division,*
c. 1880 . . . . *discontinued*
Armor, *Whiting Division,*
c. 1875 . . . . *discontinued*
Arts & Crafts, *Durgin Division*
c. 1910 . . . . *special order only*
Aspen, *c. 1963* . . . . *special order only*
Athenian, *Durgin Division*
c. 1875 . . . . *discontinued*
Athenian, *Whiting Division,*
c. 1890 . . . . *discontinued*
Atlanta, *c. 1910* . . . . . . *special order only*
Aurora, *c. 1870* . . . . *discontinued*
Balzac, *c. 1910*. . . . . . *special order only*
Bamboo, *c. 1880* . . . . . *special order only*
Baronial, *c. 1896*. . . . . *available*
Baronial, old, *c. 1897* . *special order only*
Bead, *Durgin Division,*
c. 1913 . . . . *special order only*
Bead, *Whiting Division,*
c. 1880 . . . . *discontinued*
Beaded, *c. 1855*. . . . . *discontinued*
Beaumont, *c. 1915* . . . *special order only*
Bedford, *c. 1895* . . . . *discontinued*
Berlin, *c. 1885* . . . . *discontinued*
Berry, *Whiting Division,*
c. 1885 . . . . *discontinued*
Beverly, *c. 1914* . . . . . . *special order only*
Birds Nest, *c. 1885* . . . . *discontinued*
Blithe Spirit, *c. 1959* . . *special order only*
Bouquet, *Durgin Division,*
c. 1900 . . . . *discontinued*
Bradford, *Durgin Division,*
c. 1880 . . . . *special order only*
Bridal, *Durgin Division,*
c. 1880 . . . . *discontinued*
Bristol, *c. 1885*. . . . . *discontinued*
Brookdale, *c. 1916*. . . . *special order only*
Buckingham, *c. 1910* . *special order only*
Bug, *Durgin Division* . . *special order only*

PATTERNS	CURRENT STATUS
Burlington, *Whiting Division,* c. 1900 . . . . *discontinued*	
Buttercup, *c. 1900* . . . . *available*	
Byzantine, *c. 1875* . . . . *discontinued*	
Cairo, *c. 1880* . . . . *discontinued*	
Cambridge, *c. 1899* . . . *special order only*	
Camellia, *c. 1942* . . . . *available*	
Carnation, *c. 1894* . . . . *discontinued*	
Cat Tails, *Durgin Division,* c. 1890 . . . . *discontinued*	
Celeste, *c. 1956* . . . . . . *special order only*	
Cellini, *c. 1915* . . . . *special order only*	
Chantilly, *c. 1895* . . . . *available*	
Chapel Rose, *c. 1963* . *special order only*	
Chateau, *Whiting Division* . . . . *special order only*	
Chatham, *Durgin Division,* c. 1910 . . . . *special order only*	
Chatham, hammered, *Durgin Division* . . . . *special order only*	
Chatham, No. 3, engraved, *Durgin Division* . . . . *special order only*	
Chatham, No. 4, chased, *Durgin Division* . . . . *special order only*	
Chelmsford, *c. 1911* . . *special order only*	
Chelsea Manor, *c. 1966* . . . . *available*	
Cheltenham, *Durgin Division discontinued*	
Cherry Blossom, *c. 1915special order only*	
Chesterfield, *c. 1908* . . . *special order only*	
Chippendale, *c. 1890* . . . . . *discontinued*	
Christina, *c. 1935* . . . . *special order only*	
Christina, engraved, *Feather Edge,* c. 1935 . . . . *special order only*	
Christina, engraved, *Old English Scroll,* c. 1935 . . . . *special order only*	
Chrysanthemum, *Durgin Division,* c. 1890 . . . . *special order only*	
Chrysanthemum, *c. 1890* . . . . *special order only*	
Cinderlla, *c. 1925* . . . . *discontinued*	
Classic Bouquet, *c. 1972* . . . . . . *available*	
Classique, *c. 1961* . . . . *available*	
Clematis, *c. 1885* . . . . . *special order only*	
Clermont, *c. 1915* . . . . *special order only*	
Cluny, *c. 1880* . . . . . . *special order only*	
Colfax, *Durgin Division,* c. 1910 . . . . *special order only*	
Coligni, *c. 1887* . . . . . . *special order only*	
Colonial, *c. 1880* . . . . . *special order only*	
Colonial, *Whiting Division,* c. 1900 . . . . *special order only*	
Colonial A, engraved, *Whiting Division* . . . . *special order only*	

PATTERNS	CURRENT STATUS
Colonial B, engraved, *Whiting Division* . . . . *special order only*	
Colonial Eagle . . . . *special order only*	
Corinthian, *c. 1872* . . . . *discontinued*	
Cottage, *c. 1861* . . . . *discontinued*	
Covington, engraved, *c. 1914* . . . . *special order only*	
Covington (formerly Covington Plain) c. 1914 . . . . *special order only*	
Covington hammered, *c. 1914* . . . . *special order only*	
Cox, *Whiting Division* . . . . . *discontinued*	
Cromwell, *Durgin Division* . . . . *special order only*	
Cromwell, *c. 1900* . . . . *special order only*	
Crown Baroque, *c. 1975* . . . . *available*	
Daisy, *c. 1880* . . . . *discontinued*	
Damascene, *c. 1964* . . *special order only*	
Dartmouth, *Durgin Division* . . . . *special order only*	
Dartmouth, *c. 1914* . . . *special order only*	
Dauphin, *Durgin Division* . . . . *special order only*	
Decor, *c.1953* . . . . *special order only*	
Delhi, *c. 1880* . . . . *special order only*	
Diamonds, *Whiting Division* . . . . *discontinued*	
Diana, *c. 1880* . . . . . . *special order only*	
Dighton, *c. 1914* . . . . . *special order only*	
Dolly Madison, *Durgin Division* . . . . *special order only*	
Dolly Madison, *c. 1929 special order only*	
Dolly Madison, engraved, *Durgin Division* . . . . *special order only*	
Dolly Madison, engraved, *c. 1929* . . . . *special order only*	
Domestic, *c. 1880* . . . . *discontinued*	
Dorothy Vernon, *Whiting Division* . . . . *special order only*	
Douglas, *c. 1899* . . . . *discontinued*	
Dowager, *c. 1875* . . . . *discontinued*	
Dresden, *c. 1885* . . . . *discontinued*	
Dresden, *Whiting Division* . *discontinued*	
DuBarry, *Durgin Division* . . . . *special order only*	
Duchess, *Whiting Division* . *discontinued*	
Duke of York, *Whiting Division* . . . . *special order only*	
East Lake, *Whiting Division discontinued*	
Edgeworth, *c. 1922* . . . *special order only*	
Eglantine, *c. 1870* . . . . *special order only*	
Egyptian, *Whiting Division discontinued*	
Eighty Eight, *c. 1870* . . . . . . *discontinued*	
Eighty Three . . . . *discontinued*	

PATTERNS	CURRENT STATUS
Elmwood, *c. 1894*	*.... special order only*
Empire, *Durgin Division*	
	.... special order only
Empire, *Whiting Division*	*.. discontinued*
Empress, *c. 1880*	*......... discontinued*
Empress Josephine, *Durgin Division*	*...*
	.... discontinued
English Antique, *Durgin Division*	*.......*
	.... discontinued
English Gadroon, *c. 1939*	*.............*
	.... special order only
English Rose, *Durgin Division*	*.........*
	.... special order only
English Tip, *Durgin Division*	*..........*
	.... special order only
Epic, *c. 1941*	*......... special order only*
Espirit, *c. 1963*	*.............. available*
Essex, *Durgin Division special order only*	
Essex No. 5, engraved, *Durgin Division*	*..*
	.... special order only
Etruscan, *c. 1913*	*..... special order only*
Etruscan, engraved, *c. 1913*	*...........*
	.... special order only
Eva, *c. 1870*	*............. discontinued*
Eventide, *c. 1936*	*..... special order only*
Fairfax, *Durgin Division*	*...... available*
Fairfax, No. 1, engraved, *Durgin Division,*	
	.... special order only
Fairfax, No. 2, engraved *Durgin Division,*	
	.... special order only
Fairfax, No 3, engraved, *Durgin Division,*	
	.... special order only
Fairfax, No. 4-B, engraved,	
Durgin Division	*.... special order only*
Fairfield, *Whiting Division*	*. discontinued*
Fancy Tip, *Whiting Division discontinued*	
Fanshawe, *c. 1922*	*... special order only*
Farnham, *c. 1914*	*..... special order only*
Fiddle, *c. 1832*	*........... discontinued*
Fiddle, *Durgin Division special order only*	
Fiddle, *Whiting Division*	*... discontinued*
Fiddle, old, *c. 1832*	*....... discontinued*
Firelight, *c. 1959*	*..... special order only*
Fleur de Lis, *c. 1865*	*.. special order only*
Fleur de Lis, *Durgin Division,*	
	.... special order only
Fleury, *c. 1909*	*....... special order only*
Floral, *1865*	*............. discontinued*
Florence, *c. 1901*	*........ discontinued*
Florentine, *c. 1901*	*... special order only*
Fontainebleau, *c. 1880 special order only*	
French	*................ discontinued*
French Antique, *Durgin Division,*	
	.... discontinued
French Thread, *Whiting Division,*	
	.... discontinued
French Tipt, *c. 1832*	*...... discontinued*
Fruit, *Whiting Division*	*.... discontinued*
Gem Leaf, *Whiting Division discontinued*	
Gibney, *Whiting Division*	*. discontinued*
Gilpen, *c. 1880*	*........... discontinued*
Glendale	*........... special order only*
Gold Cipher, *c. 1952*	*.. special order only*
Gold Tip, *c. 1952*	*..... special order only*
Golden Damascene, *c. 1964*	
	.... special order only
Golden Snowflake (formely Snowflake)	
c. 1952	*........... special order only*
Golden Stardust, *c. 1952*	
	.... special order only
Golden Wheat, *c. 1952 special order only*	
Gorham, *c. 1880*	*........ discontinued*
Gorham, plain, *c. 1933 special order only*	
Gorham, plain, chased (also known as	
Winthrop) *c. 1933*	*.. special order only*
Gorham, plain, engraved A, *c. 1933*	
	.... special order only
Gorham, plain, engraved B, *c. 1933*	
	.... special order only
Gorham, plain, engraved C, *c. 1933*	
	.... special order only
Gossamer, *c. 1965*	*........... available*
Gossamer, engraved, *c. 1965*	
	.... available
Gothic, *c. 1919*	*....... special order only*
Governor's Lady, *c. 1937*	
	.... special order only
Governor's Lady, engraved A, *c. 1937*	
	.... special order only
Governor's lady, engraved B, *c. 1937*	
	.... special order only
Grape, *c. 1880*	*........... discontinued*
Grape, *Whiting Division*	*... discontinued*
Grecian, *Whiting Division*	
c. 1861	*................ discontinued*
Greenbrier, *c. 1938*	*........... available*
Griswold, *c. 1922*	*..... special order only*
Guilford, *c. 1914*	*..... special order only*
H 83, *c. 1870*	*............. discontinued*
H 108, *c. 1900*	*............ discontinued*
H 109, *c. 1900*	*............ discontinued*
H 111, *c. 1900*	*............ discontinued*
H 200, *c. 1900*	*............ discontinued*
H 316, *c. 1900*	*............ discontinued*
H 385, *c. 1900*	*............ discontinued*
H 443, *c. 1900*	*............ discontinued*
H 451, *c. 1900*	*............ discontinued*
Hamburg, *c. 1880*	*........ discontinued*

PATTERNS	CURRENT STATUS
Hamilton, c. 1909 . . . . special order only
Hampshire, Durgin Division, ... special order only
Hampton, c. 1913 . . . . special order only
Hanover, c. 1895 . . . . . special order only
Harwick, c. 1914 . . . . . special order only
Hawthorne, c. 1885 . . . special order only
Hazelmere, c. 1914 . . . special order only
Henry II . . . . special order only
Heraldic, Durgin Division . . discontinued
Heraldic, Whiting Division . discontinued
Hindostanee, c. 1878 . . . . . discontinued
Hispana (now Sovereign) . . . . . available
Hizen, c. 1880 . . . . special order only
Home, Whiting Division . . . discontinued
Honeysuckle, Durgin Division, ... discontinued
Honeysuckle, Whiting Division, ... discontinued
Huguenot, engraved, c. 1880 . . . . special order only
Hunt Club, Durgin Division, ... special order only
Hunt Club, engraved, Durgin Division, ... special order only
Hyperion, Whiting Division discontinued
Imperial, c. 1891 . . . . discontinued
Imperial Chrysanthemum, c. 1894 . . . . special order only
Imperial Queen, Whiting Division, ... special order only
Indian, Whiting Division . . . discontinued
Ionic, c. 1865 . . . . discontinued
Iris, Durgin Division . . special order only
Italian, c. 1865 . . . . discontinued
Italian, Whiting Division . . . discontinued
Italian-J, Whiting Division . discontinued
Italian-K, Whiting Division . discontinued
Ivy, c. 1865 . . . . discontinued
Ivy, Whiting Division . . . . . . discontinued
Jac Rose, c. 1885 . . . . . special order only
Japanese, c. 1870 . . . . discontinued
Japanese, Whiting Division discontinued
Jefferson, c. 1907 . . . . special order only
Jenny Lind, Whiting Division . . . . special order only
Jonquil, Durgin Division . . . . special order only
Josephine, c. 1885 . . . . discontinued
Kensington, c. 1893 . . . . . . discontinued
Keyston, Whiting Division . discontinued
King Albert, Whiting Division . . . . special order only

PATTERNS	CURRENT STATUS
King Edward, c. 1936 . . . . available
King Edward, Whiting Division . . . . special order only
King George, c. 1894 . . special order only
Kings I . . . . discontinued
Kings II, c. 1885 . . . . . . special order only
Kings III, c. 1885 . . . . . special order only
Knickerbocker, etched, c. 1870 . . . . discontinued
Knickerbocker, plain, c. 1870 . . . . discontinued
Lady Baltimore, Whiting Division . . . . special order only
Lady Washington . . . . discontinued
Lady's, c. 1865 . . . . discontinued
La Modele, c. 1909 . . . special order only
Lancaster, c. 1897 . . . . special order only
Lansdowne, c. 1917 . . special order only
La Scala, c. 1964 . . . . available
Late Georgian, c. 1934 special order only
Laurel, c. 1885 . . . . discontinued
Le Cordon, Whiting Division . . . . discontinued
Lenox, Durgin Division special order only
Lenox, c. 1897 . . . . discontinued
Lily, c. 1870 . . . . discontinued
Lily, Whiting Division . special order only
Lily of the Valley, c. 1950 . . . . special order only
Lily of the Valley, Whiting Division . . . . special order only
Livingston, Whiting Division . . . . special order only
Livingston A, engraved, Whiting Division . . . . special order only
Livingston B, chased, Whiting Division . . . . special order only
London, c. 1880 . . . . discontinued
London, engraved, c. 1880 . discontinued
Lonsdale, c. 1916 . . . . special order only
Lotus, c. 1865 . . . . discontinued
Louis XIV, c. 1870 . . . . discontinued
Louis XV, Durgin Division . discontinued
Louis XV, Whiting Division . . . . special order only
Louis XVI, c. 1897 . . . . special order only
Luxembourg, c. 1893 . . special order only
Lyric, c. 1940 . . . . available
Madam Jumel, Whiting Division . . . . special order only
Madam Morris, Whiting Division . . . . special order only
Madam Morris A, engraved, Whiting Division . . . . special order only

PATTERNS	CURRENT STATUS
Madame Royale, *Durgin Division* . . . . *available*	
Magnolia, *Durgin Division* . . . . *special order only*	
Mandarin, *Whiting Division* . . . . *special order only*	
Marechal Niel, *Durgin Division* . . . . *special order only*	
Marguerite, *c. 1901* . . . *special order only*	
Marguerite, engraved, *c. 1885* . . . . *special order only*	
Marie Antoinette, *c. 1890* . . . . *special order only*	
Marigold, *c. 1880* . . . . *discontinued*	
Marion, *c. 1914* . . . . . . *special order only*	
Martha Washington, *c. 1907* . . . . *discontinued*	
Maryland, *c. 1885* . . . . *discontinued*	
Mask, *Whiting Division* . . . *discontinued*	
Master, *c. 1885* . . . . . *special order only*	
Meadow, *c. 1897* . . . . *discontinued*	
Medallion, *Durgin Division*. *discontinued*	
Medallion, *c. 1865* . . . . *special order only*	
Medici, *c. 1970* . . . . *available*	
Medici, old, *c. 1880* . . . *special order only*	
Melrose, *c. 1948* . . . . *available*	
Melrose, *c. 1908* . . . . . *special order only*	
Milan . . . . *discontinued*	
Modern American, *c. 1928* . . . . *special order only*	
Montclair, *c. 1908* . . . . *special order only*	
Mothers, *c. 1875* . . . . . *special order only*	
Mothers, engraved, *c. 1875* . . . . *special order only*	
Mothers, hammered, *c. 1875* . . . . *special order only*	
Mothers, new, *c. 1927*. *special order only*	
Mythologique, *c. 1894* *special order only*	
Narcissus, *Durgin Division* *discontinued*	
Navarre, *Durgin Division* . . . . *special order only*	
New Art, *Durgin Division* . . . . *special order only*	
New Empire, *c. 1895* . . . . . . *discontinued*	
New Plymouth, *c. 1900* . . . . *discontinued*	
New Queens, *Durgin Division* . . . . *special order only*	
New Queens, *c. 1895* . *special order only*	
New Standish, *Durgin Division* . . . . *special order only*	
New Tipt, *c. 1870* . . . . *discontinued*	
New Vintage, *Durgin Division* . . . . *special order only*	

PATTERNS	CURRENT STATUS
Newcastle, *c. 1895* . . . *special order only*	
Newport, *Whiting Division*. *discontinued*	
Nocturne, *c. 1938* . . . . *special order only*	
Norfolk, *c. 1904* . . . . . . *special order only*	
No. 19-B, *Durgin Division* . . . . *special order only*	
No. 19-C, *Durgin Division* . . . . *special order only*	
No. 19-E, *Durgin Division* . . . . *special order only*	
No. 19-G, *Durgin Division* . . . . *special order only*	
No. 19, plain, *Durgin Division* . . . . *special order only*	
Nuremburg, *c. 1880*. . . *special order only*	
Oak & Acorn, *c. 1894* . . . . *available*	
Old Bead, *Whiting Division* *discontinued*	
Old Colony, new . . . . . *special order only*	
Old Colony, old, *c. 1896* . . . *discontinued*	
Old Dominion, *c. 1912*. *special order only*	
Old Empire, *Whiting Division* . . . . *discontinued*	
Old English Tipt, *c. 1870* . . . . . . *available*	
Old English Tipt, engraved A, *c. 1870* . . . . *special order only*	
Old English Tipt, engraved Wheat A, *c. 1870* . . . . *available*	
Old English Tipt, engraved Wheat B, *c. 1870* . . . . *available*	
Old French, *c. 1905* . . . *special order only*	
Old King, *Whiting Division*. *discontinued*	
Old London, engraved, *c. 1916* . . . . *special order only*	
Old London, plain, *c. 1916*. . . . . *special order only*	
Old Masters, *c. 1885* . . *special order only*	
Old Newport, *c. 1875*. . *special order only*	
Old Standish, *Durgin Division* . . . . *special order only*	
Olive, *Durgin Division* . . . . . *discontinued*	
Olive, *c. 1865* . . . . *discontinued*	
Orange Blossom, *Durgin Division* . . . . *special order only*	
Orchid, *c. 1894* . . . . *special order only*	
Oriana, *Whiting Division* . . . . *special order only*	
Orleana, *Durgin Division* . . *discontinued*	
Oval Thread, *Whiting Division* . . . . *discontinued*	
Oval Twist, *Whiting Division* . . . . *discontinued*	
Oxford, *c. 1895* . . . . *discontinued*	
Palm, *c. 1870* . . . . *discontinued*	
Paris, *c. 1900* . . . . *special order only*	

PATTERNS	CURRENT STATUS
Patrician . . . . *special order only*
Pattern A, *c. 1912* . . . . *special order only*
Pattern B, *c. 1916* . . . . *special order only*
Pattern C, *c. 1916* . . . . *special order only*
Pembroke, *c. 1895*. . . . *special order only*
Persian, *c. 1870* . . . . *discontinued*
Persian, *Whiting Division*. . *discontinued*
Perspective, *c. 1959* . . *special order only*
Piper, *c. 1880* . . . . *discontinued*
Plain Thread, *Whiting Division* . . . .
. . . . *discontinued*
Plain Tip, *Whiting Division*. *discontinued*
Play Fellow, *c. 1885* . . . . . . *discontinued*
Plymouth, *c. 1911* . . . . *special order only*
Pompadour, *Durgin Division* . . . .
. . . . *discontinued*
Pompadour, *Durgin Division* . . . .
. . . . *discontinued*
Pompeian, *Whiting Division* . . . .
. . . . *discontinued*
Pompeii, *c. 1865* . . . . *discontinued*
Poppy, *c. 1894* . . . . . . *special order only*
Portland, *Whiting Division* . . . .
. . . . *special order only*
Portland, *c. 1904* . . . . . *special order only*
Portsmouth, *c. 1918* . . *special order only*
Portsmouth, engraved, *c. 1918*. . . . .
. . . . *special order only*
Prince Albert, *Whiting Division* . . . .
. . . . *discontinued*
Princess Patricia, *Durgin Division* . . . . . .
. . . . *special order only*
Priscilla, *c. 1892* . . . . . *special order only*
Puritan, *c. 1956*. . . . . *available*
Queen Anne, *c. 1870* . . . . . . *discontinued*
Queens, *c. 1870* . . . . . . *special order only*
Radiant, *Whiting Division* . *discontinued*
Raphael, *c. 1875*. . . . . *available*
Regent, *Durgin Division* . . . .
. . . . *special order only*
Regent, *c. 1892* . . . . . *special order only*
Renaissance, *Durgin Division* . . . .
. . . . *special order only*
Revere, *Durgin Division* . . . *discontinued*
Roanoke, *c. 1913* . . . . . *special order only*
Roman, *c. 1855* . . . . *discontinued*
Rondo, *c. 1951* . . . . *available*
Rose Marie, *c. 1933*. . . *special order only*
Rose Tiara, *c. 1963*. . . . . *available*
Rosemont, *c. 1915*. . . . *special order only*
Rosette . . . . *discontinued*
Rosette, *Whiting Division* . . . .
. . . . *discontinued*
Rouen, *c. 1892* . . . . *discontinued*

PATTERNS	CURRENT STATUS
Royal Oak, *c. 1904*. . . . *special order only*
St. Cloud, *c. 1885*. . . . . *special order only*
St. Dunstan, chased, *c. 1917* . . . .
. . . . *special order only*
St. Dunstan, engraved, *c. 1917*. . . . .
. . . . *special order only*
St. Dunstan, plain . . . . *special order only*
St. Martin's, *Whiting Division*. . . . .
. . . . *special order only*
St. Martin's A, engraved, *Whiting*
Division . . . . *special order only*
Saxon Stag, *c. 1855* . . . . . . *discontinued*
Scandinavian, *c. 1898*. . . . . *discontinued*
Scroll, *Durgin Division* . . . . *discontinued*
Sea Rose, *c. 1958* . . . . *available*
Secret Garden, *c. 1959* . . . .
. . . . *special order only*
Shamrock V . . . . *special order only*
Sheaf of Wheat (formerly Tim Sheaf),
Durgin Division . . . . **special order only**
Shell, *Durgin Division* . . . .
. . . . *special order only*
Somerset, *c. 1916* . . . . *special order only*
Sovereign (formerly Hispana)
c. 1968 . . . . *available*
Sovereign, old, *c. 1941 special order only*
Spanish Tracery, *c. 1970* . . . .
. . . . *special order only*
Spotswood, *c. 1912*. . . *special order only*
Stamford, *c. 1914* . . . . *special order only*
Stardust, *c. 1957* . . . . . *special order only*
State Spoon, *c. 1896* . . *special order only*
Strasbourg, *c. 1897* . . . . *available*
Stratford, *Whiting Division* . . . .
. . . . *special order only*
Strawberry, *Durgin Division* *discontinued*
Stuart, *Whiting Division* . . . .
. . . . *special order only*
Swansea, *c. 1919*. . . . . *special order only*
Swiss, *c. 1870* . . . . *discontinued*
Theme, *c. 1954*. . . . . . *special order only*
Threaded, *c. 1855* . . . . *special order only*
Threaded Antique . . . . *special order only*
Tipt, *c. 1832* . . . . *special order only*
Touraine, *c. 1917*. . . . . *discontinued*
Trilogy, *c. 1969* . . . . . . *special order only*
Tudor, *c. 1880* . . . . *discontinued*
Tuileries, *c. 1906* . . . . . *special order only*
Tulip . . . . *discontinued*
Tulip, *Durgin Division* . *special order only*
Tuscan, *Whiting Division*. . *discontinued*
Twist, **Durgin Division** . . . . **discontinued**
Undine, *Durgin Division* . . . *discontinued*
Versailles, *c. 1888* . . . . *special order only*

PATTERNS	CURRENT STATUS
Victoria, *Durgin Division*	. . *discontinued*
Victoria (formerly Sheraton),	
Durgin Division	. . . . *special order only*
Villa, *Whiting Division*	. . . . *discontinued*
Villa-Norfolk (same as Norfolk)	
c. 1904	. . . . *special order only*
Vine	. . . . *special order only*
Violet, *c. 1890*	. . . . *discontinued*
Violet, *Whiting Division*	. . . .
	. . . . *special order only*
Virginia, *c. 1890*	. . . . *discontinued*
Virginiana, *c. 1905*	. . . . *special order only*
Walpole, *c. 1914*	. . . . . *special order only*
Wareham, *c. 1914*	. . . . *special order only*
Watteau, *Durgin Division*	. . *discontinued*
Wedgwood, *Whiting Division*	. . . .
	. . . . *special order only*
Wellington, *Durgin Division*	. . . .
	. . . . *special order only*
Wentworth, engraved, *Durgin Division*	. .
	. . . . *special order only*
Wentworth, hammered and chased	
wreath, *Durgin Division*	. . . .
	. . . . *special order only*
Wentworth No. 1822-C, chased	
Durgin Division	. . . *special order only*
Wentworth No. 18211, chased	
Durgin Division	. . . *special order only*
Weyworth, *c. 1914*	. . . . *special order only*
White Paisley, *c. 1966*	. . . . *available*
Willow, *c. 1954*	. . . . *special order only*
Windsor, *Durgin Division*	. . . .
	. . . . *special order only*
Winthrop, *Durgin Division*	. . . .
	. . . . *special order only*
Wreath, *c. 1911*	. . . . . . *special order only*
Wyndham, *c. 1912*	. . . . *special order only*
Zodiac, *c. 1906*	. . . . *available*

INTERNATIONAL SILVER COMPANY

PATTERNS	CURRENT STATUS
Abbottsford, *c. 1907*	. . . . . . *discontinued*
Acanthus, *c. 1917*	. . . . *discontinued*
Alexandria, *c. 1915*	. . . . *discontinued*
Althea, *c. 1910*	. . . . *discontinued*
Andover, *c. 1919*	. . . . *discontinued*
Angelique, *c. 1959*	. . . . *available*
Autocrat, *c. 1923*	. . . . *discontinued*
Avalon, *c. 1900*	. . . . *discontinued*
Beacon Hill, *c. 1913*	. . *special order only*
Berkeley (former Colonial), *c. 1915*	. . . . .
	. . . . *discontinued*

PATTERNS	CURRENT STATUS
Beverly, *c. 1910*	. . . . *discontinued*
Blossom Time, *c. 1950*	*special order only*
Brandon, *c. 1913*	. . . . . *special order only*
Breton Rose, *c. 1945*	. . *special order only*
Bridal Veil, *c. 1050*	. . . . *special order only*
Brocade, *c. 1950*	. . . . . *special order only*
Cambridge, *c. 1899*	. . . . *discontinued*
Cameo, *c. 1936*	. . . . *discontinued*
Cavell, *c. 1923*	. . . . *discontinued*
Charleroi, *c. 1922*	. . . . *discontinued*
Chesterfield, *c. 1914*	. . . . . . *discontinued*
Chimes	. . . . *discontinued*
Cloeta, *c. 1904*	. . . . *discontinued*
Colonial, hammered, *c. 1923*	. . . .
	. . . . *discontinued*
Colonial Shell, *c. 1941*	*special order only*
Continental, *c. 1934*	. . *special order only*
Copley, *c. 1910*	. . . . *discontinued*
Courtship, *c. 1936*	. . . . *special order only*
Coventry, *c. 1914*	. . . . . *special order only*
Crown Princess, *c. 1949*	. . . .
	. . . . *special order only*
Crystal, *c. 1966*	. . . . . . *special order only*
Davenport, *c. 1913*	. . . . *discontinued*
Dawn Rose, *c. 1969*	. . . *special order only*
Deerfield, *c. 1913*	. . . . . *special order only*
Desire, *c. 1955*	. . . . . . *special order only*
Devonshire, *c. 1914*	. . . . *discontinued*
Diana, *c. 1900*	. . . . *discontinued*
Dorchester, *c. 1910*	. . . . *discontinued*
Dorchester, old, *c. 1910*	. . . *discontinued*
Dresden, *c. 1898*	. . . . *discontinued*
Du Barry, *c. 1969*	. . . . *available*
Duchess, *c. 1907*	. . . . *discontinued*
Edgewood, *c. 1909*	. . . . *discontinued*
1810	. . . . *available*
Elegance, *c. 1934*	. . . . *special order only*
Elsinore, *c. 1913*	. . . . . *special order only*
Empress, *c. 1932*	. . . *special order only*
Empress Eugenie, *c. 1933*	. *discontinued*
Enchanted Rose, *c. 1954*	. . . .
	. . . . *special order only*
Enchantress, *c. 1937*	. *special order only*
Essex, *c. 1915*	. . . . *discontinued*
Florence, *c. 1903*	. . . . *discontinued*
Florentine, *c. 1912*	. . . . *discontinued*
Fontaine, *c. 1924*	. . . . . *special order only*
Frontenac, *c. 1832*	. . . . *discontinued*
Gadroon, *c. 1933*	. . . . . *special order only*
Georgian Maid, *c. 1923*	. . . .
	. . . . *special order only*
Golden LaStrada, *c. 1952*	. . . .
	. . . . *special order only*
Golden Tradewinds, *c. 1952*	. . . *available*

PATTERNS	CURRENT STATUS
Golden Trianon	available
Governor Bradford, c. 1913	discontinued
Governor Bradford, hammered, C. 1913	discontinued
Governor Warren, c. 1918	discontinued
Grand Recollection, c. 1956	special order only
Grand Trianon, c. 1975	available
Grande Regency, c. 1969	available
Irene, c. 1902	discontinued
Ivy, c. 1911	discontinued
Jeanne d'Arc, c. 1905	discontinued
Joan of Arc, c. 1940	available
John Alden, c. 1911	discontinued
John Winthrop, c. 1911	discontinued
Joy, c. 1952	special order only
Kenilworth, c. 1887	discontinued
Kensington, new, c. 1912	discontinued
Kensington, old, c. 1912	discontinued
King Louis, c. 1971	available
Kings, c. 1886	discontinued
Kingston, c. 1909	discontinued
Lady Betty, c. 1920	special order only
Lambeth, c. 1915	discontinued
Lambeth Manor, c. 1952	special order only
La Rochelle, c. 1909	discontinued
La Strada, c. 1972	available
Leicester, c. 1911	discontinued
Lenox, c. 1929	discontinued
Litchfield, c. 1898	discontinued
Lorraine, c. 1917	discontinued
Luzon, c. 1899	discontinued
Mademoiselle, c. 1964	special order only
Madrid, c. 1927	discontinued
Maintenon, c. 1933	special order only
Marathon, old, c. 1909	discontinued
Marcell, c. 1907	discontinued
Margaret, old, c. 1907	discontinued
Martel, c. 1925	discontinued
Masterpiece, c. 1963	special order only
May Melody, c. 1952	special order only
Milan, c. 1928	discontinued
Mille Fleurs, c. 1904	discontinued
Minuet, c. 1925	special order only
Minuet, carved, c. 1925	discontinued
Minuet, engraved, c. 1925	special order only
Monticello, c. 1924	discontinued
Moonbeam, c. 1949	discontinued
Moonglow, c. 1938	discontinued
Napoleon, c. 1910	discontinued
Nathan Hale, c. 1912	discontinued
New Marathon, c. 1912	discontinued

PATTERNS	CURRENT STATUS
New Margaret, c. 1912	discontinued
Norfolk, c. 1915	discontinued
Norse, c. 1937	special order only
Northern Lights, c. 1946	special order only
Norwood, c. 1915	discontinued
Nosegay, c. 1938	special order only
Old Charleston, c. 1951	special order only
Old English, c. 1917	special order only
Old Hampshire, c. 1916	discontinued
Orange Blossom	discontinued
Orchid, c. 1930	special order only
Pansy, c. 1909	special order only
Pantheon, c. 1920	special order only
Patria, c. 1918	discontinued
Pine Spray, c. 1951	special order only
Pine Tree, c. 1927	special order only
Prelude, c. 1939	available
Primrose, c. 1936	special order only
Processional, c. 1947	available
Queen Bess, c. 1911	discontinued
Queen's Lace, c. 1949	special order only
Quincy, c. 1917	discontinued
Radiant Rose, c. 1938	discontinued
Revere, c. 1898	discontinued
Rhapsody, new, c. 1957	available
Rhapsody, old, c. 1931	special order only
Richelieu, c. 1935	available
Richmond, c. 1910	discontinued
Riviera, c. 1936	special order only
Romance, c. 1970	available
Romance of the Stars, c. 1959	special order only
Rosalind, new, c. 1921	special order only
Rosalind, old, c. 1908	discontinued
Rose Ballet, c. 1962	special order only
Royal Danish, c. 1939	available
Salem, c. 1928	discontinued
Scarsdale, c. 1915	discontinued
Sculptured Beauty, c. 1957	special order only
Sedan, c. 1919	discontinued
Serenity, c. 1940	special order only
Shirley	discontinued
Silhouette, c. 1957	special order only
Silver Iris, c. 1955	discontinued
Silver Melody, c. 1955	special order only
Silver Rhythm, c. 1953	special order only
Simplicity, c. 1936	discontinued
Snowflake, c. 1966	special order only
Sonja, c. 1937	discontinued
Southern Colonial, c. 1945	special order only

PATTERNS	CURRENT STATUS
Southern Treasure, *c. 1953* . . . . *special order only*	
Splendor, *c. 1939* . . . . *discontinued*	
Spring Bouquet, *c. 1940* . . . . *special order only*	
Spring Glory, *c. 1942* . . *special order only*	
Springtime, *c. 1935* . . . *special order only*	
Stratford, *c. 1902* . . . . *discontinued*	
Stuyvesant, *c. 1916* . . . . *discontinued*	
Swan Lake, *c. 1960* . . . *special order only*	
Theseum . . . . *special order only*	
Tipped, *c. 1901* . . . . *discontinued*	
Torchlight . . . . *special order only*	
Tradewinds, *c. 1975* . . . . *available*	
Tranquility, *c. 1947* . . . *special order only*	
Trianon, *c. 1921* . . . . . . *special order only*	
Trousseau, *c. 1934* . . . *special order only*	
Trumbull, *c. 1908* . . . . *discontinued*	
Valencia, *c. 1965* . . . . *available*	
Van Dyke, *c. 1910* . . . . *discontinued*	
Van Dyke, applied, *c. 1910* . *discontinued*	
Vision, *c. 1961* . . . . *available*	
Warwick, *c. 1898* . . . . *discontinued*	
Wedding Bells, *c. 1948* . . . . *discontinued*	
Wedgwood. . . . . *special order only*	
Wellesley, *c. 1912* . . . . *discontinued*	
Westminster, *c. 1915* . . . . . *discontinued*	
Westover, *c. 1913* . . . . *discontinued*	
Whitehall, *c. 1938* . . . . *special order only*	
Whitehall, old, *c. 1914* . . . . *discontinued*	
Wild Rose, *c. 1948* . . . . *special order only*	
Wild Rose, old, *c. 1939* . . . . *discontinued*	
Winchester, *c. 1902* . . . . . . *discontinued*	
Windemere, *c. 1939* . . . *special order only*	

LUNT SILVERSMITHS

PATTERNS	CURRENT STATUS
Adam . . . . *discontinued*	
Alexandra . . . . *available*	
American Directoire . . *special order only*	
American Victorian . . . . *available*	
Belle Meade . . . . *available*	
Belvedere . . . . *available*	
Bridal Lace . . . . *special order only*	
Canterbury Bell . . . . . . *special order only*	
Carillon . . . . *available*	
Carolina . . . . *discontinued*	
Carolina, engraved . . . . *discontinued*	
Charles II . . . . *special order only*	
Chased Classic . . . . . . *special order only*	
Chateau (formerly Chateau-Thierry) . . . . *special order only*	

PATTERNS	CURRENT STATUS
Chatelaine (formerly Enid) . *discontinued*	
Chippendale . . . . *available*	
Colonial Manor . . . . . . *special order only*	
Colonial Theme . . . . . . *special order only*	
Colony . . . . *discontinued*	
Columbine . . . . *available*	
Coronet . . . . *special order only*	
Cortland . . . . *discontinued*	
Counterpoint . . . . *special order only*	
Delacourt . . . . *available*	
Dorothy Q . . . . *discontinued*	
Dresden Scroll . . . . *available*	
Early American, engraved. . . . . *special order only*	
Early American, plain . . . . *available*	
Early Colonial (formerly Homes) . . . . *available*	
Elaine . . . . *discontinued*	
Eloquence. . . . . *available*	
English Shell . . . . *special order only*	
Evening Rose . . . . *special order only*	
Festival . . . . *special order only*	
Fiddle . . . . *discontinued*	
Floral Lace. . . . . *special order only*	
Florentine Scroll . . . . *available*	
Garnet Rose . . . . *special order only*	
Gaycourt . . . . *discontinued*	
Georgian Manor . . . . *available*	
Golden Columbine . . . . *available*	
Granado. . . . . *special order only*	
Greenfield . . . . *discontinued*	
Jefferson . . . . *discontinued*	
Jefferson, hand hammered *discontinued*	
John Hancock . . . . *discontinued*	
Kimberly . . . . *available*	
Knickerbocker. . . . . *discontinued*	
Lace Point. . . . . *available*	
Lasting Grace. . . . . *available*	
Madrigal . . . . *available*	
Malvern . . . . *available*	
Memory Lane. . . . . *special order only*	
Mignonette . . . . *available*	
Modern American . . . . *discontinued*	
Modern Classic . . . . . . *special order only*	
Modern Victorian . . . . *available*	
Monticello . . . . *special order only*	
Mount Vernon . . . . *special order only*	
Narcissus . . . . *discontinued*	
Navarre . . . . *discontinued*	
Nellie Custis . . . . *discontinued*	
Old Colony. . . . . *discontinued*	
Old Dominion . . . . *discontinued*	
Orleans . . . . *discontinued*	
Pendant-of-Fruit . . . . . *special order only*	

PATTERNS	CURRENT STATUS
Priscilla	discontinued
Provence	discontinued
Prudence	discontinued
Pynchon	discontinued
Raindrop	special order only
Rapallo	available
Regency	special order only
Regency XH	special order only
Rondelay	special order only
Rose Elegance	special order only
Silver Poppy	special order only
Spring Serenade	special order only
Starfire	special order only
Summer Song	special order only
Sweetheart Rose	special order only
Tipped	discontinued
Tudor	discontinued
Verona	discontinued
Virginia	discontinued
Warren	discontinued
Wentworth	discontinued
William and Mary	available
Windsor	discontinued

MANCHESTER SILVER COMPANY

PATTERNS	CURRENT STATUS
Abraham Lincoln	discontinued
Amaryllis	available
American Beauty	available
Beacon	available
Beaux Art	available
Copenhagen	available
Fleetwood	available
Gadroonette	available
Manchester	available
Mary Warren	available
Mayflower	discontinued
Park Avenue	available
Pierced Handle	available
Pilgrim	available
Plymouth	available
Polly Lawton	available
Princess	available
Priscilla	available
Silverstream	available
Southern Rose	available

MOUNT VERNON COMPANY

PATTERNS	CURRENT STATUS
Adolphus	discontinued
Alden	discontinued

PATTERNS	CURRENT STATUS
Angelo	discontinued
Apollo	discontinued
Chelsea	discontinued
Dahlia	discontinued
Empire	discontinued
Florence	discontinued
Fontenay	discontinued
George II	discontinued
George Washington	discontinued
Harewood, engraved	discontinued
Harvard	discontinued
Hope	discontinued
Josephine	special order only
Kenwood	discontinued
Lady Wynn	discontinued
L'Art Nouveau	discontinued
Laurel	discontinued
Lexington	discontinued
Louis XVI	discontinued
Mauser Warren, engraved	discontinued
Medford	discontinued
Mexico	discontinued
Mount Vernon (formerly Yale)	discontinued
Old South	discontinued
Old South, engraved	discontinued
Paul Revere	discontinued
Plymouth	discontinued
Pointed Antique	discontinued
Pomona	discontinued
Pompeian	discontinued
Poppy	discontinued
Queen	discontinued
Queen Anne	discontinued
Queen Elizabeth	discontinued
Ribbed Antique	discontinued
Rose	discontinued
Round Antique	discontinued
R. W. Empire	discontinued
Salem	discontinued
Sedgwick	discontinued
Sheraton	discontinued
Strapped Antique	discontinued
Sulgrave	discontinued
Tropea	discontinued
20th Century	discontinued
Warren	discontinued
Warwick	discontinued
Wentworth	discontinued
West Point	discontinued
Westchester	discontinued
Winthrop	discontinued
Yetive	discontinued

ONEIDA, LTD.

PATTERNS	CURRENT STATUS
Afterglow	*special order only*
American Colonial	*available*
Ardsley	*discontinued*
Belle Rose	*special order only*
Botticelli	*available*
Bountiful	*special order only*
Casa Grande	*special order only*
Damask Rose	*available*
Dover	*available*
Du Maurier (former Bromley)	*available*
Engagement	*special order only*
First Frost	*special order only*
Flower Lane	*special order only*
Glenrose	*special order only*
Grand Majesty	*available*
Grandeur	*available*
Guinevere (formerly Pembrooke)	*special order only*
Heiress	*special order only*
Impresario	*available*
King Cedric	*special order only*
Lasting Spring	*available*
Mansion House	*special order only*
Martinique	*available*
Mediterranea	*available*
Melbourne	*available*
Michelangelo	*available*
Patrician	*discontinued*
Reigning Beauty	*special order only*
Rubaiyat	*special order only*
Satin Beauty	*special order only*
Sentimental	*special order only*
Silver Rose	*special order only*
Stanton Hall	*available*
Teramo	*special order only*
Twilight	*special order only*
Venetian Scroll	*special order only*
Virginian	*special order only*
Vivant	*special order only*
Will 'O' Wisp	*special order only*
Young Love	*special order only*

REED AND BARTON

PATTERNS	CURRENT STATUS
Amaryllis, *c. 1901*	*special order only*
Antique	*discontinued*
Athenian, *c. 1891*	*discontinued*
Athenian, engraved, *c. 1891*	*discontinued*
Autumn Leaves	*available*
Betty Alden	*special order only*
Burgundy	*available*

PATTERNS	CURRENT STATUS
Cameo	*available*
Cellini	*available*
Cellini, engraved	*available*
Cellini, monogrammed	*available*
Chambord, *c. 1900*	*special order only*
Classic Rose	*available*
Clovelly	*special order only*
Colonial Classic	*special order only*
Columbia	*special order only*
Copley	*special order only*
Cotillion	*special order only*
Dancing Flowers	*available*
Da Vinci	*available*
Da Vinci, engraved	*available*
Da Vinci, monogrammed	*available*
Devon, *c. 1911*	*special order only*
Diadem	*available*
Diamond	*available*
Dimension	*available*
Dorothy Quincy	*special order only*
Eighteenth Century	*available*
Elegente	*special order only*
El Greco	*available*
English Antique, *c. 1895*	*discontinued*
English Antique, etched, *c. 1895*	*discontinued*
English Provincial	*available*
Flora, *c. 1890*	*discontinued*
Florentine Lace	*available*
Four Georges	*special order only*
Four Georges, engraved	*special order only*
Fragrance	*special order only*
Francis I	*available*
French Antique, *c. 1901*	*special order only*
French Antique, engraved, *c. 1901*	*special order only*
French Antique, hammered, *c. 1901*	*special order only*
French Antique, Watteau engraved, *c. 1901*	*special order only*
French Renaissance	*available*
Georgian Rose	*available*
Golden Tree of Life	*available*
Grande Renaissance	*available*
Guildhall	*special order only*
Hampton Court	*available*
Hawthorn	*special order only*
Hepplewhite	*special order only*
Hepplewhite, chased	*special order only*
Hepplewhite, engraved	*special order only*
Heritage	*special order only*

PATTERNS	CURRENT STATUS
Intaglio	special order only
Jacobean	special order only
Jubilee	special order only
Kings, c. 1890	special order only
LaComtesse, c. 1897	special order only
La Marquise, c. 1895	special order only
La Parisienne	special order only
La Perle	discontinued
La Perle, engraved	special order only
La Reine, c. 1893	discontinued
Lark	available
Larkspur	special order only
La Rocaille, c. 1890	discontinued
La Splendide	special order only
L'Elegante, c. 1900	special order only
Les Cinq Fleurs, c. 1900	
	special order only
Les Six Fleurs, c. 1901	special order only
Liberty	special order only
Love Disarmed	special order only
Luxembourg, c. 1890	discontinued
Majestic, c. 1894	special order only
Marlborough	available
Monique	discontinued
Nancy Lee	special order only
Old Virginia	available
Oval Thread, c. 1890	discontinued
Oxford	special order only
Petite Fleur	available
Pointed Antique, c. 1895	available
Rembrandt	special order only
Renaissance Scroll	available
Riviera	discontinued
Romaine	discontinued
Rose Cascade	available
St. George	special order only
St. George, chased	special order only
Savannah	available
Serenade	special order only
Shell, c. 1900	discontinued
Silver Sculpture	available
Silver Wheat	available
Sonata	special order only
Spanish Baroque	available
Star	special order only
Tapestry	available
Tara	available
Trajan, c. 1892	special order only
Tree of Life	available
Vienna	available
Wakefield	special order only

SAMUEL KIRK & SON, INC.

PATTERNS	CURRENT STATUS
Calvert	available
Cheryl	available
Cynthia	special order only
Cynthia, plain	special order only
Ellipse	special order only
Florentine	available
Florentine, monogrammed	available
Golden Windslow	available
Kinsley	special order only
Mayflower	available
Old Maryland	available
Old Maryland, engraved	available
Primrose	available
Quadrille	available
Repousse	available
Rose	available
Severn	special order only
Signet, plain	available
Skylark	special order only
Wadefield	available
Winslow	available

SCHOFIELD COMPANY

PATTERNS	CURRENT STATUS
Baltimore Rose	special order only
Baltimore Rose, plain back	discontinued
China Lily	discontinued
Clouet	special order only
Corinthian	discontinued
Cromwell	discontinued
Elizabeth Tudor, hammered	
	special order only
Elizabeth Tudor, plain	special order only
Eugenia	special order only
Frabee	special order only
Hand Chased Rose	discontinued
Hand Chased Straight Roll	discontinued
Jac Rose	discontinued
Jenkins Repousse	discontinued
Joccard	discontinued
Josephine	discontinued
Lady Caroline	discontinued
La Rochelle	special order only
Lily	special order only
Lorraine	special order only
Martha Washington	discontinued
Mayflower	special order only
Old Baltimore	special order only
Old English	special order only
Persian	discontinued

PATTERNS	CURRENT STATUS
Raleigh	*special order only*
Revere	*special order only*
Scroll Engraved Edge	*special order only*
Talbot	*special order only*
Virginia Dare	*discontinued*
Waterford	*discontinued*

STIEFF COMPANY

PATTERNS	CURRENT STATUS
Betsy Patterson	*available*
Betsy Patterson, engraved	*available*
Carrollton	*available*
Clinton	*special order only*
Corsage	*available*
Diamond Star	*special order only*
Forget-me-not	*special order only*
Homeward	*available*
Lady Claire	*available*
Personna	*special order only*
Princess	*special order only*
Puritan	*available*
Queen Anne-Williamsburg	*available*
Royal Dynasty	*available*
Shell-Willamsburg	*available*

TIFFANY & COMPANY, INC.

PATTERNS	CURRENT STATUS
Audubon (formerly Japanese)	*available*
Bamboo	*available*
Beekman (formerly Tiffany)	*special order only*
Broom Corn	*special order only*
Castilian	*available*
Century	*special order only*
Chrysanthemum	*available*
Clinton	*special order only*
Colonial	*special order only*
Cordis	*special order only*
Faneuil	*available*
Feather Edge	*available*
Florentine	*special order only*
Fox Head	*special order only*
Gramercy	*special order only*
Hamilton	*available*
Hampton	*available*
Harlequin	*available*
King William (formerly Antique)	*available*
Lap-over-Edge	*special order only*
Linenford	*special order only*
Olympian	*available*
Palm	*special order only*
Palmette	*special order only*

PATTERNS	CURRENT STATUS
Persian	*special order only*
Provence	*available*
Queen Anne	*special order only*
Rat Tail	*available*
Reeded Edge	*available*
Renaissance	*special order only*
Richelieu	*available*
St. Dunstan	*special order only*
St. James	*special order only*
Salem	*available*
San Lorenzo	*available*
Saratoga (formerly Cook)	*special order only*
Shell and Thread	*available*
Wave Edge	*special order only*
Windham	*available*

TOWLE MFG. COMPANY

PATTERNS	CURRENT STATUS
Albany	*discontinued*
Antique	*discontinued*
Aquilla	*discontinued*
Arcadian	*discontinued*
Aristocrat	*special order only*
Arlington	*discontinued*
Auvergne	*discontinued*
Awakening	*special order only*
Benjamin Franklin	*available*
Cambridge	*discontinued*
Candlelight	*available*
Canterbury	*discontinued*
Carpenter Hall	*available*
Cascade	*special order only*
Charlemagne	*special order only*
Chased Diana	*special order only*
Chippendale	*available*
Clifton, engraved	*discontinued*
Clover	*discontinued*
Contessina	*special order only*
Contour	*special order only*
Cordova	*discontinued*
Craftsman	*special order only*
Craftsman, carved	*discontinued*
Daisy	*discontinued*
Danish Baroque	*available*
Debussy	*available*
D'Orleans	*special order only*
Dorothy Bradford	*discontinued*
Dorothy Manners	*discontinued*
Drury Lane	*discontinued*
Du Barry	*discontinued*
Essex	*discontinued*
Fiddle	*discontinued*

PATTERNS	CURRENT STATUS
French Provincial	available
Georgian	special order only
Georgian H. H.	discontinued
Glenmore	discontinued
Godroon	discontinued
Grand Duchess	available
Hampton	discontinued
King Richard	available
Kings	discontinued
Lady Constance	special order only
Lady Diana	special order only
Lady Mary	special order only
La Fayette	available
La Fayette, engraved	discontinued
Laureate	available
Legato	available
Lenox	discontinued
Louis XIV	special order only
Madame La Fayette	discontinued
Madeira	available
Mandarin	available
Mary Chilton	special order only
Mary Chilton, engraved No. 1	discontinued
Mary Chilton, engraved No. 10	discontinued
Meadow Song	special order only
Merrimack	discontinued
Monte Cristo	special order only
Novantique	special order only
No. 38, engraved	discontinued
No. 43	discontinued
No. 128	discontinued
Old Brocade	special order only
Old Colonial	available
Old English	special order only
Old Lace	available
Old Master	available
Old Mirror	special order only
Old Newbury (formerly Newbury)	special order only
Orchids	discontinued
Paul Revere	special order only
Peachtree Manor	special order only
Petit Point	special order only
Princess	discontinued
Queen Elizabeth I	available
Rambler Rose	available
Richmond	discontinued
Rose Solitaire	special order only
Royal Windsor	special order only
R.S.V.P.	special order only
Rustic	discontinued
Sculptured Rose	special order only

PATTERNS	CURRENT STATUS
Shell	discontinued
Silver Flutes	available
Silver Plumes	special order only
Silver Spray	special order only
Southwind	special order only
Spanish Provincial	available
Stuart	discontinued
Symphony	special order only
Symphony, chased	discontinued
Tipped	discontinued
Verpera	special order only
Virginia Carvel	special order only
Virginia Lee	discontinued
Warren, plain	discontinued
Windsor, plain	discontinued

TUTTLE SILVER COMPANY

PATTERNS	CURRENT STATUS
Basket-of-Flowers	discontinued
Beauvoir	available
Charles II	discontinued
Classic Antique (formerly Aberdeen)	special order only
Colonial Fiddle	special order only
Crest of Arden	special order only
Feather Edge	special order only
Georgian	discontinued
Hannah Hull	available
Lamerie	special order only
Onslow	available
Paul Lamerie	discontinued
Revere	discontinued
Windsor Castle	special order only

WALLACE SILVERSMITHS

PATTERNS	CURRENT STATUS
Aegean Weave	available
America	discontinued
Antique	special order only
Atalanta	discontinued
Beauvais	discontinued
Berain	discontinued
Bessie	discontinued
Blenheim	discontinued
Cabot	special order only
Cairo	discontinued
Campainia	discontinued
Carmel	special order only
Carnation	discontinued
Carthage	special order only
Columbia	discontinued
Corinthian	discontinued

PATTERNS	CURRENT STATUS
Custis	*discontinued*
Dauphine	*discontinued*
Dawn	*available*
Dawn Star	*special order only*
Debutante	*special order only*
Discovery	*special order only*
Eton	*discontinued*
Evening Mist	*special order only*
Faneuil	*discontinued*
Feliciana	*special order only*
Figured Shell	*discontinued*
Figured Tipped	*discontinued*
Golden Aegean Weave	*available*
Grand Colonial	*available*
Grand Victorian	*available*
Grande Baroque	*available*
Hamilton	*discontinued*
Irian	*discontinued*
Irving	*available*
Ivanhoe	*discontinued*
Juliet	*discontinued*
King Christian (formerly Miss Columbia)	*special order only*
Kings	*discontinued*
Lady Windsor (former Victoria)	*special order only*
La Reine	*available*
Larkspur	*special order only*
La Viola	*discontinued*
Le Moderne	*discontinued*
Lotus	*special order only*
Louvre	*discontinued*
Lucerne	*available*
Madison	*discontinued*
Melanie	*special order only*
Melody	*discontinued*
Michele	*special order only*
Monterey	*discontinued*
Mozart	*discontinued*
My Love	*special order only*
Nile	*discontinued*
Normandie	*special order only*
No. 45, engraved	*discontinued*
No. 80	*discontinued*
No. 300	*discontinued*
Old Atlanta	*available*
Old Lyme	*discontinued*
Orange Blossom	*discontinued*
Orchid Elegance	*special order only*
Penrose	*special order only*
Peony	*discontinued*
Pilgrim	*discontinued*
Pompeii	*discontinued*
Princess Anne	*special order only*

PATTERNS	CURRENT STATUS
Princess Mary	*special order only*
Princess Pat	*discontinued*
Priscilla	*discontinued*
Puritan	*discontinued*
Puritan, hammered	*discontinued*
Putnam	*discontinued*
Reflection	*discontinued*
Rembrandt	*discontinued*
Renaissance	*special order only*
Rheims	*discontinued*
Rhythm	*special order only*
Romance of the Sea	*available*
Rose	*discontinued*
Rose Point	*available*
Royal Rose	*special order only*
Royal Satin	*special order only*
St. George	*discontinued*
St. Leon	*discontinued*
Salem	*discontinued*
San Juan	*discontinued*
Sappho	*discontinued*
Saxon	*discontinued*
Saybrook	*discontinued*
Shenandoah	*available*
Silver Swirl	*special order only*
Sir Christopher	*available*
Soliloquy	*special order only*
Somerset	*discontinued*
Spanish Lace	*available*
Standish	*discontinued*
Sterling Rose	*special order only*
Still Mood	*special order only*
Stradivari	*discontinued*
Tipped	*discontinued*
Versailles	*discontinued*
Violet	*available*
Waltz of Spring	*special order only*
Washington	*special order only*
Waverly	*discontinued*
Windsor	*special order only*
Wishing Star	*special order only*
Wolcott	*discontinued*

FRANKLIN MINT

Of special interest to collectors and investors are objects produced by the Franklin Mint of Franklin Center, Pennsylvania. Although numerous have been made from various materials, a large number of their products have been — and continue to be — made of silver. The following is a comprehensive listing of the firm's collectors' items made from silver excluding such items such as circulating coins struck for the use of foreign governments.

The Franklin Mint was established as a private corporation (no government connections) in 1964. At first, the firm mainly produced medals, as well as coins for foreign governments. Gradually the mint expanded, adding many types of collectors' items to its line. In a short time, the Franklin Mint became the nation's leading private mint. Today, shares for this company are traded on the New York Stock Exchange. Recent productions include such diverse items as phonograph records, furniture, and other specialty merchandise. The Mint's headquarters are open to the public with guided tours.

The Franklin Mint issues only limited editions articles. They are limited in that the quantity is not fixed or announced in advance of production. Rather, a time period is set for each edition. The number of orders received during the ordering period, in most cases, determines the quantity that will be manufactured. The Mint manufactures only enough pieces to fill the orders received. Orders come primarily from collectors and the general public, but to some extent from dealers as well. There are some exceptions to this procedure as the Mint has occasionally produced limited editions with a predetermined number.

As with limited editions in general, no reissues are made. Anyone who wishes to buy a Franklin Mint issue after the ordering deadline has passed must search the open market or secondary market. These terms are often used interchangeably; but the open market refers to dealers (such as gift-shops) who bought directly from the Mint in order to sell to the public; whereas the secondary market includes all antique shops and collectibles dealers who buy from the original Franklin Mint customers and then sell to the public. Generally, the prices charged on the secondary market differ from the prices established when the items were issued. They could be either higher or lower, depending on a variety of circumstances.

The original purchasers of Franklin Mint editions — those who buy directly from the Mint — fall into several groups. First and perhaps foremost is the Franklin Mint collector, who makes a hobby of collecting the company's products. While it would be difficult to estimate the number of such collectors, they are certainly numerous. Consistently high quality articles plus the prestige of the Franklin Mint name contribute to hobbyist interest.

Collectors who specialize in other areas also buy Franklin Mint issues, usually because of some topical connection. For example, a collector of football memorabilia is apt to buy all the medals of other art relating to football. Such hobbyists account for a large share of the Mint's sales, and an even larger proportion of sales on the secondary market — because these collectors are often unaware that such items have been issued until they're already out of production. Miscellaneous purchases are made for decorating and gift-giving.

Investment buying of Franklin Mint items dates to well before the surge of silver-bullion market activity in 1979 and 1980. Investors are attracted to these pieces because of their status as limited editions, their collector appeal, and their silver content. Selling by investors has helped to create a flow of the older editions on the market.

Many readers are undoubtedly asking: what IS the investment potential of Franklin Mint editions bought from the Mint at issue prices? No simple answer can be given. Many investors have profited from the company's works. Others are presently holding on to their possessions in hopes of a profit at some future time. And certainly, there have been those who sold at a loss. To a large extent, the silver bullion market is responsible for the success of Franklin Mint investments. When silver bullion rises dramatically in value, most silver Franklin Mint items can be sold at a profit over their cost — even merely for melting. The word "dramatically" is the key here. An increase from $8 to $10 per troy ounce in the spot price is not sufficient, because the purchase price represents a premium over the actual value of the silver used in each object. The purchaser who buys from the Franklin Mint is not "buying silver," but buying a work of art or craft in which various production expenses have been involved. The Franklin Mint must buy the silver it uses; as there is no wholesale source for silver, it pays the full market price and this is only a portion of the production cost. The additional costs of manufacturing, advertising, and other expenses are also taken into account. An edition containing $50 bullion value (silver value) may carry an issue price of $100 or more. Therefore, its popularity as a bullion investment ranks much lower than silver bars or even silver bullion coins for which the buyer pays the spot price and a small commission. On the other hand, an increase in collecting interest may raise the value, possibly to the point where it returns a profit even if the value of its silver content has not increased. It is seldom easy to forecast which issues will attract the greatest collecting attention; even the Mint cannot always tell how a particular edition will be received. Editions for which there was the greatest initial response are naturally produced in the greatest quantities. Those which did not draw such heavy response are automatically scarcer because not as many specimens were made. Since the scarcer items will be more difficult to find on the secondary market, dealers will be more justified in charging a premium for them.

There have been cases of "instant profits" (on paper, at any rate) on Franklin Mint items. These occurred mainly in 1979 and early 1980 when the price of silver rose from about $12 to $50 per troy ounce in less than a year. Those who subscribed to editions in the early part of 1979 paid prices based on a very low bullion value. As their sets were being manufactured and delivered, silver was soaring in value. These collectors received more "melt" value (disregarding the collector value) than they had paid for! Of course, the Mint sustained no losses on these transactions since the silver came from stockpiles accumulated before the price rose.

One potent influence on the collector value of Franklin Mint articles is melting. From the firm's inception in 1964 until late in the 1970's, few collectors had melted their Franklin Mint articles because it was just not profitable. Then, in 1979, wholesale melting began. Medals, ingots and other works were sold to scrap dealers and melted. When dealers advertised to buy Franklin Mint items for melting, it is impossible to say how much melting was done or which specific issues were affected the most. But a great number of Franklin Mint silver items went into furnances during the Silver Rush of 1979/80. This contributed to the scarcity of Franklin Mint articles on the secondary market. Collectors never fail to be influenced by scarcity. As the scarcity of a popular item increases, its value almost always rises. In the case of Franklin Mint items, the manufactured total of any edition is seldom more than a few thousand pieces. When some are lost to melting, the original scarcity can gradually develop into acute scarcity. Hobbyists who have circulated "want lists" of Franklin Mint products to dealers are well aware of this. Many pieces which could be bought from virtually any dealer in January 1979 were impossible to find in January 1980. Some of these items have begun to drift back into circulation, but still there are many items in the hard-to-find category *whose scarcity on the market is not reflected by production figures.* Many owners — whether they be investors or not — refuse to sell their Franklin Mint silver items when the silver market is weak. They would much prefer holding, and this means that the number of specimens in actual circulation is very small.

The older editions are always the scarcest, in relation to numbers issued, having gone through more flurries of selling for melt value. Franklin Mint items produced from early 1980 to the present time have not been melted, as it has not been profitable to do so.

There are other considerations in collector value and interest, too. One of these is possessing a full set of items which were issued as sets. The full set, especially when contained in a factory-made display tray or holder, has increased value over the aggregate value of its component parts. In other words, if a set of 10 items sells (on secondary market) at $10 apiece, the complete set would not sell for $100, but for a somewhat higher sum. Because these articles are collectors' items, the state of preservation is important to their resale value. Scratches, mars, or any other evidence of careless handling diminishes their overall value, though of course it would have no influence on the bullion value.

VERSION TO USE IF WE DON'T SHOW VALUES

The following listings provide complete information on each issue, including the quantity produced, fineness, and weight. It is impossible at the present time to provide accurate market value, because of the lingering effects of the 1979/80 events. No one — including the most astute dealer — is quite certain how many specimens produced prior to 1979 are still in existence. Tempted by the prospect of tripling or quadrupling their money, many owners of Franklin Mint articles sold in 1979 and 1980, and most of what they sold was melted. But the apparent scarcity of many editions on the current secondary market may be due largely to hoarding by bullion investors. There is no way of knowing for sure. Anyone who wants to buy or sell should shop around and check the offers of various dealers.

INGOTS (SQUARE, RECTANGLE, IRREGULAR SHAPES)

☐ **Air and Space,** *set of 100 ingots, sterling silver, proof, 2¼" x 1", 95 troy ounces per set; 1) 1st balloon flight, 2) Record-setting balloon flight, 3) 1st major aeronautical success in America, 4) Octave Chanute — glider flight, 5) 1st powered airplane flight, 6) First successful dirigible, 7) Frank Lahm wins first Gordon Bennett Balloon Race, 8) Glenn H. Curtiss wins first aviation award, 9) 1st flight from a Naval vessel, 10) 1st aerial crossing, 11) World's first regularly scheduled airline, 12) Lafayette Escadrille enters combat in World War I, 13) Inauguration of air mail delivery, 14) Edward V. Rickenbacker, 15) 1st transatlantic flight, 16) Barnstormers tour U.S., 17) 1st non-stop transcontinental flight across the U.S., 18) 1st aerial refueling, 19) ZR-1 "Shennandoah", 20) 1st around-the-world flight, 21) 1st successful liquid-fuel rocket, 22) 1st flight over the North Pole, 23) General Billy Mitchell, 24) 1st Solo Transatlantic Flight, 25) 1st Instrument-Guided Flight, 26) 1st Nonstop Transpacific Flight, 27) Taylor Cub Model A, 28) Amelia Earhart, 29) 1st rocket flight of the American Rocket Society, 30) Boeing 247, 31) Wiley Post, 32) Goddard advances the science of rocketry, 33) Stevens & Anderson, record ascent into the stratosphere, 34) Introduction of DC-3, 35) China Clipper, 36) Boeing B-17, 37) P-38 Lightning, 38) Igor Sikorsky, 39) P-51 Mustang, 40) 1st flight of a rocket-powered plane, 41) Grumman TBF Avenger, 42) B-24 Liberator, 43) Grumman F6F-3 Hellcat, 44) Douglas DC-4, 45) Doolittle Bombs Japan, 46) Bell XP59A, 47) Lockheed Constellation C-89, 48) Northrop MX-324, 49) Bell 47 Helicopter, 50) V-2 Rocket, 51) Bell X-1, 52) Bumper-Wac Program, 53) 1st non-stop round-the-world flight, 54) F-86 Sabrejet, 55) Boeing B-52, 56) Viking Sounding Rocket, 57) Boeing 707, 58) Lockheed U-2, 59) Explorer, 60) F4H Phantom II, 61) Vanguard II, 62) Pioneer IV, 63) 1st round-the-world jet passenger service, 64) 1st successful launching of an Atlas ICBM, 65) Tiros I;* **2,285 sets to be issued from 1976-1984 at $25.00 each or $2500.00 a set (100).**

☐ **Airlines — Emblems of the World's Greatest Airlines,** *set of 50 ingots, sterling silver miniatures, various sizes, enameled, P/L;* **to be issued from 1981-1986 at $12.50 each or $625.00 a set (50).**

☐ **Airlines of the World Emblems,** *set of 100 ingots, sterling silver, 1¼" high, proof, 260 grains, 54 troy ounces per set; 1) Hawaiian Airlines, 2) Aeromexico, 3) British Airways, 4) Malaysian Airlines, 5) United Airlines, 6) Alaska Airlines, 7) Trans Internat. Airlines, 8) Lufthansa German Airlines, 9) Quantas Airways Ltd., 10) Pan American World Airways, 11) Thai Airways, 12) Loftleidir Icelandic Airlines, 13) North Central Airlines, 14) Delta Airlines, 15) Air Canada, 16) Air France, 17) American Airlines, 18) Northwest Airlines, 19) Aloha Airlines, 20) South Africa Airways, 21) International Air Bahama, 22) Garuda Indonesian Airways, 23) Finnair Airways, 24) Ariana Afghan Airlines, 25) Netherlands Antilles Airlines, 26) Air New Zealand, 27) National Airlines, 28) Scandinavian Airlines, 29) Trans World Airlines, 30) Western Airlines, 31) Lan-Chile Airlines, 32) Lloyd Aero Boliviano, 33) Indian Airlines, 34) Lot Polish Airlines, 35) Cyprus Airways, 36) China Airlines, 37) BWI Int'l, Airlines, 38) Avianca Airlines, 39) Aspen Airways, 40) Aerolineas Argentinas, 41) El Al Isreal, 42) Icelandair, 43) KLM Royal Dutch Airlines, 44) Cameroon Airlines, 45) Braathens S-A-F-E, 46) Britannia Airways Ltd., 47) Sabena Belgian World Airlines, 48) None, 49) Martinair Holland, 50) Polynesian Airlines Ltd.;* **1,777 sets issued from 1977-1980 at $18.50 each or $1,850.00 a set (100).**

☐ **Airplanes,** *set of 50 ingots, sterling silver, proof, 30.5 troy ounces per set; 1) Wright Flyer I, 2) Santos Dumont De Moiselle, 3) Bleriot X1, 4) Deperdussin Monocoque, 5) Sikorsky le Grand, 6) 1918 Fokker E-1, 7) Avro 504J, 8) Sopwith Camel, 9) Junkers J1, 10) Handley Page, 11) Fokker DR1, 12) Fokker D VII, 13) Vickers Vimy, 14) Navy Curtiss NC-4, 15) de Havilland Moth, 16) Fokker F VII, 17) Ryan NYP, 18) Dornier DO-X, 19) Savoia Marchetti S-55, 20) Piper Cub, 21) Lockheed Vega, 22) Gee Beee R1, 23) Douglas DC-3, 24) Boeing B-17, 25) Messerschmitt BF-109, 26) Junkers JU-87, 27) Short C Class Flying Boat, 28) Spitfire, 29) Mitsubishi Karigane, 30) ANT-25, 31) Heinkel HE-178, 32) Illyushin IL-2 Stormovik, 33) Focke-Wulf 190, 34) Mitsubishi Zero, 35) North Amer. Mustang P-51, 36) Avro Lancaster, 37) Boeing B-29, 38) Lockheed Constellation, 39) Bell X-1, 40) Mikoyan Mig-15, 41) F-86 Sabre, 42) De-Havilland Comet;* **1,799 sets issued from 1978-1982 at $19.50 each or $975.00 a set (50).**

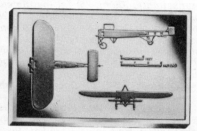 

Airplanes, *Bleriot XI, ingot #3.*

☐ **America in Space,** *sterling silver, proof-like, 1¾" x ⅞", 1,000 grains, 2.08 troy ounces;* **37,528 issued in 1977 at $12.50 each.**

☐ **Automobile Emblems,** *set of 50, hand-enameling on sterling silver, P/L, 2" x 1⅛", 38 troy ounces; 1) Lamborchini—Italy, 2) Dusenberg—U.S., 3) Pierce Arrow—U.S., 4) M.G.—England, 5) Cadillac—U.S., 6) Stutz—U.S., 7) Panhard-Levassor—France, 8) Holden—Australia, 9) Toyota—Japan, 10) Packard—U.S., 11) Napier—England, 12) Austro-Daimler—Austria, 13) Benz—Germany, 14) Buick—U.S., 15) Spyker—Netherlands, 16) Alfa Romeo—Italy, 17) Lincoln—U.S., 18) Renault—France, 19) Mercedes—Germany, 20) Aston Martin—England, 21) Citroen—France, 22) Rolls Royce—England, 23) Volkswagen—Germany, 24) Chevrolet—U.S., 25) Rover—England, 26) Volga—Soviet Union, 27) Datsun—Japan, 28) Chrysler—U.S., 29) Peugeot—France, 30) BMW—Germany, 31) Maserati—Italy, 32) Cord—U.S., 33) Delage—France, 34) Jaguar—England, 35) Isotta Franschini—Italy, 36) Willys—U.S., 37) Volvo—Sverige, 38) Opel—Germany;* **4,954 sets issued from 1979-1982 at $35.00 each or $1,750.00 a set (50).**

☐ **Bank Ingots — International,** *set of 50 ingots, sterling silver, proof, 1⅞" x 1⅛", 104 troy ouncers per set; 1) Banco de Galicia y Buenos Aires, 2) Bank of South Wales, 3) Creditanstalt-Bankverein, 4) World Banking Corp. Ltd., 5) Societe Generale de Banque, 6) Banco Boliviano Americano, 7) Banco Boavista S.A., 8) Toronto Dominion, 9) Banco O'higgins, 10) Banco Cafetero, 11) Privatbanken, 12) Banco de Guayaquil, 13) Banco Salvadoreno, 14) Barclays Bank) 15) Nordiska Foreningsbanken, 16) Banque Nationale de Paris, 17) Richard Daus & Co., Bank, 18) Comm. Bank of Greece, 19) Hong Kong & Shanghai Bank. Corp., 20) Bank Ekspor Impor Indonesia, 21) Iranians' Bank, 22) Bank of Ireland, 23) Israel Discount Bank, Ltd., 24) Banco Di Roma, 25) Royal Bank Jamaica Ltd., 26) Dai-Ichi Kangyo Bank, 27) Korea Exchange Bank, 28) Credit Libanais S.A.L., 29) Banco de Comercio, 30) Algemene Bank Nederland, N.Y., 31) Bank of New Zealand, 32) Banco Nicaraguense, 33) Den Norske Credit Bank, 34) Habib-Bank Ltd., 35) BANCO*

*FIDUCIARIO de Panama S.A., 36) Banco Paraguagyo de Comercio Sudamerica',
37) Banco Continental, 38) Bank of the Philippine Isl., 39) Develop. Bank of Singapore Ltd., 40) Trust Bank of Africa, Ltd., 41) Banco Central, S.A., 42) Skandinaviska
Enskilda Banken, 43) Schweizerische Volksbank, 44) Internat. Comm. Bank of
China, 45) Bangkok Bank Limited, 46) Turkiye Is Bankasi A.S., 47) Morgan Guaranty Trust, 48) Banco Commercial, 49) Banco Union, 50) Jugobanka;* **1,480 sets
issued in 1974 at $28.00 each or $1,400.00 a set (50).**

⊔ **Bank Ingots — United States,** set of 50, sterling silver, proof, 1¾" x ⅞", 104 troy
ounces per set; **ALABAMA** 1) 1970-1st National Bank of Birmingham, 2)
1971-Merchants National Bank, Mobile, 3) 1972-American National Bank, Gadsden, 4) 1973-1st Western Bank, Bessemer, 5) 1974-1st National Bank, Huntsville;
ALASKA 1) 1970-Alaska National Bank, Fairbanks, 2) 1971-B. M. Behrends Bank,
Juneau, 3) 1972-National Bank of Alaska of Anchorage, 4) 1973-1st National Bank,
Anchorage, 5) 1974-Alaska Statebank, Anchorage; **ARIZONA** 1) 1970-Thunderbird
Bank, Glendale, 2) 1971-Great Western Bank & Trust, Phoenix, 3) 1972-Southern
Arizona Bank, Tucson, 4) 1973-Union Bank, Tucson, 5) 1974-The Arizona Bank,
Phoenix; **ARKANSAS** 1) 1970-1st National Bank in Little Rock, 2) 1971-McIlroy
Bank, Fayetteville, 3) 1972-Worthen Bank and Trust Co., Little Rock, 4) 1973-Twin
City Bank, No. Little Rock, 5) 1974-First National Bank, Hot Springs; **CALIFORNIA**
1) 1970-Imperial Bank, Los Angeles, 2) 1971-Bank of America, San Francisco, 3)
1972-Wells Fargo Bank, San Francisco, 4) 1973-United California Bank, Los
Angeles, 5) 1974-Crocker Bank, San Francisco; **COLORADO** 1) 1970-Colorado
Springs National Bank, 2) 1971-1st National Bank, Boulder, 3) 1972-Greeley National Bank, 4) 1973-United Bank of Denver, 5) 1974-1st National Bank, Colorado
Springs; **CONNECTICUT** 1) 1970-Hartford National Bank & Trust Co, 2) 1971-Union
Trust, Stamford, 3) 1972-Connecticut Bank & Trust Co., Hartford, 4) 1973-Plainville
Trust Co., 5) 1974-Society for Savings, Hartford; **DELAWARE** 1) 1970-Wilmington
Trust Co., 2) 1971-Farmers Bank of Delaware, Wilmington, 3) 1972-Milford Trust
Co., 4) 1973-Bank of Delaware, Wilmington, 5) 1974-Baltimore Trust Company,
Bridgeville; **FLORIDA** 1) 1970-1st National Bank of Orlando, 2) 1971-Tallahassee
Bank and Trust Co., 3) 1972-United Banking Groups, Miami, 4) 1973-Marine Bank &
Trust Co., Tampa, 5) 1974-Florida National Bank & Trust Co. at Miami; **GEORGIA**
1) 1970-Citizens & Southern Nat. Bank, Savannah, 2) 1971-Georgia Railroad Bank
and Trust, Augusta, 3) 1972-Trust Company Bank, Atlanta, 4) 1973-Peoples Bank
and Trust Co. of Macon, 5) 1974-4th National Bank, Columbus; **HAWAII** 1) 1970-City Bank of Honolulu, 2) 1971-Central Pacific Bank, Honolulu, 3) 1972-First
Hawaiian Bank, Honolulu, 4) 1973-Bank of Hawaii, Honolulu, 5) 1974-Hawaii National Bank, Honolulu; **IDAHO** 1) 1970-Twin Falls Bank & Trust Co., 2) 1971-Idaho
Bank of Commerce, Rexberg, 3) 1972-Bank of Idaho, Boise, 4) 1973-1st National
Bank, Wallace, 5) 1974-Idaho First National Bank, Boise; **ILLINOIS** 1) 1970-Amalgamated Trust & Savings, Chicago, 2) 1971-Harris Trust and Savings Bank,
Chicago, 3) 1972-Continental Ill. Nat. Bank of Chicago, 4) 1973-City National Bank
& Trust Co. of Rockford, 5) 1974-1st National Bank of Chicago; **INDIANA** 1) 1970-St. Joseph Valley Bank, Elkhart, 2) 1971-Ft. Wayne National Bank, 3) 1972-Security
Bank & Trust Co., Vincennes, 4) 1973-Amer. Fletcher Nat. Bank, Indianapolis, 5)
1974-Indiana National Bank, Indianapolis; **IOWA** 1) 1970-Bankers Trust Co., Des
Moines, 2) 1971-Central Nat. Bank, Des Moines, 3) 1972-Peoples Bank & Trust Co.,
Cedar Rapids, 4) 1973-1st National Bank of Perry, 5) 1974-1st National Bank,
Dubuque; **KANSAS** 1) 1970-Exchange National Bank, Atchison, 2) 1971-4th National Bank and Trust Co., Wichita, 3) 1972-1st National Bank of Topeka, 4)
1973-Garden National Bank, Garden City, 5) 1974-Commercial National Bank,
Kansas; **KENTUCKY** 1) 1970-Central Bank & Trust Co., Lexington, 2) 1971-2nd National Bank, Ashland, 3) 1972-Citizens Fidelity Bank & Trust Co., Louisville, 4)
1973-1st National Bank of Louisville, 5) 1974-1st Security Bank, Lexington; **LOUI-**

SIANA *1) 1970-Fidelity National Bank, Baton Rouge, 2) 1971-Hibernia National Bank, New Orleans, 3) 1972-Central Bank, Monroe, 4) 1973-1st Nat. Bank of Commerce, New Orleans, 5) 1974-Rapides Bank & Trust Co., Alexandria;* **MAINE** *1) 1970-Federal Trust Co., Waterville, 2) 1971-Northeast Bankshare Assoc., Farmington, 3) 1972-Maine National Bank, Portland, 4) 1973-Merrill Bank, Bangor, 5) 1974-Canal National Bank, Portland;* **MARYLAND** *1) 1970-Farmers & Mechanics Nat. Bank, Frederick, 2) 1971-Eutaw Savings Bank, Baltimore, 3) 1972-Maryland National Bank, Baltimore, 4) 1973-Mercantile-Safe Deposit, Baltimore, 5) 1974-The Peoples Bank of Elkton;* **MASSACHUSETTS** *1) 1970-Harvard Trust Co., Cambridge, 2) 1971-1st Bank, Springfield, 3) 1972-State Street Bank and Trust Co., Boston, 4) 1973-Valley Bank, Springfield, 5) 1974-Plymouth Home National Bank, Brockton;* **MICHIGAN** *1) 1970-Pontiac State Bank, 2) 1971-Amer. Nat. Bank & Trust Co., Kalamazoo, 3) 1972-Detroit Bank and Trust, 4) 1973-Bank of the Commonwealth, 5) 1974-Michigan National Banks;* **MINNESOTA** *1) 1970-Fidelity Bank & Trust Co., Minneapolis, 2) 1971-1st Minneapolis, 3) 1972-Marquette National Bank, Minneapolis, 4) 1973-1st National Bank of Winona, 5) 1974-New Amer. Nat. Bank & Trust Co., St. Paul;* **MISSISSIPPI** *1) 1970-1st National Bank, Jackson, 2) 1971-Bank of Clarksdale, 3) 1972-Hancock Bank, Gulfport, 4) 1973-Grenada Bank, 5) 1974-Deposit Guaranty National Bank, Jackson;* **MISSOURI** *1) 1970-Boatman's National Bank of St. Louis, 2) 1971-1st National Bank, Kansas City, 3) 1972-Commerce Bank, Kansas City, 4) 1973-St. Johns Community Bank, St. Louis, 5) 1974-First National Bank, St. Louis;* **MONTANA** *1) 1970-Midland National Bank, Billings, 2) 1971-1st Metals Bank and Trust Co., Butte, 3) 1972-Great Falls National Bank, 4) 1973-1st National Bank & Trust Co., Helena, 5) 1974-Western Montana National Bank, Missoula;* **NEBRASKA** *1) 1970-1st National Bank of Omaha, 2) 1971-Omaha National Bank, 3) 1972-United States National Bank of Omaha, 4) 1973-Cornhuster Bank, Lincoln, 5) 1974-First National, Lincoln;* **NEVADA** *1) 1970-Bank of Nevada, Las Vegas, 2) 1971-1st National Bank of Nevada, Reno, 3) 1972-Valley Bank of Nevada, Las Vegas, 4) 1973-Pioneer Citizens Bank of Nevada, Reno, 5) 1974-Nevada National Bank, Reno;* **NEW HAMPSHIRE** *1) 1970-Cheshire National Bank, Keene, 2) 1971-Amoskeag Banks, Manchester, 3) 1972-Concord National Bank, 4) 1973-Indian Head Banks, Nashua, 5) 1974-Nashua Trust Co.;* **NEW JERSEY** *1) 1970-National State Bank, Elizabeth, 2) 1971-New Jersey National Bank, Trenton, 3) 1972-Citizens National Bank, Englewood, 4) 1973-1st National State Bank of N.J., Newark, 5) 1974-1st Nat. Bank of Central Jersey, Somerville;* **NEW MEXICO** *1) 1970-Clovis National Bank, 2) 1971-Alburquerque National Bank, 3) 1972-1st National Bank of Santa Fe, 4) 1973-New Mexico Bank & Trust Co., Hobbs, 5) 1974-Deming National Bank;* **NEW YORK** *1) 1970-Franklin National Bank, NYC, 2) 1971-Rochester Savings Bank, 3) 1972-Manufacturers Hanover Trust, NYC, 4) 1973-Marine Midland Banks, Buffalo, 5) 1974-First National City Bank, NYC;* **NORTH CAROLINA** *1) 1970-Mechanics and Farmers Bank, Durham, 2) 1971-Planters National Banks, Rocky Mount, 3) 1972-North Carolina National Bank, Charlotte, 4) 1973-1st Citizens Bank & Trust Co., Raleigh, 5) 1974-Wachovia Bank & Trust, Winston-Salem;* **NORTH DAKOTA** *1) 1970-1st National Bank in Grand Forks, 2) 1971-Bank of North Dakota, Bismark, 3) 1972-1st National Bank & Trust Co. of Fargo, 4) 1973-1st National Bank, Minot, 5) 1974-1st National Bank & Trust Co. of Bismark;* **OHIO** *1) 1970-Central National Bank of Cleveland, 2) 1971-1st National Bank of Toledo, 3) 1972-Bancohio Corporation, Columbus, 4) 1973-National City Bank of Cleveland, 5) 1974-Society National Bank, Cleveland;* **OKLAHOMA** *1) 1970-1st National Bank & Trust Co. of Tulsa, 2) 1971-Liberty Bank, Oklahoma City, 3) 1972-National Bank of Tulsa, 4) 1973-Commercial Bank & Trust Co., Muscogee, 5) 1974-1st Nat. Bank & Trust Co., Oklahoma City;* **OREGON** *1) 1970-U.S. Nat. Bank of Oregon, Portland, 2) 1971-Commercial Bank, Salem, 3) 1972-1st National Bank of Oregon, Portland, 4) 1973-Western Bank, Coos Bay, 5) 1974-The Oregon Bank,*

Portland; **PENNSYLVANIA** *1) 1970-Provident National Bank, Philadelphia, 2) 1971-Equimark, Pittsburgh, 3) 1972-Continental Bank, Philadelphia, 4) 1973-The Fidelity Bank, Philadelphia, 5) 1974-National Central Bank, Lancaster;* **RHODE ISLAND** *1) 1970-R.I. Hospital Trust Nat. Bank, Providence, 2) 1971-Greater Providence Trust, 3) 1972-Old Stone Park Bank, Providence, 4) 1973-Columbus National Bank of R.I., Providence, 5) 1974-People's Bank, Providence;* **SOUTH CAROLINA** *1) 1970-1st Citizens Bank & Trust Co., Columbia, 2) 1971-Peoples National Bank, Greenville, 3) 1972-Citizens & Southern Nat. Bank, Charleston, 4) 1973-South Carolina National Bank, Columbia, 5) 1974-National Bank of South Carolina, Sumter;* **SOUTH DAKOTA** *1) 1970-Pierre National Bank, 2) 1971-Aberdeen National Bank, 3) 1972-Farmers and Merchants Bank, Huron, 4) 1973-National Bank of South Dakota, Sioux Falls, 5) 1974-1st Western Bank, Wall;* **TENNESSEE** *1) 1970-1st National Bank of Memphis, 2) 1971-1st Peoples Bank, Johnson City, 3) 1972-Union Planters National Bank of Memphis, 4) 1973-3rd National Bank, Nashville, 5) 1974-Hamilton National Bank, Chattanooga;* **TEXAS** *1) 1970-Texas Commerce Bank, Houston, 2) 1971-1st National Bank of Abilene, 3) 1972-1st National Bank of Amarillo, 4) 1973-Fort Worth National Bank, 5) 1974-1st State Bank, Abilene;* **UTAH** *1) 1970-Box Elder County Bank, Brigham City, 2) 1971-Tracy Collins Bank & Trust, Salt Lake City, 3) 1972-Commercial Security Bank, Ogden, 4) 1973-Central Bank & Trust Co., Provo, 5) 1974-First Security Bank, Salt Lake City;* **VERMONT** *1) 1970-Proctor Trust Co., Poultney, 2) 1971-Chittenden Trust Co., Burlington, 3) 1972-Vermont National Bank, Brattleboro, 4) 1973-Montpelier National Bank, 5) 1974-Howard Bank, Burlington;* **VIRGINIA** *1) 1970-United Virginia Bank, Richmond, 2) 1971-Burke & Herbert Bank, Alexandria, 3) 1972-Alexandria National Bank, 4) 1973-1st & Merchants National Bank, Richmond, 5) 1974-Colonial American National Bank, Roanoke;* **WASHINGTON** *1) 1970-Bank of Yakima, 2) 1971-Seattle 1st National Bank, 3) 1972-National Bank of Commerce, Seattle, 4) 1973-Puget Sound National Bank, Tacoma, 5) 1974-Old National Bank of Washington, Spokane;* **WEST VIRGINIA** *1) 1970-Charleston National Bank, 2) 1971-Kanawha Valley Bank, 3) 1972-Wheeling Dollar Bank, 4) 1972-Parkersburg National Bank, 5) 1974-Mountain State Bank, Parkersburg;* **WISCONSIN** *1) 1970-Marine Bank, Milwaukee, 2) 1971-American Bank & Trust Co., Racine, 3) 1972-1st Wisconsin National Bank of Milwaukee, 4) 1973-People Marine Bank, Green Bay, 5) 1974-First National Bank of Kenosha;* **WYOMING** *1) 1970-1st Nat. Bank & Trust Co., Cheyenne, 2) 1971-1st Nat. Bank, Laramie, 3) 1972-Wyoming National Bank, Casper, 4) 1973-1st National Bank of Casper, 5) 1974-Cheyenne National Bank.*

☐ **Bible Tablets,** *set of 100 ingots, sterling silver, 25mm x 38mm, 83 troy ounces per set; 1) The Creation, 2) The Annunciation, 3) The Sin, 4) Birth of John, 5) Cain and Abel, 6) Birth of Jesus, 7) The Flood, 8) The Wise Men, 9) Tower of Babel, 10) Flight into Egypt, 11) God's Promise to Abram, 12) Jesus in the Temple, 13) Abram and Lot, 14) John Baptizes Jesus, 15) Sodom & Gomorrah Destroyed, 16) Jesus in the Desert, 17) Sacrifice of Isaac, 18) Wedding at Cana, 19) Rebecca at the Spring, 20) Jesus Heals a Paralized Man, 21) Jacob's Ladder, 22) 12 Apostles Appointed, 23) Reconcilation of Jacob & Esau, 24) Sermon on the Mount, 25) Joseph in Potiphars' House, 26) Calmed Storm, 27) Joseph's Brothers, 28) Death of John the Baptist, 29) Birth of Moses, 30) The Sower, 31) The Burning Brush, 32) Jesus & the Children, 33) Pharoah & the Israelites, 34) Miracle of the Loaves, 35) Night of Passover, 36) Resurrection of Lazarus, 37) Passage through the Red Sea, 38) Jesus Enters Jerusalem;* **1,000 sets to be issued from 1978-1985 at $35.00 at $3,500.00 a set (100).**

☐ **Biblical Wildlife Treasury,** *set of 24 ingots, sterling silver, proof, 2.22" x 1.25", 37 troy ounces; 1) Camel, 2) Ostrich, 3) Persian Onager, 4) Asiatic Lion, 5) Cheetah, 6) Serpent, 7) White Ass, 8) Stork, 9) Fox, 10) Rock Hyrax, 11) Arabian Horse, 12) Crocodile, 13) Sheep, 14) Saluki Dog, 15) Nubian Ibex, 16) Wild Boar, 17) Indian*

Wolf, 18) Fallow Deer, 19) Syrian Bear, 20) Arabian Oryx, 21) Roe Deer, 22) Dorcas Gazelle, 23) Wild Ox, 24) Dove; **250 sets issued from 1974-1979 at $42.00 each or $900 a set (24).**

☐ **Bill of Rights,** *set of 10 ingots, sterling silver, proof, 1.8" x 1.3", 11 troy ounces per set; 1) Prevents the government from passing laws restricting the right of free expression, 2) Guarantees that the right of the people to keep and bear arms will not be infringed, 3) Without the consent of the owner, no soldier can be quartered in a private home, 4) Protects citizens' homes and personal effects against unreasonable search and seizure, 5) Guarantees that no persons will be prosecuted without due process of law, 6) Grants the right to a speedy and public trial before an impartial jury in criminal cases, 7) Preserves the right to trial by jury for citizens engaged in civil suits, 8) Protects against cruel and unusual punishment — prevents excessive bail and fines, 9) Reserves to the people all rights not stated in the Constitution, 10) Reserves to the states powers not delegated to the federal government by the Constitution;* **4,166 sets issued in 1975 at $26.00 each or $260.00 a set (10).**

☐ **Books of the Bible,** *set of 73 ingots, sterling silver, proof, 2³⁄₁₆" x 1¹⁄₁₆", 75 troy ounces per set; 1) Adam & Eve, 2) Moses & 10 Commandments, 3) Aaron and his Sons, 4) Moses Smites the Rock, 5) The Promised Land, 6) The Walls of Jericho, 7) The Death of Samson, 8) Ruth and Naomi, 9) David and Goliath, 10) David and Bathsheba, 11) Solomon's Wisdom, 12) Elijah Ascends, 13) David Institutes Temple Music, 14) Isaiah Destroys False Idols, 15) The Return from Exile, 16) Walls of Jerusalem, 17) Cure of Tobit's Blindness, 18) Judith Slays Holofernes, 19) Esther Saves Israelites, 20) Judas Recaptures Jerusalem, 21) Divine Intervention, 22) Job Visited by Friends, 23) The 23rd Psalm, 24) The Education of Youth, 25) The Joys of Life, 26) Human Love, 27) Words of Wisdom, 28) Honor your Father & Mother,*

Books Of The Bible, *Moses and 10 Commandments, ingot #3.*

29) The Messianic Kingdom, 30) Jeremiah in the Muddy Pit, 31) Jeremiah Laments, 32) Vessels for the Temple, 33) Ezekiel's Vision, 34) Daniel in the Lions' Den, 35) Hosea's Erring Wife Returns, 36) Invasion of the Locusts, 37) Role of the Prophet, 38) Treachery of Edom, 39) Jonah and the Whale, 40) Swords into Plowshares, 41) Downfall of Nineveh, 42) The Lord's Message, 43) Israel United, 44) Rebuilding the Temple, 45) Jerusalem Restored, 46) Offerings to the Lord, 47) The Sermon on the Mount, 48) The Crucifixion, 49) The Birth of Jesus, 50) The Resurrection, 51) Paul

Converted to Christianity, 52) The Olive Tree, 53) Faith, Hope and Charity, 54) The Cheerful Giver, 55) The Christian Faith, 56) The Christian Marriage, 57) Paul Writes from Prison, 58) Things created through Jesus, 59) The Second Coming, 60) With Quietness they Work, 61) Duties of Church Leaders, 62) All Scripture is Inspired, 63) Titus Preaching on Crete, 64) Paul Seeks Forgiveness, 65) Men & Women of Faith in O.T., 66) Be Doers of the Word, 67) Christian Life, 68) Basis of True Knowledge, 69) Love Essence of Christianity, 70) Counsel against False Teachers, 71) Helping fellow Christians, 72) The true Faith, 73) The New Jerusalem; **665 Protestant versions, issued from 1975-1981 at $25.00 each or $1,650 a set (73); 508 Catholic versions issued from 1975-1981 at $25.00 each or $1,825 a set (73); 289 Hebrew versions issued from 1975-1981 at $25.00 each or $975.00 a set (73).**

☐ **British Monarchy, 1000 Years,** *set of 50 ingots, sterling silver, P/L, 1 3/4" x 15/16", 104 troy ounces; 1) Edgar, 2) Edward the Martyr, 3) Athelred the Redeless, 4) Edmund Ironside, 5) Canute, 6) Harold Harefoot, 7) Hardicanute, 8) Edward the Confessor, 9) Harold, 10) William the Conqueror, 11) William Rufus, 12) Henry I, 13) Stephen, 14) Henry II, 15) Richard I, 16) John, 17) Henry III, 18) Edward I, 19) Edward II, 20) Edward III, 21) Richard II, 22) Henry IV, 23) Henry V, 24) Henry VI, 25) Edward IV, 26) Edward V, 27) Richard III, 28) Henry VII, 29) Henry VIII, 30) Edward VI, 31) Mary I, 32) Elizabeth I, 33) James I, 34) Charles I, 35) Oliver Cromwell, 36) Charles II, 37) James II, 38) William and Mary, 39) Anne, 40) George I, 41) George II, 42) George III, 43) George IV, 44) William IV, 45) Victoria, 46) Edward VII, 47) George V, 48) Edward VIII, 49) George VI, 50) Elizabeth II;* **695 sets issued from 1973-1976 from $16.00 each or $800 a set (50).**

British Monarchy, 1000 years, *Victoria, ingot #45.*

☐ **Centennial Car,** *set of 100 ingots, proof, 2.22" x 1.25", 208 troy ounces each set; 1) 1875 Marcus, 2) 1885 Benz, 3) 1886 Daimler, 4) 1893 Duryea, 5) 1895 Panhard-Levassor, 6) 1896 Ford, 7) 1898 Winton, 8) 1899 Packard, 9) 1899 Renault, 10) 1900 De Dion Bouton, 11) 1901 Mercedes, 12) 1901 Oldsmobile, 13) 1903 Cadillac, 14) 1903 Lanchester, 15) 1905 Napier, 16) 1905 Peerless, 17) 1906 Rolls Royce, 18) 1907 Thomas, 19) 1909 Buick, 20) 1909 Ford, 21) 1909 Lozier, 22) 1909 Stanley, 23) 1909 White, 24) 1910 Austro-Daimler, 25) 1910 Chadwick, 26) 1911 Marmon, 27) 1911 Simplex, 28) 1912 Cadillac, 29) 1912 Hispano-Suiza, 30) 1913 Locomobile, 31) 1913 Mercer, 32) 1913 Peugeot, 33) 1913 Stutz, 34) 1916 Dodge, 35) 1916 Hudson, 36) 1916 Morris, 37) 1916 Packard, 38) 1916 Pierce-Arrow, 39) 1923 Chevrolet, 40) 1924 Chrysler, 41) 1924 Lancia, 42) 1924 Vauxhall, 43) 1925 Austin, 44) 1925 Bentley, 45) 1925 Doble, 46) 1925 Franklin, 47) 1925 Lorraine-Dietrich, 48) 1927 Amilcar, 49) 1928 Ford, 50) Mercedes-Benz, 51) 1929 Alfa Romeo, 52) 1929 Chevrolet, 53) 1930 Hispano-Suiza, 54) 1930 Isotta Fraschini, 55) 1931 Bugatti, 56) 1931 Cadillac, 57) 1931 Invicta, 58) 1931 Marmon, 59) 1931 Stutz, 60) 1932 Delage, 61) 1932 Ford, 62) 1932 Lincoln, 63) 1933 Duesenberg, 64) 1934 Chrysler, 65) 1934 Citroen, 66) 1934 Lagonda, 67) 1935 Auburn, 68) 1935 Bugatti, 69) 1936 Fiat, 70) 1936 Maybach, 71) 1937 Cord, 72) 1937 Delahaye, 73) 1937 Mercedes-Benz, 74) 1938 Alfa Romeo, 75) 1938 Volkswagen, 76) 1939 BMW, 77) 1941 Lincoln, 78) 1946 M.G., 79) 1948 Jaguar,*

80) 1949 Citroen, 81) 1949 Ferrari, 82) 1950 Aston Martin, 83) 1950 Rover, 84) 1953 Porsche, 85) 1954 Mercedes-Benz, 86) 1956 Citroen, 87) 1958 Lotus, 88) 1959 Rolls-Royce, 89) 1960 Austin, 90) 1961 Jaguar, 91) 1963 Chevrolet, 92) 1964 Porsche, 93) 1965 Ford, 94) 1966 Lamborghini, 95) 1967 Jensen, 96) 1970 Datsun, 97) 1970 Ferrari, 98) 1970 Mercedes-Benz, 99) 1974 Jaguar, 100) 1975 Volkswagen; **5,330 sets issued from 1973-1978 at $13.50 each or $1350.00 a set (100).**

☐ **Chai,** set of 18 ingots, sterling silver, proof, 2.22" x 1.25", 37 troy ounces per set; 1) Chanukah, 2) Pidyon Ha-Ben, 3) Tu bi'Shevat, 4) Purim, 5) Pesach, 6) Shavuot, 7) Brith Milah, 8) Tisha b'Av, 9) Rosh Hashanah, 10) Yom Kipper, 11) Succot, 12) Simchat Torah, 13) Bar Mitzvah, 14) Chupah, 15) Yizkor, 16) Lag Ba-Omer (error), 16a) Lag Ba-Omer (corrected), 17) Yom Atzmaut (error), 17a) Yom Atzmaut (corrected), 18) Shabbat; **1,005 sets issued from 1973-1975 at $27.50 each or $495 a set (18).**

Chai, Chanukah, ingot #1.

☐ **Christmas,** sterling silver, proof, 1.75" x .88" x 2.9", 1,000 grains, 2.08 troy ounces each; 1) 1970 The Skaters, **28,897 issued at $12.00 each;** 2) 1971 Sleighing Scene, **47,912 issued at $12.00 each;** 3) 1973 Hauling in the Yule Log, **72,407 issued at $12.00 each;** 4) 1973 The Carolers, **135,619 issued at $13.50 each;** 5) 1974 The Snowman, **85,331 issued at $25.00 each;** 6) 1975 The Open Sleigh, **25,052 issued at $30.00 each;** 7) 1976 Christmas Landscape, **20,211 issued at $30.00 each;** 8) 1977 Making Gingerbread, **issued at $32.00 each;** 9) 1978 Waiting for Santa, **14,481 issued at $32.00 each;** 10) 1979 Bringing Home the Tree, **issued at $37.50 each;** 11) 1980 Bringing in the Gifts, **issued at $80.00 each;** 12) 1981 First Snow, **issued at $80.00 each;** sterling silver, proof, 1.75" x .88" x .15", 500 grains, 1.04 troy ounces each; 5) 1974 The Snowman, **72,612 issued at $14.00 each;** 6) 1975 The Open Sleigh, **22,239 issued at $15.00 each;** 7) 1976 Christmas Landscape, **18,084 issued at $15.00 each;** 8) 1977 Making Gingerbread, **issued at $16.00 each;** 9) 1978 Waiting for Santa, **issued at $16.00 each;** 10) 1979 Bringing Home the Tree, **issued at $19.50 each;** 11) 1980 Bringing in the Gifts, **issued at $42.00 each;** 12) 1981 First Snow, **issued at $42.00 each.**

Christmas, 1974, The Snowman, ingot #5.

☐ **Classic Cars,** *set of 63 ingots, sterling silver; 1) Bugatti Royale-1927; 2) Duesenberg-1934; 3) Rolls Royce-1926; 4) Isotta Fraschini-1928; 5) Packard-1939; 6) Stutz-1932; 7) Bentley-1931; 8) Horch-1936; 9) La Salle-1927; 10) Hispano-Suiza-1928; 11) Brewster-1935; 12) Sunbeam-1929; 13) Chrysler-1932; 14) Mercedes-1924; 15) Peerless-1931; 16) Vauxhall-1927; 17) Lincoln Coupe-1938; 18) Auburn-1933; 19) Lagonda-1939; 20) Delage-1927; 21) None; 22) Cunningham-1928; 23) Renault-1925; 24) Alvis-1938; 25) Cord-1937; 26) Lincoln Continental-1941;* **1,500 sets to be issued from 1979-1985 at $21.50 each or $1,354.50 a set (63).**

☐ **Currier and Ives,** *set of 12 ingots, 3" x 2", proof, 33 troy ounces per set; 1) Central Park, Winter — 'the Skating Pond' by Charles Parsons, 2) 'Wooding Up' on the Mississippi by Fanny Palmer, 3) Home to Thanksgiving by George Henry Durrie, 4) Clipper Ship 'Flying Cloud' by James Butterworth, 5) The Life of a Hunter. A Tight Fix by Arthur Fitzwilliam Tait, 6) Trotting Stallion 'George M. Patchen, Jr.' of California by John Cameron, 7) Winter in the Country. 'The Old Grist Mill' by George Henry Durrie, 8) The Road, Winter by Otto Knirsch, 9) American Express Train by Fanny Palmer, 10) Haying Time. The First Load by Fanny Palmer and John Cameron, 11) Catching Trout 'We Hab You Now, Sar!' by Arthur Fitzwilliam Tait, 12) Yosemite Valley — California (Unknown Artist);* **4,241 sets issued from 1974-1975 at $40.00 each or $480.00 a set (12).**

Currier and Ives, — *'the Skating Pond' by Charles Parsons, ingot #1.*

☐ **Dow-Jones,** *sterling silver, proof-like, 4¾" x 2", 1,000 grams (more than 32 troy ounces);* **1,092 issued in 1973 at $100.00 each.**

Dow-Jones, *New York Stock Exchange, November 1972.*

☐ **El Greco Apostles,** *set of 13 ingots, sterling silver, proof, 2" x 1½", 16 troy ounces per set; 1) St. Peter, 2) St. Andrew, 3) St. James the Great, 4) St. John the Evangelist, 5) St. Philip, 6) St. Bartholomew, 7) St. Thomas, 8) St. Matthew, 9) St. James the Less, 10) St. Simon, 11) St. Jude, 12) St. Paul, 13) Christ;* **3,849 sets issued from 1976-1977 at $25.00 each or $325.00 a set (13).**

☐ **Father's Day,** *set of 8 ingots, sterling silver, proof, 1¾" x ¹⁵⁄₁₆", 2.08 ounces per set; 1) 1971-Presentation Case,* **10,259 issued at $12.50 each;** *2) 1972-Presentation Case,* **10,510 issued at $12.50 each;** *3) 1973-Presentation Case,* **8,943 issued at $12.50 each;** *4) 1974-Presentation Case,* **8,678 issued at $25.00 each;** *5) 1975-Presentation Case,* **5,806 issued at $30.00 each;** *6) 1976-Presentation Case,* **3,656 is-**

sued at $30.00 each; *7) 1977-Presentation Case,* **1,876 issued at $32.50 each;** *8) 1978-Presentation Case,* **1,374 issued at $32.50 each;** *proof-like, 3) 1973-Presentation Case,* **8,093 issued at $12.50 each;** *4) 1974-Presentation Case,* **2,384 issued at $25.00 each.**

Father's Day, *1976, ingot #6.*

☐ **Flags of America,** *set of 42 ingots, sterling silver; 1) Flag of Spain, 2) Flag of France, 3) Flag of Great Britain, 4) Flag of the Netherlands, 5) Flag of Sweden, 6) Continental Colors, 7) 1st Official U.S. Flag, 8) 2nd U.S. Flag, 9) Flag of the Republic of West Florida, 10) 3rd U.S. Flag, 11) 4th U.S. Flag, 12) 5th U.S. Flag, 13) Flag of Mexico, 14) 6th U.S. Flag, 15) 7th U.S. Flag, 16) 8th U.S. Flag, 17) 9th U.S. Flag, 18) Flag of the Republic of Texas, 19) 10th U.S. Flag, 20) Flag of the California Republic, 21) 11th U.S. Flag, 22) 12th U.S. Flag, 23) 13th U.S. Flag, 24) 14th U.S. Flag, 25) 15th U.S. Flag, 26) Flag of Confederacy, 27) 16th U.S. Flag, 28) Official Flag of Confederacy, 29) 17th U.S. Flag, 30) Last Flag of Confederacy, 31) 18th U.S. Flag, 32) 19th U.S. Flag, 33) Flag of the Russian Empire, 34) 20th U.S. Flag, 35) 21st U.S. Flag, 36) 22nd U.S. Flag, 37) 23rd U.S. Flag, 38) The Hawaiian Flag, 39) 24th U.S. Flag, 40) 25th U.S. Flag, 41) 26th U.S. Flag, 42) 27th U.S. Flag;* **4,892 sets issued from 1972-1977 at $13.50 each or $567.00 a set (42).**

☐ **Flags (American) of the Revolution,** *set of 64 ingots, sterling silver, regular size, 52 troy ounces per set; 1) Fort Johnson, 2) Stamp Act Protest, 3) New England, 4) Liberty Tree, 5) Hanover Associator's Color, 6) Rebellious Stripes, 7) Taunton, 8) Sons of Liberty, 9) George Rex, 10) Bedford Cornet, 11) Forster-Knight Color, 12) Bunker Hill, 13) Cambridge Common, 14) 2nd Conn. Regiment Color, 15) Pine Tree, 16) Phila. Light Horse Color, 17) Fort Moultrie, 18) Newburyport, 19) Proctor's Inde. Battle, 20) Culpepper County Color, 21) Hopkins, 22) Continental Colors, 23) 1st Penn. Regiment Color, 24) Massachusetts Navy, 25) 3rd N.Y. Regiment Color, 26) 2nd S.C. Regiment Color, 27) Huntington, 28) Appeal to Heaven, 29) First Jack, 30) Light Lagoons, 2nd Regiment Color, 31) White Plains Color, 32) 11th Va. Regiment Color, 33) 2nd N.H. Regiment Color, 34) Betsy Ross, 35) Stars and Stripes, 36) Enoch Poor Color, 37) Green Mt. Boys Color, 38) Bennington, 39) Dansey Regiment Color, 40) 1st R.I. Regiment Color, 41) Valley Forge, 42) Providence Art'y Color, 43) French Alliance, 44) Striped Ensign, 45) Newport, 46) Texel, 47) Knoll, 48) John Paul Jones, 49) 2nd R.I. Regiment Color, 50) Pulaski Standard, 51) Bucks of America Color, 52) Benjamin Tallmedge's Color, 53) 3rd Md. Regiment Color, 54) Eutaw Standard, 55) Washington's Headquarters, 56) Fort Independence, 57) L'Enfant, 58) Great Seal, 59) Schuyler, 60) 1st Conn. Reg't Color, 61) second jack, 62) Commander-in-Chief's Guard Color, 63) Society of the Cincinnati, 64) Peace Flag;* **2,289 sets issued at $19.50 each or $1,248.00 a set (64);** *mini-size,* **10,488 sets issued at $2.50 each or $160.00 a set (64).**

☐ **Flags of Royalty,** *set of 50 ingots, sterling silver, proof; 1) Franz-Josef — Austria-Hungary, 2) Henry I — Haiti, 3) Mutsuhito — Japan, 4) Ivan the Terrible — Russia, 5) Constantine — Roman Empire, 6) Arthur — England, 7) Charles VI — Holy Roman Empire, 8) Robert I the Bruce — Scotland, 9) Akbar the Great — Moghul Empire, 10) Wilhelm I — Germany, 11) Mansa Musa — Mali, 12) Richard II — England, 13) Ghengis Khan — Mongol Empire, 14) Skanderbeg — Albania, 15)*

Queen Isabella — Spain, 16) Ranavglona I — Hova Empire, 17) Charles V — Holy Roman Empire, 18) Charlemagne — Holy Roman Empire, 19) Philip II — Spain, 20) Francis I, 21) Louis XIV — France, 22) Tsar Peter — Russia, 23) Charles I, 24) William III — Great Britain, 25) Louis IX — France, 26) Christian X — Denmark, 27) Manuel I — Portugal, 28) Catherine II — Russia, 29) Henry IV — France, 30) Napoleon I — France, 31) William I — England, 32) Haile Selassie — Ethiopia, 33) Pedro II — Brazil, 34) Charles XIII — Sweden, 35) George I — Greece, 36) Maximilian — Mexico, 37) Fredrick II — Prussia, 38) Ibor Saud — Saudi Arabia, 39) Roma V — Thailand, 40) Wilhelmina — Netherlands, 41) Sultan Selim III — Ottom. Empire, 42) Liliuokalani — Hawaii, 43) Victor Emmanuel II — Italy, 44) Kang-te — Manchuria, 45) Salote — Tonga, 46) Uzleck, 47) Amanullah — Afghanistan, 48) Farouk I — Egypt, 49) Mutesa II — Buganda; **1,443 sets issued in 1977 at $29.50 each or $1,475.00 a set (50).**

☐ **Flags of the States,** *set of 50 ingots, regular, proof, 104 troy ounces per set; 1) Delaware, 2) Pennsylvania, 3) New Jersey, 4) Georgia, 5) Connecticut, 6) Massachusetts, 7) Maryland, 8) South Carolina, 9) New Hampshire, 10) Virginia, 11) New York, 12) North Carolina, 13) Rhode Island, 14) Vermont, 15) Kentucky, 16) Tennessee, 17) Ohio, 18) Louisiana, 19) Indiana, 20) Mississippi, 21) Illinois, 22) Alabama, 23) Maine, 24) Missouri, 25) Arkansas, 26) Michigan, 27) Florida, 28) Texas, 29) Iowa, 30) Wisconsin, 31) California, 32) Minnesota, 33) Oregon, 34) Kansas, 35) West Virginia, 36) Nevada, 37) Nebraska, 38) Colorado, 39) North Dakota, 40) South Dakota, 41) Montana, 42) Washington, 43) Idaho, 44) Wyoming, 45) Utah, 46) Oklahoma, 47) New Mexico, 48) Arizona, 49) Alaska, 50) Hawaii;* **5,803 sets issued from 1973-1975 at $17.50 each or $875 a set (50).**

☐ **Flags of the U.N.,** *set of 135 ingots, sterling silver, proof, 65,000 grains (135 troy ounces) per set; 1) Afghanistan, 2) Albania, 3) Algeria, 4) Argentina, 5) Australia, 6) Austria, 7) Bahamas, 8) Bahrain, 9) Bangledesh, 10) Barbados, 11) Belgium, 12) Bhutan, 13) Bolivia, 14) Botswana, 15) Brazil, 16) Bulgaria, 17) Burma, 18) Burundi, 19) Byelorussia S.S.R., 20) Cameroon, 21) Canada, 22) Cape Verde, 23) Central African Republic, 24) Chad, 25) Chile, 26) China, 27) Colombia, 28) Congo, 29) Costa Rica, 30) Cuba, 31) Cyprus, 32) Czechoslovakia, 33) Dahomey, 34) Democratic Yemen, 35) Denmark, 36) Dominican Republic, 37) Ecuador, 38) Egypt, 39) El Salvador, 40) Equatorial Guinea, 41) Ethiopia, 42) Fugi, 43) Finland, 44) France, 45) Gabon, 46) Gambia, 47) German Democratic Rep., 48) Germany, Federal Rep., 49) Ghana, 50) Greece, 51) Grenada, 52) Guatemala, 53) Guinea, 54) Guinea-Bissau, 55) Guyana, 56) Haiti, 57) Honduras, 58) Hungary, 59) Iceland, 60) India, 61) Indonesia, 62) Iran, 63) Iraq, 64) Ireland, 65) Israel, 66) Italy, 67) Ivory Coast, 68) Jamaica, 69) Japan, 70) Jordan, 71) Kenya, 72) Khmer Rep. (Cambodia), 73) Kuwait, 74) Laos, 75) Lebanon, 76) Lesotho, 77) Liberia, 78) Libya, 79) Luxembourg, 80) Madagascar, 81) Malawi, 82) Malaysia, 83) Maldives, 84) Mali, 85) Malta, 86) Mauritania, 87) Mauritius, 88) Mexico, 89) Mongolia, 90) Morocco, 91) Mozambique, 92) Nepal, 93) Netherlands, 94) New Zealand, 95) Nicaragua, 96) Niger, 97) Nigeria, 98) Norway, 99) Oman, 100) Pakistan, 101) Panama, 102) Papua New Guinea, 103) Paraguay, 104) Peru, 105) Philippines, 106) Poland, 107) Portugal, 108) Qatar, 109) Romania, 110) Rwanda, 111) Sao Tome & Principe, 112) Saudi Arabia, 113) Senegal, 114) Sierra Leone, 115) Singapore, 116) Somalia, 117) South Africa, 118) Spain, 119) Sri Lanka, 120) Sudan, 121) Swaziland, 122) Sweden, 123) Syria, 124) Thailand, 125) Togo, 126) Trinidad & Tobago, 127) Tunisia, 128) Turkey, 129) Uganda, 130) Ukranian S.S.R., 131) United Arab Emirates, 132) United Kingdom, 133) Tanzania, 134) United States, 135) Upper Volta, 136) Uruguay, 137) U.S.S.R., 138) Venezuela, 139) Yemen, 140) Yugoslavia, 141) Zaire, 142) Zambia;* **7,731 sets issued from 1974-1976 at $9.50 each or $1282 a set (135).**

☐ **Flags of the U.S. Territories,** *set of 8 ingots, sterling silver, proof, 1½" high, 19 troy ounces per set; 1) U.S. Virgin Islands, 2) Northern Mariana Islands, 3) Puerto Rico, 4) Guam, 5) District of Columbia, 6) Panama Canal Zone, 7) Trust Territory of the Pacific Islands, 8) American Samoa;* **117 sets issued in 1977 at $35.00 each or $280.00 a set (8).**

☐ **Gems,** *set of 30 ingots, sterling silver with gemstones, 3.5mm in diameter, 23 troy ounces per set; 1) Ruby, 2) Labradorite, 3) Blue Sapphire, 4) Rodocrosite, 5) Andulusite, 6) Flourite, 7) Emerald, 8) Amber, 9) Garnet, 10) Peridot, 11) Diamond, 12) Garmet, 13) Nephrite, 14) Quartz, 15) Opal;* **8,586 sets to be issued from 1978-1983 at $45.00 each or $1,350.00 a set (30).**

☐ **Genius of America,** *set of 100 ingots, sterling silver, proof, 2.1" x 1", 104 troy ounces per set; 1) Benjamin Franklin, 2) Eli Whitney, 3) Benjamin Thompson, 4) Nathaniel Bowditch, 5) Robert Fulton, 6) William Beaumont, 7) Peter Cooper, 8) Joseph Henry, 9) Cyrus Hall McCormick, 10) Samuel Colt, 11) Asa Gray, 12) Samuel F. B. Morse, 13) John Deere, 14) Charles Goodyear, 15) John W. Draper, 16) Jean Louis Agassiziz, 17) Elias Howe, 18) W. T. G. Morton, 19) Richard M. Hoe, 20) Maria Mitchell, 21) George Corliss, 22) James B. Francis, 23) Elisha Graves Otis, 24) Gail Borden, 25) Edwin L. Drake, 26) John Ericsson, 27) Cyrus W. Field, 28) Christopher L. Sholes, 29) John W. Hyatt, 30) George Westinghouse, 31) Luther Burbank, 32) Joseph F. Glidden, 33) Alexander Graham Bell, 34) Josiah Willard Gibbs, 35) Edward C. Pickering, 36) Samuel Langley Pierpont, 37) Albert A. Michelson, 38) Thomas Alva Edison, 39) William Le Baron Jenney, 40) George Eastman, 41) Ottmar Mergenthaler, 42) William Stanley, 43) Charles M. Hall, 44) Frank J. Sprague, 45) George Ellery Hale, 46) Herman Hollerith, 47) Charles Francis Jenkins, 48) Nikola Tesla, 49) Charles Duryea, 50) Daniel Hale Williams, 51) Harvey Williams Cushing, 52) George Washington Carver, 53) Charles G. Curtis, 54) Walter Reed, 55) Reginald A. Fessenden, 56) Alexis Carrel, 57) Wilber & Orville Wright, 58) Albert Einstein, 59) Lee de Forest, 60) Irving Langmuir, 61) Robert A. Millikan, 62) Elmer A. Sperry, 63) Casimir Funk, 64) Henry Ford;* **987 sets to be issued from 1976-1984 at $22.50 each or $2,250.00 a set (100).**

☐ **Historic Silver,** *sterling silver, 4⅝" x 1⅞", 20.8 troy ounces, mint;* **7,452 issued in 1970 at $105.00 each.**

☐ **History of the U.S.,** *set of 100 ingots, sterling silver, proof, 2.1" x 1.4", 156 troy ounces per set; 1) 1776 Declaration of Independence, 2) 1776 Hessians Defeated at Trenton, 3) 1777 Americans Victorious at Saratoga, 4) 1977-1978 Troops Winter at Valley Forge, 5) 1781 Victory at Yorktown Ends War, 6) 1783 Peace Treaty Signed in Paris, 7) 1787 Constitution Adopted and Signed, 8) 1789 Washington Inaugurated First President, 9) 1789 Bill of Rights Adopted, 10) 1794 Eli Whitney Patents the Cotton Gin, 11) 1803 Judicial Review Established, 12) 1803 Louisiana Purchase, 13) 1805 Lewis & Clark Reach the Pacific, 14) 1807 Robert Fulton's Clermont, 15) 1808 End of the Legal Slave Trade,. 16) 1812 War of 1812, 17) 1820 Missouri Compromise, 18) 1821 First Public High School, 19) 1823 Monroe Doctrine, 20) 1825 Completion of the Erie Canal, 21) 1828 First Democratic Candidate Elected, 22) 1831 McCormick Introduces His Reaper, 23) 1831 'The Liberator' Attacks Slavery, 24) 1836 Fall of the Alamo, 25) 1841 Wagon Train Reaches California, 26) 1844 Morse Demonstrates the Telegraph, 27) 1846 Howe Patents the Sewing Machine, 28) 1847 Americans Capture Mexico City, 29) 1848 Seneca Falls Convention, 30) 1849 California Gold Rush, 31) 1851 Uncle Tom's Cabin, 32) 1854 Opens Trade with Japan, 33) 1854 Formation of Republican Party, 34) 1857 Dred Scott Decision, 35) 1858 Lincoln-Douglas Debates, 36) 1859 First Successful Oil Well in U.S., 37) 1859 John Brown Seized at Harpers Ferry, 38) 1860 Harriet Tubman & the Underground Railroad, 39) 1861 Attack on Fort Sumter, 40) 1861 Passage of Homestead Act, 41) 1863 Emancipation Proclamation, 42) 1863 Lincoln's Gettysburg Address, 43) 1865 Lee Surrenders at Appomattox, 44) 1865*

Assassination of Lincoln, 45) 1866 Completion of Atlantic Cable, 46) 1867 Purchase of Alaska, 47) 1867 Opening of Chisholm Trail, 48) 1868 Passage of the 14th Amendment, 49) 1869 Rails Link East and West, 50) 1876 Bell Patents the Telephone, 51) 1879 Edison Perfects Electric Light, 52) 1881 American Red Cross Formed, 53) 1882 Standard Oil Trust Organized, 54) 1884 Ground Broken for First Skyscraper, 55) 1886 American Federation of Labor, 56) 1887 Interstate Commerce Act Passed, 57) 1889 Thousands Join Great Land Rush, 58) 1890 Sherman Anti-Trust Act Passed, 59) 1890 Battle of Wounded Knee, 60) 1895 Atlanta Compromise, 61) 1896 Separate But Equal Statute Upheld, 62) 1898 Battle of San Juan Hill, 63) 1903 Wright Brothers' First Flight, 64) 1907 Immigrants Welcomed to U.S.A., 65) 1911 Supreme Court Dissolves Oil Trust, 66) 1914 Ford Starts Mass Production, 67) 1915 Pacific International Exposition, 68) 1917 U.S. & Germany at War, 69) 1918 Battle of Meuse-Argonne, 70) 1919 Treaty of Versailles, 71) 1920 Prohibition, 72) 1920 Women Gain Right to Vote, 73) 1920 Birth of Modern Broadcasting, 74) 1921 Passage of the Quota Act, 75) 1925 Scopes Trial, 76) 1927 Lindbergh Lands in Paris, 77) 1927 First Motion Picture with Sound, 78) 1929 Stock Market Crash, 79) 1933 Roosevelt's First Hundred Days, 80) 1935 The Social Security Act; **3,231 sets to be issued from 1975-1983 at $30.00 each or $3,000.00 a set (100).**

History Of The U.S., *Declaration of Independence, ingot #1.*

☐ **Homer's America,** *set of 12 ingots, pure (.999) silver, proof, 3" x 2", 31 troy ounces per set; 1) A Sharpshooter on Picket Duty-1862, 2) The Morning Bell-1866, 3) Croquet Scene-1866, 4) The Bridle Path, White Mountain-1868, 5) Long Branch, N.J.-1869, 6) Snap the Whip-1872, 7) Breezing Up-1876, 8) The Life Line-1884, 9) The Fog Warning-1885, 10) The Herring Net-1885, 11) Eight Bells-1886, 12) Huntsman and Dogs-1891;* **430 sets issued in 1977 at $40.00 each or $480.00 a set (12).**

☐ **Independence Hall Portraits,** *set of 24 ingots, sterling silver, proof, 1.8" x 1.4", 26 troy ounces per set; 1) John Adams, 2) Samuel Adams, 3) Ethan Allen, 4) Benjamin Franklin, 5) Horatio Gates, 6) Nathanael Greene, 7) Nathan Hale, 8) Alexander Hamilton, 9) John Hancock, 10) Patrick Henry, 11) John Jay, 12) Thomas Jefferson, 13) John Paul Jones, 14) Henry Knox, 15) Richard Henry Lee, 16) James Madison, 17) John Marshall, 18) Robert Morris, 19) Thomas Paine, 20) Paul Revere, 21) Caesar Rodney, 22) Benjamin Rush, 23) Anthony Wayne, 24) George Washington;* **1,470 sets issued from 1975-1977 at $26.00 each or $624.00 a set (24).**

☐ **Kabuki,** *set of 18 ingots, pure (.999 fine) silver, proof-like, 1" x 1½", 14 troy ounces per set; 1) Fuwa, 2) Narukami, 3) Shibaraku, 4) Fudo, 5) Uwanari, 6) Zohiki, 7) Kanjincho, 8) Sukeroku, 9) Uiro Uri, 10) Oshimodoshi, 11) Yanone, 12) Kan-U, 13) Kagekiyo, 14) Nanatsumen, 15) Kenuki, 16) Gedatsu, 17) Jayanagi, 18) Kamahige;* **408 sets issued from 1976-1978 at $25.00 each or $450.00 a set (18).**

☐ **Last Supper,** *.999 fine silver, 5.20 troy ounces,* **1,811 issued in 1977 at $75.00 each.**

☐ **Locomotives,** *set of 50 ingots, proof, 3" x 1½", 93 troy ounces per set,; 1) Trevithick's Pen-Y-Daren, 2) Puffing Billy, 3) The John Stevens, 4) Locomotion I, 5) The*

Rocket, 6) Seguin, 7) Tom Thumb, 8) Best Friend of Charleston, 9) Adler, 10) Hercules, 11) Camel, 12) John Stevens, 13) Seraing, 14) Continent, 15) General, 16) Tiger, 17) Pennsylvania, 18) Thatcher Perkins, 19) Consolidation, 20) Jupiter, 21) Little Wonder, 22) Old Peppersass, 23) Stirling's Eight Footer, 24) Rigi, 25) Countess Of Dufferin, 26) Locomotive Number 510, 27) Forney Type Locomotive, 28) Gladstone, 29) El Gobernador, 30) Mallet, 31) Engine '999', 32) Atlantic, 33) Johnson Spinner, 34) Mikado, 35) Locomotive Number 382, 36) LAG 1, 37) 4-4-0 Superheated, 38) Pacific Type Locomotive, 39) Adriatic Railway, 40) Pacific Type Locomotive, 41) Matt Shay, 42) Penna. RR K-42 Pacific, 43) CNJ Diesel - Electric, 44) Degoichi - 51, 45) Pioneer Zephyr, 46) Pennsylvania RR Class GG1, 47) Big Boy, 48) S.N.C.F. 7100, 49) V-200 Locomotive, 50) Tokaido Train; **3,763 sets issued from 1974-1977 at $25.00 each or $1,250.00 a set (50).**

☐ **Mocatta & Goldsmid,** *(.999 fine) silver, P/L, 1 3/4" x 7/8", 1,000 grains, 2.08 troy ounces;* **1,500 issued in 1970 at $52.00 each.**

☐ **National Governors' Conference State,** *set of 50 ingots, sterling silver, proof, 1.5" x 2.1", 62 troy ounces per set; 1) Delaware-Blue Hen Chicken/Peach Blossom, 2) Pennsylvania-Ruffled Grouse/Mountain Laurel, 3) New Jersey-Eastern Goldfinch/Violet, 4) Georgia-Brown Thrasher/Cherokee Rose, 5) Connecticut-American Robin/Mountain Laurel, 6) Massachusetts-Black-capped Chickadee/Mayflower, 7) Maryland-Baltimore Oriole/Black-eyed Susan, 8) South Carolina-Carolina Wren/Yellow Jessamine, 9) New Hampshire-Purple Finch/Purple Lilac, 10) Virginia-Cardinal/American Dogwood, 11) New York-Bluebird/Rose, 12) North Carolina-Cardinal/Dogwood, 13) Rhode Island-Rhode Island Red/Violet, 14) Vermont-Hermit Thrush/Red Clover, 15) Kentucky-Cardinal/Goldenrod, 16) Tennessee-Mockingbird/Passion Flower, 17) Ohio-Cardinal/Scarlet Carnation, 18) Louisiana-Brown Pelican/Magnolia, 19) Indiana-Mockingbird/Peony, 20) Mississippi-Mockingbird/Magnolia, 21) Illinois-Cardinal/Violet, 22) Alabama-Yellow-shafted Flicker/Camellia, 23) Maine-Chickadee/Pine Cone and Tassel, 24) Missouri-Bluebird/Hawthorn, 25) Arkansas-Mockingbird/Apple Blossom, 26) Michigan-Robin/Apple Blossom, 27) Florida-Mockingbird/Orange Blossom, 28) Texas-Mockingbird/Bluebonnet, 29) Iowa-Goldfinch/Wild Rose, 30) Wisconsin-Robin/Violet, 31) California-Golden Poppy/Valley Quail, 32) Minnesota-Pink & White Lady Slipper/Loon, 33) Oregon-Oregon Grape/Western Meadowlark, 34) Kansas-Sunflower/Western Meadowlark, 35) West Virginia-Rhododendron/Cardinal, 36) Nevada-Sagebrush/Mountain Bluebird, 37) Nebraska-Goldenrod/Western Meadowlark, 38) Colorado-White & Lavender Columbine/Lark Bunting, 39) North Dakota-Wild Prairie Rose/Western Meadowlark, 40) South Dakota-American Pasque Flower/Ring-Necked Pheasant, 41) Montana-Bitterroot/Western Meadowlark, 42) Washington-Rhododendron/Willow Goldfinch, 43) Idaho-Syringa/Mountain Bluebird, 44) Wyoming-Indian Paint Brush/Meadowlark, 45) Utah-Sego Lily/Sea Gull, 46) Oklahoma-Mistletoe/Scissor-Tailed Flycatcher, 47) New Mexico-Yucca/Road Runner, 48) Arizona-Saguaro Cactus/Cactus Wren, 49) Alaska-Forget-Me-Not/Willow Ptarmigan, 50) Hawaii-Hibiscus/Nene Goose;* **2,988 issued from 1974-1978 at $30.00 each or $1,500.00 a set (50).**

☐ **Olympics,** *set of 10 ingots, sterling silver, proof, 1 1/4" x 7/8"; 1) Speed Skating, 2) Alpine Skiing, 3) Ski Jumping, 4) Ice Hockey, 5) Track, 6) Swimming, 7) Rowing, 8) Equestrian, 9) Javelin Throw, 10) High Jump;* **26,831 sets issued in 1980 at $29.50 each or $295.00 a set (10).**

☐ **100 Greatest Americans,** *set of 100 ingots, sterling silver, 500 grains, 104 troy ounces per set; 1) Benjamin Franklin, 2) George Washington, 3) Daniel Boone, 4) Paul Revere, 5) John Adams, 6) Patrick Henry, 7) John Hancock, 8) Thomas Jefferson, 9) John Jay, 10) John Paul Jones, 11) James Madison, 12) George Rogers Clark, 13) Alexander Hamilton, 14) John Marshall, 15) Gilbert Stuart, 16) James Monroe, 17) Noah Webster, 18) Robert Fulton, 19) Eli Whitney, 20) Andrew Jackson, 21) Henry Clay, 22) Daniel Webster, 23) Washington Irving, 24) John*

James Audubon, 25) James Fenimore Cooper, 26) Samuel Morse, 27) Horace Mann, 28) Brigham Young, 29) Ralph Waldo Emerson, 30) John Deere, 31) Nathaniel Hawthorne, 32) Robert E. Lee, 33) Henry Wadsworth Longfellow, 34) Jefferson Davis, 35) Edgar Allen Poe, 36) Abraham Lincoln, 37) Cyrus McCormick, 38) Horace Greeley, 39) John Charles Fremont, 40) Henry David Thoreau, 41) Julia Ward Howe, 42) Walt Whitman, 43) Susan B. Anthony, 44) Harriet Tubman, 45) Clara Barton, 46) Ulysses S. Grant, 47) Stephen Foster, 48) Emily Dickinson, 49) Andrew Carnegie, 50) Mark Twain, 51) George Dewey, 52) John D. Rockefeller, Sr., 53) Oliver Wendell Holmes, Jr., 54) George Westinghouse, 55) Thomas Alva Edison, 56) Alexander Graham Bell, 57) Joseph Pulitzer, 58) Samuel Gompers, 59) John Philip Sousa, 60) Booker T. Washington, 61) Robert Edwin Peary, 62) Woodrow Wilson, 63) Julia Clifford Lathrop, 64) Theodore Roosevelt, 65) William Jennings Bryan, 66) Elmer Sperry, 67) George Washington Carver, 68) O. Henry-William S. Porter, 69) Henry Ford, 70) Frank Lloyd Wright, 71) Wright Brothers, 72) Robert A. Millikan, 73) Robert Frost, 74) Mary McLeod Bethune; 1,693 sets to be issued from 1975-1983 at $19.50 each or $1,950.00 a set (100); sterling silver, proof-like, 500 grains; **13,992 issued at $19.50 each or $1,950.00 a set (100).**

☐ **100 Greatest Stamps of the World,** set of 100 ingots, sterling silver, various sizes; 1) France — 1 franc, 1849, 2) Germany — 5 marks, 1915; **to be issued at $4.75 each or $475.00 a set (100).**

☐ **Personalized Ingots,** sterling silver, 3" x 1½" x ½", 5,000 grains (10.41 troy ounces); **issued from 1972 at $60.00 each.**

☐ **Presidential,** set of 36 ingots, sterling silver, proof, 5,000 grains, 374 troy ounces per set; 1) George Washington, 2) John Adams, 3) Thomas Jefferson, 4) James Madison, 5) James Monroe, 6) John Quincy Adams, 7) Andrew Jackson, 8) Martin Van Buren, 9) William Henry Harrison, 10) John Tyler, 11) James Polk, 12) Zachary Taylor, 13) Millard Fillmore, 14) Franklin Pierce, 15) James Buchanan, 16) Abraham Lincoln, 17) Andrew Johnson, 18) Ulysses S. Grant, 19) Rutherford Hayes, 20) James Garfield, 21) Chester Arthur, 22) Grover Cleveland, 23) Benjamin Harrison, 24) William McKinley, 25) Theodore Roosevelt, 26) William H. Taft, 27) Woodrow Wilson, 28) Warren G. Harding, 29) Calvin Coolidge, 30) Herbert Hoover, 31) Franklin D. Roosevelt, 32) Harry S. Truman, 33) Dwight D. Eisenhower, 34) John F. Kennedy, 35) Lyndon B. Johnson, Richard M. Nixon; **906 sets issued from 1972-1974 at $44.50 each or $1,602.00 a set (36);** 37) Gerald R. Ford, **295 issued in 1974 at $125.00 each;** 38) Jimmy Carter, **203 issued in 1977.**

☐ **Profiles in Courage Cameo,** set of 9 ingots, sterling silver, 500 grains; 1) John Quincy Adams, 2) Daniel Webster, 3) Thomas Hart Benton, 4) Edmund G. Ross, 5) Sam Houston, 6) Lucius Q. C. Lamar, 7) George Norris, 8) Robert A. Taft, 9) John F. Kennedy; **3,103 sets issued in 1976 at $25.00 each or $225.00 a set (9).**

☐ **Racing Cars, World's Greatest,** set of 75 ingots, sterling silver, proof, 2⅛" x 1⅛", 71 troy ounces per set; 1) 1902-Panhard, 2) 1895-Panhard-Levassor, 3) 1895-Duryea, 4) 1898-Panhard, 5) 1901-Mors, 6) 1902-Napier, 7) 1903-Mors, 8) 1905-Brasier, 9) 1906-Renault, 10) 1907 Itala, 11) 1907-Christie, 12) 1907-Fiat, 13) 1907/1906-Stanley, 14) 1908-Old Locomobile, 15) 1908-Benz, 16) 1909-A.L.C.O., 17) 1910-Blitzen-Benz, 18) 1910-Hispano-Suiza, 19) 1911-Marmon Wasp, 20) 1912-Sunbeam, 21) 1913-Mercer, 22) 1913-Peugeot, 23) 1914-Delage, 24) 1914-Mercedes, 25) 1919-Ballot, 26) 1921-Frontenac, 27) 1924-Duesenberg, 28) 1927-Bentley, 29) 1923-Chenard-Walcker, 30) 1923-Voisin, 31) 1923-Sunbeam, 32) 1925-Alfa Romeo P2, 33) 1926-Miller '91', 34) 1926-Bugatti Type 35B, 35) 1927-Delage, 36) 1928-Bluebird, 37) 1922-Bugatti Brescia, 38) 1931-Mercedes-Benz SSKL, 39) 1933-Maserati 8CM-3000, 40) 1932-Alfa Romeo P3 Type B, 41) 1936-Auto-Union Type C, 42) 1933-M.G.K. 3 Magnette, 43) 1935-E.R.A., 44) 1937-Talbot Lago, 45) 1937-Mercedes Benz W125, 46) 1939-Maserati 8CTF, 47) 1947-Blue Crown Special, 48) 1949-Ferrari 166, 49) 1950-Alfa Fomeo 158/159; **2,095 sets issued from 1977-1982 at $19.50 each or $1,462.50 a set (75).**

☐ **Railroad Emblems,** *set of 50 ingots, sterling silver, hand-enameled, 38 troy ounces per set; 1) Western Pacific, 2) Illinois Central, 3) Penn Central, 4) Burlington Northern, 5) Atchison, Topeka & Santa Fe, 6) Conrail, 7) Louisville & Nashville, 8) Bessemer & Lake Erie, 9) St. Louis, San Francisco, Frisco, 10) Delaware & Hudson, 11) Great Northern, 12) Missouri Pacific, 13) Seaboard Coastline, 14) Spokane, Portland & Seattle, 15) Western Maryland, 16) Central RR of N.J., 17) Amtrak, 18) Soo, 19) Chesapeake & Ohio, 20) Missouri-Kansas-Texas, 21) Alaska, 22) Atlantic Coast Line, 23) Chicago Rock Island & Pacific, 24) Delaware, Lackawanna & West, 25) Erie, 26) New York Central, 27) Denver & Rio Grande Western, 28) Illinois Central Gulf;* **2,647 sets to be issued from 1979-1983 at $35.00 each or $1,750.00 a set (50).**

☐ **Regimental Emblems,** *set of 50 ingots, sterling silver, proof, hand-enameled, various sizes; 1) Royal Marines (U.K.), 2) 475th Infantry (U.S.), 3) Life Guards (U.K.), 4) 1st Foreign (France), 5) Fusilier Guards (Netherlands), 6) 1st Guides (Belgium), 7) 1st Cavalry (U.S.), 8) Royal Scots Greys (U.K.), 9) Brunswick Infantry (Germany), 10) Special Air Service (U.K.), 11) 107th Infantry (U.S.), 12) Sharp-shooters (Italy), 13) Princess Patricia's Canadian Light Infantry, 14) Royal 22nd (Canada);* **1,577 to be issued from 1980-1984 at $35.00 each or $1,750 a set (50).**

☐ **Rockwell's Favorite Moments from Twain,** *sterling silver, proof, 2" x 1⅝", 14 troy ounces per set; 1) Adventures of Tom Sawyer, 2) Advertures of Huckleberry Finn, 3) Life on the Mississippi, 4) Roughing It, 5) A Connecticut Yankee in King Arthur's Court, 6) Prince and the Pauper, 7) Celebrated Jumping Frog of Calaveras County, 8) Innocents Abroad, 9) Pudd'nhead Wilson, 10) Tom Sawyer, Detective;* **4,544 sets issued in 1975 at $29.00 each or $290.00 a set (10).**

☐ **Rockwell's Fondest Memories,** *set of 10 ingots, sterling silver, proof ('73), proof-like ('76), 2" x 2½", 31 troy ounces per set; 1) At the Barber, 2) Holiday Dinner, 3) The Checker Game, 4) Fun on the Hill, 5) The First Date, 6) The Knitting Lesson, 7) The Patient, 8) Playing Hookey, 9) Day Off, 10) The Big Parade;* **23,532 proof sets issued in 1973 at $25.00 each or $250.00 a set (10); 1,282 proof-like sets issued in 1976 at $37.50 or $375.00 a set (10).**

☐ **Sailing Ships of History,** *set of 50 ingots, sterling silver, 2½" x 1¾", 155 troy ounces per set; 1) Reed Hull Egyptian Ship, 2) Pharaoh Sahure's Ship, 3) Hatshepsut's Punt Ship, 4) Phoencian Trading Ship, 5) Warship of Ramses III, 6) Greek Merchantman, 7) Greek Trireme, 8) Roman Grain Ship, 9) Oseberg Ship, 10) William the Conqueror's Mora, 11) Hansa Cog, 12) Caravel, 13) Santa Marie, 14) Grande Hermine, 15) Henry Grace a Dieu, 16) Spanish Galleon, 17) Golden Hind, 18) The Ark Royal, 19) Nippon Maru, 20) Mayflower, 21) Sovereign of the Seas, 22) East Indiaman, 23) Venetian Galleass, 24) Endeavor, 25) Bounty, 26) H.M.S. Victory, 27) U.S.S. Constitution, 28) Baltimore Clipper, 29) Packet Ship, 30) Pilgrim, 31) La Belle Poule, 32) Blackwall Frigate, 33) Flying Cloud, 34) Yacht America, 35) Cutty Sark, 36) Mary Celeste, 37) Charles W. Morgan, 38) Barkentine, 39) Henry B. Hyde, 40) Coastal Schooner, 41) Lancing, 42) Otago, 43) Spray, 44) Thomas W. Lawson, 45) Preussen, 46) Pechili Junk, 47) Bluenose, 48) Dhow, 49) The Skipjack, 50) The Intrepid;* **4,386 sets issued from 1973-1976 at $25.00 each or $1,250.00 a set (50); sterling silver, ¾₀ x ½₀, mini-size; 18,933 sets issued at $3.00 each or $150.00 a set (50).**

☐ **Ships — Ocean Liners,** *set of 50 ingots, sterling silver, proof, ⅞" x 1¾", 104 troy ounces per set; 1) S.S. President Cleveland, 2) S.S. President Wilson, 3) M.V. Freeport, 4) S.S. Empress of Canada, 5) R.H.M.S. Amerikanis, 6) R.H.M.S. Atlantis, 7) M.S. Boheme, 8) T.S. Carla C., 9) T.S. Flavia, 10) T.S. Federico C., 11) M.V. Cunard Adventurer, 12) R.M.S. Queen Elizabeth 2, 13) S.S. Ariadne, 14) S.S. New Bahama Star, 15) M.S. Sea Venture, 16) S.S. France, 17) T.S. Hanseatic, 18) T.S. Hamburg, 19) T.S.S. Queen Anna Maria, 20) T.S.S. Olympia, 21) T.S. Bremen, 22) M.S. Europa, 23) S.S. Nieuw Amsterdam, 24) S.S. Rotterdam, 25) S.S. Statendam, 26) S.S. Homeric, 27) S.S. Oceanic, 28) M.S. Victoria, 29) S.S. Christoforo Colombo,*

30) S.S. Michelangelo, 31) S.S. Leonardo de Vinci, 32) S.S. Raffaello, 33) M.S. Sagafjord, 34) M.S. Skyward, 35) M.S. Southward, 36) M.S. Starward, 37) M.S. Sunward, 38) S.S. Mariposa, 39) S.S. Monterey, 40) M.S. Mermoz, 41) M.S. Renaissance, 42) S.S. Canberra, 43) S.S. Iberia, 44) S.S. Oriana, 45) S.S. Oronsay, 46) S.S. Orsova, 47) S.S. Arcadia, 48) M.S. Song of Norway, 49) M.S. Gripsholm, 50) M.S. Kungsholm; **4,277 sets issued in 1971 at $11.00 each or $550.00 a set (50).**

☐ **Ships — Register of American Fighting Ships,** *set of 50 ingots, sterling silver, proof, 1½" wide x 1¼" high; 1) Bonhomme Richard, 2) Langley, 3) Johnston, 4) Constitution, 5) Chicago, 6) Fulton, 7) Oneida, 8) Holland, 9) Oregon, 10) Sea Gull, 11) Independence, 12) Hornet, 13) Mississippi, 14) Enterprise, 15) Newark, 16) Princeton, 17) Archerfish, 18) Wasp, 19) Connecticut, 20) Michigan, 21) Lawrence, 22) Joseph P. Kennedy, Jr., 23) Yorktown, 24) Powhatan, 25) Vincennes, 26) New York, 27) Lexington;* **2,296 sets to be issued from 1979-1983 at $29.50 each or $1,475.00 a set (50).**

☐ **Signing of the Declaration,** *pure (.999 fine) silver, proof, 4.16 troy ounces;* **9,555 issued from 1975-1976 at $75.00 each.**

☐ **States of the Union Silverseals,** *set of 50 ingots, sterling silver, 1"-2" in diameter, page size 8¼" x 11";* **2,905 sets to be issued from 1979-1983 at $14.50 each or $725.00 a set (50).**

☐ **23rd Psalm,** *set of 10 ingots, sterling silver, 1.4" x 2.3", 20 troy ounces per set; 1) The Lord is my shepherd, I shall not want, 2) He maketh me to lie down in green pastures, 3) He leadeth me beside the still waters. He restoreth my soul, 4) He leadeth me in the paths of Righteousness for His names sake, 5) Yea, though I walk through the valley of the shadow of death I will fear no evil for Thou art with me, 6) Thy rod and thy staff they comfort me, 7) Thou preparest a table before me in the presence of mine enemies, 8) Thou anointest my head with oil, my cup runneth over, 9) Surely goodness and mercy shall follow me all the days of my life, 10) And I will dwell in the house of the Lord forever;* **1,618 sets issued in 1977 at $40.00 each or $400.00 a set (10).**

☐ **Western Silver Mines,** *set of 10 ingots, (.999 fine) silver, 2½" x 1½", 41 troy ounces per set; 1) Sunshine Mine-Kellogg, Idaho (Sunshine Mining Co.), 2) Galena Mine-Wallace, Idaho (Callahan Mining Corp.; Owner-American Smelting & Refining Co.; Operator), 3) Lucky Friday Mine-Mullan, Idaho (Hecla Mining Co.), 4) Utah Mine-Bingham Canyon, Utah (Kennecott Copper Corp.), 5) Bulldog Mine-Creede, Colorado (Homestake Co.), 6) Butte Mines-Butte, Montana (Anaconda Co.), 7) Bunker Hill Mine-Kellogg, Idaho (Gulf Resources Co.), 8) Crescent Mine-Kellogg, Idaho (Gulf Resources Co.), 9) Burgin Mine-Eureka, Utah (Kennecott Copper Corp.), 10) Copper Queen Mine-Bisbee, Arizona (Phelps Dodge Corp.);* **1,455 sets issued from 1973-1974 at $25.00 each or $250.00 a set (10).**

☐ **World's Greatest Historic Seals,** *set 50 ingots, sterling silver, 39mm Presentation 8¼" x 11";* **to be issued from 1981-1985 at $22.50 each or $1,125.00 a set (50).**

☐ **World's Greatest Stamps,** *set of 50 ingots, sterling silver, proof; 1) French, 1 Franc, 2) Japan, 500 Mon, 3) British Guiana, 1$C, 4) U.S., 24$C Airmail, 5) Canada, 12$C Penny Black, 6) Ceylon, 4 Pence, 7) Hawaii, 2$C, 8) Romania, 27 P, 9) Baden, 9 Kreuzer, 10) Newfoundland, 1 Shilling, 11) Switzerland, Double Geneva, 12) Natal, King Edward, 13) Switzerland, 5 Rapper, 14) Sweden, 3 SK, 15) France, 1 Franc Napoleon, 16) Canal Zone, 4$C, 17) Argentina, 15$C, 18) U.S., $1, 19) Western Australia, 4P, 20) Virgin Islands, 1 Shilling, 21) Tuscany Italian States, 3 Lire, 22) Ceylon, 1000 Rupee, 23) Mauritus, 1 Penny, 24) U.S., 2 cents, 25) Bavaria, 1 KR, 26) Bermuda, 1 Pence, 27) France, 5 Francs, 28) Spain, 2 Reals, 29) Great Britain, Penny Block, 30) Straits Settlements, 500 D, 31) India, 4 A. Queen, 32) Switzerland, 2¼R 'Basel Dove', 33) Italy, ½ Tornese Trinacrie, 34) U.S., 5 cents, 35) Newfoundland, 60$C A.M., 36) Italy, 15$C Parma, 37) Austria, 6 Kr 'Red Mercury', 38) U.S., 1$C Franklin 'Z' Grill, 39) India, ½ Anna 'Dawk' Sc., 40) Vancouver*

Island, 41) Newfoundland, 3$C Air Post, 42) U.S., 20$C Post Prov., 43) Great Britian, 6 Pence, 44) U.S., 5$C Franklin, 45) Honduras, 25$C 'Black Hon.'; **issued from 1977-1981 at $14.50 each or $725.00 a set (50).**

MINIATURES

☐ **Animals at Play Napkin Rings,** set of 8, antiqued silverplate; 1) Deer, 2) Rabbit, 3) Lion, 4) Duck, 5) Fox, 6) Squirrel, 7) Bear, 8) Raccoon; **2,146 sets issued in 1977 at $45.00 each or $360.00 a set (8).**

☐ **Cars, Great Vintage,** set of 12, sterling silver, 3½" x 2½"; 1) 1903-Fiat, 2) 1904-Mercedes-Simplex, 3) 1904-Oldsmobile, 4) 1911-Stanley Steamer, 5) 1907-Rolls Royce, 6) 1907-Thomas Flyer, 7) 1911-Renault Taxi, 8) 1911-Delauny-Belleville, 9) 1905-Vauxhall, 10) 1913-Cadillac Coupe, 11) 1908-Lanchester, 12) 1912-Hispano-Suiza; **2,819 sets issued from 1977-1981 at $180.00 each or $2,160.00 a set (12).**

☐ **Eagle — Great American Eagle by Roberts,** sterling silver, 11" x 19½"; **200 issued in 1975 at $2,500.00 each.**

☐ **Holiday Silver Miniatures,** set of 3, sterling silver; 1) '78 Sled, 4¼" x 2¼", **issued at $295.00 each;** 2) '79 Rocking Horse, 3" high, **issued at $345.00 each;** 3) '79 Weathervane, 3¾" high, **issued at $45.00 each.**

☐ **Horned Owl by Roberts,** sterling silver; **500 issued in 1978 at $2,300.00 each.**

☐ **Lindbergh's Spirit of St. Louis,** sterling silver, 7" base diameter, 12" wingspan, 5" high; **90 issued in 1977 at $1,500 each.**

☐ **Ships of Columbus,** set of 3, sterling silver, 7½" high; 1) Santa Maria, 2) Nina, 3) Pinta; **361 issued from 1977-1978 at $1,740.00 a set (3).**

☐ **Startled Yearling by Snell,** sterling silver, 3½" high; **53 issued in 1977 at $675.00 each.**

☐ **Toro by Cobo,** sterling silver, 5½" long, 35.2 troy ounces; **750 issued from 1981-1982 at $2,500.00 each.**

PLATES

☐ **Annual — Franklin Mint,** set of 2 plates, 24K gold vermeil on sterling silver, 8" in diameter, bas-relief; 1) 1977-Tribute to the Arts, 1,901 issued; 2) 1978-Tribute to Nature, **435 issued, both at $280.00 each.**

☐ **Antique English Silver,** set of 25 plates, sterling silver, 1" in diameter, antique; 1) Jacobean, 2) Med-Georgian, 3) Renaissance, 4) Rococo; **to be issued from 1981-1983 at $9.75 each or $243.75 a set (24).**

☐ **Arabian Nights,** set of 12 plates, sterling silver on brushed copper, inlaid with 24K gold, 2½" in diameter; 1) Sinbad the Sailor, 2) Aladdin & his Wonderful Lamp, 3) Ali Baba & the 40 Thieves, 4) The Magic Horse; **to be issued from 1981-1982 at $27.50 each or $330.00 a set (12).**

☐ **John James Audubon,** set of 4 plates, sterling silver, 8" in diameter, etched; 1) The Wood Thrush, 5,273 issued; 2) The Bald Eagle, 3,040 issued; 3) The Night Heron, 3,005 issued; 4) Audubon's Warbler, 3,034 issued; **all issued from 1973-1974 at $150.00 each.**

☐ **Audubon Society,** set of 4 plates, sterling silver, 8" in diameter, etched; 1) The Goldfinch, 2) The Wood Duck, 3) The Cardinal, 4) The Ruffled Grouse; **10,193 plates issued from 1972-1973 at $125.00 each.**

☐ **Bicentennial,** set of 4 plates, sterling silver electroplated and inlaid with 24K gold, 8" in diameter, bas-relief; '73 Jefferson Drafting the Declaration of Independence, **issued 8,556;** 2) '74 John Adams Champions Cause of Independence, **issued 8,442;** 3) '75 Caesar Rodney decides Vote on Independence, **issued 8,319;** 4) '76 John Hancock Signs Declaration of Independence, **issued 10,166;** issued at $175.00 each.

☐ **Birds — by Younger,** *set of 4 plates, sterling silver, etched, 8" in diameter, etched; 1) Cardinal, 2) Bobwhite, 3) Mallards, 4) American Bald Eagle;* **13,939 plates issued from 1980-1982 at $125.00 each.**

☐ **Birds of the World,** *set of 25 plates, .500 fine silver, proof-like, 1' in diameter; 1) Steamertail Hummingbird, 2) Bird of Paradise, 3) Cuvier's Toucan, 4) Hawaiian Honeycreeper, 5) Blackhead Plover, 6) Tawny Owl, 7) European Green Woodpecker, 8) Masked Lovebird, 9) Trumpeter Swan, 10) Alpine Swift, 11) Cardinal, 12) Sulphur-crested Cockatoo, 13) American Robin, 14) Rainbow Lorikeet, 15) Black-capped Chickadee, 16) Quetzal, 17) Pintail Duck, 18) Gannet, 19) Herring Gull;* **2,642 plates to be issued from 1980-1982 at $19.50 each or $487.50 a set (25).**

☐ **Bernard Buffet,** *set of 5 plates, sterling silver, etched, 8" in diameter; 1) '73 Gazelle,* **570 issued;** *2) '74 Panda,* **408 issued;** *3) '75 Giraffe,* **333 issued;** *4) '76 Lion,* **263 issued;** *5) '77 Rhinoceros,* **200 issued; all issued at $150.00 each.**

☐ **Butterflies of the World,** *set of 6 plates, sterling silver inlaid with enamels, 8" in diameter; 1) South America, 2) Australia, 3) North America, 4) Europe, 5) Africa, 6) Asia;* **481 plates issued from 1977-1979 at $240.00 each or $1,440.00 a set (6).**

☐ **Christmas in Silverplate,** *silverplate, embossed, 10" in diameter;* **908 issued in 1977 at $55.00 each.**

☐ **Columbus' Landing,** *sterling silver, bas-relief, 8¾" in diameter;* **1,000 plates issued in 1972 at $250.00 each.**

☐ **Easter,** *set of 3 plates, sterling silver and 24 K gold on sterling, 8" in diameter, bas-relief; 1) '73 The Resurrection of Evangelos Frudakis,* **7,116 plates issued at $175.00 each;** *2) '74 He is Risen by Abram Belski,* **3,719 plates issued at $185.00 each;** *3) The Last Supper by Oriol Sunyer, sterling silver, 8" in diameter, bas-relief,* **2,004 plates issued at $200.00 each.**

☐ **First Ladies of the U.S.,** *set of 42 plates, gold on sterling, 39 mm, proof;* **2,108 plates to be issued from 1979-1983 at $19.50 each or $735.00 a set (42).**

☐ **Floral Alphabet,** *set of 26 plates, sterling silver, 39, proof; 1) A-Aster, 2) B-Begonia, 3) C-Chrysanthemum, 4) D-Dahlia, 5) E-Edelweiss, 6) F-Fuchsia, 7) G-Gladiolus, 8) H-Hyacinth, 9) I-Iris, 10) J-Jasmine, 11) K-Kerria, 12) L-Lily, 13) M-Magnolia, 14) N-Narcissus, 15) O-Orchid, 16) P-Petunia, 17) Q-Quince, 18) R-Rose, 19) S-Sunflower, 20) T-Tulip, 21) U-Ulex, 22) V-Violet, 23) W-Wisteria, 24) X-Xeranthenum, 25) Y-Yucca, 26) Z-Zinnia;* **32,007 plates issued from 1978-1981 at $19.50 each or $507.00 a set (26).**

☐ **Four Seasons Champleve,** *set of 4 plates, sterling silver inlaid with enamels, 8" in diameter; 1) Spring Blossoms, 2) Summer Bouquet, 3) Autumn Garland, 4) Winter Spray;* **2,648 plates issued at $240.00 each.**

☐ **Freedom,** *24K gold on sterling silver, 8" in diameter, bas-relief; '77 Lafayette & Washington;* **546 plates issued at $275.00 each.**

☐ **Judaic Heritage Society,** *set of 3 plates, sterling silver, etched, 8" in diameter; 1) 1972-Pesach,* **5,000 issued;** *2) 1973-Chanukah,* **2,000 issued;** *3) 1974-Purim,* **1,000 issued; all issued at $150.00 each.**

☐ **Mother's Day by Belskie,** *sterling silver, bas-relief, 8" in diameter;* **290 plates issued in 1977 at $210.00 each.**

☐ **Mother's Day by Spencer,** *set of 5 plates, sterling silver, etched, 8" in diameter; 1) 1972-Mother & Child,* **21,987 issued at $125.00 each;** *2) 1973-Mother & Child,* **6,154 issued at $125.00 each;** *3) 1974-Mother & Child,* **5,116 issued at $150.00 each;** *4) 1975-Mother & Child,* **2,704 issued at $175.00 each;** *5) 1976-Mother & Child,* **1,858 issued at $180.00 each.**

☐ **Presidential Inaugural,** *set of 3 plates, sterling silver, bas-relief, 8" in diameter; 1) 1973-Nixon/Agnew,* **10,483 issued at $150.00 each;** *2) Ford,* **1,141 issued at $200.00 each;** *3) 1977-Carter,* **928 issued at $225.00 each.**

☐ **Presidential — White House Historical Association,** *set of 38 plates, sterling silver inlaid with 24K gold, etched, 8" in diameter; 1) G. Washington,* **10,304** issued; *2) J. Adams,* **4,859 issued;** *3) T. Jefferson,* **4,933 issued;** *4) J. Madison,* **3,058 issued;** *5) J. Monroe,* **2,722 issued;** *6) J. Q. Adams,* **2,501 issued;** *7) A. Jackson,* **2,408 issued;** *8) M. Van Buren,* **2,291 issued;** *9) W. H. Harrison,* **2,182 issued;** *10) J. Tyler,* **2,144 issued;** *11) J. K. Polk,* **2,083 issued;** *12) Z. Taylor, 2,023 issued;* *13) M. Fillmore,* **1,967 issued;** *14) F. Pierce,* **1,907 issued;** *15) J. Buchanan,* **1,841 issued;** *16) A. Lincoln,* **2,955 issued;** *17) A. Jackson,* **1,777 issued;** *18) U. S. Grant,* **1,754 issued;** *19) R. B. Hayes, 1,705 issued;* *20) J. A. Garfield,* **1,675 issued;** *21) C. A. Arthur,* **1,604 issued;** *22) G. Cleveland,* **1,644 issued;** *23) B. Harrison,* **1,619 issued;** *24) W. McKinley,* **1,571 issued;** *25) T. Roosevelt,* **1,555 issued;** *26) W. H. Taft,* **1,592 issued;** *27) W. Wilson,* **1,563 issued;** *28) W. G. Harding,* **1,544 issued;** *29) C. Coolidge,* **1,527 issued;** *30) H. Hoover,* **1,520 issued;** *31) F. D. Roosevelt,* **1,770 issued;** *32) H. S. Truman,* **1,493 issued;** *33) D. D. Eisenhower,* **1,494 issued;** *34) J. F. Kennedy,* **1,494 issued;** *35) L. B. Johnson,* **1,483 issued;** *36) R. M. Nixon,* **1,475 issued;** *37) G. R. Ford,* **1,486 issued;** *38) J. Carter, 1,276 issued; all issued from 1972-1976. Subscribers to single plates paid $200.00 each; active charter subscribers paid $150.00 each.*

□ **Roberts Zodiac,** *set of 12 plates, sterling silver, bas-relief, 8″ in diameter; 1) Aries, 2) Taurus, 3) Gemini, 4) Cancer, 5) Leo, 6) Virgo, 7) Libra, 8) Scorpio, 9) Sagittarius, 10) Capricorn, 11) Aquarius, 12) Pisces;* **issued from 1973-1980. Advance subscription price was $125.00 per plate, open stock price was $150.00 per plate.**

□ **Rockwell Christmas,** *set of 6 plates, sterling silver, etched, 8″ in diameter; 1) '70 Bringing Home Tree,* **18,321 issued at $100.00 each;** *2) '71 Under the Mistletoe,* **24,792 issued at $100.00 each;** *3) '72 The Carolers,* **29,074 issued at $125.00 each;** *4) '73 Trimming the Tree,* **18,010 issued at $125.00 each;** *5) '74 Hanging the Wreath,* **12,822 issued at $175.00 each;** *6) '75 Home for Christmas,* **11,059 issued at $180.00 each.**

□ **Rockwell Thanksgiving,** *sterling silver, etched, 8″ in diameter, 1) '77 Old Fashioned Thanksgiving;* **1,361 plates issued at $185.00 each.**

□ **Thanksgiving by Dohanos,** *set of 5 plates, sterling silver, etched, 8″ in diameter; 1) '72 The First Thanksgiving,* **10,142 issued at $125.00 each;** *2) '73 American Wild Turkey,* **3,547 issued at $125.00 each;** *3) '74 Thanksgiving Prayer,* **5,150 issued at $150.00 each;** *4) '75 Family Thanksgiving,* **3,025 issued at $175.00 each;** *5) '76 Home From the Hunt,* **3,474 issued at $175.00 each.**

□ **University, Fraternal and Commemorative,** *set of 65 plates, sterling silver inlaid with 24K gold, etched, 8″ diameter; 1) Univ. of Texas,* **422 issued;** *2) Univ. of Virginia,* **475 issued;** *3) Univ. of Minnesota,* **82 issued;** *4) Univ. of Pennsylvania,* **647 issued;** *5) Univ. of Wisconsin,* **93 issued;** *6) Univ. of Pittsburgh,* **215 issued;** *7) Case Inst. of Technology,* **61 issued;** *8) Univ. of Nebraska (Seal),* **115 issued;** *9) Univ. of Nebraska,* **92 issued;** *10) Tufts Univ. (Seal),* **110 issued;** *11) Tufts Univ. (Ballou Hall),* **86 issued;** *12) Louisiana State Univ. (Seal),* **122 issued;** *13) Louisiana State Univ. (Memorial Tower),* **174 issued;** *14) Univ. of North Carolina (Seal),* **168 issued;** *15) Univ. of North Carolina (Well),* **269 issued;** *16) Univ. of Oklahoma (Seal),* **150 issued;** *17) Univ. of Oklahoma (Library),* **112 issued;** *18) Univ. of Cal. at Berkeley,* **777 issued;** *19) Kansas State Univ.,* **474 issued;** *20) Univ. of Kansas,* **555 issued;** *21) College of William and Mary,* **663 issued;** *22) Northeaster Univ.,* **398 issued;** *23) Auburn Univ. (Seal),* **279 issued;** *24) Auburn Univ. (Sanford Hall),* **388 issued;** *25) Univ. of Mississippi,* **482 issued;** *26) Oklahoma State Univ. (Seal),* **119 issued;** *27) Oklahoma State Univ. (Library),* **223 issued;** *28) Univ. of Louisville (Seal),* **118 issued;** *29) Univ. of Louisville (Admin. Bldg.),* **93 issued;** *30) Brown Univ.,* **447 issued;** *31) Baylor Univ.,* **485 issued;** *32) Univ. of Cincinnati,* **353 issued;** *33) Univ. of Wyoming,* **447 issued;** *34) Univ. of South Carolina,* **272 issued; all issued from 1972-1973 at $150.00 per plate.**

□ *35) Univ. of Colorado (Old Main),* **577 issued;** *36) Duke Univ. (Seal),* **709 issued;** *37) Univ. of Idaho (Admin. Bldg.),* **329 issued;** *38) Univ. of Illinois (Seal),* **1,007 issued;** *39) Univ. of Kentucky (Memorial Hall),* **543 issued;** *40) Newcomb Univ. (Seal),* **112** issued; *41) Ohio Univ. (Cutler Hall),* **221 issued;** *42) Tulane Univ. (Seal),* **428 issued;** *43) Virginia Tech Univ. (Buruss Hall),* **473 issued;** *44) Southern Methodist Univ. (Dallas Hall),* **299 issued;** *45) Temple Univ. (Old Gates),* **599 issued;** *46) Univ. of Arizona (Old Main),* **467 issued;** *47) Colorado State Univ. (Seal),* **160 issued;** *48) Delta Upsilon Frat. (Crest),* **166 issued;** *49) Georgetown Univ. (Healy Bldg.),* **660 issued;** *50) Indiana Univ. (Seal),* **482 issued;** *51) Mississippi State Univ. (Chapel),* **280 issued;** *52) Univ. of Rochester (Rush Rhees Lib.),* **273 issued;** *53) Bowling Green State Univ. (Seal),* **149 issued;** *54) Univ. of Houston (Cullen Bldg.),* **229 issued;** *55) Michigan State Univ. (Beaumont Tower),* **705 issued;** *56) Univ. of Pittsburgh (Cathedral of Learning),* **290 issued;** *57) Univ. of Toledo (Univ. Hall),* **121 issued;** *58) Union College (Nott Memorial),* **166 issued; all issued in 1974 at $175.00 each.**

☐ *59) Univ. of Miami,* **274 issued;** *60) Univ. of South Carolina,* **194 issued;** *61) Vanderbilt Univ.,* **419 issued;** *62) Brown Univ.,* **260 issued;** *63) Univ. of Georgia,* **321 issued;** *64) Univ. of Mississippi,* **120 issued;** *65) Univ. of Virginia (Chapel),* **410 issued; all issued in 1975 at $200.00 each.**

☐ *Set of 131 plates, sterling silver, 8" in diameter; 1) Univ. of Delaware,* **412 issued;** *2)* **Lambda Chi Alpha Frat.,** **431 issued;** *3) Phi Delta Theta Frat.,* **480 issued;** *4) Villanova Univ.,* **412 issued;** *5) The Citadel,* **570 issued;** *6) Kent State Univ.,* **176 issued;** *7) Texas Tech Univ.,* **199 issued;** *8) Univ. of Utah,* **244 issued;** *9)* **Utah State Univ.,** **143 issued;** *10) Virginia Military Inst.,* **654 issued;** *11) Wake Forest Univ.,* **167 issued;** *12) Western Michigan Univ.,* **194 issued; all issued in 1974 at $150.00 each.**

☐ *13) Baylor Univ.,* **184 issued;** *14) Bucknell Univ.,* **239 issued;** *15) Florida State Univ.,* **278 issued;** *16) Furman Univ.,* **292 issued;** *17) Georgia Inst. of Technology,* **497 issued;** *18) Univ. of Michigan,* **517 issued;** *19) Oregon State Univ.,* **361 issued;** *20) Pi Kappa Alpha Frat.,* **222 issued;** *21) Purdue Univ.,* **477 issued;** *22) Randolph-Macon Woman's College,* **192 issued;** *23) Saint Louis Univ.,* **354 issued;** *24) Colgate Univ.,* **216 issued;** *25) Univ. of Dayton,* **267 issued;** *26) U.S. Merchant Marine Academy,* **310 issued;** *27) U.S. Naval Academy,* **2,249 issued;** *28) Univ. of Oregon,* **441 issued;** *29) St. Lawrence Univ.,* **169 issued;** *30) Univ. of Santa Clara,* **326 issued;** *31) Univ. of Washington,* **178 issued; all issued in 1975 at $150.00 each.**

☐ *32) Allegheny College,* **141 issued;** *33) Boston Univ.,* **201 issued;** *34) Cal. State Polytechnic Univ., Pomona,* **85 issued;** *35) Catholic Univ. of America,* **139 issued;** *36) Univ. of Massachusetts,* **238 issued;** *37) Middlebury College,* **191 issued;** *38)* **Muskingum College,** **97 issued;** *39) Northwestern Univ.,* **681 issued;** *40) Ohio Wesleyan Univ.,* **174 issued;** *41) Univ. of the Pacific,* **188 issued;** *42) Sigma Alpha Epsilon Frat.,* **485 issued;** *43) U.S. Military Academy,* **1,520 issued;** *44) Univ. of Virginia,* **410 issued;** *45) Virginia Military Inst.,* **506 issued;** *46) West Virginia Univ.,* **470 issued;** *47) Univ. of Wyoming,* **153 issued;** *48) U.S. Air Force Academy,* **415 issued;** *49) Carnegie-Mellon Univ.,* **259 issued;** *50) Chi Phi Frat.,* **147 issued;** *51) The Citadel,* **326 issued;** *52) Univ. of Delaware,* **120 issued;** *53) Farleigh Dickinson Univ.,* **141 issued;** *54) Kappa Alpha Order,* **326 issued;** *55) U.S. Marine Corps,* **1,995 issued;** *56) Univ. of Richmond,* **162 issued;** *57) San Diego State Univ.,* **158 issued;** *58) State Univ. of New York at Albany,* **68 issued;** *59) Washington and Lee Univ.,* **350 issued; all issued in 1976 at $175.00 each.**

☐ *60) Univ. of Cal. at Los Angeles,* **755 issued;** *61) Franklin and Marshall College,* **277 issued;** *62) Univ. of Michigan,* **697 issued;** *63) Cal. State Univ. at Los Angeles,* **144 issued;** *64) Univ. of Iowa,* **367 issued;** *65) Univ. of Missouri,* **485 issued;** *66) Ohio State Univ.,* **701 issued;** *67) Phi Chi Frat.,* **123 issued;** *68) San Jose State Univ.,* **301 issued;** *69) South Dakota State Univ.,* **188 issued;** *70) Univ. of South Dakota,* **120 issued;** *71) Sons of the American Revolution,* **284 issued;** *72) Air Force Assoc. (Seal),* **2,134 issued;** *73) American Fund for Dental Health,* **580 issued;** *74) Delta Kappa Epsilon (Coat of Arms),* **134 issued;** *75) Univ. of Florida (Century Tower),* **405 issued;** *76) Univ. of Illinois Medical Ctr.,* **202 issued;** *77) U.S. Merchant Marine Acad. (Insig.),* **183 issued;** *78) U.S. Naval Acad. (Seal),* **1,016 issued;** *79) Univ. of*

Northern Iowa (Campanile), **138 issued;** *80) Psi Omega Frat. (Coat of Arms),* **56 issued;** *81) Randolph-Macon College (Chapel),* **82 issued;** *82) Univ. of Rhode Island (Green Hall),* **138 issued;** *83) Tau Kappa Epsilon Frat. (Coat of Arms),* **289 issued;** *84) Univ. of Vermont (Billings Center),* **210 issued; all issued in 1977 at $175.00 each.**

☐ *85) Indiana State Univ.,* **99 issued;** *86) Descendants of the Mayflower Soc.,* **725 issued;** *87) Marine Scholarship Fund (Seal),* **571 issued;** *88) Univ. of Maryland (Memorial Chapel),* **180 issued;** *89) Arizona State Univ. (Gammage Aud.),* **177 issued;** *90) Fraternal Order of Police (Emblem),* **335 issued;** *91) Howard Univ. (Founders Library),* **661 issued;** *92) National Guard (Concord Minuteman),* **630 issued;** *93) Texas Christian Univ. (Seal),* **103 issued; all issued in 1978 at $175.00 each.**

☐ *94) Aircraft Owners & Pilots Assoc.,* **2,127 issued;** *95) Butler Univ.,* **87 issued;** *96) Cal. Polytechnic State Univ.,* **399 issued;** *97) Duquesne Univ.,* **349 issued;** *98) Eastern Washington Univ.,* **80 issued;** *99) Epsilon Sigma Alpha,* **71 issued;** *100) Montana State Univ.,* **202 issued;** *101) Phi Kappa Theta Frat.,* **70 issued;** *102) Ruritan National,* **93 issued;** *103) St. Bonaventure Univ.,* **125 issued;** *104) Seattle Univ.,* **75 issued;** *105) Univ. of Texas (El Paso),* **116 issued;** *106) Theta Chi Frat.,* **162 issued;** *107) U.S. Trotting Association,* **650 issued;** *108) Mary Washington College,* **80 issued;** *109) Alpha Kappa Psi, 111) Buffalo State, 112) Central Michigan State, 113) Dartmouth Univ., 114) Fisk Univ., 115) Kappa Psi, 116) Kappa Sigma, 117) Morehouse College, 118) Morgan State, 119) Reserve Officer Assoc., 120) St. Mary's Univ. of San Antonio, 121) Sam Houston State, 122) Southwest Texas State, 123) Weber State, 124) Weber State;* **all issued in 1979 at $195.00 each.**

☐ *125) Accountants of Ontario, 126) Cheyney State College,* **79 issued;** *127) Northern Colorado, 128) Pi Kappa Phi Frat., 129) Ryerson Polytechnical Inst., 130) Southern Cal.,* **1,638 issued;** *131) Stanford Univ.,* **168 issued; all issued in 1980 at $195.00 each.**

☐ **Western,** *set of 4 plates, sterling silver, bas-relief, 8" in diameter, 11 troy ounces per set; 1) Horizons West by Richard Baldwin, 2) Mountain Man by Gordon Phillips, 3) Prospector by Gus Shaefer, 4) Plains Hunter by John Weaver;* **5,860 sets issued from 1972-1973 at $150.00 each or $600.00 a set (4).**

☐ **James Wyeth,** *set of 5 plates, sterling silver, etched, 8" in diameter; 1) '72 Along the Brandywine,* **19,670 issued at $125.00 each;** *2) '73 Winter Fox,* **10,394 issued at $125.00 each;** *3) '74 Riding to the Hunt,* **10,751 issued at $150.00 each;** *4) '75 Skating on Brandywine,* **8,058 issued at $175.00 each;** *5) '76 Brandywine Battlefield,* **6,968 issued at $180.00 each.**

SPOONS

☐ **Apostles by Winfield,** *set of 13 spoons, sterling silver, 5⅛" long; 1) St. Peter, 2) St. Andrew, 3) St. James the Greater, 4) St. John, 5) St. Philip, 6) St. James the Less, 7) St. Thomas, 8) St. Bartholomew, 9) St. Matthew, 10) St. Simon Zelotes, 11) St. Matthias, 12) St. Jude, 13) Jesus Christ;* **9,749 sets issued from 1973-1974 at $17.50 each or $227.50 a set (13).**

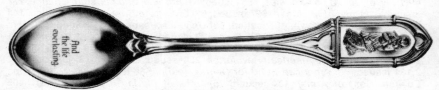

Apostles by Winfield, *St. Jude, spoon #12.*

☐ **Christmas,** *set of 5 spoons, sterling silver (gold electroplate on brass in 1977 only), 4½"-5⅜" in length; 1) '77 Golden Angel,* **issued at $37.50 each;** *2) '78 Kiss Under the Mistletoe,* **issued at $45.00 each;** *3) '79 The Carolers,* **issued at $55.00 each;** *4) '80 Plum Pudding,* **issued at $85.00 each;** *5) '81 Building the Snowman,* **issued at $85.00 each.**

☐ **Composers,** *set of 12 spoons, 24K gold on sterling silver, 4" long; 1) Johannes Brahms, 2) Franz Peter Schubert, 3) Johann Sebastian Bach, 4) George Frideric Handel, 5) Fryderyk Chopin, 6) Franz Joseph Haydn, 7) Ludwig von Beethoven, 8) Igor Stravinsky, 9) Richard Wagner, 10) Peter Ilyich Tchaikovsky, 11) Wolfgang A. Mozart, 12) Nicolay Rimsky-Korsakov;* **402 sets issued in 1977 at $32.00 each or $384.00 a set (12).**

☐ **English Flowers,** *set of 12 spoons, sterling silver, 5⅛" long; 1) Rose, 2) Freesia, 3) Daffodil, 4) Anemone, 5) Dahlia, 6) Gladiolus, 7) Iris, 8) Chrysanthemum, 9) Gentian, 10) Tulip, 11) Columbine, 12) Viola;* **2,550 sets issued from 1974-1976 at $30.00 each or $360.00 a set (12).**

☐ **Flowers of the Months,** *set of 12 spoons, silverplate, 5¾" long; 1) January-Snowdrop, 2) February-Jonquil, 3) March-Easter Lily, 4) April-Crocus, 5) May-Lily of the Valley, 6) June-Wild Rose, 7) July-Water Lily, 8) August-Poppy, 9) September-Daisy, 10) October-Hop Vine, 11) November-Chrysanthemum, 12) December-Holly;* **issued in 1980 at $295.00 a set (12).**

☐ **Love,** *set of 8 spoons, sterling silver, 4½" long; 1) Lovebird, 2) Roundel, 3) Tulip, 4) Love Knot, 5) Commas, 6) Chain, 7) Keyhole, 8) Hearts & Flowers;* **4,146 sets issued from 1976-1977 at $29.50 each or $236.00 a set (8).**

☐ **State Bird Miniatures,** *set of 50 spoons, sterling silver, 2½" long;* **3,059 sets to be issued from 1979-1983 at $12.50 each or $625.00 a set (50).**

☐ **State Flower Miniatures,** *set of 50 spoons, sterling silver, 2½" long;* **14,394 sets to be issued from 1978-1982 at $9.75 each or $487.50 a set (50).**

☐ **Twelve Days of Christmas,** *set of 12 spoons, sterling silver, Signature edition; 1) Partridge in a Pear Tree, 2) 2 Turtle Doves, 3) 3 French Hens, 4) 4 Calling Birds, 5) 5 Golden Rings, 6) 6 Geese a Laying, 7) 7 Swans a Swimming, 8) 8 Maids a Milking, 9) 9 Drummers Drumming, 10) 10 Pipers Piping, 11) 11 Ladies Dancing, 12) 12 Lords a Leaping;* **3,306 sets issued from 1972-1973 at $12.08 each or $145.00 a set (12); Regular edition issued at $12.08 each or $145.00 a set (12).**

☐ **Zodiac,** *set of 12 spoons, 5⅛" long, Signature edition; 1) Aries, 2) Taurus, 3) Gemini, 4) Cancer, 5) Leo, 6) Virgo, 7) Libra, 8) Scorpio, 9) Sagittarius, 10) Capricorn, 11) Aquarius;* **5,386 sets issued in 1972 at $11.25 each or $135.00 a set (12); Regular edition issued at $12.50 each or $135.00 a set (12).**

MEDALS (ROUND)

☐ **America in Space,** *set of 60 medals, sterling silver; 1) The Goddard Rocket, 2) Freedom 7, 3) Explorer I, 4) Friendship 7, 5) Pioneer V, 6) Faith 7, 7) Tiros I, 8) Gemini 3, 9) Telstar, 10) Gemini 4, 11) Mariner II, 12) Gemini 7/6, 13) Relay I, 14) Gemini 8, 15) Syncom II, 16) Apollo 7, 17) Mariner IV, 18) Apollo 8, 19) Ranger VII, 20) Apollo 9, 21) Surveyor I, 22) Apollo 10, 23) Lunar Orbiter I, 24) Apollo II (error), 24a) Apollo II (corr.);* **20,377 sets issued from 1969-1971 at $7.50 each or $180.00 a set (24).**

☐ *Sterling silver, 25) Apollo 12, 26) ITOS 1, 27) Apollo 13, 28) Mariner IX, 29) Apollo 15, 30) Pioneer X, 31) Apollo 16, 32) ERTS I, 33) OAO III, 34) Transit Satellite, 35) Apollo 17, 36) Nimbus V;* **6,676 sets issued in 1973 at $9.50 each or $114.00 a set (12).**

☐ *Sterling silver, 37) Pioneer XI, 38) Skylab II, 39) Skylab III, 40) Mariner X, 41) Skylab IV, 42) AE-C Atmospheric Explorer, 43) SMS I, 44) ATS VI, 45) Hawkeye I, 46) NOAA IV, 47) LANDSAT II, 48) SMS II, 49) GEOS III, 50) SAS III, 51) Nimbus VI, 52) Apollo-*

Soyuz, 53) Viking I, 54) Viking II, 55) AE-D, 56) TRANSIT, 57) GOES I, 58) LAGEOS, 59) Gravity Probe A, 60) NOAA V; **1,196 sets issued in 1977 at $19.50 each or $468.00 a set (24).**

America In Space, *Freedom 7, medal #2.*

☐ **1-60)** sterling silver, 13mm, P/L; **1,192 sets issued from 1976-1978 at $3.75 each or $225.00 a set (60).**

☐ **America the Beautiful,** *set of 8 medals, sterling silver, antique/proof, 16.6 troy ounces per set; 1) O Beautiful for Spacious Skies, 2) For Amber Waves of Grain, 3) For Purple Mountain Majesties, 4) Above the Fruited Plain, 5) America! America!, 6) God Shed Thy Grace on Thee, 7) And Crown Thy Good with Brotherhood, 8) From Sea to Shining Sea;* **2,945 sets issued in 1976 at $40.00 each or $320.00 a set (8).**

☐ **Americn Art Treasures,** *set of 100 medals, sterling silver, 96 troy ounces per set; 1) The Copley Family by John Singleton Copley, 2) Peaceable Kingdom by Edward Hicks, 3) Chez Mouquin by William Glackens, 4) Penn's Treaty with the Indians by Benjamin West, 5) The Boating Party by Mary Cassatt, 6) Coming Through the Rye by Frederic Remington, 7) The Gross Clinic by Thomas Eakins, 8) Madame X by John Singer Sargent, 9) Passion Flowers & Hummingbirds by M. J. Heade, 10) Eight Bells by Winslow Homer, 11) The Torn Hat by Thomas Sully, 12) Dempsey and Firpo by George Bellows, 13) Washington Crossing the Delaware by E. Leutze, 14) Mrs. Richard Yates by Gilbert Stuart, 15) The Greek Slave by Hiram Powers, 16) Kindred Spirits by Asher B. Durand, 17) The American School by Matthew Pratt, 18) Fleurs-de-lys by Robert Reid, 19) American Gothic by Grant Wood, 20) Battle of Bunker's Hill by John Trumbull, 21) The Lackawanna Valley by George Inness, 22) The Artist in his Museum by C. W. Peale, 23) Steelworkers Noontime by Thomas P. Anshutz, 24) Gas by Edward Hopper, 25) Man with a Cat by Cecilia Beaux, 26) Kee-O-Kuk, Chief of the Sauk & Foxes by G. Catlin, 27) The Spielers by George Luks, 28) Watson & the Shark by John Singleton Copley, 29) Lady in White by Thomas Dewing, 30) Central Park by Maurice Prendergast, 31) Diana by Augustus Saint-Gaudens, 32) Portrait of Miss Dora Wheeler by William M. Chase, 33) Carnation, Lily, Lily Rose by John Singer Sargent, 34) The Voyage of Life: Youth by Thomas Cole, 35) The Blue Clown by Walt Kuhn, 36) Still Life by Raphaelle Peale, 37) July Hay, 1942 by Thomas Hart Benton, 38) Death of Jane McCrea by John Vanderlyn, 39) Child in Straw Hat by Mary Cassatt, 40) Painting No. 4 Black Horse by Marsden Hartley, 41) The Skater by Gilbert Stuart, 42) Little Girl in Lavender by John Bradley, 43) The Death of Wolfe by Benjamin West, 44) Hollyhocks by Eastman Johnson, 45) Henry Pelham (Boy with a Squirrel) by J. S. Copley, 46) The Appeal to the Great Spirit by Cyrus Dallin Copley, 47) Belshazzar's Feast by Washington Allston, 48) Arrangement in Black and Gray No. 1, The Artist' Mother by James M. Whistler, 49) The Wyndham Sister by John Singer Sargent, 50) The Buffalo Hunt by Charles Marion Russell, 51) The Passion of Sacco* *and Vanzetti by Ben Shahn, 52) The Banjo Lesson by Henry O'Tanner, 53) The Return of Rip Van Winkle by John Quidor, 54) After the Hunt by William M. Harnett, 55) Eel Spearing at Setaucket by William Sydney Mount, 56) In the Orchard by Edmund C. Tarbell, 57) Holy Mountain III by Horace Pippen, 58) Baptism in Kansas by John Stuart Curry, 59) George Washington by John Trumbull, 60) The Schuylkill Freed by William Rush, 61) Country Wedding by John Lewis Krimmel, 62) Presidents' Portraits by Gutzon Borglum, 63) Ten Cents a Dance by Reginald Marsh, 64) Symphony in White, No. 1 by Whistler, 65) Buffalo Bill's Back Fat by George Catlin, 66) Pat Lyon at the Forge by Neagle, 67) Jolly Flatboatmen in Port by Bingham, 68) Still Life: Fruit by Roesen, 69) The Muse by Morse, 70) The Fairman Rogers Four-in-Hand by Thomas Eakins, 71) Athenaeum Portrait of George Washington by Stuart, 72) Sunday Afternoon in Union Square by Sloan, 73) Bronco Buster by Remington, 74) Bone Player by Mount, 75) The Bath by Cassatt, 76) War News from Mexico by Woodville, 77) Paul Revere by Copley;* **2,929 sets to be issued from 1975-1983 at $25.00 each or $2,500.00 a set (100).**

☐ **American Hall of Fame,** *set of 100 medals, 24K gold on sterling silver, proof, 32mm, 37.6 troy ounces per set; 1) Benjamin Franklin, 2) George Washington, 3) Daniel Boone, 4) Patrick Henry, 5) Charles Wilson Peale, 6) Thomas Jefferson, 7) James Madison, 8) Nathan Hale, 9) John Marshall, 10) Noah Webster, 11) Charles Bulfinch, 12) Robert Fulton, 13) Eli Whitney, 14) Lewis & Clark, 15) Henry Clay, 16) John James Audubon, 17) James F. Cooper, 18) Peter Cooper, 19) Samuel F. B. Morse, 20) Sam Houston, 21) Horace Mann, 22) William Holmes McGuffey, 23) Brigham Young, 24) John Deere, 25) Robert E. Lee, 26) Henry Wadsworth Longfellow, 27) Dorothea Dix, 28) Abraham Lincoln, 29) Cyrus McCormick, 30) Edgar Allen Poe, 31) Isaac Merritt Singer, 32) Harriet Beecher Stowe, 33) Currier & Ives, 34) Samuel Colt, 35) Susan B. Anthony, 36) Harriet Tubman, 37) Clara Barton, 38) Ulysses S. Grant, 39) Stephen Foster, 40) Mark Twain, 41) Andrew Carnegie, 42) Oliver Wendell Holmes, 43) Aaron Montgomery Ward, 44) George Westinghouse, 45) Alexander Graham Bell, 46) Thomas Alva Edison, 47) Joseph Pulitzer, 48) Samuel Gompers, 49) George Eastman, 50) John Philip Sousa, 51) Robert Edwin Peary, 52) Booker T. Washington, 53) Woodrow Wilson;* **695 sets to be issued from 1977-1985 at $15.75 each or $1,575.00 a set (100).**

☐ **American Heritage Treasury of American History,** *set of 20 medals, sterling silver, proof, 39mm, 20.8 troy ounces per set; 1) Columbus reaches America, 2) Settlement at Jamestown, 3) Paul Revere Sounds Alert, 4) Independence Declared, 5) Pres. Washington takes Office, 6) Lewis and Clark, 7) Jackson at New Orleans, 8)*

American Heritage Treasury Of American History, *Columbus reaches America, medal #1.*

Alamo Defended, 9) California Gold Rush, 10) Gettysburg Address, 11) Golden Spike, 12) Wright Bros. at Kitty Hawk, 13) Panama Canal, 14) Armistice brings Peace, 15) Lindbergh Solos to Paris, 16) Television, 17) Sustained Nuclear Reaction, 18) D-Day, 19) U.N. Charter Signed, 20) Moon Landing; **3,134 issued from**

1971-1972 at $9.50 each or $190.00 a set (20); *sterling silver, proof-like, 39mm,* **151 issued at $9.50 each or $190.00 a set (20).**

☐ **American Negro Commemorative Society,** *set of 70 medals, sterling silver, proof, 39mm, 60.2 troy ounces per set;* **Series I:** *1) Dr. Martin Luther King, Jr., 2) Dr. Daniel Hale Williams, 3) J. B. Pointe du Sable, 4) Benjamin Banneker, 5) Matthew A. Henson, 6) Frederick Douglass, 7) Harriet Tubman, 8) George W. Carver, 9) 369th Infantry Regiment, 10) Paul Laurence Dunbar, 11) W. C. Handy, 12) Paul Cuffe, 13) Crispus Attucks, 14) Mary McLeod Bethun, 15) John B. Russwurm, 16) Nat Turner, 17) Carter G. Woodson, 18) Prince Hall, 19) Dr. Charles Drew, 20) Thomas 'Fats' Waller, 21) Phillis Wheatley, 22) Jan Matzeliger, 23) Henry O. Flipper, 24) Henry Ossawa Tanner, 25) P. B. S. Pinchback, 26) W. E. B. Dubois, 27) 9th & 10th Cavalries, 28) Jack Johnson, 29) Bessie Smith, 30) Dr. Alain LeRoy Locke, 31) Malcolm X, 32) Norbert Rillieux, 33) Booker T. Washington, 34) Peter Salem, 35) Sojourner Truth, 36) Blanche K. Bruce, 37) Langston Hughes, 38) William Still, 39) Whitney Young, Jr., 40) Louis Armstrong, 41) Benjamin O. Davis, Sr., 42) Maggie L. Walker, 43) Ira Frederick Aldridge, 44) Martin R. Delany (error), 44a) Martin R. Delany (corr.), 45) Ernest Everett Just, 46) Richard Allen, 47) Robert Smalls, 48) William Monroe Trotter, 49) Fisk Jubilee Singers, 50) Scott Joplin;* **Series II:** *1) Ralph J. Bunche, 2) Mahalia Jackson, 3) Elijah McCoy, 4) Mary Church Terrell, 5) Granville T. Woods, 6) Richard Wright, 7) Jackie Robinson, 8) Isaac Murphy, 9) James A. Bland, 10) Walter White, 11) Bishop James A. Healy, 12) Bill Bojangles Robinson, 13) James Weldon Johnson, 14) Roberto Clemente, 15) Dorie Miller, 16) Adam Clayton Powell, Jr., 17) Marcus Garvey, 18) Garret A. Morgan, 19) Lorraine Hansberry, 20) Edmonia Lewis;* **issued from 1968-1974;** *Series I, 1-50,* **1,380 issued at $75.00 each or $375.00 a set (50);** *Series II, 1-12,* **1,380 issued at $9.00 each;** *13-20,* **900 issued at $9.00 each or $180.00 a set (7);** *1-70 Series I & II,* **issued at $555.00 a set (70).**

☐ **American Numismatic Association,** *set of 8 medals;* **A Salute to the ANA,** *1) 1969-78th Ann., Philadelphia, Pa.,* **500 issued;** *2) 1971-80th Ann., Washington, D.C.,* **706 issued;** *3) 1972-81st Ann., New Orleans, La.,* **582 issued;** *4) 1973-82nd Ann., Boston, Ma.,* **1,200 issued;** *5) 1974-83rd Ann., Bar Harbour, Fl.,* **1,000 issued;** *6) 1975-84th Ann., Los Angeles, Ca.,* **916 issued;** *7) 1976-85th Ann., New York, N.Y.,* **897 issued;** *8) 1977-86th Ann., Atlanta, Ga.,* **1,000 issued;** **A Salute to the Young Numismatists,** *1) 1974-83rd Ann., Bar Harbour, Fl.,* **150 issued;** *2) 1975-84th Ann., Los Angeles, Ca.,* **244 issued;** *3) 1976-85th Ann., New York, N.Y.,* **159 issued;** *4)* **1977-86th Ann., Atlanta, Ga., 200 issued.**

☐ **American Victories,** *set of 24 medals, sterling silver, proof, 39mm, 25 troy ounces per set; 1) Concord-1775; 2) Trenton-1776, 3) Saratoga-1777, 4) Flamborough Head-1779, 5) Yorktown-1781, 6) Lake Erie- 1813, 7) New Orleans, 1815, 8) Monterrey-1846, 9) Buena Vista-1847, 10 Manila Bay-1898, 11) Chateau Thierry-1918, 12) Belleau Wood-1918, 13) St. Mihiel-1918, 14) Meuse-Argonne-1918, 15) Midway-1942, 16) Guadalcanal-1942, 17) Salerno-1943, 18) Marianas-1944, 19) St. Lo-1944, 20) Leyte Gulf-1944, 21) Iwo Jima-1945, 22) Remagen-1945, 23) Ruhr-1945, 24) Okinawa-1945;* **1,017 issued from 1971-1972 at $9.50 each or $228.00 a set (24);** *sterling silver, 39mm, P/L,* **1,314 issued at $9.50 each or $228.00 as set (24).**

☐ **America's Cup,** *sterling silver, 32mm, .39 troy ounces;* **548 issued at $30.00 each.**

☐ **Antique Cars,** *set of 75 medals, sterling silver, 26mm, 17.2 troy ounces per set;* **Series I:** *1) White Steamer, 2) Studebaker Electric, 3) Winton Touring Car, 4) Autocar Type VIII, 5) Apperson Model B Tourer, 6) Franklin Barrel Hood, 7) Locomobile Cup Racer, 8) Stanley Steamer, 9) Ford Model T, 10) Sears High Wheeler, 11) Mercer Raceabout, 12) Simplex Speedster, 13) Lozier Light Six Sedan, 14) Stutz Bearcat, 15) Packard Twin 6, 16) Dodge Sedan, 17) Pierce Arrow Model 66, 18) Cadillac Landaulet, 19) Buick Sedan, 20) Dupont Tourer, 21) Detroit Electric, 22) Daniels Town Brougham, 23) Oldsmobile 6, 24) Chevrolet Superior Coach, 25) Lincoln Sport Sedan; issued from 1969-1970;* **Series II: 1901-1925,** *26) Phelps Tractor,*

27) Oldsmobile Curved-Dash, 28) Ford Model A Runabout, 29) Packard Touring Car, 30) Cadillac Model D Coupe, 31) Maxwell Speedster, 32) Thomas "Flyer," 33) Lambert Friction Drive, 34) Rambler Model 44, 35) Stevens-Duryea Model K, 36) Standard Electric, 37) Reo 'The Fifth', 38) Marmon Six, 39) Hupmobile, 40) White Town Car, 41) Chevrolet '490', 42) Moon Touring Car, 43) Hudson Super 6, 44) Winton 6, 45) Chandler Sedan, 46) Duesenberg Straight 6, 47) Lexington Minuteman, 48) Rickenbacker Sedan, 49) Willys-Knight, 50) Chrysler 6; issued from 1969-1970; **Series III: 1901-1925,** 51) National Stanhope, 52) Conrad Steam Car, 53) Peerless Tourer, 54) Royal Tourist, 55) Pope Toledo Victoria, 56) Columbia Phaeton, 57) Premier 24, 58) Mitchell Touring Car, 59) Stearns Laudaulet, 60) Woods Electric, 61) McFarlan Six, 62) Matheson Silent Six, 63) American Underslung, 64) Saxon Runabout, 65) Dort Roadster, 66) Pullman Coupe, 67) Scripps-Booth V-8, 68) Doble-Detroit, 69) Owen Magnetic, 70) Kissel Speedster, 71) Dorris Model 6-80 Coupe, 72) Davis Fleetaway, 73) Jordan Playboy, 74) Nash Roadster, 75) Velie Sedan; issued from 1969-1970; **5,627 sets issued for $3.00 each or $226.00 a set (70).**

☐ **Apollo Flight,** set of 13 medals, sterling silver, 32mm, 14 troy ounces per set; A) Keynote Medal, 1) Apollo 1, 2) Apollo 2, 3) Apollo 3, 4) Apollo 4, 5) Apollo 5, 6) Apollo 6, 7) Apollo 7, 8) Apollo 8, 9) Apollo 9, 10) Apollo 10, 11) Apollo 11, 12) Apollo 12; **75 sets issued in 1970.**

☐ **Apollo Project,** set of 20 medals, sterling silver, 32mm, 9 troy ounces per set; 1) Lift Off to the Moon, 2) Second Stage Ignition, 3) Earth Orbit, 4) Lunar Trajectory, 5) Command Ship Separation, 6) Docking Maneuver, 7) LM Extraction, 8) Lunar Orbit, 9) LM Launched to the Moon, 10) Descent to the Moon, 11) Lunar Landing, 12) Lunar Exploration, 13) Lunar Lift-Off, 14) Rendezvous in Space, 15) LM Jettisoned, 16) Return to Earth, 17) Final module separation, 18) Fiery Re-entry, 19) Splashdown, 20) Recovery; **1,269 sets issued in 1970 at $4.25 each or $85.00 a set (20).**

☐ **Army History,** set of 24 medals, sterling silver, proof, 39mm, 17.2 troy ounces per set; 1) George Washington Assumes Command of Army, 2) Battle of Trenton — First Major American Victory, 3) British Troops Surrender at Yorktown, 4) U.S. Military Academy Founded at West Point, 5) Andrew Jackson's Troops Repel British at New Orleans, 6) Storming of Chapultepec in the Mexican War, 7) Lee Surrenders to Grant at Appomattox, 8) Battle of San Juan Hill, 9) American Infantrymen Liberate Peking, 10) Walter Reed Discovers Cause of Yellow Fever, 11) Army Corps of Engineers Builds Panama Canal, 12) Orville Wright Conducts First Army Test Flight, 13) Meuse-Argonne Offensive Crushes German Resistance, 14) John J. Pershing — U.S. Commander in World War I, 15) Engineers Plan Mississippi River Flood Control, 16) Atomic Bomb Development — Manhattan Project, 17) Invasion of North Africa, 18) George C. Marshall — Chief of Staff in World War II, 19) Eisenhower Addresses Normandy Troops — D-Day, 20) Ridgeway Commands Liberation of Seoul, Korea, 21) Douglas MacArthur — Allied Commander in Pacific, 22) Free World's First Satellite Launched — Explorer I, 23) Formation of the First Cavalry Airmobile Division, 24) Dwight D. Eisenhower — General of the Army; **1,420 set issued from 1974-1975 at $15.00 each or $360.00 a set (20).**

☐ **Belgian Sportsmen,** set of 15 medals, sterling silver, proof, 32mm; 1) Gaston Roelants, 2) Willy Steveniers, 3) Raymond Caulemans, 4) Serge Reding, 5) Joel Robert, 6) Eddy Merckx, 7) Patrick Sercu, 8) Roger De Vlaeminck, 9) Herman Van Springel, 10) Wilfried Van Moer, 11) Paul Van Himst, 12) Roger Claessen, 13) Christian Piot, 14) Pierre Carteus, 15) Nico Dewalque; **6 sets issued in 1970.**

☐ **Bicentennial Day,** sterling silver, proof, 32mm; **238,192 issued in 1976 at $12.00 each.**

☐ **Bicentennial Medal,** sterling silver, 64mm, 4.1 troy ounces; **18,849 issued from 1975-1976 at $75.00 each.**

☐ **Bicentennial Medals — July 4, 1976,** set of 12 medals, sterling silver, 39mm, 7.4 troy ounces per set; 1) Atlanta, Ga.-Peachtree Road Race, 2) Boston, Ma.-Arthur Fiedler & Boston Symphony, 3) Chicago, Il.-Immigrants Take Oath of Allegiance *to U.S., 4) Greeley, Co.-Rodeo & Independence Stampede, 5) Los Angeles, Ca.-'All Nations, All Peoples' Parade, 6) New Orleans, La.-Statue of Louis Armstrong, 7) New York, N.Y.-Operation Sail, 8) Philadelphia, Pa.-Pres. Ford at Independence Hall, 9) San Francisco, Ca.-50-Gun Salute to the States, 10) St. Louis, Mo.-Spectacular Air Show, 11) Valley Forge, Pa.,-Rendezvous of Covered Wagons, 12) Washington, D.C.-Fireworks Display;* **4,675 sets issued in 1976 at $20.00 each or $240.00 a set (12).**

☐ **Bicentennial Medals of the 13 Original States,** *set of 13 medals, sterling silver, 39mm, 8 troy ounces per set; 1) Delaware (Caesar Rodney & Liberty Bell), 2) Pennsylvania (Lone Patriot at Valley Forge), 3) New Jersey (Colonial Troops.& British Warships), 4) Georgia (Georgia Families Who Fought in the Revolution), 5) Connecticut (Rev. Thomas Hooker), 6) Massachusetts (Soldier & Student), 7) Maryland (Great Seal of the State of Maryland), 8) South Carolina (Sargeant William Jasper), 9) New Hampshire (General John Stark), 10) Virginia (8 U.S. Presidents Born in Virginia, & Williamsburg), 11) New York (Colonial Citizen), 12) North Carolina (Sir Walter Raleigh, Tuscarora Indians and Wright Bros. Plane) 13) Rhode Island (Colonial Navy Frigate 'Providence');* **10,264 issued in 1975 at $19.00 each or $247.00 a set (13).**

☐ **Bicentennial Visits,** *set of 13 medals, sterling silver, proof, 51mm, 20 troy ounces per set; 1) Liam Cosgrave, Ireland, 2) Carl XVI Gustaf, Sweden, 3) Margrethe II, Denmark, 4) Valery Giscard Estaing, France, 5) Juan Carlos I, Spain, 6) Elizabeth II, England, 7) Helmut Schmidt, W. Germany, 8) Malcom Fraser, Australia, 9) Urho Kekkonen, Finland, 10) Yitzhak Rabin, Israel, 11) Hussein I, Jordan, 12) W. R. Tolbert, Jr., Liberia, 13) Giulio Andretti, Italy;* **2,693 sets issued in 1976 at $29.00 each or $377.00 a set (13).**

☐ **Big Game Animals,** *set of 20 medals, sterling silver, 51mm, 41.6 troy ounces per set; 1) Elephants, 2) Impalas, 3) African Buffalo, 4) Thomson's Gazelles, 5) Black Rhinoceros, 6) Roan Antelope, 7) Lions, 8) Kongoni Hartebeests, 9) Leopard, 10) Sable Antelopes, 11) Reticulated Giraffes, 12) Klipspringers, 13) Cheetahs, 14) Warthogs, 15) Eland, 16) Gorillas, 17) Hippopotami, 18) Gerenuks, 19) Wildebeests, 20) Grevy's Zebras;* **3,208 sets issued from 1971-1972 at $20.00 each or $400.00 a set (20).**

Big Game Animals, *Elephants, medal #1.*

☐ **Britannia Commemorative Society,** *set of 60 medals, pure (.999 fine) silver, proof, 45mm, 79.2 troy ounces per set; 1) William I, 2) Magna Carta, 3) Lord Nelson, 4) Canada Confed. Centen., 5) Winston Churchill, 6) William Shakespeare, 7) Spanish Armada, 8) Battle of Britain, 9) Queen Victoria, 10) Charge of the Light Brigade, 11) Great Fire of London, 12) Charles Dickens, 13) Dunkirk, 14) Captain James Cook, 15) Battle of Agincourt, 16) Prince Charles Investiture, 17) Stonehenge, 18) Elizabeth I, 19) Alfred the Great, 20) Isaac Newton, 21) Richard I, 22) Battle of the Marne, 23) Battle of Waterloo, 24) Mayflower Land., 350th Ann., 25) Geoffrey Chaucer, 26) Oliver Cromwell, 27) War of the Roses, 28) King Arthur, 29)*

Sir Walter Scott, 30) Stanley & Livingstone Cent., 31) Benjamin Disraeli, 32) Henry VIII, 33) John and Sarah Churchill, 34) Richard III and Princes in the Tower, 35) Francis Bacon, 36) Lawrence of Arabia, 37) Boadicea, 38) Edward VIII, 39) Westminster Abbey, 40) Gilbert and Sullivan, 41) Black Prince, 42) Royal Navy, 43) Conquest of Mt. Everest, 44) Indigo Jones & Christopher Wren, 45) London, 46) C. Gordon & H. Kitchener, 47) The First Plantagenets, 48) Christopher Marlowe & Ben Johnson, 49) Robert Bruce, 50) George Bernard Shaw, 51) 4 Patron Saints of Britain, 52) Monmouth's Rebellion, 53) Lord Clive of India, 54) Battle of El Alamein, 55) Julius Caesar—Hadrian, 56) Rudyard Kipling, 57) Gulliver's Travels, 250th Ann., 58) Stuarts—Jacobites, 59) Henry the Fifth-Agincourt, 60) Queen Elizabeth II, Silver Jubilee; **1,395 sets issued from 1967-1976 at $664.30 a set (60).**

☐ **Calendar/Art Medals,** *set of 13 medals, 4,500 grains each; 3) '72 Franklin Head, sterling silver,* **1,656 issued at 50.00 each;** *4) '73 Tree of Time, sterling silver,* **3,666 issued at $50.00 each;** *5) '74 Zodiac, sterling silver,* **3,155 issued at $60.00 each;** *6) '75 Zodiac, sterling silver,* **1,689 issued at $100.00 each;** *7) '76 Bicentennial, sterling silver,* **1,753 issued at $110.00 each;** *8) '77 Janus, .999 fine silver,* **605 issued at $125.00 each;** *9) '78 Aztec, sterling silver,* **689 issued at $125.00 each;** *10) '79 Time, sterling silver,* **220 issued at $135.00 each;** *11) '80 Harvest & Seasons, sterling silver,* **issued at $175.00;** *12) '81 Rip Van Winkle, sterling silver,* **issued at $360.00 each;** *13) '82 Zodiac/4 Seasons, sterling silver,* **issued at $360.00 each.**

☐ **California History,** *set of 60 medals, sterling silver, 50 troy ounces per set; 1) Cabrillo in San Diego Bay, 2) The Golden Hind, 3) Drake Claims California, 4) The Apostle of California, 5) First California Mission, 6) First Christian Baptism, 7) Portola in San Francisco Bay, 8) Anza Expedition, 9) San Carlos, 10) Mission San Juan Capistrano, 11) The 'Lelia' Byrd, 12) Russians Establish Ft. Ross. 13) Monterey Custom House, 14) Mission, Solano San Fran, 15) Jedediah Strong Smith, 16) Hide Traders, 17) First Covered Wagon, 18) Bear Flag Revolt, 19) Mexico Loses California, 20) Donner Party, 21) Gold at Sutter's Mill, 22) California Gold Rush, 23) Forty-Niners, 24) Governor Peter Burnett, 25) Giant Redwoods, 26) First Public School, 27) Sacramento — State Capitol, 28) California First Locomotive, 29) Butterfield Stage Line, 30) Pony Express, 31) Black Gold, 32) Vineyards of California, 33) Univ. of Calif. Founded, 34) Golden Spike, 35) Modoc War, 36) Wash. Navel Orange, 37) Cable Cars, 38) Borax in Death Valley, 39) 1st Tournament of Roses, 40) Yosemite National Park, 41) San Francisco Earthquake, 42) Hollywood Born, 43) Bombing of the L.A. Times, 44) 1st Transcont. Air Flight, 45) Panama-Pacific Expo., 46) "Okies' & 'Arkies" Migrate, 47) Tenth Olympic Games, 48) Death Valley Monument, 49) Central Valley Project, 50) Golden Gate Bridge, 51) Population Growth, 52) Steel Mill in Fontana, 53) United Nations Charter, 54) Warren App. Chief Justice, 55) Oroville Dam, 56) Giants and Dodgers, 57) Space Develop. in California, 58) Watts Riot, 59) Reagan Elected Governor, 60) Nixon Inaug. President;* **930 sets issued from 1970-1972, at $11.00 each or $660.00 a set (60).**

☐ **Call to Battle — April 1775,** *sterling silver, proof, 57mm, 1500 grains;* **2,229 issued in 1975 at $50.00 each.**

☐ **Calling of the Apostles (La Chiamata Degli Apostoli),** *set of 12 medals, sterling silver, 57mm, 49.3 troy ounces per set; 1) Saint Matthew, 2) Saint Peter, 3) Saint Matthias, 4) Saint Simon, 5) Saint Bartholomew, 6) Saint Andrew, 7) Saint Thomas, 8) Saint John, 9) Saint Philip, 10) Saint Jude Thaddeus, 11) Saint James the Greater, 12) Saint James the Less;* **1,225 issued from 1972-1973 at $24.00 each or $288.00 a set (12).**

☐ **Catholic Art Guild,** *set of 12 medals, sterling silver, 39mm, 10 troy ounces per set; 1) Miraculous Medal, 2) Scapular Medal, 3) St. Joseph, 4) St. Christopher, 5) SS Peter & Paul, 6) St. Jude, 7) St. Patrick, 8) St. Francis of Assisi, 9) St. Anthony of Padua, 10) Infant of Prague, 11) St. Therese, 12) St. Benedict;* **2,626 sets issued from 1970-1972 at $9.95 each or $114.00 a set (12).**

☐ *13) **St. Therese (special medal):** sterling silver, 39mm;* **1,900 issued in 1974 at $20.00 each.**

☐ **Catholic Commemorative Society,** set of 6 medals, sterling silver, proof, 39mm, 5 troy ounces per set; **Ecumenical Popes:** 1) St. Peter, 2) St. Sylvester I, 3) St. Damasus I, 4) St. Leo I, 5) Pope John XXIII, 6) Pope Paul VI; **1,890 sets issued in 1967 at $6.90/7.45 each or $43.05 a set (6).**

☐ **Special Issues:** 1) Francis Cardinal Spellman, sterling silver, proof, 39mm; 3,796 issued $10.00 each; nickel silver, 39mm, P/L; 2,081 issued at $3.50 each; 2) Prince of Peace, sterling silver, proof, 39mm; **3,796 issued at $9.50 each; nickel silver, 39mm, P/L; 5,000 issued at $10.00 each; all issued from 1968-1971.**

☐ **Churchill Centenary,** set of 24 medals, sterling silver, 16 troy ounces per set; 1) Born-30 Nov. 1874, 2) Schooldays at Harrow, 3) Battle of Omdurman, 4) Escape from the Boers, 5) Elected M.P. for Oldham, 6) Marriage-12 Sep 1908, 7) Siege of Sidney Street, 8) Mobilization of the Fleet, 9) Development of the Tank, 10) In the Trenches-World War I, 11) Victory Parade-World War I, 12) Writing at Chartwell, 13) Churchill the Artist, 14) World War II-"Blood, Toil, Tears & Sweat" Speech, 15) The Battle of Britain, 16) The Blitz, 17) Addresses U.S. Congress, 18) D-Day-6th June 1944, 19) Yalta Conference, 1945, 20) VE-Day-8th May 1945, 21) European Unity, 22) Knight of the Order of the Garter, 23) Honorary Citizen U.S.A., 24) Funeral Cortege-1965; **637 sets issued in 1974 at $17.50 each or $420.00 a set (24).**

☐ **Civil War History,** set of 50 medals, sterling silver, 36mm; 1) Fort Sumter, 2) Call to Arms-Union, 3) Call to Arms-Confederate, 4) Battle of Bull Run, 5) Fts. Henry & Donelson Captured, 6) Jefferson Davis Inaug, 7) Battle of Pea Ridge, 8) Monitor vs. Merrimack, 9) Battle of Shiloh, 10) Great Locomotive Chase, 11) Capture of New Orleans, 12) Peninsular Campaign, 13) Naval Battle of Memphis, 14) Jackson's Valley Campaign, 15) The Seven Days Campaign, 16) Second Battle of Bull Run, 17) Battle of Antietam, 18) The Wounded, 19) Emancipation Proclamation, 20) Battle of Fredericksburg, 21) Battle of Murfreesboro, 22) Running the Blockade, 23) Battle of Chancellorsville; **2,000 sets to be issued from 1980-1984 at $29.50 each or $1,475.00 a set (50).**

☐ **Collectors Society, Membership Medals:** regular-sterling silver, 26mm. P/L/ (20mm in 1980); 3) '71, 51,283 issued, 5) '72, 49,477 issued, 7) '73, 80,394 issued, 9) '74, 95,509 issued, 11) '75, 98,357 issued, 13) '76, 105,188 issued, 15) '77, 17) '78, 19) '79, 21) '80, 23) '81, at $7.00 each, 25) '82 at $7.00 each.

☐ **Tour & Cruise Medals & Ingots,** set of 10, sterling silver; 1) '71-Bahamas, 39mm, **906 issued;** 2) '72-London, 45mm, **205 issued;** 3) '72-Montego Bay, 39mm, **429 issued;** 4) '73-Mexico, 45mm, **360 issued;** 5) '74-Barbados, 39mm, **512 issued;** 6) '75-Spain, 39mm, **353 issued;** 7) '76-Hawaii, 39mm, **285 issued;** 8) '77-Panama Canal, 39mm, **590 issued;** 9) '78-Mediterranean, 39mm; 10) '79-Viennese & Bavarian Festival & 10th Ann., 39mm, **600 issued.**

☐ **Annual Gifts:** 1) '71-2-Apollo 14 mini-coin, sterling silver, 13mm, P/L, 129,449 issued; 2) '73-The Collector by Norman Rockwell, fine art print, 20" x 14", **136,056 issued;** 3) '74-Jewery-tie tack or ladies pin, gold on sterling, 48,393 issued, also sterling silver, 95,509 issued; 4) '75-Personal Seal, 140,940 issued; 5) '76-Leather Bookmark, **144,478 issued;** 6) '77-Letter Opener; 7) '78-The Franklin Key, 8) '79-Diary, 10) '81-Cuff Links or Stickpin, gold on sterling.

☐ **Dentistry, History,** set of 50 medals, sterling silver; 1) Pierre Fauchard, 2) Saint Apollonia, 3) G. V. Black, 4) Willoughby D. Miller, 5) Horace A. Wells, 6) Lucy Beaman Hobbs, 7) Abulcasis, 8) Balt. Coll. of Dent. Surg., 9) Amer. Acad. of Hist. of Dent., 10) Hesi-Re, 11) Zene Artzney, 12) John Hunter, 13) Sir John Tomes, 14) Giuseppangelo Fonzi, 15) Alfred Gysi, 16) William H. Taggart, 17) Charles Edmund Kells, 18) George B. Snow, 19) William John Gies, 20) Robert Bunon, 21) Solyman Brown, 22) Inter. Assoc. for Dent. Res., 23) Fluoridation, 24) Ambroise Pare, 25) Truman W. Brophy, 26) Alfred C. Fones, 27) Arthur D. Black, 28) Fed'n. Dent. Inter. 29) Jonathan Taft, 30) Hulihen & Garretson, 31) Norman W. Kingsley, 32) Amer. Dental Assoc., 33) Philip Pfaff, 34) William T. G. Morton, 35) Rodrigues Ottolengui, 36) Amer. Coll. of Dentists, 37) Kirk & Johnson, 38) Vincenzo Guerini, 39) Amer.

Jour. of Dent. Sci., 40) Leonardo da Vinci, 41) Hermann Prinz, 42) Robert Arthur, 43) Samuel S. White, 44) Nathan Cooley Keep, 45) J. Greenwood & J. Flagg, 46) James Leon Williams, 47) Edward Hartley Angle, 48) The Vienna School, 49) Harvey J. Burkhart, 50) Eleazar Parmly; **449 sets issued from 1971-1973 at $12.50 each or $625.00 a set (50).**

☐ **Drugs, History,** *set of 36 medals, sterling silver, 425 grains each; 1) Iatrochemicals, 2) Cinchona, 3) Theriac, 4) The Unicorn, 5) Antibiotics, 6) Calomel, 7) Opium, 8) Andrenocorticosteroids, 9) Rauwolfia, 10) Ergot, 11) Arsenic, 12) Polio Vaccines, 13) Radio-Pharmaceuticals, 14) Vegetable Alkaloids, 15) Precious Stones, 16) The Sulfonamides, 17) The Early Galenicals, 18) Salvarsan, 19) Ephedra, 20) Diuretics, 21) Mandrake, 22) Digitalis, 23) Psychotropic Drugs, 24) Anesthetic Agents, 25) Animalium Partes, 26) The Later Galenicals, 27) Hormones, 28) Halogens, 29) Smallpox Vaccine, 30) Antimony, 31) Ipecacuanha, 32) Aspirin, 33) Antiseptics & Disinfectants, 34) Cardiac Drugs, 35) Terra Sigillata, 36) Vitamins;* **235 sets issued from 1973-1976 at $12.50 each or $325.00 a set (36).**

☐ **Egyptian Golden Treasures,** *set of 36 medals, sterling silver; 1) 2nd Mummiform Coffin of Tut., 2) The Dog Anubis, 3) Head of a Sacred Cow, 4) Human-Headed Winged Cobra, 5) Crouching Figure of a King, 6) Ostrich-Feather Fan, 7) Tut. the Harpooner, 8) Mirror Case, 9) Panel from Golden Shrine, 10) The God Path, 11) Cartouche-Shaped Box, 12) Figure of a King on Staff, 13) Head of a Leopard, 14) Golden Buckle, 15) Statuette of Horus, 16) Throne with Tut. and Queen, 17) Shawbty, 18) Gold Dagger and Sheath, 19) Pendant with Vulture, 20) The Goddess Selket, 21) The Royal Scepter, 22) The Goddess Isis, 23) Bed with Hippo. Head, 24) Djed Pillar, 25) Funerary Mask of Tut., 26) Serpent Deity Netjer-ankh, 27) Shawabty, 28) Panel-Child's Armchair, 29) Statuette of Sekhmet, 30) Double Cartouche Box, 31) Cow from a Funerary Bed, 32) Amulet-Tut's. Mummy, 33) Scarab Bracelet, 34) Pectoral, 35) Gold Earring, 36) Head of a Cheetah;* **4,695 sets issued from 1976-1978 at $35.00 each or $1,260.00 a set (36).**

☐ **Endangered Wildlife,** *set of 4 medals, sterling silver; 1) California Condor, 2) Texas Red Wolf, 3) Peregrine Falcon, 4) Devils Hole Pupfish;* **739 sets issued in 1970 at $5.00 each or $20.00 a set (4).**

☐ **Eyewitness,** *1) First Step on the Moon, '69-metal, sterling silver,* **329 issued;** *Apollo 15—August '71, '71-medal, 3) President Nixon's Journey to China, '72-medal, sterling silver, 45mm,* **28,098 issued at $15.00 each;** *4) President Nixon's Journey to Russia, '72-medal, sterling silver, 45mm,* **16,334 issued at $15.00 each;** *5) Apollo 17—December '72, '72-medal, sterling silver,* **30,126 issued at $12.50 each;** *6) Viet-Nam Peace Agreement, '73-medal, sterling silver, 45mm,* **12,357 issued at $15.00 each;** *7) Skylab I—May '73, '73-medal, sterling silver,* **15,438 issued at $15.00 each;** *8) Skylab II—July 28-Sep. 25, '73, '73-medal, sterling silver,* **10,243 issued at $15.00 each;** *9) Cornet Kohoutec '73, '73-medal, sterling silver, 45mm,* **15,354 issued at $17.50 each;** *10) Skylab III—Nov. 16, '73, '74-medal, sterling silver,* **10,021 issued at $15.00 each;** *11) Pres. Gerald Ford Inaug., '74-medal, sterling silver,* **29,550 issued at $20.00 each;** *12) Viking I Landing on Mars, '76-medal, sterling silver,* **14,323 issued at $17.50 each;** *13) First Presidential Debate, '76-medal, sterling silver,* **issued at $17.50 each;** *14) Pres. Jimmy Carter Inaug., '77-medal, sterling silver,* **9,262 issued at $17.50 each;** *15) Royal Silver Jubilee—1952-1977, '77-medal, sterling silver,* **4,924 issued at $19.50 each;** *16) Sadat's Visit to Israel, '77-medal, sterling silver,* **4,667 issued at $19.50 each;** *17) Pope John Paul I, '78-medal, sterling silver,* **10,562 issued at $22.50 each;** *18) Pope John Paul II, '78-medal, sterling silver,* **9,245 issued at $22.50 each;** *19) Egyptian Israeli Peace Treaty, '79-medal, sterling silver,* **9,371 issued at $22.50 each;** *20) Pope John Paul II, '79-medal, sterling silver,* **issued at $29.50 each;** *21) Pres. Ronald Reagan Inaug., '81-medal, sterling silver,* **9,393 issued at $37.50 each;** *22)*

Columbia Space Shuttle Landing, '81-medal, sterling silver, **7,566 issued at $37.50 each; 23)** Supreme Court Justice - Sandra Day O'Connor—Sept. 25, '81, '81-medal, sterling silver, **issued at $37.50 each.**

☐ **Faith Symbols,** sterling silver, proof, 39mm, .34 troy ounces; 1) Christian, **294 issued; 2)** Hebrew, 200 issued; **issued in 1976 at $25.00 each.**

☐ **Fifty-State Bicentennial,** set of 50 medals, sterling silver, proof, 52 troy ounces per set; **20,440 issued from 1972-1976 at $12.50 each or $625.00 a set (50).**

☐ **First Ladies of the U.S.,** 1-40) set of 40 medals, sterling silver, proof, 41 troy ounces per set, **7,373 issued in 1971 at $9.50 each or $380.00 a set (40).**

☐ **41) Elizabeth Ford,** sterling silver, proof; **3,811 issued in 1974 at $20.00 each.**

☐ **42) Rosalyn Carter,** sterling silver, proof; **3,104 issued in 1977 at $25.00 each.**

☐ **Flag — History of the American Flag,** set of 12 medals, sterling silver, proof, 36mm, 10 troy ounces per set; 1) First Stars and Stripes, 2) Fort Moultrie Flag, 3) First Navy Jack, 4) Rhode Island Flag, 5) Phila. Light Horse Color, 6) Bunker Hill Flag, 7) Grand Union Flag, 8) Washington's Cruisers Flag, 9) Bennington Flag, 10) Fort McHenry Flag, 11) Flag over Iwo Jima, 12) Planted on the Moon; **4,943 sets issued in 1977 at $22.50 each or $270.00 a set (12).**

☐ **Flight, History,** set of 100 medals, sterling silver, 125 troy ounces per set; 1) 1st Manned Flight, 2) 1st Aerial Crossing of English Channel, 3) Battle of Fleurus, 4) 1st Human Descent by Parachute, 5) Father of Aerial Navigation-G. Cayley, 6) 1st Navigable Airship, 7) 1st Great Altitude Record Established, 8) 1st Aeronautical Exhibition, 9) 1st Inherently Stable Airplane-A. Penaud, 10) 1st Powered Airplane Leaves the Ground, 11) 1st Electric-Powered Airship, 12) 1st to Master Glider Flight, 13) Foundation of Modern Wing Design, 14) Steam Driven Aerodrome, 15) 1st von Zeppelin Dirigible, 16) 1st Powered Airplane Flight, 17) 1st European Airplane Flight, 18) 1st Cross Country Flight, 19) 1st Airplane Crossing of English Channel, 20) 1st Shipboard Landing, 21) 1st Successful Seaplane, 22) 1st Aerial Crossing of U.S., 23) Deperdussin Sets New World Speed Record, 24) 1st 4-Engine Airplane, 25) Junkers Designs All-Metal Plane, 26) Nieuport 17, 27) Spad 13, 28) S.E.5a, 29) Gothias Used to Bomb London, 30) Fokker D-VII, 31) Post Office Initiates Air Mail Service, 32) 1st Transatlantic Flight 33) 1st Nonstop Flight Across Atlantic, 34) Barnstormers Tour U.S., 35) Verville-Sperry Racer, 36) 1st Successful Autogiro, 37) 1st Nonstop Flight Across U.S., 38) 1st Midair Refueling, 39) 1st Around-the-World Flight, 40) Birth of Modern Rocketry, 41) 1st Flight Over North Pole, 42) 1st Solo Transatlantic Flight, 43) 1st Flight from U.S. to Australia, 44) Graf Zeppelin Circles the Globe, 45) 1st Instrument-Guided Flight, 46) 1st Flight Over South Pole, 47) Gipsy Moth Popularizes Private Flying in England, 48) 1st Nonstop Transpacific Flight, 49) Famous Aviator-Amelia Earhart, 50) 1st Modern Airliner, 51) 1st Flight over Mt. Everest, 52) Mass Flight Across Atlantic, 53) 1st Solo Around-the-World Flight, 54) Record Ascent into the Stratosphere, 55) Douglas DC-3, 56) Messerschmidt 109, 57) Heinkel III, 58) Boeing B-17, 59) Supermarine Spitfire, 60) China Clipper begins Transpacific Service, 61) Piper Cut Spurs Civil Aviation, 62) Mitsubishi Zero-Sen, 63) Heinkel 178, 64) 1st Practical Single-Rotor, 65) Boeing 307, 66) Chance Vought F4u Corsair, 67) De Havilland Mosquito, 68) Messerschmitt 163, 69) Consolidated B-24 Liberator, 70) North American P-51 Mustang, 71) Lockheed Constellation, 72) The 'Truculent Turtle', 73) 1st Man to Fly Faster than Sound, 74) Boeing B-47, 75) MIG-15, 76) Vickers Viscount, 77) 1st Nonstop Around-the-World Flight, 78) The Berlin Airlift, 79) North American F-86 Sabre, 80) De Havilland Comet, 81) 1st Woman to Break Sound Barrier, 82) Zlin Z226, 83) Convair FY-1, 84) 1st South Pole Landing, 85) 1st Man-Made Satellite, 86) McDonnell Phantom 11, 87) North American X15, 88) Convair B-58 Hustler, 89) Lockheed U-2, 90) Yuri Gagarin, 91) Sikorsky S-64 Skycrane, 92) Gemini 3, 93) Hawker Siddeley Harrier, 94) 1st Manned Landing on the Moon, 95) Boeing 747, 96) Skylab III, 97) Super Guppy, 98) Apollo Soyez, 99) Concorde SST, 100) Viking 1; **4,000 sets issued from 1973-1977 at $12.50 each or $1,250.00 a set (100).**

☐ **Founding Fathers,** *set of 50 medals, sterling silver, 20 troy ounces per set; 1) John Adams, 2) John Marshall, 3) David Rittenhouse, 4) Benjamin Franklin, 5) Rufus King, 6) Robert Morris, 7) John Hancock, 8) Richard Henry Lee, 9) James Monroe, 10) Roger Sherman, 11) George Mason, 12) George Wythe, 13) James Madison, 14) Samuel Adams, 15) James Otis, 16) Charles Wilson Peale, 17) Benjamin Rush, 18) Robert R. Livingstone, 19) Samuel Chase, 20) Thomas Paine, 21) George Clymer, 22) John Dickinson, 23) Nathaniel Gorham, 24) Thomas Jefferson, 25) Robert Treat Paine, 26) Benjamin Harrison, 27) Caesar Rodney, 28) Gouverneur Morris, 29) John Jay, 30) Stephen Hopkins, 31) William Paterson, 32) Haym Salomon, 33) Joseph Hewes, 34) Noah Webster, 35) James Iredell, 36) Francis Lewis, 37) Joseph Warren, 38) Charles Pinckney, 39) Francis Hopkinson, 40) William S. Johnson, 41) Josiah Bartlett, 42) Thomas Mifflin, 43) James Wilson, 44) John Hanson, 45) Patrick Henry, 46) George Read, 47) John Witherspoon, 48) Alexander Hamilton, 49) William Livingston, 50) George Washington;* **1,719 sets issued from 1976-1980 at $12.50 each or $625.00 a set (50).**

☐ **14 Stations of the Cross,** *set of 14 medals, sterling silver; 1) Condemned to Death, 2) Carries His Cross, 3) Falls the First Time, 4) Meets His Mother, 5) Simon Helps Jesus Carry His Cross, 6) Veronica Wipes the Face of Jesus, 7) Falls the Second Time, 8) Speaks to the Women, 9) Falls the Third Time, 10) Stripped of His Garments, 11) Nailed to the Cross, 12) Dies on the Cross, 13) Taken Down From the Cross, 14) Laid in the Tomb;* **1,900 sets issued from 1972-1976 at $14.00 each or $196.00 a set (14).**

☐ **Gallery of Great Americans,** *set of 12 medals, sterling silver, each set 9.8 troy ounces per set;* **1970:** *1) George Washington, 2) Thomas Edison, 3) Samuel Clemens, 4) Jane Addams, 5) Daniel Boone, 6) Booker T. Washington, 7) Henry Ford, 8) John J. Pershing, 9) Jim Thorpe, 10) John J. Audubon, 11) Will Rogers, 12) Albert Einstein;* **8,575 sets issued for $8.75 or $105.00 a set (12).**

☐ **1971:** *Sterling silver; 1) Benjamin Franklin, 2) Richard E. Byrd, 3) Alexander Graham Bell, 4) Walter Reed, 5) Oliver Wendell Holmes, 6) Helen Keller, 7) Andrew Carnegie, 8) Edgar Allan Poe, 9) George Gershwin, 10) W. C. Fields, 11) George 'Babe' Ruth, 12) Douglas MacArthur;* **8,757 sets issued at $8.75 each or $105.00 a set (12).**

☐ **1972:** *Sterling silver; 1) Abraham Lincoln, 2) Lewis and Clark, 3) Wilbur & Orville Wright, 4) George Washington Carver, 5) Horace Mann, 6) Susan B. Anthony, 7) John D. Rockefeller, Sr., 8) Henry W. Longfellow, 9) Walt Disney, 10) Gary Cooper, 11) Lou Gehrig, 12) Dwight D. Eisenhower;* **2,226 sets issued at $8.75 each or $105.00 a set (12).**

☐ **1973:** *Sterling silver; 1) Alexander Hamilton, 2) Davy Crockett, 3) George Eastman, 4) C. H. & Wm. J. Mayo, 5) John Marshall, 6) Fiorella La Guardia, 7) J. P. Morgan, 8) Ralph Waldo Emerson, 9) Oscar Hammerstein II, 10) P. T. Barnum, 11) Connie Mack, 12) John Paul Jones;* **1,514 set issued at $9.50 each or $114.00 a set (12).**

☐ **1974:** *Sterling silver; 1) Henry Clay, 2) John Charles Fremont, 3) Charles P. Steinmetz, 4) William C. Gorgas, 5) William H. McGuffey, 6) William Lloyd Garrison, 7) Cornelius Vanderbilt, 8) Jack London, 9) John Philip Sousa, 10) Douglas Fairbanks, Jr., 11) John L. Sullivan, 12) William F. Halsey;* **1,489 sets issued at $11.00 each or $132.00 a set (12).**

☐ **1975:** *Sterling silver; 1) Thomas Jefferson, 2) Amelia Earhart, 3) Samuel F. B. Morse, 4) Robert H. Goddard, 5) Clarence Darrow, 6) Clara Barton, 7) Andrew Mellon, 8) Ernest Hemingway, 9) Frank Lloyd Wright, 10) Humphrey Bogart, 11) Knute Rockne, 12) Robert E. Lee;* **1,114 sets issued at $16.50 each or $198.00 a set (12).**

☐ **1976:** *Sterling silver, 1) Harry S. Truman, 2) Charles A. Lindbergh, 3) Robert Fulton, 4) Luther Burbank, 5) Felix Frankfurter, 6) Eleanor Roosevelt, 7) Marshall Field, 8) Robert Frost, 9) Stephen Foster, 10) Jack Benny, 11) Babe Didrickson Zaharias,*

12) George C. Marshall; **1,254 sets issued at $16.50 each or $198.00 a set (12).**

☐ **Gannon Collections,** *set of 12 medals, sterling silver, proof, 39mm, 10 troy ounces per set; 1) Lockheed P-38 Lightning,* **300 issued;** *2) Convair B-48 Hustler,* **250 issued,** *3) Curtis P-40 Warhawk,* **300 issued;** *4) Chance Vought F-40 Corsair,* **300 issued;** *5) Republic P-47 Thunderbolt,* **250 issued;** *6) Republic F-102 Thunderchief,* **250 issued;** *7) Boeing B-17 Flying Fortress,* **250 issued;** *8) F6F Grumman Hellcat,* **250 issued;** *9) Boeing B-52 Stratofortress,* **250 issued;** *10) McDonnell F-4 Phantom II,* **250 issued;** *11) Consolidated B-24 Liberator,* **250 issued;** *12) North American P-15 Mustang;* **issued from 1969-1970 at $12.50 each or $150.00 a set (12).**

☐ **Girl Scouts by Rockwell,** *set of 12 medals, sterling silver, 7 troy ounces per set; 1) On My Honor, 2) Honest, 3) Fair, 4) Helpful, 5) Cheerful, 6) Kind, 7) Sisters, 8) Respectful, 9) Resourceful, 10) Concerned, 11) Considerate, 12) Prepared;* **2,182 sets issued in 1977 at $19.50 each or $234.00 a set (12).**

☐ **God and Country,** *set of 2 medals, sterling silver, 39mm, P/L; 1) Pledge to the Flag, 2) Lord's Prayer/Praying Hands;* **36,211 sets issued from 1968-1972.**

☐ **Good Luck,** *set of 12 medals, sterling silver, 8 troy ounces per set; 1) Chinese Dragon, 2) Irish Four-Leaf Clover, 3) Egyptian Cat, 4) Amish Hex Sign, 5) Persian Simurgh, 6) Roman Cornucopia, 7) Indian Elephant, 8) Hebrew Chai, 9) Japanese Hotei, 10) English Cricket, 11) Assyrian Scarb, 12) Greek Fish;* **3,959 sets issued from 1976-1977 at $19.50 each or $234.00 a set (12).**

☐ **Government Issues,** *1) nickel silver, 39mm, mint,* **48,864 issued at $2.00 each;** *2) sterling silver, proof, 39mm,* **600 issued at $16.50 each; issued in 1967.**

☐ **History of the American Revolution,** *set of 50 medals, sterling silver, 20 troy ounces per set; 1) James Otis Attacks Taxation Without Representation, 2) Proclamation Bars Colonists from West, 3) Patriots Convene to Oppose Stamp Act, 4) Townsend Acts Lead to Violence in Colonies, 5) British Soldiers Land to Enforce Customs Laws, 6) Pent-up Tension Triggers Boston Massacre, 7) Dispute Over Tax Leads to Boston Tea Party, 8) Congress Issued Declaration of Rights, 9) Patrick Henry Calls for Liberty, 10) Paul Revere Alers Fellow Patriots, 11) War Begins with Skirmish at Lexington, 12) Ethan Allen's Men Capture Fort Ticonderoga, 13) Second Congress Assembles in Philadelphia, 14) Bunker Hill Defense Inspires Patriots, 15) Washington Takes Command of His Troops, 16) King George III Proclaims Rebellion, 17) Americans Fail in Assault on Quebec, 18) Congress Seeks Support from Aboard, 19) Washington Unfurls First Flag of Freedom, 20) Paine's 'Common Sense' Assails the King, 21) British Troops Evacuate Boston, 22) Lee Demands Freedom for Colonies, 23) Hancock Signs Declaration of Independence, 24) British Occupy New York City, 25) Redcoats Hang Nathan Hale as a Spy, 26) Arnold's Ships Delay British at Valcour, 27) Washington Crosses the Delaware, 28) Patriots Surprise Redcoats at Princeton, 29) Lafayette Joins Fight for Freedom, 30) Congress Flees as British Take Philadelphia, 31) Burgoyne's Men Lay Down Arms at Saratoga, 32) Congress Adopts Confederation Plan, 33) Americans Suffer Cruel Winter at Valley Forge, 34) Franklin Gains Support of France, 35) Molly Pitcher Helps to Win Key Battle, 36) Indians Massacre Pennsylvania Settlers, 37) British Move South, Take Savannah, 38) Frontiersman Clark Captures Vincennes, 39) John Paul Jones Defeats the Serapis, 40) British Crush Garrison at Charleston, 41) Blockade Seals French in at Newport, 42) Americans Learn of Arnold's Treason, 43) Backwoodsmen Thrash Tories in South, 44) Howe's Troops Put Down Mutiny, 45) Congress Names 5 to Negotiate for Peace, 46) Cornwallis Surrenders at Yorktown, 47) House of Commons Votes to End the War, 48) Both Sides Sign Peace Treaty at Paris, 49) Last British Soldiers Leave New York, 50) Washington Bids Farewell to his Army;* **6,246 sets issued in 1970, 1971, 1976 at $3.75 each or $187.50 a set (50);** *sterling silver, P/L (Pa. Bicen. edition),* **525 issued at $3.75 each or $187.50 a set (50);** *sterling silver, P/L (Bicen. edition),* **2,671 issued at $12.00 each or $600.00 a set (50).**

☐ **History of the U.S.**, *set of 200 medals, sterling silver, proof, 250 troy ounces per set; 1) 1776-Signing of the Declaration of Independence, 2) 1777-Stars and Stripes are Born, 3) 1778-Winter at Valley Forge, 4) 1779-John Paul Jones Naval Victory, 5) 1780-Washington Joined by French Army at Newport, 6) 1781-British Capitulate at Yorktown, 7) 1782-Preliminary Articles of Peace Signed, 8) 1783-Washington Takes Leave of his Officers, 9) 1784-Congress Ratifies Peace Treaty, 10) 1785-Land Ordinance Becomes Law, 11) 1786-Shays' Rebellion, 12) 1787-Constitution Approved, 13) 1788-U.S. Constitution Ratified, 14) 1789-Washington Inaugurated First President, 15) 1790-Hamilton & Jefferson Agree on Debt Retirement, 16) 1791-Bill of Rights Guarantees Individual Freedoms, 17) 1792-First U.S. Mint Established, 18) 1793-Eli Whitney Invents Cotton Gin, 19) 1794-Jay's Treaty Secures Northwest Forts, 20) 1795-Pinckney's Treaty Opens Mississippi Commerce, 21) 1796-Washington Writes His Farewell Address, 22) 1797-First Vessel of the New Navy Launched, 23) 1798-Alien & Sedition Acts Curtail Liberties, 24) 1799-Death of George Washington, 25) 1800-Federal Gov't Moves to Washington, D.C., 26) 1801-Election of Jefferson Decided by Congress, 27) 1802-U.S. Military Academy Established, 28) 1803-Louisiana Territory Purchased from France, 29) 1804-Hamilton and Burr Feud Ends in Duel, 30) 1805-Lewis and Clark Reach the Pacific, 31) 1806-Zebulon Pike Sights Pike's Peak, 32) 1807-Fulton's 'Clermont' Proves Successful, 33) 1808-Importation of Slaves Prohibited, 34) 1809-Supreme Court Defends Federal Authority, 35) 1810-First County Fair Held, 36) 1811-Battle of Tippecanoe Against Indians, 37) 1812-Constitution Defeats Guerriere, 38) 1813-Battle of Lake Erie, 39) 1814-National Anthem Inspired at Ft. McHenry, 40) 1815-Jackson Repels British at New Orleans, 41) 1816-Second Bank of the U.S. Chartered, 42) 1817-Construction Begins on the Erie Canal, 43) 1818-Northern Boundary Set at 49th Parallel, 44) 1819-Spain Cedes Florida to the U.S., 45) 1820-Missouri Compromise Limits Slavery, 46) 1821-Santa Fe Trail Opened to Trade, 47) 1822-Factory Towns Begin in America, 48) 1823-Monroe Doctrine Sets Foreign Policy, 49) Lafayette Begins Hero's Tour of America, 50) 1825-Completion of Erie Canal, 51) 1826-Nation Celebrates its 50th Anniversary, 52) 1827-Beginning of American Labor Movement, 53) 1828-First Stone Laid on Baltimore & Ohio RR, 54) 1829-Andrew Jackson Becomes President, 55) 1830-First Train Passenger Service Inaugurated, 56) 1831-'The Liberator' Published to Fight Slavery, 57) 1832-South Carolina Votes for Nullification, 58) 1833-First National Temperance Convention, 59) 1834-Cyrus McCormick Patents his Reaper, 60) 1835-Liberty Bell Tolls Death of John Marshall, 61) 1836-Texas Wins Independence, 62) 1837-Industry Paralyzed by Depression, 63) 1838-Forcible Removal of Indians to West, 64) 1839-First Use of Photography in America, 65) 1840-Wilkes Expedition Reaches Antarctic, 66) 1841-First Whig President Inaugurated, 67) 1842-Fremont Begins Mapping the West, 68) 1843-Great Migration to Oregon Begins, 69) 1844-Morse Proves Telegraph to Congress, 70) 1845-Texas Annexed as a State, 71) 1846-War Declared Between U.S. and Mexico, 72) 1847-U.S. Forces Occupy Mexico City, 73) 1848-Immigration Swelled by Famine & Revolution, 74) 1849-Forty-Niners Seek El Dorado in California, 75) 1850-Compromise of 1850 Debated in Senate, 76) 1851-Clipper Ships Vie for Supremacy of Seas, 77) 1852-'Uncle Tom's Cabin' Dramatizes Slavery, 78) 1853-Crystal Palace Exhibition Opens, 79) 1854-Perry Opens Trade with Japan, 80) 1855-Year of Engineering Feats, 81) 1856-Slave Dispute Brings Violence to Kansas, 82) 1857-Supreme Court Decision Favors Slavery, 83) 1858-Lincoln-Douglas Debates, 84) 1859-Beginning of the American Oil Industry, 85) 1860-Lincoln's Election Sped by Pony Express, 86) 1861-Civil War Opens with Attack on Ft. Sumter, 87) 1862-First Battle of Ironclads, 88) 1863-Tide Turns at Gettysburg, 89) 1864-Sherman's March Brings Destruction, 90) 1865-General Lee Surrenders at Appomattox, 91) 1866-Atlantic Cable Connects America & Europe, 92) 1867-Alaska Purchased from Russia, 93) 1868-Impeachment of President Johnson, 94) 1869-East and West Joined by Railroad, 95) 1870-15th Amendment-Right to Vote,*

96) 1871-Chicago Laid Waste by Fire, 97) 1872-Yellowstone National Park Established, 98) 1873-Thousands Ruined by Financial Panic, 99) 1874-Barbed Wire Fences the West, 100) 1875-Great Religious Revivals Begin, 101) 1876-Telephone Demonstrated at Centennial, 102) 1877-Hayes-Tilden Election Decided, 103) 1878-Knights of Labor Emerge as National Union, 104) 1879-Electric Light Comes of Age, 105) 1880-Farmer's Alliance Aids Farmers, 106) 1881-American Red Cross Organized, 107) 1882-Buffalo Nears Extinction, 108) 1883-Government Civil Service Based on Merit, 109) 1884-Skyscraper Forecasts the Changing City, 110) 1885-Washington Monument Dedicated, 111) 1886-Liberty Welcomes the World, 112) 1887-Interstate Commerce Act Passed, 113) 1888-Great Blizzard Paralyzes the East, 114) 1889-Settlers Rush to Oklahoma, 115) 1890-Battle of Wounded Knee, 116) 1891-America Legislates to Save its Trees, 117) 1892-Bicycle Craze Grows in America, 118) 1893-America Celebrates its Discovery, 119) 1894-Coxey's Army Marches on Washington, 120) 1895-America Enters Horseless Age, 121) 1896-RFD Brings the Store to the Farmer, 122) 1897-Gold Seekers Head for Klondike, 123) 1898-Spanish American War, 124) 1899-Great Homecoming of Admiral Dewey, 125) 1900-Hawaii Becomes a Territory, 126) 1901-Assassination of President McKinley, 127) 1902-Irrigation Reclaims Arid Lands, 128) 1903-First Powered Heavier Than Air Flight, 129) 1904-Baseball Becomes Big League, 130) 1905-Inauguration of Theodore Roosevelt, 131) 1906-San Francisco Earthquake, 132) 1907-Treasury and J. P. Morgan End Panic, 133) 1908-U.S. Navy on World Cruise, 134) 1909-Race to the North Pole, 135) 1910-Taft Appointees Change Supreme Court, 136) 1911-Andrew Carnegie and Philanthropy, 137) 1912-Women Strive for Right to Vote, 138) 1913-Assembly Line Revolutionizes Manufacturing, 139) 1914-Panama Canal Opened to Commerce, 140) 1915-Lusitania Sunk by Submarine, 141) 1916-Mexican Border Warfare, 142) 1917-U.S. Enters World War I, 143) 1918-American Expeditionary Forces in Europe, 144) 1919-President Wilson Signs Peace Treaty, 145) 1920-Prohibition Takes Effect, 146) 1921-America Honors her Unknown Soldiers, 147) 1922-Naval Limitation Treaty, 148) 1923-Calvin Coolidge Becomes President, 149) 1924-Immigration Restricted, 150) 1925-Scopes Trial on Evolution, 151) 1926-Sesquicentennial of American Independence, 152) 1927-Lindbergh Makes Solo Flight to Paris, 153) 1928-Movier Viewers, Flock to the Talkies, 154) 1929-Wall Street Crash, 155) 1930-Great Rise in Unemployment, 156) 1931-Dedication of Empire State Building, 157) 1932-Veterans Demand Their Bonus, 158) 1933-Franklin D. Roosevelt Inaugurated President, 159) 1934-Dust Storms Cause Migration of Farmers, 160) 1935-WPA Aids the Unemployed, 161) 1936-President Roosevelt Reelected, 162) 1937-Year of Sit-down Strikes, 163) 1938-'Men from Mars' Invasion Scare, 164) 1939-U.S. Neutrality Proclaimed, 165) 1940-First U.S. Peacetime Draft, 166) 1941-Japanese Attack Pearl Harbor, 167) 1942-Battle of Midway, 168) 1943-War of Production, 169) 1944-D-Day — Massive Assault on Europe, 170) 1945-Atomic Bomb Ends War Against Japan, 171) 1946-Trial of War Criminals, 172) 1947-Truman Asks Containment of Soviet Power, 173) 1948-U.S. Uses Airlift to Supply Berlin, 174) 1949-U.S. and Western Europe Defense Pact, 175) 1950-U.S. Enters Korean War, 176) 1951-General MacArthur's Farewell Address, 177) 1952-America Like 'Ike', 178) 1953-HEW Reflects Social Consciousness, 179) 1954-Supreme Court: Desegregate Schools, 180) 1955-Polio Vaccine Declared Effective, 181) 1956-Huge Highway Building Program Approved, 182) 1957-Rights of Blacks Protected, 183) 1958-First U.S. Earth Satellite, 184) 1959-Alaska and Hawaii Admitted to the Union, 185) 1960-Nixon/Kennedy TV Debates Sway Election, 186) 1961-Peace Corps Established, 187) 1962-First American Orbital Spaceflight, 188) 1963-America Mourns Pres. Kennedy's Death, 189) 1964-Equal Representation Means 'One Man, One Vote', 190) 1965-U.S. Becomes More Involved in Vietnam War, 191) 1966-Medicare Aids in Reducing Medical Costs, 192) 1967-Year of Racial Violence and Riots, 193) 1968-Pres. Johnson Refuses to Run for 2nd Term, 194) 1969-America Makes First Moon Landing, 195)

1970-Student Unrest Flares on College Campuses, 196) 1971-Pentagon Papers Bare Vietnam War Secrets, 197) 1972-President Nixon's Peace Mission to China, 198) 1973-U.S. Withdraws from Vietnam, 199) 1974-Gerald R. Ford Becomes 38th President, 200) 1975-America's Bicentennial: A Rededication; **10,000 sets issued from 1968-1976 at $9.75 each or $1,950.00 a set (200);** *Mini Coins, sterling silver, 10 troy ounces per set;* **5,128 issued in 1977 at 2.50 each or $500.00 a set (200).**

☐ **Holiday Medals,** *sterling silver, proof, 39mm; 1) 1965-Dove of Peace,* **250 issued at $5.00 each;** *2) 1966-a) Three Angels, b) Three Wise Men, c) Praying Hands,* **1,001 issued at $5.00 each;** *3) 1967-a) Christmas Caroler,* **505 issued,** *b) Peace on Earth,* **974 issued,** *c) Mother and Child,* **700 issued; all issued at $10.00 each;** *4) 1968-a) Manger Scene, b) Peace, c) English Coaching Scene,* **1,852 issued at $10.00 each;** *5) 1969-a) Praying Child, b) Lion & Lamb, c) Winter Scene,* **3,181 issued at $10.00 each;** *6) 1970-a) Menorah,* **3,488 issued,** *b) Nativity,* **4,062 issued,** *c) Youth for Peace,* **17,015 issued,** *d) Snow Scene,* **3,038 issued; all issued at $10.00 each;** *7) 1971-a) Hanukkah,* **7,896 issued,** *b) Nativity,* **8,764 issued,** *c) Doves of Peace,* **7,761 issued,** *d) Holiday Scene,* **9,112 issued; all issued at $10.00 each;** *8) 1972-a) Festival of Lights,* **6,048 issued,** *b) Adoration of Magi,* **7,006 issued,** *c) Dove of Peace,* **6,807 issued,** *d) Home for Christmas,* **8,415 issued; all issued at $10.00 each;** *9) 1973-a) Lighting the Menorah,* **9,869 issued,** *b) The Nativity,* **12,113 issued,** *c) Peace on Earth,* **10,054 issued,** *d) Country Christmas,* **12,846 issued; all issued at $11.00 each;** *10) 1974-a) Hanukkah Prayer,* **8,471 issued,** *b) Madonna and Child,* **11,849 issued,** *c) Peace Enduring,* **10,529 issued,** *d) Christmas Carolers,* **11,314 issued; all issued at $14.00 each;** *11) 1975-a) Prayer at Hanukkah,* **4,774 issued,** *b) The Christ Child,* **5,788 issued,** *c) Dove of Peace,* **6,162 issued,** *d) Holiday Gala,* **4,954 issued; all issued at $15.00 each;** *12) 1976-a) Hanukkah,* **4,489 issued,** *b) The First Christmas,* **5,856 issued,** *c) The Toymaker's Shop,* **4,927 issued,** *d) Peace,* **4,779 issued; all issued at $15.00 each;** *13) 1977-a) Hanukkah,* **2,707 issued,** *b) Christ is Born,* **3,330 issued,** *c) Peace (Lion and Lamb),* **2,914 issued,** *d) Snow Scene, 1877,* **3,208 issued; all issued at $16.50 each;** *14) 1978-a) Hanukkah, b) The Holy Birth, c) Peace, d) Winter Magic,* **issued at $16.50 each;** *15) 1979-a) Hanukkah, b) Tidings of Joy, c) Peace, d) Under the Mistletoe,* **issued at $19.50 each;** *16) 1981-a) Sign to the Shepherds, b) Peace, c) Trimming the Tree, d) Hanukkah Driedel,* **issued at $25.00 each.**

☐ **Hollywood Hall of Fame,** *set of 10 medals, sterling silver, proof, 39mm, 8 troy ounces per set; 1) Humphrey Bogart, 2) Gary Cooper, 3) W. C. Fields, 4) Errol Flynn, 5) Clark Gable, 6) Judy Garland, 7) Jean Harlow, 8) Charles Laughton, 9) Marilyn Monroe, 10) Spencer Tracy;* **521 sets issued in 1971 at $10.00 each or $100.00 a set (10).**

☐ **Indian Chiefs of America,** *set of 36 medals, sterling silver, proof, 36mm; 1) Quetzalcoati, 2) Massasoit, 3) Hiawatha & the Peacemaker, 4) Powhattan, 5) King Philip, 6) Pope, 7) Pontiac, 8) Handsome Lake, 9) Red Jacket, 10) Black Hawk, 11) Little Turtle, 12) Sequoya, 13) Tecumseh, 14) Seathl, 15) Osceola, 16) Nana, 17) Black Kettle, 18) Red Cloud, 19) Manuelito, 20) Geronimo, 21) Satanta, 22) Kintpuash, 23) Sitting Bull, 24) Chief Joseph, 25) Crazy Horse, 26) Wovoka, 27) Louis Riel, 28) Cochise, 29) Roman Nose, 30) Dull Knife, 31) Standing Bear, 32) Quanah Parker, 33) Black Elk, 34) Mina Bonmana Kanse, 35) Leon Shenandoah, 36) Frank Foolscrow;* **1,923 sets issued at $19.50.50 each or $702.00 a set (36).**

☐ **Indian Tribes,** *4 sets of 10 each, pure (.999 fine) silver, proof, 39mm, 7.2 troy ounces per set; 1) Havasupai, 2) Hopi, 3) Apache, 4) Rosebud Sioux, 5) Paiute, 6) Navajo, 7) Crow, 8) Osage, 9) Papago, 10) Yakima, 11) Choctaw, 12) Mescalero, 13) Cherokee, 14) Muscogee, 15) Seminole, 16) Kalispel, 17) Chickasaw, 18) Three Affiliated Tribes — Mandan, Arikara, Hidatsa, 19) Oneida, 20) Cocopah, 21) Comanche, 22) Southern Ute, 23) Kenaitze, 24) Chitimach, 25) Ponca, 26) Kickapoo, 27) Quapaw, 28) Kaw, 29) Minnesota Chippewa, 30) Narragansett, 31) Seneca, 32) Hualapia, 33) Couschatta, 34) Missouri Tribe, 35) Pawnee, 36) Eskimo, 37) Ottawa,*

38) Modoc, 39) Oklahoma, 40) Wichita; 1-10 issued in 1973, 1-8 14,513 issued, 9-10 13,413 issued at $16.00 each or $160.00 each; 11-20 10,383 to 11,433 issued in 1974 at $20.00 each or $200.00 a set; 21-30 11,634 issued in 1975 at $22.50 each or $225.00 a set; 31-40 7,260 issued in 1976 at $22.50 each or $225.00 a set.

☐ **Indians — History of the American Indians,** set of 50 medals, sterling silver, proof, 45mm, 48 troy ounces per set; 1) Migration to New World, 2) Development of Agriculture, 3) Founding of Iroquois League, 4) Columbus Reaches N. Amer., 5) Introduction of Tobacco, 6) Coronado Explores Southwest, 7) Dutch Establish Indian Trade, 8) J. Rolfe Marries Pocohontas, 9) Survival at Plymouth Colony, 10) Sale of Manhattan, 11) Uncas, 12) Marquette & Joliet, 13) Pueblo Revolt of 1680, 14) Penn's Treaty, 15) Father Kino, 16) Horses Introduced to Indians, 17) The Walking Purchase, 18) Contact with NW Indians, 19) French and Indian War, 20) Pickering Treaty of 1794, 21) The Longhouse Religion, 22) Lewis & Clark Expedition, 23) Tecumseh, 24) First Indian Alphabet, 25) Petalasharo, 26) The Trail of Tears, 27) Seminole Wars, 28) Railroads Threaten Buffalo, 29) The Sioux Uprising, 30) Bosque Redondo, 31) Fort Laramie Treaty, 32) First Indian Commissioner of Indian Affairs, 33) Battle of Little Big Horn, 34) Chief Joseph, 35) Carlisle Indian School, 36) Standing Bear, 37) Peyote Religion, 38) Apache Campaign, 39) The Dawes Act, 40) Wounded Knee, 41) Wild West Shows, 42) Athletics, 43) Ishi, 44) Indian Citizenship, 45) Indian Reorganization Act, 46) Indians in WW II, 47) First Institution of Higher Learning on Reserv'n, 48) First Indian Pulitzer Prize Winner, 49) Blue Lake returned to Taos Pueblo, 49a) Blue Lake Returned to Taos Pueblo (corr.), 50) Alaska Native Claims Act; **2,294 issued from 1975-1979 at $25.00 each or $1,250.00 a set (50).**

☐ **International Fraternal Commemorative Society,** set of 50 medals, sterling silver, proof, 39mm, 41 troy ounces per set; 1) George Washington, 2) John Hancock, 3) Benjamin Franklin, 4) Paul Revere, 5) John Paul Jones, 6) Marquis de Lafayette, 7) James Madison, 8) James Monroe, 9) Joseph Brant, 10) Ethan Allen, 11) Winfield Scott, 12) George Edward Pickett, 13) Winfield Scott Hancock, 14) Albert Pike, 15) Ely S. Parker, 16) Nathan B. Forrest, 17) Kit Carson, 18) John Cabell Breckinridge, 19) Daniel Butterfield, 20) Alexander W. Campbell, 21) William McKinley, 22*) Theodore Roosevelt (error), 22a*) Theodore Roosevelt (corr.), 23) Richard E. Byrd, 24) John A. LeJeune, 25) John J. Pershing, 26) William H. Taft, 27) Horatio H. Kitchener, 28) Will Rogers, 29) William Jennings Bryan, 30) John Philip Sousa, 31) Henry Ford, 32) Franklin D. Roosevelt, 33) Joseph W. Stilwell, 34*) Claire L. Chennault (error), 34a*) Claire L. Chennault (corrected version), 35) Ernest J. King, 36) King George VI, 37) Jonathan M. Wainwright, 38) George M. Cohan, 39) Rudyard Kipling, 40) Harold Lloyd, 41) Henry H. Arnold, 42) Harry S. Truman, 43) George C. Marshall, 44) J. Edgar Hoover, 45) Douglas MacArthur, 46) Eddie Rickenbacker, 47) Charles H. Mayo, 48) Theodore Roosevelt, Jr., 49) John R. Hodge, 50) Leonard Ewing Thomas; **1,293 issued from 1966-1974 at $7.55 each or $377.50 a set (50).**

☐ **Jefferson's Genius,** set of 12 medals, sterling silver, 7.5 troy ounces per set; 1) Architect, 2) Diplomat, 3) Scientist, 4) Patriot, 5) Pioneer, 6) Lawyer, 7) Planter, 8) Statesman, 9) Scholar, 10) Inventor, 11) Educator, 12) Author; **956 issued from 1976-1977 at $19.50 each or $234.00 a set (12).**

☐ **Jewish People's History,** set of 120 medals, sterling silver, 100 troy ounces per set; 1) Abraham, 2) Moses, 3) Canaan, 4) 12 Tribes of Israel, 5) Deborah, 6) Samson, 7) Samuel, 8) Saul, 9) David, 10) Solomon, 11) Elijah, 12) Jonah, 13) Isaiah, 14) Amos, 15) Micah, 16) Jeremiah, 17) Rachel's Tomb, 18) Ezekiel, 19) Job, 20) Return From Exile, 21) The Temple, 22) Simon the Just, 23) Ben Sira, 24) Maccabean Revolt, 25) Hillel and Shammai, 26) Philo of Alexandria, 27) Mount of Olives, 28) Josephus, 29) Yohanan Ben Zakkai, 30) Masada, 31) Rabbi Akiva, 32) Bar Kochba, 33) Judah Ha-Nasi, 34) Meron, 35) Peki'in, 36) The Karaites, 37) Saadian Gaon, 38) H. Ibn Shaprut, 39) Rashi, 40) A. Ibn Ezra, 41) Rabbi Gershom, 42) Samuel HaNagid, 43) Elijah Gaon, 44) Maimonides, 45) Ibn Gabirol, 46) Yehuda Halevi, 47) Nahmanides, 48) Machpelah, 49) I. Abravanel, 50) Joseph Caro, 51) The Inquisition, 52) The Ghetto, 53) Gracia Nasi, 54) Isaac Luria, 55) M. Ben Israel, 56) Shabbetai Zvi, 57) Spinoza, 58) The Wandering Jew, 59) Baal Shem Tov, 60) Hasidism, 61) M. Mendelssohn, 62) G. M. Seixas, 63) Grand Sanhedrin, 64) I. A. Cremieux, 65) Heinrich Heine, 66) Leopold Zunz, 67) M. Montefiore, 68) Disraeli, 69) A. Geiger, 70) H. Graetz, 71) Isaac Mayer Wise, 72) Baron DeHirsch, 73) Emma Lazarus, 74) S. Schechter, 75) Shalom Aleichem, 76) Shtetl, 77) Simon Dubnow, 78) Western Wall, 79) Dreyfus, 80) Pioneers, 81) I. Zangwill, 82) Pogrom, 83) Leon Pinsker, 84) Ahad Ha-Am, 85) Theodor Herzl, 86) A. D. Gordon, 87) Deganyah, 88) Balfour Declaration, 89) The Rothchilds, 90) Louis D. Brandeis, 91) Ben Yehudah, 92) H. N. Bialik, 93) S. Y. Agnon, 94) Marc Chagall, 95) Vladimir Jabotinsky, 96) Tel Hai, 97) The Holocaust, 98) Warsaw Ghetto, 99) Henrietta Szold, 100) Stephen S. Wise, 101) Jewish Defense, 102) Hannah Szenes, 103) Albert Einstein, 104) Martin Buber, 105) Exodus, 106) David Ben-Gurion, 107) Birth of Israel, 108) War of Liberation, 109) Ingathering of the Exiles, 110) Chaim Wiezmann, 111) Ernest Bloch, 112) Moshe Sharett, 113) Sinai Campaign, 114) Moshe Dayan, 115) Yitzhak Ben-Zvi, 116) Zalman Shazar, 117) Levi Eshkol, 118) Six Day War, 119) Golda Meir, 120 Jerusalem The Eternal; 1,858 sets issued from 1969-1975 at $9.50 each or $1,140.00 a set (120).

☐ 1) **Annual Award Medals, 1973:** Harry S. Truman, sterling silver, 2,590 issued at $15.00 each; 2) **1974:** Golda Meir, sterling silver, 1,600 issued at $20.00 each; 3) **1975:** Scoop Jackson, sterling silver, 500 issued at $25.00 each.

☐ **Jews of America History,** set of 120 medals, sterling silver, 125 troy ounces per set; 1) Arrival of the 23, 2) Asser Levy, 3) Mill Street Synagogue, 4) Georgia Settlement, 5) Lancaster, Pa., 6) Touro Synagogue, 7) Jacob Franks & Family, 8) Aaron Lopez, 9) Jewish Publishing, 10) The Gratz Brothers, 11) Mordecai Sheftall, 12) Haym Salomon, 13) Gershom M. Seixas, 14) Francis Salvador, 15) Aaron Levy, 16) Rabbi Carigal, 17) Benjamin Nones, 18) Myer Myers, 19) Manuel Josephson, 20) Washington & the Jews, 21) Jacob Henry, 22) Maryland Jew Bill, 23) Uriah Levy, 24) Isaac Harby, 25) Joseph Jonas, 26) Mordecai M. Noah, 27) Penina Moise, 28) Judah Touro, 29) Adah L. Menken, 30) Judah P. Benjamin, 31) Burial Societies, 32) Isaac Leeser, 33) Palestine Relief, 34) Isaac M. Wise, 35) Benevolent Societies, 36) Rebecca Gratz, 37) Orphan Asylums, 38) Samuel M. Isaacs, 39) Jewish Hospitals, 40) David Einhorn, 41) Ernestine Rose, 42) B'nai B'rith, 43) The Occident, 44) Hear O Israel, 45) Board of Delegates, 46) Isidor Bush, 47) August Bondi, 48) Rosanna Ostermann, 49) Lincoln & the Jews, 50) Jewish Chaplaincy, 51) Medal of Honor Winners, 52) F. Knefler, 53) Sigmund Shlesinger, 54) Jospeh Seligman, 55) S. N. Carvalho, 56) B. F. Peixotto, 57) Hebrew Union College, 58) Bernard Felsenthal, 59) Levi Strauss, 60) Sabato Morais, 61) Emma Lazarus, 62) Union of Amer. Hebrew Cong., 63) Michael Heilprin, 64) Rabbi Jacob Joseph, 65) Kaufmann Kohler, 66) David Lubin, 67) Solomon Schechter, 68) Jewish Theol. Seminary of Amer., 69) Samuel Gompers, 70) Jacob Henry Schiff, 71) Jewish Publication Soc., 72) Jacob Gordin, 73) Oscar S. Straus, 74) Louis Marshall, 75) Morris Rosenfeld, 76) Amer. Jewish Historical Soc., 77) Louis D. Brandeis, 78) Abraham Cahan, 79) Nat. Council of Jewish Women, 80) Julius Rosenwald, 81) Henrietta Szold, 82) Simeon & Abraham Flexner, 83) Lillian Wald, 84) Publishing, 85) Cyrus Adler, 86) Samson Benderly, 87) Ludwig Lewisohn, 88) Benjamin N. Cardozo, 89) Felix M. Warburg, 90) Louis Ginzberg, 91) Stephen Samuel Wise, 92) Judah L. Magnes, 93) American Jewish Comm., 94) Albert Einstein, 95) Herbert H. Lehman, 96) Motion Pictures, 97) The 'Joint', 98) Sidney Hillman, 99) Bernard M. Baruch, 100) Hadoar M. Histadrut Ivrit, 101) Bernard Revel, 102) Music, 103) Albert D. Lasker, 104) Felix Frankfurter, 105) Aaron Kotler, 106) Abba Hillel Silver, 107) Medical Science, 108) David Sarnoff, 109) Fine Arts, 110) Nelson Glueck, 111) A. J. Heschel, 112) Literature, 113) Sports, 114) Theatre, 115) Humor, 116) Hadassah, 117) Women in Rabbinate, 118) Dr. Jacob Rader Marcus, 119) National Leaders, 120) American Youth; **630 sets issued from 1971-1979 at $12.50 each or $1,500.00 a set (120).**

☐ **Jonathan Livingston Seagull,** *sterling silver, .82 troy ounces;* **issued in 1973 at $67.50 each.**

☐ **Kennedy Memorial,** *sterling silver;* **31,171 issued in 1973 at $25.00 each.**

☐ **Kings and Queens of England,** *set of 44 medals, sterling silver, proof, 45mm, 55 troy ounces per set; 1) Edward the Confessor, 2) Harold II, 3) William I, 4) William II, 5) Henry I, 6) Stephen, 7) Henry II, 8) Richard I, 9) John, 10) Henry III, 11) Edward I, 12) Edward II, 13) Edward III, 14) Richard II, 15) Henry IV, 16) Henry V, 17) Henry VI, 18) Edward IV, 19) Edward V, 20) Richard III, 21) Henry VII, 22) Henry VIII, 23) Edward VI, 24) Lady Jane Grey, 25) Mary I, 26) Elizabeth I, 27) James I, 28) Charles I, 29) Charles II, 30) James II, 31) William II, 32) Mary II, 33) Anne, 34) George I, 35) George II, 36) George III, 37) George IV, 38) William IV, 39) Victoria, 40) Edward VII, 41) George V, 42) Edward VIII, 43) George VI, 44) Elizabeth II;* **6,713 issued from 1970-1974, 1977 at $12.00 each or $516.00 a set (44).**

☐ **Kings of France,** *set of 48 medals, sterling silver; 1) Clovis, 2) Clotaire 1er, 3) Dagoberti, 4) Pepin III, 5) Charlemagne, 6) Louis I, 7) Charles II, 8) Louis II, 9) Louis III, 10) Charles III, 11) Robert 1 er, 12) Lothaire, 13) Louis V, 14) Hugues Capet, 15) Robert II, 16) Henri I, 17) Philippe, 18) Louis VI, 19) Louis VII, 20) Philip II, 21) Louis VIII, 22) Louis IX, 23) Philippe III, 24) Philippe IV, 25) Louis X, 26) Philippe V, 27) Charles IV, 28) Phillipe VI, 29) Jean II, 30) Charles V, 31) Charles VI, 32) Charles VII, 33) Louis XI, 34) Charles VIII, 35) Louis XII, 36) Francois I, 37) Henri II, 38) Francois II, 39) Charles IX, 40) Henry III, 41) Henry IV, 42) Louis XIII, 43) Louis XIV, 44) Louis XV, 45) Louis XVI, 46) Louis XVII, 47) Charles X, 48) Louis Philippe I;* **764 sets issued from 1977-1981 at $22.00 each or $1,056.00 a set (48).**

☐ **Landmarks, Great American,** *set of 20 medals, sterling silver, 500 grains each; 1) Air Force Academy, 2) The Alamo, 3) Cape Kennedy, 4) U.S. Capitol, 5) The French Quarter, 6) Gateway Arch, 7) Golden Gate Bridge, 8) Grand Canyon, 9) Hoover Dam, 10) Independence Hall, 11) Lincoln's Log Cabin, 12) Mackinac Island, 13) Mount Rushmore, 14) Mount Vernon, 15) Niagara Falls, 16) Old Faithful, 17) Old Ironsides, 18) Space Needle, 19) Statue of Liberty, 20) Stone Mountain;* **1,337 sets issued in 1971 at $9.50 each or $190.00 a set (20) and 2,482 sets issued at $9.50 each or $190.00 a set (20).**

☐ **Legal Heritage Society,** *set of 60 medals, sterling silver; 1) Cicero, 2) Moses & 10 Command., 3) Magna Carta, 4) John Marshall, 5) Code of Hammurabi, 6) Sir William Blackstone, 7) Charlemagne, 8) Scopes Trial, 9) Trial of Socrates, 10) Oliver W. Holmes, Jr., 11) Sir Edward Coke, 12) Emancipation Proclamation, 13) Confucius, 14) Trial of John Peter Zenger, 15) Jesus, 16) Justinian Code, 17) Decretum Gratiani, 18) Charles Evans Hughes, 19) Hadrian, 20) John Jay, 21) John Locke, 22) William the Conqueror, 23) Declar. of Independence, 24) Louis D. Brandeis, 25) Solon, 26) Jeremy Bentham, 27) Henry II, 28) Joseph Story, 29) Sir Francis Bacon, 30) Benjamin N. Cardozo, 31) Dred Scott Trial, 32) Plato, 33) St. Thomas Aquinas, 34) Montesquieu, 35) Lord Mansfield, 36) Geneva Conventions, 37) 12 Tables of Roman Law, 38) Portia, 39) Henry de Bracton, 40) James Kent, 41) The Talmud, 42) The United Nations, 43) The Koran, 44) Bill of Rights, England, 45) Constitution of the U.S., 46) Westminster Hall, 47) Hugo Grotius, 48) Napoieonic Code, 49) American Bar Assoc., 50) Bologna, 51) U.S. Bill of Rights, 52) Nuremberg Trial, 53) The Federal System, 54) Colonial Amer. Const., 55) Sherman Anti-Trust Act, 56) Inns of Court, 57) Cesare Beccaria, 58) 1st Amer. Law School, 59) Uniform Commercial Code, 60) Brown vs. Board of Educ.;* **304 issued from 1970-1973 at $12.50 each or $750.00 a set (60).**

☐ **Leonardo da Vinci's Genius,** *set of 50 medals, sterling silver, 104 troy ounces per set; 1) The Archangel Gabriel — Detail From the Annunciation, 2) Study of a Horse For the Trivulzio Monument, 3) The Virgin and Child with St. Anne, 4) Portrait of a Musician, 5) Youth With a Lance, 6) Star of Bethlehem and Other Flowers — Detail, 7) Portrait of Ginevra de' Benci, 8) Pointing Angel and the Infant Christ — Detail from the Virgin of the Rocks, 9) Shouting Man — Study For the Battle of*

Anghiari, 10) Apostles Bartholomew, James the Less and Andrew — Detail from the last Supper, 11) Saint Jerome, 12) Benois Madonna, 13) Neptune With Four Sea Horses, 14) Kneeling Angel — Contributed by Leonardo to Verrochio's Baptism of Christ, 15) Saint John the Baptist, 16) The Virgin Mary — Detail From the Annunciation, 17) Portrait of Isabella D'este, 18) Apostles Judas, Peter and John, 19) The Fight for the Standard, 20) Head of a Pharisee, 21) Nude Figure of a Man, 22) Study For the Head of Leda, 23) Adoration of the Magi, 24) Oak Leaves With Acorns and a Spray of Dyer's Greenweed, 25) An Antique Warrior, 26) Apostles Thomas, James the Greater, Philip — Detail from the Last Supper, 27) Portrait of a Girl With a Cap, 28) Virgin of the Rocks, 29) Self-Portrait, 30) Studies and Positions of Cats, 31) Studies For the Kneeling Leda, 32) Lady With an Ermine, 33) Figure of Christ — Detail from the Last Supper, 34) Dancing Maidens, 35) The Vitruvian Man, 36) Portrait of a Youth, 37) Horseman Attacking a Fallen Foe, 38) Mona Lisa, 39) The Virgin and Child with St. Anne and the Infant St. John, 40) Young Man on Horseback, 41) Apostles Matthew, Thaddeus & Simon, 42) Head of a Man with Leaves in Hair, 43) Allegory of the Wolf Directing a Boat to a Crowned Eagle on a Globe, 44) Madonna Litta, 45) St. John the Baptist, 46) The Pointing Lady, 47) Five Grotesque Heads, 48) Profile of a Young Woman, 49) A Dragon Fight, 50) Study for Saint Anne; **issued from 1974-1978 at $30.00 each or $1,500.00 a set (50).**

☐ **Life of Christ,** *set of 12 medals, sterling silver, 400 grains each; 1) The Nativity/Glory to God in the Highest, 2) Christ in the Temple/The Holy Family, 3) The Baptism/The First Miracle, 4) The Divine Healer/The Good Shepherd, 5) Sermon on the Mount/The Lord's Prayer, 6) The Temptation/Choosing the Twelve Apostles, 7) Feeding the Multitude/Ministry of Christ, 8) Cleansing of the Temple/ Jesus Walks on the Sea, 9) The Raising of Lazarus/The Last Supper, 10) Agony in the Garden/Way of the Cross, 11) The Crucifixion/The Resurrection, 12) The Ascension/Descent of the Holy Spirit;* **1,898 sets issued from 1968-1970 at $7.55 each or $90.50 a set (12).**

☐ **Life of Mary,** *set of 12 medals, sterling silver, 400 grains each; 1) Mary is Born, 2) The Annunciation, 3) Mary & Joseph are Married, 4) The Visitation, 5) Jesus is Born, 6) The Presentation, 7) Holy Family Flees to Egypt, 8) Jesus in the Temple, 9) Marriage Feast of Cana, 10) Mary See Jesus Die, 11) The Assumption, 12) The Coronation;* **1,898 sets issued from 1972-1973 at $9.50 each or $114.00 a set (12).**

☐ **Louvre Treasures,** *set of 50 medals, sterling silver, 62.5 troy ounces per set; 1) Mona Lisa by da Vinci, 2) St. Michael Slaying the Dragon - French Romanesque Art, 3) Study for a Medal by Pisanello, 4) Portrait of a Man Called the Condottiere by de Messine, 5) The Code of Hammurabi - Mesopotamian Art, 6) Victory of Samothrace - Greek Art, 7) Portrait of Old Man and His Grandson by Ghirlandaio, 8) Head of a Saint by Memling, 9) Seated Scribe - Egyptian Art, 10) Portrait of the Artist by Durer, 11) Charles V - French Gothic Art, 12) Portrait of Francis I by Clouet, 13) Winged Ibex - Persian Art, 14) Portrait of Erasmus by Durer, 15) Portrait of Anne of Cleaves by Holbein, 16) Rebellious Slave by Michelangelo, 17) Woman Bearing Offerings - Egyptian Art, 18) The Gypsy Girl by Hals, 19) Eve Offering the Apple by Correggio, 20) Diana of Anet - French Art, 21) Portrait of Charles I of England by Van Dyck, 22) The Venus de Milo - Greek Art, 23) Portrait of Helene Fourment & 2 of her Children by Rubens, 24) Milo of Crotona by Puget, 25) The Inspiration of the Poet by Poussin, 26) The Eagle of Sugar - French Art, 27) Saint Joseph the Carpenter by de la Tour, 28) Portrait of Claude Deruet and His Son by Callot, 29) The Peasant Meal by Le Nain, 30) Bust of Countess du Barry by Pajou, 31) The Young Beggar by Murillo, 32) Head of an Amarnian Princess - Egyptian Art, 33) Christ at Emmaus by Rembrandt, 34) Half-Nude Woman by Watteau, 35) The Lacemaker by Vermeer, 36) Head of Michelangelo - Italian Art, 37) The Blessing by Chardin, 38) Bust of Alexandre Brongniart as a Child by Houdon, 39) Diana Resting After Her Bath by Boucher, 40) Leda and the Swan by Gericault, 41) Psyche Receiving the First Kiss of Love by Gerard, 42) The Age of Bronze by Rodin, 43)*

The Coronation of Napoleon by David, 44) Irma Brunner by Manet, 45) Napoleon at Eylau by Gros, 46) The 28th of July. Liberty Guiding the People by Delacroix, 47) Crispin and Scapin by Daumier, 48) Dancer on the Stage by Degas, 49) Self-Portrait by Van Gogh, 50) Jane Avril, Dancing by Toulouse-Lautrec; **7,792 sets issued from 1971-1975 at $12.00 each or $600.00 a set (50).**

Louvre Treasures, Mona Lisa by da Vinci, medal #1.

☐ **Love Tokens,** set of two medals, sterling silver, 1) 1976-Lover's Knot, **issued at $43.50 each;** 2) 1977-Fleur d'Amour, **413 issued at $43.50 each.**

☐ **Marine Corps History,** set of 24 medals, sterling silver, 16.8 troy ounces per set; 1) First Marine Recruits at Tun Tavern, 2) First Marine Landing - New Providence Island, 3) Derna, Tripoli Captured from Barbary Pirates, 4) Lt. John Gamble Leads U.S.S. Greenwich, 5) Marine Forces Defend New Orleans, 6) Archibald Henderson - Grand Old Man of the Corps, 7) Marines Occupy the Halls of Montezuma, 8) Marines Suppress U.S. Railroad Riots, 9) John Philip Sousa - Leader of Marine Corps Band, 10) First Landing of the Spanish-American War, 11) Marines Establish Beachhead at Guantanamo Bay, 12) Marines Defend Panama's Independence, 13) Marine Officers School Established at Quantico, Va., 14) Marine Aviators Patrol for Enemy Submarines, 15) Battle of Belleau Wood, 16) First Aerial Resupply Mission, 17) Marines Protect Against U.S. Mail Robberies, 18) Peace Keeping Mission in China, 19) Marines Invade Guadalcanal, 20) U.S. Takes Offensive with Landing at Bougainville, 21) Marines Secure Marianas Islands in Pacific, 22) Marines Take the Strategic Island of Iwo Jima, 23) Marines Spearhead Landing at Inchon, Korea, 24) 'Operation Golden Fleece,' Protects Vietnamese Farmers; **1,725 sets issued from 1974-1975 at $15.00 each or $360.00 a set (24).**

☐ **Mayor's Medals,** set of 50 medals, sterling silver, 52 troy ounces per set; 1) New York, New York, 2) Philadelphia, Pennsylvania, 3) Detroit, Michigan, 4) New Orleans, Louisiana, 5) Louisville, Kentucky, 6) Nashville, Tennessee, 7) Baltimore, Maryland, 8) Cincinnati, Ohio, 9) Washington, D.C., 10) Norfolk, Virginia, 11) Cleveland, Ohio, 12) Pittsburgh, Pennsylvania, 13) Indianapolis, Indiana, 14) Boston, Massachusetts, 15) St. Louis, Missouri, 16) Memphis, Tennessee, 17) Buffalo, New York, 18) Jacksonville, Florida, 19) Newark, New Jersey, 20) Columbus, Ohio, 21) Rochester, New York, 22) Toledo, Ohio, 23) Chicago, Illinois, 24) Houston, Texas, 25) San Antonio, Texas, 26) Milwaukee, Wisconsin, 27) Atlanta, Georgia, 28) San Francisco, California, 29) San Diego, California, 30) San Jose, California, 31) Los Angeles, California, 32) Kansas City, Missouri, 33) Portland, Oregon, 34) Oakland, California, 35) St. Paul, Minnesota, 36) Tampa, Florida, 37) Dallas, Texas, 38) Omaha, Nebraska, 39) Denver, Colorado, 40) Minneapolis, Minnesota, 41) Seattle, Washington, 42) Birmingham, Alabama, 43) Fort Worth, Texas, 44) El Paso, Texas, 45) Phoenix, Arizona, 46) Oklahoma City, Oklahoma, 47) Miami, Florida, 48) Long Beach, California, 49) Tulsa, Oklahoma, 50) Honolulu, Hawaii; **2,109 sets issued in 1971 at $9.50 each or $475.00 a set (50).**

☐ **Medallic Commemorative Society International,** *2 sets of 12 medals each, sterling silver, 7.4 troy ounces per set; 1) H.M. Queen Elizabeth II - 25th Ann. of Her Reign, 2) John Steinbeck - 75th Ann. of His Birth, 3) Ludwig von Beethoven - Tribute to the Great Composer, 4) Joseph Lister - 150th Ann. of His Birth, 5) Lindberg's Solo Transatlantic Flight - 50th Ann. 6) Stars and Stripes - 200th Ann., 7) Alexandre Dumas -175th Ann. of his Birth, 8) Victor Hugo - 175th Ann. of his Birth, 9) Tennis Championship at Wimbledon - 100th Ann., 10) Phonograph - 100th Ann., 11) Sir Isaac Newton - 250th Ann. of his Death, 12) Sir Francis Drake - 400th Ann. of Around the World Voyage;* **2,549 sets issued at $19.50 each or $234.00 a set (12).**

☐ *1) Wright Brothers - 75th Ann. Flight of Kitty Hawk, 2) Jules Verne - 150th Ann. of his Birth, 3) Queen Elizabeth II - 25th Ann. of Her Coronation, 4) Martin Luther King, Jr. - 10th Ann. of his Death, 5) Sir Edmund Hillary - 25th Ann. of Conquest of Mt. Everest, 6) Amelia Earhart - 50th Ann. of Transoceanic Flight, 7) Sir Alexander Fleming - 50th Ann. of Discovery of Penicillin, 8) Leo Tolstoy - 150th Ann. of his Birth, 9) Catacombs of Rome - 400th Ann. of their Rediscovery, 10) La Salle - 300th Ann. of his Great Lakes Exploration, 11) La Scala Opera - 200th Ann., 12) Nobel Peace Prize - 75th Ann.;* **1,176 sets issued at $19.50 each or $234.00 a set (12).**

☐ **Medallic Yearbook,** *5 sets of 12 medals each, all medals are sterling silver, proof, 45mm, 15 troy ounces per set; 1) Viet-Nam Peace Agreement, 2) Devaluation of the Dollar, 3) Incident at Wounded Knee, 4) In Memoriam, Pablo Picasso, 5) 25th Anniversary of Israel, 6) Brezhnev's Mission, 7) Watergate Investigation, 8) Cambodia Bombing Ceased, 9) Military takes over Chile, 10) V.P. Agnew Resigns, 11) Energy Crisis, 12) Ford Becomes 40th V.P.;* **1,648 sets issued in 1973 at $12.50 each or $150.00 a set (12).**

☐ *1) Egypt and Israel Sign Treaty of Disengagement, 2) Nobel Laureate Writer Exiled from the Soviet Union, 3) Britain Changes its Government, 4) Aaron Breaks Ruth's Home Run Record, 5) Israel and Syria Reach Disengagement, 6) Summit Meeting in Moscow, 7) Supreme Court Rules Against the President, 8) Nixon Resigns, 9) Emperor Haile Selassie of Ethiopia is Deposed, 10) Nobel Prizes Announced, 11) World Food Conference, 12) Rockefeller Becomes 41st V.P.;* **2,162 sets issued in 1974 at $12.50 each or $150.00 a set (12).**

☐ *1) Chinese National People's Congress, 2) First Woman to Head British Political Party, 3) King Faisal Assassinated, 4) South Viet-Nam Surrenders, 5) U.S. Rescues the "Mayaguez", 6) Suez Canal Reopens, 7) First Joint U.S.-Soviet Space Mission, 8) Delegates from 35 Nations Meet at Helsinki, 9) Emperor Hirohito Tours U.S., 10) Prince Juan Carlos Assumes Power in Spain, 11) Douglas Retires From Supreme Court, 12) Federal Aid Averts N.Y. Default;* **1,793 sets issued in 1975 at $17.50 each or $210.00 a set (12).**

☐ *1) Chou En-Lai Dies, 2) Bull Market on Wall Street, 3) Junta Ousts Argentina's Isabel Peron, 4) Callaghan Elected P.M. of Britain, 5) Concorde SST Lands at Dulles Airport, 6) European Communists Challenge Russia's Leadership, 7) Viking I Lands on Mars, 8) Synthesis of Working Gene Announced, 9) Mao Tse-Tung Dies, 10) Americans Sweep Nobel Prizes, 11) Jimmy Carter Wins Election, 12) Oil Spills Threaten Marine Life;* **2,446 sets issued in 1976 at $18.50 each or $222.00 a set (12).**

☐ *1) Carter & Mondale Take Office, 2) Human Rights Becomes a Diplomatic Issue, 3) Gandhi Voted Out of Office, 4) Carter Announces Energy Plan, 5) Begin Elected P.M. of Israel, 6) Silver Jubilee of H.M. Queen Elizabeth II, 7) Blackout Triggers Crisis in New York City, 8) Chinese Congress, 9) U.S. and Panama Sign New Canal Treaties, 10) 1976 Nobel Peace Prize, 11) Sadat & Begin Meet to Discuss Peace, 12) Death of Charles Chaplin;* **1,409 sets issued in 1977 at $18.50 each or $222.00 a set (12).**

☐ **Medals of America,** *set of 13 medals, sterling silver; 1) Washington Crossing the Delaware/Star Spangled Banner, 2) Salute to Old Glory/Iwo Jima, 3) Declaration of Independence, 4) Constitution of the U.S., 5) General Dwight D. Eisenhower, 6)*

President Dwight D. Eisenhower, 7) Executive Branch of Government, 8) Legislative Branch of Government, 9) Judicial Branch of Government, 10) Inauguration of Harry S. Truman, 11) Harry S. Truman, Man of Independence, 12) John F. Kennedy, Leader of Senate, 13) Lyndon B. Johnson, Citizen of Texas; **600 sets issued from 1970-1973 at $15.00 each or $195.00 a set (13).**

☐ **Medical Heritage Society,** set of 60 medals, sterling silver; A) Aesculapius, 1) Early Clinical Laboratory, 2) Edward Jenner, 3) Joseph Lister, 4) Herman Boerhaave, 5) R. T. H. Laennec, 6) Andreas Vesalius, 7) Florence Nightingale, 8) Sir William Osle, 9) Morton-Warren, 10) Claude Bernard, 11) Robert Koch, 12) Lower-Landsteiner, 13) Richard Bright, 14) Ephraim McDowell, 15) James Lind, 16) Rudolf Virchow, 17) Galen, 18) Albrecht Von Haller, 19) Louis Pasteur, 20) Ambroise Pare, 21) William Harvey, 22) Paracelsus, 23) Ivan Pavlov, 24) John Hunter, 25) School of Salerno, 26) Marie Curie, 27) Holmes-Semmelweis, 28) Charles Sherrington, 29) Daniel Drake, 30) Benjamin Rush, 31) Black Death, 32) John Billings, 33) Chinese Medicine, 34) Walter Reed, 35) Sigmund Freud, 36) William Withering, 37) Hooke & Leeuwenhoek, 38) Samuel Gross, 39) Thomas Sydeham, 40) Sir Alexander Fleming, 41) Ancient Egypt Medicine, 42) John Morgan, 43) Percival Pott, 44) Dominique Jean Larrey, 45) Hippocrates, 46) Giovanni Morgagni, 47) Gaspare Tagliacozzi, 48) Paul Ehrlich, 49) Moses Maimonides, 50) William H. Welch, 51) William Hunter, 52) Johannes Muller, 53) Indian Medicine, 54) Philippe Pinel, 55) Girolamo Fracastoro, 56) William Beaumont, 57) Marcello Malpighi, 58) Frederick G. Banting, 59) Wilhelm C. Roentgen, 60) Avicenna; **1,385 sets issued from 1969-1972 at $12.50 each or $750.00 a set (60).**

☐ **Michelangelo's Genius,** set of 60 medals, sterling silver, 45mm, 75.5 troy ounces per set; 1) The Creation of Adam, 2) The Temptation, 3) Gathering of the Waters, 4) Noah's Sacrifice, 5) The Prophet Jonah, 6) The Delphic Sibyl, 7) The Universal Flood, 8) Judith and Holofernes, 9) The Death of Haman, 10) The Head of God, 11) Creation of Sun & Moon, 12) The Prophet Jeremiah, 13) David and Goliath, 14) The Creation of Eve, 15) Ignudo, 16) The Cumaean Sibyl, 17) The Expulsion, 18) The Prophet Isaiah, 19) The Libyan Sibyl, 20) The Forefathers of Christ, 21) Christ the Judge with Mary, 22) Charon's Boat, 23) Doni Tondo, 24) Tityus, 25) The Resurrection, 26) Angels Supporting Cross, 27) St. Bartholomew, 28) Crucifixion of St. Peter, 29) The Damned Man, 30) The Fall of Phaethon, 31) David, 32) Battle of the Centaurs, 33) Dawn, 34) Mask of Night, 35) The Bearded Prisoner, 36) Little Satyr of Bacchus, 37) Day, 38) David-Apollo, 39) Kneeling Angel, 40) The Dying Slave, 41) Moses, 42) Rachel, 43) Lorenzo de Medici, 44) Saint Petronius, 45) Saint Paul, 46) Saint Peter, 47) Giuliano de Medici, 48) Leah, 49) St. Matthew, 50) Brutus, 51) Pieta of St. Peter's, 52) Risen Christ, 53) Taddei Tondo, 54) The Medici Madonna, 55) Bruges Madonna Head, 56) Madonna of the Stairs, 57) Head of Child From Bruges Madonna, 58) Pitti Tondo, 59) Pieta of Florence, 60) Head of Santo Spirito Crucifix; **19,412 sets issued from 1970-1976 at $10.00 each or $600.00 a set (60).**

Michelangelo's Genius, Gathering of the Waters, medal #3.

☐ **Miscellaneous Private Issues,** *1) Dodge Steel Co., 50th Ann.*, *sterling silver, 39mm, P/L,* **100 issued;** *2) Shell Sales Incentive, sterling silver, proof, 39mm,* **40 issued;** *11) Age of Aquarius, sterling silver, 39mm, P/L,* **2,500 issued at $9.75 each;** *14) Cedar Point, 100th Ann., sterling silver, proof, 32mm,* **51 issued;** *17) White Sands Missile Range, 25th Ann., sterling silver, proof, 39mm,* **1,000 issued;** *18) Safeco/ ABA Conv., sterling silver, 32mm, P/L,* **6 issued;** *19)* **Three Rivers Stadium Ded., sterling silver, mint, 39mm, 100 issued;** *21) Del. State Fireman's Assoc. 50th Ann., sterling silver, proof, 39mm,* **1,000 issued;** *22) Petersburg-Lincoln Survey, sterling silver, 39mm, P/L,* **1,000 issued;** *23) Westminster, Calif., sterling silver, proof, 39mm,* **500 issued at $7.50 each;** *24) Burroughs Wellcome Co., Bldg, Ded., sterling silver, proof, 39mm,* **113 issued;** *25) Univ. Coin Club, 10th Ann., fine silver, proof, 39mm,* **200 issued;** *26) Maria Montessori Centen., fine silver, proof, 39mm,* **150 issued;** *27) Pueblo, Colo., Centen., sterling silver, 39mm, P/L,* **5,000 issued;** *28) Santa Catalina Island, Telephone Service, 50th Ann., sterling silver, proof, 39mm,* **150 issued;** *29) Adlai Stevenson III, Campaign, sterling silver, mint, 39mm,* **100 issued;** *30) Mayflower Crossing, 350th Ann., sterling silver, proof, 39mm,* **168 issued;** *31) Cathedral de Santo Domingo, 1,000 issued; 32)* **Nixon-Agnew, 1970, sterling silver, proof, 39mm, 750 issued at $25.00 each;** *33)* **Shapp-Kline Inaugural, sterling silver, proof, 39mm, 500 issued at $500.00 each;** *34) Farmers Nat. Bank, 125th Ann., fine silver, 39mm, P/L,* **20 issued at $4.10 each;** *35) RMS Queen Elizabeth, fine silver, proof, 39mm,* **100 issued at $25.00 each;** *36) Free Enterprise Inst., 10th Ann., sterling silver, proof, 39mm,* **2,204 issued;** *37) St. Nicholas Green Orthodox Church Ded., sterling silver, 39mm, P/L,* **200 issued at $50.00 each;** *38) Solvang, Calif., 60th Ann., fine silver, proof, 39mm,* **500 issued;** *39) The Benny Bufano Peace Medal, sterling silver, proof, 39mm,* **100 issued at $16.00 each;** *40) Mayor Daley Inaugural, sterling silver, mint, 39mm,* **1,000 issued;** *41) Favell Museum, fine silver, proof, 39mm,* **1,000 issued at $15.00 each;** *43) Shriners Council, sterling silver, 39mm, P/L,* **100 issued;** *44) U.S. Conf. of Mayors, sterling silver, 39mm, P/L,* **704 issued;** *45) Philadelphia — Official City Seal, sterling silver, 39mm, P/L,* **1,006 issued;** *46) Twin Falls Nat. H.S. Rodeo, sterling silver, 39mm, P/L,* **200 issued;** *48) Lakehurst Naval Air Station, 50th Ann., sterling silver, 39mm, P/L,* **170 issued;** *49) First Co. Governors Foot Guard, 200th Ann., sterling silver, proof, 39mm; 50) Midland Empire State Fair — 1971, fine silver, proof, 39mm,* **250 issued at $7.50 each;** *53) New Hope-Lambertville Bridge, sterling silver, proof, 39mm,* **2,000 issued at $10.00 each;** *54) Davis Gun Museum, sterling silver, proof, 39mm,* **100 issued at $10.00 each;** *55) Chicago Zoological Soc., 50th Ann., fine silver, 39mm, P/L,* **2,006 issued at $12.00 each;** *56) Dubuque, Iowa, Town Clock Plaza Ded., fine silver, 39mm, P/L,* **1,006 issued;** *57) Allied Radio Shack, 1000th Store, sterling silver, 39mm, P/L,* **166 issued;** *59) Shepherd College, 100th Ann., sterling silver, 39mm, P/L,* **700 issued at $10.00 each;** *60) El Pico Cafe (Coffee) Promo., sterling silver, mint, 32mm,* **20 issued;** *61) Milwaukee World Festival, 1971 Summerfest, sterling silver, 39mm, P/L,* **1,250 issued at $7.50 each;** *62) Alcazar de Colon, sterling silver, 39mm, P/L,* **1,000 issued;** *63) Chanukah Medal — 1971, sterling silver, proof, 39mm,* **695 issued at $16.00 each;** *64) Christmas at the White House — 1971, sterling silver, proof, 39mm,* **250 issued at $25.00 each;** *65) Miami — Winter Coin Conv., 1972, sterling silver, proof, 39mm,* **85 issued;** *66) Torre del Homeaje, sterling silver, 39mm, P/L,* **1,000 issued;** *67) Governor Charles L. Terry, sterling silver, 39mm, P/L,* **1,200 issued at $10.00 each;** *68) Burroughs Wellcome Co. Research Triangle Park, sterling silver, proof, 39mm,* **200 issued;** *151) Bergelt Advertising, 10th Ann., fine silver, proof, 51mm,* **250 issued;** *152) Capitol Bank of Commerce, sterling silver, proof, 45mm,* **900 issued;** *155) Token & Medal Soc., 1980 Conv., sterling silver, proof, 39mm,* **95 issued at $25.00 each;** *156) Token & Medal Soc. — Arlie Slabaugh, sterling silver, proof, 51mm,* **25 issued at $70.00 each;** *158) Hong Kong & Shanghai Banking Corp. Postage Stamp Replicas, sterling silver, proof,* **500 issued;** *159) Western Heritage Savings — Mt. St. Helens,* *sterling silver, proof, 26mm,* **1,000 issued;** *160) World Tourism Conf., Manila, sterling silver, proof, 45mm,* **170 issued;** *161) Grand Bahamas Port Authority, 25th Ann., sterling silver, proof, 39mm,* **100 issued;** *162) Israeli Center for Coins & Medals, Hanukkah, .500 silver, proof, 39mm,* **100 issued;** *163) Israel Num. Soc. of Brooklyn, sterling silver, proof, 39mm,* **40 issued.**

☐ **Mother's Day,** *1971-1975, 1977: sterling silver, proof, 39mm; 1976: sterling silver (cameo), proof, 43mm; 1) 1971,* **5,083 issued at $9.50 each;** *2) 1972,* **7,089 issued at $9.50 each;** *3) 1973,* **8,823 issued at $9.50 each;** *4) 1974,* **11,085 issued at $12.50 each;** *5) 1975,* **6,504 issued at $15.00 each;** *6) 1976,* **4,254, issued at $15.00 each;** *7) 1977,* **2,304 issued at $22.00 each.**

☐ **Mountbatten History of Great Britain & the Sea,** *set of 100 medals, sterling silver, 125 troy ounces per set; 1) Henry Grace a Dieu, 2) Trinity House, 3) Sir Martin Frobisher, 4) Sir Francis Drake, 5) Sir Walter Raleigh, 6) The First Ark Royal, 7) Howard of Effingham, 8) Sir Richard Grenville, 9) Captain John Davis, 10) East India Company, 11) Sovereign of the Seas, 12) Robert Blake, 13) Samuel Pepys, 14) Hudson's Bay Company 15) Davis Backstaff, 16) H.M.S. Resolution, 17) Barfleur and La Hogue, 18) 1st Eddystone Lighthouse, 19) Capture of Gibralter, 20) William Farmer — Steering Compass, 21) Hadley and Cuningham — Quadrant and Telescope, 22) Commodore George Anson, 23) Capture of Quebec, 24) Admiral Edward Hawke, 25) Captain James Cook, 26) Harrison's Chronometer, 27) Act of Navigation, 28) Samuel Enderby, 29) Colonizing Australia, 30) George Vancouver, 31) Earl Howe, 32) Battle of Camperdown, 33) Battle of the Nile, 34) Matthew Flinders, 35) Admiral Nelson, 36) P.S. Comet 1812, 37) Herefordshire, 38) Algiers, 39) Sir Stamford Raffles, 40) Aaron Manby, 41) The Great Migration under Sail, 42) R.N.L.D., Saving Life at Sea, 43) East Indiamen, 44) Charles Darwin, 45) Cape Breton, 46) Lloyd's Register, 47) P.S. "Hindostan", 48) P.S. "Great Western", 49) Grace Darling, 50) Scottishmaid, 51) P.S. "Britannia", 52) Navy against the Slaves, 53) St. James Clark Ross, Antarctica, 54) S.S. "Great Britain", 55) North West Passage/ McClintock searches for Franklin, 56) Triumph of screw propulsion, 57) S.S. John Bowes, 58) The first transatlantic cable laid by HMS "Agamemnon", 59) H.M.S. Warrior, 60) Clipper Ship 'Cutty Sark', 61) S.S. Ocianic, 62) H.M.S. Captain, 63) H.M.S. Challenger, 64) H.M.S. Devastation, 65) Samuel Plimsoll, 66) Greenwich Meridian, 67) Tilbury Dock, 68) S.S. 'Bakuin', 69) Sir Charles Parsons & 'Turbinia', 70) The A Class Submarine, 71) H.M.S. 'Dreadnought', 72) T.S. 'Mauretantia', 73) Captain Scott — Antarctic, 74) Prince Louis of Battenberg, 75) Viscount Jellicoe of Scapa, 76) H.M.S. 'Queen Elizabeth;* **2,818 sets to be issued from 1974-1982 at $25.00 each or $2,500.00 a set (100).**

☐ **Napoleon's Epic,** *set of 12 medals, .950 French silver, 15 troy ounces per set; 1) General of the Armies of the Republic, 2) First Consul of the Republic, 3) At St. Barnard Pass, 4) Awarding the Cross of Honor, 5) Crowned Emperor, 6) Battle of Austerlitz, 7) Napoleon and his Epoque at the Battle of Friedland, 8) Marriage to Marie-Louis of Austria, 9) General Bonaparte by Painter David, 10) Retreat from Moscow, 11) Waterloo, 12) At St. Helena;* **952 sets issued in 1972 at $14.25 each or $171.00 a set (12).**

☐ **Nation's Monuments,** *set of 3 medals, sterling silver, proof; 1) Washington Monument, 2) Jefferson Memorial, 3) Lincoln Memorial;* **800 sets issued in 1970 at $15.65 each or $46.95 a set (3).**

☐ **National Commemorative Society,** *set of 150 medals, sterling silver, 124.5 troy ounces per set; 1) Douglas MacArthur, 2) In God We Trust, 3) The American Indian, 4) Francis Scott Key, 5) John F. Kennedy, 6) Statue of Liberty, 7) Pilgrims Landing, 8) Herbert Hoover Memorial, 9) Iwo Jima, 10) Declaration of Independence, 11) Churchill Memorial, 12) Abraham Lincoln, 13) Civil War Centennial, 14) Washington Crossing the Delaware, 15) Wright Brothers, 16) Four Chaplains, 17) Paul Revere, 18) Gemini 4, 19) Thomas A. Edison, 20) Dr. Albert Schweitzer, 21) Pony Express, 22) Battle of the Alamo, 23) Discovery of America, 24) Thomas Jef-*

ferson, 24a) Thomas Jefferson, 25) Custer's Last Stand, 26) Charles A. Lindbergh, 27) Benjamin Franklin, 28) Lewis & Clark Expedition, 29) Pearl Harbor, 30) Tomb of the Unknowns, 31) American Fighting Men, 32) Three Astronauts Memorial, 33) John Paul Jones, 34) Daniel Boone, 35) Patrick Henry, 36) Will Rogers, 37) Walt Disney, 38) Alaska Centennial, 39) Boston Tea Party, 40) Amer. Canadian Friendship, 41) Franklin D. Roosevelt, 42) Transcontinental RR, 43) Chief John Big Tree, 44) Carl Sandburg, 45) New Orleans, 250th Ann., 46) Memorial Day Centen., 47) Robert E. Lee, 48) World War I Armistice, 49) Theodore Roosevelt, 50) Albert Einstein, 50a) Albert Einstein, 51) Alexander Graham Bell, 52) Gen. John J. Pershing, 53) R. F. Kennedy Memorial, 54) Babe Ruth, 55) Alexander, 56) Richard E. Byrd, 57) Mount Rushmore, 58) Dwight D. Eisenhower, 59) Woodrow Wilson, 60) Samuel Clemens, 61) Apollo 8, 62) D-Day Memorial, 63) Baseball Centennial, 64) Nathan Hale, 65) Apollo, 66) Ulysses S. Grant, 67) George S. Patton Jr., 68) Jim Thorpe, 69) Henry Ford, 70) Everett Dirksen, 71) Robert Peary, 72) Andrew Jackson, 73) David Crockett, 74) World War II Armistice, 75) United Nations, 25th Ann., 76) John Hancock, 77) Mayflower Land., 350th Ann., 78) John J. Audubon, 79) Samuel F. Morse, 80) Daniel Webster, 81) Knute Rockne, 82) Charles M. Russell, 83) Louisiana Purchase, 84) Edgar Allan Poe, 85) John Barry, 86) Santa Fe Trail, 87) Panama Canal, 88) H. W. Longfellow, 89) Robert Fulton, 90) Dr. Tom Dooley, 91) Calif. Gold Discov. 92) William Cody, 93) Apollo 15, 94) William Penn, 95) Valley Forge, 96) George Gershwin, 97) The American Farmer, 98) Stephen C. Foster, 99) Yellowstone Nat. Park, 100) Amer. Clipper Ships Bicen., 101) George Washington, 102) J. Edgar Hoover, 103) Frederic Remington, 104) Alaskan Gold Rush, 105) Sam Houston, 106) Truman Memorial, 107) Niagara Falls, 108) Chester W. Nimitz, 109) Jamestown, 110) Walter Reed, 111) Apollo XVII, 112) Peace in Vietnam, 113) Johnson Memorial, 114) Battle of the Ironclads, 115) 1st Cont. Cong. Bicen., 116) Eli Whitney, 117) John Philip Sousa, 118) E. V. Rickenbacker, 119) Skylab I, 120) 13 Original States, 121) Betsy Ross, 122) Stonewall Jackson, 123) Christopher Columbus, 124) Independence Hall, 125) Amelia Earhart, 126) A. York & A. Murphy, 127) Mount Vernon, 128) Paul Revere's Ride Bicen., 129) Lexington & Concord Bicen., 130) U.S. Army Bicen., 131) Lindbergh Memorial, 132) Battle of Bunker Hill, 133) 2nd Cont. Cong. Bicen., 134) Patrick Henry's Speech, 135) U.S. Navy Bicen., 136) Jack Benny Memorial, 137) U.S. Marine Corps, 138) Marquis de Lafayette, 139) Thomas Paine's "Common Sense", 200th Ann., 140) Settling of the Amer. West, 141) Manhattan Purch., 350th Ann., 142) Apollo-Soyuz, 143) Bicen. of Amer. Indepen., 143a) Bicen. of Amer. Indepen., 144) 1st Telephone Message Cent., 145) Caesar Rodney, 146) Amer. Policemen & Firemen, 147) Battle of Trenton Bicen., 148) Lou Gehrig, 149) Overland Exped. to Calif., 150) Joseph M. Segel; **5,252 sets issued from 1964-1976 at $6.60 to $7.25 each.**

☐ **Navy History,** set of 24 medals, sterling silver, 17 troy ounces per set; 1) Flagship Alfred Leads Continental Navy to Sea, 2) John Paul Jones Victory at Flamborough Head, 3) Constellation Defeats L'Insurgente in French Quasi War, 4) U.S.S. Philadelphia Destroyed in Tripoli Harbor, 5) Constitution Defeats Guerriere in War of 1812, 6) Founding of U.S. Naval Academy at Annapolis, 7) Commodore Perry Opens Trade with Japan, 8) Battle of Ironclads — Monitor vs. C.S.S. Virginia, 9) Launching of First Battleship — U.S.S. Maine, 10) Comm. Dewey Crushes Spanish Fleet at Manila Bay, 11) Navy Commissions First Submarine, 12) Commander Robert E. Peary Reaches North Pole, 13) First Flight from Navy Ship, 14) U.S. Destroyers Arrive at Queenstown, Ireland, 15) NC-4 Completes First Transatlantic Flight, 16) U.S.S. Langley — First Aircraft Carrier Commissioned, 17) Byrd Completes First Flight Over South Pole, 18) Naval Forces Wage Battle of the Atlantic, 19) Battle of Midway Cripples Japanese Fleet, 20) Official Signing of Japanese Surrender Documents, 21) Nautilus Reaches North Pole, 22) Trieste Dives to

Greatest Ocean Depth, 23) First American Astronaut Launched into Space, 24) Blockage of Cuba Forces Withdrawal of Russian Missiles; **1,867 sets issued at $15.00 each or $360.00 a set (24).**

☐ **Nobel Prize,** sterling silver, proof, 51mm, 2.08 troy ounces; **988 issued in 1976 at $50.00 each.**

☐ **Old Testament by Monti,** set of 24 medals, sterling silver, 40 troy ounces per set; 1) The Creation, 2) Adam & Eve, 3) Cain and Abel, 4) Noah's Ark, 5) Tower of Babel, 6) Lot's Choice, 7) Abraham offers Isaac, 8) Jacob buys his Birthright, 9) Jacobs Sees the Ladder, 10) Joseph Sold into Slavery, 11) Moses and the Burning Brush, 12) Moses & 10 Command., 13) The Golden Calf, 14) Joshua & Walls of Jericho, 15) Samson and Delilah, 16) Marriage of Ruth & Boaz, 17) David Plays for King Saul, 18) David and Goliath, 19) Solomon Building Temple, 20) Elijh Entering Heaven, 21) Esther pleads for her people, 22) The Testing of Job, 23) Daniel in the Lion's Den, 24) Jonah and the Whale; **1,269 sets issued in 1973 at $12.50 each or $300.00 a set (24).**

☐ **Olympic Games History,** set of 50 medals, sterling silver, 31 troy ounces per set; 1) '96-Spirdon Louis, 2) '00-Ray Ewry, 3) '08-Dorando Pietri, 4) '12-Duke Kahanamoku, 5) '20-First Olympic Flag, 6) '24-First Winter Olympics, 7) '24-Paavo Nurmi, 8) '24-Johnny Weissmuller, 9) '28-Sonja Henie, 10) '28-Lord Burghley, 11) '32-Mildred (Babe) Didrikson, 12) '32-Westergren & Johansson, 13) '32-First Olympic Village, 14) '36-Ivan Ballangrud, 15) '36-Jesse Owens, 16) Hendrika Mastenbroek, 17) '36-Torch Relay, 18) '48-Dick Button, 19) '48-Fanny Blakers-Koen, 20) '48-Bob Mathias, 21) '48-Karoly Takacs, 22) '48-Paul Elvstrom, 23) '52-Ice Hockey, 24) '52-Emil Zatopek, 25) '52-Adheimer F. de Silva, 26) '52-Bob Richards, 27) '56-Cortina D-Ampezzo, 28) '56-Laszlo Papp, 29) '56-Olga Fikatova, 30) '56-Joaquin Capillia, 31) '60-Wagner & Paul, 32) '60-Abebe Bikila, 33) '60-Rafer Johnson, 34) '64-Nash & Dixon, 35) '64-Dawn Fraser, 36) '64-Vallery Brumel, 37) '64-Peter Snell, 38) '64-Gunter Winkler, 39) '68-Peggy Fleming, 40) '68-Jean-Claude Killy, 41) '68-Al Oerter, 42) '68-Bob Beamon, 43) '72-Yukio Kassaya, 44) '72-Ard Schenk, 45) '72-Olga Korbut, 46) '76-Rosi Mittermaier, 47) '68-Eugenio Monti, 48) '76-Vaslii Alexeev, 49) '04-John Flanagan, 50) '76-Nadia Comaneci; **5,382 sets issued from 1976-1980 at $19.50 each or $975.00 a set (50).**

☐ **Olympic Moments,** set of 17 sets, sterling silver; A) Olympic Games Medal, 1) Olympic Tribute, 2) Spiridon Louis, 3) Alvin Kraenzlein, 4) Charles M. Daniels, 5) Ray Ewry, 6) Erik Lemming, 7) Paavo Nurmi, 8) Johnny Weissmuller, 9) Sonja Henie, 10) Mildred 'Babe' Didrikson, 11) Jesse Owens, 12) Francina Blankers-Koen, 13) Robert Mathias, 14) Victor Chukarin, 15) Wilma Rudolph, 16) Donald Schollander, 17) Peggy Flemming; **365 sets issued in 1972 at $10.00 each or $170.00 a set (17).**

☐ **Olympic Summer Games,** set of 18 medals, sterling silver, 11 troy ounces per set; 1) Munich, 2) Yachting Contests, Kiel, 3) Canoe Slalom, Augsburg, 4) Yachting, 5) Running, 6) Pole Vault, 7) Broad Jump, 8) Rowing, 9) Basketball, 10) Hurdles, 11) Shot Put, 12) Swimming, 13) Soccer, 14) Gymnastics, 15) Equestrian, 16) Fencing, 17) Cycling, 18) Boxing; **2,457 sets issued in 1972 at 7.00 each or $126.00 a set (18).**

☐ **Olympic Team Medals,** set of 3 medals, sterling silver, proof, 39mm, 2.1 troy ounces per set; **9,377 sets issued from 1971-1972 at $8.33 each or $25.00.**

☐ **Olympic Winter Games,** set of 11 medals, sterling silver, 7.7 troy ounces per set; 1) Cross-Country Skiing, 2) Downhill Skiing, 3) Slalom, 4) Biathlon, 5) Ski Jumping, 6) Ice Hockey, 7) Figure Skating, 8) Speed Skating, 9) Bobsled Racing, 10) Toboggan Racing, 11) Sapporo; **1,537 sets issued in 1972 at $7.00 each or $77.00 a set (11).**

☐ **100 Greatest Masterpieces,** sterling silver, 208 troy ounces per set; 1) Queen Nefertiti, Egyptian, 2) Virgin of the Rocks by Leonardo da Vinci, 3) Sunflowers by Vincent Van Gogh, 4) Ecstacy of St. Theresa by Gianlorenzo Bernini, 5) Birth of Venus by Sandro Botticelli, 6) Marcus Aurelius, Roman, 7) Breezing Up by Winslow Homer, 8) Book of Kells, Irish, 9) The Kiss by Auguste Rodin, 10) T'ang Dynasty Horse, Chinese, 11) The Expulsion from Paradise by Massaccio, 12) Laughing

Cavalier by Frans Hals, 13) The Death of Marat by Jacques-Louis David, 14) The Return of the Hunters by Peter Bruegal the Elder, 15) Poseidon, Greek, 16) The Garden of Delights by Hieronymus Bosch, 17) Erasmus of Rotterdam by Hans Holbein the Younger, 18) Liberty Leading the People by Eugene Delacroix, 19) Portrait of Charles I of England by Anthony Van Dyck, 20) Pastoral Concert by Giorgione, 21) Charioteer, Greek, 22) The Raft of the Medusa by Theodore Gericault, 23) Mona Lisa by Leonardo da Vinci, 24) The Annunciation by Fra Angelico, 25) A Sunday Afternoon on the Grande Jatte by Georges Seurat, 26) Portrait of Francis I by Jean Clouet, 27) Fur Traders on the Missouri by George Caleb Bingham, 28) Burial of Count Orgaz by El Greco, 29) Water Nymph by Jean Goujon, 30) Horseman, Greek, 31) The Third of May, 1808 by Goya, 32) Praying Hands by Albrecht Durer, 33) The Ram in the Thicket, Sumerian, 34) The Discus Thrower by Myron, 35) Giovanni Arnolfini and His Bride by Jan van Eyck, 36) The Bather by Jean-Auguste-Dominique Ingres, 37) The Last Supper by Tintoretto, 38) Henry VIII by Hans Holbein the Younger, 39) Hermes by Praxiteles, 40) The Gleaners by Jean-Francois Millet, 41) The Descent from the Cross by Rogier van der Weyden, 42) Beau Dieu, French, 43) Mary Magdalene with a Night Light by Georges de la Tour, 44) David by Donatello, 45) The Last Judgement by Michelangelo, 46) The Burial of Phocion by Poussin, 47) The School of Athens by Raphael, 48) The Apollo Belvedere, 49) Max Schmitt in a Single Scull, 50) The Crucifixion, 51) Christ Healing the Sick, 52) Ama-no-hashidate, 53) Madonna and Child with Angels, 54) Pauline Borghese as Venus, 55) The Night Watch, 56) St. Sabastian, 57) The Venus de Milo, 58) Oath of the Horatii, 59) Duke of Urbino, 60) Flight into Egypt, 61) The Artist's Studio, 62) The Story of Jacob and Esau, 63) Prima Ballerina, 64) The Blue Boy (Jonathan Buttall), 65) Luncheon on the Grass, 66) Apollo of Veii, 67) Still Life by Cezanne, 68) The Last Supper by Leonardo da Vinci, 69) La Dame a la Licorne, French, 70) Portrait of Susanna Fourment by Peter Paul Rubens, 71) The Four Horsemen of the Apocalypse by Albrecht Durer, 72) Nude Maja by Francisco Goya, 73) The Victory of Samothrace, Greek, 74) The Wave by Katsushika Hokusai, 75) Where do we come from? What are we? Where are we going? by Paul Gauguin, 76) Portrait Bust of Voltaire by Jean-Antoine Houdon, 77) The Battle of San Romano by Pacio Uccello, 78) Bacchus by Caravaggio, 79) Nike Adjusting Her Sandal, Greek, 80) David by Michelangelo, 81) Le Moulin de la Martini and Memmi, 83) Self-Portrait by Van Gogh, 84) The Maids of Honor by Velazquez, 85) Battle of the Ten Naked Men by Del Pollaiuolo, 86) Venus of Urbino by Titian, 87) Augustus of Prima Porta, Roman, 88) Empress Theodore & Her Attendants, Byzantine, 89) Equestrian Monument of Colleoni by Verrocchio, 90) The Letter by Vermeer, 91) George Washington by Stuart, 92) The Pieta by Michelangelo, 93) The Fighting Temeraire by Mallord & Turner, 94) Standing Hornblower, African, 95) The Sistine Madonna by Raphael, 96) April from Les Tres Riches Heures du Duc de Berry, 97) Prince Baltasar Carlos on Horseback by Velazquez, 98) The Swing by Fragonard, 99) The Creation of Adam by Michelangelo, 100) Standing Budda from Mathura, Indian; **3,798 sets issued from 1973-1981 at $25.00 each or $2,500.00 a set (100).**

☐ **Parables of Jesus,** set of 20 medals, sterling silver, 2,000 grains each; 1) Sower, 2) Weeds Among the Wheat, 3) Mustard Seed, 4) Hidden Treasure, 5) Net Cast Into the Sea, 6) Two Builders, 7) Blind Leading the Blind, 8) Lost Sheep, 9) Good Shepherd, 10) Good Samaritan, 11) Unmerciful Servant, 12) Foolish Rich Man, 13) Rich Man and Lazarus, 14) Godless Judge, 15) Pharisee and the Publican, 16) Prodical Son, 17) Vine-Dressers, 18) Marriage Feast, 19) Wise and Foolish Virgins, 20) Talents; **1,195 sets issued in 1974 at $30.00 each or $600.00 a set (20).**

☐ **Patriots Hall of Fame,** 5 sets of 20 medals each, sterling silver, 20.8 troy ounces per set; **Series I:** 1) Samuel Adams, 2) Patrick Henry, 3) Paul Revere, 4) Ethan Allen, 5) Peter Salem, 6) George Washington, 7) John Barry, 8) Thomas Jefferson, 9) John Adams, 10) John Hancock, 11) Nathan Hale, 12) Benjamin Franklin, 13) Thomas Paine, 14) George Rogers Clark, 15) Molly Pitcher, 16) Anthony Wayne, 17)

John Paul Jones, 18) Francis Marion, 19) John Jay, 20) Alexander Hamilton; **2,648 sets issued in 1971 at $9.50 each or $190.00 a set (20).**

☐ **Series II:** sterling silver; 1) James Madison, 2) Eli Whitney, 3) John Marshall, 4) Stephen Decatur, 5) Lewis and Clark, 6) Robert Fulton, 7) James Lawrence, 8) Oliver Hazard Perry, 9) Andrew Jackson, 10) Henry Clay, 11) John Quincy Adams, 12) James Monroe, 13) Daniel Webster, 14) Sam Houston, 15) Osceola, 16) Horace Mann, 17) William Henry Harrison, 18) Zachary Taylor, 19) Winfield Scott, 20) John C. Calhoun; **1,336 sets issued in 1972 at $9.50 each or $190.00 a set (20).**

☐ **Series III:** 1) Harriet Beecher Stowe, 2) Abraham Lincoln, 3) Joshua Chamberlain, 4) David Farragut, 5) Philip H. Sheridan, 6) William H. Sherman, 7) Ulysses S. Grant, 8) William Lloyd Garrison, 9) Robert E. Lee, 10) William Henry Seward, 11) Horace Greeley, 12) Edmund G. Ross, 13) Susan B. Anthony, 14) Carl Schurz, 15) Frederick Douglas, 16) Clara Barton, 17) Booker T. Washington, 18) George Dewey, 19) Walter Reed, 20) Frederick Funston; **1,620 sets issued in 1973 at $11.00 each or $220.00 a set (20).**

☐ **Series IV:** 1) Oliver Wendell Holmes, 2) Orville & Wilbur Wright, 3) Mary Mcleod Bethune, 4) Theodore Roosevelt, 5) Louis D. Brandeis, 6) Jane Addams, 7) Andrew Carnegie, 8) Bernard M. Baruch, 9) John J. Pershing, 10) Herbert Hoover, 11) Woodrow Wilson, 12) Robert A. Millikan, 13) Robert H. Goddard, 14) Richard E. Byrd, 15) Will Rogers, 16) Charles A. Lindbergh, 17) Franklin D. Roosevelt, 18) Charles Evans Hughes, 19) George W. Carver, 20) Carl Sandburg; **1,316 sets issued in 1974 at $15.00 each or $300.00 a set (20).**

☐ **Series V:** 1) J. Edgar Hoover, 2) Bob Hope, 3) Ernie Pyle, 4) Dwight D. Eisenhower, 5) George S. Patton, Jr., 6) Douglas MacArthur, 7) Helen Keller, 8) Eleanor Roosevelt, 9) Harry S. Truman, 10) George C. Marshall, 11) Omar Bradley, 12) Louis Armstrong, 13) Tom Dooley, 14) Robert Frost, 15) John F. Kennedy, 16) Pearl S. Buck, 17) Martin Luther King, Jr., 18) Lyndon Baines Johnson, 19) Richard M. Nixon, 20) Gerald R. Ford; **1,273 sets issued in 1975 at $20.00 each or $400.00 a set (20).**

☐ **Personalized Coins,** sterling silver, proof-like, 1) 100 grains, 26mm; **issued from 1971-1974 at $1.50 each;** 250 grains, 32mm; **issued at $3.75 each;** 3) 500 grains, 39mm; **issued at $7.50 each.**

☐ **Pharmacy History,** set of 36 medals, sterling silver; 1) Carl Wilhelm Scheele, 2) Arabic Pharmacy, 3) Pedanios Dioscorides, 4) Apothecary Jars, 5) Martin H. Klaproth, 6) Kremers & Urdang, 7) Sir Henry S. Wellcome, 8) Emperor Frederick II, 9) Pelletier & Caventou, 10) Feder. Internat. Pharmaceut., 11) Valerius Cordus, 12) Antoine-Jerome Bafard, 13) Banting & Best, 14) J. J. De Manlius de Bosco, 15) Paul Ehrlich, 16) Sumerian Clay Tablet, 17) Philippus A. T. Paracelsus, 18) Radiopharmaceuticals, 19) Claudius Galenus, 20) J. A. A. Parmentier, 21) Johannes B. Trommsdorff, 22) Frederick G. Hopkins, 23) Francois Magendie, 24) Al-Kohen Ben Al'attar, 25) F. W. A. Serturner, 26) Monastic Pharmacy, 27) Friedrich A. Fluckiger, 28) J. B. A. Chevallier, 29) Carl Friedrich Mohr, 30) Univ. of Montpellier, 31) Antoine Baume, 32) Secundum Artem, 33) William Procter, Jr., 34) Stanislaw Limousin, 35) E. F. A. Fourneau, 36) Emil Von Behring; **711 sets issued from 1970-1972 at $12.50 each or $450.00 a set (36).**

☐ **Portraits of Greatness Selected by Kissinger,** set of 50 medals, sterling silver, proof, 27.5 troy ounces per set; 1) Benjamin Franklin, 2) Robert Livingston, 3) Thomas Jefferson, 4) Alfred Thayer Mahan, 5) John Jay, 6) George Washington, 7) James T. Shotwell, 8) James Madison, 9) Douglas MacArthur, 10) Alexander Hamilton, 11) John Adams, 12) Thomas Pinckney, 13) Theodore Roosevelt, 14) John Quincy Adams, 15) Arthur H. Vandenberg, 16) Townsend Harris, 17) Woodrow Wilson, 18) Daniel Webster, 19) Charles Francis Adams, 20) James Buchanan, 21) Robert A. Taft, 22) Herbert Hoover, 23) Bernard M. Baruch, 24) Franklin D. Roosevelt, 25) William H. Seward, 26) Harry S. Truman, 27) W. Averell Harriman, 28) Charles Evans Hughes, 29) Dwight D. Eisenhower, 30) Hamilton

Fish, 31) Walter Lippmann, 32) David K. E. Bruce, 33) Robert Daniel Murphy, 34) John F. Kennedy, 35) John Milton Hay; **180 sets to be issued from 1978-1982 at $19.50 each or $975.00 a set (50);** *sterling silver, mint,* **190 sets to be issued at $19.50 each or $975.00 a set (50).**

☐ **Presidency, History of the American,** *set of 100 medals, sterling silver, proof, 55 troy ounces per set; 1) Inauguration of George Washington, 2) First Presidential Veto, 3) George Washington quells the Whiskey Rebellion, 4) Washington's Farewell Address, 5) Franco-American Convention of 1800, 6) The Presidential Election of 1800, 7) The Louisiana Purchase, 8) The 12th Amendment, 9) The War of 1812, 10) The Monroe Doctrine, 11) Election of 1828, 12) Jackson Calls for National Unity, 13) President Jackson Vetos Bank Bill, 14) Martin Van Buren Proposes Independent Treasury System, 15) William Henry Harrison, the "Hero of Tippecanoe", 16) Vice President Tyler becomes President, 17) All except Daniel Webster resign from Tyler's Cabinet, 18) Annexation of Texas, 19) Congress overrides presidential veto, 20) Polk settles border dispute with Mexico, 21) Taylor urges admission of California as a Free State, 22) Millard Fillmore — Perry Arrives in Japan, 23) Gadsden Purchase Treaty signed by Franklin Pierce, 24) Supreme Court decides the Dred Scott case, 25) Abraham Lincoln elected President, 26) Civil War begins, 27) Habeas Corpus privilege challenged, 28) Unlimited freedom of the press is restricted, 29) Lincoln issues Emanicipation Proclamation, 30) Lincoln's Gettysburg Address, 31) Lincoln's Proclamation of Amnesty, 32) Lincoln Assassinated, 33) Andrew Johnson — Tenure of Office Act, 34) Andrew Johnson Challenges the Tenure of Office Act, 35) Impeachment Proceedings against Andrew Johnson, 36) Ulysses S. Grant — Treaty of Washington, 37) Hayes vetoes Appropriation Act, 38) James Garfield Assassinated, 39) Chester A. Arthur — Passage of the Pendleton Act, 40) Tenure of Office Act Repealed, 41) First Internal. Conf. of Amer. States — Benjamin Harrison, 42) Grover Cleveland repeals the Sherman Silver Purchase Act, 43) Pullman Strike, 44) Wm. McKinley urges Congress to declare war on Spain;* **1,758 sets to be issued 1978-1986 at $19.50 each or $1,950.00 a set (100).**

☐ **Presidential Campaign,** *1) 1972-Richard M. Nixon, silver;* **5,007 issued at $15.00 each;** *2) 1972-George S. McGovern, silver;* **2,629 issued at $15.00 each;** *3) 1976-Gerald R. Ford, silver;* **1,721 issued at $22.50 each;** *4) 1976-Jimmy Carter, silver;* **1,659 issued at $22.50 each.**

☐ **Presidential Inaugural,** *sterling silver, 64mm, proof;* **16,302 issued in 1973 at $50.00 each;** *.999 silver, 64mm, proof;* **6,229 issued in 1977 at $85.00 each.**

☐ **Presidential Medals — White House Historical Assoc.,** *set of 37 medals, sterling silver, 46.2 troy ounces per set;* **4,088 sets issued from 1972-1975 at $12.50 each or $462.50 a set (37).**

☐ **Presidential Treasury,** *set of 36 medals, sterling silver, 39mm, regular editions;* **2,525/1,597 sets issued from 1967-1970 at $5.75 each or $207.00 a set (36).**

☐ *Mini Coins, sterling silver;* **88,750 issued at .52 each or $18.75 a set (36).**

☐ *President Gerald R. Ford, (#37): sterling silver, proof, 39mm;* **605 issued in 1974 at $20.00 each.**

☐ *President Jimmy Carter (#38): sterling silver, proof, 39mm;* **issued in 1977 at $20.00 each.**

☐ *President Ronald Reagan (#39): sterling silver, proof, 39mm;* **issued in 1981 at $25.00 each.**

☐ **Presidents & First Ladies,** *set of 80 medals, sterling silver, 4.1 troy ounces per set;* **9,061 sets issued from 1977-1978 at $3.00 each or $240.00 a set (80).**

Presidents And First Ladies, *John F. Kennedy and Jacqueline Kennedy.*

☐ **Pro Football's Immortals,** *set of 50 medals, sterling silver, proof, 39mm; 1) Jim Thorpe, 2) Joe Carr, 3) Wilbur 'Pete' Henry, 4) John 'Paddy' Driscoll, 5) Guy Chamberlain, 6) Harold 'Red' Grange, 7) Ernie Nevers, 8) Steve Owen, 9) Jimmy Conzelman, 10) Earl 'Curly' Lambeau, 11) Johnny 'Blood' McNally, 12) Robert 'Cal' Hubbard, 13) Bronco Nagurski, 14) Bill Hewitt, 15) Ken Strong, 16) Earl 'Dutch' Clark, 17) Clark Hinkle, 18) Cliff Battles, 19) Mel Hein, 20) Dan Fortman, 21) Sid Luckman, 22) George McAfee, 23) Clyde 'Bulldog' Turner, 24) Sammy Baugh, 25) Don Hutson, 26) Bob Waterfield, 27) Bill Dudley, 28) Charley Trippi, 29) Steve Van Buren, 30) Pete Pihos, 31) Marion Motley, 32) Elroy 'Crazylegs' Hirsch, 33) Hugh McElhenny, 34) Bobby Layne, 35) Joe Perry, 36) Otto Graham, 37) Chuck Bednarik, 38) Leo Nomellini, 39) Art Donovan, 40) Bert Bell, 41) Norm Van Brocklin, 42) Emlen Tunnell, 43) Andy Robustelli, 44) Y. A. Tittle, 45) Gino Marchetti, 46) Ollie Matson, 47) Lamar Hunt, 48) Vince Lombardi, 49) Paul Brown, 50) George Halas;* **1,946 sets issued from 1972-1974 at $9.50 each or $475.00 a set (50);** *sterling silver, P/L,* **issued at $9.50 each or $475.00 a set (50);** *12½mm (mini), sterling silver,* **2,735 sets issued from 1976-1977 at $2.75 each or $137.50 a set (50).**

☐ **Rembrandt's Genius,** *set of 50 medals, sterling silver, 51mm, 104 troy ounces per set; 1) Aristotle Contemplating a Bust of Homer, 2) Jeremiah Lamenting the Destruction of Jerusalem, 3) Jacob Wrestling with the Angel, 4) Anatomy Lesson of Dr. Tulp, 5) Prophetess Hannah, 6) Jacob Blessing the Sons of Joseph, 7) Portrait of Saskia, 8) The Money Changer, 9) The Noble Slave, 10) Tobit and Anna with the Kid, 11) Prodigal Son in the Tavern, 12) Polish Rider, 13) Portrait of Jan Uytenbogaert, Remonstrant Preacher, 14) Wedding Feast of Samson, 15) Portrait of Hendrickji Stoffels, 16) Bathsheba with King David's Letter, 17) Night Watch*

(Militia Co. of Capt. Frans Banning Cocq), 18) Saint Jerome Reading, 19) Rembrandt's Son Titus at his Desk, 20) Presentation in the Temple, 21) Three Trees, 22) Shipbuilder and his Wife, 23) Christ Healing the Sick (100 Guilder Print), 24) Self-Portrait, 25) Christ in the Storm on the Sea of Galilee, 26) Portrait of Agatha Bas, Wife of Nicolaes van Bambeeck, 27) Sampling Officials of the Draper's Guild (The Syndics), 28) Good Samaritan, 29) Boy in Fanciful Dress, 30) Portrait of Jan Six, 31) The Flight into Egypt, 32) Danae, 33) Christ Driving Money-Changers out of the Temple, 34) Two Scholars Disputing, 35) Sophonisba Receiving the Poisoned Cup, 36) The Return of the Prodigal Son, 37) Portrait of Nicolaes Ruts, 38) A Woman Bathing in a Stream, 39) Christ before Pilate, 40) Portrait of Cornelis Claeszoon Anslo, 41) Raising of the Cross, 42) Descent from the Cross, 43) The Conspiracy of the Batavians under Claudius Civilis, 44) Self-Portrait, 45) The Bridal Couple, 46) Incredulity of the Apostle Thomas, 47) Portrait of Nicolaas van Bambeeck (Husband of Agatha Bas), 48) Apostle Paul in Prison, 49) The Visitation, 50) Apostle Peter Denying Christ; **5,242 issued from 1972-1976 at $17.00 each or $850.00 a set (50).**

☐ **Roberts Birds,** *10 sets of 5 medals, sterling silver, 10.4 troy ounces per set;* **Series I:** *1) Great Horned Owls,* **14,995 issued;** *2) Chickadees,* **13,448 issued;** *3) Ring-necked Pheasants,* **12,227 issued;** *4) Swallows,* **11,577 issued;** *5) Ospreys,* **12,435 issued; issued in 1970 at $20.00 each or $90.00 a set (5).**

☐ **Series II:** *6) Greater Flamingo,* **11,015 issued;** *7) Peregrine Falcon,* **12,113 issued;** *8) Ruby-Throated Hummingbird,* **12,540 issued;** *9) Ruffed Grouse,* **11,441 issued;** *10) Roadrunner,* **13,124 issued; issued in 1971 at $20.00 each or $90.00 a set (5).**

☐ **Series III:** *11) Bald Eagles,* **11,164 issued;** *12) Black Skimmers,* **7,671 issued;** *13) Pileated Woodpeckers,* **8,000 issued;** *14) Nightingales,* **7,704 issued;** *15) Avocets,* **7,580 issued; issued in 1971 at $20.00 each or $90.00 a set (5).**

☐ **Series IV:** *16) Skylark,* **7,437 issued;** *17) Goshawk,* **8,259 issued;** *18) European Robin,* **7,955 issued;** *19) Woodcock,* **7,544 issued;** *20) Albatross,* **7,474 issued; issued in 1971 at $20.00 each or $90.00 a set (5).**

☐ **Series V:** *21) Blue Jays,* **8,618 issued;** *22) Pelicans,* **8,515 issued;** *23) Brown Thrashers,* **8,550 issued;** *24) Quail,* **9,055 issued;** *25) Barn Owls,* **8,954 issued; issued in 1971 at $20.00 each or $90.00 a set (5).**

☐ **Series VI:** *26) American Egret,* **6,589 issued;** *27) Cardinal,* **7,868 issued;** *28) Swallow-Tailed Kite,* **6,711 issued;** *29) Mourning Dove,* **7,050 issued;** *30) Scissor-Tailed Flycatcher,* **6,642 issued; issued in 1972 at $20.00 each or $90.00 a set (5).**

☐ **Series VII:** *31) House Wren,* **7,029 issued;** *32) California Quail,* **6,460 issued;** *33) Belted Kingfisher,* **6,446 issued;** *34) Marsh Hawk,* **6,436 issued;** *35) Mockingbird,* **7,229 issued; issued in 1973 at $25.00 each or $100.00 a set (5).**

☐ **Series VIII:** *36) Baltimore Oriole,* **6,547 issued;** *37) Wild Turkey,* **5,427 issued;** *38) Black-Necked Stilt,* **5,734 issued;** *39) Sparrow Hawk,* **5,617 issued;** *40) Yellow-Shafted Flicker,* **5,758 issued; issued in 1974 at $30.00 each or $140.00 a set (5).**

☐ **Series IX:** *41) Cedar Waxwing,* **4,455 issued;** *42) Wood Duck,* **4,347 issued;** *43) Great Blue Heron,* **4,404 issued;** *44) Elf Owl,* **4,516 issued;** *45) White-Breasted Nuthatch,* **4,314 issued; issued in 1975 at $40.00 each or $180.00 a set (5).**

☐ **Series X:** *46) White Ibis,* **4,250 issued;** *47) Hawaiian Goose,* **4,246 issued;** *48) Purple Martin,* **4,436 issued;** *49) Bluebird,* **4,677 issued;** *50) Rough-Legged Hawk,* **4,365 issued; issued in 1976 at $40.00 each or $180.00 a set (5).**

☐ **Roberts Zodiac,** *set of 12 medals, sterling silver, proof, 39mm, reeded edge, regular edition; 1) Aries, 2) Taurus, 3) Gemini, 4) Cancer, 5) Leo, 6) Virgo, 7) Libra, 8) Scorpio, 9) Sagittarius, 10) Capricorn, 11) Aquarius, 12) Pisces;* **5,406 sets issued from 1968-1970 at $10.00 each or $120.00 a set (12);** *sterling silver, proof, 39mm, plain edge;* **issued at $18.50 each or $222.00 a set (12);** *sterling silver, proof-like, 39mm;* **1,115 sets issued at 10.00 each or $120.00 a set (12);** *sterling silver, proof, 32mm, reeded edge;* **1,221 issued at $6.50 each or $78.00 a set (12);** *Mini coins,* sterling silver, proof, 13mm; **6,917 sets issued in 1970 at $1.60 each or $19.20 a set (12)**; sterling silver, proof-like, **issued at $1.60 each or $19.20 a set (12).**

☐ **Rockwell's Spirit of Scouting,** set of 12 medals, sterling silver, 9.5 troy ounces per set; 1) A Scout is Trustworthy, 2) A Scout is Loyal, 3) A Scout is Helpful, 4) A Scout is Friendly, 5) A Scout is Courteous, 6) A Scout is Kind, 7) A Scout is Obedient, 8) A Scout is Cheerful, 9) A Scout is Thrifty, 10) A Scout is Brave, 11) A Scout is Clean, 12) A Scout is Reverent; **26,971 sets issued in 1972 at $9.75 each or $117.00 a set (12).**

☐ **Rockwell's Tribute to Robert Frost,** set of 12 medals, sterling silver, 11.5 troy ounces per set; 1) 'After Apple-Picking', 2) 'The Road Not Taken', 3) 'Dust of Snow', 4) 'Stopping by Woods on a Snowy Evening', 5) 'Going for Water', 6) 'Mending Wall', 7) 'The Gift Outright', 8) 'Birches', 9) 'A Mood Apart', 10) 'The Pasture', 11) A Time to Talk', 12) 'The Grindstone'; **12,544 issued in 1974 at $25.00 each or $300.00 a set (12).**

☐ **Saint Christopher Medal,** sterling silver, proof; **1,000 issued from 1968-1974 at $13.00 each.**

☐ **Sandburg's Lincoln,** set of 24 medals, sterling silver, 14.8 troy ounces per set; 1) Lincoln's Childhood, 2) Move to New Salem, 3) Black Hawk War, 4) Elected Member of 9th General Assembly, 5) Lawyer in Springfield, 6) Lincoln & Todd Wedding, 7) Lincoln in Congress, 8) Lincoln-Douglas Debates, 9) Rail Splitter Candidate for President, 10) Lincoln Elected President, 11) Lincoln Grows a Beard, 12) Assassination Plot, 13) Inauguration, 14) Civil War Begins, 15) Lincoln's Son Willie Dies, 16) Lincoln Visits McClellan in Antietom, 17) Emancipation, 18) Gettysburg Address, 19) 13th Amendment, 20) Hampton Roads Conf., 21) Second Inauguration, 22) Civil War Ends, 23) Assassinated, 24) Funeral Train; **407 sets issued from 1977-1978 at $19.50 each or $468.00 a set (24).**

☐ **Science, History,** set of 100 medals, sterling silver, 62 troy ounces per set; 1) Thales of Miletus, 2) Pythagoras, 3) Democritus, 4) Hippocrates, 5) Aristotle, 6) Euclid, 7) Archimedes, 8) Apollonius of Perga, 9) Galen, 10) Ptolemy, 11) Ibn al-Haytham, 12) Ch'In Chiu-Shao, 13) Thomas Bradwardine, 14) Nicole Oresme, 15) Leonardo da Vinci, 16) Nicolaus Copernicus, 17) Paracelsus, 18) Andreas Vesalius, 19) William Gilbert, 20) Tycho Brahe, 21) Francis Bacon, 22) Galileo Galilei, 23) Johannes Kepler, 24) William Harvey, 25) Rene Descartes, 26) Pierre de Fermat, 27) Christiaan Huygens, 28) Robert Boyle, 29) Robert Hooke, 30) Isaac Newton, 31) Gottfried Wilhelm Leibniz, 32) Georg Ernst Stahl, 33) Daniel Bernoulli, 34) Benjamin Franklin, 35) Carl Linnaeus, 36) Leonhard Euler, 37) Georges-Louis Leclerc, Count of Buffon, 38) Albrecht von Haller, 39) James Hutton, 40) Joseph Black, 41) Joseph Priestly, 42) Joseph Louis Lagrange, 43) William Herschel, 44) Antoine L. Lavoisier, 45) Jean Baptiste Lamarck, 46) Alessandro Volta, 47) Gaspard Monge, 48) Pierre Simon de Laplace, 49) John Dalton, 50) Joseph Fourier, 51) George Cuvier, 52) Thomas Young, 53) Andre Ampere, 54) Karl F. Gauss, 55) Joseph Louis Gay-Lussac, 56) Jons Jacob Berzelius, 57) Augustin Fresnel, 58) Augustin Cauchy, 59) Michael Faraday, 60) Karl Ernst von Baer, 61) Joseph Henry, 62) Charles Lyell, 63) Justus von Liebig, 64) Charles Darwin, 65) Claude Bernard, 66) Hermann von Helmholtz, 67) Louis Pasteur, 68) Rudolf Clausius, 69) Gregor Mendel, 70) William Thomson, 71) Bernhard Riemann, 72) James Clark Maxwell, 73) Dmitri Mendelyev, 74) Josiah Willard Gibbs, 75) John William Strutt, 76) Ludwig Boltzmann, 77) Georg Cantor, 78) Wilhelm Conrad Roentgen, 79) Henri Becquerel, 80) Hendrik Antoon Lorentz, 81) Henri Jules Poincare, 82) Joseph John Thomson, 83) Sigmund Freud, 84) Heinrich Rudolph Hertz, 85) Charles Scott Sherrington, 86) Max Planck, 87) Svante August Arrhenius, 88) David Hilbert, 89) Marie Curie, 90) Ernest Rutherford, 91) Albert Einstein, 92) Niels Bohr, 93) Erwin Schrodinger, 94) Otto Heinrich Warburg, 95) John Von Newman, 96) Werner Karl

Heisenberg, 97) Francis Crick, 98) James Dewey Watson, 99) John Bardeen, 100) Paul A. M. Dirac; **1,968 sets issued from 1974-1980 at $14.50 each or $1,450.00 a set (100).**

☐ **Sculptors' Studio,** *set of 20 medals, sterling silver,* **Series I:** *1) Pastorale by Philip Nathan, 2) Lisa by Clayton Blaker, 3) Horses by Jane Lunger, 4) Dutch Country by Vincent Miller, 5) Aeronaut by Ernest Schroeder, 6) Joy and Woe by Ernest Lauser, 7) Big Top by William Shoyer, 8) Maverick by Richard Baldwin, 9) The Opening Door by Norman Nemeth, 10) Steelscape by Herman De Roos, 11) Crown of Thorns by Daniel Caimi, 12) Pandora's Box by Gilroy Roberts, 13) Primavera by Caesar Rufo, 14) Mankind Uber Alles? by Anthony Jones, 15) Albert Schweitzer by James Ponter, 16) Joy of Music by James Ferrell, 17) Father and Mother by Clifford Schule, 18) Kosmos by Harold Faulkner, 19) Charioteer by Richard Renninger, 20) The Sculptor by William Cousins;* **902 sets issued from 1973-1977 at $20.00 each or $400.00 a set (20).**

☐ **Series II:** *set of 26 medals, sterling silver; 1) Metamorphosis by Caesar Rufo, 2) Four Freedoms by Gilroy Roberts, 3) The Voyager by Charles Ross, 4) St. George by Georgann Schroeder, 5) Mummers by James Ferrell, 6) Indelibertypendence by Anthony Jones, 7) Mustangs by James Lunger, 8) Peace by Daniel Stapleford, 9) Lincoln — Charity For All by Clifford Schule, 10) Navajo Sheep-Herder by Richard Baldwin, 11) Alice in Wonderland by Neila Kun, 12) The Guitar Player by Donald Everhart II, 13) Mother Goose by Daniel Caimi, 14) Carousel by Clayton Blaker, 15) Spring Ride by Ernest Schroeder, 16) Double Play by William Shoyer, 17) First Step by Vincent Miller, 18) Communication by George Connelly, 19) The Agony by Richard Renninger, 20) The Puppet Master's Gift by Norman Nemeth, 21) Bird Watcher by Ernest Lauser, 22) Over the Hill by Harold Faulkner, 23) Gift of Life by James Ponter, 24) Nez Perce Squaw and Papoose by Albert F. Michini, 25) The Lord of Life Washes Feet by Alfred Maletsky, 26) Children of the World by Deborah Bell;* **334 sets issued from 1975-1977 at $40.00 each or $1,040.00 a set (26).**

☐ **Shakespeare,** *set of 38 medals, sterling silver, 45mm; 1) Romeo and Juliet, 2) Midsummer Night's Dream, 3) King John, 4) Hamlet, 5) Twelfth Night, 6) King Richard II, 7) Macbeth, 8) Taming of the Shrew, 9) King Henry IV — Part I, 10) King Lear, 11) The Winter's Tale, 12) King Henry IV — Part II, 13) Coriolanus, 14) As You Like It, 15) King Henry V, 16) Timon of Athens, 17) The Tempest, 18) King Henry VI — Part I, 19) Titus Andronicus, 20) Merry Wives of Windsor, 21) King Henry VI — Part II, 22) Pericles, 23) The Comedy of Errors, 24) King Henry VI — Part III, 25) Othello, 26) Merchant of Venice, 27) King Richard III, 28) Cymbeline, 29) Love's Labour's Lost, 30) King Henry VIII, 31) Julius Caesar, 32) Measure for Measure, 33) Trolius and Cressida, 34) 2 Gentlemen of Verona, 35) Anthony and Cleopatra, 36) Much Ado About Nothing, 37) Two Noble Kinsmen, 38) All's Well That Ends Well; 4,053 sets issued from 1971-1974 at $12.00 each or $456.00 a set (38); sterling silver, 32mm;* **639 sets issued from 1979-1982 at $19.50 each or $741.00 a set (38).**

☐ **Signers of the Constitution,** *sets of 40 medals, sterling silver, proof, 36mm; 1) George Washington, 2) John Langdon, 3) Nicholas Gilman, 4) Nathaniel Gorham, 5) Rufus King, 6) William Samuel Johnson, 7) Roger Sherman, 8) Alexander Hamilton, 9) William Livingston, 10) David Brearley, 11) William Paterson, 12) Jonathan Dayton, 13) Benjamin Franklin, 14) Thomas Mifflin, 15) Robert Morris, 16) George Clymer, 17) Thomas Fitzsimmons, 18) Jared Ingersoll, 19) James Wilson, 20) Gouverneur Morris, 21) George Read, 22) Gunning Bedford, Jr., 23) John Dickinson, 24) Richard Bassett, 25) Jacob Broom, 26) James McHenry, 27) Daniel of St. Thomas Jenifer, 28) Daniel Carroll, 29) John Blair, 30) James Madison, Jr., 31) William Blount, 32) Richard Dobbs Spaight, 33) Hugh Williamson, 34) John Rutledge, 35) Charles Cotesworth Pinckney, 36) Charles Pinckney, 37) Pierce Butler, 38) William Few, 39) Abraham Baldwin, 40) William Jackson;* **1,218 sets issued from 1977-1980 at $17.50 each or $700.00 a set (40).**

☐ **Signers of the Declaration of Independence,** *set of 56 medals, sterling silver; 1) John Hancock, 2) Josiah Bartlett, 3) Stephen Hopkins, 4) Roger Sherman, 5) William Floyd, 6) Richard Stockton, 7) Robert Morris, 8) Caesar Rodney, 9) Samuel Chase, 10) Thomas Jefferson, 11) William Hooper, 12) Edward Rutledge, 13) Lyman Hall, 14) William Whipple, 15) Samuel Adams, 16) William Ellery, 17) Samuel Huntington, 18) Philip Livingston, 19) John Witherspoon, 20) Benjamin Rush, 21) George Read, 22) William Paca, 23) Benjamin Harrison, 24) Joseph Hewes, 25) Thomas Heyward, Jr., 26) George Walton, 27) Matthew Thornton, 28) John Adams, 29) William Williams, 30) Francis Lewis, 31) Francis Hopkinson, 32) Benjamin Franklin, 33) Thomas McKean, 34) Thomas Stone, 35) Thomas Nelson, Jr., 36) John Penn, 37) Thomas Lynch, Jr., 38) Robert Treat Paine, 39) Oliver Wolcott, 40) Lewis Morris, 41) John Hart, 42) John Morton, 43) Button Gwinnett, 44) Charles Carroll, 45) Francis Lightfoot Lee, 46) Arthur Middleton, 47) Elbridge Gerry, 48) Abraham Clark, 49) George Clymer, 50) Carter Braxton, 51) James Smith, 52) George Wythe, 53) George Taylor, 54) Richard Henry Lee, 55) James Wilson, 56) George Ross;* **14,035 sets issued from 1972-1976 at $9.50 each or $532.00 a set (56);** *Mini coins, sterling silver;* **14,535 issued at $2.50 each or $140.00 a set (56).**

☐ **Societe Commemorative de Femmes Celebres,** *set of 50 medals, sterling silver, 41.5 troy ounces per set; 1) Joan of Arc, 2) Betsy Ross, 3) Marie Curie, 4) Florence Nightingale, 5) Amelia Earhart, 6) Clara Barton, 7) Pioneer Women of Amer. 8) Dolly Madison, 9) Queen Isabella I, 10) Susan B. Anthony, 11) Women's Armed Forces, 12) Sacajawea, 13) Queen Victoria, 14) Sister Elizabeth Kenny, 15) Molly Pitcher, 16) Evangeline Cory Booth, 17) Helen Keller, 18) Queen Christina of Sweden, 19) Anne Sullivan Macy, 20) Queen Maria Theresa, 21) Jane Addams, 22) Martha Washington, 23) Maria Montessori, 24) Juliette Gordon Low, 25) Mildred Babe Didrikson, 26) Elizabeth Blackwell, 27) Emily Dickinson, 28) Catherine II The Great, 29) Statue of Liberty, 30) Sarah Bernhardt, 31) Pocahontas (Rebecca Rolfe), 32) Queen Elizabeth I, 33) Rachel Carson, 34) Clara Louise Maass, 35) Queen Wilhelmina, 36) Eleanor Roosevelt, 37) Queen Liliuokalini, 38) Julia Ward Howe, 39) Cleopatra, 40) Helen of Troy, 41) Mary E. Walker, 42) Maria Mitchell, 43) Mary, Queen of Scots, 44) Eve, 45) Pearl S. Buck, 46) Louisa May Alcott, 47) Grandma Moses, 48) Laura Secord, 49) Belva Ann Lockwood, 50) The Bronte Sisters;* **3,220 sets issued from 1966-1974 at $6.60/7.25 each or $282.75 a set (50).**

☐ **Societe de la Sculpture de Medalles,** *set of 15 medals, sterling silver, 6.2 troy ounces each; 1) Sports in Sweden by Berndt Helleberg,* **1,002 issued;** *2) New Zealand by James Berry,* **1,561 issued;** *3) Creation of the World by Dagoberto Vasquez,* **1,060 issued;** *4) Noh Player by Takanori Matsuoka,* **872 issued;** *5) Lapland in Summer by J. Leo Holmgren,* **914 issued;** *6) Modern Design by Yves Millecamps,* **742 issued;** *7) Progression by Gustave Fischweiler,* **354 issued;** *8) Boat Against the Waves by Louisa Metz,* **557 issued;** *9) Samba School by Waldir Granado,* **361 issued;** *10) Man in the Field by Francisco Delgado,* **368 issued;** *11) Peace and Tranquility by Julian Harris,* **376 issued;** *12) Copenhagen Castle by Frode Bahnsen,* **308 issued;** *13) Crest of the Wave by Cecil Thomas,* **318 issued;** *14) Bunraku by Shigemi Kawasumi,* **387 issued;** *15) Spirit of Portugal by Joao Fragoso,* **287 issued; issued from 1971-1972 at $50.00 each or $750.00 a set (15).**

☐ **Spacecraft Medals,** *set of 12 medals, fine silver; 1) Gemini, GT-10, 2) Gemini, GT-11, 3) Mercury, Friendship 7, 4) GT-7/6, 5) Mercury, Sigma 7, 6) Apollo 7, 7) Apollo 8, 8) Apollo 9, 9) Mercury, Freedom 7, 10) Gemini 9, 11) Apollo 10, 12) Apollo 11;* **500/600 issued from 1969/1970 at $10.00/12.50 each.**

☐ **Space Flight Emblems, NASA Manned,** *set of 25 medals, sterling silver, 15.7 troy ounces per set; 1) 1) Gemini V, 2) Gemini VI, 3) Gemini VII, 4) Gemini VIII, 5) Gemini IX, 6) Gemini X, 7) Gemini XI, 8) Gemini XII, 9) Apollo VII, 10) Apollo VIII, 11) Apollo IX, 12) Apollo X, 13) Apollo XI, 14) Apollo XII, 15) Apollo XIII, 16) Apollo XIV, 17) Apollo XV, 18) Apollo XVI, 19) Apollo XVII, 20) Skylab Mission, 21) Skylab I, 22)*

Skylab II, 23) Skylab III, 24) Apollo/Soyuz, 25) Apollo/Soyuz; **5,290 sets issued from 1977-1979 at $19.50 each or $487.50 a set (25).**

☐ **Special Commemorative Issues,** *set of 30 medals, sterling silver;* **1970:** *1) Boston Massacre, Bicen.-Bostonian Society, 2) Ringling Brothers & Barnum & Bailey Circus, Centennial, 3) Mayor John V. Lindsay, 2nd Term Inauguration, 4) Ohio State Univ., Centennial, 5) Governor William T. Cahill, Inauguration, 6) American Airlines 747 Astroliner-Inaugural Flight, 7) Apollo XIII, 8) King Memorial Bldg. Ded.-Wilberforce University, 9) Organization of Intenat'l. Numismatics Convention, 10) Pioneers of Space-German-Amer. National Congress, 11) Carpenters' Hall Bicen.-Phila. Conv. & Tourist Bureau, 12) Global Stk. Quotations Ctr., Ded.-Ultronic Systems Corp., 13) Atomic Energy, 25th Ann.-Los Alamos Kiwanis Club, 14) Miss America Pageant, 50th Anniversary, 15) Token & Medal Soc. (TAMS)-10th Annual Convention, 16) Salute to Mexico-Milwaukee World Festival, 17) Edgar Lee Masters, Centen.-Fulton County, Ill. Hist. Soc., 18) America's Cup Races, Centen.-Amer. Prestige Arts, 19) English Speaking Union of the U.S., Golden Jubilee, 20) Surrender of Japan, 25th Ann.-MacArthur Mem. Fdn., 21) Mayflower Landing-Sons & Daughters of the Pilgrims, 22) Beethoven Bicen.-Lincoln Center, 23) Great Mississippi Steamboat Race-Miss. Hist. Soc. of Amer., 24) 1st Scheduled Radio Broadcast, Golden Anniversary-Group W Westinghouse Broadcasting, 25) Voting Rights for Amer. Women, 50th Anniversary-League of Women Voters of the U.S., 26) Robert E. Lee Centen.-Museum of the Confederacy, 27) Martyrdom of Thomas A. Becket, 800th Ann.-American British Numismatic Society, 28) IOTS-TIROS Ded.-RCA Defense Electronic Products, 29) Army & Air Force Exchange Service, 75th Anniversary, 30) General George S. Patton-Cavalry-Armor Foundation;* **7,507 sets issued in 1970 at $6.25 each or $187.50 a set (30).**

☐ **1971:** *sterling silver, set of 36 medals; 1) Phila. Bicen.-Phila. Conv. & Tourist Bureau, 2) Governor Evans Inaug.-Virgin Islands, 3) Dante, 650th Ann.-Italian Culture Council, 4) Governor David Hall Inaug.-Oklahoma, 5) Friendly Sons of St. Patrick, Bicen., 6) Sante Fe Trail, 150th Ann.-New Mexico Hist. Soc., 7) Apollo 14, 8) Greek Independence, 150th Ann.-Order of Ahepa, 9) Johannes Kepler-Hayden Planet., Amer. Museum of Nat. Hist., 10) Walter Reuther-United Auto Workers, 11) Big Brothers of Amer., 25th Anniversary, 12) Lord Rutherford Centen.-Royal Soc. of New Zealand, 13) Arkansas River Waterway Dedication, 14) Disabled Amer. Vet., 50th Anniversary, 15) Sir Walter Scott, 200th Anniversary, 16) Florida Sesquicen.-Pensacola Historical Soc., 17) Igor Stravinsky-Lincoln Center, 18) CARE, 25th Anniversary, 19) Amer. Stock Exchange, 50th Anniversary, 20) Inter.-Tribal Indian Ceremonial, 50th Anniversary, 21) Token & Medal Soc. (TAMS), 1971 Convention, 22) Apollo 15, 23) Peace Corps, 10th Anniversary, 24) DuPont Bicen.-Hagley Museum, Eleutherian Fdn., 25) Clara Barton, 150th Ann.-Amer. Red Cross, 26) Multiple Sclerosis Soc., 25th Anniversary, 27) 26th Amend.-Votes National Committee, 28) Louis Armstrong-New Orleans Jazz Museum, 29) Tob of the Unknown Soldier, 50th Anniversary-Arlington National Cemetery, 30) Pilgrims 1st Thanksgiving, 350th Ann.-Sons & Daughters of the Pilgrims, 31) Whistler's Mother, 100th Ann.-Lowell Art Assoc., 32) South Polar Exped., Diamona Ann.-Canterbury Museum, 33) Mexican Indepen., 150th Ann.-Azteca Numis. Soc., 34) Elizabeth Blackwell-Amer. Medical Women's Assoc., 35) British Columbia Centennial, 36) U.S. Figure Skating Assoc., 50th Anniversary;* **6,281 sets issued in 1971 at $6.60 each or $237.00 a set (36).**

☐ **1972:** *sterling silver, set of 36 medals; 1) Mardi Gras-Mayor of New Orleans, 2) Samuel Adams, 250th Ann.-Bostonian Society, 3) Irish Free State, 50th Ann.-Friendly Sons of St. Patrick, 4) Marshall Plan, 25th Ann.-G. C. Marshall Research Fdn., 5) Castillo de San Marcos, Tricentenary, 6) Maryland State House, Bicen.-Hist. Annapolis Inc., 7) U. S. Grant Sesquicen.-Galena, Ill., C. of C., 8) Watauga Assoc., Bicentennial, 9) Yellowstone Nat. Park, Centen.-Wyoming State Archives, 10) Apollo 16, 11) Amer. Public Health Assoc., 100th Ann., 12) Burning of* the Gaspee, Bicen.-Rhode Island Hist. Soc., 13) Eleanor Roosevelt Library Wing, Dedication, 14) Fiddler on the Roof-Harold Prince Productions, 15) Chief Red Cloud, 150th Ann.-Red Cloud Indian School & Sioux Indian Museum, 16) Pres. Comm. on Employ. of the Handicapped, 25th Ann., 17) Calvin Coolidge, Centennial, 18) Narrow Gauge R.R., Centien.-Nat. R.R. Hist. Assoc., 19) Northbrook, Ill., Skaters, Sapporo Gold Medal Winners, 20) Settlement of the Pig War, Centennial-San Juan Island Historical Park, 21) 1st Supersonic Flight, 25th Ann.-Amer. Aviat. Hist. Soc., 22) U.S. Air Force, 25th Ann.-Air Force Sergeants Assoc., 23) Louis Pasteur, Sesquincen.-Phila. Coll. of Physicians, 24) Communications Satellite Corp., 10th Ann., 25) Discovery of the Dead Sea Scrolls, 25th Ann.-International Bible Collectors Society, 26) Lincoln Memorial, 50th Ann.-Lincoln Memorial Univ., 27) Lawn Tennis, 100th Ann.-U.S. Lawn Tennis Assoc., 28) Brazilian Indepen., 150th Ann.-Brazilian-Amer. Soc., 29) Bismarck, N.D., 100th Ann.-State Hist. Soc. of N.D., 30) Harlan Fiske Stone, 100th Ann.-Chesterfield, N.H., Historical Society, 31) Jackie Robinson, 32) Roman Colosseum, 1900th Ann.-Coloss. Restor. Fund, 33) Rutherford B. Hayes, Sesquicentennial, 34) Igor Sikorsky-Amer. Helicopter Society, 35) Governor Arch A. Moore, Jr., Inaug., West Va., 36) Apollo XVII; **3,861 sets issued in 1972 at $6.60 each or $237.60 a set (36).**

☐ **1973:** set of 36 medals, sterling silver; 1) Old North Church, 250th Ann.-Christ Church in Boston, 2) Birth of Nicholas Copernicus, 500th Ann.-Amer. Museum-Hayden Planetarium, 3) Texas Rangers, 150th Anniversary, 4) Nat. Conf. on Social Welfare, 100th Anniversary, 5) 1st Transcontinental Flight, 50th Anniversary-American Aviation Historical Society, 6) Marquette & Jolliet's Exploration of the Mississippi River, 300th Anniversary-St. Ignace Hist. Soc., 7) Harry S. Truman-Missouri Bicen. Comm., 8) King of Sports Award, 1972, Mark Spitz-Kiwanis Inter., 9) Lyndon B. Johnson-Texas Hist. Association, 10) 1st Numismatic Study Exchange with U.S.S.R.-Citizen Exchange Corps & Numismatic Inter., 11) Miami Dolphins, 1972 NFL Champions-Heart Assoc. of Greater Miami, 12) Bahamas Indepen.-Ranfurly Homes for Children, 13) Conquest of Mt. Everest-Himalayan Trust, New Zealand, 14) Royal Canadian Mounted Police Centennial-Ft. Macleod Historical Assoc., 15) Enrico Caruso, Centen.-Italian Culture Council, 16) Turkish Republic, 50th Ann.-Fdn. of Amer.-Turkish Soc., 17) Birth of Blaise Pascal, 350 Anniversary-Society des Amis de Port Royal, 18) Nat. Gov. Conf., 65th-Nev. Dept. of Econ. Devel., 19) Ben Franklin Arrives in Philadelphia, 250th Ann.-Philadelphia Convention & Tourist Bureau, 20) Birth of Sir Joshua Reynolds, 250th Anniversary-Royal Society of British Sculptors, 21) Monroe Doctrine, 150th Ann.-James Monroe Mem. Lib., 22) Boston Tea Party, Bicen.-Bostonian Society, 23) Token & Medal Society, (TAMS) 1973 Convention, 24) Nat. League of Cities, 50th Congress-Mayor of San Juan, Puerto Rico, 25) 1st Nursing School in the U.S., Centennial-Hunter College-Bellevue School of Nursing, 26) Bosphorus Intercon. Bridge, Dedication-Foundation of Turkish-American Society, 27) 'Night Before Christmas', 150th Ann.-Santa Claus, IN., 28) 1st Transatlantic Broadcast, 50th Ann.-Station KDKA, 29) Discovery of Troy, Centen.-Univ. Museum, Univ. of Pa., 30) Cathedral Church of St. John the Divine, Centen., 31) Senator Hugh Scott, Distinguished Pa. Repub. of the Year, 1973-Pa. Republican Finance Committee, 32) Charleston Museum, Bicentennial, 33) Comet Kohoutek-Adler Planetarium, 34) Birth of Sir William Blackstone, 250th Ann.-American Judicature Society, 35) Birth of Inigo Jones, 400th Ann.-Soc. of Arch. Hist., 36) Pablo Casals Memorial-U.N. International School; **3,955 sets issued in 1973 at $6.60 each or $237.60 a set (36).**

☐ **1974:** set of 36 medals, sterling silver; 1) Franklin Institute, 150th Anniversary, 2) Governor Brendan T. Byrne, Inauguration (N.J.), 3) Confraternity of the Holy Name of Jesus, 700th Ann.-Nat. Assoc. of the Holy Name Soc. (Pope Gregory X), 4) Governor George C. Wallace, 5) Birth of Harry Houdini, Centen.-Soc. of Amer. Magicians, 6) North Atlantic Treaty Org. (NATO), 25th Ann., 7) 1st Around-the-World Flight, 50th Ann. (Douglas World Cruiser)-Amer. Aviation Historical Soc., 8)

Birth of Thomas J. 'Stonewall' Jackson, 150th Ann.-United Daughters of the Confederacy, 9) Birth of Robert Frost, Centen.-Poetry Soc. of Amer., 10) Lawn Tennis, Centen.-U.S. Lawn Tennis Assoc., 11) Discovery of Oxygen, Bicen.-Amer. Chemical Soc., 12) Nat. Coin Week, 50th Ann.-Amer. Numismatic Assoc., 13) 1st Permanent Settlement in the Colony of New Netherlands, 350th Ann.-Holland Soc. of N.Y., 14) Signing of the 1st Wts. & Measures Law, 175th Ann.-Nat. Conf. on Wts. & Measures (U.S. Comm. Dept.), 15) Nat. Woman's Christian Temperance Union, Centen., 16) Dwelling built by Father Marquette at Chicago, 300th Ann., 17) Sec.-Gen. Kurt Waldheim, Inter. Statesman Award-World Affairs Council, Phila. Pa., 18) King of Sports Award, 1973, O. J. Simpson-Kiwanis Inter., 19) Birth of Guglielmo Marconi, Centen.-Centro Radioelettrico Sperimentale, Bologna, Italy, 20) Token & Medal Soc. (TAMS), 1974 Convention, Florida, 21) The Lambs, Centennial, New York City, 22) Expo '74-Spokane World's Fair, 23) Raid on Ft. William & Mary, Bicen.-Sons of the Amer. Revol., 24) Birth of Herbert Hoover, Centen.-Hoover Institution on War, Revolution & Peace, 25) Discov. of the Great Salt Lake, 150th Ann.-Utah Hist. Soc., 26) Desig. of Virginia as Royal Colony, 350th Ann. (James I)-Jamestown Foundation, 27) Birth of Sir Winston Churchill, Centennial, 28) Children to Children, 10th Ann. (Jean Dixon), 29) Duke Ellington Memorial, 30) Carpenters' Co. of Phila., 250th Anniversary, 31) U.S. Governors' Tour of China-Nat. Governors' Conf., 32) Army-Navy Game, 75th Ann.- Naval Academy Athletic Assoc. & Army Athletic Assoc., 33) Birth of Chaim Weizmann, Centen.-Magen David Adom, 34) Arrival of Shakers in America, Bicentennial, 35) Birth of Robert the Bruce, 700th Ann.-Amer. Scottish Fdn., 36) Scouter of the Year Award, 1974, President Gerald R. Ford-Boy Scouts of America; **3,074 issued in 1974 at $7.25 each or $261.00 a set (36).**

☐ **1975:** *set of 36 medals, sterling silver; 1) Shot Heard Round the World-Concord, Mass., 2) N.Y. Soc. for the Prevention of Cruelty to Children, Centen., 3) U.S. Marine Corps Bicentennial, 4) Bldg. of the Wilderness Road, Bicen.-Knox County, Ky., 5) Birth of Albert Schweitzer, Centennial, 6) Open. of the Erie Canal, 150th Ann.-Amer. Canal Soc., 7) Paul Revere's Ride, Bicen.-Bostonian Soc., 8) Bob Hope 5-Star Civilian Award-Valley Forge Military Academy & Junior College, 9) Society of American Foresters, 75th Anniversary, 10) William T. Kerr, Founder of Flag Day-Yeadon, Pa., 11) Battle of Bunker Hill, Bicentennial, 12) U.S. Governors' Tour of Russia-Nat. Governors' Conf., 13) Cities of N.Y. & Amsterdam, 350th Ann.-New Amsterdam Anniversary Foundation, 14) Birth of Andre Ampere, Bicentennial, 15) Jack Benny Memorial, 16) Patrick Henry's Speech, Bicen.-Hist. Richmond Fdn., 17) Tribute to Project Hope—People-to-People Fdn., 18) Token & Medal Society (TAMS), 1975 Convention, 19) Canoniz. of Elizabeth A. Seton-Daughters of Charity, 20) First Ford Air Reliability Tour, 50th Ann.-American Aviation Historical Society, 21) Washington's Appointment as Commander in Chief of the Continental Army, Bicen.-Freedoms Foundation, 22) Nat. Conf. of State Legislatures-1st Meeting, 23) United Service Org. (U.S.O.), Bicentennial, 24) Marco Polo Arrives in China, 700th Ann.-Explorers Club, 25) 2nd Continental Congress, Bicen.-Indepen. Hall Assoc., 26) Hirohito, Emperor of Japan, Visits U.S., 27) Birth of Vasco Nunez de Balboa, 500th Ann.-American Geographical Society, 28) Birth of D. W. Griffith, Centen.-Lillian Gish, 29) Ben Franklin's Appointment as 1st Postmaster Gen., Bicen-Pa. Postal Association, 30) Birth of Michelangelo, 500 Ann.-Amer.-Italy Society, 31) 1st Practical Submarine, 100th Ann.-Paterson Museum, 32) Stockton and Darlington Railway, 500th Anniversary-Railway & Locomotive Historical Society, Inc., 33) Birth of Jane Austen, 200th Ann.-Jane Austen Soc., 34) 1st Printing of the Canterbury Tales, 500th Ann.-Great Books, 35) Rebuilding of St. Paul's Cathedral, 300th Ann., 36) 1st Swim Across the English Channel, 100th Ann.-Channel Swimming Assoc.;* **1,872 sets issued in 1975 at 11.50 each or $414.00 a set (36).**

☐ **1976:** *set of 36 medals, sterling silver; 1) Mummers Parade, 75th Ann.-Phila String Bands, 2) Thomas Paine's Pamphlet 'Common Sense' 200th Ann.-Huguenot-Thomas Paine Historical Assoc., 3) Stephen Foster's Birth, 150th Ann., 4) 1st Flight over the North Pole, 50th Ann.-American Aviation Historical Society, 5) Bacon's Rebellion, 300th Ann.-Jamestown Fdn., 6) Common. of Australia, 75th Ann.-Australian Numis. Soc., 7) American Chemical Society, 100th Ann., 8) Invention of the Telephone, 100th Ann.-Telephone Pioneers of America, 9) Birth of Nurse Clara Maass, 100th Ann.-RN Mag. & Clara Maass Memorial Hospital, 10) Amer. Library Assoc., 100th Ann., 11) 1st Liquid-Fuel Rocket, 50th Ann.-Nat. Space Inst., 12) Va. Becomes an Indepen. Commonwealth-Williamsburg James City Co. Bicen. Comm., 13) Pub. of 'Gulliver's Travels', 250th Ann.-Irish American Cultural Institute, 14) Bldg. of Main Line Canal, 150th Ann.-Amer. Canal Soc., 15) St. Photios Shrine-Greek Orthodox Arch. of Amer. 16) Common Faith-Common Law-American Bar Assoc., 17) Nationwide Student Comp. 'My America'-Bicentennial Committee of Pennsylvania, 18) Hampden-Sydney College, 200th Ann., 19) Token and Medal Soc. Convention, 1976, 20) Death of St. Francis of Assisi, 750th Ann.-Franciscan Fathers of U.S., 21) Green Bay's Tank Cottage, 200th Ann.-Brown County Historical Society, 22) Amer. Humane Assoc., 100th Ann. Meet., 23) Pub. of 'Tom Sawyer', 100th Ann.-Mark Twain Mem., 24) No Greater Love, 25) Marquis de Lafayette Joins Amer. Cause for Freedom-American Friends of Lafayette, 26) 1st Use of Sound in Motion Picture Industry-Warner Bros., 27) San Juan Capistrano, 200th Ann., 28) Gertrude Ederle 1st Woman to Swim English Channel-Channel Swimmer Assoc., 29) John Hopkins, 100th Ann.-John Hopkins Univ., 30) Duke Paoa Kahanamoku, Father of Modern Surfing-American Surfing Assoc., 31) Consec. of St. Peter's Basilica, 350th Ann., The Vatican, 32) Field Marshal Viscount Montgomery-Middle East Forces Veteran's Assoc., 33) New York's Central Park, 100th Ann.-National Recreation and Park Assoc.-Wheelman, 34) Bicycling, 35) America's First Railroad Steam Locomotive, 150th Ann., 36) Meeting Susan B. Anthony & Eliz. C. Stanton, 125th Ann.;* **1,596 sets issued in 1976 at 13.50 each or $486.00 a set (36).**

☐ **Special Franklin Mint Issues, 1966,** *fine silver, proof, 39mm,* **177 issued;** *fine silver, P/L, 39mm,* **60 issued;** *sterling silver, proof, 39mm,* **350 issued at $5.00 each;** *sterling silver, P/L, 39mm,* **100 issued;** *nickel silver, proof, 39mm,* **3,255 issued at $2.00 each;** *nickel silver, P/L, 39mm,* **789 issued;** *fine silver, proof, 6mm,* **708 issued at $1.00 each;** *fine silver, P/L, 6mm,* **1,387 issued at .50 each. 1967,** *fine silver, proof, 39mm,* **705 issued;** *fine silver, P/L, 39mm,* **5 issued;** *fine silver, antique, 39mm,* **5 issued;** *fine silver, mint, 39mm,* **5 issued; nickel silver, proof, 39mm,** **700 issued;** *nickel silver, P/L, 39mm,* **2,100 issued;** *nickel silver, antique, 39mm,* **100 issued. 1968,** *sterling silver, proof, 39mm,* **110 issued;** *nickel silver, P/L, 39mm,* **872 issued;** *nickel silver, antique, 39mm,* **111 issued; sterling silver, P/L, 10mm,** **4,032 issued at $1.00 each. 1969,** *nickel silver, P/L, 39mm,* **5,252 issued;** *sterling silver, proof, 39mm,* **200 issued. 1970,** *sterling silver, proof, 39mm,* **200 issued;** *nickel silver, P/L, 39mm,* **4,250 issued;** *nickel silver, mint, 39mm,* **500 issued. 1971,** *sterling silver, proof, 39mm,* **1,000 issued;** *sterling silver, P/L, 39mm,* **28,050 issued; nickel silver, mint, 39mm,** **2,650 issued; sterling silver, P/L, 26mm,** **75 issued;** *sterling silver, mint, 26mm,* **75 issued. 1972,** *sterling silver, proof, 39mm,* **180 issued; sterling silver, P/L, 39mm,** **300 issued;** *nickel silver, mint, 39mm,* **550 issued;** *nickel silver, mint, 32mm,* **550 issued;** *sterling silver, P/L, 26mm,* **75 issued. 1973,** *sterling silver, proof, 39mm,* **800 issued; sterling silver, P/L, 39mm,** **50 issued;** *sterling silver, mint, 39mm,* **100 issued;** *nickel silver, P/L, 39mm,* **250 issued;** *sterling silver, P/L, 26mm,* **156 issued. 1974,** *sterling silver, proof, 39mm,* **300 issued;** *sterling silver, P/L, 39mm,* **300 issued;** *sterling silver, mint, 39mm,* **300 issued;** *sterling silver, P/L, 26mm,* **150 issued. 1975,** *sterling silver, P/L, 26mm,* **150 issued. 1976,** *sterling silver, P/L, 26mm,* **150 issued. 1977,** *sterling silver, proof, 39mm,* **100 issued;** *sterling silver, P/L, 26mm,* **100 issued. 1978** *(without date), sterling silver, proof, 39mm,*

51 issued; *sterling silver, P/L, 26mm,* **25 issued.** *1966, sterling silver, P/L, 45mm,* **545 issued;** *fine silver, proof, 39mm,* **25 issued;** *sterling silver, proof, 39mm,* **100 issued;** *fine silver, proof, 39mm,* **200 issued;** *sterling silver, proof, 39mm,* **10 issued;** *nickel silver, P/L, 39mm,* **501 issued;** *nickel silver, P/L, 39mm, 802 issued.* **1967,** *sterling silver, proof, 39mm,* **376 issued;** *nickel silver, P/L, 39mm,* **3,750 issued.** *1969, sterling silver, proof, 39mm,* **266 issued;** *nickel silver, mint, 39mm,* **1,215 issued;** *sterling silver, proof, 39mm,* **526 issued;** *nickel silver, mint, 39mm,* **3,028 issued.** *1970, sterling silver, proof, 39mm, (PNC),* **10,323 issued at $10.00 each;** *nickel silver, P/L, 39mm,* **3,550 issued.** *1972, sterling silver, proof, 39mm,* **75 issued.** *1973, sterling silver, proof, 39mm, (PNC),* **5,856 issued at $12.50 each;** *sterling silver, proof, 39mm,* **202 issued.** *1974, sterling silver, proof, 39mm,* **500 issued.**

☐ **Special Private Issues,** *7) Pres. James Buchannan-Red Rose Coin Club, fine silver, proof, 39-mm,* **400 issued at $3.00 each;** *11) Prince Philip, Royal Visit-Variety Clubs of N. Amer., fine silver, proof, 37mm,* **2,002 issued at $10.00 each;** *13) Diamond Jubilee-Collingdale, Pa., sterling silver, proof, 39mm,* **100 issued at $2.50 each;** *21) Crown of Liberty-Dalai Lama, fine silver, proof, 39mm,* **100 issued at $20.00 each;** *23) Royal Coin of Liber.-Yugoslav. Gov't. in Exile, fine silver, proof, 39mm,* **803 issued at $25.00 each;** *sterling silver, proof, 39mm,* **738 issued at $5.00 each;** *24) New York Lions Club, 50th Ann., fine silver, proof, 39mm,* **250 issued at $2.50 each;** *nickel silver, P/L, 39mm,* **551 issued at $1.00 each;** *nickel silver, mint, 39mm,* **2,499 issued at $1.00 each;** *29) Hays, Kansas, Centen. $1-Ft. Hays Coin Club, fine silver, proof, 39mm,* **400 issued at $3.00 each;** *31) Ft. Walters, Tx.-Mineral Wells Coin Club, fine silver, proof, 32mm,* **250 isissued at $3.00 each;** *32) State of Ill., Sesquicen., fine silver, proof, 39mm,* **10,050 issued at $3.00 each;** *34) C. C. Sanderson-West Chester Coin Club, fine silver, proof, 39mm,* **300 issued at $3.00 each;** *36) Oak Ridge, Tenn., 25th Ann., fine silver, P/L, 39mm,* **800 issued at $3.00 each;** *37) Aberdeen Proving Ground, Md., Diamond Jub., sterling silver, proof, 39mm,* **101 issued at $2.50 each;** *38) Mystery Car Winner, 1967-Gates Rubber Co., nickel silver, P/L, 39mm,* **551 issued at .80 each;** *nickel silver, mint, 39mm,* **32,208 issued;** *40) Token & Medal Soc. (TAMS), 1967 Conv., sterling silver, proof, 39mm,* **100 issued at $5.00 each;** *41) Atkinson, N.H., Bicen., sterling silver, antique, 39mm,* **509 issued at $7.50 each;** *42) Father Flanagan's Boys' Home, 50th Ann., fine silver, proof, 39mm,* **516 issued at $15.00 each;** *44) Peace & Friendship-Miccosukee Tribe, fine silver, proof, 39mm,* **401 issued at $20.00 each;** *47) Moshe Dayan-Internat. Numis. Agency, fine silver, proof, 39mm,* **501 issued at $20.00 each;** *sterling silver, proof, 39mm,* **1,016 issued at $5.00 each;** *48) Itzhak Rabin-Internat. Numis. Agency, fine silver, proof, 39mm,* **506 issued at $20.00 each;** *49) Project Apollo Memorial-Spacecraft Medals, fine silver, proof, 39mm,* **511 issued at $10.00 each;** *50) Phila. Flyers, Opening Game, 1967, nickel silver, P/L, 39mm,* **964 issued at $1.00 each;** *nickel silver, mint, 39mm,* **24,306 issued at $1.00 each;** *51) Fulton Opera House-Red Rose Coin Club, fine silver, proof, 39mm,* **400 issued at $5.00 each;** *52) Biosciences Info. Serv., 40th Ann., sterling silver, P/L, 32mm,* **1,050 issued;** *53) St. Louis Cardinals, World Series Victory, fine silver, proof, 39mm,* **110 issued at $10.00 each;** *55) Kosciuszko-Pilsudski-Internat. Numis. Agency, fine silver, proof, 39mm,* **502 issued at $20.00 each;** *57) Abba Eban-Journal of Israel Numis., sterling silver, proof, 39mm,* **1,010 issued at $20.00 each;** *sterling silver, P/L, 39mm,* **1,500 issued at $16.00 each;** *58) $1 Coin-Auburn, Wash., C. of C., nickel silver, P/L, 32mm,* **676 issued at $1.00 each;** *nickel silver, mint, 32mm,* **5,000 issued at $1.00 each;** *60) Columban Fathers, 50th Ann., nickel silver, P/L, 39mm,* **625 issued at .95 each;** *nickel silver, mint, 39mm,* **6,186 issued at .90 each;** *61) U.S. Bronze Powders, Inc., 50th Ann., sterling silver, mint, 39mm,* **239 issued;** *63) Cain Township, Pa., Centen., fine silver, P/L, 39mm,* **1,277 issued at $10.00 each;** *64) 2nd Delaware Memorial Bridge Opening, sterling silver, proof, 39mm,* **1,457 issued;** *65) Clifton Precision Prod., sterling silver, P/L, 32mm,* **25 issued;** *66) Summerfest*

1968-Milwaukee World Fest., nickel silver, mint, 39mm, **1,024 issued at $1.00 each;** *68) Landsteiner Centen.-Ortho Diagnostics, sterling silver, P/L, 39mm,* **450 issued at $2.50 each;** *nickel silver, P/L, 39mm,* **695 issued at $1.00 each;** *nickel silver, mint, 39mm,* **7,580 issued at** *.75 each; 69) Citizens Nat. Bank, Tx., Centen., sterling silver, P/L, 39mm,* **125 issued at $2.50 each;** *71) 1968 Dollar-Midland Empire State* ☐ *Fair, sterling silver, P/L, 39mm,* **250 issued at $2.50 each;** *nickel silver, P/L, 39mm,* **1,149 issued at $1.00 each;** *nickel silver, mint, 39mm,* **15,063 issued at** *.90 each; 72) Token & Medal Soc. (TAMS), 1968 Conv., sterling silver, P/L, 39mm,* **710 issued at $5.00 each;** *73) Lavan Island Terminal Inaug., sterling silver, P/L, 39mm,* **305 issued at $2.50 each;** *74) Lancaster, Pa., Sesquicen.-Red Rose Coin Club, fine silver, proof, 39mm,* **503 issued at $3.00 each;** *76) Palatine Nat. Bank, 25th Ann., sterling silver, P/L, 39mm,* **211 issued at $2.50 each;** *78) Colonial Heights Aeries (F.O.E.), Tenn., nickel silver, P/L, 39mm,* **785 issued at** *.90 each; nickel silver, mint, 39mm,* **2,500 issued;** *80) YF-12 Aircraft-Lockheed Employ. Coin Club, sterling silver, proof, 39mm,* **1,059 issued at $2.50 each;** *81)Medal of Meditation-Medallascopes, sterling silver, proof, 39mm,* **256 issued at $20.00 each;** *nickel silver, P/L, 39mm,* **702 issued at $7.50 each;** *nickel silver, mint, 39mm,* **2,500 issued at $5.00 each;** *82) Ft. Sil Centen., sterling silver, proof, 39mm,* **3,716 issued at $2.50 each;** *84) Johnson City, Tn., Centen. sterling silver, P/L, 39mm,* **999 issued at $2.50 each;** *nickel silver, P/L, 39mm,* **680 issued at $1.00 each;** *nickel silver, mint, 39mm,* **19,654 issued at $1.00 each;** *85) Chanuka, 1968-Journal of Israel Numis., sterling silver, proof, 32mm,* **1,109 issued at $16.00 each;** *88) Lithuanian Restoration, 50th Ann., sterling silver, P/L, 39mm,* **2,060 issued at $5.00 each;** *90) Gift Coin-Basco Jewelers (Bird), nickel silver, mint, 32mm,* **1,504 issued;** *92) Micro Tool Co., nickel silver, P/L, 39mm,* **1,094 issued;** *93) Metroliner Inaug.-Penn Central Trans. Co., sterling silver, proof, 39mm,* **2,181 issued at $6.00 each;** *sterling silver, P/L, 39mm,* **200 issued at $6.00 each;** *nickel silver, P/L, 39mm,* **500 issued at $2.00 each;** *nickel silver, mint, 39mm,* **9,649 issued at $2.00 each;** *94) Colorado Recreation Land, sterling silver, proof, 39mm,* **2,181 issued at $6.00 each;** *nickel silver, mint, 39mm,* **5,000 issued at $1.50 each;** *95) Summit, N.J., Centen. sterling silver, proof, 39mm,* **2,181 issued at $6.00 each;** *sterling silver, P/L, 39mm,* **126 issued at $6.00 each;** **nickel silver, P/L, 39mm,** **137 issued at $2.00 each;** *96) Refinery Ded.-Liberia Refin. Co., sterling silver, proof, 36mm,* **3,405 issued at $6.00 each;** *97) NATO-SACLANT, 20th Ann.-Supr. All. Comm., Atlantic, sterling silver, proof, 39mm,* **2,231 issued at $6.00 each;** **nickel silver, P/L, 39mm,** **5,200 issued at $2.00 each;** *98) Coach Adolph Rupp-Univ. of Ky. Wildcats, sterling silver, proof, 39mm,* **2,881 issued at $6.00 each;** *99) Derby, Kansas, Centen., sterling silver, proof, 39mm,* **2,681 issued at $6.00 each;** *nickel silver, mint, 39mm,* **250 issued at $1.00 each;** *100) Wayne, Mich., Centen., sterling silver, proof, 39mm,* **2,186 issued at $6.00 each;** *nickel silver, mint, 39mm,* **5,000 issued at $1.50 each;** *101) Gen. Develop. Corp., Hdqtr. Ded, sterling silver, proof, 39mm, 2,181 issued at $6.00 each; 102) 1st Transatlantic Flight, 50th Ann.-Dep. Chief of Naval Oper. for Air, sterling silver, proof, 39mm,* **2,181 issued at $6.00 each;** *nickel silver, mint, 39mm,* **800 issued at $1.50 each;** *103) Sister Cities of Indep.-Jnl. of Israel Numis., sterling silver, proof, 39mm,* **3,181 issued at $20.00 each;** *104) Golden Spike Centen.-Rlwy. & Loco. Hist. Soc., sterling silver, proof, 39mm,* **3,181 issued at $20.00 each;** *105) Michelson Hall Ded.-U.S. Naval Acad. Alumni Assoc., sterling silver, proof, 39mm,* **2,237 issued at $6.00 each;** *106) Norwich Univ., Vt., Sesquicen., sterling silver, proof, 39mm,* **2,181 issued at $6.00 each;** *107) Elko, Nevada, Centen., sterling silver, proof, 39mm,* **2,481 issued at $6.00 each;** *108) Air Force Inst. of Tech., 50th Ann., sterling silver, proof, 39mm,* **2,281 issued at $6.00 each;** *109) Upland, Pa., Centen., sterling silver, proof, 39mm,* **2,181 issued at $6.00 each;** *nickel silver, mint, 39mm,* **2,600 issued at $1.50 each;** *110) Ft. Mifflin-Shackamaxon Soc., sterling silver, proof, 39mm,* **2,205 issued at $6.00 each;** *111) Eisenhower/D-Day-Amer. Legion, sterling silver, proof,*

39mm, **2,326 issued at $6.00 each;** *nickel silver, mint, 39mm,* **10,205 issued at $1.50 each;** *112) Summerfest, 1969-Milwaukee World Fest. sterling silver, proof, 39mm,* **2,181 issued at $6.00 each;** *nickel silver, proof, 39mm,* **1,250 issued at $1.00 each;** *113) Amer. Indian Marine-4th Marine Div., sterling silver, proof, 39mm,* **2,181 issued at $6.00 each;** *nickel silver, mint, 39mm,* **2,500 issued at $1.00 each;** *114) Gulfstream Drift Mission-Grumman Aircraft Corp., sterling silver, proof, 39mm,* **2,181 issued at $6.00 each;** *115) Gov. Richard Oglivie Inaug.-Ill. State Repub. Central Comm., sterling silver, proof, 39mm,* **3,181 issued at $6.00 each;** *116) Orange County, Ca., Bicen., sterling silver, proof, 39mm,* **4,681 issued at $6.00 each;** *117) Santa Catalina Island, 50th Ann. of Air Service, sterling silver, P/L, 39mm,* **2,281 issued at $6.00 each;** *118) Ft. Wayne, Indiana, 175th Ann., sterling silver, proof, 39mm,* **2,256 issued at $6.00 each;** *nickel silver, mint, 39mm,* **1,100 issued at $1.00 each;** *119) Delaware State Educ. Assoc., 50th Ann., sterling silver, proof, 39mm,* **2,301 issued at $6.00 each;** *120) Calif. Mission Country, Bicen., sterling silver, proof, 39mm,* **2,181 issued at $6.00 each;** *121) Inter. Assoc. of Ptg. House Craftsmen, 50th Ann., sterling silver, proof, 39mm,* **2,481 issued at $6.00 each;** *122) 1969 Dollar-Midland Empire State Fair, sterling silver, proof, 39mm,* **2,481 issued at $6.00 each;** *123) Reded. of 'Old Dorm'-Gettysburg, Coll., sterling silver, proof, 39mm,* **3,182 issued at $6.00 each;** *124) Nat. Easter Seal Soc., 50th Ann., sterling silver, proof, 39mm,* **2,201 issued at $6.00 each;** *nickel silver, mint, 39mm,* **2,100 issued at $1.00 each;** *125) New Zealand Bicen.-Nuphil Assoc., sterling silver, proof, 39mm,* **2,183 issued at $6.00 each;** *nickel silver, mint, 39mm,* **2,000 issued at $2.00 each;** *126) Alum. Co. of Amer., 50 Years of Research, sterling silver, proof, 39mm,* **2,181 issued at $6.00 each;** *127) Daniel Boone, Bicen., sterling silver, proof, 39mm,* **2,581 issued at $6.00 each;** *128) Return of the A.E.F. 50th Ann.-Int. Numis. Agency, fine silver, proof, 39mm,* **700 issued at $10.00 each;** *sterling silver, proof, 39mm,* **2,181 issued at $6.00 each;** *nickel silver, mint, 39mm,* **600 issued at $1.00 each;** *129) 1st Moon Landing-99 Co., sterling silver, proof, 39mm,* **2,181 issued at $6.00 each;** *130) Dwight D. Eisenhower-Korean Cultural & Freedom Fdn. sterling silver, proof, 39mm,* **2,281 issued at $6.00 each;** *131) N.Y. Jets World Champs, 1969-Comm. Corp. of N.A., sterling silver, proof, 39mm,* **2,381 issued at $6.00 each;** *132) Flying Scotsman-McCormick-Goldsmith Mrktg., sterling silver, proof, 39mm,* **2,181 issued at $6.00 each;** *133)* **William Penn-Phila. Conv. & Tourist Bur., & Continental Bk. & Trust Co., sterling silver, proof, 39mm, 750 issued at $10.00 each;** *134) Corpus Cristi, Texas, 450th Ann., fine silver, proof, 39mm,* **750 issued at $10.00 each;** *135) Tokens & Medals Soc. (TAMS), 1969 Conv., sterling silver, proof, 39mm,* **2,356 issued at $6.00 each;** *136) Good Shepherd Lutheran Home of the West, sterling silver, proof, 39mm,* **2,331 issued at $6.00 each;** *137) United Daughters of the Confed., 75th Ann., sterling silver, proof, 39mm,* **2,181 issued at $6.00 each;** *sterling silver, mint, 39mm,* **24 issued at $5.00 each;** *138) Curacao Neth. Antilles, Demo. Party, 25th Ann., sterling silver, proof, 39mm,* **2,181 issued at $6.00 each;** *nickel silver, mint, 39mm,* **10,000 issued at $1.00 each;** *139) Admiral Arleigh Burke-Boy Scouts of Amer., sterling silver, proof, 39mm,* **2,181 issued at $6.00 each;** *140) Boston Univ., 100th Ann., sterling silver, proof, 39mm,* **2,193 issued at $6.00 each;** *141) Club Cal-Neva, Premium Token, sterling silver, proof, 39mm,* **2,181 issued at $6.00 each;** *142) Apollo XI-20th Cent. Fox Film Corp., sterling silver, proof, 39mm,* **2,281 issued at $6.00 each;** *143) 1st Transcont. Rail-Air Service, sterling silver, proof, 39mm,* **2,205 issued at $6.00 each;** *nickel silver, mint, 32mm,* **10,100 issued at $1.00 each.**

☐ **Sports History, American, 100 Greatest Events,** *set of 100 medals, sterling silver, 35 troy ounces per set; 1) Rutgers vs. Princeton, 2) Sullivan vs. Kilrain, 3) Christy Mathewson, 4) Cy Young, 5) Jim Thorpe, 6) Rube Marquard, 7) Dorais to Rockne, 8) Francis Quimet, 9) Boston Braves, 10) Ty Cobb, 11) Bill Wambganas, 12) Earle Sande-Man O'War, 13) Original Celtics, 14) Dempsey-Firpo, 15) Red Grange, 16) John B. Kelly, 17) Johnny Weissmuller, 18) Grover Cleveland Alexander, 19) Ger-*

trude Ederle, 20) Dempsey vs. Tunney, 21) Walter Johnson, 22) Bobby Jones, 23) Babe Ruth (60 homers), 24) Knute Rockne, 25) Lester Patrick, 26) Bill Tilden, 27) Babe Ruth (world series), 28) Babe Didrikson, 29) Lou Gehrig, 30) Helen Hull Jacobs, 31) Gene Sarazon, 32) Jesse Owens (Track & Field), 33) Jesse Owens (Olympics), 34) Budge vs. Von Gramm, 35) Seabiscuit vs. War Admiral, 36) Bob Feller, 37) Lou Gehrig, 38) Bears vs. Redskins, 39) Wilbur Shaw, 40) Ted Williams, 41) Maurice Richard, 42) Byron Nelson, 43) West Point vs. Notre Dame, 44) Cookie Lavagetto, 45) Jack Kramer, 46) Jackie Robinson, 47) West Point vs. Columbia, 48) Eddie Arcaro; 1,196 sets to be issued from 1977-1985 at $12.50 each or $1,250.00 each.

☐ **States of the Union,** set of 50 medals, sterling silver, 32mm, proof; 30,422 sets issued from 1969-1970 at $3.75 each or $187.50 a set (50); sterling silver, P/L, 1,853 sets issued at $4.25 each or $212.50 a set (50); Governor's Editions, sterling silver, 866 sets issued from 1970-1972 at $8.75 each or $437.50 a set (50); Mini-coins, sterling silver, 23,449 sets issued in 1969 at .75 each or $37.50 a set (50).

☐ **States of the Union Silverseals,** set of 50 medals, sterling silver, 1" - 2" in diameter, page size 8¼" x 11"; 2,905 sets issued at $14.50 each or $725.00 a set (50).

☐ **States of the Union Treasures,** set of 50 medals, sterling silver, proof, 39mm; 743 sets to be issued from 1979-1983 at $25.00 each or $1,250.00 a set (50).

☐ **Ten Greatest Men of American Business,** set of 10 medals, sterling silver, 8.3 troy ounces per set; 1) Benjamin Franklin, 2) John D. Rockefeller, Sr., 3) Andrew Carnegie, 4) Alexander Graham Bell, 5) George Eastman, 6) Thomas Alva Edison, 7) Henry Ford, 8) Thomas J. Watson, Sr., 9) Bernard Baruch, 10) Walt Disney; 266 sets issued in 1977 at $9.50 each or $95.00 a set (10).

☐ **Texas Under Six Flags,** set of 50 medals, sterling silver, 64.5 troy ounces per set; 1) dePineda Explores Texas Coastline, 2) deVaca Shipwrecked on Galveston Island, 3) deVaca Escapes into Texas Interior, 4) Coronado in Search of 7 Cities of Cibola, 5) Ysleta, Oldest Permanent Settlement in Texas, 6) LaSalle Landing at Matagorda Bay, 7) Fort St. Louis Established by LaSalle, 8) LaSalle Ambushed and Slain While Exploring, 9) San Francisco de Los Tejas Mission Founded, 10) El Camino Real, The Old San Antonio Road, 11) Jane Long, 'the Mother of Texas', 12) Stephen Austin, 'the Father of Texas', 13) Mexican Independence, Texas a Mexican State, 14) Texas Rangers Activated, 15) Anahuac Disturbances, 16) Battle of Gonzales, 17) Henry Smith, 1st Amer. Governor, 18) Texas Navy Organized, 19) Texas Declaration of Independence, 20) Goliad Massacre, 21) James Bowie, 22) James B. Bonham, 23) David Crockett, 24) William Barret Travis, 25) Siege & Fall of the Alamo, 26) Battle of San Jacinto, 27) Sam Houston, Comm. in Chief, Texas Army, 28) Surrender of Santa Anna, 29) Sam Houston, 1st Pres. Republic of Texas, 30) Lone Star Flag, 31) Mier Expedition, 32) Texas Annexed to U.S.A., 33) U.S. Declared War Against Mexico, 34) Buffalo, Bayou, Brazos & Colo. R.R. Chartered, 35) San Antonio-San Diego Mail Route Established, 36) Texas Seceded from Union, 37) Battle of Sabine Pass, 38) Battle of Palmito Ranch, 39) Great Trail Drives of Longhorns, 40) Reconstruction, Readmission to Union, 41) Second Battle of Abode Walls, 42) Judge Roy Bean, 43) Present Capitol Building Erected in Austin, 44) 1st U.S. Cavalry Volunteers-Rough Riders, 45) Galveston Storm and Flood, 46) Lucas Gusher, Spindletop Oil Field, 47) Joiners No. 3 East Texas Oil Field Discovered, 48) NASA Manned Spacecraft Center, 49) Lyndon B. Johnson, 50) Hemisfair & Astrodome; 777 sets issued from 1968-1971 at $11.00 each or $550.00 a set (50).

☐ **Thomason Medallic Bible,** set of 60 medals, sterling silver, 75 troy ounces per set; 1) Adam Names Animals, 2) Eve Presenting the Fruit, 3) Expulsion of Adam and Eve, 4) Cain Slaying Abel, 5) Enoch Carried into Heaven, 6) Noah's Ark, 7) Noah Buildeth an Altar, 8) Tower of Babel, 9) Lot Parting from Abraham, 10) Lot and his 2 Daughters, 11) Abraham Offering Isaac, 12) Rebecca Drawing Water, 13) Abraham

Buried in Cave, 14) Isaac Blessing Jacob, 15) Jacob and Esau, 16) Joseph Sold by Brethren, 17) Joseph's Interpretation, 18) Joseph Maketh Himself Known, 19) Jacob on his Deathbed, 20) Moses Discovered, 21) Rod of Moses, 22) First Born Slain, 23) Pharaoh Drowned, 24) Moses Smote the Rock 25) Worshipping Molted Calf, 26) Ark of the Covenant, 27) Moses' Brazen Serpent, 28) Balaam Smiting the Ass, 29) Sacrifice of the Red Heifer, 30) Joshua Dividing Waters, 31) Joshua Commanding Sun, 32) Travels of the Children of Israel, 33) Jael Driving the Nail, 34) Jephthah's Rash Vow, 35) Samson Killing the Lion, 36) Samson & Gates of Gaza, 37) David Defeats Goliath, 38) Saul Visits the Witch, 39) Absalom Slain, 40) Solomon's Temple, 41) Judgement of Solomon, 42) Jeroboam Ordering Man of God Seized, 43) Elijah Fed by Ravens, 44) Elijah Carried into Heaven, 45) Son Restored to Life, 46) Jonah and the Whale, 47) Army of Sennacherib, 48) Shadrach, Meshach & Abednego in Furance, 49) Job in Distress, 50) Divine Psalmist, 51) Daniel in the Lion's Den, 52) Murder of Julius Caesar, 53) Adoration of the Wise Men, 54) Flight into Egypt, 55) Baptism of Christ, 56) Raising of Lazarus, 57) Last Supper, 58) Agony of Christ, 59) Crucifixion, 60) Ascension; **2,090 sets issued from 1967-1970 at $9.50 each or $570.00 a set (60).**

☐ **Twelve Apostles,** *set of 12 medals, sterling silver, 10 troy ounces per set; 1) St. Peter, 2) St. Andrew, 3) St. James the Greater, 4) St. John, 5) St. Philip, 6) St. Bartholomew, 7) St. Matthew, 8) St. Thomas, 9) St. James the Less, 10) St. Simon, 11) St. Jude Thaddeus, 12) St. Matthias;* **1,898 sets issued from 1970-1972 at $7.55 each or $90.60 a set (12).**

☐ **Twelve Caesars,** *set of 12 medals, sterling silver, 15 troy ounces per set; 1) Julius Caesar, 2) Augustus, 3) Tiberius, 4) Caligula, 5) Claudius, 6) Nero, 7) Galba, 8) Otho, 9) Vitellius, 10) Vespasian, 11) Titus, 12) Domitian;* **1,496 sets issued in 1972 at $15.40 each or $184.50 a set (12).**

☐ **United Nations,** *United Nations 25th Anniversary, set of 5 medals, sterling silver;* **11,362 sets issued in 1970 at $11.00 each or $55.00 a set (5).**

☐ **UNICEF 25th Anniversary,** *sterling silver;* **8,498 issued in 1971 at $12.00 each.**

☐ **Five Language Sets,** *set of 5 medals each, sterling silver, proof, 39mm;* **1972:** *1) Nuclear Non-Proliferation Treaty, 2) World Health Day, 3) Human Environment Conference, 4) Economic Commission for Europe, 5) Art at the U.N.-Great Mural by J.M. Sert;* **2,261 sets issued in 1972 at $12.00 each or $300.00 a set (5).**

☐ *1973: 1) Disarmament Decade, 2) Stop Drug Abuse, 3) U.N. Volunteers Programme, 4) Namibia, 5) Universal Declaration of Human Rights;* **1,596 sets issued in 1973 at $12.00 each or $300.00 a set (5).**

☐ *1974: 1) International Labour Organization, 2) Universal Postal Union, 100 Ann., 3) Brotherhood & Understanding Among Men, 4) World Population Year, 5) Law of the Sea Conference;* **1,191 sets issued in 1974 at $12.50 each or $312.50 a set (5).**

☐ *1975: 1) Peaceful Uses of Outer Space, 2) International Women's Year, 3) U.N., 30th Ann., 4) Namibia, 5) U.S. Peace-Keeping Operations;* **706 sets issued in 1975 at 14.00 each or $350.00 a set (5).**

☐ *1976: 1) World Federation of U.S. Assoc.-30th Ann., 2) U.N. Conference on Trade & Development, 3) U.N. Conference on Human Settlements, 4) U.N. Postal Administration-25th Ann., 5) U.N. World Food Council;* **546 sets issued in 1976 at $20.00 each or $500.00 a set (5).**

☐ *1977: 1) World Intellectual Property Org., 2) U.N. Water Conference, 3) U.N. Security Council, 4) Combat Racism, 5) Peaceful Uses of Atomic Energy;* **348 sets issued in 1977 at $20.00 each or $500.00 a set (5).**

☐ *1978: 1) Global Eradication of Smallpox, 2) Namibia: Liberation, Justice-Co-Operation, 3) IACO: Safety in the Air, 4) General Assembly, 5) Technical Co-Operation among Developing Countries;* **96 sets issued in 1978 at $25.00 each or $625.00 a set (5).**

☐ *1979: set of 5 medals, 1) UNDRO Against Disaster, 2) International Year of the Child, 3) Donaupark, Vienna, 4) For a Free & Independent Namibia, 5) Interna-*

tional Court of Justice; 1980: set of 6 medals, 1) New International Economic Order, 2) U.N. Decade for Women, 3) U.N. Peace-Keeping Opeations, 4) U.N. 35th Anniversary, 5) U.N. Flag Series, 6) Economic & Social Council; 1981: set of 5 medals, 1) Inalienable Rights of the Palestinian People, 2) International Year of Disabled Persons, 3) Art at the United Nations, 4) New & Renewable Sources of Energy, 5) U.N. Flag Series.

☐ **United Nations Peace,** *1971, sterling silver, P/L,* **4,001 issued at $12.00 each;** *1972, sterling silver, proof,* **25,645 issued at $12.00 each;** *sterling silver, P/L,* **7,383 issued at $12.00 each;** *1973, sterling silver, proof,* **33,663 issued at $13.00 each;** *sterling silver, P/L,* **8,130 issued at $13.00 each;** *1974, sterling silver, proof,* **31,368 issued at $20.00 each;** *sterling silver, P/L,* **3,162 issued at $20.00 each;** *1975, sterling silver, proof,* **20,314 issued at $22.00 each;** *sterling silver, P/L,* **2,815 issued at $22.00 each;** *1976, sterling silver, proof,* **9,321 issued at $27.50 each;** *sterling silver, P/L,* **1,091 issued at $27.50 each;** *1977, sterling silver, proof,* **10,579 issued at $29.50 each;** *sterling silver, P/L,* **1,324 issued at $29.50 each;** *1978, sterling silver, proof,* **5,174 issued at $29.50 each;** *sterling silver, P/L,* **1,877 issued at $29.50 each;** *1979, sterling silver, proof,* **5,580 issued at $32.50 each;** *sterling silver, P/L,* **2,066 issued at $32.50 each;** *1980, sterling silver, proof,* **issued at $55.00 each;** *sterling silver, P/L,* **issued at $55.00 each;** *1981, sterling silver, proof,* **issued at $55.00 each;** *sterling silver, P/L,* **issued at $55.00 each.**

☐ **Vatican Art Treasures,** *set of 100 medals, sterling silver, 96 troy ounces per set; 1) Constantine the Great by Bernini, 2) Saints - Detail from Madonna of San Niccolo del Frari by Titian, 3) Laocoon by Agesander, Polydorus, and Athenodorus of Rhodes, 4) The Delphic Sibyl by Michelangelo, 5) The Entombment by Caravaggio, 6) The Good Shepherd (Anonymous), 7) The Founding of the Vatican Library by da Forli, 8) St. Francis Xavier by Van Dyck, 9) The Madonna of Foligno by Raphael, 10) The Thinker by Rodin, 11) The Rest on the Flight into Egypt by Barocci, 12) Christ the Redeemer by Giotto, 13) After Scopas by Meleager, 14) Saint Joan of Arc by Redon, 15) Pieta by Bellini, 16) Joshua Roll (detail) (Anonymous), 17) The Mars of Todi (Anonymous), 18) Madonna and Child with Saints and Angels by Fra Angelico, 19) Venus Bathing-After Doidalsas, 20) The Fall of Man by Raphael, 21) Pope Clement IX by Maratta, 22) Niobide Chairamonti (Anonymous), 23) Gideons Victory Over the Midianites by Poussin, 24) Sarcophagus of Constantia (Anonymous), 25) Cross of Emperor Justin (Anonymous), 26) Jethro's Daughters by Cappella Sistina, 27) The Dioryphorus by Braccio Nuova, 28) The Expulsion of Heliodorus from the Temple by Raphael, 29) Saint Jerome by da Vinci, 30) Coronation of the Virgin by Fra Filippo Lippi, 31) Sleeping Ariadne (Anonymous), 32) The Discus Thrower after Myron, 33) The Miraculous Draught of Fishes after Raphael, 34) Death of the Virgin (Anonymous), 35) The Countess Matilda by Bernini, 36) Achilles and Ajax Playing Dice by Exekias, 37) Deity of the River Nile (Anonymous), 38) Apollo and Muses-Detail from Parnassus Raphael by Stanza della Segnatura, 39) Madonna and Child by Pinturicchio, 40) Dome of St. Peter's Basilica by Michelangelo, 41) Marsyas after Myron, 42) Crucifixion-(Anonymous), 43) Disputation of St. Catherine of Alexandria by Borgia, 44) Moses Rescued From the Waters by Romano, 45) St. Rernard by del Piombo, 46) Lamentation by Da Cortona, 47) Pope Paul III-detail of Tomb-Guglielmo Della Porta, 48) Triumph of the Cross by Lanfranco, 49) St. Longinus by Bernini, 50) Vulcan's Forge by Penni, 51) Apostle by Goya, 52) The Crucifixion of St. Peter by Michelangelo, 53) Annunciation, Anonymous, 54) The Augustus of Prima Porta, Anonymous, 55) Vision of St. Thomas Aquinas by Sassetta, 56) Moses Proclaiming the Law by Signorelli, 57) St. Stephen Preaching by Fra Angelico, 58) Emperor Caracalla, Anonymous, 59) Nativity by di Paolo, 60) Cathedra Petri by Bernini, 61) The School of Athens by Raphael, 62) Allegorical Scene by Veronese, 63) Pope Sixtus IV by Pollaiuolo;* **3,347 sets issued from 1976-1986 at $25.00 each or $2,500.00 a set (100).**

☐ **Victory at Princeton,** *sterling silver, proof;* **305 issued in 1977 at $60.00 each.**

☐ **Vita Christi (Life of Christ)**, *set of 12 medals, sterling silver, 50 troy ounces per set; 1) The Annunciation, 2) The Nativity, 3) The Flight into Egypt, 4) The Baptism of Jesus, 5) The Sermon on the Mount, 6) The Entry into Jerusalem, 7) The Last Supper, 8) Jesus Before Pilate, 9) The Crucifixion, 10) The Descent from the Cross, 11) The Resurrection, 12) The Ascension;* **2,588 sets issued from 1971-1972 at $24.00 each or $288.00 a set (12).**

☐ **Washington Crossing the Delaware**, *sterling silver, 3.12 troy ounces;* **893 issued in 1976 at $60.00 each.**

☐ **Washington's Life**, *set of 12 medals, sterling silver, 7.4 troy ounces per set; 1) First Surveying Expedition, 2) Marriage to Martha Dandridge Custis, 3) Taking Command of the Continental Army, 4) Crossing the Delaware, 5) First Meeting with LaFayette, 6) Winter at Valley Forge, 7) Rallying Troops at Monmouth, 8) Victory at Yorktown, 9) Farewell Address to His Officers, 10) Presiding Over Constitutional Convention, 11) Inauguration as First U.S. President, 12) Formation of Nation's First Cabinet;* **1,313 sets issued from 1975-1976 at $19.50 each or $234.00 a set (12).**

☐ **Waterloo by Pistrucci**, *sterling silver;* **5,000 issued at $50.00 each.**

☐ **Wildlife of North America**, *set of 6 medals, sterling silver, 5.7 troy ounces per set; 1) Bighorn Sheep,* **1,498 issued;** *2) Red Fox,* **1,485 issued;** *3) Grizzly Bear,* **1,535 issued;** *4) Mountain Lion,* **1,529 issued;** *5) American Elk,* **1,493 issued; 6) Bison, 1,506 issued; issued in 1977 at $30.00 each or $165.00 a set (6).**

☐ **Women of American History, 100 Greatest**, *set of 100 medals, sterling silver, 300 grains each medal; 1) Abigail Adams, 2) Jane Addams, 3) Louisa May Alcott, 4) Susan B. Anthony, 5) Virginia Apgar, 6) Mary Austin, 7) Sarah Josephine Baker, 8) Ethel Barrymore, 9) Clara Barton, 10) Ruth Benedict, 11) Alice Bennett, 12) Mary McLeod Bethune, 13) Elizabeth Blackwell, 14) Amelia Jenks Bloomer, 15) Nellie Bly, 16) Evangeline Cory Booth, 17) Margaret Bourke-White, 18) Pearl S. Buck, 19) St. Frances Xavier Cabrini, 20) Annie Jump Cannon, 21) Rachel Carson, 22) Mary Cassatt, 23) Willa Cather, 24) Carrie Chapman Cart, 25) Edna Woolman Chase, 26) Imogen Cunningham, 27) Charlotte Cushman, 28) Alice Brown Davis, 29) Eleonora DeCisneros, 30) Emily Dickinson, 31) Dorothea Dix, 32) Mary Mapes Dodge, 33) Suzanne Douvillier, 34) Isadora Duncan, 35) Amelia Earhart, 36) Mary Baker Eddy, 37) Fannie Farmer, 38) Geraldine Farrar, 39) Margaret Fuller, 40) Sarah Fuller, 41) Alice Hamilton, 42) Lorraine Hansberry, 43) Harriet Boyd Hawes, 44) Billie Holiday, 45) Karen Horney, 46) Julia Ward Howe, 47) Anne Hutchinson, 48) Helen Hunt Jackson, 49) Mahalia Jackson, 50) Gertrude Santon Kasebier, 51) Helen Keller, 52) Margaret E. Knight, 53) Rose Markward Knox, 54) Julia Clifford Lathrop, 55) Emma Lazarus;* **351 sets to be issued from 1977-1985 at $19.50 each or $1,950.00 a set (100).**

☐ **Wonders of Mankind**, *set of 24 medals, sterling silver, 25 troy ounces per set; 1) Taj Mahal, 2) Eiffel Tower, 3) Karlstein Castle, 4) Itsuki Island Torii, 5) Alcazar in Segovia, 6) Parthenon, 7) Great Pyramids, 8) Shwe Dagon Pagoda, 9) Temple of the Dawn, 10) Aztec Ruins, 11) Old Quebec City, 12) Houses of Parliament, 13) Easter Island Monoliths, 14) Great Wall, 15) Mount Rushmore, 16) Rock of Cashel, 17) Coloseum, 18) Uhrturm, 19) Kremlin, 20) Lion Monument, 21) Cologne Cathedral, 22) Panama Canal, 23) Potala Palace, 24) Christ the Redeemer;* **3,563 sets issued from 1971-1972 at $9.50 each or $228.00 a set (24);** *sterling silver, P/L,* **186 sets issued at $9.50 each or $228.00 a set (24).**

How did your plates do?

Reco's "Little Boy Blue" by John McClelland

UP 214% in 1 Year

Some limited edition plates gained more in the same year, some less, and some not at all . . . But Plate Collector readers were able to follow the price changes, step by step, in Plate Price Trends, a copyrighted feature appearing in each issue of the magazine.

Because The Plate Collector is your best source guide . . . has more on limited editions than all other publications combined . . . and gives you insight into every facet of your collecting . . . you too will rate it

Your No. 1. Investment
In Limited Editions.

In 1972, Plate Collector was the first to feature limited editions only. It's expanded, adding figurines, bells and prints, earning reader raves like you see below.

To bring you the latest, most valuable information, our editors crisscross the continent. Sometimes stories lead them to the smaller Hawaiian Islands, or to the porcelain manufactories of Europe.

Their personal contact with artisans, hobby leaders, collectors, artists and dealers lets you share an intimate view of limited editions.

Each fat, colorful issue brings you new insight, helps you enjoy collecting more.

You'll find Plate Collector a complete source guide. Consider new issue information and new issue announcements, often in full color. Use the ratings of new releases and wide array of dealer ads to help you pick and choose the best.

Read regular columns, including one on Hummels, and check current market values in Plate Price Trends to add to your storehouse of knowledge.

You'll profit from tips on insurance, decorating, taxes . . . just a sample of recurring feature subjects.

Read Plate Collector magazine to become a true limited edition art insider. Order now. See new and old plates in sparkling color. Enjoy 2 issues every month, delivered to your home at savings up to 37% from newsstand price.

12 issues (6 months) $17.50
24 issues (year) $30
The PLATE COLLECTOR
P.O. Box 1041-HC   Kermit, TX 79745

To use VISA and MasterCard, include all raised information on your card.

Here is Plate Collector, as viewed by our readers in unsolicited quotes . . .

"Objective and Impartial," has *"great research,"* yet is warm and personal . . . *"I am delighted in 'our' magazine."* A New York couple says flatly, *"It is the best collector magazine on the market."*

"Quality printing is valuable to me because there are no stores near me where I can view and decide," says an Arizona reader. It is *"a major guide to the plates I buy,"* says a Massachusetts reader, while *"It is the best investment in a magazine I ever made,"* comes from Illinois.

"I enjoy your articles on artists," *"The full-color pictures are great,"* *"Your staff was most helpful,"* *"I depend on Plate Collector,"* and *"I look forward to receiving it twice a month,"* are other reader reactions.

A California reader said simply, *"I am glad there is a Plate Collector."*

PRICE GUIDE SERIES

Collector Plates
Destined to become the ''PLATE COLLECTORS' BIBLE.'' This unique price guide offers the most comprehensive listing of collector plate values — *in Print! Special information includes: company histories; artist backgrounds; and helpful tips on buying, selling and storing a collection.* ILLUSTRATED.
$9.95-1st Edition, 640 pgs., 5⅜" x 8", paperback, Order #: 349-X

Collector Prints
Over *14,750 detailed listings* representing over 400 of the most famous collector print artists from Audubon and Currier & Ives, to modern day artists. *Special feature includes gallery/artist reference chart.* ILLUSTRATED.
$9.95-4th Edition, 544 pgs., 5⅜" x 8", paperback, Order #: 189-6

Comic & Science Fiction Books
Over *30,000 listings with current values* for comic and science fiction publications *from 1903-to-date. Special sections on Tarzan, Big Little Books, Science Fiction publications and paperbacks.* ILLUSTRATED.
$9.95-5th Edition, 512 pgs., 5⅜" x 8", paperback, Order #: 183-7

Hummel Figurines & Plates
The most complete guide ever published on every type of Hummel — including the most recent trademarks and size variations, with *4,500 up-to-date prices. Plus tips on buying, selling and investing.* ILLUSTRATED.
$9.95-3rd Edition, 448 pgs., 5⅜" x 8", paperback, Order #: 325-X

Military Collectibles
This detailed historical reference price guide covers the largest accumulation of military objects — 15th century-to-date — listing over *12,000 accurate prices. Special expanded Samuri sword and headdress sections.* ILLUSTRATED.
$9.95-2nd Edition, 544 pgs., 5⅜" x 8", paperback, Order #: 191-8

PUBLISHED BY: *THE HOUSE OF COLLECTIBLES, INC.*
1900 PREMIER ROW, ORLANDO, FL 32809   PHONE: (305) 857-9095

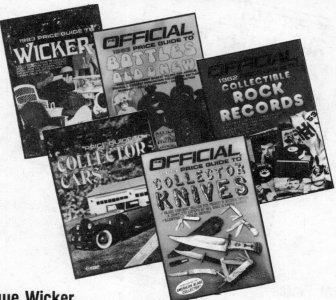

MINI PRICE GUIDE SERIES

Pete Rose Baseball Cards

This guide lists *over 44,000 current market values* for baseball cards – Bowman, Burger King, Donruss, Fleer, O-Pee-Chee and Topps. *Includes a full color PETE ROSE limited edition collector card. ILLUSTRATED.*
$2.50-2nd Edition, 288 pgs., 4″ x 5½″, paperback, Order #: 322-8

Comic Books

Young and Old are collecting old comic books for fun *and Profit!* This handy ''pocket-sized'' price guide lists current market values and detailed descriptions for the most sought-after ''collectible'' comic books. *Buying, selling and storing tips are provided for the beginning collector. ILLUSTRATED.*
$2.50-1st Edition, 240 pgs., 4″ x 5½″, paperback, Order #: 345-7

O.J. Simpson Football Cards

The world famous O.J. Simpson highlights this comprehensive guide to football card values. *Over 21,000 current collector prices* are listed for: Topps, Bowman, Fleer, Philadelphia and O-Pee-Chee. *Includes a full color O.J. SIMPSON limited edition collector card. ILLUSTRATED.*
$2.50-2nd Edition, 256 pgs., 4″ x 5½″, paperback, Order #: 323-6

Antiques & Flea Markets

Discover the fun and profit of collecting antiques with this handy pocket reference to *over 15,000 types of collectibles.* Avoid counterfeits and learn the secrets to successful buying and selling. *ILLUSTRATED.*
$2.50-1st Edition, 240 pgs., 4″ x 5½″, paperback, Order #: 308-2

Paperbacks & Magazines

Old discarded paperbacks and magazines could be worth 50-100 times their original cover price. Learn how to identify them. *Thousands* of descriptions and prices show which issues are rare. *ILLUSTRATED.*
$2.50-1st Edition, 240 pgs., 4″ x 5½″, paperback, Order #: 315-5

Scouting Collectibles

Discover the colorful history behind scouting, relive childhood memories and profit from those old family heirlooms. *Thousands of prices* are listed for all types of Boy and Girl Scout memorabilia. *ILLUSTRATED.*
: Edition, 240 pgs., 4″ x 5½″, paperback, Order #: 314-7

PUBLISHED BY: *THE HOUSE OF COLLECTIBLES, INC.*
1900 PREMIER ROW, ORLANDO, FL 32809   PHONE: (305) 857-9095